The Cambridge Handbook of Linguistic Anthropology

The field of linguistic anthropology looks at human uniqueness and diversity through the lens of language, our species' special combination of art and instinct. Human language both shapes, and is shaped by, our minds, societies, and cultural worlds.

This state-of-the-field survey covers a wide range of topics, approaches, and theories, such as the nature and function of language systems, the relationship between language and social interaction, and the place of language in the social life of communities. Promoting a broad vision of the subject, spanning a range of disciplines from linguistics to biology, from psychology to sociology and philosophy, this authoritative handbook is an essential reference guide for students and researchers working on language and culture across the social sciences.

N. J. ENFIELD is a Professor at the University of Sydney and Radboud University Nijmegen, and is a Senior Staff Scientist at the Max Planck Institute for Psycholinguistics.

PAUL KOCKELMAN is a Professor in the Department of Anthropology at Yale University.

JACK SIDNELL is Associate Professor in the Department of Anthropology and the Department of Linguistics at the University of Toronto.

CAMBRIDGE HANDBOOKS IN LANGUAGE AND LINGUISTICS

Genuinely broad in scope, each handbook in this series provides a complete state-of-the-field overview of a major subdiscipline within language study and research. Grouped into broad thematic areas, the chapters in each volume encompass the most important issues and topics within each subject, offering a coherent picture of the latest theories and findings. Together, the volumes will build into an integrated overview of the discipline in its entirety.

Published titles

The Cambridge Handbook of Phonology, edited by Paul de Lacy
The Cambridge Handbook of Linguistic Code-switching, edited by Barbara E. Bullock and Almeida Jacqueline Toribio
The Cambridge Handbook of Child Language, edited by Edith L. Bavin
The Cambridge Handbook of Endangered Languages, edited by Peter K. Austin and Julia Sallabank
The Cambridge Handbook of Sociolinguistics, edited by Rajend Mesthrie
The Cambridge Handbook of Pragmatics, edited by Keith Allan and Kasia M. Jaszczolt
The Cambridge Handbook of Language Policy, edited by Bernard Spolsky
The Cambridge Handbook of Second Language Acquisition, edited by Julia Herschensohn and Martha Young-Scholten
The Cambridge Handbook of Biolinguistics, edited by Cedric Boeckx and Kleanthes K. Grohmann
The Cambridge Handbook of Generative Syntax, edited by Marcel den Dikken
The Cambridge Handbook of Communication Disorders, edited by Louise Cummings
The Cambridge Handbook of Stylistics, edited by Peter Stockwell and Sara Whiteley
The Cambridge Handbook of Linguistic Anthropology, edited by N. J. Enfield, Paul Kockelman, and Jack Sidnell

Further titles planned for the series

The Cambridge Handbook of English Corpus Linguistics, edited by Douglas Biber and Randi Reppen
The Cambridge Handbook of Morphology, edited by Andrew Hippisley and Gregory Stump
The Cambridge Handbook of Historical Syntax, edited by Adam Ledgeway and Ian Roberts
The Cambridge Handbook of Formal Semantics, edited by Maria Aloni and Paul Dekker
The Cambridge Handbook of English Historical Linguistics, edited by Merja Kytö and Päivi Pahta

The Cambridge Handbook of Linguistic Anthropology

Edited by
**N. J. Enfield,
Paul Kockelman,**
and
Jack Sidnell

CAMBRIDGE
UNIVERSITY PRESS

University Printing House, Cambridge CB2 8BS, United Kingdom

One Liberty Plaza, 20th Floor, New York, NY 10006, USA

477 Williamstown Road, Port Melbourne, VIC 3207, Australia

314-321, 3rd Floor, Plot 3, Splendor Forum, Jasola District Centre, New Delhi - 110025, India

79 Anson Road, #06-04/06, Singapore 079906

Cambridge University Press is part of the University of Cambridge.

It furthers the University's mission by disseminating knowledge in the pursuit of education, learning and research at the highest international levels of excellence.

www.cambridge.org
Information on this title: www.cambridge.org/9781009014618

© Cambridge University Press 2014

This publication is in copyright. Subject to statutory exception and to the provisions of relevant collective licensing agreements, no reproduction of any part may take place without the written permission of Cambridge University Press.

First published 2014
First paperback edition 2021

A catalogue record for this publication is available from the British Library

Library of Congress Cataloging in Publication data
The Cambridge handbook of linguistic anthropology / [edited by]
N. J. Enfield, Paul Kockelman, Jack Sidnell.
  pages   cm. – (Cambridge handbooks in language and linguistics)
ISBN 978-1-107-03007-7 (hardback)
1. Anthropological linguistics.   I. Enfield, N. J.   II. Kockelman,
Paul.   III. Sidnell, Jack.
P35.C25   2014
306.44–dc23   2013048936

ISBN 978-1-107-03007-7 Hardback
ISBN 978-1-009-01461-8 Paperback

Cambridge University Press has no responsibility for the persistence or accuracy of URLs for external or third-party internet websites referred to in this publication, and does not guarantee that any content on such websites is, or will remain, accurate or appropriate.

For Sula and Ginger,
Zeno and Mia,
Nyssa and Nonnika

Contents

List of figures	page ix
List of tables	xii
List of contributors	xiii

1 Introduction: Directions in the anthropology of language *N. J. Enfield, Paul Kockelman, and Jack Sidnell*   1

Part I System and function   25
2 Basics of a language *R. M. W. Dixon*   29
3 The item/system problem *N. J. Enfield*   48
4 Language and the manual modality: The communicative resilience of the human species *Susan Goldin-Meadow*   78
5 Linguistic diversity and universals *Balthasar Bickel*   102
6 Denotation and the pragmatics of language *Michael Silverstein*   128
7 Language function *Sandra A. Thompson and Elizabeth Couper-Kuhlen*   158

Part II Process and formation   183
8 Language acquisition and language socialization *Penelope Brown and Suzanne Gaskins*   187
9 Language, society, and history: Towards a unified approach? *Paja Faudree and Magnus Pharao Hansen*   227
10 Language emergence: Al-Sayyid Bedouin Sign Language *Wendy Sandler, Mark Aronoff, Carol Padden, and Irit Meir*   250
11 Endangered languages *Keren Rice*   285
12 Language evolution *Stephen C. Levinson*   309
13 Causal dynamics of language *N. J. Enfield*   325

Part III Interaction and intersubjectivity 343
14 Intentionality and language   *Robert B. Brandom* 347
15 The architecture of intersubjectivity revisited   *Jack Sidnell* 364
16 Language and human sociality   *Alan Rumsey* 400
17 The ontology of action, in interaction   *Jack Sidnell and N. J. Enfield* 423
18 Conversation across cultures   *Mark Dingemanse and Simeon Floyd* 447

Part IV Community and social life 481
19 Poetics and performativity   *Luke Fleming and Michael Lempert* 485
20 Ritual language   *David Tavárez* 516
21 Oratory, rhetoric, politics   *Bernard Bate* 537
22 Language and media   *Ilana Gershon and Paul Manning* 559
23 The speech community and beyond: Language and the nature of the social aggregate   *Shaylih Muehlmann* 577

Part V Interdisciplinary perspectives 599
24 Linguistic anthropology and critical theory   *Paul Kockelman* 603
25 Linguistic anthropology and sociocultural anthropology   *Rupert Stasch* 626
26 Sociolinguistics: Making quantification meaningful   *Penelope Eckert* 644
27 Language and archaeology: State of the art   *Roger M. Blench* 661
28 Language and biology: The multiple interactions between genetics and language   *Dan Dediu* 686
29 Linguistic anthropology in the age of language automata   *Paul Kockelman* 708

Index 734

Figures

3.1 Darwin's illustration of a dog in hostile frame of mind
(Figure 5 from *The Expression of the Emotions in Man and Animals*) *page* 51
3.2 A "functional," indexical association between observable behavior and frame of mind (after Darwin) 51
3.3 Darwin's illustration of a dog in an affectionate attitude
(Figure 6 from *The Expression of the Emotions in Man and Animals*) 52
3.4 A secondary indexical association between observable behavior and frame of mind (after Darwin) 52
3.5 Sections (Northern Australia), from McConvell (1985: 32), after Radcliffe-Brown (1931) 57
3.6 Loci for transmission in a four-stroke engine model (building on Sperber 1985, 1996, 2006): exposure (world-to-mind transition), representation (mind structure), reproduction (mind-to-world transition), and material (world structure) 64
6.1 The Basic "Lockean Rectangle" (U of C: Quadrangle), "solved" in folk-intuition and enshrined in much philosophy of language and mind 133
6.2 More granular view of the phenomena along the lower edge of the Lockean rectangle (see Figure 6.1) 138
6.3 Micro-contextual semiotic of indexicality 151
10.1 Change of intonational arrays at the intonational phrase boundary in ISL: (a) raised brows and head forward signal continuation in the *if*-clause of a conditional; (b) complete change of array in the *then*-clause that follows 259
10.2 Change of facial expression and body posture at the juncture of two intonational phrases in an ABSL conditional sentence meaning 'If he says no, then there's nothing to be done.' 260

10.3	A coded example of a conditional sentence produced by a younger signer	260
10.4	Two different ABSL compounds meaning 'kettle', each found in a different familylect. (a) TEA^POUR; (b) TEA^ROUNDED-OBJECT	265
10.5	Two SASS compounds in ABSL: (a) WRITE^LONG-THIN-OBJECT ('pen'), and (b) TELEVISION^RECTANGULAR-OBJECT ('remote control')	266
10.6	Structural tendency in SASS compounds: Number of SASS-final and SASS non-final compounds in the production of each signer	267
10.7	Structure of endocentric compounds in ABSL: Head–Modifier order in the production of each signer	267
10.8	Percentage of different Head–Modifier orders in our data	268
10.9	The ISL minimal pair (a) TATTLE and (b) SEND	269
10.10	Two variations of DOG in ABSL: (a) articulation near the mouth; (b) articulation in neutral space in front of the torso	270
10.11	Change of handshape within the ABSL sign DONKEY	270
10.12	The conventionalized compound sign EGG in ABSL (CHICKEN^OVAL-OBJECT)	271
10.13	The sign EGG with handshape assimilation: three fingers assimilated to CHICKEN from OVAL OBJECT	271
10.14	The reduced compound sign EGG: only the counter-iconic assimilated version of the first member of the compound survives	272
10.15	(a) The ISL sign EXACTLY with fingertip prominence and (b) the borrowed sign with dorsal hand prominence in the ABSL accent	273
15.1	Human infant showing object to camera person	367
15.2	Detail from *The Anatomy Lesson of Dr. Nicolaes Tulp*, Rembrandt Harmenszoon van Rijn, 1632 © Fine Art/Alamy	367
16.1	Young boy playing with his sister, Paris. Photo by Alan Rumsey	406
16.2	Mother and children at home in the Papua New Guinea Highlands	407
18.1	Depiction of Kofi's movements in line 5 from Extract 1 (two stills superimposed)	451
18.2	Household settings in which Mead and Bateson used film to compare body behavior across cultures; they compared bathing practices to families in Bali (pictured here) to those seen in New Guinea and the Midwestern USA. Photo by Gregory Bateson, April 30, 1937. Mead-Bateson collection item 204e, Manuscript Division, Library of Congress	455
18.3	Two visual-gestural signs in Cha'palaa	466

27.1	An example of the Raga writing system	674
27.2	Launching the Eda alphabet chart	675
27.3	Multi-language inscription, Durbar Square, Kathmandu, Nepal	676
29.1	Automata as text-generated and text-generating devices	710
29.2	Some ways of framing secondness and thirdness	712
29.3	Relative scope of languages recognized by different kinds of automata	717
29.4	Comparison of Cartesian and Polar coordinate systems	720

Tables

1.1	Some observed correlations between relations in language systems, where causality is proposed or implied	page 10
3.1	Grammatical profile of Munda versus Mon-Khmer (i.e., Austroasiatic except Munda); after Donegan and Stampe (1983: 337–8)	56
13.1	Four distinct causal/temporal frames for studying animal behavior (after Tinbergen 1963)	327
16.1	Relations of parallelism in two lines from example 1	413
17.1	Some practice–action mappings (drawn from Schegloff 1996; see other references there; this figure adapted from Enfield 2013: 96)	430
19.1	Name taboos and the avoidance of iconic phonetic sequences	501
24.1	Some core moves of linguistic anthropology (or What the discipline foregrounds)	604
24.2	Some key modes of mediation	607
24.3	Some key modes of meta-mediation	615
27.1	Four processes of language dispersal and diversification (after Renfrew 1992: 457)	668
29.1	Intermediaries, mediation, and intermediation	714

Contributors

Mark Aronoff, Professor, Stony Brook University
Bernard Bate, Associate Professor, Yale University
Balthasar Bickel, Professor, University of Zurich
Roger M. Blench, Kay Williamson Educational Foundation
Robert B. Brandom, Professor, University of Pittsburgh
Penelope Brown, Senior Researcher, Max Planck Institute for Psycholinguistics
Elizabeth Couper-Kuhlen, Professor, University of Helsinki
Dan Dediu, Senior Researcher, Max Planck Institute for Psycholinguistics
Mark Dingemanse, Senior Researcher, Max Planck Institute for Psycholinguistics
R. M. W. Dixon, Professor, James Cook University
Penelope Eckert, Professor, Stanford University
N. J. Enfield, Professor, Max Planck Institute for Psycholinguistics, Radboud University Nijmegen, and University of Sydney
Paja Faudree, Assistant Professor, Brown University
Luke Fleming, Assistant Professor, Université de Montréal
Simeon Floyd, Staff Researcher, Max Planck Institute for Psycholinguistics
Suzanne Gaskins, Professor, Northeastern Illinois University
Ilana Gershon, Associate Professor, Indiana University
Susan Goldin-Meadow, Professor, University of Chicago
Magnus Pharao Hansen, PhD candidate, Brown University
Paul Kockelman, Professor, Yale University
Michael Lempert, Assistant Professor, University of Michigan
Stephen C. Levinson, Professor, Max Planck Institute for Psycholinguistics and Radboud University Nijmegen
Paul Manning, Associate Professor, Trent University
Irit Meir, Senior Lecturer, University of Haifa

Shaylih Muehlmann, Assistant Professor, University of British Columbia
Carol Padden, Professor, University of California, San Diego
Keren Rice, Professor, University of Toronto
Alan Rumsey, Professor, Australian National University
Wendy Sandler, Professor, University of Haifa
Jack Sidnell, Associate Professor, University of Toronto
Michael Silverstein, Professor, University of Chicago
Rupert Stasch, Associate Professor, University of California, San Diego
David Tavárez, Associate Professor, Vassar College
Sandra A. Thompson, Professor, UC Santa Barbara

1

Introduction

Directions in the anthropology of language

N. J. Enfield, Paul Kockelman, and Jack Sidnell

> The bringing-forth of language is an inner need of human beings, not merely an external necessity for maintaining communal intercourse, but a thing lying in their own nature, indispensable for the development of their mental powers and the attainment of a worldview, to which man can attain only by bringing his thinking to clarity and precision through communal thinking with others.
> (Wilhelm von Humboldt 1988: 27)

1.1 The anthropology of language

It is a truism that humans would be different creatures entirely were it not for the possession of language. One of anthropology's tasks is to find out what this means. A contention of this handbook is that anthropology must be able to specify what it is about language that helps us answer the two overarching research questions of the discipline:

(1) What distinguishes humankind from other species?
(2) Within our species, what is the nature and extent of diversity?

One way in which human groups are alike is that none are without language. This universally distinguishes humans from other species. Yet the same human groups are radically *unalike* insofar as languages show considerable diversity at all levels of their structure (Boas 1911, Comrie 1989, Ladefoged and Maddieson 1996, Van Valin and La Polla 1997, Croft 2001, 2003, Evans and Levinson 2009, Dixon 2010, and many references in those works). To truly understand – and demonstrate – the significance of this, the anthropology of language needs to confront some major conceptual and empirical challenges, including: (1) to define *language* (and describe *languages*); (2) to show how language is related to the special properties of the human *mind*; (3) to show how language is related to the processes and structures of *society* and social life; and (4) to show how language is related to the knowledge, values, technologies, and practices that make up *culture*. Taken together, the contributions to this handbook address these challenges, drawing from a wide range of disciplines, literatures, theories, and methodologies.

In this introductory chapter, we want to point to some issues that we see as central to the anthropology of language, motivating the choices we have made as editors, and offering something of a preview of the book as a whole. We do not attempt a comprehensive survey of the handbook's themes. Nor do we offer an essay outlining our editorial account of the issues. One reason is that our own versions of the story are already in print (see Enfield 2002c, 2009, 2013; Kockelman 2005, 2010, 2013; Sidnell 2005, 2010; Sidnell and Enfield 2012, and indeed our chapters in this book). But more importantly with respect to this volume, our goal as editors is to allow the contributing authors' many voices to come forward and explicate the core concerns of research on language within the scope of anthropology.

1.1.1 Two senses of "linguistic anthropology"

The term *linguistic anthropology* is as contested, negotiated, reflexive, and indexical as any other. While extensive discussion of this term falls outside the scope of this introductory chapter, we would nevertheless like to register the issue of disciplinary terminology in this handbook's title, and address expectations that the reader might have.

The term that describes our given topic – *linguistic anthropology* – can be understood in at least two ways. A first reading of the term is rather specific, and is subsumed within the broader scope of this book. It predominantly refers to a subfield within the modern discipline of anthropology in its American context. There is a journal associated with the subfield (the *Journal of Linguistic Anthropology*), a section of the American Anthropological Association devoted to it (the Society for Linguistic Anthropology), and a set of scholars who self-consciously work under its banner – though, to be sure, members of this group come from different research traditions, and often hold quite different (even contentious) commitments. Perhaps most importantly as background to this handbook, the work of these scholars has been anthologized, summarized, and historicized numerous times (see Lucy 1993, Blount 1995, Brenneis and Macaulay 1996, Silverstein and Urban 1996, Hanks 1996, Duranti 1997, 2001, 2004, Agha 2007, Ahearn 2011, Blum 2012; cf. also Foley 1997).

Duranti (2003) outlines three paradigms that have fed into this relatively focused and well-institutionalized tradition in the anthropology of language: (1) Boasian *linguistic description* and documentation, and associated work on the comparative psychology of language, including *linguistic relativity* (e.g., Boas 1911, Sapir 1949, Whorf 1956, with antecedents in scholars like Herder, von Humboldt, and Wundt); (2) Gumperz and Hymes' related traditions of the *ethnography of speaking* and *interactional sociolinguistics*, respectively (e.g., Hymes 1964, Bauman and Sherzer 1974, Gumperz 1982, Gumperz and Hymes 1986), and (3) *practice* approaches to language in social life, and related social constructivist approaches (e.g., Silverstein 1976, Bourdieu 1977, 1990, Hanks 1990, 1996, 2005).

Framed another way, linguistic anthropology in this narrow sense brings together Jakobson-inspired understandings of the importance of reflexivity; practice theory-inspired notions of the dialectical relations between linguistic practice (parole, interaction, discourse), language structure (grammar, code, langue), and language ideology (culture, worldview, beliefs and values); and a principled, and often relatively conservative, vision of the social sciences. Silverstein's Chapter 6 in this volume outlines an accordingly broad vision of the subdiscipline's key concepts, and the kinds of claims they allow one to make. And many of the chapters in this volume are authored by self-identifying linguistic anthropologists. Kockelman's Chapter 24 takes up and characterizes some of the core commitments of this subdiscipline, with an analysis, and critique, of their logic and origins. Kockelman's Table 24.1 lists some of the subdiscipline's core moves, including "Discourse as much as grammar, diachrony as much as synchrony, motivation as much as arbitrariness"; "Language as action as much as language as reflection"; "Meta-language as much as language, and reflexive language as much as reflective language"; and "Anthropology and linguistics before the 60s as much as anthropology and linguistics since the 60s."

The subdiscipline of linguistic anthropology in the narrow sense is an indispensable source of questions, methods, and solutions in the anthropology of language, though its coverage of the intended scope of this handbook is only partial. Much relevant research is clearly both linguistic and anthropological yet is not normally considered part of linguistic anthropology in the sense just described. Hence we have conceived the scope of this handbook in terms of a second, broader reading of the phrase in our title. This second sense of the term – perhaps best labeled *the anthropology of language* – encompasses any work that attempts to answer the research questions of anthropology (see 1–2, above) by focusing on the structure, use, development and/or evolution of language. This of course subsumes all of the work discussed in this chapter so far.

In (3) below we list a range of interrelated questions that are posed – and, at least provisionally, answered – in the full set of chapters that follow. Many chapters also detail the history of such questions, and the successes and shortcomings of the answers they have received in the past.

(3) Some central research questions within the anthropology of language, and chapters in this handbook that address them (see the chapters for many further references on these topics):

- What is the human-specific social cognition that is a prerequisite for language? What possible cultural variation is there? Are there primate-specific forms of social cognition that relate to it? (Rumsey, Dingemanse and Floyd, Brown and Gaskins)
- What are the human-specific biological capacities for vocal imitation? What are the genetic underpinnings for, and the ontogenetic development of, the vocal capacity? (Dediu)
- What is the relationship between language and thought – either speaking a particular language (say, English versus Japanese), or speaking human language per se? And how does one even pose such a question productively? (Goldin-Meadow, Brandom, Brown and Gaskins, Sidnell, Silverstein)
- What might diversity in human genetics tell us about the history and diversification of languages and cultures? Does this converge with evidence from the archaeological record? How to classify languages historically? What can this classification tell us about the history of human cultural diversification? (Blench, Dediu, Levinson)
- How does linguistic structure (e.g., grammar) relate to language use (e.g., what ends people use language as a means for) and linguistic ideology (e.g., speakers' understandings of their own usage patterns and language structure)? (Couper-Kuhlen and Thompson, Brandom, Sidnell and Enfield, Fleming and Lempert)
- Are there universal principles of grammatical organization in languages? What are the constraints on these? If there are few universal grammatical patterns, are there quasi-universal patterns of grammaticalization? (Bickel, Dixon, Couper-Kuhlen and Thompson)
- Are there universal principles in the underlying semantic organization of languages, thus accounting for variation in systematic ways? What is the relevance of grammatical hierarchies that reflect cognitive preferences such as an interest in self and addressee over other, agent over patient, animate over inanimate? or semantic fields such as color, biological categories, spatial relations? What types of meanings get encoded in grammatical and lexical categories (e.g., in "rules" and "words")? And what are the conditions and consequences of language-specific and cross-linguistic patterns of such encodings? (Dixon, Bickel, Sandler *et al.*, Goldin-Meadow)
- What is the art and craft of descriptive and documentary linguistics? What are the best practices, core methods, and key resources for collecting, transcribing, analyzing, storing and communicating linguistic findings? (Dixon, Rice)

- What are the structures of social interaction in conversation? What is the infrastructure for language in interaction? (Sidnell, Dingemanse and Floyd, Enfield and Sidnell)
- What do we mean by "meaning," and how is meaning essential to being human (if not specific to human beings)? (Silverstein, Rumsey)
- How does human language compare to other modes of communication – such as animal languages, computer languages, or pidgin languages? What makes human language both unique and comparable as a semiotic system? (Levinson, Silverstein, Kockelman [Chapter 29])
- How did language evolve? How do languages evolve? (Levinson, Dediu, Goldin-Meadow, Enfield, Sandler et al.)
- What are the sociocultural conditions for, and consequences of, language vitality, or for its tragic counterpart, language death? (Rice, Sandler et al., Eckert)
- How does inter-language diversity (e.g., the historical and geographic distribution of languages), and intra-language difference (e.g., ways of speaking particular to subgroups of people), relate to political, ethnic, economic, gender, and cultural differences? (Muehlmann, Bate, Eckert)
- What is the relation between ritual language and poetic language, or between highly condensed and formally constrained language and so-called everyday or spontaneous language practices? (Tavárez, Fleming and Lempert)
- How do processes occurring on ontogenetic, interactional, historical, and phylogenetic timescales interact to give rise to the emergent phenomena we tend to reify as "language," "culture," "reality," and "mind"? (Brown and Gaskins, Enfield, Faudree and Hansen)
- What is the effect of different media on language (interaction, society, culture)? And how do different linguistic and sociocultural practices mediate our uptake and use of different media? (Gershon and Manning, Kockelman [Chapter 29])
- What is the relation, however tense or unnoticed, between different disciplines (themselves cultural formations par excellence) that have historically taken "language" in some guise as an object of study? And how have such differences, and such submerged resonances, affected the study of language and culture? (Kockelman [Chapter 24], Stasch, Blench, Eckert)

A comprehensive survey of the anthropology of language would fully address and explicate all of these questions and the lines of work that handle them (among many more questions and lines of work). We cannot do more than touch on each of these issues in this handbook, but in doing at least this we hope that the volume contributes to a broader characterization of our topic. So, it should be clear, this book is not about Eskimo words for snow, nor is it about the exotic patterns of speaking exhibited by far-flung peoples. It is intended as a timely exploration of what meaning is, how it is manifest, and why it matters – when seen through the lens of language, culture, and cognition. Now, to see how the seemingly disparate lines of inquiry in (3) may be connected, let us consider some challenges that crosscut them.

1.2 Four challenges for an anthropology of language

In the above sections, we have raised some challenges that linguistic anthropology must meet. We now try to articulate the questions that define these challenges. To some extent, the challenges are addressed in the chapters of this volume. But to some extent, these challenges remain open: They should continue to be encountered and explored for years to come.

1.2.1 What is language?

Linguistic anthropology cannot be seriously undertaken without a clear idea of the ontology of language and a full command of the formal and technical aspects of scientific approaches to language. We are dealing with a phenomenon that is unique in the animal world. Language is exceedingly complex, and the details of this complexity matter deeply for understanding how language defines us. When we refer to "language," we cannot mean animal communication more generally – though of course language is one form of animal communication – nor can we mean to include metaphors, as in "body language," "the language of dance," or "the language of the bees." The properties of human language show beyond doubt that it is unique.

For example, to cite classic structuralist criteria, there is the *double articulation* or *duality of patterning* that links a generative phonological system to a generative semantico-syntactic system (Hockett 1960, Martinet 1980); there is the *generative capacity* that arises from paradigmatic relations in combination with syntagmatic relations, and the *hierarchical/recursive properties* of constituency (Bloomfield 1933, Harris 1951); there is the *displacement* by which speech events can be decoupled from narrated events and other non-immediate, including imagined, states of affairs (Jakobson 1990b); and of course, there is the *referential capacity* by which we can thematize entities and assert things about them in ways that are relatively truth-conditioned; and so on (cf. Hockett 1960, Vygotsky 1962, 1978, Halliday and Hasan 1976, Goffman 1981, Chafe 1994).

A different kind of definitive criterion for language has been found in comparative research on the non-language-possessing creatures most close to us – that is, human infants and non-human primates – to see what they lack that language users have. This criterion is a form of uniquely human social cognition known as *shared intentionality* (Tomasello 2006, 2008, Tomasello *et al.* 2005; cf. Astington 2006), a psychological capacity that allows us to achieve the primitive prerequisite for making reference in language, namely the joint attentional behavior that underlies the use of the pointing gesture. This is not merely a matter of looking where someone is pointing, but rather of the very ability to point such that another will look. This, Tomasello argues, is the definitive property of human cognition for language, and the thing from which all else in language follows (see Tomasello 2008; cf. this volume, Chapters 15 and 16, Moore and Dunham 1995, Sperber and Wilson 1995, Kita 2003, Enfield and Levinson 2006).

A last line of work on the definitive properties of language we want to note here comes from the rationalist tradition of generative linguistics, which in its most radical recent form defines language with exclusive reference to the basic property that Humboldt (1988) famously observed – language allows infinite expression from finite means – filtered by the idea that the only thing of interest is the operation of this system in the mind. The "externalization" of language – both in the sense of the motoric/perceptual/inferential processes involved in language production and comprehension, and in the more general sense of communication and the pursuit of goals in social interaction – is seen as an irrelevant distraction (see Chomsky 2011, Berwick et al. 2013). The latter stance, in particular, has alienated this approach from most research that would characterize itself as connected in any way to anthropology. But aside from the most radical versions of generative work, there is nevertheless plenty of useful work being done on linguistic structure within such frameworks broadly understood (Foley and Van Valin 1984, Van Valin and La Polla 1997, Talmy 2000, Bresnan 2001, Jackendoff 2002).

Whatever one's convictions are with respect to the uniquely distinguishing properties of language, where these properties come from, and what follows from them, when we pay serious attention to language as a domain of study, this demands that we draw on pretty much all of the fundamental questions and findings of the discipline of linguistics: from phonetics and phonology, to morphology and syntax, to semantics and pragmatics, including the psychology and typology of all these. Together, these properties of language give rise to extraordinarily complex, even baroque, systems that present formidable descriptive, analytic, and conceptual challenges. Attempts to assess their significance for human affairs without understanding their details are unlikely to succeed. As Dixon forcefully states in Chapter 2 of this handbook, a command of the technicalities of language and its description is indispensable to any work that purports to use the study of language as a means to its ends.

1.2.2 How is language related to the special properties of the human mind?

One of the central themes of research on what makes us human is the question of mind. There is no general consensus on what our minds are like, but most would agree that they would not be this way if it were not for language. (And, conversely, language would not be this way, and indeed would not exist, were it not for our kind of mind – see below.) Let us now note some of the many connections between the two.[1]

According to a set of what might be termed *rationalist* perspectives on language and mind, conceptual categories of thought are in some sense inborn, given to us as members of the human species, and thus universal, and relatively independent of influence from individual languages (proposals differ widely in kind, from Descartes to Chomsky, Pinker, Jackendoff, Lakoff, Talmy, and Wierzbicka, among many others). This can mean a lot of things, from the possession of abstract mental devices such as the "merge" operation proposed by Chomsky to underlie the syntax of all constructions in all languages (Chomsky 1995, Hauser *et al.* 2002, Berwick *et al.* 2013), to the pan-mammalian prelinguistic cognition that underlies the basic subject–predicate or topic–comment structure of propositions (Hurford 2003, 2007, 2012), to inborn concepts ranging from the rich and non-decomposable meanings proposed by Fodor (1975, 1998) to proposed semantically general and universal primitive concepts out of which language-specific meanings are argued to be composed (Jackendoff 1983, 2002, Wierzbicka 1996). Finally, there are proposals for universal principles of cognition that underlie the interpretation of utterances in communicative contexts, via generic principles of inference that use simple heuristics grounded in natural meaning (Grice 1989, Levinson 1983, 2000, Sperber and Wilson 1995).

These so-called rationalist positions are often contrasted with versions of a *relativist* position (though they are not always incompatible with linguistic relativity; see for example Wierzbicka 1992; see also Chapter 29 in this handbook by Kockelman on artificial languages, examining the origins of, and to some extent the problems with, this rationalist/relativist distinction). Lines of work on *linguistic relativity* have explored the idea that some conceptual categories or patterns of thought are given by or shaped by specific languages, and thus can vary across human groups. We speak of linguistic relativity when a person's knowledge or usage of a specific language influences the person's (cultural) cognition. The idea is that the language a person speaks can contribute in non-trivial ways to how that person thinks and/or behaves. On one interpretation of this, our patterns of thought and behavior are shaped by the fact that we possess language in the most general sense – i.e., that we are language-possessing creatures (Wierzbicka 1989, Lucy 1992; Tomasello and Call 1997). But most work is concerned with effects of knowing or using *a* language, as opposed to other languages – e.g., cognitive effects of being a Hopi speaker as opposed to being an English speaker (Sapir 1949; Brown and Lenneberg 1954, Whorf 1956; Lucy 1992, cf. Gumperz and Levinson 1996, Boroditsky 2000, 2001, Gentner and Goldin-Meadow 2003, Majid *et al.* 2004).

One domain of relativity effects, known as *thinking for speaking*, involves a direct online influence of language on thought and action (Boas 1911;

Slobin 1996), in the sense that the language one speaks can have a definable effect on the way in which one thinks or acts, where this thinking or acting has to do with the planning and production of language itself. For example, speakers of a certain language might be required to distinguish between grammatical marking for singular versus plural, and, accordingly, these speakers are more likely to notice whether entities in a scene are singular or plural. Another domain of relativity in psychological processing is suggested by research in cognitive psychology on *overshadowing* effects from language (Schooler and Engstler-Schooler 1990). This is where linguistic labeling can influence cognitive processes like memory and perceptual judgments. If you witness a collision between two vehicles, your memory of the scene can be biased depending on the words chosen to describe it – e.g., English *bumping into* versus *crashing into* (Loftus and Palmer 1974). The point of interest here is that the distinction between *bump* and *crash* happens to be made in the English language but not in other languages. This leads to the prediction that if languages have markedly distinct semantic systems – which we know to be the case – then such influences should give rise to linguistic relativity effects.

These effects of linguistic categorization are the subject of a significant line of work in comparative psychology and cognitive anthropology that is grounded in the developmental psychological research on the acquisition of linguistic and conceptual categories carried out by Roger Brown (1958a, 1958b). Brown's impact was far-reaching, with seminal research on linguistic categorization in semantic domains including color, basic-level categorization, and pronouns (see Pinker 1998). The implications of Brown's work on linguistic characterization were more famously developed by his student Eleanor Rosch (1978), among many others since, who applied the ideas to indigenous knowledge and categorization of the natural world. This opened up a range of debates about whether tendencies of such categorization are grounded in universal properties of perception and cognition, versus locally specific principles of utility and preference (cf. Berlin 1992 versus Hunn 1982, cf. Enfield in press). Brown's original observations about referential formulation were explicitly instrumentalist. His idea was that semantic categories emerge from communicatively practical needs, ultimately being the way they are because they have been selected by their efficacy in achieving ends in social coordination (Brown 1958a, Vygotsky 1962, cf. Clark 1996), thus hinting more at the possibility of relativity in the conceptual/semantic structure of languages.

A final example of a type of linguistic relativity effect is related to the use of language in the flow of social interaction. Languages provide different lexico-syntactic resources for formulating speech acts (Sidnell and Enfield 2012 and Chapter 17 of this volume). These different resources can have different *collateral effects* on the kinds of speech acts that can be produced, whereby speech acts in different languages will differ in terms of the kinds of normatively constrained responses that can or should be produced within the context of conversation. Note that this does not merely mean that different communities conventionalize different speech acts. The kind of relativity proposed here is not merely about the main business of a given speech act, but also about the interactional side-effects of the language-specific resources through which the social business is carried out (see Sidnell and Enfield 2012).

Linguistic relativity raises the question of causality. What leads to what? A range of work on language and mind has noticed correlations between relations in language systems, and has argued or implied that these correlations in publicly shared and thus collective systems are caused by psychological biases in individual agents. Table 1.1 lists a few sample claims of such correlations, where each correlation implies a causal relation between psychological or behavioral processes and synchronic structures.

Correlations among features and elements of language systems such as those shown here are sometimes assumed to be the result of cognitive biases (Hawkins 2004, 2011). The Greenbergian correlations are often said to arise from the preference for a kind of "harmony" that comes from having head-modifier structures aligned the same way in a language system. In his account of grammatical change by *drift*, Sapir (1921) argued that grammatical paradigms tend towards balance, thus avoiding the "psychological shakiness" that out-of-balance paradigms may cause. Similarly,

Table 1.1 Some observed correlations between relations in language systems, where causality is proposed or implied

Relation A	Correlates with Relation B	Example references
Some words are shorter than others	Those words are more frequently used than others	Zipf 1935, 1949
Some words change slower than others	Those words are more frequently used than others	Pagel *et al.* 2007
Some words are shorter than others	Those words are less informative than others	Piantadosi *et al.* 2011
Verbs come after their objects	Adpositions come after their nouns	Greenberg 1966
Speakers of Lg A attend to and notice plurality of entities, speakers of B don't	Plurality is obligatorily marked in the grammar of A, not in B	Slobin 1996
Speakers of Lg A make certain categorization decisions, speakers of B don't	Certain semantic categories are structured differently in Lg A than in B	Whorf 1956, Lucy 1992
Meanings that are grounded in a cultural value V of speakers of Lg A are encoded in linguistic structure/practice X in A	Meanings that are grounded in V of speakers of Lg A are also encoded in linguistic structures/practices Y, Z, etc. in A	Hale 1986, Wierzbicka 1992
Speech act X is formulated using interrogative syntax in Lg A, not in B	Normative response to speech act X is formulated as an "answer to a question" in Lg A, not in B	Sidnell and Enfield 2012

accounts of the correlations between frequency and length of items invoke cognitive preferences of individual agents (such as the preference for minimizing effort where possible) and relate these to formal features of community-wide systems. The issue of explicating causal connections between relations such as those listed in Table 1.1 is taken up further in Enfield's Chapter 13.

To finish this section, let us mention work that focuses on the implications of a causal account of linguistic transmission, given that the human mind is the niche in which language is propagated and to which language systems come to be adapted (Boyd and Richerson 1985, 2005, Chater and Christiansen 2010, Christiansen and Chater 2008, Enfield 2003, Kirby 2013, Kirby et al. 2008, Smith and Wonnacott 2010). After many generations, the forms of language that propagate best in populations will be the ones that are best fitted to our psychology; because, for example, the most easily learnt structures will – by definition – be more easily learnt than others, and will, all things being equal, be more likely to be adopted and thus become conventionalized at the population level. We noted at the beginning of this section the possibility that our minds would not be this way if it were not for language and the way it is. The work just cited suggests a reversal: Language would not be this way were it not for the way our minds are.

1.2.3 How is language related to the structures and processes of society and social life?

Just as language makes possible distinct forms of cognition, so it makes possible distinct forms of social arrangement. One proposal along these lines has been developed by John Searle (e.g., 1969, 2010) in his elaboration of some basic ideas coming out of the analytic tradition in philosophy, especially from the work of Austin (1962) and Anscombe (1957); though also traceable to Maine 2002 (1861) and Mead (1934), who made similar claims but in different frames. As Searle notes, for humans, shared intentionality extends well beyond singular acts of reference. In combination with the semantico-syntactic properties of any human language, shared intentionality allows for declarative acts by which we "impose functions on objects and people where the objects and the people cannot perform the functions solely in virtue of their physical structure" (2010: 7). Thus a person can come to be the President of the United States. A delimited area of the earth's surface can come to be the United States of America. The age of 21 years can come to be the legal drinking age, and so on. And, to each of these status functions are attached deontic powers: "rights, duties, obligations, requirements, permissions, authorizations, entitlements, and so on." In short, these status functions constitute a basis for the normative framework of institutional reality that is the human social world (Linton 1936, Garfinkel 1967, Heritage 1984, Kockelman 2006, 2013, Enfield 2013).

Searle's analysis is powerful and elegant but ultimately static. It deals best with structure rather than practice and process, and thus handles more explicit modes of role-recruitment and status regimentation. Searle's vision of the linguistic underpinning of society, itself really a wedding of Austin's theory of performativity and Hobbes' understanding of sovereignty, needs to be complemented by a vision that emphasizes verbal activity and social interaction. As Goffman famously argued (1963, 1964, 1976, 1981; following Mead 1934), social interaction is both an institution of its own and that which underlies all the rest. The basic sense in which this is the case is described in the chapter by Sidnell in this volume. Talk-in-interaction provides for a distinctive form of human intersubjectivity, one that builds upon specific properties of human language described above such as reference, semanticity, discreteness, reportability, and so on. The very fact that an utterance can be repeated and/or reported provides for a special kind of accountability that is surely unique in the animal world. If we think of social interaction as a dynamic unfolding of social relations (between speaker and hearer, story-teller and audience, etc.) we can see that the relevant types of social relations made possible are unique to humans, and are only made manifest through particular uses of language.

There is a more elaborate way in which to think of this language–society dependency. As anthropologists such as Evans-Pritchard, Malinowski, and Gluckman point out, specific verbal activities, uses of language – such as gossip, cross-examination, lecturing, and praise-singing – support and underwrite particular social relations and structures at higher levels. Azande social relations are built upon a set of practices for making accusations, for consulting an oracle, and so on (Evans-Pritchard 1937). Social relations among the Nuer, and anywhere else that anthropologists have studied, are supported by specific forms of address and self-reference (Sidnell and Shohet 2013). Further examples abound.

Much of human social reality (and all of what Searle calls institutional reality) is constituted through language but perhaps more importantly all of it rests upon a foundation of talk. A key idea here is *normative accountability*. Searle's notion of deontic powers gets at only one aspect of this. For whatever institutionally defined role a speaker (or hearer) may inhabit, there are norms or expectations that govern it, which means that a person's actions *as president* (or mother, or professor, or vegan etc.) can be discussed and evaluated as good, bad, fitting, inappropriate, adequate, problematic, and so on. That is, the whole edifice of institutional reality that Searle describes (the logical structure of what he describes) is supported by talk about it. It is important to understand the breadth of this kind of account: the relevant statuses that define normative accountability in institutionalized social relations run the gamut from permanent and long-term statuses (husband, Dutch, etc.) to more transitory statuses (acquaintance, friend, close friend), to highly fleeting but still normatively and morally binding statuses such as being the one who has just been asked a question. Any person who inhabits a status, at any of these scales, must orient to the possibility, indeed probability, that their conduct as an incumbent of that status will be evaluated, assessed, critiqued, commended, praised, etc. Thus accountability exerts both a projective and a retrospective force. People feel its power both as an after-effect of conduct, and in their anticipation of such effects. One manifestation of this is seen in speakers' explicit accounting for their behavior: when a speaker says, for instance, "Need more ice" as she gets up from the table and thus exits momentarily from the conversation taking place, she is accounting for her departure and thereby encouraging others not to read into her conduct unwanted inferences, e.g., that she was insulted, bored, or embarrassed by what was just said (see Goodwin 1987 on this case).

Now clearly language is central in all this. Its unique properties of, for instance, displacement and reference are what allow for the description and, through this, public assessment of conduct. These same properties make it possible to "narrate" one's conduct (e.g., with "Need more ice") in such a way as to guide its interpretation, and thus to account for it. Examples like this show that language is a tool of accountability. But crucially, language is also often the *object* of accountability. Just as we may narrate what is being done in order to allow others to make sense of it, so we may narrate what is *said*: hence, the utility of our linguistic resources for describing speech acts, and thus for casting a single speech event in different ways (cf. "He *told* me about that," "He *complained* to me about that," "He *informed* me of that"). So, conduct accomplished through language – in a word, *talk* – has properties that make it the object of a special kind of accountability (and flexibility, to invoke the other side of the coin of agency). Features that Hockett described as discreteness and semanticity (which, when understood within a relational totality, Saussure described in terms of *identity*) allow utterances to be repeated and reported, and thus make them available as targets for accountability. Moreover, as Austin noted, linguistic acts are decomposable in special ways by virtue of their specifically linguistic character, and as such can be talked about in ways that are at least more difficult, if not impossible, for other forms of conduct. Thus, we can describe the way someone gestured but not its referential meaning or locutionary force. The reflexive, meta-semiotic features of language and talk thus open up unique possibilities for highly complex forms of social accountability and, as a result, for richer and more sophisticated social processes than anything else known in the animal world.

1.2.4 How is language related to the knowledge, values, and practices of culture?

Obviously, to even pose the question as to whether language and culture are related, there must be a sense in which the two can be distinguished. If we define language technically as a set of terms, rules, and principles for expressing propositions, then language remains distinct from culture in the sense of a complex of knowledge, values, technologies, and practices that coexist with language and its usage.

A way to look at the language–culture relation is to examine how the grammatical structures and sub-systems of different languages encode semantic distinctions that appear to correlate with special cultural concerns of the language's speakers. Hale (1986), for example, argued that in the culture of those who speak the Warlpiri language of Central Australia, there are two "fundamental themes in Warlpiri philosophy": the *eternal logic* (the logic of "cyclical perpetuity, or unbroken circles," including themes such as the "persistence of entities through transformation" and the "unity of the actual and the potential") and the *logic of complementarity* (or "the unity of the opposites"). Hale related these two themes to a number of lexico-grammatical features of the Warlpiri language. Wierzbicka (1992) argues that in the Russian language, a cultural theme of *fatalism* is manifest not only in lexicon and idioms but also in morphosyntax, especially in the form of an array of impersonal constructions. Further studies (see for example Simpson 2002 and other chapters in Enfield 2002a, Evans 2003) argue for links between culture and language structure, typically implying cause from culture on language. Given how easily and how often such language–culture links are made, it's important to tread with care around the multiple ways that specifiable domains in linguistic and cultural systems – grammatical category, discourse practice, cognitive frame, and cultural value, say – may mediate each other (see Kockelman 2010 for case studies). It is easy to propose links, but it is exceedingly difficult to conclusively establish them. One has to control enough data in the relevant domains, isolate them in the necessary ways, and track influences from one to the other on various timescales, while (a) being causally explicit about the linking mechanisms involved (see Enfield 2002b:15 and Chapter 13 of this volume), (b) avoiding essentialization, and (c) avoiding the elision of domains and patterns that happen not to be the point of focus, but which in fact matter crucially to the story.

There are ways in which language can be considered as a phenomenon of culture, thus blurring the assumed distinction between the two. Both language and culture are historically cumulative and locally conventional sets of behaviors that are emblematic of commonality, and of difference, among human groups. From a Lévi-Straussian perspective, culture is just like language understood in structuralist terms: arbitrary, abstract, semiotic, relational, paradigmatic, synchronic. Or from a Geertzian perspective, both language and culture are complicated and mutually constitutive ensembles of practices, conventions, values, tools, and so forth. Many sociocultural anthropologists see things in this latter way, i.e., culture not as structure but as webs of signification, and so see culture as inherently semiotic, and language as just one particularly important, and closely related, semiotic system.

So, different ways of framing the language–culture relation are possible. Framed in one way, language and culture are distinct, framed in another way they are the same, or at least part of the same larger thing. But, as is clear to anyone who has looked, it's not possible to neatly separate the two, nor can they be satisfactorily lumped together as one. Their complex relationship has been the topic of abundant research, and a central topic in linguistic anthropology in the narrow sense. To take one prominent example, Silverstein (1976) grappled with the relationship in a way that has had lasting consequences for lines of work that have been undertaken since in the subdiscipline:

> At one level, language has long served anthropologists as a kind of exemplar for the nature of things cultural. It seems to display these "cultural" properties with clarity in the tangible medium of articulate phonetic speech. Thus, and at another level, could the analytic lessons of linguistics be transferred analogically to other social behavior, giving a kind of structuralized anthropology, or, more remarkably, could the actual linguistic (especially lexicographic) structures of language be called culture. I will be developing the argument that this received point of view is essentially wrong. That aspect of language which has traditionally been analyzed by linguists, and has served as model, is just the part that is functionally unique among the phenomena of culture. Hence the structural characteristics of language in this traditional view cannot really serve as a model for other aspects of culture, nor can the method of analysis. Further, linguistic (or lexicographical) structures that emerge from the traditional grammatical analysis must of necessity bear a problematic, rather than isomorphic, relationship to the structure of culture.

So, just as culture clearly cannot be simplified, neither can language, let alone the question of culture–language relations. Rather than taking the approach "Here is language, there is culture, how might they relate?," we could ask: Here is a radically complex and irreducible relational ensemble of human practices, values, institutions, instruments, and affordances; how is it that humans so easily, and often so erroneously, bound off parts of it as autonomous domains to be studied as such? And, how can we, as scholars, identify other modes of consequential relationality, emergent on other scales, that cross-cut the usual claims?

We finish this section with reference to a conception of the relation between language and culture that focuses on social action. This is expressed in the following passage from Malinowski's masterpiece of intuitive linguistics, *Coral Gardens and Their Magic* (1935:7):

> (T)here is nothing more dangerous than to imagine that language is a process running parallel and exactly corresponding to mental process, and that the function of language is to reflect or to duplicate the mental reality of man in a secondary flow of verbal equivalents.

> The fact is that the main function of language is not to express thought, not to duplicate mental processes, but rather to play an active, pragmatic part in human behavior. Thus in its primary function it is one of the chief cultural forces and an adjunct to bodily activities. Indeed, it is an indispensable ingredient of all concerted human action.

The key idea here is that language is as much a mode of action as it is an instrument of reflection. The remarkable and important propositional (i.e., referential, predicational) function of language – its capacity to serve as a symbolic system that purports to reflect a world out there – has often been treated as the locus of human culture in language whether in the form of narratives, accounts provided in response to an interviewer's question, or as a structure that replicates or manifests culture in its purest form. But in fact this is what makes language unique with respect to all other human capacities (see the Silverstein quote above; and see, in particular, Jakobson's 1990a and 1990b seminal statements). If we want to understand language as a part of culture, Malinowski suggests, we need to see it for what it is – a vehicle of action in the sociocultural world.

1.3 Conclusion

Contributors to this book include scholars who take their linguistics as seriously as their anthropology; scholars from anthropology who do not belong to the official subdiscipline of *linguistic* anthropology, but to other subdisciplines such as biological anthropology, archaeology, and cultural anthropology; scholars who use methods far beyond ethnography and descriptive linguistics; scholars who study processes far beyond the historical and cultural, bringing ontogenetic, phylogenetic, and enchronic dynamics into view; scholars from sister disciplines such as sociolinguistics and cousin disciplines such as conversation analysis; and scholars with one foot in linguistics and another in a discipline related to, but not part of, anthropology – psychology, philosophy, computer science, biology, and beyond. This breadth, we feel, is a key quality of what is offered in this book. But it also makes the book difficult to summarize, due to precisely the heterogeneity and richness of the contributions. Luckily, we think, the contributions – both individually and as a set – speak for themselves.

Our way of organizing the book has been to group the chapters into five parts, as follows. Part I focuses on aspects of language as a formal and functional system; Part II on processes of formation that apply to language in different scales and domains; Part III on language's role in social interaction, and the intersubjectivity required; Part IV on language in communities and their sociocultural practices; and Part V surveys language from the perspective of some specific disciplinary perspectives. In this introductory chapter, we have not previewed the chapters individually, as this is done in the brief chapters that we have included at the beginning of each Part. Our goal in these introductory remarks has been to provide some framing for a handbook that is wide-ranging, that incorporates diverse perspectives, and that might be taken as non-canonical with respect to the subdisciplinary tradition often associated with the term used in our title. Together, we think, the chapters can be seen to constitute some central elements of an anthropology of language but they are not all obviously representative of "linguistic anthropology" as the term is sometimes understood. This is what we felt would be the most useful contribution from a new handbook.

We are delighted to present this collection of new essays and reviews on the study of humankind through the lens of language. Each of the chapters helps build the case for an anthropology of language that explains its role in defining our species. And each chapter does so from a different perspective, spanning disciplines from biology to linguistics to philosophy to sociology, and across the fields of anthropology proper. This is as it should be if we are to have any chance of solving the highly diverse puzzles that language presents. We hope that this contribution, while modest, will point to fruitful new avenues and connections in the anthropology of language.

Note

1. We concentrate in this section on links with that aspect of mind that might be called *cognition*, and we acknowledge here that *mind* has far broader reference, also encompassing intentional states, beliefs, desires, ethnopsychology, affect and emotion, selfhood, and more; cf. Shweder and LeVine (1984), Holland and Quinn (1987), Stigler, Shweder, and Herdt (1990), Schwartz, White, and Lutz (1992), Strauss and Quinn (1997), Kockelman (2010, 2013).

References

Agha, Asif. 2007. *Language and Social Relations*. Cambridge: Cambridge University Press.

Ahearn, Laura M. 2011. *Living Language: An Introduction to Linguistic Anthropology*. Malden, MA: Wiley-Blackwell.

Anscombe, Gertrude Elizabeth Margaret. 1957. *Intention*. Cambridge, MA: Harvard University Press.

Astington, Janet W. 2006. The Developmental Interdependence of Theory of Mind and Language. In *Roots of Human Sociality: Culture, Cognition, and Interaction*, ed. N. J. Enfield and Stephen C. Levinson, 179–206. Oxford: Berg.

Austin, J. L. 1962. *How to Do Things with Words*. Cambridge, MA: Harvard University Press.

Bauman, Richard, and Joel Sherzer. 1974. *Explorations in the Ethnography of Speaking*. Cambridge: Cambridge University Press.

Berlin, Brent. 1992. *Ethnobiological Classification: Principles of Categorization of Plants and Animals in Traditional Societies*. Princeton, NJ: Princeton University Press.

Berwick, Robert C., Angela D. Friederici, Noam Chomsky, and Johan J. Bolhuis. 2013. Evolution, Brain, and the Nature of Language. *Trends in Cognitive Sciences* 17: 89–98.

Bloomfield, Leonard. 1933. *Language*. New York: Holt.

Blount, Ben G., ed. 1995. *Language, Culture, and Society: A Book of Readings*. Prospect Heights, IL: Waveland.

Blum, Susan D., ed. 2012. *Making Sense of Language: Readings in Culture and Communication*. 2nd ed. Oxford: Oxford University Press.

Boas, Franz. 1911. *Handbook of American Indian languages*, Vol. 1. Bureau of American Ethnology, Bulletin 40. Washington: Government Print Office (Smithsonian Institution, Bureau of American Ethnology).

Boroditsky, L. 2000. Metaphoric Structuring: Understanding time through spatial metaphors. *Cognition* 75(1): 1–28.

2001. Does language shape thought? English and Mandarin speakers' conceptions of time. *Cognitive Psychology* 43(1): 1–22.

Bourdieu, Pierre. 1977. *Outline of a Theory of Practice*. Cambridge: Cambridge University Press.

1990. *The Logic of Practice*. Stanford, CA: Stanford University Press.

Boyd, Robert, and Peter J. Richerson. 1985. *Culture and the Evolutionary Process*. Chicago: University of Chicago Press.

2005. *The Origin and Evolution of Cultures*. New York: Oxford University Press.

Brenneis, Donald, and Ronald K. S. Macaulay. 1996. *The Matrix of Language: Contemporary Linguistic Anthropology*. Boulder, CO: Westview.

Bresnan, Joan. 2001. *Lexical-functional Syntax*. London: Routledge.

Brown, Roger. 1958a. How Shall a Thing Be Called? *Psychological Review* 65: 14–21.

1958b. *Words and Things*. Glencoe: The Free Press.

Brown, Roger, and Eric H. Lenneberg. 1954. A Study in Language and Cognition. *Journal of Abnormal and Social Psychology* 49: 454–62.

Chafe, Wallace. 1994. *Discourse, Consciousness, and Time: The Flow and Displacement of Consciousness in Speech and Writing*. Chicago: Chicago University Press.

Chater, Nick, and Morten H. Christiansen. 2010. Language Acquisition Meets Language Evolution. *Cognitive Science* 34 (7): 1131–57. doi:10.1111/j.1551-6709.2009.01049.x.

Chomsky, Noam A. 1995. *The Minimalist Program*. Cambridge, MA: MIT Press.

2011. Language and Other Cognitive Systems: What Is Special About Language? *Language Learning and Development* 7 (4): 263–278. doi:10.1080/15475441.2011.584041.

Christiansen, Morten H., and Nick Chater. 2008. Language as Shaped by the Brain. *Behavioral and Brain Sciences* 31 (5): 489–509.

Clark, Herbert H. 1996. *Using Language*. Cambridge: Cambridge University Press.

Comrie, Bernard. 1989. *Language Universals and Linguistic Typology*, Vol. 2. Chicago: University of Chicago Press.

Croft, William. 2001. *Radical Construction Grammar: Syntactic Theory in Typological Perspective*. Oxford: Oxford University Press.

2003. *Typology and Universals*. 2nd ed. Cambridge: Cambridge University Press.

Dixon, R. M. W. 2010. *Basic Linguistic Theory*. Oxford: Oxford University Press.

Duranti, Alessandro. 1997. *Linguistic Anthropology*. Cambridge: Cambridge University Press.

2001. *Linguistic Anthropology: A Reader*. Malden, MA: Blackwell.

2003. Language as Culture in U.S. Anthropology: Three paradigms. *Current Anthropology* 44(3): 323–47.

2004. *A Companion to Linguistic Anthropology*. London: Blackwell.

Enfield, N. J., ed. 2002a. *Ethnosyntax: Explorations in Culture and Grammar*. Oxford: Oxford University Press.

2002b. Ethnosyntax: Introduction. In *Ethnosyntax: Explorations in Culture and Grammar*, ed. N. J. Enfield, 1–30. Oxford: Oxford University Press.

2002c. Cultural Logic and Syntactic Productivity: Associated Posture Constructions in Lao. In *Ethnosyntax: Explorations in Culture and Grammar*, ed. N. J. Enfield, 231–58. Oxford: Oxford University Press.

2003. *Linguistic Epidemiology*. London: Routledge.

2009. *The Anatomy of Meaning*. Cambridge: Cambridge University Press.

2013. *Relationship Thinking*. Oxford: Oxford University Press.

In press. *The Utility of Meaning: What Words Mean and Why*. Oxford: Oxford University Press.

Enfield, N. J., and Stephen C. Levinson. 2006. *Roots of Human Sociality: Culture, Cognition, and Interaction*. London: Berg.

Evans, Nicholas D. 2003. Context, Culture, and Structuration in the Languages of Australia. *Annual Review of Anthropology* 32: 13–40.

Evans, Nicholas D., and Stephen C. Levinson. 2009. The Myth of Language Universals: Language Diversity and Its Importance for Cognitive Science. *Behavioral and Brain Sciences* 32 (5): 429–48.

Evans-Pritchard, E. E. 1937. *Witchcraft, Oracles and Magic Among the Azande*. Oxford: Oxford University Press.

Fodor, Jerry A. 1975. *The Language of Thought*. Cambridge, MA: Harvard University Press.

1998. *Concepts: Where Cognitive Science Went Wrong*. Oxford: Oxford University Press.

Foley, William A. 1997. *Anthropological Linguistics*. London: Blackwell.
Foley, William A., and Robert D. Van Valin Jr. 1984. *Functional Syntax and Universal Grammar*. Cambridge: Cambridge University Press.
Garfinkel, Harold. 1967. *Studies in Ethnomethodology*. New Jersey: Prentice-Hall.
Gentner, Dedre, and Susan Goldin-Meadow. 2003. *Language in Mind: Advances in the Study of Language and Thought*. Cambridge, MA: MIT Press.
Goffman, Erving. 1963. *Behaviour in Public Places: Notes on the Social Organization of Gatherings*. New York: The Free Press.
——— 1964. The Neglected Situation. *American Anthropologist* 66 (6): 133–6.
——— 1976. Replies and Responses. *Language in Society* 5 (03): 257–313.
——— 1981. *Forms of Talk*. Philadelphia: University of Pennsylvania Press.
Goodwin, Charles. 1987. Unilateral Departure. In *Talk and Social Organisation*, ed. G. Button and J. R. Lee, 206–16. Clevedon, England: Multilingual Matters.
Greenberg, Joseph H. 1966. Some Universals of Grammar with Particular Reference to the Order of Meaningful Elements. In *Universals of Language*, 2nd edition, ed. Joseph H. Greenberg, 73–113. Cambridge, MA: MIT Press.
Grice, H. Paul. 1989. *Studies in the Way of Words*. Cambridge, MA: Harvard University Press.
Gumperz, John J. 1982. *Discourse Strategies*. Cambridge: Cambridge University Press.
Gumperz, John J., and Dell Hymes. 1986. *Directions in Sociolinguistics: The Ethnography of Communication*. London: Basil Blackwell.
Gumperz, John J., and Stephen C. Levinson, eds. 1996. *Rethinking Linguistic Relativity*. Cambridge: Cambridge University Press.
Hale, Kenneth L. 1986. Notes on World View and Semantic Categories: Some Warlpiri Examples. In *Features and Projections*, ed. Pieter Muysken and Henk van Riemsdijk, 233–54. Dordrecht: Foris.
Halliday, Michael A. K., and Ruqaiya Hasan. 1976. *Cohesion in English*. London: Longman.
Hanks, William F. 1990. *Referential Practice: Language and Lived Space Among the Maya*. Chicago: University of Chicago Press.
——— 1996. *Language and Communicative Practices*. Boulder, CO: Westview Press.
——— 2005. Pierre Bourdieu and the Practices of Language. *Annual Review of Anthropology* 34: 67–83.
Harris, Zellig. 1951. *Methods in Structural Linguistics*. Chicago: Chicago University Press.
Hawkins, J. A. 2004. *Efficiency and Complexity in Grammars*. Oxford Linguistics. New York: Oxford University Press.
——— 2011. Processing Efficiency and Complexity in Typological Patterns. In *Oxford Handbook of Language Typology*, ed. J. J. Song, 206–26. New York: Oxford University Press.
Hauser, Marc D., Noam A. Chomsky, and W. Tecumseh Fitch. 2002. The Faculty of Language: What Is It, Who Has It, and How Did It Evolve? *Science* 298: 1569–79.

Heritage, John. 1984. *Garfinkel and Ethnomethodology*. Cambridge, MA: Polity Press.
Hockett, Charles F. 1960. The Origin of Speech. *Scientific American* 203: 89–96.
Holland, Dorothy, and Quinn, Naomi, eds. 1987. *Cultural Models in Language and Thought*. Cambridge: Cambridge University Press.
Humboldt, Wilhelm von. 1988. *On Language: The Diversity of Human Language-structure and Its Influence on the Mental Development of Mankind*. Cambridge: Cambridge University Press.
Hunn, Eugene. 1982. The Utilitarian Factor in Folk Biological Classification. *American Anthropologist* 89: 146–9.
Hurford, James R. 2003. The Neural Basis of Predicate-argument Structure. *Behavioral and Brain Sciences* 26 (3): 261–82.
  2007. *The Origins of Meaning*. Oxford: Oxford University Press.
  2012. *The Origins of Grammar*. Oxford: Oxford University Press.
Hymes, Dell H. 1964. *Language in Culture and Society: A Reader in Linguistics and Anthropology*. New York: Harper and Row.
Jackendoff, Ray. 1983. *Semantics and Cognition*. Cambridge, MA: MIT Press.
  2002. *Foundations of Language: Brain, Meaning, Grammar, Evolution*. New York: Oxford University Press.
Jakobson, Roman. 1990a. The Speech Event and the Functions of Language. In *On Language*, ed. L. R. Waugh and M. Monville, 69–79. Cambridge, MA: Harvard University Press.
  1990b. Shifters and Verbal Categories. In *On Language*, ed. L. R. Waugh and M. Monville-Burston, 386–92. Cambridge, MA: Harvard University Press.
Kirby, Simon. 2013. Transitions – The Evolution of Linguistic Replicators. In *The Language Phenomenon: Human Communication from Milliseconds to Millennia*, ed. P. M. Binder and K. Smith, 121–38. Berlin and Heidelberg: Springer Press.
Kirby, Simon, Hannah Cornish, and Kenny Smith. 2008. Cumulative Cultural Evolution in the Laboratory: An Experimental Approach to the Origins of Structure in Human Language. *Proceedings of The National Academy of Sciences of the USA*. 105(31): 10681–86.
Kita, Sotaro. 2003. *Pointing*. Mahwah, NJ: Erlbaum.
Kockelman, Paul. 2005. The Semiotic Stance. *Semiotica* 157: 233–304.
  2006. Residence in the World: Affordances, Instruments, Actions, Roles, and Identities. *Semiotica* 162 (1–4): 19–71.
  2010. *Language, Culture, and Mind: Natural Constructions and Social Kinds*. Cambridge: Cambridge University Press.
  2013. *Agent, Person, Subject, Self: A Theory of Ontology, Interaction, and Infrastructure*. Oxford: Oxford University Press.
Ladefoged, Peter, and Ian Maddieson. 1996. *The Sounds of the World's Languages*. Oxford: Blackwell.
Levinson, Stephen C. 1983. *Pragmatics*. Cambridge: Cambridge University Press.

2000. *Presumptive Meanings: The Theory of Generalized Conversational Implicature*. Cambridge, MA: MIT Press.

Linton, Ralph. 1936. *The Study of Man: An Introduction*. New York: Appleton-Century-Crofts.

Loftus, Elizabeth F., and John C. Palmer. 1974. Reconstruction of Automobile Destruction: An Example of the Interaction Between Language and Memory. *Journal of Verbal Learning and Verbal Behavior* 13 (5): 585–9.

Lucy, John. 1992. *Language Diversity and Thought: A Reformulation of the Linguistic Relativity Hypothesis*. Cambridge: Cambridge University Press.

1993. *Reflexive Language*. Cambridge: University of Cambridge Press.

Maine, Henry Sumner. 2002 [1861]. *Ancient Law*. New Brunswick, NJ: Transaction.

Majid, A., M. Bowerman, S. Kita, D. B. M. Haun, and S. C. Levinson. 2004. Can Language Restructure Cognition? The case for space. *Trends in Cognitive Sciences* 8(3): 108–14.

Malinowski, Bronislaw. 1935. *Coral Gardens and their Magic*, Vol. 2: *The Language of Magic and Gardening*. London: George Allen and Unwin.

Martinet, André. 1980. *Eléments de linguistique générale*. Paris: Armand Colin.

Mead, George Herbert. 1934. *Mind, Self, and Society*, ed. Charles W. Morris. Chicago: University of Chicago Press.

Moore, C. and Dunham, P. 1995. *Joint Attention: Its Origins and Role in Development*. Mahwah, NJ: Lawrence Erlbaum Associates.

Pagel, Mark, Quentin D. Atkinson, and Andrew Meade. 2007. Frequency of Word-use Predicts Rates of Lexical Evolution Throughout Indo-European History. *Nature* 449: 717–20. doi:10.1038/nature06176.

Piantadosi, S. T., Harry Tily, and Edward Gibson. 2011. Word Lengths Are Optimized for Efficient Communication. *Proceedings of the National Academy of Sciences* 108 (9): 3526.

Pinker, Steven. 1998. Obituary: Roger Brown. *Cognition* 66: 199–213.

Rosch, Eleanor. 1978. Principles of Categorization. In *Cognition and Categorization*, ed. Eleanor Rosch and B. B. Lloyd, 27–48. Hillsdale, NJ: Lawrence Erlbaum.

Sapir, Edward. 1921. *Language: An Introduction to the Study of Speech*. Orlando, FL: Harcourt Brace Jovanovich.

1949. *Selected Writings*. Berkeley: University of California Press.

Schooler, Jonathan W., and Tonya Y. Engstler-Schooler. 1990. Verbal Overshadowing of Visual Memories: Some Things Are Better Left Unsaid. *Cognitive Psychology* 22 (1): 36–71.

Schwartz, Theodore, Geoffrey M., White, and Catherine A. Lutz, eds. 1992. *New Directions in Psychological Anthropology*. Cambridge: Cambridge University Press.

Searle, John R. 1969. *Speech Acts: An Essay in the Philosophy of Language*. Cambridge: Cambridge University Press.

2010. *Making the Social World: The Structure of Human Civilization*. New York: Oxford University Press.

Shweder, Richard A., and Robert A. LeVine, eds. 1984. *Culture Theory: Essays on Mind, Self, and Emotion*. Cambridge: Cambridge University Press.

Sidnell, Jack. 2005. *Talk and Practical Epistemology*. Amsterdam: Benjamins.

2010. *Conversation Analysis: An Introduction*. Chichester, UK: Wiley-Blackwell.

Sidnell, Jack, and N. J. Enfield. 2012. Language Diversity and Social Action. *Current Anthropology* 53 (3): 302–33.

Sidnell, Jack, and Merav Shohet. 2013. The Problem of Peers in Vietnamese Interaction. *Journal of the Royal Anthropological Institute* 19(3): 618–38.

Silverstein, Michael. 1976. Shifters, Linguistic Categories, and Cultural Description. In *Meaning in Anthropology*, ed. K. Basso and H. Selby, 11–55. Albuquerque: University of New Mexico Press.

Silverstein, Michael, and Greg Urban, eds. 1996. *Natural Histories of Discourse*. Chicago: Chicago University Press.

Simpson, Jane. 2002. From Common Ground to Syntactic Construction: Associated Path in Warlpiri. In *Ethnosyntax: Explorations in Grammar and Culture*, ed. N. J. Enfield, 287–308. Oxford: Oxford University Press.

Slobin, Dan. 1996. From 'Thought and Language' to 'Thinking to Speaking'. In *Rethinking Linguistic Relativity*, ed. J. J. Gumperz and Stephen C. Levinson, 70–96. Cambridge: Cambridge University Press.

Smith, Kenny, and Elizabeth Wonnacott. 2010. Eliminating Unpredictable Variation through Iterated Learning. *Cognition* 116: 444–9.

Sperber, Dan, and Deirdre Wilson. 1995. *Relevance: Communication and Cognition*, 2nd ed. Oxford: Blackwell.

Stigler, James W., James A. Shweder, and Gilbert Herdt, eds. 1990. *Cultural Psychology: Essays on Comparative Human Development*. Cambridge: Cambridge University Press.

Strauss, Claudia, and Naomi Quinn. 1997. *A Cognitive Theory of Cultural Meaning*. Cambridge: Cambridge University Press.

Talmy, Leonard. 2000. *Toward a Cognitive Semantics*. 2 vols. Cambridge, MA: MIT Press.

Tomasello, Michael. 2006. Why Don't Apes Point? In *Roots of Human Sociality: Culture, Cognition, and Interaction*, ed. N. J. Enfield and Stephen C. Levinson, 506–24. London: Berg.

2008. *Origins of Human Communication*. Cambridge, MA: MIT Press.

Tomasello, Michael, and Josep Call. 1997. *Primate Cognition*. New York: Oxford University Press.

Tomasello, Michael, Malinda Carpenter, Josep Call, Tanya Behne, and Henrike Moll. 2005. Understanding and Sharing Intentions: The Origins of Cultural Cognition. *Behavioral and Brain Sciences* 28 (5): 664–70.

Van Valin, R. D., and R. J. LaPolla. 1997. *Syntax: Structure, Meaning, and Function*. Cambridge: Cambridge University Press.

Vygotsky, L. S. 1962. *Thought and Language*. Cambridge, MA: MIT Press.

1978. *Mind in Society: The Development of Higher Psychological Processes.* Chapter 6: Interaction between learning and development, 79–91. Cambridge, MA: Harvard University Press.

Whorf, Benjamin Lee. 1956. *Language, Thought, and Reality.* Cambridge, MA: MIT Press.

Wierzbicka, Anna. 1989. Baudouin De Courtenay and the Theory of Linguistic Relativity. In *Jan Niecislaw Baudouin De Courtenay a Lingwistyka Swiatowa*, 51–7. Wroclaw: Ossolineum.

1992. *Semantics, Culture, and Cognition.* New York: Oxford University Press.

1996. *Semantics: Primes and Universals.* Oxford: Oxford University Press.

Zipf, G. K. 1935. *The Psycho-biology of Language.* Boston, MA: Houghton Mifflin.

1949. *Human Behaviour and the Principle of Least Effort.* Cambridge, MA: Addison-Wesley Publishing.

Part I

System and function

N. J. Enfield, Jack Sidnell, and Paul Kockelman

Language is real, students of linguistics are taught, but *languages* are only imagined. Things we call languages – Japanese, for instance – can readily be identified insofar as one might hear a person talking and say "She's speaking Japanese." But as soon as one tries to define the full contents and precise borders of "the Japanese language," one comes up short. No two speakers' idiolects are exactly the same. Still, the idea of a language is a useful way of capturing the obvious fact that when some people talk, you understand it all, whereas with others you get nothing. The idea has political utility as well. If a language can be imagined, it can be an emblem of identity, defining the commonality we have with one group of people, and the contrast between us and some other group. This emblematic function of labels often trumps definable sameness or difference between the way two groups speak. Hence, well-known distinctions such as those between Dutch and Flemish, Thai and Lao, or Serbian and Croatian are not defined by a lack of mutual intelligibility – these pairs of languages are essentially dialects – but have to do with salient distinctions in the political identities of those people who would describe themselves as speakers of one but not the other. None of this means, however, that distinctions between languages are wholly arbitrary or imagined. The limits are obvious. If someone from a remote village of the Philippines were dropped into a remote village of the Gambia, it's unlikely they would be able to use words to communicate.

Professional descriptive linguists have long shown that it is possible to supply comprehensive – though never *fully* comprehensive – descriptions of the vocabularies and sets of grammatical rules that people in a community will have at their common disposal. The great sets of thousands of words and hundreds of rules and norms that define an individual's linguistic and communicative competence are not only specifiable but cohere in an almost tangible sense. **Dixon**'s chapter – a micro-précis of his recent three-volume set, *Basic Linguistic Theory* – makes the case that a commonsense but nevertheless technical set of analytic linguistic tools is necessary and sufficient for the descriptive and analytic work that linguistics must deliver, and that anthropological work on language is so deeply dependent on. Just as a linguist "must invoke a fair dose of anthropology," so must an anthropologist "harness the essentials of linguistics." The days when this went without saying are long gone.

Among the seldom-questioned commitments of linguistics is the idea that each language has a "holistic structure," as Dixon terms it. This idea that languages hang together as systems is fundamental to descriptive and comparative linguistics. But if it is true that "languages" are merely imagined, then we have a paradox. Are language systems real or not? Or can we only study the items – including the relations – out of which the systems are built? It is the same problem we find for culture: Can we speak about cultures as whole systems or only about the *elements* that we recognize as cultural in nature? The **Enfield** chapter in this Part addresses this *item/system problem*, framed in terms of a *transmission criterion* that all of language and culture has to meet. This criterion states that if something in language and culture is real, it must have been successfully transmitted within a human population. The chapter argues that once we define the notion of cultural/linguistic item in the right way – that is, as a kind of relation to context, rather than as a kind of thing – then the holistic structures we recognize as linguistic and cultural systems can emerge. There must, of course, be causal explanations for this emergence (see the chapters in Part II on the underlying processes of linguistic formations in multiple distinct frames).

The work that linguists do, and the intuitions that many language users themselves have, suggest that we can be fairly confident about what qualifies as a bit of language and what doesn't. But a healthy line of research, going back to pioneers like David Efron and Ray Birdwhistell, among others, and over recent years most visibly represented by authors such as Adam Kendon, David McNeill, Charles Goodwin, and Susan Goldin-Meadow, forces us to confront the question of just where the limits of language lie. People who talk will at some point also move their bodies and hands with expressive intent. These expressive movements are clearly connected to language. But are they part of language? When we nod our heads when speaking English in conversation, is our nodding part of the English language? We are still far from answering this question, but in recent years we have learnt a great deal about the connections between gesture and (the rest of) language. **Goldin-Meadow**'s chapter reviews some of the ways in which movements of the hands serve communicative and conceptual functions when they occur alongside speech. This naturally leads us to consider situations in which visible movements of the hands and the rest of the body are the *sole* modality in which language emerges. Goldin-Meadow surveys the case of children who are born deaf and who do not have the option of using the audible channel (see also the chapter in Part II by **Sandler et al.**), demonstrating what she calls the resilience of language. Language, it seems, cannot be prevented from fully flowering, even when its normally dominant modality is unavailable.

Systematic comparative research on the world's linguistic systems has yet to incorporate serious attention to such "paralinguistic" elements as hand gestures. But within the scope of what is traditionally included in reference grammars, linguistic typology has made significant progress. **Bickel**'s chapter assesses the state of the art in research on diversity and universals in languages worldwide. He reviews the major categories of linguistic systems – phonology, morphology, syntax, semantics – and details great diversity across languages. He also clears some of the fog around claims to universality, by, for example, clarifying the distinction between absolute versus statistical universals. An important caution he gives is not to lean too heavily on our comparative categories, as they are not able to carry much weight. They start out as little more than practical working assumptions to facilitate metalinguistic description, and so the common practice of then using them as language-independent points for direct comparison across languages is seldom warranted.

We can describe and compare the richness and complexity of linguistic systems, but then we have to wonder why they are that way. Each language has evolved through enormous processes of language transmission and change in historical populations through selection on the basis of communicative success. At the centre of those processes are the *functions* to which language is put in the course of social interaction. What are these functions? As **Silverstein** explains in his chapter, a socially pragmatic perspective on language contrasts with the denotational model that has tended to dominate in the culture of Western scholarship. "Language," he writes, "manifests a tension between [1] what is encompassed in a denotational model so central to the intuitions of both laypersons and professional students of language in the West, and [2] discourse as practice (or 'praxis') in a sociologically or socioculturally informed perspective." He suggests a resolution of this tension: "These two functionalities engage reciprocally via [3] several planes of metapragmatic reflexivity ... This tension can be displayed and examined by developing a (meta-)semiotic from generally Peircean principles." A towering figure in modern linguistic anthropology, Silverstein articulates some of the key concerns of that tradition, and surveys some of the key theorists, with a particular focus on denotation as a species of reflexive praxis from a semiotic and social stance.

Language function in a broad sense is the focus of a cluster of kindred lines of work under the rubric of *functionalist linguistics*, reviewed in the chapter by **Thompson and Couper-Kuhlen**. The authors trace functionalist linguistics to a range of influences, including those of American anthropologists between the wars who were documenting and analyzing American languages. From around the mid 1970s especially, evidence mounted that aspects of language systems could be explained by appealing to the communicative and social functions of language. The same sorts of functions were argued to explain generalizations that were being made about language on the basis of typological comparison. This was in sharp contrast to a widespread appeal in linguistics to abstract mental devices that had no functional relation to communication, as in the work of Noam Chomsky and many others. The idea that language function determined its form gave rise to a vibrant, and now enduring, community of functionalist researchers. Thompson and Couper-Kuhlen discuss the history of this movement, and survey its literature, before presenting a case study of grammatical *constituency* – a key testing ground for deciding whether abstract categories of grammar are functionally motivated, or whether they are "autonomous." Their conclusion is that synchronically observable grammatical structures are fitted for, and indeed created by, their functions in social interaction (see the **Sidnell and Enfield** chapter in Part III), as a result of causal processes in multiple processual frames, to be taken up in the chapters of Part II.

2
Basics of a language

R. M. W. Dixon

Sometimes one hears anthropologists saying that linguistics is rather hard. Or that it is not relevant. Or else not important.

A lot of what goes under the name of linguistics (so-called "generative" and allied theories) is truly irrelevant. But the real cumulative science of linguistics is absolutely pertinent to any anthropological endeavor. It is not at all difficult, if explained in a straightforward manner (as I attempt to do in this chapter). In essence, an understanding of the basic principles of linguistics – and of how to apply them – is of inestimable benefit to any scholar investigating aspects of social organization.

Linguistics should not be regarded as an alien discipline. Viewed as the scientific study of the social phenomenon called language, linguistics is closely allied to anthropology. In days of yore, one would enroll for a degree in "the anthropological sciences," studying social anthropology, biological anthropology, archaeology, and linguistics.

Social anthropology and linguistics have moved apart, to the detriment of both. A major aim of this volume is to encourage reunification. In this chapter, I will try to show why any decent linguist must invoke a fair dose of anthropology, and that, in order to achieve significant results, an anthropologist should harness the essentials of linguistics.

2.1 What is linguistics?

Linguistics can be regarded as the general science of language, just as mathematics is the general science of number. The principles set forth in pure mathematics are applied to particular problems in physics, astronomy, every kind of engineering, communication theory, economics, actuarial work, and many other ventures. In similar fashion, the principles of general linguistics are applied in philosophy, psychology, literary analysis, translation theory, language teaching, the treatment of communicative disorders, language planning, sociology, anthropology, and more besides.

Linguistics has an extended pedigree, commencing with the work of Indian and Greek grammarians more than two-and-a-half millennia ago. However, during the past half-century there has arisen an aberration, into a cul-de-sac away from the central path of scientific endeavor. This has involved the postulation of a number of competing "formal theories" (many associated with Chomsky and his disciples). Each of these puts forward a number of a priori assertions concerning some limited area of language structure. Their program does not include the formulation of complete grammatical descriptions of languages (nor would any "formal theory" be equal to the task), just the suggestion of a number of "theoretical" insights.

These "formalists" shout loud, often creating the impression that this is it. But their work is of little or no use for the many applications of linguistics summarized just above. The "formal theories" are akin to economic theories, literary theories, and political theories. There are, at any time, several of them, each with its own diehard adherents. Old ones sink into faint memory and newcomers arise – "Theory X is dead, long live Theory Y!"

In fact, that is not all there is. The present chapter focuses on "real linguistics," the cumulative paradigm in terms of which grammars are written, programs of language teaching expounded, and the social role of language examined. In this view, linguistics is a science, just like chemistry or geology. There is *one* scientific theory, in terms of which all practitioners work. In the last couple of decades, this has come to be called "basic linguistic theory." It puts forward a number of parameters, which are available for providing scientific description of a language, its internal structure, and the way in which it is employed within the speech community. A parameter will only be invoked if it is useful in a particular instance. For many languages, it is useful to recognize a distinction between derivation (such as, in English, adding suffix *-en* to adjective *deep*, forming verb *deepen*) and inflection (adding past tense suffix *-ed*, producing *deepened*). But for other languages such a distinction is not appropriate; it would be difficult to apply, and it would explain nothing. So in this instance it is not used. (In marked contrast, "formal theories" demand that each of their components must be identified for every language.)

There is continued feedback between theory and description. A grammatical or sociolinguistic account is framed in terms of the current state of basic linguistic theory. Each description is likely to reveal new insights which may entail refinement of some part of the theory. Basic linguistic theory is thus built up inductively. It summarizes the present state of our understanding of the nature of human language, and also provides a template through which the structure of individual languages can be described and explained.

There is no such thing as a "simple language." Each language has a pretty developed structure, but the areas of complexity vary. (No language is intricate in every possible way; the human brain just wouldn't be able to handle such a degree of complication.) To illustrate this, we can compare English and Fijian.

English has a rich inventory of derivations. There are almost two hundred suffixes and prefixes each of which derives a new word. They may create an adjective from noun or verb (for example, *child-ish*, *migrat-ory*), or a verb from noun or adjective (*class-ify*, *equal-ize*), or a noun from verb or adjective (*admir-ation*, *warm-th*). Many do not change word class, but just add an element of meaning (*extra-terrestrial*, *mis-understand*, *friend-ship*). In contrast, Fijian is relatively destitute of derivational affixes. There are just half-a-dozen (some of which are widely used). For example, from verb *sele* 'cut, slice' is derived noun *i-sele* 'knife'; prefix *'ai-* can be added to any place name to indicate "native of that place," as in *'ai-Suva* 'person from Suva'; and collective prefix *vei-* combines with *'au* 'tree' to form *vei-'au* 'forest'.

Grammatical richness goes in the opposite direction when we look at the marking of possession. Compare corresponding English and Fijian expressions:

(1) Mary's shoulder   *a taba-i Mere*

(2) Mary's tea   *a tii me-i Mere*

(3) Mary's taro   *a dalo 'e-i Mere*

(4) Mary's knife   *a isele we-i Mere*

(5) the tree's branch   *a taba ni 'au*

It will be seen that English has the same construction for all of (1–5), "POSSESSOR's POSSESSED," but Fijian is different in each instance.

Like many other languages, Fijian makes a distinction between inalienable and alienable possession:

(a) A part of a human being's body is inalienably possessed by them. "X's bodypart" is stated as "BODYPART-*i* X," as in (1). (The initial *a* is a kind of article, indicating that the head of the noun phrase is a common noun, here *taba* 'shoulder'.)
(b) Anything which can be given away, or sold, is said to be alienably possessed. The construction to use is:
    POSSESSED CLASSIFIER-*i* POSSESSOR

There are three possibilities for the classifier slot:

- If the "possessed" item is to be drunk, sucked, or licked – use prefix *me-*, as in (2).
- If the "possessed" item is to be eaten, chewed, or smoked – use prefix *'e-*, as in (3).
- If none of these applies – use prefix *we-*, as in (4).

The noun *yaca* is particularly interesting. It functions as 'name' and is then treated as inalienably possessed (just like a body part), and also as 'namesake', being then treated as alienably possessed. We can compare *yaca* 'name', in a construction of type (1), and *yaca* 'namesake' in one of type (4):

a yaca-i Mere 'Mary's name'
a yaca we-i Mere 'Mary's namesake'

The inalienable possession construction is only employed for parts of a human. Noun *taba* is used for "shoulder of a person," in (1), and "branch of a tree," in (5). But, for the latter sense, a different construction must be used; that is, it is not permissible to say **a taba-i 'au* for 'tree's branch'. One has to say "PART *ni* WHOLE," as in (5).

In grammars of Fijian, *ni* is sometimes said to mean 'of', but this is misleading. A better gloss is 'associated with'. For example, *a bilo* ('cup') *ni tii* does not refer to 'a cup of tea'. What it means is 'a teacup'; that is, 'a cup associated with tea'. To ask for a cup of tea one requests *a bilo tii* (with no *ni*) where *bilo* is here functioning as a measure word, indicating how much tea is required.

It will be seen that although Fijian is a little light on derivational affixes, by comparison with English, it makes intricate and revealing distinctions in the area of possession.

2.2 Getting under the skin of a language

A first step is to develop appreciation of the subtleties of a language. Start off in one's home community, extend a little further, and then fully develop this awareness in your chosen field situation.

The English verbs *want* and *wish* have similar meanings. One can say either *John wants to impress* or *John wishes to impress*. What is the difference – perhaps just degree of emphasis? No, it's more than that. Someone might say *I wish that I could have shaken hands with Abraham Lincoln* but not **I want that I could have shaken hands with Abraham Lincoln*. The verb *want* is only used of something which is achievable, and it is restricted to a complement clause introduced by *to*, as in *I want to meet Barack Obama*. There is a more wistful sense associated with *wish*, relating to something that is not possible, and it will then take a complement clause introduced by *that* (see Dixon 2005: 266–7).

Each word has a range of meanings – those of *wish* and *want* overlap, but do not coincide. It is important to realize that a word in one language never has an exact translation equivalent in another language. Consider the verb *esperar* in Spanish. In some contexts it is translated into English by *hope (for)*, in others by *expect*, in yet others by *wait (for)*. Looking from the opposite direction, English verb *wait* may be translated into Spanish by *esperar*, or by *servir* (in the sense 'wait on table').

When commencing fieldwork on the Australian language Dyirbal (in 1963), I noticed verb *jilwan* being used to refer to the action of kicking and wrote "kick" against it. What I should have done was enquire about all the situations in which *jilwan* might be used. Much later, I heard the action of shoving someone with the knee also being described by *jilwan*. A proper characterization of this verb is: 'deliver a sharp blow with a rounded protuberance in the lower part of the body'. (A different verb, *bijin*, is used for 'punch with the fist'.)

Every language has a certain number of homonyms – words which are pronounced the same, or written the same (or both), but have different meanings. An example from English is *ear*, the organ of hearing, and *ear*, seed-bearing part of a cereal plant (as in *ear of corn*). These have distinct genetic origins – the first developed from proto-Indo-European *ous-* or *aus-* 'ear', via *auzan* and then *ēare* in Old English, and the second from *ak-* 'sharp' in proto-Indo-European, via *ahuz* and then *ēar* in Old English. Phonological change down the ages has produced identical forms. But these are separate words, and must be distinguished.

Some languages have just a few homonyms (Dyirbal is like this). In contrast, Jarawara – a language spoken in the Amazonian jungle, on which I did immersion fieldwork over a period of a dozen years – has absolutely oodles of them. There are two verbs with the form *-ita-*, one meaning 'sit, stay, be located' and the other 'pierce, spear'. And there are three verbs *saa -na-*: 'vomit', 'let go of, stop fighting', and 'shoot with an arrow'. In a language like this, it can be a tricky matter to decide whether one is dealing with a single verb which has a range of related meanings, or with homonyms.

I encountered several examples of the verb *hasi -na-*. It can mean 'have a rest', or 'an animal escapes when being hunted', or 'breathe', or 'be left over (food at the end of a meal)'. I read out these sentences to several consultants, separately. Every one of them assured me that it was the same verb each time. After a bit of thinking, it became apparent that the basic meaning of *hasi -na-* is 'breathe'. The verb is used for 'have a rest', since one is then just breathing (doing nothing else). When an animal escapes an arrow fired at it, it is still breathing; there is life left over. And, as a metaphor based on this, *hasi -na-* is also used for '(food) being left over'.

Languages, and their speakers, divide up the world in differing ways. This can be seen in taxonomic schema for classifying plants and animals. And also in the way actions are described. Some languages have a single verb 'eat, drink'; one can tell from the statement of what is consumed which sense of the verb is involved. And there are languages with several different verbs for kinds of eating. The "kinds" can vary. In the Girramay dialect of Dyirbal, there are different verbs depending on the sort of foodstuff involved:

rubima-   eat fish
burnyja- eat meat
nanba-   eat vegetables

Jarawara also has a number of verbs of eating. However, these describe not what is being consumed but rather the nature of the activity:

- -kaba-   eat where a lot of chewing is involved; this would be used of meat, fish, sweet corn, yams, manioc, biscuits, etc.
- jome -na-   eat where little or no chewing is needed; e.g., eating an orange or banana (also used for swallowing a pill)
- komo -na-   eating which involves spitting out seeds; e.g., *jifo*, the fruit of the murity palm, *Mauritia vinifera*
- bako -na-   eating by sucking; e.g., water melon, cashew fruit

Throughout the lexicon of Jarawara, we find verbs referring to a type of action, with little regard for the nature of the participants. Comparison of Girramay and Jarawara demonstrates the different fashions in which these two communities view the world.

A language has two interlocking components – vocabulary (or lexicon) and grammar. The way in which speakers view the world around them is reflected in the structure and organization of vocabulary. In addition, it underlies and explains many categories within a grammar. A prime example is gender, which can be illustrated for Dyirbal.

Each noun in Dyirbal belongs to one of four genders. These are shown not through the form of the noun itself, but by an article which accompanies it (a bit like the articles in German, French, and Spanish). The major composition of the genders is:

I   "Masculine gender" – male humans, most animals, a few birds, moon, storms, rainbow

II   "Feminine gender" – female humans, most birds, sun, anything to do with fire, with water, and with fighting (e.g., fighting spears, shield, fighting ground)

III   "Edible vegetable gender" – all plants with edible parts, honey

IV   "Neuter gender" – all else: bees, wind, body parts, meat, plants with no edible parts, stones

Assignment of nouns to the gender classes depends in part on the traditional beliefs and legends of this ethnic group:

- Non-human animates are generally in class I. But birds are believed to be the spirits of dead Aboriginal women and are, as a consequence, placed with female humans in class II. In the early 1980s, I used to record stories from Ida Henry and songs from her husband Spider. Then Ida died. I visited Spider and he said: "I knew you were coming. My wife, she's a bird up there in the sky, and she told me."
- However, a number of birds (such as *jigirrjigirr*, the willy wagtail, *Rhipidura leucophrys*) were men in age-old legends and are thus placed in class I, with male humans.
- Sun and moon are believed to be wife and husband. On this basis they are in class II (human female) and I (human male) respectively.

- Storms and rainbow are anthropomorphized as men, and thus placed in class I. But wind is considered inanimate and goes into the neuter class, IV.
- All fruit and vegetables are in class III and the trees and vines they come from are in class IV when just described in terms of their timber. Honey is regarded as vegetable food and is thus in class III. Bees produce honey in the way that a tree produces fruit, and so bees are in class IV (they are the only animate beings not in class I or II).

The moral of this example is that a linguist must do a fair amount of anthropological work in order to explain features of the language. And, contrariwise, an anthropologist will miss a good deal if they do not acquire a good knowledge of the grammar. These are important priorities of fieldwork.

2.3 In the field

A linguistic fieldworker goes to a community which has indicated a wish for its language to be described. The fieldworker will provide feedback in the form of word lists, stories, and primers for use in the local school (if there is one). They will spend an extended period – six or nine months – in a village where the traditional language is still actively spoken (rather than just remembered by a few old people).

Working out a description of the language and learning to speak it go hand in hand. A wide spectrum of texts will be recorded, transcribed, and analyzed, with the cooperation of native speaker consultants. The fieldworker should become accepted as a (rather unusual) member of the community. People will tell them what to say, in every kind of circumstance. The fieldworker's first attempts at speaking will be amicably corrected (and all this noted down). Progress will be slow at first, but will gradually escalate. Data comes from two sources – the texts, and what the fieldworker hears said around them (and immediately writes down) in the course of daily interaction.

For an anthropologist, linguistic work is background to the main task. But it is a most important background. Cultural values and parameters are encoded in the grammar and vocabulary of each language. To understand how a society thinks and operates, a basic competence in their language is a *sine qua non*. I have observed anthropologists of inferior quality spend many months in a New Guinea village, communicating with the people entirely in what is for them a second language – Tok Pisin, the national creole, or else English. The work that they do will, as a consequence, be culturally shallow and likely to lack insight.

There are various techniques for learning a language. One is by just living in a community and picking up the language along the way, as you hear it spoken around you. Another is by combining this with some explicit knowledge of grammatical constructions and rules. The first alternative works well for children, but for adults the second is necessary. Surveys have been conducted of adult immigrants to Australia and the competence they attain in English. One group attended a series of evening lectures on pronunciation and grammar and lexicon. They came to speak pretty good English, with just a bit of a foreign accent. The other group forswore explicit instruction and picked it up as it came. Their competence was so low as often to impede understanding – ragged pronunciation, unkempt grammar, and poor choice of words.

It is difficult for an outsider to assess the degree of competence an anthropologist has achieved in the language of a community they study. (But native speakers know.) By devoting a little time to systematic study of the vocabulary, and working out a grammatical sketch, a better competence will be achieved. This will lead to greater respect from the community, and will most certainly pave the way for fine anthropological insights.

The best way to organize an ever-growing accumulation of vocabulary is in thesaurus fashion. Place together words with similar meaning. Rather than being scattered anonymously through an alphabetical dictionary, it is most revealing to organize words semantically. (Adding to this, of course, alphabetical finder lists in the language under consideration, and in English.) For example, my thesaurus of Yidiñ (Dixon 1991: 247), an Australian language, groups together four verbs of 'pulling' – *munda-l* 'pull or drag with a steady motion (for example, pulling a canoe across land, pulling a horse by its reins, pulling on a pipe when smoking)', *dalji-l* 'jerk (for instance, if one throws a vine rope over a branch, one would jerk it to make sure the rope was strong enough)', *burrga-l* 'pull off, e.g. leaves or fruit from a tree, feathers from a bird', and *wirrnga-l* 'pull or snap something from where it is attached, including pulling something from a person's hand'. Each of these meanings can only be properly appreciated if contrasted with the meanings of related verbs.

The great linguistically oriented anthropologist Bronislaw Malinowski (1935: 17) emphasized the importance of (his italics) "*defining a term by ethnographic analysis*, that is, by placing it within its context of culture, by putting it within the set of kindred and cognate expressions, by contrasting it with its opposites, by grammatical analysis and above all by a number of well-chosen examples."

Look up *want* and *wish* in any English dictionary. Each is defined in an ad hoc way, neither being compared with the other, and no contrasting of their meanings in the way that I did at the beginning of section 2.2. Don't take standard dictionaries as any sort of model – prefer Malinowski!

The remainder of this chapter will outline a number of important grammatical principles. But first we need to take a quick peek at phonology.

2.4 Phonology

In the mid-1970s, an anthropologist (of some renown), having just had a stint in the Pacific, wanted to spend a little time with an Australian Aboriginal group, and chose Yidiñ. Before flying back to the States, she called me up and enthused that a staple foodstuff in traditional times, 'rickety bush' (*Cycas media*), had the same name as the color 'white', which she pronounced as [badəl]. (She had evolved an ingenious anthropological explanation for this.) I informed her that 'rickety bush' is *badil* and 'white' is *badal*, words as different from each other as are *simple* and *sample* in English. This error was particularly egregious since in a Yidiñ word each vowel is clearly pronounced; there is no indistinct central vowel like English schwa (the last vowel in *common* /kɔmən/ and *African* /afrikən/).

One must attune ears and tongue to the sounds (and rhythm) of a fieldwork language. The velar nasal /ŋ/ occurs at the ends of words in English – *sing* /siŋ/, *bang* /baŋ/ and so on – but never at the beginning. Very many languages do begin words with /ŋ/. If a fieldworker cannot pronounce this, they will be laughed at. It is, in fact, not at all difficult. Say *bang* /baŋ/, add an *a* to the end (taking care not to also insert a g) and then drop off the initial *ba-*. Say *banga, banga, nga, nga*. An alternative is to put the tongue into position to say 'g', keep it there and say 'n' instead; it will come out as 'ng' /ŋ/.

Languages differ concerning which sound distinctions are contrastive, creating words of different meaning. In English, voicing establishes distinctive speech sounds (or "phonemes"). *Bin* and *pin* are different words, showing that in this language /b/ and /p/ are contrasting phonemes. When I was learning the Australian language Nyawaygi, I couldn't tell whether the word for 'ear' was /bina/ or /pina/. In best fieldwork style, I repeated the word. First /bina/ – "that's alright," my teacher said. Then /pina/ – "that's alright too." In Nyawaygi, /b/ and /p/ are alternative pronunciations (what are called "allophones") of a single phoneme. Substituting one for the other does not change the meaning of the word.

'Swallow (something)', I was told, is /rubi/, the initial "r" sound being rather like that in British English but with the tongue tip turned back a bit more. My teacher, Willie Seaton, was a fine intuitive linguist. "That /rubi/ for 'swallow'," he warned, "don't muddle it up with the word for 'earthworm', which is /rrubi/!" The initial 'r' is here a trilled sound, as in Scottish English. In English /b/ and /p/ are different phonemes but /r/ and /rr/ are variants of one phoneme. Things go the opposite way round in Nyawaygi, with /r/ and /rr/ contrasting, while /b/ and /p/ are non-contrasting.

It is important to take note of every phonetic distinction that affects meaning. The difference between short and long versions of the same vowel is often overlooked, although it is in most cases perfectly easy to discern. A description of English would be sadly lacking if *dip* /dip/ and *deep* /di:p/, *full* /ful/ and *fool* /fu:l/, were not distinguished (":" indicates a long vowel).

Languages differ in the complexity of their phonemic systems. However many vowels there are – whether three or ten – they must all be mastered (or you might as well not bother trying to speak the language at all). Similarly if there is a system of tones. One invaluable aid can be descriptions produced by members of the Summer Institute of Linguistics. The missionary body has worked on more than a thousand languages worldwide and their phonemic statements (produced under expert supervision) are generally – although not absolutely always – sound.

2.5 Clause and predicate, argument and noun phrase

The main unit of every language is the clause. A clause may make up a complete sentence. Or several clauses may be joined together to form a complex sentence. The way in which this is done is often a matter of style – for instance, the previous two sentences of this paragraph (the second commencing with *or*) could equally well have been written as one sentence.

Each clause is centered on a predicate, which is typically a verb. Each verb requires a number of core arguments. An intransitive verb requires one core argument, which is in intransitive subject function (abbreviated to "S"), as in:

(6) [John's friend who works in a bank]$_{NP:S}$
    [drowned]$_{INTRANSITIVE.PREDICATE}$

A transitive verb requires two core arguments, one in transitive subject function ("A") and the other in transitive object function ("O"). For example:

(7) [The clever angler]$_{NP:A}$ [caught]$_{TRANSITIVE.PREDICATE}$ [a salmon]$_{NP:O}$

The core arguments are necessary (one can't say just *The clever angler caught*). In addition, there may be a number of optional peripheral elements. For instance, to either (6) or (7) may be added some specification of time – such as *on New Year's day* or *yesterday* – or of location – such as *in the big river* or *over there* (accompanied by pointing). Sentence (7) can be expanded by a benefactive phrase such as *for his wife*. And an adverb can be added – *almost* or *really* may be placed before the predicate in each of (6) and (7).

Each argument slot is filled by a noun phrase (NP). In English, this may be a pronoun, a demonstrative, a proper name, or a common noun. An NP with a common noun as its main element (called the "head" of the NP) may be modified by a possessive phrase or an adjective – exemplified by *John's* and *clever* in the NPs of (6) and (7). A head noun can be followed by a relative clause (such as *who works in a bank*) or a phrase (for example, *from across the road*). And in English each common noun (with singular reference) must be preceded by either a possessor (such as *John's*) or a definite or indefinite article (*the* or *a*).

Each language has its own structural possibilities for NPs. Unlike English, some languages may combine pronoun and demonstrative, literally 'this you'. And there may be other – perhaps unexpected – possibilities.

2.6 Word classes

Every language has a number of word classes (sometimes called "parts of speech"). There will be a number of small closed classes – pronoun and demonstrative in all languages, article, preposition, postposition in some. They are called "closed" since no new items may be added to them.

Then there are classes of noun, verb, and adjective. Every language has thousands of nouns; this is an open class to which new words are continually being added. Recent additions in English are *e-mail* (or *email*) and *blog*, short for *electronic-mail* and *web-log* respectively. Verbs are almost always also an open class with many hundreds of members (just a few languages have only a few verbs, but these enter into many compounds). Adjectives are discussed a little later.

A very important point is that word classes must be recognized separately for each language, based on internal grammatical criteria in that language. This can be shown by comparison of Latin and English. In Latin, each noun has different forms for number (whether singular or plural) and case (showing what its function is in a clause). For instance:

(8)
	'girl' (FEMININE)	'slave' (MASCULINE)
Singular number, nominative case (S and A functions)	puell-a	serv-us
Singular number, accusative case (O function)	puell-am	serv-um

For Latin, the word class "noun" is defined as "those words which inflect for number and case."

English is rather different. Countable nouns can take plural marking (*cat-s*) but other nouns cannot (there is no plural of *mud*). A different criterion is used here: "any word which should – in non-plural form – be preceded by an article or a possessor (*the cat/mud, my cat/mud*) is taken to be a noun." Similarly for verbs, varying criteria apply in different languages.

There is also the question of function. A noun can always be head of NP, which fills an argument slot in clause structure; a verb can always be head of a predicate.

What about meaning, you may ask? Well, meaning is a concomitant property, not a defining one. The noun class always includes words referring to people, animals, and things (boy, dog, stone) and the verb class always includes words referring to activities (jumping, eating, talking). The important point is that the semantic content of word classes *does not exactly coincide* between languages. Words expressing notions such as "mother" must surely be nouns, you might suggest. Well, in most languages they are, but not in all. Yuman languages, from southern California, express these notions by transitive verbs, 'be mother of' (Halpern 1942). Once you think about it, this is quite natural – the relationship necessarily involves two people, the mother and the child.

Most nouns in Latin correspond to nouns in English, but not all. For example, the idea of needing to eat is expressed through noun *hunger* in English, and by verb *ēsurio* in Latin. (Interestingly, English has a derived adjective, *hungry*, formed from the noun; and Latin also has an adjective, *ēsuriens*, derived from the verb.) In the Australian language Nyawaygi, this idea is expressed by an adjective, *ŋami*. The important point to note is that word class membership *does not depend on semantics* (although it does roughly correlate with it). The assignment of words to classes cannot be inferred from meaning, but must be based on grammatical criteria internal to each language.

2.6.1 Noun and verb

A noun can always be head of an NP, and a verb can always be head of a predicate. In some languages – including Latin and Nyawaygi – they are restricted to these functions. Other languages permit some degree of cross-functioning. In English, for instance, some nouns have secondary function as predicate – besides *John$_A$ has$_{PREDICATE}$ [a knife]$_O$* one can say *John$_A$ knifed$_{PREDICATE}$ [the burglar]$_O$*. This also applies to *table*, *market*, and *sugar*, but not to other nouns such as *kidney*, *library*, and *duty*. Similarly, some verbs can also be head of an NP – including *break*, *exchange*, *surround* – but not others – such as *destroy*, *owe*, *contain*.

In Fijian, the canonical function of a noun is to be head of an NP and of a verb is to be head of a predicate, as in:

(9) [e   aa   yaco   mai]$_{INTRANSITIVE.PREDICATE}$ [a   marama]$_{NP:S}$
    3sgS PAST arrive HERE   ARTICLE married.woman
    'The married woman arrived here.'

Note that the predicate is clause-initial. An NP commences with an 'article' – *a* if the NP head is a common noun, and *o* if it is a proper noun – as in (10) – or a pronoun.

Every noun in Fijian can also function as head of a predicate, as *marama* 'married woman' does in:

(10) [e   marama]$_{INTRANSITIVE.PREDICATE}$ [o   Mere]$_{NP:S}$
     3sgS married.woman   ARTICLE Mary
     'Mary is a married woman.'

And every verb may also function as head of an NP, as *yaco* 'arrive' does in:

(11) [au   aa   rogo-ca]_{TRANSITIVE.PREDICATE}
    1sgA PAST   listen-TRANSITIVE.3sgO
    [a   yaco   mai   we-i   Mere]_{NP:S}
    ARTICLE arrive   HERE   CLASSIFIER-POSSESSOR   Mary
    'I heard Mary's arriving here.'

Note that, within the NP in O function, *Mere* 'Mary' is marked like the possessor in an alienable possessive construction, illustrated by (4) in section 2.1 above.

It might now be asked: if both noun and verb can be head of an NP and head of a predicate, how can one distinguish between them? Don't we just have one macro word class "noun-verb"? There is in fact a clear distinction. It was mentioned, in section 2.1, that derivational prefix *i-* may be added to a verb (never to a noun) and derives a noun; for example, noun *i-sele* 'knife' from verb *sele* 'slice'. A noun can occur as NP head with or without a possessive modifier, but when a verb is NP head there must be a possessor (coding the underlying subject, as *Mere* in (11)). And there are several other criteria.

In many languages the distinction between noun and verb is very clear. In others it is more subtle, but it is always there. A noun is most frequently used as NP head. Only rather occasionally does it function as predicate head; when it does so, tense–aspect possibilities may be more limited than when a verb is predicate head. And so on.

2.6.2   The adjective class

It seems that every language has an adjective class but in some languages its distinctive properties are slightly hidden. There are four possibilities. The first is when adjectives have very similar grammatical properties to nouns, as in Latin. The following paradigm for adjective 'good' corresponds to that for nouns, in (8):

(12)

	'good'	
	FEMININE AGREEMENT	MASCULINE AGREEMENT
Singular number, nominative case (S and A functions)	bon-a	bon-us
Singular number, accusative case (O function)	bon-am	bon-um

For the first 1,500 years of writing grammars of Latin, noun and adjective were regarded as a single word class, since they both inflect for number and case. It wasn't until the twelfth century that adjective was recognized as a separate class, similar in its properties to nouns but with one important difference – each noun belongs to just one gender, but an adjective has a form in each gender (used according to the gender of the noun it is modifying).

The second kind of adjective class can function as head of a predicate, just like a verb. Fijian is of this type and it has been suggested that there is no distinction between verb and adjective. This is unwarranted. Although adjectives are very similar to verbs in their grammatical properties, there are significant differences – for example, only verbs and not adjectives (or nouns) may be used in transitive predicates, only adjectives and not verbs (or nouns) as predicate head may be modified by *rui* 'to a high degree'.

The third kind of adjective class has grammatical properties different from both nouns and verbs. This applies for English – adjectives cannot take plural *-s* as many nouns do, and they cannot take endings *-ed* and *-ing* as verbs do. Adjectives can form comparatives with *-er* or *more*, unlike nouns and verbs. Berber languages from North Africa represent the fourth type – adjectives show grammatical properties similar to nouns when used in an NP, and properties similar to verbs when used in a predicate.

Many languages are like English, Latin, Fijian, and Nyawaygi in having large open adjective classes with hundreds of members (to which new items can be added). But there are a fair number of languages, scattered right across the world, whose adjective class is small and closed. There may be only eight or ten members, typically referring to Dimension (e.g., 'big', 'little'), Age ('new', 'old'), Value ('good', 'bad'), and Color ('black', 'white', 'red'). Slightly larger classes, with twenty or thirty members, may include some Physical Property items ('raw', 'heavy', 'wet', etc.). Only when an adjective class has forty or so members is it likely to include Human Propensity terms ('happy', 'kind', 'clever', and so on).

One might ask: in languages with a small adjective class, what has happened to all the other concepts which are expressed by adjectives in a language such as English? The answer is that Physical Property terms are generally verbs (one says "It heavies" rather than "It is heavy") and Human Propensity terms are most often nouns ("She has happiness"), sometimes verbs ("She happies," rather than "She is happy").

2.7 Who does it to whom: accusative and ergative systems

A transitive clause has two core arguments. How does a speaker distinguish between them? One way is by order of elements. In English the subject (A function) precedes the verb and the object (O) follows it, as in [*The girl*]$_{NP:A}$ *saw*$_{PREDICATE}$ [*the slave*]$_{NP:O}$.

In Latin, words can occur in any order. The function of an NP in its clause is shown by the case ending – nominative, for S function (in an intransitive clause) and also for A function (in a transitive one), and accusative for O function (in a transitive clause). It is important to have different cases for A and O, because these both occur in a transitive clause. However, an NP in S function, since it occurs in an intransitive clause, could be marked like A, as it is in Latin; this is a (nominative-)accusative system. The alternative is for S to be marked like O (this is called absolutive case) and differently from A (which is shown by ergative case). About one-quarter of languages from across the world have an (absolutive-)ergative system, including Nyawaygi from Australia. Accusative and ergative patterns of case marking can be diagrammed:

(13)

	A [TRANSITIVE SUBJECT]	S [INTRANSITIVE SUBJECT]	O [TRANSITIVE OBJECT]
Latin	nominative case (feminine singular -*a*, masculine singular -*us*)		accusative case (f sg, -*am*, m sg -*um*)
Nyawaygi	ergative case (suffix -*ŋgu*)	absolutive case (zero ending, ∅)	

The accusative system in Latin is demonstrated in:

(14) *puell-a*_{NP:S}   *it*_{PREDICATE}
    girl-NOMINATIVE.SG   go.PRESENT.3sgS
    'The girl is going.'

(15) *serv-us*_{NP:S}   *it*_{PREDICATE}
    slave-NOMINATIVE.SG   go.PRESENT.3sgS
    'The slave is going.'

(16) *puell-a*_{NP:A}   *serv-um*_{NP:O}   *videt*_{PREDICATE}
    girl-NOMINATIVE.SG   slave-ACCUSATIVE.SG   see.PRESENT.3sgA
    'The girl sees the slave.'

In (16), *puella* 'girl' is in nominative case, as it is in (14), and so must here be in A function. That is, it is the girl who does the seeing. Now compare this with the ergative profile of Nyawaygi:

(17) *mujumuju-∅*_{NP:S}   *ya-ña*_{PREDICATE}
    woman-ABSOLUTIVE   go-PRESENT
    'The woman is going.'

(18) *jayŋgurru-∅*_{NP:S}   *ya-ña*_{PREDICATE}
    kangaroo-ABSOLUTIVE   go-PRESENT
    'The kangaroo is going.'

(19) jayŋgurru-∅_{NP:O}   mujumuju-ŋgu_{NP:A}   ña:-ña_{PREDICATE}
kangaroo-ABSOLUTIVE   woman-ERGATIVE   see-PRESENT
'The woman sees the kangaroo.'

In (19) *jayŋgurru* 'kangaroo' is in absolutive case, as it is in (18), and so must be in O function. That is, it is the kangaroo that is seen. (Note that words can occur in any order in a clause in both Latin and Nyawaygi, their functions being shown by case endings.)

Quite a few languages have a mix of systems. In Nyawaygi, for example, nouns show an ergative profile and pronouns basically use an accusative one.

2.8 Pronouns and demonstratives

Pronouns in English can be ambiguous. Suppose that John Smith says to his good friend Tom Jones: *The Senator has invited us for dinner tomorrow.* Tom does not know how to respond. Does John's use of *us* here include the addressee, with the invitation being for John and Tom? Or does this use of *us* exclude the addressee, with the invitation being for John and his wife (not for Tom)?

Nyawaygi and Fijian, and many other languages, avoid such difficulties by having separate inclusive and exclusive non-singular first person pronouns. In Nyawaygi, for instance (quoting nominative forms):

ŋali	1st dual inclusive (speaker and addressee)
ŋaliliɲu	1st dual exclusive (speaker and one other person, who is not the addressee)
ŋana	1st plural inclusive (speaker and one or more other people, including the addressee)
ŋanaliɲu	1st plural exclusive (speaker and one or more other people, not including the addressee)

Nyawaygi shows a {singular, dual, plural} system for pronouns, where "plural" indicates "three or more." Fijian has a four-term system {singular, dual, paucal, plural}. Here "paucal" refers to "a relatively smaller number, greater than two" and "plural" to "a relatively larger number, greater than two." The actual references of paucal and plural are relative to each other, and vary according to the context of speaking. For example, in one story paucal referred to five people and plural to eight, in another narrative, paucal was used for a group of twenty people and plural for sixty.

Sometimes one encounters a pronoun system which appears, on the surface, to have an untidy structure. Consider the eight pronouns of Hanunóo, an Austronesian language from the Philippines. If we try to arrange these in a "1st/2nd/3rd person," "singular/dual/plural," "inclusive/exclusive" matrix, the result is:

(20) 1sg *kuh* $\begin{cases} \overline{\text{1du.inc } \textit{tah} \quad \text{1pl.inc } \textit{tam}} \\ \text{1du/pl.exc } \textit{mih} \end{cases}$

    2sg *muh*   2du/pl *yuh*
    3sg *yah*   3du/pl *dah*

However, the anthropological linguist Harold C. Conklin (1962: 134–5) suggested that a better model of this pronoun system would be:

(21)
SPEAKER	HEARER		minimal	non-minimal
✓	–	1	kuh	mih
✓	✓	1+2	tah	tam
–	✓	2	muh	yuh
–	–	3	yah	dah

That is, the eight terms in this pronoun system are expressed in terms of three binary contrasts: ± speaker, ± hearer, and ± minimal. The critical point here is that 1st person dual inclusive "me and you" is put in the same column as the three singular pronouns.

Some languages have a system of this type but with more distinctions. Alongside the minimal column, we have "unit augmented" (minimal plus one further person) and "augmented" (minimal plus more than one further person). Minimal-type pronoun systems are found in many languages of the Philippines and Australia, and quite a few from North and South America and northern Africa.

Every language has a closed word class of "(personal) pronouns." And there is also a closed class of "demonstratives," which have deictic (or pointing) reference to something in the context of speech. There is always a system of local adverbal demonstratives, with at least two members (roughly corresponding to English *here* and *there*).

The number of nominal demonstratives, and their meanings, varies a good deal. In Dyirbal there is only one, with the meaning 'this' (it has four forms, corresponding to the four genders described in section 2.2 above). Many languages are like English with just two nominal demonstratives – 'this' (near speaker) and 'that' (not near speaker).

There are two basic varieties of a three-term system, exemplified by Basque and Ponapean:

(22) Nominal demonstratives (absolutive singular form) in Basque (Saltarelli 1988: 214)
    hau   proximal – 'this (near to speaker)'
    hori   medial – 'that (mid-distance from speaker)'
    hura   distal – 'that (far from speaker)'

(23) Nominal demonstratives (singular non-emphatic form) in Ponapean (Oceanic branch of Austronesian family, Rehg 1981: 152)
 me(t) 'this (near to speaker)'
 men   'that (near to addressee)'
 mwo   'that (distant from both speaker and addressee)'

There may also be demonstratives referring to something that is non-visible – perhaps it was visible until a few moments ago, or it may be not visible but audible. Languages spoken in hilly terrain sometimes – but not always – include demonstratives 'that (higher)', 'that (lower)' and 'that (on same level as speaker)'.

2.9 Envoi

Language is a vital cultural tool. It is, in large part, what characterizes us as human beings, compared with animals of a lower order. A real linguist cannot begin to understand the nature and significance of the grammar and vocabulary of a language unless they achieve a fair understanding of the cultural milieu in which it is used. In similar fashion, an anthropologist must realize that the social parameters they aim to study can only be fully understood in terms of how they are expressed within the holistic structure of the local language. A language is the emblem of its community of users. Its structure reflects the speakers' life-style, social organization, way of viewing the world, and also their environment.

2.10 Further reading

The editors of the volume invited me to contribute this chapter because they appreciated my three-volume work *Basic Linguistic Theory* (Dixon 2010a, b, 2012) as an accessible introduction to the discipline for non-specialists. The chapter is a summary of some points from those volumes. Volume 1 includes a 90-page overview of grammar (Chapter 3), an introduction to phonology (7), and an essay on fieldwork (9). Fuller discussions of other topics mentioned here will be found in the chapters of Volume 2 – noun and verb classes (Chapter 10), adjective classes (11), pronouns and demonstratives (15), and possession (16). Two important topics are scarcely discussed in *Basic Linguistic Theory* – genders and classifiers, and imperatives and commands. There are exemplary user-friendly accounts of these in Aikhenvald (2000, 2010).

 I have given many examples from my own immersion fieldwork – on Australian languages Dyirbal (Dixon 1972), Yidiñ (1977, 1991) and Nyawaygi (1983), on the Boumaa dialect of Fijian (1988), and on Jarawara from the Arawá family in Brazil (2004). Also from my grammatical study of English (2005).

References

Aikhenvald, Alexandra Y. 2000. *Classifiers: A Typology of Noun Categorization Devices*. Oxford: Oxford University Press
    2010. *Imperatives and Commands*. Oxford: Oxford University Press.
Conklin, Harold C. 1962. Lexicographical Treatment of Folk Taxonomies. In *Problems in Lexicography*, ed. Fred W. Householder and Sol Saporta, 119-41. Bloomington: Indiana University Research Center in Anthropology, Folklore and Linguistics.
Dixon, R. M. W. 1972. *The Dyirbal Language of North Queensland*. Cambridge: Cambridge University Press.
    1977. *A Grammar of Yidiɲ*. Cambridge: Cambridge University Press.
    1983. Nyawaygi. In *Handbook of Australian Languages*, Vol. 3, ed. R. M. W. Dixon and Barry J. Blake, 430-523. Canberra: ANU Press, and Amsterdam: John Benjamins.
    1988. *A Grammar of Boumaa Fijian*. Chicago: University of Chicago Press.
    1991. *Words of Our Country: Stories, Place Names and Vocabulary in Yidiny, the Aboriginal Language of the Cairns/Yarrabah Region*. St Lucia: University of Queensland Press.
    2004. *The Jarawara Language of Southern Amazonia*. Oxford: Oxford University Press.
    2005. *A Semantic Approach to English Grammar*. Oxford: Oxford University Press.
    2010a. *Basic Linguistic Theory*, Vol. 1: *Methodology*. Oxford: Oxford University Press.
    2010b. *Basic Linguistic Theory*, Vol. 2: *Grammatical Topics*. Oxford: Oxford University Press.
    2012. *Basic Linguistic Theory*, Vol. 3: *Further Grammatical Topics*. Oxford: Oxford University Press.
Halpern, A. M. 1942. Yuma Kinship Terms. *American Anthropologist* 44: 425-41.
Malinowski, Bronislaw. 1935. *Coral Gardens and Their Magic*, Vol. 2: *The Language of Magic and Gardening*. London: George Allen and Unwin.
Rehg, Kenneth L. 1981. *Ponapean Reference Grammar*. Honolulu: University of Hawaii Press.
Saltarelli, Mario. 1988. *Basque*. London: Routledge.

3

The item/system problem

N. J. Enfield

3.1 Introduction

3.1.1 The problem

When accounts of social-cultural transmission are explicit about the causal processes involved, we see that they often take cultural *items* – rather than systems – as their unit of analysis.[1] This works well but it is awkward because we know that cultural items don't exist in isolation. We can only make sense of cultural items in the context of a *system* or field of cultural meaning. Higher-level systems like languages and cultures show such a coherence of structure that we are seduced into thinking of them as organisms with bodies (see classic statements of philologists von der Gabelentz 1891 and Meillet 1926: 16). Compare this to the situation in vertebrate biology. Genes are distinct entities yet they "caucus" and "form alliances" thanks to the bodies and body plans in which they are instantiated (Gould 1977, cited in; Dawkins 1982: 117). The difference is that vertebrates actually do have bodies while cultural systems don't. The pieces of a cultural system aren't held together by physical attachment to a shared material whole. So this is our puzzle. If languages and other cultural systems "hang together," what is the binding force? If cultural transmission involves causal processes that apply only to small parts of the larger whole, what explains the coherence of that larger whole? This is the item/system problem.

3.1.2 A possible solution

I want to propose that the ideas of "cultural item" and "cultural system" are reconciled by something that they have in common: Neither idea exists without the simpler idea of a *functional relation*. A word – *kangaroo*, for example – is easily thought of as a distinct cultural item. One can cite it or borrow it without having to also cite or borrow the language system that it comes from. But the word cannot be defined or understood – nor can it exist – except in terms of its functional relation to other things, things like the words it co-occurs with, the conversations in which it is used for referring to kangaroos, and so on. Ditto for technology. A spoke can be designed, named, bought, and sold, but as a cultural item, a spoke doesn't make sense without a wheel. And while a wheel is a whole when thought of with reference to a spoke, it is a *part* when thought of with reference to a vehicle, and so on. In sum: An item doesn't make sense without functional relations to other things, just as a system doesn't make sense without the functional relations it incorporates. Functional relations are the interface that joins items and systems together, and we can look to them for a solution to the item/system problem.

3.1.3 A transmission criterion

In the causal ontology of culture, there is a *transmission criterion*. Since – by definition – social facts cease to exist if individual people stop behaving as if they exist,[2] and since social facts endure with relative stability beyond individual people's lifetimes, then social facts must be transmitted among individuals in human populations in order to (i) exist and (ii) endure with relative stability. Transmission is a necessary part of what makes culture and language the way they are. A causal account of culture depends, then, in part at least, on an account of how culture is transmitted within human groups and across generations. Much is known about how *items* are transmitted (Rogers 2003, inter alia), but macro-level cultural systems cannot be transmitted in the same way. Do we need two separate accounts of transmission, one for items, one for systems? I am going to argue that we can derive system transmission from item transmission, on the condition that we have a more accurate definition of items. We can define items not as cultural things but as cultural things with functional relations to other cultural things. Cultural items are specified for – and advertise – their relations to the contexts into which they fit (where, it must be said, this "fit" can be quickly and easily re-tooled). As Kockelman (2013: 19) writes: "there are no isolated environments and organisms, there are only *envorganisms*."

3.2 Systems

To understand what a cultural system is, first consider the notion of item. A cultural item is any seemingly detachable conceived entity such as a piece of technology, a technique, a way of saying something, a value. An item can be readily defined and labeled, and can be learned and borrowed from one human group into another (though typically with some transformation of significance in the new context). Object-like things such as tomahawks might be prototypical items, but the notion of item intended here also includes train tracks, AC current, and mother-in-law avoidance.

By contrast, a cultural system is a coherent set of such items, each item related to the others.[3] A system has a higher-level holism that goes beyond the sum of the parts, in the sense that the full meaning of any individual cultural item is determined in the context of a set of relations into which it fits, and within which it serves a function. Often, we cannot observe the system directly or in one go, as for example in the case of a language or a telecommunications infrastructure, though this is sometimes made virtually possible by means of *signs of* these systems that scale them down in such a way as to produce a "tangible expression," as Durkheim put it (1912: 208), of the more diffuse phenomenon. A book can contain a grammatical description of a language, or a diagram can portray the elements of a telecommunications system in miniature. In these cases a representation of the system is created and/or inferred from an aggregate of encounters with context-situated items. These itemized emblems have different affordances from the real systems they represent, and they have different collateral effects as a result of their form. A grammar book, for example, promotes the idea that a language is a finite, bounded thing; in short, an item.

As we now turn to examine systems in more detail let me emphasize in advance that neither items nor systems can be understood, nor indeed can they exist, without the *relations* that are inherent in both. Relations are definitive for both items and systems. For an item, relations define its *functions*. For a system, relations define its *structure*.

3.2.1 System defined

A system should have at least these three properties: (1) it can readily be construed as a thing with multiple inter-related parts; (2) effects on one part should have effects on other parts; and (3) the parts should together form a whole in the sense that they are more closely related to each other than they are to other things, outside the system. Good examples are biological or ecological systems. In a food chain, populations of different species are inter-related, where changes in the frequency or behavior of one species will affect the frequency or behavior of others. While each species in the ecosystem will ultimately be connected to entities outside the focal food chain system, the integration *within* the system is greater. Clearly, on all three counts, whether or not we are looking at a system is ultimately a matter of construal (see n. 3, above). To say that a set of entities forms a system is partly just a way of looking at those entities.

3.2.2 Relations between relations as a kernel for system emergence

Culture and language hinge on shared meaning, and so our focus in this chapter is on *semiotic* systems. The idea of a semiotic system is well illustrated in Darwin's account of the expression of emotion in animals.

Figure 3.1 Darwin's illustration of a dog in hostile frame of mind (Figure 5 from *The Expression of the Emotions in Man and Animals*)

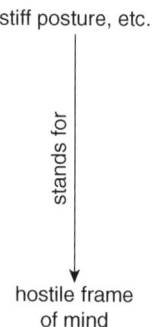

Figure 3.2 A "functional," indexical association between observable behavior and frame of mind (after Darwin)

Darwin introduces a principle of *functional connection* between a sign and what it stands for. In his example, the visible features of a dog in a "hostile frame of mind" – upright, stiff posture, head forward, tail erect and rigid, bristling hairs, ears forward, fixed stare – are intelligible because they recognizably "follow from the dog's intention to attack." Figure 3.1 is Darwin's illustration.

These behaviors are functionally connected to the aggressive attitude, and thus come to signal it. This can be illustrated as in Figure 3.2.

This is only a first step toward establishing a semiotic system. Figure 3.2 shows a relatively simple relation, a positive association between an observable behavior and a frame of mind, from which one might produce a range of relevant interpretants (e.g., running away, grabbing a big stick, etc.). From this, Darwin argues for a second signaling principle, called *antithesis*. By exploiting the already-established semiotic relation shown

Figure 3.3 Darwin's illustration of a dog in an affectionate attitude (Figure 6 from *The Expression of the Emotions in Man and Animals*)

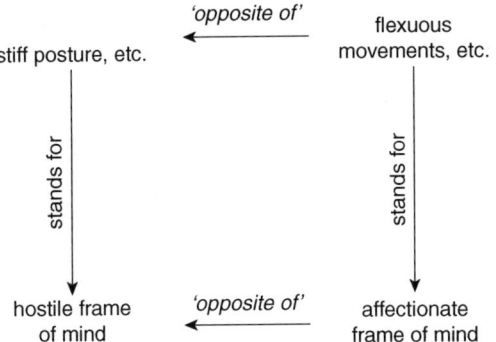

Figure 3.4 A secondary indexical association between observable behavior and frame of mind (at right), deriving its meaning only in connection with the established relation illustrated in Figure 3.2 (and incorporated at left of this Figure), assuming the interpreter's knowledge of a limited range of possible bodily behaviors, on the one hand, and a limited set of frames of mind, on the other (after Darwin)

in Figure 3.2, the dog can express the *opposite* of aggression by "reversing his whole bearing," that is, doing the "opposite" of what one would do when aggressive. Thus, when approaching his master in an affectionate attitude, visible behaviors include body down, "flexuous movements," head up, lowered wagging tail, smooth hair, ears loosely back, loose hanging lips, eyes relaxed. Figure 3.3 is Darwin's illustration.

"None of [these] movements," wrote Darwin, "so clearly expressive of affection, is of the least direct service to the animal. They are explicable, as far as I can see, solely from being in complete opposition to the attitude and movements which are assumed when a dog intends to fight, and which consequently are expressive of anger" (Darwin 1872: 15–16). This can be illustrated as shown in Figure 3.4.

As depicted in Figure 3.4, antithesis is a secondary relation. As Darwin pointed out, it depends on the interpreter's already-established recognition of a specific functional relation. But there is something more that it depends on, something crucial to the idea of a semiotic system. It is entailed by the term "opposite." To recognize that a certain behavior is *the opposite* of some other behavior, as opposed to simply *not* that other behavior, one must be able to consider alternative possibilities within a restricted set. Flexuous movements can be recognized as the opposite of the aggression-signaling behavior only when one knows, or can predict, a limited range of postures that a dog can make. And for this to work in the way depicted in Figure 3.4, one must also understand that there is a limited set of relevant frames of mind that the dog may have, such that aggressive is at one end and affectionate at the other. This basic type of semiotic system arising from Darwin's principle of antithesis sets up relations-between-relations (Kockelman 2013: 12ff.) by presupposing the interpreter's access to other systems such as body posture and emotional state, with some sense of their component elements and the logical-causal relations between them (e.g., that if one is being affectionate one is necessarily not being aggressive, or that if one's body is stiff it cannot also be flexuous).

3.2.3 Incorporation and contextualization

Central to the notion of functional relation to context that I have argued for so far are the concepts of *incorporation* and *contextualization*. These are defined in semiotic terms by Kockelman (2006: 29), as follows:

> **Incorporation**
> For any two semiotic processes, A and B, A will be said to incorporate B (and hence be an interpretant of it) if the sign of B relates to the sign of A as part-to-whole, and the object of B relates to the object of A as means-to-ends. For example, in the case of instruments (semiotic processes whose sign is an artificed entity and whose object is a function), a wheel incorporates a spoke.
>
> **Contextualization**
> For any two semiotic processes, A and B, A will be said to contextualize B, if A is required to interpret B, or at least assists in interpreting B. For example, a hammer contextualizes a nail. And a sword contextualizes a sheath. That is, nails make no sense without the existence of hammers; and sheaths make no sense without the existence of swords.

Incorporation and contextualization are widely applicable concepts in defining functional relations. They hold, for example, for the relations between a verb and a clause, a handle and a knife, a marriage rule and a kinship system. They are the basis of combinatoric rules, and as such they ultimately account for grammar in the complete sense (assuming a semantically based approach to grammar; cf. Langacker 1987; Wierzbicka 1988; Croft 2000, inter alia).

3.2.4 More complex systems: the case of linguistic grammars

The basic relations-between-relations structure depicted in Figure 3.4, combined with the functionally recursive embedding relation of incorporation, is the essence of the kinds of semiotic systems that characterize the grammatical organization of any natural language (Saussure 1916; see Dixon, this volume, Chapter 2; Bickel, this volume, Chapter 5). All languages have systems of form classes, by which the thousands of words and other meaningful elements that one must learn in order to speak the language can be grouped and categorized in terms of their distribution relative to each other. Thus, we find open classes of content words like nouns and verbs versus closed classes of function words like prepositions (e.g., in English) and case-marking affixes (e.g., in Finnish). Then there are constructional systems defined by combinatoric principles. As an example consider the system for describing motion events in Lao (Enfield 2007: 387ff.), consisting of three consecutive slots in a multi-verb construction, where each slot may be filled with a verb from three distinct sets, the first referring to the manner of motion (this is an open set), the second referring to the path of motion (from a closed set of ten verbs), and the third referring to the direction of motion in relation to the deictic centre (from a closed set of three verbs):

(1) Lao directional verb system

SLOT 1	SLOT 2	SLOT 3
Verb of MANNER	**Verb of PATH**	**Verb of DIRECTION**
OPEN CLASS	CLOSED (n=10)	CLOSED (n=3)
lèèn1 'run'	khùn5 'ascend'	paj3 'go'
ñaang1 'walk'	long2 'descend'	mùa2 'return'
king4 'roll'	khaw5 'enter'	maa2 'come'
lùan1 'slide'	qòòk5 'exit'	
tên4 'jump'	khaam5 'cross.over'	
lòòj2 'float'	lòòt4 'cross.under'	
khii1 'ride'	taam3 'follow'	
khaan2 'crawl'	phaan1 'pass'	
taj1 'creep'	liap4 'go along edge'	
com1 'sink'	qòòm4 'go around'	
doot5 'leap'		
etc.		

With this system, Lao speakers can generate utterances like the following:

(2) khaan2 qòòk5 paj3
    crawl exit   go
    '(S/he/it) crawled out/away.'

(3) doot5 long2   maa2
    leap descend come
    '(S/he/it) leapt down here.'

(4) lòòj2 phaan1 mùa2
    float pass   return
    '(S/he/it) floated back past.'

This little linguistic sub-system illustrates the fundamental intersection between a syntagmatic axis (the left-to-right axis along which separate elements combine) and a paradigmatic axis (the slots which may be filled by alternative members of a set, with contrast effects between possible values not unlike the way a dog's stiff posture is opposed to a flexuous posture).

Sub-systems in language interact with each other and show dependencies in higher-level systems such as those defined in comprehensive grammatical descriptions. Aikhenvald and Dixon (1998) describe dependencies among grammatical sub-systems. They show, for example, that the system of polarity (positive versus negative in relation to a predicate or clause) constrains many other systems in the grammars of the world's languages. In Estonian, there is a system in which person and number are distinguished by morphological marking on the verbs, but these distinctions are only realized in positive polarity. The distinctions are lost in the negative:

(5) Verb 'to be' in Estonian
    POSITIVE   **NEGATIVE**
    olen (1SG), *oleme* (1PL)
    oled (2SG), *olete* (2PL)   *ei ole* (1/2/3SG/PL)
    on (3SG/PL)

Aikhenvald and Dixon (1998) present a cross-linguistic hierarchy of such dependencies between sub-systems. Such inter-connectedness between paradigm sets and combinatoric rules, and between sub-systems in a language, is evidence for the higher-level system properties of linguistic behavior.

What follows from these facts about linguistic systems is that we cannot view any piece of language as a mere item. "A living language is not just a collection of autonomous parts," say Donegan and Stampe (1983: 337). A language is "a harmonious and self-contained whole, massively resistant to change from without, which evolves according to an enigmatic, but

Table 3.1 Grammatical profile of Munda versus Mon-Khmer (i.e., Austroasiatic except Munda); after Donegan and Stampe (1983: 337–8)

	MUNDA	MON-KHMER
Phrase accent	Falling (initial)	Rising (final)
Word order	Variable – SOV, AN, Postpositional	Rigid – SVO, NA, Prepositional
Syntax	Case, verb agreement	Analytic
Word canon	Trochaic, dactylic	Iambic, monosyllabic
Morphology	Agglutinative, suffixing, polysynthetic	Fusional, prefixing or isolating
Timing	Isosyllabic, isomoric	Isoaccentual
Syllable canon	(C)V(C)	unaccented (C)V, accented (C)(C)V(G)(C)
Consonantism	Stable, geminate clusters	Shifting, tonogenetic, non-geminate clusters
Tone/register	Level tone (Korku only)	Contour tone/register
Vocalism	Stable, monophthongal, harmonic	Shifting, diphthongal, reductive

unmistakably real, inner plan" (Donegan and Stampe 1983: 337). They illustrate their point in explaining how it is that the languages of two sides of the Austroasiatic language family – Munda and Mon-Khmer – show a list of typological distinctions that are "exactly opposite at every level of structure" (Donegan and Stampe 2002: 111) despite being demonstrably descended from the same proto-language. They argue that when speakers of Munda innovated a new prosodic profile, they were tampering with something that "pervades every level of language structure" (1983: 351). A simple change from iambic to trochaic stress had systemic knock-on effects that changed the entire morphosyntactic profile of the language. Table 3.1 is adapted from Donegan and Stampe (1983: 337–8).

As the examples discussed here show, there are good reasons to believe in the higher-level system properties of language. Yet there is no single causal event in which a language as a whole system is transmitted (cf. the single causal event of sexual reproduction by which a full set of genetic information is transmitted). Below, we will return to the transmission problem. But first, let us broaden our scope and show that the point we have just made for language also holds for social and cultural systems.

3.2.5 Systems in culture

As an illustration of the system concept in culture, consider sections and subsections in Aboriginal Australia (Radcliffe-Brown 1931). In a section system, all members of a community belong in one of four categories. Each category has a name in the local language (e.g., in the Alyawarre language of Central Australia they are *Kngwarriya, Upurla, Pitjarra,* and *Kimarra*). For descriptive purposes we can label them A, B, C, and D. As

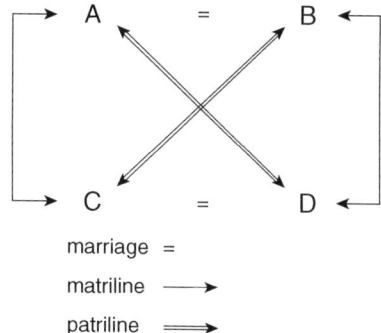

Figure 3.5 Sections (Northern Australia), from McConvell (1985: 32), after Radcliffe-Brown (1931)

McConvell (1985: 2) describes it, in a four-term section system "a man of A marries preferentially a woman of B; their children are D. A man of B marries a woman of A; their children are C. C and D similarly marry each other, and their children are A if the mother is C and B if the mother is D." After two generations of this, one ends up in the same section as one's father's father or mother's mother. (See Figure 3.5.)

McConvell also describes the doubly complex subsection systems, in which the four categories of an erstwhile section system are each divided in two (see McConvell for diagram and discussion). There are structural consequences. For example, a cross-cousin is a possible wife in a section system, but not in a subsection system. This kind of system is widespread in Aboriginal Australia, shared by groups that have completely different languages. Evans (2012) likens the situation to that of the modern system of military ranks as officially standardized by the Geneva Convention: those groups who are members of the same culture area have direct translations for the same offices in the same system. In Northern Australia, a common cultural context has facilitated the widespread and stable nature of particular types of kinship systems and vocabularies.

But there are many aspects of culture that seem more like items and less like systems. Eckert (2008) gives the example of a particular cut of jeans that happens to be fashionable among high school kids one year, though she urges us not to be tempted by the apparent individuability of such cultural elements. Something like the wearing of pegged pants or a way of pronouncing a certain vowel is always situated in an indexical field, as she puts it. When such things are borrowed or adopted into new social settings they may be "segmented" out from a historical and indexical constellation of signs and meanings. People who do this segmenting may know little of the larger (especially historical) connections, but they will nevertheless also give the item a place in a new system. Parry and Bloch (1989) make this point with reference to the historical adoption of money around the world: "in order to understand the way in which money is viewed it is vitally important to understand the cultural matrix into which it is incorporated" (Parry and Bloch 1989: 1).

Similarly, Sahlins (1999) says that when new elements – everything from money to snowmobiles – are incorporated into cultural contexts, they are adopted for local purposes and given a "structural position" in "the cultural totality." Sahlins celebrates the appropriation by neotraditional cultures/societies of elements from other societies (and note we can distinguish between processes of appropriation that alter the item so as to assimilate it into the receiving system versus those that alter the system so as to accommodate the incoming item; of course most of the time it is a combination of the two). Sahlins was critiquing the idea that cultures such as that of the Yupik are being contaminated by their borrowing of innovations associated with globalization. His point is that once borrowed, the items in question take on different meanings because of their new system context.

3.2.6 Are cultural totalities illusory?

The kinds of systems and relations of incorporation in language and culture just discussed demonstrate that we are never dealing with detached cultural items. It does not follow, however, from the striking coherence of sub-systems like Australian sections and subsections that these ramp up into cultural totalities. It's possible that they do, and indeed the idea is supported by the fact that ethnographers have succeeded in writing reference descriptions of the knowledge, practices, values, and technologies of defined social/cultural groups (see, e.g., Radcliffe-Brown 1922; Malinowski 1922; Firth 1936; Evans-Pritchard 1940; Fortes 1945, among many others). Similarly, linguists have succeeded in describing languages as totalities, not in the way a layperson might discretely label an imagined language (Dutch, Flemish, Serbian, Croatian, Thai, Lao, etc.), rather in the technical sense of listing the lexicon and set of grammatical rules that any speaker will know. But what is our evidence that such totalities exist?

Both the "whole systems" and the "parts" of language seem clearly identifiable at first glance, but both ideas crumble upon close inspection (Le Page and Tabouret-Keller 1985; Hudson 1996, inter alia). Any linguist knows that "a language" – in the sense of a community-wide system like French or Korean – is impossible to define extensionally, that is, by pointing at it: "as a totality it is inaccessible and indefinable; each of us has only partial experience of it" (Le Page and Tabouret-Keller 1985: 191). A language in the sense that we normally mean it constitutes a system insofar as it is a set of interrelated items, such as words, each of which appears to be a single unit or element. The system idea is especially clear in the case of language because, firstly, the set of interrelated items in a language is a large set; secondly, we have strong intuitions about what is part of language and what is not; and thirdly, this set contains multiple small or medium-sized sub-systems. But still we never encounter a language as such, only fragments of languages, items such as words and grammatical constructions, as instantiated in spoken utterances or in pieces of writing.

In their masterpiece on the nature of language, Le Page and Tabouret-Keller (1985: 8–9) challenge us to face the problem of "how to know when to speak of separate systems":

> If we start from the concept of an underlying system this becomes an extremely difficult, if not insoluble, problem; if however we approach it from the point of view of the degree of coherence evidenced in the behaviour of a group of individuals, the problem is seen to be one of relationships and of stereotypes inherent in each individual. We do not ourselves then need to put a boundary around any group of speakers and say "These are speakers of Language A, different from Language B", except to the extent that the people think of themselves in that way, and identify with or distance themselves from others by their behaviour.

Metalinguistic stances are real, but this does not mean that the systems they believe in are real in the same way. How, then, can we have a clear causal account of linguistic systems? The answer – to bring us back to the item/system problem – is in the causality of social behavior at the micro level.

3.2.7 Our behavior at the micro level supports the macro level cultural system

While as members of a group we may feel subjectively convinced that there is a cultural totality around us, we never directly observe it. As Fortes put it, "structure is not immediately visible in the 'concrete reality'. It is discovered by comparison, induction and analysis based on a sample of actual social happenings in which the institution, organization, usage etc. with which we are concerned appears in a variety of contexts" (Fortes 1949: 56). This mode of discovery belongs not only to the ethnographer, but also to the child whose task is to become a competent adult (see Brown and Gaskins, this volume, Chapter 8). If our experience of culture is in the micro, how, then, do we extrapolate to the macro? Parry and Bloch, in their discussion of money and its status, stress local differences between cultures and the effects on the meaning that money comes to have, but they acknowledge a certain unity across cultures. This unity is "neither in the meanings attributed to money nor in the moral evaluation of particular types of exchange, but rather in the way the totality of transactions form a general pattern which is part of the reproduction of social and ideological systems concerned with a time-scale far longer than the individual human life" (Parry and Bloch 1989: 1). In terms that apply more generally to the micro/macro issue, there is, they argue, "something very general about the relationship between the transient individual and the enduring social order which transcends the individual" (Parry and Bloch 1989: 2). It brings to mind Adam Smith's (1776: bk. 4, chap. 2) discussion of the relation between the motivations of individuals and the not-necessarily-intended population-level aggregate effects of their behavior (see also Schelling 1978; Hedström and Swedberg 1998; Rogers 2003). Parry and Bloch (1989: 29) contrast "short-term order" with "long-term reproduction," and suggest that the two must be linked.

This brings us back to the transmission criterion, a key issue for bridging the micro/macro divide.[4] If the individual is to function as a member of a social group, he or she needs to construct, as an individual, the capacity to produce and properly interpret locally normative meaningful behavior. Not even a cultural totality is exempt from the transmission criterion. Individual people must learn the component parts of a totality during their lifetimes,[5] and they must be motivated to reproduce the behaviors that stabilize the totality and cause it to endure beyond their own lives and lifetimes. This motivation can of course be in the form of a salient external pressure such as the threat of state violence, but most often it is in the form of a less visible force, namely the regimenting currents of normative accountability (Enfield 2013: Chapters 3, 9, and passim). We find ourselves in social/cultural contexts in which our behavior will be interpreted as meaningful. "The big question is not whether actors understand each other or not," Garfinkel wrote (1952: 367; cited in Heritage 1984: 119). "The fact is that they do understand each other, that they *will* understand each other, but the catch is that they will understand each other regardless of how they *would* be understood." So, if you are a member of a social group, you are not exempt from having others take your actions to have meanings, whether or not these were the meanings you wanted your actions to have. As Levinson (1983: 321) phrases it, also echoing Goffman and Sacks, we are "not so much constrained by rules or sanctions, as caught up in a web of inferences." We will be held to account for others' interpretations of our behavior and we know this whether we like it or not. This is a powerful force in getting us to conform. Accountability to norms "constitutes the foundation of socially organized conduct as a self-producing environment of 'perceivedly normal' activities" (Heritage 1984: 119). The thing that tells us what is "normal" is of course the culture.

> With respect to the production of normatively appropriate conduct, all that is required is that the actors have, and attribute to one another, a reflexive awareness of the normative accountability of their actions. For actors who, under these conditions, calculate the consequences of their actions in reflexively transforming the circumstances and relationships in which they find themselves, will routinely find that their interests are well

> served by normatively appropriate conduct.[6] With respect to the anarchy of interests, the choice is not between normatively organized co-operative conduct and the disorganized pursuit of interests. Rather, normative accountability is the "grid" by reference to which *whatever* is done will become visible and assessable. (Heritage 1984: 117)

One might ask what is "normatively appropriate conduct." The answer must include any of the kinds of behaviors discussed in the section 3.2.5 above: for example, behaving in accordance with the rules of a section system by marrying someone of the right category (or being able to produce an account for why one has done otherwise). They would not be cultural behaviors if they were not regimented in a community by accountability to norms (and laws).

So the path that is both the least resistant and the most empowering for an individual is to learn the system that generates a shared set of normative interpretations of people's behavior, and then go with the flow. This is how the totality cannot exist without the individuals, while – paradoxically – appearing to do just that. The close relationship between short-term order and long-term reproduction is an asymmetrical one. Short-term order is where the causal locus of transmission is found; it is where acceleration, deceleration, and transformation in cultural transmission occurs (Enfield 2014; cf. Schelling 1978; Sperber 1985; Sperber 1996; Rogers 2003).

From all of this it is clear that cultural systems exist and they both constrain us and influence us. The question is: How are systems *transmitted*? The regulation of individual behavior in the cultural totality is not achieved by mere emergence like the behavior of a bird in the seemingly concerted movement of a flock. Individuals' behavior is regulated by norms, in an effectively telic way, and a good deal of cultural regimentation is done through explicit instruction, often with reference to norms, and sometimes to punishable laws. Where can we find an account of how whole systems are transmitted? As we shall now see, the only good causal account we have for social transmission through populations and across generations is one that works in terms of cultural items, not whole systems.

3.3 Biased transmission

The diffusion of cultural items, including their adoption, retention, and loss, is a population-level phenomenon that can be well handled by analytical tools that are already available. There is a well worked-out *biased transmission* model of the distribution of cultural knowledge and practice within and across human groups and generations, within a general framework of cultural epidemiology (cf. Sperber 1985; Boyd and Richerson 1985, 2005; Enfield 2003, 2008, 2014). In a biased transmission model, fashions of cultural practice in a population will spread, decline, change, or remain as they are, as determined by the cumulative effect of a range of biases which ultimately serve as filters or pumps in a competition for cultural uptake, and ultimately in the actuation of change in cultural systems (cf. Weinreich, Labov, and Herzog 1968: 102 and passim, Milroy and Milroy 1985).

3.3.1 Previously proposed transmission biases

Different researchers have described different biases, sometimes in quite specific terms, sometimes in more general terms. For example, Chater and Christiansen (2010) propose four factors that mostly have to do with properties of the individual human body, especially the brain: (1) perceptuo-motor factors, (2) cognitive limitations on learning and processing, (3) constraints from mental representations, (4) pragmatic constraints. These factors can make it more or less likely that one linguistic variant is selected over another and can thereby ultimately determine the nature of the observed population-level practices.

Boyd and Richerson (1985) make distinctions that are broader in kind. They illustrate with an example from table tennis. For the function of hitting the ball, one may choose between holding the bat with a pencil grip or a handle grip. Choosing one of these variants at any given moment necessarily rules out choosing the other. They discuss different biases that might cause a person to select one grip over the other. A *direct bias* concerns the relationship between the variant and the adopter, and thus it concerns affordances (Gibson 1979). An individual should choose variant A if it is somehow more advantageous than variant B for a proximate function in a given context. Thus, by a direct bias we should choose the grip that is easier, more effective, feels better, gives better results. There are also social mechanisms that play a necessary role in the process. While the Chater and Christiansen account leaves these implicit, Boyd and Richerson include them, at least in part, under the rubric of an *indirect bias*. An *indirect bias* works with reference to a notion of social identity, assuming that the variant a person selects will be seen by others and that this selection will lend a certain status to both the adopter (as the kind of person who adopts that variant) and the variant (as a variant of the kind that is adopted by that person or someone like that). We adopt ways of doing things not only because they are of immediate advantage, but also because they can improve the way others view us. This has the potential for longer-term advantages. So by an indirect bias we should choose the same grip as those people who we identify with, or want to emulate. A final bias offered by Boyd and Richerson is a *frequency-dependent bias*. This simply favors variants that occur more frequently in the population.

Similar biases to those just discussed have been described in a vast literature in sociology on the diffusion of innovations (Rogers 2003). Here, we can discern three sets of conditioning or causal factors in the success or failure of a cultural practice. First, *sociometric factors* concern the network structure of demographic groups. Different individuals are differently socially connected, especially in terms of the number of their points of connection to others in a social network, as well as the quality (e.g., intensity) of these connections. A cultural practice is more likely to spread if it is being modeled by someone who is widely connected in a network, simply because he or she will expose a greater number of people to the practice. This is the law of the few (Gladwell 2000). Second, *personality factors* concern differences between individuals in the population that can have consequences for the success or failure of an innovation. Some people are more willing than others to innovate and to adopt others' innovations (e.g., early adopters versus laggards). And these differences may correlate with social categories such as age, class, and sub-culture. Some people are better admired or better known in their social milieu and may thus be more likely to be imitated. Third, there is the sheer *utility* of an innovation, more or less what Boyd and Richerson (1985) mean by direct bias. The innovation will spread and succeed if it is more advantageous to potential adopters.

Each of the biases that we have just reviewed plays an important role in the mechanisms of transmission that drive the circulation of bits of culture in human populations. But how to explain them? Where do these biases come from and how are they related to each other? What theory generates them? How can we constrain the possibilities? To solve these puzzles, we need to motivate the set of biases by locating them directly in the causal anatomy of transmission. We can begin with the simplest imaginable causal mechanism for transmission and see where a bias might act as a filter or pump for an item to be diffused or not. The next section explicates this.

3.3.2 A minimal causal scheme for transmission biases: the four-stroke engine model

I propose a minimal causal scheme for biased transmission which has four functionally defined loci at which any transmission bias may contribute to regulating the cumulative transmission of culture (the scheme is explicated in more detail in Enfield 2014). Each locus is an opportunity for a practice to be (further) transmitted in a human population by means of social interaction. Assuming a Sperber (2006)-style open-ended social-interactional process that oscillates between public events (practices, utterances, etc.) and private events (moments of learning, interpretation, representation), there will be four and only four causal loci where transmission biases may exert their influence: exposure (relating to the world-to-mind transition), representation (relating to mind structure), reproduction (relating to the mind-to-world transition), and material (relating to world structure). These are illustrated in Figure 3.6.

Now to summarize. While there may be a large, if not open set of possible biases, as discussed in the previous section, I submit that each bias should have its effects in ways that can be exhaustively defined in

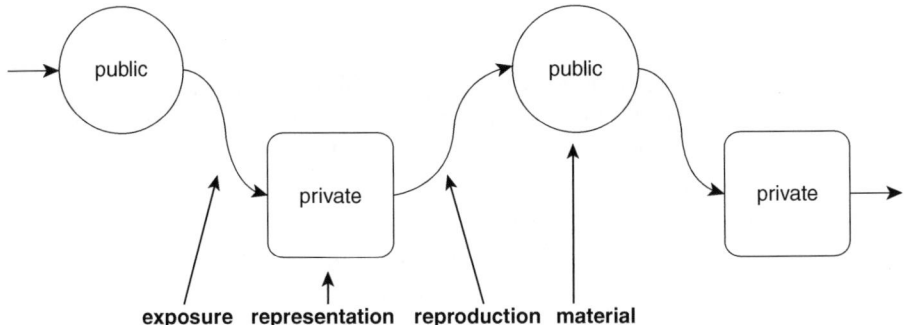

Figure 3.6 Loci for transmission in a four-stroke engine model (building on Sperber 1985, 1996, 2006): exposure (world-to-mind transition), representation (mind structure), reproduction (mind-to-world transition), and material (world structure)

terms of the basic causal structure represented in Figure 3.6. Different specific biases may affect the transmission of a practice in qualitatively different ways, but they will always and only exert their effect within one or more of the four functionally defined loci. This allows us to take the known biases listed above and re-cast them in terms of a conceptual scheme that explains all of them in the same causal terms. As discussed above, some of the biases will have to do with facts about social networks, some with individual personality traits, some with properties of human perception, attention, and memory, some with the nature of the human body, some with the culture-specific means and ends that are integral to any culturally evolved activity, some with the organization of complex information in cognition. These biases can all be understood in terms of how they causally affect the transmission of cultural items either at the point of *exposure* (affecting the likelihood that a person will come into contact with, and pay attention to, the practice: these biases include salience of variants and social identity or connectedness of the person modeling the practice), *representation* (affecting the likelihood that, or the manner in which, a practice will be learnt or stored by a person), *reproduction* (anything that affects the likelihood that a person will employ the practice themselves, going on to expose others), or *material* (anything that affects the manner in which a practice will be physically instantiated in the perceptible world). See Enfield (2014) for further explication.

3.4 The common core of both items and systems: the functional relation

The preceding section laid out a causal process that works upon items, the kinds of things that can be produced and encountered in one go. Let us now consider the implications of the points made earlier on, that an item is more accurately to be considered a kind of relation of a thing to some functional context. If the ontology of an "item" is in fact relational, and if such relations can be embedded in further such relations, then this suggests an account for how an item-based model might ultimately also be able to handle the special properties of higher-level linguistic systems or grammars – that is, if we view those higher-level systems as made up entirely of embedded sets of relations.

3.4.1 The context bias as a relational force

A key step toward seeing how this works is to invoke a *context bias*. This bias increases the likelihood of transmission of a practice when there is a good-fitting context for the practice. At the representational locus, for example (see Figure 3.6), the psychological context into which a practice must be embedded can have effects on the transmission of the practice. Practices are partly constituted by knowledge. This knowledge is caused by, and in turn causes, public behavior and associated states of affairs. Like any structured domain, knowledge is characterized by part–whole relations, hierarchical relations, and other sorts of dependency. So when we learn something, we relate it to other things we know, at the very least because the thing was related to other things in the context in which we learnt it. As an example, if I learn a new word such as *deplane*, I relate it to other words I already know, both in terms of similarity (*debone, derail, decode, decommission*) and association (e.g., the fact that *deplane* is a verb and can be used only with specific grammatical roles in English sentences). Or if I learn about the possibility of downloadable ringtones I will naturally contextualize this in terms of my existing knowledge of mobile phones and the Internet. Through a context bias I am more readily able to learn and psychologically represent those things that have an existing "place" in which to fit. This accounts, for example, for the borrowing hierarchies that have been discovered in research on language contact (cf. Matras 2009: 153ff.): the likely reason that interjections are more easily borrowed than inflectional affixes is that the context for interjections – not a grammatical structure but a discourse sequence – is more likely to be available across languages than the grammar-situated contexts required by bound morphology.

In language, items are structured into conceptual frames, systems of categorization, semplates, conceptual metaphors, structural paradigms, and syntagms. Something that happens in one place will have effects in another place, and when it comes to the densely structured linguistic systems of lexicon and grammar, system-internal perturbations may lead to a certain "psychological shakiness," as Sapir (1921: 168) put it, even when the system appears "logically and historically sound." Such shakiness is presumably undesired, and can lead to reorganization of a system, in the private realm of the mind, and then potentially in the public realm of community convention.

3.4.2 The combinatoric nature of cultural items in general

The context bias is grounded in the fact that one cannot behold any so-called item without beholding it *in relation to* something else, including not only things of similar kinds, but, perhaps especially, the social norms and intentions associated with items and the contexts in which they appear. So, I cannot know what a hammer is without seeing it in relation to, among other things, the human body, timber and nails, people's intentions to build things, conventional techniques for construction, and so on. These relations – which themselves are interrelated – form an indispensable part of what I'm referring to by the term "item." When a cultural item diffuses, what is actually diffusing is something less like an object and more like a combinatoric relation. Thus, a hammer incorporates a handle or grip. The handle or grip has a combinatoric relation to the human hand insofar as the handle and the hand are practically and normatively designed to go together. The handle is designed that way because of how the human hand is. The handle only makes sense in terms of the hand. This going together of the handle and the hand is like a grammatical relation. In a similar way, the handle of the hammer and the head of the hammer are combinatorically related, again fitting together both practically and normatively. The head of the hammer stands, in turn, in a combinatoric relation to a nail. The nail, in turn, has a combinatoric relation to the timber, and so forth. So we see how the cultural "items" that diffuse in historical populations in interaction necessarily incorporate – and advertise – their combinatoric relations.

The sprawling yet structured systems that we call languages have exactly the kinds of properties of incorporation and contextualization that I have just described for concrete objects. Thus, if speakers of a language have borrowed a word from another language, they have not merely adopted a pairing of "sound image plus thought image," but must also have adopted a way of relating the word to the existing system (whether or not this relation resembles the one used in the source system). The word will not be usable if it does not have combinatoric properties. The norms for combining the word in usage may be borrowed along with the word itself, or may be provided by existing structures in the borrowing language, or may even be innovated in the process of incorporation. It is not that the combinatoric relations surrounding a cultural item must also diffuse along with that item. Rather, it is that a cultural element cannot function or circulate if it does not have *some* combinatoric relation to other cultural items in the same domain. This is the point that authors such as Sahlins and Eckert, mentioned above, have stressed for culture.

So, structuralist linguists like Donegan and Stampe are right when they say that a language "is not just a collection of autonomous parts," but this does not necessarily mean that a language is "a self-contained whole" (both quotes 1983: 337). Similarly, when cultural anthropologists refer to the "cultural totality" (Sahlins 1999), it is not yet clear what this really means. We never encounter whole systems except one fragment at a time. Our "partial experience" (Le Page and Tabouret-Keller 1985: 191) is not experience of the whole system, but nor is it experience of stand-alone items. Our direct experience of culture is of meaningful items in relations of functional incorporation and contextualization with other such items. Each such relation is, effectively, a combinatoric principle, like a norm for forming a grammatical sentence or for using a hammer and nail in the appropriate way. These relations are at the centre of the framework being proposed here. These relations are what is transmitted. Their inherent connection to some sort of system or field is entailed, but there is no pre-given size or outer limit of the relevant system or field.

Bloch (2000) says that old critiques of diffusionism in anthropology also serve as critiques of today's item-based accounts. I suggest that the problems are handled by the simple but crucial conceptual shift being proposed here. The relevant unit of cultural transmission (meme or whatever) is not "a piece." The relevant unit is "a piece and its functional relation to a context." This might seem obvious. But when we make it explicit, the fear of a disembodied view of cultural units go away. To be clear, the required conceptual move is not just to take items and put them in a context. Their relation to a context is part of what *defines* them.

3.5 Solving the item/system problem in language

Identifying the *relation to context* as the common unit of analysis in items and systems is necessary but not yet sufficient. We need an account of how this scales up into large structured sets of such relations. Let us consider the question in connection to language. As a product of general mechanisms of social diffusion, each linguistic convention in a community has its own individual history. Each word, each morpheme, each construction has followed its own historical path to population-level conventionality. As Bloomfield (1933: 444) put it, "individual forms may have had very different adventures." But as shown earlier, languages are not bundles of items. They are large, structured, systematic wholes, with psychological and intersubjective reality. Psychologically, languages exist as idiolects, cognitively represented and neurologically instantiated in individual speakers' bodies. Intersubjectively, languages exist at a community level to the extent that individuals' idiolects are effectively alike in structure and content, as demonstrated by the evidently tolerable degree of communicative success of normative practices of signifying and interpreting. We can now specify some forces that bring items together and structure them into systems.

3.5.1 Centripetal and systematizing forces

When we say that two people speak the same language, we mean that two individuals' knowledge of a language system is effectively (though never exactly) shared. This sharedness has come about because a large proportion of the same linguistic variants have been channeled, in a giant set, along the same historical pathways.[7] The impression is that a language is passed down as a whole, transcending lifetime after lifetime of the individuals who learn and embody the system. This is the point made by Thomason and Kaufman (1988): Normal social conditions enable children, as first language learners, to construct idiolects which effectively match the idiolects of the people they learn from – i.e., those who share the same household and immediate social environment, and, incidentally, who are most likely to share their genes. Normal transmission is what allows historical linguists to abstract from the fact that each linguistic variant has its own career, instead treating the whole language as having a single spatial-historical trajectory. In many cases this is a reasonable – indeed successful – methodological presumption (cf. Haspelmath 2004). But work such as Le Page and Tabouret-Keller (1985) and Thomason and Kaufman (1988) shows that in situations other than those of normal transmission, linguistic items do not always travel together, but may follow separate paths, making visible what is always true but usually obscured by items' common destiny in practice, namely: Each item has its own history.

Genealogical continuity in language change is typically taken to be the norm, and whenever we see that linguistic systems are relatively permeable, for instance in certain language-contact situations where the components of languages are prized apart, special explanations are demanded. But we must also ask: How to explain the relative *impermeability* of linguistic systems in *normal* circumstances? *Stability* in conventional systems is no less in need of explanation than variation or change (Bourdieu 1977; Sperber 1996; Sperber and Hirschfeld 2004). What are the forces which cause linguistic variants to follow en masse a single path of diffusion and circulation, and to cohere as structured systems? Let us briefly consider three such forces.

3.5.1.1 Sociometric closure

A first centripetal force is *sociometric closure*, arising from a trade-off between strength and number of relationship ties in a social network. If a person is to maintain a social relationship, she has to commit a certain amount of time to this, and since time is a finite resource, this puts a structural constraint on the possible number of such relationships one can maintain (Hill and Dunbar 2003). The result is a relatively closed circulation of currency within a social economy of linguistic items, causing individuals' inventories of items (i.e., their vocabularies, etc.) to overlap significantly, or to be effectively identical, within social networks.

This helps to account for how individuals in regular social association can have a common set of variants, but it does not account for the tightly structured nature of the sets of relations among those items. We turn now to two reflexive forces of relational systematization inherent to grammar, in both the paradigmatic (§3.5.1.2) and syntagmatic (§3.5.1.3) dimensions.

3.5.1.2 Trade-off effects

One systematizing force comes from functional trade-off effects that arise when a goal-oriented person has ongoing access to a set of alternative means to similar ends. When different items come to be used in a single functional domain, those items can become formally and structurally affected by their relative status in the set. This happens because the items compete for a single resource – namely, our selection of them as means for our communicative ends. When Zipf (1949: 19ff.) undertook "a study of human speech as a set of tools," he compared the words of a language with the tools in an artisan's workshop. Different items have different functions, and thus different relative functional loads. In a vocabulary, Zipf (1949) argued, there is an "internal economy" of words (p. 21), with trade-offs that result in system effects such as the observed correlation between the length of a word (relative to other words) and the frequency of use of the word (relative to that of other words).[8] Zipf reasoned that "the more frequent tools will tend to be the lighter, smaller, older, more versatile tools, and also the tools that are more thoroughly integrated with the action of other tools" (Zipf 1949: 73). He showed that the more we regard a set of available means as alternatives to each other in a functional domain, the more they become defined in terms of each other, acquiring new characteristics as a result of their role in the economy they operate in. The upshot is this: The more we treat a set of items as a system, the more it becomes a system.

3.5.1.3 Item–utterance fit, or content–frame fit

Another key conduit and filter for grammatical structure is grammatical structure itself. The *utterance* is a core structural locus in language, providing narrow contextualization for the interpretation of linguistic variants, and serving as an essential ratchet between item and system.[9] As Kirby writes, although "semantic information" is what linguistic utterances most obviously convey, "there is another kind of information that can be conveyed by any linguistic production, and that is information about the linguistic system itself" (Kirby 2013: 123). He adds: "When I produce the sentence 'these berries are good' I may be propagating cultural information about the edibility of items in the environment via the content of the sentence. At the same time I may also be propagating information about the construction of sentences in my language" (Kirby 2013: 123). In this way, the utterance is a basic frame for replication of linguistic variants

(Croft 2000). Item–utterance fit is the structural fit between diffusible types of linguistic item and the token utterances in which they appear. It is an instance of the more general "content–frame" schema (Levelt 1989) also observed in phonology (MacNeilage 1998; see Enfield 2013: 54–5), and a case of the "functional relation to context" defined above as the core common property of items and systems. Here we see it is not just a common property, but it is the very property that *links* them. In this way, an utterance provides an incorporating and contextualizing frame for the diffusion of replicable linguistic variants, *and* a frame for the diffusion of the combinatoric rules from which the higher-level system is built.

3.5.2 A solution to the item/system problem?

The above considerations suggest that the item/system problem can be solved with reference to three forces that apply in the context of the biased transmission of cultural items: (1) bundling of items arising from the population-level effects of sociometric biases, (2) system-forming effects arising from the treatment of elements in a set as alternative means to related functional ends, and (3) transmission of the combinatoric properties of items via context biases and the relation of item–utterance fit. We can expect there to be analogous relations to item–utterance fit in the domain of culture (think, for instance, of systems of social relations in kinship, or systems of material culture and technology in households and villages).

Zipf's (1949) analogy is useful here. For his "economy of tools-for-jobs and jobs-for-tools" to get off the ground, one first needs a *workshop*, somewhere the set of tools can be assembled in one place and made accessible to an agent with a set of goals. In language and culture, this is achieved by sociometric closure (see 3.5.1.1, above). Then one begins to work with the set of tools, using them as alternative means to similar ends (3.5.1.2 above). These tools will, whether by design or by nature, enter into relations of incorporation and contextualization that define their functional potential (3.5.1.3 above). In short, once we get an *inventory* of items that are functional within a given domain, they will naturally enter into the *paradigmatic* and the *syntagmatic* relations that define semiotic systems in the classical sense.

3.6 Conclusion

Ever since Darwin's earliest remarks on the uncanny similarity between language change and natural history in biology, there has been a persistent conceptual unclarity in evolutionary approaches to cultural change. This unclarity concerns the units of analysis. In some cases the unit is said to be the language system as a whole. A language, then, is "like a species"

(Darwin 1871: 60; cf. Mufwene 2001: 192–4). One reading of this is that we are working with a population of idiolects that is coterminous with a population of bodies (allowing, of course, that in the typical situation – multilingualism – one body houses two or more linguistic systems). On another view, the unit of analysis is any unit that forms *part* of a language, such as a word or a piece of grammar. "A struggle for life is constantly going on amongst the words and grammatical forms in each language" (Müller 1870, cited in Darwin 1871: 60). In contrast with the idea of populations of idiolects, this suggests that there are populations *of items* (akin to Zipf's economy of word-tools), where these items are reproduced, and observed, in the context of spoken utterances.

While some of us instinctively think first in terms of items, and others of us in terms of systems, we do not have the luxury of ignoring either. Neither items nor systems can exist without the other, and the challenge is to characterize the relation between the two – this relation being the one thing that defines them both. The issue is not just the relative status of items and systems but the causal relations between them (see Enfield, this volume, Chapter 13). If the distinction between item and system is a matter of framing, it is no less consequential for that. We not only have to define the differences between item phenomena and system phenomena, we must know which ones we are talking about and when, and we must show whether, and if so how, we can translate statements about one into statements about the other. In this chapter we have adopted a causally explicit model for the transmission of cultural items, and we have approached a solution to the item/system problem that builds solely on these item-based biases. I claim that the biases required for item evolution – never forgetting that "item" here really means "something-and-its-functional-relation-to-a-context" – are sufficient not only to account for how and why certain cultural items win or lose, they also account for the key relational forces that *link* items and systems.

We started with the puzzle of the item/system problem. To solve it, we reached for the most tangible causal mechanism we have for the existence of linguistic and cultural reality: item-based transmission. The idea I have tried to put forward here is that by defining items more accurately – as always having a functional relation to context – we can have an item-based account for linguistic and cultural reality that gives us a system ontology for free.

Acknowledgements

In writing this chapter I have benefited greatly from conversations with Morten Christiansen, Dan Dediu, Mark Dingemanse, Daniel Dor, Bill Hanks, Jennifer Johnson-Hanks, Simon Kirby, Chris Knight, Paul Kockelman, Steve Levinson, Hugo Mercier, Pieter Muysken, Jack Sidnell, Kenny Smith, Dan Sperber, and Monica Tamariz. I also thank participants at the conference "Social Origins of Language" (London, 2011), the conference "Naturalistic Approaches to Culture" (Balatonvilagos, Hungary, 2011), and the "Minerva-Gentner Symposium on Emergent Languages and Cultural Evolution" (Nijmegen, 2013) for comments and reactions. This chapter draws on sections of Enfield (2008; 2013: chap. 11; 2014), and section 12.3.2 (pp. 358–65) of Enfield *et al.* (2013). This work is supported by the European Research Council (grant "Human Sociality and Systems of Language Use," 2010–2014), and the Max Planck Institute for Psycholinguistics, Nijmegen.

Notes

1. Schelling (1978); Boyd and Richerson (1985, 2005); Sperber (1985, 2006); Rogers (2003); Enfield (2003, 2008, 2014); cf. Bloch (2000); Aunger (2000).
2. I mean this in Searle's (2010) sense of social facts (cf. Enfield 2013: Chapter 8 and passim). Suppose that we share an apartment and for convenience we declare that on even-numbered days it's me who takes the trash out, while on odd-numbered days it's you. The fact that I have to take out the trash on a given day is a fact because we declared it to be a fact. We can make it untrue just by declaring that it isn't true any more. These are unlike facts defined by natural causes. You can't change the fact that water boils by declaring that it doesn't. This suggests a diagnostic: If it's a natural fact, it cannot be made untrue by declaration.
3. A caveat: Let us acknowledge that the item and system concepts are both ultimately a matter of framing. Something can be seen as an item in one frame but a system in another. A mobile telephone, for example, is a good example of an item insofar as it is an object that can be handled, transported, learnt about, desired, bought, and sold. But we can just as well focus on its internal structure and see that it is made up of many parts each with distinct functions relative to others. Or we can focus on how the phone doesn't make sense except insofar as it is a part of, and dependent on, large and complex systems that include the infrastructure of electricity, telecommunications, corporate management of subscriptions and advertising, as well as the societal preconditions for telephone use that include people's habits, desires, patterns of dependencies on phones, and the fact that many other people also have phones.
4. Agha (2007: 10–13) says that the distinction between micro and macro is "unproductive." This might have been true were the distinction based on differences of "scale" alone. But micro/macro is not a distinction of big versus small, but rather it turns on qualitatively distinct causal processes (Schelling 1978; Hedström and Swedberg 1998; for discussion of this point in relation to language cf. Enfield 2003: 2–21

and 364–6, 2005: 193–8, 2008, 2011; see also Enfield, this volume, Chapter 13).

5. Of course no individual learns the system in its entirety. Our trick to maintaining the effective existence of the system is *distributed cognition* (Hutchins 1995, 2006) and other forms of distributed agency (Enfield 2013: 115 and passim).

6. It is interesting to compare this to Adam Smith's suggestion, which seems – deceptively – similar: "Every individual is continually exerting himself to find out the most advantageous employment for whatever capital he can command. It is his own advantage, indeed, and not that of the society, which he has in view. But the study of his own advantage, naturally, or rather necessarily, leads him to prefer that employment which is most advantageous to society" (Smith 1776: 352).

7. When a full set of variants is not exactly shared by two people, this will not necessarily be taken to signal that they speak two different languages. Within ethnic or other social group boundaries, such differences might go undetected or might be ignored, or may mark mere sociolinguistic distinctions. When detected *across* social group boundaries, the same differences may be sufficient for making the metasemiotic claim that different languages are spoken.

8. See also related findings such as those by Piantadosi *et al.* (2011), that the relative degree of informativeness/predictability of a word is what correlates with its relative length; or by Pagel *et al.* (2007), that words which are more frequent will change more slowly.

9. By "utterance" I mean a burst of articulatory activity which lasts typically for a few seconds, with recognizable formal and pragmatic completeness, constituting a single move or communicative action in discourse (Enfield 2013: chap. 6). This corresponds loosely to the primitive unit of speech production in psycholinguistics (e.g., Levelt 1989), the intonation unit in research on spoken discourse (e.g., Chafe 1994), the turn-constructional unit in conversation analysis (Sacks *et al.* 1974), and the clause in syntactic typology (e.g., Foley and Van Valin Jr 1984).

References

Agha, Asif. 2007. *Language and Social Relations*. Cambridge: Cambridge University Press.

Aikhenvald, Alexandra Y., and R. M. W. Dixon. 1998. Dependencies Between Grammatical Systems. *Language* 74(1): 56–80.

Aunger, Robert. 2000. *Darwinizing Culture: The Status of Memetics as a Science*. Oxford: Oxford University Press.

Bloch, Maurice. 2000. A Well-disposed Social Anthropologist's Problems with Memes. In *Darwinizing Culture: The Status of Memetics as a Science*, ed. Robert Aunger. Oxford: Oxford University Press.

Bloomfield, Leonard. 1933. *Language*. New York: Holt.
Bourdieu, Pierre. 1977. *Outline of a Theory of Practice*. Cambridge: Cambridge University Press.
Boyd, Robert, and Peter J. Richerson. 1985. *Culture and the Evolutionary Process*. Chicago: University of Chicago Press.
— 2005. *The Origin and Evolution of Cultures*. New York: Oxford University Press.
Chafe, Wallace. 1994. *Discourse, Consciousness, and Time: The Flow and Displacement of Conscious Experience in Speaking and Writing*. Chicago: University of Chicago Press.
Chater, Nick, and Morten H. Christiansen. 2010. Language Acquisition Meets Language Evolution. *Cognitive Science* 34(7): 1131–57.
Croft, William. 2000. *Explaining Language Change: An Evolutionary Approach*. Harlow: Longman.
Darwin, Charles. 1871. *The Descent of Man, and Selection in Relation to Sex*. London: John Murray.
— 1872. *The Expression of the Emotions in Man and Animals*. London: J. Murray.
Dawkins, Richard. 1982. *The Extended Phenotype: The Long Reach of the Gene*. Oxford: Oxford University Press.
Donegan, Jane, and David Stampe. 1983. Rhythm and the Holistic Organization of Language Structure. In *The Interplay of Phonology, Morphology, and Syntax*, ed. John F. Richardson, Mitchell Marks, and Amy Chukerman, 337–53. Chicago: Chicago Linguistic Society.
— 2002. South-East Asian Features in the Munda Languages: Evidence for the Analytic-to-synthetic Drift of Munda. In *Proceedings of the 28th Annual Meeting of the Berkeley Linguistics Society, Special Session on Tibeto-Burman and Southeast Asian Linguistics, in Honor of Prof. James A. Matisoff*, ed. Patrick Chew, 111–29. Berkeley, CA: Berkeley Linguistics Society.
Durkheim, Emile. 1912. *The Elementary Forms of the Religious Life*. Oxford: Oxford University Press.
Eckert, Penelope. 2008. Variation and the Indexical Field. *Journal of Sociolinguistics* 12(4): 453–76.
Enfield, N. J. 2003. *Linguistic Epidemiology: Semantics and Grammar of Language Contact in Mainland Southeast Asia*. London: RoutledgeCurzon.
— 2005. Areal Linguistics and Mainland Southeast Asia. *Annual Review of Anthropology* 34: 181–206.
— 2007. *A Grammar of Lao*. Berlin: Mouton de Gruyter.
— 2008. Transmission Biases in Linguistic Epidemiology. *Journal of Language Contact* THEMA 2: 295–306.
— 2011. Linguistic Diversity in Mainland Southeast Asia. In *Dynamics of Human Diversity: The Case of Mainland Southeast Asia*, ed. N. J. Enfield, 63–80. Canberra: Pacific Linguistics.
— 2013. *Relationship Thinking: Agency, Enchrony, and Human Sociality*. New York: Oxford University Press.

2014. Transmission Biases in the Cultural Evolution of Language: Towards an Explanatory Framework. In *The Social Origins of Language: Studies in the Evolution of Language*, ed. Daniel Dor, Chris Knight, and J. Lewis. Oxford: Oxford University Press.

Enfield, N. J., Mark Dingemanse, Julija Baranova, Joe Blythe, Penelope Brown, Tyko Dirksmeyer, Paul Drew, *et al.* 2013. Huh? What? – A First Survey in 21 Languages. In *Conversational Repair and Human Understanding*, ed. Makoto Hayashi, Geoffrey Raymond, and Jack Sidnell, 343–80. Cambridge: Cambridge University Press.

Evans, Nicholas D. 2012. An Enigma Under an Enigma: Unsolved Linguistic Paradoxes in a Sometime Continent of Hunter-gatherers. (Talk given in Amsterdam.)

Evans-Pritchard, E. E. 1940. *The Nuer: A Description of the Modes of Livelihood and Political Institutions of a Nilotic People*. Oxford: Clarendon Press.

Firth, Raymond. 1936. *We The Tikopia: A Sociological Study Of Kinship In Primitive Polynesia*. London: Routledge.

Foley, William A., and Robert D. Van Valin Jr. 1984. *Functional Syntax and Universal Grammar*. Cambridge: Cambridge University Press.

Fortes, Meyer. 1945. *The Dynamics of Clanship Among the Tallensi*. Oxford: Oxford University Press.

1949. *Social Structure*. Oxford: Clarendon Press.

Gabelentz, Georg von der. 1891. *Die Sprachwissenschaft, Ihre Aufgaben, Methoden Und Bisherigen Ergebnisse*. 2nd ed. London: Routledge/Thoemmes Press.

Garfinkel, Harold. 1952. *The Perception of the Other: A Study in Social Order*. PhD dissertation, Harvard University.

Gibson, James J. 1979. *The Ecological Approach to Visual Perception*. Boston: Houghton Mifflin.

Gladwell, Malcolm. 2000. *The Tipping Point*. Boston: Little and Brown.

Gould, Stephen Jay. 1977. *Ontogeny and Phylogeny*. Harvard University Press.

Haspelmath, Martin. 2004. How Hopeless Is Genealogical Linguistics, and How Advanced Is Areal Linguistics? *Studies in Language* 28(1): 209–23.

Hedström, Peter, and Richard Swedberg. 1998. *Social Mechanisms: An Analytical Approach to Social Theory*. Cambridge: Cambridge University Press.

Heritage, John. 1984. *Garfinkel and Ethnomethodology*. Cambridge: Polity Press.

Hill, R. A., and Robin I. M. Dunbar. 2003. Social Network Size in Humans. *Human Nature* 14: 53–72.

Hudson, R. A. 1996. *Sociolinguistics*. 2nd ed. Cambridge: Cambridge University Press.

Hutchins, Edwin. 1995. *Cognition in the Wild*. Cambridge, MA: MIT Press.

2006. The Distributed Cognition Perspective on Human Interaction. In *Roots of Human Sociality: Culture, Cognition and Interaction*, ed. N. J. Enfield and Stephen C. Levinson, 375–98. Oxford: Berg.

Kirby, Simon. 2013. Transitions: The Evolution of Linguistic Replicators. In *The Language Phenomenon*, 121–38. Berlin, Heidelberg: Springer Verlag.

Kockelman, Paul. 2006. Residence in the World: Affordances, Instruments, Actions, Roles, and Identities. *Semiotica* 162(1–4): 19–71.

———. 2013. *Agent, Person, Subject, Self: A Theory of Ontology, Interaction, and Infrastructure*. Oxford: Oxford University Press.

Langacker, Ronald W. 1987. *Foundations of Cognitive Grammar*, Vol. 1: *Theoretical Prerequisites*. Stanford, CA: Stanford University Press.

Le Page, R. B., and Andrée Tabouret-Keller. 1985. *Acts of Identity: Creole-based Approaches to Language and Ethnicity*. Cambridge: Cambridge University Press.

Levelt, Willem J. M. 1989. *Speaking: From Intention to Articulation*. Cambridge, MA: MIT Press.

Levinson, Stephen C. 1983. *Pragmatics*. Cambridge: Cambridge University Press.

MacNeilage, Peter F. 1998. The Frame/content Theory of Evolution of Speech Production. *Behavioral and Brain Sciences* 21(04): 499–511.

Malinowski, Bronislaw. 1922. *Argonauts of the Western Pacific: An Account of Native Enterprise and Adventure in the Archipelagoes of Melanesian New Guinea*. London: Routledge.

Matras, Yaron. *Language Contact*. 2009. Cambridge: Cambridge University Press.

McConvell, Patrick. 1985. The Origin of Subsections in Northern Australia. *Oceania* 56(1): 1–33.

Meillet, Antoine. 1926. *Linguistique Historique et Linguistique Générale*. Paris: Champion.

Milroy, James and Lesley Milroy. 1985. Linguistic Change, Social Network and Speaker Innovation. *Journal of Linguistics* 21(2): 339–84.

Mufwene, Salikoko S. 2001. *The Ecology of Language Evolution*. Cambridge: Cambridge University Press.

Müller, Max. 1870. Darwinism Tested by the Science of Language. *Nature* 1(10): 256–9.

Pagel, Mark, Quentin D. Atkinson, and Andrew Meade. 2007. Frequency of Word-use Predicts Rates of Lexical Evolution Throughout Indo-European History. *Nature* 449: 717–20. doi:10.1038/nature06176.

Parry, J., and Maurice Bloch, eds. 1989. *Money and the Morality of Exchange*. Cambridge: Cambridge University Press.

Piantadosi, S. T., Harry Tily, and Edward Gibson. 2011. Word Lengths Are Optimized for Efficient Communication. *Proceedings of the National Academy of Sciences* 108(9): 3526.

Radcliffe-Brown, A. R. 1922. *The Andaman Islanders: A Study in Social Anthropology*. Cambridge: Cambridge University Press.

———. 1931. The Social Organization of Australian Tribes: Part III. *Oceania* 1(4): 426–56.

Rogers, Everett M. 2003. *Diffusion of Innovations*. 5th ed. New York: The Free Press.

Sacks, Harvey, Emanuel A. Schegloff, and Gail Jefferson. 1974. A Simplest Systematics for the Organization of Turn-taking for Conversation. *Language* 50(4): 696–735.

Sahlins, Marshall. 1999. What Is Anthropological Enlightenment? Some Lessons of the Twentieth Century. *Annual Review of Anthropology* 28(1): i–xxiii. doi:10.1146/annurev.anthro.28.1.0.

Sapir, Edward. 1921. *Language: An Introduction to the Study of Speech*. Orlando/San Diego/New York/London: Harcourt Brace Jovanovich.

Saussure, Ferdinand de. 1916. *Cours de Linguistique Générale*. Paris: Payot.

Schelling, Thomas C. 1978. *Micromotives and Macrobehaviour*. New York: W. W. Norton.

Searle, John R. 2010. *Making the Social World: The Structure of Human Civilization*. New York: Oxford University Press.

Smith, Adam. 1776. *An Inquiry into the Nature and Causes of the Wealth of Nations*. Strahan.

Sperber, Dan. 1985. Anthropology and Psychology: Towards an Epidemiology of Representations. *Man* 20: 73–89.

——— 1996. *Explaining Culture: a Naturalistic Approach*. London: Blackwell.

——— 2006. Why a Deep Understanding of Cultural Evolution Is Incompatible with Shallow Psychology. In *Roots of Human Sociality: Culture, Cognition, and Interaction*, ed. N.J. Enfield and Stephen C. Levinson, 431–49. Oxford: Berg.

Sperber, Dan, and Lawrence A. Hirschfeld. 2004. The Cognitive Foundations of Cultural Stability and Diversity. *Trends in Cognitive Sciences* 8(1): 40–6.

Thomason, Sarah Grey, and Terrence Kaufman. 1988. *Language Contact, Creolization, and Genetic Linguistics*. Berkeley: University of California Press.

Weinreich, Uriel, William Labov, and Marvin Herzog. 1968. Empirical Foundations for a Theory of Language Change. In *Proceedings of the Texas Conference on Historical Linguistics*, ed. W. Lehmann, 97–195. Austin: University of Texas Press.

Wierzbicka, Anna. 1988. *The Semantics of Grammar*. Amsterdam: Benjamins.

Zipf, G. K. 1949. *Human Behaviour and the Principle of Least Effort*. Cambridge, MA: Addison-Wesley.

4

Language and the manual modality

The communicative resilience of the human species

Susan Goldin-Meadow

All known cultures whose members are hearing exploit the oral modality – the mouth and ear – for language. But the manual modality – the hand and eye – also has a role to play in language, in two very different ways. First, individuals who use the oral modality for language move their hands when they talk – they gesture – and these co-speech gestures form part of the conversation. Second, individuals whose hearing losses prevent them from using the oral modality for language use their hands to communicate – they invent sign languages – and these languages serve all of the functions served by spoken languages. My goal in this chapter is to describe what happens to the manual modality under two distinct circumstances: (1) when it accompanies speech, and thus forms part of language; and (2) when it is used instead of speech as the primary modality for communication, and thus is itself language.

4.1 When the manual modality is used along with speech: Co-speech gesture

4.1.1 The robustness of co-speech gesture

In all cultures that have been examined thus far, speakers have been found to gesture when they talk, even very young speakers. In fact, before children use meaningful words, their meaningless vocalizations, particularly those that are syllabic and therefore speech-like in form, are more likely to be coordinated with manual movements than with other limb movements (Iverson and Fagan, 2004). When children then begin to produce meaningful words, they immediately combine those words with gestures and the combinations are temporally synchronized (i.e., the vocalization occurs on the stroke of the gesture or at its peak, the farthest extension before the hand begins to retract, Butcher and Goldin-Meadow, 2000).

Even more striking, individuals who are blind from birth, and thus have never seen anyone gesture, move their hands when they talk. Moreover, these blind speakers gesture even when talking to blind listeners, and their gestures resemble the gestures that sighted speakers produce when they talk (Iverson and Goldin-Meadow, 1998). Another compelling example of gesture's close tie to speech comes from IW (Cole, 1991). IW suffered an illness at age 19 that affected the nerves of his spinal cord and resulted in loss of the sense of touch and proprioception below the neck, as well as loss of all motor control that depends on proprioceptive feedback. Over time and with great effort, IW learned to control his arm and leg movements using visual attention, and can now exercise control over his posture and movement *if* he can see his limbs – in the dark, he cannot move. Interestingly, however, IW is able to move his unseen hands when he talks – that is, he can gesture, even though he is unable to move his unseen hands voluntarily, for example, when asked to pick up a block (Gallagher et al., 2001).

Gesturing is thus clearly not just hand waving – it's an inseparable part of the act of talking. Although traditionally linguists have not considered gesture to be integral to language, the fact that it is a robust part of the speech act suggests that we need to understand the role gesture plays in our conversations. We turn next to the form co-speech gesture assumes and then explore its functions.

4.1.2 The form of co-speech gesture

Nonverbal behavior, including gesture, has traditionally been assumed to reflect a speaker's feelings or emotions (Wundt, 1973 [1900]; see review in Feyereisen and de Lannoy, 1991). More recently, however, researchers have argued that the gestures speakers produce while talking can convey substantive information about the speaker's thoughts (Kendon, 1980; McNeill, 1992). For example, McNeill (1992) has found that speakers use hand gestures to portray concrete images (such as the actions or attributes of cartoon characters), as well as abstract mathematical concepts (such as quotients, factors, or limits in calculus). Indeed, speakers can even use their hands to convey the complex hierarchical structures found in kinship relations (e.g., to explain why the marriage between two individuals is permitted, or forbidden, within their system of kinship relations, Enfield, 2005).

But gesture and speech convey meaning differently. Speech segments and linearizes meaning. A thought that is likely to be instantaneous is divided up and strung out through time. A single event, say, somebody running across a field, must be conveyed in segments: the runner, the field, the running movement, the direction, and so forth. These segments are organized into a hierarchically structured string of words. The total effect is to present what had been a single instantaneous picture in the form of a hierarchically organized string of segments. Segmentation and linearization are essential characteristics of all linguistic systems (even sign languages, see section 4.2.1).

In contrast, the gestures that accompany speech can present meaning without undergoing segmentation or linearization. Unlike spoken sentences in which lower constituents combine to form higher constituents, each gesture is a complete expression of meaning unto itself (McNeill, 1992). For example, in describing an individual running, a speaker might move his hand forward while wiggling his index and middle fingers. The gesture is a symbol whose parts are meaningful in the context of the whole. The wiggling fingers mean "running" only because we know that the gesture, as a whole, depicts someone running and not because this speaker consistently uses wiggling fingers to mean running. Indeed, in other gestures produced by this same speaker, wiggling fingers may well have a very different meaning (e.g., "indecision between two alternatives"). In order to argue that the gesture for running is composed of separately meaningful parts, one would have to show that the components that comprise the gesture are each used for a stable meaning across the speaker's gestural repertoire (e.g., that the V handshape consistently represents a person, the wiggling fingers consistently represent manner, and the forward motion consistently represents path). The data suggest that there is no such stability in co-speech gesture (McNeill, 1992; Goldin-Meadow et al., 1995).

In addition to the fact that co-speech gestures do not appear to be composed of meaningful parts and thus are not wholes created from parts, these gestures also do not themselves combine to create larger wholes. Most of the time, gestures are "one to a clause," that is, a spoken clause is accompanied by a single gesture (McNeill, 1992). Moreover, even when more than one gesture occurs within a single clause, those gestures do not form a more complex gesture "clause." Each gesture depicts the content from a different angle, bringing out a different aspect or temporal phase, and each is a complete expression of meaning by itself. For example, while uttering the clause, "and she grabs the knife," a speaker produced two gestures: The hand first groped in a circle with the palm facing down and the finger extended (produced as the word "she" was uttered) and then the hand turned up and closed to a fist as though gripping a knife (produced along with the words "grabs the knife"). The gestures are related but do not combine into a single higher unit characterized by the same properties as a spoken clause. Rather, the gestures present successive snapshots of the scene. The spoken words also describe this scene, but whereas the words – "she," "grabs," and "the knife" – combine to form the clause, the gestures – groping and grabbing – do not combine to form anything resembling a clause. Rather, each gesture represents a predicate unto itself (McNeill 1992).

Co-speech gesture is thus not structured like a conventional linguistic system. It has its own representational properties, which work together with speech to form an integrated system. For example, co-speech gestures typically rely on the words they accompany for their interpretation. The same gesture – a twirling motion in the air – can refer to a dancer performing a pirouette when accompanied by the sentence, "she's a lovely dancer," but to a person's lack of progress when accompanied by the sentence, "he seems to be going nowhere." Even the form of co-speech gesture seems to be influenced by the structural properties of the language it accompanies. For example, English expresses manner and path within the same clause, whereas Turkish expresses the two in separate clauses. The gestures that accompany manner and path constructions in these two languages display a parallel structure – English speakers produce a single gesture combining manner and path (a rolling movement produced while moving the hand forward), whereas Turkish speakers produce two separate gestures (a rolling movement produced in place, followed by a moving forward movement) (Kita and Özyürek, 2003; Kita et al., 2007).

4.1.3 The functions of co-speech gesture

4.1.3.1 The communicative functions co-speech gestures serve

As described earlier, co-speech gesture is not meaningless hand waving but can convey substantive information. Moreover, the information gesture conveys can be quite different from the information conveyed in the speech it accompanies. For example, consider a child asked to participate in a Piagetian conservation task. The child is shown two rows that have the same number of checkers in them. The checkers in one row are then spread out, and the child is asked whether the rows still have the same number of checkers. The child says, "they're different because you moved them," indicating that she is a non-conserver. However, her gestures suggest that she does have some insight into conservation – she moves her index finger between the checkers in the two rows, aligning the first checker in row 1 with the first checker in row 2, and so on. Her gestures suggest that she is beginning to understand one-to-one correspondence and, in fact, a child who produces gesture–speech "mismatches" of this sort is particularly likely to profit from instruction in conservation, more likely than a child who does not produce mismatches on this task prior to instruction (Church and Goldin-Meadow, 1986; see also Perry et al., 1988; Alibali and Goldin-Meadow, 1993; Pine et al., 2004). Gesture can thus provide a second, important window onto a speaker's thoughts.

Not only can researchers armed with video cameras and slow-motion devices glean information from a speaker's gestures, but ordinary listeners are also sensitive to information conveyed in gesture, both adults (e.g., Graham and Argyle, 1975; Cook and Tanenhaus, 2009) and children (McNeil et al., 2000). Listeners are faster to identify a speaker's referent when speech is accompanied by gesture than when it is not (Silverman et al., 2010). Listeners are also *more* likely to glean information conveyed in a speaker's words if those words are accompanied by matching gesture than by no gesture (Graham and Argyle, 1975; Thompson and Massaro, 1994; Goldin-Meadow and Sandhofer, 1999; McNeil et al., 2000; Beattie and Shovelton, 2002). Conversely, listeners are *less* likely to glean information conveyed in a speaker's words if the words are accompanied by mismatching gesture than by no gesture (Kelly and Church, 1998; Goldin-Meadow and Sandhofer, 1999; McNeil et al., 2000; see Kelly et al., 2004, Wu and Coulson, 2007, and Özyürek et al., 2007, for evidence from event-related potentials [ERPs] that gesture plays a role in how speech is understood). Moreover, in addition to influencing the information that listeners glean from speech, gesture also conveys its own information that listeners understand. For example, a listener is more likely to attribute one-to-one correspondence to a child who expresses that rationale uniquely in gesture (i.e., not in speech) than to a child who does not express the rationale in either gesture or speech (Goldin-Meadow et al., 1992; see also Alibali et al., 1997).

Listeners are thus able to glean information from a speaker's gestures, and they act on this information – they change how they react to a speaker as a function of the gestures that the speaker produces. For example, when providing instruction on mathematical equivalence problems (e.g., 4+3+6=__+6), teachers offer different problem-solving strategies to children who produce gesture–speech mismatches when they explain how they solved the problems than to children who do not produce gesture–speech mismatches. In particular, teachers provide more different types of problem-solving strategies, and more of their own gesture–speech mismatches, to mismatching children than to matching children (Goldin-Meadow and Singer, 2003). The teachers' mismatches were different from the children's in that both strategies (the one produced in speech and the one produced in gesture) were correct; in contrast, in the child mismatches, at least one strategy (and often two) was incorrect. Teachers thus vary the instruction they give children in response to the children's gestures. And those gestures make a difference. In an experimental study designed to determine whether the instruction teachers spontaneously gave mismatching children was good for learning, Singer and Goldin-Meadow (2005) found that providing children with two different strategies, one in speech and another in gesture (i.e., a mismatch), was particularly effective in teaching them how to solve the mathematical equivalence problems, more effective than providing the same two strategies entirely in speech. Gesture is thus part of the conversation and, as such, can be harnessed in the classroom and other situations (e.g., an interview, Broaders and Goldin-Meadow, 2010) to bring about change.

4.1.3.2 The cognitive functions co-speech gestures serve

Gesture affects not only listeners but also the speakers themselves, and does so in a variety of ways. First, gesturing may help speakers find their words, that is, to access lexical items that feel as though they are on the "tip of the tongue" (Rauscher et al., 1996). Speakers are, in fact, more likely to gesture when they are saying something new (Chawla and Krauss, 1994), when they are saying something unpredictable (Beattie and Shovelton, 2000), and when word-finding is made more difficult (Rauscher et al., 1996). In addition, brain-damaged patients with difficulties in finding words (i.e., patients with aphasia) gesture at a higher rate than patients with visuospatial difficulties (Hadar et al., 1998). Gesturing is thus associated with having difficulties in lexical access. More convincing still is the fact that speakers are more successful at resolving a tip-of-the-tongue word-finding state when they are permitted to gesture than when they are not permitted to gesture, for both adult (Frick-Horbury and Guttentag, 1998) and child (Pine et al., 2007) speakers (but see Beattie and Coughlan, 1999, for a different view).

Second, gesturing may help link the words the speaker produces to the world. Deictic gestures, in particular, may help the speaker make use of the surrounding space (Ballard et al., 1997). For example, gesturing seems to be important in coordinating number words with objects for children learning to count, and also in keeping track of which objects have already been counted (Saxe and Kaplan, 1981). Children make fewer errors coordinating number words and objects when they gesture while counting than when they watch a puppet gesture while they count, or than when they are told not to gesture while counting (Alibali and DiRusso, 1999). However, a speaker's gestures do not have to be directed at visible objects in order for that speaker to benefit from gesturing (Ping and Goldin-Meadow, 2010), suggesting that gesturing need not be tied to the physical environment in order to be effective.

Third, gesturing can reduce demands on thinking and remembering. Speakers gesture more on conceptually difficult problems, even when the lexical demands of the problem are equivalent (Alibali et al., 2000; Hostetter and Alibali, 2007; Melinger and Kita, 2007; Kita and Davies, 2009). For example, when adult speakers are asked to describe dot patterns, they gesture more when talking about patterns that are more difficult to conceptualize (i.e., patterns that do not have lines connecting the dots) than about patterns that are easier to conceptualize (i.e., patterns that do have lines, Hostetter and Alibali, 2007). As a second example, children gesture more when they are asked to solve problems that require conceptualization (e.g., Piagetian conservation problems) than when they are asked to describe a scene (e.g., to describe the materials used in a conservation problem, Alibali et al., 2000). Since gesture is a natural format for capturing spatial information, it is not surprising that it is particularly effective in reducing conceptual demands in visuospatial tasks. Gesturing has been shown to maintain visuospatial information in memory (Wesp et al., 2001; Morsella and Krauss, 2005), facilitate packaging of visuospatial information for spoken language (Kita, 2000), and facilitate transformation of spatial information in memory (when performing mental rotation tasks, adults are particularly successful if they produce gestures consistent with the actual rotation that is to be performed, Wexler *et al.*, 1998; Wohlschläger and Wohlschläger, 1998; Schwartz and Black, 1999). Although consistent with the idea that gesturing reduces demands on conceptualization, all of these studies manipulate problem difficulty and observe the effects of the manipulation on gesturing. But to definitively demonstrate that gesturing plays a role in reducing conceptualization demands (as opposed to merely reflecting those demands), we need to manipulate gesture and then find that the manipulation reduces demands on conceptualization.

This type of gesture manipulation has been done with respect to working memory. Goldin-Meadow *et al.* (2001) asked speakers to remember an unrelated list of items while explaining how they solved a math problem. Half of the speakers were permitted to gesture during their explanations, and half were prevented from gesturing. Speakers (both adults and children) were able to maintain more items in verbal working memory, and thus recall more items, when they gestured during their explanations than when they did not gesture. This effect held even for problems on which the speakers chose not to gesture (as opposed to being told not to gesture), thus making it clear that the effect was not due to being instructed not to gesture (see also Wagner *et al.*, 2004). Gesturing reduces demand on working memory even when the gestures are not directed at visually present objects (Ping and Goldin-Meadow, 2010), suggesting that gesturing confers its benefits by more than simply tying abstract speech to objects directly visible in the environment. Importantly, it is not just moving the hands that reduces demand on working memory – it is the fact that the moving hands are meaningful. Speakers remember more when asked to gesture during their explanations than when asked to produce meaningless rhythmic movements or no movements at all during their explanations (Cook *et al.*, 2010).

Finally, gesturing can affect speakers by activating old thoughts or forming new ones. Broaders *et al.* (2007) asked children to explain how they solved six mathematical equivalence problems with no instructions about what to do with their hands. They then asked the children to solve a second set of comparable problems and divided the children into three groups: some were told to move their hands as they explained their solutions to this second set of problems; some were told not to move their hands; and some were given no instructions about their hands. Children who were told to gesture on the second set of problems added strategies to their repertoires that they had not previously produced; children who were told not to gesture, and children given no instructions at all, did not. Most of the added strategies were produced in gesture and not in speech and, surprisingly, most were correct. In addition, when later given instruction in mathematical equivalence, it was the children who had been told to gesture, and had added strategies to their repertoires, who profited from the instruction and learned how to solve the math problems.

Being told to gesture thus encouraged children to express ideas that they had previously not expressed, which, in turn, led to learning.

To determine whether gesture can create new ideas, we need to teach speakers to move their hands in particular ways. If speakers can extract meaning from their hand movements, they should be sensitive to the particular movements they are taught to produce and learn accordingly. Alternatively, all that may matter is that speakers move their hands. If so, they should learn regardless of which movements they produce. To investigate these alternatives, Goldin-Meadow et al. (2009) manipulated gesturing during a math lesson. They found that children required to produce *correct* gestures instantiating the *grouping* strategy learned more than children required to produce *partially correct* gestures, who learned more than children required to produce *no* gestures. Moreover, after the lesson, the children who improved began producing the *grouping* strategy in speech. Note that, during training, the children produced *grouping* only in gesture (and not in speech) and the teacher did not produce it in either modality. Gesturing thus plays a role not only in processing old ideas, but also in creating new ones.

To summarize thus far, when speakers talk, they move their hands and those hand movements form an integrated system with the speech they accompany, at times conveying information that is not found in speech. These gestures have an impact on communication through the listener and an impact on cognition through the speaker. We turn next to the hand movements people produce in the absence of speech, beginning with conventional sign languages created by deaf communities.

4.2 When the manual modality is used instead of speech: Sign language

We have seen that the manual modality assumes an imagistic form when it is used in conjunction with a segmented and combinatorial system (i.e., speech). But what happens when the manual modality must fulfill all of the functions of language on its own? Under these circumstances, the manual modality changes its form and itself becomes segmented and combinatorial. We see these form changes not only in established sign languages that have been handed down from generation to generation within a deaf community, but also in newly emerging sign languages.

4.2.1 Established sign languages

Sign languages of the deaf are autonomous languages, independent of the spoken languages of hearing cultures. The most striking example of this independence is that American Sign Language (ASL) is structured very differently from British Sign Language (BSL), despite the fact that English is the spoken language used by the hearing communities surrounding both sign languages. Even though sign languages are processed by the hand and eye, rather than the mouth and ear, sign languages have the defining properties of segmentation and combination that characterize all spoken language systems (Klima and Bellugi, 1979; Sandler and Lillo-Martin, 2006). Sign languages are structured at the sentence level (syntactic structure), at the sign level (morphological structure), and at the level of sub-sign, and have meaningless elements akin to phonemes ("phonological" structure). Just like words in spoken languages (but unlike the gestures that accompany speech, Goldin-Meadow et al., 1996), signs combine to create larger wholes (sentences) that are typically characterized by a basic order, for example, SVO (Subject-Verb-Object) in ASL; SOV in Sign Language of the Netherlands. Moreover, the signs that comprise the sentences are themselves composed of meaningful components (morphemes).

Many of the signs in a language like ASL are iconic. However, iconicity is not unique to sign languages and can be found in spoken languages as well (e.g., Shintel and Nusbaum, 2008). Moreover, the iconicity found in a sign language does not appear to play a significant role in the way the language is processed or learned. For example, young children are just as likely to learn a sign whose form does not resemble its referent as a sign whose form is an iconic depiction of the referent (Bonvillian et al., 1983). Similarly, young sign learners find morphologically complex constructions difficult to learn even if they are iconic (e.g., although moving the sign *give* from the chest toward the listener seems to be an iconically transparent way of expressing *I give to you*, the sign is, in fact, morphologically complex as it is marked for both the agent *I* and the recipient *you* and, as such, turns out to be a relatively late acquisition in ASL learners, Meier, 1987).

Moreover, sign languages do not always take advantage of the iconic potential that the manual modality offers. For example, although it would be easy enough to indicate the manner of motion in a sign describing a skate boarder circling around, to be grammatically correct, the ASL signer must produce separate, serially linked signs for the manner and for the path (Supalla, 1990). As another example, the sign for *slow* in ASL is made by moving one hand across the back of the other hand. When the sign is modified to be *very slow*, it is made more rapidly since this is the particular modification of movement associated with an intensification meaning in ASL (Klima and Bellugi, 1979). Thus, modifying the meaning of a sign can reduce its iconicity in a conventional sign language simply because the meaning of the sign as a whole is made up of the meanings of the components that comprise it.

In contrast, as described earlier, the gestures that accompany speech are not composed of parts but are instead non-compositional wholes. Since the gesture as a whole must be a good representation of its referent, the addition of semantic information to a spontaneous gesture always increases its iconicity – if something is thought of as very slow, the gesture for it is also very slow (McNeill, 1992). The gesture *as a whole* represents *very slow* and, although one could, in principle, break up the gesture into two parts (such as *slow*, a movement across the back of the hand, and *very*, an exaggerated and slowed movement), there is no evidence that these particular forms have independent and consistent meaning across a range of gestures – as they would have to if they were part of a combinatorial system in a conventional sign language.

Whether the modality in which sign language is produced shapes how the language is structured is an open (and contested) question. The sign languages that have been studied thus far are, on the whole, morphologically rich and thus comparable to a subset, and not the entire range, of spoken languages (we have not yet discovered, for example, an established sign language that has very little morphology, a characteristic of some spoken languages, e.g., Mandarin Chinese). Sign languages might occupy only a piece of the continuum along which spoken languages are arrayed because of pressures from the manual modality. However, other factors, such as the fact that sign languages tend to be relatively young and to evolve under unusual social circumstances, might also influence the way sign languages are structured.

4.2.2 Emerging sign languages

Spoken languages have long histories and, although we can fruitfully examine how these languages change over time, we cannot go back to their roots. And new spoken languages are not really new. For example, *pidgin* languages arise when speakers of two or more mutually unintelligible languages come into contact and need to communicate; the language becomes a *creole* once children are born into the pidgin-speaking households (McWhorter, 1998; Mufwene, 2001). But pidgins and creoles are grounded in at least two existing spoken languages and, in this sense, are built on previously existing languages. In contrast, languages do arise *de novo* in the manual modality. When deaf people who have not been exposed to a sign language and are unable to learn spoken language come together to form a community, a new sign language is often born. These sign languages are of two types, distinguished by the social conditions under which they emerge (Woll and Ladd, 2003; Sandler, 2005; Meir, Sandler *et al.*, 2010) – *village sign languages*, which emerge when deaf children are born into existing communities, and *deaf community sign languages*, which emerge when deaf individuals are brought together to form a community.

4.2.2.1 A village sign language: Al-Sayyid Bedouin Sign Language

An example of a village sign language is Al-Sayyid Bedouin Sign Language (ABSL, Sandler *et al.*, 2005). A community, now in its seventh generation and containing 3,500 members, was founded 200 years ago in Israel by the

Al-Sayyid Bedouins. Within the last three generations, 150 deaf individuals were born into this community, all descended from two of the founders' five sons. ABSL was thus born. The language now has three generations of signers and offers the opportunity to not only observe a language in its infant stages but also watch it grow.

ABSL is not yet a mature language and thus is still undergoing rapid change. As a result, signers from each of the three generations are likely to differ, and to differ systematically, in the system of signs they use. By observing signers from each generation, we can therefore make good guesses as to when a particular linguistic property first entered the language. Moreover, because the individual families in the community are tightly knit, with strong bonds within families but not across them, we can chart changes in the language in relation to the social network of the community. We can determine when properties remained within a single family and when they did not, and thus follow the trajectory that particular linguistic properties took as they spread (or failed to spread) throughout the community. This small and self-contained community consequently offers a unique perspective on some classic questions in historical linguistics (Labov, 1994, 2001).

It is important to note, however, that even the first generation of signers used a system of signs characterized by segmentation and linearization (Meir et al., 2010). In other words, the initial sign language did not look like co-speech gesture. In addition, highly regular sign order evolved to mark grammatical relations within the first generation; the particular order used is SOV. Interestingly, however, the language appears to have developed very little, if any, complex morphology (Aronoff et al., 2004), a property found in all established sign languages studied thus far.

4.2.2.2 A deaf community sign language: Nicaraguan Sign Language

An example of a deaf community sign language is Nicaraguan Sign Language (NSL). NSL was created by deaf individuals who were brought together for the first time in the late 1970s and became the first-generation cohort (Kegl et al., 1999; Senghas and Coppola, 2001). The signs that the first cohort uses are segmented, with each semantic primitive represented as an independent element. For example, first-cohort signers are more likely to convey manner and path in separate signs than in a single sign (the hand makes a circular movement *followed by* a downward movement, rather than the hand making a circular movement *simultaneously with* the downward movement, Senghas et al., 2004). Moreover, first-cohort signers combine their signs, adhering to consistent word orders to convey who does what to whom (Senghas et al., 1997).

But NSL has not stopped there. Every year, new students enter the school and learn to sign among their peers. This second cohort of signers has as its input the sign system developed by the first cohort and, interestingly, changes that input so that the product becomes more language-like. For example, although first-cohort signers occasionally describe events using individual manner and path signs presented sequentially, second-cohort signers do it more often (Senghas *et al.*, 2004). Similarly, first-cohort signers occasionally produce verbs with two or more arguments, but second-cohort signers use them more often (Senghas, 1995). Given this additional complexity, it seems quite natural that second-cohort signers go beyond the small set of basic word orders used by the first cohort, introducing new orders not seen previously in the language (Senghas *et al.*, 1997). Moreover, the second cohort begins to use spatial devices invented by the first cohort, but they use these devices consistently and for contrastive purposes (Senghas *et al.*, 1997; Senghas and Coppola, 2001). The second cohort, in a sense, stands on the shoulders of the first. They do not need to invent properties like segmentation and linearization – those properties are already present in their input. They can therefore take the transformation process one step further.

Like ABSL, NSL has arisen with no influence from any established language, either signed or spoken. However, NSL differs from ABSL in that the community within which it is developing is less socially stable, and the children learn their language from other members of the deaf community at school rather than from their parents at home. The differences and similarities between the two systems can thus provide useful information about the trajectories that emerging sign languages follow as they grow into a fully formed conventional system.

4.2.3 Homesign: The first step toward becoming a language

Emerging sign languages like ABSL and NSL hold a unique position between established sign languages and what has come to be known as *homesign* (Goldin-Meadow, 2003; 2009), a gesture system developed by a deaf child whose hearing losses prevent that child from acquiring spoken language and whose hearing parents have not exposed the child to a conventional sign language; that is, an individual gesture system not shared even with the hearing family members within that home. Established sign languages tell us where emerging sign languages are going. Homesign tell us where they may have started.

Despite their lack of a usable model of conventional language (and often despite intensive oral education), homesigners communicate and do so using gestures characterized by many, although not all, of the properties found in natural languages (Goldin-Meadow, 2003). For example, homesigners' gestures form a lexicon, and these lexical items are composed of parts, comparable in structure to a morphological system (Goldin-Meadow *et al.*, 1995; 2007). Moreover, the lexical items combine to form structured sentences, comparable in structure to a syntactic system (Feldman *et al.*, 1978; Goldin-Meadow and Mylander, 1984; 1998). In addition, homesigners use gestural lexical markers that modulate the meanings of their gesture sentences (negation and questions, Franklin *et al.*, 2011) and grammatical categories (nouns, verbs, and adjectives, Goldin-Meadow *et al.*,

1994). Homesigners display hierarchical structure in their sentences by building structure around the nominal constituent (Hunsicker and Goldin-Meadow, 2012) or by adding a second proposition to create a complex sentence (Goldin-Meadow, 1982). Finally, homesigners use their gestures not only to make requests of others, but also to comment on the present and non-present (Butcher et al., 1991; Morford and Goldin-Meadow, 1997); to make generic statements about classes of objects (Goldin-Meadow et al., 2005); to tell stories about real and imagined events (Morford, 1995; Phillips et al., 2001); to talk to themselves (Goldin-Meadow 2003); and to talk about language (Goldin-Meadow, 1993) – that is, to serve typical functions that all languages serve, signed or spoken.

In countries like the United States, homesigners are likely to learn a conventional sign language at some later point in their lives, often around adolescence. However, in Nicaragua, many homesigners continue to use the gesture systems they create as children as their sole means of communication. Analyses of adult homesign in Nicaragua have uncovered linguistic structures that may turn out to go beyond the structures found in child homesign: the grammatical category subject (Coppola and Newport, 2005); pointing devices representing locations vs. nominals (Coppola and Senghas, 2010); morphophonological finger complexity patterns (Brentari et al., 2012); and morphological devices that mark number (Coppola et al., 2013). By contrasting the linguistic systems constructed by child and adult homesigners, we can see the impact that growing older has on language.

In addition, by contrasting the linguistic systems constructed by adult homesigners in Nicaragua with the structures used by the first cohort of NSL signers, we can see the impact that a community of users has on language. Having a group with whom they could communicate meant that the first cohort of signers were both producers and receivers of their linguistic system, a circumstance that could lead to a system with greater systematicity – but perhaps less complexity, as the group may need to adjust to the lowest common denominator.

Finally, by contrasting the linguistic systems developed by the first and second cohorts of NSL (e.g., Senghas, 2003), we can see the impact that passing a language through a new generation of learners has on language. Once learners are exposed to a system that has linguistic structure (i.e., cohort 2 and beyond), the processes of language change may be identical to the processes studied in historical linguistics. One interesting question is whether the changes seen in NSL in its earliest stages are of the same type and magnitude as the changes that occur in mature languages over historical time.

4.2.4 Hearing gesture: Input to homesign

A defining feature of homesign is that it is not shared in the way that conventional communication systems are. Deaf homesigners produce gestures to communicate with the hearing individuals in their homes. But the hearing individuals, particularly hearing parents who are committed to teaching their children to talk and thus to oral education, use speech back. Although this speech is often accompanied by gesture (Flaherty and Goldin-Meadow, 2010), as we have seen earlier, the gestures that co-occur with speech form an integrated system with that speech and, in this sense, are not free to take on the properties of the deaf child's gestures. As a result, although hearing parents respond to their deaf child's gestures, they do not adopt the gestures themselves (nor do they typically acknowledge that the child even uses gesture to communicate). The parents produce co-speech gestures, not homesigns.

Not surprisingly, then, the structures found in child homesign cannot be traced back to the spontaneous gestures that hearing parents produce while talking to their children (Goldin-Meadow and Mylander, 1983, 1984; Goldin-Meadow et al., 1994, 1995). Homesigners see the global and unsegmented gestures that their parents produce. But when gesturing themselves, they use gestures that are characterized by segmentation and linearization. Although the gestures hearing individuals produce when they talk do not provide a model for the linguistic structures found in homesign, they could provide the raw materials for the linguistic constructions that homesigners build (see, for example, Goldin-Meadow et al., 2007). As such, co-speech gesture could contribute to the picture of emerging sign languages that we are building (see Senghas et al., 2004). Moreover, the disparity between co-speech gesture and homesign has important implications for language learning. To the extent that the properties of homesign differ from the properties of co-speech gesture, the deaf children themselves are likely to be imposing these particular structural properties on their communication systems. It is an intriguing, but as yet unanswered, question as to where the tendency to impose structure on homesign comes from.

Co-speech gestures do not assume the linguistic properties found in homesign. But what would happen if we were to ask hearing speakers to abandon speech and create a manual communication system on the spot? Would that system contain the linguistic properties found in homesign? Examining the gestures that hearing speakers produce when requested to communicate without speech allows us to explore the robustness of linguistic constructions created online in the manual modality.

Hearing gesturers asked to gesture without speaking are able to construct some properties of language with their hands. For example, the order of the gestures they construct on the spot indicates who does what to whom (Goldin-Meadow et al., 1996; Gershkoff-Stowe and Goldin-Meadow, 2002). However, hearing gesturers do not display other linguistic properties found in established sign languages and even in homesign. For example, they do not use consistent form–meaning pairings akin to morphemes (Singleton et al., 1993), nor do they use the same finger complexity patterns that established sign languages and homesign display (Brentari et al., 2012).

Interestingly, the gestures that hearing speakers construct on the spot without speech do not appear to be derived from their spoken language. When hearing speakers of four different languages (English, Spanish, Chinese, Turkish) are asked to describe animated events using their hands and no speech, they abandon the order typical of their respective spoken languages and produce gestures that conform to the same order – SOV (e.g., captain-pail-swings; Goldin-Meadow et al., 2008), the order found in ABSL (Sandler et al., 2005). This order is also found when hearing speakers of these four languages perform a non-communicative, non-gestural task (Goldin-Meadow et al., 2008). Recent work on English-, Turkish-, and Italian-speakers has replicated the SOV order in hearing gesturers, but finds that gesturers move away from this order when given a lexicon (either spoken or manual, Hall et al., 2010); when asked to describe reversible events involving two animates (*girl pulled man*, Meir, Lifshitz et al., 2010); and when asked to describe more complex events (*man tells child that girl catches fish*, Langus and Nespor, 2010). Studies of hearing gesturers give us the opportunity to manipulate conditions that have the potential to affect communication, and to then observe the effect of those conditions on the structure of the emerging language.

4.2.5 Do signers gesture?

We have seen that hearing speakers produce analog, imagistic signals in the manual modality (i.e., gesture) along with the segmented, discrete signals they produce in the oral modality (i.e., speech), and that these gestures serve a number of communicative and cognitive functions. The question we now ask is whether signers produce gestures and, if so, whether those gestures serve the same functions as co-speech gesture.

Deaf signers have been found to gesture when they sign (Emmorey, 1999; Sandler, 2003). But do they produce mismatches and do those mismatches predict learning? ASL-signing deaf children, asked to explain their solutions to the same math problems studied in hearing children (Perry et al., 1988), turn out to produce gestures just as often as the hearing children. Moreover, the deaf children who produce many gestures conveying different information from their signs (i.e., gesture–sign mismatches) are more likely to succeed after instruction in ASL than the deaf children who produce few mismatches (Goldin-Meadow et al., 2012).

These findings suggest not only that mismatch can occur within-modality (both sign and gesture use the manual modality), but that mismatch can predict learning in deaf signers just as it does in hearing speakers. Moreover, the findings suggest that juxtaposing different ideas across two modalities is *not* essential for mismatch to predict learning. Rather, it appears to be the juxtaposition of different ideas across two distinct representational formats – an analog format underlying gesture vs. a discrete and segmented format underlying words or signs – that is responsible for mismatch predicting learning. Finally, the findings pave the way for using gesture-based teaching strategies with deaf learners.

4.3 Conclusion

Humans are equipotential with respect to language-learning – if exposed to language in the manual modality, children will learn a sign language as quickly and effortlessly as they learn a spoken language. Why then has the oral modality become the modality of choice for languages around the globe? One hypothesis is that the oral modality might have triumphed over the manual modality simply because it is so good at encoding messages in the segmented and combinatorial form that human languages have come to assume. But as we have seen in our examination of sign language, the manual modality is just as good as the oral modality at segmented and combinatorial encoding. There is thus little to choose between sign and speech on these grounds. However, as we have seen in our examination of co-speech gesture, language serves another important function – it conveys information imagistically. The oral modality is not particularly well suited to this function, but the manual modality excels at it. It is possible, then, that the oral modality assumes the segmented and combinatorial format characteristic of all natural languages not because of its strengths, but to compensate for its weaknesses (Goldin-Meadow and McNeill, 1999).

Whatever role the manual modality has played in fashioning the way language looks today, it is clear that the hands have much to tell us about human functioning. The way speakers move their hands when they talk – co-speech gesture – provides insight into speakers' thoughts (thoughts they may not know they have) and can even play a role in changing those thoughts. The way signers move their hands when speech is not possible – as seen in both emerging and established sign languages – provides insight into the properties of language that define human language and the factors that have made human language what it is. How humans use the manual modality to communicate reveals a great deal about how we talk and think.

References

Alibali, M. W., and A. A. DiRusso. 1999. The Function of Gesture in Learning to Count: More than keeping track. *Cognitive Development* 14: 37–56.
Alibali, M. W., L. Flevares, and S. Goldin-Meadow. 1997. Assessing Knowledge Conveyed in Gesture: Do teachers have the upper hand? *Journal of Educational Psychology* 89: 183–93.

Alibali, M. W. and S. Goldin-Meadow. 1993. Gesture–Speech Mismatch and Mechanisms of Learning: What the hands reveal about a child's state of mind. *Cognitive Psychology* 25: 468–523.

Alibali, M. W., S. Kita, and A. J. Young. 2000. Gesture and the Process of Speech Production: We think, therefore we gesture. *Language and Cognitive Processes* 15: 593–613.

Aronoff, M., I. Meir, C. A Padden, and W. Sandler. 2004. Morphological Universals and the Sign Language Type. *Yearbook of Morphology*: 19–40.

Ballard, D. H., M. M. Hayhoe, P. K. Pook, and R. P. N. Rao. 1997. Deictic Codes for the Embodiment of Cognition. *Behavioral and Brain Sciences* 20: 723–67.

Beattie, G., and J. Coughlan. 1999. An Experimental Investigation of the Role of Iconic Gestures in Lexical Access Using the Tip-of-the-tongue Phenomenon. *British Journal of Psychology* 90: 35–56.

Beattie, G., and H. Shovelton. 2000. Iconic Hand Gestures and the Predictability of Words in Context in Spontaneous Speech. *British Journal of Psychology* 91: 473–91.

2002. What Properties of Talk are Associated with the Generation of Spontaneous Iconic Hand Gestures? *British Journal of Social Psychology* 41: 403–17

Bonvillian, J. D., M. O. Orlansky, and L. L. Novack. 1983. Developmental Milestones: Sign language acquisition and motor development. *Child Development* 54: 1435–45.

Brentari, D., M. Coppola, L. Mazzoni, and S. Goldin-Meadow. 2012. When Does a System Become Phonological? Handshape production in gesturers, signers, and homesigners. *Natural Language and Linguistic Theory* 30(1): 1–31.

Broaders, S., S. W. Cook, Z. Mitchell, and S. Goldin-Meadow. 2007. Making Children Gesture Brings Out Implicit Knowledge and Leads to Learning. *Journal of Experimental Psychology: General* 136 (4): 539–50.

Broaders, S., and S. Goldin-Meadow. 2010. Truth Is At Hand: How gesture adds information during investigative interviews. *Psychological Science* 21(5): 623–8.

Butcher, C., and S. Goldin-Meadow. 2000. Gesture and the Transition from One- to Two-Word Speech: When hand and mouth come together. In *Language and gesture*, ed. D. McNeill, 235–57. Cambridge: Cambridge University Press.

Butcher, C., C. Mylander, and S. Goldin-Meadow. 1991. Displaced Communication in a Self-styled Gesture System: Pointing at the non-present. *Cognitive Development* 6: 315–42.

Chawla, P. and R. Krauss. 1994. Gesture and Speech in Spontaneous and Rehearsed Narratives. *Journal of Experimental Social Psychology* 30: 580–601.

Church, R. B., and S. Goldin-Meadow. 1986. The Mismatch between Gesture and Speech as an Index of Transitional Knowledge. *Cognition* 23: 43–71.

Cole, J. (1991). *Pride and a Daily Marathon*. London: Duckworth.

Cook, S. W., and M. K. Tanenhaus. 2009. Embodied Communication: Speakers' gestures affect listeners' actions. *Cognition* 113: 98–104.

Cook, S. W., T. K. Yip, and S. Goldin-Meadow. 2010. Gesturing Makes Memories that Last. *Journal of Memory and Language* 63(4): 465–75.

Coppola, M., and E. Newport. 2005. Grammatical Subjects in Homesign: Abstract linguistic structure in adult primary gesture systems without linguistic input. *Proceedings of the National Academy of Sciences* 102: 19249–53.

Coppola, M., and A. Senghas. 2010. The Emergence of Deixis in Nicaraguan Signing. In *Sign Languages: A Cambridge Language Survey*, ed. D. Brentari, 543–69. Cambridge: Cambridge University Press.

Coppola, M., E. Spaepen, and S. Goldin-Meadow. 2013. Communicating about Quantity without a Language Model: Number devices in homesign grammar. *Cognitive Psychology* 67, 1–25.

Emmorey, K. 1999. Do Signers Gesture? In *Gesture, Speech, and Sign*, ed. L. S. Messing and R. Campbell, 133–59. Oxford: Oxford University Press.

Enfield, N. J. 2005. The Body as a Cognitive Artifact in Kinship Representations: Hand gesture diagrams by speakers of Lao. *Current Anthropology* 46(1): 51–81.

Feldman, H., S. Goldin-Meadow, and L. Gleitman. 1978. Beyond Herodotus: The creation of language by linguistically deprived deaf children. In *Action, symbol, and gesture: The emergence of language*, ed. A. Lock, 351–414. New York: Academic Press.

Feyereisen, P. and J.-D. de Lannoy. 1991. *Gestures and Speech: Psychological Investigations*. Cambridge: Cambridge University Press.

Flaherty, M. and S. Goldin-Meadow. 2010. Does Input Matter? Gesture and homesign in Nicaragua, China, Turkey, and the USA. In *Proceedings of the Eighth Evolution of Language Conference*, ed. A. D. M. Smith, M. Schouwstra, B. de Boer, and K. Smith, 403–4. Singapore: World Scientific Publishing Co.

Franklin, A., A. Giannakidou, and S. Goldin-Meadow. 2011. Negation, Questions, and Structure Building in a Homesign System. *Cognition* 118 (3): 398–416.

Frick-Horbury, D., and R. E. Guttentag. 1998. The Effects of Restricting Hand Gesture Production on Lexical Retrieval and Free Recall. *American Journal of Psychology* 111: 44–61.

Gallagher, S., J. Cole, and D. McNeill. 2001. The language-thought-hand system. In *Oralité et gestualité: Interactions et comportements multimodaux dans la communication*, ed. C. Cave, I. Guaitella and S. Santi, 420–4. Paris: L'Harmattan.

Gershkoff-Stowe, L., and S. Goldin-Meadow. 2002. Is There a Natural Order for Expressing Semantic Relations. *Cognitive Psychology* 45 (3): 375–412.

Goldin-Meadow, S. 1982. The Resilience of Recursion: A study of a communication system developed without a conventional language model.

In *Language acquisition: The state of the art*, ed. E. Wanner and L. R. Gleitman, 51–77. New York: Cambridge University Press.

1993. When Does Gesture Become Language? A study of gesture used as a primary communication system by deaf children of hearing parents. In *Tools, Language and Cognition in Human Evolution*, ed. K. R. Gibson and T. Ingold, 63–85. New York: Cambridge University Press.

2003. *Resilience of Language: What Gesture Creation in Deaf Children Can Tell Us about How All Children Learn Language*. New York: Psychology Press.

2009. Homesign: When gesture becomes language. In *Handbook on Sign Language Linguistics*, ed. R. Pfau, M. Steinbach, and B. Woll, 145–60. Berlin: Mouton de Gruyter.

Goldin-Meadow, S., C. Butcher, C. Mylander, and M. Dodge. 1994. Nouns and Verbs in a Self-Styled Gesture System: What's in a name? *Cognitive Psychology* 27: 259–319.

Goldin-Meadow, S., S. W. Cook, and Z. A. Mitchell. 2009. Gesturing Gives Children New Ideas About Math. *Psychological Science* 20(3): 267–72.

Goldin-Meadow, S., Gelman, S., and Mylander, C. 2005. Expressing Generic Concepts with and without a Language Model. *Cognition*, 96, 109–126.

Goldin-Meadow, S. and D. McNeill. 1999. The Role of Gesture and Mimetic Representation in Making Language the Province of Speech. In *The Descent of Mind*, ed. Michael C. Corballis and Stephen Lea, 155–72. Oxford: Oxford University Press.

Goldin-Meadow, S., D. McNeill, and J. Singleton. 1996. Silence is Liberating: Removing the handcuffs on grammatical expression in the manual modality. *Psychological Review* 103: 34–55.

Goldin-Meadow, S., and C. Mylander. 1983. Gestural Communication in Deaf Children: The non-effects of parental input on language development. *Science* 221: 372–4.

1984. Gestural Communication in Deaf Children: The effects and non-effects of parental input on early language development. *Monographs of the Society for Research in Child Development* 49: 1–121.

1998. Spontaneous Sign Systems Created by Deaf Children in Two Cultures. *Nature* 91: 279–81.

Goldin-Meadow, S., C. Mylander, and C. Butcher. 1995. The Resilience of Combinatorial Structure at the Word Level: Morphology in self-styled gesture systems. *Cognition* 56: 195–262.

Goldin-Meadow, S., C. Mylander, and A. Franklin. 2007. How Children Make Language out of Gesture: Morphological structure in gesture systems developed by American and Chinese deaf children. *Cognitive Psychology* 55: 87–135.

Goldin-Meadow, S., H. Nusbaum, S. D. Kelly, and S. Wagner. 2001. Explaining Math: Gesturing lightens the load. *Psychological Sciences*: 12: 516–22.

Goldin-Meadow, S. and C. M. Sandhofer. 1999. Gesture Conveys Substantive Information About a Child's Thoughts to Ordinary Listeners. *Developmental Science* 2: 67–74.

Goldin-Meadow, S., A. Shield, D. Lenzen, M. Herzig, and C. Padden. 2012. The Gestures ASL Signers Use Tell Us When They Are Ready to Learn Math, *Cognition* 123, 448–453.

Goldin-Meadow, S., and M. A. Singer. 2003. From Children's Hands to Adults' Ears: Gesture's role in teaching and learning. *Developmental Psychology* 39 (3): 509–20.

Goldin-Meadow, S., W.-C. So, A. Özyürek, and Mylander, C. (2008). The Natural Order of Events: How speakers of different languages represent events nonverbally. *Proceedings of the National Academy of Sciences* 105(27): 9163–8.

Goldin-Meadow, S., D. Wein, and C. Chang. 1992. Assessing Knowledge Through Gesture: Using children's hands to read their minds. *Cognition and Instruction* 9: 201–19.

Graham, J. A., and M. Argyle. 1975. A Cross-Cultural Study of the Communication of Extra-Verbal Meaning by Gestures. *International Journal of Psychology* 10: 57–67.

Hadar, U., A. Burstein, R. Krauss, and N. Soroker. 1998. Ideational Gestures and Speech in Brain-Damaged Subjects. *Language and Cognitive Processes* 13: 59–76.

Hall, M., R. Mayberry, and V. Ferreira. 2010. Communication Systems Shape the Natural Order of Events: Competing biases from grammar and pantomime. Abstracts of the 4th conference of the International Society for Gesture Studies, Frankfurt.

Hostetter, A. B., and M. W. Alibali. 2007. Raise Your Hand If You're Spatial: Relations between verbal and spatial skills and gesture production. *Gesture* 7, 73–95.

Hunsicker, D., and S. Goldin-Meadow. 2012. Hierarchical Structure in a Self-Created Communication System: Building nominal constituents in homesign. *Language* 88(4): 732–63.

Iverson, J. M., and M. K. Fagan. 2004. Infant Vocal-Motor Coordination: Precursor to the gesture-speech system? *Child Development* 75: 1053–66.

Iverson, J. M., and S. Goldin-Meadow. 1998. Why People Gesture as they Speak. *Nature* 396: 228.

Kegl, J., A. Senghas, and M. Coppola. 1999. Creation through Contact: Sign language emergence and sign language change in Nicaragua. In *Language Creation and Language Change: Creolization, Diachrony, and Development*, ed. M. DeGraff, 179–237. Cambridge, MA: MIT.

Kelly, S. D., and R. B. Church. 1998. A Comparison Between Children's and Adults' Ability to Detect Conceptual Information Conveyed Through Representational Gestures. *Child Development* 69: 85–93.

Kelly, S. D., C. Kravitz, and M. Hopkins. 2004. Neural Correlates of Bimodal Speech and Gesture Comprehension. *Brain and Language* 89: 253–60.

Kendon, A. 1980. Gesticulation and Speech: Two aspects of the process of utterance. In *Relationship of Verbal and Nonverbal Communication*, ed. M. R. Key, 207–28. The Hague: Mouton.

Kita, S. 2000. How Representational Gestures Help Speaking. In *Language and Gesture: Window into Thought and Action*, ed. D. McNeill, 162–85. Cambridge: Cambridge University Press.

Kita, S., and T. S. Davies. 2009. Competing Conceptual Representations Trigger Co-Speech Representational Gestures. *Language and Cognitive Processes* 24: 761–75.

Kita, S., and A. Özyürek. 2003. What Does Cross-Linguistic Variation in Semantic Coordination of Speech and Gesture Reveal? Evidence for an interface representation of spatial thinking and speaking. *Journal of Memory and Language* 48(1): 16–32.

Kita, S., A. Özyürek, S. Allen, A. Brown, R. Furman, and T. Ishizuka. 2007. Relations Between Syntactic Encoding and Co-Speech Gestures: Implications for a model of speech and gesture production. *Language and Cognitive Processes* 22: 1212–36.

Klima, E., and U. Bellugi. 1979. *The Signs of Language*. Cambridge, MA: Harvard University Press.

Labov, W. 1994. *Principles of Linguistic Change*, Vol. 1: *Internal Factors*. Oxford: Blackwell.

——— 2001. *Principles of Linguistic Change*, Vol. 2: *Social Factors*. Oxford: Blackwell.

Langus, A., and M. Nespor. 2010. Cognitive Systems Struggling for Word Order. *Cognitive Psychology* 60: 291–318.

McNeil, N., M. W. Alibali, and J. L. Evans. 2000. The Role of Gesture in Children's Comprehension of Spoken Language: Now they need it, now they don't. *Journal of Nonverbal Behavior* 24: 131–50.

McNeill, D. 1992. *Hand and Mind: What Gestures Reveal About Thought*. Chicago: University of Chicago Press.

McWhorter, J. 1998. Identifying the Creole Prototype: Vindicating a typological class. *Language* 74: 788–818.

Meier, R. P. 1987. Elicited Imitation of Verb Agreement in American Sign Language: Iconically or morphologically determined? *Journal of Memory and Language* 26: 362–76.

Meir, I., A. Lifshitz, D. Ilkbasaran, and C. Padden. 2010. The Interaction of Animacy and Word Order in Human Languages: A study of strategies in a novel communication task. In *Proceedings of the Eighth Evolution of Language Conference*, ed. A. D. M. Smith, M. Schouwstra, B. de Boer, and K. Smith, 455–6. Singapore: World Scientific Publishing Co.

Meir, I., W. Sandler, C. Padden, and M. Aronoff. 2010. Emerging Sign Languages. In *Oxford Handbook of Deaf Studies, Language, and Education*, Vol. 2, ed. M. Marschark and P. E. Spencer, 267–80. Oxford: Oxford University Press.

Melinger, A. and Kita, S. 2007. Conceptualisation Load Triggers Gesture Production. *Language and Cognitive Processes* 22, 473–500.

Morford, J. P. 1995. How to Hunt an Iguana: The gestured narratives of non-signing deaf children. In *Sign Language Research 1994: Proceedings of the*

Fourth European Congress on Sign Language Research, ed. H. Bos and T. Schermer, 99–115. Hamburg: Signum Press.

Morford, J. P., and S. Goldin-Meadow. 1997. From Here to There and Now to Then: The development of displaced reference in homesign and English. *Child Development* 68: 420–35.

Morsella, E., and Krauss, R. M. 2005. Muscular Activity in the Arm during Lexical Retrieval: Implications for gesture-speech theories. *Journal of Psycholinguistic Research* 34, 415–427.

Mufwene, S. 2001. *The Ecology of Language Evolution*. New York: Cambridge University Press.

Özyürek, A., R. M. Willems, S. Kita, and P. Hagoort. 2007. On-line Integration of Semantic Information from Speech and Gesture: Insights from event-related brain potentials. *Journal of Cognitive Neuroscience* 19(4): 605–16.

Perry, M., R. B. Church, and S. Goldin-Meadow. 1988. Transitional Knowledge in the Acquisition of Concepts. *Cognitive Development* 3: 359–400.

Phillips, S. B., S. Goldin-Meadow, and P. J. Miller. 2001. Enacting Stories, Seeing Worlds: Similarities and differences in the cross-cultural narrative development of linguistically isolated deaf children. *Human Development* 44: 311–36.

Pine, K. J., H. Bird, and E. Kirk. 2007. The Effects of Prohibiting Gestures on Children's Lexical Retrieval Ability. *Developmental Science* 10: 747–54.

Pine, K. J., N. Lufkin, and D. Messer. 2004. More Gestures than Answers: Children learning about balance. *Developmental Psychology* 40: 1059–106.

Ping, R. M., and S. Goldin-Meadow. 2010. Gesturing Saves Cognitive Resources When Talking About Nonpresent Objects. *Cognitive Science* 34: 602–19.

Rauscher, F. H., R. M. Krauss, and Y. Chen. 1996. Gesture, Speech, and Lexical Access: The Role of Lexical Movements in Speech Production. *Psychological Science* 7: 226–31.

Sandler, W. 2003. On the Complementarity of Signed and Spoken Language. In *Language Competence Across Populations: On the Definition of SLI*, ed. Y. Levy and J. Schaeffer, 383–409. Mahwah, NJ: Earlbaum Associates.

— 2005. An Overview of Sign Language Linguistics. In *Encyclopedia of Language and Linguistics*, ed. K. Brown, 2nd ed., 328–38. Oxford: Elsevier.

Sandler, W. and D. Lillo-Martin. 2006. *Sign Language and Linguistic Universals*. Cambridge: Cambridge University Press.

Sandler, W., I. Meir, C. Padden, and M. Aronoff. 2005. The Emergence of Grammar: Systematic structure in a new language. *Proceedings of the National Academy of Sciences of America* 102: 2661–5.

Saxe, G. B., and R. Kaplan. 1981. Gesture in Early Counting: A developmental analysis. *Perceptual and Motor Skills* 53: 851–4.

Schwartz, D. L., and Black, T. 1999. Inferences through Imagined Actions: Knowing by simulated doing. *Journal of Experimental Psychology: Learning, Memory, and Cognition* 25, 116-136.

Senghas, A. 1995. The Development of Nicaraguan Sign Language via the Language Acquisition Process. *Proceedings of Boston University Child Language Development* 19: 543-52.

——— 2003. Intergenerational Influence and Ontogenetic Development in the Emergence of Spatial Grammar in Nicaraguan Sign Language. *Cognitive Development* 18: 511-31.

Senghas, A., and M. Coppola. 2001. Children Creating Language: How Nicaraguan Sign Language acquired a spatial grammar. *Psychological Science* 12: 323-8.

Senghas, A., M. Coppola, E. L. Newport, and T. Supalla. 1997. Argument Structure in Nicaraguan Sign Language: The Emergence of grammatical devices. In *Proceedings of Boston University Child Language Development*, 21(2), ed. E. Hughes, M. Hughes, and A. Greenhill, 550-61. Somerville, MA: Cascadilla Press.

Senghas, A., S. Kita, and A. Özyürek. 2004. Children Creating Core Properties of Language: Evidence from an emerging Sign Language in Nicaragua. *Science* 305: 1779-82.

Shintel, H., and H. C. Nusbaum. 2008. Moving to the Speed of Sound: Context modulation of the effect of acoustic properties of speech. *Cognitive Science* 32(6): 1063-74.

Silverman, L., L. Bennetto, E. Campana, and M. K. Tanenhaus. 2010. Speech-and-Gesture Integration in High Functioning Autism. *Cognition* 115: 380-93.

Singer, M. A., and S. Goldin-Meadow. 2005. Children Learn When Their Teachers' Gestures and Speech Differ. *Psychological Science* 16: 85-9.

Singleton, J. L., J. P. Morford, and S. Goldin-Meadow. 1993. Once Is Not Enough: Standards of well-formedness in manual communication created over three different timespans. *Language* 69: 683-715.

Supalla, T. 1990. Serial Verbs of Motion in American Sign Language. In *Issues in Sign Language Research*, ed. S. Fischer, 127-52. Chicago: University of Chicago Press.

Thompson, L. A., and D. W. Massaro. 1994. Children's Integration of Speech and Pointing Gestures in Comprehension. *Journal of Experimental Child Psychology* 57: 327-54.

Wagner, S., H. Nusbaum, and S. Goldin-Meadow. 2004. Probing the Mental Representation of Gesture: Is handwaving spatial? *Journal of Memory and Language* 50: 395-407.

Wesp, R., Hesse, J., Keutmann, D., and Wheaton, K. 2001. Gestures Maintain Spatial Imagery. *American Journal of Psychology*, 114, 591-600.

Wexler, M., Kosslyn, S. M., and Berthoz, A. 1998. Motor Processes in Mental Rotation. *Cognition* 68, 77-94.

Wohlschläger, A., and Wohlschläger, A., 1998. Mental and Manual Rotation. *Journal of Experimental Psychology: Human Perception and Performance* 24 (2), 397–412.

Woll, B., and P. Ladd. 2003. Deaf Communities. In *Oxford Handbook of Deaf Studies, Language, and Education*, ed. M. Marschark and P. E. Spencer, 151–62. Oxford: Oxford University Press.

Wu, Y. C., and S. Coulson. 2007. How Iconic Gestures Enhance Communication: An ERP study. *Brain and Language* 101: 234–45.

Wundt, W. 1973. *The Language of Gestures*. The Hague: Mouton and Co. (Originally published in 1900.)

5

Linguistic diversity and universals

Balthasar Bickel

5.1 Introduction

The phenomenon of human language appears in two opposite manifestations: on the one hand, the phenomenon manifests itself in thousands of individual languages, dialects, and sociolects, and these come with differences that are often so obvious and easy to notice (e.g., different sounds, words, ways of saying things) that people can debate about them and deploy them for marking social or national boundaries. On the other hand, language manifests itself as a universal phenomenon that is shared by our entire species, processed by a brain that is in many fundamental aspects identical for all members of the species, learned efficiently by every infant in the first few years, and used for universally comparable purposes in communication.

Understanding how these two opposite manifestations can be reconciled has been at the core of linguistic research for a long time, and the pendulum has swung back and forth between emphasizing one or the other side. In the first half of the twentieth century, it was taken for granted that diversity is enormous and constantly evolving, while in the second half, linguistics has sent a strong message that despite all diversity, languages are built on a single universal grammar. From outside linguistics, it is difficult to find one's way in this opposition, especially so because the opposition is often fraught with ideological assertions, social factions in the scientific community, and a bewildering proliferation of theories that try to sell the right way of studying language (such as "the Minimalist Program," "Lexical-Functional Grammar," "Cognitive Grammar," and dozens more; see Heine and Narrog 2012 for a recent collection).

But for anthropology, just like for any other discipline in the neighborhood of linguistics, the dual nature of language as both a diverse and universal phenomenon is of key importance: for example, if we want to

I thank Sabine Stoll, Larry Hyman, Martin Haspelmath and Nick Enfield for helpful comments on an earlier draft.

understand the role that language plays in shaping society and ideas, we need to know where variation is played out in language and where it is constrained, and what forces determine universal trends and patterns. The present chapter aims to chart out the relevant issues, trying to stay away from the thickets of ideologies and competing theories in order to highlight what I see as the more fundamental questions. I begin by illustrating the various ways in which languages differ from each other (section 5.2) and then raise the question in what sense one can talk about universals despite this apparent diversity and variation (section 5.3). The concluding section (5.4) summarizes the current state of the art in universals research.

5.2 Diversity

One of the few undisputed universals of language is, ironically, that no language is completely stable across generations. This leads to substantial diversification in virtually all dimensions. In the following I review the extent of the diversity that we know from today's languages in the world. I do this by walking through what are traditionally assumed to be the core domains of language – phonology, morphology, syntax, and semantics – but I exclude issues in pragmatics as these are amply discussed in other chapters of this handbook. What is most striking about linguistic diversity is that it is not limited to the details of what individual languages have within each of these domains. Languages even differ from each other in whether or not they have the defining units of some of the domains: there are languages without phonemes (the key ingredient of phonology), without words (the key ingredient of morphology), without recursive phrase structure, parts-of-speech categories, or grammatical relations (the key ingredients of syntax).

Before we proceed, a word needs to be said about the units of variation. What varies and diversifies is basically individual structures and their organization. In (non-applied) linguistics the term "language" is mostly meant as no more than a rough identifier, a label, for some variants of structures that are sampled (e.g., a set of specific relative clause structures, identified as English structures) and there is no theoretical interest associated with this labeling. The term "language" sometimes does enter theoretical analysis (e.g., in historical linguistics), but then it is understood as a gradient notion: a set of variants of structures that are relatively similar to each other and therefore understandable or relatively easy to learn to understand across users of each variant (then called "dialects," "sociolects"). For the relevant gradient, there are no standard metrics, and therefore, it is not possible to count the number of languages beyond ballpark estimates (which cluster about 6,000–7,000). There are of course yet other uses of the term "language," most notably ideological ones, as when two groups of speakers start to declare that their sets of variants are distinct languages (as has happened in the case of Serbian and Croatian) or when large and widely diverse sets of structural variants are declared to belong to a single language (as is the case of Chinese).

In this chapter, I use the term "language" in the sense of a structure identifier, and so I apply it to any kind of variant set of structures, including dialects, sociolects, idiolects.

5.2.1 Phonology

The most obvious way in which languages differ is in the nature of their sounds. There are languages with only very few sound distinctions, the known minimum being eleven in Rotokas, a language of Papua New Guinea (Firchow and Firchow 1969). The largest inventory is known from languages in Southern Africa. !Xõõ (from the !Ui-Taa family), for example, has (under one analysis) thirty-seven consonants plus a complex set of eighty-three click sounds and a rich inventory of forty-four vowel qualities (including, e.g., pharyngealized or breathy vowels) and four tones (Traill 1985). Differences like these are abundant,[1] but diversity goes far beyond this, and affects even the very elements that constitute phonology.

The single most important element here is the phoneme: the smallest meaning-differentiating units, which do not themselves bear meaning but recombine to create meaningful expressions. Such units are constitutive in all known spoken languages, and also in most sign languages.[2] For example, in Israeli Sign Language, the signs meaning "send" and "scold" differ only in the location of the sign ("send" being signed near the signer's torso, "scold" near the face), the signs meaning "profit" and "restraint" only in the shape of the hand during signing, etc. This is equivalent to minimal pairs like *send* vs. *lend* in English which differ only in the shape of the tongue in the initial sound. But not all sign languages use phonemes. Sandler *et al.* (2011) demonstrate that although it is operative as a fully fledged language in the third generation, the Al-Sayyid Bedouin Sign Language lacks minimal pairs and stable phonemes. Each sign is basically a holistic unit, although young third-generation signers are now beginning to develop phonemic structure, perhaps self-organized in response to increased conventionalization and a growing lexicon size (also see Sandler *et al.*, Chapter 10, this volume). While no spoken language has been demonstrated to lack phonemic structure, some languages come close (Blevins 2012): given sufficiently rich sound inventories, a spoken language could well create its lexicon directly from meaning-bearing segments, dispensing with phonemes.

For other key elements of phonology the case is clearer: for example, there are languages without syllables, and languages without words. First, consider syllables. In most languages, syllables are the minimal unit that regulate (among other things) the possible distribution of consonants and vowels when these segments are joined together. Mandarin Chinese, for example, allows twenty-one consonants at the beginning of such units but only n and ŋ at their end. A comparable differentiation is found in Gokana (Niger-Congo, Nigeria; Hyman 1983, 2011), but here it holds not for syllables but for larger, word-like units (stems plus suffixes): in initial position, any consonant of the language is allowed, but later in the unit, only a subset: e.g., gɔɔmáá 'cowrie' and zaari 'scatter' are well-formed, but not, say, * gɔɔzaa. These constraints cannot be stated in terms of syllables because if one were to split, say, zaari into zaa.ri, one couldn't specify where the constraint holds (as both z and r would be syllable-initial); if one were to split into zaar.i, this would create a CVVC (consonant-vowel-vowel-consonant) syllable that would not occur on its own. Similar issues arise for other phonological rules in Gokana: unlike in other languages, they do not "work" in terms of syllables (but see section 5.3.1 for further discussion).

The unit "word" can also be absent in a language. Words normally constrain the application of certain rules or constraints in phonology. For example, in English the assignment of main stress is constrained by phonological words. Each word has exactly one main stress, and everything that belongs to the same stress group is within the phonological word ("PW"), no matter how this is usually written, thus: [PW an' argument], [PW 'take it] etc. The same unit also constrains for example where the voiced fricative zh can appear: only internally, never at the beginning of words (although zh can appear at the beginning of syllables, as in luxurious). The larger-than-syllable unit that we encountered in Gokana above is also an instance of phonological word:[3] it constrains the distribution of consonants and other features (e.g., there can be at most two different tones within this unit), and it also has a maximum length (four vowels and two consonants and no more; Hyman 1983, 2011). While most languages deploy such domains (indeed often in multiple versions: Bickel et al. 2009), there are languages for which there is no phonological evidence for words at all. A case in point is Vietnamese (Schiering et al. 2010). In this language, phonological rules and constraints all operate on either the syllable or on sequences of two or three syllables, but it does not matter whether these sequences are lexical units or syntactic phrases: e.g., an expression like hoa hồng does not phonologically differentiate between a single-lexeme reading 'rose' and a phrasal reading 'pink flower'. This is different from most languages, where such contrasts play out for example in terms of phonological rules that assign one stress to each word (compare double-stressed black board with single-stressed blackboard).

5.2.2 Morphology

Languages also differ widely in the type and range of morphological processes that they use for expressing various grammatical categories. Most languages realize categories by segmental affixes, but many languages in Africa rely on tonal distinctions, e.g., Kinyarwanda (Niger-Congo, Rwanda) differentiates between moods by tone alone (indicative *mukora* 'we work', subjunctive *múkora* 'that we work', relative *mukorá* 'which we work (at)'; Overdulve 1987). The range of categories that are expressed also varies widely. Some languages express only tense morphologically (English *work* vs. *worked*) while others add various distinctions depending on whether the speaker has witnessed an event or not (e.g., in Turkish), is familiar with it or not (e.g., in Tibetan), whether the event should be thought of as a single whole or in the way it unfolded over time (e.g., in Russian), etc. Some languages allow intricate combinations here: Chechen, for example, requires speakers to decide about the internal temporal constituency of events (e.g., whether the event repeated itself or took a long time) even when at the same time declaring that one hasn't witnessed the event (Molochieva 2010). The combinatorial potential in some languages is impressive. In Chintang (Sino-Tibetan, Nepal), for example, we counted in a corpus over 1,800 distinct verb forms, expressing a large variety of categories in complex and variable ways (Stoll et al. 2012).

Like in phonology, languages also vary in whether or not, or to what extent, they have the very building blocks of morphology: words, now in the sense not of phonological rule domains, but in the sense of the primary building blocks of syntax. One usually posits this type of word ("grammatical words") in order to capture the fact that some sequences of meaningful elements ("morphemes") form tight units that cannot be altered by syntax. For example, we cannot insert another word between the stem *work* and the suffix *ed* in the word form *worked*. Some languages tolerate limited insertions. In Chintang, for example, some clitics (but not full words) can be intercalated in the middle of stems (e.g., *lak=ta-luse* 's/he danced', based on the stem *laklus-* 'dance', the past tense suffix *-e* and the focus clitic *=ta*, Bickel et al. 2007). In other languages, however, there is no limit to such insertions, and then there is no evidence for grammatical words (and hence, no morphology). This is so in Vietnamese, for which we already noted that there are no phonological words either (Nhàn 1984, Schiering et al. 2010). For example, strings of syllables can be interrupted by syllables that express another morpheme. It does not matter for this whether the strings themselves constitute an unanalyzable morpheme or a sequence of morphemes. For example, one can insert words like *với* 'and' or *không* 'not' inside polysyllabic strings consisting of a single morpheme like *cà phê* 'coffee' (a French loan) just like in bi-morphemic creations like *đo đỏ* 'reddish' (from *đỏ* 'red'), cf. *cà với phê* 'coffee and the like', *đo không đỏ* 'not reddish'. Even verbs can occur in the middle of lexical units, e.g., the verb *xây* 'build' in the middle of the bisyllabic noun *nhà cửa* 'house' (*Tôi xây nhà xây cửa* 'I build a house').

5.2.3 Syntax

The most obvious ways in which languages differ with regard to syntax is in their range of rules and constructions: some languages have elaborate rules of case government (Russian), some have reduced versions (English), and some have no trace of it (Vietnamese). Another variable concerns constraints on interpretation: for example, some languages impose constraints on reference in clause-combining: in an English sentence like *she smashed the bottle to the ground and broke*, the syntax demands that we identify the second (unexpressed) referent with the agent of the first clause, against all situational odds (and so we'd rather not drop the second referent and say *... and it broke*). Some languages don't have such a constraint and referential expressions can be freely dropped (e.g., in Chinese or in Chintang). Another well-established variable is the ordering of words and phrases: e.g., some languages place possessors before, some after the head; others allow both, depending on the construction (as in English *my brother's house* vs. *the house of my brother*) or on what one wants to put emphasis on.

But as in the other domains surveyed so far, variation goes beyond these relatively obvious variables and affects the very core of syntax. I briefly survey three such issues. First, for many languages, if one wants to describe how words are put together, one needs to assume recursive stacking of phrases, e.g., the noun phrases (NPs) in [$_{NP}$[$_{NP}$[$_{NP}$*John's*] *mother's*] *car*]. But some languages impose severe limits here, so that there is no descriptive need, and hence no empirical evidence, for recursion. With regard to possession constructions, most ancient and some modern Indo-European languages, for example, frequently use structures with adjective derivations (Russian *mamina kniga* 'mother's book', where *mamin-* 'belonging to mother' is an adjective) that block recursive stacking (** Ivanova mamina kniga* 'Ivan's mother's book', Witzlack-Makarevich, p.c.). Pirahã (Brazil; Everett 2005) allows only one NP inside another (*xipoógi hoáoii* 'Xipoogi's shotgun'), but not two (**kó'oí hoagí kai* 'Kooi's son's daughter'). Similar issues arise with clause embedding, such as in: *I told you that [I was there]*. Many languages avoid this in favor of juxtaposition: *I told you that. I was there* (Mithun 1984). There is ample evidence that recursion is a historical variable, gradually developing from juxtaposition over time (Deutscher 2007, Viti 2012).

A second area of fundamental variation concerns the role of parts of speech in syntax. In most languages, syntax is to a significant extent driven by parts-of-speech (and related) categories in the lexicon, i.e., one can predict much syntactic behavior from lexical properties (in some theories in fact almost all syntactic behavior). For example, in English, the lexical unit *see* is a verb and its use predicts the creation (technically called a "projection") of a verb phrase (VP) used for predication: [$_{VP}$ [$_V$ *sees*] $_{NP}$]. The unit *tree* is a noun and this predicts projection of a noun phrase used for reference: [$_{NP}$ *a* [$_N$ *tree*]]. But not all languages work this way. Some languages use syntactic phrases that are defined independently of the lexicon. In Kharia (Austroasiatic, India; Peterson 2011 and p.c.), for example, the syntactic functions of predication and reference are formally distinguished by dedicated series of clitics that mark off the relevant phrases. These phrases are not projected from the lexicon. In fact they are totally independent of lexical choices and can be filled by any word. The full meaning results compositionally from a fairly abstract lexical content and the clitics: in a referential phrase (RefP), for example, the proper name *Aʔghrom* refers to a town, but in a predication phrase (PredP) it denotes an event: [PredP *Aʔghrom=ki*] 'it became (came to be called) Aghrom', with middle voice past *=ki*. Similarly, a word like *kayom* 'talk' identifies an event as an object when used in a referential phrase: [RefP *u kayom*] *onḍor=ki* '(someone) overheard this (*u*) talk'. But the same word expresses the event itself when used in a predication phrase: [PredP *kayom=ki*], 'it became talk', i.e., 'someone talked'.[4]

A third area of variation concerns grammatical relations, i.e., constrained sets of arguments. In most languages, if one wants to state what is possible in syntax and what not, one needs to refer to specific sets of arguments. For example, the constraint on reference in English clause combination that we noted above is best captured by the set comprising the sole argument of intransitive verbs ("S") and the most agent-like argument of transitive verbs ("A"). The same set defines the range of arguments that occur directly before the verb in English and that can trigger third-person agreement (S in *she works*, A in *she sees me*, but not, e.g., patients of transitive verbs: *I sees her*). Cross-linguistic variation here is enormous (Bickel 2011a) because some languages arrange roles in different ways (e.g., treating S arguments like patients, not agents, a phenomenon called "ergativity"), or they define their grammatical relations not, or not only, in terms of argument roles, but in terms of reference (e.g., the argument that is most topical) or rely on different relations depending on the construction and verb used. A more fundamental question is whether some languages may lack any constraints on arguments whatsoever, i.e., where arguments and adjuncts are all treated the same way, regardless of their role, reference, or whatever. Above, we noted that languages may lack specific constraints, such as the one on reference in coordination. In addition, languages may lack fixed word-order rules, case assignment, verb agreement, etc. If all of these are lacking, there is no evidence for argument sets and grammatical relations to exist. This has been claimed for the Riau (and a few other) varieties of Indonesian (Gil 1999, 2005). Clause positions are not constrained to specific argument roles or types, and so a sentence like *ayam makhan*, literally 'chicken eat', can mean 'the chicken is eating' (with first word being an agent) just as well as 'someone is eating chicken' (with the first word being a patient). So far, no constructions have been observed in Riau that would delimit one set of arguments from all other arguments or adjunct. Relative clauses, for example, use the same syntax for all purposes: compare, e.g., *yang di-pukul Ali* [REL PAT-hit Ali] 'the one who was hit by Ali' with *yang di-cari wang* [REL PAT-look.for money] 'the one who is looking for money' (the latter would be out in

Standard Indonesian because this language has grammatical relations and these constrain the *yang*-construction to patient arguments if the verb contains the patient marker *di-*, as it does here).

5.2.4 Semantics

Substantial variation in semantics is obvious to anyone trying to translate between languages: every language has words with meanings that do not correspond to similar meanings in other languages and that need lengthy circumlocutions if we want to recast them. Such differences can even be observed between closely related languages or dialects: e.g., Zurich German has a word *schärme* denoting a place where it does not rain when it rains all around. There is no equivalent in Standard German. Every language has lexical peculiarities of this kind.

More interesting are differences that are systematic across entire lexical fields: in kinship terminology, for example, languages are well known to differ substantially in how they group people. Chintang, for example, differentiates between elder and younger siblings but for younger siblings it does not distinguish between the sexes (*-nisa* 'younger brother or sister'), and this term also includes cousins. Some languages have color words exhausting the range of visible colors, others don't (e.g., Yélî Dnye, Rossel Island; Levinson 2001) and when they fully partition the range of colors, languages differ in how they do this more substantially than has often been thought (Roberson *et al.* 2000, Roberson 2005).

Variation in semantics reaches furthest, however, when it is linked to differences in morphology and syntax. As noted above, languages differ in the range and type of categories they express by morphology (or through periphrastic constructions) and therefore in what they force speakers to attend to ("thinking for speaking" in Slobin's 1996 terms). An example of the impact of syntax comes from noun-phrase syntax: in some languages (especially in Southeast Asia and Mesoamerica), most nouns have the semantics of what are called mass nouns in English grammar: they denote "stuff," not "things." In Yukatek Maya, for example, a word like *k'éek'en* denotes any "material" related to pigs and is neutral as to what kind of reference it is used for. The concrete referential meaning is only established in the syntax through the use of what are called classifiers in combination with numerals (e.g., *'un-túul k'éek'en* 'a pig (alive)', *'um-p'éel k'éek'en* 'a whole pig (dead or alive)', *'un-shóot' k'éek'en* 'a slice of pork', etc.; Lucy 1992). A similar but potentially even more radical abstraction arises in languages that lack a noun vs. verb distinction in the lexicon (as in Kharia). In these languages, the lexical semantics of individual words abstracts away not only from the specific type of reference or predication that a word is used for but even from the difference between things and events; e.g., a word like *kayom* 'talk' is general across these ontological types. All further specification arises only from use of the word in a specific syntactic environment.

Interactions with syntax are particularly important because they suggest that languages differ not only in the kind of semantic units they employ, but also in the principles of how they combine these units to form full concepts: lexically (English *pig* entails not only relevant properties associated with pigs but also reference to an identifiable entity with a definite shape) or syntactically (e.g., Yukatek *k'éek'en* only denotes the relevant properties, leaving reference and shape concerns to syntax).

5.3 Universals

From a biological and psychological perspective the diversity we find is less surprising than one might think. As Levinson (2003, 2012) and Evans and Levinson (2009) have emphasized, human cognition is fundamentally tuned to variation: our brain is extremely flexible and open to environmental input (e.g., Jäncke 2009); its development and expression is fundamentally affected by genetic variation (e.g., Thompson *et al.* 2010); the physiology of language processing is highly variable (e.g., Bornkessel-Schlesewsky and Schlesewsky 2009); children's learning strategies are geared towards extracting key grammar information from distributional signals in whatever speech environment they happen to grow up in (e.g., Tomasello 2003).

Given this, it comes a bit as a surprise that over the past fifty years linguistics has managed to send a strong message that languages are far less diverse than meets the eye and that behind the apparent diversity there is a richly articulated universal grammar. In order to understand this message we need to distinguish two senses of "universal": the absolute (exceptionless) and the statistical (tendency-based) universal. As we will see, these concepts are more complex than they would seem (and than how they are sometimes treated in the literature). Absolute universality does not simply mean "found in all languages" and the concept is deeply intertwined with the theoretical foundations of modern linguistics. Statistical universality too cannot simply be translated "found in the vast majority of languages" and instead refers to complex models of probabilistic trends anchored in the social and physiological eco-system that languages are embedded in.

5.3.1 Absolute universals

Absolute universals are exceptionless. However, since we cannot survey all possible human languages, it is not clear how one would categorically establish that a universal has no exception.[5] More importantly, how can we actually *decide* whether a given language really has syllables or not, or whether it has recursive phrase structure or not? Unless this is clear, we cannot even remotely hope to know whether syllables or recursive phrase structures are universal. The issue reflects a fundamental problem identified by Chomsky (1964, 1965, 1975): how can we justify any specific analysis (or even a whole grammar) among a range of possible analyses (grammars)? I illustrate the problem with one of the examples of diversity surveyed above.

We noted that Gokana lacks evidence for syllables as constitutive elements of phonology. This was based on Hyman's insight that all relevant phonological rules and constraints in Gokana can be best captured in terms of a larger unit than the syllable, the phonological word. As in quite a few other languages, this unit has a maximum size. The size can be described as a sequence of consonants and vowels that match the template CV(V)(C)(V)(V) and an additional constraint against CVVC words (which are allowed by the template but not possible in Gokana). However, as Hyman (2011) points out, one could in principle analyze Gokana also by positing syllables and thereby assume the syllable to be an absolute universal: the maximum word could then be analyzed as allowing maximally two syllables, each at most weighing in what is known as two moras (CVV or CVC). In addition one would need a constraint limiting C-final syllables to monosyllabic words (because strings like CVV.CVC or CVC.CVV are impossible). The asymmetry in the range of consonants in the first vs. second syllable can then be accounted for by positing a trochaic (strong before weak) ordering of syllables.

The issue is typical for many linguistic analyses: there are competing ways of analyzing structures, and the different analyses go together with different sets of universals. For example, it is perfectly possible to posit phonological words in Vietnamese and then to declare phonological words an absolute universal (as is done for example by Vogel 2009). If one does, the variation will no longer consist in whether or not languages have words, but in what kinds of audible effects these domains have on phonology (none in Vietnamese, many in English). Also, one can posit grammatical words in Vietnamese, or indeed any other, language: the variation would then consist in the fact that in some languages, grammatical words cannot be interrupted by free morphemes while in Vietnamese they can (recall the *cà với phê* 'coffee and the like' example from above). The same issues arise in syntax and semantics: one can declare recursion a universal (e.g., Nevins *et al.* 2009) and posit it for Pirahã as well, even though it has no direct syntactic effects; the variation will then concern the depth of recursion allowed by individual languages (limited to 1 in Pirahã, and some other limit elsewhere: cf. Karlsson 2010 for a survey). Also, one can posit universal parts of speech and universal grammatical relations and declare them valid for Kharia and Riau Indonesian; in return one would have to add specific rules and constraints that explain why phrase structure is not exhaustively projected from parts of speech in Kharia, and why grammatical relations range over all argument and adjunct roles in Riau but not in other languages. For semantics too, one can posit English-like noun types for Yukatek and declare them to be absolute universals if one specifies rules that explain why Yukatek nouns behave differently from English nouns in phrases with numerals. And so on and so forth.

As a result, the range and nature of absolute universals depends entirely on the nature of the analysis and the descriptive metalanguage that one uses for a particular phenomenon. The choice between alternative sets of absolute universals is not about "more" vs. "fewer" universals; it is only a choice as to where the diversity is located. This brings us back to Chomsky's problem: how can we justify one analysis over the other? In order to develop an answer, it is useful to distinguish what Chomsky (1964, 1965) has called "levels of adequacy" (though in slightly different ways than Chomsky originally proposed). The first level of adequacy is relatively trivial: an analysis obviously needs to describe the phenomena correctly, i.e., capture all and only structures that native speakers accept as part of their language. For example, saying that tonal melodies in Gokana operate on C(V)(C)(V)(C)(V) (rather than on CV(V)(C)(V)(V)) strings would simply be incorrect, as it would predict tonal melodies that Gokana speakers wouldn't produce and would reject as not being part of Gokana.[6]

Another level that is fairly uncontroversial is that the analysis of a language should aim at using only concepts (such as "C" and "V") that are also found in other languages, i.e., concepts that are cross-linguistically applicable. This criterion of cross-linguistic adequacy means that analytical concepts must come from a universal inventory and must be licensed by a universal theory of how this inventory is structured.[7] Obeying such a constraint automatically limits the absolute range of possible languages: only those with structures that can be covered by the universal theory; everything else is ruled out as violating the universal theory. Of course it is difficult to know exactly what such a universal theory should look like. There are many proposals, and this is where the many theories of grammar differ (e.g., Lexical-Functional Grammar vs. Construction Grammar vs. Role and Reference Grammar, etc.; see Heine and Narrog 2012 for a survey). In addition, there is a fairly consolidated stock of traditional, non-formalized analytical concepts that most linguists would agree as being part of the inventory (see, e.g., Shopen 2007 for one collection) and that is sometimes called Basic Linguistic Theory (Dryer 2006, Dixon 2010–12). The criterion of cross-linguistic adequacy would rule out an analysis of Gokana in terms of lists of Gokana phonemes (e.g., as set strings like {p, t, k^j, k, kp, ...}{a, e, i, ...}). But both an analysis with syllables and one without would fare equally well: most theories would allow both syllables and CV-templates.[8] This is true in fact of most of the alternative analyses mentioned above. To the extent that one theory is just as good as the other (e.g., a theory with and one without requiring syllables to be universal), one set of universals is just as good as another one.

Still, is there a way to decide? Chomsky's (1964, 1965, 2004) key insight is that there are relevant criteria for this, and that these criteria are cognitive and biological in nature, i.e., that they are about whether or not a particular theory fits with what one needs in order to explain how language is embedded in the nature of our brain/mind.[9] Specifically, analytical concepts and the set of absolute universals they imply are considered adequate only if they

(i) allow formulating grammars that are learnable by children;
(ii) are psychologically realistic;
(iii) are biologically and evolutionarily realistic;
(iv) account for the creative use of language.

The criteria themselves are not really controversial since they are relatively abstract. But heavy controversies arise whenever the criteria are made more concrete. With regard to (i), for example, it has for a long time been taken as a given that grammars are learnable only if we assume a rich set of absolute universals that are innate (e.g., Chomsky 1965, 1980). This has been challenged by empirical research on how children actually acquire language (Tomasello 2003) and by computational learnability theory (Clark and Lappin 2011, Perfors et al. 2011). Both suggest that innate universals of grammar are not needed for learnability (because children apply powerful probabilistic learning strategies).

With regard to (ii), it is often assumed in the Chomskyan tradition (e.g., Chomsky 1980) that psychological reality is already ensured if a grammar captures all generalizations that a speaker intuitively "knows" (in the sense of "has the competence of"). Under a stronger reading, criterion (ii) requires that the theory is in line with our understanding of language processing. This has been a foundational point for Lexical-Functional Grammar (Bresnan and Kaplan 1982) and similarly-minded theories (e.g., Jackendoff 2002). Processing research is advancing quickly, and it is difficult to predict which kinds of analytical concepts and thereby which representations will eventually fare best on this criterion. For example, in Chomskyan models, the properties of arguments are typically defined in phrase structure, but Bornkessel and Schlesewsky (2006) suggest on the basis of neurophysiological evidence that we need independent, non-phrase-structural dependencies for defining these properties.

With regard to (iii), it has been argued that the evolution of language requires a very specific universal, namely that grammars are modeled as the most efficient link between sign production and thinking (Chomsky 1995). But there are alternative accounts that are equally compatible with plausible evolutionary models and that do not require specific universals of grammar – for some recent perspectives see, for example, Tomasello (2008), Evans and Levinson (2009), Chater and Christiansen (2010), or Hurford (2011).

Finally, with regard to (iv), it has long been taken for granted that in order to allow for creativity one needs to assume that the set of sentences in a language is infinite and that infinitude can only be ensured by taking recursive phrase structure as an absolute universal (allowing stacks like [she said [that he knew [that she said [that...]]]]). But Pullum and Scholz (2010) note that creativity does not require the possibility of infinitude (as witnessed by the creativity in, say, Haiku poetry) and that, even if infinitude were needed for creativity, it could be achieved without recursive phrase structure (e.g., by iteration with a Kleene star, or by constrained combination of constructions and template matching) and, conversely, recursive phrase structure alone does not guarantee infinitude. And of course, hierarchical or symmetrical structure does not by itself entail recursion. Criterion (iv) is therefore not very useful in distinguishing the adequacy of theories.

The overall conclusion from this is that if one wants to know the best candidates of well-motivated absolute universals, one needs to look at the latest developments in psychology and biology. Note that this implies that once we have the relevant nonlinguistic evidence, a universal can be considered demonstrated. No individual language or set of data could falsify such a universal, because, as we have seen, any counterexample can be removed by reanalyzing the data so as to fit the universal (e.g., by reanalyzing Gokana with syllables, if syllables were demonstrated to be universal on the basis of psychological or biological evidence). The problem is of course that psychology and biology do not easily give clear evidence for or against specific analytical concepts in linguistics (words, syllables, nouns vs. verbs, etc.) because our understanding of how grammar is embedded in the brain is still limited and what evidence there is typically allows multiple interpretations. This limits the practical use of Chomsky's approach to criteria of adequacy. The standard way out is to simply *assume* a universal and then to see how far one gets (e.g., Chomsky 2004, 2010).[10] The risk is of course that assumptions (e.g., about recursive phrase structure as a universal) quickly become dogmas (e.g., when they are taught to students), and many linguists therefore reject this research strategy.

But there is a completely different perspective on language that bears more promise for deciding between analyses and how one allocates the balance between universals and diversity. To see this we need to move beyond static representations and investigate another fundamental dimension of human language: its dynamics, i.e., the way representations change and diversify. This dynamics defines another criterion of adequacy: a good analysis should also be *historically realistic*, i.e., match with what we know about how languages change over time. More than the others, this criterion is utilitarian and systematically favors theories that minimize universals and maximize the potential for diversity. We prefer analyses that maximize the detection of pathways of change and general patterns in development over time. From this point of view, some analyses clearly seem to fare better than others. For example, if the existence of words is taken to be variable rather than an absolute universal, we can see strong patterns in historical development (e.g., noting that the existence and importance of phonological words is a surprisingly stable family-specific trait: Bickel et al. 2009; for many similar examples, see Blevins 2004). Likewise, if we take the existence of phonemes as a variable rather than a universal, we can gain insight into the emergence of phonological patterning when the lexicon grows and becomes ever more conventionalized in a newly established language (Sandler et al. 2011, and Chapter 10, this volume). And for syntax, if we take recursive phrase structure to be a variable rather than an absolute universal, we can study fundamental changes in the syntax of many languages (e.g., Deutscher 2007, Sampson et al. 2009, Viti 2012).

5.3.2 Statistical universals

The criterion of historical realism is foundational for research on statistical as opposed to absolute universals because statistical universals are fundamentally historical in nature. The basic idea of statistical universals is this: when languages change over time, these historical processes are influenced by a large array of factors and because these factors are in highly dynamic competition, universal effects manifest themselves only statistically, never categorically. Let us explore this idea a bit more closely.

The relevant factors underlying statistical universals draw from the same psychological and biological issues that also matter to the theory of absolute universals, and it is no surprise therefore that research on statistical universals is also labeled "cognitive" or "biological" (e.g., Givón 2001, 2010, Croft 2003).[11] But the sense is a different one. For statistical universals, psychological and biological facts define causal theories that predict how languages tend to develop over time. A classic example comes from word-order research: Hawkins (1994, 2004) proposes that the way languages are processed by the brain causes languages to favor certain structures over others, for example "harmonic" over "disharmonic" patterns. Harmonic patterns are ones where nested phrase structures are oriented in the same way, e.g., in English, the head (constitutive element) of noun phrases is initial (*the development* in *the development of science*) and so is the head of verb phrases (*study* in *study the development*); in Turkish or Hindi, both heads are final.[12] This is indeed what we find in most languages, but there are exceptions (e.g., Chinese, which puts verbs before objects like English, but has head-final noun phrases like *kēxué de fāzhǎn* 'the development of science', where *fāzhǎn* means 'development'). Rather than trying to reanalyze the exceptions so as to fit an absolute universal, in research on statistical universals, the exceptions are taken at face value and the relevant universal is taken to be probabilistic. Why?

The reason is that language change is not only affected by psychological (or biological) demands such as ease of processing. The dynamics of languages is also deeply embedded in the social eco-system within which speakers communicate: we tend to adjust our ways of speaking to how others speak. Words and grammars can become fashion and fall out of fashion again for reasons that have nothing to do with how language is processed or represented in the brain. For example, English loan words have become fashionable in many languages around the world (sometimes triggering cultural discomfort or even outright political protest, sometimes not). Similarly for grammar: some time during the great migrations after the fall of the Roman Empire it became increasingly fashionable in Europe to coin new expressions of the perfect tense, built on an auxiliary verb meaning 'have', e.g., *I have eaten* or Italian *ho mangiato* (Heine and Kuteva 2006). Effects of this kind pervade the world: whenever speakers learn another language, they tend to adapt their grammar to this other language, a process known as "(areal) diffusion." And there are many reasons for learning other languages: for example, speakers migrate to another place, they want to establish trade or other relations, or they give up their ancestral language. There are thousands of opportunities for diffusion.

A prominent example is again word order. This aspect of syntax is particularly prone to diffusion (e.g., Thomason and Kaufman 1988, Johanson 1992, Dryer 1992, Nettle 1999). As Heine (2008) shows, in most cases the relevant process consists in turning an alternative order pattern that was previously special (less frequent, carrying overtones) into the normal way of speaking so as to minimize the difference between languages in contact (as if a special construction like *Beans I like* were to become the norm in English). As a result of many such processes over hundreds and often thousands of years, specific word-order patterns spread over large geographical regions. For example, statistical analysis suggests that the odds for a linguistic family of showing a diachronically significant preference towards object-after-verb (VO) order is on average 5.4 times higher in Europe, Africa, and the coastal area around the Pacific than in the interior parts of Eurasia, Australia, and the Americas (and the difference is statistically highly significant).[13]

Given such strong effects of historically and geographically contingent events, universals of historical change cannot be expected to be categorical and must be statistical instead. However, the strong effects of historical contingencies also mean the statistics cannot simply consist in counting what is most frequent in the world. For example, looking at the raw figures given in the *World Atlas of Language Structures* (Dryer 2005), one is tempted to hypothesize a statistical universal against putting the verb first in a clause, i.e., languages like Welsh, Maa (the language of the Maasai), Tagalog, or Yukatek would seem exceptional and dispreferred (Baker 2001), perhaps because they would be more difficult to process or require exceedingly complex representations. However, such a conclusion is not warranted. The current distribution could just as well result from the accidents of history. For example, if Insular Celtic had spread throughout Europe and beyond, or if it hadn't been Bantu but Nilotic speakers (say, the ancestors of the Maasai) who expanded into the better part of the Sub-Saharan regions, verb-initial languages might be far more common now.

For establishing statistical universals it has therefore become standard (since at least Dryer 1989 and Nichols 1992) to control for historical contingencies like areal diffusion. For the example of harmonic word-order patterns mentioned above, prospects look good: all analyses so far that control for historical contingencies reveal strong worldwide preferences for harmonic head placement (e.g., Dryer 1992, Haspelmath and Siegmund 2006, Bickel 2011b, each using different methods; but also see Dunn *et al.* 2011 for dissent and Bickel in press for further discussion).

Unlike in the case of absolute universals, establishing the validity of statistical universals is not an issue of theory choice. It is an empirical question. As such it requires appropriate statistical methodology just like empirical questions do in other sciences. Settling on the right methods here is of course not trivial. Various options are currently debated, mostly concerned with the best ways in which we can estimate diachronic trends and probabilities of language change on the basis of synchronic data, and with how we can in fact mine synchronic data for trends without missing important signals from variation.[14]

For a better understanding of statistical universals, one issue in this debate is particularly important, however: universal effects are often quite weak (perhaps not as weak as the statistical signals of certain particles in physics, but nevertheless weak enough to require large datasets). The reason is this: given the many contingencies that influence language change, it is easily possible that languages end up in a situation that appears to contradict a universal principle. Chinese is a case in point, since it places heads initially in the verb phrase, but finally in the noun phrase. And this has been so for generations, not impeding the acquisition or use of the language. Unlike absolute universals, statistical universals do not declare dispreferred structures unlearnable or unusable. Instead, they state that, given the choice between two structures (say between a harmonic and a disharmonic one), there is a very slight preference in language change for speakers to (unconsciously) choose the one structure that is better in line with the universal (the harmonic one) and make it the dominant structure in language use. This can happen either by keeping a structure if it already is in line with the universal or by changing it so as to become in line with the universal. The result and the statistical signal is the same. However, what is critical in this is that the relevant choices are given at all. Choices can arise from many different sources – for example, through developing a new structure from scratch, by borrowing it in language contact, or through fashion-driven expansion of the use of specialized constructions (e.g., one that puts objects before verbs even though the other order would be more common), etc. But, importantly, there is no need for any such choices to arise in the first place, and then the universal cannot exert any effect. Moreover, an individual may select a universally preferred variant in usage, but unless such a usage spreads and becomes a social norm in the community,[15] the selection may remain a one-off phenomenon and the universal may have no effect either. Averaged over thousands of cases of language change, therefore, a universal may leave only small statistical signals.

Not all universal effects are weak, however. For some patterns, the pressure from psychological and biological factors seems to be so strong as to yield universal effects that are virtually never canceled out by other factors. For example, Dryer (2011) finds only one out of nearly 1,000 languages that have no overt signal that would mark the difference between a statement and a question. There seems to be heavy pressure from efficient processing in communication that favors overt signaling of the distinction. Or take the case of syllables discussed above: there seems to be a very strong trend towards organizing the distribution of consonants (and vowels) in terms of syllables and Gokana seems quite exceptional. A likely cause of this trend is grounded in aspects of speech rhythm, and constraints here appear to be very strong. Note that any insights into such factors, indeed any research on them, is impossible if syllables (or question vs. statement distinctions, for that matter) are declared absolute universals and the whole discussion is locked in debates of adequacy. As a result, one would lose an important avenue for studying how language is embedded into its speakers.

Current research has established many hypotheses on statistical universals.[16] However, only a small fraction has received detailed testing. Also, many hypotheses may turn out to be spurious correlations (like the infamous correlation between the declining number of pirates in the world and global warming), because obviously any statistical pattern is only as good as the explanatory theory behind it. Where they are worked out in any detail, the relevant theories are mostly grounded in language processing (e.g., Hawkins 1994, 2004) or in principles of communication (e.g., economy, iconicity, and markedness; Croft 2003 for extensive review), conceptualization (e.g., optimizing the partition of perceptual spaces; Regier et al. 2007) or social structuration (adapting languages to social structures; Evans 2003). What is shared by all theories is the idea that languages tend to develop in such a way as to fit into the natural and social eco-system of speakers: that they are easy to process, that they map easily to patterns in nonlinguistic cognition, and that they match the social and communicative needs of speakers.

This fundamental and intrinsic connection to other disciplines makes research on statistical universals particularly rewarding: instead of exploring the natural and social basis of human language by means of theoretical working assumptions (as is typical for absolute universals), we can now explore this basis empirically and in close partnership with other disciplines. For example, it becomes possible to take neurophysiological findings on principles of language processing and test the statistical footprints that such principles might leave in the historical development of languages. One study along these lines (Bornkessel-Schlesewsky et al. 2008) currently explores the effects that certain measurable preferences in the processing of clause-initial noun phrases across languages (namely the preference for interpreting these agents) have on the way grammatical relations develop in languages worldwide (namely in such a way as to group agents with intransitive subjects, avoiding what is called ergativity).

What facilitates such undertakings is that work on statistical universals relies on the same mathematical toolkit that is standardly used in other sciences, from data-mining techniques to regression modeling. While research on absolute universals often proceeds along strictly theory-bound argumentation in arcane formalisms, statistical universals are explored in the same theory–hypothesis–statistics triangle that characterizes most sciences.

5.4 Summary

On the face of it, languages differ from each other in every aspect of their phonology, grammar, and lexicon. When linguists nevertheless speak of universals of language they mean one of two things: absolute or statistical universals.

Understood as "absolute," universals are whatever is posited as a necessary ingredient of the metalanguage that we need for describing and analyzing languages. This ranges from trivial notions of linearization (one sentence precedes another one) to sophisticated and highly controversial ideas like recursive phrase structure. Thus, the right answer to a question about absolute universals is: "It depends on the metalanguage you use!" The evidence for or against a specific metalanguage is hard to get within linguistics alone since metalanguages are hopelessly underdetermined by the data. In response, evidence is often sought in the extent to which a given metalanguage fits criteria or psychological and biological adequacy. But assessing this fit is difficult and controversial. As a result, proponents of absolute universals often proceed by assuming universals as working hypotheses and then explore how well these hypotheses allow them to analyze languages. A central problem of this approach is that working assumptions easily become dogmas.

Understood as "statistical," universals are probabilistic inequalities stating that it is more likely for languages to develop over time into some preferred state than to develop away from this state. Hypotheses on preferred states are in turn grounded in causal theories of how the nature of the human brain, the nature of societies and of our communicative needs determine language change. A well-established (though not uncontroversial) example is the preference for harmonic word-order patterns, which is grounded in processing ease. However, any such universal preference is constantly confounded by historical contingencies, above all by diffusion of structures across languages. Diffusion is mostly motivated not by choosing what might best fit our nature, but simply by what happens to be around and fashionable at a given time and place. In order to detect clear signals among all these confounding factors, statistical universals can thus normally only be tested against large-scale global databases. Developing these has become a prime issue for many linguists, especially also because we are currently witnessing an unprecedented loss of linguistic diversity in the wake of globalization.

Notes

1. For a survey, see Maddieson (2011).
2. It has become a convention to extend phonological terminology to sign languages despite the etymology in the Greek word for "sound." This move is motivated by the rich parallelism between the formal grammar of signed and spoken languages (e.g., Sandler and Lillo-Martin 2006 for review).
3. More accurately, a specific subtype of the phonological word, technically called a prosodic stem. The difference is irrelevant for current purposes.
4. English allows some flexibility too (cf. *to talk* and *a talk*), but unlike in Kharia, this involves lexical derivation between noun and verb. Evidence: the meaning effects are not predictable from the syntax, e.g., the semantic relation between *to talk* and *a talk* is very different from that between *to shovel* and *a shovel*. In Kharia, these relations are determined by the rules of syntax (Peterson 2011).
5. Piantadosi and Gibson (2013) have recently shown that given the number of languages we know, we normally cannot even *estimate the probability* that a universal can be reasonably assumed to be exceptionless. The number of languages we know is indeed very small: assuming that a language stays the same for maximally about 1,000 years, that on average there have been at least 5,000 languages in the world, and that human language emerged at least 100,000 years ago, there would have been at least half a million languages so far – perhaps many more! The total sample we know now, i.e., that we normally think of when talking about "all languages," makes up less than 1% of this.
6. What I call here the first level of adequacy corresponds to "descriptive adequacy" in Chomsky (1965). Chomsky (1964) also speaks about "observational" adequacy, which only requires that there is an analysis for every string in a corpus and, unlike descriptive adequacy, does not require that analyses capture all underlying regularities and native speaker intuitions about them. The distinction is not relevant for our purposes.
7. See Chomsky (1975: 81) for an early explication of this, and Haspelmath (2010) vs. Newmeyer (2010) for recent debate. Controversies mostly arise when terms are very coarse, as for example with a term like "noun," because such terms hide much (in fact, too much) variation across languages (Bickel 2007, in press).

8. In fact, if formulated as a regular expression like \bCV([BDG]|V{1,3}|(V?([BDG]V{1,2})?))\b, all formal grammars (in the sense of formal language theory) would have to accept the template analysis because regular expressions are necessarily a subpart of any formal grammar (Chomsky 1975).
9. Chomsky (1965) analyzes these criteria as requests for "explanatory adequacy," emphasizing the idea that they explain why we find only those structures that are licensed by a given universal theory.
10. From this perspective, absolute universals might as well be called "theoretical universals." This would highlight the fact that absolute universals are justified solely by assumptions about the best universal theory of the analytical concepts we need. But the term is also misleading because, as we will see, statistical universals are also based on theories.
11. Unlike in research on absolute universals, there is no single father figure for this research tradition, although perhaps the work of Greenberg – especially his 1963 article and the monumental four-volume oeuvre from 1978 – can be said to have played one of the most decisive roles in developing the current state of the field. For state-of-the-art surveys, see a 2007 special issue of the journal *Linguistic Typology* or the *Oxford Handbook of Linguistic Typology* (Song 2011).
12. Correlations between the properties of two structures (here, the linear organization of verb phrases and noun phrases) are traditionally called "implicational universals" and stated in the form "If the head is initial in the verb phrases, then it is also initial in the noun phrase." The terminology is misleading because the universal is a statistical correlation, not a logical implication (Dryer 1997, Cysouw 2003, Bickel in press).
13. For the analysis I applied the methods proposed in Bickel (2011b, 2013) to the data collected by Dryer (2005). The geographical regions are defined as in Nichols and Bickel (2009).
14. A glimpse of the current state of the art can be obtained from the 2007 and 2011 special issues of the journal *Linguistic Typology*.
15. For detailed discussion of the complex mechanisms behind this, see Enfield, this volume, Chapter 3.
16. The *Universals Archive* at http://typo.uni-konstanz.de/archive (Plank and Filimonova 2000) catalogues over 2,000 hypotheses that have been proposed so far (with or without good empirical support).

References

Baker, Mark C. 2001. *The Atoms of Language: The Mind's Hidden Rules of Grammar*. Oxford: Oxford University Press.
Bickel, Balthasar. 2007. Typology in the 21st Century: Major current developments. *Linguistic Typology* 11: 239–51.

2011a. Grammatical Relations Typology. In *The Oxford Handbook of Language Typology*, ed. Jae Jung Song, 399–444. Oxford: Oxford University Press.

2011b. Statistical Modeling of Language Universals. *Linguistic Typology* 15: 401–14.

2013. Distributional Biases in Language Families. In *Language Typology and Historical Contingency: Studies in Honor of Johanna Nichols*, ed. Balthasar Bickel, Lenore A. Grenoble, David A. Peterson, and Alan Timberlake, 415–44. Amsterdam: Benjamins.

In press. Distributional Typology: Statistical inquiries into the dynamics of linguistic diversity. In *The Oxford Handbook of Linguistic Analysis*, 2nd edition, ed. Bernd Heine and Heiko Narrog. Oxford: Oxford University Press [pre-print available at www.comparativelinguistics.uzh.ch/bickel/publications].

Bickel, Balthasar, Goma Banjade, Martin Gaenszle, Elena Lieven, Netra Paudyal, Ichchha P. Rai, Manoj Rai, Novel K. Rai, and Sabine Stoll. 2007. Free Prefix Ordering in Chintang. *Language* 83: 43–73.

Bickel, Balthasar, Kristine Hildebrandt and René Schiering. 2009. The Distribution of Phonological Word Domains: A probabilistic typology. In *Phonological Domains: Universals and Deviations*, ed. Janet Grijzenhout and Barış Kabak, 47–75. Berlin: Mouton de Gruyter.

Blevins, Juliette. 2004. *Evolutionary Phonology: The Emergence of Sound Patterns*. New York: Cambridge University Press.

2012. Duality of Patterning: Absolute universal or statistical tendency? *Language and Cognition* 4: 275–96.

Bornkessel, Ina, and Matthias Schlesewsky. 2006. Generalized Semantic Roles and Syntactic Templates: A new framework for language comprehension. In *Semantic Role Universals and Argument Linking: Theoretical, Typological and Psycholinguistic Perspectives*, ed. Ina Bornkessel, Matthias Schlesewsky, Bernard Comrie and Angela D. Friederici, 327–53. Berlin: Walter de Gruyter.

Bornkessel-Schlesewsky, Ina, Kamal Kumar Choudhary, Alena Witzlack-Makarevich, and Balthasar Bickel. 2008. Bridging the Gap Between Processing Preferences and Typological Distributions: Initial evidence from the online comprehension of control constructions in Hindi. In *Scales* (Linguistische ArbeitsBerichte 86), ed. Andrej Malchukov and Marc Richards, 397–436. Leipzig: Institut für Linguistik [www.uni-leipzig.de/~asw/lab/lab86/LAB86_Bornkessel_et_al.pdf].

Bornkessel-Schlesewsky, Ina, and Matthias Schlesewsky. 2009. *Processing Syntax and Morphology: A Neurocognitive Perspective*. Oxford: Oxford University Press.

Bresnan, Joan, and Ronald M. Kaplan. 1982. Grammars as Mental Representations of Language. In *The Mental Representation of Grammatical Relations*, ed. Joan Bresnan, xvii–liii. Cambridge, MA: MIT Press.

Chater, Nick, and Morten H. Christiansen. 2010. Language Acquisition Meets Language Evolution. *Cognitive Science* 34: 1131–57.

Chomsky, Noam. 1964. The Logical Basis of Linguistic Theory. In *Proceedings of the 9th International Congress of Linguists, Cambridge, Mass., August 27–31, 1962*, ed. Horace G. Lunt, 914–1008. The Hague: Mouton.

1965. *Aspects of the Theory of Syntax*. Cambridge, MA: MIT Press.

1975. *The Logical Structure of Linguistic Theory*. New York: Plenum Press [first circulated in 1955].

1980. *Rules and Representations*. Oxford: Blackwell.

1995. *The Minimalist Program*. Cambridge, MA: MIT Press.

2004. Beyond Explanatory Adequacy. In *Structures and Beyond: The Cartography of Syntactic Structure*, ed. Adriana Belletti, 104–31. Oxford: Oxford University Press.

2010. Some Simple Evo Devo Theses: How true might they be for language? In *The Evolution of Human Language: Biolinguistic Perspectives*, ed. Richard K. Larson, Viviane Déprez, and Hiroko Yamakido, 45–62. Cambridge: Cambridge University Press.

Clark, Alexander S., and Shalom Lappin. 2011. *Linguistic Nativism and the Poverty of the Stimulus*. Malden, MA: Wiley-Blackwell.

Croft, William. 2003. *Typology and Universals*. 2nd ed. Cambridge: Cambridge University Press.

Cysouw, Michael. 2003. Against Implicational Universals. *Linguistic Typology* 7: 89–110.

Deutscher, Guy. 2007. *Syntactic Change in Akkadian: The Evolution of Sentential Complementation*. Oxford: Oxford University Press.

Dixon, R. M. W. 2010–12. *Basic Linguistic Theory*. 3 vols. Oxford: Oxford University Press.

Dryer, Matthew S. 1989. Large Linguistic Areas and Language Sampling. *Studies in Language* 13: 257–92.

1992. The Greenbergian Word Order Correlations. *Language* 68: 81–138.

1997. Why Statistical Universals Are Better Than Absolute Universals. In *Papers from the 33rd Annual Meeting of the Chicago Linguistic Society*, 123–45.

2005. Order of Subject, Object, and Verb. In *The World Atlas of Language Structures*, ed. Martin Haspelmath, Matthew S. Dryer, David Gil and Bernard Comrie, 330–41. Oxford: Oxford University Press.

2006. Descriptive Theories, Explanatory Theories, and Basic Linguistic Theory. In *Catching Language: Issues in Grammar Writing*, ed. Felix Ameka, Alan Dench, and Nicholas Evans, Berlin: Mouton de Gruyter.

2011. Polar Questions. In *The World Atlas of Language Structures Online*, ed. Matthew S. Dryer and Martin Haspelmath. Munich: Max Planck Digital Library [http://wals.info/].

Dunn, Michael J., Simon J. Greenhill, Stephen C. Levinson, and Russell D. Gray. 2011. Evolved Structure of Language Shows Lineage-Specific Trends in Word-Order Universals. *Nature* 473: 79–82.

Evans, Nicholas. 2003. Context, Culture, and Structuration in the Languages of Australia. *Annual Review of Anthropology* 32: 13–40.

Evans, Nicholas and Stephen C. Levinson. 2009. The Myth of Language Universals: Language diversity and its importance for cognitive science. *Behavioral and Brain Sciences* 32: 429–48.

Everett, Daniel L. 2005. Cultural Constraints on Grammar and Cognition in Pirahã: Another look at the design features of human language. *Current Anthropology* 46(4): 621–46.

Firchow, Irwin, and Jacqueline Firchow. 1969. An Abbreviated Phoneme Inventory. *Anthropological Linguistics* 11: 271–6.

Gil, David. 1999. Riau Indonesian as a Pivotless Language. In *Tipologija i teorija jazyka*, ed. Ekatarina V. Rakhilina and Jakov G. Testelec, 187–211. Moscow: Jazyk Russkoj Kultury.

— 2005. Word Order Without Syntactic Categories: How Riau Indonesian does it. In *Verb First: On the Syntax of Verb-Initial Languages*, ed. Andrew Carnie, Heidi Harley, and Sheila Ann Dooley, 243–64. Amsterdam: Benjamins.

Givón, Talmy. 2001. *Syntax*. Amsterdam: Benjamins.

— 2010. The Adaptive Approach to Grammar. In *The Oxford Handbook of Linguistic Analysis*, ed. Bernd Heine and Heiko Narrog, 27–49. Oxford: Oxford University Press.

Greenberg, Joseph H. 1963. Some Universals of Grammar with Particular Reference to the Order of Meaningful Elements. In *Universals of Language*, ed. Joseph H. Greenberg, 73–113. Cambridge, MA: MIT Press.

— ed. 1978. *Universals of Human Language*. Stanford, CA: Stanford University Press.

Haspelmath, Martin. 2010. Comparative Concepts and Descriptive Categories: Consequences for language description and typology. *Language* 86: 663–87.

Haspelmath, Martin, and Sven Siegmund. 2006. Simulating the Replication of Some of Greenberg's Word Order Generalizations. *Linguistic Typology* 10: 74–82.

Hawkins, John A. 1994. *A Performance Theory of Order and Constituency*. Cambridge: Cambridge University Press.

— 2004. *Efficiency and Complexity in Grammars*. Oxford: Oxford University Press.

Heine, Bernd. 2008. Contact-Induced Word Order Change Without Word Order Change. In *Language Contact and Contact Languages*, ed. Peter Siemund and Noemi Kintana, 33–60. Amsterdam: Benjamins.

Heine, Bernd, and Tania Kuteva. 2006. *The Changing Languages of Europe*. Oxford: Oxford University Press.

Heine, Bernd, and Heiko Narrog, eds. 2012. *The Oxford Handbook of Linguistic Analysis*. 2nd ed. Oxford: Oxford University Press.

Hurford, James. 2011. Linguistics From an Evolutionary Point of View. In *Handbook of the Philosophy of Science: Linguistics*, ed. Ruth M. Kempson, Tim Fernando, and Nicholas Asher, 473–98. Amsterdam: Elsevier.

Hyman, Larry M. 1983. Are There Syllables in Gokana? In *Current Approaches to African Linguistics*, ed. Jonathan Kaye, Hilda Koopman, and Dominique Sportiche, Vol. 2, 171–9. Dordrecht: Foris.

2011. Does Gokana Really Have No Syllables? Or: what's so great about being universal? *Phonology* 28: 55-85.

Jackendoff, Ray. 2002. *Foundations of Language: Brain, Meaning, Grammar, Evolution.* Oxford: Oxford University Press.

Jäncke, Lutz. 2009. The Plastic Brain. *Restorative Neurology and Neuroscience* 27: 521-38.

Johanson, Lars. 1992. *Strukturelle Faktoren in türkischen Sprachkontakten.* Stuttgart: Steiner.

Karlsson, Fred. 2010. Syntactic Recursion and Iteration. In Harry van der Hulst (ed.), *Recursion and Human Language*, 43-67. Berlin: De Gruyter Mouton.

Levinson, Stephen C. 2001. Yélî Dnye and the Theory of Basic Color Terms. *Journal of Linguistic Anthropology* 10. 3-55.

2003. Language and Mind: Let's get the issues straight. In *Language in Mind: Advances in the Study of Language and Thought*, ed. Dedre Gentner and Susan Goldin-Meadow, 25-46. Cambridge, MA: MIT Press.

2012. The Original Sin of Cognitive Science. *Topics in Cognitive Science* 4: 1-8.

Lucy, John A. 1992. *Grammatical Categories and Cognition.* Cambridge: Cambridge University Press.

Maddieson, Ian. 2011. Consonant and Vowel Inventories. In *The World Atlas of Language Structures Online*, ed. Matthew S. Dryer and Martin Haspelmath. Munich: Max Planck Digital Library [http://wals.info/].

Mithun, Marianne. 1984. How to Avoid Subordination. In *Proceedings of the 10th Annual Meeting of the Berkeley Linguistics Society*, 493-509.

Molochieva, Zarina. 2010. *Tense, Aspect, and Mood in Chechen.* Leipzig: University of Leipzig dissertation.

Nettle, Daniel. 1999. *Linguistic Diversity.* Oxford: Oxford University Press.

Nevins, Andrew, David Pesetsky, and Cilene Rodrigues. 2009. Pirahã Exceptionality: A reassessment. *Language* 85: 355-404.

Newmeyer, Frederick J. 2010. On Comparative Concepts and Descriptive Categories: A reply to Haspelmath. *Language* 86: 688-95.

Nhàn, Ngô Thanh. 1984. *The Syllabeme and Patterns of Word Formation in Vietnamese.* New York: NYU dissertation.

Nichols, Johanna. 1992. *Linguistic Diversity in Space and Time.* Chicago: The University of Chicago Press.

Nichols, Johanna, and Balthasar Bickel. 2009. The AUTOTYP Genealogy and Geography Database: 2009 release. Electronic database.

Overdulve, C. M. 1987. *Kwiga ikinyarwanda: manuel d'apprentissage de la langue rwanda.* Kabgayi.

Perfors, Amy, Joshua B. Tenenbaum, and Terry Regier. 2011. The Learnability of Abstract Syntactic Principles. *Cognition* 118: 306-38.

Peterson, John. 2011. *A Grammar of Kharia.* Leiden: Brill.

Piantadosi, Steven T., and Edward Gibson. 2013. Quantitative Standards for Absolute Linguistic Universals. *Cognitive Science* 1-21 [DOI: 10.1111/cogs.12088].

Plank, Frans, and Elena Filimonova. 2000. The Universals Archive: A brief introduction to prospective users. *Language Typology and Universals* 53: 109-23.

Pullum, Geoffrey K., and Barbara C. Scholz. 2010. Recursion and the Infinitude Claim. In *Recursion and Human Language*, ed. Harry van der Hulst, 113-37. Berlin: De Gruyter Mouton.

Regier, Terry, Paul Kay, and Naveen Khetarpal. 2007. Color Naming Reflects Optimal Partitions of Color Space. *Proceedings of the National Academy of Sciences* 104: 1436-41.

Roberson, Debi. 2005. Color Categories are Culturally Diverse in Cognition As Well As in Language. *Cross-cultural Research* 39: 56-71.

Roberson, Debi, Jules Davidoff, and Ian Davies. 2000. Color Categories are Not Universal: Replications and new evidence from a stone-age culture. *Journal of Experimental Psychology: General* 129: 369-398.

Sampson, Geoffrey, David Gil, and Peter Trudgill, eds. 2009. *Language Complexity as an Evolving Variable*. Oxford: Oxford University Press.

Sandler, Wendy, Mark Aronoff, Irit Meir, and Carol Padden. 2011. The Gradual Emergence of Phonological Form in a New Language. *Natural Language and Linguistic Theory* 29: 503-43.

Sandler, Wendy, and Diane Lillo-Martin. 2006. *Sign Language and Linguistic Universals*. Cambridge: Cambridge University Press.

Schiering, René, Balthasar Bickel, and Kristine Hildebrandt. 2010. The Prosodic Word Is Not Universal, But Emergent. *Journal of Linguistics* 46: 657-709.

Shopen, Timothy, ed. 2007. *Language Typology and Syntactic Description*. 2nd ed. Cambridge: Cambridge University Press.

Slobin, Dan I. 1996. From "Thought and Language" to "Thinking for Speaking". In *Rethinking Linguistic Relativity*, ed. John J. Gumperz and Stephen C. Levinson, 70-96. Cambridge: Cambridge University Press.

Song, Jae Jung, ed. 2011. *The Oxford Handbook of Linguistic Typology*. Oxford: Oxford University Press.

Stoll, Sabine, Balthasar Bickel, Elena Lieven, Goma Banjade, Toya Nath Bhatta, Martin Gaenszle, Netra P. Paudyal, Judith Pettigrew, Ichchha P. Rai, Manoj Rai, and Novel Kishore Rai. 2012. Nouns and Verbs in Chintang: Children's usage and surrounding adult speech. *Journal of Child Language* 39: 284-321.

Thomason, Sarah Grey, and Terrence Kaufman. 1988. *Language Contact, Creolization, and Genetic Linguistics*. Berkeley: University of California Press.

Thompson, Paul M., Nicholas G. Martin, and Margaret J. Wright. 2010. Imaging Genomics. *Current Opinion in Neurology* 23: 368-73.

Tomasello, Michael. 2003. *Constructing a Language: A Usage-Based Theory of Language Acquisition*. Cambridge, MA: Harvard University Press.

2008. *Origins of Human Communication*. Cambridge, MA: MIT Press.

Traill, Anthony. 1985. *Phonetic and Phonological Studies of !Xóõ Bushman*. Hamburg: Buske.
Viti, Carlotta. 2012. *Variation und Wandel in der Syntax der alten indogermanischen Sprachen*. Zurich: UZH Habilitationsschrift.
Vogel, Irene. 2009. Universals of Prosodic Structure. In *Universals of Language Today*, ed. Sergio Scalise, Elisabetta Magni, and Antonietta Bisetto, 59–82. Berlin: Springer.

6

Denotation and the pragmatics of language

Michael Silverstein

We can – reflexively – locate linguistic anthropology and other language sciences and arts within the European cultural tradition, itself powerfully refocused by the Enlightenment on the instrumentality of language as a communicable, and hence sharable, representation of experienced and cognized universes. (See Aarsleff 1982; Eco 1994; Stillman 1995; Bauman and Briggs 2003; Losonsky 2006.) Within this tradition, and even before and beyond it, three powerful intuitions inform people's orientations to language signs, both their own and others'.

One is the intuition that "words" as abstract or at least aggregate entities stand for or even descriptively substitute for "things" as instances of such "words" recur on particular occasions of use. Intuitively, people think of themselves as users of particular word- and expression-forms differentially to single things out by appropriately describing them; in-and-by this act the users classify things as entities of certain experienceable and/or imaginable classes or categories. That, for example, on some occasion I called something I was simultaneously pointing at "(this) table" rather than "(that) shelf" must, to such intuition, have invoked and made relevant to communication a distinction of at least two classes or categories of phenomena, tables and shelves – that is to say (as so-called form-based relativism asserts) in such a language community where the two terms, table and shelf, are directly contrasted (on which more below).

A second intuition is that we can use another, more encompassing particular type of expression-form, the (actually or recoverably complete) sentence, to describe happenings, situations, or states-of-affairs as actual, or "true," or non-actual, or "false," in some experienced or projectively imaginable sphere or universe. To such an intuition, each turn at talk (in whatever actual medium: speech, writing, manual signing, etc.) when evaluated as – parsed as – a sentence, however simple or complex, seems to make a claim about the world as cognized; each multi-sentence turn at talk should therefore make coherent – or at least non-incoherent – claims as to the truth or falsity of states-of-affairs as so described, to whatever level of delicacy suggested by grammatico-semantic form.

The first of these intuitions, refined, revised, and parceled out ultimately to many different disciplinary studies in linguistics, philosophy, psychology, anthropology, to name only some, involves the notion that the descriptive forms of language are in essence labels giving evidence of a vast classification of seemingly nonlinguistic experience and imagination, an affordance to the users of a language as they communicate about particular individual things singled out as exemplars by use of sometimes highly constructionally complex expressions developed out of such classificatory categories. Given that language forms are recurrently manifested in spatiotemporally discrete events of communication, the obvious problems here involve such matters as *the stability of the categorizing effect* – particular word- and expression-forms reliably and determinately cueing particular classes of entities – across discrete events and even discrete phases of single communicative events, across types of users even of "the same" language, as well, of course, as across what are understood to be distinct languages. Centuries of theorizing and empirical research in several disciplinary lines have tried to clarify these matters, centering on the concept of LINGUISTICALLY CONSUMMATED REFERENCE, our human cognitive ability to 'extend' entities via 'referring expressions' and what this may reveal about any 'intensional' categories by which we seem, perhaps even systematically, to engage such universes of extendables as categorizable objects of discourse. (See Quine 1960; Searle 1969: 72–96, 157–74; Linsky 1971 [1967]: 76–86; Lyons 1977: 174–229.)

Refining the second of these intuitions vis-à-vis natural human languages got its impetus from the nineteenth century's multi-faceted concern with modeling syllogistic and patterns of logical inference as an idealized "symbolic logic" to formalize functional human rationality, the "laws of thought" (G. Boole) as it were, and from the twentieth century's philosophical turn to evaluating natural human language and particularly its scientifically usable registers against such models, a constructive linguistic philosophy of the so called "analytic" type. (See Carnap 1937; Morris 1938; Searle 1969: 97–127; Strawson 1971; Rosenberg and Travis 1971: 219–82.) Of course, since sentence-sized chunks of natural human language are, to this intuition, manifest in communicative events, the task entailed is to determine how "logical," that is, transparent to and consistent with a formalizable calculus of propositional inference, are our sentence-chunked turns at talk and longer stretches of discourse. One part of a sentence-as-communicated is, by the first intuition, to be taken as a referring expression, indicating the focal individuable(s) at that moment in communication. Then the rest of a sentence-as-communicated is intuitively associable with MODALLY PREDICATING certain states-of-affairs as 'true/false-of' the referent(s), the modality indicating how to calibrate the sphere in which something can be 'true' or 'false' relative to the sphere in which the users experience the framing communicative event. The default modality is presumed to be statemental or declarative, used in acts of asserting the factuality of states-of-affairs in the episteme of the communicative act.

In this connection, it should be noted that one of the central contemporary senses of the term 'pragmatics' derives from such an approach, in which, insofar as natural human discourse is to be propositionally interpreted and evaluated, its quirks necessitate a corrective overlay to what would be a more conformably "logical" interpretability of its linguistic form. Hence, to a 'logical semantics' of sentence-expressions, it has been found that we must append a '[logical] pragmatics' to account for inferential consequences of communication – propositional meanings apparently conveyed – that seem askew relative to the specific sentence-expression form used under particular circumstances. (See Grice 1989; and Horn and Ward 2004 for a revealing survey.)

It will be noted that if the study of linguistic form as such corresponds to and develops medieval "grammar," and if the study of the classificatory, truth-functional, and syllogistic-inferential counterparts of using language develops and corresponds to medieval "logic," then what is missing is the third subject of the medieval trivium, "rhetoric." Indeed, the effect of (and in many respects, the impetus for) much of the Enlightenment project for understanding the nature of language was to reform and refine it in form as an autonomous instrumentality of (logical) human thought and to direct the resulting semiotic machinery as so understood to particular representational and thereby ultimately sociopolitical ends, rationalizing (and "disenchanting") natural human language for the evolving modern institutional forms congruent with such views of it and promoting such views of it by its users as a basis of modern institutional authority. Hence, the ultimately evolved tripartite model of mid-twentieth-century theorizing (see Morris 1946) about natural human languages sees its semiotics in this light: an autonomous 'syntax' (= grammar) interpretable in terms of – that is, projectable into – a referential-and-modally-predicational 'semantics' that sometimes requires adjustment relative to "context" (see below) by a '[logical] pragmatics' of usage.

Here, then, we approach the third Enlightenment-derived intuition about language: that the practical role of language in human affairs – what we might term, with J. L. Austin (1962), "what we do with words" – depends on, yet is a separate and distinct function of "what we say in words," that is, the referentially and predicationally interpretable forms of language in communicative context. The semiotic ideology of the Enlightenment project focused a suspicious, indeed somewhat negative intuitive regard on how language essentially mediates the majority of interpersonal human phenomena, in the Western tradition those mediations having long since been subsumed under the rubric of rhetoric. Rhetoric addressed such questions as: How does poetic "eloquence" in verbal performance cause interlocutors so addressed to align with a particular societal interest on behalf of which the eloquence is mobilized? How does language-as-used serve individuals as the medium of mutual social and attitudinal self-revelation and thus social coordination, and even as a consequential medium of ascriptive definition directed at the "other" in the course of interaction? How can the use of one from among several distinct expressions that from a "logical" semantic point of view appear to be synonymous, powerfully (and differentially) effectuate certain social ends in events of discursive interaction?

Such "rhetorical" phenomena, universal in human social groups, are, to be sure, the subject matter of a second and wider sense of the 'pragmatics' of language, beyond the logical one: discourse understood as social practice or praxis inextricably intertwined and intercalated, it turns out, with anything we might wish to identify as the manifestation of linguistic form on the axis of grammar-and-logic. So what I shall term the DENOTATIONAL VIEW of natural language (adopting Lyons's [1977: 206–15] cover term) of the modernizing Enlightenment project construes as distinct and separable the very sociocultural phenomena of sociolinguistics and linguistic anthropology, but as will be seen remains incomplete and unconvincing precisely by excluding them. As will be seen below, denotation is, in fact, incoherent except when socioculturally framed and institutionally licensed, notwithstanding the fact that engaging such wider pragmatic phenomena reveals the narrowest Enlightenment project for what it is. As will be seen, immanent in and essential to language as the central sociocultural semiotic is, its peculiar character is as a *dialectical* socio-semiotic phenomenon in which denotation, to be sure, plays several roles. Language manifests a tension between (1) what is encompassed in a denotational model so central to the intuitions of both laypersons and professional students of language in the West (§**6.1**), and (2) discourse as practice (or 'praxis') in a sociologically or socioculturally informed perspective (§**6.2**). These two functionalities engage reciprocally via (3) several planes of metapragmatic reflexivity, about which more below (§**6.3**). This tension can be displayed and examined by developing a (meta-)semiotic from generally Peircean principles.

6.1 Elaborating the semiotics of denotation

In the denotational view, referring and modally predicating can thus be thought of as at least analytically distinguishable partials of a communicative – Austin's (1962: 92–8) "locutionary" – act, instantiated in-and-by the occurrence of certain linguistic signs. Referring and modally predicating are, it is postulated, one way among numerous others in which people engage semiotically with one another in social interactions, however else they may be concurrently engaging, verbally and otherwise. In this sense, indeed, each Sender of a message seems, at that moment in interactional history during which utterance takes place, to be "doing things with words" insofar that Sender is understood to be agentively responsible for intentionally precipitating a particular linguistic signal that the Receiver cannot but respond to by discerning (a) referent(s) and modally evaluating some state-of-affairs as "true"/"false" in respect of it or them. Indeed, universally people seem to have strong intuitions that their default goal is deploying linguistic forms to get participating interactants to focus differentially on entities to be discerned in actual or (under calibratable conditions) actualizable states-of-affairs, that is, that the default functionality of language is referential and predicational or, as we shall term it here, compositely DENOTATIONAL. Even if we narrow the phenomenal realm of the pragmatic or practical use of language to such denotational functionality, we encounter two traditions that have attempted to systematize it: at one extreme, a Platonic declaration that denotational usage in communicational context is merely a distorted counterpart to something more essential and deep in the way human language works; or, at the other extreme, a naïve and faux empiricist inductivism that dissolves human language into the vicissitudes of event-bound discursive interactions the very stability of which in relation to recurrence of denotational linguistic forms is rendered problematic.

Notwithstanding such extremes of theorizing, these folk intuitions underlie and animate the Enlightenment project for natural language, conceptualized as a denotational semiotic technology that can be refined and stabilized independent of the phenomena of "rhetoric." But perhaps the most important corollary – whether it was actually dependent on that project or not, it is difficult to tell in our state of historical retrospection – is the 'foundationalist' DOCTRINE OF "LITERAL" DENOTATION that posits an autonomous denotational mechanism to anchor referring and modally predicating. To explain this doctrine, I refer (!) the reader to Figure 6.1, which from the point of view of an adequate semiotics of communication sets out what I term the basic "Lockean rectangle" of elements of denotational literalism.

In the rectangle's horizontal dimension, the left side of the rectangular array pictures LINGUISTIC SIGNS; the right side PHENOMENA OF EXPERIENCE AND IMAGINATION differentially represented during communication in-and-by the use of language (including here focused thought of an inferential kind). Of course, some of these phenomena of experience and imagination may themselves be essentially linguistic, as for example when language – forms on the left side – is used (as in this entire book) as its own DENOTATIONAL METALANGUAGE to describe linguistic phenomena – now playing the role of entities and states-of-affairs on the right side. (We return to this important special case below.) In the rectangle's vertical dimension, the upper side of the rectangular array pictures whatever stability or normativity across events of language usage may be inherent in language and/or in the phenomena of the universes of experience and imagination, the realm of LINGUISTIC EXPRESSION-FORM-TYPES and

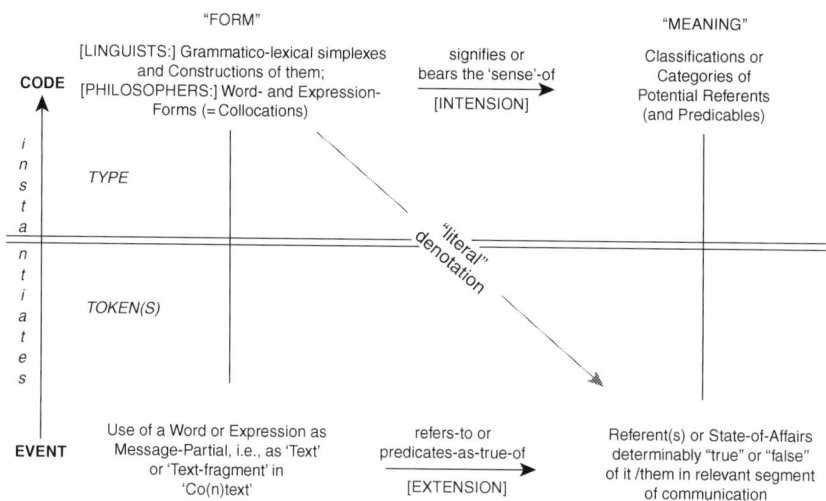

Figure 6.1 The Basic "Lockean Rectangle" (U of C: Quadrangle), "solved" in folk-intuition and enshrined in much philosophy of language and mind

CATEGORIES OF POTENTIAL REFERENTS AND PREDICABLES; the lower side pictures the event-bound instances of denotational communication in which linguistic SIGN-TOKENS are used to pick out REFERENTS and modally to predicate-as-"true"/"false" STATES-OF-AFFAIRS in modally calibratable worlds involving such referents (and possibly other denotata).

The relationships from upper to lower side and those between left and right sides need some elaboration. The vertex at the lower left represents occurring instances of language signs, word- and expression-forms precipitated by signaling and perceiving behaviors in the context of events of language use. Any empirical study of language begins with corpora of such instances or tokens, whether finite and "found," as was the case during an older philological period of collecting text inscriptions; or developed by systematic, annotated sampling of ongoing usage (and absence of usage), as in contemporary computer-assisted creation of dynamic corpora; or by systematically stimulating occurrences achieved by infinitely iteratable elicitation in interviews with speakers (so-called "fieldwork") or in laboratory experimentation with them. The point is that one can collect tokens of form as data-points for many different kinds of investigation of denotation. Now, from such material it is possible to move to the upper left vertex, the type-level or covering-law concept of linguistic form, only by assuming that there is something recurrent or constant about all of the tokens or instances of linguistic form *qua* form (Bloomfield 1970[1926]: 130, def.6); what is constant is, moreover, presumed to be replicated in each instantiation of an indefinitely large set of such, documentable in all the phenomena represented in the lower left vertex of the diagram. Linguistic phenomena conceptualized as of the upper left vertex are, in essence, abstract objects like any covering law – Peirce (1931–58: 2.142–3,

§246) termed them Legisigns for this reason – in contradistinction to the phenomena of the lower left, which are Replicas of each other insofar each is an instance, token, or 'Sinsign', as Peirce noted, of the Legisign. Such Sinsigns INSTANTIATE Legisigns, as Legisigns thus occur IMMANENT IN each of their Sinsigns; by virtue of this relationship, Legisigns such as abstract linguistic form-types can be said to recur in each event of usage instantiating them.

The left edge of our diagram is connected to the right one by relationships of SIGNIFICATION, the lower right vertex and the upper right one each corresponding to their respective left-edge vertices in the following sense. When a linguistic token is successfully used as a denotational sign, the effect is either to differentiate a referent or referents, under whatever discursive conditions this takes place, or differentially to predicate some state-of-affairs in some universe calibrated to the universe experienceable in the event of communication. Referent(s) and states-of-affairs thus constitute the phenomena signaled in-and-by deployment of some token signal on some occasion of communication in which it occurs. Correspondingly, under the presumption of denotation, the sign relationship of the upper edge of our rectangle depicts the situation where the abstract linguistic form-type, the Peircean Legisign, stands for some principle of grouping entities, something like a class characteristic by which potential referents and states-of-affairs can be sorted as members of coherently differentiable sets. The intuition is that Legisigns correspond to classificatory principles, however simple or complex, by which potential referents and predicable states-of-affairs can be – and in fact, in-and-as we communicate, are – differentiated by language, "concepts," as it were, wherever these can be figuratively said to "live."

This (as Peirce termed it [1931–58: 2.143–4, §249]) Symbolic relationship of the upper edge of the rectangle is never straightforwardly experienced as immanent in any individual event of communication – the phenomena of the lower edge of the figure – except under one specific assumption – as I have termed it, a corollary intuition: the doctrine of so-called "literal" or non-"metaphorical" extensions for type-level words and expressions of language, indicated by the diagonal that runs from upper left vertex to lower right. This intuition is that for every Legisign expression we can distinguish those referents or states-of-affairs that properly (normatively) or "literally" ("correctly") can be signaled by token Sinsigns of the Legisign, from all other referents or states-of-affairs that, on some occasion of use or other, have been or might be extended by use of a Sinsign of that expression. So, on some occasion of use of the expression (this) table while pointing at the referent in question, I may have in fact successfully extended what should have properly or "literally" been referred to with the expression (this) shelf – not having seen, for example, that the horizontal wooden surface was not resting on the floor with legs, so much as it was affixed to a wall by mounting brackets not visible to me. And yet:

(a) I did successfully refer to the entity in perceptual focus, differentiating it for my interlocutor, and (b) there is, after all, something table-like about the referent, so that, not intending to pun, one can see that I "extended the meaning" of the Legisign table in the act of extending a shelf using a token of the term. My event of referring had a certain non-"literal" or a creeping "metaphorical" character under the doctrine of literal denotation.

But it can be seen, the doctrine of literal denotation actually solves the problem of the relationship between the upper and lower edges of the Lockean rectangle. It suggests, first, that instead of focusing on token word- and expression-forms in actual events of communication, we can unproblematically focus on type word- and expression-forms, that is, that we can contemplate and analyze Legisign forms themselves, however the abstraction from and generalization over tokens is to be achieved. (We will return to this point subsequently.) Secondly, the doctrine of literal denotation seems to suggest that we can collect (at least a sufficiently large sample of) the "literal" referents and predicable states-of-affairs that correspond to type word- and expression-forms and study them (independent of their being denotata of language) for some common property or properties that distinguish them, *qua* "literally" denotable set of entities or states-of-affairs, from all those other, non-"literal" ones that may – like our hypothetical example of tables and shelves – creep into everyday usage, whether by happenstance, by mistake, or by "metaphorically" intended design. Were we able to stipulate what is common to the "literal" denotata of a word- or expression-type, that is, were we able to formulate a covering law predicable-as-'true' for all and only the word- or expression-type's denotata, generally termed the DESIGNATUM (designation) or (LITERAL) SENSE of the word or expression, we would be able to stipulate what kind of entities or states-of-affairs are rightly included among the "literal" denotata; we could identify the designatum – really a criterion for membership in a logical class – with the vertex at the upper right of the Lockean rectangle. Then, for "literal" denotational use of language, every referent or state-of-affairs at the lower right vertex instantiates the designatum of the Legisign to which, on the upper edge, it corresponds.

We have, in this view, "solved" the Lockean rectangle. But let us consider what it has taken so to do, starting from upper left and lower right vertices in the attempt to stabilize the two others. First, it must be unproblematic how word- and expression-tokens at the lower left vertex instantiate word- and expression-types at the upper left vertex. This problem for discourse in general is rendered somewhat tractable only by assuming that the referring-and-modally-predicating Sentence-type is the natural and inevitable unit of using language – to be sure, the intuitive assumption underlying modern linguistics and related views of language and enshrined even in the punctuational graphics of modern typography and related secondary linguistic practices. This assumption amounts to the immanence of systematically analyzable Sentence-grammar in every occurring chunk of discourse, now parsed into what we term, with Lyons (1995: 259–62), TEXT SENTENCES (as opposed to the SYSTEM SENTENCES that stipulate their recurrent parsability), even if discursive "turns-at-talk" may consist of only fragments of a text-sentence or, in lengthy monologue, of multiple text-sentences. (We will return to the problematic entailments of the assumption below.) Second, we have assumed that for any given word- or expression-type in a particular language, those who "know" the language have strong and clear intuitions of what "literally" can serve as denotatum of an instance of its use, and therefore of what cannot so serve. Certainly at the word level, this has proved to be a state of affairs very problematic to demonstrate empirically, and all evidence suggests rather that even people thinking of themselves as speaking the "same" language have widely divergent understandings of the "literal" meaning of particular word- and expression-types under the intuitive assumptions described. (See Putnam 1975; Labov 2004[1973].) Third, our solution of the Lockean rectangle has depended upon having a language-independent way of discovering if (or, that) the "literal" denotata of a word- or expression-type, collectible, say, through a sufficiently large sampling of use, can, in fact, be shown to share some property or properties – other than being denotata of a particular form at issue – that can be described as the criterion for membership in the set of entities/states-of-affairs that can serve as its "literal" denotatum. It is sometimes assumed that the phenomena even of the perceivable universe come in – literally! – "natural" classes or categories, with which, then, "literal" denotation must be in harmony as a "natural" function of the classifications immanent in the non-semiotic world (Kripke 1972; Rosch 1978; Kay and McDaniel 1978). Then why are all systems of intuitively "literal" denotation of that world not the same? And is there any non-circular way to determine what those "natural" classes are, with their dimensions of contrast determining inclusion and exclusion of potential "literal" denotata, without any appeal or essential role for linguistic communication? Only a completely language-independent determination of such classes or categories would be a valid grounding of the right edge of the Lockean rectangle so as to anchor the intuition of denotational literalness in an autonomous explanatory phenomenon.

Now, as it turns out, much of cognitive psychology, methodologically taking its cue from positivist philosophy, has tried just such a method of solution of the right edge of the Lockean rectangle to triangulate the doctrine of literal denotation. Using laboratory techniques that are, ultimately, no more sophisticated than the assumption of literalness, researchers have attempted to demonstrate that an autonomous "natural" world organized by perceptual dimensions underlies conceptual categorization, and that it is this world that is reflected at least in systems of word- and expression-types considered as terminological differentiae. Given the variation in terminological systems for any domain available for (intuitively "literal") denotation, such an approach is either based on a particular terminological system, whether knowingly or unknowingly, or it depends on calibrating and thus mutually anchoring all known (or possible) terminological systems in respect of their "literal" – strictly non-"metaphorical" – denotational relationships, were these universally applicable and determinate phenomena in every language community. As we can see, the approach winds up, without further refinement, being completely circular. (See John Lucy's [1997] remarks on "universals of color [=hue-saturation-brightness]" lexicalization.)

Modern linguistic structuralism or formalism, by contrast, has taken an orthogonal approach to implementing the doctrine of literal denotation, concentrating almost entirely on anchoring the signifying relationship of the phenomena of the upper side of the rectangle. That is, linguists start at the upper left vertex with the assumption of a syntax or GRAMMAR of system-sentence scope, a complex and recursive combinatoric calculus that determines an internally systematic and autonomous organization of Legisign form in which classes or categories of ultimate Legisigns under the calculus, lexical and other morphemic simplexes, combine or concatenate in larger and larger Legisign structures, up to the phrasal boundaries of the system-sentence. Classes or categories of Legisign form are defined "distributionally," that is, as a function of their relational roles in the combinatorics. The presumption is that insofar lexical simplexes in the upper left vertex of our diagram correspond to (or bear) senses in the upper right vertex, the sense of any phrase made up of such simplexes should be a computable function of the senses of the simplexes plus the rules for their combination into the particular concatenational structure in which they occur one with another. This is the grammarian's assumption of the "COMPOSITIONALITY" OF SENSE.

Note also that insofar the very same Legisign form – here exemplified by a phrasal projection of a common noun – may be instantiated in either referring or predicating segments of corresponding text-sentences (*Round smooth rocks were lying everywhere.* vs. *I saw a number of round smooth rocks.*), the senses of Legisigns are assumed to be, for purposes of linguistic analysis, stable as such across their instantiation in event-partials of reference or of predication. In other words, while at the lower edge of our figure we are concerned with events of actual reference and modalized predication, at the top edge we are concerned with a completely autonomous relationship of signification where the quasi-propositional senses of units up to and including system-sentences determine "literalness" of actual events of referring and modally predicating, but the latter are only in this special way instantiations of sense-bearing Legisigns. (This is the import of the Chomskyan discernment of "logical form" corresponding to syntactic structure, as opposed to propositional reference-and-modalized-predication. See Jackendoff 1990.) In fact, we might say that insofar senses in the upper plane of system-sentencehood constitute a propositionally relevant semantic universe, they are indeed essentially incomplete, requiring what we termed above a logical pragmatics to describe what text-sentences actually do as the frames in which referring and modally predicating expressions actually occur as language users engage in referring and predicating under particular contextual conditions.

This motivates our consideration of the nature of pragmatics, logical and otherwise.

6.2 Discursive practices in a semiotic pragmatics

Let us direct attention now to Figure 6.2 (elaborating Jakobson 1960: 353) to develop a more granular view of the phenomena along the lower edge of the Lockean rectangle.

It can be seen that the MESSAGE of this diagram is equivalent to the word- and expression-forms at the lower left vertex of the earlier figure; the GRAMMAR stipulates any regularities by which thus-definable Legisign-forms are immanent in the way parsable messages can "literally" correspond to lower-right vertex denotata (represented as the undifferentiated REFERENT

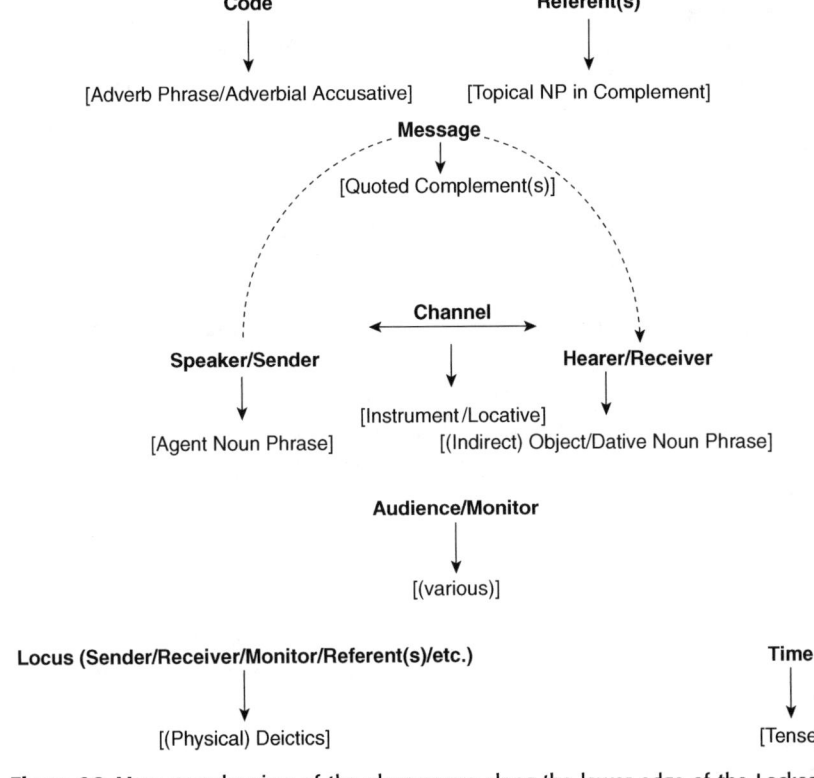

Figure 6.2 More granular view of the phenomena along the lower edge of the Lockean rectangle (see Figure 6.1)

in this figure, for simplicity's sake), i.e., how sign-types underlying sign-tokens bear what philosophers term 'senses'. It is important to note that the message *qua* denotational communication bears an indexical relationship to any grammatical principles defining whatever regularity the message manifests in-and-by occurring; the message if normatively con-form-ing presumes upon (indexically presupposes) its principles of internal structuration. As well, the message bears an indexical relationship to its corresponding determinate referent. The denotational message thus (co-)occurs as such in its relevant CHANNEL(s) of transmission only by presuming upon the existence of a grammar by which it is (in)formed and upon the existence of a denotational universe in which an entity or state-of-affairs can be determinately differentiated in-and-by use of some expression-form that one can evaluate as by-degree "appropriate" to so doing in the moment (and, by inscriptional techniques, at some future point).

But, as can be seen in the diagram, these are not the only indexical relationships contracted between a message – or any parsed fraction of a message – and other dimensions of communication. Indeed, the total set of such indexical relationships is the CONTEXT of any isolable message (or message-fraction), which latter can thus, by contrast, also be termed the precipitated TEXT (a term especially – traditionally – used for messages of complex internal structure). Text and context are constantly in a process of relational becoming by reciprocal determination (more on this below), for which reason it has recently become customary to speak of the coordinated processes of ENTEXTUALIZATION – the way that any message-segment comes to constitute part of a more complex textual organization – and CONTEXTUALIZATION – the way the message-fractions in such a text are incrementally involved in indexical relations that point beyond it to an ever "thickening" context of describable co-occurrents. (See Silverstein and Urban 1996.) Insofar something about the form of the message indexically signals one or more of these other aspects of what, at least conceptually, "surrounds" or frames it, we know that message-form is a function not merely of regularities of grammar as described earlier, but of the other conditions of the form-token's use. For example, who – that is, sociologically speaking, what definable type of individual or even biographical individual – seems to be inhabiting the relational role of SENDER for some phase of a communication, and who the role of RECEIVER, with consequences for how a message is formed and/or what it denotes? Is there someone inhabiting the role of MONITOR/AUDIENCE whose social characteristics determine which of a set of alternative, though semantically equivalent, forms occurs? With attention to local socioculturally relevant space-time schemata that "locate" events of discursive interaction, when – at what TIME, schematically speaking – does a message occur (for example, in relation to the event or state-of-affairs a message denotes), and where, in what relevant scheme(s) of LOCUS, particularly in respect of the locational topology of role inhabitance of some referent in relation to sender, receiver, audience, etc. in the ongoing configuration of a communicative event as a text-in-context?

As everyone who uses a language intuitively knows, the normative, unproblematically acceptable message-form with unproblematic contextual "appropriateness" and denotational interpretability depends on – and thus has an indexical meaning pointing to – such ever-shifting contextual conditions; as well, message-form is, normatively, a token instantiation – and thus index – of the contextual factor immanent in all denotation, grammar. All of the study of contextual variability, no matter the particular disciplinary name by which known and through which pursued – sociolinguistics, interactional linguistics, discourse functionalism, "critical" discourse analysis, etc. – is thus concerned with the pragmatics, the indexical relations, of messages/texts in relation to the dimensions of their contexts; the special tripartite relationship of grammar–message–referent (denotatum) that is a kind of self-limiting, abstract, and idealized pragmatics of Enlightenment folk theory and its disciplinary unfoldings, determines a subsidiary study of grammatico-semantic regularity forever incomplete in such wider pragmatic terms that encompass what we may term the wider "sign's-eye view" of the context in which it occurs.

Yet we need to elaborate four further aspects of indexicality as the basis for such a more general and adequate pragmatics: concurrent autonomy of form and scope of indexicals; CO-TEXTUALITY and hence the existence of texts ("texture" of Halliday and Hasan [1976]) as an indexical property; "performativity" or INDEXICAL ENTAILMENT; and the laminations of contextual scale.

Form and Scope. One of the more important things to observe about the indexical pragmatics of the message/text is that various stretches and features of message, not necessarily coinciding one with another in denotationally parsed form, may simultaneously bear relatively autonomous indexical relations to particular aspects or configurations of context. This obtains, it should be noted, independent of any parsing of message into text-sentences under the grammatico-semantic hypothesis.

For example, among non-denotational indexical signals, choice of a denotational REGISTER (in a set of such alternative ways of "saying the same thing"; see Agha 2004; 2007: 79–144) that consistently and continuously occurs across the time-course of a whole discursive interaction may index a sender's demographic status as of such-and-such socioeconomic class or professional identity over every contribution made by that individual as speaker in a discursive interaction. (The interaction overall can, for example, turn out to be a reciprocating one of alternating role inhabitance for this individual as sender, then receiver, then sender again, ..., in an alternating-turn, bidirectional adjacency-pair textual structure [Schegloff 2007:13–14]. Thus any 'first person' and 'second person' participant-deictic denotational forms – participant A being "I/me/my" during his or her turn-at-talk, "you/your" during participant B's; and vice versa – would be constantly shifting as an indexical function of the state of allocation of the role dyad during any given turn-at-talk – in complete independence of the register-based indexicality, note.) Such register usage can, in turn, form the textual (as well as "textural") proscenium or backdrop for certain momentary highly salient departures in register usage, that themselves become interpretable in-and-at the moment they occur with respect to the continuously occurring register (for example an obscenity thrown in while otherwise communicating in a hypertechnical standard register).

Most deictic (indexical-denotational; "shifter" [Jakobson 1971(1957)]) categories – for example Tense, Mood, Evidentiality associated with predicating functions; Locus, Person, Coreference associated with referring ones – are signaled by slight, morpheme-sized chunks of message – affixes, clitics, etc. – or lexical simplexes that pass by quickly as a phase of the communicative event, but indexically anchor whole stretches of message of which they appear as constituent parts definable by the overall grammatico-semantic parsing (such as phrasal projections of nouns and even clauses or other typical projections of verbs) over the duration of which these context-specifying indexed dimensions remain constant and relevant to the meaning of the message-segment containing them. Grammarians frequently have spoken of such deictics as "having scope over" such a constituent of grammatico-semantically parsed message-form in which they occur or with which they are in construction, in the sense that insofar the larger constituent projects into a propositional sense, the effect of the deictic is to anchor that sense in a determinate way to a particular referent and/or state-of-affairs in relation to factors obtaining in the context of communication, to which are calibrated entities on the plane of denotata (lower right vertex of Figure 6.1).

Thus, Tense, minimally a two-way distinction of a 'past' and a 'non-past', indexically locates the predicated event or state-of-affairs projectable from a finite clause in which the Tense marker occurs: for 'past' in an interval that precedes the interval being experienced in-and-at the event of communicating that clausal stretch of message; for 'non-past', by contrast, vulgarly identified as 'present' Tense, any other kind of interval in relation to the communicative event, for example concurrent, concurrently expected, or recurrent and hence including the concurrent (thus: 'true present', 'future', and 'habitual'). Tense systems with three contrasting members grammatically distinguish both the vectorially 'prior-and-non-concurrent (past)' from 'subsequent-and-non-concurrent (future)' from the residual 'concurrent (present)'; more complicated systems are documented as well (see Bull 1960).

So-called "Demonstratives" denote a referent of the phrase in which it occurs (in some languages, possibly comprising a nominal phrase all by itself) within a radial topology centered on the socio-spatial location of the individual inhabiting the role of speaker: 'distal' Demonstratives locate the referent beyond a certain boundary (which can be made more precise by invoking a specifically denoted framework, and even numerical degree within such a framework); 'proximal' Demonstratives, by failing to invoke such a boundary, place the referent within a region close by. Note in this connection the "presentational" use of the English 'proximal' Demonstrative <u>this</u> – cf. the use of 'non-past' Tense for futurities in two-category systems – with hypo-stressed and pre-stressed-syllable low tone for introducing a topic-worthy denotatum for the first time in some vernacular ways of narrating ("So this gúy comes up to us on the street.").

So the point is that the various relevant dimensions of context are *independently indexed* by aspects of message-form that have *distinct conditions of manifestation* relative to – and frequently in addition and sometimes in contradistinction to – grammatico-semantic text-sentencehood as such; as well, there are a variety of effects of such indexicalities, both deictically effectuated ones and non-deictic, in defining and shaping whatever domain of context – whatever configuration of values of any of the co-occurring variable "components" of the communicative event – is made salient – is put "on the record," as it were – as a function of their occurrence. At first blush, then, it would appear to the naïve view that if we abandon the unifunctional grammatico-semantic parsing of message, indexicality is merely a welter of signals standing indeterminately for anything at all one might term "context." We will see why this is not so and why humans are, with a high degree of regularity, able to formulate and interpret messages as texts-in-context.

Co-textuality. A second characteristic of message/text is this. In addition to the way that the organization of a complex message is a function of how text-sentences instantiate and conform to the system-sentence grammar, there seems to be another whole realm of organization of the very same sign material, one involving a set of indexical relationships of segments of the message/text one with another. This non-grammatical but text-internal indexicality, which of course demarcates text as such as opposed to context, is a property of every message with more than trivial internal structure. It means that projected from the point of view of any segment or fraction of a more encompassing textual message, the co-occurring and thus indexed other segments or fractions constitute the CO-TEXTUAL surround or message-internal "context" of that segment. In this sense, *the "poetic"* (Jakobson 1960: 356–8) *structure of any complex message is a measure of its very autonomy as a text, as opposed to its being merely the instantiation of grammatically determinate form.* By virtue of stabilizing what semiotic material is "inside" the text and what, therefore, "outside," creating two realms of indexicality, co-textual poetics acts as a REFLEXIVELY CALIBRATED METAPRAGMATIC (see below) – the ultimate one – in facilitating language users' coming to intuitive agreement on what the message has cumulatively become at any given moment of discursive interaction, as opposed to what the forms in such a message have been indexically indicating in the way of dimensions of text-external context.

The most obvious expression of autonomous principles of co-textuality in contradistinction to a message-form's dependence on – and instantiation of – grammatico-semantic principle is, of course, the METRICALIZATION of text, its measurability in the linear chronotope of the unfolding of discourse in terms of recurring, equal-valued segments of whatever characterizable kind, whether phonological, morphological, lexical, or syntactic. Patterns of recurrence of same or similar forms, sometimes with variation in metrically determinate positions (a metricalization termed PARALLELISM [Jakobson 1966]); the concurrent operation of multiple principles of metricalization of segments of different scope, yielding the perceptual illusion of nested metricalizations defining tiered segmentations of text; the special salience in effect of forms that come to have direct indexical connections by virtue of such structures: all these phenomena are explicitly attended to by those concerned with the aesthetics of language, such as poets and narrative artists, to be sure. But all pragmatic evidence suggests that they are intuitively attended to by ordinary users of language in the very locally engaged formulation and interpretation of discourse, where people function as "co-textuality maximizers," as it were, to yield a determinate overall text relative to which non-co-textual contextualization can be construed. Such metrical anchoring of the constituent features of discourse one to another cumulating in entextualization is in effect an implicit "meta-"phenomenon in respect of indexicality more generally, thus serving a metapragmatic functionality that helps indirectly to regiment the various (text-external) contextualizing indexical meanings in the very discourse in which the metricalized entextualization unfolds over discourse time.

Textual and thus discursive genres can thus be defined on the basis of normativities of metricalization, as can guidelines implicit in discursive style. The alternating role-inhabitance of sender and receiver described above, for example, defines a metricalization of turns-at-talk into so-called ADJACENCY PAIRS, linked contributions of two interacting partners that, while sometimes occurring separated by intervening material, are specifically and saliently related one to another in the way that people conceptualize them (Levinson 1983: 332–7); adjacency pairs are metrical genres of a lexically explicit folk metapragmatics, such as "invitation" followed by "acceptance/decline." (Of course, the critical question is what actualizable forms of text-segments come to 'count-as' the performance of either, a matter to which we return below.) So much so, that when the first of an adjacency pair is contributed to the flow of discourse, there is a compelling, metrically derived sense that the second one ought and should follow, the INTERACTIONAL TEXTUAL STRUCTURE of interaction remaining metrically fragmentary or deficient to the extent it does not.

Again, some of the most striking segments of interactionally consequential discourse are organized around parallelistic repetition of syntactically similar text segments with variation of lexical forms or grammatical categories. This textual style generates rhetorical figures that bring into confrontation the denotational values of such sense-bearing units in ways that vary from the conventional – as in Mayan-language lexical couplets used in parallelism (Bricker 1974; Haviland 1996) – to the refreshingly unique (at least until copied in a subsequent interdiscursively linked re-use). So many of the irreversible binomials (Malkiel 1959) of English – <u>bread and butter</u>, <u>milk and honey</u>, <u>peaches and cream</u>, etc. – have this quality of being now conventional – frequently interdiscursive – metrical ready-mades that have entered denotational use as "idioms," the denotational meanings of which are not simple additive concatenations of the constituents.

In speaking of metricalization as the fundamental and irreducible metapragmatic metric of stabilizing the entextual/contextual indexical divide, and in discussing such examples as adjacency pairs, we come to a third important property of indexicality, yet one relatively under-stressed by as profound a thinker as Peirce, on whose work notwithstanding the whole enterprise rests.

Indexical Entailment. The third property is this. Every message, in-and-by occurring as the mediation between sender and receiver, INDEXICALLY ENTAILS some reaffirmation or some transformation of the context. This reaffirming effect can be the minimal one of "making salient," i.e., putting "on the record" some state-of-affairs in the communicative situation that at that point, by virtue of being indexed, requires attending to, while a maximal, transformational one would be the entailment of a rather profound reordering of the statuses and thus the role relationships (other than the communication-event roles) of those present and/or referred-to. Insofar such indexical entailment is normatively or conventionally expected, in-and-by the occurrence of some particular message form – an instantiation of a formulaic aspect of message, then – there is a strongly felt expectation of certain consequences, ones that compellingly constrain, if not determine, what is likely to happen next in the time-course of discursive interaction.

Within the modern analytic philosophical tradition, it was J. L. Austin (1962), as noted, who identified the general property of indexical entailment under the banner of "performativity," but by not dissociating this indexical mode of semiosis from the received grammar-school tradition of system- and text-sentence grammatico-semantic unitization, Austin confounded the problem with the problem of the necessary metasemiotic – in this case, metapragmatic – regimentation of indexicality. That is, Austin and his followers err by starting from the "explicit primary performative" formula, in the general form of a fully syntactically conforming text-sentence with 'first person' Agentive grammatical subject, 'second person' Recipient grammatical (indirect) object, and a *verbum dicendi vel sentiendi* (a hyponym of <u>say-</u> [to] or <u>think-</u>/<u>feel-</u> [that]) with such minimal (unmarked) obligatory inflection as to render it grammatical as a highest clause. In this approach, the specific conventionally – normatively expected – entailing indexical "force" of using a token of such a formula – its so-called "illocutionary force" – is identified with the meaning of the verb, which, insofar as it is a semantically understood lexeme, does in fact denote the type of event that the use would instantiate, if a token in the proper formula were performed by the proper sender directed at a proper receiver – were it successful in its indexical entailment in the asymptotic situation of no contextual complications beyond sender and receiver having knowledge of the grammatico-semantic code.

Thus, say, absent all consideration of pre-existing contextual conditions, in the event of A's uttering to B "I$_A$ promise you$_B$ that [...]," A has, it is thought, performed an (intentional, volitional, agentive) act of 'promising' because that is the type of act that, semantically speaking, the verb lexeme promise- denotes under the doctrine of literal denotation. As one can see, the denotational meaning of the verb, as a hyponym of say- (to), is a metapragmatic descriptor of a type of event, the offer of a 'promise' to B by A, in which, however, A is not performing an act of description – Austin terms this a "constative" use, one that in English would actually require a 'present progressive' Tense and Aspectual construction (am promising) – so much as an act of committing the self to bring about a certain state-of-affairs (the one described in a complement clause or equivalent) by appropriate means.

And what of indexical entailments when the so-called performative formula is neither "explicit" – containing a minimally inflected highest-clause verb that denotes the type of act at issue during the course of this communicative segment – nor "primary" – as for example when the performance of a formula counts as an act nowhere denoted by its "literal" grammatico-semantic form? And how to recognize non-explicit, non-primary – or even non-explicit, primary, for that matter! – illocutionary forces associated with text-sentence forms of another language and culture than one's own? None of this is easily, nor even satisfactorily addressed in the "pragmatics" literature, alas, mired in post-Enlightenment folk theories of (literal) denotation and sentence-grammar.

While it is not possible to elaborate all the numerous insufficiencies of this – as it were – promising lead into the realm of indexical entailment (for a start, see Rosaldo 1982; Levinson 1983: 226–83; Silverstein 1987, 2010; 2012), we should just point out that so-called "performativity" – social consequentiality, i.e., indexical entailment in the contextual use of language – emerges as a surprising phenomenon only from the point of view of narrow denotationalist doctrines of language. As a consequence, the theoretical developments consequent upon recognizing the phenomenon only tangentially get to the central issues about indexical entailment. All messages, i.e., emergent segments of texts-in-context, are consequential, that is, have indexical entailments as a function of their occurrence; the question is the degree to which in-and-at its moment of occurrence a message determines, or at least constrains under a principle of normativity, what is consequent upon its having occurred. From the denotationalist (and individual-centered) perspective, reflexively to name the act an agent wants to perform in-and-by communicating a token of a certain grammatico-semantically conforming formula (resembling a text-sentence) would seem to be the best way to determine or constrain the formula's contextual consequentiality; this is about the best this folk-theoretic perspective can do. So long as the participants in a communicative event know the denotational sense of the verbal "name," then, they have at least an intuition of what normatively is entailed by the use of a token in the proper formula: normative 'illocution' is, as Sadock (1974: 153) notes, the asymptotic state of "sense perlocution," that is, what would now be the state of the context just by knowing the denotational semantics of the highest-clause verb reflexively applied in-and-at the instant of its occurrence to denote a social act.

So here is the larger point. All indexical entailment must be constrained or 'regimented' by some meta-indexical – we say 'metapragmatic' – functionality, to be sure: an index must "point" to something interpretable within a definable framework. Most of that metapragmatic functionality involves features of the message as such, for example the poetics of co-textuality, deixis (indexical denotation), phenomena of enregisterment of (non-deictic) indexicals (on which see below), etc. By contrast, verbal labels for event-types belong to a much more restricted, and socio-historically very local, lexical machinery for engaging in EXPLICIT METAPRAGMATIC DISCOURSE, that is, denotational use of language to talk about language-in-use. In so-called performative use, anchored by the first- and second-person deictics, a kind of ritual invocation of an event-type-name suggests that the particular moment is an actualization of whatever the name suggests in the way of entailments. But the idea that one can reflexively name the event happening in-and-at its phase of actualization is only asymptotically realizable, paradoxically enough, only *absent context*, i.e., if every message-segment were to be parsed as a disconnected and autonomous "explicit primary performative" text-sentence conforming to the formula (or its whole family of equivalent non-explicit and/or non-primary versions, if such could be rigorously identified and discretely categorized).

Rather than an idealization of how indexical entailment works in general, then, performative or illocutionary theory as such promises no empirical or operational approach to the inherently duplex or Janus-faced character of indexicality. For what permits discursive interaction to happen by-degrees smoothly is on the one hand the way that an intuitive metapragmatic sense of "appropriateness to (pre-existing/-cognizable) context" informs the predictability of what message forms ought to or are licensed to occur in the flow of discursive interaction, and on the other hand people's ability to bring a normative metapragmatic intuition to bear on interpreting the way messages-as-indexical are determinately "effective in" contexts that are, to various degrees of specificity, defined by those very message forms. The conventional or socioculturally specific Legisign indexical relationships between aspects of message form and their co(n)texts, as experienced and experienceable, require, as Peirce adumbrated, a regimenting METAPRAGMATIC INTERPRETANT; but explicit primary performative constructions, incorporating bits of metapragmatic denotational lexical form but not counting as predications of anything, are not obviously or necessarily those interpretants.

Co(n)textual Scale. The fourth characteristic of pragmatics in "message's-eye" perspective that needs elaboration involves the scale and scope of factors that are to be considered in what we term the 'co(n)text' of a message. To be sure, Fig. 6.2 very much suggests that context is an immediate surround of a physically occurring signal form in a face-to-face interaction – or at least a prototypical image of such proximity of components is vivid to our phenomenal memory of everyday discursive interaction. Face-to-face interaction – and even just the communicative behavior of a sender of messages – provides a kind of default model, then, for much work on indexical phenomena. There is, indeed, a "metaphysics of presence" involved in such presumptions. Yet, as more careful and sociologically acute study of indexicality reveals, co(n)text is an indeterminately capacious frame relative to which the indexical aspects of message must of necessity be studied, an affordance within what we should term the 'socio-space-time' of a social formation.

For example, consider the inhabitable roles of sender and receiver of a message. While in the strictly denotationalist view, anyone in a language community freely inhabits either of these roles, it is in fact the case that there are systematic distinctions as to who is recruitable to such roles in the production of "appropriate" and "effective" messages of various sorts. That is, from the "message's-eye" perspective, the occurrence of such a message indexes the existence of frameworks of social identities from which individuals are differentially recruited to serve in such roles in a particular communicative event. While the norms can be observed in the unproblematic occurrence of certain message forms under particular conditions of recruitment, norm-violating occurrence generally leads to conversational "repair" (Levinson 1983: 339–45; Schegloff 2007: 100–106) or other metapragmatic interactional work. Contemporary Western language communities have so-called "curse words" and "dirty words," for example, highly salient lexical shibboleths of register, and even in the much-decried "socially permissive" era, there are metapragmatic norms of who is licensed to serve as sender and receiver of such and under what further conditions of institutional site and mode of transmission. (In the United States, the Federal Communications Commission temporally restricts their occurrence in broadcast media, for example, literally – and negatively – "licensing" the possibilities for senders and receivers according to broadcast market and time of day!) Names and titles of beings, especially humans, both in direct address of a referent and otherwise, reveal elaborate conditions of use defined by who is communicating to whom about whom before whom (Brown and Ford 1961; Murphy 1988).

Indeed, the lexicons of all languages are shot through with paradigms of normatively differentiated, indexically distinguished lexical forms taken to be denotationally equivalent but contextually contrastive, such as distinctions of so-called "speech levels" in systems of honorification (Errington 1988; Agha 2007: 301–39). More generally, to the degree to which we can define co-textual compatibilities and/or non-compatibilities of members of such pragmatic paradigms within or across planes of linguistic form, we can characterize the structure of grammatico-semantic registers, context-specific ways of otherwise "communicating the same thing," that loom large in folk intuition and consciousness of contextual appropriateness. (More on this below.)

Again, variationist sociolinguistics has long studied social, as opposed to geographical, indexicality (see now Eckert 2012). Frequencies of occurrence of a range of closely related forms (generally tokens of phonetic realization of phonologically and lexically recurrent Legisigns in a sample of speech) are measured with a view to correlating distinct frequency ranges, means and variance, etc. with various demographic characteristics of speakers/senders, and sometimes as well those of addressees/receivers (so-called "audience design" [Bell 1984; Meyerhoff 2006: 42–51]; cf. all work on forms of [vocative] address). Where there exists a 'standard' or equivalent target register that informs the norm of the (literacy-oriented) language community, such frequencies correlate as well with the register demands of the conditions of language use (Labov's [1972: 70–109] "stylistic variation"), for example unscripted in-group oral-aural communication vs. explicitly observed graphic-to-phonic transduction, a.k.a. "reading aloud." Such demographic characterizations – age (chronological cohort, generation, etc.); sex or sometimes gender; socioeconomic or consumption-class category; transactional network position; etc. – are, of course, in no sense definable with respect to the face-to-face contexts of chatting or of an interview in which, say, verbalized utterance occurs. These are MACRO-SOCIOLOGICAL POSITIONS within perduring social-organizational and social-structural forms, statuses, then, in such collective formations in the complex intersections of which individuals can be at least analytically located. (We eschew discussing the degree to which they are in any sense "objective" characteristics.) Such characteristics of senders, receivers, etc., such large-scale institutional forms of performance recognized in a community, such as "reading aloud," are all *rendered indexically pregnant* in-and-at the moment of production in the modeling of the variationist approach, in essence a theory of an implicit metapragmatic regimentation of the indexical value of phonetic and other linguistic variance that only sometimes surfaces to explicit conscious awareness about one's own and about others' language use. The idea is that such indexicality of variance both (a) allows us to "place" ourselves – mostly unknowingly, as it turns out – as having been recruited from such-and-such demographic under such-and-so conditions of production, and (b) allows others as addressees or audiences intuitively to "place" us as well. (Things do, of course, become exceedingly complex when explicit metapragmatic consciousness of such matters is taken into account, a point to which we return below.)

Finally, as emphasized by Mikhail Bakhtin, no face-to-face micro-context of discursive interaction is an island. One of the central components of indexicality in any particular context is defined by strands of 'interdiscursivity' (see Agha and Wortham 2005) that link a current message segment-in-co(n)text to other occasions of use – to emphasize: linked not just by the existence of an underlying grammatico-semantic type – through which identities of role incumbents emerge in degrees and kinds of congruent alignment across occasions, and as well as do the generic (< genre) characteristics of the current communication. Like Benveniste's (1966: 277–85) 'delocutionary' predicates, metapragmatic descriptors that reproduce indexically pregnant forms so as to denote the social act of using them, textual ready-mades iconically reproduce or "cite" and thereby remotely index (in a "renvoi") the contextual conditions under which they have earlier occurred, or those under which they ought later to occur, placing a current communicative situation in a kind of chain of interdiscursivity as such cited (or to-be-cited) material comes to structure the co-textuality of form. Indeed, such chained interdiscursivity with recognizably genred text interacts with the deictics of evidentiality in the plane of denotation already described; here, too, one is making indexical claims about how the personnel of a current communicative event participate in and align with/against various institutional networks of communication and the values maintained in-and-through them.

Autonomy of form and scope of indexicals; co-textuality as indexically emergent; "performativity" or indexical entailment; and the socio-spatio-temporal laminations of contextualizing scale: All of these kinds of contextuality and co-textuality are always involved in using language in events of discursive interaction. In the face of this, that the Enlightenment view recognizes units of system-sentencehood and functions based only on grammar in the semantico-denotational mode reveals one particularly egregious limitation of this folk ideology. However, to the extent that this is the folk ideology by which users adapt to their languages (and to some extent vice-versa), we must elaborate the role of such necessary but not sufficient "misrecognition" of semiosis in the actual pragmatics of use.

6.3 Indexical dialectics: intersections of denotation and pragmatic functionality

Certainly within the Enlightenment episteme, and even more broadly, there is a strong intuition that "what we say" comes to count, in the instance of discursive interaction, as "what we do," i.e., what we effectuate, in the way of social action. Stripped of its fiercest individualist, agentive, volitional misrecognition, as in Western philosophy, of intentional action centered on the text-sentence identified with the turn-at-talk, we may more appropriately say that the "performativity" of usage amounts to this: the speaking agent's reflexive sense that, licensed by social convention, he or she can attempt by degrees to constrain or to limit what is entailed by a contribution to discursive interaction, the effect verifiable by noting what, if anything, follows as its sequelae. That is, from an analytic point of view, "what we say," i.e., a model of denotational entextualization in socio-space-time, comes to count as "what we do" with language insofar as the message precipitated in-and-by denotational communication seems to occur with consequentiality for various kinds of social coordination of persons concerned. That is, the denotational entextualization serves as the instrumentality of a dynamic social cause-and-effect.

"What we say" is, of course, a model of denotational text-in-context, "what we do" a model of interactional text discerned of the social context of the denotationally conceived message. So while, in the Enlightenment episteme, there is a massive ideological formation that informs language users' intuitions to the effect that they are the unmediated conceptualizers, planners, executors, and thus volitional agents of what they say/do, the situation in pragmatic perspective is much more indirect, as should be clear from the preceding. We may, for example, have a conscious metapragmatic model of something like Austinian "speech acts" elaborated on the basis of the happenstance, but salient, socio-historically specific set of metapragmatic verbs like promise-, but this is nothing more than one factor in an actually dialectical process of how, in-and-by behaviorally precipitating an occurrent message(-fraction), its indexical presuppositions are transduced into indexical entailment, both in the token instance of some particular historical communicative event and in the type normativities in terms of which expectant imaginaries shape potential performability and interpretability. So long as all of the other pragmatic factors remain occluded to folk-theoretical discourse, the latter is an insufficient model for how discursive interaction works, when it does. Yet folk intuition in the form of a Peircean metapragmatic interpretant is always immanent in the indexical functioning of language and other cultural semiotics; sometimes it is partially revealed in an explicit metapragmatic consciousness of indexical forms and functional significance, and sometimes even in metapragmatic discourse, denotational language used to refer to and predicate states-of-affairs about pragmatic phenomena (see Lucy 1993).

Indeed, if we consider the structural analysis of language suggested by the commitment to a denotational functionality, and the pragmatic dynamics of the multiple planes of indexicality within interactional text, there are numerous ways that a semiotic dialectic – a mutual, reciprocal influencing – obtains between the two semiotic partials, mediated by

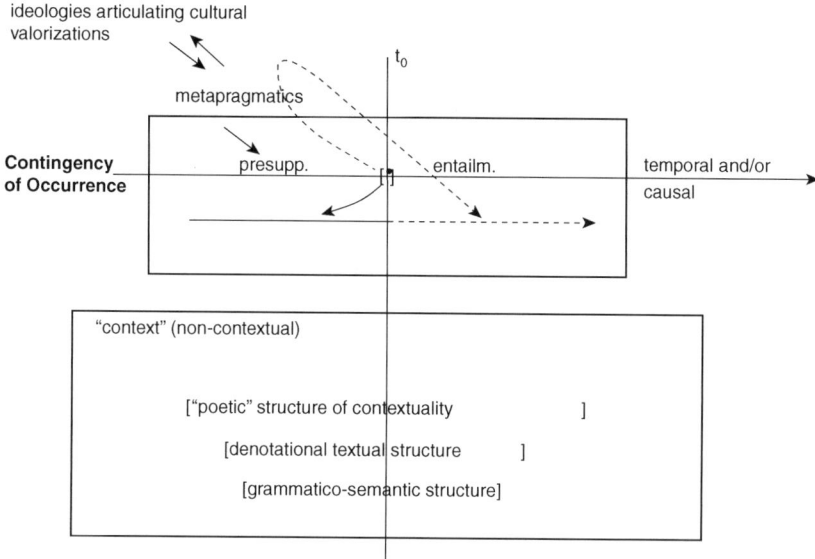

Figure 6.3 Micro-contextual semiotic of indexicality

a metapragmatic functionality at least partly constituted by an explicit metapragmatic discourse. This can best be conceptualized by explicating Figure 6.3 (reproduced from Silverstein 2003: 195), intended as a momentary snapshot diagram from "the sign's eye point of view" of indexical presupposition mapped into indexical entailment in-and-by the occurrence of some message-fraction.

In Figure 6.3, the lower block notes that a cumulatively non-incoherent denotational text emerges in its context as a function, minimally, of (a) grammatico-semantic structural principles by which any text-sentence can be parsed according to a system of grammar, (b) the operational scope and projectability of deictics, (c) the components of denotational meaning of words and expressions beyond the grammatico-semantic (see below), that contribute to the referring and modally predicating character of denotational text, and (d) the metricalized structuredness of the emergent signal (including its text-sentence parsing). All of these factors organize the denotational material beyond the grammatico-semantic "literal" into denotational figurations or tropes. A vertical axis projects upward in the diagram to highlight our focus on a particular local interval of discursive-interactional real time in the emergence of such a denotational text-in-context, the "moment"-interval over which an isolable indexical sign-vehicle is being produced, here labeled as t_0. The upper portion of the figure diagrams the semiotic processes by which in-and-at the moment of emergence of such an indexical, it presumes upon – indexically presupposes – such textuality and contextuality as have been established up to the moment, as indicated by a solid arrow pointing to the text unfolded up to that moment.

Now we noted above the necessity for some meta-indexical interpretant to regiment the entailments of indexical signs for their contexts: in the figure the broken arrow pointing to the entailed context is therefore not straightforward; such entailment depends on – hence, in the figure, loops back to – that necessary metapragmatic component of indexical function. The diagram illustrates, moreover, that the intuitive metapragmatic understanding of the language-user is in turn shaped by explicit ascriptions of cause-and-effect relations of linguistic signs, such ascription being in essence IDEOLOGICAL, that is, non-randomly distributed over the population of language users in potentially non-disinterested ways and to the ends of particular social projects identifiable with social groups and interests. (See Schieffelin *et al.* 1998; Kroskrity 2000.) Both the metapragmatic "unconscious" and the discourse of metapragmatic consciousness are ideologically informed in this sense, in large measure a function of an individual's biography in society, centrally his or her membership in and alignment with certain categories differentiated in social process and with various primary, ..., and *n*-ary reference groups.

The asymmetry of indexical presupposition and indexical entailment thus rests on the asymmetric bi-directionality of the indexical ("pragmatic")–meta-indexical ("meta-pragmatic") relationship, in which denotational textuality and its particular formally segmentable units lurk. For example, as has now long been a heuristically reliable guide, metapragmatic consciousness and hence LINGUISTIC IDEOLOGY, as we can term language-focused ideologies of indexicality, tends ascriptively and interpretatively to focus on segments that emerge to denotational and even grammatico-semantic parsing (Silverstein 1981; Gal and Irvine 1995). This seems to be the case even where the functionality ascribed to such indexicals is not denotational as such. The very units of denotational textual form seem to be the anchors of consciousness of contextual – that is, indexical – variation in language, especially lexical units, words and expressions, that constitute the identifiable linear flow of discourse rendered into textual structure.

This is particularly true as language users conceptualize contextual variability as "different [context-indexing] ways of [denotationally] saying 'the same' thing," at whatever plane and level of analysis, the isolable formal differences constituting, as was noted above, a (sometimes gradient) paradigm of indexical signs appropriate to distinct contextual conditions, in short a PRAGMATIC PARADIGM. Speakers have intuitions – sometimes even explicit normative stipulations – of how one or more elements of such paradigmatically differentiated indexes can appropriately – congruently – co-occur across textual stretches. Such principles define a DENOTATIONAL-TEXTUAL REGISTER for the users of language, an intuition (or stipulation) of which textual elements go together with which others, and which ought to be excluded from textual co-occurrence – save for producing (entailing) special effects by violation.

Registers are always projected from REGISTER SHIBBOLETHS, which serve as salient anchors or pillars of co-occurrence for other, less salient areas of denotational textual form to which users pay less attention. Registers of 'honorification', for example, ways of communicating so as to perform an act of deference to the receiver, audience, and/or referent – all these kinds of systems and their overlaps are attested – tend to focus ideological attention on deictics of ("second" or "third") person, personal proper names, and other address terms derived from status nominals, and verbs predicating 'transfers' of things, including messages (hence, metapragmatic verbs as well as "donatory" [Martin 1964: 408] ones), though much more is involved in using what people evaluate as well-formed honorific discourse.

Among such modes of ideological ENREGISTERMENT of indexical variability, common has been the appearance of STANDARD REGISTER as the very definiens of people's sense of their having a "language" (as opposed to their using mere "dialect"). Standardization, the achievement of a pervasive and ubiquitous orientation of language users to the correctness of standard register and the gradient incorrectness of any linguistic production that falls short, has been a major project of the modernist nation-state insofar projecting a language community into a polity in the Enlightenment order of things. (See Bloomfield 1970[1927]; Garvin 1964 [1959]; Ray 1968[1962]; Shaklee 1980; Silverstein 1996[1987]; Inoue 2006.) Though standard registers are composed of ever-changing and sociohistorically specific prescriptions for and proscriptions of certain denotational variance within pragmatic paradigms of such, the standard forms have ever been ideologically justified in terms of myriad ascribed virtues, intensional properties, that come to be identified with the very indexical forms themselves as well, in a certain logic of iconic consubstantiality (Gal and Irvine 1995), with those who use them properly; the opposite vices, needless to say, come to be identified with non-standard forms and their users.

Enregistered forms, especially certain register shibboleths, such as those of standard registers and their negations, become EMBLEMS OF IDENTITY (that is, within the conventions of a language community, naturalized iconic indexicals of stereotypical categories of persons; see Agha 2007: 190–232) within differentiated social orders. Deployable as such, emblems, endowed with all this naturalizing ideological infusion, are the indexical foci of now intentionally performable identities, that is, identities *indexically entailed* in-and-by the use of certain language forms. This is the paragon of performativity (metapragmatically stipulative indexical entailment) in Figure 6.3, in which the complex, inner function of ideologically infused metapragmatic consciousness, itself already biased by the salience to it of denotational form, is revealed in its dialectical counter-direction as the ever creative socio-semiotic force behind such emblematicity.

References

Aarsleff, Hans. 1982. *From Locke to Saussure: Essays on the Study of Language and Intellectual History*. Minneapolis: University of Minnesota Press.

Agha, Asif. 2004. Registers of Language. In *The Blackwell Companion to Linguistic Anthropology*, ed. Alessandro Duranti, 23-45. Malden, MA: Blackwell.

——— 2007. *Language and Social Relations*. New York: Cambridge University Press.

Agha, Asif, and Stanton Wortham, eds. 2005. Special Issue: Discourse across Speech Events: Intertextuality and Interdiscursivity in Social Life. *Journal of Linguistic Anthropology* 15(1).

Austin, John L. 1962. *How To Do Things With Words*, ed. J. O. Urmson and Marina Sbisà. Cambridge, MA: Harvard University Press. [2nd ed., 1975.]

Bauman, Richard, and Charles L. Briggs. 2003. *Voices of Modernity: Language Ideologies and the Politics of Inequality*. Cambridge: Cambridge University Press.

Bell, Allan. 1984. Language Style as Audience Design. *Language in Society* 13(2): 145-204.

Benveniste, Emile. 1966. *Problèmes de linguistique générale*. Paris: Editions Gallimard.

Bloomfield, Leonard. 1970 [1926]. A Set of Postulates for the Science of Language. In *A Leonard Bloomfield Anthology*, ed. Charles F. Hockett, 128-38. Bloomington: Indiana University Press.

——— 1970 [1927]. Literate and Illiterate Speech. In *A Leonard Bloomfield Anthology*, ed. Charles F. Hockett, 147-56. Bloomington: Indiana University Press.

Bricker, Victoria R. 1974. The Ethnographic Context of Some Traditional Mayan Speech Genres. In *Explorations in the Ethnography of Speaking*, ed. Richard Bauman and Joel Sherzer, 368-88, 470-71, 492-3. New York: Cambridge University Press.

Brown, Roger, and Marguerite Ford. 1961. Address in American English. *Journal of Abnormal and Social Psychology* 62(2): 375-85.

Bull, William E. 1960. *Time, Tense, and the Verb: A Study in Theoretical and Applied Linguistics, with Particular Attention to Spanish*. University of California Publications in Linguistics, 19. Berkeley: University of California Press.

Carnap, Rudolph. 1937. *The Logical Syntax of Language*. London: Routledge and Kegan Paul; New York: Harcourt, Brace.

Eckert, Penelope. 2012. Three Waves of Variation Study: The emergence of meaning in the study of sociolinguistic variation. *Annual Review of Anthropology* 41: 87-100.

Eco, Umberto. 1994. *The Search for the Perfect Language*. Oxford and Cambridge, MA: Blackwell.

Errington, J. Joseph. 1988. *Structure and Style in Javanese: A Semiotic View of Linguistic Etiquette*. Philadelphia: University of Pennsylvania Press.

Gal, Susan, and Judith T. Irvine. 1995. The Boundaries of Languages and Disciplines: How ideologies construct difference. *Social Research* 62(4): 967–1001.

Garvin, Paul. 1964 [1959]. The Standard Language Problem – Concepts and Methods. In *Language in Culture and Society: A Reader in Linguistics and Anthropology*, ed. Dell Hymes, 521–4. New York and Evanston, IL: Harper and Row.

Grice, [H.] Paul. 1989. *Studies in the Way of Words*. Cambridge, MA and London: Harvard University Press.

Halliday, M. A. K. and Ruqaiya Hasan. 1976. *Cohesion in English*. London: Longman.

Haviland, John B. 1996. "We Want to Borrow Your Mouth": Tzotzil marital squabbles. In *Disorderly Discourse: Narrative, Conflict, and Inequality*, ed. Charles L. Briggs, 158–203. New York: Oxford University Press.

Horn, Laurence R., and Gregory Ward, eds. 2004. *The Handbook of Pragmatics*. Malden, MA: Blackwell.

Inoue, Miyako. 2006. Standardization. In *Encyclopedia of Language and Linguistics*, 2nd ed., ed. Keith Brown, 12.121–7. Oxford: Elsevier.

Jackendoff, Ray. 1990. *Semantic Structures*. Current Studies in Linguistics, 18. Cambridge, MA and London: MIT Press.

Jakobson, Roman. 1960. Closing Statement: Linguistics and poetics. In *Style in Language*, ed. Thomas A. Sebeok, 350–77. Cambridge, MA: MIT Press.

  1966. Grammatical Parallelism and its Russian Facet. *Language* 42(2): 399–429.

  1971 [1957]. Shifters, Verbal Categories, and the Russian Verb. In *Selected Writings of Roman Jakobson*, 2.130–47. The Hague and Paris: Mouton.

Kay, Paul, and Chad K. McDaniel. 1978. The Linguistic Significance of the Meanings of Basic Color Terms. *Language* 54(3): 610–46.

Kripke, Saul A. 1972. Naming and Necessity. In *Semantics of Natural Language*, 2nd ed., ed. Donald Davidson and Gilbert Harman, 253–355. Dordrecht and Boston: D. Reidel.

Kroskrity, Paul V., ed. 2000. *Regimes of Language: Ideologies, Polities, and Identities*. Santa Fe, NM: School of American Research Press and Oxford: James Currey.

Labov, William. 1972. *Sociolinguistic Patterns*. Conduct and Communication, 4. Philadelphia: University of Pennsylvania Press.

  2004 [1973]. The Boundaries of Words and their Meanings. In *Fuzzy Grammar: A Reader*, ed. Bas Aarts, David Denison, Evelien Keizer, and Gergana Popova, 67–89. Oxford: Oxford University Press.

Levinson, Stephen C. 1983. *Pragmatics*. Cambridge: Cambridge University Press.

Linsky, Leonard. 1971 [1967]. Reference and Referents. In *Semantics: An Interdisciplinary Reader in Philosophy, Linguistics, and Psychology*, ed. Danny D. Steinberg and Leon A. Jakobovits, 76–85. Cambridge: Cambridge University Press. (Excerpted from Leonard Linsky, *Referring*, 116–31. London: Routledge and Kegan Paul [1967].)

Losonsky, Michael. 2006. *Linguistic Turns in Modern Philosophy*. New York: Cambridge University Press.

Lucy, John A., ed. 1993. *Reflexive Language: Reported Speech and Metapragmatics*. Cambridge: Cambridge University Press.

⸺ 1997. The Linguistics of 'Color'. In *Color Categories in Thought and Language*, ed. C. L. Hardin and Luisa Maffi, 320–46. Cambridge: Cambridge University Press.

Lyons, John. 1977. *Semantics*. 2 vols. Cambridge: Cambridge University Press.

⸺ 1995. *Linguistic Semantics: An Introduction*. Cambridge: Cambridge University Press.

Malkiel, Yakov. 1959. Studies in Irreversible Binomials. *Lingua* 8(2): 113–60.

Martin, Samuel E. 1964. Speech Levels in Japan and Korea. In *Language in Culture and Society: A Reader in Linguistics and Anthropology*, ed. Dell Hymes, 407–15. New York and Evanston, IL: Harper and Row.

Meyerhoff, Miriam. 2006. *Introducing Sociolinguistics*. London and New York: Routledge.

Morris, Charles. 1938. *Foundations of the Theory of Signs*. International Encyclopedia of Unified Science, 1(2). Chicago: University of Chicago Press.

⸺ 1946. *Signs, Language, and Behavior*. Englewood Cliffs, NJ: Prentice-Hall.

Murphy, Gregory L. 1988. Personal Reference in English. *Language in Society* 17(3): 317–49.

Peirce, Charles S. 1931–58. *Collected Papers*, ed. Charles Hartshorne and Paul Weiss. Cambridge, MA: Harvard University Press.

Putnam, Hilary. 1975. The Meaning of 'Meaning'. In *Philosophical Papers*, Vol. 2: *Mind, Language, and Reality*, 215–71. Cambridge: Cambridge University Press.

Quine, Willard Van Orman. 1960. *Word and Object*. Cambridge, MA: MIT Press.

Ray, Punya Sloka. 1968 [1962]. Language Standardization. In *Readings in the Sociology of Language*, ed. Joshua A. Fishman, 754–65. The Hague and Paris: Mouton.

Rosaldo, Michelle Z. 1982. The Things We Do With Words: Ilongot speech acts and speech act theory in philosophy. *Language in Society* 11(2): 203–37.

Rosch, Eleanor. 1978. Principles of Categorization. In *Cognition and Categorization*, ed. Eleanor Rosch and Barbara B. Lloyd, 27–48. Hillsdale, NJ: Lawrence Erlbaum Associates.

Rosenberg, Jay F. and Charles Travis. eds. 1971. *Readings in the Philosophy of Language*. Englewood Cliffs, NJ: Prentice-Hall.

Sadock, Jerrold M. 1974. *Toward a Linguistic Theory of Speech Acts.* New York and London: Academic Press.

Schegloff, Emanuel A. 2007. *Sequence Organization in Interaction.* Vol. 1 of *A Primer in Conversation Analysis.* Cambridge: Cambridge University Press.

Schieffelin, Bambi B., Kathryn A. Woolard, and Paul V. Kroskrity, eds. 1998. *Language Ideologies: Practice and Theory.* New York and Oxford: Oxford University Press.

Searle, John R. 1969. *Speech Acts: An Essay in the Philosophy of Language.* Cambridge: Cambridge University Press.

Shaklee, Margaret. 1980. The Rise of Standard English. In *Standards and Dialects in English*, ed. Timothy Shopen and Joseph M. Williams, 33-62. Cambridge, MA: Winthrop.

Silverstein, Michael. 1981. *The Limits of Awareness.* Sociolinguistic Working Paper no. 84. Austin, TX: Southwest Educational Research Laboratory.

1987. The Three Faces of 'Function': Preliminaries to a psychology of language. In *Social and Functional Approaches to Language and Thought*, ed. Maya Hickmann, 17-38. Orlando, FL: Academic Press.

1996 [1987]. Monoglot 'Standard' in America: Standardization and metaphors of linguistic hegemony. In *The Matrix of Language: Contemporary Linguistic Anthropology*, ed. Donald Brenneis and Ronald H. S. Macaulay, 284-306. Boulder, CO: Westview Press.

2003. Indexical Order and the Dialectics of Sociolinguistic Life. *Language and Communication* 23(3-4): 193-229.

2010. 'Direct' and 'Indirect' Communicative Acts in Semiotic Perspective. *Journal of Pragmatics* 42(2): 337-53

2012. Does the Autonomy of Linguistics Rest on the Autonomy of Syntax? An alternative framing of our object of study. In *Pragmaticizing Understanding: Festschrift for Jef Verschueren*, ed. Michael Meeuwis and Jan-Ola Östman, 15-38. Amsterdam and Philadelphia: John Benjamins.

Silverstein, Michael, and Greg Urban. 1996. The Natural History of Discourse. In *Natural Histories of Discourse*, ed. Michael Silverstein and Greg Urban, 1-17. Chicago: University of Chicago Press.

Stillman, Robert E. 1995. *The New Philosophy and Universal Languages in Seventeenth-Century England: Bacon, Hobbes, and Wilkins.* Lewisburg, PA: Bucknell University Press.

Strawson, Peter F. 1971. *Logico-Linguistic Papers.* London: Methuen.

7

Language function

Sandra A. Thompson and Elizabeth Couper-Kuhlen

> It is characteristic of our language that the foundation on which it grows consists in steady ways of living, regular ways of acting. Its function is determined above all by action, which it accompanies.
>
> (Ludwig Wittgenstein 1976: 420)

7.1 A brief history of functionalism in linguistics

"Functionalism" in linguistics can be said to have arisen in the late 1960s, though its roots can readily be found much earlier. The primary assumption shared by functional linguists has consistently been that the forms and structures of language are adapted to, and shaped by, grammar-external principles, namely their communicative functions. That is, since language is fundamentally an instrumental tool, it is reasonable to assume that its structures are informed by the structure of our experience and our cultural models of experience. Functionalists take the internal organization of language to be a complex adaptive response to the ecological settings in which language is found, the interactional functions which it serves, and the full cognitive, social, and physiological properties of the human user. Functional linguistic research is aimed at clarifying the relationship between linguistic form and function, and at determining the nature of the functions which appear to shape linguistic structure, foremost among which are facilitating effective communication and assisting cognition. Functional linguistics has always included both scholars who are working on description (what languages are like) and those working on explanation (why languages are the way they are).

In this chapter, we will offer a brief overview of scholarship in functional linguistics, and then focus on constituency, a specific problem which has attracted significant attention from functionalists. In the second part of the chapter, we will examine constituency from the perspective of a natural outgrowth of functionalism in linguistics, namely a concern with the function of grammar in its ecological habitat, conversational interaction.

Prominent early proponents of a functionalist perspective include Bolinger (e.g., 1952, 1965), Firbas (e.g., 1964, 1992), Halliday (e.g., 1967–68), and Sapir (e.g., 1921, 1949), inter alia. A community of functionalist linguists, however, didn't begin to form until the 1970s, focused around the work of such scholars as Comrie, Dixon, and Givón. The growing ascendency and cohesion of this community can be traced to at least five related factors:

- the careful and thoughtful work of American anthropologists in the 1930s and 40s striving to understand the structure of indigenous American languages
- a growing conviction that beneath the enormous variability among languages is their common function as tools of human communication, so that linguistic variability must be constrained to a significant extent by the commonalities of human cognition, culture, and social structure
- concern over the neo-Bloomfieldian deliberate lack of attention to any aspect of language use or human sociality in much of the linguistic research of the time
- the ground-breaking research on cross-linguistic patterns of Joseph Greenberg (cf. Greenberg 1957a, b, 1966), who thought of them as "language universals"
- the publication of Fillmore (1968), which awakened an interest in the semantic, as opposed to the strictly grammatical, roles of noun phrases in a clause.

Scholars accordingly began to seriously study functional motivations for cross-linguistic regularities in language; highly influential were, e.g., Comrie (1976, 1978), Li (1976), the four volumes of Greenberg (1978), Dixon (1979), Givón (1979a), Hawkins (1983), Haiman (1983, 1985a, b), Craig (1986), Dryer (1986, 1988), and Dik (1989). More researchers, including some returning from service in the American Peace Corps, began to carry out fieldwork providing the basis for grammars of under-studied languages, which were increasingly informed by a cross-linguistic perspective shared among members of the growing community, allowing for a growing convergence in the ways in which languages are described (Dryer 2006).

Looking for cross-linguistic patterns in terms of linguistic typology is consequential for revealing what kinds of data require functional explanation. Isolated arbitrary facts of a particular language may have many different sorts of explanation. But patterns of structure, and of structure–function correlation, that repeat themselves across languages throughout the world, must be motivated. On the grounds that explanations for regularities within a system cannot be found within that system, functionalists have long recognized that explanations must be sought *outside* grammar (Bybee 2010). In other words the motivations can largely be shown to lie in facts about human sociality and cognition (e.g., Evans and Levinson 2009). The process by which this happens is the diachronic one known as grammaticization (or grammaticalization).[1]

Discoveries of cross-linguistic regularities in word order (Tomlin 1986), noun–verb relations within the clause, including grammatical relations, case-marking systems, and "voice" (Shibatani 1976, Cole and Sadock 1977, Comrie 1978, Dixon 1979), relative clauses (Keenan and Comrie 1977), transitivity (Hopper and Thompson 1980), reflexive constructions (Faltz 1985), and adjectives (Dixon 1977) contributed substantially to the appreciation of cross-linguistic patterns and the emergence of such domain-general explanations within functional linguistics.[2]

As these forces were gathering momentum, starting in the late 1970s there emerged a development that provided strong new support to the functional view of linguistic structure. One group of functionalists became fascinated with the ways in which specific regularities in the organization of discourse could be drawn on to explain cross-linguistic grammatical regularities. Some of the "functions" of linguistic patterns, in other words, were to be found in the patterning of discourse organization. Early pioneers included Chafe (e.g., 1980), Du Bois (1987), Givón (e.g., 1979a, b, 1984), and Hopper (e.g., 1979); for an overview, see Cumming *et al.* (2011).

The 1980s saw a new focus on grammar as emergent structure (Hopper 1987, 1988; see also Lindblom *et al.* 1984), that is, as a self-organizing system operating in real time, in a manner reminiscent of the emergence of structure in biological and ecological systems such as termite colonies, sand dunes, and cloud formations (e.g., Camazine *et al.* 2001).[3]

Part of the understanding of emergent structure necessarily involves a recognition of the role of frequency of occurrence in shaping linguistic structure (Hooper 1976, Bybee 1985, Du Bois 1987). Central to frequency as a motivation for structural patterns is routinization, or ritualization (Haiman 1994). A task which has to be carried out frequently eventually becomes routinized – it requires little thought, because anything that needs to be figured out about how to do it has been figured out long before. If the task is one which must be regularly carried out by many or all people in a particular community, over time the community will develop a set, streamlined way, or a specially designed tool, for doing it. Since the late 1980s, these two foci have strongly influenced research into linguistic function (e.g., Bybee 1998, 2001a, 2002, 2006, 2007, Hopper 1998, 2011a, b, Bybee and Hopper 2001, Helasvuo 2003). Bybee (2006) makes the specific proposal that "grammar is the cognitive organization of one's experience with language" (711), and that "both grammatical meaning and grammatical form come into being through repeated instances of language use" (712).

Over the past fifteen years or so, growing out of this focus on grammar as emergent structure arising from ordinary language use, a burgeoning body of research has been attempting to more directly relate specific grammatical findings to the findings of scholars devoting themselves to the study of talk-in-interaction, particularly those working in Conversation Analysis.

These scholars have integrated into their research programs the idea that the very linguistic patterns that have been the deepest concern of functional linguists are emergent phenomena arising from everyday interactions. Coming to be known as "interactional linguistics," this research aims to show how linguistic regularities are dependent on, and shaped by, not just the context in which they occur, but more specifically by the actions which the speakers are undertaking with their talk. For participants in interaction, accomplishing these actions means moment-by-moment attention to the developing trajectory of the turn in progress, both in order to predict what action that turn is being used in the service of, and in order to know when it might be relevant for someone else to take a turn to further their projected actions. Recurrent regularities of turn organization and turn sequences are the primary way in which participants' actions are organized and negotiated, and these, in turn, are shown by interactional linguists to be the primary motivations for the development of grammatical patterns. The regularities of linguistic phenomena are then seen as practices which serve as solutions to recurrent needs in the real-time, situated, everyday human business of interacting and accomplishing actions.

It follows, then, that, to understand grammar, linguists' attention must also be on temporality and the developing trajectory of a turn-at-talk and the actions which such turns are accomplishing.

7.2 Constituency: Autonomous or functional?

It is in the context of these observations that we turn to the question of constituency. A "constituent" has been understood by most linguists as a word or a group of words that forms a "single unit" within a *hierarchical structure*; this hierarchical structure in turn has been taken to define the basic structure of a clause. For example, the following utterance could be hierarchized as illustrated in (1):

(1) [you [just [like [the pictures]]]]

The first American linguist to draw attention to the hierarchical structure of clauses was Bloomfield (1933), who conceived of it as a method for the structural analysis of imagined "sentences"; it was then developed further by Wells (1947) and Chomsky (1957). In this highly mechanical, and non-functional, structural tradition, constituents were seen as "building blocks" for sentences; little attention was paid to the cognitive underpinnings of constituents, let alone to their function in discourse. Furthermore, except for structurally ambiguous strings, it was understood that a given sequence of words would generally have a unique, discrete constituent analysis, such that constituent structures are a relatively fixed arrangement of nested containers.

In early functional work, these hierarchical relations were thought of as primarily conceptual (for summaries, see, e.g., Langacker 1995, Clark and van der Wege 2002). Thus, illustrating with the example above and working from the "inside out," we can see that *the pictures* is a canonical "Noun Phrase." Furthermore, it is an instance of an abstract constituent schema with the internal composition of [Article + Noun]. Moving "up" one "level," we see that *like the pictures* can also be seen as an instance of an abstract constituent, also with internal structure, this one [Verb + NP]; with the adverb *just*, another constituent is formed, *just like the pictures*. The entire clause could itself be a constituent, of course, if it occurred embedded within another clause. Evidence that these elements function "as a unit" can be found in the fact that they can be substituted for by a single item. So *the pictures* could be replaced by *avocados*, *(just) like the pictures* by *(just) cry*, and so forth.

But the functional linguists who were reacting against this tradition, and who were committed to viewing linguistic patterning as adaptive and self-organizing, began probing into the functional basis for constituent structure. Thus, Bybee and her colleagues soon realized that "conceptual unity" itself was related to linear *sequentiality*, and that constituent structure must be understood as emerging from the domain-general processes of "chunking" and categorization in discourse, that is, as a special case of the broader, domain-general phenomenon of *contiguity relations* in actual everyday language use. That is, "chunking" results as certain linear *sequences* of linguistic forms are found useful in communication and develop a sequential relation. The "chunks" come to be stored and processed, with varying degrees of abstractness, as single units, and are produced as prosodic gestalts (Bybee 2010).[4]

Bybee and her colleagues have further shown that many familiar "chunks" are sequences of repeated forms which would not have been considered as hierarchically defined "constituents" in earlier formulations. For example, the English expression *I don't know* in conversational discourse has diachronically come to be a single "chunk," complete with significant reduction/compression of sounds and syllables, thus obliterating the constituent "boundary" that would be required in a hierarchical approach between what we call the subject and the verbal expression,[5] as illustrated by the "erasure" of the boundary between *I* and *don't know* shown in (2):

(2) [I [don't know]]

Bybee (2002: 110) argues that:

> ...[linear: SAT/EC-K] sequentiality is basic to language and constituent structure emerges from sequentiality because elements that are frequently used together bind together into constituents.

So far, then, we have seen that early non-functional views of constituent structure treated it as a formal, strictly hierarchical feature of constructed utterances. From a functional perspective, a more grounded picture emerges of constituent structure as one type of "chunk" that can result from frequent collocations in discourse.

Functional approaches to patterning in language, then, have recently shifted the focus away from synchrony to diachrony and grammaticization. In the following section, we will turn to a third timescale, what Enfield (2011) has termed "enchrony," as we explore the role of constituent schemas in allowing conversational interactants to produce and monitor turns at talk for their trajectories and what it might take for them to be finished.

7.3 Constituents as a resource for social interaction

With the advent of conversation-analytic and interactional studies of mundane conversation, and the realization that the home environment of all language use is the turn-at-talk (Schegloff 1989), scholars working with usage-based approaches have become increasingly aware that the primordial functions of language are those that arise, not from monologic or written discourse, but from social interaction.[6]

Linguistic forms, among them constituents, are now being thought of as resources for interaction deployed in the service of sequential and interactional tasks (e.g., Ochs et al., 1996; Couper-Kuhlen and Selting 1996; Couper-Kuhlen and Ford 2004; Hakulinen and Selting 2005; Auer 2005, 2009a; Barth-Weingarten et al. 2010; Fox et al. 2012). In the following subsections we consider how constituent structure contributes to the conduct of interaction, using examples from everyday English conversation for illustration.

As noted above, in considering an interactional approach to linguistic patterning, one might compare the synchronic and diachronic views we have outlined above with an "enchronic" view. Enfield suggests that "enchrony" can be roughly understood as "conversational time,"

> a level of temporal-causal grain ... that an analyst of communication can adopt, as distinct from other possible perspectives, ...; these include phylogenetic, diachronic, ontogenetic, epigenetic, and synchronic perspectives ...

> An enchronic perspective is grounded in trajectories of co-relevant actions, ... [and] focuses on sequences of interlocking or interdependent communicative moves that are taken to be co-relevant, and causally-conditionally related. (2011: 287)

This enchronic perspective informs the remainder of the discussion in this chapter. To return to (1), for example, we note that this utterance is not in fact an imagined one, but comes from the recording of a natural conversation, in which it was produced with particular phonetic and prosodic properties. We will distinguish, then, between (i) "constituent schemas," or the schematic "templates," that are continuously stored and updated in memory with varying degrees of abstractness, and which serve as resources for specific realized exemplars (Bybee 2010), and (ii) the specific "constituent exemplars," which occur in enchronic time. Constituent schemas create prosodic and syntactic trajectories which allow interactants to predict possible completion and provide the grounds upon which participants are able to project what is coming next as they instantiate these schemas in interacting with one another in real time.[7] That is, as participants recognize a bit of talk as an exemplar of a particular constituent schema, they are able to narrow down the possible trajectories which it might take, when it might end, and thus when it might be time for them to talk next.[8]

7.3.1 Constituents and turn completion

Turn-taking in social interaction is self-orchestrated: current speakers must design their talk in a way that displays when their turn is potentially complete; would-be next speakers must monitor ongoing talk in order to anticipate when it could be time for their entry into the talk (Sacks *et al.* 1974). Constituent schemas are important tools for this task, allowing (i) the current speaker to display the provisional end of a turn-at-talk, and (ii) a would-be next speaker to be ready to take over the floor smoothly, without undue overlap or delay. Constituent schemas make this possible by virtue of their projective capacity: they have trajectories which allow interlocutors, at a given moment in time, to anticipate whether a turn-at-talk is close to completion and/or to predict roughly when and how it will reach possible completion. To see this, let us look at an example from English conversation:

(3) Mary Garcia (SBL 010)

(Bea, a registered nurse, has called Rosalyn to ask if she would be willing to replace her on a full-time nursing job. Rosalyn has refused on the grounds that her family commitments preclude her having the time. In the following fragment Rosalyn is wrapping up an explanation of why she would find working full-time "too much.")

```
01  Ros:    So I'm sorry to have to say no:,
02  Bea:    Yeah. hhh Well, khh ^Oka:y **if you know of ~anyone**.
03  Ros:    **If I: ^hear ~of somebody. or-or think of somebody good<**
04          hh ^Say u:: ^what about Mary Ga:rcia. What is she doing now.
05  Bea:    I don't kno:w.
06          (0.4)
07  Ros:    You know[she's a ]
08  Bea            [I haven't] seen her for yea:rs.
09  Ros:    Oh really?=She's a ~good ~nu:rse,
10  Bea:    Ah-hah,
11          (0.9)
```

This fragment consists of a number of pieces that could be considered exemplars of constituent schemas. Thus, for example, in line 4 we find *What about Mary Garcia*, an exemplar of the schema [What about X?], and in lines 5 and 9, we see exemplars of the highly specific pre-fab schemas [I don't know] and [oh really?]. In line 9, *She's a good nurse* is an instantiation of the constituent schema [Pro COPULA Noun Phrase]. By contrast, line 7, *you know she's a*, is remarkable precisely because it is *not* an exemplar of a constituent schema in English: it must therefore be analyzed as incomplete. But the focus here will be on the real-time exemplars of the constituent schemas in lines 1–3.

Rosalyn begins her turn (line 1) by saying *so*, which foreshadows more to come. At this point in time a range of different things could be said next, e.g., "That's why I've decided not to take on full-time work" or "I appreciate your thinking of me." In the event, Rosalyn continues with *I'm sorry*. This phrase has the potential to be a constituent exemplar, but it is not produced as one: lacking final lengthening and/or a major pitch accent, its prosody signals that still more will follow. Now, however, the range of syntactic options is narrower: based on one of the constituent schemas in which *I'm sorry* participates, we can predict that what will come next will either be a phrase, e.g., "for that"; a clause with finite syntax "I can't help you out"; or, as actually transpires, a clause with infinitive syntax *to have to say no*. At this juncture the pitch accent and final lengthening on *no* suggest that a major prosodic boundary has been reached (Barth-Weingarten forthcoming), marking a point of possible turn completion. The boundary of the constituent exemplar accompanied by a major prosodic break thus marks the moment at which Bea will have an opportunity to talk. Put differently, in planning and timing her incoming, Bea can recognize *I'm sorry* as a potential exemplar of several different constituent schemas. As the actual exemplar emerges in real time, syntactic information contributes to inferring which constituent schema is in play and phonetic-prosodic information conspires to mark its constituent boundary as a transition relevance place, a point in time when a next speaker can legitimately come in.

In line 2 Bea's turn unit *Okay if you know of anyone* is an exemplar (with an initial *okay*) of the constituent schema [*if* + REALIS CLAUSE]. *If*-clauses are often exemplars of a constituent schema in which they are *dependent*, projecting a main clause such as "then let me know" to follow. However, this particular constituent exemplar can be seen to belong to a different constituent schema with *if*, namely to an *independent* constituent schema with a realis clause, one which is frequently found in conjunction with certain kinds of requests and proposals (cf. also Laury 2012). When this schema occurs with a major prosodic boundary – as here, where Bea uses a final fall to low, accompanied by creaky voice – the constituent exemplar is treated as interactionally sufficient on its own.

Rosalyn's well-timed and unproblematic incoming *If I hear of somebody* in line 3 is thus cued by Bea's major prosodic boundary on a constituent exemplar in line 2 of the independent constituent schema [*if* + REALIS CLAUSE]. Note that both of Rosalyn's turn units in line 3, *If I hear of somebody* and *or (if I) think of somebody good*, can also be analyzed as constituent exemplars of this independent schema; they are also prosodic wholes that do not project more to come, although they lack the strong prosodic boundary found in line 2.

In sum, constituent schemas provide powerful means of projection. Particularly telling testimony of this will be seen in the continuation of the extract above:

(4) Mary Garcia, cont'd (SBL 010)
```
13   Ros:      An:d um=
14   Bea:      = hh [h h h h h h ]
15   Ros:           [I know she] was: (.) relieving sta:ff (.) at (.) Saint
16                 Francis afternoons for several months but she didn't (say any
17                 ^mo˘:re. but)
18   Bea:      Mm-hm,
19   Ros:      I ^think, I'll ˘ca:ll her an ask her if she's interested because
20                 ^she's a good nu:rse and I think they would ˘li:ke her don't you?
21   Bea:      t hh We:ll I'll ^tell you I haven't seen Mary for ^yea:rs.=I
22                 should- as I re^member ^ye:s.=
23   Ros:      =Well do you think she would fit i:n?
24                 (0.5)
25   Bea:      ˘Uh: t hh- hh (0.2) uh I don't know uh what I'm: uh-hesitating
26                 ab˘ou:t is: uh (.) t hh uh: (0.6) maybe she wou:ld. hh (0.8)
27                 uh but **I would hesita:te to uhm** (0.2)
28   Ros: →    **reco[mmend her.**
29   Bea:           [I-
30   Bea:      ehYe:s. You know what I mean,[ hhh
31   Ros:                                   [Yes,
```

Pressed by Rosalyn to take a stance on Mary Garcia's appropriateness as a substitute nurse, *well do you think she would fit in?* (line 23), Bea now somewhat haltingly summarizes her standpoint as *maybe she would hh (0.8) uh but I would hesitate to uhm*. At this point in time, the last part of Bea's turn, *I would hesitate to uhm*, as an exemplar of a constituent schema [PRO *to* Verbal Expression], is not syntactically or prosodically complete. Yet its trajectory is far enough developed for Rosalyn to surmise where it is going. She can now provide a candidate completion for Bea's provisionally halted turn: *recommend her* (line 28), which, as Bea confirms in line 30, is indeed what she had in mind. Again, what Bea has done is to set the terms for Rosalyn to provide a candidate verbal expression for the infinitival schema which Bea has begun. Together with her hesitations and the semantics of the verb *hesitate*, Rosalyn in fact has no trouble providing, in line 28, just the verbal expression that Bea had clearly had in mind.

In this section, we have presented examples of participants using the syntactic and prosodic trajectories created by constituent schemas (a) to display to interlocutors if and when ongoing turns are possibly complete, and (b) as ongoing turns unfold, to anticipate when possible points of completion will come and what they will consist of. In the next section we show that constituent schemas provide equally effective means for continuing one's turn past a point of possible completion in the absence of uptake (or appropriate uptake) by an interlocutor.

7.3.2 Constituents and turn continuation

One of the most fundamental facts about language as used in unprompted social interaction is that the linguistic forms emerge bit by bit, in real time (Hopper 1992, Auer 2009a). Thus, a conversationalist who initially completes a turn-at-talk can later decide to continue the same turn, talking past its prior syntactic and prosodic (as well as pragmatic) completion point. It has been noted that when this happens, speakers have different options for continuing. For one, they can add a "turn increment," a constituent exemplar which expands and/or completes the prior exemplar, transforming their turn into an exemplar of a further constituent schema (Auer 1992; Schegloff 1996; Ford *et al.* 2002, Couper-Kuhlen and Ono 2007). This is shown in the following extract: the added-on exemplar is understood to be an extension of the speaker's prior exemplar.

(5) Work full time (SBL 10)

(Rosalyn is explaining to Bea why she can't take on the full-time nursing job, although she is only working as a temporary employee for very low pay at Saint Francis hospital.)

01	Ros:	But I ^think I:'ll (1.0) stick with this: pie:ce at Saint Francis for
02		a while because (1.0) I mean I'm sure of my (.) days there.
03	Bea:	Ye:s ah-hah.
04	Ros:	Uh an:d uh I've: gone temporarily onto this (because I've
05		been suffering from) hh ruinous ba:ck pai:n.
06	Bea:	Ye:s,
07	Ros:	And uhm (0.9) uh:: (.) uh ^I've had uh some little
08		problems with my children and **I found that it was: (0.7)**
09		**^jus:t (.) just too ^mu:ch**.
10		(0.7)
11	Bea:	Ye:s.=
12	Ros:→	**=to work full time**,
13	Bea:	°Ah-huh,°=
14	Ros:	=h An:d uhm hhh so I'm ^not making much money right now
15		but the hours suit me.
16	Bea:	Mm hm,=
17	Ros:	=An' I think I'll just stick with it as long as they're willing
18		to keep me o:n tha[t bas]is.
19	Bea:	[Ye:s.] hh Well that yes ^that's ˜far more
20		important.˜

Having explained that she has gone into temporary staff nursing because of her back pain (lines 04–05) and problems with her children (lines 07–08), Rosalyn now brings her account to a close by saying *and I found that it was (0.7) just (.) just too much* (lines 08–09), with a major prosodic boundary created by the high pitch peak and strong fall on *much*. At this point Bea could be expected to provide some display of affiliation, yet she allows a 0.7-second pause to ensue. This intimates a possible problem of understanding.[9] In fact, Rosalyn's prior turn is unclear: what is it she finds too much? Bea passes the turn with a simple continuer *Ye:s* (line 11). So Rosalyn uses this opportunity to clarify her turn by adding another constituent exemplar: *to work full time* (line 12). Syntactically, this verbal expression could readily be recognized as an exemplar of an infinitival verbal expression. However, such a constituent schema is generally not realized in English standing alone; accordingly, it is here interpreted as a continuation of Rosalyn's earlier *it was just too much*. In this way Rosalyn has created a new exemplar, one which instantiates a constituent schema made up of a main clause and an infinitival complement.[10] Prosodically, she designs her infinitival complement as a continuation as well: it continues the low pitch at the end of *it was just too much*, with low register and a major falling pitch accent beginning on *work*, and it ends in creaky phonation.[11] Thus, both syntactically and prosodically, *to work full time* is designed to extend and re-complete Rosalyn's prior constituent exemplar.

Alternatively, however, speakers who talk beyond their own point of possible turn completion can do so by producing a constituent exemplar that is syntactically unattached and prosodically independent of the prior unit. Rather than re-completing the prior constituent, an independent constituent exemplar, e.g., a noun phrase or an adjective phrase, will allow the speaker to take up an evaluative stance towards the prior exemplar and show what an appropriate response to it would be (Ford et al. 2002). This is what happens in the following extract:

(6) Too bad (SBL 011)

(Dinah has been telling her friend Bea about a bad car accident she witnessed on the freeway the day before.)

```
01   Dinah:   We were s:-: (.) parked there for °quite a° whi:le but I was
02            going to (.) listen to the loca:l:: (.) ne:ws and haven't done it.
03   Bea:     No:, I haven't had my radio o:n either, t hh[hh
04   Dinah:                                                [Well I had my
05            television on but I was listening to: uh the blast-off you
06            ˋkno:w.
07   Bea:     Mm hm,
```

((18 lines omitted dealing with the absence of any report in the news))

```
26   Dinah:      Boy it was a bad one thou:gh,
27   Bea:        Well that's too ba::d.
28   Dinah: →   K[ind[of]↑ creepy.]¹²
29   Bea:         [hh[Y]ou know I  ] looked and looked in the paper <I think I
30               to:ld you f-for tha:-t uh:: f- (.) fa::ll over at the
31               ^Bow:l that ni:ght. hh And I never saw a ^thing a^bout it,
32               (.) and [I looked in the n]ext (0.4) couple of evenings,=
33   Dinah:              [ M m h m :      ]
34   Bea:        =hh'hhhh (0.3) Never saw a th- a me:ntion of it.
35   Dinah:     I didn't see that either.
36   Bea:       °Uh huh°
```

Earlier in this sequence, Dinah has detailed her experience of the car wreck, but Bea has displayed little empathy (not shown here). When Dinah now proposes to close down the sequence with an affect-laden summary assessment, *boy it was a bad one though* (line 26), Bea produces an expression of sympathy that comes off as rather pro-forma, *well that's too ba::d* (line 27). Dinah may have been expecting a stronger display of empathy and/or affect here, however, and adds on the phrasal constituent exemplar *kind of creepy* (line 28). Syntactically, this adjectival constituent exemplar is not attachable to anything in Dinah's prior turn, *boy it was a bad one though*, and it is produced with a reset of pitch and volume as compared to Dinah's turn. That is, both syntactically and prosodically Dinah's *kind of creepy* does not prolong the prior turn unit incrementally, but is produced as a separate and independent constituent exemplar that makes explicit her own stance towards the events she witnessed.

Continuing a turn with an independent constituent exemplar, as in (6), then, accomplishes something different from continuing a turn with a constituent exemplar that expands the prior exemplar, as in (5). In the latter case a speaker extends the syntactic and prosodic *form* of a prior turn, e.g., to address a potential problem of understanding and pursue *alignment*, that is, a next turn. But with an independent constituent exemplar, the speaker produces an exemplar of a different schema, taking up a stance toward the *content* of the prior turn, e.g., to address a problem of *affiliation* and pursue a specific kind of response.[13] Thus, the distinction between presence vs. absence of constituent-schema dependency in turn continuation is crucial for meaning-making in conversation. In either case, however, these extracts illustrate the strong tendency in our data for such incremental turn continuations to be just those exemplars instantiating very frequently documented constituent schemas.

In this section we have seen how constituent exemplars serve as resources for the accomplishment of two different sorts of work in turn continuation, pursuit of response (alignment) and pursuit of affiliative response (affiliation). As the next section will show, constituent exemplars also serve as resources when turns need repair.

7.3.3 Constituents and turn repair

The fact that language is produced in real time in contexts of social interaction is responsible for another of its distinctive features, namely its repairability. Speakers who produce talk spontaneously in interaction with others need strategies both for marking their speech as requiring repair (repair initiation) and for marking a stretch of speech as doing repair (repair proper). As it turns out, language-users' skills at "chunking" and storing constituent schemas provide resources for both these tasks (Schegloff *et al.* 1977, Schegloff 1979, Fox and Jasperson 1995).

Cutting off a syllable or a word with glottal closure, for instance, is one phonetic practice for temporarily halting the production of a constituent exemplar and indicating that it is repairable (Jasperson 2002). A cut-off delays the production of the word or syllable due next and is conventionally understood to mean "what I just said needs fixing." The material that follows is understood to do the fixing. We can observe this happening in the following extract:

(7) Little Rock (**SBL 010**)

(Rosalyn is explaining to Bea that she has heard about the nursing case for which Bea needs a substitute.)

```
01  Bea:       Have you been out °^there?°
02  Ros:       ^No:. I haven't met (him)
03             (XXX) we lived on Little Rock.
04             (1.0)
05  Bea:       t- h 0h: uh hah,
06             (0.2)
07  Ros: →     A:nd uh (.) u-uh she- and I ^heard ab˘out it at
08             the˘ ti:me,
09             (.)
10  Bea:       Ye-es.
```

Rosalyn's turn beginning in line 07 displays some disfluency with two *uhs* separated by a micro-pause, which is indicative of a problem in finding the right word to use next. When the next word does come (*she-*), it is cut short with a glottal stop, conveying that there is a problem with completing the constituent schema [*and* PRO Verbal Expression]. What follows *and I heard about it* is understood as fixing the problem. The word *she* has now been replaced by *I* in the exemplar of the recycled constituent schema [PRO Verbal Expression].

The success of self-repair depends heavily on prosodic and syntactic cues to constituent schematicity. Bea must understand that *I* is a replacement for *she* and not an addition to it, or in other words, that Rosalyn is not saying "she and I heard about it." This would be the more likely interpretation if there were no prosodic cut-off. But the cut-off on *she* suggests the need for repair. Recognition and comprehension of repair in extract (7) is also facilitated by the fact that the constituent schema [PRO Verbal Expression] is recycled and by the knowledge that *she* and *I* belong to the same syntactic category labeled "PRO" in the constituent schema [*and* PRO Verbal Expression]. On other occasions, a {repairable + repair} will be recognized because the string produced would otherwise be difficult to relate to any recognizable English constituent schema. For instance, in (5) we can identify self-repair in Bea's turn unit *Well that yes ↑ ˘ that's ^far more important.* (lines 19–20) because the string *that yes that's* is not an exemplar of a familiar constituent schema of English.

Constituent schematicity not only provides useful cues for the identification and recognition of *repairables*; self-repairing speakers also make systematic use of it in designing *repairing segments*. Prosodically, the repairing segment is likely to be set off from the repairable by a break in rhythm, pitch, and/or loudness (Cutler 1983). Syntactically, when repairing, for instance, a noun, English speakers typically re-do the whole noun or noun phrase exemplar (Fox and Jasperson 1995), as in the following extract:

(8) Measuring cup **(SBL 018)**

(Bea is explaining to her friend Tes how she handles making and serving coffee at her bridge parties.)

```
16   Bea:              [Eh- N o::]but I kno:w but uh I
17                have- m-u-usually ma:de just allowing hhh uh::̆:
18                ( ): ::
19                (0.3)
20   Bea: →    u-a regular mea-cuh- measuring cup fu::ll,=
21   Tes:     =Ye::s,=
22   Bea: →    =And which will make two tea- eh two tea˘cu:ps
23                you kno[˘:w.
24   Tes:            [That's ˘ri:ght.=
25   Bea:     = hhh An:d (0.2) I have:: (0.2) over half of it to throw
26                away every ti˘::me=
27   Tes:     =Ah °hah.°
```

In line 20 Bea re-does the faulty *mea-cuh-* as *measuring cup*; that is, she fixes the compound noun as a whole, not just one part of it, *-suring*. In line 22, the cut-off after the first *tea-* shows that there is something problematic with this word or the compound of which it is a part. In the event it is the compound *teacups* that Bea is aiming for, but rather than simply adding the noun exemplar itself *-cups* or recycling the compound-noun exemplar *teacups*, Bea says *two teacups* when implementing the repair, recycling an exemplar of the entire "noun phrase" constituent schema.

In principle, the same two options (re-doing the word or re-doing the phrase) should be available when speakers are repairing verbs and verbal expressions. However, empirical studies of English conversation have found that in the case of verbs and verbal expressions, speakers prefer to recycle back to the beginning of the whole clause when self-repairing (Fox and Jasperson 1995, Fox et al. 1996). This is what happens in the following:

(9) Four hearts (SBL 025)

(Clare and her friend Chloe are reviewing the bidding in a game of bridge they recently played together.)

```
01   Cla:     Well I: I never (.) n-denie:d[them I uh s]et a s[pa]:::[de.
02   Chl:                     [N o : : : ]b u t [eh]  [she:
03                [ju:mped ]Yah<]
04   Cla: →   [And then] she ] ju:mped [and then I
05   Chl:                          [She
06                (.)
07   Cla: →   put uh- I took ni:neteen and with: my two a:[ces and a ja:ck?=
08   Chl:                                  [°Yes.°
09   Cla:     =we had twenty six so I hhhh I just ˘said four
10                hea˘:r[ts you kno[w
```

In line 07 it becomes apparent that Clare has a problem when she cuts off with *uh-* an incipient complement to the verb *put*. Her subsequent repair replaces the verb *put* with the past tense of *take*. But although she could have simply replaced the verb: "put uh- took," Clare repairs by "backing up" to instantiate the entire clause in her repair: *I took nineteen*. According to Fox and Jasperson (1995), this is the most frequently encountered pattern for verb- and verbal-expression self-repair in English.

In this section we have seen brief evidence that participants rely on constituent schemas for making repairables recognizable and for implementing self-repair. What is crucial for present purposes is the realization that language provides, through these schemas, the wherewithal for recognizing and dealing with repairables when they arise in talk in social interaction.

7.4 How does language reflect interactional functions?

Let us take stock of what we have seen so far. We have discussed three ways in which constituency works to help speakers manage interactional tasks:

(i) Constituent-schema trajectories allow for projectability in turn construction, providing powerful cues for when would-be next speakers can legitimately come in.
(ii) Constituent exemplars may be added on in turn continuation to extend a turn-at-talk and re-complete it. Independent constituent exemplars, by contrast, especially unattached noun phrases and adjective phrases, continue the prior turn by taking up a stance toward it and showing what an appropriate response to it would look like.
(iii) The prosodic and syntactic properties of constituent schemas allow recipients to recognize and parse self-repair. Speakers doing a self-repair make differential use of constituent exemplars in designing repair segments.

In sum, we have shown that linguistic constituent schemas, reflecting highly frequent patterns of greater or lesser schematicity, serve as resources for the accomplishment of a range of interactional tasks in conversation. This insight does not come as a surprise, nor is it mere happenstance. Since language is central to social interaction, and since social interaction is omnipresent, we can expect *all* languages to provide their speakers with means for accomplishing basic interactional tasks. In other words, the interactional tasks discussed here stem from more general demands placed on all social interactants who are deploying language in real time:

(i) *Projection:* How to convey that what I am saying is almost complete (or not) so that a would-be next speaker can know when to legitimately come in (or not)?

(ii) *Continuation after possible completion:* How to indicate that what I am saying now is an extension of something that was provisionally completed earlier?
(iii) *Repair:* How to convey that the words I am producing now are re-doing prior talk rather than continuing it?

These demands correspond to Auer's (2005, 2009a, b) three principles, projection, expansion, and retraction, which, as he claims, can be considered the basic operations of *online syntax*, i.e., syntax understood as an inherently temporal, emergent phenomenon. As the discussion here has shown, the operations of projection, expansion, and retraction are first and foremost interactional tasks, for which constituent schemas afford a solution.

7.5 Conclusion

The study of language within its social environment, then, reveals the many ways in which human language reflects universal basic functions arising from social interaction, and also shows how these may be manifested through constituent schemas and exemplars.

We have taken one aspect of linguistic structure, namely "constituency," as a point of departure to illustrate several more general properties of language as understood through a functionalist perspective on linguistic structure:

(a) Language has evolved in diachronic time to meet the needs of its users, providing an environment in which grammaticizations of specific linear sequences emerge as constituent schemas.
(b) Language structure exists in synchronic time as a resource for communication.
(c) Language serves in enchronic time to address sequential and interactional tasks in social interaction, illustrated by the prominent role of constituent schemas in turn completion, turn continuation, and turn repair.

Notes

1. For more on the mechanisms of grammaticization, see Lehmann (1982), Bybee (1985, 1998, 2001a, 2006, 2007), Heine *et al.* (1991), Traugott and Heine (1991a, b), Hopper and Traugott (1993), Haiman (1994), Bybee *et al.* (1994), Heine and Kuteva (2002).
2. For a useful contemporary encapsulation of the tenets of this approach to grammar, see Dixon (2010–12). On the importance of domain-general explanations, see Bybee (2010).
3. For a useful contemporary discussion, see Auer and Pfänder (2011).

4. Such "constituent schemas" can be seen as comparable to what many linguists view as "constructions" (see, e.g., Fillmore et al. 1988, Fillmore 1989, Goldberg 1995, 2006).
5. For further discussion, see Bybee and Scheibman (1999), Bybee (2001a, b, 2002), Beckner and Bybee (2009), and Frank et al. (2012).
6. See Linell 2005 on the written-language bias in linguistics.
7. Our words "syntax" and "syntactic" should be understood as convenient short forms of "morphosyntax" and "morphosyntactic."
8. On "projection" in conversation, see, e.g., Local and Kelly (1986), Auer (2005, 2009b), Mondada (2006), and Hopper and Thompson (2008).
9. We acknowledge that Bea's 0.7 delay in line 10 could also be due in part to her already-displayed disaffiliation with Rosalyn's refusal to take on the nursing job Bea has called about.
10. For further discussion of the emergence of such "extraposition" exemplars, see Couper-Kuhlen and Thompson (2008).
11. See Walker (2004) for a phonetic description of other turn increments in English conversation.
12. Since this turn is overlapped, Dinah's last word is difficult to hear; however, the two of us and the original transcriber of this phone conversation hear it as *creepy*, and our analysis assumes that that is what she said.
13. See Stivers (2008) for more on how alignment and affiliation play out differently in conversation.

References

Auer, Peter. 1992. The Neverending Sentence: Rightward expansion in spoken language. In *Studies in Spoken Languages: English, German, Finno-Ugric*, ed. Miklós Kontra and Tamás Váradi, 41–59. Budapest: Linguistics Institute, Hungarian Academy of Sciences.
  2005. Projection in Interaction and Projection in Grammar. *Text* 25 (1): 7–36.
  2009a. On-Line Syntax: Thoughts on the temporality of spoken language. *Language Sciences* 31: 1–13.
  2009b. Projection and Minimalistic Syntax in Interaction. *Discourse Processes* 46(2–3): 180–205.
Auer, Peter, and Stefan Pfänder, eds. 2011. *Constructions: Emerging and Emergent*. Berlin: De Gruyter.
Barth-Weingarten, Dagmar. Forthcoming. *Intonation Units Revisited*. Amsterdam: John Benjamins.
Barth-Weingarten, Dagmar, Elisabeth Reber, and Margret Selting. 2010. *Prosody in Interaction*. Amsterdam: Benjamins.
Beckner, Clay, and Joan Bybee. 2009. A Usage-Based Account of Constituency and Reanalysis. *Language Learning* 59: 27–46.

Bloomfield, Leonard. 1933. *Language*. New York: Henry Holt.
Bolinger, Dwight L. 1952. Linear Modification. *Publications of the Modern Language Association of America* 67: 1117–44.
　1965. *Forms of English: Accent, Morpheme, Order*. Cambridge, MA: Harvard University Press; Tokyo: Hokuou.
Bybee [=Hooper], Joan. 1985. *Morphology*. Amsterdam: Benjamins.
　1998. The Emergent Lexicon. *CLS* 34: 421–35.
　2001a. *Phonology and Language Use*. Cambridge: Cambridge University Press.
　2001b. Frequency Effects on French Liaison. In *Frequency and the Emergence of Linguistic Structure*, ed. Joan L. Bybee and Paul J. Hopper, 337–359. Amsterdam: Benjamins.
　2002. Sequentiality as the Basis of Constituent Structure. In *The Evolution of Language from Pre-Language*, ed. T. Givon and Bertram Malle, 109–32. Amsterdam: Benjamins.
　2006. From Usage to Grammar: The mind's response to repetition. *Language* 82(4): 711–33.
　2007. *Frequency of Use and the Organization of Language*. Oxford: Oxford University Press.
　2010. *Language, Usage and Cognition*. Cambridge: Cambridge University Press.
Bybee, Joan, and Paul J. Hopper, eds. 2001. *Frequency and the Emergence of Linguistic Structure*. Amsterdam: Benjamins.
Bybee, Joan L., Revere Perkins, and William Pagliuca. 1994. *The Evolution of Grammar: Tense, Aspect and Modality in the Languages of the World*. Chicago: The University of Chicago Press.
Bybee, Joan, and Joanne Scheibman. 1999. The Effect of Usage on Degrees of Constituency: The reduction of *don't* in English. *Linguistics* 37(3): 575–96.
Camazine, Scott, Jean-Louis Deneubourg, Nigel R. Franks, James Sneyd, Guy Theraulaz, and Eric Bonabeau. 2001. *Self-Organization in Biological Systems*. Princeton: Princeton University Press.
Chafe, Wallace, ed. 1980. *The Pear Stories: Cognitive, Cultural, and Linguistic Aspects of Narrative Production*. Norwood, NJ: Ablex.
Chomsky, Noam 1957. *Syntactic Structures*. The Hague/Paris: Mouton.
Clark, Herbert H., and M. Van Der Wege. 2002. Psycholinguistics. In *Stevens' Handbook of Experimental Psychology*, ed. D. L. Medin, 3rd ed., 209–59. New York: John Wiley.
Cole, Peter, and Jerry Sadock, eds. 1977. *Syntax and Semantics 8: Grammatical Relations*. New York: Academic Press.
Comrie, Bernard. 1976. *Aspect*. Cambridge: Cambridge University Press.
　1978. Ergativity. In *Syntactic Typology*, ed. Winfred P. Lehmann, 329–94. Austin: University of Texas Press.
Couper-Kuhlen, Elizabeth, and Cecilia E. Ford, eds. 2004. *Sound Patterns in Interaction: Cross-linguistic Studies from Conversation*. Studies in Linguistic Typology. Amsterdam: Benjamins.

Couper-Kuhlen, Elizabeth, and Tsuyoshi Ono. 2007. "Incrementing" in Conversation. A comparison of practices in English, German and Japanese. *Pragmatics* 17(4): 513-52.

Couper-Kuhlen, Elizabeth, and Margret Selting, eds. 1996. *Prosody in Conversation*. Cambridge: Cambridge University Press.

Couper-Kuhlen, Elizabeth, and Sandra A. Thompson. 2008. On Assessing Situations and Events in Conversation: Extraposition and its relatives. *Discourse Studies* 10(4): 443-67.

Craig, Colette, ed. 1986. *Noun Classes and Categorization*. Amsterdam: John Benjamins.

Cumming, Susanna, Tsuyoshi Ono, and Ritva Laury. 2011. Discourse, Grammar and Interaction. In *Discourse Studies: A Multidisciplinary Introduction*, ed. Teun A. Van Dijk, 2nd ed., 8-36. London: Sage Publications.

Cutler, Anne. 1983. Speaker's Conceptions of the Functions of Prosody. In *Prosody: Models and measurements*, ed. Anne Cutler and D. R. Ladd, 79-91. Heidelberg: Springer.

Dik, Simon. 1989. *The Theory of Functional Grammar*. Dordrecht: Foris. [Now revised as Simon C. Dik. 1997. *The Theory of Functional Grammar*. Part 1: *The Structure of the Clause*, 2nd rev. ed., ed. Kees Hengeveld. Berlin: Mouton de Gruyter.]

Dixon, R. M. W. 1977. *A Grammar of Yidiny*. Cambridge Studies in Linguistics, 19. Cambridge: Cambridge University Press.

   1979. Ergativity. *Language* 55(1): 59-138.

   2010-12. *Basic Linguistic Theory*. 3 vols. Oxford: Oxford University Press.

Dryer, Matthew. 1986. Primary Objects, Secondary Objects, and Antidative. *Language* 62(4): 808-45.

   1988. Object-Verb Order and Adjective-Noun Order: Dispelling a myth. *Lingua* 74: 185-217.

   2006. Descriptive Theories, Explanatory Theories, and Basic Linguistic Theory. In *Catching Language: Issues in Grammar Writing*, ed. Felix Ameka, Alan Dench, and Nicholas Evans, 207-34. Berlin: Mouton de Gruyter.

Du Bois, John W. 1987. The Discourse Basis of Ergativity. *Language* 63: 805-55.

Enfield, N. J. 2011. Sources of Asymmetry in Human Interaction: Enchrony, status, knowledge and agency. In *The Morality of Knowledge in Conversation*, ed. Tanya Stivers, Lorenza Mondada, and Jakob Steensig, 285-312. Cambridge: Cambridge University Press.

Evans, Nicholas, and Stephen C. Levinson. 2009. The Myth of Language Universals: Language diversity and its importance for cognitive science. *Behavioral and Brain Sciences* 32(5): 429-92.

Faltz, Leonard. 1985. *Reflexivization: A Study in Universal Syntax*. New York: Garland.

Fillmore, Charles J. 1968. The Case for Case. In *Universals in Linguistic Theory*, ed. Emmon Bach and Robert T. Harms, 1–88. New York: Holt, Rinehart, and Winston.

1989. Grammatical Construction Theory and the Familiar Dichotomies. In *Language Processing Social Context*, ed. Rainer Dietrich and Carl F. Graumann, 17–38. North Holland: Elsevier Publishers.

Fillmore, Charles, Paul Kay, and Catherine O'Connor. 1988. Regularity and Idiomaticity in Grammatical Constructions: The Case of let alone. *Language* 64: 501–38.

Firbas, Jan. 1964. On Defining the Theme in Functional Sentence Analysis. *Travaux linguistiques de Prague* 1: 267–80.

1992. *Functional Sentence Perspective in Written and Spoken Communication*. Cambridge: Cambridge University Press.

Ford, Cecilia E., Barbara A. Fox, and Sandra A. Thompson. 2002. Constituency and the Grammar of Turn Increments. In *The Language of Turn and Sequence*, ed. Cecilia E. Ford, Barbara A. Fox, and Sandra A. Thompson, 14–38. Oxford: Oxford University Press.

Fox, Barbara A., and Robert Jasperson. 1995. A Syntactic Exploration of Repair in English Conversation. In *Alternative Linguistics: Descriptive and Theoretical Modes*, ed. P. W. Davis, 77–134. Amsterdam: Benjamins.

Fox, Barbara A., Makoto Hayashi, and Robert Jasperson. 1996. A Cross-Linguistic Study of Syntax and Repair. In *Interaction and Grammar*, ed. Elinor Ochs, Emanuel A. Schegloff, and Sandra A. Thompson, 185–237. Cambridge: Cambridge University Press.

Fox, Barbara A., Sandra A. Thompson, Cecilia E. Ford, and Elizabeth Couper-Kuhlen. 2012. Conversation Analysis and Linguistics. In *Handbook of Conversation Analysis*, ed. Jack Sidnell and Tanya Stivers, 726–40. Oxford: Wiley-Blackwell.

Frank, Stefan L., Rens Bod, and Morten H. Christiansen. 2012. How Hierarchical is Language Use? *Proceedings of the Royal Society B: Biological Sciences* 279: 4522–31. http://rspb.royalsocietypublishing.org/content/279/1747/4522.full.pdf+html

Givón, Talmy. 1979a. *On Understanding Grammar*. New York: Academic Press.

ed. 1979b. *Discourse and Syntax*. New York: Academic Press.

1984. *Syntax: A Functional-Typological Introduction*, Vol. 1. Amsterdam: John Benjamins.

Goldberg, Adele. 1995. *Constructions: A Construction Grammar Approach to Argument Structure*. Chicago: University of Chicago Press.

2006. *Constructions at Work*. Oxford: Oxford University Press.

Greenberg, Joseph H. 1957a. Order of Affixing: A study in general linguistics. In Greenberg 1957b, 86–94.

1957b. *Essays in Linguistics*. Chicago: University of Chicago Press.

1966. Some Universals of Grammar with Particular Reference to the Order of Meaningful Elements. In *Universals of Grammar*, ed. Joseph H. Greenberg, 2nd ed., 73–113. Cambridge, MA: MIT Press.

1978. *Universals of Human Language*. Stanford, CA: Stanford University Press.
Haiman, John. 1983. Iconic and Economic Motivation. *Language* 59(4): 781-819.
  ed. 1985a. *Iconicity in Syntax*. Amsterdam: John Benjamins.
  1985b. *Natural Syntax*. Cambridge: Cambridge University Press.
  1994. Ritualization and the Development of Language. In *Perspectives on Grammaticalization*, ed. William Pagliuca, 3-28. Amsterdam: Benjamins.
Hakulinen, Auli, and Margret Selting, eds. 2005. *Syntax and Lexis in Conversation*. Amsterdam: Benjamins.
Halliday, M. A. K. 1967-68. Notes on Transitivity and Theme in English. *Journal of Linguistics* 3(1) [1967]: 37-82; 3(2) [1967]: 199-244; 4(2) [1968]: 179-215.
Hawkins, John. 1983. *Word Order Universals*. New York: Academic Press.
Heine, Bernd, and Tania Kuteva. 2002. *World Lexicon of Grammaticalization*. Cambridge: Cambridge University Press.
Heine, Bernd, Ulrike Claudi, and Friederike Huennemeyer. 1991. *Grammaticalization: A Conceptual Framework*. Chicago: University of Chicago Press.
Helasvuo, Marja-Liisa. 2003. Emergent Grammar. In *Handbook of Pragmatics*, ed. Chris Bulcaen, Jef Verschueren, and Jan-Ola Östman (online). Amsterdam: Benjamins.
Hooper, Joan B. 1976. *An Introduction to Natural Generative Phonology*. New York: Academic Press.
Hopper, Paul 1979. Aspect and Foregrounding in Discourse. In *Syntax and Semantics*, ed. T. Givón, Vol. 12: *Discourse and Syntax*, 213-41. New York: Academic Press.
  1987. Emergent Grammar. *Berkeley Linguistics Society* 13: 139-57.
  1988. Emergent Grammar and the A Priori Grammar Constraint. In *Linguistics in Context: Connecting Observation and Understanding*, ed. Deborah Tannen, 117-34. Norwood, NJ: Ablex.
  1992. Times of the Sign: On temporality in recent linguistics. *Time and Society* 1(2): 223-38.
  2011a. Emergent Grammar and Temporality in Interactional Linguistics. In *Constructions: Emerging and Emergent*, ed. P. Auer and S. Pfänder, 22-44. Berlin: de Gruyter.
  2011b. Emergent Grammar. In *The Routledge Handbook of Discourse Analysis*, ed. James Paul Gee and M. Handford. London: Routledge.
Hopper, Paul, and Sandra A. Thompson. 1980. Transitivity in Grammar and Discourse. *Language* 56: 251-99.
  1998. Emergent Grammar. In *The New Psychology of Language: Cognitive and Functional Approaches to Language Structure*, ed. Michael Tomasello, 155-75. Mahwah, NJ: Lawrence Erlbaum.
  2008. Projectability and Clause Combining in Interaction. In *Crosslinguistic Studies of Clause Combining: The Multifunctionality of Conjunctions*, ed. Ritva Laury, 99-124. Amsterdam: John Benjamins.

Hopper, Paul J., and Elizabeth Traugott. 1993. *Grammaticalization*. Cambridge: Cambridge University Press. [Revised edition, 2003.]

Jasperson, Robert. 2002. Some Linguistic Aspects of Closure Cut-off. In *The Language of Turn and Sequence*, ed. Cecilia E. Ford, Barbara A. Fox, and Sandra A. Thompson, 257–86. Oxford and New York: Oxford University Press.

Keenan, Edward L. and Bernard Comrie. 1977. Noun Phrase Accessibility and Universal Grammar. *Linguistic Inquiry* 8: 63–99.

Langacker, Ronald W. 1995. Cognitive Grammar. In *Handbook of Pragmatics*, ed. Jef Verschueren, Jan-Ola Östman, and Jan Blommaert, 105–11. Amsterdam and Philadelphia: John Benjamins.

Laury, Ritva. 2012. Syntactically Non-Integrated Finnish 'jos' (if)-conditional Clauses as Directives. *Discourse Processes* 49: 213–42.

Lehmann, Christian. 1982. *Thoughts on Grammaticalization: A Programmatic Sketch*, Vol. 1. Arbeiten des Kölner Universalien-Projekts, 48. Cologne Working Papers. [Revised 2002 as *Thoughts on Grammaticalization*, Vol. 2. Rev. ed. Arbeitspapiere des Seminars für Sprachwissenschaft der Universität Erfurt, 9. Erfurt.]

Li, Charles N., ed. 1976. *Subject and Topic*. New York: Academic Press.

Lindblom, Bjorn, Peter MacNeilage, and Michael Studdert-Kennedy. 1984. Self-organizing Processes and the Explanation of Phonological Universals. In *Explanations for Language Universals*, ed. B. Butterworth, B. Comrie, and O. Dahl, 181–203. Berlin: Mouton de Gruyter.

Linell, Per. 2005. *The Written Language Bias in Linguistics: Its Nature, Origins and Transformations*. London: Routledge.

Local, John, and John Kelly. 1986. Projection and "Silences": Notes on phonetic and conversational structure. *Human Studies* 9: 185–204.

Mondada, Lorenza. 2006. Participants' Online Analysis and Multimodal Practices: Projecting the end of the turn and the closing of the sequence. *Discourse Studies* 8(1): 117–29.

Ochs, Elinor, Emanuel A. Schegloff, and Sandra A. Thompson, eds. 1996. *Interaction and Grammar*. Cambridge: Cambridge University Press.

Sacks, Harvey, Emanuel A. Schegloff, and Gail Jefferson. 1974. A Simplest Systematics for the Organization of Turn-Taking for Conversation. *Language* 50(4): 696–735.

Sapir, Edward. 1921. *Language: An Introduction to the Study of Speech*. New York: Harcourt, Brace and company.

  1949. *Selected Writings in Language, Culture and Personality*, ed. David Mandelbaum. Berkeley: University of California Press.

Schegloff, Emanuel A. 1979. The Relevance of Repair to Syntax-for-Conversation. In *Discourse and Syntax*, ed. Talmy Givón, 261–86. New York: Academic Press.

  1989. Reflections on Language, Development, and the Interactional Character of Talk-in-interaction. In *Interaction in Human Development*, ed. M. H. Bornstein and J. S. Bruner, 139-53. New York: Lawrence Erlbaum Associates.

1996. Turn Organization: One intersection of grammar and interaction. In *Interaction and Grammar*, ed. Elinor Ochs, Emanuel Schegloff, and Sandra A. Thompson, 52-133. Cambridge: Cambridge University Press.

Schegloff, Emanuel A., Gail Jefferson, and Harvey Sacks. 1977. The Preference for Self-Correction in the Organization of Repair in Conversation. *Language* 53: 361-82.

Shibatani, Masayoshi. 1976. *The Grammar of Causative Constructions*. Syntax and semantics 6. New York: Academic Press.

Stivers, Tanya. 2008. Stance, Alignment, and Affiliation during Storytelling: When nodding is a token of affiliation. *Research on Language and Social Interaction*, 41(1): 31-57.

Tomlin, Russell. 1986. *Basic Word Order: Functional Principles*. London: Croom Helm.

Traugott, Elizabeth Closs, and Bernd Heine, eds. 1991a. *Approaches to Grammaticalization*, Vol. 1. Amsterdam: John Benjamins.

eds. 1991b. *Approaches to Grammaticalization*, Vol. 2. Amsterdam: John Benjamins.

Walker, Gareth. 2004. On Some Interactional and Phonetic Properties of Increments to Turns in Talk-in-interaction. In *Sound Patterns in Interaction*, ed. Elizabeth Couper-Kuhlen and Cecilia E. Ford, 147-69. Amsterdam: John Benjamins.

Wells, Rulon S. 1947. Immediate Constituents. *Language* 23: 81-117.

Wittgenstein, Ludwig. 1976. Cause and Effect. *Philosophia* 6 (3-4): 409-25.

Part II

Process and formation

Paul Kockelman, N. J. Enfield, and Jack Sidnell

The formations of meaning explored in Part I include not only languages and cultures as highly complex systems, they also include linguistically competent and culturally socialized agents, as well as the capacities to speak languages and to inhabit cultures. What explains the nature of those formations? D'Arcy Thompson (*On Growth and Form*, Cambridge University Press, 1917) famously stressed the role of development: "Everything is this way because it got this way." The chapters in Part II explore the processes that create linguistic and cultural formations. These processes include diverse causal mechanisms, affecting different sites and unfolding on various scales, among which are the evolutionary, historical, developmental/biographical, interactional, and psychological. In surveying broad literatures, the chapters in Part II offer a rich picture of the causal mechanisms and temporal dynamics of human-specific modes of meaning.

We begin our lives surrounded by language but unable to use it. One of the most remarkable developmental processes in our earliest years is the acquisition of a first language, through which in a few years we go from having zero linguistic competence to having mastered a significant proportion of the grammar of whatever language is being spoken in our community. The chapter by **Brown and Gaskins** treats first language learning in terms of two concomitant processes. First, how do different languages and cultures influence the process of language acquisition? Second, how do increasingly competent speakers become socialized into particular cultural worlds? In answering these questions, the authors review and synthesize two extensive and often divergent literatures: language acquisition (itself often divided into formalist and functionalist-oriented work) and language socialization (with roots in the ethnography of communication and linguistic pragmatics). They foreground comparative work, arguing that a theoretical focus on language universals and child-centered interaction, often grounded in English grammar and Western child-care practices, has imported unwarranted assumptions, and has led to unwarranted conclusions, about the nature of the acquisition of language and of our socialization through it. And, with particular relevance to the chapters in Part III, Brown and Gaskins foreground the way children are not just socialized into language structure, but also into modes of social interaction more generally.

The acquisition of a first language is facilitated not only by the enchronic processes that drive social interaction but also by the historical processes that created the form and content of any individual's social networks. The issue of historical process is taken up in the chapter by **Faudree and Hansen**, who explore the nexus of language, society, and history, reviewing a broad literature. One focus is on the linguistic mediation of history, for example taking linguistic practices as a window onto events that occurred in the past. Another is the linguistic mediation of metahistory, for example taking linguistic practices as a means through which events become historicized. The authors thereby move between history as an interpretive method – focusing on textuality, mediation, language ideologies, dialogicality, and the chronotope – and history as a fact-finding endeavor, focusing on topics like historical linguistics and the comparative method, and ethnohistory. Linguistic anthropology, they argue, is well positioned to make progress with these issues, as it can tack between, and tie together, both forms of mediation by foregrounding the semiotic processes through which peoples, narratives, and events are bound.

The processes in which languages evolve historically, and are acquired in the socialization of individuals, presuppose populations of a certain size, with certain dynamics for transmission of traditions within their population. Is there a lower limit on the size of a population that would support the evolution of a linguistic system? The chapter by **Sandler, Aronoff, Padden, and Meir** examines the emergence of a sign language in villages of the Al-Sayyid Bedouin of Israel. The authors use this unique situation as an opportunity to ask what are the essential ingredients of human languages. Complementing the chapter by Goldin-Meadow in Part I, Sandler and colleagues detail the social conditions under which sign languages can arise, discussing various kinds of sign language, with various degrees of conventionalization and coherence. They outline the formal properties of Al-Sayyid Bedouin Sign Language, from syntax (word order, argument structure, the function of prosody) to lexicon (the notion of subject, the role of conventional vocabulary versus gesticulation) to phonology (handshape, location, movement). The facts lead them to conclude that languages emerge gradually, not within the scope of a single generation. They emphasize how difficult it is to give criteria for defining what a full-fledged language is, especially because different domains within a language (lexicon, syntax, morphology, phonology, semantics) do not develop in a unified fashion or at the same pace, and also because we must distinguish between the formal and functional properties of a system (see chapters by Dixon and by Thompson and Couper-Kuhlen in Part I).

Studies such as these reveal valuable lessons from the birth of languages about the limiting possibilities of a language system's existence. A natural complement to this work is the poignant and politicized phenomenon of language endangerment and extinction, taken up in the chapter by **Rice**. In part, she offers a condensed history of the last twenty years of work by linguists on the problem: their understanding of the reasons for it, the best responses to it, and the very real (and sometimes rhetorical) stakes at issue. And, in part, she highlights many of the sticking points of such an endeavor. These range from difficulties in quantifying the extent and rate of loss, to understanding its manifold causality – caught up, as it is, in sociopolitical issues far outside of linguistics as traditionally understood. And they also involve issues that go to the heart of linguistic anthropology, and that touch upon ethical questions. What forms of life are lost when we lose a language? How to theorize and minimize such loss? Rice details the ways in which linguists, governments, and the speakers themselves have responded to such loss, foregrounding what are emerging as the best practices and most realistic prognoses.

The interrelated processes and formations discussed so far take place at historical and shorter timescales. Beyond these are the evolutionary timescales that frame our accounts for the very capacity for language in humans as a species. **Levinson**'s chapter discusses the last ten years of research on language evolution, focusing on the rise of new methods, and the data these have generated. Such data include the discovery of newly emergent languages and larger typological studies of existing languages, as well as archaeo-DNA and new fossil finds. New methods range from bioinformatic analysis of typological data to MRI scanning of fossil structure, and from the extraction and insertion of ancient DNA to laboratory simulation of evolutionary processes. The concept of *niche construction* allows us to see the ways in which processes underlying biological and cultural evolution – the two lines of dual inheritance – are interlocked. Levinson offers new evidence that points to the relative antiquity of the human language capacity in evolutionary time. The chapter also has links to issues dealt with in a number of other chapters in this handbook, including the cultural evolution of language(s) in historical time (see Enfield's chapter in Part II), the historical emergence of new languages (see chapters by Sandler *et al.*, and by Goldin-Meadow) and the links and interactions between genes and culture (see chapter by Dediu).

The chapters in this Part, along with many other chapters in this book, invoke distinct explanatory/causal frames that tend to correlate with distinct temporal scales. In his chapter in this Part, **Enfield** argues for a scheme of six basic causal frames that organize distinct disciplinary approaches to language: microgenetic, ontogenetic, phylogenetic, enchronic, diachronic, and synchronic ('M.O.P.E.D.S.' for short). Each frame provides the analyst with a way of foregrounding key causal processes that underlie the emergence and propagation of linguistic and cultural phenomena. Questions can be clearly posed and answered only when several frames are taken into account at once, and a full account must work in terms of all the frames in combination. But different research traditions have tended to emphasize different frames, while eliding others. The problem has a history of scholarly attention, where various schemes distinguishing such frames have been proposed. Enfield gives a sketch of some of the representative ideas, before illustrating their application using the case study of Zipf's Law – morphological size scales inversely with discourse frequency – and pointing to the elements of a causal account from the standpoint of all six frames. The other chapters in this part also make reference to distinct causal-temporal frames, however implicitly, and so provide concrete instances of the value of bringing multiple frames and scales into a single purview.

8

Language acquisition and language socialization

Penelope Brown and Suzanne Gaskins

8.1 Introduction

Language is one of the defining traits of humans. It rests on a set of uniquely human competencies in social interaction – an instinct for cooperation, an awareness of other minds, abilities to read others' intentions and coordinate mentally – which together comprise an "interaction engine" (Levinson 2006) that develops in each child during the first year of life (Clark 2001; Tomasello *et al.* 2005). Children all over the world learn the language(s) they are exposed to with remarkable facility, and are fluent – if not mature – speakers by the age of three or four. Along with the language, they learn the cultural practices, attitudes, ways of thinking and feeling and behaving that are embodied in the interactional environment in which they are immersed. Understanding this process of socialization into language and culture is critical to understanding the biological bases, learning, and cross-cultural variability of social interaction, as well as the role of culture more broadly in children's social, cognitive, and language development.

Studying the process through which this happens has been a preoccupation of scholars in disciplines across the spectrum spanning psychology, linguistics, sociology, and anthropology, with a variety of motivations. For some, the nature of the language capacity itself is the intriguing puzzle, and these researchers – mostly developmental psychologists – tend to describe what they study as the process of *language acquisition*. Work here has diverged into two increasingly irreconcilable theoretical camps, differing profoundly in their views of the nature of language and of mind. One set consists of those adopting Chomsky's theory of universal grammar (UG), which posits an inbuilt "language acquisition device" enabling children's language to develop as a process of maturation largely immune to cultural and language variation (e.g., Guasti 2004; Lust 2006). The other set comprises those who adopt a "usage-based" or constructionist theory of language development that rejects the idea of a language acquisition device and insists that language development is a piece-by-piece achievement governed by statistically reliable aspects of speech to and around small children (the "input") (Barlow and Kemmer 2000; Tomasello 2003; Behrens 2009). An excellent and balanced assessment of evidence and issues in relation to each of these two positions can be found in Ambridge and Lieven (2011); other useful overviews are Bowerman (1981); Bavin (2009).

More compatible with an anthropological perspective are approaches where the central questions are not about the language capacity and its relation to mind, but on how the child as a novice embedded in a culturally constituted environment through social interaction gradually develops both communicative competence and sociocultural membership. A first formulation of this approach in the 1960s came out of the Gumperz and Hymes (1964) program for the *ethnography of communication*, studying communicative competence in different cultural settings. Early work based on a field manual for guiding cross-cultural research (Slobin 1967) produced doctoral dissertations reporting on child language in Mexico (Stross 1969), Kenya (Blount 1969), Samoa (Kernan 1969), and California (Mitchell-Kernan 1969).

In the 1970s and 1980s two developments added to the burgeoning stream of child language research. Work in *linguistic pragmatics* investigated children's developing pragmatic skills (e.g., Bates 1976; Ochs and Schieffelin 1979). At the same time, the paradigm of *language socialization* was articulated by anthropologists Elinor Ochs and Bambi Schieffelin, based on their fieldwork in Papua New Guinea and Samoa, respectively. Their work looked not only at the exposure to and acquisition by children of pragmatic meaning but also the role of speech as a conveyer of cultural information, especially in everyday interactions. Schieffelin and Ochs (1986a) argue for a comparative approach to the process of socialization into language through language and its use in interaction. The goal is to examine particular interactional practices in different cultural settings, to show how these proceed in situated interaction and how they influence both the development of children's communicative skills and their ability to think, feel, act, and interact like others in their social world. A snapshot of the potential contributions of the field was provided by a short article (Ochs and Schieffelin 1984), which tells "three developmental stories" illustrating why language socialization might be important to study across cultures.

While the field of language socialization in anthropology has been heavily influenced by Ochs and Schiefflin and their students and colleagues, it has multiple roots across disciplines. At about the same time that Ochs and Schieffelin were working on their ethnographies of small-scale societies, Heath (1983) considered language as a powerful socialization tool that varied across class and ethnicity in the southern United States, with important influences in education, and Miller (1982) was describing language socialization practices in lower-class homes in

Baltimore. Language socialization has matured over the past three decades into a truly cross-disciplinary research endeavor. Beyond its ability to address basic questions about language practices and socialization, it is used in a wide range of applied fields, most notably education in general and second-language learning in particular (see Duff and Hornberger 2008). There have been a number of significant reviews of the field that, from different perspectives, go into much more detail about the field's foundations and current issues than is possible here (e.g., Schieffelin and Ochs 1986a, b; Garrett and Barquedano-López 2002; Kulick and Shieffelin 2004; Ochs and Schieffelin 2008; Sterponi 2010; Duranti et al. 2011).

A distinct but complementary approach developed in work in the sociologically inspired framework of conversation analysis, which, while not for the most part explicitly comparative, is committed to the study of social interaction as social process via close examination of naturally occurring talk-in-interaction (Sidnell 2009); child language studies in this framework include Wootton (1997); Kidwell (2005).

These three independent but inter-communicating schools all take actual language use in its natural context as the data to be explained, and all have very different views of language from that of UG theorists, emphasizing language use (performance) and language as action, and interaction, rather than language as a capacity of individual human minds.

A rather different interest in child language comes from the insights it can provide into the evolution of language, and human evolution in general. The enormous variability of human languages (Evans and Levinson 2009) provides a major challenge to UG theorists. Suggestions for the evolution of language derive from recent developments in evolutionary biology and evolutionary anthropology (Sperber 1996, Whitehouse 2001; Chater and Christiansen 2010), and from comparative studies of human vs. ape cognition and communication (Tomasello 1999, 2008; Blake 2000), looking to apes and children to pinpoint aspects of the precursors to language. Other research focuses on specific aspects of the "interaction engine" – universals of conversational turn-taking (Stivers et al. 2009), mechanisms for repairing misunderstandings (Hayashi et al. 2013), and the semiotics of gesture (Kita 2003, 2009; Liszkowski et al. 2012). Informed by new views of what development consists of – a process of pruning neural connections (Whitehouse 2001) – this work provides provocative suggestions about the nature and origins of language, cooperation, and human cognition.

Given this diversity of disciplines, theoretical interests, and commitments, there is an immense literature on child language and its development. Here we take an interdisciplinary, international perspective, focusing on studies with cross-linguistic and culturally embedded approaches to how children learn language and culture. We provide a selective review emphasizing a number of themes: effects of variable language structures and of variable interactional styles on the acquisition of language, socialization through language into culturally shaped ways of thinking and feeling, and some methodological considerations in studying child language socialization.

8.2 The cultural process of acquiring a language

A child's task in learning a first language has several distinct aspects. She has to create phonological categories, in order to know what sound differences affect meaning differences in the speech around her. She has to segment the speech stream into recognizably recurring sound chunks (words, morphemes), map these sound sequences onto meanings, and create syntactic structures that allow her to say anything, including things she has never heard uttered. She must also do some social learning: she must learn to coordinate interaction with another, jointly attend with an interlocutor to a third thing (object, event), and understand that others have minds and intentions like her own and that the words people utter "refer" to things in the world (Carpenter *et al.* 1998; Tomasello 1999; Masataka 2003).

How do children achieve this? Do they use the same strategies and pursue the same timetable regardless of the structure of their language and the cultural setting? Research addressing these questions has boomed over the past thirty years, and much of it is organized around one core issue: How much is language an innate capacity? How much – and how – is its development shaped by the social and interactional environment of the learner? Proposed answers to these questions have evolved over these thirty years in response to evidence from children learning different languages. There are some 7,000 languages currently spoken in the world, and they vary enormously in both grammatical and semantic structure (Evans and Levinson 2009). Cultural patterns of interaction with children and cultural attitudes towards children as social beings also vary widely in different societies and indeed within subcultural groups within a society (LeVine and New 2008, Montgomery 2008). In this section we discuss a range of evidence bearing on how both language typology and cultural variations in caregiver–child interaction make a difference to children's language acquisition. (See Slobin and Bowerman 2007, Stoll 2009, Bowerman 2011, for more detailed discussions.)

8.2.1 Effects of language structure on language learning

Comparative evidence of the characteristics of early child language comes very largely from children learning Indo-European languages. There have been relatively few longitudinal studies of children's acquisition of non-European languages; these are mainly drawn from languages spoken in large-scale industrialized societies, for example Japanese, Korean, Mandarin Chinese, Hindi. There are even fewer studies of language learning in indigenous small-scale societies. These include work by Allen (1996) on Inuktitut (northern Quebec) and Fortescue and Olsen (1992) on Western Greenlandic, Pye (1992), Pye et al. (2007), Pfeiler (2007), Brown et al. (2013), and Pye and Pfeiler (2013) on Mayan and other Mesoamerican languages of Mexico and Guatemala, Demuth (1992; 2003) on Sesotho (South Africa), Kernan (1969) and Ochs (1988) on Samoan, Bavin (1992) on Warlpiri (Australia), Stoll et al. (2012) and Lieven et al. (in prep.) on Chintang (Nepal), and several on languages of Papua New Guinea, including Schieffelin (1990) on Kaluli, Kulick (1992) on Taiap (Gapun), and Rumsey et al. (2013) on Ku Waru. One centralized source summarizes the results of some of this work: Slobin's edited volumes (1985a,b, 1992a, 1997a,b) are an indispensable reference for what is known about the acquisition of widely different types of languages.

Here we provide examples of the kinds of language differences that have had an influence on universalist theories of language learning.

8.2.1.1 Phonological development

Work on phonological development suggests a strong biological component to the process. Infants' prelinguistic vocal development goes through an ordered set of stages, which look quite similar across languages (Menn and Stoel-Gammon 1996): attuning their auditory system to the sounds of the ambient language, producing coos and burbles coordinated with sounds produced by a caregiver, and babbling in identifiable CV syllables and intonation patterns. By the age of six months infants tune in to the sounds of the language they are exposed to, losing their inborn sensitivity to discriminate sounds that the language does not treat as separate phonemes (Kuhl 2009). Babbling begins around six months, and by the time first words are produced encompasses many of the syllable sounds of the ambient language. An early proposal by Jakobson (1968[1941]) made the universalist claim that the child's inventory of phonemic oppositions develops according to strict rules governed by the same universal hierarchy of features that organizes the phonological structure of adult languages. However, cross-linguistic empirical work on the acquisition of phonology has shown that children deviate in many ways from the universals Jakobson predicted. For example, there is no sharp discontinuity between babbling and early word learning, there is a great deal of individual variation rather than a fixed order for phonemes, and some phonological patterns rare in the language of adults are frequent in child language (Bowerman 2011: 595).

This conclusion is apparent from comparative work just on Indo-European languages. But we do not know the effect of very complex phonological systems on this process, or on the child's later language learning. Some languages have extremely complex sound systems, for example Yélî Dnye, spoken on Rossel Island off the coast of Papua New Guinea, has ninety phonemes including many multiply articulated consonants. Other languages have sounds rare in the world's languages, like the clicks of the Khoisan languages of southern Africa. We simply don't know how children approach these complex systems or whether they pose major difficulties for their learners.

8.2.1.2 First words

When it comes to children's first words, we know considerably more. Children start producing recognizable words sometime after their first birthday, but what those words sound like depends partly on the child's individual style – some children start by producing whole unanalyzed chunks, others single words – and partly on the language type. An isolating language like English favors single-word utterances with no grammatical morphemes, but children learning an agglutinative language like Turkish can have productive morphology even at the one-word stage. Children learning a polysynthetic language like Inuktitut often produce chunks of a long multi-morphemic word. Similarly, the phonological pattern of the language as stress-timed or syllable-timed makes a difference to the form of first words (Peters 1997).

Another issue raised by cross-linguistic variability is the status of nouns vs. verbs in children's early vocabulary. English-learning children start speaking with words that they use as object labels (nouns in adult speech), directional particles (e.g., "up"), deictics ("this") and adverbials ("more"). Once they have about fifty words, the vocabulary acquisition of many of them suddenly takes off with a "noun-spurt," adding nouns at a rapid rate while relying on a handful of verbs for several months (Bornstein *et al.* 2004). This "noun bias" pattern led Gentner (1982; Gentner and Boroditsky 2001) to propose a "natural categories" explanation for the primacy of nouns in early child speech: the concrete objects denoted by nouns are for the most part highly individuable, well bounded, and easily conceptualized, while verbs label relational notions connecting participants and actions or events (e.g., someone does something to something else) which are harder to grasp and indeed cross-linguistically more variable.

This position has been challenged by languages which appear to be verb-friendly for learners: e.g., Korean, Mandarin, and some Mayan languages. Children learning these languages do not show a noun spurt, but acquire verbs and nouns at an equal rate from very early on (Choi and Gopnik 1995, Tardif 1996; Choi 1997; Brown 1998a; de León 1999; Tardif *et al.* 2008). Both language typology (e.g., word order, and the possibility and frequency of argument-drop) and interactional style (especially interactional emphasis on activities rather than on object labeling) contribute to the likelihood of children finding a language to be verb-friendly.

8.2.1.3 Early morphology

Much child language research has focused on grammatical morphemes, which of course vary radically across languages. The first systematic comparison of their acquisition was by Roger Brown (1973), who studied the acquisition of fourteen early acquired morphemes in three children acquiring English, characterized the initial stages of language acquisition, and found that across children there was a highly stable order of acquisition of these morphemes, and that semantic and grammatical complexity, but not frequency in parental speech, predicted this order.

Brown's work set the pattern for language acquisition research and motivated others to link cross-linguistic patterns with developmental patterns in acquisition. Slobin's coordinated cross-linguistic study of nearly thirty languages (Slobin 1985a,b, 1992a, 1997a,b) is the most comprehensive assessment of the effects of different language structures on language learning to date. On the basis of this comparative data, Slobin (1985c) initially proposed that cognitive maturation drives language acquisition and accounts for children's "Basic Child Grammar" that grows out of two tendencies: (1) children follow "Operating Principles" (OPs) about surface forms of utterances and semantic coherence, allowing them to break into language, and (2) children orient to a core set of meanings that are "privileged" for grammatical forms.

Over the next decades, comparative work showed that there is no clear set of universally privileged grammatical meanings, and that children are highly sensitive to how grammatical meanings are semantically organized in the language they are learning. This motivated Slobin (2001) to retract his original claim, arguing instead that frequency and psycholinguistic processes in discourse can account for the child language patterns observed. He concluded further that the meanings of grammatical morphemes do not reflect cognitive predispositions, which instead are shaped by the psycholinguistic processes operating among fluent speakers.

Summing up the cross-linguistic findings, Slobin (1992b: 10–11) argued for the interplay of cognitive development (e.g., maturing "processing span" and short-term memory) and linguistic development over time. The timing of the acquisition of morphological forms is tied to their conceptual content – for example, early past tenses tend to have perfective/telic/resultative meanings, early locatives express basic notions of containment and support. When the range of grammatical options increases around the age of 3 to 4, errors increase, including paradigm simplification and over-regularization of irregulars (e.g., English *buyed* instead of *bought*) and double marking of morphemes (e.g., with both of two allophones). These errors reveal children's creative mental activity in formulating a grammar, going well beyond what they hear in input speech. Where local cues are clear, children are good at acquiring language-specific details like noun gender, noun-class prefixes, obligatory morpheme orders, and clear phonological cues to grammatical categories (e.g., Mandarin tone, Warlpiri vowel harmony). Typological patterning helps the child to home in on language-specific patterns (e.g., prefixing in Bantu languages, and the consonant frame plus V alternations of Hebrew).

This last conclusion is supported by a range of cross-linguistic data showing that constructions deemed difficult based on English child data appear early in child speech in some languages, for example early passives in Inuktitut (Allen and Crago 1996) and Sesotho (Demuth et al. 2010). The same is true for "applicative" constructions that add an argument: Demuth (1998) found that 2- to 3-year-old Sesotho children use the applicative with a full range of verb classes and demonstrate appropriate semantic knowledge of the construction (see also Brown 2007, for early Mayan ditransitives; Clark and Kelly 2006, for other constructions).

One difficulty of comparing morpheme acquisition across unrelated languages is that so many factors differ – sounds, morpheme order, meaning – it is hard to establish which ones have a crucial influence in constraining the acquisition order of grammatical morphemes. Evidence from studies *within* a language family – for example the Scandinavian languages (Strömqvist et al. 1995), or the Mayan languages (Pye et al. 2007; Brown et al. 2013) – allows much more detailed comparison of cognate affixes across the languages. These studies have shown that prosodic salience explains a large part of the variability in children's morpheme acquisition in closely related languages.

8.2.1.4 Semantics

Early analyses of the semantics of children's first utterances suggested considerable universality. First utterances in many different languages tend to express a limited set of notions relevant to early childhood experience: notions of action, agency, location, possession, and existence, recurrence, nonexistence, and disappearance of objects (Bowerman 2011). Here again the theoretical preference was cognition first, with the view that children first get concepts, then attach words to them. Yet over the years Bowerman and her colleagues (Choi and Bowerman 1991; Bowerman 1996; Choi et al. 1999; Bowerman and Choi 2001; Slobin et al. 2011) have shown clearly, for the spatial domain, that children very early tune in to the language-specific semantics of the words they use, well before the age of 2. Again, children's emergent category errors show that children are *active* learners, constructing a language system, not just parroting back what they hear. Their developmental progressions and error patterns are revealing evidence of the human blueprint for language (Bowerman 2011: 592).

8.2.1.5 Grammar

Much of the debate about what is innate vs. what must be learned has focused on the syntax/semantics interface, and how children learn to mark the arguments of verbs (agents, patients, recipients, etc.). Languages do this in one or some combinations of three basic ways: word order (as in English "John saw Mary" vs. "Mary saw John"), case marking on nouns (as in Turkish), and agreement marking on verbs (as in subject–verb agreement in Romance languages). Children learn to mark agent and patient roles with these markers generally by the end of their third year; the speed is influenced by the frequency and regularity of the markers, their distributional and semantic transparency, and how they relate to other linguistic cues (Lieven and Stoll 2009).

But how do children break into the system that links sounds with grammatical roles to establish a phrase-structure for an utterance? How do they decide which word or morpheme in the segmented speech stream instantiates the different syntactic functions (subject, object) and categories (N, V)? Two proposals have been made for innate knowledge which helps children to "bootstrap" into syntax/semantics mapping. One is Pinker's (1984) semantic bootstrapping hypothesis, which argues that meaning can predict syntax. Children are credited with innate knowledge of word classes and syntactic relations (N, V, NP, VP, and subject, object) and of rules that link thematic roles like agent and patient to syntactic functions such as subject and direct object, respectively. This helps guide the child to establish the basic word order of her language and the morphology associated with verbs vs. that for nouns, which in turn then can help the child identify instances of N, V, subject, object, even in those cases when the canonical semantics are absent. A related process can help children acquire subcategorization frames of verbs.

An alternative proposal is Gleitman's (1990) syntactic bootstrapping hypothesis, with syntax used to predict meaning. Assuming that syntax and semantics are systematically linked such that a verb's meaning projects how many arguments, and what type of arguments, the verb has, then children should be able to predict the meaning of a novel verb by noticing the different syntactic frames it occurs in. This narrowing of the hypothesis space allows the child to home in on the verb's more precise meaning by observing its use in different contexts. There is considerable evidence that young learners of English can indeed use syntax to guess a new verb's meaning (Fisher and Gleitman 2002 provide an overview), but it is not at all clear whether the linking information they draw on is innate or learned (Bowerman and Brown 2008b).

Both bootstrapping proposals require universal consistencies in the way languages link semantic functions to syntactic categories and relations. Several kinds of evidence cast doubt on this assumption. In a study based on detailed diary data of two English-learning children, Bowerman found that in their early productions the children did not match Pinker's expectations. They actually had more difficulty with verbs with canonical linking patterns like "hit" or "break" that according to Pinker should be easy to link, than with those that by Pinker's semantic bootstrapping account should be harder ("stay," "have"). There was also no evidence in the child data that correctly ordered strings for prototypical agent–patient relationships preceded those expressing other kinds of argument relations (e.g., theme-locative/source/goal) in child speech (Bowerman 1990, 2002: 525). Further, late errors that seem to be due to over-regularizations of statistically predominant linking patterns (e.g., "Can I fill some salt into the bear?"; Bowerman 2002: 524) suggest that these linking patterns are learned from the patterns in the input.

Non-Indo-European languages raise additional problems for semantic bootstrapping. Not all languages are readily analyzable as having a grammatical role of subject. Another difficulty is raised by ergative languages, which have a different pattern of linking from that of the familiar English "accusative" pattern with subjects of both transitive and intransitive sentences treated the same (e.g., receiving the same case marking). In ergative languages, the subject of an intransitive verb is treated like the object of a transitive verb, with the subject of a transitive verb receiving distinct treatment. Some languages are also syntactically ergative, with particular syntactic processes tied to the same collapsing of intransitive subject and transitive object arguments (van Valin 1992). Both types violate the link between agents and subjects, and hence present problems for bootstrapping theories. Cross-linguistic comparison of children learning some ten languages with ergative morphology has shown that ergative and accusative morphology are equally easy to learn and virtually error-free – children learning ergative languages do not extend ergative morphology to agentive intransitive subjects or make other errors which would be expected if they were assuming canonical linking (Pye 1990; Slobin 1992a; van Valin 1992; Allen 1996; Narasimhan 2005; Bavin and Stoll 2013).

Other difficulties are raised by a cross-linguistic project that examined verb argument structure and its implications for acquisition in fourteen languages (Bowerman and Brown 2008a), and showed that many languages do not have the reliable syntax/semantics mapping required for these bootstrapping proposals. For example, Wilkins (2008) demonstrates that the central Australian Aboriginal language Arrernte does not display the expected pattern that verbs of object transfer (e.g., "put") have different argument structures from verbs of perception (e.g., "see"). Arrernte has a three-argument frame for the verbs meaning both "see" and "put." Danziger (2008) shows that Mopan Maya does not display the predicted link between action word semantics and verbs – many single-participant action concepts like "run," "jump," "yell," are encoded as nouns (e.g., "My running continues," to mean "I run"). And Essegbey (2008) shows that the contrast between transitive and intransitive verbs in the Ghanaian language Ewe does not always correspond to one- vs. two-participant events; instead it reflects a single participant's degree of control over the action, with one argument indicating lack of control, two indicating control.

Such deviations from the patterns predicted by semantic and syntactic bootstrapping hypotheses undermine their applicability and suggest, instead, that linking regularities are gradually learned from the input, with neither semantic nor syntactic information unilaterally predicting the other (Bowerman 2011: 604).

8.2.1.6 Pragmatics, language usage

One realm in which there appears to be evidence for universal patterning is in conveying the information structure of an utterance – what is assumed in the context, what is made explicit. Based on Du Bois's (1987) discovery of a cross-linguistically general Preferred Argument Structure (PAS) pattern in adult speech, with agent arguments being assumed (and hence their arguments dropped or represented with a pronoun) much more frequently than those for objects and intransitive subjects, a number of child language researchers have looked at argument expression in non-European languages. Studies of PAS in child speech in Japanese (Clancy 1985), in Korean (Clancy 1993, 2003; Kim 1997), in Inuktitut (Allen and Schroder 2003), in Hindi (Narasimhan *et al.* 2005), and in Tzeltal Maya (Brown 2008) all found children following this PAS pattern by the age of 3 or 4, suggesting that already at this age children are sensitive to what their interlocutor can be taken to know about what they are saying. Language-specific factors are revealed in the contextual details constraining this pattern – for example verb-specific semantics in Tzeltal (Brown 2008), interacting contextual factors in Inuktitut (Allen 2008).

In another domain, a large-scale cross-linguistic study of narrative styles (Berman and Slobin 1994; Strömqvist and Verhoeven 2004) revealed the early influence of language-specific features on children's structuring of events in narratives. In over twenty languages children related the story depicted in Mercer Meyer's (1969) "Frog, where are you?" picture book, and their motion event descriptions were systematically compared. The findings are clear: children as young as 3 have already tuned in to language-specific ways of expressing the path in motion events – as "verb framed" (where the verb expresses the path, e.g., "he entered"), or "satellite framed" (where a satellite expresses the path, as in "he went in") (Talmy 1985). The conclusion is that languages have an effect on how children conceptualize and express events, revealing "thinking for speaking" (Slobin 1996) by age 3.

In short, cross-linguistic acquisition research over the past three decades has produced ample evidence for the influence of specific language features – in phonology, morphology, semantics, and syntax – on children's learning of those languages. This prompted Slobin (1996) to propose a typological bootstrapping hypothesis: if a language presents a pattern consistently and clearly, children will tune in early to that pattern, regardless of how the analogous phenomena are structured in other languages. An alternative perspective is suggested by the typological preference hypothesis (Gentner and Bowerman 2009), which proposes that the frequency of a pattern in the world's languages relates to children's ease of learning the pattern. Supporting evidence comes from the acquisition of spatial prepositions in two closely related languages (English, Dutch); Dutch has a typologically rare distinction in the categorizing of ON relations (contact/support), with one preposition (*op*) for canonical support from below and adhesion relations, a second preposition (*aan*) for situations of hanging and attachment, and a third (*om*) for situations of encirclement with contact. Bowerman and Gentner found that, indeed, Dutch children had more difficulty than English children in learning to express these semantic relations. This suggests that children are more predisposed toward some ways of categorizing space than others, and that cognition as well as language plays a role in children's semantic acquisition.

The comparative work reviewed here makes it clear that the theoretical focus on universals of language learning has led to unwarranted assumptions about the nature of language acquisition based solely on English and closely related languages. English is not a typical language in many ways, and the cultural contexts characteristic of middle-class Americans are certainly not typical of language learners in most of the world. Both biology and input influence language learning, and they interact in complex ways in the first few years of language development.

8.2.2 Effects of input and interaction

One of the great contributions of work on language socialization has been to document in detail the many kinds of differences in social interaction with small children, and the many different attitudes to childhood and childrearing, that occur around the world (e.g., Schieffelin and Ochs 1986b; Duranti et al. 2011). Childhood researchers in other disciplines have also produced evidence for cultural diversity in childrearing patterns and "input" or "child-directed" speech (CDS) (see e.g., Snow and Ferguson 1977; Snow 1993; Lieven 1994; Harkness and Super 1996; Blum-Kulka and Snow 2002; Gaskins 2006). There is variation in the amount of interaction with infants, the positioning of infants as interlocutors whose "utterances" are taken to be intentional communications (Ochs and Schieffelin 1984), amount of eye contact (Brown 2011), turn-taking practices (Takada 2005), and the kinds of participant structures into which infants are drawn (de León 1998, 2011), as well as in interlocutors' tendency to respond to the child's initiatives and for example to label the objects that infants point to (Brown 2011). This research makes it clear that the "child-centered" interaction style typical of middle-class American families is not present in many societies, where interaction is more "situation centered," with children being expected to fit into the activities of adults around them rather than being catered to in a child-focused way (Ochs and Schieffelin 1984).

The evidence that interactional practices with infants widely differ and are culturally shaped by beliefs about what infants need and what they can understand at different ages has challenged certain claims of developmental psychologists that there are universals in childhood experiences which are crucial to children's development of language. Here we review a few of these challenges.

8.2.2.1 Interactional style and Child-Directed Speech (CDS) with infants and small children

In response to UG claims about an innate Language Acquisition Device, several theorists have made the counter claim that children enter into language learning through interaction with others, highlighting in particular face-to-face interaction, a simplified baby-talk register (sometimes called "motherese"), baby games like pattycake that teach turn-taking and sequencing, and the use of direct address and eye contact as a way of securing the child's attention (Tomasello 1999, 2003; Masataka 2003; Gergely and Csibra 2006).

Yet studies of socialization have shown that, for many cultures, these strategies do not characterize caregiver–infant interaction, particularly in the first year of life. Face-to-face interaction with primary caregivers is much less common in cultures where children spend the day strapped on the back or held outward to engage with multiple interlocutors in addition to the primary caretaker (Martini and Kirkpatrick 1981; de León 1998). Simplified registers are not used universally in conversations with children (Pye 1986; Schieffelin 1990). Simple games are not always taught to children. And eye contact and direct address is in some cultures forbidden or discouraged (LeVine et al. 1996). In fact, in many cultures, until they start speaking children are not considered conversational partners. And in every case, children learn to talk.

Research on Western infants' development has also established a set of important developmental milestones that occur, beginning soon before the age of 12 months: babies reliably look where adults are looking, they use adults as social reference points (gazing at them to check what to do in uncertain situations), they act on objects like adults do, and they actively direct adult attention through indicative gestures and pointing (Carpenter et al. 1998). All of these are claimed to be essential prerequisites for coordinated interaction and later for referential communication.

To the limited extent that these developmental processes have been studied cross-culturally, they appear to follow a similar time course in the first year. In particular, the process of coming into joint attention with someone over a third object or event (the Referential Triangle, Tomasello 1999) also looks remarkably similar in different cultures, including those where interaction with young infants is minimal (Brown 2011; Callaghan et al. 2011; Liszkowski et al. 2012). That is, in radically different cultures infants by around the age of 12 months draw others into joint attention by index-finger pointing and uttering something like "ee." This has been taken as support for the view that these early developments necessary for human social interaction and language learning are part of our biological endowment, part of the "interaction engine" (Levinson 2006) that underlies our human communicative abilities.

How these new capacities get expressed in the second year of life and beyond is not as well documented, but, like caregiver behavior, there is evidence that children's patterns of social interaction vary widely across cultures. Perhaps the best studied example of the cultural expression of early communicative capacity is pointing. Yet the frequency with which small children point to draw an interlocutor into joint attention varies radically in different cultures, and the interactional consequences – the interlocutor's response (if any) – also differs (Brown 2011; Salomo and Liszkowski 2012). Very little infancy research has examined the contextualized sequential details of naturally occurring infant–caregiver interactions during the first year of life, nor have developmentalists done the careful comparative study of joint attention in interaction necessary to establish whether the processes observed in Western societies are visible in interactions with infants elsewhere.

Resources for drawing an interlocutor's attention everywhere include speech, gaze, body touching and postures, pointing gestures, and other actions, but it is well known that there are cross-cultural differences in adult deployment of these resources so we cannot assume that they are deployed in comparable ways with infants everywhere. To pin down the biologically driven vs. culturally shaped aspects of early social interaction we need a more qualitative and comparative approach, one that can provide evidence of the interactional processes through which infants come to coordinate attention in interaction in different cultural settings.

8.2.2.2 Child-directed vs. overheard speech

The developmentalists' assumption of child-centered and face-to-face interaction being the norm raises another issue: what counts as relevant input to the child? It has been shown that the amount and quality of "input" language – usually taken to be speech directly addressed to the child while caregiver and child are in joint attention – influences the child's early language and is directly correlated with vocabulary level at age 2;0 (Huttenlocher et al. 1991, 2010; Hoff 2003). A current debate concerns not just the amount of input but also its nature as directed to the child vs. other-directed (or "overheard") speech. In societies where small children are not often directly addressed, can listening to other people talking around them give them a comparable kind of input? The finding that differences in the quantity and quality of child-directed speech in different families predict the children's lexical development is in conflict with research findings in societies where small children are not often spoken to, yet children in these communities reach major milestones of language development at ages that are comparable with those of Western children (e.g., Crago et al. 1997, on Inuktitut children).

A possible resolution of this conundrum is suggested by arguments that, in a number of such societies – for example, Mayans (Chavajay and Rogoff 1999; Rogoff et al. 1993, 2003, 2007; Rogoff 2003; Gaskins and Paradise 2010), Samoans (Ochs 1988), and Kaluli (Schieffelin 1990) – infants are socialized from early on to attend keenly to what is going on all around them, rather than focusing intently on one activity. Such infants may pick up word meanings from hearing others use words, not necessarily in joint attention with them. We might then predict they would be attuned to attend to others' language and interactions, and be able to profit from overheard speech in ways unlike those of infants in societies where child-centered face-to-face interactions are the norm.

Initial results from research into the different efficacy of child-directed vs. overheard speech has produced mixed results. Some studies (e.g., Akhtar et al. 2001) found that 2-year-old children are equally good at learning words from overheard and directly addressed speech. Other studies have found that child-directed speech correlates with later vocabulary but overheard speech does not (for Spanish-speaking low SES families, see Weisleder and Fernald, in press; for Yucatec Mayan vs. American families, see Shneidman and Goldin-Meadow 2012; Shneidman et al., 2012). However, these studies treat all speech not directly addressed to the child as "overheard," ignoring the fact that much of that speech (e.g., of adults on the phone, or adult–adult conversations) is irrelevant to the child who may well not be actually "overhearing" it. Such studies need to have more sensitive assessments of what the child is potentially attending to (actually overhearing) and more subtle analysis of the target vocabulary set in the different settings, before this issue will be clarified.

Establishing that these kinds of differences make a difference, or not, to the language-learning process is greatly complicated by the fact that there are very large individual differences in children's rate and pattern of language acquisition (Bates et al. 1988; Snow 1993; Lieven 1997). With small sample sizes it is difficult to establish that any observed differences in language learning are due to cross-cultural differences in interactional style, amount or nature of input speech, as opposed to the normal pattern of individual variation. More and larger samples of child language data than have hitherto been feasible need to be obtained, in different cultural settings, in order for any cultural-linguistic differences to stand out from the background of individual differences.

8.2.2.3 Situational variation

A third kind of difference in the contexts for children's language learning arises in every cultural setting: there are different contexts requiring different kinds of language usage, speech appropriate to particular settings (e.g., home vs. church vs. school) or to particular kinds of relationships (e.g., to mother vs. granny vs. friends vs. the doctor or schoolteacher), and children have to learn to adapt their developing speech skills to the setting. The range of such contexts and their requirements varies enormously: in some cultural contexts this involves learning more than one language, in others learning an honorific register, in others particular kinds of interactional routines. Cultural expectations differ in how, and at what age, children are expected to show sensitivity to this kind of contextual variability.

There is relatively little work demonstrating effects of these kinds of situational variations on first-language learning (for bilingual learning see Pears 2010; for honorifics see Kim 1997 for Korean, Odden 2011 for Samoan). There may be effects of particular conversational styles: Brown (1998b), for example, argues that the Tzeltal Maya conversational practice of repeating part of the prior utterance – usually the verb – as a confirmatory response to it creates conditions that foreground the structure of the verb, helping small children to segment the verb root from surrounding material. The same kind of highlighting of the verb may occur in a different but comparable practice documented in Turkish child–caregiver interaction: caregivers express communicative intentions in multiple ways, using "variation sets" to rephrase them across turns (Küntay and Slobin 1996). Brown (2002) suggests further that the Tzeltal Maya routine practice of fake threats or lies (e.g., "Don't do that or I'll take you for an injection") – a widespread feature of caregiving in different cultures – may give Tzeltal children early access to the idea that utterances are not necessarily accurate descriptions of the world, and perhaps help them to an early recognition of indirect speech acts, lying, mistaken beliefs, and "theory of mind."

To date, these kinds of observations are only suggestive. More work is needed to pin down specific kinds of interaction patterns and input patterns to the particular effects they can be shown to have on language learning. One important goal is to identify recurring types of language socialization variables and create a typology of language socialization styles with predictions for their effects on vocabulary or on grammatical development.

We have reviewed two kinds of differences in the environments in which children learn language – differences in the language they are learning and differences in the input speech they hear around them – and considered their potential impact on language acquisition. We turn now to focus on how language use in interaction in a particular cultural setting socializes children into the local patterns and habits of speaking, of interacting, of thinking, and of feeling.

8.3 Socialization through language into the rest of culture

Socialization is a broad term used by various disciplines with slightly different emphases, but Maccoby's definition (2007: 13) would probably be accepted by most: "the process whereby naïve individuals are taught the skills, behavior patterns, values and motivations needed for competent functioning in the culture." Grusec and Hastings' definition in the same volume (2007: 1) emphasizes the active role of the learner (see below): "the way in which individuals are assisted in becoming members of one or more social groups," which involves "a variety of outcomes, including the acquisition of rules, roles, standards, and values across the social, emotional, cognitive and personal domains."

The field of language socialization asserts the centrality of language in this process. Its contributions to the study of socialization are substantial, but it often fails to be in dialogue with research on socialization that does not focus on language and talk in particular. In this section, we review the field's contributions to understanding the process of socialization through language into the rest of culture. However, we argue that there is value in distinguishing two distinct kinds of language socialization into a culturally specific worldview: *socialization through mastering language forms* and *socialization through participating in interaction*. The first of these is a more limited claim about how the internalization of specific language forms by becoming a speaker of a language leads to particular understandings; the second is a more general claim about the role of interaction in the socialization process and is the area that most closely parallels the socialization literature from other fields.

8.3.1 Socialization through mastering language forms

An inherent consequence of becoming competent speakers is being socialized in the values and practices of the culture itself, since cultural information about social roles, relationships, hierarchy, knowledge ownership, etc., is often indexed by the forms (e.g., lexicon and grammar) and uses of language (e.g., deictics, honorifics, address forms, and evidentials). Ochs (1988: 2–3) makes this central claim at the beginning of her book on Samoan language socialization: "Many formal and functional features of discourse carry sociocultural information, including phonological and morphosyntactic constructions, the lexicon, speech-act types, conversational sequencing, genres, interruptions, overlaps, gaps, and turn length. In other words, part of the meaning of grammatical and conversational structures is sociocultural."

The causal order of the effect of socialization is important here: rather than claiming that in order to be competent speakers of any language, children must have first internalized the full range of cultural meanings where the language is spoken, the claim is that cultural meanings are internalized *through becoming competent speakers*. This perspective echoes the claim of both Sapir (1949) and Whorf (1956), commonly known as *linguistic relativity*, that speakers of a particular language hold a common world view and patterns of habitual thought that have been shaped by that language (Lucy 1992a; Levinson 2012). In this sense, language – especially as a key component in interaction – can be thought of as a developmental *leading edge* of cultural understanding (Vygotsky 1978). As children master rules of grammar and discourse required for interaction, they must also construct the cultural meanings embedded in and indexed by these rules of language.

The claim about linguistic relativity being an important component of language socialization is central to the theory, and the evidence for the effects of language on thought in adults has grown since the field was founded. Unfortunately, there is still little evidence that demonstrates the developmental trajectory of such effects, but two examples demonstrate the promise of this area of research. Brown and Levinson (Brown and Levinson 1993, Levinson 2003) showed that Tzeltal Maya adults use an absolute ("geocentric") linguistic system of spatial reckoning. On a number of nonlinguistic tasks, Tzeltal adults consistently give responses in line with their absolute spatial system. Brown and Levinson also showed (2000, 2009) that Tzeltal children show early use of the absolute linguistic system of spatial language and display evidence for use of this absolute system in novel contexts by age 4–5. (Since they were tested in their home environments – with environmental cues to where "uphill/south and downhill/north" are, it is difficult to determine whether they had generalized an absolute system or simply learned to apply it in their home environment.) And Lucy (1992b) showed for adult speakers of Yucatec Maya and English that their language's treatment of grammatical number (+/– plural and +/– numeral classifiers) influenced how they responded on related nonverbal tasks. Subsequently, Lucy and Gaskins (2001, 2003) showed that children gave similar language-organized responses by age 9, but not before, even though they had mastered grammatical markings of number in their talk much earlier. Miller and Hoogstra (1992) have argued for the developmental study of "functional linguistic relativity" (Lucy: 1997) as well, looking at the impact of the uses of languages rather than their grammatical structures and the influences such uses have on affective and cognitive understandings.

The general claim about socialization through learning language forms was developed in the context of studying relatively stable, small-scale, monolingual societies. It becomes more complex when language socialization is expanded to include bilingual and multilingual communities with rapid culture change or recent culture contact. In such cases, socialization through language forms expands to include code-switching, language shift, syncretism, and other phenomena associated with contact between two or more languages and cultures (Kulick 1992, Schieffelin 1993, Rymes 2001, Garrett and Baquedano-López 2002, Bayley and Schecter 2003).

Children are socialized through language forms not only in their everyday lives at home, but in specialized contexts that rely on specific language registers. Perhaps the best example of such context-specific socialization (and certainly the most studied) is in the classroom (see Rymes 2008 and Genishi and Dyson 2009 for reviews). There are particular expectations in school settings for such things as reliance on verbal instruction (Philips 1983), quiz-like questions (Mehan 1979), narrative practices (Michaels 1991), and individual or shared responsibility for communication (Rogoff *et al.* 2007). How long it takes for a child to master such specialized registers depends on how similar or different they are from those they use in their homes and other everyday environments (Corsaro *et al.* 2002). Their degree of mastery, in turn, influences how successful their participation is in such contexts.

Thus, socialization occurs in part through the internalization of language forms and functions as children become competent speakers of particular languages and in particular contexts. This claim constitutes a unique contribution of language socialization to the more general understanding of the process of socialization. But the evidence so far is only preliminary and scattered. More research is needed on the developmental trajectory of linguistic relativity, the effects of more than one language on children's understanding of themselves and their worlds, and the impact of mastery of special linguistic registers on engagement in specialized contexts such as school.

8.3.2 Socialization through participating in interaction

In addition to being socialized into ways of thinking and behaving through making a commitment as a speaker to the cultural organization indexed in the language, there is a second, more activity-based sense of how children are socialized through language: cultural information is communicated through talk during everyday interactions. Children get socialized through interaction not only to language practices but also to the full range of cultural practices and their meanings.

Language as an intentional socializing tool – used for teaching – has been studied in its many forms of verbal feedback. The most direct verbal feedback mechanisms include praise, criticism, and verbal explanation. More indirect (but usually still intentional) mechanisms include questioning (Rogoff *et al.* 1993), teasing (Miller 1986), shaming (Lo and Fung 2012), and narrative (Miller *et al.* 2012). Even the absence of talk can be considered feedback, informative of social rules, as when children are ignored or not allowed to participate in conversations during everyday activities or special ceremonies, even though they are allowed to be present.

Parents in different cultures emphasize different verbal feedback mechanisms based on their ethnotheories about how children learn and develop and what needs to be taught. There are many studies about the particular cultural messages that are transmitted to children through talk. Two noteworthy examples are Briggs (1998), who shows how intimate conversations between a 3-year-old Inuit child and her close family members teach her to develop an Inuit sense of self and position herself in her social world, and Miller *et al.* (2012), who demonstrate how everyday narratives of transgressions co-constructed between children and their caregivers in the US and Taiwan are used to communicate very different messages in the two cultures.

Language also serves as an unintentional socializing tool during daily interactions. In all cultures, many – if not most – everyday events where children are present are primarily motivated not by socialization goals but from a desire to achieve a concrete goal through action, for example, to complete a work task. Since talk is an inherent part of such interactions, children can extract cultural information as interlocutors. In addition, children can be exposed to a wide range of cultural information from overheard adult conversations in context (e.g., learning about the legal system [Lancy 1996] or the significance of virginity [Fernea 1991]).

Beyond the use of language in interaction, language socialization researchers have embraced looking at the multi-modal aspects of communicative acts and demonstrating the integration of language with other modes of interaction, such as gesture, eye contact, body "language," and social positioning of bodies. Work on multi-modal communication in adults makes it clear that language shares the communicative burden with non-verbal modes of communication in complex semiotic relationships (Brown and Levinson 2005, Kita 2009, Rossano *et al.* 2009, Enfield 2009). With recent technological advances (e.g., high-quality portable videorecorders and eye-tracking machines), exploring how children are socialized into cultural activity through this broader definition of communication has become increasingly central to child language research. Examples include Kidwell (2005), Filipi (2009), Clark (2012). Studies of multi-modal interaction often exhibit the same methodological commitments of language socialization research more generally, especially a focus on looking at small samples of children using micro-analysis of interaction, and their interpretation of behavior is often well grounded in the ethnographic specificity of a single culture.

Despite the value of such multi-modal studies, it is important not to lose sight of the unique characteristic of verbal language as a socializing force – the ability of language to make denotational and indexical reference to objects, events, ideas, and emotions that lie beyond the immediate context. Using words, people can refer in more complex ways to such things as events happening in another time (past or future) or place, to contrary-to-fact propositions, irrealis (no commitment or uncertainty about existence) events, and metalanguage about itself. The range of things that can be communicated through interaction is vastly wider through language than through other modes of interaction, and this potential for promoting children's understanding by contrasting the present conditions with the past, future, or possible, is powerful. For instance, Taiwanese caregivers invite children through co-constructed narratives of past, shared events to generalize about moral behavior and to get children's commitment to different actions in the future (Miller et al. 2012). Decontextualized information such as that received (through language) in school, when put in dialectical tension with children's contextualized knowledge developed through experience, has been identified by Vygotsky (1987[1934]; 1978) as leading to a more complex cognitive organization of knowledge.

As the field of language socialization expands its commitment to multimodal interaction, there is a temptation to conceptualize the language socialization research agenda as being superior to all others for understanding all socialization and learning. Kulick and Schieffelin (2004: 350) argue that this perspective is appropriate: "Hence, language is not just one dimension of the socialization process, it is the most central and crucial dimension of that process. The language socialization paradigm makes the strong claim that any study of socialization that does not document the role of language in the acquisition of cultural practices is not only incomplete. It is fundamentally flawed."

This perspective has led the field of language socialization to exist somewhat isolated from other approaches to the study of socialization. Its practitioners do not integrate into their work those studies that fail to give a privileged position to language per se, even those that share their methodological commitment to ethnography (if not to micro-analysis of interaction) (e.g., in anthropology [LeVine et al. 1994, LeVine and New 2008], sociology [Corsaro 2010], and cultural psychology [Shweder et al. 2006]). In turn, despite the obvious centrality of language in the process of becoming a member of a cultural group, their work is often omitted in other socialization traditions. This segregation, in spite of common interests, is unfortunate for the field of socialization as a whole.

8.4 Three methodology comments

Here we offer methodological observations in three realms especially pertinent to the field of language socialization: the importance of focusing on children's own creative role in their socialization, the dilemma of breadth vs. depth in language acquisition and socialization research, and the pros and cons of two different styles of research, individual case studies vs. comparative studies. In all three realms, the issues we raise have to do with what counts as data in the study of child language and socialization.

8.4.1 Children's roles in socialization

One important question is this: Whose behavior influences the socialization process? Early models of socialization viewed children as passive recipients of information, given their immaturity and limited understanding (Clausen 1968). At the time that the field of language socialization developed in the 1970s and 1980s, new models of socialization were recognizing children's roles in the process, arguing that children not only receive the information offered but also interpret, improve, recreate, negate, resist, comment on, and transform it (Kuczynski and Parkin 2007). In the process, children's constructed understandings can vary from the original intentions of the socializing agents. However, while individual variation and generational change are now considered, socialization continues to be construed as primarily a normative process with the goal of producing members who function effectively in the group and are able to transmit the group's cultural practices to the next generation (Maccoby 2007).

Kulick and Schieffelin (2004) specifically articulated the role of children in language socialization; children are recognized as "active and selective agents" (Watson-Gegeo and Nielsen 2003: 165). Such attribution of agency to children is congruent with the view that socialization occurs through interaction in communities of practice (Bourdieu 1977, Giddens 1979). Children, as *legitimate peripheral participants* (Lave and Wenger 1991), are thought to learn about their shared world through shared activity. Recognizing that socialization occurs through participation in interaction highlights the dynamics of child agency, as children not only comply with, but also resist, expand, transform, or ignore the intent of their conversational partners (Gaskins et al. 1992), and studies that carefully consider detailed behavior in interaction abundantly illustrate this (e.g., Heath 1983, Sperry and Sperry 1996, Briggs 1998, De León 1998, 2012, Ochs and Capps 2001, Miller et al. 2012). From this perspective, using more intentionally child-centered methods (Clark 2010) in conjunction with current methodologies could be potentially productive.

In some cultures and contexts, children are permitted or encouraged to structure interaction and thereby become the active socializing force. In some "child-centered" cultures, children may use interactions with caregivers for their own purposes, e.g., interrupting or asking endless "why" questions (Callanan and Oakes 1992, Maratsos 2007) – as if the caregivers are being socialized by the children to prioritize the child's needs and interests. Orellana's (2009) work on bilingual children serving as translators for their monolingual parents provides a different kind of example of children using the host language as a socialization tool to teach their parents about the new culture, even as their parents are socializing the children using the home language. And in most cultures, children socialize each other through peer interactions (Corsaro 1992; Reynolds 2008; Goodwin and Kyratzis 2012).

When children exhibit non-canonical or unexpected behavior, it is difficult to distinguish among intentional assertion of power, expression of personal meaning, or merely incomplete understanding. While the first two are difficult enough to distinguish (Briggs 1998), there is also a lack of attention in much of the literature on language socialization to the milestones of human development, making it difficult to identify intentional and unintentional nonconformity in interaction. A partial list of potentially universal changes from infancy through adolescence that could influence socialization includes the following: becoming mobile, coming to share attention and intention with interlocutors, developing a "theory of mind" (an understanding that others' minds are distinct from one's own and may hold different beliefs about the world than one's own beliefs), a widening of children's social worlds beyond the family into the world of peers and cultural institutions, and a flowering of interest in potential sexual partners. As is the case in much of the ethnography of childhood, in most studies of language socialization such developmental factors are missing or left as implicit and unanalyzed.

8.4.2 Balancing breadth and depth

Kulick and Schieffelin (2004) argue that language socialization research must meet three criteria: (1) be ethnographies of speaking to and by a small sample of children in the context of their everyday lives, (2) use a longitudinal design, documenting change in children's behavior and understanding, and (3) show how children come to acquire (or not) linguistic practices and related cultural practices over time and across contexts. Ochs' (1988) and Schieffelin's (1990) original studies (and many others that followed) meet these criteria. In addition, they relied on micro-analysis of particular interactions. Ochs and Schieffelin (1984) and Schieffelin and Ochs (1986a) also emphasized the value of comparing systems of language socialization across cultures. Taken together, their approach reflects Vygotsky's three levels of analysis (1987[1934]) needed to understand developmental change: micro-analysis of change moment-to-moment, longitudinal analysis of change over developmental time, and historical analysis of change in societies (or, as in this case, across cultures).

Such work is extremely intensive and laborious. Understandably, most research in the field has not managed to meet these criteria. Instead, many studies preserve only one of these methodological approaches: the micro-analysis of naturally occurring interactions of short durations. Such analysis is often interpreted by a particular linguistic or cultural characteristic that is not generated by the study itself. Garrett and Baquedano-Lopez have called this micro-analysis "empirically grounded access to broader issues of sociocultural reproduction and transformation" (2002: 342).

These studies can provide great insight into the complexity of conversation, and the subtle coordination with other modes of interaction. They demonstrate what *can* happen, but taken alone, without evidence that the interactions analyzed represent consistent patterns in everyday behavior, they may not represent what *does* happen repeatedly in the course of daily interactions that results in socialization. Since the theory of language socialization relies heavily on practice theory, it is crucial that events singled out for micro-analysis are representative of patterns in everyday behavior. One solution to this problem is to combine a broad sampling of the distribution of types of behaviors with more in-depth analysis of specific types that appear frequently. Brown (2011) and Miller *et al.* (2012) provide examples of this approach. Another solution is to identify specific recurrent cultural events and focus the analysis on them, e.g., "dinnertime" (Ochs and Capps 2001, Pontevorvo *et al.* 2001), or playground behavior (Goodwin 2006).

Further, researchers need to be able to have their data speak to two more areas. It must inform interpretations about *why* certain kinds of interactions happen – that is, they need to be able to provide a "thick explanation" that takes into account "all relevant and theoretically salient micro- and macro-contextual influences that stand in systematic relationship to the behavior or events" that are to be explained (Watson-Gegeo 1992: 54). And they must be able to demonstrate how patterns in daily interactions lead to cultural competencies over time (or not). While a full monograph can provide a rich ethnographic context for the specific behaviors being analyzed in detail and demonstrate their consequences over time, it is more difficult to do so in a shorter, more focused analysis that stands alone as a chapter or article. Such work runs the risk of being so focused on the analysis of interaction that it is unable to address adequately the socialization outcomes of the recurrence of such experiences.

8.4.3 Case studies vs. comparison

A third methodological issue is how to combine the rich description of a single culture's socialization practices with meaningful comparison of such practices across cultures. While field-research-based cross-cultural comparison has been carried out on childhood and parenting (e.g., Whiting and Whiting 1975; Munroe *et al.* 1984; Harkness *et al.* 2011), this is a much less common strategy in language socialization research. It has occasionally been done through collaboration, either loosely (e.g., Ochs and Schieffelin 1984), through an integrated research partnership (Miller *et al.* 2012), or by a single researcher working in two communities (e.g., Heath 1983, Brown 2011). Because systematic comparison requires quantification, this goal is often in direct competition with achieving the ethnographic depth discussed above. By and large, the field remains one of individual case studies. The power of those comparative studies that do exist, however, suggest that this should be a strategy used more in the future. Inhibitions on such studies involve problems not only of competing theoretical perspectives but also of available resources.

8.5 Conclusions

Why study child language development? There are different answers from the point of view of developmental psychology, of anthropology, of linguistics, and of social interaction. There are many disagreements about what the interesting phenomena are, about theory, and about method. But it is clear that major theoretical issues are at stake: the nature of language, the cultural flexibility of child development, the role of input in language acquisition, the relation of language and cognition, whether or not there is a unified developmental outcome for cognition, the effects of interactional processes on linguistic structure and on cognitive development, and the evolution of human nature.

Because the stakes are so high, it is important to ask a second question: how is child language development best studied? Linguistic anthropologists have a unique two-part contribution to the answer to this question. They have focused on the importance of documenting the variability of linguistic structure and of caregiver–child interactions across different cultures and demonstrating when and how linguistic and cultural differences matter in the language acquisition process. Equally important, they have focused on how children's use of linguistic structures and their interactions with others lead them to become competent members of a social group. Language and the interactions in which its use is embedded are the formative locus for culture, recreated and revised by each generation via socialization.

The insights gained by the study of children's language socialization are not limited to addressing questions about how children develop. Because children are novices learning the system, language socialization is a window into cultural meanings. Looking at how language is used to children and by children as they develop highlights some of the central cultural characteristics of the communicative system – for example, how honorifics are used and acquired illuminates which social categories are most basic. Similarly, one can see the cultural importance of particular beliefs and values by what gets emphasized (or ignored) in talk to, with, and about children. Because children are not yet competent participating members of the group, many things that are not marked in adult interactions are marked for children through selection, repetition, elaboration, and explicitness. Through the dual processes of accommodating to children's lack of understanding and helping them learn, adults reveal not only their cultural understandings about themselves and the world, but also their theories about the process of acquiring those understandings: how the self is constructed, how the social graces are acquired, how humans come to relate to the world.

References

Akhtar, N., J. Jipso, and M. A. Callanan. 2001. Learning Words through Overhearing. *Child Development* 72(2): 416–30.

Allen, S. E. M. 1996. *Aspects of Argument Structure Acquisition in Inuktitut*. Amsterdam: John Benjamins.

  2008. Interacting Pragmatic Influences on Children's Argument Realization. In *Crosslinguistic Perspectives on Argument Structure: Implications for Learnability*, ed. M. Bowerman and P. Brown, 191–210. Mahwah, NJ: Lawrence Erlbaum.

Allen, S. E. M., and M. Crago. 1996. Early Passive Acquisition in Inuktitut. *Journal of Child Language* 23: 129–55.

Allen, S. E. M., and H. Schroder. 2003. Preferred Argument Structure in Early Inuktitut Spontaneous Speech Data. In *Preferred Argument Structure: Grammar as Architecture for Function*, ed. J. W. Du Bois, L. E. Kumpf, and W. J. Ashby, 301–38. Amsterdam: John Benjamins.

Ambridge, B., and E. V. M. Lieven. 2011. *Child Language Acquisition: Contrasting Theoretical Approaches*. Cambridge: Cambridge University Press.

Barlow, M., and S. Kemmer. 2000. *Usage-Based Models of Grammar*. Stanford: CSLI Publications.

Bates, E. 1976. *Language and Context: The Acquisition of Pragmatics*. New York: Academic Press.

Bates, E., I. Bretherton, and L. Snyder. 1988. *From First Words to Grammar: Individual Differences and Dissociable Mechanisms*. New York: Cambridge University Press.

Bavin, E. 1992. The Acquisition of Warlpiri. In *The Crosslinguistic Sudy of Language Acquisition*, ed. D. I. Slobin, Vol. 3, 309–71. Cambridge: Cambridge University Press.

  ed. 2009. *The Cambridge Handbook of Child Language*. New York: Cambridge University Press.

Bavin, E., and S. Stoll, eds. 2013. *Acquisition of Ergative Structures*. Amsterdam: Benjamins.

Bayley, R., and S. R. Schecter, eds. 2003. *Language Socialization in Bilingual and Multilingual Societies*. Bristol: Multilingual Matters.

Behrens, H. 2009. Usage-based and Emergentist Approaches to Language Acquisition. *Linguistics* 47(2): 383–411.

Berman, R., and D. I. Slobin, eds. 1994. *Relating Events in Narrative: A Crosslinguistic Developmental Study*. Hillsdale, NJ: Erlbaum.

Blake, J. 2000. *Routes to Child Language: Evolutionary and Developmental Precursors*. Cambridge: Cambridge University Press.

Blount, B. G. 1969. Acquisition of Language by Luo Children. Working paper no. 19, University of California, Berkeley. Language-Behavior Research Laboratory.

Blum-Kulka, S., and C. E. Snow, eds. 2002. *Talking to Adults: The Contribution of Multi-party Talk to Language Acquisition*. Mahwah, NJ: Erlbaum.

Bornstein, M. H., L. R. Cote, S. Maital, K. Painter, S-Y. Park, L. Pascual, M.-G. Pecheux, J. Ruel, P. Venute, and A. Vyt. 2004. Cross-linguistic Analysis of Vocabulary in Young Children: Spanish, Dutch, French, Hebrew, Italian, Korean, and American English. *Child Development* 75(4): 1115–39.

Bourdieu, P. 1977. *Outline of a Theory of Practice*. Cambridge: Cambridge University Press.

Bowerman, M. 1981. Language Development. In *Handbook of Cross-cultural Psychology*, vol. 4, ed. H. C. Triandis and A. Heron, 93–185. Boston: Allyn and Bacon.

  1990. Mapping Thematic Roles onto Syntactic Functions: Are children helped by innate linking rules? *Linguistics* 28: 1253–90.

  1996. Learning How to Structure Space for Language: A cross-linguistic perspective. In *Language and Space*, ed. P. Bloom, M. Peterson, L. Nadel, and M. Garret, 385–436. Cambridge, MA: MIT Press.

  2011. Linguistic Typology and First Language Acquisition. In *The Oxford Handbook of Linguistic Typology*, ed. J. J. Song, 591–617. Oxford: Oxford University Press.

Bowerman, M., and Brown, P., eds. 2008a. *Crosslinguistic Perspectives on Argument Structure: Implications for Learnability*. Mahwah, NJ: Lawrence Erlbaum.

  2008b. Introduction. In *Crosslinguistic Perspectives on Argument Structure: Implications for Learnability*, ed. M. Bowerman and P. Brown, 1–26. Mahwah, NJ: Lawrence Erlbaum.

Bowerman, M., and S. Choi. 2001. Shaping Meanings for Language: Universal and language specific in the acquisition of spatial semantic categories. In *Language Acquisition and Conceptual Development*, ed. M. Bowerman and S. C. Levinson, 475–511. Cambridge: Cambridge University Press.

Briggs, J. L. 1998. *Inuit Morality Play: The Emotional Education of a Three-Year-Old*. New Haven, CT: Yale University Press.

Brown, P. 1998a. Children's First Verbs in Tzeltal: Evidence for an early verb category. *Linguistics* 36(4): 713–53.

  1998b. Conversational Structure and Language Acquisition: The role of repetition in Tzeltal adult and child speech. *Journal of Linguistic Anthropology* 8(2): 197–221.

  2002. Everyone Has to Lie in Tzeltal. In *Talking to Adults; The Contribution of Multiparty Discourse to Language Acquisition*, ed. S. Blum-Kulka and C. Snow, 241–75. Mahwah, NJ: Lawrence Erlbaum.

  2007. Culture-specific Influences on Semantic Development: Acquiring the Tzeltal 'benefactive' construction. In *Learning Indigenous Languages: Child Language Acquisition in Mesoamerica*, ed. B. B. Pfeiler, 119–54. Berlin: Mouton de Gruyter.

2008. Verb Specificity and Argument Realization in Tzeltal Child Language. In *Crosslinguistic Perspectives on Argument Structure: Implications for Language Acquisition*, ed. M. Bowerman and P. Brown, 167–89. Mahwah, NJ: Lawrence Erlbaum.

2011. The Cultural Organization of Attention. In *Handbook of Language Socialization*, ed. A. Duranti, E. Ochs, and B. B. Schieffelin, 29–55. Oxford: Blackwells.

Brown, P., B. Pfeiler, L. de León, and C. Pye. 2013. The Acquisition of Agreement in Four Mayan Languages. In *The Acquisition of Ergativity*, ed. E. L. Bavin and S. Stoll, 271–306. Amsterdam: Benjamins.

Brown, P., and S. C. Levinson. 1993. Linguistic and Non-linguistic Coding of Spatial Arrays: Explorations in Mayan cognition. Cognitive Anthropology Research Group Working Paper 24, Max Planck Institute for Psycholinguistics.

2000. Frames of Spatial Reference and their Acquisition in Tenejapan Tzeltal. In *Culture, Thought, and Development*, ed. L. Nucci, G. Saxe, and E. Turiel, 167–97. Mahwah, NJ: Lawrence Erlbaum.

2005. Comparative Feedback: Cultural shaping of response systems in interaction. Paper presented at the Annual Meetings of the American Anthropological Association, Washington, DC.

2009. Language as Mind Tools: Learning how to think through speaking. In *Crosslinguistic Approaches to the Psychology of Language: Research in the Tradition of Dan Slobin*, ed. J. Guo, E. Lieven, N. Budwig, S. Ervin-Tripp, K. Nakamura, and S. Ozcaliskan, 451–64. Mahwah, NJ: Lawrence Erlbaum.

Brown, R. 1973. *A First Language: The Early Stages*. Cambridge, MA: Harvard University Press.

Callaghan, T., H. Moll, H. Rakoczy, F. Warneken, U. Liszkowski, T. Behne, and M. Tomasello. 2011. *Early Social Cognition in Three Cultural Contexts*. Oxford: Wiley-Blackwell.

Callanan, M., and L. Oakes. 1992. Preschoolers Questions and Parents' Explanations: Causal thinking in everyday activity. *Cognitive Development* 7: 213–33.

Carpenter, M, K. Nagell, and M. Tomasello. 1998. Social Cognition, Joint Attention, and Communicative Competence from 9 to 15 Months of Age. *Monographs of the Society for Research in Child Development* 63 (4, Serial No. 255).

Chater, N., and M. H. Christiansen. 2010. Language Acquisition Meets Language Evolution. *Cognitive Science* 34: 1131–57.

Chavajay, P., and B. Rogoff. 1999. Cultural Variation in Management of Attention by Children and their Caregivers. *Developmental Psychology* 35(4): 1079–90.

Choi, S. 1997. Language-specific Input and Early Semantic Development: Evidence from children learning Korean. In *The Crosslinguistic Study of Language Acquisition*, ed. D. I. Slobin, Vol. 5, 41–134. Hillside, NJ: Erlbaum.

Choi, S., and M. Bowerman. 1991. Learning to Express Motion Events in English and Korean – The influence of language-specific lexicalization patterns. *Cognition* 41: 83–121.

Choi, S., and A. Gopnik. 1995. Early Acquisition of Verbs in Korean: A cross-linguistic study. *Journal of Child Language* 22(3): 497–529.

Choi, S., L. McDonough, M. Bowerman, and J. M. Mandler. 1999. Early Sensitivity to Language-specific Spatial Categories in English and Korean. *Cognitive Development* 14: 241–68.

Clancy, P. 1985. The Acquisition of Japanese. In *The Crosslinguistic Study of Language Acquisition*, Vol. 1, ed. D. I. Slobin, 373–524. Hillside, NJ: Erlbaum.

  1993. Preferred Argument Structure in Korean Acquisition. In *Proceedings of the 25th Annual Child Language Research Forum*, ed. E. V. Clark, 307–14. Stanford, CA: Center for the Study of Language and Information (CSLI) Publications.

  2003. The Lexicon in Interaction: Developmental origins of Preferred Argument Structure in Korean. In *Preferred Argument Structure: Grammar as Architecture for Function*, ed. J. W. Du Bois, L. E. Kumpf, and W. J. Ashby, 81–108. Amsterdam: John Benjamins.

Clark, C. D. 2010. *In a Younger Voice: Doing Child-Centered Qualitative Research*. Oxford: Oxford University Press.

Clark, E. V. 2001. Grounding and Attention in Language Acquisition. In *Papers from the 37th Meeting of the Chicago Linguistic Society*, Vol. 1, ed. M. Andronis, C. Ball, H. Elston, and S. Neuvel, 95–116. Chicago: Chicago Linguistic Society.

  2012. Children, Conversation, and Acquisition. In *Cambridge Handbook of Psycholinguistics*, ed. M. Spivey, K. McRae, and M. Joanisse, 573–88. Cambridge: Cambridge University Press.

Clark, E. V., and Kelly, B., eds. 2006. *Constructions in Acquisition*. Stanford, CA: CSLI Publications.

Clausen, J. A. 1968. A Historical and Comparative View of Socialization Theory and Research. In *Socialization and Society*, ed. J. A. Clausen, 18–72. Boston, MA: Little, Brown.

Corsaro, W. A. 1992. Interpretive Reproduction in Children's Peer Cultures. *Social Psychology Quarterly* 55: 160–77.

  2010. *The Sociology of Childhood*. New York: Russell Sage.

Corsaro W. A., L. Molinary, and K. Brown Rosier. 2002. Zena and Carlotta: Transition narratives and early education in the United States and Italy. *Human Development* 45: 323–48.

Crago, M. B., Allen, S. E. M., and Hough-Eyamie, W. P. (1997). Exploring Innateness through Cultural and Linguistic Variation. In *The Biological Basis of Language*, ed. M. Gopnik, 70–90. Oxford: Oxford University Press.

Danziger, E. 2008. A Person a Place or a Thing? Whorfian consequences of syntactic Bootstrapping in Mopan Maya. In *Crosslinguistic Perspectives* on *Argument Structure: Implications for Learnability*, ed. M. Bowerman and P. Brown, 29–48. Mahwah, NJ: Lawrence Erlbaum.

Demuth, K. 1992. The Acquisition of Sesotho. In *The Crosslinguistic Study of Language Acquisition*, Vol. 3, ed. D. I. Slobin, 557–638. Hillside, NJ: Erlbaum.

———. 1998. Argument Structure and the Acquisition of Sesotho Applicatives. *Linguistics* 36(4): 781–806.

———. 2003. The Acquisition of Bantu Languages. In *The Bantu Languages*, ed. D. Nurse and G. Philippson, 209–22. Surrey, England: Curzon Press.

Demuth, K., F. Moloi, and M. Machebane. 2010. 3-yr.-olds Comprehension, Production, and Generalization of Sesotho Passives. *Cognition* 115: 238–251.

Du Bois, J. 1987. The Discourse Basis of Ergativity. *Language* 64: 805–55.

Duff, P., and N. H. Hornberger. 2008. *Encyclopedia of Language and Education: Language Socialization*, Vol. 8. Berlin: Springer.

Duranti, A., E. Ochs, and B. Schieffelin, eds. 2011. *The Handbook of Language Socialization*. Malden, MA: Wiley-Blackwell.

Enfield, N. J. 2009. *The Anatomy of Meaning: Speech, Gesture, and Composite Utterances*. Cambridge: Cambridge University Press.

Essegbey, J. 2008. Intransitive Verbs in Ewe and the Unaccusitivity Hypothesis. In *Crosslinguistic Perspectives on Argument Structure: Implications for Learnability*, ed. M. Bowerman and P. Brown, 213–30. Mahwah, NJ: Lawrence Erlbaum.

Evans, N., and S. C. Levinson. 2009. The Myth of Language Universals: Language diversity and its importance for cognitive science. *Behavioral and Brain Sciences* 32(5): 429–92.

Fernea, E. 1991. Muslim Middle East. In *Children in Historical and Comparative Perspective*, ed. J. M. Hawes and N. R. Hiner, 447–70. Westport: Greenwood Press.

Filipi, A. 2009. *Toddler and Parent Interaction: The Organisation of Gaze, Pointing and Vocalisation*. Amsterdam: John Benjamins.

Fisher, C., and L. Gleitman. 2002. Language Acquisition. In *Stevens' Handbook of Experimental Psychology, Vol 1: Learning and Motivation*, ed. C. R. Gallistel, 445–96. New York: Wiley.

Fortescue, M., and L. Olsen. 1992. The Acquisition of West Greenlandic. In *The Crosslinguistic Study of Language Acquisition*, Vol. 3, ed. D. I. Slobin, 111–219. Hillside, NJ: Erlbaum.

Garrett, P. B., and P. Baquedano-Lopez. 2002. Language Socialization: Reproduction and continuity, transformation and change. *Annual Review of Anthropology* 31: 339–61.

Gaskins, S. 2006. Cultural Perspectives on Infant-Caregiver Interaction. In *Roots of Human Sociality: Culture, Cognition and Interaction*, ed. N. J. Enfield and S. C. Levinson, 279–98. Oxford: Berg Publishers.

Gaskins, S., P. Miller, and W. Corsaro. 1992. Theoretical and Methodological Perspectives in the Interpretative Study of Children.

In *The Production and Reproduction of Children's Worlds: Interpretive Methodologies for the Study of Childhood Socialization*, ed. W. Corsaro and P. J. Miller, 5–23. San Francisco, CA: Jossey-Bass, Inc.

Gaskins, S., and R. Paradise. 2010. Learning through Observation. In *The Anthropology of Learning in Childhood*, ed. D. F. Lancy, J. Bock, and S. Gaskins, 85–117. Lanham, MD: Alta Mira Press.

Genishi, C., and A. H. Dyson. 2009. *Children, Language and Literacy: Diverse Learners in Diverse Times*. New York: Teachers College Press.

Gentner, D. 1982. Why Nouns are Learned Before Verbs: Linguistic relativity versus natural partitioning. In *Language development*, Vol. 2: *Language, Thought, and Culture*, ed. S. A. Kuczaj, 301–34. Hillsdale, NJ: Erlbaum.

Gentner, D., and L. Boroditsky. 2001. Individuation, Relativity and Early Word Learning. In *Language Acquisition and Conceptual Development*, ed. M. Bowerman and S. Levinson, 215–56. Cambridge: Cambridge University Press.

Gentner, D., and M. Bowerman. 2009. Why Some Spatial Semantic Categories are Harder to Learn than Others: The typological prevalence hypothesis. In *Crosslinguistic Approaches to the Psychology of Language: Research in the Tradition of Dan Isaac Slobin*, ed. J. Guo, E. Lieven, N. Budwig, S. Ervin-Tripp, K. Nakamura, and S. Ozcaliskan, 465–80. New York: Psychology Press.

Gergely, G., and G. Csibra. 2006. Sylvia's Recipe: The role of imitation and pedagogy in the transmission of cultural knowledge. In *Roots of Human Sociality: Culture, Cognition and Interaction*, ed. N. Enfield and S. C. Levinson, 229–55. Oxford: Berg.

Giddens, A. 1979. *Central Problems in Social Theory: Action, Structure, and Contradiction in Social Analysis*. Berkeley, CA: University of California Press.

Gleitman, L. 1990. The Structural Source of Verb Meanings. *Language Acquisition* 1: 3–55.

Goodwin, M. 2006. *The Hidden Life of Girls: Games of Stance, Status, and Exclusion*. Oxford: Blackwell Publishing.

Goodwin, M. H., and A. Kyratzis. 2012. Peer Language Socialization. In *The Handbook of Language Socialization*, ed. A. Duranti, E. Ochs, and B. B Schieffelin, 365–90. Malden, MA: Wiley-Blackwell.

Grusec, J. E., and P. D. Hastings. 2007. Introduction. In *Handbook of Socialization: Theory and Research*, ed. J. P Grusec and P. D Hastings, 1–9. New York: Guilford Press.

Guasti, M. T. 2004. *Language Acquisition: The Growth of Grammar*. Cambridge, MA: MIT Press.

Gumperz, J. J., and D. Hymes, eds. 1964. The Ethnography of Communication. *American Anthropologist* 66:6, part 2 (Special Issue).

Harkness, S., and C. Super, eds. 1996. *Parents' Cultural Belief Systems: Their Origins, Expressions, and Consequences*. New York: The Guilford Press.

Harkness, S., P. O. Zylicz, C. M. Super, B. Welles-Nyström, M. R. Bermúdez, S. Bonichini, U. Moscardino, and C. J. Mavridis. 2011. Children's Activities and their Meanings for Parents: A mixed-methods study in six Western cultures. *Journal of Family Psychology* 25(6): 799–813.

Hayashi, M., G. Raymond, and J. Sidnell, eds. 2013. *Conversational Repair and Human Understanding*. Cambridge: Cambridge University Press.

Heath, S. Brice 1983. *Ways with Words: Language, Life, and Work in Communities and Classrooms*. New York: McGraw-Hill

Hoff, E. 2003. The Specificity of Environmental Influence: Socioeconomic status affects early vocabulary development via maternal speech. *Child Development* 74(5): 1368–78.

Huttenlocher, J., W. Haight, A. Bryk, M. Seltzer, and T. Lyons. 1991. Vocabulary Growth: Relation to language input and gender. *Developmental Psychology* 27: 236–48.

Huttenlocher, J., H. Waterfall, M. Vasilyeva, J. Vevea, and L. V. Hedges. 2010. Sources of Variability in Children's Language Growth. *Cognitive Psychology* 61(4): 343–65.

Jakobson, R. 1968 [1941]. *Child Language, Aphasia, and Linguistic Universals*. Janua Linguarum 72. The Hague: Mouton.

Kernan, K. K. 1969. *The Acquisition of Language by Samoan Children*. Unpublished PhD dissertation. Berkeley, CA: Language Behavior Research Laboratory, University of California.

Kidwell, M. 2005. Gaze as Social Control: How very young children differentiate "the look" from "a mere look" by their adult caregivers. *Research on Language and Social Interaction* 38(4): 417–49.

Kim, Y. 1997. The Acquisition of Korean. In *The Crosslinguistic Study of Language Acquisition*, Vol. 4, ed. D. I. Slobin, 335–443. Hillsdale, NJ: Erlbaum.

Kita, S. 2003. *Pointing: Where Language, Culture and Cognition Meet*. Hillsdale, NJ: Erlbaum.

2009. Cross-cultural Variation of Speech-accompanying Gesture: A review. *Language and Cognitive Processes* 24(2): 145–67.

Kuczynski, L., and C. M. Parkin. 2007. Agency and Bidirectionality in Socialization: Interactions, transactions, and relational dialectics. In *Handbook of Socialization: Theory and Research*, ed. J. P. Grusec and P. D. Hastings, 259–83. New York: Guilford.

Kuhl, P. K. 2009. Early Language Acquisition: Phonetic and word learning, neural substrates, and a theoretical model. In *The Perception of Speech: From Sound to Meaning*, ed. B. Moore, L. Tyler, and W. Marslen-Wilson, 103–31. Oxford: Oxford University Press.

Kulick, D. 1992. *Language Shift and Cultural Reproduction: Socialization, Self, and Syncretism in a Papua New Guinea Village*. Cambridge: Cambridge University Press.

Kulick, D., and B. Schieffelin. 2004. Language Socialization. In *A Companion to Linguistic Anthropology*, ed. A. Duranti, 349–68. Malden, MA: Blackwell.

Küntay, A., and D. I. Slobin. 1996. Listening to a Turkish Mother: Some puzzles for acquisition. In *Social Interaction, Social Context, and Language: Essays in Honor of Susan Ervin-Tripp*, ed. D. I. Slobin, J. Gerhardt, A. Kyratzis, and J. Guo, 265–86. Hillsdale, NJ: Erlbaum.

Lancy, D. F. 1996. *Playing on the Mother Ground: Cultural Routines for Children's Development*. New York: Guilford.

Lave, J., and E. Wenger. 1991. *Situated Learning: Legitimate Peripheral Participation*. Cambridge: University of Cambridge Press.

León, L. de. 1998. The Emergent Participant. *Journal of Linguistic Anthropology* 8(2): 131–61.

  1999. Verb Roots and Caregiver Speech in Early Tzotzil Acquisition. In *Cognition and Function in Language*, ed. B. A. Fox, D. Jurafsky, and L. A. Michaelis, 99–119. Stanford, CA: Stanford University Center for Language and Information.

  2011. Language Socialization and Multiparty Participation Frameworks. In *Handbook of Language Socialization*, ed. A. Duranti, E. Ochs, and B. B Schieffelin, 81–111. Oxford: Blackwells.

  2012. "The j'ik'al is coming!" Triadic directives and emotion in the socialization of Zinacantec Mayan children. In *Maya Daily Lives. Proceedings of the 13th European Maya Conference, Paris, December 5–6, 2008*, ed. A. Breton and P. Nondédéo (= *Acta Mesoamericana* 24), 185–96. Markt Schwaben: Verlag Anton Saurwein.

LeVine, R. A., P. M. Miller, A. L. Richman, and S. LeVine. 1996. Education and Mother–Infant Interaction. A Mexican case study. In *Parents' Cultural Belief Systems*, ed. S. Harkness and C. M. Super, 254–69. New York: Guilford Press

LeVine, R., S. Dixon, S. LeVine, A. L. Richman, P. H. Leiderman, C. H. Keefer, and T. B. Brazelton. 1994. *Child Care and Culture: Lessons from Africa*. Cambridge: Cambridge University Press.

LeVine, R. A., and R. New, eds. 2008. *Anthropology and Child Development: A Cross-cultural Reader*. Malden, MA: Blackwell.

Levinson, S. C. 2003. *Space in Language and Cognition: Explorations in Cognitive Diversity*. Cambridge: Cambridge University Press.

  2006. On the Human "Interaction Engine." In *Roots of Sociality: Culture, Cognition, and Interaction*, ed. N. Enfield and S. C. Levinson, 153–78. Oxford: Berg.

  2012. Foreword. In *Language, Thought, and Reality: Selected Writings of Benjamin Lee Whorf*, ed. J. B. Carroll, S. C. Levinson, and P. Lee, 2nd ed., vii–xxiii. Cambridge, MA: MIT Press.

Lieven, E. V. M. 1994. Crosslinguistic and Crosscultural Aspects of Language Addressed to Children. In *Input and Interaction in Language Acquisition*, ed. C. Gallaway and B. J. Richards, 56–72. New York: Cambridge University Press.

  1997. Variation in Crosslinguistic Context. In *The Crosslinguistic Study of Language Acquisition*, Vol. 5, ed. D. I. Slobin, 199–264. Hillsdale, NJ: Erlbaum.

Lieven, E. V. M., and S. Stoll. 2009. Language Development. In *The Handbook of Cross-Cultural Developmental Science*, ed. M. Bornstein, 143–60. New York: Psychology Press.

Lieven, E. V. M., S. Stoll, B. Bickel, M. Gaenszle, and N. P. Paudyal. In prep. Early Communicative Development in Two Cultures.

Liszkowski, U., P. Brown, T. Callaghan, A. Takada, and C. de Vos. 2012. A Prelinguistic Universal of Human Communication. *Cognitive Science* 36: 698–713.

Lo, A., and H. Fung. 2012. Language Socialization and Shaming. In *The Handbook of Language Socialization*, ed. A. Duranti, E. Ochs, and B. B. Schieffelin, 169–80. Malden, MA: Wiley-Blackwell.

Lucy, J. 1992a. *Language Diversity and Thought: A Reformulation of the Linguistic Relativity Hypothesis*. Cambridge: Cambridge University Press.

1992b. *Grammatical Categories and Cognition: A Case Study of the Linguistic Relativity Hypothesis*. Cambridge: Cambridge University Press.

1997. Linguistic Relativity. *Annual Review of Anthropology* 26: 291–312.

Lucy, J., and Gaskins, S. 2001. Grammatical Categories and the Development of Classification Preferences: A comparative approach. In *Language Acquisition and Conceptual Development*, ed. M. Bowerman and S. C. Levinson, 257–83. Cambridge: Cambridge University Press.

2003. Interaction of Language Type and Referent Type in the Development of Nonverbal Classification Preferences. In *Language in Mind: Advances in the Study of Language and Thought*, ed. D. Gentner and S. Goldin-Meadow, 465–92. Cambridge, MA: MIT Press.

Lust, B. 2006. *Child Language: Acquisition and Growth*. Cambridge: Cambridge University Press.

Maccoby, E. E. 2007. Historical Overview of Socialization Theory and Research. In *Handbook of Socialization: Theory and Research*, ed. J. P. Grusec and P. D. Hastings, 13–41. New York: Guilford Press.

Maratsos, M. P. 2007. Commentary. *Monographs of the Society for Research in Child Development* 72 (286): 121–6.

Martini, M., and Kirkpatrick, J. 1981. Early Interactions in the Marquesas Islands. In *Culture and Early Interactions*, ed. T. M. Fields, A. M. Sostek, P. Vietze, and P. H. Leiderman, 189–213. Hillsdale, NJ: Erlbaum.

Masataka, N. 2003. *The Onset of Language*. Cambridge: Cambridge University Press.

Mehan, H. 1979. *Learning Lessons: Social Organization in the Classroom*. Cambridge, MA: Harvard University Press.

Menn, L., and Stoel-Gammon, C. 1996. Phonological Development. In *The Handbook of Child Language*, ed. P. Fletcher and B. MacWhinney, 335–59. Oxford: Wiley/Blackwell.

Meyer, Mercer. 1969. *"Frog, where are you?"* New York: Dial.

Michaels, S. 1991. The Dismantling of Narrative. In *Developing Narrative Structure*, ed. A. McCabe and C. Peterson, 303–50. Hillsdale, NJ: Lawrence Erlbaum.

Miller, P. J. 1982. *Amy, Wendy, and Beth: Learning Language in South Baltimore*. Austin: University of Texas Press.

———. 1986. Teasing as Language Socialization and Verbal Play in a White, Working-Class Community. In *Language Socialization across Cultures*, ed. B. B. Schieffelin and E. Ochs, 199–212. Cambridge: Cambridge University Press.

Miller, P. J., H. Fung, S. Lin, E. Chian-Hui Chen, and B. R. Boldt. 2012. How Socialization Happens on the Ground: Narrative practices as alternate socializing pathways in Taiwanese and European-American families. Monographs of the Society for Research in Child Development 77(1, Serial No. 302). Boston, MA: Wiley-Blackwell.

Miller, P. J., and L. Hoogstra. 1992. Language as Tool in the Socialization and Apprehension of Cultural Meanings. In *New Directions in Psychological Anthropology*, ed. T. Schwartz, G. M. White, and C. A. Lutz, 83–101. Cambridge: Cambridge University Press.

Miller, P. J., M. Koven, and S. Lin. 2012. Language Socialization and Narrative. In *The Handbook of Language Socialization*, ed. A. Duranti, E. Ochs, and B. B. Schieffelin, 190–208. Malden, MA: Wiley-Blackwell.

Mitchell-Kernan, C. I. 1969. Language Behavior in a Black Urban Community. Berkeley, CA: Language Behavior Research Laboratory Working Paper 23, University of Califonia.

Montgomery, H. 2008. *An Introduction to Childhood: Anthropological Perspectives on Children's Lives*. Malden, MA: Wiley-Blackwell.

Munroe, R. H., R. L. Munroe, and H. S. Shimmin. 1984. Children's Work in Four Cultures: Determinants and Consequences. *American Anthropologist* 86(2): 369–79.

Narasimhan, B. 2005. Splitting the Notion of "Agent": Case-Marking in early child Hindi. *Journal of Child Language* 32(4): 787–803.

Narasimhan, B., N. Budwig, and L. Murty. 2005. Argument Realization in Hindi Caregiver–Child Discourse. *Journal of Pragmatics* 37(4): 461–95.

Ochs, E. 1988. *Culture and Language Development: Language Acquisition and Language Socialization in a Samoan village*. Cambridge: Cambridge University Press.

Ochs, E., and L. Capps. 2001. *Living Narrative: Creating Lives in Everyday Storytelling*. Cambridge, MA: Harvard University Press.

Ochs, E., and B. B. Schieffelin, eds. 1979. *Developmental Pragmatics*. New York: Academic Press.

———. 1984. Language Acquisition and Socialization: Three developmental stories and their implications. In *Culture Theory: Essays on Mind, Self and Emotion*, ed. R. Shweder and R. LeVine, 276–320. Cambridge: Cambridge University Press.

———. 2008. Language Socialization: An historical overview. In *Language Socialization*, Vol. 8: *Encyclopedia of Language and Education*, ed. P. Duff and N. Hornberger, 2nd ed., 3–15. New York: Springer.

Odden, H. L. 2011. The Impact of Primary Schools on the Differential Distribution of Samoan Adolescents' Competence with Honorific Language. *Current Anthropology* 52(4): 597–606.

Orellana, M. 2009. *Translating Childhoods: Immigrant Youth, Language and Culture*. New Brunswick, NJ: Rutgers University Press.

Pears, B. Z. 2010. Children with Two Languages. In *Cambridge Handbook of Child Language*, ed. E. Bavin, 379–97. Cambridge: Cambridge University Press.

Peters, A. 1997. Language Typology, Prosody, and the Acquisition of Grammatical Morphemes. In *The Crosslinguistic Study of Language Acquisition*, ed. D. I. Slobin, Vol. 5, 135–99. Hillsdale, NJ: Erlbaum.

Pfeiler, B., ed. 2007. *Learning Indigenous Languages: Child Language Acquisition in Mesoamerica*. Berlin: Mouton de Gruyter.

Philips, S. U. 1983. *The Invisible Culture: Communication in Classroom and Community on the Warm Springs Indian Reservation*. New York: Longman.

Pinker, S. 1984. *Language Learnability and Language Development*, Cambridge, MA: Harvard University Press.

Pontevorvo, C., A. Fasulo, and L. Sterponi. 2001. Mutual Apprentices: The making of parenthood and childhood in family dinner conversations. *Human Development* 44(6): 340–61.

Pye, C. 1986. Quiche Mayan Speech to Children. *J. Child Lang.* 13: 85–100.

1990. The Acquisition of Ergative Languages. *Linguistics* 28: 1291–1330.

1992. The Acquisition of K'iche' Maya. In *The Crosslinguistic Study of Language Acquisition*, ed. D. I. Slobin, Vol. 3, 221–308. Hillsdale, NJ: Erlbaum.

Pye, C., and B. B. Pfeiler. 2013. The Comparative Method of Language Acquisition Research: A Mayan case study. *Journal of Child Language*, available on CJO2013. doi:10.1017/S0305000912000748.

Pye, C., B. Pfeiler, L. de León, P. Brown, and P. Mateo. 2007. Roots or Edges? Explaining variation in children's early verb forms across five Mayan languages. In *Learning Indigenous Languages: Child Language Acquisition in Mesoamerica*, ed. B. B. Pfeiler, 15–46. Berlin: Mouton de Gruyter.

Reynolds, J. F. 2008. Socializing Puros Pericos (Little Parrots): The negotiation of respect and responsibility in Antonero Mayan sibling and peer networks. *Journal of Linguistic Anthropology* 18(1): 82–107.

Rogoff, B. 2003. *The Cultural Nature of Human Development*. Oxford: Oxford University Press.

Rogoff, B., J. Mistry, A. Gonci, and C. Mosier. 1993. *Guided Participation in Cultural Activity by Toddlers and Caregivers*. Monographs of the Society for Research in Child Development 58(8), Serial No. 236.

Rogoff, B., L. Moore, B. Najafi, A. Dexter, M. Correa-Chavez, and J. Solis. 2007. Children's Development of Cultural Repertoires through Participation in Everyday Routines and Practices. In *Handbook of*

Socialization: Theory and Research, ed. J. E. Grusec and P. D. Hastings, 490–515. New York: The Guilford Press.

Rogoff, B., R. Paradise, R. Mejía-Arauz, M. Correa-Chávez, and C. Angelillo. 2003. Firsthand Learning through Intent Participation. *Annual Review of Psychology* 54(1): 175–203.

Rossano, F., P. Brown, and S. C. Levinson. 2009. Gaze, Questioning, and Culture. In *Conversation Analysis: Comparative Perspectives*, ed. J. Sidnell, 187–249. Cambridge: Cambridge University Press.

Rumsey, A., L. San Roque, and B. B. Schieffelin. 2013. The Acquisition of Ergative Marking in Kaluli, Ku Waru and Duna (Trans New Guinea). In *The Acquisition of Ergativity*, ed. E. L. Bavin and S. Stoll, 133–82. Amsterdam: Benjamins.

Rymes, B. R. 2001. *Conversational Borderlands: Language and Identity in an Alternative Uban High School*. New York: Teachers College Press.

  2008. Language Socialization and the Linguistic Anthropology of Education. In *Encyclopedia of Language and Education*, ed. P. Duff and N. Hornberger, 2nd revised ed., Vol. 8, 29–42. New York: Springer.

Salomo, D., and U. Liszkowski. 2012. Sociocultural Settings Influence the Emergence of Prelinguistic Deictic Gestures. *Child Development* 83(6) [online].

Sapir, E. 1949. *Selected Writings in Language, Culture and Personality*, ed. D. Mandelbaum. Berkeley: University of California Press.

Schieffelin, B. B. 1990. *The Give and Take of Everyday Life: Language Socialization of Kaluli Children*. Cambridge: Cambridge University Press.

  1993. Codeswitching and Language Socialization: Some probable relationships. In *Pragmatics: From Theory to Practice*, ed. J. Duchan et al., 20–42. Englewood Cliffs, NJ: Prentice Hall.

Schieffelin, B. B., and E. Ochs. 1986a. Language Socialization. *Annual Review of Anthropology* 15: 163–91.

  1986b. *Language Socialization across Cultures*. Cambridge: Cambridge University Press.

Schneidman, L., and S. Goldin-Meadow. 2012. Language Input and Acquisition in a Mayan Village: How important is directed speech? *Developmental Science* 15(5): 659–73.

Schneidman, L., M. E. Arroyo, S. C. Levine, and S. Goldin-Meadow. 2012. What Counts as Effective Input for Word Learning? *Journal of Child Language*.

Shweder, R. A., J. J. Goodnow, G. Hatano, R. A. LeVine, H. Markus, and P. J. Miller. 2006. The Cultural Psychology of Development: One mind, many mentalities. In *Handbook of Child Psychology: Vol. 1. Theoretical Models of Human Development*, 6th ed., ed. R. M. Lerner, 716–92. New York: Wiley.

Sidnell, J. 2009. *Conversation Analysis: An Introduction*. New York: Wiley.

Slobin, D. I. 1967. *A Field Manual for Cross-Cultural Study of the Acquisition of Communicative Competence*. Berkeley, CA.: Language Behavior Research Laboratory, University of California.

1985a. *The Crosslinguistic Study of Language Acquisition*, Vol. 1. Hillsdale, NJ: Erlbaum.

1985b. *The Crosslinguistic Study of Language Acquisition*, Vol. 2. Hillsdale, NJ: Erlbaum.

1985c. Cross-linguistic Evidence for the Language Making Capacity. In *The Crosslinguistic Study of Language Acquisition*, ed. D. I. Slobin, Vol. 2, 1157-1256. Hillsdale, NJ: Erlbaum.

1992a. *The Crosslinguistic Study of Language Acquisition*, Vol. 3. Hillsdale, NJ: Erlbaum.

1992b. Introduction. In *The Crosslinguistic Study of Language Acquisition*, ed. D. I. Slobin, Vol. 3, 1-13. Hillsdale, NJ: Erlbaum.

1996. From "Thought and Language" to "Thinking for Speaking". In *Rethinking Linguistic Relativity*, ed. J. J. Gumperz and S. C. Levinson, 70-96. Cambridge: Cambridge University Press.

1997a. *The Crosslinguistic Study of Language Acquisition*, Vol. 4. Hillsdale, NJ: Erlbaum.

1997b. *The Crosslinguistic Study of Language Acquisition*, Vol. 5. Hillsdale, NJ: Erlbaum.

2001. Form-Function Relations: How do children find out what they are? In *Language Acquisition and Conceptual Development*, ed. M. Bowerman and S. C. Levinson, 406-49. Cambridge: Cambridge University Press.

Slobin, D. I., and M. Bowerman. 2007. Interfaces Between Linguistic Typology and Child Language Research. *Linguistic Typology* 11: 213-26.

Slobin, D. I., M. Bowerman, P. Brown, S. Eisenbeiss, and B. Narasimhan. 2011. Putting Things in Places: Developmental consequences of linguistic typology. In *Event Representation in Language and Cognition*, ed. J. Bohnemeyer, and E. Pederson, 134-65. New York: Cambridge University Press.

Snow, C. E. 1993. Issues in the Study of Input: Finetuning, universality, individual and developmental differences, and necessary causes. In *The Handbook of Child Language*, ed. P. Fletcher and B. MacWhinney, 180-93. Cambridge: Blackwell.

Snow, C., and C. Ferguson, eds. 1977. *Talking to Children*. New York: Cambridge University Press.

Sperber, D. 1996. *Explaining Culture: A Naturalistic Approach*. Oxford: Blackwell.

Sperry, L. L., and D. E. Sperry. 1996. Early Development of Narrative Skills. *Cognitive Development* 11: 443-65.

Sterponi, L. 2010. Learning Communicative Competence. In *The Anthropology of Learning in Childhoood*, ed. D. F. Lancy, J. Bock, and S. Gaskins, 235-59. Lanham, MD: Altamira Press.

Stivers, T., N. J. Enfield, P. Brown, C. Englert, M. Hayashi, T. Heinemann, G. Hoymann, F. Rossano, J.-P. de Ruiter, K.-E. Yoon, and S. C. Levinson. 2009. Universals and Cultural Variation in Turn-taking in

Conversation. *Proceedings of the National Academy of Sciences of the United States of America* 106: 10587-92.

Stoll, S. 2009. Crosslinguistic Approaches to Language Acquisition. In *The Handbook of Child Language*, ed. E. L. Bavin, 89-104. New York: Cambridge University Press.

Stoll, S., B. Bickel, E. Lieven, G. Banjade, T. N Bhatta, M. Gaenszle, N. P. Paudyal, J. Pettigrew, I. P. Rai, M. Rai, and N. K. Rai. 2012. Nouns and Verbs in Chintang: Children's usage and surrounding adult speech. *Journal of Child Language* 39(2): 284-321.

Strömqvist, S., H. Ragnarsdóttir, K. Toivainen, *et al.* 1995. The Inter-Nordic Study of Language Acquisition. *Nordic Journal of Linguistics* 18: 3-29.

Strömqvist, S., and L. Verhoeven, eds. 2004. *Relating Events in Narrative: Typological and Contextual Perspectives.* Mahwah, NJ: Erlbaum.

Stross, B. 1969. Language Acquisition by Tenejapa Tzeltal Children. Language Behavior Research Laboratory Working Paper No. 20. University of California, Berkeley.

Takada, A. 2005. Early Vocal Communication and Social Institution: Appellation and infant verse addressing among the Central Kalahari San. *Crossroads of Language, Interaction, and Culture* 6: 80-108.

Talmy, L. 1985. Lexicalization Patterns: Semantic structure in lexical forms. In *Language Typology and Semantic Description, Vol. 3: Grammatical Categories and the Lexicon*, ed. T. Shopen, 36-149. Cambridge: Cambridge University Press.

Tardif, T. 1996. Nouns are Not Always Learned Before Verbs: Evidence from Mandarin speakers' early vocabularies. *Developmental Psychology* 32(3): 492-504.

Tardif, T., P. Fletcher, W. Liang, Z. Zhang, N. Kaciroti, and V. A. Marchman. 2008. Baby's First 10 Words. *Developmental Psychology* 44(4): 929-38.

Tomasello, M. 1999. *The Cultural Origins of Human Cognition.* Cambridge, MA: Harvard University Press.

2003. *Constructing a Language: A Usage-Based Theory of Language Acquisition.* Cambridge, MA: Harvard University Press.

2008. *Origins of Human Communication.* Cambridge, MA: MIT Press.

Tomasello, M., M. Carpenter, J. Call, T. Behne, and H. Moll. 2005. Understanding and Sharing Intentions: The origins of cultural cognition. *Behavioral and Brain Sciences* 28: 675-735.

Van Valin, R. 1992. An Overview of Ergative Phenomena and their Implications for Language Acquisition. In *The Crosslinguistic Study of Language Acquisition*, ed. D. I. Slobin, Vol. 3, 15-37. Hillsdale, NJ: Erlbaum.

Vygotsky, L. S. 1978. *Mind in Society: The Development of Higher Psychological Processes*, ed. M. Cole, V. John-Steiner, S. Scribner, and E. Souberman. Cambridge, MA: Harvard University Press.

1987 [1934]. *Thinking and Speech*, trans. N. Minick. New York: Plenum Press.

Watson-Gegeo, K. A. 1992. Thick Explanation in the Ethnographic Study of Child Socialization and Development: A longitudinal study of the problem of schooling for Kwara'ae (Solomon Islands) children. In *The Production and Reproduction of Children's Worlds: Interpretive Methodologies for the Study of Childhood Socialization*, ed. W. Corsaro and P. J. Miller, 51–66. San Francisco, CA: Jossey-Bass, Inc.

Watson-Gegeo, K. A. and S. E. Nielsen. 2003. Language Socialization in SLA. In *The Handbook of Second Language Acquisition*, ed. C. J. Doughty and M. H. Long, 155–77. New York: Basil Blackwell.

Weisleder, A., and A. Fernald. In press. How Social Environments Shape Children's Language Experiences and Influence Lexical Development. In *Language in Interaction: Studies in Honor of Eve V. Clark*, ed. A. Inbal, M. Casilas, C. Kurumada, and B. Estigarribia. Amsterdam: John Benjamins.

Whitehouse, H., ed. 2001. *The Debated Mind: Evolutionary Psychology vs. Ethnography*. Oxford: Berg.

Whiting, B. B., and J. W. M. Whiting. 1975. *Children of Six Cultures: A Psycho-Cultural Analysis*. Cambridge, MA: Harvard University Press.

Whorf, B. L. 1956. *Language, Thought, and Reality*. Boston, MA: MIT Press.

Wilkins, D. P. 2008. Same Argument Structure, Different Meanings: Learning 'put' and 'look' in Arrernte. In *Crosslinguistic Perspectives on Argument Structure: Implications for Learnability*, ed. M. Bowerman and P. Brown, 141–66. Mahwah, NJ: Lawrence Erlbaum.

Wootton, A. J. 1997. *Interaction and the Development of Mind*. Cambridge: Cambridge University Press.

9

Language, society, and history

Towards a unified approach?

Paja Faudree and Magnus Pharao Hansen

> ... language is the archives of history ...
> (Ralph Waldo Emerson 2000: 236)

9.1 Introduction: The language–society–history nexus

It would be difficult today to find a scholar who would not insist on engaging cultural phenomena within historical frameworks. Language is of necessity implicated in such an endeavor given how tightly it is bound to culture through shared history, the two having "grown up together, constantly influencing each other" (Whorf 1956: 156). But what does such co-evolution mean for how we approach the field shared by language, culture, and history?

Linguistic anthropologists have dedicated considerable effort to exploring how understandings of the past are the result of semiotic processes in present micro-contexts of interaction. They have also examined how trajectories of past events lead to formations of semiotic complexes (idioms, institutions, ideologies, identities) that structure and define particular pasts while influencing the present as well. Yet while these two approaches have contributed enormously to our understanding of the causal and conditional relations between language and history in social contexts, they have remained largely distinct from each other. We suggest that researchers working at the intersection of language, society, and history would benefit from an approach that more fully integrates the insights of both lines of inquiry.

Greg Urban (1996) conceptualizes the creation of collective memory as a dialectical process through which the sensible world is made intelligible through discourse. In similar terms, we see signs of the past as sensible in the present, but intelligible only once embedded in narrative. Language is doubly implicated in this process. It is a sensible object that can differentially serve as an index upon which to build our interpretations of the particular past that brought the present into being, and it is the medium in which those interpretive narratives are built. In engaging the language–society–history nexus, different ribbons of thought have tended to focus either on producing historical narratives (history) or on analyzing such historical production (metahistory). We take this division as a basis for our review of the literature, which is structured into two parts:

(1) *Metahistory: Language and the social life of history in the present.* Scholars working in this vein focus on how language produces and circulates distinct histories, understood as narratives through which the past becomes socially meaningful. Such work attends to how, through language use, particular linguistic-cultural forms become linked to selective, ideological awareness of the ties between past and present. A dominant question concerns the processes by which societies become aware of their pasts and use discourses about them to shape present norms and future paths.

(2) *History: Understanding the past through language.* Scholars working within this tradition study past events and meanings through linguistic signs available in the present. Such research involves examining different kinds of linguistic traces representing past forms of sociality within specific historical contexts. A driving question concerns how sociocultural change becomes "artifactualized" through and within language, and how such sedimentation processes can be reflexively understood as a dialectical process through which languages and societies jointly evolve.

By thus dividing our review we aim to show that each approach relies crucially on the other. Our main argument is that any engagement with the language–society–history nexus is best served by engaging both with how the past is sensible to us and how we make it intelligible through metahistory (a concept we build from ideas explored in White 1973). Drawing on a combination of empirical analysis of the traces of the past as well as metahistorical analysis of how these indexes are narrativized, such a dialogue promises a deeper understanding of the language–society–history nexus. We argue that linguistic anthropology is uniquely positioned to approach this field holistically, by analyzing the recursive semiotic processes tying peoples, narratives, and events together over time.

Our approach is based on the premise that the object of analysis is itself unified: the seemingly discrete concepts "culture" (or "society"), "history," and "language" are all constructions dependent upon relations among sets of signs, but are also simultaneously trajectories of sign relations that shift over time. The object's fundamental unity is evident in how language and history selectively become the targets of collective awareness and collective interventions to control them through semiotic processes. Languages are constructed as bounded, identifiable, standardized objects through discourse patterns that emerge and are stabilized in particular historical contexts, just as societies become selectively aware of their histories through particular events and their subsequent linguistic-discursive construction. The dialectical interaction of such past events and (narrative) constructions of the past in turn shape relations between peoples and sign systems in the present. This entire recursive process fundamentally depends upon relations among signs, temporal frames, and forms of sociality within a politically charged field of selective awareness.

9.2 The language–society–history nexus and the development of linguistic anthropology

Before the formal founding of disciplines, thinkers as diverse as Rousseau, Herder, Humboldt, and Nietzsche approached the language–society–history nexus holistically. With the rise of institutionalized disciplines, foci emerged that carved out bounded fields with distinct methods and theories geared towards investigating discrete empirical objects. Initially, history and anthropology shared the goal of understanding the history of humanity, but history privileged textual analysis while anthropology stressed comparative ethnology. This division of labor persisted in European anthropology until Radcliffe-Brown and later Levi-Strauss turned anthropology towards the synchronic study of social structures. As Saussure's synchronicity/diachronicity distinction evolved into Bloomfieldian structuralism and Chomskyan generativism, the historical study of language became severed from synchronic linguistics, which became linguistics proper. As each discipline continued refining its distinct object of study, its practitioners gave less attention to processes transecting the boundaries among language, history, and society.

Exceptions to this general tendency were found in Prague school linguistics, which continued to stress the need to study linguistic structure and change together and in relation to communicative functions. American Boasian anthropology also insisted that linguistic–cultural complexes are the result of historical trajectories recoverable through synthetic attention to ethnographic, archaeological, and linguistic evidence. These schools – through the intellectual legacies of Boas, Sapir, Jakobson, Benveniste, and others – provide much of the theoretical and methodological foundations of contemporary linguistic anthropology. While synchronic generative linguistics continues to have a strong position in the US, linguistic research elsewhere – tracing its genealogy to Prague school functionalism – studies language typology in a framework of grammaticalization, wherein synchronic structure is shaped by social interactions over time. Nonetheless, many anthropologists, including linguistic anthropologists, equate linguistics as a discipline with Chomsky's ahistorical, generative approach – a narrative producing lasting estrangement between linguistics and anthropology.

Another set of exceptions, deriving from historical materialist theory, focused on processes of social differentiation. Such approaches include history's Annales school and the sociolinguistics of Gumperz and Labov. In anthropology, historical materialism shaped political economy and world systems approaches – work by Wolf, Mintz, Wallerstein, and others – and the anti-colonial movement subverting the myth of the "ethnographic present" (Fabian 1983). This focus also broke with the tendency to view texts as the only valid object of historical knowledge, a bias circumscribing oral cultures as "people without history" (Wolf 2010[1982]). Though such approaches have created a robust tradition in anthropology of studying culture and history jointly (e.g., the work of Dirks, Sahlins, Stoler, Trouillot, and others), seminal works in this vein have paid scant attention to language.

Drawing on these legacies, linguistic anthropology has led the study of language in social context. The field examines how sign complexes move through social space and time by synthesizing an eclectic set of concepts and perspectives from diverse theoretical frameworks: Peircean pragmatic semiotics, ordinary language philosophy, Bakhtinian literary theory, Bourdieuean practice theory, and various post-structural approaches to discourse and textuality. Yet while theories of relations between language and society, and between society and history, have been well developed, the relation between language and history has been less theorized. Linguistic anthropology has more fully theorized the intersection of semiotics and temporality (e.g., Parmentier 1987, 1994, 2007; Silverstein 1993; Urban 1996; Inoue 2004; Agha 2007; Lempert and Perrino 2007; Hanks 2010; Monaghan 2011; Faudree 2012). But even here, linguistic anthropologists have frequently engaged lightly with history per se, focusing on describing semiotic events and processes in synchronic social time rather than describing how they unfold embedded in broader historical trajectories and specific historical contexts, which often remains categorized as the domain of the discipline of history. In other words, the history of linguistic anthropology itself – understood both as its conceptual genealogy and socially held narratives about those origins – continues to shape how we approach the language–society–history nexus.

9.3 Metahistory: Language and the social life of history in the present

What is the purpose of history? Answering this question depends, first, on distinguishing it from other temporal scales and indicating why it is a privileged site of analysis. In our view, history is unique in surveying change over time not by examining the emergence of the capacity for social conventions (i.e., phylogeny; see Levinson, this volume,

Chapter 12, and Enfield, this volume, Chapter 13) or variations in instantiations of conventions (as interaction). Rather, history pertains to changes in conventions themselves. Thus for linguistic anthropologists, paying attention to changing conventions also means examining how people produce and circulate histories about those changes, how they take evaluative and affective stances towards them, and how people subjectively experience history – and how language use is involved in these other processes. Histories provide explanations of causal relations between past and present; as meaning-making tools, they explain, motivate, and justify a range of present social categories. Language in turn plays a critical role in establishing narratives connecting people to the past: language is a product of history, and language structure and pragmatic norms are the sediments of past discourse and interactional patterns. Language is, furthermore, the medium through which history is transmitted, through which collective pasts are narratively positioned against the present. Even when collective memory is invested in material objects as crucial signifiers of the past, their social meanings are shared through narratives. Languages, too, may be taken as signs of group history: evidence of their passage through time is embedded in linguistic structure itself as well as in key lexemes indexing particular histories. Through metalinguistic discourses and language ideologies, languages become signs of particular pasts and tools for their interpretation in the present.

Linguistic anthropologists have tended to engage these issues by asking how traces of the past become evidence, critically examining social processes that produce and circulate historical narratives. This approach shares some interests with the vast, influential body of work in science and technology studies interrogating the processes by which facts are made, including some working at the intersection with history (e.g., Abu El Haj 2002). Linguistic anthropologists working on fact-making over time have focused on the social life of history: the meanings people make of the past and the layered social processes by which those meanings are invested with authority and put into circulation. They have less often focused on history itself: a past interpretable if not fully knowable through the analysis of interactions among people, events, and signs, particularly linguistic ones.

9.3.1 Textuality, interdiscursivity, and history

A diverse range of social theorists – including Ricoeur, Derrida, Kristeva, and Geertz – have privileged textual models for cultural interpretation. They have variously advocated viewing social formations as assemblages of texts that stand in contextual and intertextual relations to each other through time and space. Linguistic anthropologists have critiqued such culture-as-text approaches for not distinguishing between the text and the "text-artifact" – the text as physical object – and for isolating both from contexts of use while blurring the relations between discursive flows and social processes (Silverstein and Urban 1996; see also Bauman and Briggs 2003). Thus some linguistic anthropologists have foregrounded relations among discourses through attention to interdiscursivity (e.g., Silverstein 2005), which foregrounds relations among distinct discursive events. This approach reframes attention to text, integrating it into ethnographic analysis of the dynamic, diachronic processes by which discourses become entextualized and stabilized over time, facilitating connections among events through ongoing processes of recontextualization.

In linguistic anthropology, such work has focused on the social and political processes by which discourses become entextualized into discrete, manipulable "texts" whose meaning may shift when recontextualized. Urban (1996, 2001) identifies power relations and ideologies of textual authority as critical to replication, key factors "escalating" the circulatory processes through which "culture moves through the world." In the production of history, entextualization produces selective memory: by understanding why people voice one historical text rather than another, history can be seen as a generative process influenced by social and political forces. In her study (1995) of the circulation of history among the Brazilian Xavante, Graham describes how Xavante historical discourses are entextualized in specific discourse genres that differentially lend authority to specific narratives of the past even as they are reconfigured to fit new social circumstances. Other approaches have likewise privileged genre as a unique site where friction between past uses and present needs produces "interdiscursive gaps" that make history selectively visible to participants or analysts (Bauman 2004; Hill 2005; Agha 2007; Wirtz 2007; Hanks 2010).

Yet while broadly generative, this focus on the social dynamics of textuality has also proven limiting. Highlighting the iterative, potentially endless process of (re)entexualization and (re)contextualization runs the risk of producing a mechanism-driven grasp of change over time, constrained in its ability to account for how specific historical circumstances and actors are linked to change. History can become reduced to an inferred temporal trajectory, a narrative of movement through time that harnesses discrete textual events together rather than accounting for how such events, and their surrounding contexts, are wrapped up in broader historical processes.

9.3.2 Mediation, collective memory, and semiotic technologies

One solution involves stressing materiality more fully by focusing on how different semiotic technologies (see Agha 2011, Kockelman and Bernstein 2012) are linked to historical processes: how history becomes attached to and transmitted through particular objects such as texts and other material "artifacts." Parmentier has been a leading proponent of examining how semiotic processes mediate between past and present. He distinguishes "signs of history" from "signs in history" (Parmentier 1987). These two concepts analytically separate signs that are taken as referential symbols of "History" (particular "folk" narratives about the past) from relatively indexical signs embedded within the sequence of historical events as they unfold over time. The former concept, "signs of history," isolates objects that some group conventionally, explicitly, takes to be signs of the past (e.g., an ancient abandoned ruin as a sign of collective history). In contrast, the latter concept stresses the way signs function not only as representations of history but as active signifiers producing historical meaning in the present (e.g., an ancient building taken as a site of political activity whose present meaning is harnessed to the historical resonance of the specific venue). Parmentier's work thus helps elucidate how materiality is implicated in the semiotic construction of history in the present.

A more commonly used framework for studying materiality and historicity has been Halbwach's concept of "collective memory," used by archaeologists and others to understand practices through which peoples manipulate their environment, creating shared interpretations of the past while investing them in public objects (Van Dyke and Alcock 2003). An evolving trend in archaeology uses semiotic approaches to understand relations between materiality and discourse in past contexts (Alcock 2001, Abu El Haj 2002, Preucel 2006; Crossland 2009). Though archaeologists are only sometimes explicit about their linguistic underpinnings, processes by which material objects become representations of collective memory are necessarily both intersubjective and discursive, reliant upon multiple kinds of communicative events ranging from planning work prior to construction of major projects like monuments to collaboration during their construction stages to building consensus about post-completion use. Work in linguistic anthropology has been more consistently explicit in elucidating how the material world is bound, through discursive practices, to the construction of collective memory. A primary example is Basso's (1996) analysis of Western Apache place names, which describes how places become tied through narrative to history: landscapes become representations both of the past and of the meaning history holds in the present.

Linguistic anthropologists have also approached the language–society–history nexus by analyzing how developments in media technology drive historical, social, and linguistic processes. This approach is heavily influenced by thinkers ranging from Frankfurt School theorists to scholars like Anderson and Habermas who place media and publicity at the center of their theories of social history. Their emphasis on literacy and print has stimulated much research in linguistic anthropology (e.g., Besnier 1995, Eisenlohr 2007, Miller 2007, Faudree 2013). A parallel interest in cross-cultural meanings of literacy – particularly in non-Western media such as khipus, codices, hieroglyphs, and non-alphabetic scripts – has been of concern both to ethnohistorians and linguistic anthropologists attending to past and present in the same society (Jansen 1990, Boone and Mignolo 1994, Restall 1997a, 1997b, Makihara 2001, Salomon 2001 and 2004, Quilter and Urton 2002, Urton 2003, Houston 2004 and 2008, Tomlinson 2009, Boone and Urton 2011, Rappaport and Cummins 2011). Such work necessarily engages with how particular media selectively interact with particular languages as they encode narratives about the past (see also Gershon and Manning, this volume, Chapter 22).

A methodological conundrum faced by scholars extracting historical narratives from material artifacts is that even in attention to written texts, semiotic analysis requires making assumptions about the linkage of such signs to narratives in the past and the present. This requires approximating the indexical ground from which a given artifact was produced: deciphering the artifact's meaning by (re)constructing the narrative binding it to its surrounding context of use and interpretation. This endeavor requires the scholar to produce a rich image of the past based on as many sources of knowledge (signs of the past) as possible, but also requires a semiotically adequate theory of narrative and high levels of reflexivity about how artifacts are emplotted into past and present narratives.

9.3.3 Dialogicality and the chronotope: Bakhtinian approaches

Mikhail Bakhtin developed just such a theory of the narrative, and his work has given linguistic anthropologists unique tools for studying the language–society–history nexus. One of Bakhtin's fundamental insights is that language in its natural state is infinitely various, meaning every utterance is polyphonous and resounds with multiple voices. Furthermore, present utterances always exist in a complex relationship with past ones: present utterances are always a partial revoicing of past ones, their voices echoing those of the near and distant past. The dialogicality inherent in Bakhtin's vision is what brings some linguistic anthropologists to view culture as emerging out of dialogic interaction (e.g., Tedlock and Mannheim 1995). This view implies that likewise history is constructed dialogically, as are narratives about particular histories. Applying a dialogic lens to understanding the past foregrounds the creative role that language in dialogic interaction plays in constructing histories and narratives about them, while stressing the emergent, contingent, relative nature of historical processes as they take place.

Recent work has taken up Bakhtin's *chronotope*, a concept directly relevant to theorizing the language–society–history nexus given its explicit invocation of temporality. For Bakhtin, all semiotic endeavors – events through which social meaning is constructed – depend on the chronotope: "every entry into the sphere of meaning is accomplished only through the gates of the chronotope" (1981: 258). Bakhtin described the chronotope as the force by which time "thickens, takes on flesh, becomes artistically visible," and through which "space becomes charged and responsive to movements of time, plot and history" (1981: 84). Chronotopes are narrative frameworks that recruit and emplot particular social personae ("characters"), creating them through dialogic, interdiscursive interaction. One research trend has emphasized how speakers in interaction establish alignments with particular narrative chronotopes that frame the speech event, generating "cross-chronotope" alignments as interlocutors calibrate the chronotope of the interaction with the shared narrative chronotope (Irvine 2004, Silverstein 2005, Lempert 2007, Agha 2007, Lempert and Perrino 2007, Perrino 2007, Dick 2010). Recent work has also shown how individuals build identities through autobiographical narratives, constructions through which speakers situate themselves in relation to visions of the past. Though scholars have long found narrative a crucial tool through which selves are constructed, the chronotope concept adds new dimensions by foregrounding not only the spatial, temporal, and linguistic aspects of such narratives but also their contextual specificity. For example, Schiffrin (2009) stresses that while narratives promise access to intimate, almost private imaginations of (personal) history they also draw on highly public, collectively shared discursive frameworks. Thus such narratives situate entire discourse communities temporally and sociopolitically. In discussing "enregistered memory," Wirtz (2007) considers how narratives may be at once autobiographical and social, indexing shared interpretations of the past: the mere use of the register situates the speech event within a specific chronotopic narrative frame.

The chronotope concept is itself the product of a chronotope, of course, and arises out of a particular narrative interpretation within a specific spatio-historical context. Hence one problem in adapting the concept for present use is how to preserve its utility while shedding limitations born of its genesis in literary criticism. By putting texts at the center of analysis, studies relying on the chronotope risk neglecting those aspects of social life that less obviously formulate collective interpretations of the past by engaging with textuality. Yet when the key Bakhtinian insight – that language in use, hence social process, is fundamentally heteroglossic – is turned towards understanding interconnections among language, society, and history, the theory offers a framework capable of synthesizing relatively positivist and relatively representationalist approaches, thereby uniting history and metahistory. Using chronotopes as an organizational theoretical concept allows positivist and representationalist methods to become distinct yet relatable strategies, each dependent upon marshaling particular voices in constructing narrative explanations. A Bakhtinian framework thus produces not just a multi-vocal but a multi-epistemic reading of history and its social meaning.

By foregrounding narrative as productive of both meaning and material realities, the chronotope concept offers new possibilities for reflexive scholarship by encouraging scholars to think critically about their own processes of using narrative to engage with the past. In other words, the concept activates a range of productive questions: What is the genealogy of the particular chronotope in question? What is its field of use? How is it transmitted? How did it come to have the status it does, whether hegemonic, institutionalized, subaltern, or suppressed? What are the interactional dynamics in play, from the kinds of interactions the chronotope facilitates to those it prohibits? What other chronotopes is it interacting with? Such questions could be equally addressed to past contexts, present contexts, or scholars' own contexts of text production.

9.3.4 Ideologies of language, time, and history

Over the last two decades, language ideology has been and continues to be a dominant focus in linguistic anthropology. Research elucidating dimensions of the language–society–history nexus has likewise used the concept. One such line of work stresses how entire linguistic codes are read ideologically, as signs of a collective past. These interpretations are subject to further metalinguistic evaluations that influence language change and the ways speakers make ideological linkages between languages and other social entities, whether values, practices, objects, places, or historical eras. Such approaches have been especially widespread among linguistic anthropologists studying processes of language shift and language revitalization (e.g., Kulick 1992, Kroskrity 1993, Woolard 2004 and 2008, Eisenlohr 2007, Errington 2008, Perrino 2011, Stasch 2011, Meek 2011).

Irvine and Gal's work (2000) has been a foundational text for research stressing language ideology, introducing three macro-semiotic processes widely used in elucidating interactions over time among language ideologies, forms, and practices. They are *erasure* (some differences are ideologically muted or silenced, thereby erasing systematic differentiation, while corresponding equivalences are stressed), *fractal recursivity* (patterns of interpretation are repeated at different scales within a semiotic system, as when linguistic distinctions are projected onto social ones or vice versa), and *iconization* (iconic linkages are established between group identities and semiotic forms so that each becomes a direct, naturalized representation of the other). In addition to spawning these widely generative concepts, Irvine and Gal's work offered a model for how they can be used to understand historical pasts and their meaning in the present.

Other approaches have explored ideologies through attention to how they mediate linkages among conceptualizations of time and linguistic and social practices. Whorf's (1956) analysis of Hopi as lacking grammatical tense was foundational to this line of research, sparking cross-disciplinary inquiry into how languages differentially encode time and what implications such differences might have not only for cross-cultural understandings of time and history but for the social practices by which both are interpreted. Work critiquing Whorf's controversial argument has provided a wealth of data about how the Hopi language is tied to ideologies of time and history, yet disciplinary segregation has hampered a comprehensive synthesis. This problem is structural and thus exemplifies systemic deformations across myriad cases in existing scholarly literature – limitations that the holistic approach we advocate is designed to redress. Malotki (1983) describes in great detail the linguistic structures of Hopi temporal expression, but he divorces linguistic data from information about social context. Geertz (1994) provides a detailed account of how Hopi ideologies about prophesy and history have shaped Hopi social movements and historical events but pays little attention to the role of language or linguistic ideologies in these processes. Dinwoodie's (2006) brief study comes closest to integrating these strands of research by showing how multiple Hopi ideologies of time and language coexist and influence how individual Hopi people experience both conceptual fields. This work suggests how linguistic anthropologists might successfully take divergent views on a single case that might otherwise remain separated along disciplinary lines and fuse them into a rich, parallax interpretation. Indeed, one great advantage of examining history through a focus on language ideology is that the approach has sometimes successfully integrated study of historical pasts with analysis of the meaning made of those pasts in the present. At its best, emphasis on language ideology is accompanied by equally serious attention to, first, linguistic structure and social context and, second, to historical context consisting both of what we know of particular historical pasts as well as the meanings people have made of those pasts.

9.4 History: Understanding the past through language

If linguistic anthropologists have tended to understand history ethnographically, by looking at the social meanings people make of it, historians have tended to engage with history not only by asking what purpose history serves but also what methods provide the best route towards answering that question. This inquiry raises more questions about the role of empirical evidence in historiography. Should pieces of evidence be read as indexical signs of a past that is, however partially, essentially knowable, as history? Or should they be understood as signs from which narratives about the past – metahistories – are constructed, through political processes that have entextualized such narratives in particular ways? These teleological differences also align with different approaches toward how language is used to understand the past. Linguistic signs and structures may be used largely referentially, to infer facts about past events; or they may be viewed largely indexically as pieces in a vast complex of possible records of historical events whose importance lies less in the information they convey about those events than in how they have been used to construct particular narratives about them. Here we argue that these two approaches are complementary, and both must be engaged in order to achieve a full grasp of the language–society–history nexus.

9.4.1 Historical linguistics and the comparative method

Comparative historical linguistics has been a primary field in which language, culture, and history have been united analytically. It emerged in the early nineteenth century alongside theories of evolution and modern ethno-nationalism; all three shared an interest in tracking movements and relations among past ethnic groups. The synthesis of ethnology, archaeology, and historical linguistics provided the basis for Boasian anthropology, which was groundbreaking in maintaining that cultural and historical sources of evidence could be combined to provide the histories of indigenous groups for which no textual histories existed (see Sapir 1916). Such work has been criticized for its colonial and modernist trappings whereby the scientific study of non-Western languages became a means of appropriating the pasts of colonized peoples, a process proceeding alongside the creation of narratives of civilizational decay and their incorporation into a universalizing Eurocentric ideology of history (Bauman and Briggs 2003, Errington 2008). This disciplinary history remains a legacy in the present, evident in the ongoing preoccupation in comparative historical linguistics with constructing language taxonomies, reconstructing proto-languages, finding their homelands, tracking population movements, and constructing a total picture of "what actually happened" (see, e.g., Campbell 1998: 299). Such projects risk reifying languages, cultures, and populations as isomorphic, natural kinds. The relative lack of political and theoretical reflexivity in historical linguistics has contributed to enduring estrangement between that discipline and linguistic anthropology.

Research on Mesoamerica exemplifies these tensions. Knowledge of the region's pre-contact past rests almost entirely on historical linguistic and archaeological evidence, upon which histories of migrations, flows of cultural innovations, and genealogies of civilizational centers have been tracked. With the notable exception of the classic Maya period, the absence of legible textual evidence means that archaeological remains are frequently coupled to narratives of large-scale movements of ethno-linguistic groups constructed by comparative linguists, fitting material remains into larger cultural-historical narratives. The construction of these narratives is sometimes characterized by a relative lack of reflexivity born of faith in the rigorous application of the comparative method. Scholars working with the region's languages sometimes place particular ethno-linguistic groupings in whose language-histories they specialize at the center of the historical narratives they construct, whether speakers of Mayan (e.g., Coe 1968, Reilly 1991), Mixe-Zoquean and Oto-Manguean (Campbell and Kaufman 1976, Kaufman and Justeson 2009), or Uto-Aztecan languages (Hill 2001). This makes it nearly impossible for non-experts to objectively decide which narrative is more compelling, while the choice of one narrative over another may have unpredictable political ramifications for present indigenous peoples, thus raising the stakes for privileging one narrative over the other. Furthermore, such studies' contribution to the complex understanding of past discourse forms is frequently limited by the practice among historical linguists of taking isolated "culture words" and their referential meanings as primary analytic objects, rather then studying relations among past forms of discourse and grammatical structuration. Such shortcomings have kept many linguistic anthropologists, to the detriment of both disciplines, from engaging with the comparative historical linguistic method and the types of knowledge it produces.

While the lexicographic approach to historical linguistics remains active, particularly where tied to archaeological and population genetic approaches to the deep past, the growing importance of grammaticalization theory has enabled historically minded linguists to better address the processes by which linguistic structures are shaped by use over time (but see Campbell and Janda 2000 for a critical perspective). The grammaticalization perspective provides a fundamentally semiotic, dialectical understanding of processes through which discourse patterns sediment over time into linguistic structure. One important line of research involves examining the grammatical and structural effects of contact among linguistic groups (whether ethnic groups, regional populations, or social classes) as a potent catalyst for linguistic (and cultural) change (e.g., Thomason and Kaufman 1988, Labov 1994–2010, Harris and Campbell 1995, Thomason 1999, Matras 2009, Trudgill 2010). However, most historically oriented studies of grammaticalization assume that observable grammatical changes are caused by changing discourse patterns, finding the motivation for such change in presumed pragmatic universals. They usually stop short of analyzing how change relates to historically specific communicative contexts aligned with particular discourse genres, expressive media, and historical events. This is an arena where the tools and interests of linguistic anthropology might make important contributions. A promising example of such work is research on "ethnosyntax" (Enfield 2002).

A number of studies deserve special mention as exemplary syntheses of historical linguistic methods and anthropological concern for social context. Evans's (2003) study of kinship practices, discourse patterns, and kinship terms in indigenous Australia shows how processes of grammaticalization in the domain of kinship terms align with historical shifts in the social practices by which relatedness was organized in indigenous societies (see also Blythe 2013). Canger (2011) uses historical linguistic tools to argue, based on years of research into Nahuatl dialectology, that the Classical Nahuatl language of colonial documentary sources is best understood as a koineized urban variety with roots in divergent dialect areas – a reading of the past with great ramifications for Mesoamerican colonial history. Kroskrity (1993) shows how the influx of loanwords into Tewa has been conditioned by changing language ideologies and contexts of interaction between the Tewa and their neighbors over time. Irvine and Gal (2000) examine language structures (the phonemic inventories of Nguni languages), linguistic practices (the use of taboo registers), and particular language ideologies (conceptualizations of how speech should be used to mark social distance and proximity) to understand specific pre-colonial histories of southern Africa. Tuite (2006) stresses that viewing historical linguistics as a fundamentally interpretive rather than fact-seeking endeavor would foreground its narrative-constructing role, thereby bringing it in line with anthropological tendencies to take a reflexive stance towards the narratives we construct.

Thus when joined to nuanced understandings of relationships between communities and linguistic patterns, comparative historical linguistic research can produce results harmonious with anthropological inquiry into language, society, and history. At the same time, that field's methodological and theoretical orientations can encourage a level of attention to historical specificity often lacking in linguistic anthropological work.

9.4.2 Ethnohistorical approaches

Ethnohistory – understood as study of the histories of indigenous peoples, ethnic minorities, marginalized genders or classes, and other groups of peoples whose perspectives are underrepresented in official narratives of history backed by (national) institutions of power – is a field where attention to language has been employed successfully to construct complex pictures of past sociality. The field differentially integrates methods and theories from a diverse set of disciplines, including social history, historical linguistics, linguistic anthropology, and critical theory.

One such synthesis has been the rationalist empiricist framework exemplified by the New Philology school, centered around the work of Lockhart and his students (see Restall 2003 for a cogent overview). Drawing on insights from historical sociolinguistics, these scholars have asked how linguistic micro-variations in minority-language historical documents fit into larger historical patterns. New Philology developed out of research on colonial Mesoamerica, a region with abundant indigenously produced documents, though it has also influenced scholarship of other regions such as the Andes (see Durston 2008 for a comparison of ethnohistorical research in the two regions). New Philologists pay special attention to documents Lockhart termed "mundane" that prior to his influence were rarely studied, such as testaments (Kellogg and Restall 1998, Pizzigoni 2007), land documents (Wood 2003), and local government records (Haskett 1991, Lockhart 1992 and 1993, Terraciano 2001, Terraciano et al. 2005). Such analysis involves tracking the individual lives and concrete events documented in the sources. This approach facilitates narratives stressing disparity between the subjective experiences of the colonized and the colonizers as documented differentially in the texts produced by each group – what Lockhart (1999, 2007) has called "double mistaken identity." This perspective can be used to rethink both indigenous and Spanish perspectives on life under colonial rule, troubling narratives that divide the colonial social world along easy dichotomies between Spanish conquistadors and indigenous victims (e.g., Matthew and Oudijk 2007, Yannakakis 2008).

A different approach claims influences from post-modernism and critical theory, exemplified most clearly by the post-colonial and subaltern study groups of South Asia and Latin America (e.g., Spivak 1988, Mignolo 1992; see Van Young 2004 for a critical assessment of this and the New Philology, and Lockhart 2007 for an equally critical rebuttal from the New Philology perspective). Whereas the philological tradition aims to uncover the past realities out of which the texts they study were produced, critical approaches examine texts to understand how they reproduce ideological visions of those past realities. Like the New Philology, Subaltern and other post-colonial approaches to history employ sophisticated engagement with language but approach language with a different set of theoretical questions, in turn choosing and handling their historical sources differently. Drawing on theorists that explore relations between power and discourse – Nietzsche, Gramsci, Bourdieu, Derrida, and above all Foucault – these scholars have generated methodologies and concepts widely used across the human sciences. Scholars working from this approach engage with the workings of power through attention to how hegemonic ideas – particular linguistic and textual ideologies – are implicated in the performance and institutionalization of power relations. Such research focuses on discourse and discursive formations rather than specific linguistic structures, as well as on genealogies: lines of descent and inheritance through which discursive constructions in the present were born and came to have the meaning they do. Language is engaged primarily through such concepts as performativity and discourse, and rarely through linguistic structure. Work in this vein often focuses on the textual production of power by colonial authorities (e.g., Rabasa 2010, 2011), stressing how these and other historical colonial practices have left a legacy of oppression that must be addressed in the present.

Several scholars have joined interest in the discursive performance of power with linguistic and metalinguistic analysis of sources produced by colonial agents in the languages of empire. Errington's (2008) work on colonial linguistics is a prime example: his critique of the orientalism implicit in the development of historical linguistics analyzes linguistic structure but pays special attention to how the practices by which colonial linguists talked and wrote about colonial languages promoted imperial projects of racialization and domination. Other scholars have combined fine-grained analyses of changing linguistic structures with attention to the political dimensions of metalinguistic ideologies. Some of the most notable examine Christian evangelization in colonial contexts, with particular attention to how domination is made manifest through changes in linguistic structure (e.g., Rafael 1988, Burkhart 1989, Mannheim 1991, Durston 2008).

Another example in this latter category is Hanks's (2010) analysis of how colonial friars imposed Christian concepts of order through *reducción*, a process by which dispersed indigenous populations were relocated in nucleated settlements. In the Yucatán, this produced what Hanks calls *Maya reducido*, a new form of the language that come to pervade and remake all spheres of the Maya discursive universe and whose traces exist today in the speech of contemporary Yucatec Maya speakers. Hanks's masterful study shows how language change at multiple levels aligns with the historically specific reconfiguration of power relations emerging in colonial Yucatán. It is among the best models for work integrating the study of linguistic structures, practices, and ideologies alongside deep engagement with particular historical contexts and historical events. An even more complex vision of this particular language–society–history nexus emerges by reading Hanks' account alongside more traditional ethnohistorical work on the Yucatán (e.g., Chuchiak 2010, Farriss 1987, Restall 1997b), which collectively offer an account of how the Maya received and transmitted the colonially inflected language among themselves. Of course, such a capacious perspective is not possible in all places and periods: the body of historical sources related to Yucatán's colonial past is larger and richer than is available in many other cases. Nevertheless, the complex picture offered by this assemblage of approaches suggests that future research would benefit from trying to approximate a similar synthesis, one joining attention to the social dynamics of specific historical contexts with an examination of how interpretations of histories affect those histories themselves as well as our understandings of them in the present.

9.5 Looking ahead: Toward new research on language, society, and history

Linguistic anthropologists have a range of tools available for producing holistic, nuanced understandings of the field shared by language, society, and history. Taking research to a new level, however, will require synthesizing and integrating the two broad trends marking scholarship to date: research emphasizing the pursuit of history as a kind of fact-finding mission, where engagement with linguistic and cultural context provides access to information otherwise unavailable; and research emphasizing history as a primarily interpretive endeavor, entailing attention to the meanings people have made of history – history as representation – rather than to particular pasts per se. These quite different theoretical frameworks have tended to be coupled to divergent temporal foci: scholarship in the first vein has tended to focus on past historical contexts while that in the second has tended to stress present ethnographic settings. These differences have in turn mapped onto, and been deepened by, disciplinary orientations – toward history and linguistics in the first case, towards anthropology and cultural studies in the second. Such institutionalized divisions and how they facilitate the entrenchment and localization of scholarly discourses make it harder to promote synthetic approaches drawing on both lines of inquiry. It is notable that of the works reviewed here, few do so successfully.

Producing scholarship that is effective on this score will not be easy, and it would be foolish to suggest there are easy solutions. Nevertheless, we think the field's development to date suggests areas where scholars might fruitfully direct their energies in order to integrate historical and meta-historical approaches. Doing so offers the hope of more fully synthesizing the study of history with the study of social life, and of joining linguistic anthropology's ongoing interest in language use as social process with attention to how history is both made and made meaningful through such social processes.

The late Rolph Trouillot (1995) argued that in order to achieve new understandings of past events we must attend to how our narratives of history are based on both conscious and unconscious decisions about what is of historical interest, for otherwise we are at the mercy of dominant ideologies about history and received facts about the past. This admonishment demands that we be reflexive about our processes for selecting and discarding data – about, as it were, the archives we consciously and unconsciously create. Language is, of course, a peculiar kind of archive, and the selective terms on which we engage with it analytically remake the archive in ways we may fail to recognize. Bakhtin would, of course, agree with Emerson that "language is the archives of history": each linguistic sign, each utterance, is a footnoted, multivocal, polysemous entity, a palimpsest made of numerous past contexts and numerous interpretations of their meaning. The promise language holds out, however, for deeper understanding of history in social context will remain unrealized unless we also take to heart how language not only archives history but makes it as well, producing historical realities and also the narratives by which those histories are made meaningful – and not least, those narratives that we, as scholars, use language to construct.

References

Abu El Haj, Nadia. 2002. *Facts on the Ground: Archaeological Practice and Territorial Self-Fashioning in Israeli Society*. Chicago: University of Chicago Press.

Agha, Asif. 2007. *Language and Social Relations*. Cambridge: Cambridge University Press.

 2011. Meet Mediatization. *Language and Communication* 31(3): 163–70.

Alcock, Susan. 2001. *Archaeologies of the Greek Past: Landscape, Monuments and Memory*. Cambridge: Cambridge University Press.

Bakhtin, Mikhail. 1981. *The Dialogic Imagination: Four Essays*, trans. Caryl Emerson and Michael Holquist. University of Texas Press.

Basso, Keith. 1996. *Wisdom Sits in Places: Landscape and Language Among the Western Apache*. Albuquerque: University of New Mexico Press.

Bauman, Richard. 2004. *A World of Others' Words: Cross-Cultural Perspectives on Intertextuality*. Malden, MA: Blackwell.

Bauman, Richard, and Charles L. Briggs. 2003. *Voices of Modernity: Language Ideologies and the Politics of Inequality*. Cambridge: Cambridge University Press.

Besnier, Niko. 1995. *Literacy, Emotion, and Authority: Reading and Writing on a Polynesian Atoll*. Studies in the Social and Cultural Foundations of Language 16. Cambridge: Cambridge University Press.

Blythe, Joe. 2013. Preference Organization Driving Structuration: Evidence from Australian Aboriginal interaction for pragmatically motivated grammaticalization. *Language* 89(4): 883–919.

Boone, Elizabeth, and Walter Mignolo. 1994. *Writing Without Words: Alternative Literacies in Mesoamerica and the Andes*. Durham: Duke University Press.

Boone, Elizabeth, and Gary Urton. 2011. *Their Way of Writing: Scripts, Signs, and Pictographies in Pre-Columbian America*. Cambridge, MA: Harvard University Press.

Burkhart, Louise M. 1989. *The Slippery Earth: Nahuatl–Christian Moral Dialogue in Sixteenth-Century Mexico*. Tucson: University of Arizona Press.

Campbell, Lyle. 1998. *Historical Linguistics: An Introduction*. Edinburgh: Edinburgh University Press.

Campbell, Lyle, and Terrence Kaufman. 1976. A Linguistic Look at the Olmec. *American Antiquity* 41(1): 80–9.

Campbell, Lyle, and Richard Janda. 2000. Introduction: conceptions of grammaticalization and their problems. *Language Sciences* 23(2–3): 93–112.

Canger, Una. 2011. El nauatl urbano de Tlatelolco/Tenochtitlan, resultado de convergencia entre dialectos, con un esbozo brevísimo de la historia de los dialectos. *Estudios de Cultura Náhuatl* 42: 243–58.

Chuchiak, John F. 2010. Writing as Resistance: Maya Graphic Pluralism and Indigenous Elite Strategies for Survival in Colonial Yucatán 1550–1750. *Ethnohistory* 57(1): 87–116.

Coe, Michael D. 1968. *America's First Civilization*. New York: American Heritage.

Crossland, Zoe. 2009. Of Clues and Signs: The dead body and its evidential traces. *American Anthropologist* 111(1):69–80.

Dick, H. P. 2010. Imagined Lives and Modernist Chronotopes in Mexican Nonmigrant Discourse. *American Ethnologist* 37: 275–90.

Dinwoodie, David W. 2006. Time and the Individual in Native North America. In *New Perspectives on Native North America: Cultures, Histories, And Representations*, ed. Sergei Kan, Pauline Turner Strong, and Raymond Fogelson, 327–50. Lincoln: University of Nebraska.

Durston, Alan. 2007. *Pastoral Quechua: The History of Christian Translation in Colonial Peru, 1550–1650*. Notre Dame, IN: University of Notre Dame Press.

2008. Native-Language Literacy in Colonial Peru: The question of mundane Quechua writing revisited. *Hispanic American Historical Review* 88(1): 41–70.

Eisenlohr, Patrick. 2007. *Little India: Diaspora, Time, and Ethnolinguistic Belonging in Hindu Mauritius*. Berkeley: University of California Press.

Emerson, Ralph Waldo. 2000. *The Essential Writings of Ralph Waldo Emerson*, ed. Brooks Atkinson. New York: Modern Library.

Enfield, N. J., ed. 2002. *Ethnosyntax*. Oxford: Oxford University Press.

Errington, Joseph. 2008. *Linguistics in a Colonial World: A Story of Language, Meaning, and Power*. Oxford: Blackwell Publishing.

Evans, Nicholas. 2003. Context, Culture, and Structuration in the Languages of Australia. *Annual Review of Anthropology* 32: 13–40.

Fabian, J. 1983. *Time and the Other: How Anthropology Makes Its Object*. New York: Columbia University Press.

Farriss, Nancy M. 1987. Remembering the Future, Anticipating the Past: History, Time, and Cosmology among the Maya of Yucatan. *Comparative Studies in Society and History* 29: 566–93.

Faudree, Paja. 2012. Performativity and the Temporal Pragmatics of Power: Speech acts of the conquest. *Journal of Linguistic Anthropology* 22(3): 182–200.

2013. *Singing for the Dead: The Politics of Indigenous Revival in Mexico*. Durham, NC: Duke University Press.

Geertz, Armin W. 1994. *The Invention of Prophesy: Continuity and Meaning in Hopi Indian Religion*. Berkeley: University of California Press.

Graham, Laura. 1995. *Performing Dreams: Discourses of Immortality among the Xavante Indians of central Brazil*. Austin: University of Texas Press.

Hanks, William. F. 2010. *Converting Words: Maya in the Age of the Cross*. Berkeley: University of California Press.

Harris, Alice C., and Lyle Campbell. 1995. *Historical Syntax in Cross-Linguistic Perspective*. Cambridge: Cambridge University Press.

Haskett, Robert. 1991. *Indigenous Rulers: An Ethnohistory of Town Government in Colonial Cuernavaca*. Albuquerque: University of New Mexico Press.

Hill, Jane H. 2001. Proto-Uto-Aztecan: A Community of Cultivators in Central Mexico? *American Anthropologist* 103(4): 913–34.

2005. Intertextuality as Source and Evidence for Indirect Indexical Meanings. *Journal of Linguistic Anthropology* 15: 113–24.

Houston, Stephen, ed. 2004. *The First Writing: Script Invention as History and Process.* Cambridge: Cambridge University Press.

———. 2008. The Small Deaths of Maya Writing. In *The Disappearance of Writing Systems*, ed. John Baines, John Bennett, and Stephen Houston. London: Equinox.

Inoue, M. 2004. Introduction: Temporality and Historicity in and through Linguistic Ideology. *Journal of Linguistic Anthropology* 14: 1–5.

Irvine, Judith T. 2004. Say When: Temporalities in language ideology. *Journal of Linguistic Anthropology* 14: 99–109.

Irvine, Judith T., and Susan Gal. 2000. Language Ideology and Linguistic Differentiation. In *Regimes of Language: Ideologies, Polities, and Identities*, ed. Paul Kroskrity, 35–83. Santa Fe, NM: School of American Research Press.

Jansen, Maarten. 1990. The Search for History in Mixtec Codices. *Ancient Mesoamerica* 1: 99–112.

Kaufman, Terrence, and John Justeson. 2009. Historical linguistics and pre-columbian Mesoamerica. *Ancient Mesoamerica* 20(2): 221–31.

Kellogg, Susan, and Matthew Restall, eds. 1998. *Dead Giveaways: Indigenous Testaments of Colonial Mesoamerica and the Andes.* Salt Lake City: University of Utah Press.

Kockelman, Paul, and A. Bernstein. 2012. Semiotic Technologies, Temporal Reckoning, and the Portability of Meaning, Or: Modern modes of temporality – just how abstract are they? *Anthropological Theory* 12(3): 320–48.

Kroskrity, Paul V. 1993. *Language, History, and Identity: Ethnolinguistic Studies of the Arizona Tewa.* Tucson: University of Arizona Press.

Kulick, Don. 1992. *Language Shift and Cultural Reproduction: Socialization, Self, and Syncretism in a Papua New Guinean Village.* Cambridge: Cambridge University Press.

Labov, William. 1994–2010. *Principles of Linguistic Change*, Vols. 1–3. Oxford: Basil Blackwell.

Lempert, Michael. 2007. Conspicuously Past: Distressed discourse and diagrammatic embedding in a Tibetan represented speech style. *Language and Communication* 27(3): 258–71.

Lempert, Michael, and Sabina Perrino. 2007. Entextualization and the ends of temporality. *Language and Communication* 27(3): 205–11.

Lockhart, James. 1992. *The Nahuas After the Conquest: A Social and Cultural History of the Indians of Central Mexico, Sixteenth Through Eighteenth Centuries.* Stanford, CA: Stanford University Press.

———, ed. 1993. *We People Here: Nahuatl Accounts of the Conquest of Mexico.* Berkeley and Los Angeles: University of California Press.

———. 1999. *Of Things of the Indies: Essays Old and New in Early Latin American History.* Stanford, CA: Stanford University Press.

2007. Introduction: Background and Course of the New Philology. In *Sources and Methods for the Study of Postconquest Mesoamerican Ethnohistory, Provisional Version* (e-book), ed. James Lockhart, Stephanie Wood, and Lisa Sousa. Eugene, OR: Wired Humanities Project, University of Oregon, 2007. Expanded in 2010. Accessed at http://whp.uoregon.edu/Lockhart/index.html on April 19, 2012.

Makihara, Miki. 2001. Book Reviews. *Rongorongo: the Easter Island Script. History. Traditions. Text.* Steven Roger Fischer. Oxford and N.Y.: Oxford University Press. *Anthropological Linguistics* 43(1): 111-15.

Malotki, Ekkehart. 1983. *Hopi Time: A Linguistic Analysis of the Temporal Concepts in the Hopi Language.* Berlin: Mouton.

Mannheim, Bruce. 1991. *The Language of the Inka Since the European Invasion.* Austin: University of Texas Press.

Matthew, Laura E., and Michel Oudijk. 2007. *Indian Conquistadors.* Norman: University of Oklahoma Press.

Matras, Yaron. 2009. *Language Contact.* Cambridge: Cambridge University Press.

Meek, Barbra. 2011. *We Are Our Language: An Ethnography of Language Revitalization in a Northern Athabaskan Community.* Tucson: University of Arizona Press.

Mignolo, Walter. 1992. *The Darker Side of the Renaissance: Literacy, Territoriality, and Colonization.* Ann Arbor: University of Michigan Press.

Miller, Flagg. 2007. *The Moral Resonance of Arab Media: Audiocassette Poetry and Culture in Yemen.* Harvard University Middle Eastern Monographs series. Cambridge, MA: Harvard University Press.

Monaghan, Leila. 2011. Expanding Boundaries of Linguistic Anthropology: 2010 in perspective. *American Anthropologist* 113(2): 222-34.

Parmentier, Richard J. 1987. *The Sacred Remains: Myth, History, and Polity in Belau.* Chicago: University of Chicago Press.

   1994. *Signs in Society: Studies in Semiotic Anthropology.* Bloomington: Indiana University Press.

   2007. It's About Time: On the semiotics of temporality. *Language and Communication* 27(3): 272-7.

Perrino, Sabina. 2007. Cross-Chronotope Alignment in Senegalese Oral Narrative. *Language and Communication* 27(3): 227-44.

   2011. Chronotopes of Story and Storytelling Event in Interviews. *Language in Society* 40(1): 91-103.

Pizzigoni, Caterina, ed. and trans. 2007. *Testaments of Toluca.* UCLA Latin American Center Nahuatl Studies Series, 8. Stanford, CA: Stanford University Press; Los Angeles: UCLA Latin American Center Publications.

Preucel, Robert. 2006. *Archaeological Semiotics.* Oxford: Blackwell Press.

Quilter, J., and G.D. Urton, eds. 2002. *Narrative Threads: Accounting and Recounting in Andean Khipu.* Austin: University of Texas Press.

Rabasa, Jose. 2010. *Without History: Subaltern Studies, the Apatista Insurgency, and the Specter of History.* Pittsburgh, PA: University of Pittsburgh Press.

2011. *Tell Me the Story of how I Conquered You: Elsewheres and Ethnosuicide in the Colonial Mesoamerican World*. Austin: University of Texas Press.

Rafael, Vicente. 1988. *Contracting Colonialism: Translation and Christian Conversion in Tagalog Society under Early Spanish* Rule. Ithaca, NY: Cornell University Press.

Rappaport, J., and T. Cummins. 2011. *Beyond the Lettered City: Indigenous Literacies in the Andes*. Durham, NC: Duke University Press.

Restall, Matthew. 1997a. Heirs to the Hieroglyphics: Indigenous writing in Colonial Mesoamerica. *The Americas* 54(2): 239–67.

1997b. *The Maya World: Yucatec Culture and Society, 1550–1850*. Stanford, CA: Stanford University Press.

2003. A History of the New Philology and the New Philology in History. *Latin American Historical Review* 38: 113–34.

Reilly, F. Kent, III. 1991. Olmec Iconographic Influences on the Symbols of Maya Rulership: An examination of possible sources. In *Sixth Palenque Round Table, 1986*, ed. Virginia M. Fields, 151–66. Norman: University of Oklahoma Press.

Salomon, Frank 2001. How an Andean "Writing Without Words" Works. *Current Anthropology* 42(1): 1–27.

2004. *The Cord Keepers: Khipus and Cultural Life in a Peruvian Village*. Durham, NC: Duke University Press.

Sapir, Edward. 1916. *Time Perspective in Aboriginal American Culture: A Study in Method*. Canada Department of Mines, Geological Survey, Memoir 90. Anthropological Series, No. 13.

Schiffrin, Debora. 2009. Crossing Boundaries: The nexus of time, space, person, and place in narrative. *Language in Society* 38: 421–45

Silverstein, Michael. 1993. Metapragmatic Discourse and Metapragmatic Function. In *Reflexive Language: Reported Speech and Metapragmatics*, ed. J. Lucy, 33–58. Cambridge: Cambridge University Press.

2005. Axes of Evals. *Journal of Linguistic Anthropology* 15: 6–22.

Silverstein, Michael, and Greg Urban, eds. 1996. *Natural Histories of Discourse*. Chicago: Chicago University Press.

Stasch, Rupert. 2011. Textual Iconicity and the Primitivist Cosmos: Chronotopes of desire in travel writing about Korowai of West Papua. *Journal of Linguistic Anthropology* 21: 1–21.

Spivak, Gayatri Chakravorty. 1988. Can the Subaltern Speak? In *Marxism and the Interpretation of Culture*, ed. Cary Nelson and Lawrence Grossberg, 271–313. Urbana: University of Illinois Press.

Tedlock, Dennis, and Bruce Mannheim, eds. 1995. *The Dialogic Emergence of Culture*. Urbana: University of Illinois Press.

Terraciano, Kevin. 2001. *The Mixtecs of Colonial Oaxaca: Ñudzahui History, Sixteenth through Eighteenth Centuries*. Stanford, CA: Stanford University Press.

Terraciano, Kevin, Lisa Sousa, and Matthew Restall, eds. 2005. *Mesoamerican Voices: Native-Language Writings from Colonial Mexico, Oaxaca, Yucatan, and Guatemala*. Cambridge: Cambridge University Press.

Thomason, Sarah G. 1999. Speakers' Choices in Language Change. *Studies in the Linguistic Sciences* 29: 19–43.

Thomason, Sarah Grey, and Terrence Kaufman. 1988. *Language Contact, Creolization, and Genetic Linguistics*. Berkeley: University of California Press.

Tomlinson, Gary. 2009. *Singing of the New World: Indigenous Voice in the Era of European Contact*. New York: Cambridge University Press.

Trouillot, Michel Rolph. 1995. *Silencing the Past: Power and the Production of History*. Beacon Press.

Trudgill, Peter. 2010. *Investigations in Sociohistorical Linguistics: Stories of Colonization and Contact*. Cambridge: Cambridge University Press.

Tuite, Kevin. 2006. Interpreting Language Variation and Change. In *Language, Culture and Society: Key Topics in Linguistic Anthropology*, ed. Christine Jourdan and Kevin Tuite, 229–56. Cambridge: Cambridge University Press.

Urban, Greg. 1996. *Metaphysical Community: The Interplay of the Senses and the Intellect*. Austin: University of Texas Press.

2001. *Metaculture: How Culture Moves through the World*. Minneapolis: University of Minnesota Press.

Urton, Gary. 2003. *Signs of the Inka Khipu: Binary Coding in the Andean Knotted-String Records*. Austin: University of Texas Press.

Van Dyke, Ruth M., and Susan E. Alcock, eds. 2003. *Archaeologies of Memory*. Oxford: Blackwell Publishing.

Van Young, Eric. 2004. Two Decades of Anglophone Historical Writing on Colonial Mexico: Continuity and change since 1980. *Mexican Studies/Estudios Mexicanos* 20(2): 275–326.

White, Hayden. 1973. *Metahistory: The Historical Imagination in Nineteenth-Century Europe*. Baltimore: Johns Hopkins University Press.

Whorf, Benjamin Lee. 1956. The Relation of Habitual Thought and Behavior to Language. In *Language, Thought, and Reality: Selected Writings of Benjamin Lee Whorf*, ed. Benjamin Carroll, 134–59. Cambridge, MA: Technology Press of Massachusetts Institute of Technology.

Wirtz, Kristina. 2007. Enregistered Memory and Afro-Cuban Historicity in Santería's Ritual Speech. *Language and Communication* 27(3): 245–57.

Wolf, Eric. 2010[1982]. *Europe and the People without History*. Berkeley: University of California Press.

Wood, Stephanie. 2003. *Transcending Conquest: Nahua Views of Spanish Colonial Mexico*. Norman: University of Oklahoma Press.

Woolard, K. A. 2004. Is the Past a Foreign Country?: Time, language origins, and the nation in early modern Spain. *Journal of Linguistic Anthropology* 14: 57–80.

2008. Why Dat Now? Linguistic-anthropological contributions to the explanation of sociolinguistic icons and change. *Journal of Sociolinguistics* 12(4): 432–52.

Yannakakis, Y. 2008. *The Art of Being In-Between: Native Intermediaries, Indian Identity, and Local Rule in Colonial Oaxaca*. Durham, NC: Duke University Press.

10

Language emergence

Al-Sayyid Bedouin Sign Language

Wendy Sandler, Mark Aronoff, Carol Padden, and Irit Meir

10.1 The forbidden experiment

Language and culture separate humans from all other species. No human group lacks either, which must mean that both are deeply seated in human nature. What are the essential ingredients of these two most human of attributes? Our central task as linguists is to try to answer this question for language.

One strategy for tackling this problem is to trace all existing human languages back to some original and so discover the fundamental properties of language. Nineteenth-century historical linguists tried to do this, with notable success, beginning from William Jones's observation that Sanskrit was so similar to Greek, Latin, Gothic, Celtic, and Persian that they must have descended from a common ancestor. Though remarkably reliable, the methods of historical linguistics are incapable of taking us back more than a few thousand years. In the nineteenth century, when most educated people believed that the world had begun no more than six thousand years before, these limitations presented no barrier to answering the question of the origin of language, and historical linguistics flourished. But Charles Lyell, the founder of geology, destroyed all such hope when he argued successfully that the earth must be much older. We now know that the earth is billions of years old, that the human lineage split from the other great apes approximately six million years ago, and that anatomically modern humans have inhabited the earth for at least one hundred thousand years, emerging from Africa to spread across the globe at least fifty thousand years ago (see Dediu, this volume, Chapter 28). All of which means that we will never learn, using conventional historical linguistic methods, what the first human language was like.

Another tactic that linguists have advocated is to compare many modern languages. If we can discover what they all share, sometimes called *language universals*, then this may tell us what the basic structure of human languages is like. But detailed comparison of many languages has revealed that they are much more diverse, at least on the surface, than researchers had hoped. This has led some researchers (Evans and Levinson, 2009: 168–9) to conclude that while many languages have properties similar to other languages, there are no universal properties that all languages share. Others (Hauser et al., 2002) have looked for more abstract unifying principles, but in doing so they have had to jettison most of the properties that others deem central to human language (see Pinker and Jackendoff, 2005 for a description of these properties).

Both methods betray a fundamental problem that faces anyone dealing with the central question of language. Humans naturally acquire the language or languages that they are exposed to in early childhood, seemingly without effort, but these languages are different from one another and are all the product of historical change over many millennia, much of it resulting from chance. We can get at whatever is basic to human language by somehow controlling for this great diversity and historical contingency. One way to do this, termed *the forbidden experiment* by Shattuck (1980), has never been attempted scientifically because it is clearly unethical. It is to isolate a growing child from exposure to *any* existing language. Whatever language emerges under such circumstances will be untainted. There have been a number of recorded cases of children who have been deprived of human contact from infancy, but they present another problem besides the ethical one: humans are social creatures and when they are deprived of contact with others, especially in their very early years, they do not develop normally.

But what if humans were isolated from a linguistically organized model in some way that did not isolate them socially? What sort of language would they develop then? Susan Goldin-Meadow realized that deaf children born into hearing households in which exposure to sign language is prohibited presented just such a case (Goldin-Meadow and Feldman, 1977). They could not acquire the language that surrounded them and so had to create a system on their own. Goldin-Meadow (2003) has continued to provide insight from this sort of data successfully ever since.

But, as Goldin-Meadow would be the first to admit, this circumstance lacks one ingredient that characterizes all normal language communities: the opportunity for organized linguistic feedback. No matter how well intentioned the parents of a deaf child may be, the child is the only deaf person involved in the interaction. What would happen in a hearing family with more than one deaf child? Would the feedback that these children give one another exclusively in the visual medium lead to a communication system that is more like a language? And what if the parents were actively trying to interact with the deaf children in their own medium? Might this lead to a more structured system? What has been found may be even more interesting than such a scenario, and has been the subject of our own research for the past decade: a large extended family of deaf people that began with four deaf siblings.

10.2 The social conditions under which sign languages arise

Sign languages exist throughout the world, on almost every continent. Spoken languages are by far the most common human language type, but that sign languages exist at all is testament to the fact that human language can develop from very different resources – not speech primarily but elevating the hands, the body, and the face to become major articulators. Natural sign languages are social creations that emerge in communities with an acute need to communicate. Because the community has deaf members, either because of illness or genetic inheritance, the community resorts to using rich movement of hands on or around the body, accompanied by movements of the face and body, to create meaningful communication. While hearing people use such gestures as well, deaf people avail themselves solely of visually perceived signals, and, over time, these innovations become regularized and grammaticized as sign language.

Some sign languages have a relatively long history, with written records dating to as early as the sixteenth century in Spain (Plann, 1997). Many sign languages in Europe and North America developed from the establishment of schools for deaf children through the eighteenth and nineteenth centuries. We call these "deaf community" sign languages (Meir, Sandler et al., 2010; Meir, Israel et al., 2012) because they were formed out of interaction among a community of (mostly) deaf signers, over multiple generations.

Sign languages continue to emerge. New ones have appeared within the last few generations. These very young languages are reported from different parts of the world, for example, from Bali (Marsaja, 2008), Nicaragua (Senghas and Coppola, 2001), Ghana (Nyst, 2003), and Algeria (Lanesman and Meir, 2012), implying that language creation of this type has likely occurred many times through history. Because some of these languages emerged very recently, it is possible to watch a language grow from its roots in gesture and other forms of visible communication to its current linguistic form. Some of these new sign languages, such as Nicaraguan Sign Language, are deaf community sign languages, developing from cohorts of students attending a school for deaf children. Other new sign languages are "village sign languages," where signers share kinship and a geographic area. Most often the basis of deafness in a village sign language is genetic, and this has a number of consequences that figure in language emergence.[1]

10.3 Al-Sayyid Bedouin Sign Language

Village sign languages can emerge first in a single nuclear family. In the case of Al-Sayyid Bedouin Sign Language (ABSL), four deaf siblings were born into a family of hearing parents and other hearing siblings in the

1930s. Later, deaf children were born into other families. After about seventy-five years, there are approximately 130 deaf members in a village of about 4,000 people (Kisch 2012). ABSL has persisted across four generations, changing as more people use the language.[2] What is notable about many village sign languages is the large numbers of hearing people who use these languages. From studying these sign languages we learn not only how deaf people in the community can communicate with others, but how hearing people, too, contribute in large part to the creation and persistence of a sign language across multiple generations. ABSL is now entering its fourth generation of signers.

In the case of village sign languages, genetics and social conditions are deeply interconnected. In Al-Sayyid, the shared genetic condition is recessive and non-syndromic. This means that deaf people can be born into a family with two hearing parents (if both are carriers), and hearing siblings, and that most deaf people have no other genetic conditions accompanying their deafness. There is no social prohibition against their integration, so they may participate fully in the social and work life of the community. In Al-Sayyid, as in many communities throughout the Middle East, marriage between close relatives is favored. While deafness is noted as an impairment, it is not stigmatized, so deaf people in Al-Sayyid may marry. The combined result of a recessive condition and intermarriage is close kinship ties between deaf and hearing people, who feel the need to communicate in sign language as acutely as do deaf people.

Over the period of seventy-five years since the first four deaf siblings were born in Al-Sayyid, and ABSL with them, more households have acquired deaf members. We find a shared sign vocabulary within a household with several siblings and other first-order relatives. We call the language within a household a *familylect*. Across households, there may be two or more different signs for common names and objects, such as CAT, DOG, TOMATO, and EGG. Despite the existence of variation across families, signers still understand each other's signs, and tolerate differences in lexical choice. Nonetheless, all signers share a great deal of vocabulary (Meir, Sandler et al., 2012) and grammatical structure, summarized here. The emergence of linguistic structure can be seen within the household, and across households in the community.

We have often been asked whether the spoken language of the hearing people influences the sign language under these circumstances, an idea we would like to address at this point. In the case of ABSL, we have not found such influence. For example, the SOV word order of ABSL does not follow the SVO order of the local language (Sandler et al., 2005). While the local Arabic is a richly inflected language, no inflection has been found in ABSL (Padden et al., 2010a). The hearing interlocutors seem to have an intuitive understanding that the medium is different, and regard Arabic and ABSL as two different linguistic systems. Of course, cultural influence is found in meanings reflected in some signs, for example, in early names for days of the week such as 'market day' and 'prayer day' (Meir et al., 2012). However, no influence of Arabic grammatical structure has been found, and there is no evidence of creolization between the signed and spoken languages. Instead, the study of new sign languages such as ABSL offers a real-life view of how a language emerges anew, how it conventionalizes and spreads across users in a community.

10.3.1 Syntax

A fundamental property of human language is the existence of syntax, the level of organization that contains conventions for combining symbolic units, the words. Syntax provides the means for encoding the semantic content of propositions. Some of the resources available for this purpose are the relations among words and phrases, elements that mark dependency relations such as inflectional morphemes and function words, and elements that mark cross-reference such as pronouns. Which of all these elements are available for a new language, and how can a language develop them over time?

We learn from grammaticization research that function words can develop from content words. A word meaning 'head' or 'top' may evolve into a preposition meaning 'on top of', and eventually 'on'. Such processes are attested in all languages and are very common (Heine and Kuteva, 2002b). They may even be found in very early stages of a language.[3] Sign languages are no exception. In ABSL we find that the verb RUN is also used as an adverb QUICKLY, and in Israeli Sign Language (ISL) the verb BEAT/WIN has acquired the meaning 'more than'.

Inflectional morphemes often develop from function words, and constitute a final stage of the grammaticization process. A preposition such as "on" may eventually develop into a case marker (Heine and Kuteva, 2002a). Yet the process of developing first function words and then inflectional morphemes takes a long time. The Romance future inflection, for example, took several centuries to evolve. We cannot expect such machinery to accrue early in the development of a language. This leads to another question: How can a language express the semantic content of a proposition without linguistic items designated to mark grammatical relations?

One major problem in conveying propositional content is marking "who did what to whom." Sometimes such information may be inferred from the semantics of the verb, properties of the arguments, contextual clues, and general knowledge. Yet semantic and contextual clues may lead to a dead end. While the string of words *boy tree hug* can have only one plausible interpretation in our world, the string *boy girl hug* may have two plausible interpretations, which can be systematically distinguished only if a communication system develops formal means for marking the hugger and the huggee. Once this is introduced into the system, the system becomes independent of the pragmatic context, and can expand its expressive capabilities to describe events that cannot happen in our world, such as *The tree hugged/talked to the boy.*

How, then, does such a mechanism emerge in a new language? Does it show up full-blown right from the beginning, or does it take time to develop? Is there one universal course of development?

Our findings suggest some answers to these questions. We find that users of a new language initially avoid marking argument structure grammatically and instead use a variety of strategies that eliminate the need for overt marking. One is to use single-argument clauses. If a clause has only one argument, then its relationship to the verb can be inferred from the semantics of the verb and there is no possible ambiguity about which argument bears which role. If a language is restricted to one-argument clauses, there is no need to develop argument structure marking.

We find this single argument structure commonly in older signers of ABSL, and of Israeli Sign Language (ISL) as well.[4] When describing transitive events with two human participants, these older signers often break the event into two clauses, with two verb signs, each predicating of a different participant. Thus, an event in which a girl feeds a woman may be described as: WOMAN SIT; GIRL FEED. An event in which a man throws a ball to a girl can be rendered as: GIRL STAND; MAN BALL THROW; GIRL CATCH. In ISL, 33 percent of the descriptions of such events used this strategy, and in ABSL the proportion was even higher – 47 percent of the responses (Meir, 2010; Padden *et al.*, 2010a).

The same tendency towards one-argument clauses has been reported for another new sign language, Nicaraguan Sign Language, which emerged about thirty years ago, when the first school for the deaf was founded in Managua. The first group of deaf children brought to the school came from hearing families, and were not exposed to signing deaf adults. However, as they began to communicate with each other, a signing system started to emerge. The use of this system by subsequent cohorts of children who acquired it from their older peers brought changes into the language. Ann Senghas and her colleagues, who have been studying the language since its inception, report that the first cohort showed a strong tendency towards one-argument clauses if both arguments participating in an event were human. In fact, in their data they did not find *any* response consisting of two human nouns and a verb (Senghas *et al.*, 1997: 554). Typical responses were: MAN PUSH WOMAN FALL, MAN PUSH WOMAN GET-PUSHED when describing a clip showing a man pushing a woman, and MAN CUP GIVE WOMAN RECEIVE for an event in which a man is giving a cup to a woman. In the second cohort different word orders appeared, some of which had the two verbs adjacent to each other (e.g., MAN WOMAN PUSH FALL, or MAN PUSH FALL WOMAN). However, even in the second cohort no responses consisted of two human nouns and one verb.

Three young languages, then, show a very strong preference for one-argument clauses in their initial stages.[5] The strategy of producing two clauses for an event such as pushing, although efficient in terms of associating arguments with syntactic roles and avoiding ambiguities, is cumbersome. First, the number of verbs in the discourse is multiplied, since every animate argument is associated with a different verb. Secondly, it is not always clear which verbs can be used to predicate each of the different arguments of an event. For example, in the case of a seeing event, as in *The child saw the man*, what verb can be associated with the object? The only verb that comes to mind is 'be seen', so that the event is rendered as *The child sees, the man is seen*. This, again, creates a very "heavy" and, in a way, redundant discourse.

We expect a communication system that functions as a language to eventually develop a consistent device for marking argument roles. Of the three mechanisms for marking participants' roles mentioned above – word order, case marking, and verb agreement – the last two are morphological. Inflectional morphology takes time to develop, because it calls for the arbitrary association of a phonological string with a grammatical function, often through the very gradual grammaticization of a lexical element (Heine and Kuteva, 2002a). The literature on creole languages provides numerous examples of the phenomenon (Bruyn, 2008). McWhorter (1998) claims that the youngest creoles show no inflectional morphology, which only develops with time. However, word order, the relative order of the different constituents of a clause, requires no grammaticization of lexical material. It can therefore be expected to appear earlier in the development of a language. And indeed, we find that some new sign languages make use of this possibility.

Several village sign languages have developed a predominant word order. ABSL developed SOV order by its second generation. In our study of nine second-generation signers of ABSL, a consistent SOV order emerged (Sandler et al., 2005; Padden et al., 2010b). Though one-argument clauses by far outnumber multi-argument clauses (99 clauses out of 150), out of those 51 clauses containing two or more arguments, 31 (61%) were SOV, 8 (16%) were SVO, and 5 (10%) were OSV.[6]

Information about other sign languages emerging in small village communities suggests that in some of them a consistent word order had not developed by the time the studies were conducted. Kata Kolok, a village sign language of Bali, adheres to SVO order when possible ambiguities may arise (e.g., when both participants in an action can be either the subject or the object, as in *X sees Y*), but uses more flexible word order when the sentence can be disambiguated by its semantics alone (Marsaja, 2008: 168–9). In the sign language of Providence Island, Colombia, much variation in word order was reported (Washabaugh, 1986: 60). Deaf signers tended to put the verb at the end, but did not use consistent order between agents and patients. Hearing signers were more consistent: they tended to have agents before patients in 99 percent of their utterances. As for the position of the verb, those hearing signers who had deaf family members placed the verb in final position in 64 percent of their responses, while those who did not have daily contact with deaf people had verb-final order only 23 percent of the time. This difference may be interference from the spoken vernacular: Providence Island Creole, like many other creoles, is characterized by SVO order (Arends and Perl, 1995).

Deaf community sign languages have also been reported to exhibit a variety of word orders. Signers of the first two generations of ISL show no preference for any specific word order. In their responses to a set of thirty video clips, third-generation signers use SOV order more than other orders (32%), but SVO and SVOV are also found (14% and 10% respectively; Meir, 2010). The SVO order might reflect interference from Hebrew. The sign language of Nicaragua showed rapid early change in word order. First-cohort signers used mainly NV or NNV order (that is, sentences consisting of a noun or two nouns and a verb), while second-cohort signers introduced many more orders (Senghas et al., 1997). In older deaf community sign languages, both SVO and SOV orders have been reported as basic. ASL is SVO (Fischer, 1975; Liddell, 1980), and so is Brazilian Sign Language (Quadros, 1999), while German Sign Language is SOV (Glück and Pfau, 1998; Rathmann, 2000).

Although consistent word order for marking argument structure requires no development of special overt linguistic machinery, it does not appear right away in all new sign languages. The variability reported on in the literature shows that there is no one course of development that is necessarily taken by a new language. Additionally, a community might take a few generations before it settles on a specific word order.

10.3.1.1 Prosody and syntax

The syntactic ordering that we found early in the creation of ABSL operates within clauses and phrases. In order to investigate the emergence of how clauses might be organized in relation to one another, we turned to prosody, since it has been established for some sign languages that such relations may be conveyed prosodically, as we explain below. Through the comparison of short stretches of discourse in the language of older second-generation signers with those of signers about twenty years younger, we found differences that revealed more complexity as the language develops, both in the syntactic structure within the clause, and in the prosodic structure that links them (Sandler, Meir et al., 2011).

10.3.1.2 Prosody as a clue to the functions and complexity of utterances

When a linguist or anthropologist takes on the daunting task of describing and analyzing a newly encountered language, prosody is an essential tool, whether it is exploited explicitly or implicitly. Even before we understand the words, the rhythm, intonation, and stress of prosody help us separate utterances from one another in a discourse; determine whether an utterance has declarative, interrogative, or some other function; and infer when two constituents are connected to one another, through coordination or subordination of some kind.

Prosody can distinguish *Do you want an apple or banana cake?* (two kinds of cake) from *Do you want an apple? Or banana cake?* (fruit or cake) (Pierrehumbert and Hirschberg, 1990). It can signal continuation between a subordinate and matrix clause, as in the conditional sentence, *If it rains, we'll stay home and watch TV*. In this example, there is a rhythmic break between the *if-* clause and the *then-*clause, and rising intonation on *rains*, signaling the link to the next clause. Each clause here comprises a prosodic unit called an intonational phrase, marked rhythmically, for example, by phrase-final lengthening, and intonationally by pitch excursions, typically at the edge of the phrase. These cues make the boundaries of intonational phrases salient. While conditionals can be marked by "if," and by different tense marking in the two clauses, as in the "rain" example, these syntactic markers are not required. *You overcook that steak and you're fired!* spoken to a new cook in a restaurant is clearly a conditional utterance.

All natural languages have prosody, and sign languages are no exception (Sandler, 2011, 2012a). Of the three components of prosody, here we deal mainly with rhythm (timing) and intonation, leaving stress (prominence) aside. How is prosody manifested in sign languages? First, the timing, delineating constituent structure, is signaled by the hands, which convey the lexical items. At the end of an intonational phrase, for example, the hands carry phrase-final lengthening – the last sign may be slowed down and enlarged; it may be repeated; or the signing hand/s may be held in place or momentarily withdrawn from the signing space. Facial expression in sign language is comparable to intonation in spoken language (together with head position), both functionally and formally. Functionally, certain facial expressions systematically signal particular utterance types such as yes/no questions and wh-questions in many sign languages (Zeshan, 2004), topics in American Sign Language (Liddell, 1980), and shared information in Israeli Sign Language (Nespor and Sandler, 1999). Formally, the distribution of facial arrays is comparable to that of intonational excursions, aligning themselves temporally with the edges of prosodic constituents, edges that are marked in sign languages by the behavior of the hands. This alignment of manual rhythm, facial expression, and head position has been found to characterize grammatical prosody in ISL and American Sign Language, distinguishing it from emotional or affective prosody (e.g., Baker-Shenk, 1983; Dachkovsky and Sandler, 2009; Dachkovsky et al., 2013).

The face and the position of the head may also signal subordination, offering a critical cue to complex utterances. For example, in the ISL conditional sentence meaning "If it rains, we'll stay home and watch TV," the raised brows and head forward position shown in Figure 10.1a

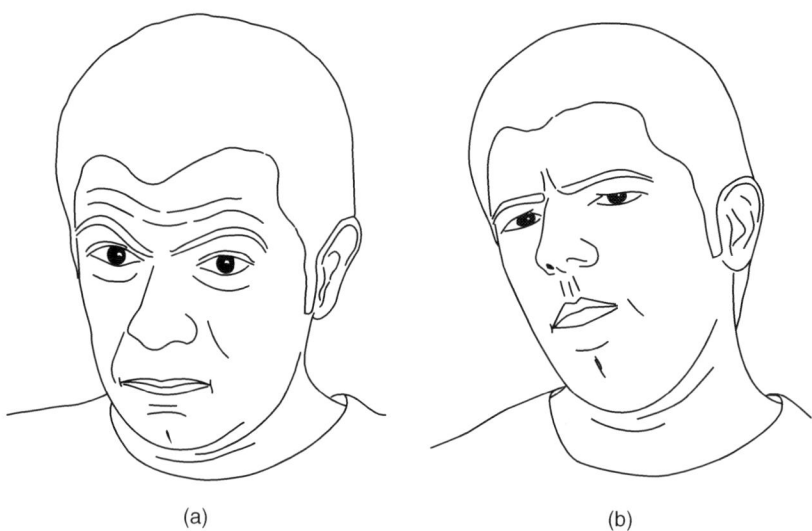

Figure 10.1 Change of intonational arrays at the intonational phrase boundary in ISL: (a) raised brows and head forward signal continuation in the *if*-clause of a conditional; (b) complete change of array in the *then*-clause that follows

are characteristic of *if*-clauses (and other dependent constituents) in that language, marking the dependency relation between it and the *then* clause, whose intonational array in this sentence is shown in Figure 10.1b (Dachkovsky and Sandler, 2009).[7] The manual and non-manual articulations of the prosodic system are recorded by detailed coding of the behavior of each articulator throughout the utterance, shown schematically in Figure 10.1.

We were interested to see whether certain types of meaning and complexity are marked prosodically in the new sign language, ABSL. Through detailed analysis of the prosody in short stretches of narrative in ABSL signers about twenty years apart in age, we discovered two impressive differences between the two age groups (Sandler, Meir et al., 2011). First, the older second-generation signers typically did not connect clauses prosodically: the majority of their utterances were prosodically equivalent to independent main clauses. Among the younger signers, half to three-quarters of the utterances were prosodically complex, with one clause marked as dependent on another. Second, where the older signers used prosodic cues of timing, facial expression, and head/body position sporadically, they were not systematically aligned at identifiable constituent boundaries. The younger signers aligned about twice as many rhythmic cues with changes in facial expression and head position, all of which serve to mark clause boundaries more systematically.

Figure 10.2 shows the final sign of the *if*-clause in a conditional sentence and the first sign of the *then*-clause in the narrative of a younger second-generation ABSL signer. Figure 10.3 shows schematically how the various

(a) NOT-AT-ALL (b) NOTHING-TO-BE-DONE

Figure 10.2 Change of facial expression and body posture at the juncture of two intonational phrases in an ABSL conditional sentence meaning 'If he says no, then there's nothing to be done.'

	HE	NOT-AT-ALL	NOTHING-TO-BE-DONE
Brow raise		———	
Wide eyes		———	
Hold		+	+
Big size		—	—
Head tilt right		———	
Head up	—		
Head down		—	
Head forward		—	
Head back			———
Torso		forward	back and up
Eye gaze		———blink	blink

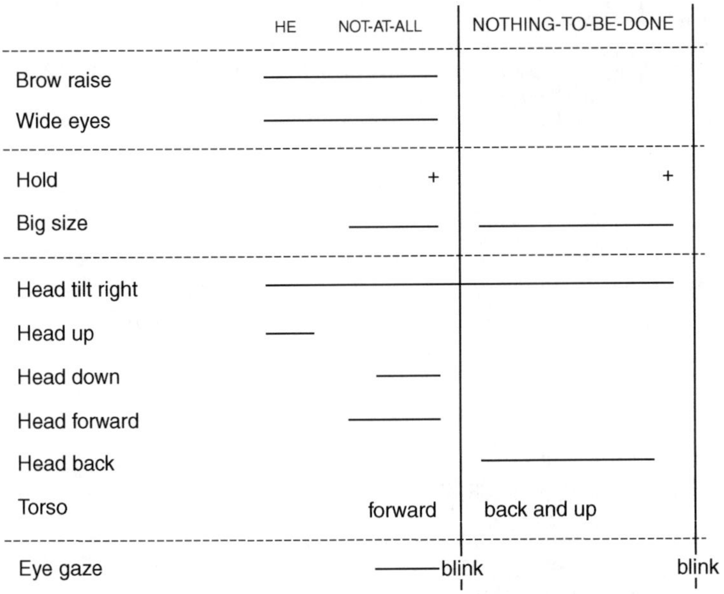

Figure 10.3 A coded example of a conditional sentence produced by a younger signer

articulations are aligned. The example shows both complexity (a conditional sentence) and systematic alignment of prosodic cues. Specifically, the hands are held in place at the end of the *if*-clause. Simultaneously, the brows are raised and the head is forward, marking continuation to the next clause. All prosodic signals change in the following clause. The sentence means *If he says "no," then there's nothing to be done*. Pictured are "no" and "nothing-to-be-done." Such marking of dependent structures was common in the younger signers and rare in the older ones. The investigation showed that prosodic structure can systematically mark complexity, and that the occurrence and co-occurrence of the elements of prosody self-organize gradually across age groups.[8]

10.3.1.3 Syntax of complex utterances

There are no overt syntactic markers in ABSL to indicate sentence complexity, and we remain agnostic about whether the prosodically marked complex propositions are complex sentences in the syntactic sense rather than just semantically linked. However, our analysis of the clauses themselves in the same study shows that the structure of simplex clauses also became more complex for the younger signers. Specifically, for the older signers, many predicates were not provided with explicit arguments, while for the younger signers, most of them were. Also, the younger signers often used pronouns, which associate verbs with arguments in a way that is abstract, with no fixed denotation, but which adds clarity and complexity to the clause. Younger signers were also more likely to use modifiers.

In the early stages of the emergence of ABSL, propositions were simple in structure and typically independent of each other. As little as twenty years later, quantifiably more structure appeared, both within the clause and in the development of dependent relations between them.

10.3.2 Lexicon

It is likely that at least some of the earliest ABSL vocabulary consisted of gestures drawn from the surrounding language environment. But the lexicon of a new sign language goes beyond gesture. Even in the first generation, sign languages start to develop a lexicon of signs that have distinctively different properties from gestures. Kendon (1988) has noted that "gesture" encompasses a range of visible representations of meaning, from gestures that are at once complex and holistic, requiring several spoken words to interpret, to more "lexicalized" gestures, such as the "okay" and "peace" signals, to the conventionalized signs of sign languages, which may become more arbitrary and general in meaning. McNeill (1992) interprets this spectrum as points along a continuum from gesture to language, with gesticulation, which is "global," or holophrastic, a single idea linked to a gesture, on one end, and, on the opposite end, sign language vocabulary items, which are segmented, fully conventional, and combine systematically in sentences.

In established languages, conventional vocabulary items have not only specific meanings, which are learned as one learns the language, they also exhibit grammatical roles, such as subject, object, predicate, and thematic roles like agent, experiencer, source, and goal. Individual vocabulary items typically belong to a grammatical category: noun, verb, adjective, etc. How does a new sign language acquire conventional features that set signs apart from gesticulation?

In ABSL, the notion of subject emerges early, at least by the second generation,[9] in the form of the body of the signer (Meir, Padden et al., 2007). The body of the signer can, but does not always represent the speaker: it can also refer to second or third person. It can represent the agent, but not always. It can alternatively represent the patient or experiencer. It is not surprising that the body represents the notion of subject, but it is somewhat surprising that it does not always represent the speaker. This is what human languages do: they have conventional grammatical structure, which marks categories and conveys, among other things, shared information in an efficient and effective way.

Established sign languages mark grammatical category in various ways. In some sign languages, the noun category is distinguished from verbs by the movement of the sign. In ASL, nouns are distinguished from semantically and formationally related verbs by a difference in the movement of the sign. Nouns are always reduplicated and have shorter and more tense movement than the related verbs (Supalla and Newport, 1978). The noun TOOTHBRUSH and the verb BRUSH-ONE'S-TEETH are differentiated only in the length and tenseness of the movement. Other sign languages distinguish these classes as well, but ABSL does not exhibit a regular distinction in form between such semantically and formationally related nouns and verbs (Tkachman and Sandler, in press.)

Transitive verbs which involve transfer of an object or a more abstract entity, e.g., GIVE, SHOW, ASK, and SEND, have a characteristic path movement where signs move from one location, the source of the action, to another location representing the goal, e.g., *she gives him* (Fischer and Gough, 1978; Padden, 1988; Meir, 2002). While ABSL uses points in space as a referential device, we have not found movement in space for verb agreement inflection in this language (Meir, Padden *et al.* 2013). Instead, the lexical pattern of body as subject persists regardless of the person categories of arguments within a sentence.

Lexicons may also accrue regularity by iconically associating the location of a sign with parts of the body. For many verbs expressing emotional or physical states, the sign contacts or is near the location on the body that is culturally associated with the state: DREAM contacts the forehead, MOURN is signed near the face, and FEEL contacts the center of the chest.

Second- and third-generation signers of ABSL consistently use a lexicalization pattern for nouns which refer to objects held by the human hand such as TOOTHBRUSH, FORK, KNIFE, SCREWDRIVER, and PAINTBRUSH (Padden, 2012; Padden *et al.*, in press). Hearing non-signers typically pantomime how to hold the object if asked to innovate a gesture for such objects. Adults will hold an imaginary toothbrush and show a back-and-forth movement as if brushing their teeth, or hold an imaginary spoon as they pretend to scoop food from a plate. In ABSL, signers likewise show the action associated with the object, but they consistently use the hands or individual fingers to also show a dimension of the object. In the ABSL sign TOOTHBRUSH, signers use the index finger (depicting the long handle of the toothbrush) while using a back-and-forth movement near the front of the mouth. The ABSL sign for 'comb' can use either two fingers or a clawed hand to show the comb itself or the teeth of a comb as it moves in a brushing motion near the head. The emergence of a lexicalization pattern by the second generation shows that consistent choice of type of handshape for a lexical category can appear early in the language's developing sign lexicon.

10.3.3 Morphology: The emergence of compounds

Compounding is the earliest type of word formation to develop in the life of a language, and it is accordingly abundant in pidgins and creoles (Plag, 2006). It has also been suggested that compounds are very early precursors to the evolution of syntax in human language (Jackendoff, 2002, 2009). ABSL, as a young language, offers us the possibility of studying the emergence and conventionalization of individual compounds and compound constructions in a community. Our data suggest a correlation between conventionalization in individual compound words and grammaticization of form: those compounds that are more conventionalized are also characterized by more clear-cut structural properties (Meir, Aronoff et al., 2010).

10.3.3.1 How do compounds arise?

Compounding expands vocabulary by drawing from the existing lexicon, using combinations of two or three words to create distinctive new meanings and new lexical items. It is a building process: lacking a lexical item, a language user draws on two or more existing words, which together convey the desired meaning. Under this scenario, three-word compounds are (more) complex, since they use more building blocks.

Our data reveal another previously unrecorded pathway by which compounds emerge, not by building but rather by carving. Signers appear to start out with long unstructured strings of words, and, as these are used more often, they become reduced, finally ending as two- or three-word units. When presented with a concept or an object that they do not have a word for, signers produce a string of words semantically related to that concept. For example, ABSL does not have a conventionalized lexical item for 'calendar', though calendars are used in the community, and one was even noticed in one of the participants' houses. In the picture-naming task, when presented with a picture of a calendar, signers produced the responses in example (1):

(1) (a) TIME + SEE + COUNT-ROWS + WRITE + TIME + CONTINUE + FLIP + SEE + COUNT-ROWS
    (b) WRITE + ROW + MONTH + ROW + WRITE
    (c) NUMBERS + ROW + MONTH + FLAT-ON-WALL + FLIP
    (d) FLIP + WRITE + FLIP

The words in these responses relate to the function of a calendar (telling the time), its arrangement (rows), its internal form (written), its shape (rectangle), how it is handled (by flipping pages). Responses vary greatly among signers, and they can also vary within a signer from one utterance to another. The example in (d) is produced by the youngest signer in this group (about 20 years old); the expression consists of only two words, encoding its form and how it is handled.[10]

'Calendar' is an extreme example: there seems to be no conventionalization at all across these tokens. Each signer recruits whatever lexical resources s/he can find in order to refer to this concept. Strings of words for other concepts are somewhat more conventionalized. Here, the signers have narrowed down the number of words related to a concept. For 'oven with cooktop', found in every household, signers draw on four lexical items: COOK, TURN, WIDE-OBJECT, INSERT. However, signers vary as to how many and which items they select from this list, as in (2):

(2) (a) TURN^COOK^WIDE-OBJECT
    (b) TURN^FIRE^FOUR^BURNER^FIRE
    (c) TURN^WIDE-OBJECT
    (d) COOK^INSERT
    (e) COOK^WIDE-OBJECT

At the other end of this continuum are compounds in which all signers use the same components in the same order. In our data, remarkably, we do not have any one compound that is signed uniformly by all signers in the study. But some signs are conventionalized within a familylect, like the sign KETTLE (Sandler, Aronoff et al., 2011). There are different sign combinations meaning KETTLE, but members of each of two different families uniformly used its own combination consistently (shown in Figure 10.4): (a) CUP^POUR (by handle) as signed uniformly by all three members recorded from one family. (b) CUP^ROUND-OBJECT as signed uniformly by all five members recorded from a different family.

There are many intermediate degrees of conventionalization. In some cases all signers share one lexical component of a compound word, but differ in the others. Signers may share components but differ in their order. Structure emerges when the types of words for describing an object are of similar function, and come in a particular order (e.g., a word describing the function, and a word describing the shape).

The variation we find in ABSL compounds is quite overwhelming.[11] However, we found two structural tendencies emerging in the language, both in more conventionalized compounds. The first, which is stronger, is characteristic of compounds containing a size-and-shape specifier (SASS). SASS signs are common in sign languages in general, though their form and distribution may vary from language to language.[12] There is a tendency in our data for the SASS member to be last. The second weaker tendency is towards a modifier–head order in non-SASS compounds containing a head and a modifier.

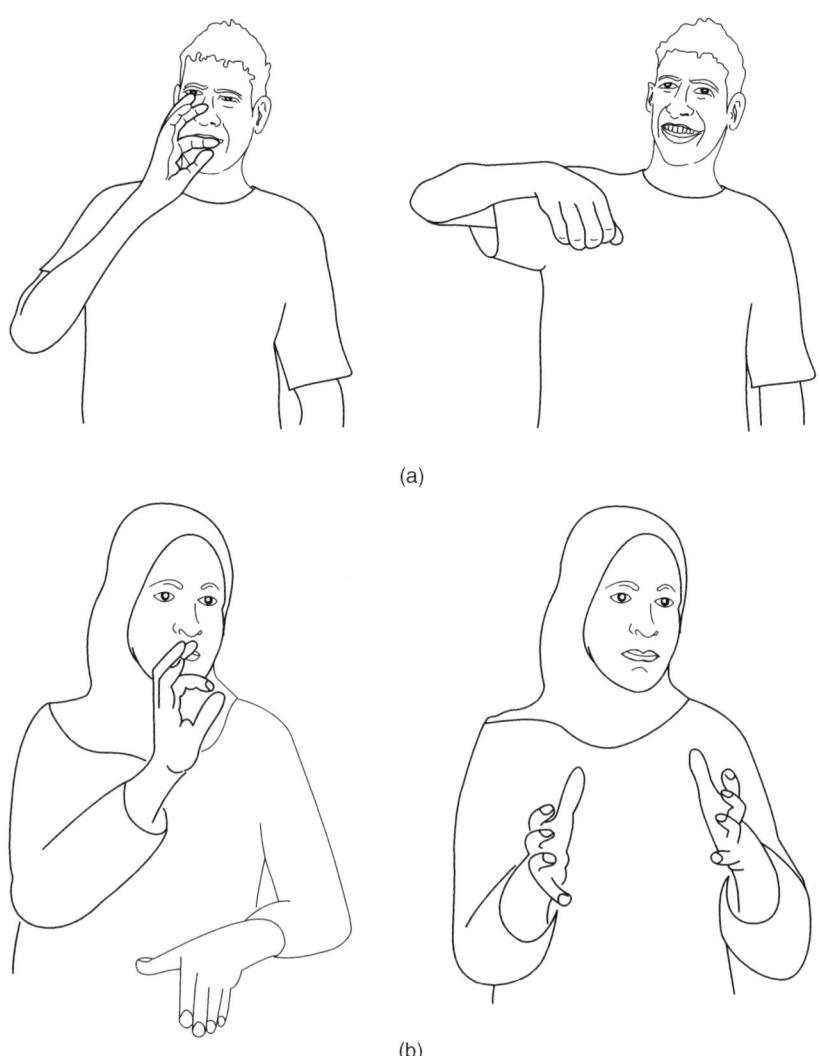

Figure 10.4 Two different ABSL compounds meaning 'kettle', each found in a different familylect. (a) TEA^POUR; (b) TEA^ROUNDED-OBJECT

10.3.3.2 SASS compounds

In many compounds, one of the signs used to refer to an object is a SASS describing the size and shape of the object that does not occur independently. Some examples follow in (3):

(3) (a) COLD^BIG-RECTANGLE 'refrigerator'
    (b) DRINK-TEA^ROUNDED-OBJECT 'kettle' (pictured in Figure 10.4b)
    (c) WATER^ROUNDED-OBJECT 'pitcher'
    (d) CUCUMBER^LONG-THIN-OBJECT 'cucumber'
    (e) PHOTO^FLAT-OBJECT 'photograph',
    (f) CHICKEN^SMALL-OVAL-OBJECT 'egg'

(g) WRITE^LONG-THIN-OBJECT 'pen'
(h) TV^RECTANGULAR-OBJECT 'remote control'

Since the SASSes do not tend to occur as independent words in the language, we may be looking at an early form of affixation. Because we cannot construct criteria for distinguishing the two in this new language, we call the complex forms with SASSes compounds. SASS compounds are widespread in the language: they constitute 37 percent of the compounds in our data set. Figure 10.5 shows two SASS compounds.

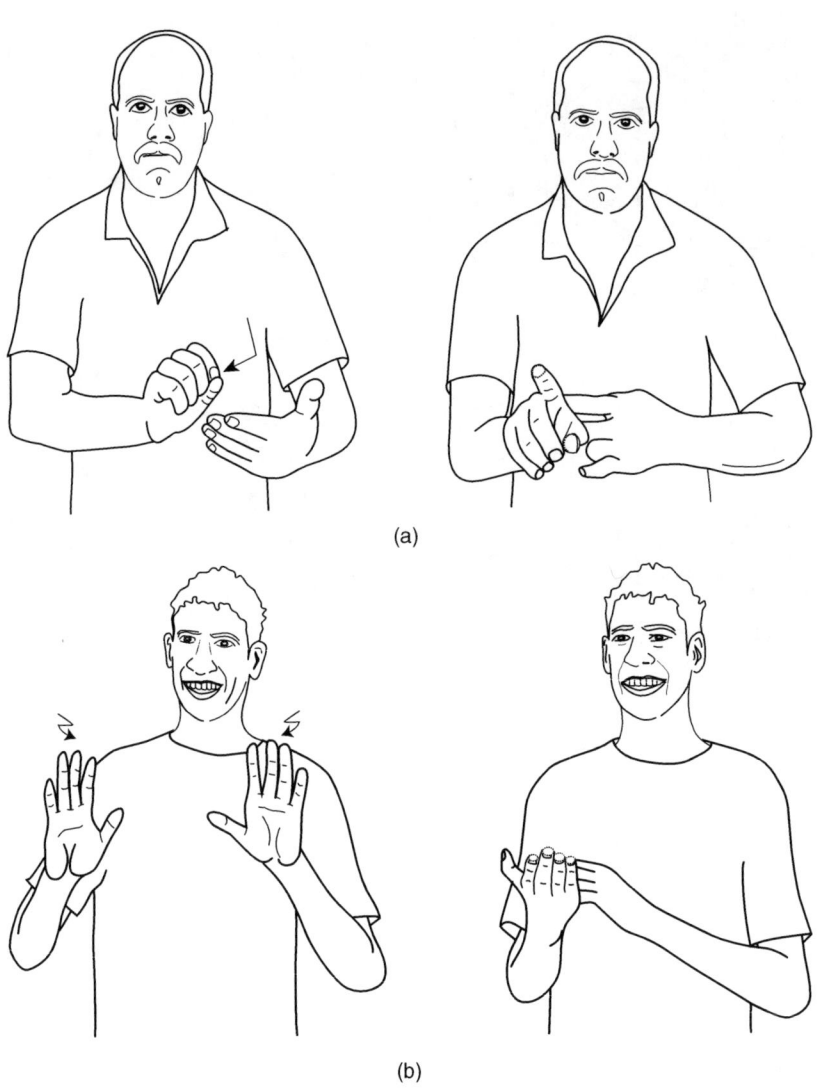

Figure 10.5 Two SASS compounds in ABSL: (a) WRITE^LONG-THIN-OBJECT ('pen'), and (b) TELEVISION^RECTANGULAR-OBJECT ('remote control')

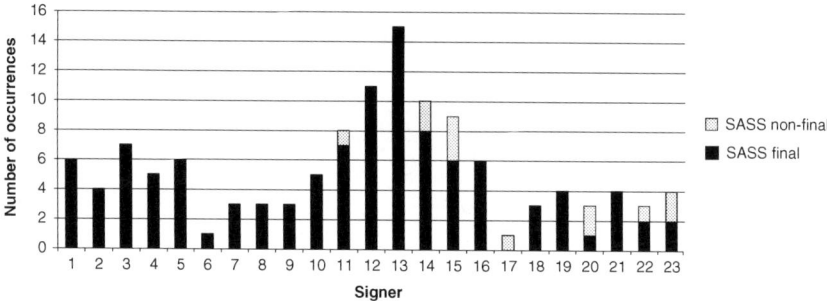

Figure 10.6 Structural tendency in SASS compounds: Number of SASS-final and SASS non-final compounds in the production of each signer

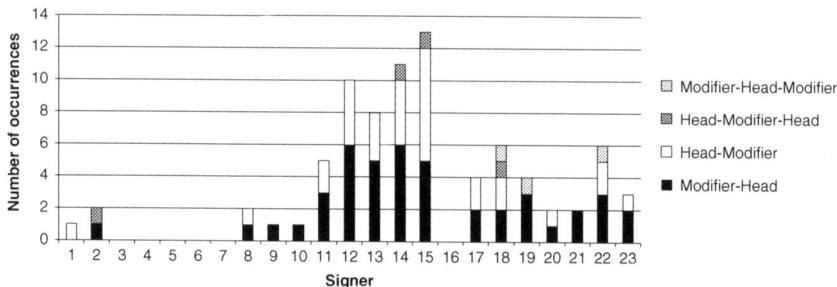

Figure 10.7 Structure of endocentric compounds in ABSL: Head–Modifier order in the production of each signer

These compounds are the most uniform, with a strong tendency for the SASS to occur finally in the compound. This holds both within and across signers (Figure 10.6).

10.3.3.3 Modifier–Head order

The other structural tendency is for a modifier–head order in endocentric compounds, as in (4):

(4) (a) PRAY^HOUSE 'mosque'
    (b) SCREW-IN^LIGHT 'light-bulb'
    (c) BABY^CLOTHES 'baby clothes'
    (d) COFFEE^POT 'coffee pot'

These are less widespread in our data set (22%) than the SASS-type compounds, and the tendency is much less pronounced, for each individual (Figure 10.7) and in the entire set of data (Figure 10.8).

As Figures 10.7 and 10.8 show, the modifier–head order occurs more often than head–modifier order, but the difference is not as striking as with SASS compounds. However, there is an interesting generalization even in this rather messy picture: the endocentric compounds that are most uniform across the population of signers tend to exhibit a modifier–head order.[13] This finding can be interpreted in the following way: there is a high degree of

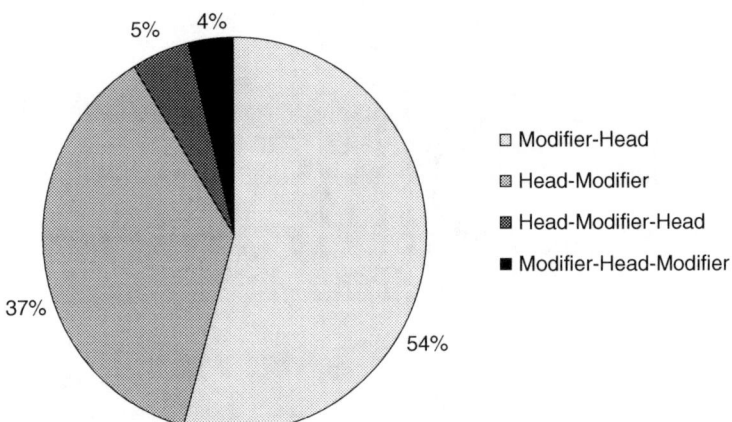

Figure 10.8 Percentage of different Head–Modifier orders in our data

variability, both within and across signers. But compounds that are agreed upon in the community, that is, the most conventionalized ones, tend to exhibit a particular structure. In a way, then, conventionalization may be detected through frequency of use within the community before conventionalization stabilizes in its individual members.

10.3.4 Phonology

The formational elements of signs serve to create contrasts (Stokoe 1960), and their form can alternate in different contexts as a result of formal constraints on the system (Liddell and Johnson, 1986; Sandler, 1989, 1993), irrespective of any iconic properties that may have motivated them. For example, the signs TATTLE and SEND in ISL are contrasted only by the place of articulation: near the mouth for TATTLE and near the torso for SEND (Figure 10.9). The two signs are otherwise identical: a five-finger handshape that opens while the hand moves outward from the body.

Handshape and movement features are also used to distinguish minimal pairs. Indeed, it was Stokoe's discovery of this previously unrecognized characteristic in American Sign Language that brought sign languages into the arena of serious linguistic investigation. Subsequently, linguists discovered other key characteristics of phonology in ASL and other sign languages. For example, although the iconic origin may be apparent in many signs, the inventory of possible locations, handshapes, and movements is as small and discrete as phoneme inventories of spoken languages, and they function in the phonological system without reference to meaning (Sandler, 1989). A good example is assimilation, which systematically alters some phonological feature/s in certain contexts on the basis of form and not meaning (Liddell and Johnson 1986; Sandler 1987, 1989). Well-formedness constraints have also been found.[14] An example of a well-formedness constraint in ASL (Mandel, 1981) is the requirement that only one finger or group of fingers be

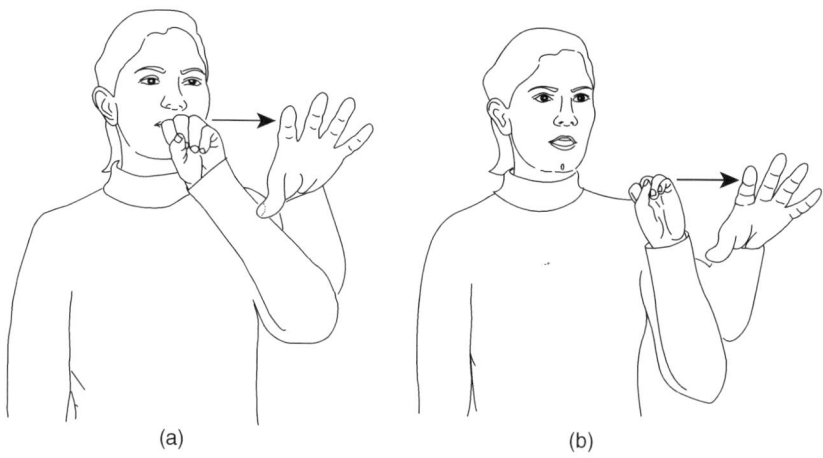

Figure 10.9 The ISL minimal pair (a) TATTLE and (b) SEND

specified for any monomorphemic sign. This constraint holds for ISL as well. In Figure 10.9 above, for example, the handshape changes from closed to open, but crucially the same fingers are selected throughout each sign, in these examples, all five fingers.

Hockett (1960) dubbed the existence of two levels of structure – one meaningful and one meaningless – "duality of patterning," and maintained that this is one of the design features that distinguishes human language from other communication systems. Presumably, manipulating forty or so contrastive sounds to create vocabularies of tens of thousands of words is more economical, and distinctions more easily perceived, than if each lexical item were comprised of a global signal.

We were interested to learn whether this property is a mandatory requirement of language, and how quickly it arises. We were especially intrigued because we had observed from the beginning that there was a good deal more lexical variation across the village than we had anticipated, as noted in Sections 10.3.2 and 10.3.3. When signers do use the same sign for a concept, we wondered, was there sublexical variation as well? Do they maintain discrete categories of handshape, location, and movement, as would be expected in a phonological system?

A comparison of the "pronunciation" of fifteen signs across ten signers of ABSL, ISL, and ASL revealed that there is significantly more variation in ABSL than in the other two languages (Israel, 2009; Israel and Sandler, 2011). The variation in ABSL sometimes crossed boundaries of what are major phonological categories in other sign languages, e.g., selected fingers and major body area, in addition to finer-grained variation that might be considered phonetic. An example of the former is seen in two exemplars of the sign for DOG, shown in Figure 10.10, one signed near the mouth and the other in front of the torso. These two categories are distinctive in ISL. Compare TATTLE and SEND in Figure 10.9 above.

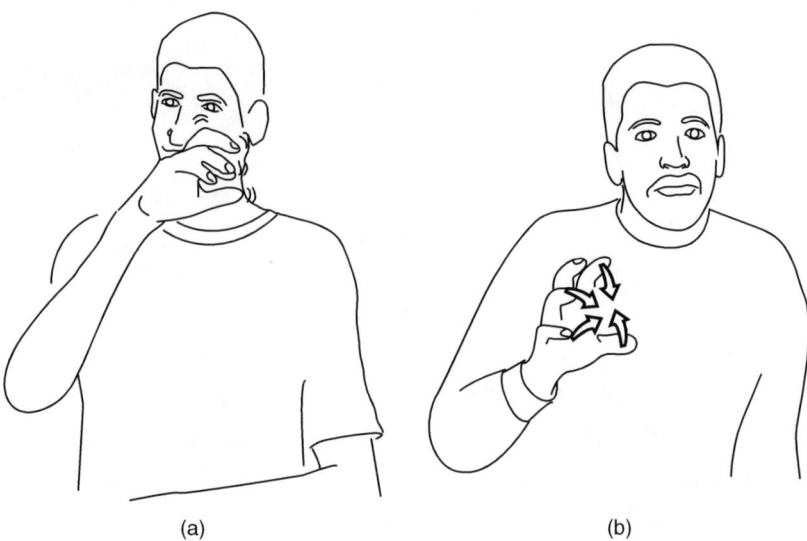

Figure 10.10 Two variations of DOG in ABSL: (a) articulation near the mouth; (b) articulation in neutral space in front of the torso

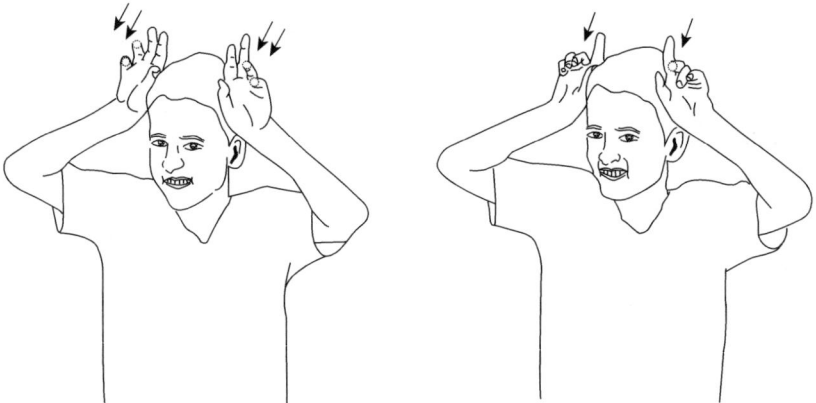

Figure 10.11 Change of handshape within the ABSL sign DONKEY

Furthermore, constraints that are quite robust in other sign languages can be violated in ABSL. In signing DONKEY, for example, a young signer switches from two fingers to one mid-stream, shown in Figure 10.11. Such findings led us to conclude that a full-fledged phonological system has not yet crystallized in the community (Sandler, Aronoff et al., 2011).

Nevertheless, there is an indication that such a system is beginning to evolve. For example, we report instances in young third-generation signers of signs that were produced in a less iconic but more easily articulated fashion, with more comfortable palm orientations or more symmetrical movements than the transparently iconic but cumbersome versions of older people.

Figure 10.12 The conventionalized compound sign EGG in ABSL (CHICKEN^OVAL-OBJECT)

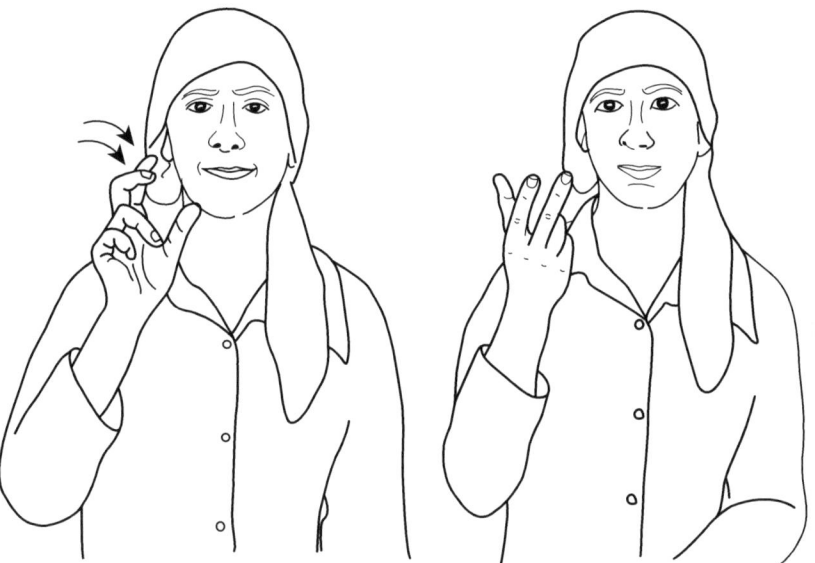

Figure 10.13 The sign EGG with handshape assimilation: three fingers assimilated to CHICKEN from OVAL OBJECT

We also found the beginnings of assimilation and lexicalization that favored meaningless formal elements over global iconicity. The most striking example involves a chicken and an egg. The conventional sign for EGG in ABSL is a compound: CHICKEN^OVAL-OBJECT, shown in Figure 10.12. Each sign is iconic: CHICKEN invokes the pecking beak, while OVAL-OBJECT invokes the shape of an egg and the manner in which it is held. In one familylect, assimilation of handshape occurs in this compound, so that the handshape for OVAL-OBJECT assimilates regressively to the handshape for CHICKEN, the first part of the compound, shown in Figure 10.13. A young

Figure 10.14 The reduced compound sign EGG: only the counter-iconic assimilated version of the first member of the compound survives

girl in this same family, who at the age of about 6 signed EGG like her sister in Figure 10.13, a few years later signed it as in Figure 10.14. The compound had become lexicalized into a single monosyllable whose iconic origin is opaque, combining the handshape of OVAL-OBJECT and the movement of CHICKEN.

While this is an isolated example, we find it interesting because the signer is a third-generation signer with a deaf mother and deaf siblings. Such intensive social interaction in a native language setting is likely to foster the conventionalization and automaticity that we argue underlie the emergence of phonology.[15]

10.3.5 Linguistic identity of the group: accent

Younger deaf people of Al-Sayyid have had varying degrees of exposure to ISL, the language of the majority deaf population in Israel. This exposure has mostly been in deaf education programs in schools, where the contact situation is quite complex. But one thing is clear: there is a good deal of borrowing of signs from ISL into ABSL, mostly among third-generation signers. However, their signing does not look like ISL; there is a signature ABSL "accent."

Contact with ISL began in the 1980s, and has increased with the third generation, when deaf children of Al-Sayyid began to be exposed to signs from Israeli Sign Language at school, where teachers typically use bare (uninflected) signs from ISL to accompany their speech, either Hebrew or Arabic. That is, the input is pidgin-like and does not convey the grammar of ISL.

In their late teens, a number of boys from Al-Sayyid were exposed to native ISL from deaf teachers at a residential vocational school, while some teenaged girls and young women were exposed to ISL at social meetings for deaf women, whose organizers are ISL signers. In both environments, young deaf people have been exposed to ISL proper (not only to signs from ISL). However, both exposures took place in the late teens and early twenties – long after the critical period for language acquisition.[16] And within the village, older deaf people, pre-school deaf children, hearing family members, and other hearing people maintain ABSL. Communication patterns also favor maintenance of ABSL. Apart from forays into ISL environments, the young deaf people of Al-Sayyid reside in the village, and the vast majority of their communicative interactions take place with their family members, spouses, and neighbors – deaf and hearing. This may not be typical pidginization or creolization, but rather rapid language change in a very young language, affected by borrowing. Still there is no question that many ISL signs have been borrowed into ABSL.

The signature Al-Sayyid accent has several features, the most notable of which is a characteristic rhythmic pattern, which we are currently analyzing. Other features include lax handshapes and wrist and dorsal hand-part prominence. An example of hand-part prominence is found in a young woman's conversation with her sister. She signed the borrowed sign EXACTLY with dorsal hand prominence (Figure 10.15b), while the ISL sign has fingertip prominence (Figure 10.15a). What we find most

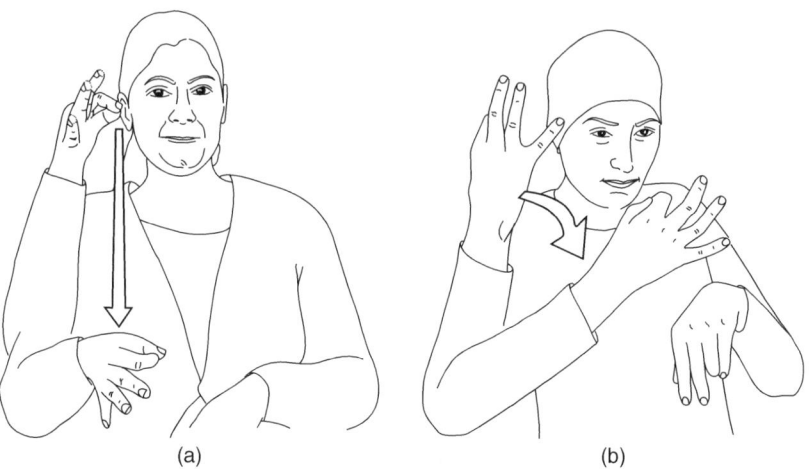

(a)   (b)

Figure 10.15 (a) The ISL sign EXACTLY with fingertip prominence and (b) the borrowed sign with dorsal hand prominence in the ABSL accent

interesting here is the reflection of group identity through accent, even before a full-fledged phonological system has crystallized.

10.4 Language emerges gradually

When can we call a communication system "a language"? Does language emerge gradually, or is the emergence abrupt, as suggested by some researchers regarding the development of creoles out of pidgins? According to Bickerton (1999: 49), in the plantation-colonies situation, "new languages are formed in the space of a single generation." Kegl et al. (1999: 180) write that in Nicaragua, "a signed creole abruptly came into being when the symmetric pidgin/jargon ... became the linguistic input to very young children." Our research on ABSL suggests more gradual development. Yet these questions lead to a more basic question: Is there a set of necessary and sufficient conditions for identifying what a language is? And if so, are these conditions structural or functional?

The literature on the evolution of language makes frequent references to the notion of *protolanguage* vs. *language*. Protolanguage is described as a communication system that is not quite language. Bickerton (1990) suggests that protolanguage is language without syntax. Others (e.g., Jackendoff, 1999; Arbib, 2012) have elaborated on this idea, stating more specifically what it is that differentiates between language and its earlier form as protolanguage. Arbib, for example, defines language as "an open-ended system in which words and then phrases can be assembled according to some grammar that makes it possible to infer plausible meaning for novel utterances created 'on the fly'" (Arbib, 2012: 252). This definition refers to the combinatory nature of language, to hierarchical syntactic structures (words and then phrases), but also to a functional property of language, the fact that novel combinations of words arise effortlessly, "on the fly." However, this definition leaves open what it actually means for a communication system to "have syntax." Does it have to have a basic word order? Not all languages do. Case marking or verb agreement? Overt complementizers? Dependency markers such as anaphors? Parts of speech? Passivization? Relative clauses? For any suggested feature, it is possible to find a language that does not have it (cf. Evans and Levinson, 2009; Bickel, this volume, Chapter 5). Therefore, it seems impossible to define what it means "to have syntax." And if we cannot define that, we cannot identify the point at which a communication system transitions to a language on that basis.

Though having syntax is the main feature referred to when discussing the transition to language, syntax is not the only level of linguistic structure that characterizes language. Languages have lexicons, phonology, morphology, and semantics (Pinker and Jackendoff, 2005). Are these additional levels of structure also necessary conditions for language? Can we identify a point at which they appear?

Our investigation of the development of ABSL makes two noteworthy contributions to this discussion. First, it underscores the need to distinguish between functional properties of a system and its structural properties. Second, it shows that language does not develop in a unified fashion across all of its domains. Rather, different sub-domains organize at different paces, and therefore a communication system may have some clear characteristics of language in some domains but not in others. We must conclude that the transition into language is gradual and not abrupt.

The need to make a distinction between complexity in the intent and interpretation of a message and complexity in grammatical form was brought home to us by a story told by a first-generation signer, which was videotaped by a villager in 1994, later shared with us. The signer, now deceased, was one of the first four deaf siblings born in Al-Sayyid. He narrates an event that happened a long time ago, probably before he was born. His narration is therefore characterized by displacement, the ability to refer to events not in the "here and now," a hallmark of human languages (Hockett, 1960). In his narration, he reports on two different discussions between different parties. Though he usually does not use overt reported speech elements, such as "he said that…," he manages to clearly convey that he is reporting what others say, and who is speaking, through contextual and mimetic cues. We can say, then, that content-wise he uses reported speech, which is often thought of as a recursive structure. In two instances, his utterances were translated (by his son) as conditional sentences, i.e., embedded structures. Yet the recursion is in the pragmatics, and not in overt syntactic or prosodic structure.

The narration consists of conventionalized signs, and the signer seems to convey the information in a fluent manner. From a functional perspective, this is language. However, there is not much explicit structure in the narrative. Most propositions contain one or two words, there are no function words except for two negators, and the prosodic structure that marks syntactic or semantic boundaries is often hard to identify. In addition, in some cases the meaning of the signing is unclear. For example, when the signer signs: SHOOT. HORSE FALL. EYE FALL-OUT, it is not clear (not even to his son) whether it is the eye of the horse or the eye of the rider that fell out. It is certain that shared context and cultural memory of the narrative goes a long way toward facilitating intelligibility, as one would expect to have been the case at the dawn of language in our species.

Narratives of second-generation signers are more fluent and much less ambiguous than that of the first-generation signer. Although we find only basic clausal structures in these narratives, functionally, they are rich and interesting accounts, referring to old customs of the tribe, to abstract concepts, such as dreams, and to reports on what other people have said. Are these narratives manifestations of language? They certainly act like language, even though the structural complexities are not evident.

We turn now to the second point, that languages develop in a gradual and non-unified way. Our study of ABSL compounds illustrates this point. First, the variation in compound production in the community shows that conventionalization takes time, and that some items are conventionalized more quickly than others. In addition, structure emerges in some types of compounds, but not in others. The compounds that include a SASS component tend to be SASS-final. Compounds for place names containing a locative pointing sign are also consistent in order of signs: the pointing sign is always final (Meir, Aronoff et al., 2010). Yet other compounds in which a head can be identified are much less consistent. These data show that even within a very restricted domain of grammar, compounding, conventionalization, and structure emerge gradually. Different items exhibit different degrees of conventionalization, and some sub-domains show clear structural preferences while others do not.

The SASS components are good candidates for developing into derivational affixes, since they recur with many different bases, and they do not occur as independent lexical items. Since they refer to objects, they may be nominal affixes. If we find good evidence for such an analysis, the implication is that there are formational differences between nouns and verbs in a specific lexical domain. In other words, we would have evidence for the emergence of parts-of-speech distinctions in the language. Yet once again, this grammatical machinery characterizes only a very restricted domain in the ABSL lexicon. Other distinctions or markers may emerge in other language domains.

The picture that emerges is one of varying developments in the language, taking place at different paces. Eventually many of them can interact, and create larger linguistic sub-domains. But by looking at the way ABSL develops and changes, we find evidence for gradual and non-uniform emergence of linguistic structure. We find no evidence for the idea of a sharp leap from non-language to complex language in the first or second generation of signers.[17]

10.5 Conclusions

When we first visited the village of Al-Sayyid a decade ago, we came with strong preconceptions of what a language emerging in such an intensive linguistic environment would look like and of how its structure would unfold across generations. In the context of ambient notions about universal grammar, about rapid creolization, and about what we took to be sign language universal properties, we expected specific types of complex grammatical structure to develop quickly and uniformly across the

Al-Sayyid village. Few of those ideas have survived our years of research on the ground.

We have concentrated on the most surprising of our findings: the differences in the pace of structuration across the components of the language. Word order emerged early and robustly, and other aspects of syntactic structure, evidenced mostly in prosody, have been slower to organize, although we see major differences between older and younger signers in the extent to which prosodic signals align with constituents and mark dependency relations among them. We have not found the agreement morphology that we thought would arise quickly because it is so iconic and pervasive among established sign languages (Aronoff et al., 2005). We have found compounds but the apparent paths to structure among them have again been gradual and unexpected, with islands of regularity both in individual compound words and in the constructions around which compounds cluster. Here the roles of the family and community in shaping the language are also clearest. The organization of the sign medium itself has held the greatest surprises. We have not found evidence of phonological structure in the earliest forms of the new sign language, structure that is well documented in more established sign languages: systematic manipulation of meaningless features in phonological categories of handshape, location, and movement. Instead, the degree and types of variation in sign form we have found suggest that signers are often aiming for a holistic image. At the same time, ABSL signers appear to have a characteristic accent that cuts across the various signs and extends to the signs that they borrow from ISL. Finally, although ABSL lacks complex grammatical structure, its signers never appear stymied. Driven by the human need to communicate with others and armed with the cognitive capacity to do so and with a wealth of shared experience, they use their language to express all the aspects of their lives.

While the specific details of these findings are couched in structural descriptions of sign language, the only kind of contemporary language that arises *de novo*, the findings offer a rare glimpse into the emergence of language more generally. They show that complex communicative interaction arises almost immediately, while the development of conventionalized linguistic structure to scaffold it is gradual, uneven across different components of grammar, and sensitive to social factors such as familylect, community identity, and frequency of use.

Acknowledgments

This research is funded by the US National Institutes of Health grant number R01 DC006473 and the Israel Science Foundation grants number

553/04 and 580/09. We thank Shai Davidi for video images, Debi Menashe for illustrations, and Calle Börstell for editorial assistance.

Notes

1. Kisch (2008) coined the term *shared signing community* to refer to what we, following Zeshan (2004) and subsequent work, call *village sign language*. Kisch (2012) emphasizes the undoubted fact that these languages are shared among both deaf and hearing people and criticizes the use of the term *village* as of little value.
2. For simplicity's sake, we use the term *generation* in a strictly genetic structural sense, sometimes termed *familial generation*. Kisch (2012) provides a nuanced description of the social generations or cohorts of signers in the Al-Sayyid community.
3. For a vivid description of a scenario of how a new language may develop function words, see Deutscher (2006: ch. 7).
4. Israeli Sign Language is about the same age as ABSL, but arose under conditions of creolization and has different grammatical characteristics (Meir and Sandler, 2008).
5. Du Bois (1987) found a related phenomenon in spoken language discourse, in which there is a strong tendency for clauses to contain only one lexical NP, while additional arguments are expressed as pronouns or as inflectional affixes on verbs. Givón (1979) argues that the tendency towards one-to-one ratio of verbs and arguments is typical of the "pragmatic mode" of communication, which characterizes pidgins and creoles inter alia.
6. This result collapses two word orders reported in Padden et al. (2010b): SOV, and SCV, where C is a complement which is not a straightforward object, such as WOMAN PAPER WRITE ('The woman wrote on a piece of paper').
7. The raised brows convey meanings similar to those typically signaled by high tone in spoken languages.
8. See Sandler (2012c) for a treatment of the relation between the gradual organization of the body and the gradual organization of prosody and other linguistic forms in ABSL.
9. Unfortunately, we have only a short videotaped narrative from one of the first four deaf siblings born in the village, all of whom are now deceased. Our evidence for subject, or other grammatical forms in the first generation, is limited.
10. Nick Enfield pointed out to us that this kind of reduction is reminiscent of Clark's tangram experiment (Clark and Gibbs, 1986) in which people start out with long-winded descriptions and quickly converge on simple labels.

11. The variation in the ABSL community is not restricted to compounds. See Israel (2009) and Sandler, Aronoff et al. (2011) on variation in sign formation in ABSL.
12. Size and Shape Specifiers in ASL are described in Klima and Bellugi's 1979 seminal volume and are generally considered to be a type of classifier (Supalla, 1986). We find that the SASS morphemes in ABSL differ from those in ASL in form and distribution, but seem to bear some similarity to "measuring stick signs" reported to be found in Adamorobe Sign Language, a village sign language of Ghana (Nyst, 2007).
13. Noticeable counterexamples to modifier–head order are the signs for 'grandmother' and 'grandfather', MOTHER^OLD-PERSON and FATHER^OLD-PERSON. This order is quite consistent across signers, and the fluidity of the transitional movement between the signs is evidence for their lexicalization.
14. See Brentari (2012) and Sandler (2012b) for recent overviews of sign language phonology.
15. See special issue of *Language and Cognition*, ed. de Boer *et al.* (2012), for recent phonological, experimental, and computational treatments of the issue of duality of patterning and its emergence.
16. See Newport (1990) for a study of the critical period for sign language.
17. In the current phase of our work, we are beginning to focus particularly on signers under the age of 25. Preliminary findings suggest the emergence of certain types of complexity not found in earlier stages of ABSL, but we do not yet know whether the devices we have begun to notice are systematic or widespread among these young ABSL signers.

References

Arbib, M. 2012. *How the Brain got Language*. New York: Oxford University Press.
Arends, J., and M. Perl. 1995. *Early Suriname Creole Texts*. Madrid: Iberoamericana.
Aronoff, M., I. Meir, and W. Sandler. 2005. The Paradox of Sign Language Morphology. *Language* 81(2): 301–44.
Baker-Shenk, C. 1983. *A Microanalysis of the Nonmanual Components of American Sign Language*. PhD dissertation, University of California, Berkeley.
Bickerton, D. 1990. *Language and Species*. Chicago: University of Chicago Press.
　1999. How to Acquire Language without Positive Evidence: What acquisitionists can learn from Creoles. In *Language Creation and Language Change: Creolization, Diachrony and Development*, ed. M. DeGraff, 49–74. Cambridge, MA: MIT Press.

Brentari, D. 2012. Sign Language Phonology. In *Handbook of phonological theory*, ed. J. Goldsmith, J. Riggle, and A. C. L. Yu, 2nd ed., 691-721. Oxford: Blackwell.

Bruyn, A. 2008. Grammaticalization in Pidgins and Creoles. In *The Handbook of Pidgin and Creole Studies*, ed. S. Kouwenberg and J. Singler, 383-410. Malden, MA: Wiley-Blackwell.

Clark, H., and D. Wilkes-Gibbs. 1986. Referring as a Collaborative Process. *Cognition* 22: 1-39.

Dachkovsky, S., C. Healy, and W. Sandler. 2013. Visual intonation in two sign languages. *Phonology* 30(2): 211-52.

Dachkovsky, S., and Sandler, W. (2009). Visual Intonation in the Prosody of a Sign Language. *Language and Speech* 52: 287-314.

de Boer, B., W. Sandler, and S. Kirby, eds. 2012. New Perspectives on Duality of Patterning: Introduction to the special issue. *Language and Cognition* 4(4): 251-9.

Deutscher, G. 2006. *The Unfolding of Language: The Evolution of Mankind's Greatest Invention*. New York: Metropolitan Books, Henry Holt.

Du Bois, J. W. 1987. The Discourse Basis of Ergativity. *Language* 63: 805-55.

Evans, N., and S. Levinson. 2009. The Myth of Language Universals: Language diversity and its importance for cognitive science. *Behavioral and Brain Sciences* 32: 429-92.

Fischer, S. 1975. Influences on Word Order Change in ASL. In *Word Order and Word Change*, ed. C. Li and S. Thompson, 1-25. Austin: University of Texas Press.

Fischer, S., and B. Gough. 1978. Verbs in American Sign Language. *Sign Language Studies* 18: 17-48.

Givón, T. 1979. From Discourse to Syntax: Grammar as a processing strategy. In *Discourse and syntax*, ed. Givón, T., 81-112. New York: Academic Press.

Glück, S., and Pfau, R. (1998). On Classifying Classification as a Class of Inflection in German Sign Language. In *ConSole VI Proceedings*, ed. T. Cambier-Langeveld, A. Lipták, M. Redford, and E. van der Torre, 59-74. Leiden: SOLE.

Goldin-Meadow, S. 2003. *The Resilience of Language: What Gesture Creation in Deaf Children Can Tell Us About How All Children Learn Language*. New York: Psychology Press.

Goldin-Meadow, S., and H. Feldman. 1977. The Development of Language-like Communication Without a Language Model. *Science* 197(4301): 401-03.

Hauser, M., N. Chomsky, and W. T. Fitch. 2002. The Faculty of Language: What is it, who has it, and how did it evolve? *Science* 298: 1569-79.

Heine, B., and T. Kuteva. 2002a. On the Evolution of Grammatical Forms. In *The Transition of Language*, ed. Wray, A., 376-397. Oxford: Oxford University Press.

2002b. *World Lexicon of Grammaticalization*. Cambridge: Cambridge University Press.

Hockett, C. 1960. The Origin of Speech. *Scientific American* 203: 88-96.

Israel, A. 2009. *Sublexical Variation in Three Sign Languages*. Masters' thesis, University of Haifa.

Israel, A., and W. Sandler. 2011. Phonological Category Resolution in a New Sign Language: A comparative study of handshapes. In *Formational Units in Sign Languages*, ed. R. Channon, and H. v.d. Hulst, 177–202. Berlin: Mouton de Gruyter.

Jackendoff, R. 1999. Possible Stages in the Evolution of the Language Capacity. *Trends in Cognitive Sciences* 3(7): 272–9.

——— 2002. *Foundations of Language: Brain, Meaning, Grammar, Evolution*. New York: Oxford University Press.

——— 2009. *Language, Consciousness, Culture: Essays on Mental Structure*. Cambridge, MA: MIT Press.

Kegl, J., A. Senghas, and M. Coppola. 1999. Creation Through Contact: Sign language emergence and sign language change in Nicaragua. In *Language Creation and Language Change: Creolization, Diachrony, and Development*, ed. M. DeGraff, 179–237. Cambridge, MA: MIT Press.

Kendon, A. 1988. How Gestures Can Become Like Words. In *Cross-Cultural Perspectives in Nonverbal Communication*, ed. F. Poyatos, 131–42. Lewiston, NY: C. J. Hogrefe.

Kisch, S. 2008. The Social Construction of Deafness in a Bedouin Community in the Negev. *Medical Anthropology* 27(3): 283–313.

——— (2012). Demarcating Generations of Signers in the Dynamic Sociolinguistic Landscape of a Shared Sign Language: The case of Al-Sayyid. In *Sign Languages in Village Communities*, ed. U. Zeshan and C. De Vos, 127–52. Berlin: Mouton; Nijmegen: Ishara Press.

Klima, E. S., and U. Bellugi. 1979. *The Signs of Language*. Cambridge, MA: Harvard University Press.

Lanesman, S., and I. Meir. 2012. The Survival of Algerian Jewish Sign Language alongside Israeli Sign Language in Israel. In: *Sign Languages in Village Communities*, ed. U. Zeshan and C. De Vos, 153–180. Berlin: Mouton; Nijmegen: Ishara Press.

Liddell, S. 1980. *American Sign Language Syntax*. The Hague: Mouton.

Liddell, S., and R. E. Johnson. 1986. American Sign Language Compound Formation Processes, Lexicalization, and Phonological Remnants. *Natural Language and Linguistic Theory* 4: 445–513.

Mandel, M. 1981. *Phonotactics and Morphophonology in American Sign Language*. PhD thesis, University of California, Berkeley.

Marsaja, G. 2008. *Desa Kolok, A Deaf Village and its Sign Language in Bali, Indonesia*. Preston: Ishara Press.

McNeill, D. 1992. *Hand and Mind: What Gestures Reveal about Thought*. Chicago: University of Chicago Press.

McWhorter, J. H. 1998. Identifying the Creole Prototype: Vindicating a typological class. *Language* 74(4): 788–817.

Meir, I. 2002. A Cross-Modality Perspective on Verb Agreement. *Natural Language and Linguistic Theory* 20(2): 413–50.

2010. The Emergence of Argument Structure in Two New Sign Languages. In *Syntax, Lexical Semantics and Event Structure*, ed. M. R. Hovav, E. Doron, and I. Sichel, 101-23. Oxford: Oxford University Press.

Meir, I., M. Aronoff, W. Sandler, and C. Padden. 2010. Sign Languages and Compounding. In *Compounding*, ed. S. Scalise, and I. Vogel, 301-322. Amsterdam: John Benjamins.

Meir, I., A. Israel, W. Sandler, C. Padden, and M. Aronoff. 2012. The Influence of Community on Language Structure: Evidence from two young sign languages. *Linguistic Variation* 12(2): 247-91.

Meir, I., C. Padden, M. Aronoff, and W. Sandler. 2007. Body as Subject. *Journal of Linguistics* 43: 531-63.

Meir, I., C. Padden, M. Aronoff, and W. Sandler. 2013. Competing Iconicities in the Structure of Languages. *Cognitive Linguistics* 24(2): 309-43.

Meir, I., and W. Sandler. 2008. *A Language in Space: The Story of Israeli Sign Language*. New York: Lawrence Erlbaum Associates.

Meir, I., W. Sandler, M. Aronoff, and C. Padden. 2012. *A Dictionary of Al-Sayyid Bedouin Sign Language*. University of Haifa and University of California, San Diego.

Meir, I., W. Sandler, C. Padden, and M. Aronoff. 2010. Emerging Sign Languages. In *Oxford Handbook of Deaf Studies, Language and Education*, Vol 2, ed. Marschark, M., and Spencer, P., 267-280. Oxford: Oxford University Press.

Nespor, M., and W. Sandler. 1999. Prosody in Israeli Sign Language. *Language and Speech* 42(2&3): 143-76.

Newport, E. 1990. Maturational Constraints on Language Learning. *Cognitive Science* 14: 11-28.

Nyst, V. 2003. The Phonology of Name Signs: A comparison between the sign languages of Uganda, Mali, Adamarobe and The Netherlands. In *Cross-linguistic Perspectives in Sign Language Research*, ed. A. Baker, B. van den Bogaerde, and O. Crasborn, 71-80. Hamburg: Signum Press.

2007. *A Descriptive Analysis of Adamorobe Sign Language*. Utrecht: LOT. PhD thesis, University of Amsterdam.

Padden, C. 1988. *Interaction of Morphology and Syntax in American Sign Language*. New York: Garland Publishers.

2012. *From Gesture to Sign: The Emergence of a Lexicalization Pattern in a New Sign Language*. Unpublished manuscript. University of California, San Diego.

Padden, C., I. Meir, M. Aronoff, and W. Sandler. 2010a. The Grammar of Space in Two New Sign Languages. In *Sign Languages: A Cambridge Language Survey*, ed. D. Brentari, 570-90. New York: Cambridge University Press.

Padden, C., I. Meir, W. Sandler, and M. Aronoff. 2010b. Against All Expectations: The encoding of subject and object in a new language. In *Hypothesis A/Hypothesis B: Linguistic Explorations in Honor of David M. Perlmutter*, ed. D. Gerdts, J. Moore, and M. Polinsky, 383-400. Cambridge, MA: MIT Press.

Padden, C., I. Meir, S. Hwang, R. Lepic, S. Seegers, and T. Sampson. In press. Patterned Iconicity in Sign Language Lexicons. In *Where Do Nouns Come From?*, ed. J. Haviland (special issue of *Gesture*).

Pierrehumbert, J., and J. Hirschberg. 1990. The Meaning of Intonational Contours in the Interpretation of Discourse. In *Intentions in Communication*, ed. P. Cohen, J. Morgan, and M. Pollack, 271–331. Cambridge, MA: MIT Press.

Pinker, S., and R. Jackendoff. 2005. *The Faculty of Language: What's special about it? Cognition* 95(2): 201–36.

Plag, I. 2006. Morphology in Pidgins and Creoles. In *The Encyclopedia of Language and Linguistics*, ed. K. Brown, 305–8. Oxford: Elsevier.

Plann, S. 1997. *A Silent Minority: Deaf Education in Spain, 1550–1835*. Berkeley: University of California Press.

Quadros, R. 1999. *Phrase Structure of Brazilian Sign Language*. PhD dissertation, Pontifícia Universidade Católica do Rio Grande do Sul.

Rathmann, C. 2000. *The Optionality of Agreement Phrase: Evidence from Signed Languages*. Master's thesis, University of Texas.

Sandler, W. 1987. Assimilation and Feature Hierarchy in American Sign Language. In *Chicago Linguistics Society Parasessions on Autosegmental Phonology*, ed. A. Bosch, B. Need, and E. Schiller, 266–78. Chicago: Chicago Linguistic Society.

1989. *Phonological Representation of the Sign*. Dordrecht: Foris.

1993. Sign Language and Modularity. *Lingua* 89(4): 315–51.

2011. Prosody and Syntax in Sign Language. *Transactions of the Philological Society* 108(3): 298–328.

2012a. Visual Prosody. In *Sign Language: An International Handbook*, ed. R. Pfau, M. Steinbach, and B. Woll, 55–76. Berlin: De Gruyter.

2012b. The Phonological Organization of Sign Languages. *Language and Linguistics Compass* 6(3): 162–82.

2012c. Dedicated Gestures and the Emergence of Sign Language. *Gesture* 12(3): 265–307.

Sandler, W., M. Aronoff, I. Meir, and C. Padden. 2011. The Gradual Emergence of Phonological Form in a New Language. *Natural Language and Linguistic Theory* 29: 503–43.

Sandler, W., I. Meir, S. Dachkovsky, C. Padden, and M. Aronoff. 2011. The Emergence of Complexity in Prosody and Syntax. *Lingua* 121(13): 2014–33.

Sandler, W., I. Meir, C. Padden, and M. Aronoff. 2005. The Emergence of Grammar: Systematic structure in a new language. *Proceedings of the National Academy of Sciences* 102(7): 2661–5.

Senghas, A., and M. Coppola. 2001. Children Creating Language: How Nicaraguan Sign Language acquired a spatial grammar. *Psychological Science* 12(4): 323–8.

Senghas, A., M. Coppola, E. Newport, and T. Supalla. 1997. Argument Structure in Nicaraguan Sign Language: The emergence of grammatical devices. In *Proceedings of the Boston University Conference on Language Development, 21*, ed. E. Hughes, and A. Greenhill, 550–61. Boston: Cascadilla Press.

Shattuck, R. 1980. *The Forbidden Experiment: The Story of the Wild Boy of Aveyron*. New York: Farrar Straus Giroux.

Stokoe, W. 1960. Sign Language Structure: An outline of the visual communication systems of the American deaf. *Studies in Linguistics, Occasional Papers 8*.

Supalla, T. 1986. The Classifier System in American Sign Language. In *Noun Classification and Categorization*, ed. C. Craig, 181–214. Amsterdam: John Benjamins.

Supalla, T., and E. Newport. 1978. How Many Seats in a Chair? The derivation of nouns and verbs in American Sign Language. In *Understanding Language through Sign Language Research*, ed. P. Siple, 181–214. Academic Press.

Tkachman, O. and W. Sandler. In press. The Noun-Verb Distinction in Two Young Sign Languages. In *Where Do Nouns Come From?*, ed. J. Haviland (special issue of *Gesture*).

Washabaugh, W. 1986. *The Acquisition of Communicative Skills by the Deaf of Providence Island*. Amsterdam: Mouton de Gruyter.

Zeshan, U. 2004. Interrogative Constructions in Signed Languages: Cross-linguistic perspectives. *Language* 80(1): 7–39.

11

Endangered languages

Keren Rice

Some time in the early 1990s, terms such as language endangerment and language death began to be heard in the linguistics community. The sense of impending language loss was important for Franz Boas, Edward Sapir, Leonard Bloomfield, and other Americanists of the early twentieth century, and spurred their focus on language documentation, with the recording of texts playing a primary role. While much work on language documentation and the linguistic effects of language obsolescence was carried on in the middle part of the century (e.g., Dorian 1981, 1989), the notion of language endangerment did not really become a major focus in linguistics again until the 1990s.[1]

Himmelmann (2008: 339) cites a talk given by Johannes Bechert (1990) as a trigger for events that led to language endangerment becoming a core concern in linguistics over the 1990s. Bechert spoke at the International Congress of Linguists in 1987, where, drawing on observations about language loss in Australia, he asked why linguists were not concerned with the imminent loss of a major part of their empirical base. Following this, a volume, Robins and Uhlenbeck (1991), was published, and a session on endangered languages was held at the International Congress of Linguists in 1992. UNESCO established an Endangered Languages Program in 1993. The Linguistic Society of America established the Committee on Endangered Languages and their Preservation in 1992, and the German linguistic society organized a summer school on endangered languages in 1994 and began work on the "Dokumentation bedrohter Sprachen" (DoBeS) program sponsored by the Volkswagen Foundation, inaugurated in 1999. As Himmelmann writes (2008: 340), by 2000, "language endangerment was firmly established as an active field of research in linguistics as evidenced by the usual indicators such as regular and manifold conferences, a steady stream of articles and books, new societies and funds dedicated to the documentation and maintenance of endangered languages, and a special mailing list."

The activity has only increased since the date that Himmelmann gives, 2000. Moore *et al.* (2010) carried out a Lexis-Nexis search of the English-language press in 2009, showing that the phrase "endangered languages" had appeared in 1,552 separate articles, most of them since the year 2000. Linguists with a wide variety of interests direct at least some of their research efforts towards endangered languages, and there has been an increasing focus on language conservation and revitalization. Endangered languages have also received much public attention, with regular media coverage.

In this chapter, I address a number of questions that have become prominent as language endangerment has became a topic of concern. The chapter is divided into two major sections. In section 11.1, I review background material, including the language situation around the world, causes of language endangerment, reasons why language endangerment has garnered the concern that it has in the past few decades, and responses to language endangerment. In section 11.2, I turn to some of the questions that language endangerment has raised in anthropological linguistics.

11.1 Foundations

11.1.1 The language situation worldwide

Romaine (2007: 116) writes that the world was "close to linguistic equilibrium" for most of human history, with a balance between the number of languages lost and those created. Over the past 10,000 years, however, "various events have punctured this equilibrium forever" – she notes in particular the invention and spread of agriculture, the rise of colonialism, the Industrial Revolution, globalization, electronic technology, and other factors that have allowed for vast language spread, particularly of Eurasian languages.

While Romaine identifies the past 10,000 years as a time of language spread, it is generally agreed that the rate of language loss has increased dramatically in recent times. In particular, recent decades have seen a decrease in the inter-generational transmission of a large number of languages. It is often said that of the approximately 7,000 languages spoken around the world, "at least half of them may no longer continue to exist after a few more generations as they are not being learnt by children as first languages" (Austin and Sallabank 2011b: 1). While counting languages and speakers is problematic (see §11.2.1), the widely recognized predicted rapid loss of linguistic diversity has been viewed as alarming by many scholars, speakers, and would-be speakers alike.

Romaine (2007; see also Nettle and Romaine 2000) also considers the distribution of languages worldwide, suggesting that the distribution is uneven, with a small number of languages spoken by a large percentage of the global population; similarly languages are unevenly distributed in terms of numbers of speakers. (See §11.2.1 on counting.) To be more concrete, Romaine notes an inverse relationship between the number of languages and the numbers of speakers of those languages, with the 3,894 smallest languages that Romaine (2007: 118) identifies spoken by 0.13 percent of the world's population, and the 75 largest languages spoken by 79.5 percent of the population.

The geographic distribution of languages is also worthy of mention. Some parts of the world are what have been termed hotbeds for linguistic diversity while others are more uniform. For instance, Europe has about 3 percent of the world's languages, with 26.3 percent of the speakers; most of these languages are spoken outside Europe as well. Africa, on the other hand, houses approximately 30 percent of the world's languages, but only 11.8 percent of the speakers. Romaine (2007: 120) notes that Papua New Guinea has 11.9 percent of the world's languages, but only 0.1 percent of the world's population. Romaine (2007: 122) estimates that, if the viability threshold for a language is 10,000 speakers, 60 percent of the world's languages are endangered, with an uneven distribution around the world – 33 percent of the languages in Africa, 53 percent in Asia, 30 percent in Europe, but 78 percent in North America, 77 percent in South America, and 93 percent in Australia and the Pacific.

See section 11.2.1 for discussion of numbers, and section 11.2.2 for what it means to be a language.

11.1.2 What does it mean to be endangered?

How do we know if and when a language is "endangered"? In attempting to address this difficult question, linguists have drawn on various ideas about language "vitality." As Romaine (2007: 121) observes, it is common to use size as a proxy for degree of endangerment. Krauss (1992: 7) takes 100,000 speakers as a rough estimate of what it means for a language to be safe. Romaine notes, however, that "size does not tell the whole story," even if "it may be the best surrogate at the moment."

Others have attempted to define degree of endangerment by somewhat more refined criteria. One well-known classification is that of UNESCO (2003). UNESCO classified languages as to their degree of endangerment, taking factors of intergenerational transmission and ages of speakers into account. Degrees of endangerment are recognized, ranging from a language being safe, with the language spoken by all generations with ongoing intergenerational transmission, to a language being extinct, with no speakers left. Four intermediate levels are identified: vulnerable languages are generally spoken by children but are restricted to certain domains; definitely endangered languages are those where children do not learn the language as their mother tongue; severely endangered languages are spoken by older generations, but are not spoken by parents to children or among themselves; and critically endangered languages are those where grandparents speak the language partially and infrequently (definitions summarized from Austin and Sallabank 2011b: 3).

UNESCO (2003) also attempted to determine factors that can be used to assess endangerment, identifying nine factors.

Factor 1.   Intergenerational language transmission
Factor 2.   Absolute number of speakers
Factor 3.   Proportion of speakers within the total population
Factor 4.   Trends in existing language domains
Factor 5.   Response to new domains and media
Factor 6.   Materials for language education and literacy
Factor 7.   Governmental and institutional language attitudes and policies, including official status and use
Factor 8.   Community members' attitudes toward their own language
Factor 9.   Amount and quality of documentation

Identifying agreed-upon criteria for defining language endangerment continues to be of debate, even as the notion of language endangerment has taken hold in both academic and popular literature. See also section 11.2.2 for additional discussion.

11.1.3   Causes of language endangerment

Much attention has been devoted to the causes of language endangerment. The most common causes are easy to pinpoint – people shift the language that they use due to contact and colonization. These involve factors such as power and prestige, as well as urbanization and globalization. I draw the following list from Austin and Sallabank (2011b), who in turn synthesize it from Nettle and Romaine (2000), Crystal (2000), and Grenoble (2011).

Austin and Sallabank divide the causes of language endangerment into four broad types:

- Natural catastrophes, famine, disease
- War and genocide
- Overt repression, often in the name of "national unity" or assimilation
- Cultural/political/economic dominance

Natural catastrophes, famine, and disease might lead to the loss of a people, and, with this, the extinction or endangerment of a language. Crystal (2000: 71) cites the 1998 earthquake in Papua New Guinea, an event that left the population of speakers of some languages at low numbers; with the destruction of villages and relocation of peoples, language loss was highly likely. Crystal (2000: 71) further notes the Irish potato famine as an important factor in the reduction in number of speakers of Irish – the impact of the famine was greatest in rural areas, where Irish was chiefly spoken. Crystal (2000: 75) discusses the effect of World War II on the people of the Andaman islands, noting that language loss was one of the consequences of invasions and battles.

While natural catastrophes, famine, disease, war, and genocide play a role in language endangerment, all things considered, it is a relatively minor one. The major factors involve the latter two given by Austin and Sallabank: repression, and cultural, political, and economic dominance.

Pressure towards assimilation has been a major force in language shift in many places; Austin and Sallabank (2011b: 5) identify Kurdish, Welsh, and Native American languages as examples.

Austin and Sallabank (2011b: 6) divide the fourth category into five factors: economic, cultural, political, historical, and attitudinal. These factors are complex and intertwined – it is rarely possible, excepting cases of natural catastrophe, to isolate a single factor as implicated in language loss.

While the first two factors, natural catastrophes and war and genocide, may result in the total loss of a people, and with this language extinction, in the case of repression and domination the result is generally language loss over time.

11.1.4 What is lost?

While there is debate about numbers (§11.2.1), what it means to be a language (§11.2.2), and what it means for a language to disappear, one cannot help but be struck by the magnitude of language loss discussed in section 11.1.1.

One might ask, with respect to languages, whether anything is really lost in language shift beyond the linguistic code itself. This question has been addressed in recent years, and is the topic of this section.

A major reason that linguists began to be concerned about language endangerment was professional. Woodbury (1998: 234), for instance, writes that the loss of linguistic diversity affects the ability of linguists to reconstruct linguistic prehistory and to determine the nature, range, and limits of communicative behavior and grammatical competence. (See §11.1.5 for additional discussion.)

Woodbury (1998) examines in detail what might be lost beyond the linguistic code. He asks in particular about the impact of language loss on individuals and communities. As he says, "as language choice becomes politically and socially polarized, many locate in their ancestral language their social identity, their cultural traditions, their aesthetic and expressive achievements and potential, and the texture of their daily interactions with those around them. Perhaps due to the naturalness of such identifications, it is usually assumed that the loss of language *entails* a loss of social identity or culture" (1998: 234–5). Woodbury (1998: 235) points out that there is little research on this question, and he asks if, under conditions of radical language shift, it might be that the language of wider communication can be "adapted ideologically, if not always structurally, to communicative ends that are continuous with those earlier fulfilled by an ancestral language." Woodbury cites research that suggests that this type of adaptation takes place. For instance, research by Eades (1988) in Australia and Kwachka (1992) in Alaska points to cultural continuity in the face of language shift; Woodbury sees this as a "welcome, even empowering, political message" (1998: 237). He asks a different question, what might be lost in language shift beyond the lexicogrammatical code, or what he calls form-dependent expression. Woodbury studies affective suffixes in Cup'ik, and argues that aestheticized and emotionalized traditions are not translated into the dominant language. He concludes that radical language shift can "drastically disturb" community values (1998: 257). Woodbury suggests that the failure to translate form-dependent expression might be some of the source of the perception that language loss means cultural loss (see §11.1.5). Thus, while much of language is translatable, parts are the basis of "community-specific rhetorical, aesthetic, and expressive practices" (1998: 257), and this is something important that is lost.

While Woodbury focuses on the loss of community-specific language, others focus on the loss of linguistic diversity worldwide. For instance, Mithun (2004) provides a rich discussion of language use in languages of North America, focusing on lexical and grammatical categories and their relationship to culture and language use. Sidnell and Enfield (2012) review the literature on linguistic relativity, addressing three versions of relativity: one involving language conceptualized as a system of thought or cognition, a second involving language as meaningful social behavior, and the third involving language and social action. While the claims are debated, nevertheless there is evidence that there are fundamental differences in the resources available in languages and in how those resources are deployed.

In response to what is lost when a language is no longer spoken, then, not only is the linguistic code lost, but so are community-specific rhetorical, aesthetic, and expressive practices, to use Woodbury's words. Such loss is both local to a community, and global, with a potential loss in diversity of many linguistically deployed resources.

11.1.5 Why be concerned about language endangerment?

The high number of languages already lost or in danger, as discussed in section 11.1.1, inspired the linguistic community to think about language endangerment in a more sustained way, and led to a consideration of whether language endangerment is something to be concerned about, or if it is simply something that is to be accepted. Woodbury (1998) identifies one reason for concern – not everything is translatable between languages. Others discuss other reasons for concern, and these are summarized in this section.

Crystal (2000) provides an overview of reasons for concern about language endangerment, as do Austin and Sallabank (2011b) and others. Crystal (2000), in a chapter entitled "Why should we care?," discusses the following broad reasons: because we need diversity, because languages express identity, because languages are repositories of history, because languages contribute to the sum of human knowledge, because languages are interesting in themselves. Austin and Sallabank (2011b) also identify reasons for being concerned about language endangerment: value to linguistic science, cultural heritage, language and ecology, language and identity, linguistic human rights, education policy. It is worthwhile looking at some of these reasons in a little more detail.

As noted earlier, the current focus on language endangerment arose for professional reasons. For instance, it is not possible to study typological relations between languages in the absence of data from a variety of languages, both related and unrelated genealogically and areally. Linguists have long been concerned with cataloguing and studying the linguistic diversity found in the world. Many cite Krauss (1992: 10), who suggested the need for "some rethinking of our priorities, lest linguistics go down in history as the only science that has presided obliviously over the disappearance of 90% of the very field to which it is dedicated."

A number of scholars identify parallels between biological diversity and linguistic diversity. In his section on biological diversity, Crystal (2000: 32) says that arguments which are relevant for biological diversity are applicable to language, drawing a parallel between species decline and language loss.

Cultural heritage is often given as a reason for concern about language endangerment. Austin and Sallabank (2011b: 7) quote the UNESCO website, where linguistic diversity is cited as a "pillar of cultural diversity"; UNESCO further states that "When languages fade, so does the world's rich tapestry of cultural diversity. Opportunities, traditions, memory, unique modes of thinking and expression – valuable resources for ensuring a better future are also lost." Linguists have also discussed cultural reasons for sustaining languages; see, for instance, Mithun (1998), Hale (1998), and, for in-depth discussion, Harrison (2007) and Evans (2010). Mithun (1998: 189), for instance, writes, "Language represents the most creative, pervasive aspect of culture, the most intimate side of the mind. The loss of language diversity will mean that we will never even have the opportunity to appreciate the full creative capacities of the human mind" and Hale (1998: 192) says that language "endangerment and progressive extinction amount to a catastrophe for human intellectual and cultural diversity, a disaster comparable in its extent to losses in other aspects of our environment." See section 11.2.5.

Language and its relationship to identity is a major reason for concern about language loss. Languages are symbols of identity. Crystal (2000: 39–40) says, "Identity is what makes the members of a community recognizably the same. It is a summation of the characteristics which make it what it is and not something else – of 'us' vs 'them'. These characteristics may be to do with physical appearance, but just as often ... they relate to local customs ..., beliefs, rituals, and the whole panoply of personal behaviours. And of all behaviours, language is the most ubiquitous." The Canadian Royal Commission on Aboriginal Peoples (RCAP 1996) echoes this, saying "Language is usually seen as an essential component of ethnic identity, and it is commonly understood that the loss of a minority language automatically entails assimilation with the dominant group." RCAP goes on to write that language shift does not automatically imply ethnic assimilation, but that "In deploring the loss of its ancestral language, an Aboriginal group may be deploring the loss of a symbol of its identity rather than an instrument of communication. Hence, the motivation to revive the ancestral language is not communication, since the dominant language fulfils that need, but stems from the desire to revive or protect a tangible emblem of group identity." Identity is a complex issue; see section 11.2.2 for brief discussion.

Some have focused on linguistic human rights, or the right to use one's own language. Skutnabb-Kangas *et al.* (1995) and Skutnabb-Kangas (2001) discuss the protection of linguistic human rights, and write of linguicism, with languages being rendered invisible or as non-resources. They argue that change of mother tongue should be voluntary rather than state-imposed. Some of the argument for linguistic human rights follows from research in education – many have found that children get off to the best start if their early education is in the mother tongue (e.g., Cummins 1979, 1991; Baker 2006).

In general, many of the concerns about language endangerment come from an academic perspective. Yet the needs of the linguistic profession are very likely not sufficient for speakers to choose to transmit a language rather than shift languages. Indeed, in many cases, the needs of linguists are simply irrelevant to the speakers of an endangered language. What if we shift to the perspective of the speaker or would-be speaker of the endangered language? It is unlikely that speakers or communities would be concerned about diversity for the sake of diversity, one of the arguments for sustaining languages that is often found in the academic literature.

Speakers are concerned with language endangerment for many reasons. McKay and McKay (1987: 80) write of language as a symbol of ethnic identity and as a source of knowledge and history (McKay and McKay 1987, Battiste 1987), and see language loss as contributing to shift or loss of identity. Speakers may mourn that the children do not understand them (e.g., RCAP 1996), seeing language loss as an inability to pass on the core of who and what they are. People speak to the deep connection between their language and the land, and how their culture changes along with language change, with language loss coinciding with the loss of traditional ways.

See, for instance, Harrison (2007) and Evans (2010) for the development of these kinds of arguments.

While people whose language is endangered often mourn its loss, this is not always the case. The sense of language loss appears to be most frequent in cases of severe language loss; in cases with reduced language transmission, but with a larger number of speakers, people might make the choice to not speak the language with their children, or might select a language for its effectiveness in achieving particular ends (for instance, they might use one language in disciplining children and another language in praising them; one in traditional settings and the other in a work place), with the language chosen for its pragmatic effectiveness rather than its symbolic value, with shift resulting. See, for example, Kulick (1992) and Garrett (2005) for discussion. In making such choices, consciously or not, a person or a community most likely does not realize that future generations might regret such decisions. See Hill (2002) for discussion.

11.1.6 Is language shift inevitable?

Language shift occurs for many reasons, and there are many reasons for responding to language shift. However, it is important to ask if it is actually possible to prevent a shift.

Some argue that language shift is inevitable. For instance, Grenoble and Whaley (1998), Mufwene (2004), Harbert (2011), and others talk about the socioeconomic factors involved in language shift – speakers choose to speak a language that will help them get ahead or help them achieve some other locally understood benefit (see, for instance, Gal 1978 for a case study). Harbert (2011: 404) further examines cultural capital, stating that

> The cultural capital assigned to one language relative to others is to a considerable degree determined by the need or desirability of employing it in the material marketplace. Speakers of dominant languages tend to have, or are perceived as having, greater access to material resources and the things that lead to them, such as education, jobs, information and "networks" (Grin 2007: 275), and these languages thus tend to accrue symbolic value, often at the expense of minority languages. The connection between the perceived value of a language and its actual value in securing economic advancement is not rigid though ...

Harbert (2011: 422) proposes a typology of economic disruptions of language communities, looking at both language shift resulting from population movement and language shift without movement. He concludes "It is not fully clear so far what economic and development intervention measures can be best applied in minority- and endangered-language contexts to ensure the continued presence of these languages on the world stage."

Crystal (2000: 130), drawing on the important work of Fishman (1991), concludes that several factors are important if a language is to be sustained, "being used in the home and neighbourhood as a tool of intergenerational communication." These include the following. An endangered language will progress if its speakers

- increase their prestige within the dominant community
- increase their wealth relative to the dominant community
- increase their legitimate power in the eyes of the dominant community
- have a strong presence in the educational system
- make use of electronic technology.

In addition, he suggests that an endangered language will progress if its speakers can write their language.

This is a tall order that places a heavy burden on the speakers and communities whose language is shifting. Fishman (2001: 481) asks "Why is it so hard to save a threatened language?" He gives five reasons; the following are quoted directly from Fishman:

- The loss of a traditionally associated ethnocultural language is commonly the result of many long-ongoing departures from the traditional culture, thereby robbing that culture of most of its erstwhile and potential defenders and establishing a rival identity that does not require the traditionally associated language.
- Organizing on behalf of a traditionally associated but weakened language is competitively depicted and regarded as social mobility contraindicated, parochial, and anti-modern.
- In order to defend a threatened language some of its functions must be both differentiated from and shared with its strong competitor – a tactically difficult allocation to arrive at and to maintain.
- Any functions to be regained by the threatened language must be simultaneously reinforced both from "below" and from "above" in terms of power considerations.
- The opposition to RLS (i.e., reversing language shift) is both statist and supra-statist, thereby labeling RLS efforts as simultaneously disruptive of local civility and of higher-order international advantage.

Fishman (2001: 481) concludes by asking if threatened languages can be saved, and responding with what he calls an "informed though uncertain answer" – yes, "but only by following careful strategies that focus on priorities and on strong linkages to them, and only if the true complexity of local human identity, linguistic competence and global interdependence are fully recognized." Hinton (2011: 311) concludes a recent article on language revitalization by quoting a language activist: "Yes, the language may die. But it won't be on my watch."

Despite the hurdles, there has been interest in trying to sustain languages, as is evident in the quote from Hinton immediately above. What has come to be called language revitalization is discussed in sections 11.1.7.2 and 11.2.4, but here I introduce the concept of sleeping languages (see Amery 2000, Hinton 2001). These are languages that have not been spoken for some time, but for which there is documentation. In writing about the reclamation of Miami, Leonard (2008) asks what it means for a language to be extinct. He writes of how, given the documentation on Miami, it has been possible to bring the language back, with some intergenerational transmission reestablished.

Leonard talks of challenges involved in reawakening Miami, focusing on purist ideologies about what it means to speak a language as a major one. At the same time, Leonard concludes: "Formerly sleeping languages such as Miami serve communicative and social functions, and among other factors, I believe that our recognition of the fallacy of extinction has facilitated our coming as far as we have in awakening *myaamia* – both the language and the culture" (2008: 32). This raises an interesting and important question: What does it mean to speak a language? See section 11.2.2.

11.1.7 Responses to language endangerment

As linguists became aware of the situation affecting languages around the world, research focused on a select set of questions. In his 2000 book on language death for instance, Crystal has chapters titled, "What is language death?," "Why should we care?," "Why do languages die?," "Where do we begin?," and "What can be done?" It was not long, though, before the realization of language endangerment served to mobilize active research. Evans captures this in the following quote from his recent book on what we have to learn from endangered languages:

> Never before in history have languages and the knowledge they hold been disappearing at a faster rate. But, equally, never before have we been aware of the dimensions of what is being lost, or had the curiosity, appreciation and technology to document what is still hanging on. Bringing this knowledge out on the scale it deserves, … is a quest that must call scholars of many types – both insiders and outsiders – from right around the world. (Evans 2010: 231)

The increasing recognition among linguists of how many languages were endangered encouraged a greater emphasis on fieldwork. This in turn promoted discussions of language documentation, language revitalization, and the ethics of fieldwork.

11.1.7.1 Language documentation
Himmelmann (2006: 1), building on Himmelmann (1998), defines language documentation in a simple, and what he calls preliminary, way – "a

language documentation is a lasting, multipurpose record of a language." This would include, ideally, "all registers and varieties, social or local; it would contain evidence for language as a social practice, as well as a cognitive faculty; it would include specimens of spoken and written language, and so on" (2006: 2).

Woodbury (2011: 157) offers a recent definition of language documentation – "the creation, annotation, preservation and dissemination of transparent records of a language." As Woodbury points out, this concept may seem simple, but language documentation is complex and multi-faceted. Woodbury notes the following points, quoted from him directly:

- LANGUAGE encompasses conscious and unconscious knowledge, ideation and cognitive ability, as well as overt social behaviour;
- RECORDS of these things must draw on concepts and techniques from linguistics, ethnography, psychology, computer science, recording arts, and more;
- the CREATION, ANNOTATION, PRESERVATION, and DISSEMINATION of such records poses new challenges in all the above fields, as well as in information and archival science and;
- above all, humans experience their own and other people's languages viscerally and have differing stakes, purposes, goals and aspirations for language records and language documentation.

(Woodbury 2011: 159)

In the ideal then, language documentation aims to capture a language in its fullness. See section 11.2.3 for additional discussion.

11.1.7.2 Language revitalization

Language documentation involves the recording of as broad a corpus as possible. Language revitalization is different – it refers to what Fishman (1991) terms reversing language shift, or "attempting to bring endangered languages back to some level of use within their communities (and elsewhere) after a period of reduction in usage" (Hinton 2011: 291). Hinton (2011: 293) outlines two major tasks for revitalization – to teach the language to those who do not know it, and to get learners and those who know the language to use it in a broadening set of situations. Another consequence of the recognition of language endangerment is that linguists have become involved in work beyond documentation and description of endangered languages, also striving to be involved with communities in efforts to sustain and revitalize languages.

11.1.7.3 Ethics

In early work recognizing the language endangerment situation, there was a focus on ethics with respect to languages. This is evident in the quote from Krauss given earlier, that linguists were presiding over the loss of 90 percent of their subject matter; we also see it in the title of the 2006 book by Grenoble and Whaley, *Saving Languages*. Dobrin and Berson (2011) write that many linguists have begun to devote attention to the social processes that result from their work, and have become concerned about power imbalances. Cameron *et al.* (1992) identify different models of fieldwork, basically involving research *on*, research *for*, and research *with* people and communities. The major issues that arise have to do with who controls the research agenda and what responsibilities the fieldworker has to the communities with which they work. Since 2000 a rich literature has emerged on this topic; for recent overviews see Dwyer (2006), Rice (2006, 2012), Yamada (2007), Czaykowska-Higgins (2009), Holton (2009), and others.

11.2 Challenges

In section 11.1 I reviewed some responses to the recognition of language endangerment. These responses have raised additional questions and prompted important discussions, many of which are of interest to linguists and anthropologists. In this section, I examine some of these questions.

11.2.1 Counting

Almost any introduction to language endangerment begins with an estimate of the number of languages spoken in the world, and, based on a rough estimate of the number of speakers of a language, an estimate of the number of languages that are likely to cease to be spoken in the coming decades. This, clearly, involves counting numbers of languages and numbers of speakers of each of those languages, as discussed in sections 11.1.1 and 11.1.2.

This information makes for good media. At the same time, as Hill (2002), Romaine (2007), Moore *et al.* (2010), Austin and Sallabank (2011b), Grenoble (2011), Muehlmann (2012a, 2012b), and others note, these numbers raise complex problems such as "Who counts as a speaker?" and "What counts as a language?"

Different issues arise around counting. For one, there are not reliable sources about numbers of languages and speakers. As Austin and Sallabank (2011b: 4) write: "complete information on all of the world's languages is not available: the majority have not been recorded or analysed by linguists, have no dictionaries or even written form, and are not recognized officially in the countries in which they are spoken. What information there is available, is often out of date."

In addition, many languages have more than one name (e.g., Spolsky 2011), and it may be unclear what should be considered a language and what a variety. Mutual intelligibility is often used to determine what is a language, but this is itself complex, and is often shaped as much by attitudes and politics as by the structures and lexicon of the languages in question (e.g., Austin and Sallabank 2011b: 4). Language names too are sociocultural and political facts, and this further complicates what may seem like a simple matter of counting (e.g., Moore *et al.* 2010).

Even if sources existed that were both reliable and up to date, there were dictionaries, and issues around names and dialects were resolvable, problems would remain in counting languages and speakers. This is the heart of the issue – the definition of a language is not straightforward, with what is a language determined by a mix of linguistic, social, and political factors, nor is it straightforward what it means to speak a language.

Moore *et al.* (2010: 2), among others, further argue that the use of counts is predicated on a fundamentally misconstrued assumption about language, with counts privileging "a conception of 'languages' as neatly-bounded, abstract, autonomous grammatical systems (each of which corresponds to a neatly-bounded 'worldview')." This raises important questions of what a language is and what it means to speak a language.

11.2.2 What does it mean to speak a language? What is a language?

As discussed in section 11.1.6, Leonard (2008: 28) concludes that Miami is not a dead language, but a reawakened language. At the same time, he remarks that the six members of the Baldwin family (Daryl Baldwin is a linguist and Miami tribal member who instituted the reclamation of the language) speak Miami on a daily basis, with the youngest two acquiring it in the home, thus reestablishing intergenerational transmission. Leonard goes on to say that reclamation is a multigenerational process that will likely involve "levels of proficiency lower than 'fluent' for quite some time."

Grinevald and Bert (2011) propose a typology of seven types of speakers – fluent speakers, semi-speakers, terminal speakers, rememberers, ghost speakers, neo-speakers, and last speakers (with this last being, they say, partly mythological). These authors develop this system in thinking about linguistic fieldwork on endangered languages as an attempt to sensitize someone planning to undertake fieldwork to the types of speakers they might encounter.

This hierarchy seems simple, but many questions arise. What does "fluent" mean? How do we define a semi-speaker as opposed to a fluent speaker? In short, what does it mean to speak a language? There are no simple responses, as many have noted. Evans (2001), for instance, talks about perceptions of speakerhood, and how a person's response to whether they speak a language or not is not a simple one, but depends on social, cultural, and political factors; see Muehlmann (2012a, 2012b) for an interesting case study.

Dobrin and Berson (2011) tell a noteworthy story of research carried out by Dobrin in Papua New Guinea with speakers in an area where Arapesh and Tok Pisin are spoken. They write that the speech is "ubiquitously multilingual, with constant switching to Tok Pisin from the matrix vernacular, as is 'the rule rather than the exception in the case of endangered languages' (Schultze-Berndt 2006: 231)." Are people speaking Arapesh? Tok Pisin? Something else? Language, the object of study, is itself dynamic.

The nature of language is much discussed in the anthropological responses to the endangerment literature. While cognitive aspects of language can, perhaps, be captured through traditional kinds of linguistic research, a language is much more than this. It is ultimately a social construction that is constituted through local social practices of naming and describing and, indeed, in some cases through the products of linguistic research such as dictionaries, grammars, and texts.

11.2.3 Language documentation

Language documentation often begins with the assumption that it is important to preserve a language in its fullest state, working with older speakers to capture the language in the most conservative form possible. This conception of language, Moore *et al.* (2010) and others argue, is problematic in its assumptions that language is an immutable object that preserves cultural values and local knowledge. Dobrin and Berson (2011: 191), among others, argue that the issue is made more complex in that it is "not simply the fact that we are trafficking in idealizations..., but rather that the idealizations in question lead to a hierarchization of speakers measured with respect to a 'pre-contact' form of linguistic competence: complete mastery of a pure ancestral code." They go on to say "Even when speakers are willing and able to speak a particular language, they may not always monitor the boundaries between it and other languages in their repertoire, meaning that decisions must be made about how and to what extent the documentary products linguists create will distill the embedded code" (2011: 191). Dobrin and Berson (2011: 194) further remark that "in fostering this kind of metalinguistic consciousness, the linguist was asking speakers to adjust their approach to deploying linguistic resources to culturally foreign ideas about the proper use of languages-as-codes." This, they suggest, is problematic in not taking into account issues such as mobility, diffusion, and mixing, and treating language mixing as aberrant and unstable (2011: 195–6). In short, language becomes viewed as something preserved, rather than something that is dynamic in use.

Current methods of language documentation focus on audio and video recordings of natural speech, both narrative and conversation, as well as structured elicitation. Such methods offer the potential of capturing the language use that Dobrin and Berson (2011) discuss. The notion of language use of a community is core to the notion of language documentation, as defined by Himmelmann (1998; see above, §11.1.7.1), and studying language use is the explicit goal of funding programs such as the Hans Rausing Endangered Languages Documentation Program (www.hrelp.org/documentation/) and the Documentation of Endangered Languages program (http://dobes.mpi.nl/). At the same time, as noted earlier, language documentation often begins with the concept of a language and with the assumption that it is important to preserve a language in its fullest state, with another goal being maintenance and revitalization. In as much as there is a focus on a language and its use rather than on language use in a community, language documentation may still privilege one conception of language as well as one group of speakers. Language documentation work captures an important piece of the complex of language use, but it can remain one piece depending on the assumptions about what should be documented that are made by the researcher and by a community.

11.2.4 Ethics in linguistic fieldwork and language revitalization

As discussed in sections 11.1.7.2–3, one consequence of the recognition of language endangerment is an increased attention by linguistic fieldworkers to the practices of fieldwork, and to the responsibilities of linguists to the people with whom they work. This focus on process came about for many reasons, including issues of social justice and indigenous rights, as well as by a shift in the social sciences more generally towards participatory research. Collaborative work and its relevance have been much discussed, and along with them issues of power and control (e.g., Cameron *et al.* 1992, and references in §11.1.7.3). Collaboration brings challenges with it, as Makoni and Pennycook (2006: 32), among others, write – achieving true collaboration is a challenge, and conflicts in perspective may have "unexpected adverse effects on exactly those same people whose interests we think we are promoting or safeguarding."

The role of linguists in language revitalization is also debated. Nevins (2004) examines a language maintenance program on the White Mountain Apache Reservation in New Mexico, addressing a controversy that arose around this program. She writes that the Apache people had different ideologies about concepts of language loss and desirable language survival. There was both a "discourse on language loss defined in terms of Apache cultural values of speaking, and modeled on ideals of communication within the family" and an engagement with the international discourse on language endangerment, with the tribal government having a political interest in defining the language in nationalist terms (Nevins 2004: 272). Nevins asks why language preservation programs are often controversial, arguing that a conflict arises between the school environment and the environments defined by Apache forms of relationships, and speaks to the importance of recognizing local ideologies, a point brought out in the papers in Kroskrity and Field (2009) as well.

In general, then, while ethics and language revitalization are important components of linguistic fieldwork, they raise many questions including what it means to be revitalized, whose ethics are at stake, and what the relationship is between language revitalization and research.

11.2.5 The rhetoric of language endangerment

Questions about counting, speakers, documentation, revitalization, ethics, and ideologies figure prominently in the language endangerment literature. The rhetoric of language endangerment has also been under scrutiny. Many authors, (e.g., Hill 2002, Errington 2003, Mufwene 2004, Duchêne and Heller 2007, Moore *et al.* 2010) critique this rhetoric.

In an influential article, Hill (2002) focuses on aspects of the endangered languages discourse. She identifies what she calls universal ownership, or the sense that "endangered languages in some sense 'belong' to everyone in the world" (Hill 2002: 120). Hill argues that the idea of universal ownership is rooted in particular notions and environmental and ecological logics. These logics, she argues, may not be shared by communities whose languages are endangered – there might not be a sense of a language belonging to someone outside of that community and unknown to the community, for instance. Hill notes that speakers based in local communities do not talk about universal ownership, but speak about "my language" and "our language" (2002: 122), contradicting the rhetoric common in the literature.

Hill also addresses hyperbolic valorization, or the use of language such as "Endangered languages are priceless treasures" (Hill 2002: 120). Errington (2003: 724) gives an example of hyperbolic valorization from the Endangered Languages Fund homepage – "every time a language dies, we lose thousands of unique insights, metaphors, and other acts of genius." Hill (2002: 123) remarks that it is "very difficult to convince most ordinary people that it is true" that language is a "resource" with "value." As she says, the languages that are endangered today were "universally viewed as barbarous and deficient," a view that was shared by some speakers. A consequence of hyperbolic valorization, Hill notes (2002: 125), is that endangered languages become so valuable that they are placed in highly restricted spheres of exchange, being inaccessible to ordinary speakers. This, she points out, "may seem to have little to do with the linguistic marketplace where everyday people negotiate with one another about everyday matters in the fleeting signals of the spoken language, which, unlike the enduring golden hoard, is in constant change." Hill continues that speakers may view their language as precious in this way. For instance, Meek (2007) argues that among the Kaska, people may consider the language to be of special dignity and more appropriate for use by elders than by youth. Dobrin and Berson (2011: 197) cite work by Moore (1988) with the Wasco-Wishram in Oregon. He writes about how speakers "understood linguistic elicitation sessions as an occasion for the display of cultural wealth, and so as a potential source of moral hazard."

On the other hand, Hill (2002: 126–7) speaks of her work with speakers of Mexicano (Nahuatl). Language shift was advanced in some towns but not in others, and, Hill writes, "There was not a widespread sense among speakers or their neighbors that the language was 'endangered.'" While speakers talked of their language in many ways, few used economic terms such as priceless. Hill notes that anecdotes of hyperbolic valorization in indigenous communities exist largely in communities at late stages of language shift, where the language is not in daily use.

11.3 Summary

The awareness of endangered languages is part of a larger picture, arising out of social and political changes in the past decades. This awareness has brought about many changes in linguistics. For one thing, it has created an increased awareness of the responsibility to languages, as in the quote from Krauss (1992) above, through the development of documentary linguistics.

The documentation imperative, as it is sometimes called, has led to work on many languages that had been understudied. It has led to new designs for research. These include designs that privilege the collection of data; see, for instance, Woodbury (2011) on the one hand, and Boerger (2011), on the other, for different models. While Woodbury advocates a "broad and inclusive view of endangered-language documentation" (2011: 184), Boerger describes BOLD (Basic Oral Language Documentation), a method recognized as an efficient way to obtain a core language data corpus. This method is designed to document a language "effectively with minimal investment of human, temporal, and financial resources" (Boerger 2011: 231). As Boerger says, something is better than nothing, and she proposes a strategy that focuses on the collection of primary oral data.

While the recognition of endangerment has led to the consideration of responsibilities to languages, it has also led to consideration of responsibilities to people and to communities, rebuilding connections between linguistics and anthropology, and other disciplines as well (see, for instance, Thieberger 2012). Many speak of the need to connect linguistic work with ethnographic work (e.g., Dorian 2002, Fishman 2002, Hill 2002, Dobrin and Berson 2011, Granadillo and Orcutt-Gachiri 2011, Woodbury 2011). Woodbury (2011) concludes that work on endangered languages must recognize the importance of community context, and its bearing on deeper intellectual and ideological questions that underlie such work. Dobrin and Berson (2011: 204) remark that an unprecedented disciplinary conversation about ethics is taking place, as is a rethinking about presentation of the products of documentary material. They too suggest that linguists work towards an ethnographic understanding, this time of their research encounters. Granadillo and Orcutt-Gachiri (2011) stress the need to understand what is happening to the speakers of a language, not just to a language. Writing in 2000, Moore (2000: 67) stresses the need for

> an anthropologically sophisticated understanding of language obsolescence and 'death' as complicated social, cultural, and historical processes that usually unfold within small speech communities during periods of socio-economic and political transformation (accompanied, virtually always, by societal bi- or multilingualism of an increasingly unstable sort). Much more ethnography needs to be done before 'losses' can be properly counted, or even understood.

Since the time that Moore wrote this, there has been a greater awareness of the need to understand language use as well as structure, and language use in its larger context. There rightly remains a concern about the local and what a language tells about the past, but there is ever increasing attention to the place of a language in the present, and, perhaps, the future.

Debates continue, and I close with a few of the many questions that will continue to animate discussion. What are the social, cultural, and political factors that lead to language shift? What does it mean to speak a language? What is the appropriate object(s) of study? How can language documentation begin to capture the complexities of language in use? How do language ideologies affect language documentation and language revitalization? What is the role of the outsider in this type of work? These are challenging questions without easy answers. I leave the reader with the conclusion that Michael (2011: 139) draws in a paper on language and culture –

> language documentation and scholarship on the language–culture nexus both stand to benefit from addressing the pressing question of what constitutes adequate documentation and description of communicative practices; the former field from the theoretical sophistication of the latter, and the latter from the resulting increased prominence of the social dimension of language within linguistics.

Note

1. Much of this background paragraph is drawn from Himmelmann (2008). There are excellent overviews of language endangerment. For recent work see Himmelmann (2008) and, especially, Austin and Sallabank (2011a). I draw on these, as well as on Crystal (2000). See Rogers and Campbell (2011) for a brief discussion of the Americanist tradition as well as for an extensive bibliography on endangered languages.

References

Amery, Rob. 2000. *"Warrabarna Kaurna!" Reclaiming an Australian language.* Multilingualism and Linguistic Diversity 1. Lisse, The Netherlands: Swets and Zeitlinger.

Austin, Peter, and Julia Sallabank. 2011a. *The Cambridge Handbook of Endangered Languages.* Cambridge: Cambridge University Press.

2011b. Introduction. In *The Cambridge Handbook of Endangered Languages*, ed. Peter K. Austin and Julia Sallabank, 1–24. Cambridge: Cambridge University Press.

Baker, Colin. 2006. *Foundations of Bilingual Education and Bilingualism*, 4th ed. Clevedon: Multilingual Matters.

Battiste, Marie. 1987. Mi'kmaq Linguistic Integrity: A Case Study of Mi'kmawey School. In *Indian Education in Canada, Vol. 2: The Challenge*, ed. Jean Barman, Yvonne Hébert, and Don McCaskill, 107–25. Vancouver: University of British Columbia Press.

Bechert, J. 1990. Universalienforschung und Ethnozentrismus. In *Proceedings of the 14th International Congress of Linguists 1987*, ed. W. Bahner, J. Schildt, and D. Viehweger, 2350–2. Berlin: Akademie Verlag.

Boerger, Brenda H. 2011. To BOLDly go where no one has gone before. *Language Documentation and Conservation* 5: 208–33.

Cameron, Deborah, Elizabeth Frazer, Penelope Harvey, M. B. H. Rampton, and Kay Richardson. 1992. *Researching Language: Issues of Power and Method.* London: Routledge.

Crystal, David. 2000. *Language Death.* Cambridge: Cambridge University Press.

Cummins, Jim. 1979. Linguistic Interdependence and the Educational Development of Bilingual Children. *Review of Educational Research* 49: 221–51.

1991. Interdependence of First- and Second Language Proficiency in Bilingual Children. In *Language Processing in Bilingual Children*, ed. Ellen Bialystok, 70–89. Cambridge: Cambridge University Press.

Czaykowska-Higgins, Ewa. 2009. Research Models, Community Engagement, and Linguistic Fieldwork: Reflections on working with Canadian indigenous communities. *Language Documentation and Conservation* 3(1): 15–50.

Dobrin, Lise M., and Josh Berson. 2011. Speakers and Language Documentation. In *The Cambridge Handbook of Endangered Languages*, ed. Peter K. Austin and Julia Sallabank, 187–211. Cambridge: Cambridge University Press.

Dorian, Nancy C. 1981. *Language Death: The Life Cycle of a Scottish Gaelic Dialect.* Philadelphia: University of Pennsylvania Press.

1989. *Investigating Obsolescence.* Cambridge: Cambridge University Press.

2002. Commentary: Broadening the rhetorical and descriptive horizons in endangered-language linguistics. *Journal of Linguistic Anthropology* 12: 134–40.

Duchêne, Alexandre, and Monica Heller. 2007. *Discourses of Endangerment: Ideology and Interest in the Defence of Languages*. Advances in Sociolinguistics. London: Continuum.

Dwyer, Arienne M. 2006. Ethics and Practicalities of Cooperative Fieldwork and Analysis. In *Essentials of Language Documentation*, ed. Jost Gippert, Nikolaus P. Immelmann and Ulrike Mosel, 31–66. Berlin: Mouton de Gruyter.

Eades, Diana. 1988. They Don't Speak an Aboriginal Language, Or Do They? In *Being Black: Aboriginal Culture in "Settled" Australia*, ed. Ian Keen, 97–115. Canberra: Aboriginal Studies Press.

Errington, Joseph. 2003. Getting Language Rights: The rhetorics of language endangerment and loss. *American Anthropologist* 105(4): 723–32.

Evans, Nicholas. 2001. The Last Speaker Is Dead – Long Live the Last Speaker! In *Linguistic Fieldwork*, ed. Paul Newman and Martha Ratliff, 250–81. Cambridge: Cambridge University Press.

2010. *Dying Words: Endangered Languages and What They Have to Tell Us*. Oxford: Blackwell.

Fishman, Joshua A. 1991. *Reversing Language Shift: Theoretical and Empirical Foundations of Assistance to Threatened Languages*. Clevedon: Multilingual Matters.

2001. From Theory to Practice (and Vice Versa). In *Can Threatened Languages Be Saved? Reversing Language Shift, Revisited: A 21st Century Perspective*, ed. Joshua A. Fishman, 451–83. Clevedon: Multilingual Matters.

2002. Commentary: What a Difference 40 years make! *Journal of Linguistic Anthropology* 12(2): 144–9.

Gal, Susan. 1978. Peasant Men Can't Get Wives: Language change and sex roles in a bilingual community. *Language in Society* 7(1): 1–16.

Garrett, Paul. 2005. What a Language is Good For: Language socialization, language shift, and the persistence of code-specific genres in St. Lucia. *Language in Society* 34(3): 327–61.

Granadillo, Tania, and Heidi A. Orcutt-Gachiri. 2011. *Ethnographic Contributions to the Study of Endangered Languages*. Tucson: University of Arizona Press.

Grenoble, Lenore A. 2011. Language Ecology and Endangerment. In *The Cambridge Handbook of Endangered Languages*, ed. Peter K. Austin and Julia Sallabank, 27–44. Cambridge: Cambridge University Press.

Grenoble, Lenore A., and Lindsay J. Whaley. 1998. Toward a Typology of Language Endangerment. In *Endangered Languages: Current Issues and Future Prospects*, ed. Lenore A. Grenoble and Lindsay J. Whaley, 22–54. Cambridge: Cambridge University Press.

2006. *Saving Languages*. Cambridge: Cambridge University Press.

Grin, François. 2007. Economics and Language Policy. In *Handbook of Language and Communication: Diversity and Change*, ed. Marlis Hellinger and Anne Pauwels, 271–9. Berlin: Mouton de Gruyter.

Grinevald, Colette and Michel Bert. 2011. Speakers and Communities. In *The Cambridge Handbook of Endangered Languages*, ed. Peter K. Austin and Julia Sallabank, 45-65. Cambridge: Cambridge University Press.

Hale, Kenneth. 1998. On Endangered Languages and the Importance of Linguistic Diversity. In *Endangered Languages: Current Issues and Future Prospects*, ed. Lenore A. Grenoble and Lindsay J. Whaley, 192-216. Cambridge: Cambridge University Press.

Harbert, Wayne. 2011. Endangered Languages and Economic Development. In *The Cambridge Handbook of Endangered Languages*, ed. Peter K. Austin and Julia Sallabank, 403-22. Cambridge: Cambridge University Press.

Harrison, David. 2007. *When Languages Die: The Extinction of the World's Languages and the Erosion of Human Knowledge*. Oxford: Oxford University Press.

Hill, Jane. 2002. "Expert Rhetorics" in Advocacy for Endangered Languages: Who is listening and what do they hear? *Journal of Linguistic Anthropology* 12(2): 119-33.

Himmelmann, Nikolaus. 1998. Documentary and Descriptive Linguistics. *Linguistics* 36(1): 161-95.

2006. Language Documentation: What is it and what is it good for. In *Essentials of Language Documentation*, ed. Jost Gippert, Nikolaus P. Himmelmann, and Ulrike Mosel, 1-30. Berlin: Mouton de Gruyter.

2008. Reproduction and Preservation of Linguistic Knowledge: Linguistics' response to language endangerment. *Annual Review of Anthropology* 37: 337-50.

Hinton, Leanne. 2001. Sleeping Languages. Can they be awakened? In *The Green Book of Language Revitalization in Practice*, ed. Leanne Hinton and Ken Hale, 217-26. San Diego: Academic Press.

2011. Revitalization of Endangered Languages. In *The Cambridge Handbook of Endangered Languages*, ed. Peter K. Austin and Julia Sallabank, 291-311. Cambridge: Cambridge University Press.

Holton, Gary. 2009. Relatively Ethical. A comparison of linguistic research paradigms in Alaska and Indonesia. *Language Documentation and Conservation* 3(2): 161-75.

Krauss, Michael. 1992. The World's Languages in Crisis. *Language* 68(1): 4-10.

Kroskrity, Paul V., and Margaret C. Field. 2009. *Native American Language Ideologies: Beliefs, Practices, and Struggles in Indian Country*. Tucson: University of Arizona Press.

Kulick, Don. 1992. Socialization, Self and Syncretism in a Papua New Guinean village. Cambridge: Cambridge University Press.

Kwachka, Patricia. 1992. Discourse Structures, Cultural Stability, and Language Shift. *International Journal of Society and Language* 93: 67-73.

Leonard, Wesley. 2008. When is an "Extinct Language" not Extinct? Miami, a formerly sleeping language. In *Sustaining Linguistic Diversity: Endangered and Minority Languages and Language Varieties*, ed. Kendall

A. King, Natalie Schilling-Estes, Lyn Fogle, Jia Jackie Lou, and Barbara Soukup, 23–33. Washington, DC: Georgetown University Press.

Makoni, Sinfree, and Alistair Pennycook, eds. 2006. *Disinventing and Reconstituting Languages*. Clevedon: Multilingual Matters.

McKay, Alvin, and Bert McKay. 1987. Education as a Total Way of Life: The Nisga'a Experience. In *Indian Education in Canada, Vol. 2: The Challenge*, ed. Jean Barman, Yvonne Hébert, and Don McCaskill, 64–85. Vancouver: University of British Columbia Press.

Meek, Barbra A. 2007. Respecting the Language of Elders: Ideological shift and linguistic discontinuity in a Northern Athapascan community. *Journal of Linguistic Anthropology* 17(1): 23–43.

Michael, Lev. 2011. Language and Culture. In *The Cambridge Handbook of Endangered Languages*, ed. Peter Austin and Julia Sallabank, 120–40. Cambridge: Cambridge University Press.

Mithun, Marianne. 1998. The Significance of Diversity in Language Endangerment and Preservation. In *Endangered Languages: Current Issues and Future Prospects*, ed. Lenore A. Grenoble and Lindsay J. Whaley, 163–91. Cambridge: Cambridge University Press.

2004. The Value of Linguistic Diversity: Viewing other worlds through North American Indian languages. In *A Companion to Linguistic Anthropology*, ed. Alessandro Duranti, 121–40. Oxford: Blackwell.

Moore, Robert E. 1988. Lexicalization and Lexical Loss in Wasco-Wishram Language Obsolescence. *International Journal of American Linguistics* 52(4): 453–68.

2000. Endangered. *Journal of Linguistic Anthropology* 9(1–2): 65–8.

Moore, Robert E., Sari Pietikäinen, and Jan Blommaert. 2010. Counting the Losses: Numbers as the language of language endangerment. *Sociolinguistic Studies* 4(1): 1–26.

Muehlmann, Shaylih. 2012a. Von Humboldt's Parrot and the Countdown of Last Speakers in the Colorado Delta. *Language and Communication* 32(2): 162–8.

2012b. Rhizomes and Other Uncountables: The malaise of enumeration in Mexico's Colorado River Delta. *American Ethnologist* 39(2): 339–53.

Mufwene, Salikoko. 2004. Language Birth and Death. *Annual Review of Anthropology* 33: 201–22.

Nettle, Daniel, and Suzanne Romaine. 2000. *Vanishing Voices: The Extinction of the World's Languages*. Oxford: Oxford University Press.

Nevins, M. Eleanor. 2004. Learning to Listen: Confronting two meanings of language loss in the contemporary White Mountain Apache speech community. *Journal of Linguistic Anthropology* 14(2): 269–88.

Rice, Keren. 2006. Ethical Issues in Linguistic Fieldwork: An overview. *Journal of Academic Ethics* 4: 123–55.

2012. Ethical Issues in Linguistic Fieldwork. In *The Oxford Handbook of Linguistic Fieldwork*, ed. Nicholas Thieberger, 407–29. Oxford: Oxford University Press.

Robins, R. H., and E. M. Uhlenbeck. 1991. *Endangered Languages*. Oxford and New York: Berg Publishers Ltd.

Rogers, Chris, and Lyle Campbell. 2011. Endangered Languages. Online: Oxford Bibliographies. Doi: 10.1093/OBO/9780199772810-0013.

Romaine, Suzanne. 2007. Preserving Endangered Languages. *Language and Linguistics Compass*. 1(1–2): 115–32.

RCAP. 1996. *Report of the Royal Commission on Aboriginal Peoples*. Ottawa: Canada.

Schultze-Berndt, Eva. 2006. Linguistic Annotation. In *Essentials of Language Documentation*, ed. Jost Gippert, Nikolaus P. Himmelmann, and Ulrike Mosel, 213–51. Berlin: Mouton de Gruyter.

Sidnell, Jack, and N. J. Enfield. 2012. Language Diversity and Social Action: A third locus of linguistic relativity. *Current Anthropology* 53(3): 302–33.

Skutnabb-Kangas, Tove. 2001. *Linguistic Genocide in Education – or Worldwide Diversity and Human Rights?* Mahwah, NJ: Lawrence Erlbaum.

Skutnabb-Kangas, Tove, Robert Phillipson, and Mart Rannut, eds. 1995. *Linguistic Human Rights*. Berlin: Mouton de Gruyter.

Spolsky, Bernard. 2011. Language and Society. In *The Cambridge Handbook of Endangered Languages*, ed. Peter K. Austin and Julia Sallabank, 141–56. Cambridge: Cambridge University Press.

Thieberger, Nicholas. 2012. *The Oxford Handbook of Linguistic Fieldwork*. Oxford: Oxford University Press.

UNESCO. 2003. Language Vitality and Endangerment. Online: www.unesco.org/culture/ich/doc/src/00120-EN.pdf

Woodbury, Anthony C. 1998. Documenting Rhetorical, Aesthetic, and Expressive Loss in Language Shift. In *Endangered Languages: Current Issues and Future Prospects*, ed. Lenore A. Grenoble and Lindsay J. Whaley, 234–58. Cambridge: Cambridge University Press.

2011. Language Documentation. In *The Cambridge Handbook of Endangered Languages*, ed. Peter K. Austin and Julia Sallabank, 159–86. Cambridge: Cambridge University Press.

Yamada, Racquel-Maria. 2007. Collaborative Linguistic Fieldwork: Practical applications of the empowerment model. *Language Documentation and Conservation* 1(2): 257–82.

12

Language evolution

Stephen C. Levinson

12.1 Introduction

In the wake of the success of Darwin's ideas, speculative papers on the evolution of language became such a rage that they were officially banned by the Société de Linguistique de Paris in 1866, and unofficially by the new Linguistic Society of America in 1924 (its journal *Language* did not publish a paper on the subject till 2000; see Newmeyer 2003). The rationale for exclusion was that there was no possible evidence that could bear on the problem: Language does not fossilize, and we cannot bring comparative biological evidence to bear because our closest primate cousins exhibit nothing like language.

In the 1990s, this extraordinary self-censorship was broken by a diverse group of pioneering scholars, who advanced a range of largely speculative but interesting ideas, nicely summarized in the collection by Christiansen and Kirby (2003). Perhaps language evolved to replace primate grooming in groups too large to do the physical thing (Dunbar 2003); perhaps it began as a gestural system (Corballis 2003), aided by the pre-adaptation of the neural mechanisms for action recognition (Arbib 2003). Whatever the beginnings, perhaps it involved a chance mutation that allowed advanced syntax (Bickerton 2003, Chomsky 2010), or perhaps the latter evolved in response to the preceding evolution of the capacity for vocal learning and production (Lieberman 2003). And what is the essential development, the essence of language as it were, that made all the rest possible? Is it the basic notion of semiosis (Deacon 2003), perhaps viewed as a triangle between speaker, hearer, and referent (Tomasello 2003)? Or is recursive syntax the crucial advance (as Hauser *et al.* 2002 have argued)? Can one spell out all the pre-adaptations and steps through which the ascent to language passed (Hurford 2003)? These are the kinds of questions that preoccupied the first decade of the renaissance of studies in language evolution.

However, in the last decade, the subject of language evolution has experienced a boom in international conferences (see, e.g., www.evolang.org/), monographs, textbooks, and learned papers – in fact, far too much has happened to be adequately reviewed here. Crucially, in that time, the subject has been transformed from a speculative enterprise to one where critical new data and new methods have completely overturned the apple cart. The new data include archaeo-DNA, large typological databases of existing languages, the discovery of contemporary emerging languages, the discovery of the relevance of animal models, and a range of new fossils. New methods include ways of extracting ancient DNA without contamination, its insertion into mice to see the effects on brain and behavior, the application of bioinformatics to typological data, laboratory simulations of evolutionary processes, the MRI scanning of the internal structure of fossils, and much more besides. These developments, missing from anthropological linguistic textbooks, are likely to rapidly accelerate, transforming the subject into a core part of the curriculum. Linguistic anthropology can surely no longer ignore these developments: Language is the key factor in making us a cultural species, and how that happened is a saga that should be told in every introductory course.

This review covers two subjects that many would consider essentially unrelated: the evolution of the underlying biology that makes language possible on the one hand, and the processes underlying language change and diversification on the other. But the two need to be considered hand in hand for a number of reasons. First, biological and cultural evolution is an interlocked process. A new model for conceptualizing this is *niche construction* (Odling-Smee *et al.* 2003). Many animals alter their ecology so fundamentally that the selecting environment has now been constructed by the species. Consider for example the beaver, whose dams make watery fastnesses which then select for specialized aquatic and woodworking skills. In these cases, along with the genetic mode of inheritance, the environment becomes a second inheritance channel, with the two in mutual interaction (better teeth, more felled trees, more water...). For humans, this second channel has been exploited on a unique scale, for culture is this second channel: a new human enters a world that is highly structured by the cultural environment. That includes the material culture, the habitat, and of course the language(s) a child must learn, which pervades the acoustic environment. The cultural ecology has a direct impact on genes, e.g., through the vectors of disease: wet-rice agriculture breeds malaria, which selects for resistance. In this perspective, culture is as much part of biology as the genome.

A second reason for seeing cultural and biological evolution as a single process is that there are clear feedback relations to observe. Consider the human hand, with its extreme motor control and opposing thumb: this clearly evolved hand in hand (to pun) with human tool use, which now seems (on indirect evidence) to date to over 3.5 mya (and 2.5 mya on direct evidence). That motor control was likely inherited by the cortical strip that happens to lie next to hand in the motor cortex: the tongue. The vocal apparatus is an impressive retrofit to the basic primate system: the supra-laryngeal tract is bent at right angles, the larynx lowered at the risk of choking, cortical (rather than midbrain) control allows voluntary breath control, the tongue, the palate, and the velum are reconfigured to allow a wide range of filters that give us our speech sounds (Fitch 2010). This retrofit was driven by the increasing cultural exploitation of the speech channel – presumably for language. It largely took place somewhere between 1.5 mya and 0.5 mya, but the interaction between language and vocal tract continues to this day (see §12.4). Finally, there are model systems – micro-speech communities – where this kind of ongoing interaction between genes and biology on the one hand and culture and language on the other can be directly observed today.

This review is therefore structured as follows. We first consider (§12.2) the range of new data that gives insights into the time course of the biological evolution of language capacities. We then turn (§12.3) to cultural evolution and introduce the new methods that are revolutionizing this area. Finally, we consider the evidence for ongoing relations between biological and cultural evolution, and point to many avenues where future research is likely to rapidly expand our horizons.

12.2 Biological evolution and the antiquity of language

Until ten years ago, there had been a majority of linguists, paleontologists. and archaeologists who subscribed to a very recent origin of language, with mention of dates between 70 kya (kilo years ago) and as low as 50 kya. The reasoning was based largely on the archaeological and paleontological record in Western Europe, where the Upper Paleolithic (from *c.* 40 kya) ushered in a huge burst of technological and symbolic creativity which suggested some qualitative change in human cognition associated with modern humans arriving in this rich ecology about that time. In addition, the paleontologists viewed the Neanderthal forebears, who had inhabited the same area for some hundreds of thousands of years, as premodern in anatomy and primitive in technology and resource exploitation. There was an influential theory too that Neanderthals lacked a fully modern vocal tract, and as a result would not have had the vowel contrasts typical of modern languages. Chomsky (2010, Berwick *et al.* 2013) influentially continues to hold this model, arguing that some freak mutation suddenly made available the recursive syntax that typifies modern languages.

But in fact this position is now undercut on almost every front. We now know that Neanderthals were not a separate species and interbred with modern humans (Green *et al.* 2010), that anatomically modern humans had lived with Neanderthal-level technology for 150,000 years in Africa

(McBrearty and Brooks 2000), that Neanderthal technology has been underrated, and Neanderthals seem to have all (or virtually all) of the genetic and anatomic preconditions for modern speech (Dediu and Levinson 2013). Modern humans up to the modern era have occasionally exhibited (e.g., in Tierra del Fuego, or Tasmania) simpler technologies and less traces of symbolic activity than Neanderthals (Henrich 2004). In short, the European Upper Paleolithic now looks like just one of those epochal leaps in cultural complexity that we associate with such periods as the Greek city states, the Renaissance, the Industrial Revolution, or Mayan civilization.

This section therefore sketches the modern synthesis of information from different contributory sciences (see Dediu and Levinson 2013 for a full review). Let us start with paleontology. The discovery of a Neanderthal hyoid bone, structured within the modern range, undermined the idea that the larynx had a different structure with higher position (Arensburg et al. 1989). A low location for the larynx is essential for the structure and function of the modern vocal tract: the larynx is the vibratory source at the base of the vocal tract, allowing the flexibility of the upper tract to provide a variable filter to encode speech sounds (Fitch 2010).

If modern humans and Neanderthals had the same vocal tract, this can be attributed to their common ancestor, *Homo heidelbergensis*, who flourished roughly half a million years ago. Recently a huge cache of fossils of this species was found in Spain, and it has yielded invaluable information about anatomy. Especially interesting has been the preservation of the middle ear, which allows the reconstruction of audiograms, reflecting the sensitivities to specific wave-lengths. It turns out that the hearing of *H. heidelbergensis* seems to be within the range for modern humans, and distinctly different from the sensitivities of chimpanzees (Martínez et al. 2004). The range is ideally suited for sensing the formant structure of vowels. For almost all species the hearing range matches the broadcast range for vocal communication, and this allows us to be reasonably confident that *H. Heidelbergensis* was making sounds similar to modern speech. Other features are in line with this assumption, like the hypoglossal canal that serves the tongue.

Bones, especially from cold locations, can preserve ancient DNA, and we now have fully reconstructed genomes for Neanderthals and a sister race, the Denisovans (who diverged perhaps 600 kya, Meyer et al. 2012). These genomes present protein-coding differences from modern humans in only a handful of locations, mostly to do with skin and bone structure. The gene that (at the time of writing) seems most intimately connected with language is FOXP2, which seems involved in fine motor control (see Dediu, this volume, Chapter 28). Neanderthals and Denisovans had exactly the same variant as modern humans, which is unique to the *Homo* genus. Breaking news suggests that one way in which most (but not all) modern humans differ, however, may be a gene that binds to FOXP2, and which may therefore effect its quantitative expression. Although caution is in order, as the recovery and interpretation of archaeo-DNA is a rapidly developing field, the implication seems to be that humans of various lineages half a million years ago seem to have differed at most quantitatively in their genetic foundations for language.

There is one other crucial piece of evidence. Chimpanzees have little if any voluntary control of vocalization, which is produced both on the in- and out-breath. For human speech, very fine voluntary control of breathing is required: this involves a separate control pathway to the involuntary system controlled by the medulla or mid-brain which is triggered chemically by oxygen levels. This breath control allows a sharp in-breath in proportion to the length of an utterance, and controlled release of air that allows sufficient more or less constant pressure to power the source (larynx) and filters (vocal tract) that encode speech. The cortical pathway necessary for this passes directly down the vertical column to the intercostal muscles, requiring an enlarged vertebral canal which can be picked up in the fossil record (MacLarnon and Hewitt 1999). Once again it turns out that Neanderthals had the modern system, and thus the common ancestor at *c.* 500 kya. This vertebral evidence also puts a top limit on the modern speech system, since it is not found in *Homo erectus* at about 1.4 mya (at least in the one intact column found so far).

All the evidence thus tends to point modern speech capacities by half a million years ago. Various commentators have pointed out that speech – the capacity to produce something like modern speech sounds – does not necessarily imply language, interpreted say as words combined syntactically. Fitch (2010), for example, argues that various deer species have permanently lowered larynxes, and corresponding formant-structured vocalizations, without exhibiting anything like language; the motivation in this case, he argues, is to extend the perceived size of the animal, a mating adaptation specialized in males. There is nothing exclusive to humans in the production and comprehension system for speech, Fitch argues. This helps to motivate the Chomskyan view that it is something else that is the magic bullet for language, namely recursive syntax (Hauser *et al.* 2002). But this and other such arguments miss the point: the structure of the vocal tract is an elaborate adaptation for speech, involving a highly flexible and relatively small tongue, domed palate, voluntary control of the velum for nasal sounds, and above all the fine motor control that may be empowered by the human variant of FOXP2. And although size-exaggeration may well have been a pre-adaptation for speech, the complex system as a whole is clearly adapted to language – that is, complex and rapid human communication. It is worth bearing in mind that it is peripheral motor and sensory systems that drive neural development: the structure of the brain adapts to the available input and output systems (so that, e.g., in the blind, language is served by the visual areas of the brain). That is why the evidence for the full system for modern speech at half a million years ago should be interpreted as an adaptation for language, carrying with it much re-wiring of the brain which unfolds during infant development.

The other evidence for early language is much more indirect, but nevertheless compelling. It is the complexity of cultural traditions, passed on across many generations. Apes may pass on rudimentary gestural and grooming habits, even some kinds of tool using (e.g., sticks for "fishing" in termite mounds), but this is controversial since chimpanzee groups also differ ecologically and genetically. Nothing like the systematic traditions of human tools exist in any primate species. To take an example: Neanderthal stone-tool technology involved the elaborate preparation of a large flint core, trimmed around the edges to make a 90-degree percussion angle; from this large flakes could be struck, and then trimmed to fit the job, as awls, scrapers or points. It will take an average archaeology student at least a month of practice to achieve this (even without having to learn where to procure the raw material), and then only under constant verbal instruction. Skeletally modern humans used the identical technology up to c. 40 kya. Neanderthals systematically controlled fire, something that some modern human groups may actually have lost from time to time (for example the Tasmanians). Most of the stone tools seem to have been machine-tools as it were: they were used largely on wood, and fine aerodynamic javelins have been recovered from 400 kya in Europe. Add to this that Neanderthals lived in sub-Arctic conditions (presumably with clothing and footwear), hunting large game like mammoths, and it seems overwhelmingly likely that all of this cultural elaboration was empowered by an advanced communication system based on speech.

Combining these lines of evidence argues for something close to the modern capacity for language in our premodern forebears at half a million years ago. But why does the antiquity of language matter? For the same reason that Charles Lyell's (1830–33) demonstration of the antiquity of the earth opened up the way for Darwin's theory of evolution – the time-depth radically changes how we should think about language. If language really evolved in the last 100,000 years there would be hardly time for any significant biological reorganization. Consider for example the case of bat echolocation: a substantive re-tooling of basic mammalian vocalization for the purposes of spatial cognition. It has an antiquity of around 50 million years. Even half a million years for the antiquity of language makes it a biologically recent and rapid adaptation, which would have occurred mostly in the preceding one million years or so (using the vertebral evidence from *Homo erectus* as a terminus post quem). This relatively recent development suggests that language capacity has been cobbled together from pre-existing aspects of human biology and cognition. Moreover, it suggests that much of what we think about as the complexity of language is actually carried in the cultural channel, a point to which we now turn.

12.3 Cultural evolution of language over deep time

As Darwin (1871) observed, there is a strange parallel between the biological evolution of species and the historical development of languages. In both cases, species and languages split over time, evolving in distinct lines, so generating family trees. There are roughly as many languages as mammals, and they are phylogenetically related in similar ways, except that we have extreme difficulties connecting together the great language families, at the apex of the language tree. How many such families are there, of unproven relationship to one another? The answer depends on whether you are a "lumper" (like Joseph Greenberg) or a "splitter" like most historical linguists – splitters might estimate 300+ independent stocks, including many isolate languages (Nichols 1997). Historical linguistics, which has studied the processes involved in language change and diversification, is the oldest and perhaps the most scientific branch of linguistics, and played a role in inspiring Darwin's ideas. The "comparative method" – the gold standard in historical linguistics – involves finding cognates (words or morphemes with similar sounds and meanings) across languages and reconstructing the mother forms from which the descendant forms are derived by systematic sound changes (Durie and Ross 1996).

The parallel between biological and linguistic, and more broadly cultural, diversification has been explored from different perspectives. Efforts have been made to find detailed parallels between the particulate "genes" as it were, the origins of variation and the selective forces that work upon them, but there is no consensus on how best to view this exactly (see, e.g., Croft 2008, and Enfield, this volume, Chapter 13). Nor does that seem to hamper research. The fact is languages change generally slowly at their core, while peripheral words and structures change faster. The differential rate of change allows one to see both the common ancestry of languages and the ways in which they have diversified, and thus to trace out the family tree of related languages. Most of this work has been done on core vocabulary, using for example Swadesh's wordlist of conservative vocabulary, or on grammatical morphemes. It relies on the fact that detailed form–meaning pairings are unlikely to be due to chance. This kind of research presupposes a family-tree model of diversification, but it has been recognized for well over a century that languages change also through contact and diffusion from neighboring languages that may not be related at all phylogenetically. And words diffuse more often and more rapidly than structure (Thomason and Kaufman 1988). In rare cases, such diffusion can obscure whether two languages are actually related by descent or not (as in the case of Quiche and Aymaran), but mostly the two processes can be readily distinguished. In an earlier phase of anthropological theory, very similar processes of both descent and diffusion were noted in technology, ornament, and ritual, suggesting that linguistic evolution and cultural evolution in general follow similar principles.

In the last decade there has been a methodological revolution in the study of linguistic and cultural evolution (McMahon and McMahon 2005, Holden and Mace 2005, Levinson and Gray 2012). Methods developed in biology to trace the genetic similarities between species or the hybridization of plant or microbial lineages have been fruitfully applied to linguistic and cultural material. If a set of languages are known to be related, the tree-like nature of that relation can be extracted computationally, by searching for the most likely tree that underlies the present pattern of features in the descendants. All that is required is a large number of features for each language, some resistant to change and some less so. The favored technology at the time of writing is Bayesian phylogenetics, which involves making basic assumptions of, e.g., rates and directionalities of change, and seeing whether the most likely trees under those assumptions predict back the observed distribution of features across languages. If not, the assumptions are minimally changed, the computations repeated, and so on for thousands of iterations until no improvements are found. If some dates are known (e.g., for ancient Hittite or Linear B), then these methods allow the dates to be factored in, and rates of change varied across the tree in proportion to the number of feature changes in each branch. Using these methods, for example, the age of Indo-European as a language family seems robustly established as about 9,000 years (much older than many philologists had thought; Gray and Atkinson 2003).

Many linguists have assumed that these bioinformatics methods are undercut by the facts of language contact or diffusion. But this is not so. Methods exist for estimating the degree to which the data for a language family exhibit tree-like structure, and network models for analyzing hybridization have developed in parallel to computational phylogenetics. Work on bacterial evolution, where hybridization is a constant force, has provided bioinformatic models that may prove more appropriate for language. Recently, using the same techniques used to trace the source and diffusion of influenza types, it has been shown that Indo-European arose in Anatolia and not much later in the northern Kurgan steppes as many philologists had argued (Bouckaert *et al.* 2012). The success and generality of these methods have transformed the study of cultural evolution generally; there are intriguing studies of the development of Turkic carpet patterns, kinship systems, stone-tool traditions, and so forth. But in the case of language at least, a limiting factor has been a ceiling on the time-depth that we seem to be able reach back to, due to the erosion of word forms and meanings over time. The ceiling for the comparative method has been put at 10,000 years (close to the estimate of the age of Indo-European by the new methods mentioned above).

An alternative resource is to look not at the vocabulary of languages but at their abstract structure – their word order, their grammatical categories, their phoneme inventories, and so forth. There are limitations here:

there are limited numbers of word-orders (for transitive sentences, subjects, objects, and verbs can be in one of six orders for example), so having the same word order is much more likely than having the same or similar sounds meaning "water," for example. However, the chances of having the same or similar word orders, specific phonemes, and specific grammatical categories entirely by chance are quite remote: the combination of features can carry the signal of phylogenetic relatedness very well (Dunn et al. 2008, Levinson et al. 2011). One interesting thing that has come out of this work is the timescale for the cultural evolution of language. For vocabulary, the stability of word forms varies widely, and is closely related to their frequency. Using this as a yardstick, one can estimate the age of word forms, and it may be that some date right back to the Paleolithic (Pagel 2009). For the structural features of language, one can examine the pattern of diversification through the largest extant language families (like Austronesian, Indo-European, or Bantu). Once a split has occurred, e.g., Italic vs. Gothic, all further changes in both lines are independent. If one adds up all the independent lineages in Indo-European one arrives at something like 200,000 years of language evolution. One can then ask how many and which structural changes have occurred per unit time. The answer is that structural changes are actually very slow, varying from say one change per 10,000 years to none at all in 200,000 years. This contrasts of course with other aspects of cultural evolution like technology, and for principled reasons: change in language is stabilized by the parity problem (what I say must be understandable to you, unlike my fishing techniques which don't depend on yours). If these computations are correct, they suggest that language typology – the overall structure of languages – is on the whole very stable over deep time, offering the possibility that the 300-odd language families of the world may be provably related to one another using structural features. It may be possible to rank the structural features of language according to their stability, just as one can rank vocabulary according to its conservatism (Dediu and Cysouw 2013). It is also possible to discern that specific language families have a tell-tale "stability profile" – being especially conservative about specific features. Using these profiles it is possible to suggest very ancient connections between language families, e.g., between those in Siberia and North America (Dediu and Levinson 2012).

Another interesting payoff from this work is that once one has established the most probable family trees, it is possible to look at the interconnections between structural features – their systemic properties. For example, Greenberg suggested that languages tend to "harmonize" their features, so that, for example, if they have SOV (subject object verb) basic order, they will have postpositions rather than prepositions, thus harmonizing with head elements of phrases at the end (see Bickel, this volume, Chapter 5). Greenberg tested this by looking cross-linguistically (see the online WALS atlas for a modern update), but if there is some causal mechanism at play then it should also channel language change. This can now be tested, and initial tests show that the causal effect is in fact very weak if present at all (see Levinson and Gray 2012).

12.4 Language emergence

Languages are changing all the time, and sociolinguists have shown how to catch these changes in the process (although this work is confined to Western languages). But a more intriguing question is: What would a language soon after its birth look like? Bickerton (2003) believes that creole languages provide such insight, allowing us a glimpse of a stripped down innate language system. But creole languages are amalgams of other languages, and emerge in multilingual situations where everyone is already a speaker of some language. It is possible, however, to see the birth of languages absolutely or nearly from scratch, by observing deaf children, either isolated in hearing communities, or where there are other deaf individuals with whom to construct a sign language. The emergence of language-like properties in the signing of isolated deaf individuals has been studied in the US, China, and Turkey, in particular, under the rubric of "home sign" (Goldin-Meadow 2003, and this volume, Chapter 4). In these cases, one observes the rather rapid emergence of a structured signing system distinct from gesture, e.g., with a systematic word or phrase order. In industrial societies deaf children are rather rapidly institutionalized, where the chances occur for more systematic transformation of the signing system into a full-blown language. In the case of Nicaragua, there has been recent institutionalization of this kind with the provision of centralized deaf schools; here the transformation of individual homesigners into sharers of a common, jointly constructed system can be observed (Senghas *et al.* 2004). This work shows that these first-generation signers of a common language remain somewhat handicapped, for the simple reason that it takes time (generations indeed) for a fully expressive language to emerge; they may thus fail to communicate fully satisfactorily even about spatial locations, and find it difficult to express and even reason about other minds (Pyers *et al.* 2010).

In more rural circumstances, a local community where there is a strand of hereditary deafness may develop its own sign language. Such systems, known as village sign languages, are known from, e.g., Ghana, Israel, Mexico, Thailand, and Bali, where the languages may be five to seven generations old (Zeshan and de Vos 2012). This gives us the nearest glimpse into early-stage languages that we are ever likely to get – the urban systems like that in Nicaragua are rapidly creolized with developed sign languages through the importation of teachers and professionals.

The properties of these village sign languages are thus of very great scientific interest (see Meir *et al.* 2010; Zeshan and de Vos 2012, and

Sandler *et al.* this volume, Chapter 10). One of the surprising findings is that they may lack many of the features that linguists have judged to be essential characteristics of language, while still performing as fully adequate, sole languages for many individuals. They often seem to lack "duality of patterning," i.e., the construction of words out of recombinable segments or features. They may or may not have developed a fixed word order that allows "who did what to whom" in a transitive sentence to be disambiguated. They may lack proper names for places, making do with pointing instead. And they may lack features that scholars had presumed to be universal for sign languages, like the so-called classifier constructions, the use of arbitrary loci for anaphoric reference, or grammatical agreement on verbs. From this it is clear much of the grammatical machinery that we take for granted in languages takes many (perhaps a dozen or more) generations to evolve. These reports therefore qualify the findings from Nicaragua, where second generation signers in institutional settings already showed rapid development of the linguistic system. In both emerging urban and emerging rural sign languages there are special conditions: in the urban case, the building of a deaf culture in opposition to a hearing one, together with the hot-house conditions of institutionalized schooling and imported language structures; in the rural case, if the deaf population is of any size, the whole community participates in the sign language, although to varying degrees. Thus in the Balinese sign language studied by de Vos (2012) and others, some sixty congenitally deaf members of the village are complemented by over a thousand signers, whose second-language skills in sign may hold back the fast development of complex grammatical machinery.

Insights into the emergence of grammar can also come from simulating these processes, either by getting individuals to learn simple constructed languages and pass them on, or by computer simulations that can mimic thousands of repeated transmissions of this sort. Both paradigms involved iterated learning – transmission of a simplified language to another agent, who then passes it on to a third (Kirby and Hurford 2002). Under these conditions, unexpected simplifications and regularizations occur: regularization, double articulation, and recursive compositionality, for example, can be emergent properties in both computational simulations and experimental outcomes of iterated learning (Kirby *et al.* 2008).

12.5 Genes and culture in interaction

A common assumption is that the evolution of the language capacity and the cultural evolution of language have nothing to do with one another: at some distant point in the past we evolved the language capacity and then, on this platform, cultural evolution took off. In fact, of course, the two processes are interconnected: language is a kind of bio-cultural hybrid, with the cultural part evolved to exploit the biological part, and vice versa (Richerson and Boyd 2005). This tandem evolution is how we have been able, in some half a million years, to evolve such a complex system of communication, unparalleled in the animal world since the mammals evolved some 100 mya. The process can perhaps be understood best in terms of "niche construction," the way in which animals often construct the environments that then select for biological features: the environment becomes another track of inherited material, with the genetic and environmental tracks in constant interaction. In this way, we don't invent our languages (except in the rare cases involving sign languages mentioned above), we inherit them from our social environments. We know of a number of cases where these interactions between culturally constructed environments and our biology are attested. For example, dairying peoples have evolved greater adult lactose tolerance, or cultural processes for modifying lactose (e.g., through bacterial processing as in yoghurt), or both.

In the case of village sign languages, the feedback relations between biology and culture are rather visible. A strand of hereditary deafness creates the need for cultural innovation: as an expressive sign language emerges, and the speaking population also masters it, deaf people become fully competent central players in the community, intermarrying, and producing more offspring with genes conducive to deafness in the general population. That spread of the genes generates the further generations who can further elaborate the sign language. Both the biology and the culture depend on one another (see Levinson and Dediu, in press).

Ongoing interactions between genes and spoken languages are less visible, but almost certainly in play. It has been shown that even slight biological or cognitive biases can become amplified through cultural transmission, so that cultural evolution can be channeled by slight differences in population genetics. Take the case of contrastive tone in languages. This inversely correlates with the distribution of certain rather recent variants of genes involved in brain development: populations without these relatively recent alleles or variants seem more likely to have developed tone languages (Dediu and Ladd 2007). We don't know the mechanisms involved, but in the case of the more recent alleles they may involve slight changes in auditory cortex, which might make tone marginally harder to process. Additional arguments of this kind have been advanced for different shapes and sizes of the vocal tract which may make the production of some sounds easier or harder to produce. In all cases, the presumption is that the biological biases are weak, and represented only as slight differences in frequency distributions in the populations. Any child can master a tone language, but perhaps not every child finds it equally easy.

12.6 Conclusion

Both fields of language evolution – the evolution of the biological capacity for language and the cultural elaboration of languages – are vibrant fields of current study. It is a matter for regret that linguistic anthropology has played such a small role in either the first decade of speculative work, or the last decade of more empirical work in both subjects. Linguistic anthropologists are uniquely placed to contribute to these debates, since they have empirical information about what language is actually primarily used for in small-scale societies, how it is transmitted, the effects of divisions of labor, varying demographics and social organizations. It is to be hoped that their voice will be heard in the next decade.

References

Arbib, M. A. 2003. The Evolving Mirror System: A neural basis for language readiness. In *Language Evolution*, ed. M. Christiansen and S. Kirby, 182-200. Oxford: Oxford University Press.

Arensburg, B., A. M. Tillier, B. Vandermeersch, H. Duday, L. A. Schepartz, and Y. Rak. 1989. A Middle Palaeolithic Human Hyoid Bone. *Nature* 338: 758-60.

Berwick, R. C., A. D. Friederici, N. Chomsky, and J. J. Bolhuis. 2013. Evolution, Brain, and the Nature of Language. *Trends in Cognitive Sciences* 17: 89-98.

Bickerton, D. 2003. Symbol and Structure: A comprehensive framework. In *Language Evolution*, ed. M. Christiansen and S. Kirby, 77-93. Oxford: Oxford University Press.

Bouckaert, R., P. Lemey, M. Dunn, S. J. Greenhill, A. V. Alekseyenko, A. J. Drummond, R. D. Gray, M. A. Suchard, and Q. D. Atkinson. 2012. Mapping the Origins and Expansion of the Indo-European language family. *Science* 337(6097): 957-60. (doi:10.1126/science.1219669.)

Chomsky, N. 2010. Some Simple Evo-Devo Theses: How true might they be for language? In *The Evolution of Human Language*, ed. R. Larson, V. Déprez and H. Yamakido, 54-62. Cambridge: Cambridge University Press.

Christiansen, M., and S. Kirby, eds. 2003. *Language Evolution*. Oxford: Oxford University Press.

Corballis, M. 2003. From Hand to Mouth: The gestural origins of language. In *Language Evolution*, M. Christiansen and S. Kirby, 201-18. Oxford: Oxford University Press.

Croft, W. 2008. Evolutionary Linguistics. In *Annual Review of Anthropology*, Vol. 37, ed. W. H. Durham, D. Brenneis, and P. T. Ellison, 219-34. Palo Alto, CA: Annual Reviews.

Darwin, C. 1871. *The Descent of Man, and Selection in Relation to Sex*. London: John Murray.

Deacon, T. W. 2003. Universal Grammar and Semiotic Constraints. In *Language Evolution*, ed. M. Christiansen and S. Kirby, 111–39. Oxford: Oxford University Press.

De Vos, C. (2012). *Sign-spatiality in Kata Kolok: How a Village Sign Language of Bali Inscribes its Signing Space*. PhD dissertation, Radboud University Nijmegen.

Dediu, D., and M. A. Cysouw. 2013. Some Structural Aspects of Language are More Stable than Others: A comparison of seven methods. *PLoS One* 8: e55009. (doi:10.1371/journal.pone.0055009.)

Dediu, D., and D. R. Ladd. 2007. Linguistic Tone is Related to the Population Frequency of the Adaptive Haplogroups of Two Brain Size Genes, ASPM and Microcephalin. *PNAS* 104: 10944–9.

Dediu, D. and S. C. Levinson. 2012. Abstract Profiles of Structural Stability Point to Universal Tendencies, Family-Specific Factors, and Ancient Connections Between Languages. *PLoS One* 7: e45198.

——— 2013. On the Antiquity of Language: The Reinterpretation of Neandertal Linguistic Capacities and its Consequences. *Frontiers in Language Sciences* 4: 397. (doi:10.3389/fpsyg.2013.00397.)

Dunbar, R. 2003. The Origin and Subsequent Evolution of Language. In *Language Evolution*, ed. M. Christiansen and S. Kirby, 219–34). Oxford: Oxford University Press.

Dunn, M., S. C. Levinson, E. Lindström, G. Reesink, and A. Terrill. 2008. Structural Phylogeny in Historical Linguistics: Methodological Explorations Applied in Island Melanesia. *Language* 84: 710–59.

Durie, M., and M. Ross, eds. 1996. *The Comparative Method Reviewed: Regularity and Irregularity in Language Change*. Oxford: Oxford University Press.

Fitch, W. T. 2010. *The Evolution of Language*. Cambridge: Cambridge University Press.

Goldin-Meadow, S. 2003. *The Resilience of language: What Gesture Creation in Deaf Children Can Tell Us About How All Children Learn Language*. New York: Psychology Press.

Gray, R. D. and Q. Atkinson. 2003. Language-tree Divergence Times Support the Anatolian Theory of Indo-European Origins. *Nature* 426: 435–9. (doi.org/10.1038/nature02029.)

Green, R. E., J. Krause, A. W. Briggs, T. Maricic, U. Stenzel, M. Kircher, N. Patterson, et al. 2010. A draft Sequence of the Neandertal Genome. *Science* 328: 710–22.

Hauser, M., N. Chomsky, and W. T. Fitch. 2002. The Faculty of Language: What is it, who has it, and how did it evolve? *Science* 298: 1569–79.

Henrich, J. 2004. Demography and Cultural Evolution: Why adaptive cultural processes produced maladaptive losses in Tasmania. *American Antiquity* 69(2): 197–221.

Holden, C. J., and R. Mace. 2005. "The Cow is the Enemy of Matriliny": Using phylogenetic methods to investigate cultural evolution in Africa.

In *The Evolution of Cultural Diversity: A Phylogenetic Approach*, ed. R. Mace, C. J. Holden, and S. J. Shennan, 217-34. London: UCL Press.

Hurford, J. R. 2003. The Language Mosaic and its Evolution. In *Language Evolution*, ed. M. Christiansen and S. Kirby, 38-57. Oxford: Oxford University Press.

Kirby, S., H. Cornish, and K. Smith. 2008. Cumulative Cultural Evolution in the Laboratory: An experimental approach to the origins of structure in human language. *PNAS* 105(31): 10681-6. doi:10.1073/pnas.0707835105.

Kirby, S., and J. Hurford. 2002. The Emergence of Linguistic Structure: An overview of the Iterated Learning Model. In *Simulating the Evolution of Language*, ed. Angelo Cangelosi and Domenico Parisi, 121-48. London: Springer Verlag.

Levinson, S. C., and D. Dediu. In press. The Interplay of Genetic and Cultural Factors in Ongoing Language Evolution. In *Cultural Evolution*, ed. M. Christianssen and P. Richerson. Cambridge, MA: MIT Press.

Levinson, S. C., and R. Gray. 2012. Tools from Evolutionary Biology Shed New Light on the Diversification of Languages. *Trends in Cognitive Science* 16(3): 167-73.

Levinson, S. C., S. J. Greenhill, R. D. Gray, and M. Dunn. 2011. Universal Typological Dependencies Should Be Detectable in the History of Language Families. *Linguistic Typology* 15: 509-34. (doi:10.1515/LITY.2011.034.)

Lieberman, P. 2003. Motor Control, Speech, and the Evolution of Human language. In *Language Evolution*, ed. M. Christiansen and S. Kirby, 255-71. Oxford: Oxford University Press.

Lyell, C. 1830-3. *Principles of Geology, Being an Attempt to Explain the Former Changes of the Earth's Surface, by Reference to Causes Now in Operation*, Vol. 1. London: John Murray.

MacLarnon, A. M., and G. P. Hewitt. 1999. The Evolution of Human Speech: The role of enhanced breathing control. *Am. J. Phys. Anthr.* 109: 341-63.

Martínez, I., M. Rosa, J.-L. Arsuaga, P. Jarabo, R. Quam, C. Lorenzo, A. Gracia, J.-M. Carretero, J.-M. B. de Castro, and E. Carbonell. 2004. Auditory Capacities in Middle Pleistocene Humans from the Sierra de Atapuerca in Spain. *PNAS* 101: 9976-81.

McBrearty, S., and A. S. Brooks. 2000. The Revolution That Wasn't: A new interpretation of the origins of modern human behavior. *Journal of Human Evolution* 39: 453-563.

McMahon, A., and R. McMahon. 2005. *Language Classification by the Numbers*. Oxford: Oxford University Press.

Meir, I., W. Sandler, C. Padden, and M. Aronoff. 2010. Emerging Sign Languages. In *Oxford Handbook of Deaf Studies, Language, and Education*, Vol. 2, ed. M. Marschark and P. Spencer, 267-80. Oxford: Oxford University Press.

Meyer, M., M. Kircher, M.-T. Gansauge, H. Li, F. Racimo, S. Mallick, and S. Pääbo. 2012. A High-Coverage Genome Sequence from an Archaic Denisovan Individual. *Science* 338: 222–6.

Newmeyer, F. J. 2003. What Can the Field of Linguistics Tell Us About the Origins of Language? In *Language Evolution*, ed. M. Christiansen and S. Kirby, 58–76. Oxford: Oxford University Press.

Nichols, J. 1997. Modeling Ancient Population Structures and Population Movement in Linguistics and Archeology. *Annual Review of Anthropology*, 26: 359–84.

Odling-Smee, J. F., K. N. Laland, and M. W. Feldman. 2003. *Niche Construction: The Neglected Process in Evolution.* Monographs in Population Biology 37. New Jersey: Princeton University Press.

Pagel, M. 2009. Human Language as a Culturally Transmitted Replicator. *Nat. Rev. Genet.* 10: 405–15.

Pyers, J. E., A. Shusterman, A. Senghas, E. S. Spelke, and K. Emmorey. 2010. Evidence from an Emerging Sign Language Reveals that Language Supports Spatial Cognition. *PNAS* 107(27): 12116–20. doi: 10.1073/pnas.0914044107.

Richerson, Peter J., and Robert Boyd. 2005. *Not By Genes Alone: How Culture Transformed Human Evolution.* Chicago: Chicago University Press.

Senghas, A., S. Kita, and A. Özyürek. 2004. Children Creating Core Properties of Language: Evidence from an emerging sign language in Nicaragua. *Science* 305(5691): 1779–82.

Thomason, S. G., and T. Kaufman. 1988. *Language Contact, Creolization, and Genetic Linguistics.* Berkeley: University of California Press.

Tomasello, M. 2003. On the Different Origins of Symbols and Grammar. In *Language Evolution*, ed. M. Christiansen and S. Kirby, 94–110. Oxford: Oxford University Press.

Zeshan, U., and C. De Vos, eds. 2012. *Sign Languages in Village Communities: Anthropological and Linguistic Insights.* Berlin: Mouton de Gruyter; Nijmegen: Ishara Press.

13

Causal dynamics of language

N. J. Enfield

> An especially powerful form for theory is a body of underlying mechanisms, whose interactions and compositions provide the answers to all the questions we have.
> (Newell 1990: 14)

13.1 Introduction

Consider some of the different types of process that one might focus on in studying language. There are the finely timed perceptual, cognitive, and motoric processes involved in producing and comprehending language (Levelt 1989, 2012; Emmorey 2002; McNeill 2005; Cutler 2012). There are the early lifespan processes by which children acquire linguistic and communicative knowledge and skills (see Brown and Gaskins, this volume, Chapter 8; Schieffelin and Ochs 1986; Tomasello 2003), and the evolutionary processes that led to the unique emergence of the requisite cognitive capacities for language in our species (Hauser *et al.* 2002; Hurford 2007, 2012; Tomasello 2008; Chomsky 2011). There are the ways in which linguistic utterances are involved in the sequential interlocking of social actions (Schegloff 1968; Goffman 1981a; Goodwin 2000, 2006; Sidnell and Stivers 2012; Enfield 2013; Enfield and Sidnell 2014; Sidnell and Enfield, this volume, Chapter 17). There are the processes, and the products, of language change (Hopper and Traugott 1993; Harris and Campbell 1995; Dixon 1997; Hanks 2010), with links between processes at historical timescales and evolutionary timescales (e.g., Boyd and Richerson 1985, 2005; Durham 1991; Smith *et al.* 2003). There is linguistic variation and its role in how historical change in language is socially conducted in human populations (e.g., Eckert 2000; Trudgill 2010; Labov 2011). And there are phenomena that can be described without reference to process or causation at all, as seen in linguistic grammars, dictionaries, ethnographies, and typologies, where relationships rather than processes tend to be the focus.

These different kinds of foci correspond roughly with distinct research perspectives. But they do not merely represent disciplinary alternatives. The different perspectives suggested above can be seen to fit together as parts of a larger conceptual apparatus. In this chapter I try to sketch that apparatus by defining a set of six frames that I suggest are useful for orienting our work in the anthropology of language, and that should remind us of the perspectives that are always available and relevant, but that we might not be focusing on. They do not constitute a definitive set of frames – there is no definitive set – but I suggest that they correspond well to the most important causal domains, that they conveniently group similar or tightly interconnected sets of causal mechanisms under single rubrics, and that together they cover most of what we need for providing answers to our questions in research on language. The frames are referred to here as *Microgenetic, Ontogenetic, Phylogenetic, Enchronic, Diachronic,* and *Synchronic*; or M.O.P.E.D.S. for short. While such frames are sometimes referred to as "timescales," the differences between them are not defined in terms of abstract or objective units of time such as seconds, hours, or years. The frames are qualitatively distinguished in terms of the different types of underlying processes and causal-conditional mechanisms that define them. For each frame, what matters most is how it works, not how long it takes.[1]

By offering a scheme of interrelated causal frames as a conceptual framework for research on language in the context of this handbook, I want to stress two points. The first is that these frames are most useful when we keep them conceptually distinct. Kinds of reasoning that apply within one frame do not necessarily apply in another, and data that are relevant in one frame might not be relevant (in the same ways) in another. We need to avoid the chronic confusions that arise from mixing up these frames. The second point is that in order to get a full understanding of the phenomena we study in the anthropology of language it is not just necessary to understand these phenomena from within all of the different frames. The ideal is also to show how each frame is linked to each other frame, and, ultimately, how together the frames point to the existence of a system of causal forces that define linguistic reality.

13.2 Distinct frames and forces

The ethologist Niko Tinbergen, in a 1963 paper "On aims and methods in Ethology," emphasized that different kinds of research question may be posed within different theoretical and methodological frames, and may draw on different kinds of data and reasoning. When studying animal behavior, Tinbergen argued, some questions may be answered with reference to the development of an individual organism, others with reference to the evolution of a species, others may concern the proximal mechanism

Table 13.1 Four distinct causal/temporal frames for studying animal behavior (after Tinbergen 1963)

Causal	What is the mechanism by which the behavior occurs?
Functional	What is the survival or fitness value of the behavior?
Phylogenetic	How did the behavior emerge in the course of evolution?
Ontogenetic	How does the behavior emerge in an individual's lifetime?

of a pattern of behavior, and yet others may have to do with the survival or fitness value of the behavior, independent from the other three kinds of question. See Table 13.1.

Tinbergen's four questions were applied to the study of the behavior of non-human animals. These distinctions were designed to handle communication systems such as the mating behavior of stickleback fish, not the far greater complexities of language, nor the rich cultural contexts of language systems. If linguistic anthropology is going to capture the spirit of Tinbergen's idea, we need a scheme that better covers the phenomena specific to language and its relation to human diversity.

As it happens, many researchers of language and culture have emphasized the need to monitor and distinguish different causal frames (often called "timescales") that determine our perspective. These include researchers of early last century (Saussure 1959; Vygotsky 1962) through to many of today (Lemke 2000, 2002; Tomasello 2003; Macwhinney 2005; Cole 2007; Donald 2007; Larsen-Freeman and Cameron 2008; Rączaszek-Leonardi 2010; Uryu et al. 2014). Let us consider some of the distinctions they have offered.[2]

The classical two-way distinction made by Saussure (1959) between the *synchronic* study of language – viewing language as a static system of relations – and the *diachronic* study of language – looking at the historical processes of change that give rise to the synchronic relations observed – is the tip of the iceberg. Those who have looked at the dynamic nature of language have quickly noticed that diachrony – in the usual sense of the historical development and divergence of languages – is not the only dynamic frame. Vygotsky distinguished between *phylogenetic, ontogenetic,* and *historical* processes, and stressed that these dynamic frames were distinct from each other yet interconnected. His insight has been echoed and developed in much subsequent work, from psychologists of communication like Cole (2007) and Tomasello (1999) to computational linguists like Steels (1998; 2003) and Smith et al. (2003), among many others. Smith et al. (2003: 540) argue that to understand language we must see it as emerging out of the interaction of multiple complex adaptive systems, naming three "time-scales" that need to be taken into account – *phylogenetic, ontogenetic,* and *glossogenetic* (= "cultural evolution," i.e., diachronic) – thus directly echoing Vygotsky. Language is, they write, "a consequence of the interaction between biological evolution, learning and cultural evolution" (Smith et al. 2003, 541). Rączaszek-Leonardi, arguing that multiple frames need to be addressed simultaneously in psycholinguistic research, invokes three frames – *online*, *ontogenetic*, and *diachronic* – thus not invoking the phylogenetic frame, but adding the "online" frame of cognitive processing. Cole (1996: 185) expands the list of dynamic frames to include *microgenesis*, *ontogeny* (distinguishing early learning from overall lifespan), *cultural history*, *phylogeny*, and even *geological time*. And Macwhinney (2005: 193ff.) offers a list of "seven markedly different time frames for emergent processes and structure," citing Tinbergen's mentor Konrad Lorenz (1958). MacWhinney's frames are *phylogenetic*, *epigenetic*, *developmental*, *processing*, *social*, *interactional*, and *diachronic*.

Newell (1990: 122) proposes a somewhat more mechanical division of time into distinct "bands of cognition" (each consisting of three "scales"), taking the abstract/objective temporal unit of the second as his key unit, and defining each timescale on a gradient from 10^{-4} seconds at the fast end to 10^7 seconds at the slow end: the *biological band* (= 10^{-4}–10^{-2} seconds), the *cognitive band* (= 10^{-1}–10^1 seconds), the *rational band* (= 10^2–10^4 seconds), and the *social band* (= 10^5–10^7 seconds). He also adds two "speculative higher bands": the *historical band* (= 10^8–10^{10} seconds), and the *evolutionary band* (= 10^{11}–10^{13} seconds; 1990: 152), thus suggesting a total of eighteen distinct timescales. Like Newell (though without reference to him), Lemke (2000: 277) takes the second as his unit and proposes no less than twenty-four "representative timescales," beginning with 10^{-5} seconds – at which a typical process would be "chemical synthesis" – through to 10^{18} seconds – the scale of "cosmological processes." Lemke's discussion is full of insights, but the taxonomy is generated by an arbitrary carving-up of an abstract gradient rather than being established in terms of research-relevant qualitative distinctions or methodological utility, or being derived from a specific theory (cf. Larsen-Freeman and Cameron 2008: 169; Uryu et al. 2014). It is not clear why a distinction between units of 3.2 years versus 32 years should necessarily correlate with a distinction between processes like institutional planning versus identity change; nor why the process of evolutionary change should span three timescales (3.2 million years, 32 million years and 317 million years) or why it should not apply at other timescales.

Larsen-Freeman and Cameron (2008: 169) propose a set of "timescales relevant to face-to-face conversation between two people": a *mental processing* timescale of milliseconds, a *microgenetic* timescale of online talk, a *discourse event* timescale, a *series of connected discourse events*, an *ontogenetic* scale of an individual's life, and a *phylogenetic* timescale. Uryu et al. (2014) critique this model for not explaining why these timescales are the salient or relevant ones, and for not specifying which other timescales are "real but irrelevant." Uryu et al. propose a principled "continuum" of timescales running from "fast" to "slow" (eleven distinctions in the order *atomic, metabolic, emotional, autobiographical, interbodily, microsocial, event, social systems, cultural, evolutionary, galactic*) that are orthogonal to a set of "temporal ranges" running from "simple" to "complex" (six distinctions in the order *physical universe, organic life forms, human species, human phenotype, dialogical system, awareness*). Uryu et al.'s approach applies the notion of ecology to the dynamics of language and its usage (see also Steffensen and Fill 2014).

Some of these schemes are well motivated but incomplete: Saussure gives us just one dynamic frame, leading us to wonder, for example, whether we should regard speech processing as nano-diachrony. Vygotsky, similarly, gives us three dynamic frames, but does not single out or sub-distinguish the "faster" frames of microgeny and enchrony; are we to think of these as pico-ontogeny? On the other hand, some schemes give us finer differentiation than we seem to need, or offer weak or arbitrary motivations for the distinctions made. What is needed is a middle way.

13.3 M.O.P.E.D.S.: A basic-level set of causal frames

From the array of frames discussed in the previous section, defined in different ways and for different purposes, I'm going to suggest that six float to the top. I outline these below, and I suggest that they capture what is most useful about previous proposals. These six frames are relatively well understood, are known to be relevant to research, are well grounded in prior work on language and culture, and are known to be related to each other in important ways. I suggest that this set is what we need: a basic-level set of conceptually distinct but interconnected causal frames for understanding language.

Each of the six frames – microgenetic, ontogenetic, phylogenetic, enchronic, diachronic, synchronic – is distinct from the others in terms of the kind of causality it implies, and thus in its relevance to what we are asking about language and its relation to culture and other aspects of human diversity. One way to think about these distinct frames is that they are different sources of evidence for explaining the things that we want to understand. I now briefly define each of the six frames.

13.3.1 Microgenetic (action production and perception/comprehension)

In a microgenetic frame, we consider the processes by which linguistic behaviors such as simple utterances are psychologically processed.[3] For example, in the production of spoken utterances there is a set of cognitive processes – concept formulation, lemma retrieval, phonological encoding, etc. – that take us "from intention to articulation" (Levelt 1989). Or in the perception and comprehension of others' utterances (Cutler 2012), there are cognitive processes by which we parse the speech stream, recognize distinct words and constructions, and infer others' communicative intentions. These processes tend to take place at timescales between a few milliseconds and a few seconds. The causal mechanisms involved at this level include working memory (Baddeley 1986), application of rational heuristics (Gigerenzer et al. 2011), balancing of processing effort (Zipf 1949), online categorization, motor routines, inference, possession and attribution of mental states such as beliefs, desires, and intentions (Searle 1983; Enfield and Levinson 2006), and the fine timing of motoric control and action execution.

13.3.2 Ontogenetic (biography)

In an ontogenetic frame, we are considering the processes by which an individual's linguistic capabilities and habits are acquired and/or change during the course of that individual's lifetime. Many of the phenomena that are studied within this frame come under the general rubric of language acquisition and socialization, referring primarily to the learning of a first language by infants (see Brown and Gaskins, this volume, Chapter 8; Clark 2009), but also referring to the learning of a second language by adults. The kinds of causal processes observed in this frame include strategies for learning and motivations for learning. Some of these strategies and motivations can be complementary, and some may be employed at distinct phases of life. The causal processes involved in this frame include conditioning, statistical learning, and associated mechanisms like entrenchment and pre-emption (Tomasello 2003), adaptive docility (Simon 1990), a pedagogical stance (Gergely and Csibra 2006), and long-term memory.

13.3.3 Phylogenetic (biological evolution)

A phylogenetic frame considers the processes by which our species came to acquire the capacity for learning and using language, including the cultural context of language. The study of the evolution of the language capacity in humans fits firmly within the broader field of study of the biological evolution and origin of species. It is a difficult topic to study, but this has not stopped a vibrant bunch of researchers from making progress (see Levinson, this volume, Chapter 12). The kinds of causal processes that are at play within a phylogenetic frame are those typically described in evolutionary biology. They invoke concepts such as survival, fitness, and reproduction of biological organisms (Ridley 1997, 2004), which in the case of language means members of our species. The processes involved at this level include the basic elements of Darwinian natural selection: competition among individuals in a population, consequential variation in individual characteristics, heritability of those characteristics, and so forth (Darwin 1859; Dawkins 1976; Mayr 1982).

13.3.4 Enchronic (interactional)

An enchronic frame views language in the context of the interactional sequences of moves, as Goffman termed them, that constitute typical communicative interaction.[4] In an enchronic frame, the causal-conditional processes of interest involve both structural relations of sequence organization (practices of turn-taking and repair which organize our interactions; Schegloff 1968; Sacks et al. 1974; Schegloff et al. 1977; Sidnell and Stivers 2012; Enfield and Sidnell 2014) and ritual or affiliational relations of appropriateness, effectiveness, and social accountability (Heritage 1984; Atkinson and Heritage 1984; Stivers, Mondada, and Steensig 2011; Enfield 2013). The linguistic phenomenon of turn-taking operates in the enchronic frame, as do the range of speech act sequences such as question-answer, request-compliance, assessment-agreement, and suchlike (see Sidnell and Enfield, this volume, Chapter 17). Enchronic processes tend to take place at a temporal granularity around the one-second mark; from fractions of seconds up to a few seconds and minutes (though as stressed here, time units are not the definitive measure; exchanges made using email or surface mail may be stretched out over much greater lengths of time). Enchronic processes and structures are the topic of research in conversation analysis and other traditions of research on communicative interaction. Some key causal elements in this frame include relevance (Garfinkel 1967; Grice 1975; Sperber and Wilson 1995), local motives (Schutz 1970; Leont'ev 1981; Heritage 1984), sign-interpretant relations (Kockelman 2005, 2013; Enfield 2013: ch. 4), and social accountability (Garfinkel 1967; Heritage 1984).

13.3.5 Diachronic (social/cultural history)

In a diachronic frame, we look at elements of language as historically conventionalized patterns of knowledge and/or behavior. If the question is why a certain linguistic structure is the way it is, a diachronic frame looks for answers in terms of processes that operate in historical communities. While of course language change has to be "actuated" at a micro level (Weinreich et al. 1968; Milroy 1980; Labov 1986; Eckert 2000; see also Enfield, this volume, Chapter 3), for a linguistic item to be observed in a language, that item has to have been diffused and adopted throughout a population before it can have become conventionalized. Among the causal processes of interest in a diachronic frame are the adoption and diffusion of innovations, and the demographic ecology that supports cultural transmission (Rogers 2003). Population-level transmission is modulated by the microgenetic processes of conceptual extension, inference, and reanalysis that feed grammaticalization (Hopper and Traugott 1993). Of central importance in a diachronic frame are social processes of community fission and fusion (Aureli et al. 2008), migration (Manning 2005), and sociopolitical relations through history (Smith 1776; Marx and Engels 1947;

Runciman 2009). The timescales of interest in a diachronic frame are often stated in terms of years, decades, and centuries.

13.3.6 Synchronic (representational)

Finally, a synchronic frame is distinct from the other frames mentioned so far because time is removed from consideration, or at least theoretically so.[5] One might wonder if it is a causal frame at all. But if we think of a synchronic system as a veridical statement of the items and relations in a person's head, as coded, for example, in their memory, then this frame is real and relevant, with causal implications, even if we see it as an abstraction (e.g., as bracketing out near-invisible processes that take place in the fastest levels of Newell's "biological band").

In Saussure's famous metaphor, language is a game of chess. If we observe the state of the game at the halfway point, a diachronic account would describe what we see in terms of the moves that had been made up to that point, and that had created the situation we observe, while a synchronic account would simply describe the positions and interrelations of the pieces on the board at that point in time. For an adequate synchronic description, one does not need to know how the set of relations came to be the way they are. There are two ways to take this. One is to see it as a purely methodological move, an abstraction that allows the professional linguist to describe a language as a whole system that hangs together. Another, which is not in conflict with the first, is to see the synchronic description of a language as a hypothesis about what is represented in the mind of somebody who knows the language. A synchronic system cannot be an entirely atemporal concept – at the very least because synchronic structures cannot be inferred without procedures that require time; e.g., the enchronic sequences that feature in linguistic elicitation with native speaker informants – but it is clearly distinct from a set of ontogenetic processes, on the one hand, and diachronic processes, on the other (though it is of course causally implied in both). We can infer an adult's knowledge of language and distinguish this from the processes of learning that led to this knowledge, and from the historical processes that created the model for this knowledge but which neither the learner nor the competent speaker need have had access to.

Because the concern here is on characterizing different frames of relevance to a natural, causal account of language, when I talk about a synchronic frame I shall mean it as a hypothesis about an adult's conceptual representation of a language that makes it possible for them to produce and interpret utterances in the language.[6] The causality in a synchronic frame is tied to the events that led to the knowledge, and the events that may lead from it, as well as how the nature and value of one convention may be dependent on the nature and value of other conventions that coexist as elements of the same system (Smith 1776; Marx and Engels 1947; Runciman 2009).

13.3.7 Interrelatedness of the frames?

A challenge that awaits us is to figure out how these frames are interrelated. As Rączaszek-Leonardi (2010: 276) says, "even if a researcher aims to focus on a particular scale and system, he or she has to be aware of the fact that it is embedded in others." Other authors (Cole 1996: 179; Macwhinney 2005: 192) have asked: What are the forces that cause these frames to "interanimate" or "mesh"? One place to begin would be to test and extend the suggestions of authors like Newell (1990), Cole (1996: 184–5), Lemke (2000: 279ff), MacWhinney (2005) and Uryu *et al.* (2014). How might the outputs of processes foregrounded within any one of these explanatory frames serve as inputs for processes foregrounded within any of the others? The answers will greatly enrich our tools for explanation.

13.4 Roles of frames in explaining synchronic facts: the case of Zipf's law

The main payoff of having a set of distinct causal frames for language is that it offers explanatory power. By way of illustration, let us consider a simple case study, the observation made by Zipf (1935; 1949), that "every language shows an inverse relationship between the lengths and frequencies of usage of its words" (1949: 66). Zipf suggested that the correlation between word length and frequency is ultimately explained by a psychological preference for minimizing effort. If we take that as a claim that synchronic structures in language are caused by something psychological – though Zipf's own claims were rather more nuanced[7] – this raises a "linkage" problem (Enfield 2002: 18, citing Clark and Malt 1984: 201). The problem is that a cognitive bias or preference, such as a desire to minimize effort, cannot directly affect a synchronic system's structure. A cognitive preference is a property of an individual while a synchronic fact is shared across an entire population. Something must link the two. While it may be a fact that the relative length of the words I know correlates with the relative frequency of those words, this fact was already true of my language (i.e., English) before I was born. The fact of a correlation cannot, therefore, have been caused by my cognitive preferences. How, then, can the idea be explicated in causal terms?

As was clear to Zipf (1949: 66ff.), to solve this problem we appeal to multiple causal frames. We can begin by bringing diachronic processes into our reasoning. The presumption behind an account like Zipf's is that all members of a population have the same biases. The key to understanding the link between a microgenetic bias like "minimize effort in processing where possible" is to realize that this cognitive tendency has an effect only in its role as a *transmission bias* in a diachronic process of diffusion of convention in a historical population (see Enfield, this volume, Chapter 3 and 2014 for explication of diachrony as an epidemiological process of biased transmission, following Sperber 1985; Boyd and Richerson 1985; Rogers 2003; Boyd and Richerson 2005, among others). The observed synchronic facts are an aggregate outcome of the individual biases multiplied in a population and through time. The bias has a causal effect precisely in so far as it affects the likelihood that the pattern will spread throughout a population.

Now, while the spread of a pattern and its maintenance as a convention in a populaton are diachronic processes, the operation of a transmission bias may occur in three other frames. In an ontogenetic frame, a correlation between the shortness of words and the frequency of words might make the system easier to learn, and might thereby introduce a bias that causes the correlation to become more widely distributed in a population. In a microgenetic frame, individuals may be motivated to save energy by shortening a word that they pronounce often, again broadening the distribution of the correlation in a population. And an enchronic frame will capture the fact that communicative behavior is not only regimented by biases in learning or individual-centered preferences of processing and action, but also by the need to be successfully understood by another person if one's communicative action is going to have the desired effect. It is the presence of an interlocutor who displays their understanding, or failure thereof, in a next move – criterial to the enchronic frame – that provides a selectional counter-pressure against the tendency to minimize effort in communicative behavior. There is a need to have one's action recognized by another person if that action is going to be consummated (Zipf 1949: 21; Enfield 2013: ch. 8).

By adopting a rich notion of a diachronic frame in which transmission biases play a central causal role, we can incorporate the ontogenetic, microgenetic, and enchronic frames in explaining synchronic facts, invoking the mechanisms of *guided variation* explicated by Boyd and Richerson (1985; 2005) and explored in subsequent work by others (e.g., Kirby 1999; Kirby et al. 2004; Christiansen and Chater 2008; Chater and Christiansen 2010). This allows us to hold onto Zipf's insight, along with similar claims by other authors such as Sapir before him, and Greenberg after him, who both also saw connections between psychological biases and synchronic facts. Greenberg (1966) implied, for example, that there is a kind of cognitive harmony in having analogous structures in different parts of a language system. Sapir (1921: 154–8) suggested that change in linguistic systems by drift can cause imbalances that produce "psychological shakiness," leading to the need for grammatical reorganization to avoid that mental discomfort. Similar ideas can be found in work on grammaticalization (cf. Givón 1984; Bybee 2010) and language change due to social contact (cf. Weinreich 1953), supporting the notion that synchronic patterns can have psychological explanations but only when mediated by the aggregating force of diachronic processes. The point is central to explaining a range of other observed correlations, for example that more frequent words change more slowly (Pagel *et al.* 2007), that differences in processes of attention and reasoning correlate with differences in the grammar of the language one speaks (Whorf 1956; Lucy 1992; Slobin 1996, inter alia), that ways of responding in conversation can be constrained by collateral effects of language-specific grammatical structures (Sidnell and Enfield 2012), and that different cultural values can give rise to different grammatical categories (Hale 1986; Wierzbicka 1992; Enfield 2002 and references therein). Most if not all of these claims bracket out some elements of the full causal chain involved. To give a complete and explicit account of the causal chain involved, a multi-frame account is needed.

13.5 Conclusion

"We might gain considerable insight into the mainsprings of human behavior," wrote Zipf (1949: v), "if we viewed it purely as a natural phenomenon like everything else in the universe." This does not mean that we cannot embrace the anthropocentrism, subjectivity, and self-reflexivity of human affairs. It does mean that underneath all of that, our analyses remain accountable to natural, causal claims. If we are going to answer the two fundamental questions "What's language like?" and "Why is it like that?" we will have to look in multiple directions for answers. Our case study of the length/frequency correlation in words invoked cognitive preferences of individual agents and related these to formal features of community-wide systems. To establish links between these, we drew on a set of frames – under the rubric of M.O.P.E.D.S. – that are distinguished from each other in terms of different types of causal process and conditional structure, and that roughly correlate with different timescales. These different types of process together account for how meaning arises in the moment.

Acknowledgments

In writing this chapter I have benefited greatly from conversations and correspondence with Stephen Cowley, Paul Kockelman, Michael Lempert, Joanna Rączaszek-Leonardi, Giovanni Rossi, Jack Sidnell, Chris Sinha, Kenny Smith, Sune Vork Steffensen, Jordan Zlatev, and Chip Zuckerman. I also thank participants at the conference "Naturalistic Approaches to Culture" (Balatonvilagos, 2011), the conference "Language, Culture, and Mind V" (Lisbon, 2012), the workshop "Rethinking Meaning" (Bologna, 2012), and the "Minerva-Gentner Symposium on Emergent Languages and Cultural Evolution" (Nijmegen, 2013) for comments and reactions. This work is supported by the European Research Council (grant "Human Sociality and Systems of Language Use," 2010–2014), and the Max Planck Institute for Psycholinguistics, Nijmegen.

Notes

1. It is nevertheless true that the frames tend to correlate with distinct timescales (see below). An open question is why and to what extent this is the case.
2. There is a large literature on anthropological and sociological approaches to time, in which authors have looked at local understandings of time, including cultural ideologies of time, and ways in which time can be experienced and measured by people of different cultural and historical backgrounds (cf. Evans-Pritchard 1939; Leach 1961; Gurvitch 1964; Bloch 1977; Adam 1990; Goody 1991; Gell 1992; Munn 1992; Hughes and Trautmann 1995; Goodwin 2002). In that work the object of study concerns the ways in which people conceptualize and categorize time, whereas in the present chapter we are more concerned with how the researcher's analytic conceptualization and categorization of time define or delimit the object of study.
3. McNeill (2005: 68) uses the term *microgenesis* for the timescale of language production, defining it as "diachronic on a scale of seconds," thus appearing to take *diachronic* to mean change per se, leaving unspecified any differences in scale or causal process.
4. The term *enchrony* is introduced in Enfield (2009: 10) and further explicated in Enfield (2013: ch. 3 and passim). Goffman (1981b: 5) mentions "sequence time." See Schegloff *et al.* (1996: 20) for the idea of "kairotic time," drawn from the Greek root *kairos* as an alternative to the instrumentally measurable notion of time referred to by *chronos*. Schegloff *et al.* are partly using the term *kairotic time* to distinguish instrumentally measurable time from "meaning-implicated" time, which can change the subjective experience of, and meaning of, time depending on context, or the "relevance of the structures of the occasion."
5. Many linguists freely include microgenetic processes under the "synchronic" rubric, apparently using *synchronic* to mean anything not diachronic.
6. Instances of production and interpretation are of course outside of the synchronic frame per se. They are handled within microgenetic and enchronic frames.
7. Zipf drew an analogy between the elements of a language and the hand tools in an artisan's workshop. He wrote, "we may expect to find at any time certain tendencies, or correlations, in any set of tools which are organized in reference to the criteria of a fixed point for the discharge of fixed jobs. Thus we may expect to find in general that *the more frequent tools will tend to be the lighter, smaller, older, more versatile tools, and also the tools that are more thoroughly integrated with the action of other tools because of their permutations with the same*" (Zipf 1949: 73; original italics). With this, Zipf points to underlying conditions for the existence of linguistic systems as we know them (see Enfield, this volume, Chapter 3).

References

Adam, Barbara. 1990. *Time and Social Theory*. Philadelphia: Temple Univ Press.

Atkinson, J. Maxwell, and John Heritage. 1984. *Structures of Social Action: Studies in Conversation Analysis*. Cambridge: Cambridge University Press.

Aureli, F., C. M. Schaffner, C. Boesch, S. K. Bearder, J. Call, C. A. Chapman, R. Connor, A. Di Fiore, R. I. M. Dunbar, and S. P. Henzi. 2008. Fission-Fusion Dynamics. *Current Anthropology* 49(4): 627–54.

Baddeley, Alan D. 1986. *Working Memory*. Oxford: Clarendon Press.

Bloch, Maurice. 1977. The Past and the Present in the Present. *Man (N. S.)* 12(2): 278–92.

Boyd, Robert, and Peter J. Richerson. 1985. *Culture and the Evolutionary Process*. Chicago: University of Chicago Press.

 2005. *The Origin and Evolution of Cultures*. New York: Oxford University Press.

Bybee, Joan. 2010. *Language, Usage and Cognition*. 1st ed. Cambridge: Cambridge University Press.

Chater, Nick, and Morten H. Christiansen. 2010. Language Acquisition Meets Language Evolution. *Cognitive Science* 34(7): 1131–57. (doi:10.1111/j.1551-6709.2009.01049.x.)

Chomsky, Noam A. 2011. Language and Other Cognitive Systems: What Is Special About Language? *Language Learning and Development* 7(4): 263–78. (doi:10.1080/15475441.2011.584041.)

Christiansen, Morten H., and Nick Chater. 2008. Language as Shaped by the Brain. *Behavioral and Brain Sciences* 31(5): 489–509.

Clark, Eve V. 2009. *First Language Acquisition*. Cambridge: Cambridge University Press.

Clark, Herbert H., and Barbara C. Malt. 1984. Psychological Constraints on Language: a Commentary on Bresnan and Kaplan and on Givón. In *Methods and Tactics in Cognitive Science*, ed. Walter Kintsch, James R. Miller, and Peter G. Polson, 191–214. Hillsdale, NJ: Lawrence Erlbaum.

Cole, M. 1996. *Cultural Psychology: A Once and Future Discipline*. Cambridge, MA: Harvard University Press.

 2007. Phylogeny and Cultural History in Ontogeny. *Journal of Physiology-Paris* 101(4): 236–46.

Cutler, Anne. 2012. *Native Listening: Language Experience and the Recognition of Spoken Words*. Cambridge, MA: MIT Press.

Darwin, Charles. 1859. *On the Origin of Species by Means of Natural Selection*. London: John Murray.

Dawkins, Richard. 1976. *The Selfish Gene*. Oxford: Oxford University Press.

Dixon, R. M. W. 1997. *The Rise and Fall of Languages*. Cambridge: Cambridge University Press.

Donald, Merlin. 2007. The Slow Process: A Hypothetical Cognitive Adaptation for Distributed Cognitive Networks. *Journal of Physiology, Paris* 101(4-6): 214–22.

Durham, William H. 1991. *Coevolution*. Stanford University Press.
Eckert, Penelope. 2000. *Linguistic Variation as Social Practice*. Oxford: Blackwell.
Emmorey, Karen. 2002. *Language, Cognition and the Brain: Insights from Sign Language Research*. Mahwah, NJ: Lawrence Erlbaum.
Enfield, N. J. 2002. *Ethnosyntax: Explorations in Culture and Grammar*. Oxford: Oxford University Press.
——— 2009. *The Anatomy of Meaning: Speech, Gesture, and Composite Utterances*. Cambridge: Cambridge University Press.
——— 2013. *Relationship Thinking: Agency, Enchrony, and Human Sociality*. New York: Oxford University Press.
——— 2014. Transmission Biases in the Cultural Evolution of Language: Towards an Explanatory Framework. In *The Social Origins of Language: Studies in the Evolution of Language*, ed. Daniel Dor, Chris Knight, and J. Lewis. Oxford: Oxford University Press.
Enfield, N. J., and Stephen C. Levinson, eds. 2006. *Roots of Human Sociality: Culture, Cognition, and Interaction*. London: Berg.
Enfield, N. J., and Jack Sidnell. 2014. Language Presupposes an Enchronic Infrastructure for Social Interaction. In *The Social Origins of Language: Studies in the Evolution of Language*, ed. Daniel Dor, Chris Knight, and J. Lewis. Oxford: Oxford University Press.
Evans-Pritchard, E. E. 1939. Nuer Time-Reckoning. *Africa* 12(02): 189–216. (doi:10.2307/1155085.)
Garfinkel, Harold. 1967. *Studies in Ethnomethodology*. Englewood Cliffs, NJ: Prentice-Hall.
Gell, Alfred. 1992. *The Anthropology of Time: Cultural Constructions of Temporal Maps and Images*. Explorations in Anthropology. Oxford; Providence, RI: Berg.
Gergely, György, and Gergely Csibra. 2006. Sylvia's Recipe: The Role of Imitation and Pedagogy in the Transmission of Cultural Knowledge. In *Roots of Human Sociality: Culture, Cognition, and Interaction*, ed. N. J. Enfield and Stephen C. Levinson, 229–55. London: Berg.
Gigerenzer, Gerd, Ralph Hertwig, and Thorsten Pachur, eds. 2011. *Heuristics: The Foundations of Adaptive Behavior*. New York: Oxford University Press.
Givón, Talmy. 1984. *Syntax: A Functional-typological Introduction*. Amsterdam/Philadelphia: John Benjamins.
Goffman, Erving. 1981a. Replies and Responses. In *Forms of Talk*. Philadelphia: University of Pennsylvania Press.
——— 1981b. *Forms of Talk*. Philadelphia: University of Pennsylvania Press.
Goodwin, Charles. 2000. Action and Embodiment Within Situated Human Interaction. *Journal of Pragmatics* 32: 1489–1522.
——— 2002. Time in Action. *Current Anthropology* 43: S19–S35.
——— 2006. Human Sociality as Mutual Orientation in a Rich Interactive Environment: Multimodal Utterances and Pointing in Aphasia. In

Roots of Human Sociality: Culture, Cognition, and Interaction, ed. N. J Enfield and Stephen C. Levinson, 97–125. London: Berg.

Goody, Jack. 1991. Time: Social Organization [1968]. In *International Encyclopedia of Social Sciences*, ed. D. L. Sills, vol. 16, 30–42. New York: Macmillan.

Greenberg, Joseph H. 1966. Some Universals of Grammar with Particular Reference to the Order of Meaningful Elements. In *Universals of Language*, ed. Joseph H. Greenberg, 2nd ed., 73–113. Cambridge, MA: MIT Press.

Grice, H. Paul. 1975. Logic and Conversation. In *Speech Acts*, ed. Peter Cole and Jerry L. Morgan, 41–58. New York: Academic Press.

Gurvitch, Georges. 1964. *The Spectrum of Social Time*. Dordrecht: D. Reidel.

Hale, Kenneth L. 1986. Notes on World View and Semantic Categories: Some Warlpiri Examples. In *Features and Projections*, ed. Pieter Muysken and Henk van Riemsdijk, 233–54. Dordrecht: Foris.

Hanks, William F. 2010. *Converting Words: Maya in the Age of the Cross*, Vol. 6. Berkeley/Los Angeles: University of California Press.

Harris, Alice C., and Lyle Campbell. 1995. *Historical Syntax in Cross-linguistic Perspective*. Cambridge: Cambridge University Press.

Hauser, Marc D., Noam Chomsky, and W. Tecumseh Fitch. 2002. The Faculty of Language: What Is It, Who Has It, and How Did It Evolve. *Science* 298: 1569–79.

Heritage, John. 1984. *Garfinkel and Ethnomethodology*. Cambridge: Polity Press.

Hopper, Paul J., and Elizabeth Closs Traugott. 1993. *Grammaticalization*. Cambridge: Cambridge University Press.

Hughes, Diane Owen, and Thomas R. Trautmann, eds. 1995. *Time: Histories and Ethnologies*. Ann Arbor: University of Michigan Press.

Hurford, James R. 2007. *The Origins of Meaning*. Oxford: Oxford University Press.

2012. *The Origins of Grammar*. Oxford: Oxford University Press.

Kirby, Simon. 1999. *Function, Selection, and Innateness: The Emergence of Language Universals*. Oxford: Oxford University Press.

Kirby, Simon, Kenny Smith, and Henry Brighton. 2004. From UG to Universals: Linguistic Adaptation Through Iterated Learning. *Studies in Language* 28(3): 587–607. (doi:10.1075/sl.28.3.09kir.)

Kockelman, Paul. 2005. The Semiotic Stance. *Semiotica* 157(1/4): 233–304.

2013. *Agent, Person, Subject, Self: A Theory of Ontology, Interaction, and Infrastructure*. Oxford: Oxford University Press.

Labov, William. 1986. On the Mechanism of Linguistic Change. In *Directions in Sociolinguistics: The Ethnography of Communication*, ed. John J. Gumperz and Dell Hymes, 2nd ed., 512–38. London: Basil Blackwell.

2011. *Principles of Linguistic Change, Cognitive and Cultural Factors*. Chichester: John Wiley and Sons.

Larsen-Freeman, D., and D. Cameron. 2008. *Complexity Theory and Second Language Learning*. Oxford: Oxford University Press.

Leach, Edmund. 1961. *Rethinking Anthropology*. London: The Athlone Press.
Lemke, J.L. 2000. Across the Scales of Time: Artifacts, Activities, and Meanings in Ecosocial Systems. *Mind, Culture, and Activity* 7(4): 273–90.
  2002. Language Development and Identity: Multiple Timescales in the Social Ecology of Learning. *Language Acquisition and Language Socialization: Ecological Perspectives*: 68–87.
Leont'ev, A. 1981. *Problems of the development of mind*. Moscow: Progress Press. (Russian original 1947.)
Levelt, Willem J. M. 1989. *Speaking: From Intention to Articulation*. Cambridge, MA: MIT Press.
  2012. *A History of Psycholinguistics: The Pre-Chomskyan Era*. Oxford University Press.
Lorenz, Konrad Z. 1958. The Evolution of Behavior. *Scientific American* 199(6): 67–83.
Lucy, John. 1992. *Language Diversity and Thought: a Reformulation of the Linguistic Relativity Hypothesis*. Cambridge: Cambridge University Press.
Macwhinney, B. 2005. The Emergence of Linguistic Form in Time. *Connection Science* 17(3-4): 191–211.
Manning, Patrick. 2005. *Migration in World History*. New York and London: Routledge.
Marx, Karl, and Friedrich Engels. 1947. *The German Ideology*. New York: International Publishers.
Mayr, Ernst. 1982. *The Growth of Biological Thought: Diversity, Evolution, and Inheritance*. Cambridge, MA: Belknap Press.
McNeill, David. 2005. *Gesture and Thought*. Chicago and London: Chicago University Press.
Milroy, Leslie. 1980. *Language and Social Networks*. Oxford: Basil Blackwell.
Munn, Nancy D. 1992. The Cultural Anthropology of Time: A Critical Essay. *Annual Review of Anthropology* 21(1): 93–123. (doi:10.1146/annurev.an.21.100192.000521.)
Newell, Allen. 1990. *Unified Theories of Cognition*. Cambridge, MA: Harvard University Press.
Pagel, Mark, Quentin D. Atkinson, and Andrew Meade. 2007. Frequency of Word-use Predicts Rates of Lexical Evolution Throughout Indo-European History. *Nature* 449: 717–20. (doi:10.1038/nature06176.)
Rączaszek-Leonardi, J. 2010. Multiple Time-Scales of Language Dynamics: An Example From Psycholinguistics. *Ecological Psychology* 22(4): 269–85.
Ridley, Mark. 1997. *Evolution*. Oxford: Oxford University Press.
  2004. *Evolution*. Chichester: John Wiley and Sons.
Rogers, Everett M. 2003. *Diffusion of Innovations*. 5th ed. New York: Free Press.
Runciman, W. G. 2009. *The Theory of Cultural and Social Selection*. Cambridge: Cambridge University Press.
Sacks, Harvey, Emanuel A. Schegloff, and Gail Jefferson. 1974. A Simplest Systematics for the Organization of Turn-taking for Conversation. *Language* 50(4): 696–735.

Sapir, Edward. 1921. *Language: An Introduction to the Study of Speech*. Orlando/San Diego/New York/London: Harcourt Brace Jovanovich.

Saussure, Ferdinand de. 1959. *Course in General Linguistics*. New York: McGraw-Hill.

Schegloff, Emanuel A. 1968. Sequencing in Conversational Openings. *American Anthropologist* 70(6): 1075-95.

Schegloff, Emanuel A., Gail Jefferson, and Harvey Sacks. 1977. The Preference for Self-correction in the Organization of Repair in Conversation. *Language* 53(2): 361-82.

Schegloff, Emanuel A., Elinor Ochs, and Sandra A. Thompson. 1996. Introduction. In *Interaction and Grammar*, ed. E. A. Schegloff, E. Ochs, and S. A. Thompson. Cambridge: Cambridge University Press.

Schieffelin, Bambi B., and Elinor Ochs. 1986. *Language Socialization Across Cultures*. Cambridge: Cambridge University Press.

Schutz, Alfred. 1970. *On Phenomenology and Social Relations*. Chicago: University of Chicago Press.

Searle, John R. 1983. *Intentionality: An Essay in the Philosophy of Mind*. Cambridge: Cambridge University Press.

Sidnell, Jack, and N. J. Enfield. 2012. Language Diversity and Social Action. *Current Anthropology* 53(3): 302-33.

Sidnell, Jack, and Tanya Stivers, eds. 2012. *The Handbook of Conversation Analysis*. Oxford: Wiley-Blackwell.

Simon, Herbert A. 1990. A Mechanism for Social Selection and Successful Altruism. *Science* 250: 1665-8.

Slobin, Dan. 1996. From "Thought and Language" to "Thinking to Speaking". In *Rethinking Linguistic Relativity*, ed. J. J. Gumperz and Stephen C. Levinson, 70-96. Cambridge: Cambridge University Press.

Smith, Adam. 1776. *An Inquiry into the Nature and Causes of the Wealth of Nations*. London: W. Strahan.

Smith, Kenny, Henry Brighton, and Simon Kirby. 2003. Complex Systems in Language Evolution: The Cultural Emergence of Compositional Structure. *Advances in Complex Systems* 6: 537-58.

Sperber, Dan. 1985. Anthropology and Psychology: Towards an Epidemiology of Representations. *Man* 20: 73-89.

Sperber, Dan, and Dierdre Wilson. 1995. *Relevance: Communication and Cognition*. 2nd ed. Oxford: Blackwell.

Steels, Luc. 1998. Synthesizing the Origins of Language and Meaning Using Coevolution, Self-organization and Level Formation. In *Approaches to the Evolution of Language: Social and Cognitive Bases*, ed. James R. Hurford, Michael Studdert-Kennedy, and Chris Knight. Cambridge: Cambridge University Press.

2003. Evolving Grounded Communication for Robots. *Trends in Cognitive Sciences* 7: 308-12.

Steffensen, Sune V., and Alwin Fill. 2014. Ecolinguistics: The State of the Art and Future Horizons. *Language Sciences* 41: 6-25.

Stivers, Tanya, Lorenza Mondada, and Jakob Steensig, eds. 2011. *The Morality of Knowledge in Conversation*. Cambridge: Cambridge University Press.

Tinbergen, Niko. 1963. On Aims and Methods in Ethology. *Zeitschrift Für Tierpsychologie* 20: 410–33.

Tomasello, Michael. 1999. *The Cultural Origins of Human Cognition*. Cambridge, MA: Harvard University Press.

2003. *Constructing a Language: a Usage-based Theory of Language Acquisition*. Cambridge, MA: Harvard University Press.

2008. *Origins of Human Communication*. Cambridge, MA: MIT Press.

Trudgill, Peter. 2010. Contact and Sociolinguistic Typology. In *The Handbook of Language Contact*, ed. Raymond Hickey. Chichester: John Wiley and Sons.

Uryu, Michiko, Sune V. Steffensen, and Claire Kramsch. 2014. The Ecology of Intercultural Interaction: Timescales, Temporal Ranges and Identity Dynamics. In *The Ecology of Language and the Ecology of Science*, ed. Sune Vork Steffensen and Alwin Fill (*Language Sciences* Special Issue on Ecolinguistics), 41: 41–59.

Vygotsky, L. S. 1962. *Thought and Language*. Cambridge, MA: MIT Press.

Weinreich, Uriel. 1953. *Languages in Contact*. New York: Linguistic Circle of New York.

Weinreich, Uriel, William Labov, and Marvin Herzog. 1968. Empirical Foundations for a Theory of Language Change. In *Proceedings of the Texas Conference on Historical Linguistics*, ed. W. Lehmann, 97–195. Austin: University of Texas Press.

Whorf, Benjamin Lee. 1956. *Language, Thought, and Reality*. Cambridge, MA: MIT Press.

Wierzbicka, Anna. 1992. *Semantics, Culture, and Cognition*. New York: Oxford University Press.

Zipf, G. K. 1935. *The Psycho-biology of Language*. Boston, MA: Houghton Mifflin.

1949. *Human Behaviour and the Principle of Least Effort*. Cambridge, MA: Addison-Wesley Publishing.

Part III

Interaction and intersubjectivity

Jack Sidnell, N. J. Enfield, and Paul Kockelman

The distinctive character of human social interaction – including the capacities that underlie it and the consequences that flow from it – forms an important pillar of research in linguistic anthropology. The five essays in this Part address a range of aspects of interaction and intersubjectivity.

A basic premise underlying the chapters in this Part is the idea that human thinking is *intentional*. As **Brandom** puts it in his chapter, "This is the idea of a kind of *contentfulness* that is distinctive of at least some of our psychological states and linguistic utterances." Many mental states, "thoughts" in common parlance, are directed at some*thing*, where "thing" receives the broadest possible construal. Brandom reviews a number of crucial distinctions within the domain of intentionality (e.g., practical vs. discursive, representational vs. propositional) before arguing for the fundamentally normative – and thus collective – character of discursive intentionality.

For people, intentional mental states do not exist in isolation from the mental states of others. There are many ways in which this is the case but perhaps most important is that many of our mental states are *about* the mental states of others. "He suspects that she thinks the movie was boring," and so on. Minds are fundamentally and irreducibly linked to other minds in this respect. Face-to-face social interaction, in all its forms, constitutes the primordial (as Schegloff often puts it) scene of social life and thus perhaps the most basic, primitive way in which minds are linked to one another. When a human infant follows the gaze of its mother toward a toy, we assume it is constructing, at some level, a representation of the mother's mental state – mother is thinking about the toy, etc. Here the mother's gaze direction (or change thereof) becomes the sign of her mental state of attention and evaluation. The relation between the two will be constituted by and constitutive of an *interpretant*. Such linking of minds (or mental states – i.e., the child's mental representation of the mother's representation) then involves treating something observable (something in the world) as a sign of something unobservable (something in the mind of another – a mental state). Interaction is in this sense non-telepathic, it is always embodied in signs. Moreover, the human capacity (and propensity) for inference means that any sign has the potential to become a sign for something else. The mother's gaze, for example, becomes a sign of her attention which in turn can convey her concern or her interest. When the child redirects its gaze to the same object as its mother, the mother now has available to her a sign of the child's attention. Intention thus leads to interaction and interaction to intersubjectivity. Along these lines, **Sidnell's** chapter in this Part reviews the ways in which notions of intersubjectivity have been applied to interaction and social life. Drawing on the conversation-analytic approach and work in this tradition, he argues that the structures of talk-in-interaction provide for a distinctive form of intersubjectivity that is universal and species-specific.

The intersubjective social relations constituted in interaction are a form of social organization. This important idea has been put forward in a range of contexts, from the sociology of Erving Goffman to the phenomenology of Alfred Schutz, and the ethology of Robert Hinde. Moreover, people can have intentional and intersubjective mental states about social relations. Developing these and other themes, **Rumsey**'s chapter asks two questions. First: How are social relations implicated in human-specific forms of communication? Second: What difference does language make to human-specific forms of sociality? To answer these questions, he focuses on the relation between shifters (referring to forms that are radically indexical, or context-specific, such as *I*, *you*, and *he*), and what he calls the "primordial social situation" (speaker, addressee, referent), a situation that is both figure and ground of such shifting forms of reference. To do this, he distinguishes between human language and animal communication systems more generally (turning on features like the relative discreteness, arbitrariness, and displacement of a sign). And he offers a detailed ethnographic explication of triadic engagement, and the ways human-specific forms of communication can transform human-specific forms of sociality. Drawing on his fieldwork among speakers of Ku Waru, in Papua New Guinea, he shows a variety of language-specific processes whereby social relations (and the actors so related) are typified, and he also shows some consequences of this typification.

In interacting with one another, people are, typically, pursuing purposive action together. Of course, unrelated persons sitting at a park bench can rightly be said to be interacting: they know of one another's presence, direct their gaze so as not to be understood as looking at one another and so on. This, arguably, is interaction without jointly purposive action. But as soon as one of them asks the other the time or even says "excuse me," they have together engaged in, and committed to, action with a readily identifiable purpose, i.e., asking a question, making a request, summoning the other's attention, and so on. Research on talk-in-interaction has shown that one of the basic ways in which such interaction is organized is through the linking of actions into sometimes quite elaborate sequences. But as revealing as such work is, it has not, for the most part, provided a definitive account of what social actions consist of or, indeed, which actions exist. What is the ontology of action in interaction? In their contribution to this Part, **Sidnell and Enfield** begin by reviewing some ways in which these problems have been addressed by anthropologists and philosophers. Most work has been based on the assumption of action-primitives such as "request", "promise," and "assertion." Sidnell and Enfield sketch an alternative, generative approach in which joint purposive action emerges from inferences based on complex configurations of sub-move practices.

Theories of social action and interaction have not been subject to the kind of systematic testing across cultures that has long been standard in grammatical typology. Yet the question of cross-cultural similarities and differences in the organization of talk-in-interaction has a basic relevance for anthropological research. **Dingemanse and Floyd** show in their chapter that as far as we have adequate records, in all communities a number of things can be said to be true about how language plays a role in social action. First, talk is organized as turns at talk. Second, these turns are composed of a set of possible turn-constructional units. Third, turns at talk are used to implement actions, and fourth, these actions are organized into sequences with identifiable relations to one another. There are of course differences in the way interaction is organized across different communities – and the kinds of possible local inflection or calibration of the underlying infrastructure is a major open line of research – but these appear to ride upon an underlying, universal interactional infrastructure common to all human groups.

14

Intentionality and language

Robert B. Brandom

14.1 Intentionality

In this essay I present a battery of concepts, distinctions, terminology, and questions that are common currency among philosophers of mind and language who think about intentionality. Together, they define a space of possible explanatory priorities and strategies. In addition, I sketch a systematic, interlocking set of commitments regarding the relations among these concepts and distinctions, which underwrites a distinctive set of answers to some of the most important of those questions. This normative, pragmatist, inferentialist approach to intentionality and language is much more controversial. I have developed and expounded it in a number of books over the past two decades. In the present context its exposition can serve at least to illustrate how one might assemble a framework within which to think about the relations among these important issues.

The contemporary philosophical use of the medieval scholastic term "intentionality" was introduced by Franz Brentano (1838–1917). His student Edmund Husserl (1859–1938) recognized it as apt to characterize a phenomenon that Immanuel Kant (1724–1804) had put at the center of our thought about mindedness, as part of what we would now call his semantic transformation of René Descartes's (1596–1650) epistemological turn in the philosophy of mind. This is the idea of a kind of *contentfulness* that is distinctive of at least some of our psychological states and linguistic utterances. Brentano characterized intentionality in terms of "reference to a content, a direction upon an object."[1] John Searle (b. 1932) offers this pretheoretical summary of the subject-matter of his book *Intentionality* (1983):

> if a state S is Intentional then there must be an answer to such questions as: What is S about? What is S of? What is it an S that?

We can specify the content of someone's belief by saying, for instance, that she believes *that* Kant's servant was named "Lampl." In that case, it is a belief *of* or *about* Kant's servant, *representing* him as being so-named.

Brentano was impressed by the thought that while things can only stand in physical or causal relations to actually existing facts, events, and objects, intentional states can "refer to contents" that are not true (do not express actual facts) and be "directed upon objects" that do not exist.[2] I can only kick the can if it exists, but I can think about unicorns even if they do not.

We should distinguish *intentionality* in this sense from *consciousness*. These phenomena only overlap. For, on the one hand, pain is a paradigmatically conscious phenomenon. But pains are not in this sense relevant to intentionality *contentful* states or episodes. They do not have contents that could be expressed by sentential "that" clauses. And they are not (at least not always) *about* anything. On the other hand, there is nothing incoherent about the concept of *unconscious* beliefs – which do have intentional contents specifiable both in terms of "that" and "of." Attributions of belief answer to two kinds of norms of evidence, which in some cases diverge. Evidence derived from sincere avowals by the believer license the attributions of beliefs of which the believer is conscious. But beliefs, desires, and other intentional states can also be attributed on the basis of what relatively stable beliefs and desires provide premises for bits of practical reasoning that make the most sense of what the believer actually does, even in the absence of dispositions sincerely to avow the intentional states in question. Where such intentional explanations are good explanations, the attributed intentional states are unconscious.

The need to make this distinction is a manifestation of a deeper distinction between two sorts of mindedness: sentience and sapience. Sentience is awareness in the sense of being awake. Anything that can feel pain is sentient. Sapience is having intentionally contentful states such as beliefs, desires, and intentions: believing, desiring, or intending *of* the dog *that* it is sitting, will sit, or should sit. An essential element of Descartes's invention of a distinctively modern conception of the mind was his assimilation of *sensations* (for instance, pain) and *thoughts* (for instance, that foxes are nocturnal omnivores). His predecessors had not been tempted by such an assimilation of sentience and sapience. His innovation, and the rationale for the assimilation, was an *epistemic* criterion of demarcation of the mental. Both sensations and thoughts, he took it, were *transparent* and *incorrigible* to their subject: they could not occur without the subject knowing that they occurred, and if the subject took it that they occurred, then they did. Apart from growing appreciation (beginning already with Gottfried Leibniz [1646–1714]) of the potential explanatory significance of unconscious mental states, concerning which subjects do not have the sort of privileged epistemic access Descartes focused on, we have come to appreciate the importance of not prejudging issues concerning the relations between sentience and sapience. In particular, we have come to see that some of the most important issues concerning the plausibility, and even the intelligibility, of artificial intelligence as classically conceived, turn on the question of whether sapience presupposes sentience (which is, as far as our understanding so far reaches, an exclusively biological phenomenon).

14.2 Representational and propositional dimensions of practical and discursive intentionality

Within the general area marked out by the term "intentionality," there are two distinctions it is important to keep in mind: the distinction between practical and discursive intentionality, and the distinction between propositional and representational intentionality. Practical intentionality is the sort of directedness at objects that animals exhibit when they deal skillfully with their world: the way a predator is directed at the prey it stalks, or the prey at the predator it flees. It is a phenomenon of sentience, with the role objects, events, and situations play in the lived life of an animal providing the practical significances (food, threat, ...) that can be perceptually afforded. At the most abstract level of description, however, biological practical intentionality is an instance of a kind of broadly teleological directedness at objects that also has non-sentient examples. For any process that has a Test–Operate–Test–Exit feedback-loop structure, where operations on an object are controlled by information about the results of previous operations on it that are repeated until a standard is satisfied, can be seen as in a distinctive way "directed at" the objects the system both operates on and is informed about. This genus includes both finite-state automata executing conditional branched-schedule algorithms, for instance, in a radar-guided tracking anti-aircraft missile, and the fly-wheel governors that regulated the boiler-pressure of the earliest steam engines. Discursive intentionality is that exhibited by concept-users in the richest sense: those that can make judgments or claims that are *about* objects in the semantic sense. The paradigm of the sort of sapience I am calling "discursive intentionality" is exhibited by language users: ones who can *say* what they are thinking and talking about.

The distinction between representational and propositional intentionality is that between the two dimensions of content that intentional states can exhibit, corresponding to two of Searle's questions, quoted above: "What is S of? What is it an S that?" The answer to the first sort of question is the specification of an object represented by the state ("It is a belief of or about ships, shoes, sealing-wax ..."), while the answer to the second sort of question is the specification of what is believed or thought ("It is the belief that ships should be sea-worthy, that shoes are useful, that sealing-wax is archaic ..."). The first expresses what we are thinking or talking *about*, and the second what we are thinking or saying (about it).

This distinction of two dimensions of contentfulness applies both to the practical and to the discursive species of intentionality. The dog believes *that* his master is home, and he believes that *of* Ben, his master. The principled difficulties we have with using the terms appropriate to discursive intentionality to specify precisely the propositional contents exhibited in practical intentionality (the dog does not really have the concepts specified by "master" and "home" – since it does not grasp most of the contrasts and implications essential to those concepts) do not belie the fact there is some content to his beliefs about that human, Ben, in virtue of which his belief that his master is about to feed him differs from his belief that his master is home, or that someone else will feed him.

Two opposed orders of explanation concerning the relations between practical and discursive intentionality are pragmatism and Platonism. Pragmatism is the view that discursive intentionality is a species of practical intentionality: that knowing-that (things are thus-and-so) is a kind of knowing-how (to do something). What is explicit in the form of a principle is intelligible only against a background of implicit practices. The converse order of explanation, which dominated philosophy until the nineteenth century, is a kind of intellectualism that sees every implicit cognitive skill or propriety of practice as underwritten by a rule or principle: something that is or could be made discursively explicit. A contemporary version of Platonism is endorsed by the program of symbolic artificial intelligence, which seeks to account for discursive intentionality as a matter of manipulating symbols according to definite rules. A contemporary version of pragmatism is endorsed by the program of pragmatic artificial intelligence, which seeks to account for discursive intentionality by finding a set of non-discursive practices (practices each of which can be exhibited already by systems displaying only practical intentionality) that can be algorithmically elaborated into autonomous discursive practices.[3] Pragmatism need not take the reductive form of pragmatic AI, however.

What about the explanatory priority of the representational and propositional dimensions of intentionality? Here, too, various strategies are available. My own approach is to give different answers depending on whether we are talking about practical or discursive intentionality. Within practical intentionality, the propositional dimension should be understood in terms of the representational dimension. Within discursive intentionality, the representational dimension should be understood in terms of the propositional. (Notice that the possibility of such a view would not even be visible to a theorist who did not make the distinctions with which I began this section.) The sort of representation that matters for understanding practical intentionality is the mapping relation that skillful dealings produce and promote between items in the environment and states of the organism. The usefulness of map representations depends on the goodness of inferences from map-facts (there is a blue wavy line between two dots here) to terrain-facts (there is a river between these two cities). The propositional content of the map-facts is built up out of representational relations that are sub-propositional (correlating blue lines and rivers, dots and cities). Such relations underwrite the representation-to-proposition order of explanation at the level of practical intentionality.

The considerations that speak for this order of explanation for *practical* intentionality are sometimes thought to speak for the same order of explanation for *discursive* intentionality. And the case could only get stronger when one conjoins that commitment with a pragmatist order of explanation relating practical and discursive intentionality. Nonetheless, I think there are strong reasons to endorse the explanatory priority of the propositional to the representational dimensions of intentionality at the level of discursive intentionality. They derive to begin with from consideration of the essentially *normative* character of discursive intentionality.

14.3 The normativity of discursive intentionality

Kant initiated a revolution in thought about discursive intentionality. His most fundamental idea is that judgments and intentional doings are distinguished from the responses of non-discursive creatures in that they are things the subject is in a distinctive way *responsible* for. They express *commitments*, or *endorsements*, they are exercises of the *authority* of the subject. Responsibility, commitment, endorsement, authority – these are all *normative* concepts.[4] In undertaking a theoretical or practical discursive commitment that things are or shall be thus-and-so, the knower/agent binds herself by rules (which Kant calls "concepts") that determine *what* she thereby becomes responsible for. For instance, in making the judgment that the coin is copper, the content of the concept copper that the subject applies determines that she is committed (whether she knows it or not) to the coin's conducting electricity, and melting at 1085° C, and that she is precluded from entitlement to the claim that it is less dense than water. The difference between discursive and non-discursive creatures is not, as Descartes had thought, an *ontological* one (the presence or absence of some unique and spooky sort of mind-stuff), but a *deontological*, that is, normative one: the ability to bind oneself by concepts, which are understood as a kind of *rule*. Where the pre-Kantian tradition had focused on our grip on concepts (is it clear, distinct, adequate?), Kant focuses on their grip on us (what must one do to subject oneself to a concept in the form of a rule?). He understands discursive creatures as ones who live, and move, and have their being in a *normative* space.

The tradition Kant inherited pursued a bottom-up order of semantic (they said "logical") explanation that began with concepts, particular and general, representing objects and properties. At the next level, they considered how these representations could be combined to produce propositions of different forms ("Socrates is a man"; "All men are mortal"). To the "doctrine of concepts" supporting the "doctrine of judgments" they then appended a "doctrine of syllogisms," which classified inferences as good or bad, depending on the kinds of judgments they involved. ("Socrates is a man, and all men are mortal, *so* Socrates is mortal.") This classical theory was a paradigm of the order of explanation that proceeds from the representational to the propositional dimensions of intentionality. In a radical break with tradition, Kant starts elsewhere. For him the fundamental intentional unity, the minimal unit of experience in the sense of sapient awareness, is the *judgment* (proposition). For that is the minimal unit of *responsibility*. Concepts are to be understood top-down, by analyzing judgments (they are, he said "functions of judgment," rules for judging), looking at what contribution they make to the responsibilities undertaken by those who bind themselves by those concepts in judgment (and intentional agency). He initiated an order of explanation that moves from the propositional to the representational dimensions of intentionality.

Pursuing that order of explanation in the context of his normative understanding of the propositional dimension of discursive intentionality led Kant to a normative account also of the representational dimension of discursive normativity. On the propositional side, the concept one has applied in judgment determines what one has made oneself responsible *for*. On the representational side, it determines what one has made oneself responsible *to*, in the sense of what sets the standard for assessments of the *correctness* of judgment. Kant sees that to treat something as a represent*ing*, as at least purporting to present something represent*ed*, is to acknowledge the *authority* of what is represented over assessments of the correctness of that representing. Discursive representation, too, is a normative phenomenon. And it is to be understood ultimately in terms of the contribution it makes to the normativity characteristic of propositional discursive intentionality.

Contemporary philosophical analyses of the normativity characteristic of discursive intentionality, along both propositional and representational dimensions, fall into two broad classes: social-practical and teleosemantic. Both are broadly *functionalist* approaches, in the sense that they look to the role discursive intentional states play in some larger system in explaining the norms they are subject to. Teleosemantic theories derive norms (what ought to follow, how the representing ought to be) from selectionally, evolutionary, adaptive explanations of the advent of states and expressions that count as intentionally contentful (typically not just in the discursive, but also the practical sense) just in virtue of being governed by those norms. Ruth Millikan (b. 1933), for instance, defines Proper Function as that function that selectionally (counterfactually) explains the persistence of a feature or structure, in the sense that if such features had not in the past performed that function, it would not have persisted (1987). Social practice theories date to Georg Hegel (1770–1831), who accepted Kant's insight into the normative character of discursive intentionality, but sought to naturalize the norms in question (which Kant had transcendentalized). He understood normative statuses, such as commitment, entitlement, responsibility, and authority, as instituted by practical normative attitudes. (Slogan: "All transcendental constitution is social institution."). On his account, genuine norms can only be instituted *socially*: as he put it, by "reciprocal recognition." The idea that discursive norms are to be understood as implicit in social practices was taken up from Hegel by the American pragmatists (C. S. Peirce [1839–1914], William James [1842–1910], and John Dewey [1859–1952]), and later on by Ludwig Wittgenstein (1889–1951), who had independently discovered the normative character of discursive content.

The idea is that social norms are instituted when practitioners take or treat performances *as* appropriate or inappropriate, take or treat each other *as* committed, entitled, responsible, authoritative, and so on. The pragmatist thought is that even if the norms in question are discursive norms, adopting the instituting normative attitudes might require only practical intentionality. Practically punishing or rewarding performances is one way of treating them as inappropriate or appropriate. So, for instance, hominids in a certain tribe might practically treat it as inappropriate for anyone to enter a certain hut without displaying a leaf from a rare tree, by beating with sticks anyone who attempts to do so. In virtue of the role they play in this practice, the leaves acquire the practical normative significance of hut-licenses. In more sophisticated cases, the reward or punishment might itself be an alteration in normative status, regardless of its actual reinforcing effect. So one might treat a performance as appropriate by giving the performer a hut-license leaf, even if he has no interest in entering the hut.

14.4 An inferential approach to discursive propositional intentional content

What makes something a specifically *discursive* norm? Discursive norms are norms governing the application of concepts, paradigmatically in judgment. Discursive norms govern the deployment of judgeable, that is, propositional intentional contents. In the context of a commitment to pragmatism, this question becomes: what kind of knowing *how* (to do something) amounts to knowing (or believing) *that* (things are thus-and-so)? What is the decisive difference – the difference that *makes* the difference – between a parrot who can reliably differentially respond to the visible presence of red things, perhaps by uttering "Rawk! That's red," on the one hand, and a human observer who can respond to the same range of stimuli by claiming and judging *that* something is red? What is it that the sapient, discursively intentional observer knows how to do that the merely sentient, practically intentional parrot does not?

The important difference is, to be sure, a matter of a distinctive kind of *understanding* that the concept-user evinces. The pragmatist wants to know: what practical abilities does that understanding consist in? We have acknowledged already the *normative* difference: the observer's performance does, as the parrot's does not, express an endorsement, the acknowledgement of a commitment. The key additional point to understand is that the content endorsed, the content the sapient observer is committed to, qualifies as a *conceptual* content (of which specifically *propositional* contents are a principal species) just insofar as it is situated in a space of other such contents to which it stands in relations of material *consequence* and *incompatibility*. The observer knows how to make inferences and so draw conclusions from his commitment: to determine what *else* he has committed himself to by the claim that the apple is red (for instance, that it is colored, that it is ripe ...). He knows how to distinguish what is *evidence* for and against that claim, and what else that commitment rules out as incompatible (for instance, that it is not wholly green). The sapient practically understands his commitment as taking up a stance in a network of related possible commitments, which stand to one another in *rational* relations of material consequence and incompatibility. He is making a move in a practice of giving and asking for *reasons*, in which one move has normative consequences for what others are obligatory, permitted, or prohibited.

Material inferential (and incompatibility) relations, by contrast to formal logical inferential and incompatibility relations, articulate the contents of non-logical concepts. These are inferences such as "*A* is to the West of *B*, so *B* is to the East of *A*," "Lightning now, so thunder soon," and "If the sample is copper, then it will conduct electricity." Part of what one must do to count as understanding the contents of concepts such as East and West, lightning and thunder, copper and electrical conductor is to endorse inferences such as these. This is not to say that for each concept there is some meaning-constitutive set of material inferences one must endorse to count as understanding it. But if one makes *no* distinction, however partial and fallible, between material inferential and incompatibility relations that do and do not articulate the content of some concept, then one cannot count as a competent user of that concept.

Another way to get at the same point about the internal connection between *conceptual* contentfulness and *inferential* articulation is to consider the difference between *labeling* or *classifying* something and *describing* it. Any reliable differential responsive disposition imposes a classification on stimuli, distinguishing those that would from those that would not elicit a response of the given kind by the exercise of that reliable practical responsive capacity. The chunk of iron rusts in some environments and not others, the beam breaks under some loads and not others, the parrot squawks "Red!" in some situations and not others. What more is needed for such a performance to count not just as discriminating or labeling what elicits it, but also as describing it *as* red? The philosopher Wilfrid Sellars (1912–1989) offers the following inferentialist answer:

> It is only because the expressions in terms of which we describe objects ... locate these objects in a space of implications, that they describe at all, rather than merely label. (Sellars 1958: 306–7 [§107])

If I discover that all the boxes in the attic I am charged with cleaning out have been labeled with red, yellow, or green stickers, all I learn is that those labeled with the same color share *some* property. To learn what they *mean* is to learn, for instance, that the owner put a red label on boxes to be discarded, green on those to be retained, and yellow on those that needed further sorting and decision. Once I know what *follows* from affixing one rather than another label, I can understand them not as *mere* labels, but as *descriptions* of the boxes to which they are applied. Description is classification with inferential *consequences*, either immediately practical ("to be discarded/examined/kept") or for further classifications.

The inferentialist semantic claim is that what distinguishes specifically *discursive* (paradigmatically, but not exclusively, propositional) commitments is that their contents are articulated by the roles they play in material inferential and incompatibility relations. Grasping or understanding such contents is a kind of practical know-how: distinguishing in practice what follows from a given claimable or judgeable content, what it follows from, what would be evidence for it or against it, and what it would be evidence for or against. The practical inferential abilities to acknowledge the consequences of one's commitments for further commitments (both those one is committed to and those one is precluded from) and to distinguish evidence that would and would not entitle one to those commitments are what distinguish sapients from mere sentients, creatures that exhibit discursive intentionality from those that exhibit only practical intentionality.

14.5 The relation of language and thought in discursive intentionality

It is obvious that there can be practical intentionality without language. Can there be discursive intentionality in the absence of language? Modern philosophers from Descartes through Kant took it also to be obvious that propositionally contentful thoughts and beliefs both antedate and are intelligible apart from their linguistic expression, which they understood in terms of symbols whose meanings are inherited from those antecedent prelinguistic discursive states and episodes. More recently, H. P. Grice (1913–1988) extended this tradition, by understanding linguistic meaning in terms of speaker's meaning, and speaker's meaning in terms of the intention of a speaker to induce a belief in the audience by an utterance accompanied by the audience's recognition that the utterance was produced with that very intention. Another prominent line of thought in the area, due to Jerry Fodor (b. 1935), is the claim that public language is made possible by a language of thought, which is innate and so does not need to be learned.

A contrary order of explanation, identified with Wittgenstein among many others, gives explanatory priority to linguistic social practices in understanding discursive intentionality. Michael Dummett (b. 1925) forcefully expresses one of the consequences of this approach:

> We have opposed throughout the view of assertion as the expression of an interior act of judgment; judgment, rather, is the interiorization of the external act of assertion. (Dummett 1973: 362)

This way of turning the traditional explanatory strategy on its head is more extreme than is needed to acknowledge the crucial role of public language. Donald Davidson (1917–2003) claims that to be a believer in the discursive sense one must be an interpreter of the speech of others. But he also claims that:

> Neither language nor thinking can be fully explained in terms of the other, and neither has conceptual priority. The two are, indeed, linked in the sense that each requires the other in order to be understood, but the linkage is not so complete that either suffices, even when reasonably reinforced, to explicate the other. (Davidson 1984: 156)

Although Davidson shares some important motivations with Dummett's purely linguistic theory, in fact these two views illustrate an important difference between two ways in which one might give prominence to linguistic practice in thinking about discursive intentionality. Davidson's claim, by contrast to Dummett's, serves to epitomize a *relational* view of the significance of language for sapience: taking it that concept use is not intelligible in a context that does not include language use, but not insisting that linguistic practices can be made sense of without appeal at the same time to intentional states such as belief.

According to such relational views, the transition from mere sentience to sapience (from practical to discursive intentionality) is effected by coming into language: coming to participate in discursive, social, linguistic practices. The capacity to *think* in the discursive sense – that is, to have propositionally or conceptually contentful thoughts, to be able to think that things are thus-and-so (a matter of knowing *that*, not just knowing *how*) – and the capacity to *talk* arise and develop together. For Wittgenstein, the essentiality of public language to the capacity for individual thought is a consequence of the normativity of discursive intentionality. He endorsed a pragmatist order of explanation that understands discursive norms as in the first instance implicit in social practices ("uses, customs, institutions" as he put it).[5] The capacity to make propositionally explicit claims and have conceptually contentful thoughts is intelligible only in the context of implicitly normative social linguistic practices.

14.6 Putting together a social normative pragmatics and an inferential semantics for discursive intentionality

An inferentialist about discursive content who understands discursive norms as implicit in social linguistic practice and holds a relational view of the priority of language and thought will take it that the core of discursive intentionality is to be found in the role *declarative sentences* play in expressing *propositional* contents in speech acts of *assertion*. This connection between the *syntactic* category of declarative sentences, the *semantic* category of propositions, and the *pragmatic* category of assertions is the iron triangle of discursiveness. A pragmatist about the relations between them takes it that the syntactic and semantic elements are ultimately to be understood in terms of the pragmatic one. It is their role in the practice of assertion, of claiming that things are thus-and-so, that is appealed to in picking out declarative sentences and propositional contents. Propositional contents are what can both serve as and stand in need of reasons – that is, can perform the office both of premise and of conclusion in inferences. So the inferentialist pragmatist takes it that what distinguishes the speech act of assertion is its role in practices of giving and asking for *reasons*.

One way of putting together a social normative pragmatics and an inferential semantics for discursive intentionality is to think of linguistic practices in terms of *deontic scorekeeping*. Normative statuses show up as social statuses. The paradigmatic deontic status is *commitment*. The idea is that we should understand what one is doing in making an assertion is undertaking a distinctive kind of commitment: making a claim is staking a claim. If acquiring the status of being committed in the way standardly undertaken by assertively uttering the sentence *p* is to be significant, it must have consequences. The inferentialist says to look for *inferential* consequences (and antecedents): what *else* one becomes committed to by asserting *p* (what follows from *p*) and what would commit one to it (what it follows from). The pragmatist says to understand that in terms of what one is obliged (or permitted) to *do*, upon asserting *p*. To understand an assertional speech act is to know how to *keep score* on the commitments the speaker has undertaken by performing that act. In undertaking commitment to *p*, the asserter has *obliged* herself to acknowledge *other* commitments: those that follow from it. She has also *authorized* other interlocutors to attribute that commitment to her. Further, she has obliged herself to offer a *justification* (give reasons) for the claim, if her authority is suitably challenged. The idea is that exercising such inferentially articulated *authority* and fulfilling such inferentially articulated *responsibility* is what one must do (the task responsibilities one must carry out) in order to count as responsible for or committed – not now to do something, but to what in this social-practical scorekeeping context shows up as the propositional content *p*.

For such an idealized assertional practice to count as one of giving and asking for reasons, there must be a difference between commitments for which one *can* give a reason (so fulfilling one's justificatory task-responsibility) and those for which one can*not*. That is, there must be a distinction between commitments to which an asserter is (rationally, inferentially, by one's evidence) *entitled*, and those to which the assertor is not entitled. So in practice to take or treat a performance *as* an assertion of a particular propositional content, other interlocutors must keep track not only of how that performance changes the score of what the asserter is committed to, but also what she (and others) are entitled to. Discursive scorekeeping requires attributing two sorts of deontic status: commitments and entitlements (to commitments), and knowing how different speech acts change the deontic "scores" of various interlocutors – who may become entitled to new commitments by relying on the authority of other asserters (to whom they can then defer their justificatory responsibility). This deontic scorekeeping story is a sketch of how discursive intentionality is intelligible as emerging from exercises of practical intentionality that have the right normative and social structure.[6]

Scorekeepers acknowledging and attributing two kinds of normative deontic status, commitments and entitlements, can distinguish three kinds of practical consequential relations among them, which generate three flavors of inferential relations, and a relation of material incompatibility. Scorekeepers who take anyone who is entitled to p to be (prima facie) entitled to q thereby practically endorse a *permissive* inferential (probatively evidential) relation between p and q. This is a generalization, from the formal-logical to the contentful material case, of *inductive* inference. (The barometer is falling, so there will be a storm.) Scorekeepers who take anyone who is committed to p to be committed to q thereby practically endorse a *committive* inferential (dispositive evidential) relation between p and q. This is a generalization, from the formal-logical to the contentful material case, of *deductive* inference. (If the sample is pure copper, it will conduct electricity.) Scorekeepers who practically take or treat anyone who is committed to p *not* to be entitled to q, and vice versa, thereby treat the two claims they express as materially *incompatible*. (The plane figure cannot be both square and circular.) Scorekeepers for whom everything incompatible with q is incompatible with p thereby practically take or treat q as *incompatibility-entailed* by p. (Everything incompatible with Pedro being a mammal is incompatible with Pedro being a donkey, so his being a donkey in this sense entails his being a mammal.) These are modally robust, counterfactual-supporting entailments.

When an interlocutor makes an assertion by uttering p, scorekeepers take or treat him as also committed to committive consequences of p, withdraw attributed entitlements to any claims incompatible with p, and if they take it that he is also entitled to p, attribute further entitlements to its permissive consequences to him and to anyone in the audience not precluded by virtue of incompatible commitments. Adopting these practical deontic scorekeeping attitudes is what those who appreciate the practical significance of the speech act must *do* in order thereby to count as implicitly taking or treating the utterance as playing the functional role in virtue of which it expresses a *propositional* discursive content. Other uses of language are built on this assertional-inferential core (the "downtown" of language), and make use of the conceptual contents conferred by it.

14.7 Logic: The organ of semantic self-consciousness

According to this inferentialist social practical story about the structure of practical intentionality (knowing *how*, abilities) that adds up to discursive intentionality (knowing or believing *that* things are thus-and-so) – a story about pragmatics, or the *use* of language (the norms implicit in scorekeeping practices) – it is being practically taken or treated *as* standing in relations of material inference-and-incompatibility in virtue of which expressions come to have propositional discursive semantic content and so are able to make something explicit, in the sense of its being sayable, claimable, thinkable. Building on this kind of basic discursive (sapient) intentional practices and abilities, it is also possible for such practitioners to make propositionally explicit those normative material inferential and incompatibility relations, which are initially implicit in the practical attitudes discursive scorekeepers adopt to one another.

Most centrally, inferential (including *material* inferential) relations can be put in claimable (propositional, explicit) form by the use of *conditional* locutions. One can explicitly express one's endorsement of the inference from *p* to *q* by asserting "If *p* then *q*." Incompatibility relations can be made explicit using *negation* operators. One can explicitly express one's taking *p* to be incompatible with *q* by asserting "Not (*p*&*q*)."[7] Conditional and negation operators are *logical* vocabulary. (Indeed, versions of them suffice to define the classical propositional calculus.) The expressive role characteristic of logical vocabulary is to make explicit the material inferential and incompatibility relations in virtue of which non-logical vocabulary expresses the semantic content that it does. It is by playing the role they do in a network of such relations that expressions acquire the propositional content that makes possible the discursive, sapient awareness that consists in explicitly claiming or judging *that* things are thus-and-so. Logical vocabulary makes possible explicit, discursive, sapient awareness of those very semantogenic material inferential and incompatibility relations. Logic is the organ of semantic self-consciousness.

On this account of the expressive role that demarcates vocabulary as distinctively logical, it is intelligible that there should be creatures that are *rational*, but not yet *logical*. To be rational is to engage in practices of giving and asking for reasons, that is, making inferentially articulated assertions and justifying them. To do that one must attribute and acknowledge commitments and entitlements, and practically keep track of their inferential relations along all three dimensions those two deontic statuses generate: permissive, committive, and incompatibility entailments. But one need not yet deploy specifically logical vocabulary, which permits one to make explicit and so be discursively aware of those material inferential and incompatibility relations. In being rational, one already knows how to do everything one needs to know how to do to introduce logical vocabulary. But until such semantically explicitating vocabulary actually is deployed, rational creatures need not be semantically self-conscious, that is, logical creatures. We are not like that, but our hominid ancestors might have been.

14.8 Pragmatic social normative perspectives and the representational dimension of discursive semantic content

Practically keeping track of inferentially articulated commitments and entitlements (that is, engaging in discursive practices) requires distinguishing between the normative statuses one *attributes* (to another) and those one *acknowledges* (oneself). This distinction of social perspective between normative attitudes means that there are two points of view from which one can assess another's consequential commitments. For the auxiliary hypotheses or collateral premises one conjoins to another's avowed commitment to extract its consequences (whether permissive, committive, or incompatibility-entailed) can be drawn either from other commitments one *attributes* to that interlocutor, or from those one *undertakes* oneself. Suppose S attributes to A commitment to the claim "Benjamin Franklin was a printer" (perhaps on the basis of hearing A make that assertion). If S also attributes to A commitment to "Benjamin Franklin is (=) the inventor of the lightning rod," then S should also attribute to A commitment to "The inventor of the lightning rod was a printer." But suppose S, but not A, is committed to "Benjamin Franklin is (=) the inventor of bifocals." Should S attribute to A commitment to "The inventor of bifocals was a printer"? Given the fact (as S takes it) that Franklin invented bifocals, that is indeed a consequence of A's original claim. In the context of that fact, a claim about Ben Franklin is a claim about the inventor of bifocals, whether or not A realizes that. So in a genuine and important sense, A has, without knowing it, committed herself to the inventor of bifocals having been a printer. But that is a different sense from that in which A has committed herself to the inventor of the lightning rod having been a printer.

When the practical adoption of a normative attitude of attributing a commitment to another interlocutor is made propositionally explicit by the use of locutions that let one *say* what commitments one practically attributes to another, this difference in social perspective manifests itself in two different kinds of ascription of propositional attitude. Consequential commitments attributed solely on the basis of commitments the target would assert are ascribed *de dicto*. S can say "A claims (believes, is committed to the claim) *that* the inventor of the lightning rod was a printer." Consequential commitments attributed partly on the basis of commitments the target would assert and partly by the use of collateral premises that the *attributor*, but *not* the target of the attribution, would assert are ascribed *de re*. S can say "A claims *of* the inventor of bifocals that he was a printer." In putting things this way, S marks that while he is *attributing* to A responsibility for the overall claim, S is himself *undertaking* responsibility for the substitution-inference licensed by the identity "Benjamin Franklin is the inventor of bifocals" (commitment to which he does *not* attribute to A).[8]

Propositional attitude-ascribing locutions, such as "claims" and "believes," let their users make explicit their practical normative scorekeeping attitudes of attributing commitments, that is, using such vocabulary empowers them to *say that* they adopt such attitudes, which otherwise remain implicit in what they practically do. Performing this expressive office with respect to social normative attitudes, on the side of pragmatics, marks them as another species of the same explicitating genus as logical vocabulary, which does corresponding service on the semantic side, by making explicit inferential commitments. What S is *doing* in making *de re* ascriptions is expressing the distinction of social perspective between commitments *attributed* (Ben Franklin was a printer) and those *undertaken* (Ben Franklin invented bifocals). But what one is *saying* is what the one to whom the commitments are ascribed was talking *about*. *De re* ascriptions of propositional attitude are the home language-game of *representational* locutions: the ones used to make explicit what one is talking or thinking *of* or *about*. What they make explicit is the representational dimension of discursive intentionality.

That representational dimension is always already implicit in the distinction of social perspective that is integral to keeping track of others' inferentially articulated commitments. For discursive deontic scorekeepers, players of the game of giving and asking for reasons, care about what follows from others' claims for two reasons. They care about the consequential commitments that would be ascribed *de dicto* because they want to know what else the target would endorse, and what she will do based on the commitments she acknowledges. They care about the consequential commitments that would be ascribed *de re* because they want to extract *information* from the claims of others – that is, premises that the attributor can use in his own inferences. If S attributes to A the intention to shoot a deer and the belief that the tawny creature in front of her is a deer, the *de dicto* ascription "A believes that the tawny creature in front of her is a deer, the shooting of which would fulfill her intention," S will predict that A will shoot. If S, but not A, believes that the tawny creature in front of

A is (=) a cow, then S's *de re* ascription "A believes *of* the cow in front of her *that* it is a deer, the shooting of which would fulfill her intention," S will predict that the result of A's action will be the shooting of a cow. That is an inference that S is in a position to extract from A's avowed commitments, even though that information is not available to A. Keeping track of what premises are available for the reasoning of others and what premises are available for our own reasoning is what we are doing when we talk or think about what we are talking or thinking *about*: the representational dimension of discursive intentionality.

Notes

1. Franz Brentano, "Psychology from the Empirical Standpoint," trans. D. B. Terrell, quoted in Morick (1970: 119-20).
2. Notice that it is at least not obvious that the first part of this claim is true. Reinforcing the dam might have averted a possible disaster. If so, the nonexistence of the disaster was presumably an effect caused by the reinforcement.
3. I discuss these programs in more detail in Brandom (2008: ch. 3).
4. According to the philosopher's convention observed here, underlining indicates mention of concepts, quotation indicates mention of linguistic expressions.
5. Wittgenstein (1991: §199).
6. I develop this model further in Brandom (1994), especially Chapter 3.
7. I suppress here consideration of what modal operators (also logical vocabulary) make explicit. Incompatibility should really be rendered as "*Necessarily* not (p and q)." Incompatibility and modal operators are discussed in Brandom (2008: ch. 5).
8. I discuss the distinction between propositional attitude ascriptions *de dicto* and *de re* in Brandom (1994: ch. 8), and Brandom (2002: ch. 3).

References

Brandom, Robert B. 1994. *Making It Explicit: Reasoning, Representing, and Discursive Commitment*. Cambridge, MA: Harvard University Press.
    2002. *Tales of the Mighty Dead: Historical Essays in the Metaphysics of Intentionality*. Cambridge, MA: Harvard University Press.
    2008. *Between Saying and Doing: Towards an Analytic Pragmatism*. Oxford: Oxford University Press.
Davidson, Donald. 1984. Thought and Talk. In *Inquiries Into Truth and Interpretation*. New York: Oxford University Press.
Dummett, Michael. 1973. *Frege's Philosophy of Language*. New York: Harper and Row.

Millikan, Ruth. 1987. *Language, Thought, and other Biological Categories*. Cambridge, MA: MIT Press.

Morick, H., ed. 1970. *Introduction to the Philosophy of Mind: Readings from Descartes to Strawson*. Glenview, IL: Scott, Foresman.

Searle, John. 1983. *Intentionality*. Cambridge: Cambridge University Press.

Sellars, Wilfrid. 1958. Counterfactuals, Dispositions, and Causal Modalities. In *Minnesota Studies in the Philosophy of Science, Vol. 2: Concepts, Theories, and the Mind-Body Problem*, ed. Herbert Feigl, Michael Scriven, and Grover Maxwell, 225–308. Minneapolis: University of Minnesota Press.

Wittgenstein, Ludwig. 1991. *Philosophical Investigations*, ed. G. E. M Anscombe, 3rd ed. Wiley-Blackwell.

15

The architecture of intersubjectivity revisited

Jack Sidnell

> Try not to think of understanding as a "mental process" at all.
> Wittgenstein 1953: §154

The structures of talk-in-interaction provide for a form of intersubjectivity or mutual understanding that is distinctive in the animal kingdom. These structures – principally turn construction, action sequencing, and repair – together constitute what John Heritage (1984) aptly describes (drawing on Rommetveit 1976) as an "architecture of intersubjectivity" in which previous, current, and next components of a sequential organization interlock and reinforce one another. Describing the architecture will take up much of this essay but I will also try to contrast the perspective developed here with another which emphasizes the diversity of local interpretive norms as well as putatively culture-specific ideas (ideologies) about the relative transparency or opacity of other minds. And finally I will address the question of whether and to what extent this architecture of intersubjectivity is unique to humans, drawing on some recent work among (other) apes.

15.1 Dimensions of intersubjectivity

Among humans and perhaps some other animals, intersubjectivity is a multi-faceted phenomenon that can be understood in different ways. While intersubjectivity, at least among humans, takes various forms, the interactional architecture which supports it appears to be relatively constant across all human societies, cultures, languages etc. (see Schegloff 2006, Sidnell 2007, Sidnell and Enfield 2012, Enfield and Sidnell 2014). I begin with a quick review of some of the ways in which intersubjectivity has been conceptualized before turning to sketch the structures of interaction through which it is constituted. In conclusion I discuss issues of cross-cultural diversity and species-uniqueness.

15.1.1 Phatic communion, attunement, involvement, engagement

Perhaps the most basic, primitive version of intersubjectivity among humans is what Malinowski described as "phatic communion." Although Malinowski (1923) had some rather peculiar ideas about this (some of which were developed in later work by Jakobson 1960 among others; see Sidnell 2009b for a review), here I want to point to the simple fact that interaction, indeed any form of "being together," involves some kind of shared attention and involvement; a "communion of mutual engagement" as Goffman (1957) so eloquently put it.

Along these lines, psychologists have shown that normally developing infants are able to tune into others, often their own mother, from a very early age, indeed, possibly within the first hour of life. Trevarthen (1977) examined the behaviors of infants when confronted with their mothers and compared these with the behaviors of the same infants when a small toy was dangled in front of them. The findings were robust and revealed that infants are attuned to other persons in a range of ways suggesting, according to Trevarthen, a pre-adaptation for interaction:

> A pronounced difference in responses to objects and persons was seen when the infants were two months old ... an exceedingly complex innate mechanism foreshadowing the cooperative intelligence of adults, and more general than the mechanism of language, was already functioning in early infancy. The responses of the infants to persons were different in kind from those to objects, and they were pre-adaptive to reception and reply by persons.

This basic form of intersubjectivity as manifested in dyadic, mutual involvement and attunement is obviously not restricted to humans. But the human animal is primed for this in a way that perhaps no other is. And of course, it is not just that human infants are primed for it – it also seems to be the case that adult members of the species are, in a range of culturally diverse forms, prepared to engage infants and make themselves available for interaction with them (see Brown 2011). Trevarthen (1977: 241) concludes that, "a correct description of this behaviour, to capture its full complexity, must be in terms of mutual intentionality and sharing of mental state."

As Goffman emphasized on many occasions, human interaction requires coordinating the attention and involvement of two or more persons – this is a minimal requirement of interaction, a *sine qua non*. In adult humans the semiotics of such coordination in face-to-face interaction can be extremely subtle; a missed "uh huh," a recipient's brief look away, a fidgeting hand can be understood as a sign of trouble, an indication that phatic contact between two persons is threatened and this can lead to various forms of remedial action. On the other hand, prolonged gaze at a speaker by a recipient or vice versa can also be treated as a sign of trouble – current or impending – and lead to remedial action. Indeed, the possible sources of "alienation from interaction" (as Goffman 1957 again put it) are everywhere and as a result participants must carefully manage their involvements (with themselves, each other, and the environment) all the while that they are pursuing the official business of talk (Sidnell 2009b, 2010b).

15.1.2 Joint attention, shared intentionality, and the roots of reference

Dyadic, mutual involvement between two individuals can be contrasted with the triadic patterns of joint attention and shared intentionality that constitute the roots of reference (see Sidnell and Enfield, in press). At about nine months of age human infants begin to engage in a suite of joint attentional behaviors such as gaze-following and joint object-engagement. These behaviors differ markedly from those of younger infants, which are primarily dyadic. At about this age, then, "infants for the first time begin to 'tune in' to the attention and behavior of adults toward outside entities ..." (Tomasello 1999: 62). As Tomasello notes, it is at around this same age – nine months – that infants also begin to *direct* adult attention to things, using deictic gestures such as pointing.

Kidwell and Zimmerman (2007), as well as Tomasello (1999) and Clark (2003), have described one of the ways young infants direct the attention of another and in so doing establish and maintain the triadic, joint attentional framework that is at the heart of all reference. In a typical showing sequence, a young child will approach another (typically an adult) with an outstretched arm and an object in hand (see Figure 15.1), the other might produce a response which identifies the object ("Watermelon"), expresses a social-relational feature of the object ("Your shoe"), or appreciates it in some way ("Oh wow, a pretty hat"). The child then withdraws the object from view and/or moves out of the recipient's line of vision, either returning to the activity she was engaged in before the showing or initiating some new activity.

Rembrandt's "Anatomy Lesson of Dr. Nicolaes Tulp" provides a stunning illustration of the joint attentional arrangement in showing (Figure 15.2). Here Tulp is presenting a part of the cadaver for the consideration of his students, some of whom look attentively at that which is being shown.

The human form of intersubjectivity, then, centrally involves joint attention and shared intentionality thus allowing two or more individuals to focus on the same object while simultaneously attending to the attention of the other. According to Tomasello (2008) this is a uniquely human behavioral pattern. While the cases of showing and pointing make this

Figure 15.1 Human infant showing object to camera person

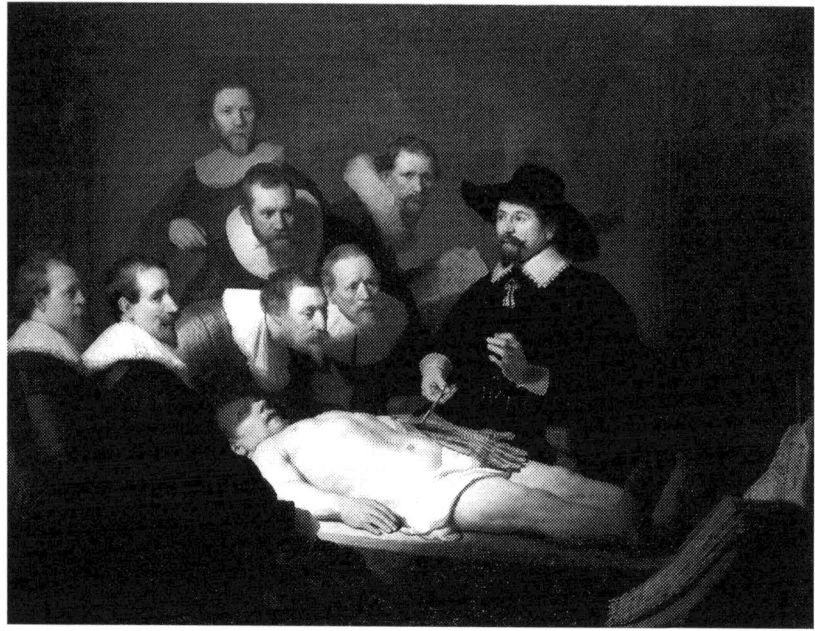

Figure 15.2 Detail from *The Anatomy Lesson of Dr. Nicolaes Tulp, Rembrandt Harmenszoon van Rijn, 1632* © Fine Art/Alamy

pattern visible in the configuration of the participants' bodies and thus particularly obvious to an observer, it is just as central to reference by verbal means. Any substantive expression (a noun, a verb, an adjective, etc.) is simply an instruction to the recipient to attend to whatever it is the speaker is attending to and thus to whatever it is to which reference is being made (i.e., an entity, an event, an action, an attribute).[1]

15.1.3 Stance sharing and coordination

In the showing sequence just discussed it is not just attention towards a third object that is shared, it is also an affective and evaluative stance (Kockelman 2004). The thing being shown is attended to as an object of interest in some respect or capacity. In human interaction, then, participants not only jointly attend to something referred to, they coordinate their stance toward it.

Stance sharing as a dimension of intersubjectivity is visible in a very wide range of behaviors. Crowds and audiences exhibit forms of collective behavior that both presuppose and convey a shared stance toward some object of attention. This is apparent in activities such as booing, laughing, and cheering for instance (see Atkinson 1984a, 1984b, Clayman 1993), where each member of the crowd or audience exhibits the same stance and differences between them are quantitative rather than qualitative (booing louder than others, etc.) and hence this is best understood as stance-sharing.

In conversational interaction stance coordination takes a variety of more subtle and nuanced forms. While stance-sharing similar to what we see in audiences and crowds is exhibited in phenomena such as "choral productions" (Lerner 2002) and perhaps laughter (see Jefferson 1979 Sidnell 2011a), in other cases stances are not shared so much as "calibrated" or coordinated. Two participants then – a teller and a recipient in a troubles telling for example – often do not share a stance in any obvious sense since their relation to the matters talked about is fundamentally different.[2]

Part of the complexity of stance coordination in conversation results from the fact that experiences are treated as "owned" by the one who experienced them (Sacks 1984). Whereas in group behaviors such as booing, all participants have essentially equivalent access to that toward which the stance is being taken, in conversation access or rights to evaluate are typically differentiated among them. Heritage (2011) develops these themes in an analysis of what he terms "empathic moments." Heritage focuses on first-person reports, noting that these introduce something of a problem for their recipients:

> Because persons conceive experience as "owned" by a subject-actor, and as owned in a singular way, a "problem of experience" arises. In

particular, when persons report first-hand experiences of any great intensity (involving, for example, pleasure, pain, joy or sorrow), they obligate others to join with them in their evaluation, to affirm the nature of the experience and its meaning, and to affiliate with the stance of the experiencer toward them. These obligations are moral obligations that, if fulfilled, will create moments of empathic communion. As Durkheim (1915) observed, such moments are fundamental to the creation of social relationships, to social solidarity, and to an enduring sociocultural and moral order. However, recipients of reports of first-hand experiences can encounter these empathic moments as a dilemma in which they are required to affiliate with the experiences reported, even as they lack the experiences, epistemic rights, and sometimes even the subjective resources from which emotionally congruent stances can be constructed.

Stance, encompassing a participant's attitude toward, feelings about, evaluation of whatever is being talked about, is centrally implicated in the human form of intersubjectivity. Indeed, in many cases (perhaps all) recognition of what a speaker is doing presupposes recognition of the stance they adopt toward something talked about. Stance, in this sense, makes the difference between complaining and proposing to end a telephone call (e.g., "I guess I'll see you sometime"), or between asking a question and making an accusation (e.g., "What is the deal?").

15.1.4 Perceiving a world in common: The reciprocity of perspectives

The notion of intersubjectivity is most famously associated with the phenomenologists, especially Husserl (1970a, 1970b) and Schutz (1962, 1967). While exactly what Husserl meant to convey by the term remains somewhat controversial (see Duranti 2010), Schutz's usage is fairly straightforward. For Schutz (1962, 1966, 1967) intersubjectivity is linked to the possibility of persons sharing a world in common. It is of course undeniable that each of us sees the world from a unique perspective – one shaped not only by our actual physical location in it but moreover by our unique personal biography which influences how we interpret what we see and, in some cases at least, what we see in the first place (e.g., after taking Biology 101 you see a sycamore or *Platanus occidentalis*, whereas for me, having not taken the class, it's just a tree). And yet for the most part we assume that what we see (or more generally perceive) is what anyone else would see if they were "in our shoes" as the saying goes. Indeed, we assume a general "reciprocity of perspectives" even where we know very well that what another sees differs from what we do. For instance, we assume that two persons watching a football game see the same goal even if one of them is high in the stands and another is behind the net.

Garfinkel (1967) expanded and developed these ideas, showing that "the reciprocity of perspectives" and a handful of other assumptions underlie the procedures by which we make sense of the world and other people in the course of our everyday activities. A central idea from Garfinkel is that, in the vast majority of ordinary situations, we do not question reality and our perception of it too vigorously – we let things pass, we assume that things are as they appear, we apply an etcetera principle to situations as a way out of radical indeterminacy and infinite indexicality, we treat the talk of others as adequate for all practical purposes, and so on. And these procedures are supported by a massive normative infrastructure such that pointed inquiry into the ordinary assumptions that give the lifeworld the appearance of solidity are hearable as moral challenges and are sanctionable as such (see Heritage 1984, Pollner 1987).

15.1.5 Collective intentionality and institutional reality

John Searle has proposed that human society is distinguished from all others by the existence within it of "institutional facts."[3]

> The distinctive feature of human social reality, the way in which it differs from other forms of animal reality known to me, is that humans have the capacity to impose functions on objects and people where the objects and the people cannot perform the functions solely in virtue of their physical structure. The performance of the function requires that there be a collectively recognized status that the person or object has, and it is only in virtue of that status that the person or object can perform the function in question. Examples are pretty much everywhere: a piece of private property, the president of the United States, a twenty-dollar bill, and a professor in a university are all people or objects that are able to perform certain functions in virtue of the fact that they have a collectively recognized status that enables them to perform those functions in a way they could not do without the collective recognition of the status.

Wolves live in groups, packs that are organized by social relations (see, e.g., Mech 1981). For instance, wolf packs have leaders who earn (and maintain) their position through various means, e.g., physically dominating others, success in hunting, and so on. Humans also live in groups that are organized by social relations. However, in contrast with wolves, the leader of a human group is, often at least, the leader because the members of the group collectively recognize that s/he is the leader by virtue of some set of rules which specify this. He may have won an election or she may have killed off all other possible claimants to the throne but ultimately in human societies leadership is typically a product of collective recognition. Rules of royal succession may be manipulated (see Comaroff 1978) but, crucially, they cannot be ignored if a *legitimate* claim to the throne is to be made. And once a coronation has taken place anyone is free to doubt that the person anointed *should* be the king but not that he *is* the king. One can easily see then that a complex social arrangement such as kingship is underwritten by a whole host of institutional facts which specify not only who is the king today, but what a king is in the first place, what his rights and duties are and so on. And of course each of these institutional facts will be tied (by links of entailment and presupposition) to many others. The human social world is then constituted by a massive web of epistemically subjective, yet ontologically objective, facts. According to Searle, these are established through a special kind of speech act that he terms the status function declarative (Searle 2010).

What makes institutional reality possible, and thus what gives human society its distinctive character, is the capacity for "collective intentionality" – meaning that two or more persons can coordinate both their mental states (intentionality in the sense of being directed at or about something) and their actions (intentionality in the more vernacular sense of intending to do something). Collective intentionality, according to Searle, lies at the heart not only of cooperative behavior like sailing a ship across the Atlantic (which requires the coordinated contributions of several persons) but also of the institutional facts that make up much of the human social world. Searle himself has noted the possible connections to notions of intersubjectivity. He writes (2006):

> It is common in social philosophy, and perhaps in the social sciences as well, to use the notion of "intersubjectivity". I have never seen a clear explanation of the concept of intersubjectivity, and I will have no use for the notion. But I will use "collective intentionality" to try to describe the intentionalistic component of society; and I suspect that if intersubjectivity is a legitimate notion at all, it must amount to collective intentionality.

So, another sense of intersubjectivity then emphasizes collective recognition of social (or institutional) facts (see also Sidnell 2011b for an application of these ideas to interaction among young children).

15.1.6 Action and mutual understanding

Ryle (1949) characterized the prevailing view of understanding as a kind of psychological divining which involves inferring hidden mental operations from visible behaviors and went on to write, if "understanding does not consist in inferring, or guessing, the alleged inner-life precursors of overt actions, what is it?" (Ryle 1949: 54). Ryle's penetrating critique of the concept of mind along with Wittgenstein's (1953, 1969) aphoristic remarks on the topic of understanding (e.g., "Try not to think of understanding as a 'mental process' at all." – Wittgenstein 1953: §154) suggest a radically alternative perspective – one in which understanding does not happen in the dark recesses of individual minds but rather the publicly visible arena of human interaction. In their empirical investigation of conversation, Sacks *et al.* (1974) arrived at a remarkably similar view. In a paper jointly authored with Michael Moerman, Sacks wrote, "participants must continually, there and then – without recourse to follow up tests, mutual examination or memoirs, surprise quizzes and other ways of checking on understanding – demonstrate to one another that they understood or failed to understand the talk that they are party to" and further that these understandings are "done locally, immediately, publicly, accessibly, sanctionedly, and continually" (Moerman and Sacks 1988: 185). In the turn-taking paper (1974), Sacks *et al.* elaborated on this idea, noting that:

> The turn-taking system has, as a by-product of its design, a proof procedure for the analysis of turns. When A addresses a first pair-part such as a "question" or a "complaint" to B, we have noted, A selects B as next speaker, and selects for B that he next perform a second part for the "adjacency pair" A has started, i.e. an "answer" or an "apology" (among other possibilities) respectively. B, in so doing, not only performs that utterance-type, but thereby displays (in the first place to his co-participants) his understanding of the prior turn's talk as a first part, as a "question" or "complaint" . . . It is a systematic consequence of the turn-taking organization of conversation that it obliges its participants to display to each other, in a turn's talk, their understanding of other turns' talk. . . . Regularly, then, a turn's talk will display its speaker's understanding of a prior turn's talk, and whatever other talk it marks itself as directed to.

Investigation into the structures of interaction (conversation) then suggested a radically alternate way to think of "understanding" and, ultimately, intersubjectivity – one in which understanding emerges from and is maintained by the very sequential organization of action in interaction – this is an interactional architecture of intersubjectivity. On this view, understanding applies, in the first instance not to mental states but rather to conduct. As Schegloff (1992a) writes:

> An alternative, or supplementary, stance might take the conduct of other social actors as not, in effect, random or inaccessible to affirmative inquiry, but, rather, together with interpretive procedures, coshaping an appreciated grasp of the world. Such a view would allow for the intervention by the accountable authors of conduct in what would come to be stabilized as the effective understanding of that conduct. Intersubjectivity would not, then, be merely convergence between multiple interpreters of the world (whether understood substantively or procedurally) but potentially convergence between the "doers" of an action or bit of conduct and its recipients, as coproducers of an increment of interactional and social reality.

Sacks, Schegloff, and Jefferson proposed an alternative account of intersubjectivity, one which emphasizes the central role of interaction. On their account, intersubjectivity is a product of the structures of interaction – it is to a more detailed view of this account that we now turn.

15.2 The interactional architecture of intersubjectivity

15.2.1 Enchrony, turn-organization, sequential position

Key to our contemporary understanding of talk-in-interaction is the idea that it unfolds in time. Enfield (2011) describes this as the "forward-feeding temporal, causal-conditional trajectory of relevance relations" and proposes to name it with the term enchrony, on analogy with diachrony and synchrony.[4] When we think about interactional time, or enchrony, it is important to distinguish two, partially independent, unit types which can be conceptualized as endogenous "standards of measure" or metrics. First, talk in interaction unfolds in turns-at-talk and more precisely in turn-constructional units. As Sacks *et al.* (1974) noted, these have a property of projectability and participants use them to locate points of possible completion in a current turn. There's a great deal of evidence to show that such units are indeed a robust social fact to which participants in interaction are oriented.

While they are talking in turn-constructional units, participants are of course producing actions – "moves" if you prefer – in a sequence of alternating actions (see Sidnell and Enfield, this volume, Chapter 17). These sequences of action again have various well-known properties (described, e.g., by Schegloff 1968 and 2007); perhaps most important for present purposes they are linked together by relations of relevance both prospectively and retrospectively – thus a current action can reveal how a prior was understood while at the same time establishing what would be an appropriate next.

It is an important, and somewhat underappreciated, fact that these two levels of structure are partially independent of one another. Notice then that whether a person is complaining, inviting, requesting, agreeing, excusing, accepting, granting, or whatever else, the current turn constructional unit will eventually reach a point of possible completion and when it does that may be heard as a place at which transition to a next speaker is relevant.[5] In this sense the turn-taking machinery marches on independently of whatever actions are being accomplished in and through its operation. Of course, the details of turn construction play an important, indeed crucial, role in conveying to the recipient what action is being done (see Enfield and Sidnell, this volume, Chapter 17) but the essential design features of the overall turn-taking (and turn-constructional) system operate independently of whatever actions the participants are engaged in.

Recognizing this we can notice that a current utterance displays an understanding of a prior utterance both in terms of its status as a turn *and* in terms of its status as an action. These are quite distinct. So we can identify many cases in which the next speaker correctly parsed the emerging talk and responded in such a way as to show a correct understanding that the TCU had reached possible completion, while at the same time displaying a problematic understanding of what action it was that the first speaker meant to accomplish. And the reverse also occurs. A next speaker's beginning to talk can reveal that they misprojected the completion of the current turn even though the action that they produce (or begin to produce) is perfectly well fitted to the prior.

Consider a simple case to begin. This is an example from Sacks' recordings of the Group Therapy Sessions.

```
(1)  (Sacks 1992: 1.281)⁶
01   Roger:      On Hollywood Boulevard the other night they were
02               giving tickets for dirty windshields ((door opens))
03   Jim:        hh
04   Thera:      Hi, Jim [c'mon in.
05   Jim:               [H'warya
06   Thera:      Jim, this is uh Al,
07   Jim:        Hi
08   Thera:      Ken,
09   Jim:        Hi
10   Ken:        Hi
11   Thera:      Roger.
12   Roger: →    Hi
13   Jim:        Hi
14   Thera:      Jim Reed.
```

Sacks (1992) draws attention to "the *prima facie* evidence afforded by a subsequent speaker's talk" in his analysis of the therapist's turns at 8 and 11 as recognizable introductions. Thus, when, at line 12, Roger responds to the

> utterance with his name ... not with "What" (as in an answer to a summons), indeed not with an utterance to the therapist at all, but with a greeting to the newly arrived Jim, he shows himself (to the others there assembled as well as to us, the analytic overhearers) to have attended and analyzed the earlier talk, to have understood that an introduction sequence was being launched, and to be prepared to participate by initiating a greeting exchange in the slot in which it is he who is being introduced. (Schegloff 1992b: xliii)

A current utterance then displays a hearing or analysis of the utterance to which it responds and this is "publicly available as the means by which previous speakers can determine how they were understood" (Heritage 1984: 254–5). The discussion of this example has focused on the sequencing of actions but the same ideas can be applied, *mutatis mutandis*, to the practices of turn-organization. So, by beginning to talk at the precise moment he does at line 12, Roger displays to the co-participants an analysis of the turn-constructional organization of the prior turn and specifically an analysis of its possible completion.

These are familiar observations about the role that a next turn plays in the display of understanding in interaction. But participants do not produce TCUs as simple, unanalyzable chunks and, in fact, there is good evidence that even a single TCU is the product of an interaction between speaker and recipient. This entails that intersubjectivity is established and maintained not only between turns but also within them. Goodwin and Goodwin (1987) write:

> One very productive strategy for uncovering the interactive organization of talk has focused on ways in which subsequent utterances display an analysis of prior ones (Sacks *et al.* 1974: 728). However, despite the great power of this methodology and in particular its ability to reveal how participants themselves analyze prior talk in a way relevant to the activities they are engaged in, there are limitations to it ... while subsequent utterances can reveal crucial features of the analysis participants are making of prior talk they do not show how participants hear the talk as it is emerging in the first place, what they make of it then, and what consequences this has for their actions, not in a next turn, but within the current turn ... In brief it would be valuable to begin to uncover the types of organization that a strip of talk provides, not simply for subsequent talk, but for the organization of action as it is being spoken.

In order to appreciate the importance of what Goodwin and Goodwin are pointing to here we need first to recognize that many forms of conduct in interaction are *not* turn-organized and as such can operate simultaneously with unfolding turns-at-talk. Turns, as described by Sacks *et al.*, are units built up out of talk and, as a result, have certain affordances and impose certain constraints on their use. Particularly important here is the fact that talk can be impaired by overlap. It is this that underlies the basic design feature of the conversational turn-taking system: As Sacks put it, "For conversation, preservation of 'one party talking at a time' is organizationally primary" (Sacks 2004: 37).

Gesture, in contrast, can be used to display a recipient's understanding within a current turn-at-talk in such a way that the display does not compete with or impair that talk (see Sidnell 2005). Similarly with gaze, speakers routinely treat a co-participant's gaze at them as indicating recipiency – that is, another's gaze at speaker is taken to mean that person is attending to the talk being produced. Conversely, gaze away from speaker is routinely treated as evidence that the recipient is not attending and speakers may try to secure that gaze (see Goodwin 1979, 1980, 1981). Some vocal phenomena also appear to be not turn-organized. For instance, laughter can overlay an utterance or be produced simultaneously with an ongoing utterance by a recipient without violating the basic provision for one-at-a-time that regulates turn-taking (Sacks et al. 1974, Schegloff 2000). As such, a recipient's display of understanding that something was meant non-seriously for instance can be produced in the course of a turn-at-talk; such a display need not be deferred until next position.

So far I have described practices which may be deployed by a recipient within the course of a turn-at-talk that display an understanding of what is being said or done in that turn-at-talk without thereby impairing it. Importantly, there are also practices deployed by speakers in the course of a turn-at-talk that make such responses relevant independently of, and possibly prior to, TCU completion. The clearest cases of this involve try-marked references such as the following:

```
(2)   KIDS SKT7 12:00
01    Ali:        I think I'm gonna use this [(      )]
02    Ben: →                                  [Cindy?]
03    Tea: →      Yes
04    Ben: →      Has these.
05    Tea:        Has?
06    Ben:        [The melter beads]
07    Cari:       [(              )]
08    Tea:        Oh ok, did you guys- were you guys
09                with Cindy last year?=
10    Cari:       =yeah
```

Here Ben produces the first word of a TCU with clear "try-marking" prosody (see Sacks and Schegloff 1979). The recipient confirms that he recognizes who it is being referred to in line 03 with "yes". Ben then completes the TCU bringing it to a *first* point of possible completion with "these". Examples such as this illustrate interaction *within* a TCU, interaction that provides for the establishment and maintenance of intersubjectivity.

We have so far considered the architecture of intersubjectivity in current and next turn. To summarize what has so far been proposed: during the course of a given turn-at-talk the speaker monitors various aspects of the recipient's behavior to find how that turn-at-talk is being understood. Aspects of the recipient's behavior which may be treated as revealing how they understand the talk of the moment include, for instance, their gaze direction, their body orientation, the production or non-production of laughter, continuers, assessments, and (especially in telephone talk it would appear) the audible quality of their breath. Where some aspect of a recipient's behavior suggests a problem of understanding (for instance the absence of gaze may suggest that they are not treating the talk as addressed to them, the absence of laughter may suggest they have not heard the talk as joking, the absence of a token such as "uh huh" can suggest that a referred-to person has not been recognized), speakers can redesign the talk in its course in an attempt to remedy the problem (see Sidnell 2010c: 157–67).[7] Eventually, the production of a next-positioned utterance displays a range of understandings of the prior talk as a complete turn/TCU, e.g., that it reached a point of possible completion, that it was a question, that it was a yes/no question, etc.

The result is a highly efficient system in which understandings are displayed *en passant* in the course of whatever business is otherwise being done and in which problems of understanding can be detected and dealt with more or less immediately. We can describe the architecture most effectively in terms of a series of positions. "Positions" here, though, must be understood in an appropriately situated way – that is, a turn will never be in a single, objectively identifiable position. Rather, a position is always calibrated relative to some starting point.

15.2.2 Next position and other-initiated repair

In next turn (second position), the recipient of the first-position turn can, as we have noted, respond to the action(s) it embodies and in so doing display an understanding of it. However, where the identity of the action or some other aspect of the TCU (e.g., a reference contained therein) is not clear to the recipient they have available to them a set of practices for initiating repair. With repair initiation, the progress of a current unit (a TCU, a sequence of action, etc.) is temporarily suspended and the focal activity of the interaction becomes removing whatever barrier to that unit's progress is the current source of trouble. A great deal has been written about the practices of other-initiated repair and need not be repeated here. (See for an overview Schegloff, Jefferson and Sacks 1977, Kitzinger 2012, Hayashi et al. 2013.) Instead, to give just a sketch of the possibilities, consider that there are practices of initiation that target at least the following common trouble source types:

(a) problems resulting from the use of an unfamiliar word
(b) problems of reference
(c) problems of action recognition
(d) problems relating to assumptions of shared knowledge/common ground.

The following examples illustrate each of these practices.

```
(3)  Virginia page 15 – Trouble source type = unfamiliar word
04   Virginia:                      [I KNOW::, BUT
05              A:LL THE REST OF MY: PEOPLE MY AGE ARE
06              GWAFFS. I promise. they are si:[ck.
07   Mom:  →                                   [They're what?
08                  (.)
09   Virginia:  GWAFFS.
10   ???:       (   )
11   Prud?: →   What's a gwaff.
12              (3.1)
13   Virginia:  Gwaff is jus' someb'dy who's really (1.1) I just-
14              ehh! ˙hh s- immature.>You don't wanna hang around
                people like tha:t.<

(4)  Kids_JKT8 24:21 – Trouble source type = reference
01   Michael:   I have the higher place ((looking at chairs))
02              wonder why this is higher
03              (0.8)
04              'cause it's ma::de higher. Ah:::::
05              (0.2)
06   Jude:  →   what's made higher.
07   Michael:   ((taps the chair top))
08              see 'cause look. I can't even get up 'cause it's
09              too high

(5)  Pyatt and Bush TC II(b):#28 – Trouble source type = what action?
29   Pyatt:     Well I guess I'll jus sit back an wait for
30              somebody to call me and tell me [that-
31   Bush:                                     [Yeah he'll probably
32              call you [(in the )
33   Pyatt:              [Hell I don't know what desert he's in,
34              (0.5)
35   Bush:  →   Huh?
36   Pyatt:     u- u- I don't know. He says diyou know where he
37              might be. Well- (0.2) I don't know what desert he's in.
38   Bush:      Yeah,
39   Pyatt:     I don't whether he went to S::- to the Sahara desert,
40              the Mohave, the-

(6)  Kids_GIT8 54:05 – what do you mean?
01   Olivia:    No you can't
02   Char:      What do you mea::n,
03   Olivia:    You can't do that.
04   Char:      What do you mean.
05   Olivia:    You can't skip spaces.
06   Char:      Yes you can.
```

So in (3) Virginia uses the word "gwaff" to describe "all the rest of my: people my age". Mom initiates repair using a [repeat] + [question word] format (the anaphor "they" is used to replace the complex referring expression Virginia originally employed, the verb "are" is repeated and thus frames the trouble source which is itself represented by the question word, "what?"). Virginia treats this as targeting "gwaffs" as the trouble source, which she repeats in line 09. When Mom indicates that this has not solved her problem Virginia glosses the word with "Gwaff is jus' someb'dy who's really (1.1) I just- ehh! .hh s- immature."

In (4) two 4-year-olds are playing with toys on adjacently placed chairs. At lines 01–04 Michael first asserts that he has the higher place, then wonders why this is so before concluding that "it is made higher.". Jude, apparently not able to determine what "it" in the final TCU refers to, initiates repair with "What's made higher.". Michael addresses this problem by touching the chair and going on to show Jude the difference in height.

In (5) Pyatt has called Bush to ask whether Bush knows the whereabouts of a mutual friend (Leo Bowdwin). After Bush indicates that he does not know where Leo is (see example 10 below), Pyatt tells how Leo's brother had phoned him earlier to ask him if he knew where Leo had gone. Now when, at line 33, Pyatt says, "Hell I don't know what desert he's in," he apparently means to be complaining, this action being marked, in particular, by prefacing the turn with "hell". However, Bush initiates repair with "huh?" indicating a trouble with the prior TCU. Pyatt treats this as a trouble of action-recognition and attempts to repair by providing the details and context necessary to see how it is that what he is saying constitutes a complaint. Leo's brother has asked Pyatt a question which suggests that Pyatt keeps track of Leo's whereabouts and it is to this suggestion that his complaint responds.

Finally, in (6) two children are playing checkers. When Charlotte makes a move, Olivia asserts "No you can't." Clearly with this elliptical expression Olivia presumes a good deal of shared background knowledge or common ground. When Charlotte initiates repair with "What do you mean," Olivia says "You can't do that." While this in some ways addresses the problem by providing some of the information that was presumed to be in common ground with "No you can't" – specifically directing Charlotte's attention to the game and her actions in it – it also presumes that Charlotte will be able to use shared knowledge to determine the referent of "that." When Charlotte initiates repair again with "What do you mean," Olivia replaces the [pro-verb] + [deictic] "do that" with "skip spaces" thereby explicitly naming the problem she has identified. This repair "skip spaces" allows us to see, retrospectively, what was presumed to be in common ground by the earlier formulations – specifically these did not identify what, of all the things Charlotte could have been said to have done (e.g., moved, adjusted a piece, moved diagonally on the board, etc.) Olivia had found problematic.

It's obvious that the sources of trouble are not entirely discreet – so, for example, in both (4) and (6) the problem involves ostensive reference and in both that problem results from the speaker assuming too much common ground. What we want to recognize, though, is that the repair initiation format selected foregrounds a particular aspect or feature of a complex trouble source. "What's made higher." in (4) foregrounds a problem of reference whereas "What do you mea::n," in (6) foregrounds problems resulting from assumptions about what is in the common ground.

15.2.3 Third position

A recipient may have failed to properly understand a first-position utterance but nevertheless produced a response to it, one based, that is, on a faulty understanding. Where this happens the problematic understanding is made public in the response. The speaker of the first-position utterance can then set about repairing the problem in third position. It would appear that there are three broad types of trouble that may be dealt with in this way. There are troubles of reference, there are troubles of action recognition and there are troubles relating to the serious/non-serious distinction. The first kind of case is illustrated by an example such as the following:

```
(7)  Third position repair (from Schegloff 1992)
01   Annie:       Which one:s are closed, an' which ones are open.
02   Zebr:        Most of 'em. This, this, [this, this ((pointing))
03   Annie: →                              [I 'on't mean on the
04          →     shelters, I mean on the roads.
05   Zebr:        Oh!
06                (0.8)
07   Zebr:        Closed, those're the ones you wanna know about,
08   Annie:       Mm[hm
09   Zebr:          [Broadway...
```

Here, in the turn at line 02, Zebrach displays an understanding of Annie's inquiry in responding to it. One aspect of this involves an interpretation of "ones". Zebrach has apparently understood this indexical expression to refer to the "shelters" when in fact Annie meant to refer to the "roads". Annie repairs the problem and the course of action underway is then re-engaged on the basis of the new understanding which Annie's correction provides for. Here then the trouble is one of reference.

Consider now the following case taken from a talk show in which Ellen Degeneres is interviewing Rashida Jones. Where this fragment begins DeGeneres is raising a next topic: Jones's new television show with comedian Amy Poehler, *Parks and Recreation*. DeGeneres initiates the topic by inviting Jones to tell the audience about the show. She concludes the turn with "an' you an' Amy Poehler how- how great is that.". This final part of the turn can be heard as a real information question, i.e., a request for Jones to specify how great "that" is. At the same time, the construction "How X is that?" is a familiar, idiomatic expression that, by virtue of the presupposition it carries, conveys "it's X" or, in this case, "it's great."

(8) Rashida Jones on Ellen 04, 2009
```
01  Ellen:     Al:right tell people about this hilarious
02             show. It's Parks and Recreation an' you
03             an' Amy Poehler how- How great is that.=
04  Rashida:   =It's pretty great=
05  Ellen:     =mm mh[m.
06  Rashida:        [It's- uhm- it- I just mean it- ek-
07             experientially for me it's pr(h)etty
08             [gr(h)ea(h)t(h)   [heh heh ha (    )
09  Ellen:     [yeah.            [no. an' but I mean it's
10             a- I ah- know what you mea[nt. But I: say
11  Rashida:                             [hih huh ha hah ha
12             [huh huh .hh hah
13  Ellen:     [it's really great. The two of you.=
14  Rashida:   nyeah.
15  Ellen:     yeah. [an' it's about,
16  Rashida:        [(it is)
```

The talk at line 03 (the A arrow) takes the form of a wh-question ("How great is that.") and Rashida Jones treats it as one by answering "It's pretty great" (at the B arrow). This response, by treating "How great is that.=" as an information-requesting question, reveals a problematic understanding of the action which Ellen subsequently goes on to repair at lines 09–10 and 13 (the C arrows). By saying "I: say it's really great." Ellen conveys that "How great is that.=" was not in fact meant as a question but rather an assertion (or more specifically an assessment). Here then the problem that is repaired in third position is one of action recognition and not one of reference as it was in (7).

The final kind of trouble which third position repair is routinely used to address is illustrated by the following case taken from a radio news interview:

(9) Current Dairy Board
```
04  FJ:   =.h now your timing is interesting because this does
05        come in the midst of thuh: Harper government gutting.
06        The powers. of the wheat boa:rd.uhm an' in favour of
07        a more free market approach<how hopeful are you of
08        riding on the coat-tails of the wheat board ch[anges=
09  MJ:                                                 [.hh
10        =well I ca- uh uh they didn'- they didn't give us
11        inside information about the wheat boards so we ha[d
12  FJ:                                                     [NO
13        [but >it's in been in the ne[ws.<=
14  MJ:   [we                         [.h
15        =it is- no I am teasing but in a way I kn(h)ow
16        (there)'s u:h uh serendipity in the way thet that
17        ha:ppened h. uhm (0.2) uhh I I don't know.
```

Here then the interviewer has asked a question about proposed reform of the dairy board in Canada at lines 07–08, "How hopeful are you...".[8] The interviewee, an advocate of such reform, responds by saying "=well I ca- uh uh they didn'- they didn't give us inside information about the wheat boards." "Inside information" is an expression used in the context of high-stakes, potentially criminal, financial trades and the like. Here it is apparently meant to convey a hint of irony and perhaps to suggest that the interviewer is treating the matter with more gravity than it actually warrants. In any case, the response to this in line 12–13 treats it as perfectly serious. And so we see at line 15 the interviewee produces a third position repair in which he attempts to make explicit the non-serious or "teasing" character of the talk he produced at line 10–11.

This example provides a useful illustration of the way in which positions are not "objective" but rather calibrated relative to some starting *origo* (see Schegloff 1992a). So in relation to the trouble source we have the series of positions just described but another framing that is anchored to the sequence of question and responses results in a different calibration of positions. Specifically, under this description "How hopeful are you of riding on the coat-tails of the wheat board changes" is a first-position question.

Positions vis-à-vis Third Position Repair		Positions vis-à-vis Action Sequencing
	"how hopeful are you of riding on the coat-tails of the wheat board changes"	**1st**
1st	"=well I ca- uh uh they didn'- they didn't give us inside information"	**2nd**
2nd	"NO but >it's in been in the ne[ws."	**3rd**
3rd	"no I am teasing"	

So far, then, we have identified a series of positions within an architecture of intersubjectivity: same turn/first position, transition space, next turn/second position, third position. These are arranged serially as positions within an unfolding course of talk and their organization reflects then the fact that understanding, in interaction, is not static but in a certain basic sense emergent. Understanding consists on this view of "good enough" approximations of what was meant – sufficient, as Garfinkel (1967) sometimes put it, "for all practical purposes." A key feature of these understandings is that they are publically available in interaction and thus provide a means by which participants can check to see if and how some bit of talk or other conduct has been understood.

15.2.4 Fourth position

There is a fourth position in the architecture illustrated by the following case taken from the opening of a telephone conversation.

(10) Pyatt and Bush

```
              ((ring))
01  Bush:   Hello¿
02  Pyatt:  .h m- Mister Bush,
03  Bush:   Yes.
04  Pyatt:  Mister Fiatt.
05  Bush:   Yes,
06  Pyatt:  D'Yknow where Mister Bowdwin is.
07          (0.2)
08  Bush:   Wha:t?
09          (·)
10  Pyatt:  hhuh-hhuh-°hu-° [`hhh
11  Bush:                   [Do I know where who?
12  Pyatt:  Leo is.
13  Bush:   No.
14  Pyatt:  Oh. Okay.
15          (0.2)
16  Bush:   He's down in Mexico or some'in¿
17  Pyatt:  I don't know,
18  Bush:   Oh:. Yer lookin' for him.
```

At line 06 Pyatt asks a question, "D'Yknow where Mister Bowdwin is.", which can be heard as either a real request for information or as a pre-announcement (see Schegloff 1988). After Bush twice initiates repair in next turn position he responds specifically to the turn at line 16 with, "He's down in Mexico or some'in¿". This clearly treats Pyatt as informed as to Leo Bowdwin's whereabouts and as such conveys that Bush has heard the turn at line 06 as a pre-announcement rather than a real request for information. When Pyatt responds with "I don't know" this understanding is revealed to be incorrect and, in what is the fourth position in the sequence, Bush produces the repair "Oh:. Yer lookin' for him." which expresses a revised understanding of the turn at 06.

The idea here, then, is that understanding in conversation – understanding of what the other is doing, what the other means, what the other is referring to, indeed, all the dimensions of intersubjectivity discussed in the first section of this chapter – is built up step-by-step in talk-in-interaction through turns at talk that display the speakers' understanding of what has come before *while* they are engaged in whatever action(s) it is that they are doing. Where those publically displayed understandings are found to be problematic, participants have available to them a range of practices of repair which they may deploy in an effort to fix them.

15.3 Concluding discussion: Cultural diversity and species uniqueness

Everything I have said so far appears to apply to human interaction generally. Across significant differences of linguistic structure and cultural context we find exactly the same architecture of intersubjectivity in operation with relatively minor local inflections (see inter alia Sidnell 2001, 2007, 2009a, Enfield and Levinson 2006, Levinson 2006, Schegloff 2006, Sidnell and Enfield 2012, Stivers et al. 2012). Suggesting a quite different view, Alan Rumsey (2013: 326) asks: "How and to what extent do societies differ with respect to the ways in which intersubjectivity and its manifestations are construed and enacted?" A first challenge is to clarify what is meant by "construed" and "enacted" in this context. It is beyond the scope of this essay to unpack each of these terms; however, it is worth noting that "construed and enacted" suggests an idea or concept that lurks behind and in some sense informs practice. "Construe" is linked with notions of interpretation and perspective, "enact" with putting into practice or acting out (i.e., put into act). In contrast, the focus of the present discussion has been on the ways in which intersubjectivity is achieved (or not) in interaction – I have argued that intersubjectivity is an essential part of interaction that is built into, and inseparable from, the sequential organization of talk.

With these caveats in mind we can now turn to the evidence that has been adduced in favor of the contention that intersubjectivity is subject to significant cultural diversity. There are two bodies of work by linguistic anthropologists that are particularly relevant. First, there is a literature from the 1980s and 1990s that questioned the role that intentions play in human communication cross-culturally. This line of argument was developed especially by Ochs (1982, 1984, 1988) and Duranti (1984, 1988, 1993) based on ethnographic research in Western Samoa (see also Rosaldo 1982). Second, there is a more recent literature in which these issues have been considered under the rubric of the doctrine of the opacity of minds.

In a set of related essays, Duranti and Ochs contrasted what they termed the individualist or personalist approach to meaning of Austin, Grice, and Searle with one for which they found evidence in Samoa. The following quotations are representative of this approach to the problem of intention in linguistic anthropology:

> the role assigned to the speaker's intentions in the interpretation of speech may vary across societies and social contexts. On many occasions, participants seem more interested in coordinating social action for particular ends than in reading other people's minds.   (Duranti 1984: 2)

> Rather than taking words as representations of privately owned meanings, Samoans practice interpretation as a way of publicly controlling social relationships rather than as a way of figuring out what a given

person "meant to say." Once uttered in a given context, words are interpreted with respect to some new reality they help to fashion rather than with respect to the supposedly intended subjective content.
(Duranti 1984: 2)

When *amio* leads to socially offensive behaviors, the actor is held responsible in the sense that some form of negative sanction will be imposed. However, the action itself will not be seen as an outcome of the actor's own control or direction (a product of his intention). Intention is not an issue. Only the social consequences of the action are at issue.
(Ochs 1982: 90)

The concern with intentionality is not matched in traditional Samoan society. In assessing a behavior, it is far less likely that a Samoan caregiver (or other member of the society) will consider the intention behind the behavior. If a child breaks a valued object, it is irrelevant whether he/she did so inadvertently or consciously. What counts is the consequences of the behavior.
(Ochs 1982: 99-100)

These remarks cover a good bit of ground. The first two focus specifically on the *interpretation of speech*, the latter on *assessments of behavior*. Part of the overarching argument then appears to be that, in Samoa, all action, be it communicative or otherwise, is understood according to a single set of principles. This view clearly diverges from the accounts of both Grice and Austin, who quite clearly concern themselves with communicative actions of various types – indeed, Grice's ideas about intention are tied to his notion of meaning$_{nn}$ which is by definition communicative. This is a first indication that what Duranti and Ochs are talking about here is something different from what at least Grice had in mind. Another indication is to be found in the use of the word "interpret." On Grice's account we don't, at least in the first instance, "interpret" what someone says (& co.), we understand it. What someone said may later be subject to interpretation – i.e., in terms of the motives that lie behind it, which is to say the "intention" in another sense – but this is something clearly different from what Grice was concerned with.[9]

In the more recent work addressing the so called "doctrine of the opacity of other minds" an attempt has been made to typologize societies along a continuum from extreme to moderate believers in the doctrine of the opacity of other minds:

Bosavi speakers and the Urapmin would be on one end of a continuum, at which knowing other's minds is thought to be virtually impossible, and in any case not something one ought to try to do ... There is little or no room among these people for public verbal speculation about the motives of others, and hence gossip and confession were traditionally not highly developed modalities of interaction ... At the far edge would be the Korowai, who routinely make opacity statements and find opacity issues compelling, but who at the same time believe that it is possible to know what others think and are not shy about speculating on these matters.

(Robbins and Rumsey 2008)[10]

The basic idea here in both the earlier and more recent accounts is, then, that the ability to surmise and/or the willingness to guess what is on another's mind might be a bit of culture, i.e., something that is not part of the essentially biological inheritance of the human being but rather something traditionally transmitted through processes of cultural learning and socialization. One aspect of this relates to interaction. Those that adhere to the doctrine such as the Bosavi and the Urapmin, it is supposed, do not concern themselves with the intention of a communicative action since this is considered essentially unknowable.

In all but some of the most recent discussions, there has been a tendency to slide together distinct levels or orders of phenomenon – e.g., the various senses of "intention," online/real-time interaction on the one hand and post hoc reflection about it on the other, practice and ideology, etc. – and the fact that informants refuse to speculate about what some other person intended or meant *after the fact* has been treated as evidence for the claim that intentions are not relevant in the online interpretation of talk-in-interaction. There *may* be a connection between these – indeed, many of the authors cited argue that there is – but that needs to be shown and in order to do that we must begin with clear distinctions. It is also quite possible that there is little or no causal relation here at all. The communicative infrastructure (Tomasello 2008) upon which human interaction rests and which centrally includes a capacity for ascribing/attributing intentions to others is quite likely a biological inheritance that emerged during the course of several million years of evolution.

An empirical argument for the view that beliefs about mental opacity are in some way causally related to the online comprehension and understanding of utterances in interaction would require data of several different kinds from a representative sample of languages and communities and this is currently unavailable. As such we can only make conceptual arguments. Before attempting this it is important I think to begin with the *prima facie* fact that persons, presumably everywhere, do in fact have something we can reasonably call "intentions" in both the basic sense of mental states that are directed at something and in the sense of plans to do things.

Consider then an extreme case in which speaker's intention truly plays no role in the interpretation of their talk by others. How in such a situation would a recipient be able to discern whether the speaker was actually speaking rather than involuntarily making noises with her mouth? The very concept of "speaking," at least in so far as this involves using some particular human language, entails intention – if not the intention of what Goffman might describe as the animator, then the intention of some temporary inhabitant of that animator, for instance a spirit in possession and so on.[11]

So let us admit that in this community the recipients *do* distinguish intentional from non-intentional action. But perhaps they do not distinguish between intentions. So they will recognize that a person is intending to communicate with them but they will not be able to tell or willing to guess whether this intentional wave of the arm is meant to beckon them, to greet them, or to direct their attention. Such a people would, it seems, refrain from reasoning such that all the patterns and regularities of human conduct would be ignored in order to *prevent* the making of assumptions about others' intentions. We could extend the argument but it should at this point be clear that in all human societies persons distinguish between intentional and non-intentional action and indeed between different intentions.

Notice also that both the anti-personalist account of Duranti and Ochs and the opacity-doctrine account of Robbins, Rumsey, and others can be used to generate predications and these might actually be tested to see if they hold. For instance, on both accounts, members of the community in question should not engage in third-position repair as described above and exemplified by cases (8) and (9) (see also Schegloff 1992a for a range of cases in English). On the anti-personalist account, use of such third-position repair is precluded on the grounds that a speaker does not have rights to say what s/he meant or intended. Third-position repair routinely takes the form "I didn't mean X, I meant Y" in English but such a format would presumably be completely unidiomatic in Samoan and culturally incongruous. On the opacity-doctrine account, third-position repair should be prohibited on the grounds that it requires a speaker to infer how a recipient's second-position response reveals their (mis)understanding of a first-position utterance. This would be to engage in mind-reading of the kind that adherents of the doctrine, supposedly, avoid. These are strong predications that could be tested by considering a corpus of conversational interaction in any of the relevant languages.

In any case, it is indisputable that everywhere – Samoa, Papua New Guinea, Mayan Mexico – recipients of talk are able to determine what a speaker *intended to refer to with an expression*. No one, not even the strongest "native" or "academic" advocate of the opacity doctrine, doubts this. While it may, erroneously, seem that words are transparent referring expressions that somehow obviate the question of intention, when the speaker, acting in the shadow of taboos that prevent the use of personal names, employs a series of eye-brow flashes, gaze-points, and circumlocutions to indicate who he is speaking about, it is obvious that the recipient is forced to ask themselves a version of the question – to whom that I know does the speaker *intend* to refer by producing this series of eye-brow flashes, gaze-points, and circumlocutions while intermittently gazing at me (see Levinson 2005)? And from there it should be obvious that in order to understand, for instance, the use of a name such as "John" a hearer must ask themselves, to whom, that I know, did the speaker intend to refer by saying "John"? Names provide a particularly clear example of the role that intention plays in making reference but of course they are not unique in this way – *successful reference of any kind* implies intention-attribution. A hearer must discern to what a speaker intends to draw his or her attention in making reference whether reference is made to a person, an object, an action, a quality, or anything else.

Some of the most persuasive evidence for the variable role that intentions might play in the interpretation of conduct comes from interaction with children. For instance Ochs (1982) argued that Samoans do not engage their pre-verbal children in elaborate "dialogues" through expansions of their utterances in the way that at least some English-speaking, middle-class Euro-American mothers do.[12] But again there are other ways to make sense of this. It is at least possible that the Euro-American mothers are not imputing intentional states to their infants in any serious, interactionally consequential, sense. Rather they are merely modeling possible or (culturally, situationally) appropriate states for a novice who cannot articulate them himself. Or alternatively this is simply a game that mothers with sufficient leisure time engage in as part of doing "good mothering" and so on. On the other hand, the fact that Samoan mothers *don't* do it need not be explained by a different understanding of intention – it's possible that it's simply not considered interesting or important or relevant. And even if Ochs is right that caregivers do not engage in this behavior because they do not understand the child to be an intentional agent, it is not entirely clear what relevance this might have for interaction more generally between adult members of the community. At the same time we have a great deal of evidence – from all over the world – that infants *are* treated as capable of intentional action from the very first days, if not hours, of life. They are treated as having attentional states, and actions are designed to fit those states (see Brown 2011).[13]

In a recent contribution, Duranti (2008) reviews much of the earlier literature, concluding that we need to carefully distinguish different senses of intention since there are "qualitatively distinct ways of making inferences about what others are up to." Here and elsewhere Duranti suggests that there is likely a universal and biological basis to human intention-attribution abilities. Along these lines, work done outside of linguistic anthropology by Tomasello and colleagues shows that the capacity for recognizing the intentions of others emerges very early (just how early is a matter of some debate) and serves as a platform upon which a range of other, specifically human abilities are able to develop, e.g., reference.

Indeed, I would suggest that we cannot make sense of human conduct without a notion of intentional action – we anthropologists can't, nor can participants in social interaction. On this view, intention-recognition is a basic feature of the human form of life in Wittgenstein's (1953) sense, which is to say that it is part of the background assumptions against which human social life takes place. And the evolutionary roots of this, as I summarize below, go back to a period before the emergence of our own species. Gorillas and orangs use intentional gestures to communicate with one another and as such we can assume that so did our common ancestor 16 million years ago!

The evidence reviewed to this point suggests that there is a particular human form of intersubjectivity in interaction, one that is made possible by the special properties of interaction itself. While other animals, of course, interact with one another, much of this interaction is quite unlike that between humans because it involves the use and recognition of what have been described as cues (Krebs and Dawkins 1984) or displays (Tomasello 2008) – communicative devices that are not under the intentional control of the individual who produces them (for wolves see, e.g., Mech 1981: 80–103).

However, there is now substantial evidence to indicate that the other great apes (orangs, gorillas, chimps, and bonobos) do communicate by means of intentionally controlled, flexibly used gestural signs (see Tomasello 2008, Rossano 2013). In chimps and bonobos these gestures take a wide range of forms and are used to solicit grooming from another individual, to initiate play, to request carrying, to beckon, and so on. Moreover, these gestures are used quite flexibly in the sense that if a first attempt fails to achieve the desired response from a recipient, a second subsequent version of the gesture or an alternative gesture may be used (see Rossano 2013). Another aspect of flexibility is seen in the fact that gestures are designed with a sensitivity to the recipient's attentional state. If a chimp wants to communicate with another that is not looking in the right direction he or she will often "walk-around" so as to make the gesture visible to the recipient (see Tomasello 2008). These ape gestures would, then, seem to constitute a form of communication that involves the recognition of intentions in just the same way that human communication does – indeed Tomasello argues that this is evidence of a communicative infrastructure that allows for reading others' intentions and making inferences based on aspects of the common ground that is at least partially shared by all hominids. But is communication in the other great apes undergirded by the same elaborate interactional architecture of intersubjectivity that we see in humans? Do the other apes have the same capacity for intersubjectivity as humans? The answer, it would seem, is partially yes but mostly no.

Other apes do appear to build action sequences through something like adjacency pair structures in which first and second actions are linked by a relation of conditional relevance (see Rossano 2013). We can see this in some very basic properties of the action sequences they produce. For example, a first chimp will gesture at a second, the second will begin to comply with what is being requested, and the first chimp will stop gesturing. The first has conveyed some communicative intention, the second has displayed an understanding of that intention in responding in some particular way, the first chimp recognizing that display of recognition stops gesturing. Furthermore, where a second, responsive action is *not* produced the producer of the first can "pursue a response" either through a subsequent version of the gesture or an alternative gesture. These are, then, the roots, at least, of an architecture of intersubjectivity of the same kind that we see in humans.

However, this would seem to be where the similarities end. Other apes do not have available to them a culturally transmitted system of arbitrary signs akin to human language, i.e., one in which the meaningful signs are composed of meaningless, distinctive units (i.e., duality of patterning) allowing for unconstrained growth of the lexico-semantic component, one in which meaningful signs are combinable in grammatical patterns that are themselves meaningful (i.e., grammar). Moreover, apes do not seem to do reference in anything like the same way humans do, if at all. The consequences of this for the architecture of intersubjectivity they are able to build are extremely significant.

For instance, one important feature of action sequencing in humans is that the structures it produces (i.e., adjacency pairs) are accountable. Suppose a recipient does not produce the conditionally relevant next action. This is an accountable fact, and participants orient themselves to this – recipients by actually accounting for not responding (e.g., indicating that they are not answering because they do not know) and first speakers by pursuing such accounts (see, inter alia, Sidnell 2010c, 2012). Another aspect of the accountability involved in action sequencing is seen in reports and complaints about failures – e.g., "he didn't answer me." Other apes, not having available to them a flexible semiotic code like a human language, are apparently incapable of any of this.

And at an even more basic level, as we have seen, the architecture of intersubjectivity is supported by a system of repair. While it seems at least possible that apes might be capable of something similar to open-class repair initiation in second position (see Enfield *et al.* 2013, Dingemanse *et al.* 2013) through an interjection or gestural sign, there are no reports of them doing this. Moreover, in humans, the technology of repair is built in large part around a capacity for repetition. Repeats are used not only to identify the trouble source through framing it but also to show what was heard or understood in a prior turn (see, inter alia, Jefferson 1972, Sacks *et al.* 1974, Schegloff 1997, Sidnell 2010a, Robinson and Kevoe Feldman 2010, Robinson 2013). And repetition is used in a very wide variety of responses beyond repair initiation – it is used to confirm (Schegloff 1996, Stivers 2005), to mimic, to challenge (Sidnell 2010a), to appreciate (Jefferson 1972). All of these are ways to convey if and how a prior turn was understood. Repetition then allows for flexibility in response and, as such, elaborates the architecture of intersubjectivity in crucial ways.

Whether or not repetition is possible in gestural communication between apes it does not seem to occur. And it would appear that much of what humans are able to accomplish via repetition is made possible bythe distinctive properties of human language as a semiotic code. As far as interaction and intersubjectivity go, then, language changes everything.

Acknowledgments

I used to joke that the approach taken in this chapter was "Goodwitagegloffian." All joking aside, I owe a huge debt throughout this chapter to the pioneering work of Charles Goodwin, John Heritage and Manny Schegloff. Earlier versions of this chapter were presented at the Max Planck Institute for Psycholinguistics in Nijmegen and the Kickoff Conference for the *Finnish Center of Excellence in Research on Intersubjectivity in Interaction*, Helsinki, June 6–8th, 2012. For comments, questions, suggestions, and challenges on those occasions I wish to thank especially Nick Enfield, Ceci Ford, Kobin Kendrick, Steve Levinson, Federico Rossano, Marja-Leena Sorjonen. For comments on an earlier written version I thank Nick Enfield, Paul Kockelman, and the students in a graduate seminar in Linguistic Anthropology in the fall of 2012: Taryn Blanchard, Shayne Dahl, Polina Dessiatnitchenko, Natalie Ellis, Emily Hofstetter, Siobhan MacLean, Sara Maida-Nicol, Maria Martika, Emilie Nicolas, Norielyn Romano, Victoria Sheldon. Discussions with Bianca Dahl helped to clarify and develop many of the ideas presented here.

Notes

1. I am arguing that all reference involves, and is essentially reducible to, joint attention. So, for example, when I say "John ate an apple" I am inviting you to jointly attend with me to the person we know as "John," the action we know as "eating," and the idea of any singular "apple."
2. Jefferson (1985, 1993) discussed many aspects of this in her writings on acknowledgement tokens, laughter, and troubles telling. For instance, she notes that a participant can respond to talk in a prior turn with a "minimal acknowledgement," using a token such as yes or no. Jefferson noted two standard uses of such tokens. First, where one speaker's talk (A) is overlapped by another's (B), that speaker (A) may respond to the other's overlapping talk with a minimal acknowledgment before continuing or redoing their own. Second, a speaker may respond to prior talk with a minimal acknowledgment token as a preface to topic shift. These practices evidence a normative obligation to attend to the other's stance and concerns even when this diverges from one's own

interactional goals. Such acknowledgments are "minimal" in contrast to more elaborated responses with newsmarks (such as "oh really"), assessments ("that's great"), or even more elaborate forms such as "you're kidding" or "are you serious?" etc. These later forms typically invite elaboration of the speaker's topic by conveying heightened interest in it (see also Stivers 2008).

3. Searle's account owes much not only to Austin (1962) but also to Anscombe, especially her discussion of intention (2000[1957]) and brute facts (1958).
4. And, on the other hand, on analogy with terms such enfold, enclose, envelope, entrain, entangle, endear, etc.
5. The terms "complaining, inviting, requesting, agreeing, excusing, accepting, granting" are used here for analytic convenience without implying anything about the ontology of action in interaction (see Sidnell and Enfield, this volume, Chapter 17).
6. Examples are presented using the transcription conventions originally developed by Gail Jefferson. For present purposes, the most important symbols are the period (".") which indicates falling and final intonation, the question mark ("?") indicating rising intonation, and brackets ("[" and "]") marking the onset and resolution of overlapping talk between two speakers. Equal signs, which come in pairs – one at the end of a line and another at the start of the next line or one shortly thereafter – are used to indicate that the second line followed the first with no discernible silence between them, i.e., it was "latched" to it. Numbers in parentheses (e.g., (0.5)) indicate silence, represented in tenths of a second. Finally, colons are used to indicate prolongation or stretching of the sound preceding them. The more colons, the longer the stretching. For an explanation of other symbols see Sacks *et al.* (1974) and Sidnell (2009a).
7. The next position in the architecture is what we describe as the transition space, and the form of repair we find there – transition space repair – would, in a more comprehensive account, be dealt with here (see, though, the discussion below of "the two of you").
8. The dairy board and wheat board protect the interests of producers by imposing minimum pricing constraints – thus reducing the possibilities of competitive pricing.
9. So it is possible that the phenomenon which Duranti and Ochs found to be culture-specific was simply not the same one that Grice was concerned with though both may be referred to by the same lexical item (intention) in English. Part of the confusion then may have, somewhat ironically given that the roots of the issue lie in ordinary language philosophy and the American linguistic anthropology that Boas and his students founded, resulted from the fact that the English word "intention" is used in several quite distinct ways – namely, the technical

sense of directedness of thoughts, the more vernacular sense of planning to do something, the yet more distant sense of motives or reasons. As Whorf (1956) and others suggested, we are prone to analogical thinking between different senses of a single lexical item.
10. And finally in very recent work the matter has been put in what is perhaps its most extreme version by Groark (2013) who writes:

> The Tzotzil Maya, ..., hold a distinct interpretive stance toward the knowability of other minds: the inner states of others ... are generally held to be relatively "opaque" to many forms of everyday appraisal. This sense of "social opacity" is widespread throughout the Mayan world, and appears to serve as a basic axiom of local social life. Indeed, in many interactive contexts, people disavow their ability to make explicit claims about the content of others' hearts and minds.

11. This applies to those favorite cases of anthropologists, such as possession, in which it is the intention of some being other than the animator that lies behind the talk. Indeed this is integral to the very notion of intention. I do not agree with Du Bois (1993) that the poison oracle among the Azande is bereft of notions of intention – indeed it seems crucial that the poison itself is, in some sense, an intentional agent that is capable of communicating by killing (or not) the chick to which it is administered.
12. Moreover, in clarifying a child's unclear utterances, Samoan mothers and caregivers use a "minimal grasp strategy" whereas middle-class Euro-American mothers and caregivers are more likely to use an expressed guess strategy.
13. Brown (2011: 49) concludes: "While the imputation of intentions to infants' behavior may be a universal, the disposition to do so varies radically across situations and social groups, and intentions imputed do not necessarily lead to social interaction."

References

Anscombe, G. E. M. 2000[1957]. *Intention*. Cambridge, MA: Harvard University Press.
   1958. On Brute Facts. *Analysis* 18(3): 69–72
Atkinson, J. M. 1984a. *Our Masters' Voices: The Language and Body Language of Politics*. London: Methuen.
   1984b. Public Speaking and Audience Responses: Some techniques for inviting audience applause. In *Structures of Social Action: Studies in Conversation Analysis*, ed. J. M. Atkinson and J. Heritage, 370–407. Cambridge: Cambridge University Press.
Austin, J. L. 1962. *How To Do Things with Words*. Oxford: Clarendon Press.

Brown, P. 2011. The Cultural Organization of Attention. In *The Handbook of Language Socialization*, ed. A. Duranti, E. Ochs, and B. B. Schieffelin, 29–55. Malden, MA: Wiley-Blackwell.

Clark, H. H. 2003. Pointing and Placing. In *Pointing: Where Language, Culture, and Cognition Meet*, ed. S. Kita, 243–68. Hillsdale, NJ: Erlbaum.

Clayman, S. E. 1993. Booing: The anatomy of a disaffiliative response. *American Sociological Review* 58(1): 110–30.

Comaroff, J. L. 1978. Rules and Rulers: Political processes in a Tswana chiefdom. *Man* (NS) 13: 1–20.

Dingemanse, M., F. Torreira, and N. J. Enfield. 2013. Is "Huh?" a Universal Word? Conversational infrastructure and the convergent evolution of linguistic items. *PLoS One* 8(11): e78273. doi:10.1371/journal.pone.0078273.

Du Bois, J. W. Meaning Without Intention: Lessons from divination. In *Responsibility and Evidence in Oral Discourse*, ed. Jane Hill and Judith T. Irvine, 48–71. Cambridge: Cambridge University Press.

Duranti, A. 1984. *Intentions, Self and Local Theories of Meaning: Words and Social Action in a Samoan Context*. Center for Human Information Processing Report No. 122. La Jolla.

  1988. Intentions, Language, and Social Action in a Samoan Context. *Journal of Pragmatics* 12: 13–33.

  1993. Intentions, Self, and Responsibility: An essay in Samoan ethnopragmatics. *In Responsibility and Evidence in Oral Discourse*, ed. J. Hill and J. Irvine, 24–47. Cambridge: Cambridge University Press.

  2008. Further Reflections on Reading Other Minds. *Anthropological Quarterly* 81(2): 483–94.

  2010. Husserl, Intersubjectivity and Anthropology. *Anthropological Theory* 10(1): 1–20.

Durkheim 1915 *The Elementary Forms of the Religious Life: A Study in Religious Sociology*. London: G. Allen and Unwin; New York: Macmillan.

Enfield, N. J. 2011. Sources of Asymmetry in Human Interaction: Enchrony, status knowledge and agency. In *The Morality of Knowledge in Conversation*, ed. T. Stivers, L. Mondada, and J. Steensig, 285–312. Cambridge: Cambridge University Press.

Enfield, N. J., M. Dingemanse, J. Baranova, J. Blythe, P. Brown, T. Dirksmeyer, et al. 2013. Huh? What? – A first survey in 21 languages. In *Conversational Repair and Human Understanding*, ed. M. Hayashi, G. Raymond, and J. Sidnell, 343–80. Cambridge: Cambridge University Press.

Enfield, N. J., and S. C. Levinson. 2006. Introduction: Human Sociality as a New Interdisciplinary Field. In *Roots of Human Sociality: Culture, Cognition, and Interaction*, ed. N. J. Enfield and Stephen C. Levinson, 1–38. Oxford: Berg.

Enfield, N. J., and J. Sidnell. 2014. Language Presupposes an Enchronic Infrastructure for Social Interaction. In *The Social Origin of Language*, ed. Daniel Dor, Chris Knight, and Jerome Lewis, 92-104. Oxford: Oxford University Press.

Garfinkel, H. 1967. *Studies in Ethnomethodology*. Englewood Cliffs, NJ: Prentice-Hall.

Goffman, E. 1957. Alienation from Interaction. *Human Relations* 10: 47-60.

Goodwin, C. 1979. The Interactive Construction of a Sentence in Natural Conversation. In *Everyday Language: Studies in Ethnomethodology*, ed. G. Psathas, 97-121. New York: Irvington.

 1980. Restarts, Pauses, and the Achievement of Mutual Gaze at Turn-beginning. *Sociological Inquiry* 50: 272-302.

 1981. *Conversational Organization: Interaction between Speakers and Hearers*. New York: Academic Press.

Goodwin, C., and M. H. Goodwin. 1987. Concurrent Operations on Talk: Notes on the interactive organization of assessments. *IPrA Papers in Pragmatics* 1(1): 1-52.

Grice, H. P. 1957. Meaning. *Philosophical Review* 66: 377-88.

Groark, K. 2013. Toward a Cultural Phenomenology of Intersubjectivity: The extended relational field of the Tzotzil Maya of highland Chiapas, Mexico. *Language and Communication* 33(3): 278-91.

Hayashi, M., G. Raymond, and J. Sidnell, eds. 2013. *Conversational Repair and Human Understanding*. Cambridge: Cambridge University Press.

Heritage, J. 1984. *Garfinkel and Ethnomethodology*. Cambridge: Polity Press.

 2011. Territories of Knowledge, Territories of Experience: Empathic moments in interaction. In *The Morality of Knowledge in Conversation*, ed. T. Stivers, L. Mondada, and J. Steensig, 159-83. Cambridge: Cambridge University Press.

Husserl, E. 1970a. *Logical Investigations*. 2 vols., trans. J. N. Findlay. Atlantic Highlands, NJ: Humanities Press.

 1970b. *The Crisis of European Sciences and Transcendental Phenomenology*. Evanston, IL: Northwestern University Press.

Jakobson, R. 1960. Linguistics and Poetics. In *Style in Language*, ed. T. Sebeok, 350-77. Cambridge, MA: MIT Press.

Jefferson, G. 1972. Side Sequences. In *Studies in Social Interaction*, ed. D. Sudnow, 294-338. New York: Free Press.

 1979. A Technique for Inviting Laughter and its Subsequent Acceptance/Declination. In *Everyday Language: Studies in Ethnomethodology*, ed. G. Psathas, 79-96. New York: Irvington.

 1985. Notes on a Systematic Deployment of the Acknowledgement Tokens 'yeah' and 'mm hm'. *Papers in Linguistics* 17(2): 197-216.

 1993. Caveat Speaker: Preliminary notes on recipient topic-shift implicature. *Research on Language and Social Interaction* 26: 1-30.

Kidwell, M., and D. H. Zimmerman. 2007. Joint Attention as Action. *Journal of Pragmatics* 39(3): 592-611.

Kitzinger, C. 2012. Repair. In *The Handbook of Conversation Analysis*, ed. J. Sidnell and T. Stivers, 229-56. Chichester: Blackwell/Wiley

Kockelman, P. 2004. Stance and Subjectivity. *Journal of Linguistic Anthropology* 14(2): 127–50

Krebs, J.R., and R. Dawkins. 1984. Animal Signals: Mind-Reading and Manipulation. In *Behavioural Ecology: An Evolutionary Approach The Handbook of Conversation Analysis*, ed. J.R. Krebs and N.B. Davies, 380–405. London: Blackwell.

Lerner, G.H. 2002. Turn-sharing: The choral co-production of talk-in-interaction. In *The Language of Turn and Sequence*, ed. C.E. Ford, B.A. Fox, and S.A. Thompson, 225–56. Oxford: Oxford University Press.

Levinson, S.C. 2005. Living with Manny's Dangerous Idea. *Discourse Studies* 7(4–5): 431–53.

⸺ 2006. On the Human 'Interaction Engine'. In *Roots of Human Sociality: Culture, Cognition, and Interaction*, ed. N.J. Enfield and S.C. Levinson, 39–69. Oxford: Berg.

Malinowski, B. 1923. The Problem of Meaning in Primitive Languages. In *The Meaning of Meaning*, ed. Charles K. Ogden and Ian A. Richards, 146–52. London: Routledge.

Mech, L.D. 1981. *The Wolf: The Ecology and Behavior of an Endangered Species*. Minneapolis: University of Minnesota Press.

Moerman, M., and H. Sacks. 1988 [1970]. On "Understanding" in the Analysis of Natural Conversation. In *Talking Culture: Ethnography and Conversation Analysis*, ed. M. Moerman, 180–6. Philadelphia: University of Pennsylvania Press.

Ochs, E. 1982 Talking to Children in Western Samoa. *Language in Society* 11: 77–104.

⸺ 1984 Clarification and Culture. In *GURT'84: Meaning, Form, and Use in Context: Linguistic Applications*, ed. D. Schiffrin, 325–41. Washington, DC: Georgetown University Press.

⸺ 1988 *Culture and Language Development: Language Acquisition and Language Socialization in a Samoan Village*. Cambridge: Cambridge University Press.

Pollner, M. 1987. *Mundane Reason: Reality in Everyday and Sociological Discourse*. Cambridge: Cambridge University Press.

Robbins, J., and A. Rumsey. 2008. Social Thought and Commentary Section: Anthropology and the opacity of other minds. *Anthropological Quarterly* 81(2): 407–20.

Robinson, J.D. 2013. Epistemics, Action Formation, and Other-Initiation of Repair: The case of partial questioning repeats. In *Conversational Repair and Human Understanding*, ed. M. Hayashi, G. Raymond, and J. Sidnell, 261–92. Cambridge: Cambridge University Press.

Robinson, J.D., and H. Kevoe-Feldman. 2010. Using Full Repeats to Initiate Repair on Others' Questions. *Research on Language and Social Interaction* 43: 232–59.

Rommetveit, R. 1976. On the Architecture of Intersubjectivity. In *Social Psychology in Transition*, ed. L.H. Strickland, K.J. Gergen, and F.J. Aboud, 163–75. New York: Plenum Press.

Rosaldo, M. Z. 1982. The Things We Do With Words: Ilongot speech acts and speech act theory. *Language in Society* 11: 203–37.

Rossano, F. 2013. Sequence Organization and Timing of Bonobo Mother-Infant Interactions. *Interaction Studies* 14(2): 160–89.

Rumsey, A. 2013. Intersubjectivity, Deception and the 'Opacity of Other Minds': Perspectives from Highland New Guinea and beyond. *Language and Communication* 33(3): 326–43.

Ryle, G. 1949. *The Concept of Mind*. New York: Barnes and Noble.

Sacks, H. 1984. On Doing "Being Ordinary". In *Structures of Social Action*, ed. J. M. Atkinson and J. Heritage, 413–29. Cambridge: Cambridge University Press.

1992. *Lectures on Conversation*. 2 Vols. Oxford: Blackwell.

2004. An Initial Characterization of the Organization of Speaker Turn-taking in Conversation. In *Conversation Analysis: Studies from the First Generation*, ed. G. Lerner, 35–42. Amsterdam and Philadelphia: John Benjamins.

Sacks, H., and E. A. Schegloff. 1979. Two Preferences in the Organization of Reference to Persons and their Interaction. In *Everyday Language: Studies in Ethnomethodology*, ed. G. Psathas, 15–21. New York: Irvington.

Sacks, H., E. A. Schegloff, and G. Jefferson. 1974. A Simplest Systematics for the Organization of Turn-Taking for Conversation. *Language* 50: 696–735.

Schegloff, E. A. 1968. Sequencing in Conversational Openings. *American Anthropologist* 70: 1075–95.

1988. Presequences and Indirection: Applying speech act theory to ordinary conversation. *Journal of Pragmatics* 12: 55–62.

1992a. Repair after Next Turn: The last structurally provided for place for the defense of intersubjectivity in conversation. *American Journal of Sociology* 95: 1295–1345.

1992b. Introduction. In *Harvey Sacks, Lectures on conversation (Fall 1964–Spring 1968)*, ed. G. Jefferson, Vol. 1, ix–lxii. Oxford: Blackwell.

1996. Confirming Allusions: Toward an empirical account of action. *American Journal of Sociology* 102(1): 161–216.

1997. Practices and Actions: Boundary cases of other-initiated repair. *Discourse Processes* 23(3): 499–545.

2000. Overlapping Talk and the Organization of Turn-Taking for conversation. *Language in Society* 29(1): 1–63.

2006. Interaction: The infrastructure for social institutions, the natural ecological niche for language, and the arena in which culture is enacted. In *Roots of Human Sociality: Culture, Cognition, and Interaction*, ed. N. J. Enfield and S. C. Levinson, 70–96. Oxford: Berg.

2007. *Sequence Organization in Interaction: A Primer in Conversation Analysis*. Cambridge: Cambridge University Press.

Schegloff, E. A., G. Jefferson, and H. Sacks. 1977. The Preference for Self-Correction in the Organization of Repair in Conversation. *Language* 53(2): 361–82.

Schutz, A. 1962. *Collected Papers*, Vol. 1. The Hague: Martinus Nijhoff.

1966. The Problem of Transcendental Intersubjectivity in Husserl. In *Collected Papers*, Vol. 3, 51–83. The Hague: Martinus Nijhoff.

1967. *The Phenomenology of the Social World*. Evanston, IL: Northwestern University Press.

Searle, J. R. 2006 Social Ontology: Some basic principles. *Anthropological Theory* 6: 12–29.

2010. *Making the Social World: The Structure of Human Civilization*. Oxford: Oxford University Press.

Sidnell, J. 2001. Conversational Turn-Taking in a Caribbean English Creole. *Journal of Pragmatics* 33(8): 1263–90.

2005. Gesture in the Pursuit and Display of Recognition: A Caribbean case study. *Semiotica* 156(1/4): 55–87.

2007. Comparative Studies in Conversation Analysis. *Annual Review of Anthropology* 36: 229–44.

ed. 2009a. *Conversation Analysis: Comparative Perspectives*. Cambridge: Cambridge University Press.

2009b. Participation. In *The Pragmatics of Interaction*, ed. S. D'hondt, J.-O. Östman, and J. Verschueren, 125–56. Philadelphia: John Benjamins Publishing Co.

2010a. Questioning Repeats in the Talk of Four-year-old Children. In *Analyzing Interactions in Childhood: Insights from Conversation Analysis*, ed. H. Gardner and M. A. Forrester, 103–27. Oxford: Wiley-Blackwell.

2010b. The Ordinary Ethics of Everyday Talk. In *Ordinary Ethics: Anthropology, Language and Action*, ed. M. Lambek, 123–39. Fordham University Press.

2010c. *Conversation Analysis: An Introduction*. Oxford: Wiley-Blackwell.

2011a. "D'you understand that honey": Gender and Participation in Conversation. In *Conversation and Gender*, ed. E. Stokoe and S. Speer, 183–209. Cambridge: Cambridge University Press.

2011b. The Epistemics of Make-Believe. In *The Morality of Knowledge in Conversation*, ed. T. Stivers, L. Mondada, and J. Steensig, 131–56. Cambridge: Cambridge University Press.

2012 Basic Conversation Analytic Methods. In *Handbook of Conversation Analysis*, ed. J. Sidnell and T. Stivers, 77–100. Oxford: Blackwell.

Sidnell, J., and N. J. Enfield. 2012. Language Diversity and Social Action: A third locus of linguistic relativity. *Current Anthropology* 53(3): 302–21.

In press. Deixis and the Interactional Foundations of Reference. In *The Oxford Handbook of Pragmatics*, ed. Y. Huang. Oxford: Oxford University Press.

Stivers, T. 2005. Modified Repeats: One method for asserting primary rights from second position. *Research on Language and Social Interaction* 38(2): 131–58.

   2008. Stance, Alignment, and Affiliation During Storytelling: When nodding is a token of affiliation. *Research on Language and Social Interaction*, 41(1), 31–57.

Stivers, T., N. J. Enfield, P. Brown, C. Englert, M. Hayashi, T. Heinemann, et al. 2009. Universals and Cultural Variation in Turn-Taking in Conversation. *Proceedings of the National Academy of Sciences* 106(26): 10587–92.

Tomasello, M. 1999. *The Cultural Origins of Human Cognition*. Cambridge, MA: Harvard University Press.

   2008. *Origins of Human Communication*. Cambridge, MA: MIT Press.

Trevarthen, C. 1977. Descriptive Analyses of Infant Communicative Behaviour. In Studies in Mother-Infant Interaction, ed. H. R. Schaffer. London: Academic Press.

Whorf, B. L. 1956. *Language, Thought and Reality: Selected Writings of Benjamin Lee Whorf*. Cambridge, MA: Massachusetts Institute of Technology.

Wittgenstein, L. 1953. *Philosophical Investigations*, ed. G. E. M. Anscombe and R. Rhees, trans. G. E. M. Anscombe. Oxford: Blackwell.

   1969. *On Certainty*, ed. G. E. M. Anscombe and G. H. von Wright, trans. G. E. M. Anscombe and D. Paul. Oxford: Blackwell.

16

Language and human sociality

Alan Rumsey

16.1 Introduction

We humans are of course not the only social species. Others whose social lives have been extensively studied include bees, whales, dolphins, hyenas, scrub jays, chimpanzees, and vervet monkeys. And the forms of communication used by at least some of these species have sometimes been called "language" (e.g., Frisch 1967, Savage-Rumbaugh 1986). Here I will be using that word in a stricter sense to pertain to language in its specifically human form. On that basis I will be addressing two questions: (1) "How are social relations implicated in the nature of language?" and (2) "What difference does language make for human social relations as distinct from those of other species?"

Regarding the first of these questions, John Searle has pointed out that classical European political theory in both its utopian variants (e.g., More, Bacon) and social-contract ones (Hobbes, Locke, Rousseau) erred in assuming that humans living in a pre-social "state of nature" had language, since

> to have language is already to have a rich structure of institutions. Statement making and promising are human institutions as much as property and marriage. (Searle 2010: 134)

Searle's point could have been reinforced by considering certain structural features which seem to be common to all languages, namely so-called "indexical" categories including those of "person" (as in "first person," "second person," "third person") and demonstrative reference ("this," "that," etc.).[1] These categories presuppose and install at the heart of language a primordial social situation: one in which there are established roles of speaker, addressee, and referent (thing spoken about), where the referent can be either the speaker, the addressee, or another person or object. The roles are commutable, so that the person who is a speaker at one moment can become the addressee at the next and vice versa, a third-party referent can become the (self-)indexed speaker or addressee, etc.

16.2 Language and other animal communication systems

How do the above features of language differ from the communication systems used by other species? Do those not also involve reversible roles occupied by emitters of signs, recipients of them, and objects which are neither? Indeed they do. Let us consider for example the sign system of bees as studied by Karl von Frisch (1967). Western honey bees, on finding a food source and returning to their hive, perform one of two "dances": the "round dance" or the "waggle dance." Frisch showed that certain features of these dances correlate to the distance and direction of the food source from the hive, the position of the sun in relation to the food source, and how rich the source is. Another bee who receives this message and responds it to by flying to the food and gathering more may on another occasion be the one who discovers a new food source and performs the dance for others.

Vervet monkeys have been shown to communicate with each other using a number of gestures and calls, including, for example, distinct calls for warning other members of their troupe of the presence of a snake, leopard, or eagle (Struhsaker 1967, Cheney and Seyfarth 1990). The calls are typically responded to by other vervets in different ways as appropriate: by standing on their hind legs and scanning the ground for snakes, climbing to the smallest branches of nearby trees to evade leopards (who are too heavy to follow them), or climbing a tree but staying near the trunk or diving into dense bushes to evade eagles. Here again, the individual who issues the signal on one occasion can be the one who responds to it on another.

These communication systems share some important properties with human language. A useful framework for comparing them with it is the set "design features" of language that was set out by Charles Hockett (1963). Some of those features were said to be shared with at least some other animal communication systems and others to be unique to language. Among the former, some relevant ones for the present comparison are:

- *discreteness*, whereby "the possible messages ... constitute a discrete repertory rather than a continuous one" (Hockett 1963: 10);
- *arbitrariness*, whereby "the relation between a meaningful element and its denotation is independent of any physical or geometrical resemblance between the two" (ibid.);
- *displacement*, whereby "messages may refer to things remote in time or space, or both, from the site of communication" (Hockett 1963: 11).

The predator-warning calls of the vervet are discrete and arbitrary in Hockett's sense, but show displacement to only a limited degree, since the warnings always pertain to predators in the immediate vicinity of the caller at the time of the call. The dances of the bee are discrete from one another but continuous in the range of directions and distances that are indicated, and non-arbitrary in that the direction of movement within the dance maps directly onto the direction of the food source from the hive, and the distances map proportionally. The dances show little temporal displacement, in that the dance always pertains to a food source discovered by the dancer immediately prior to his arrival back at the hive.

Among the design features that Hockett claimed were unique to human language, the one that has often been taken to be the most distinctive is what he called *duality of patterning*, whereby meaningless units can be combined in various ways to make up an open-ended range of meaningful ones (the prototypical case being the relationship between phonemes and morphemes). As expected, the bee dances do not show this property. Contrary to Hockett's claim the cries of the vervet do show it to some degree,[2] but human language undoubtedly shows it to a much greater degree than any other known communication system.

Another feature that Hockett claimed was unique to human language was *reflexiveness*, which he defined as the ability to "communicate about communication" (Hockett 1963: 13) – or, as he later put it, "communicate about the very system in which we are communicating" (Hockett and Altman 1968: 64). A similar point had been made earlier by philosophers and logicians including Quine (1940), Tarski (1944), and by linguist Roman Jakobson when he posited a class of utterances in which "the message refers to the code," as in the sentence "'Pup' means a young dog" (Jakobson 1971[1957]: 131). This reflexive capacity of language is especially important for understanding the relation between language and human sociality. Most important in this respect is not just the capacity of each language for referring to aspects of the language in general – as in Jakobson's example – but what Reichenbach (1947: 284) called *token* reflexivity: the capacity of language to treat aspects of its own use in particular contexts as that which it is about.[3]

A prime instance of this is the category of person that I have referred to above. The pronouns *I* and *you* for example are token-reflexive in that they refer respectively to "the speaker of this instance of the word *I*" and "the person who is being addressed by the speaker of this instance of the word *you*."[4] While many communication systems used by other species – including the two discussed above – are indexical in that the messages conveyed in them are interpretable only within a particular context of use (the particular beehive in which a given dance is performed, a surrounding terrain with the sun at a particular position in the sky at the time of the dance, etc.), as far as I have been able to determine from the literature on animal communication only human language is token-reflexive in the sense discussed above.

What makes that especially germane to the topic of this chapter is that the prime domain of token-reflexivity in language is a set of social relations, namely "the primordial social situation" that I have referred to above, in which parties to the speech situation interact within the commutable roles of speaker and addressee, sharing and exchanging perspectives with respect to objects to which they are jointly attending. Interestingly, this scenario corresponds exactly with what Michael Tomasello and his colleagues (e.g., Tomasello *et al.* 2005) have found to be the most distinctive of human capacities – one which is not found even in our closest primate cousins, but is present among typically developing[5] humans even as infants before they learn to use language. That is, the capacity to interact with each other in configurations of this kind more generally (with or without the use of speech), and the capacity that it presupposes for discerning and sharing intentions with fellow members of our species and for engaging in "joint attention" with them in respect of objects that we are both focusing on. While it had previously been assumed (e.g., by Benveniste 1971[1966]: 217–38, Sahlins 1997: 275–6) that the evolution of language was what made such mutuality possible, Tomasello has cogently argued that it evolved earlier, and is what made language possible. He has not, as far as I know, considered in this connection the significance of the linguistic category of person and its universality, along with deictic terms such as English *this* and *that* or French *ce* which seem to be available in every language for the interactional task of achieving joint focus on a "third person" object of attention (Himmelmann 1996, Diessel 1999).

In some respects each of the animal communication systems referred to above also presupposes a "primordial social situation." For example, expanding on what I have said above about the role of indexicality in this connection, bees' communication presupposes as context for each message: (1) the location of the hive in which the dance is being performed, as the anchoring point or "origo" (Buehler 1990[1934]) of the message; (2) the presence in the hive of other bees belonging to the same colony who are the potential recipients of the message; (3) a surrounding terrain in which there are more or less remote food sources in any direction; (4) the trajectory of the sun relative to the position of the hive and the food source; (5) a set of dimensions of the space where the dance is performed, and an implicit metric for calibrating distances within it (at different scales for each of the two dances) relative to the distances to be traversed in the surrounding terrain.

All of the above factors come into play each time a dance is performed, as the tacit ground on which communication takes place – or "primordial social situation" – of bee communication. Now let us compare it with the one I have sketched for human language above. An obvious difference is that the former is connected to the surrounding natural environment in very specific ways whereas the latter is not. A related difference is that there is only one thing that all possible messages in Bee are about: a source of food and its location and quality. By contrast, the social situation that is built into human language includes only the communicating parties themselves, the reciprocal relations between them, and their mutual relations to an open-ended range of other possible objects to which they may attend. Enabled – even compelled – by its formal token-reflexivity with respect to that situation, communicative interaction in the medium of language is always in part – and sometimes entirely – about the communicative situation in which it occurs, the relations among the interacting parties, and the ones between them and other objects of their discourse.

A related difference between language and other animal communication systems is that language allows for interaction which is much more fully dialogical. In this connection, consider once more the two animal communicative systems I have described above. In both cases I have said that the positions of message emitter and message receiver in the system are reversible, but actually this is true only in the long run, not within a single communicative event. Within any given event, there is only one message emitter. In the first example it is the bee who has found the source of food and comes back to the hive to report it to the others. The response – or, as C. S. Peirce would have called it, the "interpretant" – of the sign produced by the dancing bee is for the other bees to join in the dance with that one, thereby registering the message as a series of corresponding movements within their own bodies, and then fly off to find the food source. Similarly in the case of vervet monkeys a single monkey emits a signal and the others respond with appropriate movements as described above.[6]

By contrast, in language-based human communication a possible response to an utterance conveying a message is another utterance by the erstwhile addressee in which she conveys another message to the erstwhile speaker – in other words, a "reply." Indeed, careful empirical investigation by conversation analysts over the past four decades has shown that this is not merely a possibility, but a basic expectation and ubiquitous organizing feature of conversational interaction in every human community where it has been studied (see Dingemanse and Floyd, this volume, Chapter 18).[7]

As pointed out by Benveniste (1971[1966]), another related difference between human language and bee communication lies in the potential of language for relayed transmission of messages. In the case of bees, the dance through which the location of a food source is transmitted can only be done by a bee who has been there and returned to the hive. Another bee that has received the first bee's message, found the food source, gone there, and returned to the hive can then do the dance, thereby transmitting the message to others. But he cannot short-circuit this procedure by merely reenacting the first bee's dance, thereby relaying the message without having gone to the food source himself. Similar considerations apply to the signaling systems of vervet monkeys. Drawing an explicit contrast with bee communication in this regard, Benveniste remarked that

Human language is different; for in the dialogue the reference to the objective experience and the reaction to its linguistic manifestation [in the form of relayed message] mix freely and without limitation ... the characteristic of language is to produce a substitute for experience which can be passed on *ad infinitum* in time and space. This is the nature of our symbolism and the basis of linguistic tradition.

(Benveniste 1971[1966]: 53)

Below I will have more to say about the implications of this difference for the nature of human social relations. Before doing so I want to point out another universal feature of language that plays a central part in the relaying and "mixing" process that Benveniste refers to, namely, the grammar of "reported speech," or what I prefer to call "represented speech." It is a striking fact that every known language provides means not only for the indexical anchoring of an utterance within the immediate speech situation in which it is produced, as discussed above, but also means for representing another speech situation within the immediate one (De Roeck 1994, Güldemann and von Roncador 2002). Minimally, these means always seem to include direct quotation, whereby the indexical anchoring of the represented speech event is "transposed" into the speech event in which it is being represented: "'I'll see you tomorrow,' she said to him yesterday," etc.

I would argue that, no less than the token-reflexive indexing of participant roles in the "primordial social situation" that I have referred to above, the cross-linguistically universal possibility of represented speech builds into language a particular, distinctively human form of sociality – namely, one in which speech act participants not only share and exchange perspectives and intentions with respect to a common object, but in which they also do so with respect to other such interactions (whether real or imagined), thereby placing themselves in a dialogical relation not only with each other, but also with those other speech situations and the perspectives and intentions that are attributed to their participants.

This unique capacity of human language is reflected not only in the phenomenon of represented speech, but in the "perspectival" nature of the linguistic sign itself. As Tomasello (1999: 107) has put it, "What makes linguistic symbols truly unique from a cognitive perspective is the fact that each symbol embodies a particular perspective on some entity or event: this object is simultaneously a rose, a flower and a gift." Likewise, as we shall see below, linguistic symbols, and the configurations in which they are used, allow for multiple perspectives on the participants in the speech event and relationships between them.

Having described a number of features of language and human social relations in abstract terms, I now turn to an ethnographic exemplification of them.

16.3 Examples of triadic engagement and the difference that language makes

The first pair of examples are photographs from two otherwise quite different settings across the world that both illustrate the joint-attention scenario that I have discussed in section 16.2. The photograph in Figure 16.1 was taken in a park in central Paris. It shows a young boy playing with his infant sister in a sandbox, silently collaborating with her in scooping sand into a plastic container. The photograph in Figure 16.2 shows a woman with her 5-year-old son and 21-month-old daughter sitting by the hearth in their house in the New Guinea Highlands. The boy is blowing through a plastic tube to stoke the fire, while his younger sister reaches towards him, trying to get the tube from him (which she succeeded in doing with his cooperation a few seconds later). Neither of these collaborations involved speech. Yet both were instances of the distinctly human, triadic form of engagement that underlies our ability to use language as discussed above in connection with Tomasello's findings.

Now let us consider a case of such engagement that does involve speech. Example 1 comes from the same locale as Figure 16.2, Kailge, in the Ku Waru-speaking region of the Western Highlands of Papua New Guinea. It is an excerpt from a transcript of interaction between a woman Wapi and her two year old son Jesi.[8] Also present is Wapi's six-year-old son Alex. The interaction took place in their house, next to the hearth, much as in Figure 16.2.

Figure 16.1 Young boy playing with his sister, Paris

Language and human sociality 407

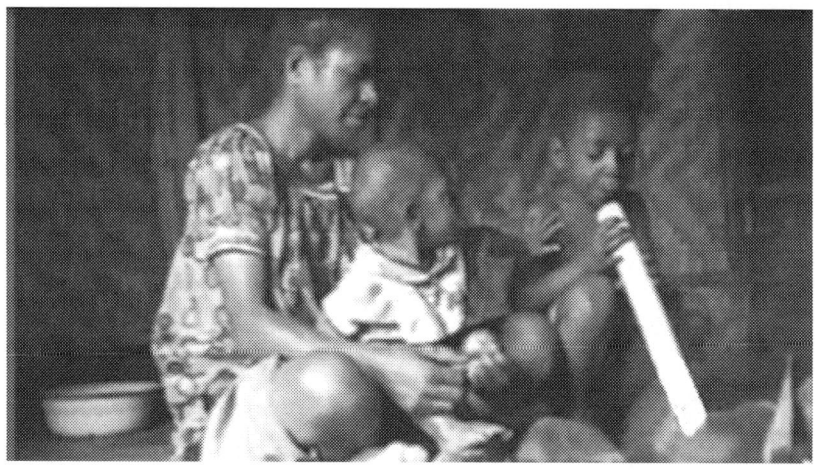

Figure 16.2 Mother and children at home in the Papua New Guinea Highlands

(1) Interaction between Wapi and her son Jesi, with Alex as targeted overhearer

(a) Wapi: ana kola naa ti=o nya
same.sex.sibling cry not do:JUS.SG=VOC say:IMP.SG
'Tell your brother not to cry.' [lit: 'Say "brother, don't cry"']

(b) Jesi: ana kola naa ti=o
same.sex.sibling cry not do:JUS.SG=VOC
'Brother don't cry.'

(c) Wapi: kali pabiyl=o
kalyke go:OPT:2DU=VOC
'Let's go to Kailge.'

(d) Jesi: teka pabi=o
kalyke pabiyl=o
Kailge go:OPT:2DU=VOC
'Let's go to Kailge.'

(e) Wapi: sispop lyabiyl pabiyl=o
cheesepop get:OPT:2DU go:OPT:2DU=VOC
'Let's go get some cheesepops.'

(f) Jesi: titopa-ti nabi
sispop-DEF nabiyl
cheesepop eat:OPT:2DU
'We'll eat a cheesepop.'

(g) Wapi: pabiyl
go:OPT:2DU
'Let's go.'

(h) Jesi: pebil=o
pabiyl=o

		go:OPT:2DU
		'Let's go.'
(i)	Wapi:	kola naa ti=o
		cry not do:JUS.SG=VOC
		'Don't cry.'
(j)	Jesi:	pike naa ti
		biket not do:JUS.SG
		'Don't be a bighead.'

As in Figure 16.1 there was in this interaction an object that was jointly attended to by two interacting persons. In this case that object was another person, Jesi's brother Alex. This joint focus may already have been established by coordinated gaze directions between the interacting parties as in Figure 16.1,[9] perhaps stimulated in part by Alex's crying, which could be understood as a call for attention. In any case, when speech enters into the picture beginning in line 1a, there is a profound transformation in the kinds of engagement that are involved. The very first word of 1a, *ana*, already belongs not only to the immediate context of interaction between Wapi and Jesi, but also to another projected one that Wapi seeks to bring about between Jesi and Alex. She does this by means of the standard Ku Waru represented-speech construction, in which the represented locution is presented first, followed by a form of the framing verb *nyi-* 'say'. In this case that verb occurs in its singular imperative form *nya*, thereby retrospectively framing the rest of the utterance, *ana kola naa tio* 'Brother, don't cry', as one that she is telling addressee Jesi to say to Alex. This is a prime instance of perspective-taking, in both of the senses discussed above.

First, it involves the speaker (Wapi) taking the perspective of the addressee (Jesi) towards a third party (Alex). In this case there is the added complication that the relevant perspective is one that pertains to an interactional frame that has not been actualized yet, in which Jesi is the speaker and Alex the addressee. Beginning in line 1b, that second frame becomes actualized when Jesi repeats in his own voice the utterance that Wapi has prompted him to say to Alex in 1a. That and everything else that is said in the entire interaction involves two triadic configurations, one embedded within the other.[10] The initial triad consists of Wapi as speaker, Jesi as addressee, and Alex as the referent, to whom Wapi directs Jesi's attention. The second, embedded triadic interaction is the one that is orchestrated by Wapi involving Jesi as speaker, Alex as addressee, and as the object of attention a proposed trip to Kailge to get some cheesepops (a kind of packaged snack food that has found its way into even remote Highland PNG trade stores).[11]

Besides the embedding, a further complexity is that from line 1c onward, all Wapi's utterances belong to both triadic frames at once, in that she is both addressing Jesi and at the same time speaking *as* Jesi – putting words in his mouth that he is in turn meant to say to Alex, which he then does. (Consistent with this double framing, in the third line Wapi uses a baby-talk pronunciation of the name Kailge, *kali* which Jesi then repeats in an even more simplified pronunciation *take*). Likewise, from line b to h, all of Jesi's utterances belong to both triadic frames, being positioned both as responses to Wapi and as utterances addressed to Alex. In line j Jesi partially breaks out of the first frame, no longer repeating after Wapi exactly, but elaborating on her utterance and at the same time showing that he understands the force of it by in effect treating Alex's crying as an instance of *biket*, i.e., selfish, inconsiderate behavior. This complex framing illustrates the power of represented speech for creating the kind of double dialogicity that I have described above, whereby relations among participants in the "representing" speech act are placed in relation to others in the "represented" one. (Incidentally, it also exemplifies a discourse strategy that is very commonly used in interactions between Ku Waru parents and their children, as also among the Kaluli approximately 150 km to the southwest of them, where it has been studied in detail by Bambi Schieffelin (1990), who shows that it figures centrally in the socialization process there.)

Besides the perspective-taking that is involved in represented speech, the other, rather different way in which line 1a involves perspective-taking is in the choice of lexical expressions by which Wapi refers to Alex. Consistent with my discussion of this dimension of language above, the word that she uses in reference to Alex within the represented utterance, *ana*, is one that contrasts with a number of others that Jesi could have used in reference to the same person (e.g., his name Aleks, *nu* 'you', *kang* 'boy'). By her choice of the vocative kin term *ana* she has directed Jesi to take a particular perspective or stance toward Alex, which is grounded not just in the immediate interaction, but in a shared set of cultural understandings about *types* of relations that people can have with each other. The type of relation entailed by *ana* is rather different than that of 'brother' – notwithstanding my gloss – since it does not specify the gender of the referent, but rather, that the people in the relationship are of the *same* gender, whether male or female. This is of special relevance here in that same-sex siblingship features as a key building-block of Ku Waru social organization (Merlan and Rumsey 1991) as elsewhere in the region (Wagner 1967, Strathern 1972).

Having identified in section 16.2 a set of features which are common to all languages and which build into them a primordial social situation, in this section I have exemplified the way in which those features are used in discursive interaction, and the difference they make for triadic interaction when speech is involved. Even from the single short stretch of interaction involving a 2-year-old child as a main participant, one could see that, while building on a prelinguistic capacity for joint attention, the use of language enables much more complex forms of perspective-taking, through which the scope of the interaction is expanded so as to relate to other perspectives besides those of the speaker and addressee in the here and now. One of the ways in which it does so is through the invocation of shared, more or less culturally specific understandings about the *types* of things, events, processes, and relationships there are in the world, and construal of the participants' ongoing interaction in relation to those types. An example would be the invocation of the type *ana* 'same-sex sibling' as discussed above. In keeping with that discussion, perspective-taking of the lexical variety discussed here can also be thought of as a process of what Alfred Schutz (1967) (after Husserl 1973[1938]: 36) called "typification."

It is important to note that the differences of perspective that are at play in processes of typification are not just matters of individual perception or "subjectivity." They can also figure crucially in the constitution of what counts as objective reality in the human social world. For example, at Ku Waru ceremonial exchange events, large numbers of live pigs and other wealth items (including, nowadays, money) are presented in transactions which can be alternatively construed as inter-personal ones or inter-group ones at various levels within a complex system of Chinese-box-like internally subdivided segmentary groups (tribes, clans, sub-clans, etc.). In the visual displays and elaborate oratory at those events, as demonstrated in detail in Merlan and Rumsey (1991), much of what goes on can be understood as a process of typification through which the socially recognized status of the transactions (e.g., as interpersonal ones vs. inter-group ones) is determined. This process has very real material consequences. For example, by establishing people's exchange obligations for future events of the same kind, it affects how they will be using their garden land, and how many pigs they will have to raise over the next few years. Within more familiar settings, similar considerations apply with respect to the operation of courts, governments, states, and everyday conversation, as will be illustrated in section 16.5.

16.4 Typification through social indexicality

In the only actual example of typification that I have discussed so far – the one involving the type *ana*, 'same sex sibling' – the relevant type is associated with a specific lexical item pertaining to its denotatum – that which it is explicitly "about." But not all linguistic typifications work that way. A basic premise of linguistic anthropology is that what gets typified in discursive interaction is not only the explicit objects or denotata of the discourse, but also the participants in the discursive interaction and their relations to each other and to the denotata. This is done not only through expressions that refer explicitly to the participants (in which case they *are* the denotata), but also through expressions that implicitly index aspects of the speech situation. Situation-indexical devices of that kind have been a major focus of linguistic anthropology and sociolinguistics over the past fifty years or more, and are one of the most extensively studied areas of connection between language and social relations. Relevant phenomena include:

Forms of personal reference and address. Even though these forms do explicitly refer to participants in the speech event they may also implicitly index aspects of the relation between them. For example, in almost all European languages (Brown and Gilman 1960) and many others from around the world (e.g., Turkish, Hindi, Tamil, Tagalog, Guugu Yimidhirr, Ainu) the same pronoun and/or person category that is used for addressing more than one person (e.g., French *vous*, Tamil *niinka*) can also be used for addressing a single person. What is signaled by the use of the second person plural vs. second person singular in such instances is nothing about the addressee per se, but rather, something about the relation between speaker and addressee, namely, a greater degree of social "distance" (Brown and Levinson 1987[1978]) or "distantiation" (Silverstein 2010) between them. Reciprocal use of the plural form indexes mutual distantiation, whereas non-reciprocal use indexes a kind of asymmetrical distantiation whereby the user of the plural form is placed in a subordinate position to the addressee. The full details of the social relationships that figure in the relevant ascriptions of distance and/or subordination vary greatly from one sociocultural setting to another. For example, in a Tamil-speaking village in southern India, Levinson (1977) found that caste was a major factor, organizing people into a fixed hierarchy, in which people at or near the bottom regularly used the plural form to a far larger number of other villagers than did those at or near the top of it. Among Guugu-Yimidhirr speaking Aboriginal people of Northeastern Australia Haviland (1979) found that the plural pronominal form was used specifically when addressing males to whom the speaker stood in a relation of real or potential wife's brother or wife's father – an open-ended set of people, since in common with Aboriginal systems of kinship and affinity all across Australia, the Guugu-Yimidhirr system is a classificatory one, encompassing everyone in the known social universe. Unlike in the Tamil case, here the relevant social relations of subordination do not comprise a fixed hierarchy, since one man's wife's brother is another man's sister's husband.

Discourse registers (a.k.a. 'speech styles'). Within every speech community, even among people who are considered to be speakers of the same language, distinctions are made among varieties of the language that are typically associated with different kinds of social setting. The relevant differences can be of many different sorts, including grammatical, lexical, phonological, or prosodic, and can be more or less clear-cut as locally recognized types. To the extent that they are so recognized they comprise "registers" – a concept aptly characterized by Asif Agha (2007: 145) as "cultural models of action that link diverse behavioral signs to enactable effects, including images of persona, interpersonal relationship and type of conduct." Well-known examples include: Australian Aboriginal "avoidance styles," which are or were used in the presence of an actual or potential wife's mother and include among their distinctive features alternative vocabularies, with most lexical items standing in a many-to-one semantic relationship with the corresponding "every day" ones, soft, slow speech, averted gaze, and other kinds of special bodily deportment (Dixon 1971, Haviland 1979, Rumsey 1982, Merlan 1997); Javanese "speech levels," of which there are three named ones, involving distinctive vocabulary and some phonological differences, which are used to index relations of deference both between speaker and addressee and between speaker and third-person referent (a.k.a. "honorifics") (Geertz 1960, Errington 1988); and the distinctive ways of speaking and writing that are associated with nearly every profession, trade, or political movement.

As with Ku Waru exchange transactions, and as is true of typification more generally, the types of social relationships and persons that are indexed by differences in form of address or register cannot be taken as "brute facts" that exist entirely independently of language use. Instead, the patterns of language use are part of what constitutes the relationships and persons as ones of particular sorts – again with very real material consequences.

16.5 Typification through discourse patterning

In section 16.4 I have made the point that typification takes place not only through lexically explicit characterization of denotata, but also through indexical characterization of speech-act participants and their relations to each other and the denotata. The examples discussed there have in common with lexical typification the fact that they draw on relatively fixed associations between specific linguistic forms and their significations in given contexts. So for example a plural pronoun used in reference to a single addressee has a relatively fixed value of speaker–addressee "distantiation," and a man's use of words from the avoidance register of an Aboriginal language within earshot of a woman has the fixed value of treating her as a potential or actual mother-in-law. But not all indexical typification works that way. Indeed, one of the most important developments in linguistic anthropology and related disciplines over the past thirty years (in keeping with the insights of Husserl and Schutz) is to show that typification is always a work-in-progress, and, furthermore, that it proceeds in part through the sequential and "metrical" organization of discursive interaction (e.g., Silverstein 2004, Agha 2007, Goodwin 2007, Du Bois 2007). This can be illustrated at a basic level by returning to example (1).

Table 16.1 Relations of parallelism in two lines from example 1

	Line b	Line c
Intentional modality	negative+jussive 'Don't ___ '	optative 'Let's ___ '
Subject	2SG 'You'	1 DU 'You and I'
Predicate	kola te- 'cry'	kali pu- 'go to Kailge'

For understanding the "metrical" organization of this text, it is important to know that the syntax of Ku Waru is strictly verb-final. Accordingly, every line in example 1 ends with a verb. Of special importance for this particular interaction is that each of those final verbs is one of a coherent set of Ku Waru verb categories that express an intention on the part of the speaker: imperative in line a, jussive (a "milder" form of the imperative) in lines b, i and j, and optative in lines c, d, e, f, g, and h (in this case first person dual optative "Let's you and me __"). Also noteworthy is that in each of the utterances that Wapi prompts Jesi to say to Alex, the final, intentional verb is followed by the vocative postposition =o, the interactional meaning of which is something like 'Listen to this'. Within that series of prompting utterances by Wapi (in lines a, c, e, and i), the clause-final intentional verb + vocative postposition constitutes a fixed point in relation to which the variation in the rest of each clause from line to line stands out as significant – a pattern of the kind known to poetics as "parallelism." More particularly, the varying elements are placed in a relation of what Roman Jakobson in his groundbreaking study of parallelism (1960) called "equivalence." To say that two or more terms are "equivalent" in this sense is not to say that they are identical, but that they are to be construed in relation to one another. The terms that are placed into such a relation in lines b and c are shown in the two rightmost columns in Table 16.1.

In order to understand the relation of co-construal that is figured by the parallelism between these two lines it is relevant to know that, like most people in the Ku Waru region, Wapi and her family live not in a village or town, but in a small family compound surrounded by their gardens, and that Kailge is a traditional display ground about ten minutes' walk away, which also serves as a local market, meeting place, and terminus for the only motor vehicle in the area, a small van which takes paid passengers to and from the provincial capital Mt. Hagen. In other words, Kailge is a hub of what are taken to be interesting activities and exciting prospects, as opposed to the everyday routine of the home compound.

Within this context, the relevant relation of co-construal between "cry" and "go to Kailge" is one of contrast, in which the latter is offered as an antidote to the former. Likewise, the conjunction of "you and I" is offered as an antidote to "you" alone. In this connection it is relevant to recall that, in response to Wapi's prompting, Jesi in line b has explicitly cast the relation between the entailed "you" and "I" of that and all the following lines as one of same-sex siblingship, and therefore one of mutual help and support. The parallel terms in lines b and c in effect expand upon that characterization by contrasting Alex's current state of unhappiness, crying alone, with what will happen when the two of them as brothers act together and go to Kailge.

In line e Wapi takes this further, filling in on the point of the proposed trip to Kailge, to "get some cheesepops." The syntax of this line is presumably too complex for Jesi to understand, making use of a Ku Waru construction that combines two optative verbs in series to mean 'do X (the action predicated by the second verb) in order to do Y (the action predicated by the first verb)'. Undaunted, Jesi responds with a parallel line in which he replaces that complex construction with his baby-talk version of a single optative verb which is different from either of Wapi's but consistent with the scenario that is being proposed: *nabi* (=*nabiyl*) 'Let's you and I eat ...'. In line g Wapi then repeats the second verb of her complex construction from line e *pabiyl*, which Jesi repeats as *pabi* 'Let's you and I go'. In the exchange across lines i and j Jesi again innovates on what he has been prompted to say, by replacing *kola* ... *ti* 'cry' with *pike* ... *ti* 'be a bighead'.

Now let us consider how social relations are created, maintained, or transformed through what Silverstein (2004: 627) would call the "figurational dynamics" of this text. As discussed in section 16.3, in terms of its framing through the use of represented speech, it comprises two triadic interactions, an initial one involving Wapi and Jesi as the interacting parties and another embedded one which is the object of the initial one and itself involves Jesi and Alex as the interacting parties, and the proposed trip to Kailge as the object. Here we need to add that, although Alex never speaks in the stretch of interaction that is shown in example 1, he is a key party to it, both as Jesi's projected addressee and as the "targeted overhearer" (Levinson 1988) of Wapi's remarks to Jesi.

Partly consistent with this represented-speech framing and partly crosscutting it, there is a set of alignments among the participants, and between them and the external referents of their discourse, which is created via the patterns of parallelism discussed above. In line b, by repeating the utterance she has proposed for him, Jesi has aligned himself with Wapi vis-à-vis Alex and the present reality of his crying. By his similar repetitions in lines d and h, and parallel, partly innovative but thematically consistent utterance in line f, Jesi has also aligned himself with his addressee Alex in the appropriate brotherly manner. But through his replacement of her *kola* in line i with *biket* in line j Jesi has introduced a new theme that partly contravenes the full mutuality of the ideal same-sex sibling relationship. Deriving ultimately from English 'big head' and/or 'pig-head(ed)'[12], and borrowed into Ku Waru from the national lingua franca Tok Pisin (in which it takes the form *bikhet*), this word is used more-or-less synonymously with a Ku Waru expression *kara pu-* 'to act in an obstinate, conceited, or disobedient manner'. It belongs to a number of such "diglossic" pairs in Ku Waru, which share in common a tendency for the Tok Pisin-derived member of the pair to be used to berate people or issue orders to them. An obvious legacy of the colonial past, this particular linguistic division of indexical value has survived into the present in modified form as an aspect of a more general opposition that is drawn between *bo ul* 'indigenous ways' and *kewa ul* 'exogenous, especially European-derived ways', and a tendency to regard the latter as more efficacious and powerful. By using the *kewa*-inflected expression *biket* in place of Wapi's *kola*, and in a parallel position with it, Jesi has in effect not only identified Alex's crying as an instance of *biket* behavior but also in effect shifted his "footing" (Goffman 1981) or "stance" (Kockelman 2005, Du Bois 2007, and see Eckert, this volume, Chapter 26) toward Alex from that of the solicitous *ana* to that of would-be enforcer of norms of proper deportment, thereby also identifying himself with those norms.

Something like the *bo/kewa* contrast is also at play in Wapi's invocation of *sispop* 'cheesepops' as the goal of the trip to Kailge that she has prompted Jesi to propose to Alex. Consistent with both that contrast and the one between home and Kailge that was explained above, *sispop* are projected as an object of desire, the prospect of which will stop Alex from crying. They are also projected as an object in relation to which Alex's and Jesi's perspectives will be aligned with each other, as happy consumers of that *kewa* commodity.

In sum, over the course of this interaction there emerge a number of typifications of the participants' behavior and aspects of their lifeworld, some of which are lexically explicit and some of which are implicit in its patterns of parallelism and the relations of co-construal that they invite. Among the latter, beginning with the two parallel lines as shown in Table 16.1, there is a consistent set of identifications made between, on the one hand, the present state of play, Alex, crying, and "biket" behavior, and on the other, a proposed new activity, the pair of Alex and Jesi, not crying, going to Kailge, and eating cheesepops. These typifications operate at two levels. First, within the immediate context of this speech event and its participants, they momentarily identify Alex with the present state of play and crying, and the pair of Jesi and Alex with the proposed new activity of going to Kailge and eating cheesepops. Second, at a more general level they identify crying as *biket* behavior and going to Kailge and eating cheesepops as the antithesis of crying – something that makes people happy. At the first of these levels, conceptual types which are already established as lexemes within the local language(s) – *kola* 'cry', *biket* 'bighead', *sispop* 'Cheesepops', *lya-* 'get', *no-* 'eat' – are brought into play for describing the present situation and a proposed new activity. At the second level, the types *kola*, *biket*, and *sispop* are brought into a relationship with each other and with the contrast I have discussed in section 16.3 between the home compound and Kailge. In effect, all of this is consistent with the pervasive theme among Ku Waru people that I have discussed above involving the contrast between *bo ul* 'indigenous ways' and *kewa ul* 'exogenous ways'.[13] And as with most or all such typifications, through its figuration in the discourse, this one is not only evoked but *enacted* by the participants, who thereby align themselves and each other in relation to it.

16.6 Conclusion

This chapter began with a description of some universal features of languages on the basis of which I argued that a certain form of sociality that I call the "primordial social situation" is built into language per se. Comparing language with the communication systems used by two other highly social species – western honey bees and vervet monkeys – I showed that each of those systems also has a primordial social situation built into it, but that language differs from them in that its inbuilt social situation is one that is not inherently linked to aspects of the natural environment other than the presence of the interacting parties. Further, language appears to be unique in building into its social situation, through token-reflexivity, the means for its users to exchange perspectives with each other in relation to a shared focus of attention, and to place them in relation to other communicative events and perspectives. Though based in part on a uniquely human capacity for triadic engagement that probably preceded it in evolutionary terms, the development of language has greatly extended the range of human sociality and depth of intersubjective engagement that we are capable of.

By the same token, it has allowed for the development of an order of social relations that is qualitatively different from that found in any other species – an order that is grounded not in specific innate behaviors such as the dance of the bees or the warning cries of the vervet, but in an innate capacity for shared representations such as those illustrated in example (1). None of these representations follows from direct sensory or motor experiences as do the cognitive representations of other animal species and human infants. Yet all belong to an order of phenomena that are as real as the bee's search for pollen or the vervet's evasion of predators – the order of human social reality, mediated by culture. It is an order that of course extends far beyond the immediate setting of any single speech event,[14] and beyond speech per se – in ways that often make it difficult or impossible to distinguish the strictly "linguistic" aspects of human communicative action from others. But the overall order of human social reality is one that, in the long run of human evolution, has been enabled by the development of language, and which is built up out of social relations of a kind that come into play every time language is used.

Acknowledgments

For their close reading and valuable feedback on the first draft of this chapter I would like to thank Aung Si, Francesca Merlan, Paul Kockelman, and Jesse Rumsey-Merlan. For their expert advice about non-human primate sociality many thanks to Colin Groves and Frans de Waal. Partial draft versions of this chapter were presented at the 2012 Annual Meeting of the American Anthropological Association and at a seminar at Griffith University in 2013. Many thanks to those who provided comments at those occasions. For funding the research in Papua New Guinea on which I draw in sections 16.3 and 16.5 I gratefully acknowledge the US National Science Foundation, the University of Sydney, the Australian Research Council, and Australian National University.

Notes

1. For further discussion of these categories, see Silverstein, this volume, Chapter 6.
2. The cries of vervets show what Cheney and Seyfarth (1990) call "phonological syntax," whereby "callers take elements from their repertoire of acoustic symbols and recombine them" so as to produce new vocalizations, in such a way as not to "require that acoustic elements being combined ever be used in isolation or that they have any meaning when presented on their own" (125). But the number of "new vocalizations" that are produced in this way is quite limited, in part because vervet communication does not include a level of what Cheney and Seyfarth call "lexical syntax," whereby "the meaning of the compound [would result] from the sum of meanings of its constituent units" (125).
3. The word "token" in this phrase is used in a technical sense to mean "particular instance," and is contrasted with "type" – the general category of which the token is an instance. For example "one Australian dollar" would be a type of which the particular gold coin that I have in my pocket would be a token. Likewise "pup" in Jakobson's example refers to a linguistic type, whereas an utterance of the word "pup" in a particular speech event is a token of the type.
4. In terms of the framework of Jabokson (1971[1957]) that is referred to above these would be instances, not of "the message referring to the code" but of "the code referring to the message," or (after Jespersen 1924) "shifters." In Silverstein's (1993: 39) terms they are "inherently metapragmatic semanticoreferential forms" (cf. Silverstein, this volume, Chapter 6).
5. I include this qualifying term in order to exclude children with autism-spectrum disorders, who are specifically impaired in this respect.
6. Based on their 14-month long study of vervets living in their native habitat in East Africa, in which they recorded vervets' alarm calls and

played them back to others, Seyfarth *et al.* (1980: 1086) report that "all observed changes in behaviour following playbacks of alarms were non-vocal in nature. In a total of 88 experiments, only once did a monkey (a juvenile) respond to an alarm call by giving an alarm itself. In contrast with the chorusing that occurs in natural predator encounters, playbacks did not increase the probability that monkeys would utter alarms. Under natural conditions, animals other than the first alarmist presumably sight the predator and then call."

7. When comparing animal communication to human language in this respect, it is important to note that more is involved in the notion of "reply" than mere "response". The difference is evident from Cheney and Seyforth's discussion of vervet "grunts". They report that, unlike their finding regarding responses to "alarm calls" (as described in note 6) "on 43 occasions [during their 14-month study] a grunt from one animal elicited a grunt from another." They add that "On 15 of those occasions we were able to tape record the exchange and to analyze the calls' acoustic features. Under these conditions, interestingly enough, the second animal always replied by repeating what the first animal had said. If a subordinate, for example, approached a dominant, giving the grunt to a dominant, the dominant individual disregarded her partner's rank and replied with the same call" (Cheney and Seyforth 1990:127). In other words, there was no evidence that vervets were engaging in the reciprocity of perspective that is built into human language and is fundamental to the kind of dialogicity that is associated with it.

8. The reader will note that in some lines of the children's transcribed speech (e.g., 1d, 1f, 1h) there is a second tier of Ku Waru. The top tier shows what the child said and second tier shows what my language assistants offered as the equivalent forms in "normal" or "adult" Ku Waru. Abbreviations and symbols used are: 2DU second person dual, IMP imperative, JUS jussive, VOC vocative, SG singular, - morpheme boundary, : morpheme boundary that is not clearly segmentable, = boundary before clitic element.

9. We can't be certain about this because this particular interaction was not videoed.

10. For sophisticated treatments of this kind of embedding and complex interplay among interactional frames see Goffman (1981), Hanks (1990), Goodwin and Goodwin (2004) and references cited therein.

11. Actually the product with the brand name Cheesepops is only one of many brands of similar snack foods that are now on the market in Papua New Guinea. But the term cheesepop / *sispop* is often used as a generic for all of them.

12. Given the phonological conflations and simplifications that have occurred under pidginization, many Tok Pisin words have arisen

from two or more similar sounding words in English (Mülhäusler 1979: 217–19).

13. Note that I have not claimed that the typification that is made here through discourse patterning is exactly the same as the lexically explicit *bo ul* and *kewa ul* contrast, or that the latter somehow underlies the former. At least from the developmental point of view, that would be putting the cart before the the horse, since the two-year old Jesi almost certainly does not know those words, and yet is able to participate competently and creatively in the typification that has been laid out for him in interactional form by Wapi. More generally, there is no reason to think that the typifications made through discourse patterning in the use of a given language will always correspond to lexical ones that are available within it. Indeed they often do not. In this case, for example, I suspect that, at least for the younger generation of Ku Waru speakers, the relevant typification of "cheesepops" has less to do with *kewa* 'foreignness' per se than with "lifestyle" considerations which are more like the ones at play in the promotion and consumption of such products in PNG urban settings such as Port Moresby, Lae or Mt. Hagen, where people are fully exposed to sophisticated forms of advertising.

14. Though is it impossible to develop this important point within the space of this chapter, a single example from it can serve to indicate what is involved – namely, the role played by *sispop* 'cheesepops' as what I have called an "object of desire" in example (1), and the way in which Ku Waru people's engagement with that object places them within a global complex of socioeconomic relations. Within their fertile, well-watered tropical highland environment where their ancestors have been practicing horticulture and animal husbandry for thousands of years, Ku Waru people are still largely self-sufficient in terms of food production. Indeed their own household produce by and large provides better nutrition than most of the foods they purchase with money (which they earn largely by growing coffee). Yet store-bought food items such as "cheesepops," Maggi noodles, and bottled soft drinks regularly feature as products that Ku Waru people wish for and appeal to as objects of desire in interactions with young children such as in example (1). Insofar as they not only fantasize about such products but actually spend a significant amount of their available cash on them, people within this seemingly remote part of the world are thereby placed in a nexus of relationships with large, mostly multinational corporations that manufacture the products, and the global economy in which they operate. For example Cheesepops (which is just one of many products nowadays known generically as *sispop*) are produced by Goodman Fielder, PNG, a subsidary of Goodman Fielder, a multinational that describes itself as

"Australasia's leading listed food company" (www.goodmanfielder.co.nz/index.php?q=node/3), with total sales during the 2010-11 fiscal year of *ca.* $2,556 million.

References

Agha, Asif. 2007. *Language and Social Relations*. Cambridge: Cambridge University Press.
Benveniste, Emile. 1971[1966]. *Problems in General Linguistics*. Coral Gables: University of Miami Press.
Brown, Penelope, and Stephen C. Levinson. 1987[1978]. *Politeness: Some Universals in Language Usage*. Cambridge: Cambridge University Press.
Brown, Roger, and Albert Gilman. 1960. The Pronouns of Power and Solidarity. In *Style in Language*, ed. T. A. Sebeok, 253-76. Cambridge, MA: MIT Press.
Buehler, Karl. 1990[1934]. *Theory of Language*. Amsterdam: John Benjamins.
Cheney, Dorothy, and Robert Seyfarth. 1990. *How Monkeys See the World*. Chicago: University of Chicago Press.
De Roeck, Marike. 1994. A Functional Typology of Speech Reports. In *Function and Expression in Universal Grammar*, ed. E. Engberg-Pedersen, L. F. Jakobson, and S. Rasmussen, 331-51. Berlin: Mouton de Gruyter.
Diessel, Holger. 1999. *Demonstratives: Form, Function and Grammaticalization*. Typological Studies in Language 42. Amsterdam: John Benjamins.
Dixon, Robert M. W. 1971. A Method of Semantic Description. In *Semantics: An Interdisciplinary Reader in Philosophy, Linguistics and Psychology*, ed. D. D. Steinberg, and L. A. Jakobovits, 436-71. Cambridge: Cambridge University Press.
Du Bois, John W. 2007. The Stance Triangle. In *Stancetaking in Discourse: Subjectivity, Evaluation, Interaction*, ed. Robert Englebretson, 139-82. Amsterdam: John Benjamins.
Errington, Joseph. 1988. *Style and Structure in Javanese: A Semiotic View of Linguistic Etiquette*. Philadelphia: University of Pennsylvania Press.
Frisch, Karl von. 1967. *The Dance Language and Orientation of Bees*. Cambridge, MA: Harvard University Press.
Geertz, Clifford. 1960. *The Religion of Java*. Chicago: University of Chicago Press.
Goffman, Erving. 1981. *Forms of Talk*. Philadelphia: Unversity of Pennsylvania Press.
Goodwin, Charles. 2007. Participation, Stance, and Affect in the Organization of Activities. *Discourse and Society* 18: 53-73.
Goodwin, Charles, and Marjorie Harness Goodwin. 2004. Participation. In *A Companion to Linguistic Anthropology*, ed. Alessandro Duranti, 222-44. Malden, MA: Blackwell.

Güldemann, Tom, and Manfred von Roncador, eds. 2002. *Reported Discourse: A Meeting Ground for Different Linguistic Domains*. Amsterdam: Benjamins.

Hanks, William F. 1990. *Referential Practice, Language and Lived Space among the Maya*. Chicago: University of Chicago Press.

Haviland, John. 1979. Guugu Yimidhirr Brother-in-law Language. *Language in Society* 8: 365–93.

Himmelmann, Nikolaus. 1996. Demonstratives in Narrative Discourse: A taxonomy of universal uses. In *Studies in Anaphora*, ed. Barbara Fox, 205–54. Amsterdam: John Benjamins.

Hockett, Charles. 1963. The Problem of Universals in Language. In *Universals of Language*, ed. Joseph Greenberg, 1–29. Cambridge, MA: MIT Press.

Hockett, Charles, and Stuart Altman. 1968. A Note on Design Features. In *Animal Communication: Techniques of Study and Results of Research*, ed. Sebeok, Thomas, 61–72. Bloomington: Indiana University Press.

Husserl, Edmund. 1973 [1938]. *Experience and Judgment*. Evanston: Northwestern University Press.

Jakobson, Roman. 1960. Concluding Statement: Linguistics and poetics. In *Style in Language*, ed. Thomas Sebeok, 350–77. Cambridge, MA: MIT Press.

   1971[1957]. Shifters, Verbal Categories, and the Russian Verb. In his *Selected Writings II*, 130–47. The Hague: Mouton.

Jespersen, Otto. 1924. *The Philosophy of Grammar*. London: Allen and Unwin.

Kockelman, Paul. 2005. The Semiotic Stance. *Semiotica* 157(1/4): 233–304.

Levinson, Stephen. 1977. *Social Deixis in a Tamil Village*. PhD Thesis, University of California, Berkeley.

   1988. Putting Linguistics on a Proper Footing: Explorations in Goffman's participation framework. In *Goffman: Exploring the Interaction Order*, ed. P. Drew and A. Wootton, 161–227. Oxford: Polity Press.

Merlan, Francesca. 1997. The Mother-in-Law Taboo: Avoidance and obligation in Aboriginal Australia. In *Scholar and Sceptic: Australian Aboriginal Studies in Honour of L. R. Hiatt*, ed. Francesca Merlan, John Morton, and Alan Rumsey, 95–122. Canberra: Aboriginal Studies Press.

Merlan, Francesca, and Alan Rumsey. 1991. *Ku Waru: Language and Segmentary Politics in the Western Nebilyer Valley*. Cambridge: Cambridge University Press.

Mühlhäusler, Peter. 1979. *Growth and Structure of the Lexicon of New Guinea Pidgin*. Series C, No 52. Canberra: Pacific Linguistics.

Quine, Willard. 1940. *Mathematical Logic*. Cambridge, MA: Harvard University Press.

Reichenbach, Hans. 1947. *Elements of Symbolic Logic*. New York: Free Press.

Rumsey, Alan 1982. Gun-gunma: An Australian Aboriginal Avoidance language and its social functions. In *Languages of Kinship in Aboriginal Australia*, ed. J. Heath, F. Merlan, and A. Rumsey, 161–82. Sydney: Oceania Publications.

Sahlins, Marshall. 1997. Contribution to R. Borofsky, 'Forum on Theory in Anthropology: Cook, Lono, Obeyesekere, and Sahlins'. *Current Anthropology* 38: 272-6.

Savage-Rumbaugh, E. S. 1986. *Ape Language: from Conditioned Response to Symbol*. New York: Columbia University Press.

Schieffelin, Bambi. 1990. *The Give and Take of Everyday Life: Language Socialization of Kaluli Children*. Cambridge: Cambridge University Press.

Schutz, Alfred. 1967. *The Phenomenology of the Social World*, trans. F. Walsh, and F. Lehnert. Evanston, IL: Northwestern University Press.

Searle, John. 2010. *Making the Social World*. Oxford: Oxford University Press.

Seyfarth, R. M., D. L. Cheney, and P. Marler. 1980. Vervet Monkey Alarm Calls: Semantic communication in a free-ranging primate. *Animal Behaviour* 28: 1070-94.

Silverstein, Michael. 1993. Metapragmatic Discourse and Metapragmatic Function. In *Reflexive Language*, ed. Lucy, 33-58. Cambridge: Cambridge University Press.

2004. "Cultural" Concepts and the Language–Culture Nexus. *Current Anthropology* 45: 621-51.

2010. "Direct" and "Indirect" Communicative Acts in Semiotic Perspective. *Journal of Pragmatics* 42: 337-53.

Strathern, Andrew. 1972. *One Father, One Blood: Descent and Group Structure among the Melpa People*. London: Tavistock.

Struhsaker, T. T. 1967. Auditory Communication among Vervet Monkeys (Cercopithecus Aethiops). In *Social Communication among Primates*, ed. S. A. Altmann, 281-324. University of Chicago Press.

Tarski, Alfred. 1944. The Semantic Conception of Truth. *Philosophy and Phenomenological Research* 4: 341-75.

Tomasello, Michael. 1999. *The Cultural Origins of Human Cognition*. Cambridge, MA: Harvard University Press.

Tomasello, M., M. Carpenter, J. Call, T. Behne, and H. Moll. 2005. Understanding and Sharing Intentions: The origins of cultural cognition. *Behavioral and Brain Sciences* 28: 1-17.

Wagner, Roy. 1967. *The Curse of Souw: Principles of Daribi Clan Definition and Alliance in New Guinea*. Chicago: University of Chicago Press.

17

The ontology of action, in interaction

Jack Sidnell and N. J. Enfield

17.1 Introduction

A central goal of linguistic anthropology is to understand the role that language and associated semiotic systems play in the carrying out of social action, that is, to understand how we pursue our goals, and especially, how we do this in collaboration with others. We define *action* here as controlled behavior that is a means for achieving a goal (see Kockelman 2013: 121-5, Enfield 2013: ch. 8 and many references therein). While this excludes things like slipping on an icy path, or sweating, it includes things like turning a key in a door to get inside, or asking someone for the time. Within the category of actions generally, we must distinguish between brute actions and social actions. Brute actions bring about their effects by means of direct natural causation. If I am physically strong enough, I can get you out of a room just by pushing you. This works even if you are unconscious. But a *social* action's effect is an interpretant of someone's sign, not a mere effect of someone's cause. Social actions only bring about effects by virtue of someone recognizing what is intended, and reacting appropriately. It is a social action, if, for example, I say "Would you mind stepping outside," or if I make threatening gestures that cause you to leave of your own accord, because in both cases the result comes about by means of your recognition of, and compliance with, my goal. To work at all, these social actions depend on your capacity to interpret and respond appropriately.

Any account of social action presupposes an ontology of action whether this is made explicit or not. At one extreme, we might propose that actions have the properties of natural kinds (as implied by Searle 1969), with clear defining properties and a kind of essential causal basis; analogous to, say, "citrus fruits." At the other extreme we might propose that actions are cultural constructions (e.g., Rosaldo 1982, Wierzbicka 2003), roughly comparable across cultures in functional terms but essentially defined by historically developed local practices; analogous to, say, "desserts" (or "games" à la Wittgenstein 1953). If social actions are natural kinds we should be able to count the number of possible actions, in the same way we are able to count types of extant life forms, and provide a comprehensive list of all observable actions (difficulties of defining species, etc., notwithstanding). If, on the other hand, actions are cultural constructions such an exhaustive listing of possible actions could not in principle be done – it would be akin to asking "How many different kinds of desserts are there?" The difference between citrus fruits and desserts is that we can create new types of dessert for local purposes and according to unique contextual conditions (e.g., availability of ingredients) any time we want.

It seems obvious to us that action realization is subject to *both* universal human contingencies grounded in phylogeny, *and* local cultural contingencies that have arisen historically. But we want to argue that if actions are natural, this is not because they are pre-given or programmed in any sense, but rather because their commonality *emerges*. And if they are culturally constructed, they are still constrained by basic imperatives of social life, and by basic affordances of our bodies and physical settings. Our view then is that social actions – such as telling, asking, and recruiting – are not natural kinds. They do not spring from innate intentional state categories (as proposed by Searle 2010) or analogous mind-located structures. Instead, social actions are the emergent products of dealing with the complex fission–fusion social organization that is characteristic of all human groups and of the need to exercise our flexibility in finding means for pursuing social goals (Enfield 2013). These are the cognitive, social, and historical conditions that precede, and undergird, the historical emergence of cultural difference.

It is a truism that language is a tool for action, but the theoretical and conceptual issues that follow from this are far from resolved. Our aim in this chapter is to review the problem of defining and analyzing action in interaction, and to propose a solution. In the following section, we deal with three points of conceptual clarification that, we suggest, are indispensable preliminaries to any discussion of social action and language. We then discuss two case studies that illustrate the core problem of this chapter: how it is that actions are recognized and thereby consummated, both by participants in social interaction and by analysts.

17.2 Three dimensions of contrast in the analysis of action

Our approach is owed partly to Austin and the analytic tradition in philosophy, which emphasizes the distinctive properties and importance of intentional or purposive action in contrast to non-intentional effects of our behavior. A first point is that both purposive action and non-intentional effects can be seen as ways to do things with words but, as we shall see, they differ in many respects. Second, there is a need to distinguish explicit from primary in action. This distinction concerns not the *kind* of action in question, but rather how it is expressed or formulated. And third, we need to distinguish between the constitution of action, on the one hand, and the ex post facto description of action, on the other. The following subsections deal with these three conceptual preliminaries before we proceed to the central issue of the chapter.

17.2.1 Purposive action vs. effect

If a speaker says to some recipient, "Sir, your lecture today was extremely informative," they will have paid that recipient a compliment and, in doing so, they will have set in motion a set of relevancies such that the recipient is normatively obliged to respond, and to respond in some particular way – for instance with appreciative acceptance (e.g., "Thank you"), with disagreement (e.g., "Not really"), with a turn that redirects the compliment elsewhere (e.g., "I had excellent sources to draw upon"; see Pomerantz 1978; Sidnell, this volume, Chapter 15). Now, of course, the speaker will have done a whole host of other things in addition to paying the recipient a compliment. For instance, the speaker will have taken a turn, perhaps initiated a larger exchange on the topic of the lecture, perhaps elicited the attention of another person thereby drawing them into a conversation. These we can describe as interactional effects. Moreover the speaker will have displayed deference to the recipient (by paying him a compliment, and by using the address term "sir"), will have claimed some knowledge of the lecture in question, will have situated the referent being talked about in relation to the current event of speaking. These we can describe as indexical effects since they are produced by relating, via presupposition or entailment, aspects of the speech signal to particular and recognizable contextual parameters. Finally, in so speaking, the speaker may also have made himself look obsequious, made his recipient feel proud, or made some third party feel awkward.

In the literature the distinction between an action and its possible effects has been described in a range of ways: e.g., as a distinction between action and collateral effects (Sidnell and Enfield 2012), illocution and perlocution (Austin 1962, Searle 1969), giving and giving off (Goffman 1983), pragmatic function$_1$ and pragmatic function$_2$ (Silverstein 1987).[1] Often the distinction between action versus effect correlates with the distinction between what is intended versus what is unintended, but there are exceptions. For instance, a speaker may purposely use a T-form pronoun either to initiate "familiar" relations or to insult a recipient (see, e.g., Jacquemet 1994). Another example is what Schegloff (2009) refers to as a *component action*. In the example he gives, a 14-year-old girl named Virginia asks her mother – in a bid for permission to get a job – "Didn't Beth get to work before she was sixteen." The mother replies "People just don't want *children* waiting on them." The main line of the mother's purposive action here is clearly to respond to the question and to anticipate a possible objection (Beth got to work, why can't I?), but by selecting the word "child" to refer, obliquely, to the recipient, the mother *effects* an insult of Virginia, who wants to be considered an adult.

While recognizing such exceptions, our view is that, in the main, people are engaged in goal-directed purposive action. Indeed, this is a fundamental assumption that guides people's reasoning about others' behavior. As a result, questions such as "What is he doing?" and "What does she mean?" become omnirelevant. Purposive actions both respond to prior actions and establish relevancies for next actions in such a way as to constitute an architecture of intersubjectivity (described by Sidnell, this volume, Chapter 15). When people are pursuing such goal-directed actions they are simultaneously producing effects such as establishing contextual parameters including the presumed social relations between participants, and thereby reproducing various aspects of the sociocultural order. As we have noted, it is true that people *can* pursue such effects purposively – e.g., by addressing an interlocutor with a T-form or by using French rather than English in a Montreal shop – but they cannot do so without also, at the same time, being understood to accomplish some purposive action of the kind sometimes identified with terms such as "request," "compliment," and so on. The framework of normative accountability for what is being done then hangs centrally on what participants in interaction recognize as a *main line* of action (Goffman 1963: 43ff.; cf. Kendon 1990, Clark 1996). This has been a central concern, for example, of work in conversation analysis, and the point has been well documented within that approach (see for instance Schegloff 1968, 2007; cf. Levinson 2013, in press).

17.2.2 Explicit vs. primary (cf. "implicit" and "indirect")

In lecture III of *How To Do Things With Words*, Austin (1962: 32) writes the following:

> The performative utterances I have taken as examples are all of them highly developed affairs, of the kind that we shall later call explicit performatives, by contrast with merely implicit performatives. That is to say, they (all) begin with or include some highly significant and unambiguous expression such as "I bet", "I promise", "I bequeath" – an expression very commonly also used in naming the act which, in making such an utterance, I am performing – for example betting, promising, bequeathing, &c. But, of course, it is both obvious and important that we can on occasion use the utterance "go" to achieve practically the same as we achieve by the utterance "I order you to go": and we should say cheerfully in either case, describing subsequently what someone did, that he ordered me to go ... Here we have primitive as distinct from explicit performatives; and there may be nothing in the circumstances by which we can decide whether or not the utterance is performative at all.

Austin went on to develop these ideas as the contrast between *explicit* performatives such as "I promise to be there at 11 o'clock" and *primary* performatives such as "I'll be there at 11 o'clock." Austin's point touched on both the hearer's problem of recognition and the speaker's problem of accountability:

> If someone says "I shall be there", we might ask: "Is that a promise?" We may receive the answer "Yes", or "Yes, I promise it" (or "that..." or "to..."), whereas the answer might have been only : "No, but I do intend to be" (expressing or announcing an intention), or "No, but I can foresee that, knowing my weaknesses, I (probably) shall be there".
> (Austin 1962: 69)

So the difference between an explicit performative and a primary performative has to do with what the speaker *may be taken as doing* by another (e.g., a recipient), and, most importantly, what he or she is then *accountable for having done*. In the case of an explicit performative there is, according to Austin, no room for interpretation – the speaker having announced in so many words what they are doing. In the same way that a police uniform leaves little room for doubt as to the set of rights and duties it signifies and bestows, the explicit performative is "maximally public and minimally ambiguous" (Kockelman 2006, 2013). In the case of the primary performative, the speaker may be taken as promising or as merely expressing an intention, or alternatively warning the recipient, etc. The key issue then for Austin is about "making plain what I am doing":

> suppose I bow deeply before you; it might not be clear whether I am doing obeisance to you or, say, stooping to observe the flora or to ease my indigestion. Generally speaking, then, to make clear both that it is a conventional ceremonial act, and which act it is, the act (for example of doing obeisance) will as a rule include some special further feature, for example raising my hat, tapping my head on the ground, sweeping my other hand to my heart, or even very likely uttering some noise or word, for example "Salaam". Now uttering "Salaam" is no more describing my performance, stating that I am performing an act of obeisance, than is taking off my hat: and by the same token (though we shall come back to this) saying "I salute you" is no more describing my performance than is saying "Salaam". To do or to say these things is to make plain how the action is to be taken or understood, what action it is. And so it is with putting in the expression "I promise that".
> (Austin 1962: 70)

This distinction between explicit and whatever contrastive category is used (primary, implicit, indirect, etc.) is a complex one and has been a source of confusion in the literature. It is often suggested or implied that Austin was primarily or even solely concerned with explicit performatives, but one only has to read Austin's book to see that this is not the case (cf. Silverstein 1979, Lee 1997, Agha 2007).[2] Austin argued, for good reason, that explicit performatives must have developed as later elaborations of primary ones – to meet the needs of explicitness and precision required by particular contexts (e.g., courtrooms, weddings, or christenings). Primary performatives obviously constitute the bulk of what we see in ordinary interaction and are of central concern to us in this chapter. Let us reiterate that explicit vs. primary as a dimension of contrast is distinct from that of purposive action vs. effect.

The matter of explicitness is clearly more complicated than Austin imagined. A speaker's use of an explicit performative formula such as "I $V_{performative}$ (you) (that) X" does not guarantee that the speaker is in fact doing the action so named. Consider for instance "I promise you'll regret that" which is more likely to be a warning or a threat than a promise. Or consider passengers in an airport being asked (i.e., requested, and certainly not "invited") to board the plane at another gate with "Passengers are invited to proceed to Gate 63 to board the aircraft," and so on. Indeed Garfinkel and Sacks (1970; see also Sacks 1995) noted that in naming or describing what one is doing one seems to be necessarily committed to doing something else either in addition or as an alternative.

17.2.3 Real-time constitution vs. ex post facto (i.e., retroactive) formulation

A final key distinction is between the actual constitution of action in interaction (and its real-time ascription by other participants) versus ex post facto or retroactive formulation or reconstruction of a piece of behavior as having been such-and-such an action (see the passage from Austin above). Much of the literature has been concerned with speech-act labels in their retroactive use to report or describe the illocutionary force of what was done, though unfortunately this has not always been made explicit. Native metalinguistic vocabulary is a form of categorization,[3] and as such it frequently involves collapsing into a single type (e.g., "asking") actions that are conceptually distinct. The retroactive formulation of an action can be done at various degrees of distance from the target object, including in next turn ("Are you asking me or telling me?" – see Sidnell 2012), in third position ("No, I was *asking* you," "But I *say* it's really great the two of you"; see discussion of example [7] below, and Sidnell, this volume, Chapter 15) and in still more distal positions as is common in various forms of reported speech ("He *told* me that X").

Metalinguistic vocabulary is clearly necessary for retroactive formulation (and note that this vocabulary can include both familiar vernacular and invented technical terms, both general and specific), though there is no evidence that such a vocabulary necessarily has consequences for the real-time constitution of action. Yet nearly all scholarship in this area has either tacitly assumed or explicitly proposed that the real-time constitution of action is organized in relation to a set of categories more or less isomorphic with the metalinguistic vocabulary of English, and perhaps other languages (cf. Wierzbicka 1987, 2003). It is not difficult to see how this has come about given not only the powerful effects of referential projection of the kind described by Anscombe (1957, 1958, who defined intention as "action under a description"), Silverstein (1979), and Rumsey (1990), but also the pervasive use of metalinguistic vocabulary by participants in interaction itself to retrospectively formulate action (e.g., "She was *complaining* about it," "He *told* me this," "She *suggested* it").

17.3 Components and types of action in interaction

With these preliminaries out of the way, we now consider two questions that have been addressed in previous literature: (1) What are actions made up of? (2) What types of actions are there, and how many?

17.3.1 Distinguishing components of an action

The first sustained attempt to analyze action rather than merely classify it was made in Austin's *How To Do Things With Words*. Austin's goal was to understand just what social action consists of. He proposed that an action could be decomposed into multiple components, including a locutionary act (itself decomposable into phonetic, phatic, and rhetic acts), an illocutionary act, and perlocutionary effects (for elaboration see Enfield 2013: 91ff.). This scheme was later updated by Clark (1996). While Austin's scheme was stated in terms of the behavior of the one who instigates the action, Clark adjusted the scheme so as to include the corresponding role of an addressee at every level. Thus, the phonetic act not only involves "uttering certain noises," as Austin put it, but has the essential counterpart of an addressee "perceiving certain noises"; and so on for the other levels (see Clark 1996 and Enfield 2013: ch. 8 for further elaboration).

The Austin/Clark "ladder of action" is not a taxonomy of action types. Rather it takes an action and prizes apart the different "layers" that make it up. In this way, Austin showed, we can take the action of saying "You can't do that" and separate it out into a phonetic act (He produced this noise: [juː kʰaːnt du ðæt]), a phatic act (He said these words: "you," "can't," "do," and "that"), a rhetic act (He said, "You can't do that"), a locutionary act (He said to me "You can't do that"; i.e., the phonetic, phatic, and rhetic acts, taken together), an illocutionary act (He protested against my doing it), and a perlocutionary act (He stopped me doing it). The perlocutionary "act" might also be described in another way, not in terms of what he did, but what the outcome was: i.e., the perlocutionary effect of his action was that I stopped doing it.[4]

Table 17.1 Some practice–action mappings (drawn from Schegloff 1996; see other references there; this figure adapted from Enfield 2013: 96)

Sample practice	Example	Possible action	Possible appropriate perlocutionary effects
negative observation	*You didn't get an ice cream sandwich*	COMPLAINT	give reason; resist
positive evaluation of feature of interlocutor or just-prior conduct	*You look good in that shirt*	COMPLIMENT	say "Thank you"; self-deprecate
tell of own limited access	*Your line's been busy*	SOLICIT ACCOUNT	provide account

Another way of prizing apart the components of an action is seen in a distinction widely made in conversation analysis between "practices" and "actions" (Schegloff 1996, 1997, Sidnell 2010a). Sidnell (2010a: 61) defines practices as "relatively stable features which recur across a wide range of utterance types and actions." Actions are the social outcomes that these practices effect, in context. So, practices are tools for carrying out actions. They are devices for getting people to understand the goal behind a piece of communicative behavior. See Table 17.1.

While practices and actions are conceptually distinct from each other, one approach is to view them as fused. This can be referred to as a "practions" approach (Enfield 2013: 100; see Schegloff 1996, 1997; Robinson 2007), where praction is defined as "a pairing of a defined practice or defined combination of practices with a defined action that these practices conventionally bring about" (Enfield 2013: 100). This approach has been developed by Sacks, Schegloff, Jefferson, and their colleagues in conversation analysis – though note that much conversation-analytic work is not practions-based; thus, for example, in research by Drew and colleagues, the researcher may look at a single action type such as "request" or "offer" and ask what are the different practices that can be used for carrying it out.

Unlike the other major perspectives discussed here, praction-based approaches begin with the data of recorded interaction, attempting to locate within it recurrent practices of speaking and the actions that they bring off. Beginning with such recordings encourages thinking in terms of tokens rather than types, giving direct access to the practices, which are identifiable by looking across a range of unique cases. As a result, in addition to the familiar and vernacularly labeled actions such as requesting, complaining, inviting, and so on, those working within this tradition have identified a range of previously undescribed, and indeed previously unknown, action types such as "confirming allusions" (Schegloff 1996), "my-side telling" (Pomerantz 1980), "possible pre-closing" (Schegloff and

Sacks 1973), among others. Many of these action types are defined in technical terms, and members of a society apparently have no conscious or explicit awareness of them (though of course they carry out and interpret them with ease). For example, when a speaker says "We:ll" at a point that could be the end of talk on a topic, that speaker can be heard as doing a "pre-closing," that is, proposing to begin the closing phase of the conversation.

In addition it has been shown that the particular practices by which an action is implemented are various, contextually specific, and, most important, consequential for how they are taken up (or not taken up) by recipients. For example, the action of making a complaint can be done by means of practices that merely project or imply the complaint (see Schegloff 2005), e.g., by producing a negatively valenced assessment (e.g., "This is disgusting"), by making a negative observation (e.g., "You didn't bring an ice-cream sandwich"; see Schegloff 1988) or by using an interrogative format (e.g., "Would you like that if she did it to you?," "Am I supposed to eat this?"). While each of these can be construed as a complaint, the different linguistic practices establish different relevancies for response (see Sidnell and Enfield 2012). They are, in this sense, different practions. This approach is the most attentive to the details of action simply because the details matter not only for what action a speaker is understood to be doing but also, within that, what relevancies are established by doing the action in some particular way. These different relevancies give rise to different perlocutionary effects and are part of what may be taken to define different actions.

As Sacks noted in his first transcribed lecture (1995), the limiting case is one in which some particular goal is accomplished without the action ever having "officially" been done. For instance, though institutional call takers can get callers to give their names by asking them directly: "What is your name?," they may also do this by merely giving their own name first, thereby making relevant a reciprocal identification by the caller with the same format.

17.3.2 Taxonomizing actions

In the last section we looked at some approaches that ask what are the components of a single action. We now turn to approaches that seek to identify the different types of action. Searle (1979, 2010) proposed a taxonomy of actions that is grounded in the set of basic human intentional states: beliefs, desires, intentions, and feelings. Searle (2010: 69 and passim) proposes an "exact analogy" between four basic speech acts and four basic intentional states or possible relations of mind to world (see Brandom, this volume, Chapter 14):

    assertives ≅ **beliefs** (judged on whether they fit the way the world is)
    directives ≅ **desires** (judged on whether the world comes to fit to them)

commissives ≅ **intentions** (judged on whether the world comes to fit to them)
expressives ≅ **emotions**

Searle begins with a basic theory of intentional states (1983), grounded in individual cognition, and derives from it a higher-level set of social/communicative actions. (In addition, Searle has a fifth type of speech act – the declarative – that is not based on a basic psychological state unless perhaps imagining; see Searle 2010.) It is a conceptual framework, and Searle does not attempt to account for any aspect of reality with it. Indeed, in a late response to Rosaldo's (1982) anthropological critique of his arguments (especially Searle 1965, 1969, 1976, 1979), he writes (2006: 26-7):

> When I published a taxonomy of the five basic types of speech acts (Searle, 1979), one anthropologist (Rosaldo, 1982) objected that in the tribe that she studied, they did not make very many promises, and, anyway, how did I think I could get away with making such a general claim on the basis of such limited data? But the answer, of course, is that I was not offering a general empirical hypothesis but a conceptual analysis. These are the possible types of speech acts given to us by the nature of human language. The fact that some tribe does not have the institution of promising is no more relevant than the fact that there are no tigers at the South Pole is relevant to a taxonomy of animal types. I am discussing the logical structure of language and getting the categorization of possible types of speech acts.

A second version of a taxonomy of speech acts begins with the lexical semantics of speech act verbs. In one sense this would seem to be closer to the work that Austin began but later elaborators have not developed the underlying conceptual account the way Austin would have presumably wanted (or the way Searle did). This account begins with the observation that all languages include a vocabulary of speech act verbs and that these have certain affordances, principal among them being that they can be used to describe what a speaker did in saying something. Moreover speech act verbs appear to be organized – within a language – into "families," such as requesting, pleading, commanding, ordering, directing, instructing, and so on (Wierzbicka 1987, 2003). There is a sense in which these various words denote variant actions within a single functional class (they are hyponyms of the technical hypernym "recruitments").

The vernacular label issue is a complex matter of categorization. If we analyzed vernacular labels for speech acts in the same way we analyzed vernacular terms for natural kinds or cultural artifacts, we'd say that they reflected the speakers' worldview. But in addition, action labels have unique affordances for action itself, and play a role in the regimentation or accountability of action, in ways that other types of categorizing words do not. The use of speech act categories, being metasemiotic as they are, should have an impact on how people behave (cf. "I'm going to complain about that").

The approach of categorizing actions by reference to vernacular labels suffers from a problem that plagued Austin, namely that it inevitably raises but seems unable to answer the basic question of the relationship between descriptions of action and action itself. In fact, most of the research in this area (e.g., in conversation analysis) either overlooks or denies the fact that vernacular speech act terms carry conceptual baggage from the historical culture from which they are derived (cf. Wierzbicka 1987, 2006, 2010, 2014, on English). We need, then, to distinguish between ideology (as enshrined in vocabulary) – i.e., the set of actions "we" think we have and think "we" do – and practice (as observed in utterances), i.e., the actions we actually do, and are treated as having done by our recipients. Note that there are occasions on which actions indeed get named in the course of doing them (e.g., saying "You're not supposed to *agree* with him," which explicitly describes a token utterance as a speech act of "agreeing"; see Schegloff 1992, Sidnell, this volume, Chapter 15). Participants in interaction sometimes say, in so many words, what they were doing in speaking the way they do, and in so saying they may be justifying, explaining, or holding others to account for, what was done. The resources for doing this vary from language to language.

17.4 An alternative account: a generative view of action

The two questions discussed in the last section – what are the components of an action, and what types of action, if any, are there – relate directly to the hearer's problem of figuring out what a speaker is trying to do by saying something. Our focus here is on the problem that faces any addressee of an utterance: What is the speaker of this utterance doing, or trying to do? How should I react? We are going to argue here that a hearer does not need to *classify an action as being of a certain type* in order to know how to deal with it. A hearer uses the components of a move to figure out on the fly an appropriate response to a particular token move. It may happen that certain token actions share features with many others, and so are readily interpreted by means of heuristics that have been successfully applied before (Schelling 1960, Gigerenzer et al. 2011, among others). But note that such heuristic-based shortcuts do not entail that type-level categorization is being done. Actions can be dealt with at the token level, and need not be seen as tokens *of action types* at all. We want to say that the taxonomy of action types is fundamentally metasemiotic in nature. It is primarily an analyst's construct.[5] An extreme version of our claim is that there are no actions, only the parts of actions. To be able to analyze interaction using action category labels is a descriptive convenience, not a veridical claim.

Our account therefore contrasts with those which suggest that for participants to ascribe an action to another person's talk, they must take a particular bit of conduct (e.g., the utterance "That's a really nice jacket") and assign it to some particular action type or category – e.g., "compliment." This is what we describe as a *binning* approach, by which the central problem is taken to involve recipients of talk (or other participants) sorting the stream of interactional conduct into the appropriate categories or bins. The mental operation might be translated as "that's a compliment" (Levinson 2013) or "that's a possible compliment" (Schegloff 2006). These accounts appear to involve a presumption about the psychological reality of action types that is somewhat akin to the psychological reality of phonemes (Sapir 1933; see also Dresher 1995). That is, for the binning account to be correct, there must be an inventory of actions just as there is a set of phonemes in a language.[6] Each token bit of conduct would be put into an appropriate pre-existing action-type category. The binning approach thus also suggests that it would be reasonable to ask how many actions there are. But we think that to ask how many actions there are is more like asking how many *sentences* there are. Here lies the key to our account: Actions are generated out of constituent elements of context and code that we already need in order to infer utterance meanings. There is no need to add another level, at which action categorization would be done.

In the following sections we present two cases to illustrate the way interpreters can figure out how to respond appropriately to others' behavior, based exclusively on components available in the talk and bodily conduct, and without us having to categorize the move to which they respond "as action X" or equivalent.

17.4.1 A nonlinguistic example: Action construal and object transfer

Consider the difference between two commonly used action type-labels: "request" and "offer." One way of conceptualizing the difference is to distinguish in terms of who is the beneficiary: if it is a request, the one who instigates the action is the beneficiary; if it is an offer, the beneficiary is the addressee. But a problem with this is that often, we cannot know – nor, it appears, can the participants – whether one is actually a beneficiary relative to the other. Indeed, it can be argued that the answer to the question "who benefits?" is always a matter of construal anyway. What matters, instead, is *the publicly claimed construal of the behavior*. Thus, we sometimes have no doubt what the action is: "Would you mind passing me that plate?" is readily labeled as a request, while "Shall I take that plate for you?" is readily labeled as an offer. The transparency of the action in each case is a product of the fact that the publically construed (claimed) beneficiary is made explicit in the coding of the utterance ("passing *me*," "for *you*," etc.). In other cases it is hard to tell whether the action should be labeled one or the other. But in just these cases – crucially for the point we want to make here – it remains clear how one ought to react, i.e., hand the plate to the other person. Consider an example.[7] At the end of a meal Mary is clearing the plates and holds her hand out across the table toward John, whose plate is in front of him. John responds by picking up his plate and putting it in her hand. What was the action that Mary did by holding out her hand? Was it a request from Mary for John to pass the plate? Or was it an offer by Mary to take the plate from John? Our point is that whether it was a request or an offer is not an issue for the participants. John's appropriate response – and thereby his *categorization* of Mary's behavior by *treating* it as something (rather than by *describing* it as something; see footnote 2 above) – did not require him to distinguish between these two possibilities, nor to explicitly commit to a construal of "which action" (as labeled by the words *request* versus *offer*) her move was. By handing the plate to her he resolved the interpretation of what she was doing to a level that was *adequate for the situation*. No further resolution was necessary.

We argue that John is able to respond in an appropriate way purely on the basis of the components of Mary's behavior, rather than by recognizing a general action category that Mary's behavior instantiated. To see how this works, we begin by noting that in the example we are considering, Mary and John face a simple, and general – surely universal – problem: that of transferring objects between people. Locally speaking, transfer of an object – the plate – is a goal. In order to achieve that goal, the people involved have available to them various means. In this particular case Mary has employed a set of signs she can readily assume John will recognize, and she has exploited the common ground that she knows that they share. Here are some of those signs:

- she is looking at John while holding out her hand and is thereby "addressing" him
- her hand shape indexes holding the plate
- her body is oriented in a certain way
- her arm has a certain trajectory
- her behavior has a relation to prior conduct, continuation of an ongoing, recognizable activity of clearing the table.
- Mary is host, John is guest.

The most relevant interpretation of this ensemble of signs in context is that John should now pick up his plate and put it in her hand. Other interpretations are thinkable (e.g., that she is doing a bodily depiction of some behavior that happened on another occasion) but are less likely. For the participants to decide whether this was an "offer" or a "request" may go beyond the requirements of the moment. For us the analysts to decide would involve us making claims for which no evidence is available – for example, who was the beneficiary of the object transfer. That's a matter of construal, and no claim to such a construal has been made here.

Now, if Mary had said "Would you mind passing me that plate?", then we would happily say it was a request or, better yet, that she had formulated it as a request which is to say that she was, by the format of the utterance, construed as the beneficiary of the projected action. But this does not mean the addressee had to, or did, categorize it as a request. (Though note, of course, that another key measure of how it was taken could be found in a linguistic component of the response, if there was one – e.g., saying "Sure" versus "Thanks" as he passes the plate.) The proper or desired response can be calculated in the same way as we've described for the earlier, seemingly ambiguous situation. The addition of explicit linguistic wording may not be in the service of making "the action" recognizable at a specific level, but may have more to do with the potential accountability of the move being made. Had Mary said "Shall I take that plate for you?," she would be making explicit her construal of the situation in action terms; i.e., that she's doing it *for John*. This would lead us to label it – if we had to label it – as an offer. The linguistic component may, though need not, make explicit some of the defining components of action recognition, bringing us back to the on-record nature of the claim of who's benefiting.

17.4.2 A linguistic example: "pre-closing," "assertion," "complaint," or "request"?

We now move into the linguistic domain, and look at an example in which a listener is faced with the task of inferring how they are to respond on the basis of elements of a complex linguistic construction, in combination with the sequential placement of the speaker's move. Our example gives further support to the idea that a binning approach cannot account for much of the data of ordinary talk-in-interaction – i.e., it will not adequately predict how participants in fact respond. We sketch an alternative account in which participants attend to a range of components of a move – both turn-constructional and sequential features – in order to assess what a prior speaker is doing in a given utterance, and in turn, how they are to react.

In our example, sisters Lottie and Emma are talking on the telephone:

```
(1)  NB:1:6:4, 4:15
01   Lottie:    °Oh I ↓love tuh gee I ride mine all [th' ti:me.°
02   Emma:                                          [°Ye:ah.°
03   Lottie:    I love it.
04   Emma:      hhh WELL honey (.) Ah:ll (.)
05              pob'ly SEE yih one a'these da:y[s,
06   Lottie:                                   [Oh: Go:d yeah
07              [(ah wish)] But I c- I jis'[couldn' git do:wn
08   Emma:      [ ehh huh ]                 [Oh-ü
```

```
09                  ↓Oh I ↓know=
10    Emma:         =I'm not as[kin' yih tih c'm dow- ]
11    Lottie:                  [J e e : z i z  I  mean  ] I jis (0.2)
12                  I didn' have five minutes yesterday.
13    Emma:         Ah don' know how yih do i:t.
14                  (0.3)
15    Lottie:       Ah don' kno:w. nh huh
16    Emma:         You wuh: work all day tihda:y.
17                  (0.3)
18    Lottie:       Ye:ah.
19                  (0.2)
20                  Jis git well I'm (.) by myself I'm kin'a cleanin
21                  up fr'm yesterday.
```

To this point the conversation has covered a range of topics and in line 01 Lottie is talking about riding her bicycle. Then at line 04 Emma produces the turn

hhh WELL honey (.) Ah:ll (.) pob'ly SEE yih one a'these da:ys,

This utterance has several properties of interest to us here:

- It comes at the analyzable end of talk on a topic (riding bicycles)
- It is prefaced with "well"
- It does not raise a possible next topic of discussion
- It looks forward to some future occasion when the sisters will see one another (albeit in an unusual way).

All of these features of the turn mark it as what Schegloff and Sacks (1973) described as a possible "pre-closing," a first move to initiate a closing sequence. Two common types of response to such possible pre-closings are (1) to produce a matching turn that similarly passes on the opportunity to raise a next topic and thereby forwards the closing sequence, (2) to raise a next topic of conversation and thereby defer the move toward the closing sequence. Lottie does neither of these things.

We can see that Lottie responds in a way that suggests she has heard in Emma's turn a *complaint* about her. Specifically, she responds by excusing herself, explaining that she "just couldn't get down," and that "she didn't have five minutes yesterday." This occasions Emma saying, "I'm not asking you to come down" at line 10.

A binning approach would have to analyze this in terms of ambiguity. Thus, Emma's talk at line 04–05 *could* have been heard as a pre-closing, a complaint, or even a request (Emma later explicitly denies this). Lottie simply picks one possibility and responds to that: here, she takes it as a complaint. But there is no need to say that the talk is one action or the other, in terms of these labels. We think it is none of these. What we see instead is that in the details of its design, Emma's turn makes available to Lottie a set of resources for building an understanding of what she is doing.

Lottie's evidence for an understanding is drawn from Emma's specific choices of words, grammatical construction, prosody, positioning of the utterance in relation to what has come before, and so on.

Returning to Lottie's response to Emma, then, we can notice that she understands this to be something new – not apparently related to the talk about bicycles and riding. Second, she seems to respond primarily to two parts of the talk in lines 04–05 – "probably" and "one of these days." This is a recurrent position in conversation where participants routinely make plans to get together at some specific time in the future. In this context, Emma indicates uncertainty by selecting "probably" and "one of these days" in designing her turn. Both expressions – one expressing doubt that they will in fact see one another, the other making reference to a time that is insufficiently precise to allow for planning – suggest a problem. It has already been established (in earlier talk) that Emma had hoped to see Lottie and so, in this context, the talk suggests that Lottie is responsible for their not getting together. We see, then, how multiple elements of the highlighted move's formulation serve as bases for an interpreter's construction of understanding, where this understanding then provides grounds for producing a response that effectively categorizes (though, importantly, does not describe or otherwise *type*-categorize) the first move in a certain way.

Consider this example now in light of the three fundamental conceptual distinctions we made in section 17.2. The first distinction was between purposive action versus given-off effects of one's behavior. Lottie's problem at line 06 is how to respond to what Emma has said. As we have noted, various features of placement and design converge to suggest that "hhh WELL honey (.) Ah:ll (.) pob'ly SEE yih one a'these da:ys," is meant to initiate pre-closing, that being Emma's possible purpose or intention in producing the utterance. But there are obvious complications here. For one thing, we can describe Emma's purposive action at different degrees of granularity. While apparently designed to accomplish possible pre-closing, Emma's utterance is simultaneously an assertion. It asserts about a likely future state of affairs. This is available to Lottie as a possible hearing of the utterance and thus as a possible target for response. Consider then what Lottie says: "Oh: Go:d yeah." In form, at least, this constitutes *agreement* with the proposition Emma has asserted. Moreover, this provides the basis from which Lottie launches her excuse. And of course the excuse, as we have already noted, treats Emma's turn not as a possible pre-closing, not as an assertion, but rather as a complaint. This suggests, then, that a given utterance makes available various understandings of a speaker's purpose or intent and that a response, or next utterance generally, targets one or more of these, thereby treating that *as the purposive action* that that utterance was doing (see Goffman 1976). Notice in this respect that, as noted, a wide variety of compositional and positional resources may bear on what an utterance is understood to be doing.

These are the elements of a generative account. It is important to note that the components of a given utterance need not necessarily point toward a single obvious action interpretation. Rather the various features may point in different directions resulting in ambiguity and so on (for studies that deal with aspects of this see, for instance, Sidnell 2010b, 2012, Heritage 2012).

As we have argued above, it is possible and, from a methodological point of view, crucial to distinguish such purposive action from the multitude of effects that any given utterance may have. Consider, again, Emma's utterance "hhh WELL honey (.) Ah:ll (.) pob'ly SEE yih one a'these da:ys,". There are ways in which the design of the utterance in question indexes the relationship between the participants. Perhaps most obviously, by addressing Lottie as "honey," Emma claims that they are related to one another in such a way that her calling Lottie "honey" is appropriate (see Enfield 2013: chs. 5 and 10). Moreover, the phonetic production of the talk here suggests a casualness and lack of formality that is appropriate to social intimates. A more complex issue here has to do with the indexical effects of the purposive action that the speaker is understood to be engaged in (whether it be complaining, asserting, or proposing closure). To do an action presupposes that the participants stand in such a relation to one another that that action is appropriate, e.g., one tells or reports something to an addressee who is uninformed, one advises an addressee who is less expert, less knowledgeable, or less experienced, one commands an addressee who is subordinate, etc. (see Rosaldo 1982 on this point). And another set of indexical effects relates to the assertive character of the utterance – that is, Emma conveys by the use of "pob'ly" a degree of uncertainty with respect to the truth-value of the proposition asserted. And of course there are effects of a more mundane sort: In speaking here, Emma displays involvement in the ongoing activity, sustains the conversational turn-taking system in operation, suggests an understanding of the point at which this conversation has arrived, and so on.

The second distinction we made in section 17.2 contrasted explicit versus primary performatives. Explicit performatives, in which the action apparently being performed is named by a speech act verb in the first person, non-past denotational structure of the utterance itself, are rare in conversation. One view might be that the action is distinct enough, it's just that there is no available word for the action being done in "hhh WELL honey (.) Ah:ll (.) pob'ly SEE yih one a'these da:ys,".[8] Schegloff and Sacks (1973) noted that the closing of a conversation can be initiated in one of two ways. Specifically, the reason (what they describe as the "warrant") for closing can either be announced (e.g., "well that's all I wanted to say."; "I should go, the kettle's boiling") or it can be embodied by reciprocal turns at talk that pass the opportunity to raise further topics of conversation, thereby conveying – giving off rather than giving – that the participants have nothing left to say. These are not explicit and primary versions of the same action. Rather they are different actions. A possible pre-closing such as saying "We:ll" at the key moment may result in the same outcome as saying "I have to go," but it is not the same. A possible pre-closing is inexplicit about what is being done. This inexplicitness is part of what defines it as a possible pre-closing. It is not equivalent to saying "I propose we initiate the close of this conversation" (something we can safely say almost never happens) despite the fact that it is, in a certain sense, just that: a proposal to initiate closing.

And finally there is the contrast between the real-time constitution of action and the ex post facto (i.e., retroactive) formulation of action. It is obvious that actions can be named (e.g., "She praised me."), described (e.g., "She talked down to me"), indexed (e.g., "Why did you do that?"), and so on. The implications of this, are however, not well understood. In our example we can note that after Lottie responds to Emma's utterance with an excuse or explanation, Emma remarks "↓Oh I ↓know= =I'm not askin' yih tih c'm dow-". Here, then, Emma treats what Lottie has said as already known to her and thereby as constituting a recipient-design error.[9] She goes on to characterize what she was doing in negative terms, as "*not asking* you to come down" (see Schegloff 1992: 1306). In the following example from a news interview panel, the formulation is positive, with the interviewer noticing that he has violated the ground-rules of the activity by "telling" rather than "asking" (see Sidnell 2012 for further explication):

```
(2)   The_Sunday_Edition_RESERVES_6_11_05_FRAG
01    Intwe:    has got to be: lo:cal, regional, and pro[vincial.
02    Intwr:                                            [.hhhhhh
03              Indian people on reserves. (.) don't own the land
04              they live on.
05              (0.4)
06    Intwe:    That's:: [(
07    Intwr:            [it's held by the crown.
08    Intwe:    wuh-uh- well: uhm:
09    Intwr:    It's owned by the crown [an' administered by [thu::h
10    Intwe:                            [yes.               [yes.
11    Intwr:→   Here I am telling you what it (h)[i(hh)-
```

In both cases just discussed, the formulation of a prior action is done in third position, but other positions are, of course, possible. So, for instance, there are cases in which an interviewee asks, in second position, "Are you telling me or asking?" (see Heritage 2012). And of course, extra-local formulations are common for instance in reports of what happened in another interaction and so on. Thus, although the vast majority of action is produced and recognized without any such ex post facto formulation, this is nevertheless an ever-present possibility and thus must figure in a comprehensive account of action in interaction. Action ascription is accomplished, in the main, without recourse to formulation and associated taxonomies. In interaction, the question of "what a speaker is doing" does not require definitive or fine-grained resolution. Rather the matter is addressed, on the fly, with understandings that are tacit, provisional, and never needing to be more than sufficient to allow for the production of appropriate and effective response.

17.4.3 Discussion

We have argued for a generative account of action ascription which focuses on the token inferences a recipient makes based on multiple components of an utterance, and where this inferred understanding is displayed in the token response that they produce. This account is superior, we argue, to one that is based on assumptions about the category or type of action – assuming some sort of action inventory – an utterance is designed by a speaker or understood by a recipient to accomplish. We want to be clear about what this does and does not entail.

First, we are not denying that speakers engage in purposive action, indeed this is central to our account. Rather we are suggesting that such purposive action is not usefully understood in terms of categories or types which constitute an *inventory*. Instead, purposive action emerges through a token-level inferential system (which may, of course, be streamlined by the use of fast and frugal heuristics). Action "types" are available through various forms of retroactive (and sometimes proactive) formulation but are not required for orderly production and recognition of action in interaction.

Second, we are suggesting that a crucial feature of action in interaction has to do with the accountability structures to which participants hold one another. In a basic sense, to paraphrase Cavell, "we must mean what we say." A speaker will be understood to be meaning – and therefore to be doing – just what his or her words conventionally imply. A speaker cannot simply choose not to mean what he or she has said. Similarly, in producing an utterance with certain components the speaker unavoidably does something and what he or she is understood to do, and is held accountable for, will certainly bear some relationship to those components. Thus, in our example, Emma's use of "probably" and "one of these days" triggered a particular inference for Lottie, as we saw from Lottie's response. As Austin was well aware, and as later commentators elaborated, more explicit performatives are designed so as to minimize ambiguity with respect to what is being done and to specify more precisely that for which the speaker is accountable (see "I promise to be there" vs. "I'll be there").

If action is conceived in terms of categories or types, then the job of the recipient is to identify the appropriate bin into which a particular turn should be put. But with a generative approach we can begin to describe, for any particular case, the specific linguistic practices used as bases for inferences about purposive action. We have focused here on a complex case – the seemingly ambiguous "Well I'll probably see you one of these days" – and the reader might object that our account does not apply to most actions most of the time. The reader might object that all sorts of actions like "requests," "offers," "invitations," "complaints," etc. are usually directly recognizable, straightforward, clear; and thus that a binning analysis is fine. But this does not follow. Our account is more parsimonious because one can still get to the straightforward response by working up from the parts. And in any case, not many moves are straightforward in interaction. Anyone who has tried the exercise of working through a conversational transcript line-by-line and labeling each line with an action category knows that it is a hopeless task. Indeed, our approach predicts that it would be hopeless to *label the action*, yet it should be straightforward to know *what an appropriate next move would be*. As we have stressed, these two things are not the same. Interactants are far from hopeless in knowing how to respond. Our point is that they can know how to respond quite reliably by working up from turn components and finding a token solution, and not by having to assign the whole turn to an action category.

Now, finally, think about this from the producer's point of view. In order to select the right elements in formulating a move, a speaker must anticipate the effect that those elements will have on the interpretive behavior of a listener. The interpreter's task is what drives the speaker's formulation (Enfield 2009, 2013). The speaker's job is to design a turn on the basis of a set of available components: phonetic, lexical, syntactic, and other resources. Speakers select components such as words, intonation patterns, and grammatical constructions, but – crucially – they don't select actions.

17.5 Conclusion

Participants in interaction do not need to recognize action types or categories in order to respond appropriately (or inappropriately for that matter). This is the central claim that we have tried to make in this chapter. Other theories that have addressed the problem of action ascription seem to assume that this involves assigning each bit of conduct to an action type category, essentially a process of labeling. Our view is that when people are analyzing such moves in the flow of interaction they are not labeling actions but rather they are considering the details of particular turns-attalk for their relevance in deciding what to do next and how to do it. And all of their details are potentially relevant to what people are understood to be doing. Action category labels are convenient but they are, ultimately, neither necessary nor sufficient. Category labels cannot substitute for practice-based analysis of situated social action.

Notes

1. Silverstein (1987: 23) writes, "There is a contrasting functionalism that grows out of ancient concerns with rhetoric; it sees function as the purposive, goal-oriented use of speech (or equivalents) by intentional individuals in specific situations of discourse, each such usage constituting a 'speech act' or 'speech event' (terminologies differ)."
2. It is also often suggested that Austin understood action primarily in explicit or referential terms. But as the quotation above and specifically the suggestion that "saying 'I salute you' is no more describing my performance than is saying 'Salaam'" makes clear, this is simply not the case.
3. When a person describes someone's behavior using metalinguistic vocabulary such as *complain, ask, insult,* or *offer,* this is a form of categorization which involves an explicit *description* of the behavior, and thus a commitment to a conceptual construal of precisely what that behavior was (as coded in the semantics of the relevant word; "complain," etc.). As should be clear from the discussion throughout this chapter, most "action categorization" in social interaction is done by an entirely different mechanism – not by how we *describe* the behavior but by how we *treat* it (see also Enfield 2013: 88–90 and Chapter 8 passim). These are two very different ways of categorizing, yet they are not always clearly distinguished in the analysis of social action in interaction; hence the central problem we are trying to address in this chapter.
4. See Silverstein (1979) for a meta-analysis which suggests that Austin's categories are projections from the grammar of reported speech in English, i.e., the possibilities for reporting what someone did when they spoke.
5. Remembering that ordinary people, i.e., participants in interaction, can also act as "analysts," e.g., in cases of third-position repair where prior talk is analyzed as having constituted some particular action.
6. The analogy should not be overextended: obviously, inventories of phonemes differ greatly from language to language.
7. Thanks to Giovanni Rossi: We have benefited from discussion with him of examples such as these in his project on recruitments in Italian interaction (cf. Rossi 2012, in press).
8. This was the case for all sorts of actions before they were described by analysts (e.g., "confirming allusions," "my-side tellings," etc.); although a "my-side telling" could easily be vernacularly glossed as "asking," but not, of course, during the course of the turn itself.
9. The "oh" obviously does not convey that Emma has been informed by what Lottie has said – that would be inconsistent with what she goes on to say – "I know". Rather the "oh" seems akin to the "oh-prefaced responses to inquiry" or "oh-prefaced responses to assessments" that

mark what the prior has said as inapposite and requiring a shift of attention (see Heritage 1998, 2002). See Schegloff (1992: 1306): "the repair-initiating component ('Oh') is followed by an acceptance of Agnes's excuse for not visiting, the B component."

References

Agha, A. 2007. *Language and Social Relations*. Cambridge: Cambridge University Press.
Anscombe, G. E. M. 1957. *Intention*. Harvard University Press.
    1958. On Brute Facts. *Analysis* 18(3): 69–72.
Austin, J. L. 1962. *How To Do Things With Words*. Oxford: Clarendon Press.
Clark, H. H. 1996. *Using Language*. Cambridge: Cambridge University Press.
Dresher, E. 1995. There's No Reality Like Psychological Reality. *Glot International* 1(1): 7.
Enfield, N. J. 2009. *The Anatomy of Meaning: Speech, Gesture, and Composite Utterances*. Cambridge: Cambridge University Press.
    2013. *Relationship Thinking: Agency, Enchrony, and Human Sociality*. New York: Oxford University Press.
Garfinkel, H., and H. Sacks. 1970. On Formal Structures of Practical Actions. In *Theoretical Sociology: Perspectives and Developments*, ed. J. C. McKinney, and E. A. Tiryakian, 337–66. New York: Appleton-Century Crofts.
Gigerenzer, G., R. Hertwig, and T. Pachur, eds. 2011. *Heuristics: The Foundations of Adaptive Behavior*. New York: Oxford University Press.
Goffman, E. 1963. *Behavior in Public Places: Notes on the Social Organization of Gatherings*. Glencoe: The Free Press.
    1976. Replies and Responses. *Language in Society* 5(3): 257–313.
    1983. Felicity's Condition. *American Journal of Sociology* 89(1): 1–53.
Heritage, J. 1998. Oh-prefaced Responses to Inquiry. *Language in Society* 27(3): 291–334.
    2002. Oh-prefaced Responses to Assessments: A method of modifying agreement/disagreement. In *The Language of Turn and Sequence*, ed. C. E. Ford, B. A. Fox, and S. A. Thompson, 196–224. Oxford: Oxford University Press.
    2012. Epistemics in Action: Action Formation and Territories of Knowledge. *Research on Language and Social Interaction* 45: 1–29.
Jacquemet, Marco. 1994. T-offenses and Metapragmatic Attacks: Strategies of interactional dominance. *Discourse and Society* 5(3): 297–319.
Kendon, A. 1990. *Conducting Interaction: Patterns of Behavior in Focused Encounters*. Cambridge: Cambridge University Press.
Kockelman, P. 2006. Residence in the World: Affordances, Instruments, Actions, Roles, and Identities. *Semiotica* 162(1–4): 19–71.
    2013. *Agent, Person, Subject, Self: A Theory of Ontology, Interaction, and Infrastructure*. Oxford: Oxford University Press.

Lee, B 1997. *Talking Heads: Language, Metalanguage, and the Semiotics of Subjectivity*. Durham, NC: Duke University Press

Levinson, S. C. 2013. Action Formation and Ascription. In *The Handbook of Conversation Analysis*, ed. J. Sidnell and T. Stivers, 103–30. Malden, MA: Wiley-Blackwell.

In press. Speech Acts. In *Handbook of Pragmatics*, ed. Yan Huang. Oxford: Oxford University Press.

Pomerantz, A. M. 1978. Compliment Responses: Notes on the co-operation of multiple constraints. In *Studies in the Organization of Conversational Interaction*, ed. J. Schenkein, 79–112. New York: Academic Press.

1980. Telling My Side: "Limited access" as a "fishing device". *Sociological Inquiry* 50: 186–98.

Robinson, J. D. 2007. The Role of Numbers and Statistics within Conversation Analysis. *Communication Methods and Measures* 1: 65–75.

Rosaldo, M. Z. 1982. The Things We Do with Words: Ilongot Speech Acts and Speech Act Theory in Philosophy. *Language in Society* 11(2): 203–37.

Rossi, G. 2012. Bilateral and Unilateral Requests: The use of imperatives and Mi X? interrogatives in Italian. *Discourse Processes* 49(5): 426–58.

In press. When Do People Not Add Language to Their Requests? In *Requesting in Social Interaction*, ed. P. Drew and E. Couper-Kuhlen. Amsterdam: John Benjamins.

Rumsey, A. 1990. Wording, Meaning, and Linguistic Ideology. *American Anthropologist* 92(2): 346–61.

Sacks, H. 1995. *Lectures on Conversation*. Oxford: Blackwell.

Sapir, E. 1933. La Réalité Psychologique des Phonèmes. *Journal de Psychologie Normale et Pathalogique (Paris)* 30: 247–265. (English version published as 'The Psychological Reality of Phonemes', in *Selected Writings of Edward Sapir in Language, Culture and Personality*, ed. D. G. Mandelbaum, 46–60. Berkeley: University of California Press.)

Schegloff, E. A. 1968. Sequencing in Conversational Openings. *American Anthropologist* 70(6), 1075–95.

1988. Goffman and the Analysis of Conversation. In *Erving Goffman: Exploring the Interaction Order*, ed. P. Drew, and A. J. Wootton, 89–135. Cambridge: Polity Press.

1992. Repair After Next Turn: The last structurally provided defense of intersubjectivity in conversation. *American Journal of Sociology* 97(5): 1295–1345.

1996. Confirming Allusions: Toward an empirical account of action. *American Journal of Sociology* 102(1): 161–216.

1997. Practices and Actions: Boundary cases of other-initiated repair. *Discourse Processes* 23(3): 499–545.

2005. On Complainability. *Social Problems* 52(3): 449–76.

2006. On Possibles. *Discourse Studies* 8(1): 141–57.

2007. *Sequence Organization in Interaction: A Primer in Conversation Analysis*. Cambridge: Cambridge University Press.

2009. *Prolegomena to the Analysis of Action(s) in Talk-in-interaction*. Paper presented at the LISO, University of California, Santa Barbara.

Schegloff, E. A., and H. Sacks. 1973. Opening Up Closings. *Semiotica* 8: 289–327.

Schelling, Thomas C. 1960. *The Strategy of Conflict*. Cambridge, MA: Harvard University Press.

Searle, J. 1965. What is a Speech Act? In *Philosophy in America*, ed. M. Black, 221–39. London: Allen and Unwin. (Reprinted in *The Philosophy of Language*, ed. J. Searle. Oxford: Oxford University Press, 1971.)

1969. *Speech Acts*. Cambridge: Cambridge University Press.

1976. The Classification of Illocutionary Acts. *Language in Society* 5(1): 1–23.

1979. *Expression and Meaning*. Cambridge: Cambridge University Press.

1983. *Intentionality*. Cambridge: Cambridge University Press.

2006. Social Ontology: Some basic principles. *Anthropological Theory* 6: 12–29.

2010. *Making the Social World: The Structure of Human Civilization*. New York: Oxford University Press.

Sidnell, J. 2010a. *Conversation Analysis: An Introduction*. Oxford: Wiley-Blackwell.

2010b. "D'you understand that honey": Gender and Participation in Conversation. In *Conversation and Gender*, ed. E. Stokoe and S. Speer, 183–209. Cambridge: Cambridge University Press.

2012. Declaratives, Questioning, Defeasibility. *Research on Language and Social Interaction* 45(1): 53–60.

Sidnell, J., and N. J. Enfield. 2012. Language Diversity and Social Action: A third locus of linguistic relativity. *Current Anthropology* 53(3): 302–21.

Silverstein, M. 1979. Language Structure and Linguistic Ideology. In *The Elements: A Parasession on Linguistic Units and Levels*, ed. P. R. Clyne, W. F. Hanks, and C. L. Hofbauer, 193–247. Chicago: Chicago Linguistic Society.

1987. The Three Faces of "Function": Preliminaries to a psychology of language. In *Social and Functional Approaches to Language and Thought*, ed. Maya Hickmann, 17–38. Orlando, FL: Academic Press.

Wierzbicka, A. 1987. *English Speech Act Verbs: A Semantic Dictionary*. Sydney: Academic.

2003. *Cross-Cultural Pragmatics: The Semantics of Human Interaction*. Expanded 2nd ed. Berlin: Mouton de Gruyter.

2006. *English: Meaning and Culture*. New York: Oxford University Press.

2010. *Experience, Evidence, and Sense: The Hidden Cultural Legacy of English*. New York: Oxford University Press.

2014. *Imprisoned in English*. New York: Oxford University Press.

Wittgenstein, L. 1953. *Philosophical Investigations*, trans. G. E. M. Anscombe. New York: Macmillian.

18

Conversation across cultures

Mark Dingemanse and Simeon Floyd

> For ethnography, there is no richer ore than everyday conversation.
> (Moerman 1988: 18)

18.1 Introduction

Informal conversation is a practice found among speakers of every language in every culture on Earth. Or is it? Is conversation just one of many culturally variable speech genres, or is it the informal baseline on which all other genres are built? Can the same type of basic turn-taking system be observed in all languages, or does it vary analogously to the ways that grammatical systems do? Are conversational actions such as "asking questions" or "giving directives" present in every culture, or are these culture-specific categories based on English, meaning that other cultures have their own distinct categories? These questions are central not only to understanding language usage, but also to conceptualizing human sociality more generally. Larger social realities are built up from thousands and thousands of small-scale interactions, so a social scientist's need to understand these tiny moments is a bit like a physicist's need to understand subatomic particles. Given its fundamental nature, it is surprising that conversational interaction has, with a few notable exceptions, mainly been treated peripherally to other domains in linguistic anthropology. Reasons for this are complex, involving both disciplinary histories as well as changing technological constraints on the collection of corpora of audio/video data in many different linguistic and cultural contexts. This history is discussed in more detail below, but initially it is worth revisiting the origins of the modern-day study of talk in interaction with respect to our present questions about conversational practices across cultures.

In the late 1960s at UCLA the ethnographer Michael Moerman witnessed first-hand and participated in the birth of the new subdiscipline of Conversation Analysis. While the early findings of Sacks and his colleagues were exclusively based on English-language recordings, Moerman had field recordings from his work in Tai/Lue-speaking communities of Thailand, and he was curious to revisit them in light of recent observations about English. He discovered that some conversational practices were strikingly similar cross-linguistically, much more so than cultural relativists might predict. At the same time, he noted that not *everything* in the data was cross-culturally comparable, and that the knowledge that he had accumulated through long-term ethnographic fieldwork was sometimes crucial in understanding specific interactions. These experiences led Moerman to pioneer an approach that took "ethnography with its concern for context, meaning, history" and connected it with the "techniques that conversation analysis offers for locating culture *in situ*" (Moerman 1988: xi). This innovative proposal arrived to much interest, as evidenced in many reviews and in a special issue of *Research on Language and Social Interaction* with contributors from several disciplines including anthropology and conversation analysis (Hopper 1990; Heritage 1990; Mandelbaum 1990; Streeck 1990; Pomerantz 1990; Beach 1990; Moerman 1990; and other articles in the same issue). However, it was not followed by a boom in studies of conversational interaction in the languages of the world. Conversation analysis stuck mainly to English, in part due to concerns that ethnographic methods would introduce data from beyond specific transcribed interactions that could not be studied in the same way (Schegloff 1992; Sanders 1999; McHoul *et al.* 2008). Descriptive linguistics continued to make great advances in documenting the world's diversity of linguistic structures, but has had less to say about language use in interaction (though see Ochs *et al.* 1996). Linguistic anthropology has always privileged the speech situation (Hymes 1974), but many of its advances have been centered on formalized language, where cultural variation tends to be especially salient, and its most recent paradigm has focused more on macro-political concerns than micro-interactional ones (Duranti 2003).

The cross-cultural comparative study of conversation has commenced only recently, but new advances suggest that we may be poised for a period of new emphasis and discoveries in this area. In this chapter we trace the origins of this emerging field and sketch some of its preliminary findings, and we assemble a set of tools and best practices from across different disciplines. We aim to aid students of language and culture in pursuing a new paradigm of ethnographic, cross-cultural, field-based studies of social interaction. The central puzzle of this chapter is: how is conversation structured, to what extent do its structures vary culturally and across various languages – and which interdisciplinary methods can contribute to resolving these questions?

18.1.1 Defining "conversation" and "culture"

Conversation is sometimes seen as a speech genre, to be contrasted with other genres such as political oratory or narrative. Here, however, we use it as a technical term to foreground a focus not on genre or text type but on the technical details of talk-in-interaction concerning a set of generic organizational problems that have to be dealt with in any occasion of social interaction: how to organize turn-taking between participants; how to work out the relations between successive turns at talk; how to deal with interactional trouble; how to compose turns out of smaller elements; and how to structure an occasion of interaction (Schegloff 2006).

Many specialized types or genres of interaction feature predetermined solutions to some or all of these problems – for instance, the explicit turn allocation procedures in court hearings, the restrictions on answers in a game of Twenty Questions, the duration of a prison visit, or the rules for interaction with spirits in a divination session. However, no society is known where social interaction happens exclusively in such predetermined ways. Instead, people across the globe dedicate substantial amounts of time to more informal spates of social interaction. It is here that we may expect to find generic, self-organizing (as opposed to specific, pre-determined) solutions to the organizational problems of social interaction. If our goal is to compare the technical organization of talk, here we may find a promising baseline for cross-cultural comparison, since the more specific formalized restrictions there are on an interaction, the less comparable it becomes. With this goal in mind, we define conversation as *maximally informal social interaction*. While not forgetting that even the most informal conversations can be studied with respect to formalized practices reflecting, for example, social asymmetries between interlocutors, the sense in which we use the term "conversation" foregrounds close attention to the organizational practices of conversational sequences. This perspective takes seriously the fact that conversation constitutes one of the most common – perhaps *the* most common – forms of language use, and is also an important medium for language acquisition and socialization (Schieffelin and Ochs 1986; Goodwin and Heritage 1990; cf. this volume, Chapters 8 and 16).

If we are interested in comparing structures of conversation cross-culturally, then we also must clarify what constitutes cross-cultural comparison. It was once common in anthropology to speak of "cultures" in the plural, but critiques of the culture concept (e.g., Abu-Lughod 1991) have problematized any simple way of talking about discrete, bounded cultural groups. Our use of the term *culture* is informed by these critiques, but instead of avoiding the word we attempt to use it in a more sensitive way.[1] The idea of cultural difference we invoke here should be understood as complex and partial, and when we advocate comparing video corpora from different cultures we really mean comparing samples recorded in particular communities at particular times, assuming that this data is representative *at some tractable level* of a larger social group. But the main reason we advocate cross-cultural studies of conversational interaction is straightforward: besides a few notable exceptions, historically the study of conversation has been dominated by work on English, and while findings on English are usually not explicitly framed as representative of all cultures, this is sometimes the implication. While this ethnocentrism is more pragmatic than dogmatic, it is still problematic, and we are hesitant to accept any of these findings as more than particularities of English speakers until similar topics have been studied cross-culturally.[2]

18.1.2 A piece of data

Informal talk can be studied across different human societies: it can be inspected for how it helps construct distinct linguistic and cultural worlds and for how it may itself be subject to linguistic and cultural inflection. Any stretch of conversation shows that participants rely on a combination of interactional, linguistic, and cultural competencies to bring off even seemingly simple sequences (Keating and Egbert 2004). Consider the following extract of everyday conversation in Siwu, a Niger-Congo language spoken in Ghana. Kofi, Aku, and some others are chatting while shelling corn by hand. Kofi launches a story about something he saw the other day.

Extract 1. Siwu (Ghana) [Neighbours_1958690][3,4]

1	Kofi	*Éi! (0.7) Ŋgɔngbe to ɔ-nyagɛ̃ kɔmakadeɔ.*
		INTJ REL.CM-this PROG SCR-contort yesterday 3SG.TP
		'Hey! (0.7) This one, she was behaving strangely yesterday.'
2	Aku	*ǹna ɔ́ de?*
		who 3SG be?
		'Who's that?'
3	Kofi	*Ɔbuafo Yawa:*
		PSN PSN
		'Obuafo Yawa:'
4	Aku	*sɔ be?* ((shifts gaze towards Kofi))
		QT what
		'What?'
5	Kofi	((3.7s: shakes upper torso and head from side to side, eyes closed; see Figure 18.1))
6		*kaɔ̀. (0.2) kpaìtiri. (0.3) [Adom i̠]yo.*
		ING-SR leave forum PSN house
		'She. (0.2) went from the forum. (0.3) to Adom's House.'
7	Aku	[*kùyɔ-*] *kùyɔ ɔ́-kpese ku-ba:?*
		spirit spirit SR-return it-come
		'The spirit – the spirit came back?'

8	Kofi	Àdom iyo-Àdom ɔre iyo kàmá-ba ma-tere-gu ũ ma-kɛ̀lɛ̀-gu kɔ̀makade.
PSN house PSN wife house ING 3PL-come 3PL-run-COM her 3PL-go-COM yesterday
'To Adom's House – Adom's wife's house, she was dragged yesterday.'
9	Aku	[Yes.]
'Yes.'
10	Beatrice	[ɔ́-sɛ ɔ-]kpa koko:?
3SG-HAB 3SG-possess before
'She's been possessed before?'
11	Aku	igɔgɔ́ ama.
year last
'Last year.'

Kofi starts a telling with an attention-calling *hey!* and a story preface. After clarifying the identity of the protagonist, Aku asks what happened (line 4). Kofi responds with a communicative move that contains no speech: he closes his eyes and shakes his upper torso and head from side to side (line 5, and see Figure 18.1). All present turn towards Kofi to look at this demonstration. In overlap with a verbal increment by Kofi (line 6), Aku presents a candidate understanding of his non-verbal enactment: "The spirit – the spirit came back?" (line 7). Kofi confirms this by continuing his description: she was being "dragged around" by the spirit yesterday. In overlap with a news receipt by Aku, Beatrice asks whether this person has been possessed before (line 10), which Aku confirms.

Various structural features of this sequence are readily recognizable as having equivalents in many languages. Examples are the story preface in line 1 with its typical "promise of interestingness" (Sacks 1992); the other-initiated repair sequence in lines 2–4 (Schegloff *et al.* 1977); the brief violation of the turn-taking norms in line 7a in the form of an overlap occurring at a place where speaker transition could have occurred (Sacks

Figure 18.1 Depiction of Kofi's movements in line 5 from Extract 1 (two stills superimposed)

et al. 1974); the quick resolution of this overlap by means of a cut-off and restart in the same line (Schegloff 2000); the candidate understanding in line 7b, which serves the progressivity of the sequence by advancing the telling (Antaki 2012); the self-repair by means of a cut-off in line 8, which recycles some just-said material and inserts some new material (Schegloff 2013); the use of a question and directional gaze in line 4 to select a next speaker (Lerner 2003); the way questions and responses form adjacency pairs in lines 2–3, 4–5, and 10–11 (Schegloff 1968; Enfield *et al.* 2010); and the structural organization of the larger sequence itself, with basic adjacency pairs like the question–answer sequences, but also the more specific pre-telling and its go-ahead response in lines 1 and 4, and the insert sequence of other-initiated repair in lines 2–3 (Schegloff 2007).

At the same time, these routinely produced conversational structures cannot be understood without reference to cultural knowledge. When Kofi starts his story in line 1, his noticing of someone's strange behavior achieves its relevance in relation to the others' understanding of what their world is normally like (Moerman 1988). The way the underspecified person reference is spelled out in line 3 presupposes knowledge of the available formats for person reference and their relative ordering in this society and for these participants (Sidnell 2005; Levinson 2007). Aku's interpretation of Kofi's wordless depiction in line 5 (Figure 18.1), and her treatment of it as a satisfactory answer to her question, crucially depends on knowing local cultural models of spirit possession (Field 1969; Cohen 2008). The places referred to by Kofi in lines 6 and 8 gain their significance from the fact that they are important landmarks in the village: the forum is the main public space, accounting for where and why Kofi saw the reported events, and Adom's House is the former residence of a well-known clan elder. The self-repair that corrects "Adom's House" to "Adom's *Wife's* House" in line 8 reflects the history of Adom's high-profile conversion to Christianity and divorce and move away from his influential priestess wife, who stayed in their old residence – highlighting the deep connections that some places can have to traditional ritual and religion (Smith 1992). In line 10, Beatrice's question whether this has happened to this person before draws attention to the out-of-the-ordinary nature of possession and the notion that such things do not happen to just everyone (Stoller 1989). And so on; these readings can be multiplied for all kinds of background understandings that come into play and help the interaction come off smoothly.

This extract therefore brings to the surface many of the issues that render conversation such a rich source for ethnography and ethnography an indispensable tool for understanding conversation across cultures. It is unclear how conversation-analytic methods would be able to entirely make sense of what is going on here without access to additional ethnographic information. What combination of deep cultural common ground, presupposed understandings, and interactional norms allow the participants in this interaction to bring off this seemingly simple sequence of communicative moves? How can the kind of ethnographic information generated by long-term participation in a society be used to complement the information that can be discovered in the transcribed instance itself, while still staying true to the intrinsic and emergent nature of the orderliness of a particular instance?

The only way to face the challenges posed by these questions is for researchers to combine anthropology's methods of long-term research participating in a community with recording and transcribing sequential data from the same community.[5] The importance of bringing ethnographic understandings to the table has not been widely appreciated in conversation analysis. One reason for this is that the majority of studies have focused on English and a few other major languages in urban settings with official status and writing systems (German, Finnish, Japanese, etc.), and have been carried out by native members of these societies (Schegloff 2005) who are able to rely on their own assumptions – and those of their readers – for providing cultural context (Moerman 1996).[6] In contrast to this small subset of well-studied languages, the greater part of the world's linguistic diversity is represented by small-scale, unwritten languages, often spoken in remote places (Nettle 1998), If languages like these are excluded from comparison, the possibilities of documenting diversity or making cross-cultural generalizations are seriously compromised. Such languages have historically been the focus of cross-linguistic grammatical typology, but rarely have they been compared in terms of interactive structures and practices in a complementary typology of language usage. Anthropological linguistic fieldworkers have an important role to play in the development of such a paradigm because their ethnographic methods are a key component that can help make recordings of specific instances in possibly unfamiliar societies penetrable to analysis in the first place.

18.2 Tools and their affordances

While trusted field-notes-based methods continue to be central to linguistic and anthropological field research, fieldworkers have also been quick to adopt new recording technologies, and replacing earlier unwieldy and poor-quality options with high-quality portable video recording has opened up a world of millisecond timings and multimodal practices that were difficult to approach through earlier methods. There is no special insight inherent in the technology itself, but the ability to catch fleeting moments for repeated close observation has introduced new kinds of data and new questions to the field, and the emergence of new areas of interaction research is intertwined with these technological developments. Today a researcher interested in conversation who refuses to use video might be seen as similar to an astronomer turning down a telescope. This section traces a few historical developments leading up to the present paradigm in which the video camera has become a standard fieldwork tool.

18.2.1 Early video analysis

As far back as the early twentieth century Franz Boas was using film and wax cylinders to document elements of native North American culture (Ruby 1980),[7] but in a "salvage anthropology" framework focused more on formalized events than mundane interactions. Boas's contemporary and gesture studies pioneer David Efron supplemented his notebook sketches of body behavior by experimenting with slow-motion film (Efron 1941: 66–7), now a basic method in multimodal analysis. Margaret Mead and Gregory Bateson also used film in the 1940s and 1950s for cross-cultural study of bodily practices, as seen in their film *Bathing Babies in Three Cultures* (Bateson and Mead 1951; see Figure 18.2), which compared the behavior of New Guinean, Balinese, and American parents by looking at similar mundane daily moments in each context (Jacknis 1988).

There were other early applications of film beyond the American anthropological tradition, but these ethnographically minded precursors are particularly relevant for current linguistic anthropological approaches to bodily behavior because they emphasized its cultural basis rather than its psychological or physiological aspects. In later decades the relationship between culture and body behavior was approached in a number of ways, including Edward Hall's program of "proxemics," which looked at cultural differences in the management of physical space (Hall 1963), and Ray Birdwhistell's approach to motor behavior, called "kinesics" (Birdwhistell 1952; cf. Davis 2001), which was applied cross-culturally in studies like that shown in the film *Microcultural Incidents in Ten Zoos* (1969), contrasting the bodily behavior during visits to the zoo of families from ten different cultural backgrounds. Other trajectories of research have had great influence on current uses of video as a part of field methodology, notably in early work of Adam Kendon, who used film to study greeting sequences at a North American social event (Kendon 1990), and in the paradigm of human ethology as seen in the work of Eibl-Eibesfeldt (1979; 1989), in which observational methods are similar to those applied to non-human animals. Spurred on by the increasing accessibility of video equipment, modern gesture and multimodality studies have developed in dozens of different directions that we cannot review here, but two important questions for researchers of conversation across cultures arise out of this history of close analysis of video data: (1) In what ways is cultural specificity and variation manifest in bodily behavior? and (2) What are the implications of the cultural elements of bodily behavior for the paradigm

Figure 18.2 Household settings in which Mead and Bateson used film to compare body behavior across cultures; they compared bathing practices to families in Bali (pictured here) to those seen in New Guinea and the Midwestern USA. Photo by Gregory Bateson, April 30, 1937. Mead-Bateson collection item 204e, Manuscript Division, Library of Congress.

of sequential, interactional analysis? The next section gives some background on the latter.

18.2.2 Talk in interaction: From audio to video data

While the use of video recording methodology was developing on one side, the study of talk in interaction had a different trajectory, linked to a 1960s break-away movement in sociology influenced by Garfinkel's ethnomethodology (Garfinkel 1967; 2002; Heritage 1984). Ethnomethodologically minded sociologists argued, contrary to the traditional approach of quantitatively analyzing large data sets based mainly on a priori categories, that the social order is best studied as it emerges through interactions among members of a society. This perspective led Harvey Sacks and his colleagues to create a paradigm for analyzing the minute details of social interactions that has over the years developed into the field of Conversation Analysis (CA) (Schegloff 1968; Sudnow 1972; Sacks et al. 1974; Sacks 1992; Sidnell 2010, among many other sources).

While some early CA work addressed bodily behavior in interaction (e.g., Schegloff's work on gesture [1984] and body torque [1998], among other studies), due to the ease of recording over the phone, practitioners initially focused to a large extent on telephone interaction, leading to classic work on phone-based practices like call openings (e.g., Schegloff 1968; see discussions in Luke and Pavlidou 2002). This audio-only approach was also sometimes used when participants were co-present, leading to the transcription of conversational sequences with attention to elements like turn-taking, pauses, and overlap at an unprecedented level of detail. Today conversation analysts have embraced video data and study all kinds of visual bodily behavior like gesture (Streeck 1993; Mondada 2007) and gaze (Egbert 1996; Kidwell 2005; Rossano *et al.* 2009) as part of sequential conversational structure (Stivers and Sidnell 2005; Enfield 2009). However, because of CA's historical focus on English and a handful of other languages, its methods are only just beginning to be applied cross-culturally in the way that early anthropological studies of bodily behavior were. Armed not with wax cylinders and cassette recorders but with portable high-definition video cameras, researchers in future paradigms of multimodal interaction analysis are set to enrich CA through confronting the linguistic and cultural diversity emphasized by comparative ethnographic approaches, while providing ethnographically minded fieldworkers with a whole range of tools for sequential analysis to be tried out and adapted to diverse sociolinguistic settings.

18.2.3 Everyday conversation in ethnographic approaches to language

Through the 1960s, 1970s, and 1980s, while much of mainstream linguistics was studying decontextualized English sentences, linguistic anthropology continued to emphasize cultural diversity and social context through paradigms like "the Ethnography of Speaking" (or later, "The Ethnography of Communication") (Hymes 1962; 1974; Gumperz and Hymes 1964; Bauman and Sherzer 1974; 1975). This explicitly relativistic approach was based on "the understanding that speaking, like other systems of cultural behavior – kinship, politics, economics, religion, or any other – is patterned within each society in culture-specific, cross-culturally variable ways" (Bauman and Sherzer 1975: 98). Many studies in this framework focused on the "poetic function" of language (Jakobson 1960), studying formalized speech genres in which cultural variation was salient, like Sherzer's *Kuna Ways of Speaking* (1983), which comprehensively describes verbal art genres like ritual curing songs and language games, but discusses everyday conversation in less detail.[8] Like conversation analysts, verbal art researchers developed specialized transcription systems (Tedlock 1983; Sammons and Sherzer 2000), but oriented around ethnopoetic questions rather than questions of turn-taking and sequence organization in the technical sense. There has certainly been some discussion of everyday conversation in this framework, but, oddly, ethnographers of communication may have historically generated more empirical information about formalized speech genres around the world than about mundane, informal conversation (cf. this volume, Chapters 19 and 20).

While linguistic anthropology has moved in many new directions since the early days of the ethnography of communication,[9] its basic concern with linguistic and cultural particularity remains part of the subdiscipline. If this focus on linguistic and cultural diversity is combined with the approach of conversation analysis, which like mainstream linguistics focused mostly on English and a few other languages during the second half of the twentieth century, a whole set of unaddressed questions arises about the cross-cultural scope of previous findings. What we suggest, and what Michael Moerman advocated decades ago when he wondered whether the turn-taking system of Tai-Lue speakers in Thailand resembled that of American English speakers (Moerman 1977, 1988), is the further development of ethnographically informed, cross-linguistic methods in conversation analysis (which some researchers are already developing; see Sidnell 2006; 2007; 2009 and references therein). This "Ethnography of Communication 2.0," while not necessarily abandoning topics like poetics (which can also be addressed with CA methods; see Jefferson 1996), would take up an array of new and unresolved questions about cultural diversity in interactive practices and sequential structures of conversation.

18.2.4 Conversational actions cross-culturally

One of the first problems that any program for the cross-cultural study of interaction must confront is the issue of the cross-cultural equivalence of actions like those discussed in terms of "speech acts" (Austin 1962; Searle 1969) or in terms of "conversational actions" (Levinson 2013). Are actions like "requesting" or "promising" things speakers of English do with words? Or should we expect to see versions of these kinds of actions among speakers of different languages all over the world?

Some studies have applied speech act categories cross-linguistically, like those that looked at speech acts like "apologies" in languages as different as Arabic, Persian, Korean, Chinese, Japanese, and Akan.[10] Much of the work in this area falls into the paradigm called "cross cultural pragmatics" (Blum-Kulka et al. 1989).[11] Most of these studies were based on interviews, surveys, and discourse completion exercises rather than on the sequential analysis of records of conversational data. A few studies have applied sequential analysis to similar questions, as in Beach and Lindstrom's (1992) comparison of acknowledgment tokens in conversational recordings of Swedish and American English, and Sidnell and Enfield's (2012) study of agreement sequences in Caribbean English Creole, Finnish, and Lao.

Ethnographic looks at local metalinguistic knowledge can offer interesting takes on the problem of cross-linguistic action types, as in a study by Edwards on insults in Guyanese creole (Edwards 1979), in which he treats "insults" as a cross-linguistic category, but then describes how Guyanese insults are locally split into two named sub-types of insult that might not be translatable into other languages. Anthropologist Michelle Rosaldo critiqued speech act theory in a discussion of Ilongot speech acts (1982) where she argued that the taxonomy of speech acts proposed by Searle (1969) was not cross-linguistically transferable; Searle (2006) later responded that she had misunderstood, arguing that his universal categories need not be found in every culture to be valid. It is increasingly obvious that the best way to settle these kinds of debates and make progress with these questions is to empirically study comparable data sets of social interaction in different languages and societies. In contrast to the elicited and mostly written data considered by many studies in cross-cultural pragmatics, however, observing conversational actions in interaction requires conversation-analytic tools to approach the sequential contexts in which they occur (cf. this volume, Chapter 17).

18.3 Conversational structures

The above sections highlight some of the challenges raised by the prospect of cross-linguistically comparative interaction studies, as well as the diverse approaches developed across the social sciences to meet these challenges. A way for researchers to begin to solve these kinds of problems is by building corpora of social interaction that can offer both qualitative and quantitative ways for comparing interactional practices of different peoples around the world, making possible a level of empirical research on natural speech practices that controlled speaking exercises and impressionistic observation cannot equal.

Some work is already heading in this direction. In the following sections we highlight three domains of conversational structure in which there has been some comparative research. From the basic mechanisms of turn-taking and timing we move to the achievement of mutual understanding through other-initiated repair, and from there we branch off into the semiotics of visible behavior. The goals are, first, to show the kinds of structures brought to light by comparative analysis of rich records of conversation, and second, to highlight some of the more salient methodological points from this literature. It will become clear that any researcher with a comparable conversational corpus can ask the same questions asked in these studies to get an idea of how the language they study compares to others – or they can pose new questions and seek collaborators with similar corpora to generate new comparisons.

18.3.1 Turn-taking

A basic structural fact about social interaction is that speakers change and that turns at talk follow each other, forming conversational sequences. Some basic features of turn-taking include a normative rule that one party speaks at a time, as well as principles of turn construction, speaker selection, and turn transition (Sacks *et al.* 1974). Strongly similar turn-taking practices have been found wherever people have looked (Moerman 1977, 1988; Hopper *et al.* 1990; Lerner and Takagi 1999; Zimmerman 1999; Sidnell 2001; Stivers *et al.* 2009). So far, claims of deviance from these systematics have not held up to empirical investigation of recorded interactions. For instance, Reisman claimed that conversations in Caribbean Creole English were "contrapuntal" and "anarchic," in direct opposition to the one-speaker-at-a-time rule proposed by Sacks and colleagues (Reisman 1974: 113). If true, this would imply a turn-taking system that is structured very differently from the one outlined by Sacks *et al.* (1974). Sidnell (2001) investigated tape-recorded multi-party conversations in a Caribbean English Creole carefully matched to the variety described by Reisman, and showed that these conversations are in fact orderly and that participants do monitor talk in progress to determine possible turn completion points, suggesting that the turn-taking aspects of informal conversation "are not open to a great deal of cultural diversification" (2001: 1287).

Recent comparative work provides evidence for a combination of strong similarities with measurable cultural variation. In a study of ten languages of varied type, geographical location, and cultural setting, Stivers *et al.* (2009) found strong commonalities in turn-taking behavior. Timing the response offsets in yes/no question–response sequences, they found that all languages showed a similar distribution of response offsets, with the highest number of transitions occurring between 0 and 200 milliseconds. They concluded that the distribution in the ten languages "reflects a target of minimal overlap and minimal gap between turns" (Stivers *et al.* 2009: 10589). At the same time, they documented measurable cultural differences in the mean response across languages. Danish has the slowest average response time (469ms), while Japanese had the fastest (7ms). Are differences like these perhaps the grounds for earlier ethnographic reports of cultural variability? As Stivers *et al.* point out, the Danish finding is in line with field reports for Scandinavian languages, which state that there can be long silences between turns (Lehtonen and Sajavaara 1985; as cited in Stivers *et al.* 2009). On the other hand, the very fast response times for Japanese are not in line with ethnographic reports, which generally emphasize the value placed on silence in Japanese conversation (Gudykunst and Nishida 1994; as cited in Stivers *et al.* 2009). This shows the importance of a continuous interaction of theory and empirical work in this field.

Comparative research in the domain of turn-taking provides us with a number of ingredients for our toolkit of cross-linguistically comparative studies of social interaction. The work on turn-taking remains one of the strongest demonstrations that conversation exhibits order, and that this order can be discovered and described on the basis of records of conversation. Even though original description of the organization of turn-taking was based on English, subsequent research has shown that it is a system with a strong claim to cross-linguistic generality.[12] The interaction between claims based on unrecorded observations and empirical verification shows the importance of basing *comparative* claims on *comparable* materials. Conversation-analytic work provides a number of useful methodological principles here. One is the requirement that analyses be grounded in data that are available for repeated inspection, to make sure that observations can be independently checked and replicated. Another is what we will call the *natural control method*. This method rests on the insight that the sequential structure of interaction can be used as a natural control, enabling systematic comparison across linguistic-cultural settings (Zimmerman 1999:198). Stivers *et al.* (2009) used this method in their study of the timing of turn-taking across languages: rather than haphazardly measuring the timing of any kinds of turn-transitions across corpora, they selected one specific sequential environment that occurred in all of the languages studied: the transition from question to response in a question–answer sequence. To determine whether this sequential environment was representative of turn-transitions in general, as a further control, they examined turn-transitions in a corpus of Dutch conversations, and found no difference between response times after questions and non-questions (Stivers *et al.* 2009: 10588). Thus, by using sequential environment as a natural control over the data, it is possible to carry out fine-grained qualitative analysis as well as large-scale quantitative studies, and to discover both candidate universals and subtle cultural variation. The following section illustrates the natural control method by comparing three instances of another sequence type, "other-initiated repair," showing how it provides a context for comparison across three unrelated languages.

18.3.2 Repair

Wherever people communicate, we can expect to find mechanisms for repair: ways of dealing with problems of speaking, hearing, and understanding (Schegloff 2006). Early work in conversation analysis detailed the basic organization of repair in conversation (Schegloff *et al.* 1977). Distinguishing who initiates repair (self or other), who carries it out (self or other), and where it is done (same turn, transition space, or subsequent turn), this work mapped out the possibility space of repair as realized in a corpus of English conversation. A comparative study by Moerman (1977) found repair to be similarly organized in a corpus of Tai/Lue conversation. Based on this, Moerman concluded that the organization of repair is essentially generic: "Since Tai is historically unrelated to English, and since a northern Thai village is (by most standards) socioculturally quite different from America, the detailed, systemic, and massive parallels between these two corpora support a claim that the domain described by Sacks, Schegloff and Jefferson is conversation – without respect to the language, nation, class, or culture in which it occurs" (Moerman 1977: 875). At the same time, he noted that "one gets the impression of languages with quite different resources being mobilised to do the same conversational jobs" (ibid.). The study of repair in conversation thus started out in an explicitly comparative fashion, and with attention to repair as at once generic in organization and potentially locally inflected (cf. Sidnell 2007).

The striking similarity of some of the basic strategies for repair can be demonstrated using the three conversational extracts below. Taken from unrelated languages spoken on three different continents (Siwu, Niger-Congo, Ghana; Lao, Tai-Kadai, Laos; Cha'palaa, Barbacoan, Ecuador), these are examples of the repair strategy that has been called *open-class other-initiated repair* (Drew 1997): repair initiated not by self but by other, and initiated on some prior talk while leaving open what or where in the turn the problem is.

Extract 2. Siwu (Ghana) [Maize3_758330a]
1   A   *mámà sɔ ba.*
        mama QT come
        'Mama says "come"!'
2   B   *aá?*
        OIR.INTJ
        'Huh?'
3   A   *mámà sɔ ba.*
        mama QT come
        'Mama says "come"!'

Extract 3. Lao (Laos) [CONV_050815c_03.10]
1   A   *nòòj4 bòò1 mii2 sùak4 vaa3 nòòj4*
        PSN NEG have rope QPLR.INFER PSN
        'Noi, don't you have any rope, Noi?'
2   B   *haa2?*
        OIR.INTJ
        'Huh?'
3   A   *bòò1 mii2 sùak4 vaa3*
        NEG have rope QPLR.INFER
        'Don't you have any rope?'

Extract 4. Cha'palaa (Ecuador) [CHSF2012_01_20S1_1457697]
1 A ***chundenashin***
      sit-PL-POS-AFF
      '(youPL are) sitting'
2 B *aa?*
      OIR.INTJ
      'Huh?'
3 A *ñuilla kera'* ***chundenahshin***
      2PL see-SR sit-PL-POS-AFF
      'YouPL (can be clearly) seen sitting.'

All three sequences come in the same three-turn structure. This structure (in which one participant initiates repair by pointing out some trouble in a prior turn and the other solves it in the next turn) is one of those sequential environments that can be located across different corpora and therefore is a fruitful locus for comparison. Following the natural control method described above, by keeping the sequential environment constant, one can compare the different formats for initiating repair available within and across languages, and the relations between types of trouble, repair initiations, and repair solutions. The three data extracts above represent the most common sequence type for open-class other-initiated repair in Siwu, Lao, and Cha'palaa.[13] They not only share the same three-turn structure but also show similarities in the formats of repair initiation and solution. For instance, in all three, the result of the repair initiation is that some material of the first turn is repeated by A in the third turn.[14] But it is the form of the interjection that is most strikingly similar in the three languages: a monosyllable with a low front vowel, viz. *aa* in Cha'palaa, *aá* in Siwu, and *haa2* in Lao. On the face of it, this would suggest that perhaps this form is not quite a word, but "a virtually pre-lexical grunt," as Schegloff (1997: 506) characterizes the phonetically similar English *huh?* [hã]. A striking difference, however, is that the intonation of the Cha'palaa interjection is falling, whereas it is rising in Siwu and Lao. The key is that in all three languages, the intonation on the item is understood to signify *questioning* intonation.[15] Thus even though on the surface, pitch patterns differ, the more revealing generalization is that the interjections for initiating repair appear to share their pitch patterns with the interrogative prosodic systems of the languages (Dingemanse et al. 2013).

Amidst the striking similarities, this, then, is a first locus of variation: the tuning of techniques of repair to the linguistic resources of a language. This tuning has been observed at several levels of linguistic organization, and in different types of conversational repair. For instance, in the context of self-repair, Fox et al.'s (1996) comparison of English and Japanese brings to light a difference due to morphosyntax. In Japanese self-repairs, speakers are sometimes found to replace one inflectional ending of a verb with another, whereas this is not observed in English.

Fox et al. (1996) connect this to several differences in the verbal morphology of English and Japanese: the fact that Japanese verb suffixes are often full syllables (e.g., -*shi*, -*soo*) whereas in English, they often are not (e.g., -*ed* [t]/[d], -*s* [s]); the fact that Japanese verb suffixes tend to have unitary meanings, whereas English verb suffixes are more semantically complex; and the fact that Japanese verb suffixes do not agree, whereas English verb suffixes do. English verb suffixes, they conclude, "are more tightly 'bonded' to the verb than are verb endings in Japanese and hence are less available for individual replacement" (Fox et al. 1996: 203).

Another locus of variation in repair techniques has been proposed to lie in differences in social norms. In a study of gossip in Nukulaelae Tuvaluan (Austronesian, Tuvalu), Besnier says that the repair initiation technique of providing a candidate understanding is "conspicuously absent" (Besnier 1989: 324). He attributes this to a social norm in this Polynesian island community to the effect that "interactants avoid guessing what is on another person's mind" (1989: 322). Social norms of this kind have been described for other Polynesian societies too (e.g., Ochs 1984; Duranti 1988 on Samoa; Duranti 2008), and so this is potentially a significant gap. However, Besnier's discussion equivocates between describing the unavailability of candidate understandings as a fact about the Nukulaelae genre of "gossip interactions" (1989: 318, 336) and as a fact about "Nukulaelae conversation" in general (1989: 322–5). These possibilities need to be kept apart. The first would involve the claim that the use or avoidance of certain practices are among the things that can serve as markers of genres or can be constitutive of such genres. The second, stronger claim would be that the inventory of repair practices itself is modified, so that the technique of presenting a candidate understanding is wholly unavailable to Nukulaelae speakers. Besnier's data provides grounds for the first claim but not the second. The data extracts cited in his paper to demonstrate the workings of other-initiated repair do in fact contain candidate understandings: in extract 11, one speaker presents a candidate understanding *te fafa?* "a fathom?" followed by a nonverbal confirmation by the other (Besnier 1989: 324), and in extract 12, a speaker presents a person reference as a candidate understanding, glossed as "(you mean) Neli?" (Besnier 1989: 324). So it appears that the technique of presenting a candidate understanding is available in Nukulaelae conversation, but that not using this technique, or using it less frequently, may be a feature constitutive of gossip interactions. A similar but inverse situation is the use of apology-based expressions for initiating repair in English, which has been observed – in a collection of 101 cases – to occur predominantly in situations where social asymmetries are foregrounded (Robinson 2006), and only very rarely in informal social interaction.

What lessons can we draw from the cross-linguistic study of repair practices? So far, the basics of the organization of repair appear to show remarkable similarities across languages, but at the same time, cross-linguistic differences that can be linked to differences in linguistic resources; and there have been suggestive claims of the possible relation between social norms and repair practices. With regard to this relation, it is worth reiterating that conversation is not a passive code influenced by social norms, but that its production can be constitutive of these norms: the choice for one repair technique over another may be one among several signals indicating, for instance, that interlocutors are now "doing gossip interaction" or "doing formality." More broadly, what the divergent claims about the shaping of repair practices suggest is that there is a need to establish common standards of evidentiary requirements and data collection. At the very minimum, this includes empirically grounding the analysis in data that is available for repeated inspection, and providing information about the nature and representativeness of the corpus and the number of cases studied. Only with such information, does proper comparison become possible.

18.3.3 Cultural variation and multimodal interactional resources

Many sequential structures, like the repair sequences discussed above, can to some extent be effectively compared in terms of spoken turns alone, but the findings of a flourishing interdisciplinary field of gesture studies over recent decades has shown us that spoken language and body behavior are two integrated aspects of a single process (Kendon 1980; McNeill 1992; and many others), and are packaged together in "composite utterances" (Enfield 2009). Sequences do not just exist as "turns," in the sense that turn-constructional units have been traditionally seen as *spoken* elements, but can be thought of as consisting of more complex multi-modal "moves" (Goffman 1981; Enfield 2009, in press). Conversation analysts are increasingly studying the visual mode's potential for simultaneity with talk that allows for a number of practices that run together with, but parallel to, turn-taking. Speakers can use gaze to help accomplish sequence closure (Rossano 2013). They can use posture to manage engagements in multiple courses of action (Schegloff 1998). They can use pointing to project upcoming turns (Mondada 2007). These observations, when considered together with the cross-cultural questions that motivate this chapter, lead us to ask to what extent such practices can be expected to vary according to cultural convention, or to what extent they are part of a general semiotics of social interaction for speakers of any language.

Ethnographers have long been interested in cultural variation in gestural and bodily behavior,[16] as seen for instance in the early cross-cultural film studies cited above (for a recent review, see Kita 2009). While there has been relatively little systematic cross-linguistic comparison in this area since that early work, some recent work has shown, for example, a degree of cultural variation in gaze behavior (Rossano *et al.* 2009). Research on pointing shows it to be a great example of a practice that occurs around the world (Kita 2003), although with cross-cultural variation. For example, while most speakers of English canonically point with the index figure, speakers of other languages may use other hand shapes or other body parts entirely, such as the lips (see for instance Sherzer 1973 on the Kuna of Panama and Enfield 2001 on Lao). What are the implications of this kind of cultural variation for cross-cultural interaction studies?

The following excerpt (Excerpt 5) from a household interaction among speakers of Cha'palaa provides a partial answer to this question. In this example, an instance of lip-pointing constitutes a distinct move in the sequential structure of a conversation. If we were to attend only to the spoken turns, this exchange between two parents and their son would seem odd, since the boy's questions in lines 2 and 4 appear to be ignored, followed only by pauses in the talk. However, analysis of the video shows that the question in line 2, the repair initiator "to whom?," was followed in 3 by the mother's lip point, directed at the father (Figure 18.3a), a perfectly fitted response of a person reference to a "who" question. Shortly thereafter, another culturally conventionalized bodily practice comes into play, because the boy offers a candidate understanding of his mother's lip point ("to father?") which is then confirmed in line 5 through a brief raising of the eyebrows, or "eyebrow flash" (Grammer *et al.* 1988; Eibl-Eibesfeldt 1989: 453ff.), closing the sequence by confirming the candidate repair solution in 4 (Figure 18.3b).

Extract 5. Cha'palaa (CHSF2012_01_20S6_2071407)
1 Mother *ajpele-nu ka'-ta-di-'mityaa   ee-tyu-i   tii-ti-ee*
            belt-ACC get-have-POS-because send-NEG-EGO say-say-DECL
            'Since he was holding a belt they said not to send him.'
2 Boy   *mu-nu-n*
            who-ACC-Q
            'To whom?'
3 Mother ((lip point towards father))   ((pause before next spoken TCU: 1.8s))
4 Boy   *apa-nu-u?*
            father-ACC-Q
            'To father?'
5 Mother ((eyebrow flash))   ((pause before next spoken TCU: 2.5s))

Speakers of English in a similar sequence might have drawn on their own conventionalized gestural resources, like index finger pointing for person reference and head nodding for confirmation (Schegloff 1982; Whitehead 2011). Despite the fact that gestural elements are not generally considered part of turn-constructional units with respect to the turn-taking system as it is technically understood, in the excerpt above these practices are indeed parts of the sequential structure. Studying cross-cultural variation

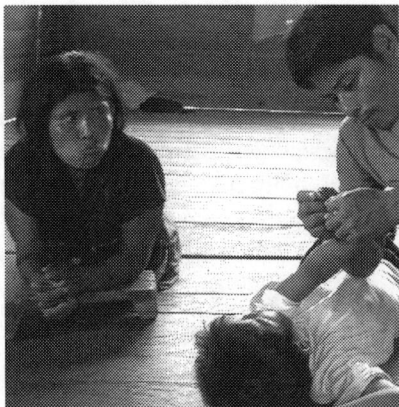

Figure 18.3 Two visual-gestural signs in Cha'palaa

in gestural practices and their interactional uses is one angle in the persistent problem of how to approach elements other than spoken turns within the turn-taking system.

Halfway around the world from Ecuador, Levinson has observed eyebrow flashes as used as confirmations among speakers of Yélî Dnye in Papua New Guinea, as in this question–answer sequence (Levinson 2006: 60):

Extract 6. Yélî Dnye (R02_V4 00:03:27)
1 J *mu dmâádî ngê? cha w:ee?*
      that girl TP you understand
      'That girl, you see?'
2 R ((eyebrow flash)) *éé*
      ((confirmation)) 'Yes.'

The fact that eyebrow flashing for confirmation and lip pointing for reference are practices that pop up in different languages around the world leads to a series of questions that should be a part of cross-cultural interaction studies: What functions do specific local bodily or multimodal practices have in conversation? To what extent is there formal and functional variation in multimodal practices cross-culturally? Why do similar practices appear in completely unrelated languages? What are the relative roles of natural meaning and conventionalization in the development of these practices? Further research in this area stands to teach us much more about the intersection between cross-cultural and multi-modal questions.[17]

18.4 Conclusions

Tools for the comparative study of social interaction are divided among different disciplines, and so a proposal for undertaking this project means assembling an eclectic toolkit. From linguistic anthropology, we need the focus on linguistic diversity and methods for analyzing language usage in different cultural settings. From sociocultural anthropology, we need ways to tap into the rich cultural understandings that enter into the construction and interpretation of everyday social interaction. From conversation analysis, we need the methods, concepts, and transcription practices developed for studying sequential structures of talk. We also need the resources of descriptive linguistics for understanding the basic morphosyntactic and phonological elements that make up the linguistic parts of interactional structures. Corpus linguistics offers methods for dealing with quantitative and comparable sets of data. And in addition to all of these interdisciplinary tools, we need the attention to visual bodily behavior provided by gesture studies and related fields, and methods for analysis of video data that complement those for analysis of talk.

The material reviewed here can be summed up in five key methodological principles for cross-cultural comparative interaction studies. Studies in this field should be:

(1) ECOLOGICALLY VALID. Language and social interaction are best studied in their natural-cultural habitat: everyday face-to-face interaction, the primordial home of language. Special ways of speaking only become special against a baseline, and understanding the workings of this baseline is a crucial part of understanding language use in all its forms.

(2) ETHNOGRAPHICALLY ENRICHED. Moments of talk never take place in a vacuum: their occurrence is embedded in, their interpretations enriched by, social, cultural, and biographical contexts. Records of interaction are artifacts that for most purposes can only be analyzed with reference to knowledge based on long-term experience in the society.

(3) EMPIRICALLY GROUNDED. Claims about interaction should be as directly accountable to the data as possible. They should be based on rich records of data that are available for repeated inspection.

(4) MULTI-MODAL. The bodily elements of interaction and the semiotics of visible behavior are part and parcel of language use around the world. This is the form in which language evolved and it therefore commands our primary attention.

(5) COMPARABLE. Claims purporting to go beyond single cases should always be based on comparable collections of data. It is not only important to collect data in comparable settings, but also to carry out comparison in carefully matched sequential environments, using the natural control method as a way to ensure that like is compared with like.

Studying conversation across cultures means taking a perspective on social interaction that is committed to linguistic as well as anthropological insights. We hope to have shown in this chapter that a truly cross-cultural comparative study of social interaction is within reach. The interdisciplinary approach outlined here offers promising avenues for not being overwhelmed by diversity but for learning from it. Similarly to the way that the cumulative record of grammatical descriptions of the world's languages made linguistic typology possible, as fieldworkers (often together with community members) record and transcribe more hours of conversational video data from diverse languages and settings, comparative studies of interaction will become more and more practical, and yield greater insights.

Acknowledgments

We thank Giovanni Rossi, Gunter Senft, and Maria Luz Garcia for helpful comments, and also the editors (Nick Enfield, Paul Kockelman, and Jack Sidnell) for giving us guidance at various stages of the process. We would also like to thank the communities in our respective fieldsites (Akpafu-Mempeasem, Ghana and Tsejpi, Ecuador). This research was funded by the Max Planck Society for the Advancement of Science and the European Research Council grant 240853.

Notes

1. In linguistics the concept of discrete languages versus dialect continua is equally problematic, but linguists generally use the concept in an informed and pragmatic way and have been able to make progress with cross-linguistic comparison. Bashkow advocates adapting some approaches from dialectology into cultural anthropology, pointing out that the fact that language boundaries are indeterminate can be dealt with pragmatically: "The lesson dialectologists draw from [unclear boundaries] is not that distinguishable languages do not exist, but that the way one draws their boundaries depends on the particular language features one chooses to emphasize" (2004: 52). We feel it is better to use the term pragmatically in this way, since avoidance of the word "culture" often leads to its substitution by other words referring to the same kinds of differences across social groups, somewhat like a speaker of an Australian language whose local norms do not permit her to mention the name of a specific relative but who can choose other more indirect words for referring to the same person.
2. Abu-Lughod points out that in anthropology "Americans who study Americans" (1991: 139) have been considered odd, but this claim is increasingly outdated. In other disciplines like sociology and psychology the norm has long been to research with members of the same culture as the researchers themselves, leading to general theories of

human behavior based on just one or a few cultures (Henrich et al. 2010). In the interest of keeping cultural concerns on the table, it may be better to risk glossing over some complexity and heterogeneity if the payoff is avoiding ethnocentrism.

3. This extract exemplifies the transcription conventions for representing conversation we use in this chapter (adapted from Jefferson 2004): pauses are marked with decisecond precision in single brackets (1.0), the beginnings and ends of overlapping turns are marked using [square brackets], non-verbal behaviour is described in ((double brackets)), uncertain hearings/readings are marked using (single brackets), and lengthening is marked with a colon. Speaker identifications and names mentioned in the conversation are anonymized where necessary.

4. Abbreviations used in glosses: ACC accusative, AFF affirmative, CM noun class marker, COM comitative, DECL declarative, EGO egophoric, ING ingressive, INTJ interjection, NEG negation, OIR other-initiated repair, PL plural, PLN place name, POS positional, PSN personal name, REL relative (pronoun), SCR subject cross-reference marker, SG singular, SR same referent, TP topic, Q question, QPLR.INFER polar question proposition inferred, QT quotative.

5. With respect to the long debate in anthropology about the ethnographer's membership status with respect to the field site, we believe that focused ethnography is useful for both "insiders" and "outsiders" in any social setting.

6. This despite the fact that in ethnomethodology (in many ways a cognate discipline to conversation analysis), researchers have commonly used ethnographic fieldwork as a way of acquiring membership competencies in order to study local routine practices (Garfinkel 1967; Garfinkel and Wieder 1992; ten Have 2002).

7. In his review of this period, Ruby points out that Boas was "one of the first anthropologists, and perhaps the first social scientist anywhere, to use the motion picture camera to generate data in natural settings (as opposed to a laboratory) in order to study gesture, motor habits, and dance as manifestations of culture" (1980: 7). Several of Boas' students also adopted these methods; for example, Zora Neal Hurston used a film camera for collecting African American folklore (Charnov 1998).

8. This approach did not ignore dialogic aspects of language, but considered these mainly in terms of poetics, like in Urban's discussions of "backchannels" (or "continuers") and of ceremonial dialogs in which listeners to narratives repeat syllables in disregard of the usual turn-constructional units (Urban 1986).

9. Duranti (2003) describes the current paradigm in linguistic anthropology as one that turns away from some of the concerns of the ethnography of communication and toward some of the socio-political questions current in social anthropology (e.g., the boom in "language ideology" studies).

10. Apology studies include: Akan (Obeng 1999), Persian (Shariati and Chamani 2010), Jordanian Arabic (Bataineh and Bataineh 2006), Sudanese Arabic (Nureddeen 2008), Japanese (Barnlund and Yoshioka 1990), Korean and Chinese (Guan et al. 2009). Other kinds of actions that have been studied include "requests" in Swahili (D'hondt 1992), Spanish (Márquez-Reiter 2000), Japanese (Fukushima 2003), and Mandarin Chinese and Korean (Rue 2008); and "compliments" and "compliment responses" in Japanese (Barnlund and Araki 1985), Finnish (Ylänne-McEwen 1993), Chinese (Tang and Zhang 2009), and Arabic (Nelson et al. 1996).
11. Some work in this paradigm was motivated by the goal of identifying problems in interethnic communication rooted in cross-cultural differences in interactive practices (e.g., Gumperz 1982).
12. The robust universality of turn-taking has led to speculation about its origins. One proposal is that the turn-taking system may be a "species-specific adaptation to the contingencies of human social intercourse" (Sidnell 2001). While this wording seems to suggest a native endowment (as does Levinson's [2006: 44] "human interaction engine"), it is an open question whether turn-taking abilities should be attributed to biological or to cultural evolution or to a combination of both. Turn-taking behaviors are found in some non-human primates (e.g., Campbell's monkeys, Lemasson et al. 2011; vervet monkeys and rhesus macaques, Hauser 1992), though not in chimpanzees (Arcadi 2000). Although the particulars of the human turn-taking system are clearly organized with reference to human linguistic abilities (such as the capacity to construct turns from linguistic units and to recognize turn-constructional units as complete), turn-taking itself may be an evolutionarily optimal solution to the generic problem of bidirectional communication, found not just in humans but in many other species (Yoshida and Okanoya 2005; Colman and Browning 2009).
13. The extracts are drawn from a corpus of about eight hours per language of video recordings of maximally informal interaction, typically between people who know each other well (family, friends, neighbors). Besides the interjection format described here, the other two formats for open-class other-initiation of repair in these three languages are, in order of frequency, a question-word format (be: 'what?' in Siwu, i'ɲaŋ 'what?' in Lao, ti 'what?' in Cha'palaa) and a non-verbal format (combining leaning forward with eyebrow action) (Enfield et al. 2013).
14. The exact operation of the repair solution is subtly different in the three cases, so that the extracts demonstrate three points about repetition in repair solutions cross-linguistically. The Siwu example shows that repetition can be exactly verbatim. The Lao example demonstrates the phenomenon known as "dispensability" (Schegloff 2004): items linking the trouble source turn to the discourse context (such as

the doubly occcurring address term *Noi* in Extract 3 line 1) can be left out in the repair solution. The Cha'palaa example shows that repair solutions may involve an analysis of the trouble: more information may be included besides the repeated material, displaying an orientation to a possible problem of underspecification. Though illustrated here with material from different languages, we have observed these three phenomena within each language as well.
15. Questioning intonation is marked in our transcripts using "?". Note that in this respect our transcription deviates from CA transcription, in which the question mark is used to mark "rising intonation," based on English.
16. For example, in the 1930s and 1940s David Efron asked questions about the cultural basis for gesture as part of a Boasian argument against the racial or hereditary determination of gestural patterns, showing that while immigrant populations in the US differed systematically from each other in terms of both form and frequency of gesture, by the second generation the groups were indistinguishable from each other, thus validating a cultural explanation for the difference (Efron 1941).
17. Languages that are expressed entirely in the visual mode have special significance for cross-cultural interaction studies, and a program of cross-linguistic conversation analysis should also be sure to take into account the diversity of the world's sign languages. We do not have space to do justice to the issues raised by cross-modal comparison here, but one important question that arises is how turn-taking can be studied in languages whose "spoken" elements are in the visual mode. There has been little research on the topic of turn-taking in signed languages (e.g., Baker 1977; Coates and Sutton-Spence 2001), but tentatively it would seem that signed languages do operate with a turn-taking system similar to that of spoken languages.

References

Abu-Lughod, Lila. 1991. Writing Against Culture. In *Recapturing Anthropology: Working in the Present*, ed. Richard G. Fox, 137–62. Santa Fe: School of American Research Press.

Antaki, Charles. 2012. Affiliative and Disaffiliative Candidate Understandings. *Discourse Studies* 14(5): 531–47. doi:10.1177/1461445612454074.

Arcadi, Adam Clark. 2000. Vocal Responsiveness in Male Wild Chimpanzees: Implications for the evolution of language. *Journal of Human Evolution* 39(2): 205–23. doi:10.1006/jhev.2000.0415.

Austin, J. L. 1962. *How to Do Things with Words*. Oxford: Clarendon Press.

Baker, C. 1977. Regulators and Turn-taking in American Sign Language Discourse. *On the Other Hand*. http://ci.nii.ac.jp/naid/10021343089/.

Barnlund, Dean C., and Shoko Araki. 1985. Intercultural Encounters: The Management of Compliments by Japanese and Americans. *Journal of Cross-Cultural Psychology* 16(1): 9–26. doi:10.1177/0022002185016001002.

Barnlund, Dean C., and Miho Yoshioka. 1990. Apologies: Japanese and American Styles. *International Journal of Intercultural Relations* 14(2): 193–206. doi:10.1016/0147-1767(90)90005-H.

Bashkow, Ira. 2004. A Neo-Boasian Conception of Cultural Boundaries. *American Anthropologist* 106(3): 443–58. doi:10.1525/aa.2004.106.3.443.

Bataineh, R., and R. Bataineh. 2006. Apology Strategies of Jordanian EFL University Students. *Journal of Pragmatics* 38(11): 1901–27. doi:10.1016/j.pragma.2005.11.004.

Bateson, Gregory, and Margaret Mead. 1951. *Bathing Babies in Three Cultures*. 16mm BW film, 11 minutes.

Bauman, Richard, and Joel Sherzer, eds. 1974. *Explorations in the Ethnography of Speaking*. London, New York: Cambridge University Press.

1975. The Ethnography of Speaking. *Annual Review of Anthropology* 4: 95–119.

Beach, Wayne A. 1990. Searching for Universal Features of Conversation. *Research on Language and Social Interaction* 24: 351–68. doi:10.1080/08351819009389347.

Beach, Wayne A., and Anna K. Lindstrom. 1992. Conversational Universals and Comparative Theory: Turning to Swedish and American acknowledgment tokens in interaction. *Communication Theory* 2(1): 24–49. doi:10.1111/j.1468-2885.1992.tb00027.x.

Besnier, Niko. 1989. Information Withholding as a Manipulative and Collusive Strategy in Nukulaelae Gossip. *Language in Society* 18(3): 315–41. doi:10.1017/S0047404500013634.

Birdwhistell, Ray L. 1952. *Introduction to Kinesics: An Annotation System for Analysis of Body Motion and Gesture*. Dept. of State, Foreign Service Institute.

Blum-Kulka, Shoshana, Juliane House, and Gabriele Kasper. 1989. *Cross-Cultural Pragmatics: Requests and Apologies*. Norwood, NJ: Ablex Pub. Corp.

Charnov, Elaine S. 1998. The Performative Visual Anthropology Films of Zora Neale Hurston. *Film Criticism* 23(1): 38–47.

Coates, Jennifer, and Rachel Sutton-Spence. 2001. Turn-taking Patterns in Deaf Conversation. *Journal of Sociolinguistics* 5(4): 507–29. doi:10.1111/1467-9481.00162.

Cohen, Emma. 2008. What is Spirit Possession? Defining, comparing, and explaining two possession forms. *Ethnos* 73(1): 101–26. doi:10.1080/00141840801927558.

Colman, Andrew M., and Lindsay Browning. 2009. Evolution of Cooperative Turn-taking. *Evolutionary Ecology Research* 11: 949–63.

D'hondt, Sigur. 1992. A Request in Swahili: On conversation analysis and non-western societies. In *SKY Yearbook of the Linguistic Association of Finland*, ed Maria Vilkuna, 127–40.

Davis, Martha. 2001. Film Projectors as Microscopes: Ray L. Birdwhistell and Microanalysis of Interaction (1955-1975). *Visual Anthropology Review* 17(2): 39-49.

Dingemanse, Mark, Francisco Torreira, and N. J. Enfield. 2013. Is "Huh?" a Universal Word? Conversational infrastructure and the convergent evolution of linguistic items. *PLoS One* 8(11): e78273. doi:10.1371/journal.pone.0078273.

Drew, Paul. 1997. "Open" class repair initiators in response to sequential sources of trouble in conversation. *Journal of Pragmatics* 28: 69-101.

Duranti, Alessandro. 1988. Intentions, Language, and Social Action in a Samoan Context. *Journal of Pragmatics* 12(1): 13-33. doi:10.1016/0378-2166(88)90017-3.

   2003. Language as Culture in U.S. Anthropology: Three Paradigms. *Current Anthropology* 44(3): 323-47. doi:10.1086/368118.

   2008. Further Reflections on Reading Other Minds. *Anthropological Quarterly* 81(2): 483-94. doi:10.1353/anq.0.0002.

Edwards, Walter F. 1979. Speech Acts in Guyana: Communicating Ritual and Personal Insults. *Journal of Black Studies* 10(1): 20-39.

Efron, David. 1941. *Gesture, Race and Culture: A tentative study of the spatio-temporal and "linguistic" aspects of the gestural behavior of eastern Jews and southern Italians in New York City, living under similar as well as different environmental conditions*. The Hague: Mouton.

Egbert, Maria M. 1996. Context-Sensitivity in Conversation: Eye gaze and the German repair initiator *bitte*? *Language in Society* 25(4): 587-612. doi:10.1017/S0047404500020820.

Eibl-Eibesfeldt, Irenäus. 1979. Human Ethology: Concepts and implications for the sciences of man. *Behavioral and Brain Sciences* 2(1): 1-57.

   1989. *Human Ethology*. New York: Aldine De Gruyter.

Enfield, N. J. 2001. "Lip-pointing": A discussion of form and function with reference to data from Laos. *Gesture* 1(2): 185-212.

   2009. *The Anatomy of Meaning: Speech, Gesture, and Composite Utterances*. Cambridge: Cambridge University Press.

   In press. A "Composite Utterances" approach to meaning. In *Handbook Body – Language – Communication*, ed Cornelia Müller, E. Fricke, Alan Cienki, and David McNeill. Berlin: Mouton De Gruyter.

Enfield, N. J., Tanya Stivers, and Stephen C. Levinson. 2010. Question-response sequences in conversation across ten languages: An introduction. *Journal of Pragmatics* 42(10): 2615-19. doi:10.1016/j.pragma.2010.04.001.

Field, Margaret J. 1969. Spirit Possession in Ghana. In *Spirit Mediumship and Society in Africa*, ed J. Beattie and John Middleton, 3-13. London: Routledge and Kegan Paul.

Fox, Barbara A., Makoto Hayashi, and Robert Jasperson. 1996. Resources and Repair: A cross-linguistic study of syntax and repair. In *Interaction and Grammar*, ed Elinor Ochs, Emanuel A Schegloff, and

Sandra A Thompson, 185–237. Cambridge: Cambridge University Press.

Fukushima, Saeko. 2003. *Requests and Culture: Politeness in British English and Japanese*. Bern, New York: P. Lang.

Garfinkel, Harold, ed. 1967. *Studies in Ethnomethodology*. Englewood Cliffs, NJ: Prentice-Hall.

——— 2002. *Ethnomethodology's Program: Working Out Durkheim's Aphorism*. Rowman and Littlefield.

Garfinkel, Harold, and D. Lawrence Wieder. 1992. Two Incommensurable, Asymmetrically Alternate Technologies of Social Analysis. In *Text in Context: Studies in Ethnomethodology*, ed. Graham Watson and Robert M. Seiler, 175–206. Newbury Park, CA: Sage.

Goffman, Erving. 1981. *Forms of Talk*. Philadelphia: University of Pennsylvania Press.

Goodwin, Charles, and John Heritage. 1990. Conversation Analysis. *Annual Review of Anthropology* 19: 283–307.

Grammer, Karl, Wulf Schiefenhövel, Margret Schleidt, Beatrice Lorenz, and Irenäus Eibl-Eibesfeldt. 1988. Patterns on the Face: The eyebrow flash in crosscultural comparison. *Ethology* 77(4): 279–99. doi:10.1111/j.1439-0310.1988.tb00211.x.

Guan, Xiaowen, Hee Sun Park, and Hye Eun Lee. 2009. Cross-cultural Differences in Apology. *International Journal of Intercultural Relations* 33(1): 32–45. doi:10.1016/j.ijintrel.2008.10.001.

Gudykunst, William B., and Tsukasa Nishida. 1994. *Bridging Japanese/North American Differences*. Thousand Oaks, CA: Sage.

Gumperz, John. 1982. *Discourse Strategies*. Cambridge/New York: Cambridge University Press.

Gumperz, John Joseph, and Dell H. Hymes. 1964. The Ethnography of Communication. *American Anthropological Association* 66(6), part 2 (Special Issue).

Hall, Edward T. 1963. A System for the Notation of Proxemic Behavior. *American Anthropologist* 65(5): 1003–26.

Hauser, Marc D. 1992. A Mechanism Guiding Conversational Turn-taking in Vervet Monkeys and Rhesus Macaques, ed. Tsukasa Nishida, Frans B. M. de Waal, William C. McGrew, P. Marler, and M. Pickford. *Topics of Primatology* 1: 235–48.

ten Have, Paul. 2002. The Notion of Member is the Heart of the Matter: On the Role of Membership Knowledge in Ethnomethodological Inquiry. *Forum Qualitative Sozialforschung / Forum: Qualitative Social Research* 3 (3). www.qualitative-research.net/index.php/fqs/article/view/834.

Henrich, Joseph, Steven J. Heine, and Ara Norenzayan. 2010. The Weirdest People in the World? *Behavioral and Brain Sciences* 33(2–3): 61–83. doi:10.1017/S0140525X0999152X.

Heritage, John. 1984. *Garfinkel and Ethnomethodology*. Cambridge/New York: Polity Press.

1990. Intention, Meaning and Strategy: Observations on constraints on interaction analysis. *Research on Language and Social Interaction* 24: 311. doi:10.1080/08351819009389345.

Hopper, Robert. 1990. Ethnography and Conversation Analysis after Talking Culture. *Research on Language and Social Interaction* 24: 161. doi:10.1080/08351819009389336.

Hopper, Robert, Nanda Doany, Michael Johnson, and Kent Drummond. 1990. Universals and Particulars in Telephone Openings. *Research on Language and Social Interaction* 24: 369-87. doi:10.1080/08351819009389348.

Hymes, Dell. 1962. The Ethnography of Speaking. In *Anthropology and Human Behavior*, ed. Thomas Gladwin and William C. Sturtevant, 13-53. Washington, DC.

1974. *Foundations in Sociolinguistics: An Ethnographic Approach*. University of Pennsylvania Press.

Jacknis, Ira. 1988. Margaret Mead and Gregory Bateson in Bali: Their Use of Photography and Film. *Cultural Anthropology* 3(2): 160-77.

Jakobson, Roman. 1960. Linguistics and Poetics. In *Style in Language*, ed Thomas A. Sebeok, 350-77. Cambridge, MA: MIT Press.

Jefferson, Gail. 1996. On the Poetics of Ordinary Talk. *Text and Performance Quarterly* 16(1): 1-61.

2004. Glossary of Transcript Symbols with an Introduction. In *Conversation Analysis: Studies from the First Generation*, ed. G. H. Lerner, 13-23. Philadelphia: John Benjamins.

Keating, Elizabeth, and Maria Egbert. 2004. Conversation as a Cultural Activity. In *A Companion to Linguistic Anthropology*, ed. Alessandro Duranti, 169-96. New York: Blackwell.

Kendon, Adam. 1980. Gesticulation and Speech: Two aspects of the process of utterance. In *The Relationship of Verbal and Nonverbal Communication*, ed. Mary Ritchie Key, 207-27. The Hague: Mouton.

1990. *Conducting Interaction: Patterns of Behavior in Focused Encounters*. Cambridge: Cambridge University Press.

Kidwell, M. 2005. Gaze as Social Control: How very young children differentiate "the look" from a "mere look" by their adult caregivers. *Research on Language and Social Interaction* 38(4): 417-49.

Kita, Sotaro, ed. 2003. *Pointing: Where Language, Culture, and Cognition Meet*. Mahwah, NJ: L. Erlbaum Associates.

ed. 2009. Cross-cultural Variation of Speech-accompanying Gesture: A review. *Language and Cognitive Processes* 24(2): 145-67. doi:10.1080/01690960802586188.

Lehtonen, Jaakko, and Kari Sajavaara. 1985. The Silent Finn. In *Perspectives on Silence*, ed. Deborah Tannen and Muriel Saville-Troike, 193-201. Norwood, NJ: Ablex Pub. Corp.

Lemasson, A., L. Glas, S. Barbu, A. Lacroix, M. Guilloux, K. Remeuf, and H. Koda. 2011. Youngsters Do Not Pay Attention to Conversational

Rules: Is this so for nonhuman primates? *Scientific Reports* 1. doi:10.1038/srep00022.

Lerner, Gene H. 2003. Selecting Next Speaker: The context-sensitive operation of a context-free organization. *Language in Society* 32(02): 177–201. doi:10.1017/S004740450332202X.

Lerner, Gene H., and Tomyo Takagi. 1999. On the Place of Linguistic Resources in the Organization of Talk-in-Interaction: A co-investigation of English and Japanese grammatical practices. *Journal of Pragmatics* 31(1): 49–75.

Levinson, Stephen C. 2006. The Human Interaction Engine. In *Roots of Human Sociality: Culture, Cognition, and Human Interaction*, ed. N. J. Enfield and Stephen C. Levinson, 39–69. Oxford: Berg.

——— 2007. Optimizing Person Reference – Perspectives from usage on Rossel Island. In *Person Reference in Interaction: Linguistic, Cultural, and Social Perspectives*, ed. N. J. Enfield and Tanya Stivers, 29–72. Cambridge: Cambridge University Press.

——— 2013. Action Formation and Ascription. In *Handbook of Conversation Analysis*, ed. Jack Sidnell and Tanya Stivers, 103–30. Malden, MA: Blackwell Publishers.

Luke, Kang Kwong, and Theodossia-Soula Pavlidou, eds. 2002. *Telephone Calls: Unity and Diversity in Conversational Structure Across Languages and Cultures*. Philadelphia, PA: J. Benjamins.

Mandelbaum, Jenny. 1990. Beyond Mundane Reason: Conversation Analysis And Context. *Research on Language and Social Interaction* 24: 333–50. doi:10.1080/08351819009389346.

Márquez-Reiter, Rosina. 2000. *Linguistic Politeness in Britain and Uruguay: A Contrastive Study of Requests and Apologies*. Amsterdam/Philadelphia: John Benjamins.

McHoul, Alec, Mark Rapley, and Charles Antaki. 2008. You Gotta Light?: On the luxury of context for understanding talk in interaction. *Journal of Pragmatics* 40(1): 42–54. doi:10.1016/j.pragma.2007.03.006.

McNeill, David. 1992. *Hand and Mind*. Chicago: University of Chicago Press.

Moerman, Michael. 1977. The Preference for Self-Correction in a Tai Conversational Corpus. *Language* 53(4): 872–82.

——— 1988. *Talking Culture: Ethnography and Conversation Analysis*. Philadelphia: University of Pennsylvania Press.

——— 1990. Exploring Talk and Interaction. *Research on Language and Social Interaction* 24: 173–87. doi:10.1080/08351819009389337.

——— 1996. The Field of Analyzing Foreign Language Conversations. *Journal of Pragmatics* 26(2): 147–58. doi:10.1016/0378-2166(96)00009-4.

Mondada, L. 2007. Multimodal Resources for Turn-taking Pointing and the Emergence of Possible Next Speakers. *Discourse Studies* 9(2): 194–225.

Nelson, Gayle, Mahmoud Al-Batal, and Erin Echols. 1996. Arabic and English Compliment Responses: Potential for Pragmatic Failure. *Applied Linguistics* 17(4): 411–32. doi:10.1093/applin/17.4.411.

Nettle, Daniel. 1998. Explaining Global Patterns of Language Diversity. *Journal of Anthropological Archaeology* 17: 354-74.

Nureddeen, Fatima Abdurahman. 2008. Cross Cultural Pragmatics: Apology strategies in Sudanese Arabic. *Journal of Pragmatics* 40(2): 279-306. doi:10.1016/j.pragma.2007.11.001.

Obeng, S. 1999. Apologies in Akan Discourse. *Journal of Pragmatics* 31(5): 709-34. doi:10.1016/S0378-2166(98)00089-7.

Ochs, Elinor. 1984. Clarification and Culture. In *GURT'84: Meaning, Form, and Use in Context: Linguistic Applications*, ed. Deborah Schiffrin. Washington, DC: Georgetown University Press.

Ochs, Elinor, Emanuel A. Schegloff, and Sandra A. Thompson, eds. 1996. *Interaction and Grammar*. Cambridge: Cambridge University Press.

Pomerantz, Anita. 1990. Mental Concepts In The Analysis of Social Action. *Research on Language and Social Interaction* 24: 299-310. doi:10.1080/08351819009389344.

Reisman, Karl. 1974. Contrapuntal Conversations in an Antiguan Village. In *Explorations in the Ethnography of Speaking*, ed. Richard Bauman and Joel Sherzer, 110-24. London/New York: Cambridge University Press.

Robinson, Jeffrey D. 2006. Managing Trouble Responsibility and Relationships During Conversational Repair. *Communication Monographs* 73: 137-61. doi:10.1080/03637750600581206.

Rosaldo, Michelle Z. 1982. The Things We Do with Words: Ilongot Speech Acts and Speech Act Theory in Philosophy. *Language in Society* 11(2): 203-37.

Rossano, Federico. 2013. Gaze in Social Interaction. In *Handbook of Conversation Analysis*, ed. Jack Sidnell and Tanya Stivers, 308-29. Malden, MA: Blackwell Publishers.

Rossano, Federico, Penelope Brown, and Stephen C. Levinson. 2009. Gaze, Questioning, and Culture. In *Conversation Analysis: Comparative Perspectives*, ed. Jack Sidnell, 187-249. Cambridge: Cambridge University Press.

Ruby, Jay. 1980. Franz Boas and Early Camera Study of Behavior. *Kinesics Report* 3(1): 6-11.

Rue, Yong-Ju. 2008. *Request Strategies: A Comparative Study in Mandarin Chinese and Korean*. Amsterdam/Philadelphia: John Benjamins.

Sacks, Harvey. 1992. *Lectures on Conversation*. 2 vols. London: Blackwell.

Sacks, Harvey, Emanuel A. Schegloff, and Gail Jefferson. 1974. A Simplest Systematics for the Organization of Turn-Taking for Conversation. *Language* 50(4): 696-735.

Sammons, Kay, and Joel Sherzer. 2000. *Translating Native Latin American Verbal Art: Ethnopoetics and Ethnography of Speaking*. Washington, DC: Smithsonian Institution Press.

Sanders, Robert E. 1999. The Impossibility of a Culturally Contexted Conversation Analysis: On Simultaneous, Distinct Types of Pragmatic Meaning. *Research on Language and Social Interaction* 32(1/2): 129.

Schegloff, Emanuel A. 1968. Sequencing in Conversational Openings. *American Anthropologist* 70(6): 1075-95.

1982. Discourse as Interactional Achievement: Some Uses of "uh huh" and Other Things That Come Between Sentences. In *Analyzing Discourse: Text and Talk*, ed. Deborah Tannen, 71–93. Washington, DC: Georgetown University Press.

1984. On Some Gestures' Relation to Talk. In *Structures of Social Action Studies in Conversation Analysis*, ed. J. M. Atkinson and John Heritage, 266–96. Cambridge/New York/Paris: Cambridge University Press / Editions de la Maison des sciences de l'homme.

1992. In Another Context. In *Rethinking Context: Language as an Interactive Phenomenon*, ed. Alessandro Duranti and Charles Goodwin, 191–227. Cambridge: Cambridge University Press.

1997. Practices and Actions: Boundary cases of other-initiated repair. *Discourse Processes* 23(3): 499–545. doi:10.1080/01638539709545001.

1998. Body Torque. *Social Research* 65(3): 535–96.

2000. Overlapping Talk and the Organization of Turn-Taking for Conversation. *Language in Society* 29(1): 1–63.

2004. On Dispensability. *Research on Language and Social Interaction* 37(2): 95–149.

2005. On Integrity in Inquiry . . . of the Investigated, Not the Investigator. *Discourse Studies* 7(4-5): 455–80. doi:10.1177/1461445605054402.

2006. Interaction: The Infrastructure for Social Institutions, the Natural Ecological Niche for Language, and the Arena in which Culture is Enacted. In *Roots of Human Sociality: Culture, Cognition, and Human Interaction*, ed. N. J. Enfield and Stephen C. Levinson, 70–96. Oxford: Berg.

2007. *Sequence Organization in Interaction: A Primer in Conversation Analysis*. Cambridge: Cambridge University Press.

2013. Ten Operations In Self-Initiated, Same-Turn Repair. In *Conversational Repair and Human Understanding*, ed. Makoto Hayashi, Geoffrey Raymond, and Jack Sidnell, np. Cambridge: Cambridge University Press.

Schegloff, Emanuel A., Gail Jefferson, and Harvey Sacks. 1977. The Preference for Self-Correction in the Organization of Repair in Conversation. *Language* 53(2): 361–82.

Schieffelin, Bambi B., and Elinor Ochs, eds. 1986. *Language Socialization Across Cultures*. Cambridge: Cambridge University Press.

Searle, John R. 1969. *Speech Acts: An Essay in the Philosophy of Language*. Cambridge: Cambridge University Press.

2006. Social Ontology: Some basic principles. *Anthropological Theory* 6(1): 12–29. doi:10.1177/1463499606061731.

Shariati, Mohammad, and Fariba Chamani. 2010. Apology Strategies in Persian. *Journal of Pragmatics* 42(6): 1689–99. doi:10.1016/j.pragma.2009.10.007.

Sherzer, Joel. 1973. Verbal and Nonverbal Deixis: The Pointed Lip Gesture Among the San Blas Cuna. *Language in Society* 2(01): 117–31. doi:10.1017/S0047404500000087.

1983. *Kuna Ways of Speaking: An Ethnographic Perspective*. Austin: University of Texas Press.

Sidnell, Jack. 2001. Conversational Turn-taking in a Caribbean English Creole. *Journal of Pragmatics* 33(8): 1263–90. doi:16/S0378-2166(00)00062-X.

2005. *Talk and Practical Epistemology: The Social Life of Knowledge in a Caribbean Community*. Amsterdam/Philadelphia: Johns Benjamins.

2006. Conversational Analytic Approaches to Culture. In *Encyclopedia of Language and Linguistics*, ed. Keith Brown, 169–72. Oxford: Elsevier. www.sciencedirect.com/science/article/B7T84-4M3C3K0-2MX/2/b93e2e9491643ddb591c655f9a277c60.

2007. Comparative Studies in Conversation Analysis. *Annual Review of Anthropology* 36(1): 229–44. doi:10.1146/annurev.anthro.36.081406.094313.

ed. 2009. *Conversation Analysis: Comparative Perspectives*. Cambridge: Cambridge University Press.

2010. *Conversation Analysis: An Introduction*. Chichester, UK: Wiley-Blackwell.

Sidnell, Jack, and N. J. Enfield. 2012. Language Diversity and Social Action. *Current Anthropology* 53(3): 302–33. doi:10.1086/665697.

Smith, Jonathan Z. 1992. *To Take Place: Toward Theory in Ritual*. Chicago: University of Chicago Press.

Stivers, Tanya, N. J. Enfield, Penelope Brown, C. Englert, Makoto Hayashi, Trine Heinemann, Gertie Hoymann, et al. 2009. Universals and Cultural Variation in Turn-taking in Conversation. *Proceedings of the National Academy of Sciences* 106(26): 10587–92. doi:10.1073/pnas.0903616106.

Stivers, Tanya, and Jack Sidnell. 2005. Introduction: Multimodal interaction. *Semiotica* 156(1/4): 1–20.

Stoller, Paul. 1989. *Fusion of the Worlds: An Ethnography of Possession Among the Songhay of Niger*. University of Chicago Press, July 10.

Streeck, Jürgen. 1990. Tao/Saó: Talking Culture With Rousseau. *Research on Language and Social Interaction* 24: 241–61. doi:10.1080/08351819009389341.

1993. Gesture as Communication I: Its coordination with gaze and speech. *Communication Monographs* 60(4): 275–99.

Sudnow, David N., ed. 1972. *Studies in Social Interaction*. New York: MacMillan/The Free Press.

Tang, Chen-Hsin, and Grace Qiao Zhang. 2009. A Contrastive Study of Compliment Responses among Australian English and Mandarin Chinese speakers. *Journal of Pragmatics* 41(2): 325–45. doi:10.1016/j.pragma.2008.05.019.

Tedlock, Dennis. 1983. *The Spoken Word and the Work of Interpretation*. Philadelphia: University of Pennsylvania Press.

Urban, Greg. 1986. Ceremonial Dialogues in South America. *American Anthropologist* 88(2): 371–86. doi:10.1525/aa.1986.88.2.02a00050.

Whitehead, Kevin A. 2011. Some Uses of Head Nods in Third Position in Talk-in-Interaction. *Gesture* 11(2): 103–22. doi:10.1075/gest.11.2.01whi.

Ylänne-McEwen, Virpi. 1993. Complimenting Behaviour: A cross-cultural investigation. *Journal of Multilingual and Multicultural Development* 14(6): 499–508. doi:10.1080/01434632.1993.9994551.

Yoshida, Shigeto, and Kazuo Okanoya. 2005. Evolution of Turn-Taking: A Bio-Cognitive Perspective. *Cognitive Studies* 12(3): 153–65.

Zimmerman, Don H. 1999. Horizontal and Vertical Comparative Research in Language and Social Interaction. *Research on Language and Social Interaction* 32(1–2): 195–203. doi:10.1080/08351813.1999.9683623.

Part IV

Community and social life

Jack Sidnell, Paul Kockelman, and N. J. Enfield

The ancient Greeks divided the study of discourse into three parts: grammar, logic, and rhetoric. The study of grammar is premised on the idea that language is structured while the study of logic acknowledges that it can be used to say things that are true or false. The study of rhetoric, on the other hand, is based on the idea that speaking is consequential. Aristotle defined rhetoric as the "faculty of observing in any given case the available means of persuasion." Language is effective to the extent that a speaker is able to affect and direct the agency of others, and language, along with associated forms of conduct, can be conceptualized as the means to accomplish this. Language, on this view, is a tool. It is a means not only for harnessing the agency of others but also for constituting the very social groups whose agency is enlisted and distributed.

The chapters in this Part are centrally concerned with the effectiveness of language in this sense – as a tool for directing others and for constituting social groups. The anthropological study of language from this perspective dates to the beginnings of the discipline. Two important strands go back to Malinowski on the one hand and Boas on the other. In *The Coral Gardens and their Magic*, Malinowski developed an argument that language is fundamentally a mode of action. The language of ritual and of magic constituted key examples here, and later scholars – especially Firth and Tambiah – elaborated the view that language was an instrument for the constitution and transformation of social reality.

The chapters by Fleming and Lempert, by Tavárez, and by Bate take up these themes in various ways. **Fleming and Lempert** ask in what ways language is effective, focusing on poetics and taboo as two aspects of *performativity*. Distinguishing their approach from one based on speech acts (see Sidnell and Enfield, this volume, Chapter 17), the authors begin with the idea that poetics involves a foregrounding of form over content. Poetics in this sense is an emergent feature of all discourse. Fleming and Lempert suggest that performativity – the capacity for language to have effects in the world – is a consequence of poetic configurations. While post hoc reconstruction/retrospection may suggest that talk amounts to "rational conscious agentivity" via speech acts, Fleming and Lempert propose that effects are produced through indexically presupposing and entailing sign configurations manifested as both poetic metricalization (i.e., patterning of form in combination with lexical content) and taboo (i.e., avoidance).

Ritual and ritual language have a number of important and cross-culturally recurrent features. In his chapter on ritual **Tavárez** suggests that any instance of social interaction is a candidate for ritualization in so far as it is repeatable. Like Fleming and Lempert, Tavárez emphasizes the importance of form here too. Grammatical parallelism, for instance, characterizes much ritual language. One of the important insights of work in this area – for example by Maurice Bloch, Judith Irvine, Jack Du Bois, and Wallace Chafe – is that the degree to which discourse is routinized and formalized is inversely related to the degree to which it is understood as the expression of individual agency. *Formalization*, as Bloch put it, results in a distribution of agency across a social field, even a dissolution or effacement of the speaker. In this sense, ritual language is a product not of a single individual but of a social group, even if it is animated by a lone voice.

Extending and elaborating many of these same themes into the domain of political language, **Bate**'s chapter explores the effectiveness of oratory. In this domain, too, poetics and form play a key role. Interestingly, as a number of linguistic anthropologists have pointed out, here actual poetic practices routinely clash with ideologies of transparency or the idea that politicians are duty-bound to speak plainly, and to articulate a clear message. Through a consideration of rhetorical practices across a range of communities Bate shows that all rhetorics are ethno-rhetorics.

While Malinowski pondered questions of linguistic effectiveness, Boas was considering the relation between language and social groups. In his landmark introduction to the *Handbook of American Indian Languages*, Boas argued that relations between physical type (i.e., "race"), language, and culture were distinct products of historical events. Countering the dominant view of the time, Boas argued that there was no inherent connection between race, language, and culture. To make the case he drew on many examples from native North America and elsewhere involving language shift and change, in the context of social contact between communities. With these arguments Boas paved the way for anthropological thinking about the relation between language and human groups. **Muehlmann**'s chapter traces the development of these ideas in work by Bloomfield and, later, Gumperz. She shows the central importance for linguistic anthropologists of the notion of community and the role that language plays in constituting the boundary between one community and another. Many of the ideas inherited from Boas and developed by Bloomfield and Gumperz were rethought, as linguistic anthropologists developed the notion of *linguistic ideology* and incorporated insights from scholars such as Benedict Anderson, Jürgen Habermas, and, later, Michael Warner. These scholars and others encouraged linguistic anthropologists to think of communities not as static social groups but as *publics* that are being continually reconstituted in and through acts of communication and the forms of media through which they are effected.

The preceding chapter by **Gershon and Manning** shows this with reference to the technologies involved in the use of language, including cassette tapes, books, blogs, and telephones. The media/medium of language and communication turn out to be deeply consequential for social life. As these technologies are integrated into the social field, they not only make possible new forms of participation in interaction but also new identities and social statuses such as transcriber, stenographer, operator, and even telephone user. Gershon and Manning question a simple dichotomy between co-present (or face-to-face) and mediated interaction, and they suggest that technologies of communication carry the potential to redefine our very sense of presence.

19

Poetics and performativity

Luke Fleming and Michael Lempert

In his posthumous *How to Do Things with Words*, John Austin (1962) introduced a wider world to "performativity," a notion which, through John Searle's (1969) systematization into "speech act theory," came to be applied to everything from literature to music theory and has continued to influence research on pragmatics within disciplinary linguistics. By performativity Austin meant, and here we simplify brutally, how an instance of speech behavior can count as a social act. "I bet you sixpence it will rain tomorrow" – counting as a "bet" (Austin 1962: 5), for instance. Austin's work responded to that of the logical positivist philosophers: "the only things that they are interested in are utterances which report facts or which describe situations truly or falsely" (Austin *et al.* 1961: 233). He was at pains to show how, in the very act of uttering performative formulae, speakers seemed to bring said affairs into being, to make them true – a feat that comes from what Austin called an utterance's "illocutionary force."[1] Here, though, a tension immediately arose, a tension that, as we shall see, has continued to surface in work on performativity: Austin conceded that the utterance itself lacked any such force. Concerning the act of "marrying," for instance, carried out with a ritual formula such as, "I do take this woman to be my lawfully wedded wife," Austin entertained this doubt: "[O]ne might protest, perhaps even with some alarm, that I seem to be suggesting that marrying is simply saying a few words, that just saying a few words *is* marrying" (Austin *et al.* 1961: 236). Not at all, he replied, for the force of the speech act depends on features of context, what he termed "felicity conditions" – such as the presence of the requisite personnel (a priest, two eligible participants, and a witness), the existence of a conventional procedure for doing the act (a liturgy), the successful execution of the procedure (the vows *before* the declaration of marriage), and so forth. Observe the tension: Austin marveled at the power of "a few words" yet conceded that these were impotent out of context. As we shall see, his equivocation betrays certain critical weaknesses in speech-act theory, weaknesses that are important to understand for an anthropology of performativity.

Speech-act theory's view of speech as social action at first inspired linguistic anthropologists, but later became a foil for defining their own approach to language. A long train of criticism has been directed at speech-act theory over the years, and include the charges that it is ethnocentric for assuming and universalizing a certain "personalist" language ideology (Hall 2000; Hill 2008), as suggested by the way it made speaker-intention and "sincerity" into felicity conditions (e.g., Rosaldo 1982; Duranti 1993; Du Bois 1993; Lee 1997); that it also neglects cultural variation by positing universal typologies of speech-acts based strictly on English material (Rosaldo 1982; but see Searle's responses in D'Andrade 2006); that it fixates on lexicalized action types (or "metapragmatic descriptors"; see below), words like "bet" and "promise" which describe action, when most of the things we do with speech have no ready-made name; that even when such lexicalized (or "explicit") speech-act forms are employed, the social act that is actually performed is rarely a direct transform of the action so named (Schegloff 2007; Sidnell 2010); that it looks at blinkered sentence-sized units of analysis rather than stretches of discourse and has an "exclusive focus ... on word-and-sentence level properties of language" (Levinson 1994; Agha 1996: 1118); that it relies on invented examples rather than richly contextualized data gathered through empirical fieldwork (Glick 1996; Schegloff 2007: 8–12); that it suffers from "the total absence of what one might term a social theory beyond folk ideology of rational conscious agentivity" (Silverstein 1993: 46).

The long list of criticisms is testimony to speech-act theory's influence. Linguistic anthropologists have moved on, no longer feeling compelled to engage this literature or reprise critiques of it except in textbooks and introductions to the field, naturally (for a recent example, see Ahearn 2012), but performativity, broadly conceived, continues to be a central preoccupation, even if it is no longer talked about in terms set by speech-act theory. A number of incisive reviews and critical engagements with speech act theory have appeared over recent decades (Levinson 1994; Hall 2000), and we see no reason to rehash those, nor will we trace here the varied appropriations of performativity (e.g., Tambiah 1981; Habermas 1984; Bohman 1986; Butler 1997; Miller 2001). Instead, we want to direct attention to two neglected forms of performativity, the "poetic" and the "taboo." These may seem like boutique topics that are unrelated to one another, but, as we shall see, they expose dimensions of variation that have been underappreciated and are instructive for an anthropology of performativity. The poetic and the taboo represent two poles of performative form and function, ranging from the most textually distributed and diffuse, the poetic, to the most localizable and essentialized, the taboo. Our focus on these topics gestures towards a resolution of the paradox that vexed Austin, that of where, but moreover of how, to locate the performative and its "force."

19.1 Poetic performativity

"Poetics means action," wrote Michael Herzfeld (1997: 142), pointedly noting that the Greek verb *poieō* ('action') gave us the word *poetics*. In saying this Herzfeld was not dismissing the long history of poetic theory since Greek antiquity or brushing aside cultural diversity in poetic practice. His point was simply that poetics is a dimension of persuasion and should not be separated out and treated as "mere" aesthetics. "[R]estoring that etymological awareness," continued Herzfeld, "would ... more effectively integrate the study of language into an understanding of the role of rhetoric in shaping and even creating social relations" (Herzfeld 1997: 145; cf. Bauman and Briggs 1990; Silverstein 2005; Bate 2009). Herzfeld's appeal was one of many meant to make poetics central to our understanding of performativity, and much of this owes a lot to the seminal work of Roman Jakobson.

In the spirit of the Russian Formalist literary critics, Jakobson defined the "poetic function" as the foregrounding of message form, a "focus on the message for its own sake" (Jakobson 1960: 356); think of how rhyme elevates "form" over "content." This focus on form was in contrast to a focus on other facets of the speech event, like a focus on the addresser (the "emotive" or "expressive" function), the addressee (the "conative" function), the communicative channel used (the "phatic" function).[2] While the poetic function was named after metricalized "poetries," featuring meter, rhyme, scansion, and the rest, this function surfaces in all sorts of oral and written discourse (Jakobson 1960, 1966), from political oratory to nursery rhymes to spells. Noting this, Banti and Giannattasio (2004: 293-4 and passim) wish to distinguish "poetically organized discourse" from culturally recognized genres of poetry (cf. Silverstein 2004).[3]

Jakobson's capsule description of the poetic function merits repeating: "The poetic function projects the principle of equivalence from the axis of selection into the axis of combination" (Jakobson 1960: 358). Here Jakobson used an idiom drawn from the renowned Genevan linguist and chief architect of modern structural linguistics, Ferdinand de Saussure (1983). For Saussure, forms that have the same distributional privileges, that normatively occur in the same linear, syntagmatic environment, share a certain semantic "equivalence," forming equivalence classes from which the speaker is imagined to "select" (e.g., the dog {cat : boy : child, etc.} dozed on the porch) – hence the "axis of selection." Equivalence classes, which "descend" along the axis of selection, cannot be directly observed; they are virtual classes, existing in absentia or in potentia, determined by co-occurrence patterns and their restrictions (e.g., which lexemes can and cannot function as the subject of a verb). Jakobson suggested that we can see a similar kind of "equivalence" along the real-time axis of combination, where signs, as they unfold over time, seem to resemble each other – like the way a single pulse of alliteration can draw together in our awareness the words alliterated, creating an emergent (and evanescent) paradigm defined upon a principle of phonetic likeness. Linearly co-occurring signs can be "scanned" – as students of metricalized poetry say – for their comparability. The poetic function is thus an expansive way of talking about equivalences in discourse that are distinct from – indeed, orthogonal to – equivalences that are a function of Saussurian language structure. To this extent, Jakobson exposed a distinct stratum of orderliness in language use, what some in recent decades have gestured toward with the broader notion of "textuality."[4]

But while Jakobson saw the poetic function as an emergent property of all discourse, scholarship on this topic in the areas of ethnopoetics and folklore – much of which drew inspiration from him – remained stuck in orbit around specialized forms of language use apprehended as out of the ordinary or "poetic," especially oral poetries and ritual speech (Bauman 1977: 19). This was true, too, of the research tradition termed the ethnography of speaking and communication. For this tradition's then nascent interest in "performance," poetics seemed doubly important. First, expectedly, it offered a window onto the aesthetic dimensions of discursive genres (Bauman and Briggs 1990; Bauman 2011, 2012). Second, and less obviously, these aesthetic qualities, especially the cardinal quality of "parallelism" (repetition with variation), helped explain how distinct discourse genres became distinct. Parallelism, that is, was said to do double reflexive duty: In creating equivalences among chunks of linearly unfolding speech, it could draw attention to message form – exhibiting a kind of first-order, small-scale reflexivity. But as it draws attention to message form over larger stretches of discourse, parallelism can also, at a higher order, help put the whole event-in-progress in sharp relief, like a gestalt erupting from the background of "ordinary" communication. (See work by Russian Formalists like Mukarovsky [1964] who thought of foregrounding in poetic language as the breaking of rules and regularities associated with the standard language.)

In subsequent decades the study of the poetic function was extended to a wider range of discursive practices, including forms of face-to-face conversation. Tannen (1987, 1989) was among the first to study systematically poetic performativity in conversational encounters (see also Erickson 1982; Silverstein 1984; on children's speech, see, for example, Keenan [Ochs] 1977). With transcripts of audio-recorded conversations, she detailed how people did all sorts of things with the help of poetic structure, such as "getting or keeping the floor," "showing listenership," "providing back-channel response," "gearing up to answer or speak," "ratifying another's contribution" (Tannen 1989: 51 and passim). A two-volume edited collection of essays (Johnstone 1994) showcased the many things repetition could do, and did so in contexts that ranged from psychotherapeutic interviews (Ferrara 1994) to air-ground communication (Cushing 1994). An unnerving quality of this literature, however, was that it wasn't always clear what role poetics played, for as the list of functions grew, one wondered how poetics could do all these things, or anything at all. Poetic performativity itself tended to be left unexplained.

A recent attempt to address the performativity problem can be found in the "stance" literature (Hunston and Thompson 2000; Englebretson 2007; Jaffe 2009). Stance has often been used as a caption for a speaker's evaluations of the propositional content expressed by an utterance: "the lexical and grammatical expression of attitudes, feelings, judgments, or commitment concerning the propositional content of a message," as Biber and Finegan (1989) once wrote – or what Agha (2007) terms simply "propositional stance." "Stance" has also meant not just assessments and evaluations of people, events, and things, but interpersonal orientations – stances toward other interlocutors; Agha calls this "interactional stance" (cf. Goffman's 1981 "footing" and Du Bois's 2007 discussions of "positioning" and "alignment" in his conception of stance).

One important way in which the poetic function has consequential social effects is by mediating propositional and interactional stances. That is, poetic structures in discourse can guide pragmatic interpretation by helping interactants map propositional stances into interactional ones (Agha 2007: 96–103; Du Bois 2007; Lempert 2008). Consider, for instance, what Conversation Analysts term "upgraded" second-position assessments, where, say, someone evaluates a comestible as *delicious* and an interlocutor chimes in with *really delicious*.[5] The parallelistic juxtaposition of evaluative predicates across speaking turns (*delicious : **really** delicious*) helps invite one to read the second gustatory stance as an "upgrade," which then has implications for interpersonal alignment; it may invite participants to infer that the second assessor "agrees."[6] The poetic function here creates a "stance differential" (Du Bois 2007: 166): "Analogical relations are established between the juxtaposed stances," so that "[t]he foregrounding of this dialogic relation potentially invites inferences based on the comparison" (Du Bois 2007: 159) (see Agha 2007 and Lempert 2008). The cross-turn parallelism of propositional stances invites comparison, and such comparison in respect of what speakers say then serves as a principle for interpreting what speakers do (cf. Anward 2004; parallelism in such cases can thus serve a reflexive, "metapragmatic" function, Silverstein 1992, 1993, 2004). (Note the movement from the propositional to the interactional, as this is also crucial in more canonical cases of performativity, discussed below.)

It would be wrong to argue that such performativity inheres "in" the poetic organization of discourse itself, however. In cases like that of the upgraded second assessment cited above, poetic structure may be understood on analogy with the familiar "double articulation" or "dual patterning" of language. Unlike morphemes, phonemes and subphonemic distinctive features do not have a positive meaning, but rather serve a "sense-discriminatory" function (Waugh 1987); in a minimal pair like *pit* and *bit*, the contrast between unvoiced and voiced bilabial plosives /p/ and /b/ conveys that these are different words but tells us nothing about what the words mean. Similarly, poetic structure helps set off chunks of discourse as similar/dissimilar units; these emergent likenesses and differences may come to function metapragmatically – that is, they may come to guide an interpretation of what is being done in the text, of what acts people are doing, what roles people are inhabiting, what definition of the situation is in progress – but this can't be said to be the "meaning" of the poetic structure itself any more than the meaning of the word "pit" can be said to be encoded in the phoneme /p/.

Consider a second, slightly more complex manifestation of the poetic function, which Goodwin has dubbed "format tying." This is a kind of cross-turn lexico-syntactic parallelism that, in her study of urban African American youth in Philadelphia, often showed up in oppositional environments (Goodwin 1993: 177; 1990; see also Goodwin 2006).

> MARTHA: I don't know what you **la**ughin' at.
> BILLY: I know what I'm laughin at.
> Your **h**ead.

What matters here is not merely some cross-turn lexico-semantic "stance differential" (Billy's substitution of *know* for *don't know* and his punchline, *your head* for *what*). Goodwin suggests that Billy exploits parallelism to do something more, to enact a socioculturally recognizable kind of move found in this peer group. Goodwin's caption "format tying" is felicitous precisely because there is presumably a move-type in play here, which uses parallelism but is more than this. Exchanges like this, explains Goodwin (1990: 181), "display their status as escalations of prior actions ... by making use of the talk of prior speaker and transforming it to their advantage; in essence, they turn the prior action on its head." An action seems to be *figurated* by means of poetic structure to a degree greater than the upgraded second assessment example, while the ability to recognize this figuration depends to a greater extent on group-relative frameworks of cultural belief and value. Poetics here does more than unitize and make comparable chunks of discourse: it helps fashion discourse into a metapragmatic icon, an image of an act imbued with cultural value (Silverstein 2004).

The more "ritualized" the interaction, the more we tend to find global poetic structures ("global," in the sense that the structure encompasses the whole event, rather than only parts of it) that aspire to transfigure the whole event into such culturally inflected metapragmatic icons (Silverstein 2004). In his work on native South American ceremonial dialogues, Urban (1986), for instance, suggested that a cultural ideology of solidarity is exemplified and enacted through poetic patterns of symmetric role alternation in the dialogic performance itself. Of the Shokleng origin-telling myth style of ceremonial dialogue (termed wãñeklèn), Urban (1990: 101–2) describes how –

> In the wãñeklèn, two men sit opposite one another in the middle of the plaza, their legs entwined … One interlocutor leads, uttering the first syllable of the origin myth. The respondent repeats that syllable, after which the first speaker utters the second syllable, and so forth, in rapid-fire succession. Speakers move their heads and upper torso rhythmically in time with the syllables, which are shouted with extreme laryngeal and pharyngeal constriction.

Drawing together various semiotic resources (discourse, kinesic movements, bodily orientation, prosody [voice quality and speech rate]), Shokleng speakers fashion a vivid, multi-dimensional "model of and for coordination more generally, this coordination in turn representing a fundamental building block of social solidarity" (Urban 1990: 106).[7] Poetic qualities of this dialogic ritual are critical, because they become the formal means by which speakers materialize and exhibit cultural ideals (cf. Graham 1993; Perrino 2002; Lempert 2012a).

Such global, cross-modal poetic structures are typical – perhaps even a hallmark – of ritual textuality. Ritual has long been argued to function as a vehicle for materializing and "reproducing" otherwise intangible cultural norms and values (Durkheim and Mauss 1963). The study of ritual has spawned a substantial literature that spans several disciplines. Here we restrict ourselves to the semiotic and linguistic anthropological literature where Stasch (2011) observes a convergence in views. "A ritual event," writes Stasch (2011: 160), "is characterized by the exceptional quantity and vividness of the general types that are felt as present in its concrete particulars." This materialization is accomplished with the help of cross-modal poetic structure. Ritual, Stasch summarizes, involves the "poetically dense figuration of macrocosmic order in microcosmic action." Public rituals' "excessive formalism" (Parmentier 1994) or "hypertrophic" qualities (Silverstein 1981b, 2004) – achieved through exploiting the poetic function – help foreground the whole event relative to ordinary communication, making it stand out and serve as a sign in its own right. This self-reflexive and self-objectifying aspect of ritual semiosis, in turn, helps to fashion the here-and-now event into a socioculturally embedded metapragmatic icon of a macrocosmic order (Silverstein 2004; Lempert 2012a). Ritual thus "intensifies features common to human activity at large" (Stasch 2011: 162), at once parasitic on ordinary interaction even as it stands apart from it. Deeply reflexive, ritual has often been shown to foreground and caricature normal features of communication, and it does this in a way that brings the seemingly macrocosmic into the here-now constructed microcosm of the ritual event.

19.1.1 Problems with poetics

A number of issues merit more reflection and research. These issues center around the way poetic patterning helps actors move from "what is said" to "what is done," and the way this movement involves orders of cultural meaning. It is here that the analogy to the phonology–morphology interface breaks down, for while a specific configuration of phonemes does or does not have a denotational meaning in a given language, poetic patterns in discourse – no matter the degree of textual cohesion – can always fail to convey a determinate interpretation. Poetic performativity, like all species of the performative, is measured by success or failure rather than by conditions of truth or falsity. Future research should show how – processually speaking – poetically organized discourse crystallizes in real time into metapragmatic icons, in a semiotically cumulative rather than instantaneous manner. Indeed, when sociocultural beliefs and values get invoked with the aid of such poetic structure, we would do well to investigate this crystallization as a precarious and gradient achievement, something people accomplish in varying degrees, from the gendered inflection of Billy's retort to Martha, to the florid acting out of a whole ideological complex in the full-tilt public ritual of Shokleng ceremonial dialogues. Just as the poetic figuration of action should be approached as a provisional, gradient, and cumulative achievement, so too should the process of uptake be troubled and studied with more care. Though not trained on the poetic function, some research has, indeed, called for an increased sensitivity to the ways signs are evaluated differently by different categories of social actors (see especially Agha's 2007 notion of "social domain"), or even by different participants in an interaction; we can't assume that all participants equally notice poetic qualities of textuality.

Attention to the poetics of ritual does not mean a retreat to the symbolic anthropology of old. Ritual events, imagined as "cultural performances" (Singer 1972), do not require that participants dutifully act out cultural scripts (as Geertz, for instance, made it sound, and as functionalist-styled analyses of ritual had often suggested, where ritual blindly did the bidding of some sociocultural order). Such performances can be, and frequently are, shot through with critical evaluation – such as stances taken by performers on their own and others' roles, and on what they and others say and act out. This alone suggests that the pragmatics of ritual poetics may be fraught and not unproblematically conservative. Insofar as poetic structure helps materialize otherwise intangible aspects of social and cultural life, this materialization also exposes these very aspects to public reflexivity (see Bauman and Briggs 1990); it makes it possible to scrutinize society and culture in multiparty events of often great visibility. In terms of its axiological (value-setting) functions, ritual may, indeed, aspire to "reproduce" institutions and their normative infrastructure, but more often it ends up akin to a crucible in which pieces of the sociocultural surround are assembled for all to see, and where the resultant construction is subject to scrutiny.

As we have seen, ritual's dense, global, cross-modal poetic integration is but an extreme, hypertrophied case of what one finds in ordinary communicative interaction. In a study of a video-recorded dinner-table interaction, Erickson (2004), for instance, detailed forms of rhythmic integration that were surprising both for the range of semiotic materials integrated and for the number of people who participated in it. It was not simply that a beat could be heard within a single speaker's stream of speech, by tracking (relatively) regular temporal intervals between prosodic prominences (this is a familiar phenomenon termed isochrony: see Wennerstrom 2001); several people at the table also worked to maintain this shared rhythm and, what is more, key kinesic activities (reaching for comestibles arrayed on the table, lifting fork to mouth or setting silverware down) were swept up in this cross-turn, multi-party rhythmic structure, such that Erickson could represent this multiplex orderliness by means of musical notation. It was as if they were reading from the same score. (On co-speech gestural integration, see also McNeill 1992, 2005; Enfield 2009.)

As cases like Erickson's dinner-table conversation show, a methodological problem that has long dogged the study of poetics stems from the fact that there's always a surfeit of poetic patterns. Recall the philosopher Nelson Goodman's (1972: 440) quip that "[a]nything is in some way like anything else." How might we constrain the search for likenesses, then? As Brown (1987) astutely observed, Jakobson often made it sound like there is a discovery procedure for finding poetic patterns in the text, as if texts were stable objects and their architectonics evident to an astute observer. (Brown's point echoed critiques leveled at the Russian Formalists, who had exaggerated the autonomy of the text – partly as a means of discipline building, just as Saussure had exaggerated the autonomy of language [la langue], and Durkheim society – thereby neglecting the normative, metadiscursive force of literary criticism as an institution; criticism is a force in its own right that guides readings of texts.) If repetitions and parallelisms are, simply put, interpretations, then we need to know for whom and under what conditions these register as patterns and do things at all. Brown's methodological advice was elegant: "[R]ather than attempt to use linguistic analysis as a technique for discovering patterns in a text, one might start from data about the effects of poetic language and attempt to formulate hypotheses which would account for these effects" (Brown 1987: 69). Indeed, the object of investigation is better thought of as a set of form-functional motivations, which mean that we independently work out the functional end – what type of action seems to be in progress – and then see what may have motivated it. For example, we might start by analyzing comments about, and tacit responses to, the stretch of discourse containing the poetic pattern, either while the event was in progress (through attention to transcripts) or after the fact (e.g., through eliciting comments in interviews, the differences among these kinds of data notwithstanding), and then work backwards, as it were, to see what may have motivated the construal.

Another methodological problem concerns the spatiotemporal distribution and "reach" of the poetically organized elements. Because poetics involves the foregrounding of message form, it is no surprise to find many students of this function staring at transcripts so intently that the periphery bleeds away. Such a textualist bias can blind us to the "interdiscursivity" of language use, to the far-reaching dialogic resonances of discourse, where signs echo or reach out to signs from other events, real or imagined, past or future (Bauman 2004; Agha and Wortham 2005). Taken seriously, this sensitivity leads us to agree with Du Bois (2007: 140), when he writes that "[d]ialogicality makes its presence felt to the extent that a stancetaker's words derive from, and further engage with, the words of those who have spoken before – whether immediately within the current exchange of stance utterances, or more remotely along the horizons of language and prior text as projected by the community of discourse" (cf. Becker 1995). In terms of stance-taking in discourse, distant stance objects, objects we evaluate but never actually mention, are common, as are distant interlocutors with whom we align or disalign when we talk. Perhaps nowhere is this penumbral interdiscursivity and stance-taking more pronounced than in mass-mediated political discourse, such as televised public oratory and debate. There discourse is styled to reach certain constituencies and not others, and to turn back attacks against one's message – attacks made not just in the immediate, here-and-now speech event but in prior events like television attack ads and speeches by opposing candidates (Lempert and Silverstein 2012).

19.2 "Explicit" performativity

The poetic function involves a species of performativity that operates by means of emergent likenesses and differences among chunks of text. Rather than being localizable, something that can be pinpointed as here or there, poetic structure is highly distributed and configurational in its formal organization. In terms of what it does, it is cumulative rather than instantaneous, and provisional rather than determinate or indefeasible – in the sense that the actions it helps bring into being can be canceled out or easily reinterpreted after the fact. We began our discussion with such cases, because they offer critical insights into performativity, understood as causal efficacy of signs in society, as a by-degrees successful but never determinate relationship between forms in co(n)texts and their sociocultural functions – what they "do."

This was not the point of departure for Austin, who took so-called "explicit" performatives as his starting point. This "explicit" classification was provisional, because he conceded, in italics no less, that the performative formulae with which he started his lectures in *How to Do Things with Words* were just a "peculiar and special case," a way to "make plain how the action is to be taken or understood, what action it is" (Austin 1962: 63–70). "Peculiar" and "special" these formulae may have been, but Austin's initial examples committed him willy-nilly to a vast category of "indirect" speech acts, which speech-act theory's systematizer John Searle later famously addressed: "In hints, insinuations, irony, and metaphor – to mention a few examples – the speaker's utterance meaning and the sentence meaning come apart in various ways" (Searle 1975: 59). There is no place here to repeat the criticism of indirect speech acts and interrogate Austin's preoccupation with denotational explicitness, nor can we survey the considerable literature on "indirectness" in fields like sociolinguistics (for two recent engagements with this problematic, see Silverstein 2010; Lempert 2012b). It must suffice to say that explicit performatives constitute a peculiar and special case, indeed.[8]

Let us recall the linguistic peculiarities of these explicit formulae. Setting aside for the moment the issue of felicity conditions, recall the design of these expressions. Formulae like *I promise you that* ... are built around certain verbs like "promise" and "baptize," which denote action types. Because these verbs characterize communicative signs as socially consequential action, they can be considered "metapragmatic" descriptors (Silverstein 1976). Each of the items of a metapragmatic vocabulary "designates a type of speech event as an enactable, accomplishable relationship between a speaker and an addressee" (Silverstein 1987: 34). The clearest examples are verbs of speaking – verbs like *say, protest, apologize,* and *promise*. In the performative expression *I promise you* ..., the verb "promise" is deployed as a token of the named metapragmatic type "promise," thereby denoting the speech act it simultaneously accomplishes.[9]

The explicit performative has other peculiarities of design; the canonical form of these expressions is that of first-person-indicative active sentences with non-past tense marking on the verb, a frame that tends to collocate with the adverb "hereby" (e.g., *I (hereby) bet you sixpence* ...). They don't "work" in the past tense or with quotative framing – which would result in a *report* of an act rather than an act executed in the here-and-now (technically put, the constituents of explicit performative utterances are hence "reflexively" rather than "reportively" calibrated to the contexts of their occurrence, Silverstein 1993). Then there is the fact that speaker and addressee are indexed through person deixis ("I" and "you"), occupying the grammatical roles of (1st person) subject and (2nd person) indirect object. For canonical performatives to work the indexical expressions which are their vital component parts (e.g., the person and temporal deictics in "I *(hereby)* promise **you** ...") must refer to the here-and-now interaction in which they are spoken.[10]

Consider, in sum, just how robust this whole frame is, how much work it does to tell us about what kind of act is done, by whom, and to whom. Each of these parameters – the relationship of what is said to the context of its occurrence (the distinction between reflexive and reportive calibration), the way participant roles of speaker and addressee are filled and related, and the way a metapragmatic descriptor serves as a token of a speech-act type – may be thought of as minimal linguistic conditions on the success of an explicit performative utterance. To this we must then add the vast array of extra-linguistic contextual conditions – the felicity conditions posited by Austin, which he argued are needed for these exquisitely crafted formulae to count as acts.

Austin's theory of denotationally explicit speech acts crystallizes the intuition of speakers that language is made up of neatly segmentable and inherently referential words and, furthermore, that it is these aspects of language that do things. It was with this in mind that Silverstein (1979: 210–15) critiqued Austin's analysis of performative "forces" (we will focus here on his analysis of "locution" and "illocution," see n. 1), arguing that the latter's analysis of performatives involves a Whorfian projection – a process whereby the grammatical categories and "fashions of speaking" of a language community influence habits of thought and behavior (Whorf 1998 [1956]). Whereas researchers interested in linguistic relativity have usually examined how the language-specific organization of grammatical categories influences habits of cognition, Silverstein extended this notion to pragmatics, to ideologies about how language works and what it does. Following the analysis of Whorf (1998 [1956]: 88ff.), Silverstein considered how covert linguistic categories inform habitual conceptualization or ideology about language use. In English a range of explicit performative verbs appear to folk-consciousness as hyponyms of the superordinate verb *to say* (e.g., "She {... said, promised, demanded ...} that ..."). As with the verb *say*, these performative verbs take sentential complements and exhibit an alternation common to reported-speech constructions in English between "direct" and "indirect" types (e.g., "He$_i$ {... said, promised ...} 'I$_i$ will ...'" versus "He$_i$ {... said, promised ...} that he$_i$ would ..."). Of course, at the same time as the focus on parallels between speech-act verbs and verbs of speaking makes them appear to be essentially linked phenomena, it also simultaneously masks other lexicogrammatical differences between them.

(For example, this folk analysis fails to reveal which ditransitive verbs allow for double-object dative constructions and which require the morphological dative [e.g., the speech-act verb allows a double object construction, "I promised John that we would ...", but the verb of speaking does not, *"I said John that we would ..." requiring the dative, "I said *to* John that ..."]; see Rappaport Hovav 2008.) But all differences as would be revealed by distributional analysis are not equally fixed upon by native metalinguistic awareness, being elided in a folk-analysis that "conclude[s] that promising is really saying ... plus something else" (Silverstein 1979: 213).

The ideological elaboration of the analogy between verbs of speaking and explicit speech-act verbs, where parallel treatment in reported-speech constructions serves as the privileged ground for the analogy, interprets direct reports as faithful to message "form" and indirect reports as faithful only to "content," a distinction which (together with other patterns in English) invites us to imagine a natural divide between an utterance's "wording" and its propositional "meaning" (Rumsey 1990). Not all languages "valorize wording as something *distinct* from meaning," argues Rumsey (1990: 354), using the indigenous Australian languages of Ngarinyin and Bunaba as his point of comparison. Because explicit performative verbs in English pattern in a partially parallel manner to verbs of speaking like *to say*, exhibiting a distinction between "indirect" and "direct" reporting types, this form–content, wording–meaning distinction comes to affect the way we reason about performativity (cf. Lee 1997). The folk-analyst tends to see the "illocutionary force" of language as residing in the "locution" of a particular propositional meaning – the "meaning" being that which is seemingly preserved across indirect and direct construction types. The tendency is to objectify "force," *qua* causal consequentiality of speech, to treat it as localized either in the segmentable metapragmatic designator itself, a word that denotes the speech act being accomplished in the instance, or in the decontextualizable (i.e., reportable) utterances in which such "force"-ful words occur. As Silverstein argued, "[g]iven Austin's concentration on lexical items, in particular on the predicates of the explicit performatives, it is almost as if these lexical forms embodied the 'force'" (Silverstein 1979: 213).

This fixation on propositionally transparent words and utterances removes from sight the myriad other co-occurring signs necessary for the "felicitous" accomplishment of the act. This example of the motivation of ideology from language structure and usage suggests how people focus on the most reportable pragmatic acts of reference and illocution (e.g., descriptors like "demand" or "promise") rather than complex configurations of signs – when they reason about the effectiveness of language use. The word, as the minimal unit of decontextualizable or reportable discourse whose meaning is still transparent, steals attention when speakers try to reflect on what language does and how it does it. While this category "error" – this treatment of symbolic predication as causally effective action – may be motivated in part by fashions of speaking in languages like English, it may also derive support from more general reflexive habits and limitations (Silverstein 1981a). Speakers (and here Austin and Searle are no exception) tend to focus upon the most decontextualizable elements of language – the words and expressions which denote speech acts – and analyze these as being imbued with "force."[11]

19.3 Taboo performativity

The folk analysis of performativity, of "illocutionary force," as immanent in decontextualizable words that describe actions still does not guarantee that performative expressions will work. While a verb like "promise" can function performatively, it normally doesn't, as when the subject is not the grammatical first person or the verb is in the past tense. Performative formulae, again, must have a specific linguistic design to work and must also be supported by a host of extra-linguistic felicity conditions.

Now compare this dependency on linguistic design and nonlinguistic context with verbal taboo, expressions normatively evaluated as having dispreferred consequences that speakers in certain contexts or engaged in certain genres of speaking seek to avoid. Verbal taboos are also a kind of performative construction, but they differ in terms of their extraordinary parsimony, both in terms of linguistic design and in terms of felicity conditions.[12] They are performatives in the sense that by uttering taboo expressions speakers accomplish socially recognized acts. To use the English metapragmatic vocabulary, by cursing and swearing we may, for instance, "insult" and "disrespect" others. However, the efficacy of taboo expressions, unlike explicit performatives, does not depend upon their occurrence in a certain co-textual or grammatical frame. Person deixis, which specifies the speech act as a relation between speaker and hearer, and qualities involving mood and temporal deixis are not required. The word alone is all one seems to need.

Indeed, verbal taboos typically require few if any co(n)textual felicity conditions in order for them to accomplish performative effects. Under strict proscriptive regimes, like the FCC ban on obscenities on broadcast television and radio, or the edicts of the royal court in Tahiti prohibiting the utterances of the king's name (Simons 1982), one can't even innocently "mention" a taboo expression without the utterance counting as a taboo "use." Utter *fuck* on the airwaves in the United States between the hours of 6 a.m. and 10 p.m. and obscenity happens – with fines to follow – no matter who says the word or how hard one tries to mitigate or cancel the word's force, such as by embedding the wayward curse in quotes. In their extreme form, verbal taboos are, properly speaking, *unmentionable* (Fleming and Lempert 2011a). For Austin, performative utterances could not count as acts without felicity conditions, but taboo utterances seem curiously free of such conditions.

What can we learn from the curious, twofold parsimony of verbal taboo? First, we can see that verbal taboos can be distinguished from explicit performatives in terms of co-occurring metapragmatic discourse. The relationship between the denoting and the doing of verbal taboos is nowhere near as convergent and transparent as it is for canonical speech-act verbs. Thus, to curse at someone by, in different words than these, telling them to engage in an anatomically impossible sex act, where they perform the roles of both semantic agent and reflexive patient, does describe something, but it doesn't describe that which is done by uttering it – to wit, the offending of one's verbally abused interlocutor. When we turn to cases of verbal taboo outside of the rarefied and rather specialized domain of cursing, such as taboos on everyday speech in the presence of one's mother-in-law in Aboriginal Australia, the relationship between the semantics and the performative effects of taboo expression types is often less motivated. To take an example from the in-law avoidance speech of the native Australian language Guugu-Yimidhirr, the meaning of *balinga*, "echidna" (i.e., spiny anteater), which must be replaced with the term *nhalngarr* when speaking to one's brother-in-law, tells us nothing about the shame and embarrassment which would be experienced if the proscribed word were to be used in such a context (Haviland 1979: 218). The meaning of tabooed words and expressions help little or not at all when it comes to figuring out what the verbal taboo, *qua* performative, does. The meanings are arbitrarily related to their pragmatic effects in avoidance contexts.

Taboo expressions count as action not because they *represent* action – as is the case for verbs that denote speech-act types, like the explicit performatives described above. This lack of fit between the semantics of verbal taboos and the pragmatics of their performative effects appears to be related to that other peculiar feature of verbal taboos as performatives – their unmentionability. By reporting the event of a baptism after the fact, you do not risk thereby naming your addressee; by describing a wedding you don't inadvertently marry your interlocutors. But, as the existence of special citational formulae (like "the F-word" in English) attest, reporting on the use of a curse word, thereby replicated, may risk replicating the social effect simultaneously reported (cf. "no-name" in central Australia, Nash and Simpson 1981). Avoidance in such reporting contexts reflects the relative "rigidity" of taboo performativity (i.e., parallel to the invariance of reference of "rigid designators" in Kripke 1972; Fleming 2011). Indeed, this seems to be a good diagnostic of verbal taboo from the perspective of performativity: They are performatives whose effects, at least for some discourse contexts, are indefeasible.

Compared in this manner to explicit performatives, verbal taboos appear as the apotheosis of a folk analysis of performativity wherein the pragmatic efficacy of discourse is felt to be localized in words and expressions. This process was at work in cases of explicit performativity but reaches its apogee here. Here the very pragmatics of avoidance – the fact that a form may be avoided even in reported speech constructions, because the speaker worries that quotes can't contain the form's "force" – implicitly frames the performative efficacy of utterances containing tokens of the expression-type as "in" the forms themselves. It is for this reason that rigid, indefeasible performativity is so pronounced among verbal taboos. Here the ideological folk analysis of verbal taboos is motivated by the pragmatics of what Rumsey (1990) calls "wording" and not, as with the idea of "illocutionary force" at work in the folk analysis of explicit performativity, by the pragmatics of a propositional "meaning" underwritten by the particularities of reported speech in languages like English. Indeed Rumsey (1990: 353) argues that indigenous Australian speech communities (like Bunaba and Guugu-Yimidhirr) do not have a clearly motivated distinction between "wording" and "meaning," that all language is primarily understood pragmatically (rather than semantically) as "wording" (rather than "meaning"). This focus on the pragmatics of language is precisely reflected, for Rumsey, in the institution of in-law avoidance speech, a register locally understood as related to everyday speech in how it enacts different kinds of social relationships, not in its ability to say "the same thing."

This productive relationship between usage and ideology, whereby speakers' practices of avoidance implicitly frame the "power" of words and expressions as inherent to them, can be seen even more vividly in processes of homophone avoidance. Just as speakers may avoid citing iconic replicas of taboo items in reported speech, so too may they avoid words iconic with other taboo expressions at the level of the lexical type. A peculiarity of rigid performatives is that signs similar in material substance to a given taboo target often themselves become taboo, exhibiting a kind of "contagion" (cf. Tylor 1913; Frazer 1959). Similar sounding words in speech, graphic words in writing, or manual gestures in signing may become secondary targets of taboo and avoidance. Table 19.1 illustrates how, for a range of unrelated languages, homophone avoidance (a phrase we use as a coverall term for all iconically motivated secondary avoidances at the level of the lexical type) is often associated with name taboos.

The second column of Table 19.1 provides examples of names tabooed for a range of speakers who stand in specific social relationships to the named individuals. The third and fourth columns present everyday words, phonetically similar to those names, which are also tabooed for those speakers. Name taboo and homophone avoidance serve as an important resource for structuring social relationships under rather different

Table 19.1 Name taboos and the avoidance of iconic phonetic sequences

Language	Tabooed name	Phonetically similar forms also avoided	
Tahitian (Simons 1982: 211)	**tu**	**tui** 'to strike'	**fetu** 'star'
Mongolian (Humphrey 1978: 94)	**tegsh**	**tegsh** 'level'	**tevsh** 'wooden platter'
Mwotlap (Codrington 1957[1891]: 44)	**pantutun**	**panei** 'hand'	**tutun** 'hot'
Kambaata (Treis 2005: 295)	**caa'mmíse**	**cancanáta** 'chatter'	**caakkíse** (woman's name)
Xhosa (Herbert 1990: 466)	**saki**	**ukusabela** 'to listen'	**iswekile** 'sugar'

conditions in these cases. For Mwotlap speakers (Banks Islands, Vanuatu) a range of affinal relationships (both same and alternate generation, and parallel and cross-sex) involve reciprocal name-tabooing. These name and homophone avoidances form part of a larger linguistic and nonlinguistic repertoire of avoidance practices most pronounced, as in Australia, in the relationship between sons-in-law and mothers-in-law. These relatives studiously keep at a distance from one another, "if the two chance to meet in a path, the woman will step out of it and stand with her back turned till he has gone by" (Codrington 1957 [1891]: 43). Name tabooing and homophone avoidance – reference-based practices employed always and everywhere – thus complement nonlinguistic avoidance practices of bodily distancing and interpersonal non-ratification employed in contexts where avoidance relations are co-present to one another. In Xhosa, Kambaata, and Mongolian, name tabooing is non-reciprocal with the daughter-in-law asymmetrically avoiding the father-in-law's name and phonologically similar words. The examples from Tahitian involve the tabooing of the name of the king and of a set of ritually purged lexemes phonetically similar to his name. But while different types of social relations and different beliefs about what uttering tabooed names will do are at work in these cases, in each the semiotic processes are similar: verbal taboo is not exclusively identified with the name, as a lexical type, but rather affects a range of words connected by phonetic likeness to the tabooed name.[13]

So what do these cases of contagion tell us about taboo performativity? Tabooed homophones illustrate the decoupling of the performative function of verbal taboos from their denotational backing. While the efficacy of explicit performatives depends upon their being built around a semantically rich metapragmatic discourse, in the cases of these name taboos, and specifically the secondarily avoided (near-) homophones, there is no relationship between the meaning of the avoided expression and the expression's performative function. The Mwotlap word for 'hand' (*panei*) or for 'hot' (*tutun*) has no semantic relationship to the name *Pantutun*. (Indeed, the fact that the avoidance of the word for "hand" in the speech of Pantutun's brother-in-law is a sign of deference to him requires a quite complex set of inferences as well as a broad base of sociological knowledge.) The words in question are not avoided because they are tokens of the personal name type, but merely because they are iconic with tokens of that type. Notice how "illocutionary force" here is treated by users as if it resided in the materiality of the semiotic token itself. That is, there is a kind of wording-based sign fetishism (Fleming and Lempert 2011a) associated with this focus on sign-tokens over sign-types. This fetishism is itself cyclically motivated by the homophone avoidance itself, since such avoidance practices frame taboo performativity as inherent in the material substance (rather than lexical form) of tokens. Here the pragmatics of avoidance – of the "wording" of utterances rather than their "meaning" – motivate ideologies of performative inherency. If unmentionability frames performative efficacy as inherent in the lexical type, the avoidance of materially similar signs (i.e., homophone avoidance) frames performative efficacy as inherent in the substance of lexical tokens (see note 13).

Note again, then, that some of the most basic felicity conditions on the success of explicit performatives do not need to be met when it comes to verbal taboos. While explicit performatives are infelicitous should they occur in quotative contexts, such a constraint does not defease the performative efficacy of verbal taboos. And while a token of the explicit performative type must occur for it to be felicitous, for verbal taboos which trigger homophone effects, the sign which has a performative effect needn't even be a token of the performative type. The indefeasibility of verbal taboos thus contrasts with the greater defeasibility (e.g., through treatment in reported speech constructions, in infelicitous contexts, etc.) of explicit performatives. This opens up a perspective on the "gradience" of performativity, a metric through which we can scale performativity in terms of its relative "strength" or indefeasibility. Excellent examples of those on the rigid, less defeasible end of the performativity spectrum include interjections (see Kockelman 2003), and especially verbal taboos,[14] the most extreme cases of which are literally unmentionable, as no reporting frame can contain their potent illocutionary force, a force which invariably "leaks" (cf. Irvine 2011). Explicit performatives, by contrast, have a "weaker" performativity, requiring many felicity conditions for their success – which is to say that their efficacy is easily defeased. As we can see, in sum, verbal taboos reveal that not all performatives are created equal, and that one dimension of variation is the relative ease or difficulty with which they are defeased. Attention to verbal taboo thus reveals a neglected dimension of variation in the study of performativity, providing us with a basis for comparison.

19.4 Conclusion

"Speech act theory," as Agha (1996: 1118) noted, "has little to say about the effectiveness or 'force'-fulness of speech at other levels of form and structure – for example, stretches of speech larger than the sentence; prosody and intonation; the 'figures' of rhetoric, formed by means of parallelistic and other types of devices in larger scale stretches of connected discourse, and across conversational turns." Poetic performativity – the idea that repetition and parallelism in discourse can "do" things, akin to the way formulae like *I bet you* or *I promise you* can – exposes this limitation well. Still, "poetic performativity" is something of a misnomer, for it isn't the poetics alone which accomplishes the actional aspect of discourse. Once our units of analysis are stretched beyond the narrow sentence-sized ones privileged in the philosophical approaches of Austin and Searle, we can see that what we're captioning as poetic performativity is but an artifact of a highly distributed and configurational semiotic assemblage (cf. Enfield 2009). (And even this expanded approach leaves out the inferential processes which are undeniably important for making sense of such assemblages; see Levinson 2000.) Such configurational, or as we have termed it, poetic performativity is ubiquitous in semiotic life, and yet speakers typically find it difficult to report and reflect upon its pragmatic efficacy. At the other extreme of performative function, reflecting and naturalizing precisely the biases of metalinguistic awareness which conceal the importance of poetic performativity for its users, are taboo expressions – discrete lexical items, words and expressions – to which much anxious attention is paid, and around which whole regimes of proscription may be built. Here performativity seems hyperlocalized, as if it resided in the lexical type or material tokens of the expression itself. As we have argued, this is directly tied to the (un)reportability of such speech – to a focus on the "wording" rather than the "meaning" of speech highlighted by the avoidance of certain words and expressions even in frames, like reported speech, where speakers are not conventionally held responsible for the "content" of their utterances (cf. Hill and Irvine 1993; Goffman 1981). The hyperlocalization of performativity in cases of verbal taboos is the result of a process of ideological fetishization, perhaps already nascent at the level of word "meaning" for the case of explicit performativity, which sees words and expressions – rather than configurational texts-in-co(n)texts – as the locus of pragmatic efficacy in discourse. Cases of poetic and taboo performativity thus make us acutely aware of the problem of "where" illocutionary force – that cardinal fiction of speech-act theory – resides.

These cases were also designed to make us aware of the way performativity is gradient, a matter of degree, and how a denotationally explicit metapragmatics is, as Silverstein (1976) has long argued, just a special case – a concession Austin made but never took seriously enough. We cite these cases not to pile more criticism on the already beleaguered speech-act theory, but rather to stimulate new lines of research. Performativity can be resolved into a number of distinct parameters that can then be used to guide comparison, parameters such as the relative "rigidity" or "defeasibility" of performatives – how hard or easy it is to annul the act; metapragmatic explicitness – the degree to which the linguistic denotation of the utterance is related to what the utterance does; discursive localizability – how discrete or distributed the sign-tokens that make up the performative assemblage are, all the way from the hyperlocalizable phonetic substance which makes up the material sign form of the token of a taboo expression type to the highly configurational, emergent patterning of cross-turn poetically organized utterance sequences. These dimensions of variation are not meant to be exhaustive, but rather are intended to inculcate a sensitivity to the diversity of performativity and thereby open up new avenues of empirical research.

Acknowledgments

Our thanks to the editors and especially Jack Sidnell for incisive comments that helped improve the quality of this chapter. While Lempert contributed the section on "poetics" and Fleming on "taboo," we worked together to synthesize our arguments and hence each of us contributed equally to this chapter. Authorship order is strictly alphabetical.

Notes

1. In the beginning of his lectures, Austin created a twofold distinction between the "performative" and the "constative" – roughly corresponding to linguistic signs functioning to causally change social conditions and facts, on the one hand, and linguistic signs functioning to describe them, on the other. As the lectures progressed, he went on to argue that describing itself is a kind of doing, and rejected his initial twofold distinction in favor of a tripartite distinction between the "locutionary," the "illocutionary," and the "perlocutionary." For Austin the "locutionary act" came to replace the "constative"; by this he meant "uttering a certain sentence with a certain sense and reference, which again is roughly equivalent to 'meaning' in the traditional sense" (Austin 1962: 108). The distinction between "illocutionary" and "perlocutionary," on the other hand, distinguished between the "conventional force" of an utterance type (e.g., commissives such as a "promise," directives such as a "request") and its causal consequences, respectively.

2. There is no place here for a nuanced account of Jakobson's discussions, nor can we situate his work in relation to Russian Formalist theory of literary analysis to which he contributed. For a review of Jakobson's contributions to anthropology, see especially Caton (1987).
3. Banti and Giannattasio want to admit "poetry" as a cross-cultural category while acknowledging considerable historical and cultural variation. This "narrower level of *poetry in a strict sense*," they write, "is autonomously defined by each culture in the course of its history on the basis of its own choice of genres, specific contents, ways of production, functions, occasions of performance, and aesthetic and social values." As they note, the study of poetries – unlike the study of manifestations of the "poetic function" in discourse generally – comes with an additional methodological burden, requiring "a careful analysis of the different poetical settings with their historical, social, and cultural backgrounds" (Banti and Giannattasio 2004: 294). Between the two poles they erected – poetically organized discourse here, official poetries there – Banti and Giannattasio admit many "intermediate forms," like spells, proverbs, ritual speech, children's taunts. So pronounced is the poetic function in these forms that it threatens to flood out the boundary between official poetries and poetically organized discourse. The many intermediary cases hint at what is perhaps the real, underlying sociohistorical variable here. It is not the contingency of categories per se that is at issue (viz. whether a category akin to the "poetic" exists for some given community at a point in time), but the degree to which the poetic function has been subject to sustained, reflexive attention by language users, producing poetic sensibilities and standards that enjoy at least some degree of institutionalization. The poetic function may "focus on the message for its own sake," but other forms of reflexivity have an eye on poetics, keeping it in check, making it an object of attention, reflection, and cultural value.
4. On textuality generally, see, for example, Halliday and Hasan (1976); Gutwinski (1976); de Beaugrande and Dressler (1982); Hanks (1989); Silverstein (1997); Martin (2001); Schiffrin (2001).
5. For pedagogical purposes, this constructed example of an "upgraded" assessment is meant to spotlight the parallelism and eliminate the complexity one finds in actual data. Assessments cannot adequately be studied in isolation like this – with no sense of context or co-text. Nor do we wish to suggest that "assessment" is the primary or sole pragmatic function in play. Such functions can only be identified with well-contextualized data. For discussions of second assessments, see especially Heritage and Raymond (2005); Sidnell (2010); Enfield and Sidnell (2012).
6. Conversation Analysts have sometimes argued that there is a pervasive underlying "preference" for agreement (Sacks 1987), and some suggest that such "upgrading" of second-position assessments is a function of this preference's strength. That is, this preference is so strong and

pervasive that if the second assessment is not markedly upgraded from the first assessment it will register to hearers as merely "going along." Such upgrades can in turn motivate other readings, such as attempts to claim more epistemic authority for the assessable (Heritage and Raymond 2005). For the purposes of the present example, we bracket Conversation Analysis' issues of preference and sequential organization and simply note that formal contrasts across chunks of text – the poetic function – play a role in making the move termed "upgrade" recognizable to interactants and to the analysts who study them, whatever else these patterns may do in any discursive instance.

7. Urban's case can be contrasted with more dynamic, "processual" figurations of action that are also well attested in the literature. Examples include Mertz's studies of law school discourse (Mertz 1996, 1998), Parmentier's (1997: 37–9) astute reanalysis of Abu-Lughod's (1986) work on the Bedouin genre of *ghinnawas*, Silverstein's (1996) analysis of Sapir's encounter with Peter McGuff, Wortham's (2001) discussion of self-transformation in autobiographical narrative, Lempert's (2012a) analysis of textual-ideological reunification in Tibetan Buddhist debate.

8. There is no place here to address debates over the utility of an analytic distinction between "explictness" and "implicitness." It is now received tradition in discourse analysis that denotational explicitness is not a good guide to action. Nevertheless, interactants themselves quite often *do* use explicitness as a guide for action, relying on denotationally explicit metapragmatic descriptors to report what just happened, as in cases of so-called "plausible deniability." In terms of reportable action and in terms of the local interpretive practices of participants themselves, "explicit" performativity does matter. Regardless of whether they actually do accomplish the actions that they "explicitly" denote or whether they accomplish wholly other types of action only metaphorically or inferentially related to those denoted, Austin's explicit performatives do purport to enact certain nameable action types. The exploitation of explicitness-implicitness also results in conventionalized and even highly ritualized discursive practices. "Residual semanticity," for instance, was Silverstein's (1976) caption for all the after-the-fact, "all-I-said-was" maneuvers that reframe action by appeal to prior denotation. And there are countless kinds of practices – all highly routinized, from insults to forms of oratory – that deliberately try to avoid being reportable as such-and-such action-type and hence aim for "indirectness" (Lempert 2012b). In fact, the very existence of metapragmatic labels like "hint" and "innuendo" – even "indirectness" itself – makes plain the relevance of explicitness-implicitness as a dimension of pragmatic life.

9. Even the relationship between a felicitously co(n)textualized, denotationally explicit speech-act verb and what it accomplishes is often itself an inferentially complex interactional achievement. This dimension of

the interactional negotiation of the act is beyond the scope of this chapter but addressed, for example, in Sidnell and Enfield's chapter in this volume. Here our focus is on what might be thought of as first-order relationships between speech-act types and their pragmatically effective tokens.

10. To use the analytical distinctions presented in Silverstein (1993) these signs must be "reflexively" rather than "reportively" calibrated to the context of their occurrence. Where, as in reported speech constructions, the speech-act verb and its accompanying indexical expressions are recentered (or "decentered," Kockelman 2010: 168) into a narrated event, the performative ceases to have a performative efficacy. In Austinian terms, it is only the reporting or "constative" function which remains.

11. Lest this seem to imply a chicken-and-egg problem – how can the performative be understood to derive from the metapragmatic term which describes it? – we should remember that diachronically the formation of "explicit" performatives typically involves a dialectical relationship between performative use and reportive mention. Just as metapragmatic descriptors may be recast as performatives when used in those specialized first-person, present-tense constructions which are maximally bound to the context of their occurrence, so too may more purely performative forms be lexicalized as metapragmatic descriptors through processes of delocutionary derivation (Benveniste 1971). For instance, the extended phonetic articulation of the postalveolar fricative "shhhhh," often accompanied by an extended pointer finger vertically bisecting the speaker's lips, is a purely performative expression (similar to an interjection) which has been "rank-shifted" (Silverstein 1987: 34) into a metapragmatic verb, "to shush." Though now capable of reporting the censorious act in question (e.g., "He shushed me"), the metapragmatic designator can, in turn, be again used performatively (i.e., "Shush!").

12. In talk about talk, the word "taboo" is often used in a rather fast and loose manner. We may say that for Republicans tax hikes are a "taboo topic," or that for evangelical Christians the discussion of safe sex in sex education classes is "strictly taboo." The common use of the term can have both a narrow and a broad meaning, covering anything from the avoidance of specific words – like curse words – to the avoidance of whole discourse topics. The plasticity of the term can mask some of the important aspects of verbal tabooing as a sociolinguistic phenomenon. In this section we focus on verbal taboo in the narrower sense of the term, as it relates to specific, relatively discrete linguistic forms (as opposed to phenomena like proscribed discourse topics) (see Fleming and Lempert 2011). There are certain form-functional criteria (conditions of "unmentionability"; see Fleming and Lempert 2011) that distinguish such taboo performativity from more canonical speech-act

performativity. Thus retention of performative effects in quotative contexts, formal similarity rather than identity to the performative type (cf. "sound symbolism") as sufficient for achievement of performative effects, and non-exclusivity of addressee but possible extension to bystanders and overhearers as potential benefactees (or malefactees) of the performative action, all serve as diagnostics of such taboo or rigid performativity.

13. The avoidance of homophones and near-homophones of a tabooed word or expression is a diagnostic of phonetic as opposed to lexical taboos (Diffloth 1980: 157–8, 162). As a rule of thumb, phonetic taboos are forms – like curse words – which always have performative effects no matter the context of their use (or mention). Lexical taboos are forms which are normally unremarkable, being tabooed only within specific contexts. For example, lexical roots of everyday Guugu-Yimidhirr are tabooed when speaking to one's brother-in-law (Haviland 1987). The everyday words have indefeasible performative effects only under particular contextual conditions; outside of these they are pragmatically unremarkable. In cases like these, taboos are restricted to the lexical type and do not affect (near-)homophones. Distinct from such examples of lexical taboos, verbal taboos whose tokens always have performative effects often trigger homophone effects. Note that English curse-words condition effects similar in kind to the homophone avoidance discussed here for personal name taboos – paradigms of euphemistic substitutes for curse-words are often determined on a basis of phonetic likeness (e.g., *fuck, fudge, fooey, frig*, etc.). (Euphemism canonically involves analogous processes of differentiation, only at the level of semantics rather than phonology; see Allan and Burridge 1991.) This distinction between phonetic and lexical taboo itself reflects a Whorfian ideological projection: where all tokens have performative effects performativity is interpreted as inherent to sign tokens (i.e., phonetic substance), where only some tokens have performative effects it is interpreted as inherent to the sign type (i.e., lexical form).

14. Note that because curse words can occur quite freely in certain contexts doesn't mean that they don't have performative effects. In the United States, the F-word is often used as an affectively charged performative resource for fashioning social solidarity in in-group speech (see, for example, Mendoza-Denton 2008). In Aboriginal Australia, the hypertrophied use of obscenities or of what would elsewhere be deemed inappropriate physical contact among joking relations is performatively effective in forging social relationships, even though they are not avoided in those contexts (see the Australianist literature on joking relationships, e.g., Thomson 1935; Garde 2008). Avoidance is a diagnostic, but by no means a necessary condition, of "rigid performativity."

References

Abu-Lughod, Lila. 1986. *Veiled Sentiments: Honor and Poetry in a Bedouin Society.* Berkeley: University of California Press.

Agha, Asif. 1996. Rhetoric. In *Encyclopedia of Cultural Anthropology*, ed. D. Levinson and M. Ember, 1115–19. New York: Henry Holt.

— 2007. *Language and Social Relations.* Cambridge: Cambridge University Press.

Agha, Asif, and Stanton E. F. Wortham. 2005. Special Issue: Discourse across Speech Events: Intertextuality and Interdiscursivity in Social Life. *Journal of Linguistic Anthropology* 15(1): 1–150.

Ahearn, Laura M. 2012. *Living Language: An Introduction to Linguistic Anthropology.* Blackwell Primers in Anthropology. Chichester, West Sussex, UK; Malden, MA: Wiley-Blackwell.

Allan, Keith, and Kate Burridge. 1991. *Euphemism and Dysphemism: Language Used as Shield and Weapon.* New York: Oxford University Press.

Anward, J. 2004. Lexeme Recycled. How categories emerge from interaction. *Logos and Language. Journal of General Linguistics and Language Theory* 5(2): 31–46.

Austin, John. 1962. *How to Do Things With Words*, ed. J. O. Urmson. London: Oxford University Press.

Austin, John, J. O. Urmson, and G. J. Warnock. 1961. *Philosophical Papers.* Oxford: Clarendon Press.

Banti, Giorgio, and Francesco Giannattasio. 2004. Poetry. In *A Companion to Linguistic Anthropology*, ed. A. Duranti. Malden, MA, 290–320: Blackwell Publishers.

Bate, Bernard. 2009. *Tamil Oratory and the Dravidian Aesthetic: Democratic Practice in South India.* New York: Columbia University Press.

Bauman, Richard. 1977. *Verbal Art as Performance.* Rowley: Newbury House Publishers, Inc.

— 2004. *A World of Others' Words: Cross-Cultural Perspectives on Intertextuality.* Malden, MA; Oxford: Blackwell Pub.

— 2011. Commentary: Foundations in performance. *Journal of Sociolinguistics* 15(5):707–20.

— 2012. Performance. In *A Companion to Folklore*, ed. R. Bendix and G. Hasan-Rokem, 94–118. Malden, MA: Wiley-Blackwell.

Bauman, Richard, and Charles L. Briggs. 1990. Poetics and Performance as Critical Perspectives on Language and Social Life. *Annual Review of Anthropology* 19: 59–88.

Becker, Alton L. 1995. *Beyond Translation: Essays Towards a Modern Philology.* Ann Arbor: University of Michigan Press.

Benveniste, Emile. 1971. *Problems in General Linguistics.* Miami: University of Miami Press.

Biber, Douglas, and Edward Finegan. 1989. Styles of Stance in English: Lexical and grammatical marking of evidentiality and affect. *Text* 9 (1): 93–124.

Bohman, James. 1986. Formal Pragmatics and Social Criticism. *Philosophy and Social Criticism* 11: 331–53.

Brown, Edward J. 1987. Roman Jakobson: The unity of his thought on verbal art. In *Language, Poetry, and Poetics: The Generation of the 1890s – Jakobson, Trubetzkoy, Majakovskij; proceedings of the First Roman Jakobson Colloquium, at the Massachusetts Institute of Technology, October 5–6, 1984*, ed. K. Pomorska, E. Chodakowska, H. McLean, and B. Vine, 233–56. Berlin/New York: Mouton de Gruyter.

Butler, Judith. 1997. *Excitable Speech: A Politics of the Performative.* New York: Routledge.

Caton, Steven C. 1987. Contributions of Roman Jakobson. *Annual Review of Anthropology* 16: 223–60.

Codrington, R. H. 1957[1891]. *The Melanesians: Studies in their Anthropology and Folk-Lore.* New Haven, CT: HRAF Press.

Cushing, Steven. 1994. "Air Cal Three Thirty Six, Go, Around Three Thirty Six, Go Around": Linguistic Repetition in Air-Ground Communication. In *Repetition in Discourse: Interdisciplinary Perspectives*, ed. B. Johnstone, 53–65. Norwood, NJ: Ablex.

D'Andrade, Roy. 2006. Searle on Institutions. *Anthropological Theory* 6(1): 5–125.

de Beaugrande, Robert-Alain, and Wolfgang Ulrich Dressler. 1982. *Introduction to Text Linguistics.* London: Longman.

Diffloth, Gerard. 1980. To Taboo Everything at All Times. *Proceedings of the Berkeley Linguistic Society* 6: 157–65.

Du Bois, John. 1993. Meaning without Intention: Lessons from divination. In *Responsibility and Evidence in Oral Discourse*, ed. J. Hill and J. T. Irvine, 48–71. New York: Cambridge University Press.

    2007. The Stance Triangle. In *Stancetaking in Discourse: Subjectivity, Evaluation, Interaction*, ed. R. Englebretson, 139–82. Amsterdam: John Benjamins.

Duranti, Alessandro. 1993. Intentionality and Truth: An ethnographic critique. *Cultural Anthropology* 8: 214–45.

Durkheim, Émile, and Marcel Mauss. 1963. *Primitive Classification.* Chicago: The University of Chicago Press.

Enfield, N. J. 2009. *The Anatomy of Meaning: Speech, Gesture, and Composite Utterances, Language, Culture and Cognition.* Cambridge: Cambridge University Press.

Enfield, N. J., and Jack Sidnell. 2012. Language Diversity and Social Action: A third locus of linguistic relativity. *Current Anthropology* 53: 302–33.

Englebretson, Robert, ed. 2007. *Stancetaking in Discourse: Subjectivity, Evaluation, Interaction.* Pragmatics and Beyond New Series 164. Philadelphia: John Benjamins.

Erickson, Frederick. 1982. Money Tree, Lasagna Bush, Salt and Pepper: Social Construction of Topical Cohesion in a Conversation Among Italian-Americans. In *Analyzing Discourse: Text and Talk (Georgetown*

University Round Table on Languages and Linguistics 1981), ed. D. Tannen, 43-70. Washington, DC: Georgetown University Press.

2004. *Talk and Social Theory: Ecologies of Speaking and Listening in Everyday Life*. Cambridge/Malden, MA: Polity Press.

Ferrara, Kathleen. 1994. Repetition as Rejoinder in Therapeutic Discourse: Echoing and Mirroring. In *Repetition in Discourse: Interdisciplinary Perspectives*, ed. B. Johnstone, 66-83. Norwood, NJ: Ablex.

Fleming, Luke. 2011. Name Taboos and Rigid Performativity. *Anthropological Quarterly* 84(1): 141-64.

Fleming, Luke, and Michael Lempert. 2011a. Introduction: Beyond Bad Words. *Anthropological Quarterly* 84(1): 5-14.

eds. 2011b. *The Unmentionable: Verbal Taboo and the Moral Life of Language*. Anthropological Quarterly 84 (Special Issue).

Frazer, Sir James George. 1959. *The New Golden Bough: A New Abridgment of the Classic Work*. New York: Criterion Books.

Garde, Murray. 2008. The Pragmatics of Rude Jokes with Grandad: Joking relationships in Aboriginal Australia. *Anthropological Forum* 18(3): 235-53.

Glick, Douglas J. 1996. A Reappraisal of Brown and Levinson's *Politeness: Some Universals of Language Use*, eighteen years later. *Semiotica* 109(1/2): 141-171.

Goffman, Erving. 1981. Footing. In *Forms of Talk*, ed. E. Goffman, 124-59. Philadelphia: University of Pennsylvania Press.

Goodman, Nelson. 1972. Seven Strictures on Similarity. In *Problems and Projects*, ed. N. Goodman, 437-47. New York: Bobbs-Merrill Company.

Goodwin, Marjorie Harness. 1990. *He-Said-She-Said: Talk as Social Organization Among Black Children*. Bloomington: Indiana University Press.

1993. Tactical Uses of Stories: Participation frameworks within girls' and boys' disputes. In *Gender and Conversational Interaction*, ed. D. Tannen, 110-43. New York: Oxford University Press.

2006. *The Hidden Life of Girls: Games of Stance, Status, and Exclusion*. Malden, MA: Blackwell.

Graham, Laura. 1993. A Public Sphere in Amazonia? The depersonalized collaborative construction of discourse in Xavante. *American Ethnologist* 20(4): 717-41.

Gutwinski, W. 1976. *Cohesion in Literary Texts: A Study of Some Grammatical and Lexical Features of English Discourse*. The Hague: Mouton.

Habermas, Jürgen. 1984. *The Theory of Communicative Action: Reason and the Rationalization of Society*, trans. T. McCarthy. 2 vols. Vol. 1. Boston: Beacon Press.

Hall, Kira. 2000. Performativity. *Journal of Linguistic Anthropology* 9(1-2): 184-7.

Halliday, M. A. K., and R. Hasan. 1976. *Cohesion in English*. London: Longman.

Hanks, William F. 1989. Text and Textuality. *Annual Review of Anthropology* 18: 95-127.

Haviland, John B. 1979. How to Talk to Your Brother-in-Law in Guugu Yimidhirr. In *Languages and Their Speakers*, ed. T. Shopen, 161-239. Philadelphia: University of Pennsylvania Press.

Herbert, Robert K. 1990. Hlonipha and the Ambiguous Woman. *Anthropos* 85: 455–73.

Heritage, John, and Geoffrey Raymond. 2005. The Terms of Agreement: Indexing epistemic authority and subordination in talk-in-interaction. *Social Psychology Quarterly* 68(1): 15–38.

Herzfeld, Michael. 1997. *Cultural Intimacy: Social Poetics in the Nation-State*. New York: Routledge.

Hill, Jane H. 2008. *The Everyday Language of White Racism*. Blackwell Studies in Discourse and Culture. Chichester, UK/Malden, MA: Wiley-Blackwell.

Hill, Jane H., and Judith T. Irvine, eds. 1993. *Responsibility and Evidence in Oral Discourse*. Studies in the Social and Cultural Foundations of Language no. 15. Cambridge/New York: Cambridge University Press.

Humphrey, Caroline. 1978. Women, Taboo, and the Suppression of Attention. In *Defining Females: The Nature of Women in Society*, ed. Shirley Ardener, 89–101. London: Croom Helm.

Hunston, Susan, and Geoff Thompson. 2000. *Evaluation in Text: Authorial Stance and the Construction of Discourse*. Oxford/New York: Oxford University Press.

Irvine, Judith T. 2011. Leaky Registers and Eight-Hundred-Pound Gorillas. *Anthropological Quarterly* 84(1): 15–39.

Jaffe, Alexandra M. 2009. *Stance: Sociolinguistic Perspectives*. Oxford/New York: Oxford University Press.

Jakobson, Roman. 1960. Closing Statement: Linguistics and Poetics. In *Style in Language*, ed. T. Sebeok, 350–77. Cambridge, MA: MIT Press.

———. 1966. Grammatical Parallelism and its Russian Facet. *Language* 42(2): 399–429.

Johnstone, Barbara, ed. 1994. *Repetition in Discourse: Interdisciplinary Perspectives*. 2 vols. Norwood, NJ: Ablex.

Keenan (Ochs), Elinor. 1977. Making it Last: Uses of Repetition in Child Language. In *Child Discourse*, ed. S. Ervin-Tripp and C. Mitchell-Kernan, 125–38. New York: Academic Press.

Kockelman, Paul. 2003. The Meanings of Interjections in Q'eqchi' Maya: From emotive reaction to social and discursive action. *Current Anthropology* 44(4): 467–90.

———. 2010. *Language, Culture, and Mind: Natural Constructions and Social Kinds*. Language, Culture and Cognition. Cambridge/New York: Cambridge University Press.

Kripke, Saul. 1972. Naming and Necessity. In *Semantics of Natural Language*, ed. Donald Davidson and Gilbert Harman, 251–355. Dordrecht: Reidel.

Lee, Benjamin. 1997. *Talking Heads: Language, Metalanguage and the Semiotics of Subjectivity*. Durham, NC: Duke University Press.

Lempert, Michael. 2008. The Poetics of Stance: Text-metricality, epistemicity, interaction. *Language in Society* 37(4): 569–92.

———. 2012a. *Discipline and Debate: The Language of Violence in a Tibetan Buddhist Monastery*. Berkeley: University of California Press.

2012b. Indirectness. In *Handbook of Intercultural Discourse and Communication*, ed. S. F. Kiesling, C. B. Paulston, and E. Rangel, 180–204. Malden, MA: Wiley-Blackwell.

Lempert, Michael, and Michael Silverstein. 2012. *Creatures of Politics: Media, Message, and the American Presidency*. Bloomington: Indiana University Press.

Levinson, Stephen C. 1994. *Pragmatics*, ed. B. Comrie *et al*. Cambridge Textbooks in Linguistics. Cambridge: Cambridge University Press.

2000. *Presumptive Meanings: The Theory of Generalized Conversational Implicature, Language, Speech, and Communication*. Cambridge, MA: MIT Press.

Martin, J. R. 2001. Cohesion and Texture. In *The Handbook of Discourse Analysis*, ed. D. Schiffrin, D. Tannen, and H. E. Hamilton, 35–53. Malden, MA: Blackwell.

McNeill, David. 1992. *Hand and Mind: What Gestures Reveal about Thought*. Chicago: University of Chicago Press.

2005. *Gesture and Thought*. Chicago: University of Chicago Press.

Mendoza-Denton, Norma. 2008. *Homegirls: Language and Cultural Practice among Latina Youth Gangs*. New Directions in Ethnography 2. Malden, MA: Blackwell.

Mertz, Elizabeth. 1996. Reconcontextualization as Socialization: Text and pragmatics in the law school classroom. In *Natural Histories of Discourse*, ed. M. Silverstein and G. Urban, 229–49. Chicago: University of Chicago Press.

1998. Linguistic Ideology and Praxis in U.S. Law School Classrooms. In *Language Ideologies: Practice and Theory*, ed. B. B. Schieffelin, K. A. Woolard, and P. V. Kroskrity, 149–62. New York: Oxford University Press.

Miller, J. Hillis. 2001. *Speech Acts in Literature*. Stanford, CA: Stanford University Press.

Mukarovsky, Jan. 1964. Standard Language and Poetic Language. In *A Prague School Reader on Esthetics, Literary Structure, and Style*, ed. P. L. Garvin, 17–30. Washington, DC: Georgetown University Press.

Nash, David, and Jane Simpson. 1981. "No-Name" in Central Australia. In *Papers from the Parasession on Language and Behavior*, ed. C. S. Masek, 165–77. Chicago: Chicago Linguistic Society.

Parmentier, Richard J. 1994. The Semiotic Regimentation of Social Life. In *Signs in Society: Studies in Semiotic Anthropology*, ed. R. J. Parmentier, 125–55. Bloomington: Indiana University Press.

1997. The Pragmatic Semiotics of Cultures. *Semiotica* 116(1): 1–114.

Perrino, Sabina M. 2002. Intimate Hierarchies and Qur'anic Saliva (Tëfli): Textuality in a Senegalese ethnomedical encounter. *Journal of Linguistic Anthropology* 12(2): 225–59.

Rappaport Hovav, Malka. 2008. The English Dative Alternation: The case for verb sensitivity. *Journal of Linguistics* 44: 129–67.

Rosaldo, Michelle Zimbalist. 1982. The Things We Do with Words: Ilongot speech acts and speech act theory in philosophy. *Language in Society* 11: 203–37.

Rumsey, Alan. 1990. Word, Meaning, and Linguistic Ideology. *American Anthropologist* 92: 346-61.

Sacks, Harvey. 1987. On the Preferences for Agreement and Contiguity in Sequences in Conversation. In *Talk and Social Organisation*, ed. G. Button and J. R. E. Lee, 54-69. Clevedon, UK: Multilingual Matters.

Saussure, Ferdinand de. 1983. *Course in General Linguistics*. La Salle, IL: Open Court.

Schegloff, Emanuel A. 2007. *Sequence Organization in Interaction: A Primer in Conversation Analysis*. Cambridge/New York: Cambridge University Press.

Schiffrin, Deborah. 2001. Discourse Markers: Language, Meaning, and Context. In *The Handbook of Discourse Analysis*, ed. D. Schiffrin, D. Tannen, and H. E. Hamilton, 54-75. Malden, MA: Blackwell.

Searle, John R. 1969. *Speech Acts: An Essay in the Philosophy of Language*. London: Cambridge University Press.

———. 1975. Indirect Speech Acts. In *Syntax and Semantics, 3: Speech Acts*, ed. P. Cole and J. L. Morgan, 59-82. New York: Academic Press.

Sidnell, Jack. 2010. *Conversation Analysis: An Introduction*. Language in Society. Chichester, UK/Malden, MA: Wiley-Blackwell.

Silverstein, Michael. 1976. Shifters, Linguistic Categories, and Cultural Description. In *Meaning in Anthropology*, ed. K. H. Basso and H. A. Selby, 11-55. Albuquerque: University of New Mexico Press.

———. 1979. Language Structure and Linguistic Ideology. In *The Elements*, ed. R. Clyne *et al*, 193-247. Chicago: Chicago Linguistics Society.

———. 1981a. *The Limits of Awareness*. Working Papers in Sociolinguistics, No. 84. Austin, TX: Southwest Educational Development Laboratory.

———. 1981b. Metaforces of Power in Traditional Oratory. Paper read at Lecture to Department of Anthropology, Yale University, at New Haven.

———. 1984. On the Pragmatic 'Poetry' of Prose: Parallelism, repetition, and cohesive structure in the time course of dyadic conversation. In *Meaning, Form, and Use In Context: Linguistic Applications*, ed. D. Schiffrin, 181-99. Washington, DC: Georgetown University Press.

———. 1987. The Three Faces of "Function": Preliminaries to a psychology of language. In *Social and Functional Approaches to Language and Thought*, ed. M. Hickmann, 17-38. New York: Academic Press.

———. 1992. The Indeterminacy of Contextualization: When is enough enough? In *The Contextualization of Language*, ed. P. Auer and A. Di Luzio, 55-76. Philadelphia: John Benjamins Publishing Company.

———. 1993. Metapragmatic Discourse and Metapragmatic Function. In *Reflexive Language: Reported Speech and Metapragmatics*, ed. J. Lucy, 33-58. Cambridge: Cambridge University Press.

———. 1996. The Secret Life of Texts. In *Natural Histories of Discourse*, ed. M. Silverstein and G. Urban, 81-105. Chicago: University of Chicago Press.

———. 1997. The Improvisational Performance of "Culture" in Real-Time Discursive Practice. In *Creativity in Performance*, ed. R. K. Sawyer, 265-312. Greenwich, CT: Ablex.

2004. "Cultural" Concepts and the Language-Culture Nexus. *Current Anthropology* 45(5): 621–52.

2005. The Poetics of Politics: "Theirs" and "Ours." *Journal of Anthropological Research* 61(1): 1–24.

2010. "Direct" and "Indirect" Communicative Acts in Semiotic Perspective. *Journal of Pragmatics* 42(2): 337–53.

Simons, Gary F. 1982. Word Taboo and Comparative Austronesian Linguistics. *Pacific Linguistics* 3 (C-76): 157–226.

Singer, Milton. 1972. *When a Great Tradition Modernizes: An Anthropological Approach to Indian Civilization*. New York: Praeger Publishers.

Stasch, Rupert. 2011. Ritual and Oratory Revisited: The Semiotics of Effective Action. *Annual Review of Anthropology* 40: 159–74.

Tambiah, Stanley. 1981. *A Performative Approach to Ritual*. London: British Academy.

Tannen, Deborah. 1987. Repetition in Conversation: Towards a poetics of talk. *Language*. 63(3): 574–605.

1989. *Talking Voices: Repetition, Dialogue, and Imagery in Conversational Discourse*. Studies in Interactional Sociolinguistics 6. Cambridge/New York: Cambridge University Press.

Thomson, Donald. 1935. The Joking Relationship and Organized Obscenity in North Queensland. *American Anthropologist* 37(3): 460–90.

Treis, Yvonne. 2005. Avoiding Their Names, Avoiding Their Eyes: How Kambaata women respect their in-laws. *Anthropological Linguistics* 47(3): 292–320.

Tylor, Edward B. 1913. *Primitive Culture: Researches into the Development of Mythology, Philosophy, Religion, Language, Art, and Custom*, Vol. 1. London: John Murray.

Urban, Greg. 1986. Ceremonial Dialogues in South America. *American Anthropologist* 87(2): 371–86.

1990. Ceremonial Dialogues in South America. In *The Interpretation of Dialogue*, ed. T. Maranhão, 99–119. Chicago: The University of Chicago Press.

Waugh, Linda R. 1987. On the Sound Shape of Language: Mediacy and immediacy. In *Language, Poetry, and Poetics: The Generation of the 1890s–Jakobson, Trubetzkoy, Majakovskij; Proceedings of the First Roman Jakobson Colloquium, at the Massachusetts Institute of Technology, October 5–6, 1984*, ed. K. Pomorska, E. Chodakowska, H. McLean and B. Vine. Berlin/New York: Mouton de Gruyter.

Wennerstrom, Ann K. 2001. *The Music of Everyday Speech: Prosody and Discourse Analysis*. New York: Oxford University Press.

Whorf, Benjamin Lee. 1998[1956]. *Language, Thought and Reality: Selected Writings of Benjamin Lee Whorf*. Cambridge, MA: Massachusetts Institute of Technology.

Wortham, Stanton. 2001. *Narratives in Action*. New York: Teacher's College Press.

20

Ritual language

David Tavárez

20.1 Introduction: Ritual, social action, and intentionality

As a quote by the poet W. H. Auden has it, "[t]o pray is to pay attention or, shall we say, to 'listen' to someone or something other than oneself" (Kirsch 2005: 159). This citation, though lapidary, does usher in two deceivingly simple questions – What is ritual language, exactly? What is it like to employ it? – that lead to two more baseline queries: How is ritual language deployed? How does it become an authoritative or efficacious event?

Ritual has been a privileged object at the heart of many foundational and ongoing inquiries not only in anthropology, but also in related social disciplines, such as sociology and religion. Linguistic performance also stands at the core of ritual practice, for it directs, shapes, and even stands in as a summary of ritual performance. Given the breadth and range of ritual language as a social and discursive phenomenon, an answer to the four questions posed above must also sketch out the relationship between speakers' consciousness and verbal ritual performances, and between ritual language and the social world. While the number of ethnographic works devoted to ritual language in anthropology is both humbling and staggering, this essay discusses a number of works published in the last two decades, and draws on a variety of examples of ritual speech from societies in the Americas, the Pacific, South Asia, the Indian Ocean, and the Mediterranean, with a particular focus on anthropological and historical research on Amerindian languages.

Any repeatable social interaction is, in latent form, a candidate for ritualization. Hence, this brief review of ritual language cannot possibly account for all instances of ritual and ritualization as a social mode of action among human beings. An expansive account would begin with an analysis of repetitive acts of social contact among primates – what Michael Tomasello (1999) brands "ontogenetic ritualization" – and might include Gregory Bateson's (1958) insistence that a structured form of social interaction with a set configuration may give rise to its very ritualization by its participants, or Edmund Leach's (1976) perception of ritual as communicative phenomena whose meanings are anchored in a highly stable semantic system. A more hierarchical and highly structured view of ritual language may follow Roy Rappaport's (1999) insistence on a distinction between self-referential and canonical messages, and on the articulation of a tripartite scheme that connects discrete objects with higher-order, cosmological meanings.

From a different perspective, the very act of approaching "ritual" and "ritual language" as an area of inquiry that is radically distinct from other social exchanges may be deeply embedded in unexamined ontological claims about human societies. This move is part of a broader, ongoing, and much-debated critique of a default ontology, or a "meta-ontology," in ethnographic accounts that present human societies as simply possessing different perspectives on what is assumed to be a uniform set of ontological claims (Course 2010, Pedersen 2011, Holbraad 2012), even if some have argued that, in such usage, "ontology" is nearly interchangeable with "culture" (Venkatesan et al. 2010). There remains ample analytic terrain for a multiplicity of views that sidestep this debate by focusing on a sustained analysis of the many epistemic assumptions that serve as a substructure for our analyses of the role of ritual discourse and literacy within shared social realities (Urcid 2011), or that are mobilized in colonial situations as forms of dissent that constitute an epistemological critique of a dominant set of ontological claims (Tavárez 2011). What follows below is one possible account of a relatively sustained – and, one might say, analytically ritualized – set of convergences on the notion of ritual language as an emergent linguistic process rooted in interdiscursivity, reflexivity, and intentionality.

Émile Durkheim's (1912) work on ritual posits a series of highly influential categories, such as the distinction between the monotony of profane time and the exalted nature of sacred time, or between positive and negative rituals, which support two central theses about ritual: that it can be understood only as a totality rather than as the sum of discrete and autonomous traits, and that ritual practice both precedes and shapes belief. Among Anglophone anthropologists, while Durkheim's focus on ritual as a collective phenomenon was granted analytical prominence, there has been a historical trend away from schemes that divided ritual language into categories such as primitive "magic" and more reflexive "religion" (Frazer 1922), a critique of the characterization of "magical words" as highly contingent and even nonsensical performances (Malinowski 1929 and 1965, as reanalyzed in Tambiah 1985: 47–54), and a distancing from a consideration of ritual language as a direct reflection of the experiences of the participants in ritual events (Turner 1977).

There is, in any case, relative agreement regarding how ritual language in many societies merges both performative and referential practices in a discrete speech event shot through with a multiplicity of indexical links to broad spatiotemporal domains. In an essay devoted to ritual oral performance, Stanley Tambiah (1985: 53) concluded that "all ritual, whatever the idiom, is addressed to the human participants and uses a technique which attempts to restructure and integrate the minds and emotions of the actors." Following John Searle – whose focus on collective action brings us back, in part, to Durkheim – one could regard ritual language as an overtly marked performance, through specific linguistic resources, of a "collective intentionality," which would be "a sense of doing (wanting, believing, etc.) something together" in which "the individual intentionality that each person has is derived *from* the collective intentionality that they share" (Searle 1995: 25). This primordial account of collective intentions in ritual may be complemented by a discussion of reflexive forms of personhood, such as the emergence of introspection and empathy among its participants (Taylor 1985).

How ritual language, collective intentions, and microcosmic actions linked to macrocosmic consequences come together is a different matter, analytically speaking. In an attempt to sketch out an explanation, this short essay defines and problematizes five domains that inform many known forms of ritual language in different societies: parallelism and repetition; representation and mimicry; enaction and personification; authority; and reflexivity and indeterminacy. My discussion of these domains follows a path from discrete linguistic phenomena to broader forms of articulating and expressing beliefs through linguistic performances. These five domains arguably have a close ideational relationship with various forms of collective linguistic intentionality embedded in ritual language. These beliefs in the efficacy of ritual language form a continuum that may range from Paul Friedrich's (1989) "linguacultural ideologies," or nebulous assumptions about language articulated both directly and indirectly, to rationalizing beliefs that contribute towards the legitimation of social and historical relations (Woolard 1998), and which can be analyzed as overt language ideologies.

Here, "ritual" is shorthand for the repetitive and highly creative performance of multilayered symbolic acts by individuals or groups in order to secure a number of pragmatic aims (Evans-Pritchard 1965, Tambiah 1990). The primary effect of ritual practices may be the reproduction of a social or cultural order, but this does not mean that ritual recreates an ahistorical ideological realm (Kelly and Kaplan 1990); instead, endogenous ritual practices may respond to and assimilate exogenous events and thus result in the transformation of endogenous cultural categories (Sahlins 1981). While collective ritual may enhance, reenact, or reproduce representations of group identity and group cohesion, or situate communities and individuals within an unfolding life or yearly cycle according to their own experiences as participants (Turner 1977), private ritual may address a much narrower range of interests, dispositions, and representations.

While distinctions between public and private rituals may be used as a baseline for contrasts in ritual action, one should bear in mind that this distinction is also a continuum of "degrees of centralization" in terms of situational focus and the identities of social participants (Irvine 1979: 786). A doctrinaire Marxist viewpoint may place ritual language in the superstructure, as a species of false consciousness. Nevertheless, if we regard structured linguistic performances that deploy authoritative knowledge as a form of work, then we can regard ritual language as a form of highly valued social and intellectual labor that is an integral part of the political economies of historicized speech practices (Irvine 1989, Friedrich 1989). Indeed, ritual language *qua* labor may be transparently labeled as such by its enactors; for instance, the commemoration of royal Sakalava ancestors through ritual forms that include obeisance and gift exchange is called *Fanompoa Be* (The Great Service) in Madagascar (Lambek 2002), and colonial Northern Zapotecs designated local ancestral worship rituals with the bivalent label *china bezelao*, "the labor of the Underworld Lord," which could also mean "the labor of the Devil" in the context of a Christian confession.

20.2 Parallelism and repetition

While ritual may be envisaged as privileged repetition, ritual language emphasizes concrete iterative structures that index register, genre, and intent. Speakers' reflexivity and self-awareness regarding ritual language as register or genre often take the salient form of paired utterances, also called couplets. In his well-known statement regarding grammatical parallelism in poetry, Roman Jakobson (1987: 146–7) suggested that these parallel forms worked at various levels of analysis – phonology, morphology, syntax, prosody, etc. – and noted that the term "repetitive parallelism" was first used in Semitic studies to indicate this device, which could also be located in ancient Hebrew and Chinese poetry. James Fox (1974, 1975, 1988) extended Jakobson's focus on parallelism both by documenting and discussing its use in poetic and ritual genres in many societies, and posited that Rotinese ritual speech in Eastern Indonesia created lexical pairings that supported a symbolic hierarchy and a fixed semantic network (see also Kuipers 1990 for Sumbanese parallelistic speech). Stylistic parallelism at this level of generality has been noted as a device in the ritual speech of various literate and non-literate societies (Tambiah 1985). To exemplify the structuring and social valence of parallelism, the section below draws brief examples from Yupik, Nahuatl, Tzotzil Maya, and Anakalang.

Amerindian oral genres employ a broad repertoire of prosodic, syntactic, semantic, and rhetorical devices to structure speech performances according to a set of aesthetic and social expectations that vary from genre to genre (Silverstein 2005, Tedlock 1987). Guided in part by Hymes's (1981) influential account of interlocking parallel syntactic, prosodic, and narrative structures in a Clackamas story, Anthony Woodbury (1987) defined four basic components in the rhetorical structure of Central Alaskan Yupik narratives at various levels in an oral performance: prosodic phrasing, based on the intonation contours of utterances; pause phrasing, which divides discourse by alternating silences with speech; syntactic constituency, sometimes correlated with prosodic phrasing, and based on a standard discrete syntactic hierarchy; and adverbial-particle phrasing, which introduces both syntactic and prosodic units.

Comparable but non-isomorphic morphological, syntactic, and semantic parallel constructions are a particularly well-attested rhetorical device in Mesoamerican oral genres. According to Miguel León-Portilla (1983: 76–7), Classical Nahuatl speech genres, recorded by native speakers in alphabetic form from the 1530s onwards, could be divided into two macrogenres: *cuicatl* (song) and *tlahtolli* (word). A recurring device in both genres was what Angel M. Garibay K. (1954: 19) called *difrasismo*, or "the pairing of two metaphors, which together yield a symbolic medium for the expression of a single thought." In essence, Nahua *difrasismos* were composed of two terms conveying a third, absent notion through metonymical reference, as in *in petlatl in icpalli* (the mat, the high-backed seat), which conveys legitimate rulership. Besides *difrasismos*, some other colonial Nahua genres also featured couplets: two or more verbal, nominal, or locative constructions exhibiting parallel features at the phonological, morphosyntactic, and/or semantic levels.

In an influential treatment of couplets, Bricker (1974: 368, 377) observed that certain Zinacanteco Tzotzil Maya speech genres, called *k'op* 'word', differ from other genres due to their use of both couplets and *difrasismos*. Bricker contended that structured speech highlights the beginning and end of important segments in a speech event, and "the wording of the speeches is not absolutely set, but the general content seems to be fairly generally known, though younger people and women often mumble their way through them"; furthermore, John Haviland (2010) explored the performative salience of Zinacanteco couplets in a careful analysis of their spatial and social context in a dispute. This apparently exuberant "stacking" of parallel forms, comparable to the Clackamas and Yupik examples mentioned above, is a metasemiotic and highly reflexive marker of poetic structure in some Mesoamerican languages, as Gossen (1974) and Tedlock (1987) noted regarding, respectively, Chamula Maya heated speech, and K'iché Maya poetics.

Diphrasic structures, of course, are found in many ritual traditions. For instance, as Webb Keane (1997a: 108–13, 119, 127, 136) asserts in his analysis of parallel forms in Amakalang formal language registers, one may refer to *laupa lai yera* 'going to visit one's wife's family' through the semantically salient couplet *tàka ta haga jara, toma ta ora ahu* 'arrive at the horse's face, come to the dog's snout', two elements which symmetrically figure one another, while asymmetrically constituting a colloquial phrase. Like archaic or opaque forms used in Nahuatl, Tzotzil Maya, Kalapalo speech registers (Basso 2009), or Christian ritual performance in Zimbabwe (Engelke 2004), certain Anakalangese couplets index the esoteric, non-quotidian nature of ritual speech. Amakalang presuppositions about ritual language do contrast with the somewhat less bounded and more creative deployment of couplets in Mesoamerica; in the former case, speakers reject literal rendering of couplets as a "true" translation, regard couplets as part of a "canonical core" which, in performance, acquire deictic elements that are rarely recorded, and focus on the formal quality of couplets, which ritual specialists may alter pragmatically only at great risk to themselves.

20.3 Representation and mimicry

A recurring concern in the analysis of ritual language has been the assumption that the recreation or mimesis of social worlds through speech acts goes a long way toward explaining its putative effectiveness. A multiplicity of examples in the anthropological literature track the reflexive and laborious representation of cosmological beliefs through ritual action and speech acts, from Frazer's (1922: 14-43) focus on "homeopathic magic" to Clifford Geertz's inquiry into religion as an overarching system (1966) or into the "poetics of power" through which the Balinese state performed its authority in public rituals (Geertz 1980), and Tambiah's (1985: 94-107, 147-50) analyses of curing rituals by a Thai *achan* (teacher) and Sinhalese exorcism rituals (Tambiah 1985). In some cases, the speech act itself constructs a meaningful spatiotemporal domain, as when Navajo prayer specialists narrate a highly detailed indexical ground indicated through a set of metonymical relationships that build a safe space around a patient (Field and Blackhorse 2002); in others, a specific sociocultural model is rendered in microcosmic form through a plurality of indexically salient visual and performative icons, as is the case with the construction of a longhouse for ritual feasting among the Korowai of West Papua, Indonesia (Stasch 2003).

Nonetheless, discursively enacted representations of the world are not mere mimicries of the universe, but domains with their own ontology, as Bruce Kapferer (1997: 36, 142-52, 180) proposes in his phenomenological approach to the Suniyama, an anti-sorcery ritual practiced by Sinhalese Buddhists in Sri Lanka. First, Sinhalese specialists possess a distinctive language ideology regarding sorcery: not only do they separate sorcery into *huniyama* (its objectified form) and *kodivina* (the actual destruction of well-being), but also employ *pranaksara*, 'life-giving letters' that are the ideal starting point for healing songs, to recreate an epochal seven-step walk undertaken by the young Buddha, in order to have the sorcery victim's mind focus on the qualities of this journey. Kapferer argues that this performance is not merely a simulacrum, but a "a reality complete unto itself and with no reference other than itself," and a form of virtuality that brings forth social reality.

Another mode of interaction is the representation, recreation, and modification of social identities through ritual language. At the level of quotidian interaction, anthropologists have long been aware of symbolic domains that are carefully enacted, represented, and reinforced by quotidian bodily and oral performances (Goffman 1967) arranged in intricate spatial and gestural domains, which are also part of an exchange through which children learn about reciprocity and social status, as Schieffelin (1990) reminds us in her study of Kaluli language socialization. Spatially and grammatically salient cues are predominant in the use of evidentiality and epistemic marking that reveals Kalapalo speakers' commitment to "social truths" in ritualized speech (Basso 2009), in the carefully orchestrated spatial meanings of Kri domestic spaces in Laos that allow speakers to "ritually regularize" what co-presence entails (Enfield 2009) and in the performative construction of three different genres of To Pamona weddings in Indonesia (Schrauwers 2000). Furthermore, ritual action and evidence of personhood may come together and crystallize at specific life-cycle rituals, as Kockelman (2007) has argued in an analysis of Q'eqchi' Maya baptism and marriage ceremonies that foreground the links between inalienable possessions and personhood.

20.4 Enaction and personification

In an article about oppositional nostalgia discourses among Eastern Nahua communities, Jane Hill (1998: 80–3) deploys Alan Rumsey's (1990) distinction between "referential" and "enactive" linguistic ideologies. From this perspective, while many Indo-European languages emphasize the distinction between wording and meaning, in contrast, in Nahuatl (as is the case for the Australian language Ungarinyin) "language is seen as embodied in action, with no distinction made between such action and reference"; thus, Nahuatl language ideologies "emphasize, not denotation, but performance: the proper accomplishment of human relationships as constituted through stereotyped moments of dialogue." If present, such an enactive ideology would tend to reinforce the illocutionary force of ritual language: a case in point would be the personification of deities and non-human entities through speech acts, as discussed below in terms of Nahua and Kuna ritual language.

A substantial corpus representing a Nahua ritual genre called *nahualtocaitl*, or "Shape-Changer Names," was compiled in the early seventeenth century (Ruiz de Alarcón 1984). An important enactive ideology informed this genre: every entity in the world, including deities, animals, and natural entities, bore a unique name associated with creation narratives, and uttering the appropriate parallelistic epithet conferred cosmological authority on practitioners. Furthermore, *nahualtocaitl* specialists used these epithets to become, in the here and now, the *iixiptla*, or "representative," of a *teotl*, or sacred being. For instance, in some agricultural rites, specialists called themselves *Nohmatca nehhuatl / nicnopiltzintli nicenteotl* 'My person, I myself / I am Orphan Child, I am Centeotl', where Centeotl named the male aspect of a maize deity, and "Orphan Child" was one of this entity's appellations. Such a practice reenacted a primordial relation between deities and nature, justified and historicized by Nahua creation narratives (Tavárez 2011). To return to enactive ideologies, while in this case stereotyped speech acts did enact an important social labor just by virtue of being performed in the "right" way, their proper performance hinged on a highly constrained referential game.

As for Kuna ritual language, Sherzer (1991: 17–22) has noted that, besides its use of parallelism, metadiscursive elements that begin or end a poetic line, and a specialized vocabulary that contrasts with common terms, it differs from colloquial speech by means of morphological resources that index its poetic qualities; in general, complex verb suffixation and the use of highly marked forms, such as the optative -*ye*, operate as reliable indices of ritual speech. Following a complementary but different trajectory, Carlo Severi (2002: 34–6) has analyzed the Nia Ikala chant, a Kuna ritual to cure madness featuring a dialogic progression in which the shaman and his auxiliary spirit eventually mimic and embrace the patient's pathogenic spirit – unseen, but encountered as an acoustic presence. At the metadiscursive level, this is a chant about the ritual itself, through which the shaman announces the progression of the ritual act. In iconic terms, the shaman includes onomatopoeic animal cries in the chant as he performs various identities – shaman, patient, the Jaguar of the Sky, a spirit of the forest, and various animal spirits. In the end, as Severi suggests, through illocutionary force alone, the shaman confronts two opposite identities, the patient-as-an-animal spirit and the shaman-as-a-vegetal-spirit, through a process of "cumulative inclusion" that allows the chanter to embrace "an entire series of contradictory identities." To invoke J. L. Austin's (1975) influential analysis of speech acts, as Severi has done, both *nahualtocaitl* specialists and Kuna shamans seem to believe that the effectiveness of their propitiation activities derived from the illocutionary force of the speech act through which they designated themselves as deities or personified a multiplicity of human and spiritual identities. Moreover, the enacting through speech forms of dense webs of social relations among and between various living entities – humans, animals, and other animated forms – could be seen as a recalibration of a "cosmological deixis" in which a sentient being's point of view activates, or "agents," other subjects (Viveiros de Castro 1998).

A more routinized instance of enactive language ideologies is in evidence in the drafting of testaments by indigenous notaries, the most common colonial textual genre in Spanish America, and one that depicts the impact of colonial language ideologies on indigenous genres. The sociopolitical and discursive context for the production of colonial wills provided a highly structured framework built around the illocutionary force that words in a testament possessed. As noted by Lockhart (1992: 369), the Nahua testament followed a highly bracketed developmental course as a ritual genre. First, it emerged by the mid-sixteenth century, following Spanish conventions; then, it became a repository of spontaneous, innovative oral rhetoric between the late sixteenth and early seventeenth century; finally, the diversity of rhetorical forms yielded to a smaller number of received formulae by the mid-seventeenth century, and toward the end of that century, the genre converged once again with Spanish conventions.

As for embodiment, ritual language in and of itself may be indexical proof, in a public performance, of a continued relationship between mediums and entire kin groups of spirits. In Brazilian Candomblé, for instance, as noted by Paul Johnson (2002), the deified African ancestors known as *orixás* are rendered present through the bodily performances of mediums that occupy structural kinship slots with respect to those whom they embody and their fellow *orixás*. These mediums manage the *axé* (life force) summoned by these relationships in sacred spaces, or *terreiros*, that contain *axé* and envelop both mediums and audiences in layers of secrecy. Furthermore, as Michael Lambek (2002) asserts, the continuous management of embodiment practices of *tromba* (royal ancestors) by mediums in Madagascar who may possess an exacting knowledge of genealogies and a specialized vocabulary for common terms, are linked to an individually assumed but collectively salient burden of important historical narratives and genealogical relations that may date back as far as the seventeenth century.

Nevertheless, the embodied authority claimed through such speech acts remains open to scrutiny and reevaluation by all parties involved, as it may derive from a form of charismatic authority (Weber 1968: 1.114). Furthermore, as Tambiah (1985: 135) noted regarding curing rituals for spirit possession in South Asia, in this case the perlocutionary effects of embodiment may be "notoriously uncertain." Hence, there is a nonverbalized source of uncertainty that haunts the divide between purported illocutionary force and instantiated perlocutionary effects. Moreover, this account focuses on ritual efficacy that is gained through the modeling of a speech event in which an authorized speaker addresses a compliant or complicit audience. A more interactional model may be derived, for instance, from Keenan's (1973) influential analysis of Malagasy *kabary*, a formal political speech genre, as a communicative act built layer by layer through obliqueness and implication, and based on a vision of social relations shared by orators and their audiences (see also Jackson 2009). Finally, the interdiscursive nature of ritual as it unfolds possesses emergent qualities regarding self-realization that are not fully anticipated in speech act analyses. Thus, in his overview of the "Spirit Power" quest among speakers of Kiksht in the US Northwest Coast, and the granting of a "great name" through which future members of a Worora-speaking Aboriginal society in Australia are announced to their genitors, Silverstein (2009: 288) asserts that rituals of life-transition are "a chain of interdiscursive events that license and legitimate 'self'-realization and 'self'-fashioning in the act of recognition."

To return to Goffman (1967), the staggering variety of ritualized social interactions that individuals as interactants perform as part of their "facework" means that, while there may be a discrete set of data regarding the ritual code, these data do not necessarily reveal in and of themselves the social actors' objectives in following this code, or the reasons they have for following such a code. Furthermore, the two sections below focus on two crucial phenomena that qualify and bracket any analysis of ritual language as a discrete series of speech acts deeply invested in self-reflexivity and firmly rooted in easily accessible intentions: the multifarious conditions for the emergence of an authoritative ritual performance, and the multiple sources for indeterminacy and ambivalence.

20.5 Authority

Another influential way of thinking about ritual, authority, and language ideologies is one that emanates from a longstanding historical association between ritual and inscribed speech. As argued in a work edited by Stephen Houston (2004), the origin of early writing systems such as the Egyptian, Mesopotamian, Elamite, Shang, Maya, and Runic scripts is tied not only to bureaucratic expediency, but also to the necessity to inscribe and memorialize oral performances that figured prominently in public and private rituals. In the West, scriptural authority may be tied to a Biblical model where God creates the Word at the beginning of time and used it to communicate with a chosen people; its antithesis, as Aquinas (1948: 482) would have it, is the emergence of false revelations after the Flood, which led to unauthorized forms of ritual practice, or idolatry, "the cause, beginning, and end of all sins." However, as James Watts asserts (2005), "trusting the text" – a belief in the ontological supremacy of the full and verbatim reproduction of inscribed speech in a ritual – is a widespread presupposition about ritual language that permeated ancient societies in the Near East and the Mediterranean, from Ugaritic and Hittite ritual texts accompanied by metadiscursive specifications about performance, to the rediscovery of the "proper" way to hold the Feast of the Tabernacles (see Nehemiah 8:14–17), to rituals devoted to Osiris in Ptolemaic Egypt. In premodern India, as Sheldon Pollock (2006) contends, Sanskrit was deployed as an elite language that rendered ritual performance authoritative through its fixity and stability, in contrast with the ever-shifting nature of vernacular languages that mapped a complementary, non-elite set of social relations.

European colonial expansion into the Americas, Asia, and Africa from the early sixteenth century onwards resulted in the emergence of many philological and lexicographic projects intimately tied to a hegemonic refashioning of the social and religious order. In particular, the expansion of colonial Christianity and the resulting confrontations and convergences over the transposition and hybridization of Christian ritual discourse is a research domain that has attracted a multiplicity of anthropological and ethnohistorical analyses. Some approaches are summarized in Joseph Errington's (2007) comparative survey of the momentous convergence of colonial administration, colonial evangelization, linguistic description, language ideologies, and philology in Africa, Asia, and the Americas. Such an emphasis is made possible, first and foremost, by the survival of thousands of documents in indigenous languages composed under colonial rule by colonial lexicographers and their indigenous coauthors. Perhaps the most ambitious such work is the manuscript now known as *The Florentine Codex*, a compendium of the ceremonies, language, rhetoric, and cosmology of the Mexica, as compiled by a Franciscan lexicographer and several Nahua co-authors (Sahagún 1950–82).

Admittedly, the semiotic and discursive distance between colonial and indigenous ideologies and expectations regarding ritual language is initially rather formidable (Keane 2006), but the intense epistemic exchanges that took place over three centuries of Iberian rule in the Americas and Asia provide multiple lines of evidence regarding the nature of ritual language as a site of debate and transformation in a colonial setting. For instance, in an influential study of the interactions that took place between Nahuas and Franciscan, Dominican, and Augustinian lexicographers in sixteenth-century Mexico, Louise Burkhart (1989) carefully documented a "moral dialogue" that resulted in the recasting of a Christian lexicon and certain semiotic fields using translating solutions that often indexed Nahua cosmological beliefs. Likewise, Bruce Mannheim (1991) focused on the sociohistorical and cultural factors that drove Southern Quechua language change in colonial Peru; Alan Durston (2007) chronicled the emergence of doctrinal genres in Quechua in the sixteenth and seventeenth centuries; and William F. Hanks (2010) authored a longitudinal analysis of the Franciscan lexicographic reengineering of Yucatec Maya grammatical categories and morphosyntax, which yielded a hybrid series of formal registers that permeated colonial Maya textual genres and were reinterpreted by native speakers themselves. Moreover, Saul Kripke's (1980) characterization of proper names as "rigid designators" associated with one and only one possible referent in the world through a "baptismal act" may help elucidate the relative successes and failures of colonial translation experiments, such as the long-term reception of the translation of Christian terms into Nahuatl (Tavárez 2000). Beyond the Atlantic arena, two studies have scrutinized the emergence of hybrid forms of ritual language: while Vicente Rafael (1993) sketched a Derridian analysis of Tagalog colonial lexicography and its development as a surprisingly unstable vehicle for Christian education, Ines Županov (1999) examined the sociocultural and linguistic underpinnings of Jesuit doctrinal translation projects in pre-colonial South India in the seventeenth century.

As for Pacific colonial Christianities, there has been a strong analytic focus on the attendant Protestant ideologies that may render Christian ritual speech a distinct phenomenon: Keane (1997b) suggested that an intention/meaning/truth model underlies both some Anglo-American analytical philosophy and Protestant Christianity, and Robbins (2001, 2007) argued that a distinctly Protestant demand for sincerity and truthfulness conflicts with a traditional Urapmin linguistic ideology in which speech is not fully trusted as a stable locus for referring to emotions and creating social meanings. However, I would argue that such a distinction between Catholic and Protestant language ideologies underestimates the degree to which pre- and post-Reformation Christian language ideologies converged. Before the schism, the popularity of the *devotio moderna* – best exemplified by the enthusiastic reception of Thomas à Kempis's *On the Imitation of Christ* in Western Europe in the fifteenth and sixteenth centuries and its translation into Nahuatl and Japanese – popularized the notion of an individual subject who constructed a subjective relation with Christ not by means of scriptural authority, but through prayer and meditation. Afterwards, Counter-Reformation policies emphasized sincerity and intentionality as an objective for Christian confessants just as they sought to implant institutional modes that surveyed their attainment (Gruzinski 1989, Klor de Alva 1999).

In any case, one can think about prayers, regardless of denomination, as indexing hierarchical relations through which subjects constitute themselves as conduits for repetitive utterances of divine origin (Engelke 2004), even if a balance is kept through text-creating strategies shifting between spontaneous and canonical prayer (Shoaps 2002), and if some genres, such as African American sermons, call for the creative use of discourse markers that index continuous spiritual performance (Wharry 2003). More markedly, in Matt Tomlinson's (2004) analysis of *masu sema* (chain prayers) conducted by Fijian Methodist congregations at various prayer sites to stave off disease-causing "ancestral malice," a Fijian minister shifts into an exorcising register mid-prayer. Even if the addressee in this shift is denoted deictically with a second-person singular pronoun, its identity remains ambiguous, and contributes to the presentation of the prayers' beneficiaries as powerless subjects. As for Islamic prayer, the cadence of the performance itself may be seen as constructing a closer emotional bond between subject and deity (Mahmood 2001), and the acoustic correlates associated with exemplary Qur'anic readings can be heard as indices of piety in action in a complex urban soundscape (Hirschkind 2006).

From a different perspective, ritual authority as an emergent property from speech structure itself – the shared recognition of a register as authoritative – has been widely discussed. Famously, Marc Bloch (1975) posited that formalized language constitutes its own, unassailable truth, and as such fetters social action and can hardly be contested through empirical evidence or logic. Bloch's insistence on ritual authority as a self-fulfilling prophecy was disarmingly questioned by a different account of formalization (Irvine 1979, Brenneis and Myers 1984).

There is, of course, a middle ground that investigates the constitution of political authority and public renown through artfully calibrated performances of ritual and poetic registers, as suggested by Steve Caton's work in Yemen (1987, 1990), or by Paul Liffman's (2011) analysis of ritual action as a modality that "binds" together the now discontinuous ancestral territory claimed by the Wixarika in Mexico. Furthermore, Duranti (1994: 107–13) has proposed a continuum between formal speech and less regimented registers in Western Samoa through a discussion of *lauga*, or ceremonial speech delivered by specialists, which has performance rules that are progressively altered to include speech acts with indexical relations to different contexts. Moreover, Duranti has also tracked social and grammatical agency in the *fono* (village council) by exploring the mutually reinforcing practice of denoting social rank through spatial placement and through the use of ergative agents and alternative case markers – a foregrounded use of morphosyntactic resources available to Samoan speakers – by prominent speakers who seek to mitigate the allocation of social responsibility when speaking about the actions of fellow villagers. Furthermore, communicative ecologies may have multivocal forms of enacting authority through ritual speech, as Shoaps (2009) demonstrates by contrasting *pixab'*, a marriage counsel genre, with a transgressive moral critique voiced by a stereotyped Ladino outsider in a Sakapultek Maya town.

20.6 Reflexivity and indeterminacy

The examples discussed above suggest that the world-making, macrocosmic effectiveness of ritual language involves a form of intentionality that should be viewed as collective, and as involving registers of ambiguous and multifarious authorship (Du Bois 1986, Keane 1997a). Nonetheless, ritual speech is not inherently authoritative or even stable in lexical or referential terms. As a practice that relies on a collective form of consciousness, ritual speech is part of a shifting constellation of genres that are easily impacted by momentous changes in language ideologies and collective beliefs, as Joel Kuipers (1998) has noted in his study of the progressive loss of respect for "the words of the ancestors" in Weweya ritual speech after mass Christian conversions took place in Sumba, Indonesia in the 1980s.

Moreover, the discursive performances that model the macrocosm should be seen as reflexive, pragmatically contingent, and subjective forms of action that frame their own conditions of production (Turner 2006). As Hanks (1984) asserts in his study of *sáantiguar*, a Yucatec Maya prayer genre in which paradigmatic relations of vertical hierarchy, order of creation, and a quincunx-shaped cosmos are embedded through systematic and indexical discursive constraints, even such a formalized genre "is contingent on irreducibly subjective features," ranging over specialist-patient relations, pragmatic assessments of the patient's health, and the instantiation of the prayer's structural features in a specific social moment.

In certain contexts, the absence of form and the semantic and referential indeterminacy of ritual speech may be an integral part of the linguistic labor performed by specialists, who thus demarcate a social field through hierarchies of knowledge (Briggs 1995, Hanks 1996, Kearney 1977). What may appear as nonsensical, lexically unrecognizable speech to an analyst (May 1956, Malinowski 1965) may be, in fact, an integral part of a ritual genre. A famous example of lexical indeterminacy is found in the transcription of syllable sequences unrecognizable as lexical items in the sixteenth-century Nahuatl songs known as *Cantares Mexicanos* and the eighteenth-century Zapotec ritual genres called *dij dola* (songs of penance) and *libana* (sermons); in both instances, syllabic sequences index stanza structure, mark topical shifts, and are closely coordinated with metapragmatic instructions regarding singing and percussion (Bierhorst 1985, Tomlinson 2007, Tavárez 2011), which may be seen as a poetic embodiment of the pragmatic framing for a ritual performance (Silverstein 2005). Furthermore, the production and elucidation of semantically indeterminate ritual language help participants focus on a genre's poetic and pragmatic functions, as Wirtz (2005, 2007) argued regarding Lucumí ritual speech in Cuban Santería, which is construed as a register whose obliqueness and unintelligibility index its authenticity and rootedness in a diasporic historical consciousness deployed across the Atlantic world.

20.7 Conclusion

To no one's surprise, anthropologists have often highlighted the role of repetition, formalization, and structure in ritual language. However, such a convergence does not lead to a default and universally shared perspective on ritual speech, and there are important analytical distinctions regarding the multiple sources of its efficacy, or even its very fixity and stability as a linguistic practice.

Nevertheless, an overarching consideration of ritual language might highlight, according to Michael Silverstein (2009: 272-3), that its relationship with social worlds runs along both performative and transformative axes; focusing on the latter, he argues that "ritual efficaciousness depends on the calibrated reflexivity of the metasemiosis" that constitutes and brackets ritual events, causally linking "the bounded microcosm of ritual social-spacetime" with "consequences in the real world as a macrocosm." Moreover, in a recent review of ritual and oratory, Rupert Stasch (2011: 158, 169) contends that Anglo-American anthropological research has moved toward a relatively stable paradigm of ritual performance as an "exceptionally dense representation of spatiotemporally wider categories and principles in an interactional here-now." In other words, ritual language embodies, mimics, indexes, and models a staggering diversity of ideational categories, epistemic stances, social action, and cosmological theories through a deeply interactional instantiation of macrocosmic presences and absences within the parameters of a discrete communicative act.

Hence, the broadest possible definition of ritual speech should depart from a baseline acknowledgment of its collective intentions, its investment in the restructuring of macrocosm–microcosm relations, and its world-changing reflexive semiosis. Regardless of genre or mode, ritual language partakes of the following three features: it is an overt structuring of speech performance, it is exercised reflexively, and it remains open to various forms of indeterminacy. As a process, it is unavoidably linked to epistemic claims about embodiment, the representation and restructuring of social identities, and the instantiation and representation of political and social authority. In the end, ritual language, while anchored in repetition, structure, formula, and cosmological insight, must possess emergent qualities that recreate and transform history, social relations, and the cosmos, as they are performed and perceived by all participants in the ritual act.

References

Aquinas, Thomas. 1948. *Summa Theologiae*. Rome: Marietti.

Austin, John Langshaw. 1975. *How to Do Things with Words*. Cambridge, MA: Harvard University Press.

Basso, Ellen. 2009. Civility and Deception in Two Kalapalo Ritual Forms. In *Ritual Communication*, ed. G. Senft, and E. Basso, 243–70. Oxford: Berg Publishers.

Bateson, Gregory. 1958. *Naven: A Survey of the Problems Suggested by a Composite Picture of the Culture of a New Guinea Tribe Drawn from Three Points of View*. 2nd ed. Stanford, CA: Stanford University Press.

Bierhorst, John. 1985. *Cantares Mexicanos: Songs of the Aztecs*. Stanford: Stanford University Press.

Bloch, Marc. 1975. Introduction. In *Political Language and Oratory in Traditional Society*, ed. M. Bloch, 1-28. New York: Academic Press.

Brenneis, Donald, and Fred Myers, eds. 1984. *Dangerous Words: Language and Politics in the Pacific*. New York: New York University Press.

Bricker, Victoria R. 1974. The Ethnographic Context of Some Traditional Mayan Speech Genres. In *Explorations in the Ethnography of Speaking*, ed. Richard Bauman, and Joel Sherzer, 368-88. New York: Cambridge University Press.

Briggs, Charles L., 1995. The Meaning of Nonsense, the Poetics of Embodiment, and the Production of Power in Warao Healing. In *The Performance of Healing*, ed. C. Laderman, and M. Roseman, 185-232. Routledge: New York.

Burkhart, Louise. 1989. *The Slippery Earth: Nahua-Christian Moral Dialogue in Sixteenth- Century Mexico*. Tucson: University of Arizona Press.

Caton, Steve C. 1987. Power, Persuasion, and Language: A critique of the segmentary model in the Middle-East. *International Journal of Middle East Studies* 19(1): 77-102.

—— 1990. *"Peaks of Yemen I Summon": Poetry as Cultural Practice in a North Yemeni Tribe*. Berkeley: University of California Press.

Course, Magnus. 2010. Of Words and Fog. Linguistic relativity and Amerindian ontology. *Anthropological Theory* 10(3): 247-63.

Du Bois, John W. 1986. Self-evidence and Ritual Speech. In *Evidentiality: The Linguistic Coding of Epistemology*, ed. W. Chafe, and J. Nichols, 313-36. Norwood, NJ: Ablex.

Duranti, Alessandro. 1994. *From Grammar to Politics: Linguistic Anthropology in a Western Samoan Village*. Berkeley: University of California Press.

Durkheim, Emile. 1912. *The Elementary Forms of the Religious Life*. Oxford: Oxford University Press.

Durston, Alan. 2007. *Pastoral Quechua: The History of Christian Translation in Colonial Peru, 1550-1650*. Notre Dame, IN: University of Notre Dame Press.

Enfield, N.J. 2009. Everyday Ritual in the Residential World. In *Ritual Communication*, ed. G. Senft, and E. Basso, 51-80. Oxford: Berg Publishers.

Engelke M. 2004. Text and Performance in an African Church: The book, "live and direct." *American Ethnologist* 31(1): 76-91.

Errington, Joseph. 2007. *Linguistics in a Colonial World: A Story of Language, Meaning and Power*. New York: Wiley, John & Sons.

Evans-Pritchard, Edward E. 1965. *Theories of Primitive Religion*. Oxford: Clarendon Press.

Field, Margaret, and Taft Blackhorse Jr. 2002. The Dual Role of Metonymy in Navajo Prayer. *Anthropological Linguistics* 44(3): 217-30.

Fox, James J. 1974. "Our Ancestors Spoke in Pairs": Rotinese views of language, dialect, and code. In *Explorations in the Ethnography of Speaking*, ed. Richard Bauman, and Joel Sherzer, 65-85. New York: Cambridge University Press.

1975. On Binary Categories and Primary Symbols: Some Rotinese perspectives. In *The Interpretation of Symbolism*, ed. Roy Willis, 99–132. London: Malaby Press.

ed. 1988. *To Speak in Pairs: Essays on the Ritual Languages of Eastern Indonesia*. Cambridge: Cambridge University Press.

Frazer, Sir James George. 1922. *The Golden Bough: A Study in Magic and Religion*. New York: MacMillan Publishing Co.

Friedrich, Paul. 1989. Language, Ideology and Political Economy. *American Anthropologist* 91: 295–313.

Garibay K., Angel María. 1954. *Historia de la literatura náhuatl*. Mexico: Editorial; aPorrú.

Geertz, Clifford. 1966. Religion as a Cultural System. In *Anthropological Approaches to the Study of Religion*, ed. M. Banton, 1–46. ASA Monographs, 3. London: Tavistock Publications.

1980. *Negara: The Theatre State in Nineteenth-Century Bali*. Princeton, NJ: Princeton University Press.

Goffman, Erving. 1967. *Interaction Ritual: Essays on Face-to-Face Behavior*. New York: Doubleday.

Gossen, Gary. 1974. *Chamulas in the World of the Sun: Time and Space in a Maya Oral Tradition*. Cambridge, MA: Harvard University Press.

Gruzinski, Serge. 1989. Individualization and Acculturation: Confession Among the Nahuas of Mexico from the Sixteenth to the Eighteenth Century. In *Sexuality and Marriage in Colonial Latin America*, ed. Asunción Lavrín, 96–117. Lincoln: University of Nebraska Press.

Hanks, William F. 1984. Santification, Structure, and Experience in a Yucatec Ritual Event. *Journal of American Folklore* 97 (384): 131–65.

1996. Exorcism and the Description of Participant Roles. In *Natural Histories of Discourse*, ed. M. Silverstein, and G. Urban, 160–202. Chicago: University of Chicago Press.

2010. *Converting Words: Maya in the Age of the Cross*. Berkeley: University of California Press.

Haviland, John B. 2010. Mu xa xtak'av: "He Doesn't Answer". *Journal of Linguistic Anthropology* 20(1): 195–213.

Hill, Jane. 1998. Today There Is No Respect: Nostalgia, "respect," and oppositional discourse in Mexicano language ideology. In *Language Ideologies: Practice and Theory*, ed. B. Schieffelin, P. Kroskrity, and K. Woolard, 68–86. Oxford: Oxford University Press.

Hirschkind, Charles. 2006. *The Ethical Soundscape: Cassette Sermons and Islamic Counterpublics*. New York: Columbia University Press.

Holbraad, Martin. 2012. *Truth in Motion: The Recursive Anthropology of Cuban Divination*. Chicago: University of Chicago Press.

Houston, Stephen D., ed. 2004. *The First Writing: Script Invention as History and Process*. Cambridge: Cambridge University Press.

Hymes, Dell. 1981. Discovering Oral Performance and Measured Verse in American Indian Narrative. In *"In Vain I tried to tell you." Essays in Native*

American Ethnopoetics, 309–41. Philadelphia: University of Pennsylvania Press.

Irvine, Judith. 1979. Formality and Informality in Communicative Events. *American Anthropologist* 81(4): 773–90.

1989. When Talk Isn't Cheap: Language and political economy. *American Ethnologist* 16(2): 248–67.

Jackson, J. L. 2009. To Tell It Directly Or Not: Coding transparency and corruption in Malagasy political oratory. *Language in Society* 38(1): 47–69.

Jakobson, Roman. 1987. *Language in Literature*. Cambridge, MA: Harvard University Press.

Johnson, Paul. 2002. *Secrets, Gossip, and Gods: The Transformation of Brazilian Candomblé*. Oxford: Oxford University Press.

Kapferer, Bruce. 1997. *The Feast of the Sorcerer: Practices of Consciousness and Power*. Chicago: University of Chicago Press.

Keane, Webb. 1997a. *Signs of Recognition: Powers and Hazards of Representation in an Indonesian Society*. Berkeley: University of California Press.

1997b. From Fetishism to Sincerity: On agency, the speaking subject, and their historicity in the context of religious conversion. *Comparative Studies in Society and History* 39(4): 674–93.

2006. *Christian Moderns: Freedom and Fetish in the Mission Encounter*. Berkeley: University of California Press.

Kearney, Michael. 1977. Oral Performance by Mexican Spiritualists in Possession Trance. *Journal of Latin American Lore* 3: 309–328.

Keenan, Elinor Ochs. 1973. A Sliding Sense of Obligatoriness: the Poly-Structure of Malagasy Oratory. *Language in Society* 2: 225–43.

Kelly, John, and Martha Kaplan. 1990. History, Structure and Ritual. *Annual Review of Anthropology* 119: 119–50.

Kirsch, Arthur C. 2005. *Auden and Christianity*. New Haven, CT: Yale University Press.

Klor de Alva, Jorge. 1999. "Telling Lives": Confessional Autobiography and the Reconstruction of the Nahua Self. In *Spiritual Encounters*, ed. Nicolas Griffiths, and Fernando Cervantes, 136–62. Lincoln: University of Nebraska Press.

Kockelman, Paul. 2007. Inalienable Possession and Personhood in a Q'eqchi'-Mayan Community. *Language in Society* 36: 343–69.

Kripke, Saul. 1980. *Naming and Necessity*. Cambridge, MA: Harvard University Press.

Kuipers, Joel. 1990. *The Power in Performance*. Philadelphia: University of Pennsylvania Press.

1998. *Language, Identity, and Marginality in Indonesia: The Changing Nature of Ritual Speech on the Island of Sumba*. Cambridge: Cambridge University Press.

Lambek, Michael. 2002. *The Weight of the Past: Living with History in Mahajanga, Madagascar*. New York: Palgrave Macmillan.

Leach, Edmund. 1976. *Culture and Communication: The Logic by which Symbols Are Connected*. Cambridge: Cambridge University Press.

León-Portilla, Miguel. 1983. Cuicatl y Tlahtolli: Las formas de expresión en náhuatl. *Estudios de Cultura Náhuatl* 16: 13-108.

Liffman, Paul. 2011. *Huichol Territory and the Mexican Nation: Indigenous Ritual, Land Conflict, and Sovereignty Claims*. Tucson: University of Arizona Press.

Lockhart, James. 1992. *The Nahuas After the Conquest*. Stanford, CA: Stanford University Press.

Mahmood, Saba. 2001. Rehearsed Spontaneity and the Conventionality of Ritual: Disciplines of salat. *American Ethnologist* 28(4): 827-53.

Malinowski, Bronislaw. 1929. *The Sexual Life of Savages in Northwest Melanesia*. London: Routledge.

  1965. *Coral Gardens and their Magic*. 2 vols. Bloomington: Indiana University Press.

Mannheim, Bruce. 2011. *The Language of the Inka Since the European Invasion*. Austin: University of Texas Press.

May, L. Carlyle. 1956. A Survey of Glossolalia and Related Phenomena in Non-Christian Religions. *American Anthropologist* 58 (1): 75-96.

Pedersen, Morten Axel. 2011. *Not Quite Shamans: Spirit Worlds and Political Lives in Northern Mongolia*. Ithaca, NY: Cornell University Press.

Pollock, Sheldon I. 2006. *The Language of the Gods in the World of Men: Sanskrit, Culture, And Power in Premodern India*. Berkeley: University of California Press.

Rafael, Vicente L. 1993. *Contracting Colonialism: Translation and Christian Conversion in Tagalog Society Under Early Spanish Rule*. Durham, NC: Duke University Press.

Rappaport, Roy A. 1999. *Ritual and Religion in the Making of Humanity*. Cambridge: Cambridge University Press.

Robbins, Joel. 2001. God is Nothing but Talk: Modernity, language, and prayer in a Papua New Guinea society. *American Anthropologist* 103(4): 901-12.

  2007. You Can't Talk behind the Holy Spirit's Back: Christianity and changing language ideologies in a Papua New Guinea society. In *Consequences of Contact: Language Ideologies and Sociocultural Transformations in Pacific Societies*, ed. M. Makihara, and B. Schieffelin, 125-39. Oxford: Oxford University Press.

Ruiz de Alarcón, Hernando. 1984. *Treatise on the Heathen Superstitions that Today Live Among The Indians Native to this New Spain (1629)*, trans. and ed., J. R. Andrews and R. Hassig. Norman: University of Oklahoma Press.

Rumsey, Alan. 1990. Wording, Meaning, and Linguistic Ideology. *American Anthopologist* 92: 346-61.

Sahagún, Bernardino de. 1950-82. *The Florentine Codex: General History of the Things of New Spain, Books 1-12*, trans. and ed. Arthur J. O. Anderson and Charles E. Dibble. 13 vols. Salt Lake City: University of Utah Press.

Sahlins, Marshall. 1981. *Historical Metaphors and Mythical Realities: Structure in the Early History of the Sandwich Islands Kingdom*. Ann Arbor: University of Michigan Press.

Schieffelin, Bambi. 1990. *The Give and Take of Everyday Life: Language Socialization of Kaluli Children*. New York: Cambridge University Press.

Schrauwers, Albert. 2000. Three Weddings and a Performance: Marriage, households, and development in the highlands of Central Sulawesi, Indonesia. *American Ethnologist* 27 (4): 855-76.

Searle, John. 1995. *The Construction of Social Reality*. New York: The Free Press.

Severi, Carlo. 2002. Memory, Reflexivity and Belief. Reflections on the ritual use of language. *Social Anthropology* 10(1): 23-40.

Sherzer, Joel. 1991. *Verbal Art in San Blas: Kuna Culture through its Discourse*. Cambridge: Cambridge University Press.

Shoaps, Robin. 2002. "Pray Earnestly": The Textual Construction of Personal Involvement in Pentecostal Prayer and Song. *Journal of Linguistic Anthropology* 12(1): 34-71.

2009. Ritual and (Im)moral Voices: Locating the Testament of Judas in Sakapultek communicative ecology. *American Ethnologist* 36(3): 459-77.

Silverstein, Michael. 2005. The Poetics of Politics: "theirs" and "ours". *Journal of Anthropological Research* 61(1): 1-24.

2009. Private Ritual Encounters, Public Ritual Indexes. In *Ritual Communication*, ed. G. Senft, and E. Basso, 271-91. Oxford: Berg Publishers.

Stasch, Rupert. 2003. The Semiotics of World-Making in Korowai Feast Longhouses. *Language and Communication* 23(3/4): 359-83.

2011. Ritual and Oratory Revisited: The semiotics of effective action. *Annual Review of Anthropology* 40: 159-74.

Tambiah, Stanley J. 1985. *Culture, Thought, and Social Action: An Anthropological Perspective*. Cambridge, MA: Harvard University Press.

1990. *Magic, Science, Religion, and the Scope of Rationality*. Cambridge: Cambridge University Press.

Tavárez, David. 2000. Naming the Trinity: From ideologies of translation to dialectics of reception in colonial Nahua texts, 1547-1771. *Colonial Latin American Review* 9(1): 21-47.

2011. *The Invisible War: Indigenous Devotions, Discipline, and Dissent in Colonial Mexico*. Stanford, CA: Stanford University Press.

Taylor, Charles. 1985. *Human Agency and Language*. Cambridge: Cambridge University Press.

Tedlock, Dennis. 1987. Hearing a Voice in an Ancient Text: Quiché Maya poetics in performance. In *Native American Discourse: Poetics and Rhetoric*, ed. Joel Sherzer, and Anthony Woodbury, 140-75. Cambridge: Cambridge University Press.

Tomasello, Michael. 1999. The Human Adaptation for Culture. *Annual Review of Anthropology* 28: 509-29.

Tomlinson, Gary. 2007. *The Singing of the New World: Indigenous Voice in the Era of European Contact*. Cambridge: Cambridge University Press.

Tomlinson, Matt. 2004. Ritual, Risk, and Danger: Chain prayers in Fiji. *American Anthropologist* 106(1): 6–16.

Turner, Terrence. 2006. Structure, Process, Form. In *Theorizing Rituals: Issues, Topics, Approaches, Concepts*, ed. J. Kreinath, J. Snoek, and M, Stausberg, 207–46. Leiden: Brill.

Turner, Victor Witter. 1977. *The Ritual Process: Structure and Anti-Structure*. Ithaca, NY: Cornell University Press.

Urcid, Javier. 2011. The Written Surface as a Cultural Code: A comparative perspective of scribal traditions from southwestern Mesoamerica. In *Their Way of Writing: Scripts, Signs, and Pictographies in Pre-Columbian America*, ed. Elizabeth Boone and Gary Urton, 111–48. Washington, DC: Dumbarton Oaks.

Venkatesan, Soumhya et al. 2010. Ontology Is Just Another Word for Culture: Motion tabled at the 2008 meeting of the Group for Debates in Anthropological Theory, University of Manchester. *Critique of Anthropology* 30(2): 152–200.

Viveiros de Castro, Eduardo. 1998. Cosmological Deixis and Amerindian Perspectivism. *Journal of the Royal Anthropological Institute* 4(3): 469–88.

Watts, James W. 2005. Ritual Legitimacy and Scriptural Authority. *Journal of Biblical Literature* 124(3): 401–17.

Weber, Max. 1968. *Economy and Society*. New York: Bedminster Press.

Wharry, Cheryl. 2003. Amen and Hallelujah Preaching: Discourse functions in African American sermons. *Language in Society* 32(2): 203–25.

Wirtz, Kristina. 2005. "Where Obscurity Is a Virtue": The mystique of unintelligibility in Santería ritual. *Language and Communication* 25(4): 351–75.

——— 2007. How Diasporic Religious Communities Remember: Learning to speak the "tongue of the oricha" in Cuban Santería. *American Ethnologist* 34(1): 108–26.

Woodbury, Anthony C. 1987. Meaningful Phonological Processes: A consideration of Central Alaskan Yupik Eskimo prosody. *Language* 63(4): 685–740.

Woolard, Kathryn. 1998. Language Ideology as a Field of Inquiry. In *Language Ideologies: Practice and Theory*, ed. B. Schieffelin, P. Kroskrity, and K. Woolard, 3–47. Oxford: Oxford University Press.

Županov, Ines G. 1999. *Disputed Mission: Jesuit Experiments and Brahmanical Knowledge in Seventeenth-Century India*. New Delhi: Oxford University Press.

21

Oratory, rhetoric, politics

Bernard Bate

Linguistic anthropologists promote a view of the human condition that places language at the center of the generation and transformation of social and cultural life. Language, this view holds, is not merely an expression of already extant social and cultural worlds but a key engine of its transformation. This is not to offer the romantic and idealist view of language as the clothing of ideas. Language in the linguistic anthropological view is a material process, a praxis of ideas-unfolding-in-genres-of-activity that are themselves stipulated in the process of communicative action. Its organizing effects extend even to the formation of politics and political fields themselves.

This chapter will examine the concept of rhetoric within anthropological studies of oratory and political practice. We will find that there have been two views of rhetoric, a broad one consisting of phenomenologies of strategic language use and a narrow one that is basically Western rhetoric, which itself has certain peculiar notions of what language is and what kinds of selves and persons that notion presupposes and entails. A final section will address the historical emergence and transformation of oratorical models of discursive interaction and the resulting formation of new kinds of politics emerging within new imagined worlds.

21.1 Two views of rhetoric

Rhetoric is simultaneously over- and under-theorized. In making appeals to rhetoric, anthropologists and others find themselves deploying concepts taken from a vast corpus of language theorizing and usage categorization produced since at least the European re-appropriation of Greek and Roman rhetoric sometime in the twelfth or thirteenth centuries (and its explosion in the Italian Renaissance in the sixteenth). It is under-theorized for the same reasons. Because rhetoric has become a doxic understanding of how language works in Western language theories, it is almost never defined or specifically theorized as an operable analytic concept (with some exceptions).

Anthropologists are participants in wider intellectual and cultural movements that today privilege the concept in unprecedented ways. We can see it applied to all manner of different domains far removed from its traditional object of the production of oratory (or textuality generally). "The rhetoric of self-making" (Battaglia 1995), the "rhetoric of exchange" (Gewertz 1984) or the "rhetoric of experienced objectivity" in ethnographic writing (Clifford and Marcus 1986: 14, or virtually any other page of their book), are the anthropological counterparts of a far broader trend in academia to include such things as "the rhetoric of science." On that latter point, rhetorician Dilip Gaonkar (1997: 26) writes that

> Rhetoric is everywhere. Never before in the history of rhetoric, not even during its glory days of the Italian Renaissance, did its proponents claim for rhetoric so universal a scope as some postmodern neosophists do today ... The rhetoric of science is simply one manifestation of this contemporary impulse to universalize rhetoric.

Gaonkar calls rhetoric the "incredibly engulfing discipline" that, while expanding its purview, has become somewhat thin, shifty, and never quite what it seems to be. Essentially, in determining what is "rhetorical" about any object of anthropological inquiry (say, self-making, exchange, or science), we find that it is precisely the reading given to the object or practice rather than anything intrinsic to it (1997: 29). As Gaonkar concludes, "if what is rhetorical is an effect of one's reading, then a master reader can produce such an effect in relation to virtually any object" (ibid.). Like Humpty Dumpty, the word means precisely what one wants it to mean, neither more nor less.

21.1.1 So what is rhetoric?

In my view, we can use the term in two senses, one broad and universal, the other narrow and culture-bound.

The Broad View. Rhetoric in the broad view comprises phenomenologies – ideologies and aesthetics – of communicative functionality or strategic language use that may be operating in any particular society (Silverstein 1979: 204–6). Basically, by phenomenologies of language function we refer to any notion (explicitly cognized or implicitly felt, ideology or aesthetic) about how language works to accomplish things in the world. Following Michael Silverstein's rather specific formulation, "the folk ream of rhetoric" involve those notions of "how language signals derive their socially-understood effects in various socially-constituted situations of discourse."

> To understand how speaking ... is effective social action, accomplishing such various social ends as warning, insulting, marrying, condemning, christening, growing yams, making sores heal, creating light in the world, etc., we must systematize the description of relationships of coexistence (understood copresence) that hold between elements of speech and elements comprising the context in which speech elements are uttered
> (Silverstein 1979: 205).

Rhetoric here constitutes some level of awareness (explicitly theorized or felt) of the functions of the indexical plane of language, i.e., the ways that language use indexes not only the participant roles and "contexts" of any interactional event but the larger sociologies, cosmologies, and histories stipulated – presupposed and entailed – in that event. Such awareness informs what kinds of actions people have available to them as well as the kinds of ends they hope to effect in their use of language.

We can take rhetoric in the broad sense, then, as an anthropological universal: to one degree or another, all people have notions of communicative functionality. Some have very limited conscious rhetoric insofar as they do not think very much about it (e.g., the Ilongot; see below) but they will nevertheless have strong feelings about how to do things with words – especially in the breach of normative rhetorical behavior. In this respect, all people have rhetoric, but they may not have a specific term that expresses what we mean by rhetoric nor a complex set of terms – a science – for the various modes of accomplishing ends with language. Contrarily, people may have very well worked-out and highly sophisticated understandings, terminologies, and traditions of rhetorical practice and analysis such as the ancient and powerful rhetorics of the Mediterranean basin (Greek, Latin, Arabic), West Africa (Irvine 1979; Yankah 1995: chs. 1–4), or Madagascar (Bloch 1975; Ochs 1998[1989]; Jackson 2008, 2009, 2013). In the broadest sense, a science of "pure rhetoric," as C. S. Peirce put it, stripped-down in aesthetic simplicity or filigreed in baroque and ideological complexity, involves those notions of how to make one thought follow from another (Peirce 1955: 99).

A great deal of contemporary linguistic anthropology concentrates precisely on this aspect of language under the rubric of language ideology (Silverstein 1979; Woolard and Schieffelin 1994; Kroskrity et al. 1998; Irvine and Gal 2000; Kroskrity 2000). Culturally and historically contingent ideas about how language functions (including ideologies of strategic language use) are the "mediating link between social structures and forms of talk" (Woolard and Schieffelin 1994) insofar as such notions track what people can do in the world based on their understandings of the kinds of social action and agencies that are available to them via certain kinds of communicative praxis. This is not the case only on the "strategic" level but on the level of speech genres (Bakhtin 1986; Hill 1995), those (frequently) named models of communicative action that people embody in their interactions with others – from "everyday" forms of speaking, such as having a conversation, gossiping, shooting the shit, *adda*, etc., to more ceremonial models, including the myriad sorts of oratorical performances for which people may gather, such as a lecture (Goffman 1983), a sermon (Hirschkind 2001, 2006; Robbins 2001; Bate 2005, 2010), a funeral oration (Seremetakis 1991, Silverstein 2003, Loraux 2006[1981]), a stump speech, or the State of the Union Address. That people may "have" these culturally and historically contingent forms enables their embodiment in interaction – for if there were nothing resembling a sermon in the world, how then would someone embody a sermonic form?

In the case of rhetoric, per se, the language ideology model focuses specifically upon notions of strategic language use that inform people's actions, agencies, and the emergence of new sociocultural and political forms. A recent example in the anthropology of political language is Silverstein's focus upon the organizing rhetoric of "message" in American political practice (2003, 2011). Developed over the latter half of the twentieth century as the consumer economy in America grew, "message" emerged alongside the expansion of advertising and marketing and shares with those fields a strong similarity to the concept of the "brand":

> "Message" in political life is parallel to what one would term in marketing language, "brand." In political life, however, "message" is the characterological aura of a persona, much like a character in realist literature, who has not only said and done things, but who has the potential, in the fictive universe of a plot, to be imaginable as acting in certain ways in situations still unrealized in plot spacetime – the character's plot-framed "future."
> (Silverstein 2011: 204)

In contrast to American ideologies of political language by which people feel politicians should speak about real-world "issues," message actually works to promote what Silverstein calls emblems of identity, that is, iconic and indexical links to an imagined biography, sociological field, and moral order. In such an imaginary, "our" candidate (in the Tea Party era of 2008–10, for instance) is a "Washington outsider," a "conservative," "a Christian," "a capitalist," "a regular guy" supported by other regular guys (plumbers and beer drinkers, for example), and "their" candidate is "elite," "liberal," "socialist," even "Muslim," "Kenyan," indeed, "non-American." That such a discourse of radical otherness – even alienness – emerges when a black man first enters the White House led the President's surrogates to brand his opponents – i.e., promote the message – that they were "racists," another negative position within a socio-ethical field. Regardless, message as an organizing phenomenology of strategic language use – a rhetoric – is at the very center of a wide range of practices such as candidates struggling to stay "on-message," exercising "message discipline," or trying to provoke their opponents to fall "off-message."

More strikingly, perhaps, message is central to the emergence of new sociological forms including surrogate advocacy (527(c)) organizations such as MoveOn.org or, in the post–Citizens United era, so-called "Super Pacs," which are now considered legal "persons" who can raise and spend unlimited funds. Lobbyists and think-tank surrogates of the candidate who are expert in national TV interviewing, reporters and producers, and of course the blooming-buzzing world of political campaign professionals in general, constitute

> a huge establishment of professionals for whom "message" as communication organizes the very conduct of electoral politics, and certainly the economics thereof. It is the presumed-upon communicative framework in terms of which everything is understood, interpreted, planned and scored. (Silverstein 2011: 206)

We should hasten to point out that the ideologies of message are frequently at odds with the actual practice of it. This is the case, first, because while professionals work to produce message, their opponents work to undermine that message with message of their own. Political professionals make message, to be sure, but not as they please. Second, the dominant ideology (if not aesthetic) of language function reduces language to the denotational function, to the process of reference and predication, to language as the deployment of symbols, in the Peircean sense, and not of the indexicality and iconicity so forefronted in the praxis of message-making in American politics.

The Narrow View. The second, or narrow, view of rhetoric amounts to one rhetorical tradition, albeit a very complex, powerful, and historically fateful one, i.e., what we might call the Standard Average European (SAE) or Western folk-understanding of language functionality. By "folk" we do not mean to belittle – all rhetorics are folk-rhetorics, after all, no matter how sophisticated they may be. We want only to add, however, that due to the complexity, power, and fateful historical position, Western rhetoric is taken as a pan-human, universally applicable science of language functionality that exists apart from its own peculiar cultural positionality and historical emergence. While such a powerful science of language function may serve a great many purposes as we will see below, it is counter-anthropological insofar as it fails to transcend its own cultural and historical specificity, i.e., it elevates cultural categories to the status of universal law.

In essence, the narrow or SAE view of rhetoric is that phenomenology of communicative functionality that presupposes an autonomous and durable self who intends to persuade someone of something denotationally.

Persuasion in this view is the key function of language. Kenneth Burke's general theory of rhetoric (1969[1945]; 1969[1950]), developed throughout the middle decades of the twentieth century and taken up in anthropology during the 1970s and 80s (MZ Rosaldo 1973; Fernandez 1974, 1986;

Crocker 1977; Paine 1981; Parkin 1984; Tyler and Strecker 2009) appears to be at the heart of a broad range of anthropology today. For Burke, rhetoric involves a whole series of practices associated with what he calls "identification" (Burke 1969[1950] as cited in Rosaldo 1973: 206), that is the process or motivation of identifying or "entitling" – N.B. to transitively "*title*" – persons, events, or objects within the overall purview of the speaker, making some things a part of our world, others distant from it. In general, identification is the process of persuasion through the entitlement of the world according to the speaker's motivation. In so far as anything may come under this process, rhetoric is vast. Rhetoric, according to Burke's famous definition, includes

> strategies for selecting enemies and allies, for socializing losses, for warding off evil eye, for purification, propitiation, and desanctification, consolidation and vengeance, admonition and exhortation, implicit commands or instruction of one sort or another.
> (Burke 1957[1941]: 262, cited in Crocker 1977: 42)

Burke's position was explicitly taken up by a broad range of anthropologists as evidenced by several of the first volumes devoted to developing an anthropology of rhetoric (Sapir and Crocker 1977; Paine 1981). One of the early practitioners of that anthropology, Robert Paine, defines it as follows:

> Rhetoric is devoted to persuasion ... This means releasing the study of politics from a study of its institutions and concentrating instead upon the way in which politicians attempt to sway, and even mold the experience and knowledge of their public. (Paine 1981: 1)

Friedrich and Redfield provided a somewhat more complicated definition that preserved persuasion as a fundamental rhetorical motive while relativizing the cultural contexts in which speaking might be evaluated as "good" (1979: 412):

> By "rhetoric" we mean simply those devices or strategies which, effectively employed, make a "good speech" and a "good speaker" ... These devices may be acquired by systematic instruction, but more often are unconsidered by the speaker and organized at a subliminal level. Rhetoric impinges on argument since it involves the selection of relevant points, and orders them into a persuasive structured relation; rhetoric also impinges on style and syntax, since it involves the organization of linguistic elements into meaningful and pointed utterance.

Rhetoric, here, is organized both at a conscious level (that "may be acquired by systematic instruction") as a rationalized ideology of strategic language use (as in the definition provided by Burke) as well as on a "subliminal level," as an aesthetic of language that we feel, that we know on a "gut" level is good or bad, beautiful or ugly, meaningful or empty. Specifically, the notion of evaluation, "good speech" and "good speakers," suggests a view that allows us to move beyond strategy and "intentionality" (without denying it, cf. Bourdieu 1977) into broader evaluative schemata that partake of culturally and historically contingent ways of feeling (Lutz and Abu-Lughod 1990).

Ethel Albert, too, defines it in terms of "persuasion" as well as evaluative criteria:

> [R]hetoric designates the norms and techniques of persuasion as well as the criteria governing styles of delivery in public speaking.
> (Albert 1964: 75)

But Albert is one of the rare anthropologists who not only specifically defines it in her writing – in fact, in 1964 she is the first anthropologist to do so – but to qualify what she means by first noting that there is a danger in using such a culturally specific term as "rhetoric" (along with "logic" and "poetics"). When applied to non-Western societies, such as those in Africa, it may well have a distorting effect by applying concepts outside of their "native cultural habitat" (ibid.)! She also quickly problematizes "rhetoric" by the inclusion of what she calls "ethno-epistemological" concerns regarding the nature of truth and falsity, "the social structural definitions of speech situations," the culturally specific kinds of persons (and subjectivities) that are instantiated within particular communicative models of speaking, and, finally, the primacy of "esthetic-emotional values" in the cultural patterning of speech behavior in Burundi.

Albert's "ethno-epistemology" anticipates the kind of rigorous anthropological inquiry into rhetoric in the broad sense that linguistic anthropologists have undertaken in recent decades, i.e., the study of speakers' own phenomenologies of strategic language use.

For the privileging of persuasion carries with it certain peculiar ethno-epistemological assumptions about language and language use in general.

The first of these, as mentioned above, is the reduction of language function to that of reference and predication, sometimes called the denotational function of language, the ability of people to use language to make propositional statements about the world. As Jane Hill has put it, western rhetoricians are subject to the broad ideological tendency to locate "the crucial nexus of representation in the relationship between reference and reality" (1992: 264). So, what the "rhetoric" may be of any particular sign or communicative practice can usually be explained by appeal to some basic "meaning" that is inherent within the sign or practice itself.

A second assumption leads rhetoricians to neglect the socio-semiotic variation of self and personhood indexed in discursive interaction. They rather impose a very specific understanding of personhood and the self that may or may not be operable among the people considered. To put this in the words of Michelle Rosaldo, "ways of thinking about language, about human agency and personhood in the world are intimately linked: our theoretical attempts to understand how language works are shaped by those culturally prevalent views about the given nature of those human beings by whom language is used" (Rosaldo n.d., quoted in Brenneis and Myers 1984: 8). Some folk do not recognize a "self" that exists through time that is stable and durable, as for instance, is considered the ethical norm of most Western societies (if not a norm that is always met in practice; indeed such a self is as much a rhetorical creation by some as an ideological presupposition, cf. Newton Leroy Gingrich, discussed below).

Further, specific genres of speaking are tightly bound up with concepts of personhood, that is the named, specific roles people can take (Sherzer 1987a; c.f. Mauss 1985). Clearly, who speaks is very much a part of what kinds of persons we are – men vs. women, nobles vs. griots, chiefs vs. linguists, junior faculty vs. Heads of departments. Indeed, one very broadly shared aspect of oratorical practice across the world is the statistically overwhelming tendency for orators to be male and for women's visible performance genres to stand in some kind of opposition to oratorical ones (Rosaldo 1973, 1984; Sherzer 1987a, 1987b; Kulick 1993, 1998; Ochs 1998[1989]; Kuipers 1999; Besnier 2009; Bate 2009). Oddly, however, until very recently with the rise of feminist studies in oratory (cf. Waggenspack 1989; Campbell 1989a, 1989b, 1995; Johnson 2000), Western academic notions of rhetoric obscure gender as a category of oratorical performance. It only becomes relevant when there is a rupture or a struggle that ruptures that veil of genderlessness, say in the women's movement in the United States. So, even in one of the most sophisticated rhetorical traditions in the world, traditional western rhetoricians have had intuitions of the gender of oratory, but our ideologies of language functionality have not necessarily taken these things into account.

Finally, and perhaps most fatefully, given the presumed universality of Western rhetoric, rhetoricians fail to take into account the historical emergence of the communicative forms and phenomenologies themselves. So, for instance, because we see oratory across the planet, we assume that oratory is panhuman and natural.

This is the problem with Rhetoric. It takes a narrow (though fateful) understanding of Western rhetoric and conflates it with the broad notion of rhetoric. Anthropologists thus elevate their own unrecognized ethnocategories to the status of universal law.

21.2 Rosaldo's change of heart

The extraordinary Michele Zimbalest Rosaldo was among the first anthropologists of rhetoric and oratory to come to this understanding, but not without first falling under the spell of a narrow view of rhetoric. In one of her first articles on Ilongot oratory (1973), among whom she had then recently completed her fieldwork, she articulates a highly sophisticated anthropology of rhetoric based on the writings of Kenneth Burke.

Over the course of the following decade, most certainly before her book, *Knowledge and Passion* (1980), and her final essay on rhetoric, which was published posthumously (1984), she appeared to have moved beyond Western rhetoric in a manner that both embodied a general shift in anthropology and pointed us to a more productive and ethnographically sensitive understanding of language phenomenologies of strategic language use generally.

Her first paper focused on the Burkean concept of the "rhetorical motive," i.e., "the universal methods of argument and persuasion" (Rosaldo 1973: 205). Central to these methods is what Burke called identification, that process by which a speaker identifies

> the objects, persons, or event of his descriptions with examples, categories, or concepts whose typical fates and motives have the sorts of moral implications which are relevant to his interest and intent. The speaker describes things, gives them names, in a way which highlights their identity with some, and opposes them to other, kinds of objects; in categorizing people, his words provide a basis for both allegiance and opposition, for closeness and for war. Through identification, the specific becomes a member of a category, which can enter certain relationships and behave and be evaluated in terms of certain norms.
> (Rosaldo 1973: 206)

Rosaldo uses the concept of identification within the new "ethnography of speaking" articulated in a programmatic essay by Del Hymes (Hymes 1995[1962]), a key forerunner of linguistic anthropology proper, which called for understanding of culturally specific modes of language use. By her own soon-to-be-adopted standards, however, there were significant slippages between Burke's rhetoric and Hymes's ethnography of language, as she sought to account "not merely for what constitutes a culturally salient mode of speaking, but also for the effectiveness of particular performances, as rhetoric ..." (Rosaldo 1973: 194). The resulting paper is a brilliant and fine-grained ethnographic description of the use of a peculiar speech genre, "crooked" speech (*qambaqan*), within oratorical performance (*purung*), particularly focusing on bride-price negotiation between two potential affines. Here, despite an allusive, metaphor-heavy, self-deprecating, and not entirely straightforward use of language, the speaker appears to "hide" his intentions at the very moment of attempting to persuade his interlocutor. The analysis takes on the ethnography-of-speaking mode of describing the cultural specificity of this form of speaking in order to provide a culturally sensitive account of persuasive oratory. She notes the formal elements of posture ("tense and studied"), the preponderance of metaphor and repetition, the frequent appeals to categories of persons and to previous talk about talk to provide an anthropologically rich description of oratorical practices unlike any that Western rhetoricians might ever have given attention to.

By privileging the rhetorical motive, however, Rosaldo produces a thick and convincing account of an entirely different culture of speaking that, in the end, appears to embody the same purpose – the same motive – as any other rhetorician with which the reader may be familiar, i.e., to persuade. All of the baroque and beautiful strangeness of the "crooked speech" of the Ilongot is actually about persuading people to see the world in the speaker's terms. To paraphrase Wallace Stevens, we traveled all the way to another world only to find ourselves, more truly and more strange.

But over the next few years, Rosaldo would change her mind about what it was that the Ilongot were doing with oratory. Alas, evidence of this change was only published after her death in an accident in the Philippines in 1981. Deploying a new translation for *qambaqan*, she offers another basis altogether for the use of "slow," "curvy" speech:

> But practically, there is, I think, an even deeper way in which "slow" speech is necessary to oratorical encounters, something I mislabeled in earlier work on oratory (cf. Rosaldo 1973) as an ability to persuade.
> (1984: 148)

Rosaldo's transformation centered on an understanding that "ways of thinking about language and about human agency and personhood are intimately linked" (Rosaldo 1980: 203). Ilongot folks do not appear to have notions of "autonomous selves whose deeds are not significantly constrained by the relationship and expectations that define their local world" (1980: 203):

> What Ilongots lack from a perspective such as ours is something like our notion of an inner self continuous through time, a self whose actions can be judged in terms of the sincerity, integrity, and commitment actually involved in his or her bygone pronouncements. Because Ilongots do not see their inmost "hearts" as constant causes, independent of their acts, they have no reason to "commit" themselves to future deeds or feel somehow guilt-stricken or in need of an account when subsequent actions prove their earlier expressions false.
> (1980: 218)

What are they doing if not persuading each other of something? Of speaking about a bride price, or a specific amount of money to be paid by one to another, etc? Despite a clear desire to achieve material success in the *purung*, Rosaldo claims the main object of such verbal dancing wasn't about persuading anything. It was rather about carefully revealing one's heart and attempting to provoke one's opponent to do the same. A man who comes to *purung* will have a heart full with anger/passion (*liget*), and the object of interlocutors there is to provoke the other to reveal their heart:

> The careful speech of *purung* is, thus, predicated upon a particular view of people's hearts and thoughts, a view that claims that troubled feelings can be quieted if their source, once hidden, is made known. One tries to find the words that will occasion revelation, just as in medicinal spells one tries

to "hit upon" the words that "find" the things that made a person ill. In both cases, the "knowledge" that leads to a success is something one assumes to be already there, requiring only revelation; and so, practitioners seek to make the "names" of troubles public because in giving voice to "hidden" founts of "anger," one makes them manipulable, subjecting them to social action and control. (1984: 150)

So, oratory is predicated upon people's understanding of knowledge and passion (*liget*), and it is predicated upon an understanding of the self and of the nature of human understanding. Traditional Ilongot oratory is more about trying to uncover a dangerous hiddenness, which is entirely due to the way that Ilongot understand what constitutes a "self."

21.3 Duranti's ethnopragmatics

Just as the notion of persuasion presupposes a durable, bounded individual, it also presupposes that individual's intention to communicate some kind of denotational text. Alessandro Duranti (1992) takes up the problem of the individual self in his research on Samoan political/deliberative meetings (*fono*). Duranti offers an analysis that critiques the related concept of meaning, what he calls (following Michael Holquist) the "personalist view of meaning," a view shared by such philosophically sophisticated approaches as Speech Act Theory (cf. Austin, Searle) and by Western rhetoricians at large for whom the autonomous individual is the post-Enlightenment basis for social reality above all others. Within such an understanding of language/personhood, the intention of the individual exists, like the individual himself, *sui generis* and prior to any social status, role, or speaking event appropriate to that role. In this view of language, autonomous selves appear to be just that and are entirely unconstrained by any social processes by which they might be formed.

Instead, Duranti, echoing Ethel Albert, argues for an ethnopragmatic approach to the study of oratory that takes into consideration what Samoans think they are doing with words. For Samoans, intentions are not really the issue involved in their evaluations of political practice. Rather, people are far more concerned with the social roles of the persons involved, their responsibilities as social actors, as well as the effects of their words/deeds (which are not really separate). This is an anti-personalist approach insofar as the intentions of what people say are not nearly as important as the effects that their words have on social order. And just as Samoans view the social world as a product of hierarchically coordinated social action, an individual may not know the true "meaning" of his own words until that meaning is ratified in social processes of all kinds – emblematic of them all being the *fono*.

The deliberative meetings Duranti described, the *fono*, involving *matai*, chiefs or "orators," is both a judicial and legislative body. Throughout his published work (see, e.g., 1994) he read the meetings as emblematic of Samoan adult life in general. In fact the spatial organizations of the meetings were themselves little icons of the social hierarchies that emerge and change over time and of the statuses, offices, and responsibilities of the people involved. In the *fono*, men engage in a kind of action that is all about who they are as adult, agentive social beings and what effects their speech has on the nature of social relations.

Duranti uses the *fono* and Samoan ethnopragmatics in general to make a far larger claim about the irreducibly social nature of meaning and its dependence upon people's understanding of what constitutes a person, a self, and their hearts.

> Given that human action, and speech as one aspect of it, is goal oriented, Samoans, like other people in the world, must interpret one another's doing as having certain ends with respect to which those doings should be evaluated and dealt with. The problem – for us, and, I would like to suggest, for them as well – lies in the extent to which, in interpreting one another's behavior, Samoans display a concern for the actors' alleged subjective reality. The fact that a society can carry on a great deal of complex social interaction without much apparent concern with people's subjective states, and with a much more obvious concern for the public, displayed, performative aspect of language is, in my opinion, an important fact which any theoretical framework concerned with the process of interpretation should take into account. (Duranti 1992: 44)

In many ways the Samoan model described by Duranti that holds people accountable for the social effects of their words rather than their intentions is not alien to American evaluations and aesthetics (if not ideologies) of language use. American public cultural insistence on a fixed, durable self on the part of our leaders occasionally erupts in claims of "flip-flopping" (in the case of Senator Kerry's run for the presidency in 2004) and in the rather stunning changes in position – what one of his opponents called the "serial hypocrisy" – of former Speaker of the House of Representatives Newton Leroy Gingrich in the Republican Primaries of 2011–12. Critics sought out a durable Gingrich that could be compared to previous positions, a self that would be seen by linking statements made in the past to those made in the present. Should we see a change, it would index a new kind of self, one marked by hypocrisy and duplicity, a self that changes due to circumstances. Such ideologies of a stable, durable self, however, can be trumped among some quarters of the electorate, through spiritual transformations, most especially in the process known as being born again among evangelical Christians by which a person's previous transgressions can be entirely forgiven. Being born again is, in effect, becoming an entirely new person whose past is irrelevant to evaluations of his current action.

21.4 Protestantization and the megarhetorics of modernity

Michele Rosaldo's work ends on a melancholy note, troubled by the changes she notes in the world of Ilongot oratory and the ways that they might speak to the darker side of the modern condition at large. A final section of her last paper offers a history of the emergence of a new style of oratory associated with Protestant missionaries and the increasingly important Philippine state authority that favored "straight," transparent, direct speech devoid of rhetorical elaboration. Rosaldo links the transformation in oratorical practice among this group of former headhunters to broader transformation in modernity, from signs that are multi-accentual (polysemic) to signs that have (or at least *should* have) a fixed denotational content; from a valuation of metaphorical and beautiful speech – "curvy" or "crooked" speech that follows a person's heart, that, like a river, winds a delicate and curvy course – to a "straight talk" that forefronts the denotational fixity of language. In this way, she argues, a new totalitarianism has emerged, one that relegates older forms of speech to the "backward," the "bush," the "traditional," the "violent," and disorderly. She offers the baleful thought that such "straight," direct language would more and more characterize the universalizing modern states with their (what we would call today) governmentalization and totalization of human life: a world in which the hearts of men need not be changed as the question of what we are to do in the world is already given in the bureaucratic rationality of the state. Recourse to rhetorically more sophisticated and subtle forms of discourse, such as the crooked, curvy speech of traditional Ilongot oratory within situations in which one man would be required to "hit" at the heart of another, would increasingly be marginalized as irrational and inefficient.

There is quite a bit of evidence to support Rosaldo's lament. Don Kulick's work among Taiap-speaking villagers in Papua New Guinea (1993, 1998), for instance, demonstrated the increasing shift toward a more plain-spoken Tok Pisin as the language of men's oratories, which were contrasted ideologically to the metaphorically rich Taiap vulgarity of women's *kroses* (angry outbursts), which index their "traditional" ways, their non-Christian arrogance (*hed*), and irrationality in general. The two languages came to index two different social and cultural aesthetics: Christian, global, masculine, and rational modernity on the one hand, and traditional, local, feminine, and irrational backwardness on the other (Kulick 1998: 99).

Similarly, Judith Irvine (e.g., 1989) describes the localization of what had been the mode of political praise-singing among Wolof-speaking griots and nobles in contrast to the universalization of French as the language of the modern state. Griots, a caste of hereditary verbal artists, sing the praise of the nobles in order to inspire the nobles into ever greater demonstrations of their largesse. Irvine describes the different bodily properties of griots and nobles as iconic of a hierarchical order within that society. "Griot speech," she writes, is not only "an index of the speaker's relatively low rank and social identity. In a larger sense, it also indexes the traditional system of ranks and sources of authority, as compared with other sources [of authority] such as the French-speaking colonial regime and the national state" (1989: 261). In this way, we can speak of a griot-in-practice as an iconic index of the event of speaking itself, the relative qualities of different kinds of persons within the sociocultural and semiotic order, and of the larger system of traditional authority itself vs. the French and modern post-colonial governmental practices in Senegal.

But perhaps the most striking example of this kind of transformation has been documented by Jennifer Jackson in her accounts of Malagasy Kabary (2006, 2008, 2009, 2013). Madagascar may be considered the single most important locus of the practice and theory of oratory outside the Western canon and tradition. About forty years ago, anthropologists and linguists – notably Maurice Bloch (1975) and Eleanor Ochs (1998[1989]) – began detailed ethnographic documentation of the Malagasy speakers' practice of *kabary*, a formal oratorical genre. Previously associated with Merina royal practice in the pre-colonial era, traditional kabary was a highly elaborate, trope- and proverb-packed circumambulation around a conclusion that it never got to. The point was to reveal the heart and character of a person, not anything actually "out there" in the world (Rasaonarison 2002). For the pre-colonial kings and their contemporary counterparts, kabary was a way of demonstrating what kind of people are speaking or coming together. During the colonial period kabary was politically "defanged" when it was restricted by the European authorities to the realm of life-cycle rituals and small-scale politics. And that is where Bloch and Ochs found it, alive and well to be sure, but nowhere near the *modus vivendi* of political practice that it had been before.

Jackson's work returns anthropology to the topic of kabary as one of the key modes of communicative practice in the post-colonial democratic nation-state, where it again became a formal political genre of communicative practice, now known as *kabary politika*. But Jackson describes other ideologies of kabary that emerged under new regimes of development and democracy: the newest speakers (*mpikabary*) eschew some of the time-worn formulas of classic kabary as a sign of a corrupt past, an image that is widely echoed in the editorial cartoons that Jackson mines as evidence of wider ideologies and aesthetics of contemporary kabary. The older registers of traditional kabary, like griot speech described by Irvine, iconically index the older system of traditional authority which was increasingly being seen as old-fashioned and corrupt – the elaborate use of poetry and thick metaphors themselves were seen as lacking "transparency," a key value of contemporary statecraft. Advised by American political professionals and speechwriters during the 2000s when Jackson was conducting her research, Madagascar's President Marc Ravolomanana used a far more direct style (syntactically and referentially) in order to embody a new, modern, transparent dispensation associated with what Jackson calls the megarhetoric of international development regimes. This megarhetoric blends the values of community solidarity (*fihavanana*) and unity of purpose (*firaisan-kina*) that were the core messages of traditional kabary with two newer registers: contemporary Protestant sermons and international development discourse which favors a straight speech that promotes denotationality as the primary function of language. In essence, "to be a developed nation is to speak as a developed nation" (Jackson 2006). As kabary reemerges as a key political communicative form, these latter registers have come more and more to dominate *kabary politika*, utterly transforming the sense of what kabary had been to previous generations.

Though situations such as the new *kabary politika* in Madagascar and those described by Rosaldo, Kulick, and Irvine have been documented around the world (cf. Robbins 2001; Makihara and Schieffelin 2007; Keane 2007; Larkin 2008), the megarhetorics of modernity need not be taken up in all modernizations – or at least not just as they please. We see, for instance, the return to older ideologies and aesthetics that may have been operating in other contexts, emerging within new oratorical traditions such as those increasingly dominating the modern soundscape in Egypt (Hirschkind 2006).

Consider in this respect our final example, Tamil oratory of southern India. Unlike west Africa or Madagascar, which had well-developed oratorical traditions associated with formal political practice, the nearly two-thousand-year literary record in Tamil demonstrates that the very form of homiletic oratory was not developed as a high-status practice in any formal institution until well into the nineteenth century. Universal interpellation, the calling out to all regardless of caste, gender, or status, was a practice associated only with the lowest-status people – indeed, the drum (*parai*), an instrument of the lowest caste (*paraiar*) due to its polluting leather (Sherinian 2013), stands as an emblem of what was considered a vulgar act: the calling out to all indiscriminately. High-status communicative events would be socially, spatially, and temporally – i.e., ritually – coherent affairs; those who recited high-value texts or gathered to hear them would be people whose caste, gender, and training would qualify them as reciters or participants.

It was only with the coming of Protestant missionaries in the early eighteenth century and the indigenization of its communicative forms in Indic religiosities, in particularly Saivism and Vaisnavism (Hudson 1992a, 1992b, 1994; Young and Jebanesan 1995; Grafe 1999; Bate 2005, 2010), that homiletic oratory was taken up broadly as a mode of higher-status formal practices. And it wasn't until the early part of the twentieth century that oratory entered formal political practice and transformed what politics could and would become in the twentieth century, i.e., the *sine qua non* of the Tamil mass political. Young activists associated with one of India's first truly modern political movements, Swadeshi (1905–8), were the first to systematically eschew English as the language of formal politics and begin deploying vernacular – or *swadeshi*, "own country" – languages such as Tamil or Telugu in mass meetings of thousands of people. These meetings drew students and educated professionals mostly, but also workers and "coolies" in a few notable places where organizers imagined that such people would be relevant to the political (Bate 2012, 2013). The Protestant communicative *cum* ethical call to universalize the Word of God – "Go ye into all the world and preach the Gospel to every creature" (Mark 16:15) – would now be applied to the whole of Indian society in a new mass political project of establishing an Indian raj in place of the British one by the power of the people. Though there would be fits and starts to this project, by 1918 and the beginnings of the labor movement in Madras, the vernacularization of political oratory was nearly complete: to be a Tamil politician was to orate in Tamil. And that would become the norm from that moment on.

But the Protestant form of the message would not carry with it its own aesthetics or ideologies. In marked contrast, again, to the megarhetorics of modernity in Madagascar which stripped kabary of its traditional communal aesthetics, mid-twentieth-century politicians in Tamilnadu had available to them an entirely different set of linguistic resources that they would deploy in the transformation of Tamil political oratory (Bate 2009).

The first generation of orators in the Swadeshi and labor movements were relatively plain-spoken folk whose language indexed the speakers as "one of us," Indians as opposed to British. They used a form of Tamil that was closer to ordinary speaking, the "bent" (*koduntamil*) or "vulgar" Tamil (*koccaittamil*), a Tamil that enabled the speaker to embody the *vox populi*. To me, an American inheritor of the Protestant expectation of plain-spokenness and linguistic (and sartorial) humility on the part of our politicians, this makes perfect sense (cf. Fliegelman 1993). But the first generation of politicians following independence in 1947 and the full-scale democratization of the political system began to deploy another register of Tamil, the "fine" or "beautiful" Tamil (*centamil*) of pundits, scholars, a language that was anything but populist. These were the founders of a new kind of national imagining, a Tamil – or Dravidian – nationalism, and their language was now shot through with archaisms and poetic allusions drawn from a newly established canon that boasted nearly two thousand years of literary production. Now, their language embodied a new kind of nationalism, a modernity to be sure, but one that viscerally evoked the greatness, purity, antiquity, and autochthony of the Tamil language and the Tamil people themselves (even if the denotationality of the utterances may not have been perfectly clear to the millions of illiterate villagers and townsfolk who gathered in great droves to hear these new verbal artists). To speak this new/old language was to become an avatar of Tamil itself, to embody that very antiquity, purity, autochthony, and power. While the Protestant form of the homiletic oration certainly formed the organizational frame of the message, the ethno-epistemology of the new megarhetorics of political language that characterize so much of modern political practice around the world was quite otherwise in the Tamil twentieth century. And, alas, when we consider the tragedy of ethnic fratricide in neighboring Sri Lanka, the Tamil epistemology was just as fateful. But that is a story for another time.

21.5 Coda

> To study political language as a preliminary to studying politics would seem a fairly obvious thing to do, since if we think about what it is that anthropologists have had in mind when they have been discussing the political, it is soon realized that it is almost exclusively speech acts. This fact, however, has been only rarely treated as relevant to the political process.
> Maurice Bloch (1975:4)

To repeat: all rhetorics are ethnorhetorics, whether they inform the fateful aesthetics and ideologies associated with what Jennifer Jackson called the megarhetoric of development and Protestant plain-spokenness in Madagascar or the communicative medium through which politicians fatefully evoked a trans-historical Tamil peoplehood and nation in twentieth-century Tamil South India and Sri Lanka. Everywhere we go we see the first rhetoric at play in the globalizing political form of the nation-state complete with elections, campaign speeches, annual states of the union, or fiery denunciations of the ruling party at the head of a mass rally about to march on the Presidential palace. That rhetoric may have emerged from place to place through Protestant missionaries in the nineteenth and twentieth centuries, or through their secularized descendants – development workers operating on different levels in institutions of global neoliberalism such as the IMF or the World Bank, or in the armies of well-intentioned and earnest young people coming out of Western colleges and universities staffing INGOs in countries around the world.

But the examples discussed in this chapter indicate, too, that each place touched by the megarhetoric also has other rhetorics at work that may be more difficult to discern, as Michele Rosaldo discovered over the course of her short and brilliant career. We might see the form of the utterance and think that they are operating with the same kinds of ideas that people the world over think about their oratorical practices. But once we probe beneath the surface we find that other ideas of truth, beauty, self, personhood, and history structure the production and reception of speeches. And these ideas of how language works, what it is, and how it binds us together or tears us apart are as fateful as the larger megarhetorical frame of the utterance itself. For it is upon the bases of these broader, more diverse rhetorics that oratory finds its power. Those rhetorics are what anthropology seeks.

References

Albert, Ethel. 1964. "Rhetoric," "Logic," and "Poetics" in Burundi: Culture Patterning of Speech Behavior. *American Anthropologist* 66(6): 35–54.

Bakhtin, M. M. 1986. The Problem of Speech Genres. In *Speech Genres and Other late Essays*. Austin: University of Texas Press.

Bate, Bernard. 2005. Arumuga Navalar, Saivite Sermons, and the Delimitation of Religion, c. 1850. In *Language, Genre, and the Historical Imagination in South India*, a special issue of the *Indian Economic and Social History Review*, 42(4): 467–82.

2009. *Tamil Oratory and the Dravidian Aesthetic: Democratic Practice in South India*. New York: Columbia University Press.

2010. The Ethics of Textuality: The Protestant sermon and the Tamil public sphere. In *Genealogies of Virtue: Ethical Practice in South Asia*, ed. Daud Ali and Anand Pandian, 101–15. Bloomington: Indiana University Press.

2012. Swadeshi Oratory and the Development of Tamil Shorthand. In *Swadeshi in the Time of Nations: Reflections on Sumit Sarkar's The Swadeshi Movement in Bengal, India and Elsewhere*, ed. Bernard Bate and Dilip Menon, a special section of the *Economic and Political Weekly*, 47(42): 70–5.

2013. "To persuade them into speech and action": Vernacular oratory in a genealogy of the Tamil political. *Comparative Studies of Society and History* 55(1): 1–25.

Battaglia, Deborah, ed. 1995. *The Rhetorics of Self-Making*. Berkeley and Los Angeles: University of California Press.

Besnier, Niko 2009. *Gossip and the Everyday Production of Politics*. Honolulu: University of Hawai'i Press.

Bloch, Maurice, ed. 1975. *Political Language and Oratory in Traditional society*. London/New York: Academic Press

Bourdieu, Pierre 1977. *Outline of a Theory of Practice*. Cambridge: Cambridge University Press.

Brenneis, Donald, and Fred R. Myers, eds. 1984. *Dangerous Words: Language and Politics in the Pacific*. Prospect Heights, IL: Waveland Press.

Burke, Kenneth. 1957[1941]. *The Philosophy of Literary Form*. Rev. abr. ed. New York: Vintage.

1969[1945]. *A Grammar of Motives*. Berkeley: University of California Press.

1969[1950]. *A Rhetoric of Motives*. Berkeley: University of California Press.

Campbell, Karlyn Kohrs. 1989a. *Man Cannot Speak for Her*, Vol. 1: *A Critical Study of Early Feminist Rhetoric*. New York: Praeger.

ed. 1989b. *Man Cannot Speak for Her*, Vol. 2: *Key Texts of the Early Feminists*. New York: Praeger.

1995. Gender and Genre: Loci of invention and contradiction in the earliest speeches by U.S. women. *Quarterly Journal of Speech* 81(4): 479-95.

Clifford, James and George M. Marcus. 1986. *Writing Culture: The Poetics and Politics of Ethnography*. Berkeley/Los Angeles: University of California Press.

Crocker, J. Christopher. 1977. The Social Functions of Rhetorical Forms. In *The Social Use of Metaphor: Essays on the Anthropology of Rhetoric*, ed. J. David Sapir and J.C. Crocker, 33-66. Philadelphia: University of Pennsylvania Press.

Duranti, Alessandro. 1992. Intentions, Self, and Responsibility: An essay in Samoan ethnopragmatics. In *Responsibility and Evidence in Oral Discourse*, ed. Jane Hill and Judith Irvine, 24-47. Cambridge: Cambridge University Press.

1994. From Grammar to Politics: Linguistic anthropology in a Western Samoan village. Berkeley and Los Angeles: University of California Press.

Fernandez, James. 1974. The Mission of Metaphor in Expressive Culture - With Comments and Rejoinder. *Current Anthropology* 15(2): 119-45.

1986. *Persuasions and Performances: The Play of Tropes in Culture*. Bloomington: Indiana University Press.

Fliegelman, Jay 1993. *Declaring Independence: Jefferson, Natural Language and the Culture of Performance*. Princeton, NJ: Princeton University Press.

Friedrich, Paul, and James Redfield. 1979. Speech as a Personality Symbol: The Case of Achilles. In *Language Context and the Imagination*, 403-40. Stanford: Stanford University Press.

Gaonkar, Dilip Parameshwar 1997. The Idea of Rhetoric in the Rhetoric of Science. In *Rhetorical Hermeneutics: Invention and Interpretation in the Age of Science*, ed. Alan Gross and William Keith, 25-85. Albany, NY: SUNY Press.

Gewertz, Deborah 1984. Of Symbolic Anchors and Sago Soup: The rhetoric of exchange among the Chambri of Papua New Guinea. In *Dangerous Words: Language and Politics in the Pacific*, ed. D. Brenneis and F. R. Myers, 192-213. Prospect Heights, IL: Waveland Press.

Goffman, Erving 1983. "The Lecture." *Forms of Talk*. Philadelphia: University of Pennsylvania Press.

Grafe, Hugald 1999. Hindu Apologetics at the Beginning of the Protestant Mission Era in India. In *Missionsberichet aus Indien im 18. Jahrhundert*, ed. Michael Bergunder, 69-93. Halle: Verlag der Franckeschen Stiftungen zu Halle.

Hill, Jane. 1995. The Voices of Don Gabriel: Responsibility and self voice in a modern Mexicano narrative. In *The Dialogic Emergence of Culture*, ed.

Dennis Tedlock and Bruce Mannheim, 97–147. Urbana/Chicago: University of Illinois Press.

Hill, Jane, and Judith Irvine. 1992. *Responsibility and Evidence in Oral Discourse.* Cambridge: Cambridge University Press.

Hirschkind, Charles. 2001. The Ethics of Listening: Cassette-Sermon audition in contemporary Cairo. *American Ethnologist* 28(3): 623–49.

——— 2006. *The Ethnical Soundscape: Cassette Sermons and Islamic Counterpublics.* New York: Columbia University Press.

Hudson, Dennis. 1992a. Arumuga Navalar and the Hindu Renaissance among Tamils. In *Religious Controversy in British India: Dialogues in Asian Languages, Albany,* ed. Kenneth W. Jones, 27–51. Albany: State University of New York Press.

——— 1992b. Winning Souls for Siva: Arumuga Navalar's Transmission of Saiva Religion. In *A Sacred Thread: Transmission of Hindu Traditions in Times of Rapid Change,* ed. Raymond B. Williams and John B. Carmen, 23–51. New York: Columbia University Press..

——— 1994. Tamil Hindu Responses to Protestants: Nineteenth-Century Literati in Jaffna and Tinnevelly. In *Indigenous Responses to Western Christianity,* ed. Steven Kaplan, 95–123. New York: New York University Press.

Hymes, Dell. 1995[1962]. The Ethnography of Speaking. *In Language, Culture and Society,* ed. Ben Blount, 248–82. Prospect Heights, IL: Waveland Press.

Irvine, Judith T. 1979. Formality and Informality in Communicative Events. *American Anthropologist* 81(4): 773–90.

——— 1989. When Talk Isn't Cheap: Language and political economy. *American Ethnologist* 16(2):248–67.

Irvine, Judith, and Susan Gal 2000. Language Ideology and Linguistic Differentiation. In *Regimes of Language: Ideologies, Politics, Identities,* ed. Paul Kroskrity, 35–84. Santa Fe: School of American Research Press.

Jackson, Jennifer. 2006. To Be a Developed Nation is to Speak as a Developed Nation: Constructing Tropes of Transparency and Development Through Syntax, Register, and Context in the Political Oratory of Imerina, Madagascar. *Texas Linguistic Forum* 49: 72–83.

——— 2008. Building Publics, Shaping Public Opinion: Interanimating registers in Malagasy Kabary oratory and political cartooning. *Journal of Linguistic Anthropology* 18(2): 214–35.

——— 2009. To Tell It Directly Or Not: Coding transparency and corruption in Malagasy political oratory. *Language in Society* 38: 47–69.

——— 2013. *Political Oratory and Cartooning: An Ethnography of Democratic Processes in Madagascar.* Chichester, UK: Wiley-Blackwell.

Johnson, Nan. 2000. Reigning in the Court of Silence: Women and rhetorical space in postbellum America. *Philosophy and Rhetoric* 33(4): 221–42.

Keane, Webb 2007. *Christian Moderns: Freedom and Fetish in the Mission Encounter.* Berkeley and Los Angeles: University of California Press.

Kroskrity, Paul, ed. 2000. *Regimes of Language: Ideologies, Politics, Identities*. Santa Fe: School of American Research Press.

Kroskrity, Paul V., Bambi B. Schieffelin, and Kathryn Woolard, eds. 1998. *Language, Ideologies, Practice and Theory*. New York: Oxford University Press.

Kuipers, Joel. 1999. Oratory. *Journal of Linguistic Anthropology* 9(1–2): 173–6.

Kulick, Don. 1993. Structure and Gender in Domestic Arguments in a New Guinea Village. *Cultural Anthropology* 8(4): 510–41.

1998. Anger, Gender, Language Shift, and the Politics of Revelation in a Papua New Guinean Village. In *Language Ideologies: Practice and Theory*, ed. B. Schieffelin, K. Woolard, and P. Kroskrity, 87–102. New York: Oxford University Press.

Larkin, Brian. 2008. Ahmed Deedat and the Form of Islamic Evangelism. *Social Text* 26(3): 101–21.

Loraux, Nicole. 2006[1981]. *The Invention of Athens: The Funeral Oration in the Classical City*. New York: Zone Books.

Lutz, Catherine A. and L. Abu-Lughod, eds. 1990. *Language and the Politics of Emotion*. Cambridge: Cambridge University Press.

Makihara, Mimi, and Bambi Schieffelin, eds. 2007. *Consequences of Contact: Language Ideologies and Sociocultural Transformations in Pacific Societies*. Oxford and New York: Oxford University Press.

Mauss, Marcel 1985. A Category of the Human Mind: The notion of person, the notion of self. In *The Category of the Person: Anthropology, Psychology, History*, ed. Michael Carrithers, Steven Collins, and Steven Lukes. Cambridge: Cambridge University Press.

Ochs, Eleanor. 1998[1989]. Norm Makers, Norm-Breakers: Uses of Speech by Men and Women in a Malagasy Community. In *The Matrix of Language: Contemporary Linguistic Anthropology*, ed. Donald Brenneis and Ronald Macaulay, 99–115. Boulder, CO: Westview.

Paine, Robert, ed. 1981. *Politically Speaking: Cross-Cultural Studies of Rhetoric*. Philadelphia: Institute for the Study of Human Issues.

Parkin, David 1984. Political Language. *Annual Review of Anthropology* 13: 345–65.

Peirce, Charles S. 1955. Logic as Semiotic: The Theory of Signs. In *Philosophical Writings of Peirce*, ed. Justus Buchler, 98–119. New York: Dover Publications.

Rasaonarison, Elie. 2002. Poetry and Politics: Malagasy Literature in the Making of Malgasy Democracy. Lecture delivered at the Department of Anthropology, Yale University, 23 October 2002.

Robbins, Joel. 2001. God Is Nothing but Talk: Modernity, Language, and Prayer in a Papua New Guinea Society. *American Anthropologist* 103(4): 901–12.

Rosaldo, Michele Z. 1973. I Have Nothing to Hide: The language of Ilongot Oratory. *Language in Society* 2: 193–223.

1980. *Knowledge and Passion: Ilongot Notions of Self and Social Life*. New York: Cambridge University Press.

1984. Words that are Moving: The social meanings of Ilongot verbal art. In *Dangerous Words: Language and Politics in the Pacific*, ed. Donald Brenneis and Fred R. Myers, 131–60. Prospect Heights, IL: Waveland Press.

Sapir, J. David, and J. Christopher Crocker, eds. 1977. *The Social Use of Metaphor: Essays on the Anthropology of Rhetoric*. Philadelphia: University of Pennsylvania Press.

Schieffelin, Bambi, Kathryn Woolard, and Paul Kroskrity, eds. 1998. *Language Ideologies: Practice and Theory*. New York: Oxford University Press.

Seremetakis, C. Nadia. 1991. *The Last Word: Women, Death, and Divination in Inner Mani*. Chicago: University of Chicago Press.

Sherinian, Zoe. 2013. *Tamil Folk Music as Dalit Liberation Theology*. Bloomington: Indiana University Press.

Sherzer, Joel. 1987a. A Discourse-Centered Approach to Language and Culture. *American Anthropologist* 89(2): 295–309.

1987b. A Diversity of Voices: Men's and women's speech in ethnographic perspective. In *Language, Gender, and Sex in Comparative Perspective*, ed. Susan U. Philips, Susan Steele, and Christine Tanz, 95–120. Cambridge: Cambridge University Press.

Silverstein, Michael. 1979. Language Structure and Language Ideology. In *The Elements: A Parasession on Linguistic Units and Levels*, ed. Paul Clyne, William Hanks, and Carol Hofbauer, 193–247. Chicago: Chicago Linguistic Society.

2003. *The Substance of Style from Abe to "W."* Chicago: Prickly Paradigm Press.

2011. The "Message" in the (Political) Battle. *Language and Communication* 31: 203–16.

Tyler, Stephen, and Ivo Strecker. 2009. *Culture and Rhetoric*. New York/Oxford: Berghahn.

Waggenspack, Beth M. 1989. *The Search for Self-Sovereignty: The Oratory of Elizabeth Cady Stanton*. New York: Greenwood Press.

Woolard, Kathryn, and Bambi B. Schieffelin. 1994. Language Ideology. *Annual Review of Anthropology* 23: 55–82.

Yankah, Kwesi 1995. *Speaking for the Chief: Okyeame and the Politics of Akan Royal Oratory*. Bloomington: Indiana University Press.

Young, Richard F., and S. Jebanesan. 1995. *The Bible Trembled: The Hindu–Christian Controversies of Nineteenth-Century Ceylon*. Vienna: Sammlung de Nobili.

22

Language and media

Ilana Gershon and Paul Manning

If we begin to think about the relationship of language and media, materiality is often at stake. Why? Media as a category has in the past often only been visible as an analytical object when one moves away from a co-present situation, and thus when media's materiality helps distinguish it from language. In the "default" case of a putatively pure spoken language, language is materialized in only one medium or channel, that is, acoustically. It is primarily when language is materialized in some other material medium that we begin to speak of "media" (with spoken language being treated sometimes as unmediated, at other times as one unmarked media among others). In turn, the fact that the mediality of language is rarely explored in media studies, Eisenlohr notes, is partially an inheritance of a view of language in which "language becomes a seemingly transparent medium of sense, not because ... the linguistic sound was considered to be the most 'immaterial' of all media" (Eisenlohr 2011: 267). This can lead one to think of the semiotic "essence" of language as belonging to whatever is left over when analysts factor out these materializations in differing media, as belonging exclusively to a dematerialized Saussurean *langue*, Peircean types or *legisigns*, or Jakobsonian *code*. Media in this sense thus might be reduced to an epiphenomenal or accidental issue of differing material realizations of the code, Saussurean *parole*, Peircean *sinsigns*, and Jakobsonian *message*.

For media scholars, media, not surprisingly, is not treated as an epiphenomenal manifestation of code. Indeed, media is so polysemous that for media scholars as well as contemporary linguistic anthropologists, media is only occasionally taken to be the opposite of language. As Spitulnik notes, while media can be defined in the sense of a "transmitter"/"medium" as mentioned above, it currently has such a wide range of additional meanings – including "communication channels, technologies, formats, genres and products" (Spitulnik 2000: 148) – that it becomes difficult to delineate a coherent object. Yet what all these uses have in common is the fact that media can move rapidly from being a visible, even intrusive, part of communication to an invisible and taken-for-granted element. As Eisenlohr points out "If one abandons the simple transmitter model of media, there is perhaps one key characteristic that unites the manifold objects and technologies that have been designated 'media.' This is their oscillation between highly obvious, visible and creative roles on one hand, and their tendency to vanish in the act of mediation on the other hand" (Eisenlohr 2011: 267). Eisenlohr persuasively argues that this propensity towards "simultaneous salience and disappearance" applies equally to language.[1] The problems of studying media (and other infrastructures), and the relation of language to media, then, are at least partly coterminous with the problem of studying the materiality of language, an area where linguistic anthropology has been particularly fruitful in recent years.

Materiality in some form often becomes the basis for analytically distinguishing language from media for many theorists, even when these scholars disagree over the basic definitions, including what language is, what media is, and thus, inevitably, what materiality is.

For example, for Charles Pierce, materiality denotes all that is "outside" of the semiotic. When defining the material qualities of the sign, he writes: "Since a sign is not identical with the thing signified, but differs from the latter in some respects, it must plainly have some characters which belong to it in itself, and have nothing to do with its representative function" (Peirce 1868). The materiality of the sign, according to Pierce, is that which is not part of the process of representing, the leftover that is unique to the way that the specific sign exists in the world. The "material qualities" of an object are precisely those real qualities *not yet* significant semiotically, for example, for the word "man" as written down, the fact that the letters are flat and without relief (Peirce 1868).

By contrast, Frederick Kittler, a German media theorist, begins with a radically different conception of language and media than Peirce does. And yet materiality (albeit a Kittlerian materiality) is also at the heart of how language and media are counterposed in Kittler's theoretical framework. For Kittler, humans ontologically are cyborgs, existing in terms of how what they communicate is transmitted and stored. Humans are one with the media they use to communicate, and thus ontologically different selves when new technologies are introduced. The people who wrote with pens prior to the introduction of the typewriter were different selves than the people who typed. In large measure, the difference for Kittler lies in the ways that the pen and the typewriter store information: the material structures of each transforms how people can exist within discourse networks. What people communicate is not as relevant for Kittler as the material structure of the tools they use to communicate. He writes: "What counts are not the messages or the content with which they equip so-called souls for the duration of a technological era, but rather (and in strict accordance with McLuhan) their circuits, the very schematism of perceptibility" (Kittler 1999: xl–xli). Kittler, in short, by beginning with media and only turning to semiotic representation as an afterthought, ends up taking the representational aspect of language to be a leftover in what is important in communication, an almost exact inverse of Peirce. Yet for both, materiality plays a central role in distinguishing language and media, although in ways that depend entirely on their starting points.

What, then, are the questions we are encouraged to ask when, as Webb Keane recommends (2003), one places the materiality of the sign front and center as the focus of analysis? In the first section, we examine the topics that one studies when focusing on the materiality of the medium itself, aspects such as entextualization, participant structure, and remediation. In the second section, we discuss analyses that result when one takes mediated communication to be the opposite of immediacy, when the central analytical dichotomy is between mediated communication and co-presence. In our third section, we discuss how a focus on materiality has the potential to transform who or what counts as a mediator, framing in unexpected ways the roles humans and non-humans might play in mediating communication.

22.1 Materiality of the Medium

Attention to materiality can allow scholars to ask: to what extent are scholars analyzing how people separate texts from the contexts for circulation, and what ideas about authorship, authenticity, and circulation accompany these processes of producing intertextuality? Entextualization is the process by which a text is bound and made available for circulation in other contexts (see Bauman and Briggs 1990, Silverstein and Urban 1996, Bauman 2004), serving to "objectify it as a discrete textual unit that can be referred to, described, named, displayed, cited *and otherwise treated as an object*" (Bauman 2004: 4, emphasis added). While the materiality of the medium in no way exhausts the different processes involved in entextualization, it remains that different media allow this binding to take place in medium-specific ways. An audiotape prepares its content to circulate in different ways than a handwritten text does. As a result, the circulation itself can be strongly affected by the medium, or media used (one can now photocopy a handwritten letter or scan it and post it on the web to ensure broader circulation). The process of removing the text from its originary context, decontextualization, relies heavily on the structure of the medium used to move a text from one context to another. The structure of the medium also affects the practices used to introduce texts into new contexts, the techniques of recontextualization. By turning to materiality, one can begin to focus on some aspects of entextualization as a process in which the ways in which a text is a material form is integral to how a text can be separated from its context and integrated into other contexts. Whether the utterances are spoken or written, typed or scribbled, recorded on analog tape or a digital MP3, all this shapes the ways in which entextualization takes place.

When texts enter into new contexts, they both are transformed and transform the contexts. The process of recontextualization always requires that texts be calibrated anew to a particular context and interwoven with the discursive strands available in that context (Bauman 2004). The degree to which recontextualization alters the text varies – sometimes the gap created is a major one, sometimes a minor one. These intertextual gaps are often affected by the material structure of the medium used in the process of entextualization. A half-remembered lyric repeated stentoriously during a political rally can be a wider intertextual gap than a karaoke performance of the same lyric. The degree to which the gap exists, however, is not something an analyst can determine simply by comparing the two contexts in question. As Eisenlohr persuasively illustrates in his 2010 discussion of why Mauritian Muslims take audiotaped prayers to be more authentic and closer to the original than written prayers, participants' semiotic ideologies are crucial in understanding the implications and degree of the intertextual gap (Eisenlohr 2010).

When people are choosing which medium to use for a communicative task, they might pay attention to how a medium enables decontextualization. Some communicative technologies allow texts to be removed from their context more easily than others. Some of the work on entextualization has focused on how people use different grammatical structures to enable decontextualization or prevent it (Silverstein and Urban 1996). People can pay the same kind of attention to their media choices, deciding that emails can be forwarded too easily and a phone call might not allow conversational turns to be removed from the larger context (ignoring wire taps).

People's understandings of a particular medium contribute to whether those involved are focused on the texts' boundaries, as well as the intertextual gaps at play. When a king's messenger announces his sovereign's proclamation, the text is clearly demarcated as a text with origins elsewhere. Indeed, this recontextualization is part of the text's metapragmatic regimentation. By contrast, when someone posts song lyrics on their Facebook status update, it is not always clear to readers that this is poetry written by someone other than the manager of that Facebook profile. The Facebook poster might need to insert additional information to indicate where the text's boundaries are and where the poster's own phrases begin.

Goffman's participant framework (Goffman 1974, 1981) is the second aspect of communication that, focusing on the materiality of a medium, encourages analysts to unpack. The materiality of the medium/channel of communication helps determine both the pragmatics of an interaction's participant structure or framework and how this framework or structure will be understood. Goffman (1974, 1981) suggests that the folk categories of "speaker" and "hearer" can be analytically decomposed, so for example, the "production format" of the "speaker" consists minimally of the **principal** ("someone whose position is established by the words that are spoken," 1981: 144), the **author of the words** ("that is, someone who has selected the sentiments that are being expressed and the words in which they are encoded," ibid.), the **animator** ("the talking machine, the body engaged in acoustic activity," ibid.), and (sometimes) the **figure** (a role which we argue usually complements the animator, namely the character animated by the animator). Similarly, the "participation framework" (1981) decomposes the hearer into a similarly subtle range of ratified and unratified recipients, though Judith Irvine (1996) and Steve Levinson (1988) point out that these roles over-simplify the many different ways in which people relate to utterances in any context.

For our purposes what is most interesting is that the medium can affect these multiple ways in which person and utterance are linked (see Agha 2011 for links between a variety of participant frameworks, media, and commodification). For example, the medium will influence who can be the author of a statement, how many people can be the author, as well as who is likely to be considered the author. The medium also helps determine who can even participate in the first place, and what the value of their participation is, as studies of different forms of literacy as well as different types of digital divides have demonstrated. As Inoue (2011) shows, initially the (male) stenographer (as male skilled worker) plays a constitutive, co-producing, role in the rise of Japanese public speaking, as *transcriber* virtually sharing authorship with the (male) public orator as *performer*: "The rise of 'the man who speaks' was simultaneously the rise of the stenographer, the man who listened to and copied him in writing" (Inoue 2011: 184). However, as stenographic writing came to be seen as a "mere" mechanical copy of anterior speech, stenography became devalued as another form of routinized, unskilled, feminized labor, a mechanically repetitive, metaphorically reproductive, "labor of fidelity." As Inoue argues, "all mechanical labors of fidelity (including dictation, typing, message taking, telephone operating) are predominantly female jobs. Modern asymmetries of labor in the workplace diagram traditional asymmetries involved in human reproduction" (Inoue 2011): 181).

Participant structure can be applied both to show the mediation within co-present interactions (for example, the many laminations involved in a simple quotation), as well as to explore the way that the various roles normally laminated into the unitary speaker are displaced onto different actual persons in non-co-present interaction (as when Bill asks his best friend Ted to break up with Ruth on Bill's behalf). Some technologies allow many more listeners than speakers to engage in a conversational exchange, some allow texts to circulate over long periods or to people far from the original exchange's location, yet others allow new roles in conversational exchange or new relationships to established roles. Technologies can function not only to augment the number and kinds of participants, but also analytically to decompose the integral unity of participants like speaker and hearer into different role fractions which can be distributed across multiple participants (for example, a person with a megaphone decomposes a speaker into human source or originator and a technological animator, and at the same time increases the number of people potentially in the audience by an order of magnitude).

These changes can shed light on why new technologies might provoke anxieties. After all, when people discuss the dangers new media introduce, be it telephones or texting, they are describing how the technology can ensure changes in the participant structures of communication. Because new technologies offer new possibilities for participating in conversational exchanges, and limit other ways, the technologies can afford new participant structures. Historian Claude Fischer describes how, when the telephone was first introduced, companies were deeply concerned about how people's participant structure might be altered, allowing many more people as passive and unseen observers on conversations: "A common concern of Bell companies, independents and rural mutual lines alike was teaching party-line etiquette. They repeatedly cautioned subscribers not to eavesdrop, both for reasons of privacy and to reduce the drain on the electrical current caused by so many open connections ... The companies also tried to teach customers to avoid occupying the line with long conversations. They printed notices, had operators intervene, and sent warning letters to particularly talkative customers" (Fischer 1992: 71). Here the participant structure changes in a number of ways. First, a party line requires several households to share a single telephone line, thus allowing single individuals from a household to join or overhear telephone conversations taking place on the line. Second, companies expected telephone operators to monitor party lines to prevent talkative people (often understood to be women) from dominating this shared medium. Telephone operators (almost all of whom were women, Fischer 1988a) had an assigned role of monitoring as company representative; the telephone line allowed not only new primarily silent participants into conversations but also a new type of participant, the operator, to engage in these conversations. The process of "technical identification" (Haring 2007) for the telephone involved creating not only new technical identities for humans like (female) operators and (stereotypically feminine) telephone users (Fischer 1988a, b), but also new identities, meanings, and uses for the telephone itself, which moved from being understood as a *masculine* technology modeled on the telegraph, for communicating discrete, entextualized utilitarian "messages," to being a *feminine* "technology of sociability" (Hutchby 2001a) whose stereotypical use was sociable conversation and stereotypical user was a woman (Fischer 1988a, b).

People often respond to the introduction of new media with concerns about how marked identity categories might be affected by changes in participant structures. In other words, confronted with a medium's new participant structures, people will often discuss the degree to which certain identities must be performed in particular ways and through particular communicative organizations. New media are seen to put at risk vulnerable people and vulnerable relationships – women, children, and fragile class distinctions. With digital media, as Dortner (1999), Livingstone (2009), Marwick (2008), and others have pointed out, children or youth are often seen as the segment of the population most vulnerable to the more hazardous interactions the Internet makes possible.

In general, people are deeply concerned that carefully established participant structures that had previously enforced certain identities, boundaries, and distinctions would no longer be possible to maintain as these new technologies shift how participant structure is organized. Carolyn Marvin, in her seminal book, *When Old Technologies were New*, writes, in this case focusing on the telephone:

> New forms of communication put communities like the family under stress by making contacts between its members and outsiders difficult to supervise. They permitted the circulation of intimate secrets and fostered irregular association with little chance of community intervention. This meant that essential markers of social distance were in danger, and that critical class distinctions could become unenforceable unless new markers of privacy and publicity could be established.
> (Marvin 1988: 69–70).

The anxieties Marvin details all revolved around how changing participant structures of the telephone would lead to new unwelcome connections and practices that undercut established gender and class hierarchies. On the other hand, various new media have been celebrated as liberating "levelers" precisely for that reason, from the normative stranger anonymity or pseudonymity of the eighteenth/nineteenth-century republic of letters made possible by the affordances of postal networks and print culture (Warner 1990, 2002, Manning 2012) to the liberating normative anonymity of sites like 2chan in Japan and 4chan in North America (Nozawa 2012, Knuttila 2011, respectively) which affords a hetero-normative non-identity politics based on "radical opacity," opposed to the mainstream identity-based "radical transparency" of sites like Facebook which seek to ground online identity in offline identity (Dibbell 2010). As Coleman (2011, 2012) has shown, the crowd-sourced non-identity politics of Anonymous can be linked to the affordances of IRC chat, where (like 2chan and 4chan) the default identity for any posting is "anonymous."

While focusing on participant structure encourages scholars to analyze people's responses to changes in social interactions, focusing on what are called "affordances" allows for explanations of changes in how surroundings are experienced and interpreted. As Hutchby summarizes Gibson's original definition of the term "affordance": "For Gibson, humans, along with animals, insects, birds, and fishes, orient to objects in their world (rocks, trees, rivers, etc.) in terms of what he called their affordances: the possibilities that they offer for action. For example, a rock may have the affordance, for a reptile, of being a shelter from the heat of the sun; or, for an insect, of concealment from a hunter" (2001b: 447). Gibson's original definition treated affordances as categories of direct perception: "for instance, it may be that a fleeing lizard perceives the shape in front of it directly in terms of its affordance as a 'place to hide' (while an observing human may equally characterise it as 'a rock')" (Hutchby 2001b: 448).

While Gibson's concept of affordance emerged within an ecological context and debates about the psychology of perception, Hutchby (2001a, b), a sociologist of communication technology, has usefully expanded the concept to include designed aspects of the environment. What is important for our purposes is the way that the range of uses we can put an object to *emerge* from what one might call a material encounter with or "trial" of their perceived affordances (for "trial" see for example Law 2008), so that the possibilities for use or action that an artifact offers are interpretations of its affordances: "We are able to perceive things in terms of their affordances, which in turn are properties of things; yet those properties are not determinate or even finite, since they only emerge in the context of material encounters between actors and objects" (Hutchby 2001a: 27). Affordances are part of the material structure of an object that reveals itself in perception and are interpreted in use, and inherently many affordances exist as potentials in any object.

The term affordance, which refers to potentialities of objects, allows one way to productively engage with the materiality of technological or media objects, avoiding both technological determinism and equally implausible forms of social constructivism (Hutchby 2001a: 3, 2001b). The term affordance, since it refers to *real* perceptual properties of objects (media) (revealed in vision) which afford them emergent functional *potentials* (interpreted in the material encounter or "trial" of use), is in some sense similar to the Peircean semiotic term "qualisign," which refers to inherent qualities that similarly afford semiotic potentials. For Peirce, as noted above, the "material qualities" of an object are precisely those real qualities *not yet* significant semiotically. In certain ways, then, as applied to media objects, the term affordance and the semiotic term qualisign have certain similarities. Moreover, since objects will always "bundle" far more "material qualities" than are relevant for their current use, this becomes a resource for emergence, as the material properties (affordances or qualisigns) bundled together in any object will shift in their relative value, utility, and relevance across contexts (Keane 2003: 414), a matter which is explored by Hull (2003, 2012) with respect to graphic artifacts like bureaucratic documents and files.

Third, the material structure of a technology often becomes a resource for people on the ground to analyze communication itself, which in turn influences, but does not predict, how people communicate. A communication technology is not only a medium, but is also a technology that people find good to think with. Joshua Barker (2008) points out that people find particular media good to think with as their language ideologies and media ideologies intertwine in their reflexive engagements with new technologies. He discusses how people using interkom networks in Indonesia see speaking on this analog chat network, pieced together by local technicians, as a different kind of communication than co-present communication. The differences perceived enable people to engage easily in less hierarchically marked dyadic conversations than one could have readily in person in Indonesia: "Like many new technologies, it provokes reflexivity. In the case of interkom, ... such reflexivity is not restricted to the meta-pragmatics of speech but extends to the broader question of the forms of sociality and community that some forms of talk can give rise to. Briefly stated, I view interkom as a kind of real world laboratory where people can learn how discourse publics are created and experiment with some of the pleasures, challenges and disappointments of participating in public life" (Barker 2008: 129). Reflecting on speaking on interkom becomes a vehicle for some Indonesians to re-imagine potential ways of being social and political in general (deserving comparison with the way that the affordances of IRC chat are a resource for the political imagining of collectivities like Anonymous; see Coleman 2011, 2012). Thus, Barker points out, people's semiotic ideologies about speaking on interkom also shape users' understandings of co-present speech. Every medium provides a rich supply of metaphors for analyzing unmediated communication, and in doing so, every technology also offers new ways of thinking about what it means to be human.

22.2 Mediation as absence of presence: Presence and telepresence

The way Indonesians contrast interkom with face-to-face conversation reminds us of another implicit sense that most uses of the word "media" have, that is, denoting any medium that is *not* face-to-face conversation (Spitulnik 2000: 148). And yet, what is excluded here, conversation, is one of the most salient genres in which language is used, and one of the largest single groups of "technologies for communication" are those which either afford technologically mediated conversations or build conversational interfaces into technologies themselves (Hutchby 2001a).

According to this sense of media, extremely influential in anthropological and sociological approaches to language, spoken language is aligned with the *immediacy* of co-present interlocutors engaging in the prototypical, indeed primordial, form of spoken language, face-to-face conversation. By comparison with the multi-media mutual monitoring possibilities that arise from sharing a perceptual field ("presence") – the immediacy of the face-to-face social "situation" – other mediated forms of communication have been treated by scholars as attenuated or derivative forms of communication (Rettie 2009). By contrast, forms of mediated communication represented by the telephone and mail, as Goffman puts it (possibly ironically), "presumably … provide reduced versions of the primordial real thing" (Goffman 1983: 2). What statements like this show us is that the term "mediation" comes to denote *what is lost* when situated conversation is removed from the multi-channel indexical moorings of the face-to-face context: "that aspect of a discourse that can be clearly transferred through writing to paper has long been dealt with; it is the greasy parts of speech that are now increasingly considered" (1964: 61).

Partially due to the success of Goffman's pioneering call to study "the neglected situation" (1964), the study of the "greasiness" of *situated* language (as opposed to mediated forms) became, under rubrics like "indexicality" and "contextualization," for quite some time the stock and trade of linguistic anthropologists: From this perspective, mediated forms, by contrast, actually involved *fewer* material media channels, in fact processes like entextualization might erase linguistic forms like deictics (indexical denotationals) that make necessary reference to contexts of utterance for interpretation. Additionally, many design features of the specific genre of communication, conversation, might be argued to derive from this sphere of presence which forms "the natural home of speech" (Goffman 1964: 135). In other words, not to belabor the point, **immediacy** here is once again about **materiality**: about the range of material channels (and associated richness of indexicality and evidential possibilities for mutual monitoring) available in face-to-face conversation. Conversations that are "mediated," then, would be those that show a reduction of this plenitude of materiality glossed by "presence" or "situation."

However, while conversation may find its "natural home" in face-to-face interaction (Goffman's "social situations"), it remains that conversation can also dwell in very different *material* forms of "situation," for example those afforded by various kinds of telephony (what Ito and Okabe 2005 call "technosocial situations"). Such forms of technologically mediated "telepresence" (Sconce 2000) confront the wholesomeness of face-to-face situations with uncanny hybrids of presence and absence, the social and the technical: just as passing notes in a classroom brings mediation into the world of face-to-face situations, so the affordances of telephone conversation, Hutchby argues, allow material qualities of the message strongly associated with intimate, warm, animating "presence," the voice, to be made present across vast distances ("intimacy at a distance") (Hutchby 2001a: 83–5).

Whether or not one embraces a foundational binary opposition between face-to-face "social situations" and mediated "technosocial situations," many scholars have found this terminology to be quite useful analytically in treating face-to-face conversation as a comparative baseline for the study of technologically mediated forms (Hutchby 2001a, Ito and Okabe 2005, Rettie 2009). Given face-to-face conversation as an analytical baseline, scholars can show how the technological affordances that constitute these new forms of technologically mediated copresence interact with a normative order of conversation, producing hybrid forms of technologized interaction. Building on a large body of work within the field of conversation analysis, Hutchby shows, for example, that conversational opening sequences of residential phone calls produce a set of novel opening sequences and novel categorical identities (caller, answerer, person called, person talked to) that are addressed to the problematic mixture of presence and absence characteristic of the technosocial situation of the residential telephone (Hutchby 2001a: chs. 5–6). The interactional genres (conversational sequences, technosocial categories of identity) built up around the affordances of the residential phone, in turn, serve as a baseline for comparison with those found with the mobile phone. As in the opposition between face-to-face and telephonic conversation, here one finds both continuities and changes. Normative practices associated with the older technology are sometimes retained even as new ones address the affordances of the new technology: Even though the "personal, portable, pedestrian" (Ito and Okabe 2005) affordances of mobile phones obviate many of the canonical opening sequences of the residential telephone related to, for example, identification (Hutchby and Barnet 2005), sometimes these persist. Meanwhile, the very same affordances occasion the relevance of locational inquiries (for example, the frequent question asked of mobile phone users, but not landline users: "Where are you?") (Laurier 2001, Weilenmann 2003, Hutchby and Barnett 2005).

However, alongside new forms of telepresence, these technologies can also foster new genres of presence. Ito and Okabe's work on the technosocial situations associated with mobile phone technologies shows how the simple opposition between social (face-to-face) and technosocial (telepresence) situation can be further recursively hybridized into what Ito and Okabe call the "augmented 'flesh meet'," a face-to-face social situation that is bracketed on both sides, and sometimes permeated throughout, by telephone-mediated technosocial situations. Here the opposition between "social situation" and "technosocial situation," instead of being mutually disruptive (as when one receives a cellphone call in the middle of some other social situation), or "disjunctive," instead become "contiguous," parts of a larger technosocial gathering (Ito and Okabe 2005: 271).

In addition, Ito et al. (2007) draw our attention to the way that the mobile phone, as part of an ensemble of other portable devices forming a "mobile kit," "reshape and personalize the affordances of urban space," producing new "genres of presence," "ways of being present in urban space that involve the combination of portable media devices, people, infrastructures, and locations" (Ito et al. 2007: 73). Mobile devices thus not only afford new forms of conversational "telepresence," they also afford new genres of presence in public which mediate relations to urban space and infrastructures, making them analytically useful in the way their use makes the often invisible domain of urban infrastructure (Star 1999, Graham 2000) powerfully present and visible for mobile technology users. Genres of "cocooning," for example, help to shelter users from physical presence and co-present others, producing private territories in public spaces ("killing time" in in-between spaces like public transportation), while "camping" instead sees mobile technology users appropriating public spaces and public infrastructures ("spending time" in desirable public places like coffee shops or parks) (Ito et al. 2007). These mobile genres of presence can also in turn have powerful effects on how and whether different forms of telepresence, particularly those related to online environments, are perceived as being disjunctive or contiguous with offline life. As Ito (2005: 8) notes, in contrast to the fantasies of absolute "cyberian apartness" between "offline" and "online" fostered by stationary PC internet platforms, "The extroverted, out-of-doors nature of mobile communication, as well as its low profile origins in the pedestrian technology of telephony, has meant that the 'online' domain of mobile communications has not been experienced as cut off from everyday reality, places, and social identities."

22.3 Media, intermediaries, and mediators

This brings us to our final point. In many contemporary understandings of media, as Bauman points out (2004: 129), "speech is unmediated, with speaker and hearer in a co-present, face-to-face relationship, while the employment of writing and the electronic media distance the sender from the receiver." We have already seen how such an understanding founders when confronted with even such ubiquitous forms of technological mediation as the telephone or mobile phone, which produce the uncanny immediacy and presence of speech despite physical absence (Sconce 2000, Hutchby 2001a, Ito and Okabe 2005). However, as Bauman shows, speech can not only be made possible across distances by technological mediation (telepresence), speech can also serve as a mediation itself, by "relaying ...spoken messages through intermediaries" (ibid.). Here we want to focus not on the relationship between each message in the citational chain, which Bauman discusses at length and we have mentioned above, but rather on the fact that human intermediaries are relaying it. Human intermediaries, in effect, are replacing non-human media, and by so doing, speech and face-to-face dialog moves from something opposed to media, or that can be mediated (telephony), to acting as a medium does, to transcend the boundaries of the face-to-face situation.

Such "mediational performances" do not simply involve the serial transmission of utterances, for example, as in folkloric transmission or gossip (Bauman 2004: 130), but in specific "implicational or indexical relationships between a sequence of dialogs," so that the whole routine cannot be analyzed as separate dialogs but as one synthetic dialog including both a "source dialog" and a "target dialog." Using a number of different ethnographic examples of such mediational performances, Bauman (2004: 133–45) shows various ways that the fact of spoken mediation not only can "extend the reach of spoken communication in physical space" (messengers, for example) but also serves "to bridge gaps in existential space" (for example, the way mediums can transcend cosmological boundaries between, say, the living and the dead), or even, by displaying the whole chain of mediation performance itself within a single situation, can also produce social distance, authority, and hierarchy between co-present interlocutors (as when Akan chiefs speak *through* their co-present mediators, and the whole mediational performance, including both the source and target dialogs, is on display within a single social situation).

But in Bauman's last example, he discusses the case of the actor in the Mexican *Coloquio* who delivers lines that are parodic reproductions of the lines of source dialog of a play. This parodic performance shows how mediational routines might normally assume the passivity of the human intermediaries, but this assumption can be reversed – the actor in the *coloquio* is behaving more like what Latour calls a "mediator." This allows us to bring in a useful Latourian distinction between intermediaries and mediators:

> An *intermediary*, in my vocabulary, is what transports meaning or force without transformation: defining its inputs is enough to define its outputs. For all practical purposes, an intermediary can be taken as a black box, but also a black box counting for one, even if it is internally made up of many parts. *Mediators*, on the other hand, cannot be counted as just one; they might count for one, for nothing, for several, or for infinity. Their input is never a good predictor of their output ... Mediators transform, translate, distort, and modify the meaning or the elements they are supposed to carry.
> (Latour 2005: 39)

The distinction between passive, invisible "blackboxed" intermediaries and active, refractory mediators draws attention to the fact that we need to pay attention to the active agency of both human *and* non-human mediation if we want to see the constitutive role of media in relation to language, to paraphrase Matthew Hull's discussion of bureaucratic documents (see also Kockelman 2010 for a discussion of this opposition in relation to Peirce and Michel Serres' category of the "parasite"):

> To analytically restore the visibility of documents, to look *at* rather than *through* them, is to treat them as mediators, things that "transform, translate, distort, and modify the meaning or the elements they are supposed to carry" (Latour 2005: 39). Just as discourse has long been recognized as a dense mediator between subjects and the world, we need to see graphic artifacts not as neutral purveyors of discourse, but as mediators that shape the significance of the linguistic signs inscribed on them. (Hull 2012: 13)

Bauman's discussion of mediational performances also points up a rather large blind spot within the conventional definition of media, not only that it excludes *spoken mediation*, but that it tends to reproduce a binary of human *actor* and non-human *media* (cf. Mcluhan's famous 1964 title *Media: the Extensions of Man*). Here we are not interested in reading the relation of human and non-human media, as Mcluhan appears to do, as a continuity within a single entity, a cyborg composed of both human and non-human extensions; rather, we wish to read it as a continuum. Unlike Mcluhan's "cyborg" reading of media, what Bauman's intervention allows us to do is avoid making a priori distinctions about what kinds of actants can count as media.

Bauman's application of the concept of mediation to spoken chains with human intermediaries draws attention to another way we can establish symmetry between human and non-human mediation: delegation. Delegation involves, essentially, the question of whether a task or competence will be assigned to a human or non-human actant. Figuration is the related ontological question of whether the actant to which the task is delegated is viewed as a human (anthropomorphism) or a non-human (technomorphism) (Latour 1988, Akrich 1992). One might say that delegation is a matter of symmetry between humans and non-humans based on mutual substitutability for the same task, while figuration has to do with whether this relation of symmetry is also grasped as similarity. As Bruno Latour (1988) and Madeleine Akrich (1992) remind us in by now classic articles, any channel of communication (medium) forms "a geography of delegation"; any competence embodied in a non-human media might equally well be delegated to a human medium, and vice versa: "As a general descriptive rule, every time you want to know what a nonhuman does, simply imagine what other humans or other nonhumans would have to do were this character not present. This imaginary substitution exactly sizes up the role, or function, of this little character" (Latour 1988: 299).

A simple example of delegation to humans: during the recent Occupy protests many municipalities quickly passed or resurrected laws that banned the use of megaphones or loudspeakers, technologies which of course allow a single human voice to be relayed to a much larger audience (in effect, the megaphone plays the role of the Goffmanian animator or "sounding box"). The ban on this technomorphic actor led to the *delegation* of the animating task of "amplification" to human actors, which took the form of the "human megaphone," several humans standing next to the speaker and relaying their speech in the manner of a town crier. The very phrase "human megaphone" draws attention to the way a specific mediation normally delegated to a non-human can under certain circumstances instead be delegated to humans. But our story does not end here: subsequent more general bans on sound amplification by human actors ("human megaphones") in turn generated other delegations, in one case, to the iPhones of those same human actors, using an "app" called "The Inhuman Microphone" to allow cell phones to act as voice amplifiers, and immediately raised the question of whether the object that it produces is a human voice or not: "while the voice started out human, a digital device is actually delivering it. A smartphone's speaker can't technically be classified as a human voice, but it sure can increase the volume of it and also spread through the crowds" (http://dvice.com/archives/2011/12/inhuman-megapho.php).

22.4 Conclusion

When linguistic anthropologists have focused on the intersection of language and media, they often found it useful to assume a fundamental distinction at play – be it a distinction between mediated and unmediated or situated and unsituated. In this sense, mediation has largely been defined by what it is not, but determining how to conceptualize the ways in which mediation is not co-presence has led to different approaches in the scholarly literature. Thus, choosing to think about the contrast in terms of mediation and absence led to productive explorations of how a "community of time and space" (Goffman 1983: 2) often presupposes certain interactive aspects (such as immediacy) that participants must compensate for when not present. Analyses of media from this perspective explore what aspects of co-present communication a particular medium occludes or amplifies, affecting how people will communicate. Choosing, by contrast, to analyze conversations in terms of situatedness led to other, equally productive, investigations of how the social and the technical are co-constructed. These co-constructions often made visible how hybrid situations can be, at the same time guiding analysts to focus on particular aspects of a situation (such as new categorical identities). In both cases, analysts could figure out what was significant precisely because they were using co-presence as an analytical baseline. As we have shown, these two epistemological choices set the terms for much of the subsequent intellectual explorations of how language and media intertwine, and how materiality plays a part.

Note

1. These same properties that Eisenlohr discusses with respect to media are similar to the defining characteristics of *infrastructures* (including all media considered as channels of communication): they are presupposed, embedded, taken-for-granted, invisible (Star 1999, see also Elyachar 2010, Kockelman 2010).

References

Agha, Asif, ed. 2011. *Mediatized Communication in Complex Societies.* Special Issue of *Language and Communication* 31(3).

Akrich, Madeline. 1992. The De-scription of a Technical Object. In *Shaping Technology/Building Society: Studies in Sociotechnical Change*, ed. W. A. Bijker and John Law, 205-24. Cambridge: The MIT Press.

Barker, Joshua. 2008. Playing with Publics: Technology, talk and sociability in Indonesia. *Language and Communication* 28: 127-42.

Bauman, Richard. 2004. *A World of Others' Words*. Malden, MA: Blackwell Publishing.

Bauman, Richard, and Charles Briggs. 1990. Poetics and Performance as Critical Perspectives on Language and Social Life. *Annual Review of Anthropology* 19: 59-88.

Coleman, Gabriella. 2011. Anonymous: From the Lulz to Collective Action. *The New Everyday*. http://mediacommons.futureofthebook.org/tne/pieces/anonymous-lulz-collective-action (accessed February 7, 2014).

——— 2012. Our weirdness is free. *Triple Canopy* 15 http://canopycanopycanopy.com/15/our_weirdness_is_free (accessed February 7, 2014).

Dibbell, Julian. 2010. Radical Opacity. *MIT Technology Review*.

Dortner, Kirstin. 1999. Dangerous Media?: Panic discourses and dilemmas of modernity. *Paedagogica Historica* 35(3): 593-619.

Eisenlohr, Patrick. 2010. Materialities of Entextualization: The domestication of sound reproduction in Mauritian Muslim devotional practices. *Journal of Linguistic Anthropology* 20(2): 314-33.

——— 2011. Media Authenticity and Authority in Mauritius: On the mediality of language in religion. *Language and Communication* 31: 266-73.

Elyachar, Julia. 2010. Phatic Labor, Infrastructure, and the Question of Empowerment in Cairo. *American Ethnologist* 37(3): 452-64.

Fischer, Claude. 1988a. Gender and the Residential Telephone, 1890-1940: Technologies of sociability. *Sociological Forum* 3(3): 211-33.

——— 1988b. "Touch Someone": The telephone industry discovers sociability. *Technology and Culture* 29 (1): 32-61.

——— 1992. *America Calling: A Social History of the Telephone to 1940*. Berkeley: University of California Press.

Goffman, Erving. 1964. The Neglected Situation. *American Anthropologist* 66 (6): 133-6.

1974. *Frame Analysis: An Essay on the Organization of Experience.* New York: Harper and Row.

1981. *Forms of Talk.* Oxford: Blackwell.

1983. Presidential Address: The Interaction Order, *American Sociological Review* 48(1): 1–17.

Graham, Stephen. 2000. Introduction: Cities and Infrastructures. *International Journal of Urban and Regional Research* 24(1): 114–19.

Haring, Kristen. 2007. *Ham Radio's Technical Culture.* Cambridge, MA: MIT Press.

Hull. M. 2003. The File: Agency, authority, and autography in an Islamabad bureaucracy. *Language and Communication* 23(3–4): 287–314.

2012. *The Government of Paper: The Materiality of Bureaucracy in Urban Pakistan.* Berkeley: University of California Press.

Hutchby, Ian. 2001a. *Conversation and Technology: From the Telephone to the Internet.* Cambridge: Polity Press.

2001b. Technologies, Texts and Affordances, *Sociology* 35(2): 441–56.

Hutchby, I. and Barnett, S. 2005. Aspects of the Sequential Organization of Mobile Phone Conversation, *Discourse Studies* 7: 147–71.

Inoue, Miyako. 2011. Stenography and Ventriloquism in Late Nineteenth Century Japan. *Language and Communication* 31: 181–90.

Irvine, Judith T. 1996. Shadow Conversations: The indeterminacy of participant roles. In *Natural Histories of Discourse*, ed. Michael Silverstein and Greg Urban, 131–59. Chicago: University of Chicago Press.

Ito, Mizuko. 2005. Introduction: Personal Portable, Pedestrian. In *Personal, Portable, Pedestrian: Mobile Phones in Japanese Life*, ed. M. Ito, M. Matsuda, and D. Okabe, 1–18. Cambridge, MA: MIT Press.

Ito, Mizuko, and Daisuke Okabe. 2005. Technosocial Situations: Emergent structuring of mobile e-mail use. In *Personal, Portable, Pedestrian: Mobile Phones in Japanese Life*, ed. M. Ito, M. Matsuda, and D. Okabe, 257–73. Cambridge, MA: MIT Press.

Ito, Mizuko, Daisuke Okabe, and Ken Anderson. 2007. Portable Objects in Three Global Cities: The Personalization of Urban Spaces. In *The Mobile Communication Research Annual, Vol. 1: The Reconstruction of Space, and Time through Mobile Communication Practices*, ed. R. Ling and S. Campbell, 67–87. Edison, NJ: Transaction Publishers.

Keane, Webb. 2003. Semiotics and the Social Analysis of Material Things. *Language and Communication* 23(3–4): 409–25.

Kittler, Friedrich. 1999. *Gramophone, Film, Typewriter.* Stanford, CA: Stanford University Press.

Knuttila, Lee. 2011. User Unknown: 4chan, Anonymity and Contingency. *First Monday* 16(10), http://firstmonday.org/htbin/cgiwrap/bin/ojs/index.php/fm/article/view/3665/3055 (accessed February 7, 2014).

Kockelman, P. 2010. Enemies, Parasites, and Noise: How to take up residence in a system without becoming a term in it. *Journal of Linguistic Anthropology* 20(2): 406–21.

Latour, Bruno. 1988. Mixing Humans and Non-Humans Together: The sociology of a door-closer. *Social Problems* 35(3): 298–310.

2005. *Reassembling the Social: An Introduction to Actor-Network-Theory*. Oxford: Oxford University Press.

Laurier, E. 2001. Why People Say Where They Are During Mobile Phone Calls, *Environment and Planning D: Society and Space* 19: 485–504.

Law, John. 2008. The Materials of STS, version of 9th April 2009. Available at www.heterogeneities.net/publications/Law2008MaterialsofSTS.pdf, (accessed February 7, 2014).

Levinson, Stephen C. 1988. Putting Linguistics on a Proper Footing: Explorations in Goffman's concepts of participation. In *Erving Goffman: An Interdisciplinary Appreciation*, ed. P. Drew and A. Wootton, 161–227. Oxford: Polity Press.

Livingstone, Sonia. 2009. *Children and the Internet*. Cambridge: Polity Books.

Manning, Paul. 2012. *Strangers in a Strange Land: Occidentalist Publics and Orientalist Geographies in Nineteenth-Century Georgia*. Brighton, MA: Academic Studies Press.

Marvin, Carolyn. 1988. *When Old Technologies Were New: Thinking about electric communication in the nineteenth century*. New York: Oxford University Press.

Marwick, Alice. 2008. To Catch a Predator? The Myspace Moral Panic. *First Monday* 13(6), http://firstmonday.org/htbin/cgiwrap/bin/ojs/index.php/fm/article/view/2152/1966 (accessed February 7, 2014).

Nozawa, Shunsuke. 2012. The Gross Face and Virtual Fame: Semiotic mediation in Japanese virtual communication. *First Monday* 17(3–5): http://firstmonday.org/ojs/index.php/fm/article/view/3535/3168

Peirce, C. S. 1868. Some Consequences of Four Incapacities. *Journal of Speculative Philosophy* 2: 140–57. (Electronic document, www.peirce.org/writings/p27.html, accessed October 10, 2011.)

Rettie, Ruth. 2009. Mobile Phone Communication: Extending Goffman to mediated interaction. *Sociology* 43(3): 421–38.

Sconce, Jeffrey. 2000. *Haunted Media*. Durham, NC: Duke University Press.

Silverstein, Michael, and Greg Urban. 1996. *Natural Histories of Discourse*. Chicago: University of Chicago Press.

Spitulnik, Debra. 2000. Media. *Journal of Linguistic Anthropology* 9(1–2): 148–51.

Star, S. L. 1999. The Ethnography of Infrastructure. *American Behavioral Scientist* 43(3): 377–91.

Warner, Michael. 1990. *The Letters of the Republic: Publication and the Public Sphere in Eighteenth Century America*. Cambridge, MA: Harvard University Press.

2002. *Publics and Counterpublics*. Cambridge, MA: Zone Press.

Weilenmann, A. 2003. "I Can't Talk Now, I'm in a Fitting Room": Formulating availability and location in mobile phone conversations, *Environment and Planning A* 35: 1589–1606.

23

The speech community and beyond

Language and the nature of the social aggregate

Shaylih Muehlmann

23.1 Introduction

This chapter examines some of the key analytical categories that have shaped understandings of the relationship between social aggregates and language. I will focus on three particular concepts, "community," "culture," and "the public," and analyze the way they emerged in relation to broader theoretical trends in linguistic anthropology and the social sciences.

The notion of the social aggregate is fundamental to linguistic anthropology because from its inception the discipline has been oriented towards a view of language as an inherently social rather than individual phenomenon. This orientation emerged both as an explicit and implicit critique of a longstanding Western-liberal ideology of language where individual voices were understood as articulating views in the public sphere (Habermas 1991[1962]). The emphasis on social aggregates also emerged as a reaction against, first, a view of language as an abstract system of rules reproduced by an "ideal speaker," as it is often represented by formal grammarians and structural linguists, and, second, Saussurian views of language that privileged abstract and arbitrary systems of meanings (*Langue*) (Saussure 1983). In contrast, what has distinguished linguistic anthropology from other approaches to language has been a focus on how linguistic conventions, performances, and situated discourses are all linguistic practices constitutive of social relationships (Sapir 1921; Austin 1962; Hymes 1974).

Despite this long-standing orientation, the problem of relating a linguistic system, or indeed any kind of communicative practice, to its speakers is complex. The question of how to relate language practices with the groups of people practicing them is, in fact, the foundational conceptual task for linguistic anthropology. Because some conceptualization of the social aggregate lies at the heart of every approach to the study of language and social life, this chapter is necessarily a highly selective and partial tracing of the way that social aggregates have been theorized in work that has focused on language. First, I examine some of the early and polemical work on the "speech community." I also trace its theoretical and political implications out to work in practice theory, on the one hand, and issues of language and broader-scale imaginings of groups on the other (such as the nation-state and "cultures"). Finally I consider how more recent work on the topic of "language and publics" in anthropology has shifted the analytical focus of efforts to theorize the relationship between language and social groups to one that attends to more subjective social imaginings of collectivities through mass-mediated discourse.

I trace this particular genealogy because it allows me to highlight themes that, I will argue, are central to the theorization of what a social group is, particularly as it pertains to language. One of these themes is the inherent fragility of any notion of a homogeneous social or linguistic group. I will explore, in particular, the kinds of fractal recursivity that ultimately undoes reified notions of bounded groups, cultures, communities, and publics (Irvine and Gal 2000). The second theme I will explore is related to this constant undoing of social collectives: that is, the resulting tension in this body of work between the impetus to identify groups as empirical objects and the counter trend to take concepts such as "community," "culture," and "public" only as analytical categories. Finally, this genealogy highlights the interaction between the way social aggregates have been "theorized" by analysts and the way they have been "imagined" by speakers, state officials, and policy makers.

As a result, this chapter is ultimately concerned with examining both the social and the scholarly production of a few key units of analysis. It follows in the recent impulse to explore the analytical categories we work with by locating their historical sources in discursive fields and social and often political processes (Woolard 1992; Silverstein 2000; Gal and Woolard 2001). The aim of such a study is to get a better sense of the way in which linguistic ideologies are intertwined with political and historical trajectories.

23.2 The speech community

One of the foundational formulations of the relationship between social aggregates and language was the concept of the "speech community." Because linguistic anthropologists share with sociolinguistics the disciplinary necessity of not just working on language varieties but on particular language varieties spoken in particular communities, they start from the assumption that any notion of a language variety presupposes a community of speakers (Bloomfield 1926; Gumperz 1962). Linguistic anthropologists also share with sociolinguists the concern for a notion of a speech community as a real group of people who share something about the way in which they use language. Because of these common research dispositions, this section primarily focuses on the concept of speech community as it developed in sociolinguistics and linguistic anthropology. Despite this focus, it is important to recognize that some notion of a speech community is at the center of any kind of empirical linguistics dealing with the realities of spoken language.

Historically, the notion of the speech community was articulated against the approach proposed by most formal grammarians, who started from an idealization of the community they work with as homogeneous and therefore prioritized the "ideal speaker-listener" within this community (Chomsky 1965: 3). The classic definition of the speech community, perhaps first articulated by Bloomfield, was developed within the framework of his postulates: "1. Definition. An act of speech is an utterance. 2. Assumption. Within certain communities successive utterances are alike or partly alike ... 3. Definition. Any such community is a speech community" (1926: 153–4).

The term "speech community" was originally used broadly to refer to linguistic distribution within any social or geographical space (Boas 1911; Bloomfield 1933: 42; Gumperz 1962: 30). Dialectologists were the first to rigorously apply the notion. Labov (1966), for example, showed in the case of New York City that despite differences in speakers' language use based on different social variables, this heterogeneity can be analyzed as the patterning of a single speech community. The term here was used for geographically bounded communities, both large (Labov 1966) and small (Putnam and O'Hern 1955; Feagin 1979). It was also used for "subgroups" such as Belfast vernacular speakers (Milroy and Margrain 1980), "minority languages" such as French-Canadian (Mougeon and Beniak 1996), and the speech patterns of immigrant groups (Haugen 1953). The term was later used to examine groups that cut across geographic boundaries to delineate other kinds of aggregates such as children (Romaine 1982: 7) as well as specific and temporary communities such as Paolillo's (1999) analysis of a virtual speech community.

While the speech community has been defined in many ways, every definition posits language as a primary criterion of community (Bucholtz 1999: 207). As Bucholtz argues, what is taken as shared in these definitions tended to reflect the varied research interests of the author. Thus, the criteria used to define a "speech community" ranged from the linguistic system (Bloomfield 1933: 42–56), participation in a set of shared norms (Labov 1972), to an emphasis on shared interactional settings and ways of speaking (Hymes 1974; Dorian 1982). Later applications of the term have focused on shared patterns of variation (Milroy 1992) or sets of sociolinguistic norms (Romaine 1982). While the emphasis in defining speech communities has generally highlighted what features are "shared" by a community (Bloomfield 1933: Labov 1966), it is noteworthy that Gumperz conceptualized the community as much by a distribution of linguistic variants, which were in turn a reflection of social facts (Gumperz 1968:

381). Significantly though, in every case, language remains the focus of all these various perspectives on speech communities (Bucholtz 1999).

One of the reasons this research was important was because the concept of the speech community helped to clearly establish the relevance of social and geographic factors in language change (Gumperz 1968: 382). Furthermore, as a language-based unit of social analysis, the speech community has allowed sociolinguists to demonstrate that many linguistic phenomena previously relegated to the realm of free variation are in fact socially structured (Bucholtz 1999: 203).

Controversies and disputes over the scope and utility of the concept of the speech community arose early on. For example, originally speech communities were considered to be coterminous with a single language, and therefore people who are bilingual were thought to "bridge" different speech communities (Soffietti 1955; Hockett 1958). This was a criterion that Gumperz reformulated in the context of his own research, redefining the speech community "as a social group which may be either monolingual or multilingual" (1962: 31; see also Gumperz 1968). This early revision of the concept highlights one of the problems that would become central to later debates, which is the question of just how homogeneous a group's language practices need to be in order to count as a single community.

Furthermore, in terms of delineating these communities' social boundaries, the notion of the speech community consistently privileges the perception of the analyst. It prioritizes the researchers' interpretations over the participants' own understandings of their practices. Therefore, most definitions of the speech community exclude speakers that do not share the analysts' criteria of membership in that community even if they count themselves as members of that community. Dorian's (1982) work on semi-speakers complicated this delineation. As Dorian pointed out, the problem of how to define and count "speakers" revolves around whether someone is a first-language speaker or a second-language speaker, fluent or semi-fluent and, crucially, whether they identify as a speaker in the first place (Dorian 1977; see also Elmendorf 1981; Urla 1993).

Therefore, one of the problems with the notion of the speech community was that it directed attention to the group and away from individuals. Insofar as individuals could be theorized in this context, there was a preference for studying central members of the community over those at the margins. Thus, ultimately the concept provided little theoretical guidance at the level of how to count or identify any given individual member of the community. These are the kinds of problems that scholars have routinely pointed out in reference to the census of language speakers (Gal 1993; Leeman 2004; Graham and Zentella 2010). For example, Urla (1993) analyzes the use of language surveys in the Basque nationalist movement and shows that there were points of difference between the ways that native speakers and the census classified people. While the census differentiated between levels of competence, locals, in contrast, differentiated between different dialects (Urla 1993: 830). In other words, residents differentiated between those who spoke different dialects of Basque, which were in turn imbued with all sorts of perceived moral and social inequalities. They did not, however, make meaningful distinctions between those who spoke well or who had an active or passive competence.

For these reasons, some authors have preferred the criteria of "regarding oneself as speaking the same language" (Corder 1973: 53) to be the only criteria necessary for defining a speech community, without necessary recourse to any other shared linguistic practice (Corder 1973; Dorian 1982). This solution does not necessarily recuperate the viability of the concept of the speech community, since it raises similar boundary-marking problems (i.e., it assumes that speakers would count themselves in a group, thus ignoring the potential for dispute among speakers themselves who may or may not count others who self-identify as speakers). However, this critique points again to the recurring problem with the concept of the speech community: the issue of homogeneity or the question of precisely how much of the linguistic features under consideration need to be "shared" in order to constitute speakers as sharing a speech community.

The problem of homogeneity, which necessarily emphasized the sharedness of linguistic features as an organizing principle of community, also served to emphasize consensus. The postulate, often associated with the Labovian definition, that speakers agree on certain linguistic forms and uphold them as normative despite differences in class and social background, assumes a consensus model of society, which has also been criticized (Rickford 1986; Milroy 1992). The expectation of consensus in the norms of a speech community assumes that the system is closed to outside influence. Therefore, the possibility of interaction between different speech communities is not taken into account (Bucholtz 1999: 209).

The problems that are posed by marginal members of the speech community, the issue of self-identification, the degree of sharedness, and the assumption of consensus are all directly related to a more fundamental problem. In many accounts, the social unit of the "community" is inserted into this formulation relatively unquestioned as an analytical category. There is a great deal of potential for circularity here with the assumption that social units can be clearly identified on nonlinguistic criteria. This raises the question of the status of the equation between shared linguistic knowledge and social membership. Is it assumed that speakers united by linguistic measures form a social group? Patrick (2004: 8) argues that confusion on this point is rampant in the work on speech communities, with the same author sometimes implying different positions at different times. The confusion also points to the fact that the social group itself, regardless of considerations of language, is also a problematic concept. In fact, as I will describe in the next section, the concept of "the community" has undergone attack from various different theoretical perspectives – on grounds that have ultimately been helpful for thinking through some of the problems presented by the more specific notion of the speech community.

23.3 Beyond the speech community

At around the same time that theorists first began using the concept of the speech community, anthropologists and sociologists were confronting problems with the use of the more general concept of "community" that resonated with some of the issues highlighted in the previous section, particularly around the assumptions about consensus and homogeneity. For example, Oscar Lewis's critique of Robert Redfield's 1930 study of a Mexican peasant community is by now considered a classic in anthropology (1951, 1969). Lewis's research, based in the same village studied by Redfield years earlier, showed that in contrast to what the latter had argued, the peasant culture in Tepoztlán was not based on "folk" solidarity but was rather highly conflictual and driven by struggles over land and power.

This famous debate was one of the first interventions into a long tradition of enlightenment thought which counter-posed harmonious communities imagined in far-off, exotic places to what has been portrayed as the highly unequal, conflict-ridden modern capitalist present (Hobsbawm 1959; Thompson 1966; O'Brien and Roseberry 1991). Over the past several decades, anthropologists have increasingly acknowledged the multiplicity of interests at stake in the constitution of communities as well as the political effects that the representations of such communities produce (Asad 1973; Fox 1991; Behar and Gordon 1995).

Therefore, the problems that arose for both traditions of research, in sociolinguistics and in anthropology more widely, had to do with how the homogenizing function involved in any representation of a social aggregate gravitates toward the reification of the analytic concept of community. For these reasons, Duranti proposes that we take the notion of speech community to be understood as an analytical category rather than an "already constituted object of inquiry" (1997: 32). He argues that this recognizes the constitutive nature of speaking as a human activity that not only assumes but also builds "community." According to this definition, to engage in linguistic anthropological research means, first of all, to look at a group of people's daily dealings with one another from the point of view of the communication they exchange and the communicative resources they employ (Duranti 1997: 32).

This is not an entirely radical suggestion – even some of the earliest theorists of the speech community made similar cautions about reifying the category. Hymes specified that the speech community should not be formulated as a naïve attempt to conceive of language as encompassing a social unit. He suggested, rather, that the speech community be taken as "an object defined for purposes of linguistic inquiry," not to be confused with "attributes of the counterpart of that object in social life ... It postulates the unit of description as a social, rather than linguistic, entity" (1974: 48).

Bloomfield conceded from the start that some of the difficulties with delineating "speech communities" had to do with the empirical impossibility of doing so. He wrote: "The difficulty or impossibility of determining exactly what people belong to the same speech-community is not accidental, but arises from the very nature of the speech community ... no two persons – or rather perhaps, no one person at different times – spoke exactly alike" (Bloomfield 1933: 45).

While all analytic objects are of course ideal types, what is at stake in the extent to which sociolinguistic aggregates are primarily treated as such is that ideologies of language are inseparable from both the scholarly and political production of categories of sociolinguistic aggregates. Therefore, treating speech communities as empirical entities brackets off the way such communities become salient for speakers, governments, and other actors (as opposed to analysts) and thus constrains the kinds of questions that can be asked about the speech community. For this reason, the relative emphasis on treating such aggregates as analytical objects as much as empirical ones will become more relevant in the discussion of "publics" in the final section.

It is noteworthy that despite the fact that doubts such as these were raised, these debates in sociolinguistics remained fairly distinct from wider debates in closely related fields. This theoretical isolation, coupled with the fact that the speech community was construed principally as a linguistic object, has meant that sociolinguistic theory was late to benefit from theoretical advances in related disciplines. It was not until scholars working on the gendered aspects of language use engaged with the notion of the speech community that it really came into conversation with other contemporary theoretical trends in the social sciences more generally. This convergence transpired largely because the notion of the speech community created dissonance with the basic insights of feminist theory, which emphasized the fluidity of identities and their contested and performative constitution, rather than viewing identities as constituted by shared features in the way that the notion of the "speech community" was largely taken up.[1]

Feminist theorizing had already been greatly influenced by work in practice theory, which challenged the view of social behavior as fundamentally ordered by rules and norms evident in many formal and certain sociolinguistic approaches to language. Instead, practice theory focused on the interplay between relatively stable schematic aspects of social life and emergent, unformalizable ones (Bourdieu 1977; de Certeau 1984; Ortner 1984; Butler 2006[1990]). Practice theory also reformulated understandings of how identities connect individuals to certain social groups, by emphasizing that such connections are not predetermined but, rather, that they vary across social, situational, and interactional contexts

(Freeman and McElhinny 1996). This work rejects categorical notions of social identities in favor of more constructivist and dynamic ones (Cameron 1990, 1997; Ehrlich 1997; McElhinny 1998). By this view, identities emerge in practice, through the dialectical interaction of structure and agency. Individuals engage in multiple identity practices simultaneously, and they are able to move from one identity to another (Bucholtz 1999: 209).

It was principally this critique of the concept of speech community that prompted the revised notion of "community of practice" (Eckert and McConnell-Ginet 1992; Holmes and Meyerhoff 1999). Following practice theory as well as the more specific research that came out of critical social theories of learning (Lave and Wenger 1991), a community of practice was conceptualized as any "aggregate of people who come together around mutual engagement in an endeavor." As a social construct, this is different from the traditional speech community, because it is defined "simultaneously by its membership and by the practice in which that membership engages" (Eckert and McConnel-Ginet 1992: 464). This was a crucial revision precisely because it emphasizes practice as central to understanding the nature of the social aggregate (Holmes and Meyerhoff 1999). Bucholtz (1999) argued that the use of "community of practice" also allows identities to be explained as the result of positive and negative identity practices and performances rather than as fixed social categories, as presented in some uses of the speech-community model (Bucholtz 1999: 203; Butler 2006[1990]).

Unlike the notion of the speech community, which prioritizes the analytic status of language, the "community of practice" framework considers language as one of many social practices in which participants engage. Therefore, while Gumperz had also underscored practices as central to any notion of the speech community (1968, 1971), he had prioritized language as the key practice of interest. Furthermore, the community of practice model treats difference and conflict, not uniformity and consensus, as the ordinary state of affairs by defining the community as a group of people oriented to the same practice, though not necessarily in the same way (Bucholtz 1999).

Practice theory, therefore, helped to pull the concept of the speech community into conversation with wider theoretical trends in the social sciences. The influence of practice theory also galvanized the looming worry expressed by some of the core theorists of the speech community: i.e., that perhaps the concept would be better taken as an analytical perspective rather than an empirical object (Bloomfield 1933; Hymes 1974; Patrick 2004). Practice theory emerged out of the conviction that it is possible to mediate between the shortcomings of subjectivism and objectivism, thus offering the potential to view social aggregates as emergent, fluid, and defined by conflict. However, the theoretical responses to this apparent antinomy are invariably met with the critique that they fail to transcend this dichotomy. Bourdieu's work has been especially susceptible to this critique (Schatzki 1997; King 2000). King argued that Bourdieu's formulation of *habitus*, defined as enduring social knowledge in the form of unreflective habits and commonsense perceptions, slipped back into the objectivism it attempted to refute since the dispositions that comprise habitus are directly derived from individuals' socioeconomic or structural positions. Similarly, despite the trend toward the rejection of the speech community as an empirical object, Patrick (2004: 4) points out that it is still referred to by most researchers as though it were either unproblematic or, at the very least, necessary.

23.4 Larger-scale imaginings: Languages, nations, cultures

While the previous sections traced the notion of the speech community from sociolinguistics to practice theory, in more general terms the concept can also be traced to a wider historical and philosophical tradition in various branches of language research. Hymes and Fought (1981) trace the sources of the notion of the speech community to the German philosophers Von Humboldt and Herder, following a continuity through to Boas, Sapir, and Whorf, which reveals a persistent link between community and language form. On the one hand, this genealogy examined how different aspects of language form reflect, and are shaped by, cultural conceptions or "worldviews" – a large body of work often characterized under the umbrella term "whorfianism" (Whorf 1964; Lucy 1992; Silverstein 2000). On the other hand, these philosophical roots branched into the work that associated language with identity groups more generally (Fishman 1982). Indeed, the links between one language, one people, one culture, and one community are often attributed specifically to a Herderian model of language and society (Hymes 1974: 123).

Not incidentally, this second branch has also led to the philosophical tradition that reinforced the importance of language in the context of larger-scale imaginings of social aggregates in relation to nationalism and culturalism. Since the rise of European nation-states in the nineteenth century, the idea of languages as homogeneous bounded units has been central to the ideological construction of an imagined "national community" (Anderson 1991; Hobsbawm 1992; Billig 1995; Hill 2002). For example, a large body of research has documented how language standardization efforts constructed monolingual national languages by objectifying and denigrating linguistic difference within what are now understood as single linguistic codes (Mühlhäusler 1996; Lippi-Green 1997; Silverstein 1998; Milroy and Milroy 1999; Agha 2003).

Because the nation-state was constructed on the premise of cultural, linguistic, even racial homogeneity, this construction problematized the role of those who could not speak the state-sanctioned language. This has resulted in ongoing debates on the constitutional rights of minority language speakers (Grillo 1989; McDonald 1989; Heller 1999; Jaffe 1999). Furthermore, as sociolinguists have documented, minority movements took over the very discourse of the centralized homogeneous nation-states that marginalized them, and created the category of the minority in the first place (Heller 1999, 2001; Jaffe 1999). These movements have done so by claiming collective rights to political autonomy, emphasizing their own linguistic homogeneity and boundedness in terms that are considered legitimate because they underlie the legitimacy of existing states (Heller 2001: 124).

As the ideology of the nation-state has been reconfigured in recent decades by the globalizing expansion of economic networks in an international capitalist system, ideologies of bounded national languages have also changed. The perception of expanding global interconnection and the accelerated circulation of people and commodities as well as the implementation of the European Union (see Gal 2006) have problematized the discourse on multilingualism that appealed to the legitimacy of the nation-state to argue for minority rights. On the one hand, this new global context has affected the way multilingualism has been debated by shifting the sites where public discourses on language are produced from state and government institutions such as schools to trans-national organizations such as the United Nations (Duchêne 2008). On the other hand, it has also affected the nature of the discourses on multilingualism, which have moved away from notions of "minority languages" and towards discourses emphasizing "linguistic diversity" and "linguistic human rights" (Skutnabb-Kangas 2000; Maffi 2005).

This new discursive framework did not manage to extricate itself from the fragmentation that the homogenizing discourses of language and the nation-state reproduced in the context of recursive minority claims to autonomy, however. The very notion of linguistic human rights is contingent upon the concept of the linguistic minority, that is, a social group which is marginalized from centers of power on the basis of linguistic difference. In turn, the concept of the linguistic minority depends on the discursive formation of the nation-state understood as linguistically and culturally homogeneous (see Muehlmann and Duchêne 2007). Therefore, the human rights framework persists as the dominant ideology through which minorities and linguistic minorities are understood in many language-policy contexts even as the ideology of the nation-state has been reconfigured in more global governance contexts.

One of the primary arenas where this ideology has persisted is in relation to language endangerment (and even "dialect endangerment" [Wolfram and Shilling-Estes 1995]). In this context, the language–culture–people triad has been most powerfully invoked in relation to indigenous language communities and their cultures. Indigenous-language competence has become a primary criterion for defining cultural difference through the assumption that there is a necessary relationship between language and culture. In the last few decades, work in anthropology has rejected just such encompassing models of culture as a coherent, bounded system (Clifford 1988; Roseberry 1989; Ortner 1996, 2000; Comaroff and Comaroff 1999). Parallel critiques in linguistic anthropology have problematized understandings of language as closed systems that correspond to cultural groups and territories. While the assumed links between bounded groups and territories had long ago been questioned by anthropologists (see for example Boas 1911 and Hymes 1968), such discourses have been reinvigorated by much of the scholarly work on language endangerment (Hill 2002; Duchêne and Heller 2007).

It is noteworthy, then, that despite the decades of theoretical work on the relationship between language and social aggregates, public conversations on this topic are largely uninformed by these theoretical advances. Many linguistic anthropologists have supported claims that speech communities and identities or cultures are explicitly linked and mapped onto each other, such that when languages are lost cultures are assumed to disappear as well (Woodbury 1993; Nettle and Romaine 2000; Harrison 2007). This language ideology has been reinvigorated in the scholarly and activist literature on language endangerment, as indigenous languages have increasingly been replaced by more dominant languages all over the world. Campaigns to "save" endangered languages have been connected to efforts to rescue cultural heritage, knowledge, and practices (Crystal 2000; Nettle and Romaine 2000; Skutnabb-Kangas 2000; Harmon and Maffi 2002).

In linguistic anthropology, critiques of the essentializing link between "cultures" and "languages" coupled with the receding specter of the nation-state in the context of dominant language ideologies, especially in Europe, were some of the developments that Cody (2011) argues moved the discussion of language and the social aggregate toward a focus on "publics."

23.5 Language and publics

The analytical and political categories that we have analyzed so far have played a number of roles both theoretically and politically. They have delineated a space for exploring how linguistic differentiation and homogeneity are organized across different geographical and social spaces as well as across different settings. Notions such as the community and national or indigenous cultures have also served as objects of ideology, which are operationalized as instruments of political agency to produce discursively drawn publics. The production of these publics has recently become a focus of specific investigation in linguistic anthropology. This work has explored how different communicative modalities serve both theoretically and practically as the grounds for constituting imaginaries of communities, cultures, public spheres, and large-scale sociopolitical orders.

It does so by investigating both the public construction of languages, the linguistic construction of publics, and the relationship between these two processes (Gal and Woolard 2001).

In anthropology and related disciplines, the surge of interest in publics was inspired first by the publication of Jürgen Habermas's (1991[1962]) *Structural Transformation of the Public Sphere* and, later, by Benedict Anderson's (1991) *Imagined Communities*. Habermas (1991[1962]) originally conceived of the "public" as a particular kind of arena, which he formulated as a category of bourgeois society. For Habermas, this was a sphere open, in principle, to all citizens and characterized as a democratic discursive space free of coercion – organized by private citizens rather than the state – where arguments were made based on rational common interest. Anderson (1991) argued that what allowed the emergence of this "sociability among strangers," which understood itself as acting collectively, was the mass circulation of texts in the form of printed books and newspapers.

Therefore, the "public sphere" was important because it drew attention to an arena distinct from the interactional field of the market, the masses, or the kin group. Instead, it drew attention to a sphere where people who live in states speak as "citizens," with reference to public affairs, yet not as agents of the state. Habermas argued that the bourgeois public sphere reached its pinnacle in the eighteenth century before it was eroded through industrialized mass cultural commodification.

This notion of a sense of a stranger sociability marks a major difference with this approach to social aggregates. The concept of the community that I have examined thus far implies the idea of shared familiarity, and evokes the idea that people, at least potentially, know each other. This is also true with the concept of a "community of practice," for the idea of "mutual engagement" also implies an immediacy in terms of the potential of interaction with others co-engaged in mutual practices. In contrast, the idea of "the public" invokes a much larger aggregate that by definition connects people that are strangers. That dimension marks one of the clear counterpoints with prior notions of the speech community.

Both Habermas and Anderson emphasize the sociability among strangers that characterizes print-mediated discourse as one of the new ways of imagining the public life enabled by capitalist production. The mass circulation of texts in the form of printed books and newspapers is what allowed for the emergence of an abstract assembly of strangers that recognized itself as self-organized. In Anderson's *Imagined Communities*, in which he focuses on publics in the form of national communities, he pushes the constitutive understanding of communication further. Specifically, he argues that language itself attained a new fixity through the objectifications produced by the rise of print technology. He argues that the standardization of languages that accompanied the rise of print capitalism also resulted in a homogenization of the means by which national publics are imagined.

Much of the recent work on publics has come out of the various critiques leveled at both Anderson and Habermas. Habermas's formulation of the public sphere has been subject to a range of criticisms for its commitment to a nostalgic conception of the freedom and rationality of the bourgeois public as well for his neglect of the ways in which this sphere functioned to exclude as much as to include (Calhoun 1992; Negt and Kluge 1993; Robbins 1993). For example, some work has critically examined the ways the public sphere has been constructed along gendered lines (Elshtain 1981; Fraser 1985; Ryan 1990) and, specifically, to exclude women (Landes 1988). Similarly, Fraser (1990) argues for the political importance of multiple "subaltern counter-publics" among subordinated groups who engage in oppositional discourses in alternative spheres. According to Fraser, those who are excluded from publics nonetheless produce discourses that are oriented toward public consumption.

These critiques of the fragility of any homogeneous formulation of publics resemble earlier discussions around the assumed homogeneity and normative conceptions of speech communities as well as the related tendency toward fractal recursion in ideologies of national and minority language ideologies. But the distinction between community and society or nation does not map neatly onto the distinction between intimates and publics that has emerged from the body of works on publics.

Indeed, Warner (2002) argues that what these critiques of the exclusionary power of publics tend to miss is the fact that in the emergence of publics there is a necessary discrepancy between claims to be addressing "everyone" and the embedding of implicit messages that define a more exclusive audience. Because of this inherent contradiction, Warner argues that publics are always both singular and multiple. He further highlights the contradictory character of publics by arguing that a public discourse must address a projected collection of already existing persons (2002: 82) with something specified as already shared or in common. He emphasizes, however, that the public is not actually created until the circulation of this discourse, which people then engage with in some way. Therefore the public is imaginary until it comes into being as an entity through the circulation of discourse.

The approach to publics that has been taken in linguistic anthropology has been less oriented toward Habermas's view of the public as a category of sociohistorical theory and more oriented to the contradictory processes highlighted by Warner. This is because the original work on publics, while clearly recognizing the importance of mass-mediated discursive practices, largely took these linguistic processes for granted in ways that linguistic anthropologists would later critique. For example, Silverstein (2000) criticized Anderson's account by arguing that he mistook the dialectically produced sense of belonging to a community for the reality, when it was precisely this construction of belonging through standard language ideologies that needs to be characterized and explained.

Therefore, the way the notion of the public was recast in linguistic anthropology was more attentive to the concrete mechanisms by which multiple publics were constructed, not only in terms of the processes of interdiscursivity, entextualization, and interpellation through which they emerge, but also through the kinds of language ideologies that allow for such publics to be recognizable to those that they ultimately either include or exclude.[2] For linguistic anthropology, the concept of the public is productive precisely because from its inception the sphere has been built, as Warner underscored, on powerful mechanisms of exclusion. Thus the concept outlines an important arena for the reproduction of exclusions in contemporary societies. Therefore, linguistic anthropology takes as its point of departure this focus on the "public" as an ideological construct, rather than an object of empirical and historical study (this position is most explicitly articulated by Hill 2009: 197).

Work in this vein has been particularly productive out of the tradition of scholarship on language ideologies. The turn to publics in this subfield has led to a focus on the specific social conditions that allow for a sense of self-organization to be constituted through mass-mediated discourse. It has also led to a focus on how the interaction between different kinds of social relations and particular communicative practices are imbricated in large-scale imaginings of publics (Schieffelin *et al.* 1998; Kroskrity 2000; Silverstein 2003; Gal 2005, 2006; Cody 2011).

Because this body of scholarship begins with the premise that any concept of a "public sphere" is ideological (while having real material effects), it avoids some of the analytical impasses that have shaped other theorizations of linguistic/social aggregates. It does not confront the ambiguity between conceptions of the public as an empirical object versus the public as an analytical category. Of course, this literature is able to avoid these pitfalls by posing a very different set of questions. Therefore, the work on publics is less concerned with how speakers use language than with how people imagine language and themselves as part of groups that engage in particular discursive practices. Some of the most compelling work in this body of scholarship examines how such ideological constructs – which shape senses of discursively mediated mass personhood – actually affect the way people engage in particular discursive practices.

For example, Susan Gal (2005) analyzes large-scale processes of discourse circulation through which the dichotomy between "private" and "public" features of social life are delineated for particular social domains by institutionalized metasemiotic processes. Jane Hill (1998), in turn, examines how the register of English known as "Junk Spanish" is a useful tool for exploring the ambiguities and the blurred boundaries between the public and the private. She argues that the ideas of the "public" and "public discourse" constitute today an ideology that mystifies and confounds the workings of race, sex, and class-based oppression in American life (1998: 210). Jackson (2008), in her analysis of a type of political oratory in

Malagasy called Kabary, shows how speakers and political cartoonists depend on the interanimation of varying registers associated with different social fields to persuade public opinion and to play off already-in-place attachments people feel with those domains of practice.

In exploring the particular mechanisms through which publics are created, some scholars have pointed out that the success of their constitution depends on what Louis Althusser (1971) termed "interpellation." The idea of interpellation refers to a primarily discursive process by which the state "calls" or "hails" its subjects into certain positions. His famous example is of a policeman calling out: "Hey, you!" When we recognize ourselves as the person addressed by this statement and turn around, we are interpellated as the subject of state discourse.[3] Warner cautions that when the model of interpellation is extracted from this example to account for public culture generally, the analysis will be skewed because the policeman who says "Hey, you!" will be understood to be addressing a particular person, not a public. When one turns around, it is partly to see whether one is that person. If not, one goes on. If so, then all the others who might be standing on the street are bystanders, not addressees (Warner 2002: 58). Briggs (2003) explores how in the circulation of public health discourses in Venezuela during the cholera epidemics of the early 1990s it was precisely this failure to interpellate targeted subjects that limited the effect of such discourses. The capacity of a projected public to inadvertently reduce some intended addressees to the status of ideologically excluded overhearers meant that such discourses did not reach their intended audience.

Perhaps one of the most important aspects of work on publics in linguistic anthropology that distinguishes it from the earlier work on communities and social groups has been its embeddedness in larger discussions in social theory, in particular in the tradition of critical work on publics. It is also noteworthy that the original work on publics, characterized by the foundational works by Habermas and Anderson, also emerged from a thorough awareness of the social salience of language, even if their attention to the role of language was limited in ways that, as we have seen, researchers of language would later critique.

23.6 Conclusion

One of the most fundamental problems in the study of society is how to understand the very notion of the social aggregate. What is a social group and how is it constituted? What is a "tribe," a "community," a "nation," a "public"? And how do groups of people come together in the construction and enactment of such collectivities to act in the world based on something "shared"? While these are certainly central questions for the study of society, they are also fundamentally political questions since social constructions such as these are what mobilize constellations of people politically, either to dominate other groups or resist forms of marginalization and injustice.

Work in linguistic anthropology and sociolinguistics that has taken up the issue of the social aggregate has shown that attention to language is key to understanding how human collectivities come together, either as ideological constructs or the political entities they constitute. In this chapter, I have reviewed some of the central concepts that have formulated the relationship between language and such social aggregates, and I have shown how an engagement with wider theoretical discussions has been crucial to the development of a nuanced understanding of the way that people are organized into collectivities through linguistic practices. However, it should also be clear from the preceding discussion that it is important that wider work in social theory on the nature of collectivities attend to linguistic processes, regardless of whether language is an explicit object of such inquiry. As the scholarship on the speech community, through nations, cultures, and publics, has clearly shown, language is both an object of focused attention, crucial to the way that people conceive of themselves as part of social collectives, and one of the most important mediums through which these conceptions are communicated.

Notes

1. While the idea of the "community of practice" emerged as an implicit critique of the "speech community" along feminist grounds, see Bucholtz (1999) for a more developed argument for the incompatibility of the concept of the "speech community" in the context of work on gender and language and in feminist theory more broadly (see also Cameron 1992; Holmes and Meyerhoff 1999).
2. This also contrasted with the emphasis in Habermas and Anderson on a single central public and particularly on official public spaces. It's noteworthy that the interest in publics in linguistic anthropology also tapped more directly into concerns that arose out of very different intellectual traditions, such as Goffman's sociological concern with how the public order is founded on individuals' "management of co-presence" according to a series of ground rules that people preform on a daily basis (1971) and the participant frameworks that divide ratified hearers and unofficial overhearers (1974).
3. Warner also points out that the necessary element of impersonality in public address is one of the things missing from view in the Althusserian notion of interpellation (2002: 58).

References

Agha, Asif. 2003. The Social Life of Cultural Value. *Language and Communication* 23(3/4): 231–73

Althusser, Louis. 1971. Ideology and Ideological State Apparatuses. In *Lenin and Philosophy, and Other Essays*, trans. Ben Brewster. New York: Ben Brewster Monthly Review Press.

Anderson, Benedict R. O'G. 1991. *Imagined Communities: Reflections on the Origin and Spread of Nationalism*. London: Verso.

Asad, Talal. 1973. *Anthropology and the Colonial Encounter*. New York: Humanities Press.

Austin, John. 1962. *How to do Things with Words: The William James Lectures delivered at Harvard University in 1955*, ed. J. O. Urmson. Oxford: Clarendon.

Behar, Ruth, and D. A. Gordon. 1995. *Women Writing Culture*. Berkeley: University of California Press.

Billig, Michael. 1995. *Banal Nationalism*. London: SAGE Publications Ltd.

Bloomfield, Leonard. 1926. A Set of Postulates for the Science of Language. *Language* 2: 153-64.

 1933. *Language*. New York: H. Holt and Company.

Boas, Franz. 1911. *Handbook of American Indian Languages*, Vol. 1. Bureau of American Ethnology, Bulletin 40. Washington: Government Print Office (Smithsonian Institution, Bureau of American Ethnology).

Bourdieu, Pierre. 1977. *Outline of a Theory of Practice*. Cambridge: Cambridge University Press.

Briggs, Charles L. 2003. Why Nation-States and Journalists Can't Teach People to Be Healthy: Power and pragmatic miscalculation in public discourses on health. *Medical Anthropology Quarterly* 17(3): 287-321.

Bucholtz, Mary. 1999. "Why Be Normal?": Language and Identity Practices in a Community of Nerd Girls. *Language in Society* 28(2): 203-23.

Butler, Judith. 2006[1990]. *Gender Trouble: Feminism and the Subversion of Identity*. New York: Routledge.

Calhoun, Craig J. 1992. *Habermas and the Public Sphere*. Cambridge, MA: MIT Press.

Cameron, Deborah. 1990. *The Feminist Critique of Language: A Reader*. London/New York: Routledge.

 1992. "Not gender differences but the difference gender makes": Explanation in research on sex and language. *International Journal of the Sociology of Language* 94: 13-26.

 1997. Performing Gender Identity: Young Men's Talk and the Construction of Heterosexual Masculinity. In *Language and Masculinity*, ed. S. Johnson and U. H. Meinhof, 47-64. Oxford: Blackwell.

Certeau, Michel de. 1984. *The Practice of Everyday Life*. Berkeley: University of California Press.

Chomsky, Noam. 1965. *Aspects of the Theory of Syntax*. Cambridge, MA: MIT Press.

Clifford, James. 1988. *The Predicament of Culture: Twentieth-Century Ethnography, Literature, and Art*. Boston, MA: Harvard University Press.

Cody, Francis. 2011. Publics and Politics. *Annual Review of Anthropology* 40(1): 37-52.

Comaroff, Jean, and John L Comaroff. 1999. Occult Economies and the Violence of Abstraction: Notes from the South African Postcolony. *American Ethnologist* 26(2): 279–303.

Corder, S. Pit. 1973. *Introducing Applied Linguistics*. Baltimore: Penguin Education.

Crystal, David. 2000. *Language Death*. Cambridge/New York: Cambridge University Press.

Dorian, Nancy. 1977. The Problem of the Semi-Speaker in Language Death. *Linguistics* 191: 23–32.

————. 1982. Defining the Speech Community to Include Its Working Margins. In *Sociolinguistic Variation in Speech Communities*, ed. S. Romaine, 25–33. London: Edward Arnold.

Duchêne, Alexandre. 2008. *Ideologies Across Nations: The Construction of Linguistic Minorities at the United Nations*. New York: Mouton de Gruyter.

Duchêne, Alexandre, and Monica Heller, eds. 2007. *Discourses of Endangerment: Interest and Ideology in the Defence of Language*. New York: Continuum International Publishing Groups.

Duranti, Alessandro. 1997. *Linguistic Anthropology*. Cambridge: Cambridge University Press.

Eckert, Penelope, and Sally McConnell-Ginet. 1992. Think Practically and Look Locally: Language and gender as community-based practice. *Annual Review of Anthropology* 21(1): 461–88.

Ehrlich, Susan. 1997. Gender as Social Practice. *Studies in Second Language Acquisition* 19(4): 421–46.

Elmendorf, William W. 1981. Last Speakers and Language Change: Two Californian Cases. *Anthropological Linguistics* 23(1): 36–49.

Elshtain Jean B. 1981. *Public Man, Private Woman: Women in Social and Political Thought*. Princeton, NJ: Princeton University Press.

Feagin, Crawford. 1979. *Variation and Change in Alabama English: A Sociolinguistic Study of the White Community*. Washington, DC: Georgetown University Press.

Fishman, J. A. 1982. Whorfianism of the Third Kind: Ethnolinguistic diversity as a worldwide societal asset. *Lang. Soc.* 11: 1–14.

Fox, Robin. 1991. *Encounter with Anthropology*. New Brunswick, NJ: Transaction Publishers.

Fraser, Nancy. 1985. What's Critical About Critical Theory? The Case of Habermas and Gender. *New German Critique* 35: 97–131.

————. 1990. Rethinking the Public Sphere: A contribution to the critique of actually existing democracy. *Social Text* 25/**26**: 56–80.

Freeman, Rebecca, and Bonnie McElhinny. 1996. Language and Gender. In *Sociolinguistics and Language Teaching*, ed. Sandra Lee Mckay, 218–80. Cambridge: Cambridge University Press.

Gal, Susan. 1993. Diversity and Contestation in Linguistic Ideologies: German Speakers in Hungary. *Language in Society* 22: 337–59.

————. 2005. Language Ideologies Compared. *Journal of Linguistic Anthropology* 15(1): 23–37.

2006. Contradictions of Standard Language in Europe: Implications for the Study of Practices and Publics. *Social Anthropology* 14(2): 163-81.
Gal, Susan, and Kathryn Ann Woolard. 2001. *Languages and Publics: The Making of Authority*. Manchester /Northampton, MA: St. Jerome Pub.
Goffman, Erving. 1971. *Relations in Public: Microstudies of the Public Order*. New York: Basic Books.
  1974. *Frame Analysis: An Essay on the Organization of Experience*. London: Harper and Row.
Graham, Laura, and Ana Celia Zentella. 2010. Language in the US Census: Problems and progress. *Anthropology News* (May): 6.
Grillo, Ralph D. 1989. *Dominant Languages: Language and Hierarchy in Britain and France*. Cambridge/New York: Cambridge University Press.
Gumperz, John Joseph. 1962. Types of Linguistic Communities. *Anthropological Linguistics* 4(1): 28-40.
  1968. The Speech Community. In *International Encyclopedia of the Social Sciences*, ed. D. L. Sills, 381-6. New York: Macmillan.
  1971. *Language in Social Groups*. Stanford, CA: Stanford University Press.
Habermas, Jürgen. 1991[1962]. *The Structural Transformation of the Public Sphere: An Inquiry into a Category of Bourgeois Society*. Cambridge, MA: MIT Press.
Harmon, David, and L. Maffi. 2002. Are Linguistic and Biological Diversity Linked? *Conserv. Biol. Pract.* 3: 26-7.
Harrison, K. David. 2007. *When Languages Die: The Extinction of the World's Languages and the Erosion of Human Knowledge*. New York: Oxford University Press.
Haugen, Einar. 1953. *The Norwegian Language in America*. 2 vols. Philadelphia: University of Pennsylvania Press.
Heller, Monica. 1999. *Linguistic Minorities and Modernity: A Sociolinguistic Ethnograpy*. London/New York: Longman.
  2001. Critique and Sociolinguistic Analysis of Discourse. *Critique of Anthropology* 21(2): 117-41.
Hill, Jane. 1998. Junk Spanish, Covert Racism, and the (Leaky) Boundary Between Public and Private Spheres. *Pragmatics* 5(2): 197-212.
  2002. "Expert Rhetorics" in Advocacy for Endangered Languages: Who is listening, and what do they hear? *Journal of Linguistic Anthropology* 12(2): 119-33.
  2009. *Everyday Language of White Racism*. Chichester: Wiley-Blackwell.
Hobsbawm, Eric J. 1959. *Primitive Rebels: Studies in Archaic Forms of Social Movements in the 19th and 20th Centuries*. Manchester: Manchester University Press.
  1992. *Nations and Nationalism since 1780: Programme, Myth, Reality*. Cambridge: Cambridge University Press.
Hockett, Charles Francis. 1958. *A Course in Modern Linguistics*. New York: Macmillan.
Holmes, Janet, and Miriam Meyerhoff. 1999. The Community of Practice: Theories and methodologies in language and gender research. *Language in Society* 28(2): 173-83.

Hymes, Dell H. 1968. Linguistic Problems in Defining the Concept of "Tribe". In *Essays on the Problem of Tribe*, ed. J. Helm, 23–48. Seattle: University of Washington Press.

———. 1974. *Foundations in Sociolinguistics; An Ethnographic Approach*. Philadelphia: University of Pennsylvania Press.

Hymes, Dell. H., and J. G. Fought. 1981. *American Structuralism*. The Hague: Mouton Publishers.

Irvine, Judith, and Susan Gal. 2000. Language ideology and Linguistic Differentiation. In *Regimes of Language*, ed. P. Kroskrity, 35–84. Santa Fe, NM: School of American Research Press.

Jackson, Jennifer L. 2008. Building Publics, Shaping Public Opinion: Interanimating registers in Malagasy Kabary oratory and political cartooning. *Journal of Linguistic Anthropology* 18(2): 214–35.

Jaffe, Alexandra M. 1999. *Ideologies in Action: Language Politics on Corsica*. Berlin/New York: Mouton de Gruyter.

King, Anthony. 2000. Thinking with Bourdieu against Bourdieu: A "Practical" Critique of the Habitus. *Sociological Theory* 18(3): 417–33.

Kroskrity, Paul V. 2000. Regimenting Languages: Language ideological perspectives. In *Regimes of Language: Ideologies, Polities, and Identities*, ed. Paul V. Kroskrity, 1–34. Santa Fe, NM: School of American Research Press.

Labov, William. 1966. *The Social Stratification of English in New York City*. Washington, DC: Center for Applied Linguistics.

———. 1972. Hypercorrection by the Lower Middle Class as a Factor in Linguistic Change. In *Sociolinguistic Patterns*, 122–42. Philadelphia: University of Pennsylvania Press.

Landes, Joan. 1988. *Women and the Public Sphere in the Age of the French Revolution*. Ithaca, NY: Cornell University Press.

Lave, Jean, and Etienne Wenger. 1991. *Situated Learning: Legitimate Peripheral Participation*. Cambridge/New York: Cambridge University Press.

Leeman, Jennifer. 2004. Racializing Language: A history of linguistic ideologies in the US Census. *Journal of Language and Politics* 3(3): 507–34.

Lewis, Oscar. 1951. *Life in a Mexican Village: Tepoztlán Restudied*. Urbana: University of Illinois Press.

———. 1969. *A Death in the Sánchez Family*. New York: Random House.

Lippi-Green, Rosina. 1997. *English with an Accent: Language, Ideology, and Discrimination in the United States*. New York: Routledge.

Lucy, John Arthur. 1992. *Language Diversity and Thought: A Reformulation of the Linguistic Relativity Hypothesis*. Cambridge/New York: Cambridge University Press.

Maffi, Luisa. 2005. Linguistic, Cultural and Biological Diversity. *Annual Review of Anthropology* 34(1): 599–617.

McDonald, Marion. 1989. *We Are Not French: Language, Culture and Identity in Brittany*. London: Routledge.

McElhinny, Bonnie. 1998. Genealogies of Gender Theory: Practice theory and feminism in sociocultural and linguistic anthropology. *Social Analysis* 42(3): 164–89.

Milroy, Lesley. 1992. *Linguistic Variation and Change: On the Historical Sociolinguistics of English*. Oxford/Cambridge, MA: B. Blackwell.

Milroy, Leslie, and Sue Margrain. 1980. Vernacular Language Loyalty and Social Network. *Language in Society* 9(01): 43–70.

Milroy, John, and Leslie Milroy. 1999. *Authority in Language: Investigating Standard English*. London: Routledge.

Mougeon, Raymond, and Édouard Beniak. 1996. Social Class and Language Variation in Bilingual Speech Communities. *Towards a Social Science of Language* 1: 69–99.

Mühlhäusler, Peter. 1996. *Linguistic Ecology: Language Change and Linguistic Imperialism in the Pacific Region*. Oxford: Routledge.

Muehlmann, Shaylih, and Alexandre Duchêne. 2007. Beyond the Nation-State: International Agencies as New Sites of Discourses on Bilingualism. In *Bilingualism: A Social Approach*, ed. Monica Heller, 96–110. New York: Palgrave Macmillan.

Negt, Oskar, and Alexander Kluge. 1993. *Public Sphere and Experience: Toward an Analysis of the Bourgeois and Proletarian Public Sphere*. Minneapolis: University of Minnesota Press.

Nettle, Daniel, and Suzanne Romaine. 2000. *Vanishing Voices: The Extinction of the World's Languages*. Oxford/New York: Oxford University Press.

O'Brien, Jay, and William Roseberry. 1991. *Golden Ages, Dark Ages: Imagining the Past in Anthropology and History*. Berkeley: University of California Press.

Ortner, Sherry B. 1984. Theory in Anthropology since the Sixties. *Comparative Studies in Society and History* 26: 126–66.

   1996. *Making Gender: The Politics and Erotics of Gender*. Boston, MA: Beacon University Press.

   2000. *The Fate Of "Culture": Geertz and Beyond*. Berkeley: University of California Press; Boston, MA: Beacon Press.

Paolillo, John. 1999. The Virtual Speech Community: Social Network and Language Variation on IRC. *Journal of Computer-Mediated Communication* 4(4). doi: 10.1111/j.1083-6101.1999.tb00109.x.

Patrick, Peter. 2004. Speech Community. In *The Handbook of Language Variation and Change*, ed. J.K. Chambers, P. Trudgill, et al., 573–97. Malden, MA: Blackwell Pub.

Putnam, George N., and Edna M. O'Hern. 1955. The Status Significance of an Isolated Urban Dialect. *Language* 31(4): 1–32.

Rickford, John R. 1986. The Need for New Approaches to Social Class Analysis in Sociolinguistics. *Language and Communication* 6(3): 215–21.

Robbins, Bruce. 1993. *The Phantom Public Sphere*. Minneapolis: University of Minnesota Press.

Romaine, Suzanne. 1982. *Sociolinguistic Variation in Speech Communities*. London: Edward Arnold.

Roseberry, William. 1989. *Anthropologies and Histories: Essays in Culture, History and Political Economy.* New Brunswick, NJ: Rutgers University Press.

Ryan, Mary P. 1990. *Women in Public: Between Banners and Ballots, 1825–1880.* Baltimore, MD: Johns Hopkins University Press.

Sapir, Edward. 1921. *Language: An Introduction to the Study of Speech.* New York: Dover.

Saussure, Ferdinand de. 1983 (1916). Course in General Linguistics. La Salle, Ill.: Open Court Press

Schatzki, Theodore. 1997. Practices and Action: A Wittgensteinian Critique of Bourdieu and Giddens. *Philosophy of the Social Sciences* 27(3): 283-308.

Schieffelin, B. B., K. A. Woolard, and P. V. Kroskrity. 1998. *Language Ideologies: Practice and Theory*, Vol. 16. New York: Oxford University Press.

Silverstein, Michael. 1998. Contemporary Transformations of Local Linguistic Communities. *Annual Review of Anthropology* 27(1): 401-26.

―― 2000. Whorfianism and the Linguistic Imagination of Reality. In *Regimes of Language Ideologies, Polities, Identities*, ed. P. V. Kroskrity, 85-139. Santa Fe, NM: School of American Research.

―― 2003. Indexical Order and the Dialectics of Sociolinguistic Life. *Lang. Commun.* 23(3/4): 193-229.

Skutnabb-Kangas, Tove. 2000. *Linguistic Genocide in Education – or Worldwide Diversity and Human Rights?* Mahwah, NJ: Erlbaum.

Soffietti, James P. 1955. Why Children Fail to Read: A linguistic analysis. *Harvard Educational Review* 25(2): 63-84.

Thompson, E. P. 1966. *The Making of the English Working Class.* New York: Vintage Books.

Urla, Jacqueline. 1993. Cultural Politics in an Age of Statistics: Numbers, nations, and the making of Basque identity. *American Ethnologist* 20(4): 818-43.

Warner, Michael. 2002. Publics and Counterpublics. *Public Culture* 14(1): 49-90.

Whorf, Benjamin Lee. 1964. *Language, Thought, and Reality: Selected Writings*, ed. and introd. John B. Carroll, with foreword by Stuart Chase. Cambridge, MA: MIT Press.

Wolfram, Walt, and Natalie Schilling-Estes. 1995. Moribund Dialects and the Endangerment Canon: The case of Ocracoke Brogue. *Language* 71(4): 696-721.

Woodbury, Anthony C. 1993. A Defense of the Proposition, "When a language dies, a culture dies". In *SALSA 1: Proceedings of the First Annual Symposium about Language and Society – Austin*, ed. Robin Queen and Rusty Barrett, 101-29. Austin: University of Texas Department of Linguistics.

Woolard, Kathryn A 1992. Language Ideology: Issues and approaches. In *Pragmatics: Special issue on Language Ideologies*, ed. P. Kroskrity, B. Schieffelin and K. Woolard, 2(3): 235-50.

Part V

Interdisciplinary perspectives

Paul Kockelman, Jack Sidnell, and N. J. Enfield

The title of Part V should immediately suggest the usual caveats. For example, disciplines are artificial entities, the products of historical happenstance and cultural commitments, rather than the rational effects of well-defined and naturally bounded subject matters. Attempts to bring them together often only succeed in reifying what was originally an erroneous separation. And most interesting work is already resolutely interdisciplinary, and so need not announce itself as such. Moreover, as may be seen by the titles of the chapters offered here, the perspectives are often intra-disciplinary rather than interdisciplinary, and thereby bring together subfields within anthropology as much as connect (linguistic) anthropology to other disciplines. Anthropologists of language have always worked across fields and perspectives, as should already be apparent from most of the chapters in this volume. Given the essential importance of language and culture to every human endeavor, and given their radical entanglement, linguistic anthropologists have often had two underlying attitudes: How could you ever expect to understand one without reference to the other? And how could you ever expect to understand any other topic of human concern without reference to both? Enough said.

There is a deep relation between linguistic anthropology and *critical theory* which, admittedly, is not really a discipline at all, but rather a set of conceptual and quasi-ethical commitments that are shared across a range of disciplines in the social sciences and humanities. To better understand, and bring to light, this relation, **Kockelman**'s first chapter in this Part takes a critical look at theory in linguistic anthropology by foregrounding its dependence on certain moves in critical theory. He begins by synthesizing a dozen or so relatively axiomatic commitments of modern linguistic anthropologists. It emerges that two key modes of mediation – *conditioning* and *representation* – when subject to processes such as framing, embedding, disturbing, and reflecting, as Kockelman terms them, straightforwardly generate almost all of the major claims made by critical theorists, as incorporated by linguistic anthropologists.

In its focus over the last decades on the relation between language and culture, linguistic anthropology in the narrow sense has understood "culture" mostly in Boasian terms, as a group-specific totality of value-oriented practices. It has studied culture, in part, through detailed ethnographic fieldwork of the kind that Malinowski introduced and championed. In this way, linguistic anthropology has tended to be most closely connected with *sociocultural anthropology* as a subfield within the larger discipline. **Stasch**'s chapter draws out these dense and long-standing connections, and the shared commitments that underlie them. In addition, he highlights differences, such as how the term *representation* is understood by both groups, and the degree to which the ethnographic monograph is valued as a form of empirical presentation. And he also shows various ways anthropologists have brought together linguistic and nonlinguistic materials. One upshot is that the two subdisciplines could be more productively linked by extending the notions of iconicity and indexicality, whereby signs seem to be connected by virtue of having qualities in common or exhibiting causal relations.

There have been long-standing connections between linguistic anthropology and its sister subdiscipline of *sociolinguistics*. As **Eckert** shows in her chapter, while the latter is often framed as standing closer to sociology than anthropology – in terms of the categories it uses, and the quantitative methods it often deploys – it has an intimate conceptual and topical relation to linguistic anthropology proper. Eckert outlines the early history of the discipline, and its tight connection to linguistic anthropology, then focusing on what is sometimes referred to as the *Third Wave* perspective in variation studies, a perspective that emphasizes "the local construction of meaning in variation." Her survey of the results of classic case studies, taking up topics such as stance and style, variation and change, and identity and iconization, foregrounds topics of central interest to linguistic anthropologists, while simultaneously showing the empirical focus and conceptual framing of sociolinguistics. Taken together, then, the chapters by Stasch and Eckert engage with historically porous disciplinary divides, highlighting the relatively wide range of shared ideas and topics, and thus the ways in which such subdisciplines are almost unconscious allies if not fellow travelers.

The chapters by Blench and Dediu, in contrast, draw out a set of relations between language (and linguistics proper) and subfields which are often maximally contrastive with cultural anthropology – in terms of timescales, methodologies, and conceptual frameworks. Blench explores connections between language and *archaeology*, with the latter's focus on the material remains of past cultures on historical timescales. Dediu foregrounds the connections between language and *biological anthropology*, with the latter's focus on changes in genetic (and phenotypic) structures on evolutionary timescales. Not only are the methods and tools radically different in both cases, so are the timescales at which salient processes occur, and about which central claims are made. Both of these chapters may thereby also be usefully read in conjunction with the chapters in Part II of this volume, with their focus on process and formation.

Blench's chapter examines gender registers, creolization, and the origins of writing, and shows the ways such topics can be more richly understood through the dual perspective of archaeology and linguistics. Some of the issues are controversial or at least fraught, such as the relation between language classification and diversification, or the proposed syntheses of linguistics, archaeology, and genetics. In line with Stasch's stance with reference to sociocultural anthropology, Blench directly addresses the skepticism of some archaeologists as to the importance of linguistics to their discipline. He argues: "Combining archaeological results with linguistic reconstruction and a nuanced understanding of social process derived from ethnography allows us to evolve a richer model of prehistory."

A similarly constructive challenge is offered in **Dediu**'s chapter. The links between language and biological anthropology are addressed through two interwoven topics. The first concerns the way in which models developed in evolutionary biology may be used to understand language. The second concerns the relation between speaker variation and linguistic diversity. Dediu's survey of a wide range of literatures intervenes in some central debates, showing the ways in which genetics and language interact at various levels. Because there are so many such relations, because they are so closely interrelated, and because they are often so indirect in their causal mediation, understanding them "will require a broad interdisciplinary approach integrating not only the language sciences, anthropology, genetics and evolutionary biology but will also require advanced data analysis and computational skills." The methodological requirements here are distinctly challenging for those who have been reared in the standard disciplinary contexts of linguistic and sociocultural anthropology.

Information science and the modern technology now associated with it tend not to be the first topics that come to mind in formulating linguistic anthropological research. But as we see in **Kockelman**'s final chapter, there is an intimate, albeit often hidden, relation between linguistic anthropology and computer science. Kockelman argues that computers, as both engineered and imagined, are essentially text-generated and text-generating devices. Computation (in the machine-specific sense) may be understood as the enclosure of interpretation – an attempt to render a highly messy and stereotypically human process relatively formal, quantifiable, and context-independent. In making these arguments, Kockelman introduces some of the key concepts and claims of computer science, and shows their fundamental importance to the concerns of linguistic anthropology. This reveals the ways some of the core contentions and methods of linguistic anthropologists can be productively applied to, and extended using the digitally mediated, computationally processed, and pervasively networked infrastructure of modern social environments – opening up not only a new set of topics, but also a new set of techniques.

24

Linguistic anthropology and critical theory

Paul Kockelman

24.1 Cages, claws, and keys

As used here, the term critical theory refers to work produced by a set of thinkers who might best be understood as shadows of the enlightenment – Bacon and Hobbes, Kant and Hegel, Marx and Freud, Darwin and Nietzsche, Saussure and Peirce, among many others.[1] While these thinkers are, to be sure, radically heterogeneous in many respects, they all pondered the limits (and sometimes the seeming limitlessness) of knowledge and power. In some sense, they all understood human-specific forms of agency, and mediation more generally, to be simultaneously cage, claw, and key.

This chapter is meant to characterize the core theoretical claims of linguistic anthropology while, simultaneously, critiquing the cultural logic underlying its practices of claim-making. The title, then, is meant to do double-work: we will take a critical look at theory in the discipline of linguistic anthropology by foregrounding its dependence on certain moves in critical theory. As will be seen, such practices turn on the repeated deployment of a small set of interrelated moves, themselves closely linked to such limits: replace any mediated relatum with a mediating relation; reframe any entity or event as the precipitate of a process; and recast seemingly mono-dimensional figures as flattenings of multi-dimensional frameworks.

The first section simply summarizes a dozen or so relatively axiomatic commitments of linguistic anthropologists, showing how they are all structurally similar in their invocation of a particular metaphor – why live (or, rather, think and theorize) in Flatland when there is affordable housing (or, rather, readily available analytic tools) in Textureville? The next six sections treat mediation in detail. They detail two key modes of mediation (conditioning and representation), and the ways these modes (when subject to processes such as framing, embedding, disturbing, and reflecting) effortlessly generate almost all of the major claims made by critical theorists (as incorporated by linguistic anthropologists). In some sense, then, my claim is that there is a very simple "grammar" that generates almost all of the major moves made in critical theory and, insofar as we have inherited many of the claims of this tradition, those of our own discipline. And the conclusion develops some of the stakes of this fact.

24.2   From Flatland to Textureville

Some of the core commitments in the last half-century of linguistic anthropology are summarized in Table 24.1.[2] Perturbing the Saussurian dichotomies (1983[1916]; and see Greenberg 1990, inter alia), we foreground discourse practice (parole) as much as grammatical structure (langue), diachronic transformation as much as synchronic relations, motivation (icons and indices) as much as arbitrariness (symbols). Building on Malinowski (1936), Austin (2003[1955]), and Jakobson (1990a; and see Hymes 1962, as well as the essays in Bauman and Sherzer 1974), we foreground language as action as much as language as reflection or description. Building on Austin again, with roots in Mead (1934) and fruits in Goffman (1959), we foreground implicit signs (e.g., gestures, signs given off) as much as explicit signs (e.g., symbols, signs given), and their effectiveness on context (protention) as much as their appropriateness in

Table 24.1 Some core moves of linguistic anthropology (or What the discipline foregrounds)

a)	Discourse as much as grammar, diachrony as much as synchrony, motivation as much as arbitrariness
b)	Language as action as much as language as reflection
c)	Implicit signs as much as explicit signs, and their effectiveness on context as much as appropriateness in context
d)	Meta-language as much as language, and reflexive language as much as reflective language
e)	Poetic regimentation (showing equivalence) as much as meta-linguistic regimentation (stating it)
f)	Semiotic collectivities (on multiple social, temporal, and ideational scales) as much as speech communities
g)	Multiplicity and concreteness of human creativity as much as abstract (or syntactic) generativity
h)	Tropic usage (etiolation, parasites, refootings, decenterings, etc.) as much as conventional usage
i)	Interactional orders (and their re-orderings) as much as speech events
j)	Processes precipitating "text" and "context" as much as text in relation to context
k)	Parole (*qua* practice), and langue and parole about langue and parole (*qua* ideology), as much as langue (*qua* structure)
l)	Competence (langue, potentia, etc.) as precipitate of process as much as condition for performance
m)	Anthropology and linguistics before the 1960s as much as anthropology and linguistics since the 1960s
n)	Methodology as theory as much as methods in relation to theory

context (rentention). Building on Austin yet again, as well as another key essay of Jakobson (1990b; and see the essays in Lucy 1993), in addition to a host of work in analytic philosophy, we foreground meta-language as much as language, and reflexive language (such as shifters, proper names, and so forth) as much as reflective language. Developing a particular insight in that first essay of Jakobson (1990a), we foreground poetic regimentation (showing equivalence) as much as meta-linguistic regimentation (stating it). Building on Gumperz (1965), and with many subsequent additions, we focus on semiotic collectivities (on multiple social, temporal, and ideational scales) as much as speech communities. Gathering often diverse claims from a range of scholars (Goffman 1981; Friedrich 1986; and see Enfield and Levinson 2006), we focus on the multiplicity and concreteness of human creativity as much as abstract (or syntactic) generativity. As developed most clearly by Goffman (1981), we focus on tropic usage (etiolation, parasites, ritualization, refootings, decenterings, etc.) as much as conventional usage. And, again with particular reference to Goffman (1964, 1983; and see Blom and Gumperz 1972), we focus on interactional orders (and their re-orderings via shifts in footing, and so forth) as much as speech events. In a tradition that runs back to Haliday and Hasan (1976; and see the particularly important essays in Silverstein and Urban 1996), we foreground processes that precipitate "text" and "context" as much as text in relation to context. Building on insights of Bourdieu (1977[1972]; and see the essays in Schieffelin et al. 1998; and, in particular, work by Silverstein 1979, 1981), we focus on parole (*qua* practice), and langue and parole about langue and parole (*qua* ideology), as much as langue (*qua* structure). Building on Hymes (1966; and see the essays in Schieffelin and Ochs 1986), we foreground communicative competence (langue, potentia, etc.) as precipitate of process as much as condition for performance. More generally, unlike many of our colleagues in related disciplines, we make use of anthropology and linguistics "before the 60s" (Ortner 1984) as much as anthropology and linguistics since the 1960s. And finally, via a pragmatic tradition that goes back to Peirce (1998[1907]), we foreground methodology as theory as much as methods in relation to theory.

As may be seen, all the moves are closely interrelated, and so might constitute a "theory" if they didn't already have a kind of axiomatic status (somewhere between best-practices and paradigmatic assumptions). As should be noted, many of the core moves aren't from linguistic anthropology proper, but have been adopted by linguistic anthropologists from other fields, making our discipline seem like an incredibly stream-lined device for sieving wheat from chaff (and then resowing its seeds in particularly fertile fields, *qua* culture-specific and ethnographically framed ways).

Before moving onto mediation as a central analytic trope, it is worthwhile saying a few words about the overarching logic of the list itself. As should be apparent from the meter (and, in particular, by the repeated use of the relational term *as much as*), one key strategy turns on a three-stroke process. First, foreground previously backgrounded dimensions (which may have been overlooked, elided, or misunderstood). For example, attend to all the functions of language beside the referential. Second, continue to carefully attend to the previously foregrounded dimension (and thus the issue is not inversion, but rather subsumption). For example, the point is not to foreground discourse instead of structure, but rather to foreground both discourse and structure (as well as each in relation to the other). And third, account for the relation between foreground and background; and thus try to understand how one relates to the other (say, as condition to consequence), or why certain dimensions more easily come to the fore. For example, as per point (j), instead of focusing on text per se, focus on textuality as a process which gives rise to such a precipitate (and focus as well on the factors that frequently lead to the elision of the former in local and expert understanding).

Crucially, such a summary of key moves in the discipline of linguistic anthropology also serves as a quick-and-dirty summary of its key failings.[3] In particular, while many linguistic anthropologists work at the level of subsumption much of the time, a substantial amount of scholarship only ever manages to invert. For example, we get a lot on ideology but, relatively speaking, not much (or at least no longer much) on structure and practice; a lot on textualization, but not much on text; and so forth. We will return to some of the conditions for these inversions in the conclusion.

24.3 Mediation

A core commitment of linguistic anthropology is the importance of *mediation*, which may be loosely (and provisionally) understood as a kind of relation between two relata ($R_1 \Rightarrow R_2$).[4] The relata in question may be figured in a variety of ways (e.g., as entities, events, qualities, processes, actors, domains, other relations, and so forth). What usually matters is that, aside from the mediating relation per se, the relata seem otherwise relatively different or disconnected.[5] For example, a word in relation to a referent, a mode of consciousness in relation to a form of communication, a practice in relation to a structure, a collectivity in relation to a value, a grammatical category in relation to a semantic feature, one identity in relation to another identity, and so forth.

Like many other disciplines, linguistic anthropology has traditionally been interested in two particular *modes of mediation*. First, one relatum may relate to the other as sign to object ($S \Rightarrow O$); or, more generally, as representation to representatum (e.g., a gesture that points and an object that is pointed to). And second, one relatum may relate to the other as cause to effect ($C \Rightarrow E$); or, more generally, as condition to consequence (e.g., the action of flipping a switch and the event of a light turning on). See Table 24.2a.

Table 24.2 Some key modes of mediation

	Expression	Paraphrase	Examples
a) Basic Modes	$S \Rightarrow O$	Sign stands for object, or representation has some representatum	Grammatical category => semantic feature, mental state => state of affairs
	$C \Rightarrow E$	Cause gives rise to effect, or condition has some consequence	Discursive practice => grammatical structure, mode of communication => mode of consciousness
b) Reframings	$(S)_C \Rightarrow (O)_E$	Sign relates to object as cause to effect	Performatives (token level), projection (type level)
	$(O)_C \Rightarrow (S)_E$	Object relates to sign as cause to effect	Constatives (token level), iconicity (type level)
	$(C)_S \Rightarrow (E)_O$	Cause relates to effect as sign to object	Clues, symptoms, natural meaning; Hobbes, Darwin, Veblen, Labov
	$(E)_S \Rightarrow (C)_O$	Effect relates to cause as sign to object	Clues, symptoms, natural meaning; Hobbes, Darwin, Veblen, Labov
c) Embeddings	$S \Rightarrow (S \Rightarrow O)_O$	Object of sign is sign–object relation	Meta-language, paraphrase, reported speech, etc.
	$C \Rightarrow (C \Rightarrow E)_E$	Effect of cause is cause–effect relation	Meta-control, conducting conduct, keys, switches, etc.
	$S \Rightarrow (C \Rightarrow E)_O$	Object of sign is cause–effect relation	Physics equation: $E=mc^2$; warning sign: Slippery when wet
	$C \Rightarrow (S \Rightarrow O)_E$	Effect of cause is sign–object relation	Grammaticalization, regimentation, entextualization, enregisterment, etc.
	$(S \Rightarrow O)_S \Rightarrow O$	Sign–object relation is sign of object	Language you speak sign of your identity
	$(S \Rightarrow O)_C \Rightarrow E$	Sign–object relation is cause of effect	Any interpretant of sign–object relation
	$(C \Rightarrow E)_S \Rightarrow O$	Cause–effect relation is sign of object	One's reaction to a situation itself a sign of one's mood or emotion
d) Disturbances	$(C \Rightarrow E)_C \Rightarrow E$	Cause–effect relation is cause of effect	Phylogenetic interpretants
	$S =/ O$	Blocked or unknown representation	Not conscious of some object; cannot articulate some object
	$S \sim\!\!> O$	Distorted or false representation	Representation of object incorrect; representation of object distorted
	$C =/ E$	Effect stopped, path blocked	Thwarting of action; channel capped
	$C \sim\!\!> E$	Effect redirected, path rerouted	Co-opting of action; channel transformed

If, in the first case, the relation may often be described as something like *standing for* (i.e., a sign stands for an object), in the second case, the relation may often be described as something like *giving rise to* (i.e., a condition gives rise to a consequence). To return to the concerns of critical theory, as raised in the introduction, these two modes of mediation may often map onto knowledge and power, respectively.

Observing, describing, and theorizing such mediating relations is hard-enough work by itself (e.g., writing a grammar of a language or an ethnography of a speech community; or analyzing the correlation between discourse patterns and grammatical structures or between semantic categories and cognitive frames), and one might think that linguistic anthropologists would content themselves with undertaking the scholarship necessary to resolve such issues. However, the nature of the mediation involved seems to be complicated in particular ways, such that many linguistic anthropologists have felt the need to become critical theorists as much as scholars and scientists. (Note, for example, the split among our contributors.)

In the next four sections we will discuss such complications in detail: framing, embedding, disturbances, and meta-mediation. As already emphasized, the issue is not so much, what are the arguments and claims per se (i.e., our representations as to what mediates what and how so, and the genealogy of such representations in our discipline). Rather, the issue is the epistemic logic (or culture, if you will) that conditions (!) such representations (!) to be more or less endlessly and effortlessly deployed. In some sense, then, the point is to understand and critique linguistic anthropology's approach to understanding and critique.

24.4 Framing

It should first be emphasized that the two modes of mediation (representation and conditioning) are best understood as poles of a continuum, rather than positions in an opposition (and even that phrasing is optimistic). In part, this is because most modes of mediation are hybrid entities, exhibiting features of both types. And so the point is not to specify where something should belong as an ideal type (Weber 1949[1904]), but rather to characterize what features it partakes of as an actual token (as compared to and contrasted with an array of such ideal types). In part, this is because each mode of mediation may often only do its work in the context of the other. For example, an infrastructure of cause–effect relations enables any sign–object relation (and usually vice versa). In part, this is because many actual modes of mediation are quite complex, turning on long chains of the two simpler kinds. Indeed, in some sense this section is precisely an account of such complex chains of mediation. In part, it is because whether some instance of mediation is understood as one mode or the other often depends on other modes of mediation. For example, our attempts to represent where causal influencing ends and semiotic representation begins is itself causally influenced by our semiotic representations. In part, it is because there are other ways to characterize the two modes of mediation. For example, in certain situations, the distinction between representation (S=>O) and conditioning (C=>E) maps not only onto distinctions like knowledge and power, but also distinctions like code and channel (Kockelman 2010), mind (or language) and world (Putnam 1975), reflection and action (Malinowski 1936), semantics and pragmatics (Levinson 1983), symbol and index (Peirce 1955a), theoretical agency and practical agency (Kockelman 2007), representing and intervening (Hacking 1983), mediator and intermediary (Latour 2007, and see Chapter 29, this volume), third and second (Peirce 1992[1868]), and even distinctions like self-consciousness and self-control. And finally, as will now be discussed in detail, and as closely related to all of the foregoing points, it is because each mode of mediation may be *reframed* in terms of the other under certain circumstances. See Table 24.2b.

Firstly, sign–object relations may often be understood in terms of cause–effect relations (either $(S)_C => (O)_E$ or $(O)_C => (S)_E$). For example, when sign-tokens are foregrounded, a performative utterance (*qua* sign) relates to the state of affairs it represents (*qua* object) as condition to consequence (recall Table 24.1c). Conversely, a constative utterance relates to the state of affairs it represents as consequence to condition. Similar claims can be made for private representations (*qua* mental states) as opposed to public representations (*qua* speech acts). For example, perceptions are, in part, caused by the states of affairs they represent; and intentions are, in part, causal of the states of affairs they represent. Such moves were crucial not only to analytic philosophers studying intentionality (Anscombe 1957, Searle 1983, Grice 1989a, Austin 2003[1955], and see Brandom, this volume, Chapter 14), but also to critical philosophers like Marx (1978[1845]) and Hegel (1977[1807]). For example, in one relatively widespread reading (however schematic and simplistic), a key question is whether mind or consciousness (*qua* ensemble of relatively representational processes) is relatively conditioning of the world (*qua* ensemble of relatively causal processes), or whether the world is relatively conditioning of mind (see, for example, Sahlins 1978, for a classic statement).

Similarly, when sign-types are foregrounded, motivation describes a process whereby signs take on, or are conditioned by, the features of their objects. Conversely, projection describes a process whereby objects take on, or are conditioned by, the features of their signs. And just as iconic-indexicality (versus symbolism), and motivated meaning (versus arbitrary meaning) more generally, was crucial to both Peircean semiotics (1955) and Saussurian semiology (1983[1916]), projection was fundamental to critical philosophy (Marx, Nietzsche, Freud, and so forth) as much as to Boasian anthropology (Sapir 1985[1927], Whorf 1956a). It is impossible to understand notions like reification and fetishization, as the systematic misrecognition of the origins of value, without it. Indeed, even relatively hoary philosophical stances (nominalism, realism, conceptualism) may be understood as particular commitments to various modes and directions of mediation (see Putnam 1975; Haugeland 1998; and Brandom, this volume, Chapter 14). For example, is the intentionality exhibited by private representations (*qua* mental states) derivative of the intentionality exhibited by public representations (*qua* speech acts), or vice versa; and how do mind and language relate to reality more generally, *qua* condition or consequence?

Secondly, cause–effect relations may often be understood in terms of sign–object relations ($(C)_S \Rightarrow (E)_O$ or $(E)_S \Rightarrow (C)_O$). In the simplest of cases, this describes processes of natural meaning (Grice 1989b): such as smoke means fire or fire means smoke.[6] More generally, insofar as I know (or assume) one thing causally leads to, or follows from, another, I can treat the former as a sign of the latter. It thereby has "meaning" for me even though it was not "meant" to by its maker. In certain domains, such as symptoms and clues, such relations may be typified – the ability to read them is disciplined into an entire collectivity (of doctors and detectives) as part of its episteme. In other cases, such clues and symptoms may be used only by particular agents in particular events (during, say, the simple sort of detective and doctor work each of us does every day). What is crucial in all cases is really the set of ontological assumptions that underlie such interpretations (as to various kinds of causality and the way they connect various kinds of qualities and events, understood as the roots or fruits of other qualities and events), such that an interpreting agent may semiotically move from one kind of quality or event (*qua* cause) to another (*qua* effect).[7] Note, for example, that linguistic anthropology, as a theory, is in part precisely a set of claims about such cause–effect relations: we don't use symptoms as indices of illnesses or clues as indices of culprits so much as linguistic tokens and types as indices of social relations and sociality-in-formation.

Theories turning on precisely these kinds of dynamics, on various sorts of scales (evolutionary, historical, developmental, etc.) are legion: Vygotsky's (1978) account of pointing; Veblen's (1971[1899]) understanding of pecuniary emulation; Labov's (2001) description of hypercorrection; Darwin's (1981[1871], 1965[1872]) theory of sexual selection and emotional expression; Hobbes's (1994[1651]) understanding of power (and its symbols and symptoms); Bourdieu's (1984) notion of distinction; Mead's (1934) theory of the gesture; Goffman's (1959) description of signs "given off"; and so forth.[8] Finally, much of this might be understood as the essence of poetic meter (Jakobson 1990a), and patterning more generally: past experiences (with relatively connected qualities, whatever the why and how of the connection) condition future expectations (*qua* interpretations), be these "expectations" embodied, enminded, or engenomed.

24.5 Embedding

Just as such relations may be reframed (sign–object to cause–effect, or cause–effect to sign–object), so too may they be *embedded*. In such cases, the key issue is that each relatum in such a relation may itself be a relation with relata (and so on, indefinitely). See Table 24.2c. In particular, there is the possibility of both left-handed embedding and right-handed embedding. For example, just as there are embedded relations of the type S => (S => O)$_O$, or a sign relates to an object which is itself a sign–object relation (at some degree of remove), so too are there embedded relations of the type (S => O)$_S$ => O, or the relation between a sign and an object is itself the sign of an object. Moreover, the embedded relation may itself be of the same type as the relation in which it is embedded, as per these two examples, or it may be of a different type. For example, just as there are embedded relations of the type S => (C => E)$_O$, or a sign relates to an object which is itself a cause–effect relation, so too are there embedded relations of the type (S => O)$_C$ => E, or the relation between a sign and an object is itself the cause of an effect.[9] Finally, these may be recursively re-embedded in each other again and again to any degrees of remove (see the discussion of context-free grammars in Chapter 29, this volume). For example, as will be discussed at length below, many articles by linguistic anthropologists are precisely complicated signs (*qua* texts) that represent conditions for (and consequences of) particular sign–object relations, where such conditions and consequences, *qua* causes and effects, are themselves other sign–object relations (and may themselves have other conditions and consequences). For example, (Text)$_S$ => ((S => O)$_C$ => (S => O)$_E$)$_O$. In the rest of this section, we will offer examples of the eight relatively simple kinds of embeddings, discuss various ways they may be disturbed, and then discuss a few multiple embeddings of particular importance and complexity.

Right-handed embeddings are the most familiar kind. Signs may stand for objects that are themselves sign–object relations. Metalanguage, and meta-semiosis more generally (Jakobson 1990a, 1990b; Lucy 1993; Silverstein 1995[1976]), was mentioned in the last section, and so needs no introduction. For present purposes, just note how over-represented it is in more popular literature (perhaps because it is just the most obvious peak of the meta-mediation mountain).[10] Signs may stand for objects that are themselves cause–effect relations. For example, just as many physics equations are signs that represent causal processes ($F=Gm_1m_2/r^2$), so are many warning signs (slippery when wet). Causes may give rise to effects which are themselves cause–effect relations. A canonical example of this is unlocking a door, or any form of meta-agency more generally: by turning on (or off) a machine, one ensures that other effects will (or will not) be caused by it; by disciplining a child one tries to ensure that other actions (including speech actions) will and will not be instigated by it. More generally, any attempt to conduct conduct (often through representations), as per Foucault's (1991a[1978], 1991b[1978]) account of governmentality, or Weber's (1978) account of domination, is of this variety. Or, closer to home, language prescriptivism and even quotidian modes of "correction." Finally, causes may give rise to effects which are themselves sign–object relations. For example, any process that gives rise to a sign–object relation, or a field of such relations, may be described in these terms: grammaticalization, conventionalization, ritualization (Goffman 1981), enregisterment (Agha 2007), typification (Peirce 1955; Berger and Luckman 1967), sexual selection for certain emblematic characteristics (Darwin 1981[1871]), etc. Here, then, might go any condition of possibility for any particular semiotic process.

Left-handed embeddings may, at first, seem less familiar; but they too are ubiquitous. The sign of an object can itself be a (relatively causal) sign–object relation. In some sense, much of linguistic anthropology (Goffman 1959; Silverstein 1995 [1976]) works through this lens: my use of a sign–object relation from some particular code may itself be a sign (itself merely "given off," and thus "not meant to mean"), to an interpreting agent with a particular ontology, of my particular sociocultural identity (class, gender, political stance, ability, etc.). The sign of an object can itself be a cause–effect relation. For example, the melting of a substance (effect) when heated to a certain temperature (cause), provides evidence (sign) that the substance is gold (object).[11] When semiotic processes are properly understood as sign–object relations that give rise to interpretant–object relations, and hence as relations between relations (Kockelman 2005), this may be framed as follows: insofar as you interpret (*qua* effect) a sign in some way (*qua* cause), that is itself a sign of a certain object. For example, because you raise your hand (interpretant) when I ask a question (sign), I infer that you think you know the answer (object). Similarly, the cause of a cause–effect relation can itself be a sign–object relation. Again, linguistic anthropologists are constantly foregrounding this, as should be obvious when phrased in slightly different terms: not, what are some of the historical (or interactional) conditions for a particular grammatical structure (*qua* code, *qua* sign–object relation), but what are some of the consequences (Whorf 1956a; Lucy 1992a, 1992b; Silverstein 1979, 1981)? And again, when semiotic processes are properly understood as relations between relations, all sign–object relations are causes of interpretant–object relations *qua* effects (essentially be definition). Finally, a cause–effect relation may itself be the cause of an effect. In certain cases, this is essentially a trivial observation: because dams relatively reliably slow the flow of rivers, beavers are disposed to build them. More generally, most of the given traits of a particular species may be understood as phylogenetic interpretants (*qua* effects) of particular cause–effect relations in their environment. This should emphasize that the issue is not, is such a meta-relation true or important, but rather, how do assumptions about such processes underwrite particular claims (say, the relation between some significant practice, e.g., dam building or oath-taking, and the processes that lead to its natural, artificial, and/or unconscious selection)?

24.6 Disturbances

Crucially, both kinds of mediation can be thwarted and diverted, perturbed and parasited, and subject to *disturbances* more generally. See Table 24.2d. Indeed, the possibility of going awry, or at least of being judged so, is arguably the essence of such processes (Serres 2007[1980], Kockelman 2010, 2012). In the case of representations, there is unconsciousness (being unable to represent some particular object) and misrepresentation (representing something incorrectly, or in a highly refracted fashion). Similarly, in the case of conditioning, there is repression (stopping a cause from having its effect) and rechanneling (creating conditions for causes to have unusual or unintended effects). Needless to say, the political stakes of these kinds of processes, especially when crossed with embedding and reframing, are, or at least seem to be, enormous.

To take up sign–object disturbances first, from the standpoint of some relatively transcendental frame, we may talk about relatively important objects for which there are no signs. In the terms of critical theory, this is understood as being unconscious of something. Similarly, sign–object relations can not only be blocked, they can also be distorted (and thus refracted instead of reflected) – we represent an object, only we do so incorrectly. This may range from falsity (our representation is false) to simple transformation (certain features are missing, added, distorted, etc.). Needless to say, there is huge literature on these sorts of topics (hegemony, false consciousness, bad faith, etc.), stemming out of ideas from Whorf (1956a, 1956b), Goffman (1959), Kant (1964[1781]); Marx (1967 [1867]), Sapir (1985[1927]), Nietzsche (1989[1887]), Boas (1989a[1889], 1989b [1910]), Hobbes (1994[1651]), Heidegger (1996[1927]), Bacon (2000[1620]), Freud (2008[1900]), and so on.

It should be stressed, and thereby subject to critique, that both of these processes may be understood in terms of Frege's (1997[1892]) *intensionality* or the *sense–reference* distinction (think indirect and direct reported speech, and meta-representations more generally), and so linguistic anthropology is hilariously well-poised (or rather suspiciously presupposedly primed) to be good at it. In particular, some relatively immanent individual or collective agent (*qua* reported speaker, local villager, or other linguist) has not represented, or has represented poorly, some representatum that some relatively transcendental agent (*qua* reporting speaker, observing analyst, or linguistic anthropologist) has represented correctly (and has represented as being unrepresented or represented poorly by the relatively immanent agent in question). Indeed, there is perfect resonance between our discipline's topical focus on issues tightly linked to reported speech (shifters, meta-language, intensionality, etc.) and language ideology as its current paradigm.[12] In particular, both the choice of topic, and the style of critique, come down to Frege-like statements: *Dave thinks he's a waiter (but I know him to be a spy)*. Indeed, our entire discipline might be summed up as follows: *They say it's a symbol (entity, intermediary, relatum, cause, mode of abstraction, etc.), but we know it's an index (process, mediator, relation, effect, mode of interaction, etc.)*.

Similarly, there are disturbances of cause–effect relations. For example, Austin's (2003[1955]) account of felicity conditions was essentially a way of describing all the ways a speech act could fail – by not having the normatively appropriate roots (*qua* conditions) or by not having the normatively effective fruits (*qua* consequences). But also, more simply, our actions (*qua* intentions that give rise to states of affairs), which include our speech acts (and conversational moves more generally), can be thwarted or co-opted. Such disturbances are especially easy to spot when cause–effect relations are intentional (or selected more generally), insofar as the function or purpose of anything may be defined in terms of its capacity to fail (to serve that function or fulfill that purpose). However, one can also obstruct and redirect relatively natural, serendipitous, or atelic cause–effect relations. For example, any time one incorporates an affordance (such as wood) into an instrument (such as the handle of a hammer) one is doing this. And so any technology that "exploits nature" (including technologies of the self, as well as technologies designed to control [dominate, exploit, surveil, etc.] the representations and actions, and hence signs and effects, of others) is of this variety. Semiotic technologies in the stereotypic sense, such as media, usually work on both forms of mediation at once, and are thus subject to both kinds of disturbances simultaneously (a fact which should really ground our theories about them).

24.7 Meta-mediation

Issues of blockage and distortion, and disturbances more generally, are particularly important (or at least particularly salient in the imaginary of linguistic anthropologists) when they reflexively feed back into the foregoing kinds of embedded and enframed processes. In particular, the real move for linguistic anthropologists is to propose forms of meta-mediation, which turn on these last kinds. For example, what are some of the conditions for, and consequences of, distorted or unrepresented objects?[13] Similarly, what are some of the conditions for, and consequences of, unintended effects or failed efforts? See Table 24.3a.

Pushing further, the objects that are distorted or unrecognized may be precisely other sign–object relations, or their conditions and consequences. For example, many want to say that metalanguage is never an adequate

Table 24.3 Some key modes of meta-mediation

	Expression	Paraphrase
a) Conditioned Disturbances	$C \Rightarrow (S=/O)_E$ or $(S=/O)_C \Rightarrow E$ $C \Rightarrow (S \sim> O)_E$ or $(S \sim> O)_C \Rightarrow E$ $C \Rightarrow (C=/E)_E$ or $(C=/E)_C \Rightarrow E$ $C \Rightarrow (C \sim> E)_E$ or $(C \sim> E)_C \Rightarrow E$	Conditions for, or consequences of, unrepresented or distorted object Conditions for, or consequences of, blocked or redirected effect
b) Embedded Disturbances	$S \sim> (S \Rightarrow O)_O$ or $S =/ (S \Rightarrow O)_O$ $S \sim> (C \Rightarrow (S \Rightarrow O))_{E/O}$, etc. $S \sim> (C \Rightarrow E)_O$ or $S =/ (C \Rightarrow E)_O$ $S \sim> (C \Rightarrow E)_{E/O}$, etc.	Misrepresented, or unrepresented, representations (and/or their conditions and consequences) Misrepresented, or unrepresented, conditionings (and/or their conditions and consequences)
c) Circular Disturbances	$Si =/ (C \Rightarrow (Si=/Oi))_{E/J}$ $Si \sim> (C \Rightarrow (Si \sim> Oi))_{E/J}$ $Si =/ ((Si=/Oi)_C \Rightarrow E)_{Oi}$ $Si \sim> ((Si \sim> Oi)_C \Rightarrow E)_{Oi}$	Distorted (or blocked) representation of conditions for distorted (or blocked) representation Distorted (or blocked) representation of consequences of distorted (or blocked) representation
d) Disturbed Frames	$S \sim> ((S)_C = (O)_E)_O$	Sign–object relations misrepresented as cause–effect relations (reification) Cause–effect relations misrepresented as sign–object relations (fetishization)
e) Inter-Domain	$((Economic\ Practice)_C \Rightarrow$ $(Legal\ Code)_E)_C \Rightarrow$ $((Grammatical\ Category)_C \Rightarrow$ $(Cultural\ Value)_E)_E$	Mediation across seemingly disparate domains
f) Intra-Domain	$...\Longleftrightarrow$ structure (e.g., langue) $\Longleftrightarrow$ practice (e.g., parole) $\Longleftrightarrow$ ideology (e.g., langue and parole about langue and parole) $\Longleftrightarrow$ ...	Mediation within seemingly simple domains
g) Projected	Is some other epistemic formation's understanding of the mediation of linguistic-cultural process itself mediated (formal linguists, cognitive scientists, other linguistic anthropologists we don't like, etc.)?	Others' theories of mediation are mediated
h) Introjected	Is our theory of mediation, involving basic kinds like S and O, or C and E, as well as notions like embedding, framing, parasites, and so forth, itself mediated – perhaps even conditioned by processes it cannot represent (or rather this form of understanding is no longer able to be applied)?	Own theory of mediation is mediated

representation of the language it represents (Silverstein 1981, Lucy 1993). Similarly, the objects that are distorted or unrecognized may be cause–effect relations, or their conditions and consequences. For example, depending on how one understands a wish or desire (*qua* mode of intentionality or *qua* causal drive, and thus in terms of representation or in terms of conditioning), Freud's (2008[1900]) unconscious can be understood in either way. See Table 24.3b.

One can get even trickier, via circular or self-referencing processes. For example, the objects that our signs distort may themselves be precisely the cause–effect relations that give rise to our distorted signs. Loosely speaking, what I cannot envision is precisely that which blocks my vision. And, more generally, one can make very bold claims, e.g., the systematic misrecognition of the origins of mediation is both cause and effect of the very system that mediates. This is one way to generalize Marx's (1967[1867]) classic statements as to the wily nature of value. See Table 24.3c.

Depending on how the distinction between sign–object relations and cause–effect relations is understood (say, as mind versus world, or as convention versus nature, or as subject versus object, or as mediator versus intermediary), two key kinds of misrecognition are often invoked, especially by scholars working in Marx- or Freud-inspired traditions: fetishization, or treating objective entities as subjective entities; and reification, or treating conventional entities as natural entities.[14] For example, to return to Grice (1989a), treating natural forms of meaning as intentional (or non-natural) modes of meaning (for example, omens, oracles, auguries, and the like), or treating intentional modes of meaning as natural. See Table 24.3d (and recall Table 24.2b). Needless to say, these sorts of claims are legion in anthropology: we used to apply them to the people we study, now we apply them to the people who think about the people we study (for example, missionaries, tourists, and colonizers, other linguists, anthropologists, and scholars, and even the community members themselves).

One can study inter-mediation: ask how any of these domains (or mediating relations between domains) mediate other domains (or mediating relations between domains). See Table 24.3e. For example, and to return to section 24.2, what about relations between modes of reproduction and modes of communication, or language acquisition and socialization? And what about the relation between modes of production and modes of communication, or between economy and language? For example, we might put Marx (1978[1845]) and McLuhan (1994[1964]) together as follows: for any particular mode of production or mode of communication, the issue is not so much what is being produced or what is being communicated (*qua* contents, in the sense of obvious effect or object), but rather how are these modes of production and communication themselves conditioned by and conditioning of social relations, cultural values, and conceptual categories? It's not so much that "mediation is the message" (which at least has the benefit of not reifying mediation as "media"), but rather that "'mediation is the message' is itself a mediated message (about mediation)."

Similarly, one can also study intra-domain mediation: take what at first seems to be a single or simple domain and ask how it is internally mediated. For example, rather than talk about the mediating relations between language and economy, ask about the ways in which language self-mediates. As an instance of this, as noted in the last section, linguistic anthropology has taken up as its foundational axiom Bourdieu's (1977 [1972]) famous claim that practice (*qua* parole) mediates both structure (*qua* langue) and ideology (*qua* langue and parole about langue and parole), which themselves mediate practice. See Table 24.3f.

Crucially, as noted above, all of these issues not only apply to the kinds of social formations we study (and the actors implicated in them), they also apply to the other scholars and scientists who study those social formations. And so linguistic anthropologists are constantly critiquing other analyses of mediation – as undertaken, say, by formal linguists, philosophers, cultural anthropologists, cognitive scientists, their own dissertation advisors, and so forth – as themselves being mediated in precisely the foregoing kinds of ways. See Table 24.3g.[15]

Finally, we can make self-reflexive claims, and thereby ask epistemic-ontological questions, such as: How is our understanding of what domains there are to be mediated, and what kinds of mediating relations there are between them, mediated? See Table 24.3h. Indeed, to even play the mediational game at all, and thereby disclose modes of representation and influence, requires that one have already enclosed two or more domains: here is language and there is culture; or here is economy and there is society; so now let us study their relations. Indeed, in some sense, to find such relations is to dissolve the boundaries between domains. And so the game is often like this: presume a distinction between two domains; find a relation between them; and so propose there is no distinction between two domains, and thus that the original distinction was an illusion or ideology.

24.8 A critique of mediation as critique

To conclude, it should first be emphasized that all the moves detailed above are really a single move, generatively applied: *treat any mediated relatum as a mediating relation*. (Indeed, we might even recast it in Freudian terms: where there is an "it," there "I" should go.) It should also be emphasized that this style of critique resonates with the other key move made by linguistic anthropologists, as described in section 24.2: take any mono-dimensional account and recast it as a multi-dimensional terms, and thereby deliver us from Flatland and lead us to Textureville.

Such moves, however simple (or simple-minded) they may be, seem to provide a huge amount of leverage. In particular, all other moves (made by other disciplines, our colleagues, our teachers, etc.) become both partial (there is some form of mediation they didn't take into account) and reifying (in so doing, they took what was relatively fluid and made it seem fixed, relatively contested and made it seem constant, relatively constructed and made it seem natural, relatively complicated and made it seem simple, relatively partial and made it seem total, relatively textured and made it seem flat).[16] This allows us to almost effortlessly generate an infinite number of critiques (you are not wide enough in your vision), while simultaneously granting some kind of "agency" to the people so studied (they are deeper than you imagined). We thereby grant agency, openness, and creativity to actors in a world that other analysts made seems structured, closed, and predictable.[17] In this way, one can almost feel as if one's work is political, in that it seems to simultaneously unmask villains (other analysts) and liberate victims (those who are so analyzed).

But there is a secondary set of payoffs as well for those who adopt this kind of critique. In particular, to really show a form of mediation (and not just state it) is very difficult work – ask anyone who have ever tried to write a careful descriptive grammar of a language, or provide a careful account of the moves made in a conversation. And so the people who really want to show such things (referred to above as scientists and scholars) by necessity bracket off a whole set of possible mediations. (Indeed, how could they not? Everything mediates everything else at some degree of remove.) And, in so doing, they prime themselves to be critiqued by critical theorists *qua* "meta-mediationalists." Concomitantly, the latter's generative system of meta-mediational critique makes stating complicated claims about mediation incredibly easy, but showing them quite difficult. It simultaneously allows meta-mediationalists to claim that "high-level" mediation is involved in research undertaken by scholars and scientists (themselves trying to show mediation at a "low level"), and protect themselves from return critiques – especially critiques from people who are committed to showing what they state in, say, nomothetic terms. In particular, such claims are often made at a level that's abstract (or vacuous) enough that it's not so much that they cannot be shown to hold, but rather that they cannot be shown to not hold. In this way, the people making such claims never have to defend themselves.[18] In short, one can simultaneously attack others and protect oneself from attack.

All that said, it should be remembered that what is at issue here is not whether some particular claim about mediation is right or wrong. My interest is only in the style of argumentation itself. With such seemingly huge political and epistemic benefits (unmask and liberate, attack and never have to defend), and with essentially minimal costs (it can be learned with a year's worth of introductory graduate courses, summarized in seven pages, and generated with a context-free grammar), it's no wonder linguistic anthropologists have adopted meta-mediationalism as the dominant frame underlying their form of life. And no small worry either.

Notes

1. Note, then, that as used here the term critical theory is meant to include the Frankfurt School (and thus the ideas of scholars like Adorno, Horkheimer, and Benjamin), but also be much wider in scope.
2. This is, of course, a highly schematic summary. With my sincere apologies to the living, and to keep this from being a citation fest, only dead authors are mentioned, or particularly salient edited collections. Chapter 29 of this volume discusses a key part of the first half-century of linguistic anthropology (linguistic relativity) as well as tries to divine a key part of the next half-century of linguistic anthropology (language automata). Many of the other chapters in this volume take up related claims in much greater depth. For example, Chapter 25 by Stasch is particularly salient in highlighting key connections between linguistic anthropology and cultural anthropology, which is the other subdiscipline most heavily indebted to critical theory.
3. There are other failings, in my opinion, but they are not so systematic, and so might simply be listed. For example, via our reliance on practice-theory, we got a blank-slate theory of mind. Via our reliance on Goffman and Bourdieu, we got a dramaturgical (and only a dramaturgical or distinction-oriented) account of the subject: as if actors' main intention is to one-up each other. Via our Saussure-directed uptake of Peirce, we mainly took on iconicity and indexicality of the latter, and forgot all about interpretants (or simplified them as "concepts" and "responses"). Via the critiques of scholars who had simple-minded understandings of language, we keep insisting that language is "material" and "embodied" (as opposed to ideational or enminded), whereas we should have said those are also folk-categories.
4. See the important essays in Mertz and Parmentier (1985) for a different take on this topic.
5. Saussure-like forms of mediation (any particular sign–object relation is mediated by an ensemble of other sign–object relations, insofar as such signs can combine with each other or substitute for each other) are a special case. As are Marx-like forms of mediation, themselves rooted in Aristotle: a relation between people is mediated by a relation between things.
6. It also is fundamentally important for intentional communication, or so-called non-natural meaning (Grice 1989b, 1989c; Sperber and Wilson 1995[1986]; Levinson 2000; Tomasello 2008), but linguistic anthropologists in the critical tradition have not spent much time on this topic.
7. For example, if I believe cats meow and have long whiskers, then I may infer that the animal that just meowed behind the sofa is a cat and also expect that, when it appears, it will have long whiskers.
8. Note that this is not the same as natural meaning versus non-natural meaning, in the usual Gricean way (Kockelman 2011), as the selectional

agencies involved are only sometimes intentional (in human terms), *qua* purposefully expressed for the sake of another's interpretant. (Crucially, the meaning-nn versus meaning-n distinction doesn't really cut it – for the real issue is the degree to which the cause–effect relation becomes a sign–object relation, on what timescale.)

9. These may seem closely related to framing.
10. Other examples include interpretants, themselves signs, which have as their dynamic objects the sign–object relations that gave rise to them. More generally, when one realizes that the sign that stands for the sign–object relation does not have to be of the same domain as the sign in the sign–object relation (*qua* meta-language and language), most semiotic processes turn on precisely this kind of relation.
11. Note, from these examples, how reframings are closely related to embeddings.
12. See, for example, the important early insights of Silverstein (1979, 1981), as well as as subsequent substantial work by scholars such as Gal and Irvine (1995), and Schieffelin *et al.* (1998), inter alia.
13. More generally, this means we can ask questions of the following kind: What are the conditions for, or consequences of, a group being able to signify (or represent to themselves and others) a particular sign–object or condition–consequence relation? That is, how conscious are they of it, and what are some of the roots and fruits of this (lack of) consciousness? Concomitantly, we can ask how accurate (as opposed to distorted) or true (as opposed to false) a representation is (in particular a representation of such condition–consequence relations); and what are some conditions for, and consequences of, this relative accuracy or distortion?
14. Compare naturalization and conventionalization, or downshifting and upshifting, as used by scholars like Parmentier (1994); and compare projection and iconicity, as described above.
15. Indeed, Boas and Sapir were the ur-theorists of this, via alternating sounds. And so, in a sort of Bacon-Marx-Freud tradition, they have taken up these kinds of questions – a kind of canonical nineteenth-century theory of the self and society, sometimes called a "hermeneutics of suspicion."
16. And we have an infinite number of buzzwords to describe this: emergent, fluid, dialogic, relational, partial, underdetermined, interactional, fractal, etc. Crucially, it is also usually fetishizing, in that they project too much causal explanatory power onto the wrong place.
17. For every scholar who does painstaking work to show how complicated the actual theories of mediation really are, and does empirical work to show how subtle the mediation can be, there a dozen other scholars who simply state X is mediated (constructed, emergent, relational, contexted, dialogic, etc.).

18. Phrased another way, because it is truly hard work to not just, say, write a grammar, write an ethnography of a people who use a grammar, write an account of the relation between the two, or between various historical conditions, but to also write an account of the distortions, and an account of the distortions of others who have studied the group, they have more or less given up on correlations of the lower types and focused their efforts on correlations of the higher types.

References

Agha, Asif. 2007. *Language and Social Relations.* Cambridge: Cambridge University Press.
Anscombe, G. E. M. 1957. *Intentions.* Oxford: Blackwell.
Austin, J. L. 2003[1955]. *How to Do Things with Words.* Cambridge: Harvard University Press.
Bacon, Francis 2000[1620]. *The New Organon.* Cambridge: Cambridge University Press.
Bauman, Richard, and Joel Sherzer, eds. 1974. *Explorations in the Ethnography of Speaking.* Cambridge: Cambridge University Press.
Berger, Peter L., and Thomas Luckmann. 1967. *The Social Construction of Reality: A Treatise in the Sociology of Knowledge.* New York: Anchor Books.
Blom, Jan-Peter, and John J. Gumperz. 1972. Social Meanings in Linguistic Structure: Code-switching in Norway. In *Directions in Sociolinguistics*, ed. John J. Gumperz and Dell H. Hymes, 231-56. New York: Holt, Rinehart and Winston.
Boas, F. 1911-. *Handbook of American Indian Languages.* Washington, DC: Bureau of American Ethnology/Smithsonian Institution/Government Printing Office.
  1989a[1889]. On Alternating Sounds. In *Franz Boas Reader*, ed. G. W. Stocking Jr., 72-7. Chicago: Midway Reprints.
  1989b[1910]. Psychological Problems in Anthropology. In *Franz Boas Reader*, ed. G. W. Stocking Jr., 243-54. Chicago: Midway Reprints.
Bourdieu, Pierre. 1977[1972]. *Outline of a Theory of Practice.* Cambridge: Cambridge University Press.
  1984. *Distinction.* Cambridge, MA: Harvard University Press.
Darwin, Charles. 1981[1871]. *The Descent of Man, and Selection in Relation to Sex.* Princeton, NJ: Princeton University Press.
  1965[1872]. *The Expression of the Emotions in Man and Animals.* Chicago: University of Chicago Press.
Enfield, N. J., and Stephen C. Levinson, eds. 2006. *Roots of Human Sociality: Culture, Cognition, and Interaction.* Oxford: Berg.
Foucault, Michel. 1991a[1978]. Politics and the Study of Discourse. In *The Foucault Effect*, ed. Graham Burchell, Colin Gordon, and Peter Miller, 53-72. Chicago: University of Chicago Press.

1991b[1978]. Governmentality. In *The Foucault Effect*, ed. Graham Burchell, Colin Gordon, and Peter Miller, 87-104. Chicago: University of Chicago Press.

Frege, Gottlob. 1997[1892]. On Sinn and Bedeutung. In *The Frege reader*, ed. Michael Beaney, 151-71. Oxford: Blackwell Publishers Ltd.

Freud, Sigmund. 2008[1900]. *The Interpretation of Dreams*. Oxford: Oxford University Press.

Friedrich, Paul. 1986. *The Language Parallax*. Austin: University of Texas Press.

Gal, Susan, and Judith T. Irvine. 1995. The Boundaries of Languages and Disciplines: How ideologies construct difference. *Social Research* 62(4): 967-1001.

Goffman, Erving 1959. *The Presentation of Self in Everyday Life*. New York: Anchor Books, Doubleday.

1964. The Neglected Situation. *American Ethnologist* 66(6): 133-6.

1981. Footing. In *Forms of Talk*, 124-59. Philadelphia: University of Pennsylvania Press.

1983. The Interaction Order. *American Sociological Review* 48(1): 1-17.

Greenberg, Joseph. 1990. *On Language: Selected Writings of Joseph H. Greenberg*. Stanford, CA: Stanford University Press.

Grice, Paul. 1989a. The Causal Theory of Perception. In *Studies in the Ways of Words*, 224-47. Cambridge, MA: Harvard University Press.

1989b. Utterer's Meaning and Intention. In *Studies in the Ways of Words*, 86-116. Cambridge, MA: Harvard University Press.

1989c. Logic and Conversation. In *Studies in the ways of words*, 22-40. Cambridge, MA: Harvard University Press.

Gumperz, John Joseph. 1965. Speech Community. *Encyclopedia of the Social Sciences* 9(3): 382-6.

Hacking, Ian. 1983. *Representing and Intervening*. Cambridge, MA: Harvard University Press.

Halliday, M.A.K., and Ruqaiya Hasan. 1976. *Cohesion in English*. London: Longman.

Haugeland, John. 1998. The Intentionality All-Stars. In *Having Thought: Essays in the Metaphysics of Mind*, 127-70. Cambridge, MA: Harvard University Press.

Hegel, Georg Wilhelm Friedrich. 1977[1807]. *Phenomenology of Spirit*. Oxford: Oxford University Press.

Heidegger, Martin. 1996[1927]. *Being and Time*. Albany: State University of New York Press.

Hobbes, E. 1994[1651]. *Leviathan*. Indianapolis, IN: Hackett.

Hymes, Dell. 1962. The Ethnography of Speaking. In *Anthropology and human Behavior*, ed. T. Gladwell and W. Sturtevant, 13-53. Washington, DC: Anthropological Society of Washington.

1966. Two Types of Linguistic Relativity. In *Sociolinguistics*, ed. W. Bright, 114-58. The Hague: Mouton.

Jakobson, Roman. 1990a. The Speech Event and the Functions of Language. In *On Language*, ed. L. R. Waugh and M. Monville-Burston, 69–79. Cambridge, MA: Harvard University Press.

1990b. Shifters and Verbal Categories. In *On Language*, ed. L. R. Waugh and M. Monville-Burston, 386–92. Cambridge, MA: Harvard University Press.

Kant, Immanuel. 1964[1781]. *Critique of Pure Reason*. New York: St. Martin's Press.

Kockelman, Paul. 2005. The Semiotic Stance. *Semiotica* 157: 233–304.

2007. Agency: The relation between meaning, power, and knowledge. *Current Anthropology* 483: 375–401.

2010. Enemies, Parasites, and Noise: How to take up residence in a system without becoming a term in it. *Journal of Linguistic Anthropology* 20(2): 406–21.

2011. Biosemiosis, Technocognition, and Sociogenesis: Selection and Significance in a Multiverse of Sieving and Serendipity. *Current Anthropology* 52(5): 711–39.

2012. *Agent, Person, Subject, Self: A Theory of Ontology, Interaction and Infrastructure*. Oxford: Oxford University Press.

Labov, William. 2001. *Principles of Linguistic Change: Social Factors*. New York: Blackwell.

Latour, Bruno. 2007. *Reassembling the Social*. Oxford: Oxford University Press.

Levinson, S. C. 1983. *Pragmatics*. Cambridge: Cambridge University Press.

2000. *Presumptive Meanings: The Theory of Generalized Implicature*. Cambridge, MA: MIT Press.

Lucy, John A. 1992a. *Grammatical Categories and Cognition*. Cambridge: Cambridge University Press.

1992b. *Linguistic Relativity*. Cambridge: Cambridge University Press.

1993. *Reflexive Language: Reported Speech and Metapragmatics*. Cambridge: Cambridge University Press.

Malinowski, Bronisław. 1936. The Problem of Meaning in Primitive Languages. In *The Meaning of Meaning*, ed. C. K. Ogden and A. I. Richards, 296–336. New York: Harcourt, Brace.

Marx, Karl. 1967[1867]. *Capital*, Vol. 1. New York: International Publishers.

1978[1845]. The German Ideology. In *The Marx-Engels Reader*, ed. Robert C. Tucker, 2nd ed., 146–200. New York: Norton.

McLuhan, Marshall. 1994[1964]. *Understanding Media*. Cambridge, MA: MIT Press.

Mead, George Herbert. 1934. *Mind, Self, and Society*. Chicago: University of Chicago Press.

Mertz, Elizabeth, and Richard Parmentier, eds. 1985. *Semiotic Mediation: Sociocultural and Psychological Perspectives*. New York: Academic Press.

Nietzsche, Friedrich. 1989[1887]. *The Genealogy of Morals and Ecce Homo*. New York: Vintage.

Ortner, Sherry. 1984. Theory in Anthropology Since the Sixties. *Comparative Studies in Society and History* 26(1): 126-66.
Parmentier, Richard J. 1994. *Signs in Society: Studies in Semiotic Anthropology*. Bloomington: Indiana University Press.
Peirce, Charles S. 1955. Logic as Semiotic: The theory of signs. In *Philosophical Writings of Peirce*, ed. Justus Buchler, 98-119. New York: Dover.
⎯⎯⎯ 1992[1868]. On a New List of Categories. In *The Essential Peirce*, Vol. 1: *1867-1893*, ed. Nathan Houser and Christian Kloesel, 1-10. Bloomington: Indiana University Press.
⎯⎯⎯ 1998[1907]. Pragmatism. In *The Essential Peirce*, Vol. 2: *1883-1913*, ed. Nathan Houser and Christian Kloesel, 398-433. Bloomington: Indiana University Press.
Putnam, Hilary. 1975. The Meaning of "Meaning". In *Philosophical Papers: Mind, Language and Reality*, Vol. 2, 215-71. Cambridge: Cambridge University Press.
Sahlins, Marshall. 1978. *Culture and Practice Reason*. Chicago: University of Chicago Press.
Sapir, Edward. 1985[1927]. The Unconscious Patterning of Behavior in Society. In *Selected Writings in Language, Culture, and Personality*, ed. David G. Mandelbaum, 544-59. Berkeley: University of California Press.
Saussure, Ferdinand de. 1983[1916]. *Course in General Linguistics*. La Salle, IL: Open Court Press.
Schieffelin, Bambi B., and Elinor Ochs, eds. 1986. *Language Socialization across Cultures*. Cambridge: Cambridge University Press.
Schieffelin, B., K.A. Woolard, and P.V. Kroskrity, eds. 1998. *Language Ideologies: Practice and Theory*. Oxford: Oxford University Press.
Searle, John. 1983. *Intentionality*. Cambridge: Cambridge University Press.
Serres, Michel. 2007[1980]. *The Parasite*. Minneapolis: University of Minnesota Press.
Silverstein, Michael. 1979. Language Structure and Linguistic Ideology. In *The Elements: A Parasession on Linguistic Units and Levels*, ed. R. Cline, W. Hanks, and C. Hofbauer, 193-247. Chicago: Chicago Linguistic Society.
⎯⎯⎯ 1981. *The Limits of Awareness*. Sociolinguistic Working Paper 84. Austin: Southwest Educational Development Laboratory,.
⎯⎯⎯ 1995[1976]. Shifters, Linguistic Categories, and Cultural Description. In *Language, Culture, and Society: A Book of Readings*, ed. Ben G. Blount, 187-221. Prospect Heights, IL: Waveland Press.
Silverstein, Michael, and Greg Urban. 1996. *Natural Histories of Discourse*. Chicago: University of Chicago Press.
Sperber, Dan, and Deidre Wilson. 1995[1986]. *Relevance: Communication and Cognition*. 2nd ed. Cambridge: Harvard University Press.
Tomasello, Michael. 2008. *Origins of Human Communication*. Cambridge, MA: MIT Press.
Veblen, Thorstein. 1971[1899]. *The Theory of the Leisure Cass*. New York: Free Press.

Vygotsky, L. S. 1978. *Mind and Society: The Development of Higher Psychological Processes*. Cambridge, MA: Harvard University Press.
Weber, Max. 1949[1904]. *The Methodology of the Social Sciences*. New York: Free Press.
　1978. *Economy and Society*, Vol. 1. Berkeley: University of California Press.
Whorf, B. L. 1956a. The Relation of Habitual Thought and Behavior to Language. In *Language, Thought, and Reality: Selected Writings of Benjamin Lee Whorf*, ed. John B. Carroll, 134–59. Cambridge, MA: MIT Press.
　1956b. Grammatical Categories. In *Language, Thought, and Reality: Selected Writings of Benjamin Lee Whorf*, ed. John B. Carroll, 87–101. Cambridge, MA: MIT Press.

25

Linguistic anthropology and sociocultural anthropology

Rupert Stasch

In an ideal world, the short version of this chapter could be, "Linguistic and sociocultural anthropology are the same thing." To analyze human diversity and sociocultural process is necessarily to analyze language, and vice versa, such that the two fields are by definition historically and intellectually coextensive. To say anything more than "they are the same" is to trivialize the common ground of these intellectual endeavors by underplaying its obviousness.

Yet in actual scholarly practice today, the two fields are not the same. Any close examination reveals that linguistic anthropology is set off from sociocultural anthropology by its distinct subject matter, methods, body of theory, and twentieth-century history. There are reasons, though, why any attempted overview of the relation between sociocultural and linguistic anthropology as distinct fields is bound to be inaccurate. Sociocultural anthropology is large and fractured. Linguistic anthropology is smaller but also heterogeneous, especially the more account is taken of its areas of exchange with language-focused disciplines beyond anthropology. Forms of intellectual distance within each of the two exceed the distance between them, and their internal heterogeneity prevents their cross-relations from stabilizing into one shape. In this kind of situation, it is not clear that coming at matters from the direction of a question about the relation between subdisciplines is even the right thing to do. The "and" in a title like "Linguistic anthropology and sociocultural anthropology" might seem innocent enough, but can easily serve as naturalizing cover for agendas of compulsory unification, or desire for one's own value and the other's reform, that may hinder rather than help clarity of vision about what is actually most intellectually important.

I rehearse these disclaimers in order that skepticism might aid realism. The statements above even in their negative character are already the beginnings of a description of the two fields' relation, and they make clear that my more positive statements to follow are ideal typifications and are necessarily partial. Many other chapters of this volume chart areas of interface between linguistic and sociocultural anthropology in more focused ways, and can be read as complements or counterpoints to my account.

I begin by outlining the general convergence of theoretical sensibilities between linguistic anthropology and sociocultural anthropology over the last four decades. Yet this general convergence has not resulted in a dense unity of conversation, and so I also explore some reasons for the fields' separateness, including imaginative limitations to the ideas of "representation" held by sociocultural anthropologists, and limitations on linguistic anthropologists' valuing of the ethnographic monograph. I then open up one important question at the heart of these two fields' relation, namely the issue of distinctions and interconnections between linguistic and more-than-linguistic layers of human worlds. I survey a few ways anthropologists today join together linguistic and more-than-linguistic materials theoretically. By way of a few ethnographic sketches, I advocate greater recognition of unity of figurational processes across human lifeworlds. I suggest this unity can be productively articulated at least in an initial way by extending the concepts of indexicality and iconicity more widely than is commonly done.

25.1 Theoretical convergences

Linguistic anthropology's special intellectual trajectory has been defined by the conjoining of two prime commitments, loosely corresponding to the two elements of its name. On the one hand, there is the "linguistic," meaning intense empirical attention to linguistic form and the total linguistic medium. This narrowing of subject matter is also a deepening. Close attention to the topic of language leads to perceptions of vast complexity and differentiation across the constituent areas and levels of language in human life. Specifically, this focus has meant that linguistic anthropology has been deeply infused by a core understanding of human worlds as composed of processes of representation, or semiotic mediation. Consider this image from non-anthropologist Roland Barthes:

> If I am in a car and I look at the scenery through the window, I can at will focus on the scenery or on the window-pane. At one moment I grasp the presence of the glass and the distance of the landscape; at another, on the contrary, the transparency of the glass and the depth of the landscape; but the result of this alternation is constant: the glass is at once present and empty to me, and the landscape unreal and full. The same thing occurs in the mythical signifier: its form is empty but present, its meaning absent but full. To wonder at this contradiction I must voluntarily interrupt this turnstile of form and meaning, I must focus on each separately, and apply to myth a static method of deciphering, in short, I must go against its own

dynamics: to sum up, I must pass from the state of reader to that of mythologist. (1972: 123-4)

Barthes's allegory can be aptly bent to a description of linguistic anthropology as well. Through commitment to the linguistic medium as a subject matter, linguistic anthropologists tend more than other types to be in continuous intellectual touch with a kind of "glass" and its many properties and modes of organization, and in continuous intellectual touch with a problematic of the glass's relations to the diverse "landscapes" it mediates.

On the other hand, there is also the "anthropology," here meaning a deep commitment to studying language not as an academic might wish or imagine it to be, but as it actually exists, for all humans, in all ways. This empirical commitment to language's *actuality* has driven linguistic anthropologists toward perceptiveness about use, as an irreducible site of language's organization. Reflexive orientations to use, encodings of use as an integral element of linguistic structure, ambiguities and instabilities of use, and all other aspects of "pragmatics" broadly conceived are major aspects of the chemical makeup and naked-eye properties of the "glass" itself. Different facets of use are integral, systematic elements in the "turnstile" of semiotic mediation that linguistic anthropologists "interrupt" in their work of documentation and interpretation. They have developed an immense network of specific findings and theoretical categories adapted to the task of giving empirically serious accounts of pragmatics as an integral site of what is systematic and consequential in language.

This network of findings and categories is broadly convergent with the main shifts in the theoretical sensibilities of many sociocultural anthropologists since at least the 1980s (see also Silverstein 2005). A common refrain in anthropology across this period has been disavowal of models of cultural order as existing independently of practical activity, time, power, materiality, and the subjectivity or interest of specific persons. This is often understood as a rejection of the approach to cultural order articulated by Claude Lévi-Strauss, whose ideas were influenced by Saussure's conception of *langue* as separable from *parole*. The turn is also often understood as a rejection of approaches set out by Clifford Geertz or David Schneider, who are taken to have followed Talcott Parsons in separating and hypostatizing the order of "symbols," in a manner parallel to the Saussurean divide. Even while many anthropologists were increasingly denouncing models of culture as a coherent body of norms and symbols, though, there was also a partial internationalization of the hitherto American and French anthropological concern with recognizing culture, consciousness, or representations as importantly constitutive of human institutions and lives, an internationalization again seemingly convergent with linguistic anthropology's grounding in an idea of irreducible semiotic mediation.

To give some specificity to my claim of convergence, let me outline a little-known core argument of Roy Wagner's *The Invention of Culture* (1981 [1975]), a prominent work of sociocultural anthropology from early in the transition.[1] Wagner's book does for "culture" as a body of norms and conventions what Lévi-Strauss (1962) had done for "totemism," and what Schneider in *American Kinship* (1980[1968]) and elsewhere was doing for "kinship" as genealogy: he argues that the idea of "culture" as a body of conventions is the selective and projective preoccupation of a particular kind of people (Wagner 1981[1975]: 28–9, 36, 41, 87–8). Wagner starts from a broadly Kantian and symbolic anthropological premise that human action and perception is a process of fitting existing "symbolic elements" to particular objects and situations (39). But he theorizes this process in a way that does not accord primacy or stability to the existing elements, centering his account instead on the fitting itself, and relativizing the pre-existing symbolic elements as themselves nodes in a network of ongoing processes of fitting and context-connecting. Thus he describes all activity as a kind of "culture shock" (9, 35), or "metaphorization." Even something like a routine application of a kinship term to a relative, on this account, is an instance of the ceaseless flow of incommensurate fitting. The constant shock of something unassimilably new generated in metaphoric extension of concept to object – something not quite concept, not quite object – is what Wagner calls "differentiation" or "invention" (43). Such a process, he suggests, is accompanied by a social pull of the communication and stabilization of new metaphors of linked concept and object, a counterpart process he calls "collectivization" or "convention" (itself an innovatory, inventive culture shock in its own way). He further argues that Westerners tend on the whole to take invention for granted, and work hard to accomplish convention. This is the distribution of ideological hiding and attention generating the received anthropological and popular idea of "culture." People like Daribi of New Guinea, by contrast, as an overall tendency take convention for granted and work hard to accomplish "differentiating symbolization," or invention (49, 58–9). All humans, in this account, are involved in the same dialectic. They vary in which part of the dialectic they focus on ideologically, and which part they "mask," meaning they precipitate it out in the shadows of inattention.

Leaving aside Wagner's interest in a typological distinction between two whole kinds of cultural emphases, the overall dialectic he describes has strong affinities to the project of linguistic anthropology. His account decenters culture as norm or convention, puts activity and temporality on a symmetric and mutually internal footing with conventions, and describes a process of systematic intermediation between norm and activity. Wagner envisions a non-reduction of signification's here-and-now that is broadly similar to the non-reduction advocated by linguistic anthropologists. For example, specific explanatory potentials of his model anticipate closely the idea of a dialectic of stabilized norm and tropic innovation on the norm that is central to Agha's (2007) important account of register formation and the linguistic field generally.

The affinities of Wagner's ideas to linguistic anthropology's guiding conception of pragmatic semiosis are all the more remarkable given the influence of Schneider on Wagner's thought, the rarity of direct uptake of the above-sketched parts of *The Invention of Culture* in other anthropologists' work, and the limited terminological commensurability between Wagner and linguistic anthropologists (though see Parmentier 1994: 101–24). To the extent there was direct conversational crossover between sociocultural and linguistic anthropology around conceptualizing practical activity as bearing an internal and symmetric relation to the normed aspect of social life and cultural categorization, this crossover has tended to be passing, and to center on loose consideration of work by third-party figures like Pierre Bourdieu, Mikhail Bakhtin, John Austin, Judith Butler, Jacques Derrida, Michel Foucault, Ben Anderson, and Bruno Latour, with the third-party figures themselves being evaluated and understood in quite different ways by scholars in the two subfields. My point in bringing up Wagner is to suggest that the broader convergence of theoretical orientations was structured less by direct interchange than by common goals of empirical adequacy in relation to similar fieldwork experiences and intellectual objects, as well as by shared post-1968 turns of broad intellectual disposition.

Another area where we can see the fields moving convergently is the entire opening of cultural anthropology to history in the 1980s, and the common integration of historical analysis into ethnographic monographs by the 1990s. The general anthropological sensibility that emerged across this time holds that there is of course a temporality to culture, and that the systematicity of social worlds is one and the same with the making of intertemporal connections and breaks. This idea is present germinally also in linguistic anthropology's interest in sign use as irreducibly foundational to language's systematicity and consequentiality.

25.2 Limits on integration

For all these predispositions toward common cause, sociocultural and linguistic anthropologists today do not densely adopt each other's terms, questions, and insights.[2] Probably the strongest curb on their integration is a large proportion of sociocultural anthropologists' indifference or antipathy toward conceiving their subject matter as consisting of processes of *representation* or *meaning*. This stance is structured by the enduring folk ideology that a representation is a secondary depiction, in an unreal ontological domain, of a pre-existing real entity that exists outside the domain of representations. Under the terms of this ideology, overenthusiastic study of representations is an error of idealism, when anthropology actually needs to study the real as the main part of its subject. If this preconception is traded for a wider sense of representation as simply "making present," then the vocabulary of representation becomes a powerful analytic for talking about sociocultural connectivity in human worlds generally, and a powerful description of everything anthropology is about. A bodily action or feeling, a sensory perception, a social institution or event, an object of collective or personal attention: these elements of human life are at once themselves *and* they make present more than themselves to the people involved. Some of these connectivities exist in ways relatively overtly felt, and some are lived in tacit or fetishized modes. Anthropologists need a framework for thinking openly about these vast networks of connectivity. The "making present" notion does not prejudge that a representation is secondary in reality to what it represents, that the effect of "making present" is one-directional, or that representation and represented are of different ontological orders. Under this construal, a linkage of causality is a representation. Representations themselves may be *more* real than what they represent, or equiprimordial in level of reality. Representations may causally bring what they represent into real existence, as well as the reverse.

Why should anthropologists bother approaching their subject in these terms? Because to do otherwise is to miss the anthropological point itself, the point of directly naming and describing the historical, cultural, and social specificity of how elements in people's lives are connected with each other. In any human process, there are deeply figural, semiotic organizations to the real and causal. Yet while the defining subject matter of linguistic anthropology can be described as "pragmatic semiosis," a lot of sociocultural anthropologists find very recognizable the "pragmatics" but not the "semiosis." (To linguistic anthropologists, though, having to imagine "pragmatics" distinct from "semiosis" would be like trying to imagine the part of snow that isn't water.) Reification of "practice" as a defining object leaves sociocultural anthropology gravitating toward nominalism, or toward functionalism organized around a tacit universal idea of rational choice or power-seeking.

On a more prosaic but also fateful level, another curb on integration between linguistic and sociocultural anthropology has been a proportional decline in sociocultural anthropologists' engagement with linguistic diversity, with language learning, and with fieldwork in a language other than an international or national lingua franca. Conversely, linguistic anthropologists' commitments to transcription-based argument, and their elaboration of technical vocabularies for specific descriptive and interpretive tasks, have made some of their scholarship alien to outsiders.

Enduring distance between the two fields is also notably due to differences in commitment to the genre of the book-length ethnography. Linguistic anthropology thrives largely as a field of articles, edited collections, and thematic journal issues. Many linguistic anthropologists have labored mightily to produce monographs, and it would be easy to list right away a hundred important and high-quality ethnographies by linguistic anthropologists. However, this genre does not hold among linguistic anthropologists the singular status of *exemplarity* that it has among sociocultural anthropologists, whose recent culture-phobia has not lessened the place of ethnographic monographs as their field's gold standard. Ethnographies that succeed in reshaping readers' knowledge continue to be ones organized as a layering together of different interconnected facts, and ones that describe their empirical topic as something systematic – even if emergently, processually, or contradictorily so.[3] A book-sized canvas subjects authors to problems of textual organization, conceptual and empirical proportion, and text-to-topic analogy that do not arise in the same way in articles. It is partly by elevating the essay as their mainstay that linguistic anthropologists have developed such high standards of precise empirical and theoretical identification, dissection, and reconstruction of topics. This same commitment lessens the immediately recognizable relevance of their core conversations to sociocultural anthropologists, whose routine largest objects of study often hold something closer to their pretheoretical shape across the anthropological process than is the case in work that does not reassemble its fragments, or reassembles them in a heavily theory-displaced manner.

25.3 Language and more-than-language

The points set out in the previous section, it may accurately be felt, are in a mode of disciplinary sportscasting that dances around the edges of certain intellectual problems without getting to their heart. What are we really wishing to talk about if we raise the issue of the relation of linguistic and sociocultural anthropology? One promising possibility for getting closer to the kernel of the issue is to come at it from a linked but different question, that of the relation between language and more-than-language as subjects of anthropological analysis.[4] The boundaries between language and non-language are not definitional of the difference between linguistic and sociocultural anthropology, since many linguistic anthropologists give serious weight to study of extralinguistic levels of people's lives, and since most sociocultural anthropologists take aspects of language as major parts of their subject. However, there are differences of proportion between the fields on this measure. More to the point, the common goal of both fields is to know and state accurately the shape of some portion of human reality, a goal which unquestionably involves somewhere at its center problems of the makeup and effects of linguistic processes and more-than-linguistic processes, and problems of the makeup and effects of interrelations between these.

The linguistic and extralinguistic layers of human lives are probably more like each other and more interdependent than current writing of linguistic and sociocultural anthropologists generally gets across. A fundamental anthropological task is to grasp the deeply *figurational* make-up of such levels of life as geography, embodiment, kinship, gender, social stratification, vision, and temporality, alongside the deeply *figurational* make-up of linguistic pragmatics. By "figurational" I mean that a given form or act in human life is not self-contained, self-same, or natural, but semiotic. The form or act is defined and supported by concepts, understandings, and other forms or acts in other layers of life, and it defines and supports them in turn.

How to organize an approach to the vast connectivities of this kind constituting a lifeworld or a social process? One option worth exploring is to scaffold outward from the analytic categories "indexicality" and "iconicity" as these have been developed in linguistic anthropology, drawing on their basic definitions by Peirce (1955) as respectively a making-present built on a notion of spatiotemporal or causal contiguity, and a making-present built on a notion of likeness. Michael Silverstein's classic essay "Shifters, Linguistic Categories, and Cultural Description" (1976) did much to launch and organize the investigation of *indexicality* as a mode of linguistic meaning. However, this article was also written against a background of widespread interest in modeling cultural analysis on analysis of language. In making the case for a reorientation of work on language to center on indexicality-focused processes of meaning alongside lexico-grammatical ones, he also suggested that it was this other face of linguistic meaning that was most relevant to theorizing culture in general (e.g., p. 54). Arguably, a sociocultural anthropology modeled on the implications of this point about linguistic meaning has yet to take explicit shape, even though other paradigms of cultural analysis built on the lexico-grammatical metaphor have certainly waned.

At least two shifts would be required for the full emergence of such an anthropology. First, we would need to explore more ambitiously than has so far been addressed the full depth of the symbolic constitution what are experienced as naturally indexical and iconic relations of making-present. Second, we would also need to explore more ambitiously the full reach of sociocultural levels at which processes of indexicality and iconicity take place. The first of these has been a concern of several interrelated linguistic anthropological categories and bodies of analysis, including work on linguistic ideologies (Schieffelin *et al*. 1998; Kroskrity 2000), on "metapragmatics" (linguistic signs and actions that reflexively portray, shape, and construe sign use itself, as per Silverstein 1998: 128 and other discussions), on the processual tiering of multiple orders of indexicality in single sign complexes (e.g., Ochs 1992; Hill 1998; Graham 2002; Silverstein 2003), on register formation as being constituted by a reflexive model or idea of the register (Agha 2007), and on the Jakobsonian poetic force of the coordinated textuality of mutually resonant sign processes across different surfaces and layers of a sign complex (e.g., Caton 1986; Stasch 2011, 2013).

The second shift of taking the explicit theoretical conversation about indexical and iconic figuration beyond linguistic pragmatics into the full expanse of the sociocultural field is also something being initiated through the idea of linguistic or semiotic ideologies, through calls to use the category of indexicality to integrate analysis of speech in a wider field of material sign processes (Irvine 1989; Keane 2003; Stasch 2003a; Agha 2007; Manning 2012: 1–29; Hull 2012, Ochs 2012), and through work on "multimodal" aspects of language use charting how the efficacy of linguistic signs is wrapped up in their coordination with gesture, sight, and other communicative channels (Stivers and Sidnell 2005; Streeck *et al.* 2011). For example, in one well-known charter passage on the topic of linguistic ideologies, Woolard writes:

> Ideologies of language are not about language alone. Rather, they envision and enact ties of language to identity, to aesthetics, to morality, and to epistemology. Through such linkages, they underpin not only linguistic form and use but also the very notion of the person and the social group, as well as such fundamental social institutions as religious ritual, child socialization, gender relations, the nation-state, schooling, and law.
>
> (1998: 3)

A particularly frequent finding pursued by scholars of linguistic ideology is that reflexive sensibilities about language are often sites for the making or reconstruction of stratification and political inequality in social relations generally.

While indexicality is the kind of sign relation that has featured most regularly in linguistic anthropologists' work and has been an important category for linking linguistic orders to more-than-linguistic ones, engagement with the additional idea of "iconicity" is an important possible step toward a more fully elaborated account of semiosis and pragmatic figuration across the boundary zones of language and non-language. One noteworthy contribution from the linguistic ideology literature in this vein has been Irvine and Gal's (2000) concern with "iconization," which they identify as one of three main processes in how linguistic ideologies create sociocultural difference. The term "iconization" designates a process in which actors take up certain linguistic forms as feeling like the very image of the human types and relations of difference those forms are indexically linked to. Relations of difference and evaluation are naturalized, through being reflected on multiple surfaces of an overall world, including the surface of specific highly ideologized linguistic features. On this broad level, this notion of iconization thus tends in the direction of the vision of cross-connection between layers of life described incidentally, for example, by Bourdieu in the midst of an explication of his well-known ideas about *habitus* and material culture:

The mind born of the world of objects does not rise as a subjectivity confronting an objectivity: the objective universe is made up of objects which are the product of objectifying operations structured according to the very structures which the mind applies to it. The mind is a metaphor of the world of objects which is itself but an endless circle of mutually reflecting metaphors. (Bourdieu 1977: 91)

The approach also aligns with Munn's (1986: 17, 74, 121) theorization of sensory qualities or sensory objects that causally result from some chain of activities (in other words, are indexically linked to those preceding activities) as further coming to be experienced as the very iconic likeness and image of those activities, with this feeling of likeness being central to the objects' overall symbolic force. To go further in describing the vast sweep of ties of indexical and iconic figuration across different media and dimensions of a human world requires the further elaboration of a crucial step that runs contrary to popular thought about symbolic likeness: namely, the step of understanding with respect to iconicity that a feeling of likeness is generally not natural but cultural. Iconic representations create the idea of the presence, shape, or character of what they represent, as often as they match their represented object in its character as a pre-existing presence. These points are parallel to linguistic anthropology's well-established understandings of indexicality as structured by circulating ideologies and sensibilities of communities of interpretation and understanding of linguistic forms as creating indexical signifieds like politeness, a hearer role, or gender qualities as often as conforming to previously existing conditions.

25.4 Indexical and iconic figuration across the lifeworld

My claim that lifeworlds are composed of vast networks of pragmatic figuration across and within all different layers of people's presence is too large to substantiate in any serious way here. But to make the terms of the claim at least a bit more concrete, let me give an illustrative example drawn from one narrow area of my own research with Korowai of West Papua, Indonesia, before then ranging across some cases from other authors' work.

The Korowai illustration I have in mind is interactional avoidance between mothers-in-law and sons-in-law. Avoiding pairs stay separate in several media at once: they do not utter each other's names, they do not refer to each other in the singular (see Rumsey, this volume, Chapter 16), they do not touch each other's bodies, they do not eat from the same food bodies, they do not catch sight of each other, and they do not relate sexually. (This last avoidance is so strong that it is generally unspoken, in contrast to the explicitness of the others.) There is little that naturally links this set of action-types. But the very fact that Korowai draw them together as a unitary suite of practices upheld by participants in a single relation suggests the strong presence of a cultural, metapragmatic understanding of these several different actions of contact as densely indexical and iconic of each other. Violation of name avoidance in particular is expected to result in bodily puncture by small sharp tree stumps or by insects, a sanction that further suggests the operation of a broader figure of transgressively impinging "touch" cutting across the whole set. The culturally elaborated indexical iconicity extends in turn to the practices' effects of creating an overall social quality of the mother-in-law relation's abstractness, importance, and constancy of presence in the lives of its protagonists. Here the concrete interactional practices are in a relation of mutual making-present with a wider *moral* sense of the mother-in-law tie as a link of obligation and beholdenness, at the level of the man's overall intrusion into the woman's life and her bond with her daughter. For Korowai, there is an overtly performative character to this fabric of indexical iconicities across person reference, touch, taste, sight, sex, and kinship morality. Persons may differently define themselves and their alters *as* mother-in-law or son-in-law through hamming up their avoidance in specific channels, scaling it back, deliberately transgressing it, or agreeing not to do it at all (Stasch 2003b).

To open up further the sense of what range of layers of human presence would need to be considered in close theoretical symmetry with language, another medium it is appropriate to draw into discussion is space on a wider scale than the body alone, including specifically landscape and people's activities on it. The semiotics of space and landscape is by now the subject of a sizable literature. Given the special significance I have claimed earlier for the ethnographic monograph, I will approach the topic via the example of a work in this genre, Anand Pandian's *Crooked Stalks: Cultivating Virtue in South India* (2009). Pandian's study centers on the historically stigmatized caste category of Kallars (lit. 'thieves') in a region of Tamil Nadu they initially migrated into just over a century ago, amidst colonial projects of their criminalization, surveillance, and reform. The book charts a pervasive figurative process in the lives of Kallar and other people in this region, in which they map between qualities of landscape (or labor on it) and humans' interior ethical character. This core pattern of intermediation between landscape and ethics is further indissociable from history, and the complicated inheritances of forgotten or submerged past events and conditions within contemporary life. The intermediation of land, ethics, and history is indissociable also from structures of social stratification, such as the troubled position of the category "Kallar" itself as an object of others' evaluative stereotypy but also as a self-affirmed identity. Links between these different layers of the lifeworld do not fall out in one specific way. In the domain of ethics, Pandian describes certain qualities and their opposites as being held up as simultaneous virtues.

Landscape, history, and ethical subjectivities of single groups or persons are each lacerated by contradictions and unreduced ambivalences. But these tensions unfold within an overall pattern of densely indexical and iconic interplay between landscape, categories of human labor on it, a historical inheritance of colonial governance, and the subjectivity of moral striving by concrete persons.

One power of space and landscape is its frequent quality of givenness, and of filling and exceeding actors' sensory surroundings (as well as being intimately known or remade by those actors). In this respect, the experience of landscape probably works allegorically as a deep indexical icon of our conditions of living in culture and history generally (Stasch 2013: 567).[5] An underexamined problem is that of partial parallels between the organization of shifters as linguistic signs charted by Benveniste, Jakobson, and Silverstein, and the more-than-linguistic organization of humans in relation to land, such as actors' physical position and trajectory of motion on a concrete stretch of land at a certain moment, a relation of ownership, or specific action-types such as cultivation, burial, dwelling, driving, or riding public transit. Pandian does not make speech itself a focus of primary analytic attention as would be the case in linguistic anthropological work (though see for example pp. 50–51), but like many of the best socioculturally oriented ethnographers he is an exceptional *listener*, and brings many features of people's speech through to his readers (see also for example Mines 2005; Vilaça 2010). Many other authors more programmatically and equivalently juxtapose speech and geography as co-enfolding semiotic media, through the interlacing of which the fuller shape of a social world is precipitated (e.g., Hoffman 2008; Hanks 2010; Mueggler 2011).

In my own writing about Korowai, I also have sought to treat indexicalities and iconicities of action in space in a manner interpretively symmetric with how linguistic anthropologists treat indexicalities and iconicities of speech. Specifically, I have sought to show how practices of dispersed living across a patchwork of clan-owned territories is reciprocally figurative with a broad sociopolitical ethos of egalitarianism and autonomy, an epistemology of the opacity of others' minds, and a sense of social relating as a project of making separateness itself a positive basis of social bonds (Stasch 2008; 2009). Specific local actions on the landscape of constructing a feast longhouse and coordinating labor and pleasure around it, for example, are complexly indexical and iconic of diverse layers of wider social space and time, including pragmatic uncertainties of food production and social cooperation faced by the feast participants (Stasch 2003a). In the last thirty years, Korowai have increasingly adopted the alien spatial form of the permanent centralized "village" as a complement to their established practices of dispersed living. As with the old spatial forms, so too the new spatial type is poetically dense in its associations of morality, language, ontology, economy, polity, and history.

Villages are linked to a new ethos of non-violence; to the Indonesian language as an intrusive lingua franca; to the dead and foreigners as radically strange actor types; to rice, clothing, and the idea of securing a livelihood just by purchase of premade consumables with money; and to the Indonesian state, Christian churches staffed by immigrant evangelists, and the social processes of international primitivist tourism. Acts of walking into or out of a village, sleeping in one, building and dwelling in one, or staying away from villages altogether are more than spatial. Such acts are made deeply indexical and iconic of all of these other levels of people's being, as they in turn are deeply indexical and iconic of organizations of space (Stasch 2013).

Historical temporalities are another range of layers composing a lifeworld, which are also deeply semiotic in constitution and merit analysis symmetric with analysis of the semiotic constitution of linguistic pragmatics. One of many excellent studies in this vein is Miyako Inoue's *Vicarious Language: Gender and Linguistic Modernity in Japan* (2006). Inoue's topic is the ideologization of "women's language" across different phases of Japanese modernity since 1880, the practical use of indexical linguistic markers construed and supported by these ideological understandings, and the understandings of the Japanese nation, its economics, and its temporality that are covertly expressed through the figure of a woman speaking what is construed as a self-evidently female register of speech. The discourse about women's language – the typification of the forms by others, for other projects – precedes and calls to life actual use of the forms by women. In the time of Inoue's fieldwork in the 1990s, women directly using the forms were not originary or seamless speakers, but through mockery, switching, and other tropic processes themselves engaged with the stereotypic *figure* of the enregistered feminine speaker: a woman indexically and iconically bearing the burden of a national idea of past order and unity contrasting with the chaotic diversity of the present, and bearing the burden of all the spectral traumas of threat and loss contained in this idea. Embodied realities of gender, the economy of labor and material welfare, the chronotopes of national belonging, and the non-referential femininity-indexing morphemes are each known and made through the others, in a vast web of the figural constitution of a mass society.

A final example I will briefly touch on is the sociocultural processes analyzed in Holly Wardlow's *Wayward Women: Sexuality and Agency in a New Guinea Society* (2006). Like Pandian and Inoue, Wardlow writes about a social position that exists as a cultural figure elaborately stereotyped by other people in movements of censure and fascination, but who also exists as a lived identity occupied from within by concrete persons. Wardlow explores the life histories of Huli "passenger women," who by engaging in transient, monetized sexual liaisons act to remove their sexuality from the dominant understanding of female reproductive potential as a possession of clans, subject to collective exchange and control. This new organization of sexuality, Wardlow documents, is not mainly prompted by economic pressure, but by the women's rage at male relatives' failures to conduct themselves morally in the terms of historical Huli norms. Under new conditions of male labor migration and rising consumerism, men in bridewealth contexts are increasingly focused on cash gain rather than on recognizing obligation and human value, and they fail to stand up appropriately for wives or sisters who suffer assault or mistreatment at the hands of other men.

Huli women's actions and life trajectories are in these ways viscerally real *and* mediations making present other layers of the surrounding social and historical world. The figure of a "passenger woman" and her illicit sexuality is indexically iconic of commoditization, labor migration, and other conditions of new times, and of a break with the model of sexuality being an accessory to reproduction and of women's fecundity being a possessed indexical icon of networks of kinspeople. One pattern Wardlow documents is how much the shape of women's break with the bridewealth system is initially organized by the terms of that system, and by the place of women's sexuality as standing in a link of mutual representation with norms of exchange and kin-group constitution. Wardlow's skills of listening, dialogic renarration, and interpretive contextualization are such that readers can trace in the remarkable life histories she records the coming into speech of forms of experience in some cases initially lived through exchange, kinship, and bodily suffering or attack, and the inchoate taking shape in speech of new sensibilities formerly beyond saying (cf. Ochs 2012).

The preceding brief sketches may only be redescriptions of a kind of connection-making that is by now definitional of ethnography itself. Endless other ethnographies and topics could be revisited in much this vein. And I am applying the categories "indexical" and "iconic" in very general ways, which would quickly need to be replaced by more precise formulations. But the initial framing offered here does accomplish a few things. First, it foregrounds that different levels and elements of a sociocultural world are densely mediative of each other, and that adequately describing such mediative links is a main anthropological task. Second, it gets language and non-language onto the same broad page – even if one point of doing so is then to specify disparities or complementarities between linguistic and nonlinguistic media, substantively or as culturally ideologized (e.g., Keane 1997; Robbins 2001). Across these areas, the terms "indexical" and "iconic" or analogs to them are at best starting points for more exact characterization of *how* one element and another are connected. What specific properties or levels of the elements are connected in these modes, in what more specific ways, and what wider trends of mediational effect do different strands of iconic and indexical linkage together produce? This process of more exact characterization would also involve inquiry into the underlying theoretical notions of "likeness" and "contiguity" as modes of relations, rather than assuming these as a primitive and adequate distinction. But another benefit of using a basic vocabulary of "indexicality" and "iconicity" is that it provides a basis for addressing the often extreme naturalness and persuasiveness of figural processes by which people live their lives. This vocabulary draws attention to the experienced *principle* of the mediational link itself, putting us in a position to understand in turn how forms of contiguity or similarity could be subject to eclipse of any overt sense that a substitution is in play: the signifying element *is* the very thing it makes present. The vocabulary also draws attention to processes of poetic multiplicity of coordinated, coexisting *kinds* of mediational links: indexical in one way and iconic in another way, proliferating at different levels such that people experience an overall movement of naturalized ideas as being reflected on all different surfaces of their experience. And finally, there is the benefit that working with categories like "indexicality" and "iconicity" in analysis of cultural materials tends on a large range of levels to foster making situated activity of persons a central element of what is analyzed.

25.5 Conclusion

The ultimate direction of my account here has been to resist framing the question of the relation of linguistic and sociocultural anthropology as one of disciplines, subdisciplines, intellectual schools, literature reviews, or theory maps, and instead to understand it as a question of ethnography, with ethnographic answers. The real answers would arise through artful conduct of the work of actually seeking to know something about the makeup of people's lives, rather than through direct consideration of the question in its own surface terms. A different, equally valuable approach would be to chart the fields' relations through a close look at specific specialized subjects about which each has recently had convergently or divergently innovative things to say, such as religion or science and technology. I have opted instead to gesture at the kind of openness and wideness of empirical attention that anthropology's interpretive categories are going to have to be adapted to, if we are actually curious about what is behind this particular question of subdisciplinary identity and interrelations.

Notes

1. All points about the *Invention of Culture* set out in the rest of this paragraph are derived from an explication by Joel Robbins in a course we co-taught, except for any mistakes, which are my own responsibility.
2. See Caton (2006: 222–4) for one thoughtful account of this non-integration somewhat different from what I sketch here.

3. For one recent collection examining the changed and ongoing status of systematicity as an anthropological object (though not concerned mainly with the monograph as genre), see Otto and Bubandt (2010).
4. I use the phrase "more-than-language" to emphasize (or leave open the possibility) that what exceeds language might very much have language inside of it, be contained by language, or be otherwise mediated and shaped by language. At the same time, against logocentrism, the expression is meant to acknowledge that there is irreducibly *more* present than language alone. When I use the less awkward forms "nonlinguistic" or "extralinguistic," I intend them as synonyms of "more-than-linguistic."
5. This point is somewhat akin to Lacan's idea that "the best image to sum up the unconscious is Baltimore in the early morning" (1972: 189).

References

Agha, Asif. 2007. *Language and Social Relations*. Cambridge: Cambridge University Press.
Barthes, Roland. 1972. Myth Today. In *Mythologies*, 109–59. New York: Noonday.
Bourdieu, Pierre. 1977. *Outline of a Theory of Practice*. Cambridge: Cambridge University Press.
Caton, Steven C. 1986. Salam Tahiyah: Greetings from the Highlands of Yemen. *American Ethnologist* 13: 290–308.
   2006. Linguistic Ideologies, Text Regulation, and the Question of Post-Structuralism. *Reviews in Anthropology* 35: 221–51.
Graham, Laura. 2002. How Should an Indian Speak? Amazonian Indians and the symbolic politics of language in the global public sphere. In *Indigenous Movements, Self-Representation, and the State in Latin America*, ed. Kay B. Warren and Jean E. Jackson, 181–228. Austin: University of Texas Press.
Hanks, William. 2010. *Converting Words: Maya in the Age of the Cross*. Berkeley: University of California Press.
Hill, Jane. 1998. Language, Race, and White Public Space. *American Anthropologist* 100(3): 680–89.
Hoffman, Katherine. 2008. *We Share Walls: Language, Land, and Gender in Berber Morocco*. Oxford: Blackwell.
Hull, Matthew. 2012. *Government of Paper: The Materiality of Bureaucracy in Urban Pakistan*. Berkeley: University of California Press.
Inoue, Miyako. 2006. *Vicarious Language: Gender and Linguistic Modernity in Japan*. Berkeley: University of California Press.
Irvine, Judith T. 1989. When Talk Isn't Cheap: Language and Political-Economy. *American Ethnologist* 16(2): 248–67.
Irvine, Judith T., and Gal, Susan. 2000. Language Ideology and Linguistic Differentiation. In *Regimes of Language: Ideologies, Polities, and Identities*, ed.

Paul V. Kroskrity, 35–83. Santa Fe, NM: School of American Research Press.

Keane, Webb. 1997. *Signs of Recognition: Powers and Hazards of Representation in an Indonesian Society*. Berkeley: University of California Press.

——— 2003. Semiotics and the Social Analysis of Material Things. *Language and Communication* 23(2–3): 409–25.

Kroskrity, Paul V., ed. 2000. *Regimes of Language: Ideologies, Polities, and Identities*. Santa Fe, NM: School of American Research Press.

Lacan, Jacques. 1972. On Structure as an Inmixing of an Otherness Prerequisite to Any Subject Whatever. In *The Structuralist Controversy: The Languages of Criticism and the Sciences of Man*, ed. Richard Macksey and Eugenio Donato, 186–94. Baltimore, MD: Johns Hopkins Press.

Lévi-Strauss, Claude. 1962. *Le totémisme aujourd'hui*. Paris: Presses Universitaires de France.

Manning, Paul. 2012. *The Semiotics of Drink and Drinking*. London: Continuum.

Mines, Diane P. 2005. *Fierce Gods: Inequality, Ritual, and the Politics of Dignity in a South Indian Village*. Bloomington: Indiana University Press.

Mueggler, Erik. 2011. *The Paper Road: Archive and Experience in the Botanical Exploration of West China and Tibet*. Berkeley: University of California.

Munn, Nancy D. 1986. *The Fame of Gawa: A Symbolic Study of Value Transformation in a Massim (Papua New Guinea) Society*. Cambridge: Cambridge University Press.

Ochs, Elinor. 1992. Indexing gender. In *Rethinking Context: Language as an Interactive Phenomenon*, ed. Alessandro Duranti and Charles Goodwin, 335–58. Cambridge: Cambridge University Press.

——— 2012. Experiencing Language. *Anthropological Theory* 12(2): 142–60.

Otto, Ton, and Nils Bubandt, eds. 2010. *Experiments in Holism: Theory and Practice in Contemporary Anthropology*. Oxford: Wiley-Blackwell.

Pandian, Anand. 2009. *Crooked Stalks: Cultivating Virtue in South India*. Cambridge: Cambridge University Press.

Parmentier, Richard J. 1994. *Signs in Society: Studies in Semiotic Anthropology*. Bloomington: Indiana University Press.

Peirce, Charles S. 1955. Logic as Semiotic: The theory of signs. In *Philosophical Writings of Peirce*, ed. Justus Buchler, 98–119. New York: Dover Publications.

Robbins, Joel. 2001. God is Nothing But Talk: Modernity, language, and prayer in a Papua New Guinea society. *American Anthropologist* 103(4): 901–12.

Schieffelin, Bambi B., Katherine A. Woolard, and Paul V. Kroskrity, eds. 1998. *Language Ideologies: Practice and Theory*. Oxford: Oxford University Press.

Schneider, David M. 1980[1968]. *American Kinship: A Cultural Account*. Chicago: University of Chicago Press.

Silverstein, Michael. 1976. Shifters, Linguistic Categories, and Cultural Description. In *Meaning in Anthropology*, ed. Keith H. Basso and Henry A. Selby, 11–55. Albuquerque: University of New Mexico Press.

1998. The Uses and Utility of Ideology: A Commentary. In *Language Ideologies: Practice and Theory*, ed. Bambi B. Schieffelin, Kathryn A. Woolard, and Paul V. Kroskrity, 123–45. Oxford: Oxford University Press.

2003. Indexical Order and the Dialectics of Sociolinguistic Life. *Language and Communication* 23(3–4): 193–230.

2005. Languages/Cultures are Dead! Long Live the Linguistic-Cultural! In *Unwrapping the Sacred Bundle : Reflections on the Disciplining of Anthropology*, ed. Daniel Segal and Sylvia Yanagisako, 109–25. Durham, NC: Duke University Press.

Stasch, Rupert. 2003a. The Semiotics of World-making in Korowai Feast Longhouses. *Language and Communication* 23(3/4): 359–83.

2003b. Separateness as a Relation: The Iconicity, Univocality, and Creativity of Korowai Mother-in-law Avoidance. *Journal of the Royal Anthropological Institute* 9(2): 311–29.

2008. Knowing Minds is a Matter of Authority: Political dimensions of opacity statements in Korowai moral psychology. *Anthropological Quarterly* 81(2): 443–53.

2009. *Society of Others: Kinship and Mourning in a West Papuan Place*. Berkeley: University of California Press.

2011. Ritual and Oratory Revisited: The semiotics of effective action. *Annual Review of Anthropology* 40: 159–74.

2013. The Poetics of Village Space When Villages are New: Settlement form as history-making in West Papua. *American Ethnologist* 40(3): 555–70.

Stivers, Tanya, and Jack Sidnell. 2005. Introduction: Multimodal Interaction. *Semiotica* 156: 1–20.

Streeck, Jürgen, Charles Goodwin, and Curtis LeBaron, eds. 2011. *Embodied Interaction: Language and Body in the Material World*. Cambridge: Cambridge University Press.

Vilaça, Aparecida. 2010. *Strange Enemies: Indigenous Agency and Scenes of Encounters in Amazonia*. Durham, NC: Duke University Press.

Wagner, Roy. 1981[1975]. *The Invention of Culture*. Chicago: University of Chicago Press.

Wardlow, Holly. 2006. *Wayward Women: Sexuality and Agency in a New Guinea Society*. Berkeley: University of California Press.

Woolard, Kathryn. 1998. Introduction: Language ideology as a field of inquiry. In *Language Ideologies: Practice and Theory*, ed. Bambi B. Schieffelin, Kathryn Woolard, and Paul Kroskrity, 3–47. Oxford: Oxford University Press.

26

Sociolinguistics

Making quantification meaningful

Penelope Eckert

26.1 The origins of sociolinguistics

The foundations of the study of sociolinguistic variation lie in anthropology, in John Gumperz's (1958) study of linguistic diversity in a north Indian village. In a paper entitled "Dialect Differences and Social Stratification in a North Indian Village," Gumperz examined the relation between phonological variation and social boundaries. This analysis was based on a broader ethnographic study, and sought explanations for patterns of differentiation among the population of the village, and particularly the maintenance of a substantial linguistic difference between Sweepers and other castes. The approach in this study reflected the dialectological questions of the time, asking how innovation spreads through populations and across space. Gumperz began with Bloomfield's claim that linguistic influence spreads by virtue of density of contact. Examining a variety of determinants of contact such as residential patterns, social networks, economic activities, and avoidances to maintain ritual purity, he found that the type of interaction was more important than simple density of contact in explaining linguistic distributions. Specifically, he pointed to friendship contacts as the avenue of linguistic influence. This made it clear that the spread of linguistic change is not mechanical, and that linguistic variability is intimately tied to social life. This study was qualitative, comparing general patterns among population groups based on close inspection of the speech of a small number of people, and it established the potential for the quantitative era that was to follow.

William Labov's study of Martha's Vineyard (1963) just a few years later followed on Gumperz's study. Based on a short-term ethnography, Labov uncovered the use of phonological variation to index speakers' stance in a local dispute over mainland incursion on the island economy. The traditional

---

I am grateful to Jack Sidnell for his thoughtfulness and patience, and for his careful reading and penetrating comments on this chapter.

island dialect had a historically conservative centralized [ɐ] pronunciation of the nucleus of the vowels in *price* and *mouth*, while most mainland dialects had a lowered nucleus [a]. For some years, speakers on the island had been following the mainland lowering trend, but with increasing resistance to economic control from the mainland, some Vineyarders were reversing the trend as they reclaimed the centralized island pronunciation. Based on quantitative analysis of Vineyarders' speech in recorded interviews, Labov found a correlation between the use of a centralized nucleus and negative attitudes towards mainland incursion, particularly among the fishing population, who were the people most under threat from the mainland economy. This reclaiming of a traditional local feature amounted to taking a linguistic stance, as a segment of the population laid claim to island authenticity and ownership. In a classic example of what Michael Silverstein some years later (2003) would term *indexical order*, these resisters moved the indexicality of centralization from "island resident" to a particular kind of island resident, redefining local authenticity in the context of a contemporary ideological struggle. If the Vineyard study showed that the kinds of insights Gumperz found in northern India could be nailed down quantitatively, it also showed that variation can carry quite local and timely social meaning.

The field did not follow up on this insight in the years that followed, but pursued quantification in larger numbers, seeking out more abstract patterns across large urban populations. A series of urban survey studies (e.g., Labov 1966; Wolfram 1969; Cedergren 1973; Trudgill 1974; Macaulay 1977; Modaressi 1978) showed broad correlations between macro-sociological categories and linguistic form, most particularly between social class and phonological variables. The roots of the study of variation in dialect geography and sound change kept the focus on the spread of sound change, with the socioeconomic hierarchy a kind of local extension of geographic space. Demographic patterns indicated that change enters communities through working-class networks, and spreads from there through the socioeconomic hierarchy, so that the class hierarchy defines a continuum from the most historically conservative, non-local standard speech in the upper middle class to the most innovative, local, and non-standard in the working class. This continuum was also found to be embedded in the speech of individuals, as each speaker produced more conservative variants when speaking with increasing carefulness. Style in this tradition was defined as the continuum from casual to careful speech, from natural to monitored, from vernacular to standard.

The vernacular played a defining role in the survey tradition. Labov (1972b) defined the vernacular as the speaker's first learned, most automatic speech, and attributed stylistic variation to the suppression of vernacular features to avoid stigma in self-conscious speech. As the direct output of the speakers' linguistic system, Labov characterized the vernacular as language at its most regular, the source of systematic linguistic change,[1] and the classic natural and non-reflexive object of scientific study. The notion of the vernacular thus kept the study of variation within the broader cognitive tradition in linguistics, reducing the explanation for variation to a purely cognitive state, attention paid to speech, and leaving theory-external the actual social practice that brings about this state.[2]

To be sure, there was a general recognition that variation had nuanced indexical value. Peter Trudgill (1972), for example, suggested that middle-class men pick up working-class sound changes by virtue of their *covert prestige*, derived from their association with the masculine working-class qualities of roughness and toughness. This intuition about meaning pointed to the link between macro-sociological categories and personal characteristics, just as Labov's account of (ay)[3] centralization on Martha's Vineyard pointed to the link between macro-geographical categories and local ideology. But these links had no theoretical status since to the extent that the use of variation was passive, it could reflect social address, but could not bring about new meaning.

One might say that the view of language as encoding predefined and enduring messages is what truly separated sociolinguistics in the early years from linguistic anthropology. The reintegration of variation study with anthropology began with an ethnographic turn introduced by Lesley Milroy's social network study (1980) of variation in Belfast. Linking the use of vernacular variants to engagement in local working-class networks, Milroy brought broader agency and the positive value of the vernacular squarely into the picture. A range of ethnographic studies followed, with an emerging focus on the relation between variation and local practice (e.g., Cheshire 1982; Rickford 1986; Eckert 1989, 2000). And while studies of macro-sociological patterns continue to great effect (e.g., Labov 2001; Tagliamonte and D'Arcy 2009), the ethnographic turn has led some to focus on the local construction of meaning in variation. What follows will be an outline of this – commonly referred to as *Third Wave*[4] – perspective in variation studies.

26.2 Quantification and meaning

A sociolinguistic variable is a set of competing linguistic forms (variants), whose patterns of occurrence are socially determined and potentially socially meaningful. The study of patterns calls for quantification, and a focus on meaning raises interesting questions in a basically probabilistic enterprise. Individual phonemes, lasting only milliseconds, pass by too quickly in the stream of speech for the speaker to control them or for the hearer to perceive them on a token-by-token basis. This makes it difficult to think of each use of a variable as controllable or meaningful. Rather, the effect is cumulative, and most likely achieved through a more general articulatory setting than a phoneme-by-phoneme control. Social differences among speakers involve differences in probabilities of occurrence of variants, and associations with predominant users of a particular variant offer meaning potential which can be realized in more intentional and creative uses. Highlighted utterances in discourse are no doubt a major means by which phonological variants come to be imbued with indexical value. Scott Kiesling (2005) has argued that variation always indexes stance, and that long-term patterns result from the accumulation of stances. Kiesling defines stance quite broadly, and indeed inasmuch as social life involves a continual process of recognizing and creating distinctions, all of social life can be seen as positioning oneself with respect to one distinction after another. But the value of talking about stance is greatest in cases where the move in question puts forward an important, possibly controversial, interest at a strategic moment in interaction. Stance-taking moves have the greatest potential for registering the meaning of a variant, since they commonly involve contextual focus. One can imagine that the re-centralization of (ay) in Martha's Vineyard gained its meaning in situations in which the struggle over local power was foregrounded.

Variables above the phonological level are more controllable and prominent, and morphology and syntax gain increased awareness through their greater regulation in education than phonology. Some grammatical variants are sufficiently emblematic to require only one occurrence to create an impression. In most dialects of English, a single occurrence of *ain't* is sufficiently salient to achieve its meaning, and depending on the context, it can be called on to index loutishness, rebelliousness, casualness, and any number of local social affiliations. It can also borrow from higher-level indexicality, as in its use by a dean at a prestigious eastern university, quoted in the *Chronicle of Higher Education*: "Any junior scholar who pays attention to teaching at the expense of research ain't going to get tenure." Geoffrey Nunberg (2002) calls this "linguistic slumming," as the dean's use within otherwise standard speech made it clear that "it was something that should be clear to anyone with an ounce of sense."

The indexical value of a variant, then, emerges in the interplay between the automatic and the intentional, as indexical orders are set down in the links between the abstract and enduring on the one hand (e.g., Vineyard birth, working-class status), and the characterological and timely on the other (e.g., resistance to mainland incursion, roughness and toughness). To the extent that the difference between the mainland and the Vineyard was socially salient, any linguistic features distinguishing the two locations could be called into service as indexical of the terms of difference. The local struggle over mainland control foregrounded the opposition between Vineyarders and mainlanders, and "native" status on Martha's Vineyard became salient in the struggle for self-determination. Political struggles on the island gave it importance, and a new indexical order emerged as the significance of an association became sufficiently consensual across the population to achieve semiotic usefulness. At the same time, the establishment of a new linguistic sign gave life to the political struggle out of which it grew, and no doubt facilitated the forging of alliances and rhetorical moves in the struggle. In this way, variation is not simply a reflection of a static social order but a resource for social change. It is probably not accidental that the residents of Martha's Vineyard reversed the mainland sound change when they did. Ian Hodder (1982) links stylistic moves in material culture to the need for legitimation, and it has been said (e.g., Hoijer 1948) that linguistic change accelerates during times of cultural change. If so, we can see one mechanism in the case of the quiet upheaval that was taking place on Martha's Vineyard at the time of Labov's 1963 study.

One cannot say when an indexical order takes off – one cannot say what meanings were associated earlier with Vineyard and mainland speech and one cannot say where it will lead. But once established, the sign becomes available for reinterpretation, yielding a chain of associations that is not linear, but can develop into an array of signs with competing and ideologically related meanings – an indexical field (Eckert 2008). For example, intervocalic /t/ in American English is normally flapped and final /t/ is normally unreleased or glottaled. Release and aspiration of this phoneme has an indexical field that builds on two aspects of its phonetic make-up. On the one hand, a strongly released stop is a hyperarticulation (a prototypical stop), making it a natural for indexing carefulness, propriety, and articulateness, and its association with British English supports these meanings. On the other hand, a strongly released stop is a fortition (a stronger articulatory gesture), making it also a natural for indexing force. (I will return to the iconic side of variation below.) Each of these can lead to other meanings – e.g., formality on the one hand, anger on the other. Which of the range of possible meanings a particular token has will depend on the larger interactional and stylistic context. For instance, an "angry" stop release may co-occur with a non-standard grammatical feature, whereas a "proper" one will not; an "angry" stop release may co-occur with (dh)-stopping (e.g., [dɪs] for *this*), whereas a "proper" one will not.

At the moment, most of what we know about the meaning of variation is gathered from observations of diverse speakers' use of variables, and individual speakers' use across situations. But meaning is constructed in the intersubjective space between production and perception, and the challenge to Third Wave studies is to learn how meaning is constructed in variation in the give and take of day-to-day discourse. Experimental work[5] shows that hearers interpret individual occurrences of phonological variables on the basis of beliefs about the speaker's identity and character. Kathryn Campbell-Kibler (2008) has found that hearers may hear the apical variant of (ING) as indexing condescension or compassion, depending on whether they believe the speaker to be more or less educated. And this belief in turn is based in a more general assessment of the speaker's style. The question of the processes by which interlocutors come to these assessments no doubt involves the relative salience of their general and momentary concerns.

26.3 Stylistic practice

Style, a socially locatable combination of linguistic features (only one modality in a broader semiotic system that includes such things as adornment, consumption, patterns of movement) connects language to the types and personae that make up the social world. The term *style* normally invokes enregistered (Agha 2003) styles – styles that are widely recognized as enduringly associated with some widely recognized character types such as *Valley Girl*, *Country* (Hall-Lew and Stephens 2012), or *Pittsburgher* (Johnstone et al. 2006). Styles can be more or less enregistered, more or less consensual across a population, as stylistic practice works below the register level,[6] in a continual recruitment of features into indexical service. In stylistic practice, speakers make social-semiotic moves, reinterpreting variants, and combining and recombining them in a continual process of bricolage (Hebdige 1984) as highly idiosyncratic resources may combine with more widespread ones to construct a nuanced persona. Widely recognized registers serve as landmarks in the sociolinguistic landscape, and their component features can be appropriated into a new indexical order based in the public understanding of the significance of that particular register. Thus stylistic practice is a continual process of enregisterment and recruitment. And it is this creativity that allows language to recirculate signs as resources that are not simply borrowed, but changed in the course of appropriation.

Stylistic practice, then, is a continual reinvention of meaning as speakers individually and severally move through situations and through time and across the life span. Robert Podesva has delved into processes of persona construction by following individuals as they modify their personae in their daily participation in widely disparate situations. Focusing on gay professionals, Podesva has landed on maximally different self-presentations, for example as a medical student ("Heath") moves from the clinic to a barbeque with his friends (Podesva 2007), or an MBA ("Regan") moves from dinner with a friend to "boys' night out" in the Castro (Podesva 2011). The personae these men construct are quite specific, making it clear that there are no "gay" or "straight" personae, but more specific personae – only some of which overtly perform sexuality – and the notion of "gay speech" emerges in the performative space, not in any correlation between speaker sexuality itself and language use (Cameron and Kulick 2003). The difference between Heath's doctor persona in the clinic and the "gay diva" persona he adopts at the barbeque draws on a variety of resources, including falsetto and the aspiration of (t). Differences in Heath's speech between the clinic and the barbeque is a prime example of movement around an indexical field. At the barbeque, Heath used falsetto twice as often as he did in the clinic, the pitch contour lasted twice as long, and the pitch excursion was significantly greater as well. Furthermore, he used falsetto differently in the two situations – almost exclusively on the discourse markers *okay* and *alright* in the clinic, but on a wide variety of utterances at the barbeque. In other words, he used falsetto in the clinic to engage patients in participating in their treatment, while at the barbeque, he used it to achieve a flamboyant persona. Similarly, Heath aspirated significantly more occurrences of (t) in the clinic than at the barbeque. But when he did aspirate (t) at the barbecue, the bursts were significantly longer than the bursts in the clinic. In fact, they were sufficiently exaggerated to amount to parody, resulting in a "prissy" style.

If variation can achieve different personae from situation to situation in a single day, it can extend to change over time as well. In an ethnographic study of high-school girls in Bolton, England, Emma Moore (2004) traced a change in patterns of variation as individuals modified their personae in the course of adolescence. She followed the split of a friendship group of mildly rebellious girls known as the *populars*, as several members moved off to join a more rebellious category, commonly known as *townies*. The populars' grammar was mildly non-standard – particularly, they tended to use a feature common to working-class speech in that part of England, leveling *was* and *were* (e.g., *I were drunk*). In the course of ninth grade, the populars who moved off to become townies showed an increase in their use of *were* leveling: while the populars' use remained essentially the same, the townies' use of the non-standard form jumped from 25 percent to 48 percent. What begins as a situated use may extend as speakers choose to foreground one of their personae, in a kind of stance accretion (Dubois 2002; Kiesling 2005).

26.4 Linguistic change, personal change, and social change

The potential for individual change, both momentary and long-term, is at the center of stylistic practice. Language is often treated as something that children acquire, and adults use. But the ability to interpret differences in styles, to segment their components, and to continually modify one's own, calls for the same linguistic practice that is at work in early acquisition. In other words, language development continues through life as we move through the social world and as that world changes around us. We are constantly called upon to interpret instances of variability – to understand an ever-changing stylistic landscape and to situate ourselves within it. Variation is learned as an integral part of language from the very earliest stages, both in its linguistic patterning (Roberts 1995) and its social meaning (Andersen 1990). An awareness of variation begins in infancy, as babies are exposed to the affective displays of their caretakers, and to differences among the people who interact with them (Andersen 1990; Foulkes et al. 2005). It is clear that speech patterns can change throughout one's life (e.g., Sankoff 2006; Sankoff and Blondeau 2007). Certain aspects of one's speech patterns will be more enduring – above all the phonological patterns that are engrained early and constitute one's native dialect. Whether a speaker has a phonological distinction between the vowels in *cot* and *caught*, for example, indicates his or her geographic origins, and is likely to follow him or her through life (Payne 1980). But the actual phonetic realization of those vowels – e.g., the extent to which a New Yorker diphthongizes and raises the vowel in *caught* – is indexical in the here and now and available for change throughout life. People aren't born thinking of themselves as gay or as fishermen, but develop styles as they continually create places for themselves in the social order. It is not surprising, then, that one's speech, while strongly affected by one's birthplace, can change significantly, and large differences can emerge quite early in life among siblings.

Children's patterns of variation change as their social worlds expand. Adolescence is the point at which speakers' patterns of variation cease to correlate neatly with their parents' social address (e.g., Macaulay 1977), as kids make definitive moves into a social market outside the family. Work in the Detroit suburbs (Eckert 1989, 2000) showed that high-school students' patterns of variation correlate not with their parents' class, but with their participation in the class-based peer social order. At the time of this study, the social order in every public school in the predominantly white suburbs of Detroit was dominated by two opposed communities of practice (Lave and Wenger 1991): *jocks* and *burnouts*. While self-identified jocks and burnouts made up barely half the student body, the hegemony of this split led the unaffiliated to refer to themselves as "in-betweens." The college-bound *jocks* based their networks and activities in the school's extracurricular sphere, while the *burnouts*, bound for the local workforce, expanded their networks and activities into the urban area. This deeply ideological split was central to the peer social order in every school in the Detroit suburban area, and was articulated through every stylistic means available – from clothing and territory (Eckert 1980) to substance use (Eckert 1983) to language (Eckert 2000). In keeping with their urban orientation, the burnouts led the jocks in every school in the use of urban phonological innovations, acting as agents in the spread of sound change outwards from the urban periphery.

The patterns within schools in turn connected local personae and ideologies to the larger socio-geographic complex, and in turn to the larger class structure. The social order of each public school in the suburban area was a fractile (Irvine and Gal 2000) of the larger socio-geography of the conurbation. Socioeconomic class increases with distance from Detroit, so that the progress of these changes through the suburbs was associated simultaneously with class and urbanness. Jocks and burnouts differed gradually across suburban space, as the jocks were more corporate as one moved farther from the city, and the burnouts were tougher and more streetwise as one moved closer. Even within each school, the most corporate and "squeaky-clean" among the jocks used the most conservative phonology, while among the burnouts, the network cluster of girls considered to be the "biggest burnouts" led the rest of the school, including the rest of the burnouts, in their use of urban phonology (and non-standard grammar). And among the in-betweens, the use of urban phonology correlated with engagement in burnout practices. Thus the mechanism of the spread of change through the Detroit suburbs was not simply a matter of contact between static populations, but the selective adoption in each place of a more urban, streetwise, anti-institutional "burnout" persona. In this way, the pattern found in survey studies, by which change spreads through and from the working class, is an accumulation of class differences in local practice.

Stylistic practice can also be an important force in social change. At the turn of the millennium, tremendous media attention was turning to the emergence of Chinese Yuppies as symptomatic of China's growing class disparity. Qing Zhang (2005) studied the new breed of young managers in the foreign-owned financial sector, who represented the vanguard in the growing class of affluent professionals, and the emergence of a new culture of consumption. These "Chinese Yuppies" stand out as distinct from their more traditional peers in state-owned and home-oriented financial businesses, as their value in the highly-paid global financial market depends on their ability to adopt a cosmopolitan lifestyle, and to project a cosmopolitan self. Through the consumption of home furnishings, clothing, toys and leisure activities, the yuppies stand out from their peers in the state-owned financial sector. Central to this life-style activity was the development of a cosmopolitan speech style.

The most widely known feature of Beijing Mandarin is rhotacization of finals (so that *hwa* 'flower' is pronounced [hwaɹ]). Zhang (2008) traces this pronunciation in popular "Beijing flavored" fiction, which regularly uses rhotacization to depict the speech of a particular male Beijing urban type – the "smooth operator." The "oily tone" popularly associated with rhotacization is associated with the smoothness of this character, yielding a particularly tight iconicized link between a variant and its perceived users. A very different urban type is associated with the interdental realization of the sibilants /s/, /ts/, and /ts^h/. This pronunciation is commonly associated with the hutongs, and one of Zhang's interviewees referred to this pronunciation as "alley saunterer" speech, referring to a feckless urban character who hangs around the hutongs waiting for something to happen. While the state managers used these Beijing features, the Yuppies largely avoided them. The yuppies also adopted a full tone on unstressed syllables, a feature of southern and non-mainland Mandarin. This latter feature is never used by the state managers, and is a matter of regular metalinguistic commentary, as the yuppies are accused of "trying to sound like Hong Kongers." By combining patterns of differential use of Beijing and non-mainland variables, each of which brings a particular meaning to the mix, the yuppies construct a new kind of mainland Chinese persona – one that is modern, affluent, elegant, and cosmopolitan. It is particularly clear in this case that the construction of new linguistic styles is central to the construction of a new social category, making linguistic variation integral to social change.

26.5 The centrality of iconicity

The multiple synesthetic associations of Beijing rhotacization with smoothness and oiliness are a particularly dramatic example of iconization (Irvine and Gal 2000), stemming from the apparent human desire to essentialize language features. I would argue that this desire is not trivial, and that sociolinguistic variation is at its very foundation iconic.

The frequentistic nature of variation is in itself iconic. An increase in frequency of a variant generally intensifies its meaning. A few occurrences of [-ən] (e.g., *walkin'*) may hint at a casual attitude, and the repeated use of this apical form will increase the casualness of the style. Quantity also plays a role in phonetic character, as vowels may be more or less high, front, rounded, etc.; consonants may be more fortis or lenis, aspirated or glottalized, etc.; pitch may be higher or lower, more or less variable, etc. Increase, whether of frequency or of phonetic character, intensifies the meaning of the variant.

Some phonetic material is iconic independently of frequency effects. Podesva's work on gay speech styles (2004, 2007, 2011) provides dramatic examples of the use of exaggeration of phonetic form to increase the intensity of the indexical value of phonological variants. The hyperarticulation and fortition that characterize (t) release are iconically related to carefulness and force respectively. And moving beyond the individual variable, phonological processes more generally can take on meaning: fortition–lenition and hyperarticulation–hypoarticulation can carry similar meanings across phonemes.

Vowel quality, the material of much of sociolinguistic variation in North American English, is rife with iconicity. The frequency code (Hinton *et al.* 1994; Ohala 1994), by which high- and low-frequency sounds tend to index smallness and largeness respectively, plays an important role in the expression of affect. The frequency code emerges across languages, engaging cultural discourses of age and size (Hamano 1994; Silverstein 1994; Joseph 1994). Eckert (2011) compared the speech of a pre-adolescent girl in two situations in which she was expressing very different kinds of affect. In one situation, she talked about the fun things she did and the people she liked. A few months later, she sought me out to complain about what pains boys were, giving an account of how she and her best friend had been fighting over a boy. In the first situation, she was not simply showing positive affect, but presenting herself as a happy and innocent young girl; while in the second, she was not simply showing negative affect, but presenting herself as a more sophisticated person with grown-up concerns. Age or life stage and affect, in other words, were inseparable, and both were indexed through the frequency code. Acoustic evidence showed a highly significant effect on the quality of the central vowel (a) and the nucleus of (ay), fronting in the positive affect situation and backing in the negative one. In an experimental study, Katherine Geenberg (unpublished) found that both male and female adults varied the acoustic frequency of their vowels when expressing affect towards stuffed animals. Given the task of telling a stuffed pig how cute she was, the participants spoke cheerfully, raising the frequency of their voice and fronting their vowels. When soothing the pig for having hurt her knee, on the other hand, they lowered the frequency of their voice and backed their vowels.

Iconicity takes on increasing importance when we consider the role of affect in variation. Affect has been absent from linguistic analysis in general, and certainly from the mainstream of variation studies. But affect is embedded in language at every level (Besnier 1990) – perhaps particularly at the level of phonological variation. Affect is commonly invoked as underlying the gender, ethnic, and class differences that dominate survey studies – certainly there are significant cultural and social differences in the expression of emotion. But perhaps more importantly, people do not engage with social distinctions that have no affective force, hence one cannot separate affect from other social meaning. The role of affect in variation requires greater study of non-segmental variation, as such things as intonation, rhythm, and voice quality are essential to the expression of affect, and particularly closely associated with iconicity. It is no doubt not accidental that prosodic patterns are the earliest ones that infants recognize, and it is most likely that affective displays first clue infants in to the indexical nature of variability. And indeed, resources for affective meaning play an important role in variation throughout life. Analyses of child-directed speech by language-acquisition researchers tend to focus on hyperarticulation, assuming that adults' primary purpose is to speak clearly with presumably instructional aims, and on high pitch and pitch variability as devices to retain children's attention. But these devices have social meaning and function in other contexts as well, in speech addressed to non-children, most particularly adult intimates and pets, presumably indexing intimacy and protectiveness. "Baby talk," in fact, is a register used by people of all ages, including older children in regressive moments.

26.6 Conclusion

Sociolinguistics is traditionally about identity – about how variability in language use indexes who we are – but the nature and breadth of that "who" has been at issue over the years. In the early studies, identity was defined in terms of membership in, or more accurately assignment to, macro-sociological categories, and sociolinguistic variation was taken to reflect that membership. Later, Le Page and Tabouret-Keller (1985) put identity more squarely in the agency of the speaker, arguing that speakers perform "acts of identity" as they adopt elements of linguistic form to align themselves with social groups or categories. The categories themselves have broken down over the years, as the treatment of identity and variation has become increasingly constructivist, as the focus has moved to the broader range of social meanings indexed in variation, and as attention has moved to intersubjective processes of social positioning (Bucholtz and Hall 2005). In the context of a linguistics of gender and sexuality, Don Kulick (2000, 2003) argued against the notion of identity altogether, arguing instead for a linguistics of desire. It is clear that identity is in large part desire, which is central to the dynamics discussed in this chapter. Identity is as much about what the individual aspires to as what the individual "is." Speakers reach out in the name of desire – to move toward not simply people but what they see in people, to pull those things into themselves. In fact, identity – if it is a person's sense of their place in the world – is constructed in that space between what one thinks one has, what one desires, and what one thinks one can have. And as variation facilitates our movements around the social landscape, it also indexes the affect that inhabits desire.

While sociolinguists have so far been concerned with a small inventory of variables, particularly sound changes in progress and a few others that stratify socioeconomically, these are only the tip of the semiotic iceberg. Variation is a vast semiotic system that enables the non-propositional expression of some of our most important information. Several properties of variables are particularly important to their functioning: implicitness, underspecification, and combinativeness.

Implicitness. Unlike much of the propositional meaning that preoccupies semantics, the meaning of variants is implicit, and only rarely overtly constructed. Rarely do speakers argue about what an individual variant means, what a person meant by pronouncing a word in a particular way. And if they do, the meanings are deniable. In this way, variation enables speakers to say things about themselves and the social world without saying them "in so many words." If I respond to a question with my native (and long suppressed) New Jersey phonology, the accusation that I'm commenting on the stupidity of the question may be valid, but eminently deniable. Conveying something stylistically is less of a commitment, less face-threatening than putting it in the content of an utterance, and it allows both speaker and interlocutor to leave things "unsaid." This also allows the speaker to make small indexical moves, to try out the waters with less risk to face.

Underspecification. Underspecification is a design feature of language more generally. It allows a small number of forms to serve a large number of purposes, it binds language to social action, and it lies at the core of language's capacity for flexibility, nuance, creativity, and change. In this sense, sociolinguistic variables are like other linguistic signs, as their specific meanings emerge only in context.

Combinativeness. Finally, variables do not occur alone, and are not interpreted on their own, but as components of holistic styles. Styles are what connect to social meaning through their relation to types, personae, or characterological figures (Agha 2003). The underspecification of variables allows them to bring meaning to styles, but only through a process of vivification as they contribute to the construction of these figures. And the deployment of individual variables across styles expands their indexical range.

The combination of underspecification, implicitness, and combinativeness makes the meaning of variation eminently mutable, and this mutability is crucial to its social functioning, allowing the means of expression to move as fast as the social world it negotiates.

Notes

1. In more traditional terminology, *vernacular* refers to everyday local speech, associated with particular speakers rather than part of every individual's repertoire. This duality of meaning surfaces in class-stratificational variation theory in the claim that everyone's personal vernacular is closer to the community vernacular. The implication that the two definitions of vernacular are related surfaces explicitly in characterizations (Labov 1972a) of middle-class speech as more self-conscious and contrived than working-class speech, and claims (Kroch 1978) that the socioeconomic stratification of language is a result of stratified resistance to innovation.
2. The notion of the vernacular also permitted the study of age differences as reflections of changes in progress. As the first learned variety, the state of the language at the time of the individual's acquisition remains stable in the individual's vernacular, allowing speakers to represent not only social address but time.
3. Parentheses indicate the status of a form as a variable.
4. For an account of this development as taking place in three waves of analytic practice, see Eckert (2012). It is not accidental that this wave corresponds to third-wave feminism, inasmuch as it contests the givenness of social categories.
5. Experimental studies of perception are older than the study of variation (e.g., Lambert 1960), and figured prominently in Labov's New York City study (1966). More recent work on perception has benefited from increasingly sophisticated experimental methods emerging in social psychology and psycholinguistics.
6. One can talk about the enregisterment of a single feature, but this turns on the verbal sense of register alone, and not on the holism of registers.

References

Agha, Asif. 2003. The Social Life of a Cultural Value. *Language and Communication* 23: 231–73.

Andersen, Elaine Slosberg. 1990. *Speaking with Style: The Sociolinguistic Skills of Children*. London: Routledge.

Besnier, Niko. 1990. Language and Affect. *Annual Review of Anthropology*. 19: 419–51.

Bucholtz, Mary, and Kira Hall. 2005. Identity and Interaction: A sociocultural linguistic approach. *Discourse Studies* 7: 585–614.

Cameron, Deborah, and Don Kulick. 2003. *Language and Sexuality*. Cambridge/New York: Cambridge University Press.

Campbell-Kibler, Kathryn. 2008. I'll Be the Judge of That: Diversity in social perceptions of (ING). *Language in Society* 37: 637.

Cedergren, Henrietta. 1973. *The Interplay of Social and Linguistic Factors in Panama, Linguistics*. PhD Dissertation, Cornell University.

Cheshire, Jenny. 1982. *Variation in an English Dialect*. Cambridge: Cambridge University Press.

Dubois, John W. 2002. Stance and Consequence. Paper presented at the Annual Meeting of the American Anthropological Association, New Orleans.

Eckert, Penelope. 1980. Clothing and Geography in a Suburban High School. In *Researching American Culture*, ed. Conrad Phillip Kottak, 45–8. Ann Arbor: University of Michigan Press.

   1983. Beyond the Statistics of Adolescent Smoking. *American Journal of Public Health* 73: 439–41.

   1989. *Jocks and Burnouts: Social Categories and Identity in the High School*. New York: Teachers College Press.

   2000. *Linguistic Variation as Social Practice*. Oxford: Blackwell.

   2008. Variation and the Indexical Field. *Journal of Sociolinguistics* 12: 453–76.

   2011. Where Does the Social Stop? In *Language Variation: European Perspectives III*, ed. Frans Gregersen, Jeffrey Parrott, and Pia Qiust, 13-30. Amsterdam and Philadelphia: John Benjamins.

   2012. Three Waves of Variation Study: The emergence of meaning in the study of variation. *Annual Review of Anthropology* 41: 87–100.

Foulkes, P., G. J. Docherty, and D. Watt. 2005. Phonological Variation in Child-Directed Speech. *Language* 81: 177–206.

Geenberg, Katherine. Unpublished. Sound symbolism in Adult Baby Talk (ABT): The role of the frequency code in the construction of social meaning. Stanford University.

Gumperz, John J. 1958. Dialect Differences and Social Stratification in a North Indian Village. *American Anthropologist* 60: 668–82.

Hall-Lew, Lauren, and Nola Stephens. 2012. Country Talk. *Journal of English Linguistics* 40: 256–80.

Hamano, S. 1994. Palatalization in Japanese Sound Symbolism. In *Sound Symbolism*, ed. L. Hinton, J. Nichols, and J. J. Ohala, 148–57. Cambridge: Cambridge University Press.

Hebdige, Dick. 1984. *Subculture: The Meaning of Style*. New York: Methuen.

Hinton, Leanne, Johanna Nichols, and John J. Ohala, eds. 1994. *Sound Symbolism*. Cambridge: Cambridge University Press.

Hodder, Ian. 1982. *The Present Past*. London: Batsford.

Hoijer, Harry. 1948. Linguistic and Cultural Change. *Language* 24: 335–45.

Irvine, Judith T., and Susan Gal. 2000. Language Ideology and Linguistic Differentiation. In *Regimes of Language: Ideologies, Politics, and Identities*, ed. P. V. Kroskrity, 35–83. Santa Fe, NM: SAR Press.

Johnstone, Barbara, Jennifer Andrus, and Andrew E. Danielson. 2006. Mobility, Indexicality, and the Enregisterment of "Pittsburghese". *Journal of English Linguistics* 34: 77–104.

Joseph, Brian. 1994. Modern Greek ts: Beyond sound symbolism. In *Sound Symbolism*, ed. L. Hinton, J. Nichols, and J. J. Ohala, 222–36. Cambridge: Cambridge University Press.

Kiesling, Scott. 2005. Variation, Stance and Style. *English World-Wide* 26: 1–42.

Kroch, Anthony S. 1978. Toward a Theory of Social Dialect Variation. *Language in Society* 7: 17–36.

Kulick, Don. 2000. Gay and Lesbian Language. *Annual Review of Anthropology* 29: 243–85.

——— 2003. Language and Desire. In *The Handbook of Language and Gender*, ed. Janet Holmes and Miriam Meyerhoff. Oxford: Blackwell.

Labov, William. 1963. The Social Motivation of a Sound Change. *Word* 18: 1–42.

——— 1966. *The Social Stratification of English in New York City*. Washington, DC: Center for Applied Linguistics.

——— 1972a. Hypercorrection by the Lower Middle Class as a Factor in Linguistic Change. In *Sociolinguistic Patterns*, ed. William Labov, 122–42. Philadelphia: University of Pennsylvania Press.

——— 1972b. Some Principles of Linguistic Methodology. *Language in Society* 1: 97–120.

——— 2001. *Principles of Linguistic Change: Social Factors*. Cambridge: Blackwell.

Lambert, W., R. Hodgson, R. Gardner, and S. Fillenbaum. 1960. Evaluative Reactions to Spoken Language. *Journal of Abnormal and Social Psychology* 60: 44–51.

Lave, Jean, and Etienne Wenger. 1991. *Situated Learning: Legitimate Peripheral Participation*. Cambridge: Cambridge University Press.

Le Page, R. B., and A. Tabouret-Keller. 1985. *Acts of Identity*. Cambridge: Cambridge University Press.

Macaulay, Ronald K. S. 1977. *Language, Social Class and Education: A Glasgow Study*. Edinburgh: University of Edinburgh Press.

Milroy, Lesley. 1980. *Language and Social Networks*. Oxford: Blackwell.

Modaressi, Yahyah. 1978. *A Sociolinguistic Analysis of Modern Persian*. PhD dissertation, University of Kansas.

Moore, Emma. 2004. Sociolinguistic Style: A multidimensional resource for shared identity creation. *Canadian Journal of Linguistics* 49: 375-96.

Nunberg, Geoffrey. 2002. Fresh Air Commentary. National Public Radio, September 11.

Ohala, John. 1994. The Frequency Code Underlies the Sound-Symbolic Use of Voice Pitch. In *Sound Symbolism*, ed. Leanne Hinton, Johanna Nichola, and John J. Ohala, 325-47. Cambridge/New York: Cambridge University Press.

Payne, Arvilla. 1980. Factors Controlling the Acquisition of the Philadelphia Dialect by Out-of-State Children. In *Locating Language in Time and Space*, ed. William Labov, 143-78. New York: Academic Press.

Podesva, Robert. 2004. On Constructing Social Meaning with Stop Release Bursts. Paper presented at Sociolinguistics Symposium 15, Newcastle upon Tyne.

  2007. Phonation Type as a Stylistic Variable: The use of falsetto in constructing a persona. *Journal of Sociolinguistics* 11: 478-504.

  2011. The California Vowel Shift and Gay Identity. *American Speech* 86: 32-51.

Rickford, John. 1986. Concord and Contrast in the Characterization of the Speech Community. *Sheffield Working Papers in Language and Linguistics* 3: 87-119.

Roberts, Julie. 1995. Acquisition of Variable Rules: A study of (-t, d) deletion in preschool children. *Journal of Child Language* 24: 351-72.

Sankoff, Gillian. 2006. Age: Apparent time and real time. In *Elsevier Encyclopedia of Language and Linguistics*, 110-16. Oxford: Elsevier.

Sankoff, Gillian, and Hélène Blondeau. 2007. Language Change Across the Lifespan: /r/ in Montreal French. *Language* 83: 560-88.

Silverstein, Michael. 1994. Relative Motivation in Denotational and Indexical Sound Symbolism of Wasco-Wishram Chinookan. In *Sound Symbolism*, ed. L. Hinton, J. Nichols, and J.J. Ohala, 40-60. Cambridge: Cambridge University Press.

  2003. Indexical Order and the Dialectics of Sociolinguistic Life. *Language and Communication* 23: 193-229.

Tagliamonte, Sali A., and Alexandra D'Arcy. 2009. Peaks Beyond Phonology: Adolescence, incrementation, and language change. *Language* 85: 58-108.

Trudgill, Peter. 1972. Sex, Covert Prestige and Linguistic Change in the Urban British English of Norwich. *Language in Society* 1: 179-95.

  1974. *The Social Differentiation of English in Norwich*. Cambridge: Cambridge University Press.

Wolfram, Walt. 1969. *A Sociolinguistic Description of Detroit Negro Speech*. Washington, DC: Center for Applied Linguistics.

Zhang, Qing. 2005. A Chinese Yuppie in Beijing: Phonological variation and the construction of a new professional identity. *Language in Society* 34: 431–66.

2008. Rhotacization and the "Beijing Smooth Operator": The social meaning of a linguistic variable. *Journal of Sociolinguistics* 12: 201–22.

27

Language and archaeology

State of the art

Roger M. Blench

27.1 Introduction: Why link two such different disciplines?

Archaeology is the reconstruction of past lifeways through the excavation and analysis of material remains, whereas linguistics is the description of human language and interpretation of patterns that can be observed. Sociocultural anthropologists may well wonder what the two disciplines have in common and their relevance to sociocultural anthropology. Archaeology can provide time-depth for the synchronic observations of sociocultural anthropology and thus add analytic richness to descriptions of social change. For example, the transition from foraging to agriculture must have occurred many times in different regions (Barker 2006). Yet a change with such momentous economic and social implications cannot now be directly observed, so archaeology must provide a window on this process. However, the development and spread of agriculture also had major consequences for the linguistic map of the world. Combining archaeological results with linguistic reconstruction and a nuanced understanding of social process derived from ethnography allows us to evolve a richer model of prehistory.

Linguistics has historically been linked to hypotheses concerning prehistory in three main ways:

(a) the correlation of linguistic reconstructions from historical linguistics with the findings of archaeology
(b) speculations concerning the origin of human language and palaeoanthropology
(c) palaeosociolinguistics, the use of language evolution models from the near present to explain both language patterning and archaeological results.

Of these, the first is the most well established, and has practitioners in almost all the major language phyla of the world. Speculations on the origin of language and whether this has osteological correlates to be found in the fossil record has a long and somewhat disreputable history. Palaeosociolinguistics is a developing area, where there is so far very limited consensus, but intriguing vistas are opening up. Ethnography plays an important role in modeling credible sociological scenarios; if we hypothesize a sociolinguistic process in the past, we should be able to point to its analog in the present.

This chapter[1] discusses the evolution of the ideas that connect linguistics with the modeling of prehistory and focuses on particular topics to illustrate the practical working out of their interactions. It begins with some of the contrasting opinions about the relationships between linguistics and archaeology, and in particular the negative views of some archaeologists. It then explores some of the main topics that have been the subject of debate, in particular claims about numerical classification of languages and the processes of language diversification. As examples of topics which should be of particular interest to sociocultural anthropologists, it considers the genesis of writing – for which there is considerable epigraphic evidence but which can also be documented ethnographically – and the evolution of gender registers, something clearly present in Sumerian but also the subject of contemporary descriptions. The final section takes on one of the most controversial issues, the proposed synthesis of linguistics, archaeology, and DNA evidence to generate new hypotheses about prehistory.

27.2 Linguistics and archaeology

The relationship between linguistics and archaeology reflects both the internal dynamic of the disciplines themselves and external political and social trends. Many archaeologists have asserted that archaeology and linguistics do not share much common ground; some for reasons internal to archaeology, while others may be traced to the sometimes startling misuse of the conjunction of disciplines by earlier scholars. Linguistics is in many ways more internally diverse than archaeology; a much greater proportion of its practitioners are engaged in high theory and fieldwork is often perceived as a low-prestige activity. The great majority of linguists are engaged in an enterprise that really does have no relevance for archaeology, whilst the reverse is not true. However, among the subset of linguists interested in historical topics, few have not at least glanced at archaeology, in the light of its potential to provide interpretative tools for their findings.

Historical linguistics suggests that we can plot the development of language families, and reconstruct particular lexical items of social and economic significance, such as hunting gear and food crops, but also social organization. It therefore seems that we should be able to map these against archaeological findings. The argument from the linguists' point of view is simply put: languages were spoken by real people in the past and indeed form striking patterns in the present. This must have been the consequence of distinct strategies of movement and diversification of peoples and somehow reflect their changing social and economic conditions. The first language phylum where this type of speculation was exercised was Indo-European, with the work of Adolphe Pictet (1859–63), who first introduced the concept of *linguistic paleontology*, the reconstruction of the social and material through linguistic reconstruction. This was picked up and expanded by the semiotician Émile Benveniste (1973) in his seminal work on Indo-European language and society. Similar observations from an entirely different region of the world are Crowley's (1987: 268 ff.) reconstruction of the concept of the meeting house in Polynesian and its cultural relatives in Oceanic, or Lynch and Fakamuria's (1994) study of moieties in Vanuatu.

Although these approaches have been highly influential elsewhere in the world, they have been treated with skepticism by many archaeologists. There are two distinct reasons for this: either because it is evident what language was spoken by the people who occupied the sites they excavate, or because they have actively rejected linguistics. The rejection of the opportunity to identify speech-communities is more interesting but also more problematic, as it seems to arise from a barely articulated background ideology. Glyn Daniel, for example, wrote:

> We must alas, for the most part, keep the builders and bearers of our prehistoric cultures speechless and physically neutral. This may seem to you an unsatisfying conclusion. And so it is but then much of our prehistory is unsatisfying and difficult, tantalisingly meagre and sketchy. We can appreciate this and accept the limitations of prehistory along with its excitements. (Daniel 1962: 114–15)

The unspoken message is undoubtedly a fear that the precision and empirical content of archaeology will be contaminated by speculation and unhealthy racial hypotheses. But this battle has been lost; if some of the speculations have touched on wilder shores, this is no reason to reject the whole spectrum of methods for reconstructing a richer past.

27.3 Historical linguistics and models of prehistory

Historical linguistics, like many another discipline, has a contested past. Some of its early practitioners developed models of world prehistory by arguing for links between geographically remote languages in the context of Biblical references, such as the location of the lost tribes of Israel (Wauchope 1962). This type of scholarship is often broadly referred to as Voltairean linguistics, from a famous apothegm attributed by Max Müller

(1871: 1.238) to Voltaire: "Etymology is a science in which the vowels count for nothing and the consonants for very little."[2]

Historical linguistics in the modern sense began as a comparison of written languages and textbooks; Sir William Jones's famous lecture in 1786 is typically cited as demonstrating the links between Sanskrit and the classical languages of Europe.[3] Precursors to historical linguistics existed, both among the Sanskrit grammarians and in the works of rabbinical scholars. Yehuda Ibn Quraysh, who lived in Fez, Morocco, in the tenth century, was the first to compare the phonology and morphology of Hebrew, Aramaic, and Arabic in his book *'Risāla'* (Téné 1980). However, Van Driem (2001: 1039 ff.) has shown that the conventional accounts (Bonfante 1953; Muller 1986) of the predecessors of Jones, notably Marcus van Boxhorn, are highly inaccurate. Boxhorn's (1647) published study of 'Scythian' (comparative Indo-European) represents the first discussion of the methodological issues in assigning languages to genetic groups. He observed that to use lexical cognates, loanwords must be first eliminated and he placed great emphasis on common morphological systems and on irregularity, *anomalien*, as an indicator of relationship. Even the expression *ex eadem origine* 'from a common source' first appears in a book by Johann Elichmann (1640: iii) – who served as a doctor at the Persian court – which uses morphology to relate European languages to Indo-Iranian. The concept of reconstructing an Indo-European proto-language appears as early as 1713 in the works of the English divine William Wotton:

> My argument does not depend on the difference of Words, but upon the Difference of Grammar between any two languages; from whence it proceeds, that when any Words are derived from one Language into another, the derived Words are then turned and changed according to the particular Genius of the Language into which they are transplanted. [...] I can easily suppose that they might both be derived from one common Mother, which is, and perhaps has for many Ages been entirely lost.   (Wotton 1730: 57)

Wotton showed that Icelandic ("Teutonic"), the Romance languages, and Greek were related, which is certainly as convincing a demonstration of Indo-European affinities as Jones's links between classical languages and Sanskrit.

Although earlier scholars worked with written languages, historical linguistics today is used principally to illuminate the evolution of unwritten or recently written languages, and it is this which has been of greatest interest to archaeologists. The recognition of the major language families is often surprisingly early. The outlines of the Austronesian family were first recognized in the early eighteenth century by the Dutch scholar Adriaan van Reeland, who compared Malay, Malagasy, and Polynesian (Relandus 1708). A contemporary of Jones, Forster, also had a clear concept of proto-etyma:

> I am ... inclined to suppose, that all these dialects preserve several words of a more ancient language, ... which gradually divided into many languages, now remarkably different. The words therefore of the language of the South Seas isles, which are similar to others in the Malay tongue, prove clearly in my opinion, that the Eastern South Sea Islands were originally peopled from the Indian, or Asiatic Northern isles; and that those lying more to the Westward, received their first inhabitants from the neighbourhood of New Guinea.
>
> (Forster 1778:190)

Another Austronesianist, Bishop Codrington, in a surprisingly satirical comment, may have been the first to disentangle race from linguistic classification:

> The Melanesian people have the misfortune to be black, to be much darker, at least, than either Malays or Polynesians; and because they are black it is presumed that their original language cannot be of the same family with that spoken by their brown neighbours; that where their language has a general resemblance to that of their neighbours they must have cast off their own and taken another in the lump, and that where the resemblance is not conspicuously apparent they must have borrowed words and expressions in commercial or other intercourse.
>
> (Codrington 1885: 12)

Remarkably, the earliest sketch of an entirely unwritten language phylum appears to be Arawakan, a language phylum spoken in the pre-Columbian Caribbean, and stretching into today's southeastern Colombia and central Brazil, which dates from 1782 (Gilij 1780–84). Gilij's insights were remarkable for their time: he recognized sound-correspondences as a key tool in classifying languages, focused on the importance of word-order patterns, and discussed the diffusion of loanwords.

Nearly a century later, Pictet (1859–63) developed the notion of linguistic paleontology, the idea that prehistory can be reconstructed from evidence drawn from modern spoken languages and the transformation of individual words. Lexicostatistics, the counting of cognate words between two or more languages in a standardized list, also was first sketched at around the same time. Dumont d'Urville (1834) compared a number of Oceanic (Austronesian) languages and proposed a method for calculating a coefficient of their relationship. When he extended his comparison to a sample of Amerindian languages he correctly concluded that they were not related to Oceanic. Lexicostatistics is associated in more modern times with the work of Morris Swadesh, and was a key tool in the armoury of historical linguists in the 1960s and 1970s, before some of its methodological problems began to surface.

A sister discipline to lexicostatistics is glottochronology, the notion that if the differentiation between languages can be assigned numerical status then it might be regularly related to the time-depth of the split between languages (Swadesh 1952). Latham (1850) first sketched the possibility of assigning a precise date to the divergence of two languages through the application of a mathematical algorithm. The attractive aspect of both lexicostatistics and glottochronology is quantification; they seem to represent a scientific approach to the dating and genetic classification of languages.

Both lexicostatistics and glottochronology have been given a new lease of life with modern mathematical methods (McMahon and McMahon 2005). Adapting statistical techniques from biology, a series of papers has proposed new models for language classification and dating and pattern of splits. Russell Gray and colleagues, for example, have published several versions of the Austronesian "tree" based on these methods, which are strongly denied the label lexicostatistics, although they make use of the cognacy judgments of conventional historical linguists (e.g., Gray et al. 2009; Greenhill et al. 2010). Gray and Atkinson (2003) and Atkinson and Gray (2006) have published a re-evaluation of the dating and splits of Indo-European, and Holden and Gray (2006) a "tree" of Bantu. More boldly, Atkinson (2011) has claimed that high phoneme inventories in Africa and relatively low inventories in Oceania show that human language gradually simplified as humans moved away from Africa.

Linguists have diametrically opposed views about this type of analysis, either viewing it as an important advance on previous techniques, or as problematic for its failure to take into account recent insights into the nature of language change and pidginization processes. A key assumption is thus uniformitarianism, that linguistic change takes place according to predictable rates. The whole enterprise of lexicostatistics and glottochronology depends on the underlying assumption that languages change at a standard rate if only the right algorithm can be uncovered. It may seem obvious that past societies exhibited complex sociolinguistic patterns in much the same way as those in the present, but historical linguistics has often taken a uniformitarian perspective. Paradoxically, the Austronesianist Robert Blust, whose data has been used for tree-like modeling of Austronesian (Greenhill et al. 2010), has been one of those to study differential erosion of core vocabulary (Blust 1999, 2009a). He found strikingly different rates of loss of core Austronesian lexemes over time, for reasons that remain unexplained. The view taken here is that uniformitarianism is not a realistic assumption about language change in the real world and we would be better modeling past societies from what we know of the present. Certainly the language networks that are increasingly common in historical accounts (cf. for example critique of hierarchical trees in Austronesian in Donohue and Denham 2010) find no place in this more dichotomous view of language. In addition, these models face the thorny issue of testability, the difficulty of showing what empirical result would falsify their findings. Archaeological calibration of claims about dating has yet to be undertaken, so the relevance for conventional models of prehistory cannot be fully assessed.

27.4 Dating and linguistic diversity

The issue of linguistic diversity and absolute dating is thrown into sharp focus by the controversies over the settlement of the New World, addressed by Nichols (1992). The Americas represent a region of exceptional linguistic diversity and the earliest classifications suggested there were at least fifty-eight distinct phyla, which would make it one of the most diverse regions of the world (cf. Campbell 1997 for an overview of scholarship and dates). Archaeologists, however, have generally considered the occupation of the Americas as relatively recent, with most dates focusing on the so-called "Clovis" horizon, ca. 12,500 BP (e.g., Lynch 1990). Even the revised dates for Monte Verde in Chile only go back to 14,600 BP (Dillehay 1997). This creates a major disconnect, since few linguists would accept such differentiation could evolve in so short a time, especially in the light of what we know about language diversification in Australia and Melanesia (Blench 2012).

Throughout most of the twentieth century, linguists have been unwilling to reduce significantly the numbers of distinct phyla of Amerindian languages, despite a major expansion in available data, and so have been rather skeptical of the archaeological position. However, Joseph Greenberg (1987), then known principally for his work in Africa, put forward a radical reclassification of the linguistic situation in the Americas which proposed to reduce the languages to just three distinct phyla. The largest of these, Amerind, would roll up most of the languages of North and South America. Amerind has been widely adopted by both archaeologists and geneticists, since it neatly solves the problem of the contradiction between language and settlement dates (e.g., Renfrew 1992). Unfortunately, there seems to be little evidence that it is even partly true. Despite the predictions of many Africanists, the years since the publication of *Language in the Americas* have not seen a single major scholar adopt Greenberg's ideas and recent large reference books now uniformly reject it (e.g., Campbell 1997; Mithun 1999; Dixon and Aikhenvald 1999). Amerind now lives on as a fossil conception outside the professional discipline of native American linguistics.

Neatness and truth are not necessarily good partners and in the case of the Americas there are several possible scenarios to explain the situation:

(a) Archaeological dates are significantly older than those currently accepted.
(b) Classifications of the languages of the New World are in error.
(c) New World languages diversify at much greater rates than elsewhere in the world.

Table 27.1 Four processes of language dispersal and diversification (after Renfrew 1992: 457)

Category	Example
a) Initial colonisation	Early forager dispersals, e.g., Khoisan
b) Agricultural dispersal	Migratory movement of farmers, e.g., Austronesian
c) Northern climate-sensitive adjustments	Migrations of polar foragers, e.g., Eskimo-Aleut
d) Elite dominance	Military expansion and domination, e.g., Indo-Iranian

(d) Multiple migrations to the Americas brought in "pre-diversified" languages.

Of these, (c) is the least likely; the resolution will probably be found with partial elements from the other three scenarios. However, the situation illustrates difficulties of reconciling archaeological and linguistic hypotheses, even when the canvas is large and the datasets dense.

27.5 Language diversification and shift

One of the major debates in the interpretation of the pattern of world language phyla is the underlying process; cf. chapters in Part II of this handbook. In other words, what type of social or technological engine drove their dispersal and can we account for this archaeologically? The first author to establish the terms of the debate was Renfrew (1987, 1992) who postulated four processes. These are listed in Table 27.1.

These hypotheses relied strongly on the account of world language phyla propounded by Ruhlen (1987) and an in-press version of Cavalli-Sforza et al. (1994) for the genetics. Although these sources are no longer widely accepted, the categories have been immensely influential among archaeologists. The rebranding of migration as *demic diffusion* and the link with agriculture has been debated for many linguistic families (see the papers in Bellwood and Renfrew 2002; Enfield 2011; Blench 2011, 2012).

The notion of demic diffusion is the unspoken subtext behind the neatly branching trees used to characterize the structure of many language phyla. In some cases, such as the expansion of Polynesian, Bantu, or Turkic peoples, it would be hard to deny a link with physical movement of populations. But language shift is one of the key processes of cultural change and indeed bound up with prestige institutions and material culture. Any convincing model of the relation between language and prehistory must take such processes into account (Ehret 1988). Bulbeck (2011) provides a complex account of the disconnect between the physical anthropology of the Orang Asli of the Malay Peninsula, their phenotypic diversity, and recently adopted Austro-Asiatic languages.

Quite different approaches to language diversification are now coming from cognitive sciences. Levinson and Gray (2012) claim that the tools which have revolutionized evolutionary biology can also be applied to language diversification. The basis of the argument appears to be that data-mining can uncover historical processes invisible to normal linguistic and archaeological investigation. Since they give no concrete examples, this is more a program than a demonstration of these new techniques.

Despite the emphasis on "neat" trees and movement of populations, ethnography points strongly to the predominance of language shift in migration. All over the world, ethnic minorities are under extreme pressure to yield their own speech to a national language and in many cases this is occurring (Blench 2007; Rice, this volume, Chapter 11). Australian and American indigenous minorities were subject to programs of forced assimilation for long periods, accounting for the precarious state of their languages. While these programs have been halted, apologies made, and the watchword is language revitalization, continuing voluntary migration to these states results in migrants rapidly losing their language. In a highly nationalist state such as India, right-wing Hindu parties have been pressing for the imposition of Hindi in a multilingual state such as Arunachal Pradesh. To this end, they have been marshaling technology, notably satellite television, to achieve acceptance. But technology can also be adapted by its intended targets; minorities such as the Koro and the Hruso are also seeking to preserve their languages in the face of this attempt at cultural bleaching.

Language shift can be seen and documented in the present, which makes it easier to model processes in the past. The consequences for material culture of interest to archaeologists can be highly variable. In many developed economies, for minority languages such as Breton, Scots Gaelic, or the Amerindian languages of North America, the shift in material culture has already occurred. Language loss trails behind it, perhaps artificially retarded by literacy programs or well-intentioned linguists. However, in the developing world, speaking a minority language is often linked to poverty and social exclusion, for example in Indonesia or Mexico. The spread of a dominant language by agencies of the state in such countries reflects as much the impulse towards political control as the inexorable tide of globalization, and consequently there may be no material change in the state of populations who lose their language, as in many Latin American countries.

To relate this to archaeological interpretation, one of the long-standing puzzles of Australian prehistory is the distribution of Pama-Nyungan languages. Although the diversity of language groupings of Australia indicates long periods of separation, it is confined to a small region of Northern Australia (Koch 1997). The rest of the continent is dominated by a single family, Pama-Nyungan, the languages of which are sufficiently close as to be almost inter-intelligible (cf. Dixon 2002 for a skeptical account and Evans 2005 for a detailed rebuttal). Given the early settlement dates for

Australia (O'Connor and Chappell 2003), Pama-Nyungan speakers must have persuaded the resident groups to switch languages. Since there is no evidence that this was achieved by violence, we have to assume that either technological superiority or prestige social institutions were the keys to this process. McConvell and Evans (1998) argue that we can see evidence for both. Pama-Nyungan speakers show an innovative type of social organization, linguistic exogamy linked to possession of song repertoires, that may well be the prestige institution that impressed the in situ populations. At the same time, some 4–5,000 years BP, a new type of microlithic technology begins to appear throughout the region, backed blades, whose distribution corresponds closely with that of Pama-Nyungan languages. The combination of tools and songs seems to have been irresistible and the languages gradually spread through most of the continent, assimilating those already present.

27.6 Palaeosociolinguistics

It may seem obvious that past societies exhibited complex sociolinguistic patterns in much the same way as those in the present. *Palaeosociolinguistics* is where documentation can be used to reconstruct the sociological elements in language use and change. The challenge of palaeosociolinguistics is to detect events that are beyond the reach of oral tradition *and* to link them with the archaeological record.

One area where this is of particular interest is in the area of language leveling, where the spread of a major language, usually among speech-forms which are already related, causes lexical and grammatical convergence and reduced typological diversity. Nichols (1992) has been a highly influential text in this area, arguing that the striking contrasts in phyletic diversity between regions, notably between Eurasia and the New World, can be explained by concepts of "spread zones" and "residual zones." Her argument is that repeated spreads of migration in the Old World have eliminated typological diversity and hence have resulted in language leveling. Nichols did not attempt to link her chronologies with absolute dating from archaeology, which continues to create problems for interpreting her claims.

Language leveling can often be the consequence of centralized political authority. For example, the spread of Khalkh Mongol following the military expansion of the Mongols in the thirteenth century has eliminated much of the diversity of Mongolic, leaving divergent dialects at the periphery (Janhunen 2003). The material correlates of this expansion are still very much present in Mongolia, in styles of livestock management, dress, music, and oral literature. The prior relatedness of the Mongolic languages means that unless there is reason to suspect this process on historical grounds its existence has to be inferred from reduced diversity, where this can be measured in comparable situations.

Island Southeast Asia (ISEA) is another region where language leveling can be hypothesized. Virtually all of ISEA and the Pacific is populated by speakers of Austronesian languages as far as New Caledonia and New Zealand, bypassing much of Melanesia. In principle, language diversity can be very great: Vanuatu has more than a hundred indigenous languages in a land area of 12,200 km^2. Blust (2005, 2009b) has observed that the lexical diversity of languages in both the Philippines and Borneo is too low, if they have indeed been diversifying in *situ* for more than 3,500 years. To account for this situation, Blust proposes that a leveling process took place in the unspecified past. In the case of the Philippines, he calls this the "Macro-Philippines" hypothesis and for Borneo the "Greater North Borneo" subgroup. As this process faltered, languages would again begin to diversify, but the leveling event would be visible in subsequent analysis. In another case, the island of Nias off the west coast of Sumatra shows astonishing genetic and linguistic uniformity, despite settlement more than 12,000 years ago (Forestier *et al.* 2005). This can be attributed to a settlement and language-leveling event as little as 600 years ago, obliquely recorded in the *hoho* or historical chants (Kennerknecht *et al.* 2012). To this list can certainly be added Malagasy, which is again very similar across the island, despite a time-depth for its occupation of at least 1,500 years (Dewar 1994).

In the case of early language leveling in the Austronesian world, one probable factor is the spread of metalworking in the region. We know that the technology of iron-smelting was introduced around 100 BC and spread rapidly in ISEA. This would have given early adopters a considerable technological advantage both in warfare and in cutting back the heavy vegetation that characterizes most islands, making more room for agriculture. The likely consequence was a sudden increase in the population of particular ethnolinguistic groups, leading the leveling events identified subsequently by linguists.

Language leveling may be the result of a wide variety of sociolinguistic processes, but the result is the same, the gradual elimination of diversity following the spread from some central source of a persuasive and characteristic lexicon. Java, Sumatra, and the Malay Peninsula have also reduced language diversity in historical times through better-documented political processes, and comparable changes today with Malay, Indonesian, and Tagalog are being induced by the nation state, education, and television. Such processes need not necessarily involve a top-down imposition of a language policy; they can be political or cultural.

27.7 Modeling creolization

As with language shift, processes of language change observable in the present clearly took place in the past, although they muddy the waters of conventional language diversification models. One important area is pidginization and the related creolization (Thomason and Kaufman 1988). The conventional definition of a pidgin is a simplified language that develops for speakers with different languages to communicate with each other, and a creole arises when such a speech-form becomes the mother-tongue of a particular group. The boundary between these two is not always clear; presumably in transitional households, the parents speak a pidgin and the children a creole. Moreover, the elevation of Pidgin Englishes to codified speech-forms in various parts of the world (e.g., Bislama in Vanuatu, or Pidgin in Cameroun) means that what linguists would call creoles are known as Pidgin.

Earlier writing on creolization tended to focus on creoles that evolved between European (i.e., colonial) languages and indigenous languages, often through conquest or slavery. But as perceptions have sharpened, it is increasingly clear that these are broad processes affecting human language at all times and places. We know about these because they have occurred in the recent, observable past. But there is every reason to think that various types of language mixing also happened prior to modern documentation. It used to be considered that "mixed" languages did not occur, that every language was essentially or underlyingly one language and was relexified from another. Thomason and Kaufman (1988:1) counterpose Max Muller's categorical assertion that there are no mixed languages with Hugo Schuchardt's claim that there are no "unmixed" languages.[4] Linguists' resistance to the idea of mixed languages has rather broken down with increasing evidence that such languages do exist (Bakker and Mous 1994). Bechhaus-Gerst (1996) documented the evolution of Nile Nubian (where written sources exist) and was able to illustrate patterns of borrowing and language mixing over time in a way that is exceptional for Africa. More recent African examples are Ma'a in Tanzania (Mous 2004) and Ilwana in Kenya (Nurse 2000).

It was also generally thought that pidgins occurred as a result of the interaction of two languages, but more complex scenarios are clearly possible. An example of a problematic language with a complex history is Laal. Laal is spoken by several hundred fishermen in Central Chad (Boyeldieu 1977). Its vocabulary and morphology seem to be partly drawn from Chadic (i.e., Afro-asiatic), partly from Adamawa (i.e., Niger-Congo), and partly from an unknown source, perhaps its original phylum, a now-vanished Central African grouping. For this to develop, Laal speakers must have been in situations of intense bilingualism with different neighbors over a long period, without being in a relationship where cultural dominance would cause them to lose their language. Similarly, this does not suggest pidginization, since Laal speakers have a very full ethnoscientific vocabulary, as would be expected from a remote inland fishing community.

Another way of regarding the multiplicity of changes that can occur is from the perspective of language restructuring. Many languages which have never been regarded as creoles have nonetheless undergone radical changes under the influence of bilingualism. Dimmendaal (2001: 97ff.) shows that Luo, a Nilotic language of Western Kenya, has acquired an incipient system of noun-classes through contact with neighboring Bantu-speakers. The degree of contact necessary for this major restructuring to occur is reflected in many aspects of Luo culture, which resembles those of the Bantu farmers more than their pastoral relatives in the Western Nilotic group.

The relevance for the interpretation of prehistory is that processes of language mixing must surely reflect cultural interpenetration and as such, should be visible in the archaeological record. This type of interaction between attested linguistic and archaeological data has been more thoroughly studied in Oceania, where the encounter between Austronesian and Papuan languages and their highly distinctive material culture has been documented in some detail. Dutton (1999) studied the relationship between language mixing and pottery in the archaeological record on the island of Mailu. The dominant group today, the Papuan-speaking Magi, turn out to have a maritime and trade vocabulary almost entirely borrowed from Austronesian. The pottery sequence, described by Irwin (1985) can be almost exactly correlated with a series of hypothetical language events.

27.8 Understanding writing

Epigraphy is a specialized branch of archaeology and immense scholarly effort goes into the processes of decipherment of fragmentary texts. Exploring relations between sound and symbol is the focus of the typical encyclopedic volumes on writing systems that have been published in recent years (e.g., Coulmas 2003). However, much less research has gone into the social context of writing and in particular understanding the social processes that lead to its adoption. Typical texts on this subject seem to be characteristically ill-informed about actual writing systems (e.g., Goody 1986). However, the potential for anthropologists to explore the creation, adoption, and spread of writing systems synchronically suggests that in principle we can illuminate past processes through present ethnography.

As an example, Figure 27.1 shows an accounting book written in the Raga script, developed on the northern coast of Pentecost Island in Vanuatu.[5] There is no reference to this script in the usual sources, but from interviews it seems it was developed in the context of the Raga cultural revival movement. It is only known to a small number of individuals who are senior in the ranking system based on pig-killing. The bases of the symbols are iconic elements taken from sand-drawing, a traditional art on Pentecost and other nearby islands. A roman orthography has long been developed

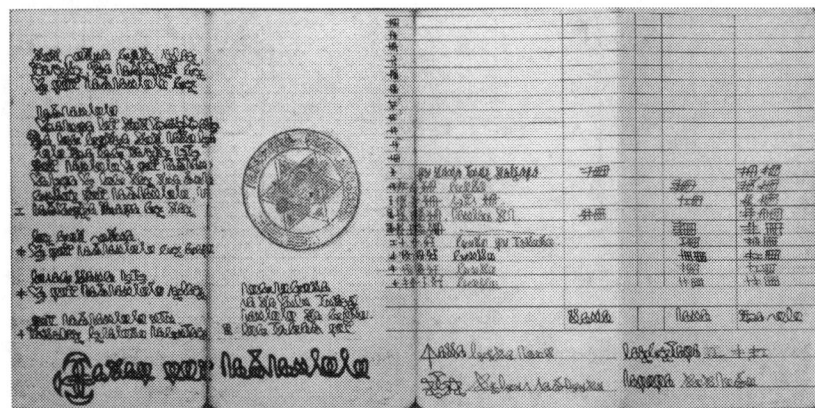

Figure 27.1 An example of the Raga writing system (*Source:* Author photo, Loltong, Vanuatu, August 2011)

for Raga, and the script follows its conventions closely, indicating it is a recent invention.

Figure 27.2 shows that it is possible to capture the introduction of writing as it happens. It shows the 2008 launching of the first alphabet chart and primer for the Eda language, spoken in northwestern Nigeria.[6] Unusually for Nigeria, the orthography was developed without outside input, and entirely funded by the community. The morning after the launching was the first time many Eda speakers had been exposed to a written form of their language, and people were walking around, primers in hand, expressing amazement at the relationship between the already familiar symbols and the sounds of their own languages. Participation in events of this type can help model the transition from the oral to the written in prehistory; the script-bearers, committed Christians, clearly parallel the priestly classes of the Ancient Near East.

Multiple language inscriptions are known from many written cultures and are often expressive of actual or intended political dominance. The role of such inscriptions in, for example, the decipherment of hieroglyphics is a well-known story. Less understood is the passion for multiple languages as an expression of intellectual curiosity. Figure 27.3 shows part of a stone inscription on the palace wall, in Durbar Square, Kathmandu, dating from the seventeenth century, where English and French can be descried, along with other languages of the subcontinent. This clearly is not primarily about politics, but rather reflects the multilingual environment of the market during the Malla period in Newar history.

27.9 The genesis of language registers

Sociocultural anthropologists have long documented marked divisions of gender roles in societies across the world, reflected in social and economic

Figure 27.2 Launching the Eda alphabet chart (*Source:* Author photo, Kadara, Nigeria, 2008)

organization. But similar divisions also have linguistic correlates. Informal differences in male and female speech registers have often been noted across the world, reflected in both choice of topics and semantics. Phonological and morphological marking of a gender register is much rarer, although it is reported sporadically across the world, notably in Sumerian (Rubio 2007), Chukchi (Dunn 2000), and Garifuna (Munro 1998). Japanese has a large repertoire of lexical variants used by women that are distinct from the politeness register, known as *onna kotoba* (女言葉 'women's words') or *joseigo* (女性語 'women's language') (Reynolds 1990). These typically interface with the politeness registers in Japanese. The Australian language Yanyuwa has separate dialects for men and for women at the morphological level (Kirton 1988). The only time men use the women's dialect is when they are quoting someone of the opposite sex, and vice versa.

Ethnographic evidence for gender registers in the present can be compared with epigraphic evidence from archaeology. For example, there were

Figure 27.3 Multi-language inscription, Durbar Square, Kathmandu, Nepal (*Source:* Author photo)

apparently two sociolects of Sumerian (Rubio 2007). The standard variety is called *eme-ŋir*, but *eme-sal* (EME.SAL, possibly 'fine tongue' or high-pitched voice) is often translated as 'women's language'. *Eme-sal* is used exclusively by female characters in some literary texts and in certain genres of cult songs. The special features of *eme-sal* are mostly phonological (e.g., m is often used instead of ŋ as in *me* vs. standard *ŋe* 'I'), but words different from the standard language are also used (e.g., *ga-ša-an* vs. standard *nin* 'lady').

Tarok, a Plateau language of East-Central Nigeria, has a morphologically marked gender register. This is quite atypical for a Niger-Congo language, although sex-gender pronominal marking is common in the adjacent languages. Longtau and Blench (under review) hypothesize that the evolution of this register arises from two factors: a strongly patrilineal and patrilocal society, where powerful secret societies have acted to reinforce male authority, and persistent bilingualism with Ngas, a neighboring and unrelated Chadic language, which does mark gender morphologically. Tarok has not borrowed segmental morphology, but has adapted the concept of direct linguistic marking of male/female relations.

27.10 Archaeology, linguistics, and genetics: New synthesis or wayward detour?

A discipline which has been the subject of great expectations and even greater claims has been genetics, specifically the analysis of mitochondrial and latterly paternal or nuclear DNA. (mt)DNA can be recovered from archaeological material and techniques to achieve this are constantly improving. Excavated bones and plant materials can also be compared with their modern relatives to develop hypotheses about palaeoenvironments and the genesis of subsistence strategies. However, more influential has been the sampling of living human populations with a view to determining their relationships. During the 1990s, it was only possible to examine single haplogroups, but advanced techniques now allow whole genome sequencing (first demonstrated in 2000 and commercially practical since 2007). An early success of this technique was "Mitochondrial Eve," the assumption that all humans had a "Most Recent Common Ancestor" who lived in Africa some 200,000 years ago (e.g., Behar *et al.* 2008). To judge by the claims of some of its exponents, the links between language, demographic movement, and genetics in prehistory are well established. These were enthusiastically promoted at the end of the 1980s and into the early 1990s as "the New Synthesis" and "Archaeogenetics" (see, for example, Cavalli-Sforza *et al.* 1988; Renfrew 1992; Renfrew 2002). The volume *The History and Geography of Human Genes* essayed a major revision of the methodology for exploring human history (Cavalli-Sforza *et al.* 1994). Linguistic classifications of human populations purport to offer a tool for outflanking simple racial models; more abstract, they appear to provide an ideal analog to the classificatory trees drawn from DNA analyses.

What is going wrong here? Human populations move, interact, spread their genes; there should be a link with the language map. The sand in the machine is language shift; human populations shift languages for reasons which have no biological analogy. Their marriage patterns may reflect notions of cultural prestige that do not mirror biological advantage. As a consequence, language affiliation and genetic composition rapidly go out of synchronization. Only where a population is expanding into previously uninhabited terrain or is otherwise unable to interact with other, genetically distinct, populations is such a correspondence likely. Genetics seems presently to be confident about its ability to provide useful hypotheses for other disciplines to test, but outside its special arena, a healthy skepticism still prevails.

Polynesian represents as simple a case history as exists: linguists agree that it is an offshoot of Central Pacific, which includes Rotuman and Fiji, and Samoa is the first island in the chain which eventually leads to New Zealand. For most accepted language groupings, notably Austronesian, of which Polynesian is but a late subset, many physical types are represented and many of the genetic interactions in prehistory are still poorly understood. Despite their racial, archaeological, and genetic accretions, terms such as Polynesian and Austronesian remain purely linguistic classifications and attempts to implant other types of meanings encounter a logical gap (hence the problems with overviews such as Friedlaender *et al.* 2008). To assume that linguistic entities can be mapped one-to-one against constructs from other disciplines is also to implicitly accept that contradictions can occur. In other words, a proposition of the form "genetics shows that Polynesians did not originate in Samoa as commonly supposed, but rather ..." has an assignable meaning. Bing Su et al. (2000) use genetics to try to decide between a Melanesian and a Taiwanese origin for the Polynesians. If geneticists claim that the Polynesians originated in Java some 17 kya (Oppenheimer and Richards 2001), and archaeology points to Fiji/Samoa around 3,000 years ago (Kirch 2000), one or the other or both are wrong, or they are using non-congruent definitions of "Polynesian." This represents a serious confusion; genetics cannot show linguistic hypotheses to be "wrong" in this way.

What, then, can such statements mean? Presumably those who say this have something in mind. The underlying statement seems to be that "certain genetic markers characteristic of the people presently identified as Polynesian are found in important concentrations in x," where x is different from the agreed homeland of the Polynesians. Whether the Polynesian-speaking peoples have really been adequately sampled remains doubtful. However, for the sake of argument, let us suppose that Polynesian-speaking peoples have been so characterized. The geneticists' claim then amounts to the observation that the genetic profile typical of a linguistic group is found among peoples who do not speak those languages today. Clearly this can have a number of possible explanations:

- Chance mutation
- Migration of a population from the present-day Polynesian-speaking region to region x and its assimilation
- Migration of a population from region x to the present-day Polynesian-speaking region and its assimilation
- Both populations deriving from a common source in a third region thus far unidentified

However, none of these options suggest that linguists are wrong or even confused in their characterization of Polynesian. There are technical problems with the results from DNA analyses, but even more important are logical gaps that are far from being addressed. Moreover, DNA is a large church, with a great variety of haplotypes and significantly different distributions of nuclear and mitochondrial DNA. So a distinctive characterization of Polynesians on this basis is probably as much a chimera as the classification of human races by head types, nasal indices, or many another now-forgotten indicator.

Skepticism on this front does not imply that a synthesis is not possible or desirable. More cautious essays in bringing together these different disciplines have begun to appear in edited volumes, confronting results from disciplinary approaches, notably Sagart et al. (2005) and Enfield (2011). Less grandiose claims may lead to more coherent accounts of the past.

27.11 Conclusions

Generally speaking, archaeologists have taken more interest than sociocultural anthropologists in adapting models from the present to interpret the past. Sociocultural anthropologists are interested in documentary evidence, but rarely in prehistory. But sociocultural anthropologists with an interest in linguistics could enrich their models of social and language change by comparison with the evidence from archaeology. Some examples given in this chapter include the early impact of writing on non-literate societies, the comparison with past and present episodes of language leveling, the modeling of creolization processes, and the genesis of language registers. Sociocultural anthropology has contributed much to the study of political and religious authority, and these were expressed through language as much in the past as in the present. Interpreting both linguistic patterning, as in palaeosociolinguistics, and hence the distribution of material culture can only be achieved when all three disciplines work together.

Notes

1. Some previous publications cover similar ground (e.g., Blench and Spriggs 1999; Blench 2004) so I have concentrated on recent developments and innovative approaches, summarizing briefly the more usual topics.
2. Leonard Bloomfield (1935: 6) noted that no direct source in Voltaire's writings has been discovered and there is more than a suspicion that this is a piece of convenient linguistic folklore.
3. The conventional narrative omits Jones's erroneous belief that Egyptian, Japanese, and Chinese were part of Indo-European while Hindi was not, which suggests that his method was seriously flawed.
4. Originals: *Es gibt keine Mischsprache* and *Es gibt keine völlig ungemischte Sprache*.
5. Thanks to Patrick Tevi for introducing me to this script and allowing me to photograph his manuscripts.
6. Thanks to Alex Maikarfi for inviting me to this event.

References

Atkinson, Q. D. 2011. Language Expansion from Africa: Phonemic diversity supports a serial founder effect model of language expansion from Africa. *Science* 332: 346–9.

Atkinson, Q. D., and R. D. Gray 2006. How Old is the Indo-European Language Family? Progress or more moths to the flame? In *Phylogenetic Methods and the Prehistory of Languages*, ed. P. Forster and C. Renfrew, 91–109. Cambridge: The McDonald Institute for Archaeological Research.

Bakker, P., and M. Mous, eds. 1994. *Mixed Languages: 15 Case Studies in Language Intertwining*. Amsterdam: IFOTT.

Barker G. W. W. 2006. *The Agricultural Revolution in Prehistory: Why Did Foragers Become Farmers?* Oxford: Oxford University Press.

Bechhaus-Gerst, M. 1996. *Sprachwandel durch Sprachkontakt am Beispiel des Nubischen im Niltal*. Cologne: Rüdiger Köppe.

Behar, D. M., R. Villems, H. Soodyall, J. Blue-Smith, L. Pereira, E. Metspalu, et al. 2008. The Dawn of Human Matrilineal Diversity. *American Journal of Human Genetics* 82(5): 1130–40,

Bellwood, P., and C. Renfrew, eds. 2002. Introduction. In *Proceedings of the Meeting on Early Farming Dispersals*, 3–16. McDonald Institute Monographs. Cambridge: McDonald Institute for Archaeological Research.

Benveniste, É. 1973. *Indo-European Language and Society*, trans. Elizabeth Palmer. London: Faber and Faber. (First published 1969.)

Bing Su, Li Jin, Peter Underhill, et al. 2000. Polynesian Origins: Insights from the Y chromosome. *Proceedings of the National Academy of Sciences USA* 97(15): 8225–8.

Blench, R. M. 2004. Archaeology and Language: Methods and issues. In *A Companion To Archaeology*, ed. J. Bintliff, 52–74. Oxford: Basil Blackwell.

——— 2007. Endangered Languages in West Africa. In *Language Diversity Endangered*, ed. M. Brenzinger, 140–62. The Hague: Mouton de Gruyter.

——— 2011. The Role of Agriculture in the Evolution of Southeast Asian Language Phyla. In *Dynamics of Human Diversity in Mainland SE Asia*, ed. N. Enfield, 125–52. Canberra: Pacific Linguistics.

——— 2012. The Role of Agriculture in Explaining the Diversity of Amerindian Languages. In *The Past Ahead: Language, Culture and Identity in the Neotropics*, ed. Christian Isendahl, 13–37. Uppsala: Acta Universitas Uppsaliensis.

Blench, R. M., and M. Spriggs. 1999. General Introduction. In *Archaeology and Language, IV*, ed. R. M. Blench and M. Spriggs, 1–20. London: Routledge.

Bloomfield, L. 1935. *Language*. London: Allen and Unwin.

Blust, R. A. 1999. Subgrouping, Circularity and Extinction: Some issues in Austronesian comparative linguistics. In *Selected Papers from Eighth International Conference on Austronesian Linguistics*, ed. E. Zeitoun and P. Jen-Kuei Li, 31–94. Taipei: Academica Sinica.

——— 2005. The Linguistic Macrohistory of the Philippines: Some speculations. In *Current Issues in Philippine Linguistics and Anthropology*, ed. H.-C. Liao, C. R. G. Rubino, K. Lawrence, and A. Reid, 31–68. Manila: The Linguistic Society of the Philippines and SIL, Philippines.

——— 2009a. *The Austronesian Languages*. Canberra: Pacific Linguistics.

——— 2009b. The Greater North Borneo Hypothesis. *Oceanic Linguistics* 49(1): 44–118.

Bonfante, G. 1953. Ideas on the Kinship of the European Languages from 1200 to 1800. *Cahiers d'Histoire Mondiale*, 1: 679–99.

Boxhorn, M. van 1647. *Antwoord van Marcus Zuerius van Boxhorn op de Vraaghen, hem voorgesteldt over de Bediedinge van de tot noch toe onbekende*

Afgodinne Nehalennia, onlancx uytgegeven. In welcke de ghemeine herkomste van der Griecken, Romeinen, ende Duytschen Tale uyt den Scythen duydelijck bewesen, ende verscheiden Oudheden van dese Volckeren grondelijck ontdeckt ende verklaert. Leyden: Willem Christiaens van der Boxe.

Boyeldieu, P. 1977. Éléments pour une phonologie de Laal de Gori. In *Études phonologiques tchadiennes*, ed. J.-P. Caprile, 186-98. Paris: SELAF.

Bulbeck, D. 2011. Biological and Cultural Evolution in the Population and Culture History of Homo sapiens in Malaya. In *Dynamics of Human Diversity in Mainland SE Asia*, ed. N. Enfield, 207-56. Canberra: Pacific Linguistics.

Campbell, L. 1997. *American Indian Languages: The Historical Linguistics of Native America*. New York/Oxford: Oxford University Press.

Cavalli-Sforza, L. L., P. Menozzi, and A. Piazza. 1994. *The History and Geography of Human Genes*. Princeton, NJ: Princeton University Press.

Cavalli-Sforza, L. L., A. Piazza, P. Menozzi, et al. 1988. Reconstruction of Human Evolution: Bringing together genetic, archaeological and linguistic data. *Proceedings of the National Academy of Science, USA* 85: 6002-6.

Codrington, R. 1885. *The Melanesian Languages: A linguistic survey of the groups of dialects and languages spread over the islands of Melanesia comprising their comparative grammar, numerals, vocabularies and phonology, and the grammars of some thirty-five languages*. Oxford: Clarendon Press.

Coulmas, F. 2003. *Writing Systems: An Introduction to their Linguistic Analysis*. Cambridge: Cambridge University Press.

Crowley, T. 1987. *An Introduction to Historical Linguistics*. Suva: University of the South Pacific.

Daniel, G. 1962. *The Idea of Prehistory*. Harmondsworth: Penguin.

Dewar, R. E. 1994. The Archaeology of the Early Settlement of Madagascar. In *The Indian Ocean in Antiquity*, ed. J. Reade, 471-86. London/New York: Kegan Paul/British Museum.

Dillehay, T. 1997. *Monte Verde: A Late Pleistocene Settlement in Chile*, Vol. 2. Washington, DC: Smithsonian Institution Press.

Dimmendaal, G. J. 2001. Language Shift and Morphological Convergence in the Nilotic Area. *Sprache und Geschichte in Afrika* 16/17: 83-124.

Dixon, R. M. W. 2002. *Australian Languages: Their Nature and Development*, Vol. 1. Cambridge: Cambridge University Press.

Dixon, R. M. W., and A. Y. Aikhenvald, eds. 1999. *The Amazonian Languages*. Cambridge: Cambridge University Press.

Donohue, M., and T. Denham 2010. Farming and Language in Island Southeast Asia Reframing Austronesian History. *Current Anthropology* 51(2): 223-56.

Dumont d'Urville, J. S. C. 1834. Philologie, par M. D'Urville. Seconde Partie. Les autres vocabulaires de langues ou Dialectes océaniens recueillies durant le voyage, et le Vocabulaire comparatif des langues françaises, madekass, malaio, *mawi, tonga, taiti et hawaii, suivis de quelques considérations générales sur ces langues*. Paris: Ministère de la Marine.

Dunn, M. J. 2000. Chukchi Women's Language: A historical-comparative perspective. *Anthropological Linguistics* 42(3): 305–28.

Dutton, T. 1999. From Pots to People: Fine tuning the prehistory of Mailu Island and neighbouring coast, south-east Papua New Guinea. In *Archaeology and Language III: Artefacts, Languages and Texts*, ed. R. M. Blench and M. Spriggs, 90–108. London: Routledge.

Ehret, C. 1988. Language Change and the Material Correlates of Languages and Ethnic Shift. *Antiquity* 62: 564–74.

Elichmann, J. 1640. *Tabula Cebetis Græce, Arabice, Latine. Item Aurea Carmina Pythagoræ cum Paraphrasi Arabica*. Leiden: Ioannis Maire.

Enfield, N. J., ed. 2011. *Dynamics of Human Diversity in Mainland SE Asia*. Canberra: Pacific Linguistics.

Evans, N. 2005. Australian Languages Reconsidered: A Review of Dixon (2002). *Oceanic Linguistics* 44 (1): 242–86.

Forestier, H., T. Simanjuntak, D. Guillaud, D. Driwantoro, K. Wiradnyana, D. Siregar, R. D. Awe, and Budiman. 2005. Le site de Togi Ndrawa, île de Nias, Sumatra Nord: les premières traces d'une occupation hoabinhienne en grotte en Indonésie. *C.R. Palevolution* 4: 727–33.

Forster, J. R. 1778. *Observations Made during a Voyage Around the World*. London: G. Robinson.

Friedlaender, J. S., F. R. Friedlaender, F. A. Reed, K. K. Kidd, J. R. Kidd, G. K. Chambers, *et al*. 2008. The Genetic Structure of Pacific Islanders. *PLoS Genetics* 4 (1): e19, doi: 10.1371/journal.pgen.0040019.

Gilij, F. S. 1780–84. *Saggio di storia americana, o sia, storia naturale, civile e sacra de'regni e delle provinzie spagnuole di Terra-Firma nell'america meridionale*. 4 vols. Rome: Perigio.

Goody, J. R. 1986. *The Logic of Writing and the Organization of Society*. Cambridge: Cambridge University Press.

Gray, R. D., and Q. D. Atkinson. 2003. Language-tree Divergence Times Support the Anatolian Theory of Indo-European Origin. *Nature* 426: 435–9.

Gray, R. D., A. J. Drummond, and S. J. Greenhill. 2009. Language Phylogenies Reveal Expansion Pulses and Pauses in Pacific Settlement. *Science* 323: 479–83.

Greenberg, J. 1987. *Language in the Americas*. Stanford, CA: Stanford University Press.

Greenhill, S. J., A. J. Drummond, and R. D. Gray. 2010. How Accurate and Robust Are the Phylogenetic Estimates of Austronesian Language Relationships? *PLoS ONE* 5(3): e9573.

Holden, C. J., and R. D. Gray. 2006. Rapid Radiation, Borrowing and Dialect Continua in the Bantu Languages. In *Phylogenetic Methods and the Prehistory of Languages*, ed. P. Forster and C. Renfrew, 19–31. Cambridge: McDonald Institute for Archaeological Research.

Irwin, G. 1985. *The Emergence of Mailu as a Central Place in Coastal Papuan Prehistory*. Terra Australis 10. Canberra: Department of Prehistory, Research School of Pacific Studies, Australian National University.

Janhunen, J. 2003. *The Mongolic Languages*. London: Routledge.

Kennerknecht, I., J. M. Hämmerle, and R. M. Blench. 2012. The Peopling of Nias, from the Perspective of Oral Literature and Molecular Genetic Data. In *Crossing Borders in Southeast Asian Archaeology: Selected papers from the 13th International Conference of the European Association of Southeast Asian Archaeologists, Berlin, 2010*, 2 vols., ed. D. Bonatz, A. Reinecke, M. L. Tjoa-Bonatz. Singapore: NUS Press.

Kirch, P. V. 2000. *On the Road of the Winds: An Archaeological History of the Pacific Islands Before European Contact*. Berkeley, CA: University of California Press.

Kirton, Jean F. 1988. Yanyuwa, a Dying Language. In *Aboriginal Language Use in the Northern Territory: 5 reports*. Work Papers of the Summer Institute of Linguistics, ed. M. J. Ray, 1-18. Darwin: Summer Institute of Linguistics.

Koch, H. 1997. Comparative Linguistics and Australian Prehistory. In *Archaeology and Linguistics: Aboriginal Australia in Global Perspective*, ed. P. McConvell and N. Evans, 27-43. Melbourne: Oxford University Press.

Latham, R. G. 1850. *The Natural History of the Varieties of Man*. London: John van Voorst.

Levinson, S. C., and R. D. Gray. 2012. Tools from Evolutionary Biology Shed New Light on the Diversification of Languages. *Trends in Cognitive Sciences* 16(3): 167-73.

Longtau, S., and R. M. Blench. Under review. A Gender Register in Tarok. *Anthropological Linguistics*.

Lynch, J., and K. Fakamuria. 1994. Borrowed Moieties, Borrowed Names: Sociolinguistic contact between Tanna and Futuna-Aniwa. *Pacific Studies* 17(1): 79-91.

Lynch, T. F. 1990. Glacial-age Man in South America? *American Anthropologist* 55: 12-36.

McConvell, P., and N. Evans 1998. The Enigma of Pama-Nyungan Expansion in Australia. In *Archaeology and Language II*, ed. R. M. Blench and M. Spriggs, 174-91. London: Routledge.

McMahon, A., and R. McMahon. 2005. *Language Classification by Numbers*. Oxford: Oxford University Press.

Mithun, M. 1999. *The Languages of Native North America*. Cambridge: Cambridge University Press.

Mous, M. 2004. *The Making of a Mixed Language: The Case of Ma'a/Mbugu*. Creole Language Library 26. Amsterdam: John Benjamins.

Müller, F. M. 1871. *Lectures on the Science of Language*. 2 vols. London: Longmans, Green and Company.

Muller, J.-C. 1986. Early Stages of Language Comparison from Sassetti to Sir William Jones (1786). *Kratylos* 31(1): 1-31.

Munro, P. 1998. The Garifuna Gender System. In *The Life of Language: Papers in Linguistics in Honor of William Bright*, ed. J. H. Hill, P. J. Mistry, and L. Campbell, 443–61. Berlin: Mouton de Gruyter.

Nichols, J. 1992. *Linguistic Diversity in Space and Time*. Chicago: University of Chicago Press.

Nurse, D. 2000. *Inheritance, Contact and Change in Two East African Languages*. Cologne: Rüdiger Köppe.

O'Connor, S., and J. Chappell 2003. Colonisation and Coastal Subsistence in Australia and Papua New Guinea: Different timing, different modes? In *Pacific Archaeology: Assessments and Anniversary of the First Lapita Excavation (July 1952) Koné, Nouméa, 2002*, ed. C. Sand, 17–32. Nouméa, New Caledonia: Les Cahiers de l'Archéologie en Nouvelle-Calédonie.

Oppenheimer, S., and M. Richards. 2001. Polynesian Origins: Slow boat to Melanesia? *Nature* 410: 166–7.

Pictet, A. 1859–63. *Les origines indo-européennes, ou les Aryas primitifs: essai de paléontologie linguistique*. Paris: Cherbuliez.

Relandus, Hadrianus [Adriaan van Reeland]. 1708. *Dissertationum Miscellanearum, Pars Tertia et Ultima*, 55–139. Utrecht: Guilielmus Broedelet.

Renfrew, C. 1987. *Archaeology and Language: The Puzzle of Indo-European Origins*. London: Jonathan Cape.

—— 1992. Archaeology, Genetic and Linguistic Diversity. *Man* 27(3): 445–78.

—— 2002. The "Emerging Synthesis": The Archaeogenetics Of Language/Farming Dispersals And Other Spread Zones. In *Proceedings of the Meeting on Early Farming Dispersals*, ed. P. Bellwood and C. Renfrew, 3–16. McDonald Institute Monographs. Cambridge: McDonald Institute for Archaeological Research.

Reynolds, K. A. 1990. Female Speakers of Japanese in Transition. In *Aspects of Japanese Women's Language*, ed. S. Ide and N. McGloin, 1–17. Tokyo: Kurosio Pub.

Rubio, G. 2007. Sumerian Morphology. In *Morphologies of Asia and Africa*, ed. Alan S. Kaye, Vol. 2, 1327–79. Winona Lake, IN: Eisenbrauns.

Ruhlen, M. 1987. *A Guide to the World's Languages*, Vol. 1: *Classification*. London: Edward Arnold.

Sagart, L., R. M. Blench, and A. Sanchez-Mazas, eds. 2005. *New Perspectives on the Phylogeny of East Asian Languages*. London: Curzon.

Swadesh, M. 1952. Lexicostatistic Dating of Prehistoric Ethnic Contacts. *Proceedings of the American Philosophical Society* 96: 453–62.

Téné, D. 1980. The Earliest Comparisons of Hebrew with Aramaic and Arabic. In *Progress in Linguistic Historiography*, ed. K. Koerner, 355–77. Amsterdam: John Benjamins.

Thomason, S. G., and T. Kaufman. 1988. *Language Contact, Creolization and Genetic Linguistics*. Berkeley: University of California Press.

Van Driem, G. 2001. *Languages of the Himalayas: An Ethnolinguistic Handbook*. Handbuch der Orientalistik. Leiden: Brill.
Wauchope, R. 1962. *Lost Tribes and Sunken Continents*. Chicago/London: University of Chicago Press.
Wotton, W. 1730. *A Discourse Concerning the Confusion of Languages at Babel*. London: Austen and Bowyer.

28

Language and biology

The multiple interactions between genetics and language

Dan Dediu

28.1 Introduction

As amply shown by the chapters in this handbook, language is a weird creature: it both defines and permeates being human, and while there might be some non-trivial aspects universally shared by the 7,000 or so languages, diversity in every aspect seems to be the norm. Languages differ in how they are produced and perceived (using airwaves, gestures, or tactile and visual marks), they vary in their structure (word order, phonological categories, etc.), vocabulary, domains of use, and so on. In turn, there has been until fairly recently an almost universal tacit assumption in modern linguistics that speakers are, for all practical purposes, identical, with the inter-speaker variation that could not be ignored relegated to the uninteresting domains of "performance" or "pathology." However, as in all cognitive science, *speaker variation* is more and more accepted as a fundamental ingredient of how language works, what language is, and how we got to have it. This chapter will try to provide an overview and summarize the complex relationships between linguistic and speaker biological diversity, on one hand, and the influence of paradigms derived from evolutionary biology – the science of diversity par excellence – on understanding language, on the other. These broad themes do not exhaust by far the richness of interactions between language and biology but they reflect the author's competences as well as the space constraints imposed on this chapter.

28.2 Linguistic and biological diversities as travel companions

Probably the simplest (apparently) and least controversial type of relationship between linguistic and biological diversities is represented by the fact that different human groups tend to speak different languages. Modern humans are a remarkably homogeneous species from the point of view of genetic variation when compared with other mammals (Templeton, 1998; Barbujani and Colonna, 2010; Jobling *et al.*, 2013), due to our recent origins in the last couple of hundred thousand years (Stringer and Andrews, 1988; Klein, 2009) and, until the agricultural revolution some 12,000–10,000 years ago (Mithen, 2003; Diamond and Bellwood, 2003), very low global population size (Barbujani and Colonna, 2010; Jobling *et al.*, 2013). This homogeneity is reflected in the oft-cited distribution of genetic variation between (about 10–15%) and within (about 85–90%) human populations (Lewontin, 1972), meaning that most of the variation in humans is to be found among the members of the same group (Barbujani and Colonna, 2010; Jobling *et al.*, 2013). Moreover, even these 15% differences are distributed as continuous clines and there seem to be no sharp boundaries marking anything like discrete human "races" (Cavalli-Sforza *et al.*, 1994; Barbujani, 2005), with the differences between groups given mostly by the relative frequencies of widespread ("cosmopolitan") genetic variants (or *alleles*) as opposed to group-specific "private" variants (Barbujani, 2005).

Nevertheless, there is genetic structure in modern humans and this can be revealed by analyses which can use simultaneously the information provided by many *genetic loci*. A genetic locus can be, for example, a whole *gene*, such as the one controlling the blood group (the *ABO* gene[1] on chromosome[2] 9; OMIM[3] 110300) and giving each one of us a unique type (*A*, *B*, *O*, or *AB*), a change in a single DNA letter (*single nucleotide polymorphisms* or *SNPs*) of which there are millions and which can happen within or between genes, or variations in the number of copies of a given strand of DNA somebody carries (*copy number variations* or *CNVs*). Methods commonly used to analyze the information provided by several loci include general techniques for summarizing complex datasets such as *Principal Components Analysis* (PCA; Tabachnick and Fidell, 2001) and *Multi-Dimensional Scaling* (MDS; Cox and Cox, 1994), which are widely used in other scientific fields including psychology and dialectology (e.g., Shackleton, 2007), as well as methods specifically developed for tackling genetic diversity, such as *STRUCTURE* (Pritchard *et al.*, 2000), which can be used to study population structure, and *Geneland* (Guillot *et al.*, 2005), which also takes into account geography.

Just as one recent and striking example of studies and findings concerning the genetic structure of modern humans, Novembre *et al.* (2008) used about half a million SNPs from individuals across Europe and found that there is a remarkable similarity between the genetic variation and Europe's geography (see their Figure 1): 90 percent of the genotyped individuals not of mixed grandparental origins could be placed within 700 km of their geographical origin! However, even if there is enough genetic structure within Europe to reconstruct its geography from genetic variation data, there are no sharp boundaries between populations; instead this genetic variation is largely gradual, highlighting the continuity of human populations across the continent. Moreover, the amount of genetic variation explained by this geographical structure is under 1 percent (Novembre et al., 2008), showing again that most genetic variation happens within small-scale groups and not between them. Similarly, when looking at continent-scale populations, about one to several hundred so-called *Ancestry Informative Markers* (AIMs) – genetic loci which show strong differences in frequency between populations – are enough for distinguishing such populations and for placing individuals with acceptable accuracy (e.g., Nassir et al., 2009; Paschou et al., 2010).

It has been shown time and again that there are large-scale patterns in our genetic structure, with Africa being home to by far the most genetically diverse human populations (Campbell and Tishkoff, 2010; Jobling et al., 2013), and with the genetic and phenotypic diversities seemingly decreasing the further away from Africa one goes (Manica et al., 2007). Interestingly, it has been recently suggested that language might also partially follow a similar pattern, with "phonemic diversity" decreasing with increasing geographic distance from Africa (Atkinson, 2011), but there are serious doubts about the validity of this claim (e.g., Cysouw et al., 2012).

However, the story told by genetic diversity is far from simple, and it has been aptly compared to a *palimpsest* (Relethford, 2003: 102) recording aspects of multiple events having happened at various times and in various places, some partially overwriting more ancient traces or leaving only the faintest marks. Importantly, such traces reveal only fragments of a larger and extremely complex story and they do *not* come with conveniently attached geographical coordinates, dates, ethnic or linguistic labels, or even "species" names (Sims-Williams, 1998; MacEachern, 2000; McMahon, 2004). On this palimpsest, aided by other sources of evidence from, among others, archaeology, palaeoanthropology, geology, and climatology, one of the most visible traces is that of the evolution of our lineage somewhere in Africa during the last several million years and of a number of dispersals from there starting roughly 1.8–2.0 million years ago across the world (Stringer, 2002; Templeton, 2002; Jobling et al., 2013), culminating around 100,000 years ago with the spread of the modern humans – that's us – first across the Old World, reaching Australia about 40–60,000 years ago (Jobling et al., 2013), the Americas probably sometime before 12,000 years ago (Waters, Forman, et al., 2011; Waters, Stafford, et al., 2011), and the remotest Polynesian islands only some thousand years ago (Friedlaender et al., 2008).

However, there are other stories embedded there, harder to discern behind the blinding glare of our *Recent Out of Africa* emergence but not less important, and ongoing advances in our ability to extract and analyze ancient DNA from fossils prove invaluable. Thus, we found not only that our cousins the *Neanderthals* contributed about 1.4% of the genetic make-up of present-day non-Africans (Green et al., 2010) – a fringe possibility entertained by some for quite a while based on fossil and genetic hints (Wolpoff and Caspari, 1997; Templeton, 2002; Relethford, 2003; Hurford and Dediu, 2009) – but that other cousins that we had no idea existed at all, the *Denisovans* (Krause et al., 2010), also did, leaving their genetic legacy especially in present-day Melanesians (Reich et al., 2010) at levels of about 4–6%. While genetic contributions of the level of 1% or 6% might seem negligible, one must keep in mind that they represent averages across the genome and are most probably downward biased by the techniques used to estimate them, as seemingly suggested by the discovery that genes involved in the immune system might show extremely high rates of *introgression* of up to 95% in Papua New Guinea (Abi-Rached et al., 2011). It would not come as a surprise then if it turns out that we have also inherited linguistic and cultural traits from these, and other, as yet undiscovered, archaic humans (Dediu and Levinson, 2013).

As argued above, the existing genetic structure of modern humans, no matter how genetically uniform we are compared to other mammals, is the result of our complex history. Several processes affect it, either increasing or decreasing it. The main source of genetic variation is *mutation*, understood here as an umbrella term covering all processes creating new genetic information, such as *point mutations* flipping one DNA letter into another one (say, an A into a G), *recombination* (creating new strings of DNA from the combination of two other strings) and *insertion/deletion* of sequences of DNA letters (Jobling et al., 2013).

In the absence of any other forces acting on them, two separated populations will slowly diverge genetically (the genetic differences between them will increase) in time due to the accumulation of random mutations, and this process goes a long way in explaining the patterning of genetic diversity in modern humans. If we consider a *mother* population P_0 at time t_0 undergoing a split into two *daughter* populations P_1 and P_2 at time $t_1 > t_0$ due, for example, to migration into a new territory, then at the time of split (t_1) the two daughter populations will be relatively similar genetically (but probably not identical; see below), and as time goes by, and assuming that they are isolated from each other, they will both accumulate different mutations in a random manner, becoming more and more genetically different. Now, if population P_0 spoke at t_0 (to keep things simple) a language, L_0, then its daughter populations P_1 and P_2 will speak at t_1 two very closely related languages L_1 and L_2 (or maybe even dialects of L_0), but as time goes by, these two languages (dialects) will keep diverging from one another, becoming less and less similar until their ancestral relatedness is unrecognizable even to expert historical linguists.

This *parallel diversification of genes and languages* was famously proposed by L. L. Cavalli-Sforza and colleagues (e.g., Cavalli-Sforza et al., 1994; Cavalli-Sforza, 2000) as an important factor in explaining the genetic and linguistic diversities and their interrelations. In this conception, the resulting relationships (correlations) between genetic and linguistic diversities reflect a deeper cause, namely *demographic processes* affecting both in parallel ways. Thus, finding that, for example, allele A_1 of a certain gene is present in populations speaking West Germanic languages, while allele A_2 of the same gene is present in North Germanic-speaking populations, does not mean that this gene is somehow involved in determining the *type* of language a population speaks, A_1 making it speak West Germanic while A_2 makes it speak North Germanic. In a more subtle version of this fallacy, this gene would determine structural, typological features of the language spoken by the population such that allele A_1 makes the population speak a typologically West Germanic-like language, while A_2 makes it speak a typologically North Germanic-like language. However, the truth behind this correlation between A_1 and West-Germanic and A_2 and North-Germanic is simply due to *shared ancestry and subsequent differentiation*, with the populations changing towards West Germanic having gained and fixed allele A_1 in their gene pool, while the other populations fixed A_2 instead. This is a case of the more general fallacy of interpreting correlations as pointing to direct causal links, known as the "chopsticks gene" when correlating genetics with behavioral, cultural, or linguistic traits (Hamer and Sirota, 2000), and is made even more dangerous by the multitude of such potential correlations: just imagine how easy it would be to find a gene for eating with chopsticks when there are literally millions of genetic markers available for testing, some of them just by pure chance different between chopstick-using populations and non-chopstick-using ones! (I will revisit these issues below when discussing multiple comparisons correction and genetic biasing.)

Intuitively, this scenario of *parallel divergence of genes and languages* seems to make a lot of sense, and the early proponents supported it by showing striking similarities between linguistic and population classifications (see, for example, Cavalli-Sforza et al., 1994). Alas, it soon transpired that despite its simplicity and beauty the idea was flawed on several levels. For example, the population trees constructed represent the genetic similarities between these populations and should not be interpreted simply in genealogical terms, given that human populations are not biological species and gene exchange between them muddles such simple interpretations (Sims-Williams, 1998; MacEachern, 2000). Moreover, the purported similarities between the language and population trees seem to be in large part due to visually arranging the trees so that their similarity is highlighted (Bateman et al., 1990), and might be helped by the usage of mostly linguistic labels in identifying the populations in the first place, thus inducing a certain degree of circularity (McMahon, 2004). Another contentious issue was the early practitioners' strong attraction to large-scale (macro-family) linguistic classifications such as Greenberg's *Amerind* (Greenberg, 1987) or the various versions of *Nostratic* (see the papers in Renfrew and Nettle, 1999 and Salmons and Joseph, 1998 for a good overview), usually as summarized and updated by Ruhlen (1991). This was justified through theoretic appeals to arguably simplistic models of language change and evolution and by the pragmatic need to match the population trees with something tree-like on the linguistic side (e.g., Cavalli-Sforza, 2000: 139–40), but such constructs are vehemently rejected by most practitioners of historical linguistics (e.g., Bateman et al., 1990; Matisoff, 1990; Sims-Williams, 1998; Campbell, 1999; Bolnick et al., 2004; McMahon, 2004; Campbell and Poser, 2008). Nevertheless, modern studies in this vein make use of much more sophisticated conceptualizations of the processes affecting both genetic and linguistic diversities through time as well as more powerful statistical techniques for looking for such similarities, while still preserving the original insights that there are complex relationships between linguistic and genetic diversities due to shared history. For example, *Monmonier's algorithm* (Monmonier, 1973) and other techniques can be used to detect regions of rapid change based on genetic and linguistic data and to estimate the correlations between them (Barbujani and Sokal, 1990; Manni et al., 2004).

An accent on uni-parentally inherited genetic markers (the Y chromosome, inherited by males from their fathers, and mitochondrial DNA, inherited by children of both genders from their mothers) helps in making clearer and stronger inferences about the genetic history of populations at the cost of providing only sex-specific stories (to give just a few examples from a rapidly expanding literature, see Nasidze and Stoneking, 2001; Wood et al., 2005; Hassan et al., 2008; Mona et al., 2009; Cruciani et al., 2010). The downside is that the histories of the female and male lines, as told by *mtDNA* and the Y chromosome respectively, can be different, as when, for example, there are gender-specific patterns of migration or selection, different marriage customs, or different post-marital residence rules. The case of Genghis Khan's genetic legacy (Zerjal et al., 2003), manifested as a disproportionate presence of a Y-chromosome lineage that originated in Mongolia about 1,000 years ago in present-day men, is well known and shows that, as opposed to women, men can experience very large differences in biological fitness which leave their specific signature in the genes. Likewise, patrilocal, matrilocal, and neolocal post-marital residence patterns will affect the genetic histories of the two genders differently (Oota et al., 2001; Wilkins and Marlowe, 2006; Jordan et al., 2009). More importantly, both these histories will diverge to various degrees from the ethnographic record and from the history of the languages, and highlight the importance of, on one hand, using all available data when making historical inferences and, on the other, specifying the history of what or whom we are reconstructing.

An important class of models derived from the principle that associations between genetic and linguistic diversities are related through shared history is represented by attempts at explaining the origins and spread of the major language families, such as *Indo-European* and *Austronesian*. Probably the best known concerns the controversies around the place of origin and subsequent spread and differentiation of the Indo-European languages, with the two most prominent proposals being (see, e.g., Mallory, 1991; Jobling et al., 2013) the "Kurgan hypothesis" championed by Marija Gimbutas proposing a relatively recent origin (about 5,000 years ago) somewhere in the steppes north of the Black and Caspian Seas and a spread driven by military conquest, and the "Anatolian hypothesis" proposed by Colin Renfrew and suggesting an older origin (about 9,000 years ago) in Anatolia, from where the Indo-European languages spread mostly due to the expansion of the agricultural populations speaking them (a process called *demic diffusion*). It is fair to say that the jury is still out, with both proposals being supported by different lines of evidence, with linguistics being used by the proponents of both theories: the recent "Kurgan origins" seems supported by *linguistic paleontology* (Mallory, 1991; Mallory and Adams, 2006) while the older "Anatolian origins" have recently received strong support from the application of modern *phylogenetic techniques* inspired by evolutionary biology to the *basic vocabulary* (Gray and Atkinson, 2003; Bouckaert et al., 2012).

Nevertheless, in this context, the proposal that Indo-European was spread by early farmers expanding from one of the origins of agriculture (the Middle East in this case) is only a particular case of a more general *language-farming co-dispersal* process which purports to explain the distribution of several major language families around the world (Diamond, 1997; Diamond and Bellwood, 2003). There are multiple ways in which agriculture can expand and they will leave different genetic, archaeological, and linguistic signatures (e.g., Cavalli-Sforza et al., 1994; Jobling et al., 2013), not necessarily easy to distinguish. For example, the *demic diffusion* model (Cavalli-Sforza et al., 1994) proposes that, due to their much higher growth, agriculturalists would expand into land inhabited by hunter-gatherers and replace or admix with them, resulting in relatively clear *genetic clines* and the accompanying expansion of large language families (such as Indo-European or Bantu; Diamond and Bellwood 2003). However, other scenarios are also possible, such as a purely *cultural diffusion* of agriculture whereby local populations take the cultural practices with minimal genetic admixture. The reality, as always, was probably messier than these extreme models would imply, leaving behind complex genetic and linguistic patterns of diversity (Diamond and Bellwood, 2003; Jobling et al., 2013). On top, we have to remember that the present-day genetic patterns are a palimpsest on which these expansions are but one of the messages written on top of previous ones and over-written in turn by more recent phenomena such as the Early Medieval population movements in Europe (e.g., Davies, 1997).

In conclusion, present-day genetic and linguistic diversities are not independent, due to common processes affecting both, but the relationship between them is far from simple. While human populations generally tend to keep their languages and genes, creating correlations between large-scale genetic and linguistic patterns, there are many situations in which this correlation is broken through, for example, language shift and population admixture. Moreover, multiple such processes have repeatedly left their mark on these patterns and the association of these patterns to conveniently labeled groups of people or historical events, while seductive both scientifically and politically, is fraught with difficulties and uncertainties.

28.3 The genetic foundations of speech and language

It is clear even without much reflection that there is something "genetic" or "innate" about language and speech in that it is only our species that possesses them. It would, therefore, seem like a logical and easy step to claim that there must be some genetic factors *specific* to language and speech, a step notoriously taken and still vigorously defended by Chomsky (e.g., 2011) and his followers. However, on closer inspection it turns out that such a naïve concept of "innateness" is in fact *extremely multifaceted* and *hard to define* in general (Mameli and Bateson, 2006, 2011) and especially so when it comes to complex phenotypes, where plasticity and environmental interactions are the norm (West-Eberhard, 2003), requiring a profound and critical re-evaluation and an increased sophistication of the discussion concerning the genetic bases of speech and language. To begin with, it is important to reiterate that genetic and environmental factors are fundamentally in *interaction* and it does not make much sense to even consider them in isolation, and that genes very rarely can be conceptualized as coding "for" a single higher-level trait (e.g., an abstract linguistic parameter) but instead are involved in *complex networks* of molecular interactions (Snustad and Simmons, 2010) influencing (among others) various aspects of speech and language (Fisher, 2006). This means that simple stories rarely hold – as amply shown by the complexities and unexpected findings of the ongoing research program centered on *FOXP2*, the gene sometimes misleadingly labeled "the language gene" (see for example, Lai *et al.*, 2001; Enard *et al.*, 2002; Spiteri *et al.*, 2007; Vernes *et al.*, 2008; Roll *et al.*, 2010) – and this is especially so when one also takes into account the population/cultural level at which language lives.

The "classic" approach to the investigation of the genetic foundations of language and speech, predating the advent of modern molecular techniques and the understanding of the complexities of our genome, is represented by estimates of *heritability* and *genetic correlations*, quantifying the relative contributions of environmental and genetic factors to the *interindividual differences* in aspects of speech and language, on one hand, and evaluating the relationships between the numerous genetic factors involved, on the other.

Heritability is essentially defined as the proportion of phenotypic variance explained by variance in the genotype, $h^2 = var(G)/var(P)$ (Lynch and Walsh, 1998; Visscher *et al.*, 2008), but we cannot compute it directly and instead need to estimate it from various types of data. Classically, this estimation is based mostly (Plomin et al., 2008) on twin studies (whereby *monozygotic* [identical] and *dizygotic* [non-identical] twins are compared) and adoption studies (where adoptees are compared to their biological and foster parents and siblings), but recently developed methods can make use of unrelated individuals as well (Yang et al., 2010; Davies et al., 2011). The heritability of a trait can vary between a maximum of 1 (all variation in trait values among the tested individuals is accounted for by variation in their genomes) and a minimum of 0 (genetic factors do not explain any of the trait variation). In the case of twin studies, the similarity between the phenotypes of monozygotic (identical; MZ) and dizygotic (non-identical; DZ) twins are compared, and on the assumption that MZ twins are genetically identical but DZ twins share on average half of their genomes, the heritability of the phenotype under study is estimated as, $h^2 = 2\,(r_{MZ} - r_{DZ})$ where r_{MZ} and r_{DZ} are the correlation between the phenotypes of the MZ and the DZ twins, respectively.[4]

Important caveats affect the interpretation that can be attached to heritability estimates in general (Visscher et al., 2008) and their validity (Charney, 2012), among which the most important are that they depend on the population under study and do not automatically generalize to other populations, they depend on the amount of environmental variation experienced by the individuals, they cannot automatically be used to explain inter-population differences, and high heritability estimates do not equate with "innateness." Finally (and needless to say), any heritability (or other type of genetic) study is only as good as the definition and measurement of the phenotype of interest it uses. Measuring speech and language is much more difficult, indirect (involving sometimes questioning the parents or teachers), and less reliable (having higher and more insidious measurement errors and requiring better psychometric approaches; Nunnally and Bernstein 1994, Furr and Bacharach 2007, Borsboom 2009) than measuring height for example, but there are no a priori reasons to think that their heritability must be less than that of more "biological" phenotypes. Thus, heritability estimates must be taken as rough and context-dependent indications of the balance between environmental and genetic factors, and must be followed by further molecular studies designed to find the genes and the exact processes (including developmental ones) involved.

There is currently a wealth of twin studies concerning multiple aspects of language and speech (Stromswold, 2001) and, taken together, they strongly suggest that most have a genetic component. Various disorders, such as *dyslexia* (Scerri and Schulte-Krne, 2010; Hensler et al., 2010), the liability to *stuttering* (Felsenfeld, 2002), and *specific language impairment* (Bishop, 2003), have moderate to high heritabilities ($h^2 > 0.50$). Similarly, certain aspects of the normal variation between individuals in speech and language, such as *vocabulary size* (Stromswold, 2001) and *second language learning* (Dale et al., 2010) also exhibit an important genetic component. Interestingly, the anatomical and physiological aspects of speech production are also under genetic influence, as indicated by heritability studies of the shape and size of the hard palate (Townsend et al., 1990), of the tongue (Klockars and Pitkranta, 2009), and of various acoustic properties of speech (e.g., Debruyne et al., 2002).

However, on top of the limitations and caveats discussed, heritability studies offer only a suggestion that genetics might play a role in phenotypic variation and, due to recent advances in molecular genetics, the focus has moved towards actually identifying the genetic loci, the specific mechanisms, and the environmental factors involved. One very productive such research program was generated by the discovery (Lai et al., 2001) that the *FOXP2* gene is involved in a complex pathology affecting speech and language (*developmental verbal dyspraxia*; OMIM 602081). While *FOXP2* is one of the most conserved genes across mammals, its modern human form (shared with our close relatives, the *Neanderthals*; Krause et al., 2007) shows two specific mutations (Enard et al., 2002) which have been proposed as linked with the emergence of speech and language (Trinkaus, 2007). Besides the catastrophic (and rare) mutations that give rise to developmental verbal dyspraxia, *FOXP2* (like most of our genes) has a number of polymorphisms (variants present in the population at frequencies above a certain threshold such as 5%). It is currently unclear if these polymorphisms influence the normal variation between individuals in what concerns speech and language, but it has been recently proposed that they have an effect at least at the neural level (Pinel et al., 2012). But probably the most important aspect is that *FOXP2* represents an entry point for (or a *molecular window* into; Fisher and Scharff, 2009) the genetic underpinnings of speech and language. The search for the genes regulated by *FOXP2* (Konopka et al., 2009) is an active scientific field, resulting in the identification of promising genes such as *CNTNAP2* (Vernes et al., 2008). Another line of research with high potential is into the genetics of dyslexia, resulting in the identification of risk factors such as *KIAA0319* (Francks et al., 2004) and *ROBO1* (Hannula-Jouppi et al., 2005), recently proposed (Bates et al., 2011) to be involved in the normal variation in a component essential for language acquisition.

Thus, there is quite a lot of variation between individuals in most aspects (both normal and pathological) of speech and language, most such aspects have a genetic component, but these genetic influences are very complex (Fisher, 2006) and can range from massive to very subtle.

28.4 The interplay between genes and language at the population level

I have said, when discussing language and genes as travel companions through history and geography, that genetic and linguistic diversities are related indirectly, being shaped by underlying population processes and, thus, there is no direct causal connection between a population's genes and its language(s). While this is generally true, the possibility that a population's genes might influence aspects of the language(s) it speaks is not a priori forbidden by what we currently know.

Probably the most convincing case that genes do *bias* language is offered by the sign languages developed by communities with a relatively high incidence of hereditary deafness, where such sign languages emerge spontaneously and spread even among hearing members of the community. Two well-studied cases are represented by the *Kata Kolok* of Bengkala, Bali (Winata et al., 1995; De Vos, 2012), and the *Al-Sayyid Bedouin Sign Language* of the Negev desert, Israel (*ABSL*; Scott et al., 1995; Sandler et al., 2005; Sandler et al., this volume, Chapter 10), where mutations were introduced relatively recently (10–20 generations ago for *Kata Kolok* and 7–8 for *ABSL*). However, the mutations are different, affecting the *DFNB3* locus (*MYO15A* gene) involved in the cochlear hair cells essential for hearing in *Kata Kolok* (OMIM 602666; Friedman et al., 1995, Liang et al., 1998), and the locus *DFNB1* (genes *GJB2* and *GJB6*) in *ABSL* (OMIM 220290; Scott et al., 1995), both resulting in *pre-lingual* (before the start of language acquisition) *non-syndromic* hearing loss (deafness not accompanied by other defects) only affecting *homozygous* individuals (with two copies of the mutation). As both loci are on *autosomes* (non-sex chromosomes), an individual will inherit one copy from each parent, being affected by deafness only if the two copies of the gene are mutated, which happens only if both parents are *heterozygous* carriers (with normal hearing) or *homozygous* deaf. In both cases there is a relatively high incidence of deafness (2% for *Kata Kolok* and 3% for *ABSL*) having persisted for several generations (Winata et al., 1995; Sandler et al., 2005) due to high levels of *inbreeding* (within-community marriages), and in both communities the deaf are well integrated socially and with normal biological fitness (i.e., marriage and reproduction).

These conditions resulted in the emergence, maintenance, and complexification of new sign languages shared by the whole community (including the hearing members) and which show little (if any) signs of structural influence from the other speaking or sign languages the communities might be exposed to. These cases also highlight the *indirectness* of the interactions between these "deafness genes" and sign language, in the sense that the specific genetic features of these populations make possible the emergence of sign language across generations, which, in turn, allows the social integration of deaf members and their increased biological fitness, allowing the persistence of the "deafness genes" in the population. Thus, this is the result of a cross-generational feedback loop between biology ("deafness genes") and culture (village sign languages). Thus, these dramatic cases of emergent "deaf village" sign languages show that language does adapt to the biological characteristics of its speakers (in this case, genetic deafness). An interesting question that still needs to be explored (but see Aoki and Feldman, 1991: 358; Feldman and Aoki, 1992; Nance et al., 2000, Nance and Kearsey 2004) concerns the number of deaf individuals, the social, cultural, and communicative characteristics, and the time-depth necessary for such a system to emerge and evolve.

As previously mentioned, even if we are a very uniform species from a genetic point of view, there is, nevertheless, quite a bit of genetic variation between human groups manifested mostly as differences between the frequency of ubiquitous alleles. Therefore there is enough variation for such genetic biases to exist and probably the most obvious place to look for them is in the production and perception of speech. A striking example was recently proposed to explain several characteristics of the Australian languages (lack of fricatives and a large number of place distinctions) through the deleterious effects on hearing of *Chronic Otitis Media* (COM; a long-term infection of the middle ear) infections affecting a large proportion of Australian aboriginal children (Butcher, 2006). If confirmed, this would represent a slightly different type of *biological biasing* of language in the sense that while there might be an increased genetic liability to COM in the Australian populations, the bias manifested as a specific type of hearing deficit ultimately has environmental causes (an infection). Preliminary and largely unsystematic data seem to point to extensive variation in the anatomy and physiology of the vocal tract, such as the reported lack of alveolar ridge in click-language speakers (Traill, 1985; Traunmüller, 2003), differences in various muscles of the larynx and the lips (Brosnahan, 1961; Catford, 1977) and differences in shape and dimensions of the hard palate (Hiki and Itoh, 1986; Kashima, 1990), to cite just a few. Some of these differences seem to have a genetic basis and to show population structure, but more systematic data collection and statistical analysis are required before any strong conclusions can be drawn.

There must be, however, "milder" cases where language adapts to smaller such genetic biases (Dediu, 2011). The idea is that these genetic biases are *very weak* at the individual level, such that any normal child acquires the language(s) of his/her community, but only become manifest when the frequency of biased individuals in a community crosses a certain threshold, and requires repeated cultural transmission across multiple generations (Ladd *et al.*, 2008). Therefore, these genetic biases are not deterministic but represent just one of many causal factors influencing the structural properties of a language. A well-known early proposal is represented by Peter Ladefoged's (1984) explanation of the differences in the second formant between the otherwise very similar vowel systems of *Yoruba* and *Italian* as being due to the differences in the shape and dimensions of the upper vocal tract between the two populations. But probably the best-supported case is represented by the genetic biasing of *linguistic tone* by two brain growth and development–related genes, *ASPM* and *Microcephalin* (Dediu and Ladd, 2007). This proposal rests on a population-level association between the population frequency of two alleles of these genes (the so-called "derived haplogroups") and the presence of linguistic tone (i.e., the use of voice pitch to convey lexical and/or grammatical meaning; Yip 2002) in the language(s) spoken by those populations, even after controlling for the effects of shared history and contact (Dediu and Ladd, 2007). Our proposal was that a *by-product* of these two alleles is to influence the acquisition, perception, processing, or production of voice pitch such that populations with many speakers carrying both alleles would be biased away from using linguistic tone (Ladd et al., 2008). It must be stressed that these would *not* in any meaningful way be construed as "genes for tone" as their putative effect on linguistic tone would be very small, indirect, and fortuitous (Dediu and Ladd, 2007; Ladd et al., 2008). After the publication of our proposal, several lines of direct and indirect evidence supporting our general proposal have appeared (see Dediu 2011 for a review, and Wong et al., 2012 for a recent behavioral experiment).

Given the above discussion, it seems safe to expect that at least some of the structural differences between languages might be due to the slight influence of cognitive biases as well as to anatomical and physiological differences in the vocal tract, amplified by repeated cultural transmission across generations (Dediu, 2011). Such biases dynamically affect the "selective landscape" of language, in the sense that language – as a cultural being – must adapt to them in order to be used and transmitted (Christiansen and Chater, 2008), and this landscape will change both through time and space. Thus, besides explaining some of the patterns of linguistic diversity, if these genetic (biological) biases are shared by all members of our species, then they might play a role in shaping universal linguistic tendencies as well (see also Nick Enfield, this volume, Chapter 13).

28.5 Conclusions

I hope I managed to make it clear to the reader that genetics (biology) and language interact on many inter-related levels, from the individual to the group to the whole species. Understanding these multi-faceted interactions and their consequences will require a broad interdisciplinary approach not only integrating the language sciences, anthropology, genetics, and evolutionary biology but also drawing upon advanced data analysis and computational skills. This effort holds the promise to help us understand not only the patterns of linguistic diversity and their history, but to shed light on the emergence and evolution of our species and one of its hallmarks, namely language.

Acknowledgments

The ideas explored in this chapter have resulted from many discussions and I cannot thank individually all involved, but special thanks go to Bob Ladd, Stephen C. Levinson, Simon Kirby, James Hurford, Didier Demolin, Bart de Boer, and Nick Enfield.

Notes

1. By convention, human genes are denoted with *ITALIC CAPITAL LETTERS* and their protein product by NORMAL TYPEFACE CAPITALS.
2. The human genetic information (the human *genome*) is composed of the mitochondrial DNA (*mtDNA*), which is inherited only from the mother, and the nuclear *chromosomes*, which come in 22 pairs of *autosomes* and one pair of *sex chromosomes* inherited from both parents. The sex chromosomes come in two forms: the X and the Y, with women having two X's (*XX*) and men having an X and a Y (*XY*). In general, a *locus* is a place on a chromosome where there can be one or more alternative forms of the DNA (*variants* or *alleles*), which can have an observable effect on the organism (the *phenotype*). For more details see any recent introductory text to genetics such as Jobling *et al.* 2013 or Snustad and Simmons 2010.
3. The *Online Mendelian Inheritance in Man* (http://omim.org) is an essential database of genetic disorders and genes, identified by unique numbers.
4. More advanced methods are in fact currently used (see for example Lynch and Walsh 1998 or Posthuma 2009).

References

Abi-Rached, L., M. J. Jobin, S. Kulkarni, A. McWhinnie, K. Dalva, L. Gragert, *et al.* 2011. The Shaping of Modern Human Immune Systems by Multiregional Admixture with Archaic Humans. *Science* 334(6052): 89–94.

Aoki, K., and M. W. Feldman. 1991. Recessive Hereditary Deafness, Assortative Mating, and Persistence of a Sign Language. *Theoretical Population Biology* 39(3): 358–72.

Atkinson, Q. D. 2011. Phonemic Diversity Supports a Serial Founder Effect Model of Language Expansion from Africa. *Science* 332(6027): 346–9.

Barbujani, G. 2005. Human Races: Classifying people vs understanding diversity. *Current Genomics* 6: 215–26.

Barbujani, G., and V. Colonna. 2010. Human Genome Diversity: Frequently asked questions. *Trends in Genetics* 26(7): 285–95.

Barbujani, G., and R. R. Sokal. 1990. Zones of Sharp Genetic Change in Europe are also Linguistic Boundaries. *Proceedings of The National Academy of Sciences of the USA*, 87(5): 1816–19.

Bateman, R., I. Goddard, R. O'Grady, V. A. Funk, R. Mooi, W. J. Kress, *et al.* 1990. Speaking of Forked Tongues: The feasibility of reconciling human phylogeny and the history of language. *Current Anthropology* 31: 1–13.

Bates, T. C., M. Luciano, S. E. Medland, G. W. Montgomery, M. J. Wright, and N. G. Martin. 2011. Genetic Variance in a Component of the Language Acquisition Device: Robo1 polymorphisms associated with phonological buffer deficits. *Behavior Genetics* 41(1): 50–7.

Bishop, D. V. M. 2003. Genetic and Environmental Risks for Specific Language Impairment in Children. *International Journal of Pediatric Otorhinolaryngology* 6751: S143–S157.

Bolnick, D. A. W., B. A. S. Shook, L. Campbell, and I. Goddard. 2004. Problematic Use of Greenberg's Linguistic Classification of the Americas in Studies of Native American Genetic Variation. *American Journal of Human Genetics* 75(3): 519–23.

Borsboom, D. 2009. *Measuring the Mind: Conceptual Issues in Contemporary Psychometrics*. 1st ed. New York: Cambridge University Press.

Bouckaert, R., P. Lemey, M. Dunn, S. J. Greenhill, A. V. Alekseyenko, A. J. Drummond, et al. 2012. Mapping the Origins and Expansion of the Indo-European Language Family. *Science* 337(6097): 957–60.

Brosnahan, L. F. 1961. *The Sounds of Language: An Inquiry into the Role of Genetic Factors in the Development of Sound Systems*. Cambridge: W. Heffer and Sons.

Butcher, A. 2006. Australian Aboriginal Languages. In *Speech Production: Models, Phonetic Processes, and Techniques*, ed. J. Harrington and M. Tabain, 187–210. New York: Psychology Press.

Campbell, L. 1999. Nostratic and Linguistic Palaeontology in Methodological Perspective. In *Nostratic: Examining a Linguistic Macrofamily*, ed. C. Renfrew and D. Nettle, 179–230. Cambridge: McDonald Institute.

Campbell, L., and W. J. Poser. 2008. *Language Classification: History and Method*. New York: Cambridge University Press.

Campbell, M. C., and S. A. Tishkoff. 2010. The Evolution of Human Genetic and Phenotypic Variation in Africa. *Current Biology* 20(4): R166–R173.

Catford, J. C. 1977. *Fundamental Problems in Phonetics*. London: Indiana University Press.

Cavalli-Sforza, L. L. 2000. *Genes, Peoples and Languages*. Berkeley, CA: Penguin.

Cavalli-Sforza, L. L., P. Menozzi, and A. Piazza. 1994. *The History and Geography of Human Genes*. Abridged paperback ed. Princeton, NJ: Princeton University Press.

Charney, E. 2012. Behavior Genetics and Post Genomics. *Behavioral and Brain Sciences* 35(05): 331–58. doi:10.1017/S0140525X11002226.

Chomsky, N. 2011. Language and Other Cognitive Systems. What is special about language? *Language Learning and Development* 7: 263–78.

Christiansen, M. H., and N. Chater. 2008. Language as Shaped by the Brain. *Behavioral and Brain Sciences*, 31(5), 489–508.

Cox, T., and M. Cox 1994. *Multidimensional Scaling*. London: Chapman and Hall.

Cruciani, F., B. Trombetta, D. Sellitto, A. Massaia, G. Destro-Bisol, E. Watson, et al. 2010. Human Y Chromosome Haplogroup R-V88: A paternal genetic record of early mid Holocene trans-Saharan connections and the spread of Chadic languages. *European Journal of Human Genetics* 18(7): 800–7.

Cysouw, M., D. Dediu, and S. Moran. 2012. Comment on Phonemic Diversity Supports a Serial Founder Effect Model of Language Expansion from Africa. *Science* 335(6069): 657.

Dale, P. S., N. Harlaar, C. M. A. Haworth, and R. Plomin. 2010. Two by Two: A twin study of second-language acquisition. *Psychological Science* 21(5): 635–40.

Davies, G., A. Tenesa, A. Payton, J. Yang, S. E. Harris, D. Liewald, *et al.* 2011. Genome-wide Association Studies Establish that Human Intelligence is Highly Heritable and Polygenic. *Molecular Psychiatry* 16(10): 996–1005.

Davies, N. 1997. *Europe: A History*. London: Pimlico.

Debruyne, F., W. Decoster, A. Van Gijsel, and J. Vercammen. 2002. Speaking Fundamental Frequency in Monozygotic and Dizygotic Twins. *Journal of Voice* 16(4): 466–71.

Dediu, D. 2011. Are Languages Really Independent from Genes? If not, what would a genetic bias affecting language diversity look like? *Human Biology*, 83(2): 279–96.

Dediu, D., and D. R. Ladd. 2007. Linguistic Tone is Related to the Population Frequency of the Adaptive Haplogroups of Two Brain Size Genes, ASPM and Microcephalin. *Proceedings of The National Academy of Sciences of the USA*, 104(26): 10944–9.

Dediu, D., and S. C. Levinson. 2013. On the antiquity of language: The reinterpretation of Neandertal linguistic capacities and its consequences. *Frontiers in Language Sciences* 4: 397. doi:10.3389/fpsyg.2013.00397.

De Vos, C. 2012. *Sign-Spatiality in Kata Kolok: How a Village Sign Language of Bali Inscribes its Signing Space*. Nijmegen: Max Planck Institute for Psycholinguistics.

Diamond, J. 1997. The Language Steamrollers. *Nature* 389: 544–6.

Diamond, J., and P. Bellwood. 2003. Farmers and their Languages: The first expansions. *Science* 300: 597–603.

Enard, W., M. Przeworski, S. E. Fisher, C. S. L. Lai, V. Wiebe, T. Kitano, *et al.* 2002. Molecular Evolution of FOXP2, a Gene Involved in Speech and Language. *Nature* 418(6900): 869–72.

Feldman, M. W., and K. Aoki. 1992. Assortative Mating and Grandparental Transmission Facilitate the Persistence of a Sign Language. *Theoretical Population Biology* 42(2): 107–16.

Felsenfeld, S. 2002. Finding Susceptibility Genes for Developmental Disorders of Speech: The long and winding road. *Journal of Communication Disorders* 35(4): 329–45.

Fisher, S. E. 2006. Tangled Webs: Tracing the connections between genes and cognition. *Cognition* 101(2): 270–97.

Fisher, S. E., and C. Scharff. 2009. FOXP2 as a Molecular Window into Speech and Language. *Trends in Genetics* 25(4): 166–77.

Francks, C., S. Paracchini, S. D. Smith, A. J. Richardson, T. S. Scerri, L. R. Cardon, *et al.* 2004. A 77-kilobase Region of Chromosome 6P22.2 Is Associated with Dyslexia in Families from the United Kingdom and from the United States. *American Journal of Human Genetics* 75(6): 1046–58.

Friedlaender, J. S., F. R. Friedlaender, F. A. Reed, K. K. Kidd, J. R. Kidd, G. K. Chambers, et al. 2008. The Genetic Structure of Pacific Islanders. *PLoS Genetics* 4(1): e19.

Friedman, T. B., Y. Liang, J. L. Weber, J. T. Hinnant, T. D. Barber, S. Winata, et al. 1995. A Gene for Congenital, Recessive Deafness DFNB3 Maps to the Pericentromeric Region of Chromosome 17. *Nature Genetics* 9(1): 86–91.

Furr, R. M., and V. R. Bacharach. 2007. *Psychometrics: An Introduction*. 1st ed. Thousand Oaks, CA: Sage Publications, Inc.

Gray, R. D., and Q. D. Atkinson. 2003. Language-tree Divergence Times Support the Anatolian Theory of Indo-European Origin. *Nature* 426: 435–9.

Green, R. E., J. Krause, A. W. Briggs, T. Maricic, U. Stenzel, M. Kircher, et al. 2010. A Draft Sequence of the Neandertal Genome. *Science* 328(5979): 710–22.

Greenberg, J. 1987. *Language in the Americas*. Stanford University Press: Stanford.

Guillot, G., A. Estoup, F. Mortier, and J. F. Cosson. 2005. A Spatial Statistical Model for Landscape Genetics. *Genetics* 170(3): 1261–80.

Hamer, D., and L. Sirota. 2000. Beware the Chopsticks Gene. *Molecular Psychiatry* 5(1): 11–13.

Hannula-Jouppi, K., N. Kaminen-Ahola, M. Taipale, R. Eklund, J. NopolaHemmi, H. Kriinen, et al. 2005. The Axon Guidance Receptor Gene Robo1 is a Candidate Gene for Developmental Dyslexia. *PLoS Genetics* 1(4): e50.

Hassan, H. Y., P. A. Underhill, L. L. Cavalli-Sforza, and M. E. Ibrahim. 2008. Y-Chromosome Variation Among Sudanese: Restricted gene flow, concordance with language, geography, and history. *American Journal of Physical Anthropology* 137(3): 316–23.

Hensler, B. S., C. Schatschneider, J. Taylor, and R. K. Wagner. 2010. Behavioral Genetic Approach to the Study of Dyslexia. *Journal of Developmental and Behavioral Pediatrics* 31(7): 525–32.

Hiki, S., and H. Itoh. 1986. Influence of Palate Shape on Lingual Articulation. *Speech Communication* 5: 141–58.

Hurford, J. R., and D. Dediu. 2009. Diversity in Language, Genes and the Language Faculty. In *The Cradle of Language*, ed. R. Botha and C. Knight, 167–88. Oxford: Oxford University Press.

Jobling, M. A., E. Hollox, M. Hurles, T. Kivisild, and C. Tyler-Smith. 2013. *Human Evolutionary Genetics*. New York: Garland Science.

Jordan, F. M., R. D. Gray, S. J. Greenhill, and R. Mace. 2009. Matrilocal Residence is Ancestral in Austronesian Societies. *Proceedings of the Royal Society B: Biological Sciences* 276(1664): 1957–64.

Kashima, K. 1990. [Comparative study of the palatal rugae and shape of the hard palatal in Japanese and Indian children]. *Aichi Gakuin Daigaku Shigakkai Shi* 28(1.2): 295–320.

Klein, R. G. 2009. *The Human Career: Human Biological and Cultural Origins*. 3rd ed. Chicago: University of Chicago Press.

Klockars, T., and A. Pitkranta. 2009. Inheritance of Ankyloglossia (tongue-tie). *Clinical Genetics* 75(1): 98–9.

Konopka, G., J. M. Bomar, K. Winden, G. Coppola, Z. O. Jonsson, F. Gao, *et al.* 2009. Human-specific Transcriptional Regulation of CNS Development Genes by FOXP2. *Nature* 462(7270): 213–17.

Krause, J., Q. Fu, J. M. Good, B. Viola, M. V. Shunkov, A. P. Derevianko, *et al.* 2010. The Complete Mitochondrial Dna Genome of an Unknown Hominin from Southern Siberia. *Nature* 464(7290): 894–7.

Krause, J., C. Lalueza-Fox, L. Orlando, W. Enard, R. E. Green, H. A. Burbano, *et al.* 2007. The Derived FOXP2 Variant of Modern Humans was Shared with Neandertals. *Current Biology* 17(21): 1908–12.

Ladd, D. R., D. Dediu, and A. R. Kinsella. 2008. Languages and Genes: Re-flections on biolinguistics and the nature-nurture question. *Biolinguistics* 2(1): 114–26.

Ladefoged, P. 1984. "Out of Chaos Comes Order": Physical, Biological, and Structural Patterns in Phonetics. In *Proceedings of the Tenth International Congress of Phonetic Sciences*, ed. C. A. Van den Broecke, Vol. 2B, 83–95. Dordrecht, Holland: Foris Publications.

Lai, C. S., S. E. Fisher, J. A. Hurst, F. Vargha-Khadem, and A. P. Monaco. 2001. A Forkhead-Domain Gene is Mutated in a Severe Speech and Language Disorder. *Nature* 413(6855): 519–23.

Lewontin, R. C. 1972. The Apportionment of Human Diversity. In *Evolutionary biology 6*, ed. T. Dobzhansky, M. K. Hecht, and W. C. Steere, 381–98. New York: Appleton-Century-Crofts.

Liang, Y., A. Wang, F. J. Probst, I. N. Arhya, T. D. Barber, K. S. Chen, *et al.* 1998. Genetic Mapping Refines DFNB3 to 17P11.2, Suggests Multiple Alleles of DFNB3, and Supports Homology to the Mouse Model Shaker-2. *American Journal of Human Genetics* 62(4): 904–15.

Lynch, M., and B. Walsh. 1998. *Genetics and Analysis of Quantitative Traits*. Sunderland, MA: Sinauer Associates Inc.

MacEachern. 2000. Genes, Tribes, and African History. *Current Anthropology* 41(3): 357–84.

Mallory, J. 1991. *In Search of the Indo-Europeans: Language, Archaeology, and Myth*. London: Thames and Hudson.

Mallory, J. P., and D. Q. Adams. 2006. *The Oxford Introduction to Proto-Indoeuropean and the Proto-Indo-European World*. New York: Oxford University Press.

Mameli, M., and P. Bateson. 2006. Innateness and the Sciences. *Biology and Philosophy* 21: 155–88.

2011. An Evaluation of the Concept of Innateness. *Philosophical Transactions of the Royal Society B: Biological Sciences* 366: 436–43.

Manica, A., W. Amos, F. Balloux, and T. Hanihara. 2007. The Effect of Ancient Population Bottlenecks on Human Phenotypic Variation. *Nature* 448(7151): 346–8.

Manni, F., E. Guerard, and E. Heyer. 2004. Geographic Patterns of (Genetic, Morphologic, Linguistic) Variation: How barriers can be detected by using Monmonier's Algorithm. *Human Biology* 76(2): 173–90.

Matisoff, J. A. 1990. On Megalocomparison. *Language* 66, 106–20.

McMahon, R. 2004. Genes and Languages. *Journal of Community Genetics* 7(1): 2–13.

Mithen, S. 2003. *After the Ice: A Global Human History.* London: Orion Books Ltd.

Mona, S., K. E. Grunz, S. Brauer, B. Pakendorf, L. Castr, H. Sudoyo, et al. 2009. Genetic Admixture History of Eastern Indonesia as Revealed by Y-Chromosome and Mitochondrial DNA Analysis. *Molecular Biology and Evolution* 26(8): 1865–77.

Monmonier, M. 1973. Maximum-Difference Barriers: An alternative numerical regionalization method. *Geographical Analysis* 3: 245–61.

Nance, W. E., and M. J. Kearsey. 2004. Relevance of Connexin Deafness (DFNB1) to Human Evolution. *American Journal of Human Genetics* 74(6): 1081–7.

Nance, W. E., X. Z. Liu, and A. Pandya. 2000. Relation Between Choice of Partner and High Frequency of Connexin-26 Deafness. *Lancet* 356(9228): 500–1.

Nasidze, I., and M. Stoneking. 2001. Mitochondrial DNA Variation and Language Replacements in the Caucasus. *Proceedings of the Royal Society B: Biological Sciences* 268(1472): 1197–1206.

Nassir, R., R. Kosoy, C. Tian, P. A. White, L. M. Butler, G. Silva, et al. 2009. An Ancestry Informative Marker Set for Determining Continental Origin: Validation and extension using human genome diversity panels. *BMC Genetics* 10: 39.

Novembre, J., T. Johnson, K. Bryc, Z. Kutalik, A. R. Boyko, A. Auton, et al. 2008. Genes Mirror Geography within Europe. *Nature* 456: 98–101.

Nunnally, J., and I. Bernstein. 1994. *Psychometric Theory.* 3rd ed. USA: McGraw-Hill.

Oota, H., W. Settheetham-Ishida, D. Tiwawech, T. Ishida, and M. Stoneking. 2001. Human mtDNA and Y-Chromosome Variation is Correlated with Matrilocal Versus Patrilocal Residence. *Nature Genetics* 29(1): 20–1.

Paschou, P., J. Lewis, A. Javed, and P. Drineas, 2010. Ancestry Informative Markers for Ne-Scale Individual Assignment to Worldwide Populations. *Journal of Medical Genetics* 47(12): 835–47.

Pinel, P., F. Fauchereau, A. Moreno, A. Barbot, M. Lathrop, D. Zelenika, et al. 2012. Genetic Variants of FOXP2 and KIAA0319/TTRAP/THEM2 Locus are Associated with Altered Brain Activation in Distinct Language-Related Regions. *Journal of Neuroscience* 32(3): 817–25.

Plomin, R., J. C. DeFries, G. E. McClearn, and P. McGuffin. 2008. *Behavioral Genetics.* 5th ed. New York: Worth Publishers.

Posthuma, D. 2009. Multivariate Genetic Analysis. In *Handbook of Behaviour Genetics*, ed. Y.-K. Kim, 47–60. New York: Springer.

Pritchard, J. K., M. Stephens, and P. Donnelly. 2000. Inference of Population Structure Using Multilocus Genotype Data. *Genetics* 155(2): 945–59.

Reich, D., R. E. Green, M. Kircher, J. Krause, N. Patterson, E. Y. Durand, et al. 2010. Genetic History of an Archaic Hominin Group from Denisova Cave in Siberia. *Nature* 468: 1053–60.

Relethford, J. 2003. *Reflections of our Past: How Human History is Revealed in our Genes*. Boulder, CO: Westview Press.

Renfrew, C., and D. Nettle, eds. 1999. *Nostratic: Examining a Linguistic Macrofamily*. Cambridge: McDonald Institute.

Roll, P., S. C. Vernes, N. Bruneau, J. Cillario, M. Ponsole-Lenfant, A. Massacrier, et al. 2010. Molecular Networks Implicated in Speech-Related Disorders: FOXP2 regulates the SRPX2/uPAR complex. *Human Molecular Genetics* 19(24): 4848–60.

Ruhlen, M. 1991. *A Guide to the World's Languages*, Vol. 1: *Classification (with a postscript on recent developments)*. London: Arnold.

Salmons, J. C., and B. D. Joseph, eds. 1998. *Nostratic: Sifting the Evidence*. Amsterdam: John Benjamins.

Sandler, W., I. Meir, C. Padden, and M. Aronoff. 2005. The Emergence of Grammar: Systematic structure in a new language. *Proceedings of The National Academy of Sciences of the USA* 102(7): 2661–5.

Scerri, T. S., and G. Schulte-Krne. 2010. Genetics of Developmental Dyslexia. *European Child and Adolescent Psychiatry* 19(3): 179–97.

Scott, D. A., R. Carmi, K. Elbedour, G. M. Duyk, E. M. Stone, and V. C. Sheffield. 1995. Nonsyndromic Autosomal Recessive Deafness is Linked to the DFNB1 Locus in a Large Inbred Bedouin Family from Israel. *American Journal of Human Genetics* 57(4): 965–8.

Shackleton, R. G. 2007. Phonetic Variation in the Traditional English Dialects: A computational analysis. *Journal of English Linguistics* 35: 39–102.

Sims-Williams, P. 1998. Genetics, Linguistics, and Prehistory: Thinking big and thinking straight. *Antiquity* 72: 505–27.

Snustad, D. P., and M. J. Simmons. 2010. *Principles of Genetics*. 5th ed. John Wiley and Sons, Inc.

Spiteri, E., G. Konopka, G. Coppola, J. Bomar, M. Oldham, J. Ou, et al. 2007. Identification of the Transcriptional Targets of FOXP2, a Gene Linked to Speech and Language, in Developing Human Brain. *The American Journal of Human Genetics*, 81(6): 1144–57.

Stringer, C. 2002. Modern Human Origins: Progress and Prospects. *Philological Transactions of the Royal Society of London B* 357: 563–79.

Stringer, C. B., and P. Andrews. 1988. Genetic and Fossil Evidence for the Origin of Modern Humans. *Science* 239: 1263–8.

Stromswold, K. 2001. The Heritability of Language: A review and metaanalysis of twin, adoption, and linkage studies. *Language* 77: 647–723.

Tabachnick, B. G., and L. S. Fidell. 2001. *Using Multivariate Statistics*. 4th ed. Needham Heights, MA: Allyn and Bacon.

Templeton, A. R. 1998. Human Races: A genetic and evolutionary perspective. *American Anthropologist* 100: 632–50.

——— 2002. Out of Africa Again and Again. *Nature* 416(6876): 45–51.

Townsend, G. C., L. C. Richards, M. Sekikawa, T. Brown, and T. Ozaki. 1990. Variability of Palatal Dimensions in South Australian Twins. *Journal of Forensic Odonto-stomatology* 8(2): 3–14.

Traill, A. 1985. *Phonetic and Phonological Studies of !x Bushman.* Hamburg: Buske.

Traunmüller, H. 2003. Clicks and the Idea of a Human Protolanguage. *PHONUM* 9: 1–4.

Trinkaus, E. 2007. Human Evolution: Neandertal gene speaks out. *Current Biology* 17(21): R917–R919.

Vernes, S. C., D. F. Newbury, B. S. Abrahams, L. Winchester, J. Nicod, M. Groszer, et al. 2008. A Functional Genetic Link Between Distinct Developmental Language Disorders. *New England Journal of Medicine* 359(22): 2337–45.

Visscher, P. M., W. G. Hill, and N. R. Wray. 2008. Heritability in the Genomics Era: Concepts and Misconceptions. *Nature Reviews Genetics* 9(4): 255–66.

Waters, M. R., S. L. Forman, T. A. Jennings, L. C. Nordt, S. G. Driese, J. M. Feinberg, et al. 2011. The Buttermilk Creek Complex and the Origins of Clovis at the Debra L. Friedkin Site, Texas. *Science* 331(6024): 1599–1603.

Waters, M. R., T. W. Stafford, Jr, H. G. McDonald, C. Gustafson, M. Rasmussen, E. Cappellini, et al. 2011. Pre-Clovis Mastodon Hunting 13,800 Years Ago at the Manis Site, Washington. *Science* 334(6054): 351–3.

West-Eberhard, M. J. 2003. *Developmental Plasticity and Evolution.* 1st ed. New York: Oxford University Press.

Wilkins, J. F., and F. W. Marlowe. 2006. Sex-Biased Migration in Humans: What should we expect from genetic data? *BioEssays: News and Reviews in Molecular, Cellular and Developmental Biology* 28(3): 290–300.

Winata, S., I. N. Arhya, S. Moeljopawiro, J. T. Hinnant, Y. Liang, T. B. Friedman, et al. 1995. Congenital Non-Syndromal Autosomal Recessive Deafness in Bengkala, an Isolated Balinese Village. *Journal of Medical Genetics* 32(5): 336–43.

Wolpoff, M., and R. Caspari. 1997. *Race and Human Evolution: A Fatal Attraction.* Boulder, CO: Westview Press.

Wong, P. C. M., B. Chandrasekaran, and J. Zheng. 2012. The Derived Allele of ASPM Is Associated with Lexical Tone Perception. *PLoS One* 7(4): e34243.

Wood, E. T., D. A. Stover, C. Ehret, G. Destro-Bisol, G. Spedini, H. McLeod, et al. 2005. Contrasting Patterns of Y Chromosome and mtDNA Variation in Africa: Evidence for sex-biased demographic processes. *European Journal of Human Genetics* 13(7): 867–76.

Yang, J., B. Benyamin, B. P. McEvoy, S. Gordon, A. K. Henders, D. R. Nyholt, et al. 2010. Common SNPs Explain a Large Proportion of the Heritability for Human Height. *Nature Genetics* 42(7): 565-9.

Yip, M. 2002. *Tone*. Cambridge: Cambridge University Press.

Zerjal, T., Y. Xue, G. Bertorelle, R. S. Wells, W. Bao, S. Zhu, et al. 2003. The Genetic Legacy of the Mongols. *The American Journal of Human Genetics* 72(3): 717-21.

29

Linguistic anthropology in the age of language automata

Paul Kockelman

29.1 Introduction

Computers, as both engineered and imagined, are essentially text-generated and text-generating devices. And computation (in the machine-specific sense) may be understood as the enclosure of interpretation – an attempt to render a highly messy and stereotypically human process relatively formal, quantifiable, and context-independent. To make these arguments, I introduce some of the key concepts and claims of computer science (language, recognition, automaton, transition function, Universal Turing Machine, and so forth), and show their fundamental importance to the concerns of linguistic anthropology.

I argue that no small part of linguistic anthropology constitutes an oppositional culture in relation to computer science: many of its core values and commitments are essentially contrastive (rather than contentful). Such contrasts have hamstrung the ability of linguistic anthropologists to engage productively with the fruits of computer science, such as pervasively networked, digitally mediated, and ubiquitously present environments that more and more constitute the infrastructure for so-called "natural" communication. Here I will show the ways some of the core claims and methods of linguistic anthropologists can be productively applied to, and extended using, such infrastructure – opening up not only a new set of topics, but also a new set of techniques.

Sections 29.2 and 29.4 describe key concepts of computer science in their own terms, developing the relation between different kinds of languages and different kinds of computers. Sections 29.3 and 29.5 show the ways these concepts relate to core concerns in linguistic anthropology, such as interaction versus abstraction and linguistic relativity versus universal grammar. And the conclusion tacks between the concerns of both disciplines, highlighting key areas of future interest.

29.2 The relation between languages and computers

As in linguistic anthropology, the notion of language is crucial to computer science (however differently it is understood). In particular, a computer (or, automaton more generally) may be abstractly understood as a sieving device that accepts certain strings of characters and rejects others (Kockelman 2011). The set of strings that it accepts is called the language that it recognizes. The rest of this section will develop these ideas at length, as grounded in standard works on this subject (Rabin and Scott 1959; Turing 2004 [1936]; Sipser 2007), describing the core operations that computers must be able to perform if they are to sieve strings in these ways.

An *alphabet* may be understood as a set of characters. Examples include: {0, 1}, {0, 1, 2, 3, ..., 9, #}, {a, b, c, ..., z}, {the characters of a standard QWERTY typewriter}, {glyphs from an ancient language}, and so forth. Most generally, an alphabet can be any set of types whose tokens are perfectly and reliably readable and writable by the computer in question.[1] A *string* may be understood as a list of characters from such an alphabet (such that a string is said to be "over" the particular alphabet whose characters it incorporates). Examples of strings, over some of the foregoing alphabets, include: "11110111100," "3#29," "hullabaloo," "What did the quick brown fox jump over?" and so forth. More generally, the strings in question may be understood as containing any amount of quantifiable information, as well as encoding any kind of imaginable meaning. And a *language* may be understood as a set of such strings. Examples include: {the set of all w, where w is a string over the English alphabet that ends in -ing}, {the set of all s, where s is a grammatically acceptable sentence in German}, {the set of all pairs x#y, where $y = x^3 + 2$}, and so forth. In this way, with its innards still suitably black-boxed, a computer may be imagined as taking in strings as its input (whatever their length or alphabet), and turning out one of two strings, and thereby instigating one of two actions, as its output ("accept" or "reject," 1 or 0, "True" or "False," "permit" or "prohibit," etc.). See Figure 29.1a.

To be able to perform the task of accepting or rejecting particular strings, and thus, ultimately, of recognizing a particular language, a generalized automaton (or *Turing Machine*, as it will be referred to below) must be able to engage in the following kinds of operations: (1) read and write tokens of particular character types; (2) move along some kind of medium (where such tokens are read and written); and (3) both ascertain and update its own internal state. See Figure 29.1b. At the heart of such a device is a *transition function* that maps a domain of values onto a range of values. And thus, depending on the current state of the device, and the character it is currently reading, the transition function specifies what character to write (if any), what direction to move in (along the medium), and what state to change into. See Figure 29.1c. In essence, that is all such a

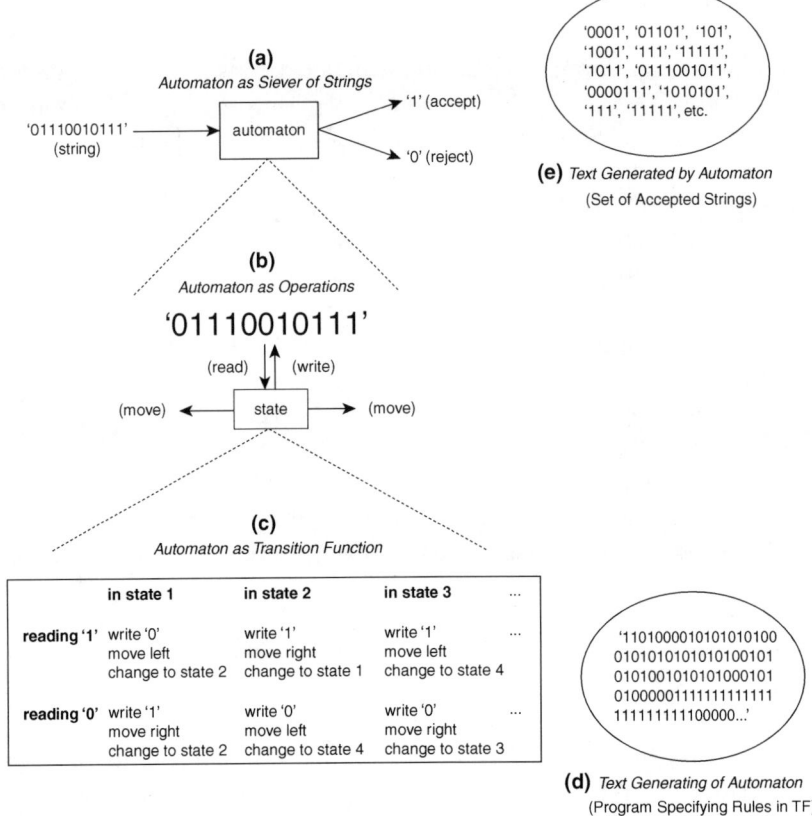

Figure 29.1 Automata as text-generated and text-generating devices

device ever does: having been given some string as its initial input (as written into the medium), and having been put in a particular state at a particular position along the string (usually the beginning), it repeats this mapping procedure (a potentially mind-numbing number of times) until it ends up in one of two particular states as its final output (accept or reject).

Phrased another way, a transition function consists of a finite set of rules which map current values (character read, current state) onto subsequent values (character written, movement undertaken, next state). To *program* such a device is essentially to specify its transition function (usually by giving the device another, more "primordial" string which encodes the rules in question). See Figure 29.1d. And such a transition function itself determines whether or not the device will accept particular strings; and thus, ultimately, whether or not the device will recognize a particular language. See Figure 29.1e. Crucially, while each rule may be trivial to specify, the list of rules (or program) can be quite complicated to formulate, and the overall behavior of such a device (e.g., the particular patterning of the language it recognizes) impossible to predict without actually observing it (if a pattern is even inferable at all). In all of these ways, then, *as both engineered and imagined, computers are essentially text-generated and text-generating devices.* Framed recursively, computers presuppose strings and create languages, where a language is a set of strings, anyone of which might be presupposed by another computer in its creation of a language.

29.3 String-sieving: Abstraction and interaction

Having characterized some of the ways computer scientists understand languages and computers, we may now begin to sketch a linguistic anthropology of strings, and the devices that sieve them. In part, this is done to show how the tools of linguistic anthropology can be applied to the concepts of computer science (as well as to the objects of computer engineering). And, in part, this is done to show and soften the fundamental tension between the culture of linguistic anthropologists and the concepts of computer science – a tension that is otherwise almost laughably overdetermined in its binary simplicity. As will be seen, the title of this chapter is meant to be ironic: for, in fact, linguistic anthropology came of age in the time of language automata, but somehow managed to studiously avoid what it is arguably destined to embrace.

As described in this section, automata are exemplary instances of relatively black-boxed, rule-bound, and deterministic intermediaries. In particular, both the localized mapping of values (e.g., character read and current state to character written, move made, and next state), and the global input–output relation (e.g., string to accept/reject) are radically deterministic,[2] such that there seems to be a maximally rigid (as opposed to flexible) mapping between inputs and outputs.[3] This characteristic puts them at odds with anthropology's strongly humanistic imaginary, which sees human agency as maximally mediated. For example, people are understood as norm-abiding, culture-inhabiting, context-sensitive, interactively emergent, and reflexively conscious agents. And so it is not surprising that linguistic anthropologists have been extremely wary of disciplines (such as cognitive science and formal linguistics) that have invoked computational metaphors in their attempts to understand key features of human behavior.

While Latour (2005: 39) is often cited in relation to this distinction between *intermediaries* (or whatever "transports meaning or force without transformation: defining its inputs is enough to define its outputs") and *mediators* (whose "input is never a good predictor of their output; their specificity has to be taken into account every time"), Michel Serres (2007 [1982]) is arguably the more originary figure. And Serres was himself developing certain ideas of Claude Shannon (1949, 1963[1949]) in regards to noise and enemies (Kockelman 2010), a thinker who – ironically enough – was the key theorist of information (as opposed to meaning, a distinction that will be returned to in the conclusion). Of particular relevance to linguistic anthropologists, an even earlier definition was offered by Peirce, in his use of a path metaphor to distinguish between what he called *secondness* and *thirdness*: "a straight road, considered merely as a connection between two places is second, but so far as it implies passing through intermediate places [themselves possibly connected by other paths to further places] it is third" (1955b: 80; Kockelman 2010: 413). That said, the distinction is really much more general and variable, as may be seen in Figure 29.2, which diagrams a variety of analogous and overlooked relations. And that said, the distinction is itself highly ontology-specific and frame-dependent (points that will be taken up below).

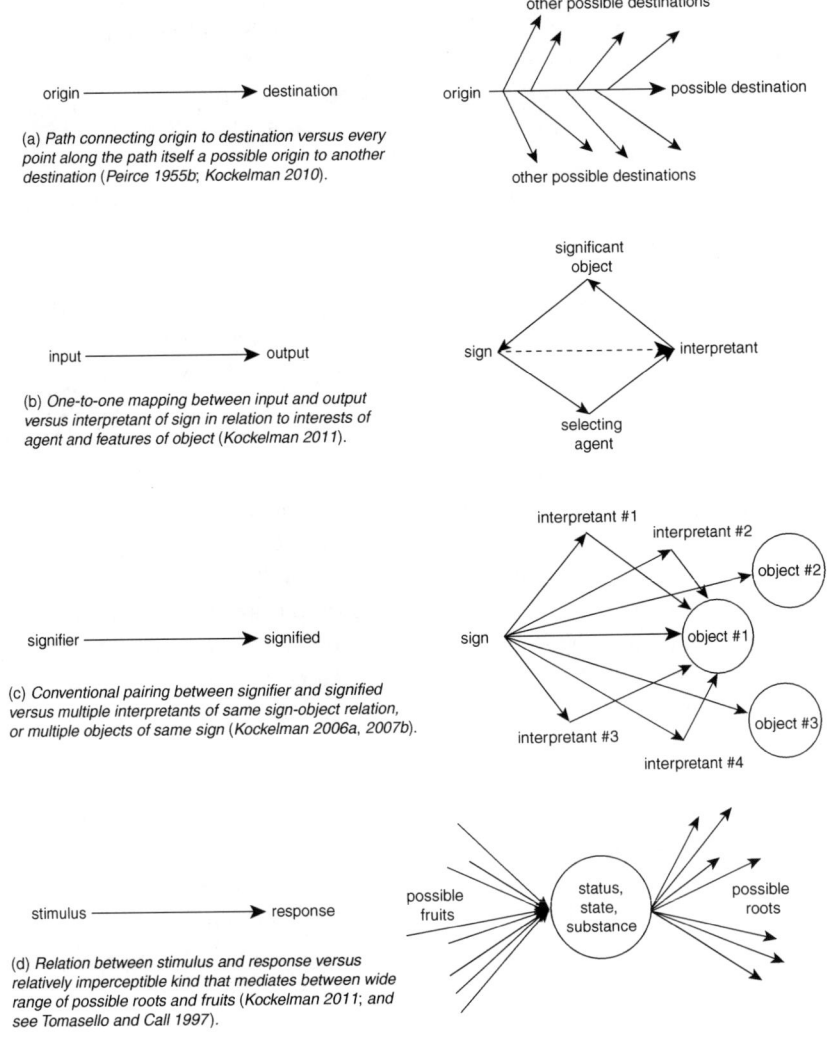

Figure 29.2 Some ways of framing secondness and thirdness

Indeed, an enormous amount of energy has gone into trying to refute any claim that people are in any way automaton-like (and thus in no way like seconds or intermediaries). Forty years of anthropology has spent its time trying to show that each and every social form (such as a practice, structure, sign, identity, or belief) is "emergent," "contested," "fluid," "embodied," "non-deterministic," "dialogic," "constructed," "distributed," "context-bound," "reflexive," "mediated," and so forth. In some sense, computers (or rather a widespread folk-theory of computers), have been the favorite bogeyman of anthropology (and social scientists more generally): where there are rules, give us practices; where there are symbols, give us indices; where there is truth-conditioning, give us poetry and performance; where there is mind, give us body; where there is abstraction give us interaction; where there are ideal languages give us forms of life.

The history of these divisions is institutional as much as intellectual, and deserves a chapter of its own; but some of the key moves are easy enough to sketch. Descartes versus Heidegger in continental philosophy (see, for example, Dreyfus 1991 and Haugeland 1998a). Early Wittgenstein (1961 [1921]) versus late Wittgenstein (1958[1953]) in analytic philosophy (and see, for example, Kripke 1982 and Kockelman 1999). The structuralism of Levi-Strauss (1969[1949]) versus the practice theory of Bourdieu (1977 [1972]) in anthropology.[4] Saussure (1983[1916]) versus Peirce (1955a, b, c) in semiotics (and see, for example, Kockelman 2006b). And formalism (Chomsky 1965) versus functionalism (Jakobson 1990a) in linguistics (and see, for example, Van Valin and LaPolla 1997).[5] Insofar as linguistic anthropology sits downstream, as it were, of all of these currents it has adopted most of their claims, such that its understanding of interpretation (and meaning) is essentially contrastive with stereotypes about automata (and information). As such, it is worth examining one of its key foils with a renewed empathy built on fifty years or so of enmity.

More important than being dismissive of, or trying to circumvent, the rule-like nature of such devices is to understand the ways such rules get coupled to norms: or, rather, the way allegedly human-specific modes of signifying and interpreting meaning (as grounded in mediation, or thirdness) are mediated by and mediating of allegedly machine-specific modes of sending and sieving information (as grounded in intermediaries, or secondness). In particular, much of the current built environment, *qua* communicative infrastructure, consists of precisely such devices. And so natural languages and culture-specific communicative practices more generally, are constantly being mediated by (encoded with and channeled through) such devices. Moreover, the distinction between mediators and intermediaries is itself grounded in mediators: and so there is a culture and history to the ways some community specifies where machine-like things end and human-like things begin; as well as a culture and history of evaluating what is essential to each, and what is good or bad when breached. Phrased another way, there is a lot of firstness in where we draw the line between secondness and thirdness (Kockelman 2013a: 141). More generally, rather than ontologize the world in such binary terms, it is much better to (1) foreground agency as a radically multidimensional, distributed, and graduated process; (2) foreground a variety of practices which not only have the effect of enclosing agency as "agents" but also dichotomizing such agents in terms of distinctions like "intermediary" and "mediator"; and (3) genealogize the recent presumption of this dichotomy among scholars (Kockelman 2007a, 2007b, 2010). And thus a key task for the linguistic anthropology of automatized languages is to trace the politics and pragmatics of such *intermediation*.[6] See Table 29.1.

Indeed, the genealogy of this division may be traced back at least as far as the industrial revolution. For example, the art critic and historian Ruskin endlessly railed against the machine, championing handicraft in the face of widespread industrialization, arguing that the latter insofar as it is massproduced rather than individually and singularly crafted loses "the traces or symptoms of a living being at work" (quoted in Gombrich 1979: 40; and note the relation to Walter Benjamin's more famous notion of "aura"). Interestingly, Rushkin often aimed his critiques at the "decorative" arts more generally, in their often mechanically produced and repetitive or

Table 29.1 Intermediaries, mediation, and intermediation

Secondness	Thirdness	Via Peirce
Intermediary	*Mediary*	Via Serres and ANT
Ideal Language	*Form of Life*	Via Wittgenstein
Universal Grammar	*Linguistic Relativity*	Via Chomsky and Sapir
Machines Talking	*Humans Talking*	Via Turing
Structure	*Agency*	Via Cultural Anthropology
Computer Science	*Linguistic Anthropology*	Via Disciplinary Boundaries
Computing Machines	*Interpreting Humans*	Via Multiple Encodings
Real Imaginaries	*Symbolic Imaginaries*	Via Ontological Mappings
Artificial Languages	*Natural Languages*	Via Possible Objects
Statistics (Math)	*Semiotics (Meaning)*	Via Possible Methods
Enclosing	*Disclosing*	Via Underlying Imperative
Sieving and Serendipity	*Significance and Selection*	Via Semiotic Framing
Redundancy	*Poetry (qua Metricality)*	Via Shannon and Jakobson

Intermediation as Obviation
(1) Secondness and thirdness are poles of a continuum, not positions in an opposition;
(2) Boundary between secondness and thirdness is itself grounded in thirdness (and secondness);
(3) Each is affecting of, and affected by, the other at various degrees of remove;
(4) Whether some process is understood as one or the other is dependent on degree of resolution and frame of relevance;
(5) Process of making (or seconding and thirding, as it were), and making seem (like secondness and thirdness), as important as the products made (seconds and thirds, per se).

highly patterned nature. This is particularly salient insofar as there is a close linkage between the patterns (*qua* languages) generated by automata and the patterns generated by decoration-producing mechanisms such as looms (which themselves were, in the age of Jacquard, programmable with punch-cards, and thus also generated by text-like patterns). Finally, these issues go back to the origins of rhetoric (and see Bate, this volume, Chapter 21): the admonishment to make one's speech simple (and thus less flowery or "decorated"), and thus less poetic and more referential. Note, then, linguistic anthropology's valorization of mediation over intermediaries is itself grounded in the oldest (or at least most famous and widespread) of language ideologies. Ironically, this is, in a certain sense, the converse of its own explicitly articulated sensibilities as to the importance of poetic regimentation and the multi-functionality of language, as discussed by Kockelman, this volume, Chapter 24.

As another example of intermediation, note that because a sieving device is, in some sense, coupled to its input (the string it is initially given) by way of its transition function (which makes reference to the possible characters on a string), the device and the string are "intimate" (Kockelman 2013a: 109–10; and see Gibson 1986[1979], Simon 1996, and Haugeland 1998b for intimacy as a metaphor). In certain respects, a stringless device is like an organism without its environment; just as a deviceless string is like an environment without an organism. Neither makes much sense except in relation to the other. In this way, such sieving devices are (inverse) iconic-indices of the strings of symbols they sort: each incorporates, creates, and complements the other. Moreover, and closely related to the first point, such devices are shifters in an expanded sense: their input-to-output mapping (string to accept/reject) only counts as a sign–interpretant relation when contextualized – such that the features of an object, and the interests of an agent, can be specified (Kockelman 2011).[7] For both these reasons, such devices are not at all "context free" or "abstract" or "meaningless" or "symbolic," but rather radically grounded, intimate, contextual, iconic-indexical, motivated, embedded, and so forth.[8] In this way, the classic techniques of linguistic anthropology (Silverstein 1976; Jakobson 1990a, 1990b; Lucy 1993; Silverstein and Urban 1996) are perfectly poised to illuminate both the string–sieve relation and the string/sieve–situation relation (not to mention the cultural and disciplinary ontologies that would otherwise figure such relations in simplistic ways). For example, modern approaches to interaction (see, for example, Enfield 2009 and Sidnell 2010) can be brought to bear on what otherwise seems to be canonical cases of abstraction.

As is well known, the actual material instantiation of such devices is "immaterial" in regards to the mathematical specification of the language in question: there is nothing inherently electronic (as opposed to mechanical, quantum mechanical, lively, etc.) about computers – even if their practical instantiation, and widespread adoption, had to await a particular technology. What matters, ultimately, is that the device be able to undertake the kinds of tasks listed above (read and write, move left or right, ascertain and update). In particular, people can do each task; and, ironically, the first "computers" were indeed people (often women), who carried out lengthy (and tedious) calculations according to a finite set of relatively simple rules (Kittler 1989[1986]; Inoue 2011). In this way, several other interrelated tensions are immediately apparent. First, claims to a timeless disembodied abstraction in relation to a history of particular material instantiations. Second, the relation between people and machines (as ontologized by any particular community, or imagined in terms of a particular technology) in relation to the relation between different kinds of people (e.g., genders, classes, ethnicities, and so forth). Third, the kinds of computational tasks asked of sieving devices and their relation to politicized notions like labor, work, and action (not to mention often highly idealized and romanticized notions like creativity, contemplation, and communication). And finally, as will be taken up in subsequent sections, the relation between such artificial languages (both generating and generated) and so-called "natural" languages – in all their forms and functions (news, philosophy, poetry, grammar, conversation, and so forth). While the scholarship relevant to such concerns is enormous, key works include: Benjamin (1968a); MacKay (1969); Kittler (1989 [1986], 1996[1993]); McLuhan (1996[1964]); Hayles (1999); Mirowski (2002); Turing (2004[1950]); Suchman (2007); Benkler (2007); and many of the essays collected in Wardrip-Fruin and Montfort (2003).

29.4 Kinds of languages, kinds of computers

Before taking up other important kinds of tensions, it is worth returning to some key claims of computer science. Particular automata (or particular programs running on a universal Turing Machine, essentially a "computer" in the stereotypic sense) may be characterized in terms of the sets of strings that they accept (and thus the languages that they recognize). And different classes of automata may be characterized in terms of the kinds of languages they can recognize – kinds of languages that can be compared in terms of their relative complexity, and thus classes of automata that can be compared in terms of their relative power.[9] See Figure 29.3.

In particular, three key classes of sieving devices are Deterministic Finite Automata (DFA), Context-Free Grammars (CFG), and Turing Machines (TM). DFAs are the simplest of the three devices. In contrast to TMs (whose innerworkings were detailed in section 29.2), such devices only move in one direction (from the beginning of the string to the end); no characters are ever written; and the medium only ever contains the string in question. Endowed with such capabilities, such devices can recognize the class of

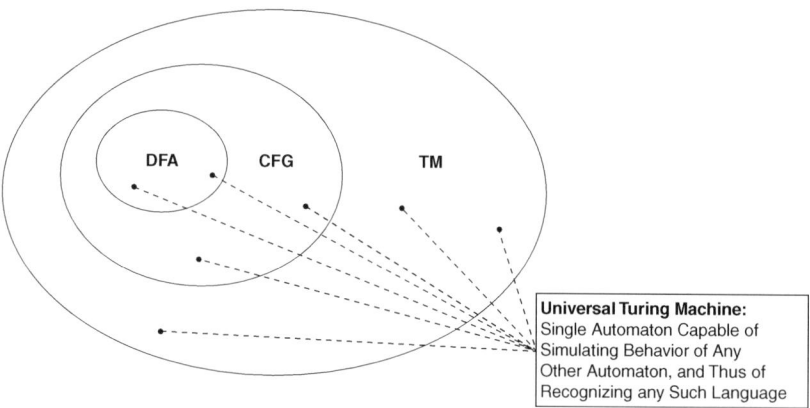

Figure 29.3 Relative scope of languages recognized by different kinds of automata

regular languages, which are essentially all languages recursively definable in terms of three simple functions. Loosely speaking, the *union* of strings from any two regular languages is itself a regular language; any possible *concatenation* of strings from any two regular languages is itself a regular language; and any possible *iteration* (or "self-concatenation") of strings from any regular language is itself a regular language. More carefully, if L_1 and L_2 are two languages recognizable by a DFA (and thus regular languages), the following languages are also recognizable by a DFA (and thus regular languages): $L_1 \cup L_2$ = {the set of all strings w, where w is a string in L_1 or L_2}; $L_1 \circ L_2$ = {the set of all strings w_1w_2, where w_1 is a string in L_1 and w_2 is a string in L_2}; and L_1^*= {the set of all strings $w_1w_2w_3 \ldots w_k$, where k >=0 and w_i is a string in L_1}. For example, if L_1={a,b} and L_2 ={c}, $L_1 \cup L_2$={a,b,c}, $L_1 \circ L_2$={ac,bc}, and L_1^*=[e,a,b,ab,ba,aa,bb,abb,aab,...}, where e is the empty string (that is, the string with no characters). And so on, recursively, for languages like $(L_1 \circ L_2) \cup L_1$, $(L_1 \cup L_2)^*$, and $L_1^* \cup (L_1 \circ L_2)$. In this way, with three relatively simple functions, and some primitive notions like empty strings and singleton languages (or languages with only one string, itself consisting of a single character), one can build up languages with great complexity. Practical applications that implement DFAs include password checks, word searches, swearword censors, and simple spam-filters; as well as devices like automatic doors, traffic lights, and elevator traffic controls.

CFGs not only recognize all regular languages, they also recognize languages like {the set of all strings w#w | where w is itself a string of any length over some alphabet}, which require an infinite amount of memory that is only accessible in a relatively restricted fashion (essentially a kind of "last-written, first-read" form of storage). In particular, in contrast to DFAs, the domain of the transition function of a CFG turns on not just the current state of the device, and the character currently being read from the string, but also (potentially) the character currently being read from the top of the "stack" (its restricted memory). And the output involves not only updating the state of the device, and moving to the next character on the string, but also (potentially) writing some other character onto the top of the stack. When understood as generating languages (as opposed to recognizing them), CFGs should be immediately familiar to linguistic anthropologists in terms of the rewrite rules (or "tree structures") of formal models of language. For example, a particular set of rules (such as S => NP-VP; NP => DET-ADJ-N; VP => V-NP; DET => *a, the*; ADJ => *short, tall*; N => *boy, girl*; V => *pinched, ticked*) may be understood to generate a particular language (which would include the following strings: *the short girl pinched the tall boy, the tall girl tickled the short girl*, and so forth). Such languages may exhibit another kind of recursion, as when the range or output of a rule ultimately makes reference to the same variable that constitutes its domain or input (for example, PP => Prep NP, NP => N PP). Practical applications that implement CFGs include most parsers (involved in compiling or interpreting the computer programs that are run on universal Turing Machines, and thus the texts that specify their transition functions), as well as many applications that either simulate or process natural languages. Indeed, as will be discussed at length in section 29.4, many of Chomsky's early intuitions about language (themselves a key foil for functional linguists and linguistic anthropologists for the last fifty years) were grounded in the structure and logic of CFGs (and related kinds of automata).[10]

Finally, TMs not only recognize all languages recognized by CFGs (and thus, all languages recognized by DFAs), but also languages like $\{w \mid$ where w is an integer root of the polynomial $x^3 + 3x^2 + 8x = 0\}$.[11] Indeed, the Church–Turing Thesis postulates that such devices are definitionally equivalent to algorithms: they can recognize any language that can be specified in terms of a finite deterministic procedure (loosely speaking, an iteratively applied, easily followed, and simply stated set of rules for undertaking a longer and more complicated calculation).[12] Not only do they have an infinite amount of memory but, in contrast to CFGs, their memory is unrestricted in its accessibility. Finally, as already mentioned, a *Universal Turing Machine* (essentially a modern-day computer with infinite memory) is an automaton that can be programmed (by giving it a string that encodes the set of instructions that specify its transition function) to model the behavior of any particular Turing Machine. In some sense, it is the one automaton that can take the place of any other automaton. Or, to invoke a comparison that will need some unpacking, and should echo Marx's (1967[1867]) notion of universal money (as well as Benjamin's 1968b notion of empty homogeneous time), it is akin to a universal language: the one language whose expressions can be used to translate the meaning of any expression from any other language (Kockelman 2006b: 100).

29.5 Universal Turing Machines: Universal grammar and linguistic relativity

Crucial to the theoretical imaginary surrounding Turing Machines is the fact that various adjustments to a TM's basic capacities do not affect its functioning (or the set of languages it can recognize) in any important way. For example, there are TMs that can stay in place at any transition (in addition to moving left and right); there are TMs that use more than one tape (where characters may be read or written); there are TMs that move in two dimensions rather than one (and thus accept two-dimensional "swatches" of text rather than one-dimensional strings of text); there are TMs that enumerate languages rather than recognize them; and so on, and so forth. And not withstanding such differences, all of these devices can be shown to be *equivalent* to the others. Put another way, with certain caveats, all the different kinds of computers out there, and any of the different programming languages used on any particular computer, are equivalent (or "commensurable"). For example, any program written in LISP can be written in Java or C; and any program run on one machine can be run on another. Because TMs are so incredibly "robust" in this way, computer scientists consider the class of languages that they recognize (i.e., the set of algorithmically solvable problems) to be relatively "natural" (Sipser 2007: 128–33). This is another way of framing the claim, introduced above, that such devices are "universal."

One issue of fundamental importance to linguistic anthropologists is closely related to this fact: the tension between universal grammar and linguistic relativity. To see how, let me both elaborate and extend a claim made by Sapir (1949[1924]; and see Lucy 1992a, 1992b; Sidnell and Enfield 2012): while all languages are arguably "formally complete," in that they are able to represent the same set of experiences (*qua* reference), each has its own "secret," which involves not only a way of orienting to a referent (*qua* "sense") but also an associated feeling of orientation (*qua* "sensability").[13] While one may or may not be particularly committed to this claim, it is worthy of careful consideration because of the foundational tensions it brings to light.

To use an example from geometry, note that both Cartesian coordinates (x,y) and polar coordinates (r,O) may be used to represent the same set of points (all points in a two-dimensional plane). See Figure 29.4.

Any expression in either system may thereby be translated into the other system (through equations like x = r cos O and y = r sin O). But that said, the equations of particular entities may be more or less aesthetically elegant when expressed in one system rather than the other (e.g., lines are relatively simple entities in Cartesian coordinates, whereas circles are relatively simple entities in polar coordinates). As physicists know (Arfken and Weber 1995), certain problems may be more or less easy to solve in one system rather than the other (insofar as the symmetry of the problem

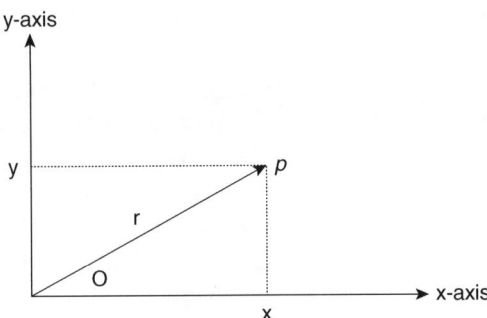

Figure 29.4 Comparison of Cartesian and Polar coordinate systems

matches the symmetry of the system). And finally, as a function of such symmetry and solvability, the intuitions of problem solvers may be more or less enabled or constrained. In this way, while the two systems are equivalent at the level of reference, they are non-equivalent at the level of sense and sensibility. More generally, and perhaps most colorfully, while different systems may allow us to "touch" the same worlds, the worlds so touched may be nonetheless "felt" in distinctly different ways.

Understood in such terms, three points may now be made. First, while Sapir was, of course, talking about natural languages, such claims may also be understood to hold for artificial languages. In particular, while any program written in any programming language may be written in any other programming language (as per our discussion above), it is likely that different programming languages (not to mention interfaces, architectures, and so forth) have different "secrets" – different symmetries built into them (that make certain problems easier or harder to solve), and different sensibilities disciplined by them (as embodied in those who habitually program in them). While this claim is a low-hanging fruit, it is worth making insofar as it shows another site where classic techniques of linguistic anthropology can be applied to classic objects of computer science – the texts that generate computation (*qua* programs) as much as the texts generated by computation (*qua* languages, in the technical sense discussed above).

Second, given the relation between the languages generated by context-free grammars and natural language, given the "naturalness" of the class of languages recognizable by Turing Machines, and given the strong referential equivalence of natural languages (not to mention the close initial disciplinary linkage between computer science, cognitive science, and formal linguistics), it is not difficult to empathize with the desire of early generative linguists to discover the "universal grammar" (a kind of ur-language) underlying all natural languages. Nor is it difficult to empathize with their intuition that it should be equally discoverable through any particular language if analyzed closely enough. In other words, if all coordinate systems (*qua* systems of signs) are equivalent (in that any one may relate to the others as interpretant to sign), why not just use one of them to understand the world (of objects) so referred to?

And third, just as it is easy to foreground equivalence of reference (as a disciplinary focus), it is also easy to foreground non-equivalence of sense and sensibility. In particular, having just characterized some key ideas underlying the analytic imaginary (or disciplinary culture) of generative linguists, it is easy to see where some of linguistic anthropology's own contrastive commitments come from. For example, if universal grammar may be understood to foreground equivalence of reference, linguistic relativity may be understood to foreground non-equivalence of sense and sensibility. And while early linguistic anthropologists like Whorf (1956 [1939], 1956[1937]) and Sapir (1985[1927], 1985[1945]) could comfortably shift between both perspectives (indeed, not withstanding contemporary readings of them, Sapir and Whorf highlighted linguistic invariance as much as relativity, as should be clear in the work just cited), the latter has been given center stage. For example, Hill and Mannheim (1992 ; and see Lee 1996), have gone so far as to argue that linguistic relativity should be understood as an "axiom" of linguistic anthropology rather than an hypothesis. In this way, two sets of scholars have passionately rallied around flags of complementary colors, themselves placed in contiguous and often overlapping terrains that were originally staked out by the same surveyors.

29.6 Conclusion

One way to reframe some of the foregoing claims is as follows: *computation is the enclosure of interpretation*. In part, this means that computation is a species of interpretation that is relatively regimented as to its use-value, truth-value, and exchange-value (Kockelman 2010). In part, this means that it is a species of interpretation that has been relatively mediated by technology, science, and economy (ibid.). And in part, this means that the values in question (be they signs, objects, or interpretants) become relatively portable: not so much independent of context, as dependent on contexts which have been engineered so as to be ubiquitous, and hence seemingly context-free (Kockelman 2007b, 2013a). In effect, the mediation is so great that it appears to be unmediated – and thus a mere intermediary. For the average denizen of such an environ, thirdness often goes about as secondness (and vice versa).

This claim may be easily generalized. While the focus has been on the relation between computation and interpretation (and thus the input–output, or sign–interpretant relation per se), we could also focus on the sign–object relation, and argue that information is the enclosure of meaning (Kockelman 2013a). And we could focus on the signer–interpreter relation, and argue that infrastructure is the enclosure of interaction

(Kockelman 2011). In this way, we could focus on *a set of concomitant processes whereby semiosis gets not only automated, but also formatted and networked.*

Hand in hand with the real-time practices and *longue durée* processes though which this occurs is a kind of reflective understanding of its occurrence – itself usually radically refracted (or so the story goes). In each kind of enclosure, a great degree of agency (power, flexibility, meta-reflexivity, progress, etc.) seems to be gained – and so there is celebration and speculation. And a great degree of authenticity (context-dependence, historical uniqueness, cultural specificity, etc.) seems to be lost – and so there is nostalgia and mourning.[14] Recall the admonitions of Ruskin.

Needless to say, such modes of refracted reflexivity should be all-too-familiar to anthropologists, as they are themselves grounded in a particular imaginary that is found again and again in critical theory (Kockelman 2007c): from Aristotle and Marx (e.g., substance and form, quality and quantity), through Maine and Toennies (e.g., status and contract, community and society), to Levi-Strauss and Bourdieu (e.g., raw and cooked, practice and structure). Indeed, anthropology has always been, in part, the disciplinization of precisely such refracted reflections: in its more sophisticated variants it proposes them; in its less sophisticated variants it presupposes them.

With these core claims and key caveats in mind, we may now sketch some future topics and techniques for a linguistic anthropology of automatized (formatted and networked) languages, one which focuses on *intermediation* (or embeddedness) rather than constantly trying to counter intermediaries by reference to mediation, and thus one which seeks to empathize with machines (and their makers), as much as with humans (and their makings). Recall Figure 29.2 and Table 29.1.

For example, an obvious topic of interest to linguistic anthropologists is the *Turing Test*, and attempts to make computers speak (and interact more generally) in ways that are more or less indistinguishable from human speech and interaction (Turing 2004[1950]; and see French 2000 and Saygin *et al.* 2001). One relatively direct route to this topic is through the lens of ontology (our assumptions as to the kinds that constitute a particular world, and how these assumptions license particular inferences) and transformativity (how such assumptions change through our indexical encounters with such kinds), as these relate to the machine-human relation (Kockelman 2013a, 2013b). And one relatively indirect route to this topic would be to study the intersection of several text-building processes. First, the texts (qua computer programs) used to make computers speak. Second, the texts (qua human–machine dialogues) generated through interactions between these programs and people. And third, the texts (qua meta-language) by humans (and perhaps machines) about these dialogues and programs (describing them, theorizing about them, categorizing them, evaluating them, commodifying them, vilifying them, and so forth). More generally, these kinds of inter-textual processes are at work in a multitude of natural language-processing projects: voice recognition, spam filtering, dialog censoring, machine translation, etc. And so there are ample opportunities for linguistic anthropologists who want to study the tensions among such texts (and their underlying processes of textualization).[15]

One important relation that shows up again and again in computer science, among other places, might be called *ontological isomorphisms*, *cross-domain diagrams*, or even, "real imaginaries." By this is meant that a set of relations found in one domain is found in another seemingly disparate domain, such that insights from each domain may be used to generate insights about the other (often licensing large-scale theoretical and technological innovation). For example, just as Boole (1958[1854]) worked out the relation between binary numbers and truth conditions (and thus math and logic), Shannon (1936) worked out the relation between truth conditions and electrical circuits (and thus logic and engineering).[16] And actual material instantiations of Turing Machines, such as the standard desktop computer we now have, itself not much different from the architecture initially proposed by von Neumann (Ceruzzi 2000; Petzold 2000), exploit precisely these relations. While closely related to metaphor (and thus able to be studied, in part, using the techniques of trope analysis), these mappings are not metaphors (in the conventional sense of, say, Lakoff and Johnson 1980) for two crucial reasons: first, there is no distinction between concrete and abstract domains (each domain is on equal par, as it were); and second, it is not, strictly speaking, a linguistic or conceptual phenomenon (the parallels exist in the domain of reference, and may be pointed to with any kind of sign). But that said, while certain mappings may be well founded and referentially motivated, other mappings may be more whimsical or social – licensed by particular imaginaries (concepts) and symbolics (signs), as much as by particular reals (reference).[17] In particular, a key kind of relation between relations to study is the relation between these real imaginaries (i.e., cross-domain diagrams) and symbolic imaginaries (i.e., metaphors in their more conventional sense, and textual and technological aesthetics more generally). These are key sites where the promises and pitfalls of automatized languages, as well as the interfaces they present to the world, and the infrastructures they depend on in the world, get refracted in reflection. And again, linguistic anthropologists, who have long been interested in the relation between culture and diagrammatic iconicity, and the relation between poetics and pragmatics more generally, are perfectly poised to analytically tap into these issues.

Intersecting the phenomenon of cross-domain diagrams is *multiple encoding* (or perhaps, "multiple interpreters"): the way a given computer language (or technology more generally) is subject to the demands and abilities of the machines that compute with it as much as of the humans that interpret with it.[18] For example, the texts that tell computers what to do (i.e., "programs"), such that they may generate further texts (i.e., "languages") can be more or less easily "read" by humans and, concomitantly, less or more easily "read" by machines. And so, there are programming languages like Assembly which stay very close to the structure of the machines that run them; and there are programming languages like Python and C, which are generally more amenable to the intuitions of people who write in them, and which have to be interpreted or compiled before they can be run by a computer.

Framed more generally, to serve a single function (or have a particular object) a given sign must be amenable to the ontologies (capacities, codes, habits, cultures, etc.) of several interpreting agents at once. Crucially, this means that each kind of interpreting agent might understand it in different ways, and so there can be issues of translation, the division of labor, relative perspicacity of encoding, and so forth, with all the usual tensions. And, needless to say, this is related to a set of more timeless topics: how a tool is crafted to the demands of the world, the body, and the mind at once; or how a practice is regimented by cultural norms and natural causes simultaneously; or how a dream may be interpretable in regards to both its manifest and latent content at the same time; and so forth.

To put this in a more critical perspective, this leads to a set of tensions that were first foregrounded by Marx: the degree to which an instrument is designed to fit the requirements of a user (e.g., a "tool"); or a user is disciplined to fit the requirements of an instrument (e.g., a "machine"). And this relation may itself be reframed in semiotic terms: the degree to which a sign (and, concomitantly, a signer) takes on features of its object (iconicity, via Saussure and Peirce); or an object takes on features of its sign (projection, via Sapir and Whorf). Again, the relevance and reach of these issues for linguistic anthropologists should be clear, especially given the discussion of reference, sense, and sensibility in section 29.3.

Another relatively obvious, but nonetheless key move would be to simply apply the usual linguistic anthropological toolkit to the study of *programming languages*. For example, descriptive grammars of such languages are waiting to be written (i.e., grammars of actual usage patterns, as opposed to language specifications, instruction manuals, and so forth). There is discourse analysis of the real-time writing of texts, *qua* programming languages – and not just coders in dialogues with other coders and users, but also coders in dialogue with CPUs and worlds so to speak (via the shell, debugging applications, and so forth). There are ethnographies of communication (Hymes 1962; Bauman and Sherzer 1975) to be written about the sub-cultures surrounding different programming languages (text editors, etc.) in their language use (e.g., users of Perl versus users of Lisp, users of VI versus users of Emacs). Cross-cutting all of these, there is an immense "historical archive" of intertextual relations that has yet to be touched regarding the multiple corpora of code that have been written: not just issues related to intellectual property, authorship, riffing, disclosure of source code, voicing, borrowing, and theft; but also simply the use of libraries, genres, well-known sub-routines, algorithm implementation, and of course the data generated by the programs themselves (e.g., all the information out there on each and every one of us). There is the relation between language ideologies (Silverstein 1979) and programming languages: for example, the politics, pragmatics, and poetics of why one language is picked up or rallied around rather than another (which turns closely on the kinds of issues discussed above). There is the relation between Goffman's interaction order (1981, 1983) and human–machine interaction, as well as human–human interaction when mediated by machines (not to mention machine–machine interaction when mediated by humans). As developed in section 29.3, there are also the classic Sapir–Whorf issues regarding the linguistic relativity of programming languages (and, more generally, of interfaces, architectures, platforms, and so forth).[19] And finally, there is a lengthy and ever-evolving set of concepts in computer science and engineering that have direct parallels and strong resonances with key concepts in linguistic anthropology: pointers, name-spaces, unmarked values, files, protocols, libraries, platforms, and so forth. While all of these are relatively obvious topics to take up (in the sense that one just applies already developed analytic concepts to new objects), they are not low-hanging fruits (insofar as they will require a great deal of expert knowledge, and thus specialization, in the domains at issue). Moreover, because of the cross-fertilization of concepts, they are likely to yield analytic insights (for both disciplines) as much as empirical knowledge.

And finally, there is a set of topics that might be best considered as staple goods: on the one hand, they are the most readily available to anthropologists (in terms of the tools they already have); and, on the other hand, they are of the most central interest to anthropologists (given the topics they are used to). Indeed, the literature on such topics is already enormous, and growing larger every day. (See Gershon and Manning, this volume, Chapter 22, for a careful and creative review.) For example, there is the culture and identity of hackers, and any other sub-community closely linked to computer science (e.g., their beliefs and values in relation to language, technology, politics, and so forth). There is the mediation of natural language via new channels and interfaces (e.g., what happens to English grammar, discourse patterns, and genre styles in the context of text-messaging, cell-phones, and so forth). More generally, there is the mediation of semiotic practices and social relations via new channels and interfaces (e.g., identity and interaction in the context of social networking sites, dating applications, the crowd-sourcing of artistic creation, etc.). There is the mediation of language and, in certain cases, talk-in-*intermediated*-interaction, in virtual worlds, video games, and so forth.

In short, there is an infinite list of topics (most of which fall under the rubric of "digital anthropology") that might be characterized as *old concerns in light of (rapidly changing) new media*. It is easy to predict that such relations will be found to change quickly enough over time, and be different enough in different places, such that anthropologists should be able to generate (!)

article after article, and dissertation after dissertation, on their local mediation somewhere: hacker culture in the former Soviet Union; diasporic identity in the context of Facebook; love in the time of relational databases; Japanese slang in NSM; property and personhood (not to mention anonymity, enmity, and amicability) in virtual worlds; gender (race, sexuality, ethnicity, etc.) in video games; space (time, value, etc.) in chat rooms; new political imaginaries and counter-cultures in the wake of new channels; and so forth. In particular, not only will the ethnographic details differ as a function of time and place, but the mediating media themselves will be constantly changing (emails, cell-phones, NSM, Skype, …; Myspace, Friendster, Facebook, Diaspora, …; mainframe, desktop, laptop, smartphone, …; and so on, and so forth), such that if linguistic anthropologists aren't strategically lazy, they will find themselves perpetually busy – passionately tracking potentially superficial topics whose ultimate empirical and theoretical allure is, I'm tempted to say, analytically *akin to* commodity fetishism. (But that is another essay.)

While there are many more potentially interesting topics (sieves in general, self-automatizing languages, data explosions, spam-filters, noise, the relation between capital and computation – for example, electronic trading –, the nature and culture of automated creativity, self-replicating automata, the relation between evolution, computation, and interpretation, Unicode, etc.), the foregoing list of potential frames (and possible pitfalls) should be enough to illuminate some of the space of possibilities, and some of the analytics of approach, for a linguistic anthropology of language automata.

And so there is only one last methodological point to be made: *the tools and techniques used by linguistic anthropologists to study such domains will, in part, have to partake of precisely the objects in such domains.* This means that the usual tools (Shoebox, Elan, etc.) won't be enough. Linguistic anthropologists will not only be writing texts (programs) to study such texts, they will also probably be writing them to write up their studies. More generally, semiotics will have to go hand in hand with statistics, or meaning with mathematics. In particular, the ap-perceiving and ap-intending ears and mouths, eyes and hands, brains and bodies, of linguistic anthropologists do not afford nearly enough power, leverage, speed, or space for the task ahead. To study automatized (networked and formatted) languages, linguistic anthropologists will need to automatize (network and format) languages.

Notes

1. Though, as is well known from information theory, complicated alphabets are not necessary, in that a simple binary alphabet like {0,1} can be used to represent the characters from all other alphabets and, indeed, the strings from all other languages.

2. There is a technical sense of deterministic, as used by computer scientists (Sipser 2007), which is not being invoked here.
3. While linguistic anthropologists have long been nervous about postulating rules to understand behavior (witness the success of practice-based approaches in anthropology), large collections of such rules can exhibit behaviors that appear – and, thus, for all intensive purposes *are* – highly flexible. (And, indeed, one can write rules for a device that enables it to update its own rules – depending, say, on the environment it finds itself in.)
4. Indeed, the claims are themselves recursively applicable. For example, within the domain of critical theory (or continental philosophy), Foucault is to Deleuze what structure is to practice.
5. Ironically and again recursively, in the domain of cognitive psychology, Chomsky is to Skinner as mediators are to intermediaries, and so sits on both sides of this contrast depending on whom he is contrasted with.
6. Linguistic anthropology has always been more formal than its cultural anthropology cousins; and so I'm hoping that they are resolute enough in their commitment to the right-hand side (thirdness), such that they can delve deeply into the left-hand side (secondness), and thus investigate intermediation, which should necessarily obviate the distinctions.
7. Phrased another way, while the input–output relation is deterministic, the "meaning" such devices have and the "function" they serve only make sense in terms of the interests of some agent and the features of some object, which themselves are usually only partially determined, and are always dependent on the placement of such a device in a particular context (a context which includes the device's own input).
8. Insofar as transition functions presume that such devices can read and write inputs which are tokens of a particular type, such devices exhibit the hallmark of digital process (Haugeland 1998b). And, as per the nature of digitality, the types in question, as well as the states and positions, are necessarily discrete: there are no partial types, quasi-states, or half-positions. Needless to say, the discreteness (or "digitality") of the mechanism, like the discreteness of the alphabet, closely aligns it with classic Saussurean understandings of the "symbolic": value (*qua* typehood of any token) only adheres in difference. Loosely speaking, a particular character can be instantiated however we like, so far as it is distinguishable, in both reading and writing, from the other characters with which it contrasts. Crucially, as discussed above, this does not entail that the meaning of such devices is "arbitrary" or conventional (as opposed to "natural" or motivated). Such devices are usually highly iconic and always highly indexical. But again, it's precisely the tension between such grounds (and the ideological claims to one or the other) that make them interesting objects of analysis. Loosely speaking, where we draw the line between the symbolic and the iconic-indexical (or the arbitrary and the

motivated), is itself grounded in convention (or so say the culturalists), which is itself grounded in nature (or so say the realists).

9. Key works on these three kinds of automata, the history of automata-theory more generally, and the nature of programming languages, include: Church (1941); McCulloch et al. (1943); Shannon (1949); Chomsky (1956); Kleene (1956); Rabin and Scott (1959); McCarthy (1960); Thompson (1968); Kernighan and Ritchie (1988[1978]); Abelson et al. (2001); Piccinini (2004); Turing (2004[1936]); Friedl (2006); Sipser (2007); Jurafsky and Martin (2008); Bird et al. (2009).

10. On the one hand, anyone who has ever tried to specify the grammar of a language in any detail will recognize the need for something like a generative capacity (in the unmarked sense): a finite number of words and rules gives rise to an infinite number of actual sentences. And so the idea of a construction (in Bloomfield's original sense) which incorporates parts which are themselves wholes with parts (potentially recursively), and so on, indefinitely, is necessary for describing syntactic processes. On the other hand, these same people will all quickly recognize that this is not sufficient. Formalists may push for further and further refinements (under banners like transformations, government and binding, principles and parameters, minimalism). And functionalists may simply accept a kind of Bloomfieldian minimalism, and then get to work on context-dependent grammars.

11. Left aside are issues related to recognizing versus deciding a language. Famously, as discussed in Sipser (2007), a TM can recognize but not decide a language like {p | p is polynomial with integer roots}.

12. Or, as famously defined by Hilbert, a "process according to which it can be determined in a finite number of operations" (quoted in Sipser 2007).

13. As Sapir put it, "All languages are set to do all the symbolic and expressive work that language is good for, either actually or potentially. The formal technique of this work is the secret of each language" (1949[1924]: 155).

14. For example, celebrations of cyborg futures are just as misplaced as lamentations about authenticities lost.

15. Also key are the framing processes that are involved in linking distinct and potentially distal "texts" and "contexts" (across different points in space-time, so to speak) as much as constituting any particular "text" or "context" (at some particular point in space-time). See, for example, Halliday and Hasan (1976); Lucy (1993); Silverstein and Urban (1996); Enfield (2009); Kockelman (2011; 2012: 202–3).

16. Curiously, Peirce had made similar claims forty years earlier (Chiu et al. 2005).

17. A more recent move with comparable importance is probably *graph theory*: a mathematical field that is used to account for the sieving patterns of automata as well as the interconnections among agents, and a field that is encoded by machines as much as imagined by people.

18. And not only expert populations of humans, but also lay populations.
19. Many of the most famous interface designers make reference to Whorf. See, for example, Englebart (1962), Victor (2006). And see Stephenson for an inspired engagement with Whorf-like ideas (1999).

References

Abelson, Harold, Gerald Jay Sussman, and Julie Sussman. 2001. *The Structure and Interpretation of Computer Programs.* Cambridge, MA: MIT Press.

Arfken, George B., and Hans J. Weber. 1995. *Mathematical Methods for Physicists.* 4th ed. San Diego: Academic Press.

Bauman, Richard, and Joel Sherzer. 1975. The Ethnography of Speaking. *Annual Review of Anthropology* 4: 95–119.

Benjamin, Walter. 1968a. The Work of Art in the Age of Mechanical Reproduction. In *Illuminations*, ed. Hannah Arendt, 217-52. New York: Schocken Books.

— 1968b. Theses on the Philosophy of History. In *Illuminations*, ed. Hannah Arendt, 253-64. New York: Schocken Books.

Benkler, Yochai. 2007. *The Wealth of Networks.* Cambridge, MA: Harvard University Press.

Bird, Steven, Ewan Kleine, and Edward Loper. 2009. *Natural Language Processing with Python.* Sebastopol: O'Reilly.

Boole, George. 1958[1854]. *An Investigation of The Laws of Thought.* New York: Dover.

Bourdieu, Pierre. 1977[1972]. *Outline of a Theory of Practice.* Cambridge: Cambridge University Press.

Ceruzzi, Paul E. 2000. *A History of Modern Computing.* Cambridge, MA: MIT Press.

Chiu, Eugene, Jocelyn Lin, Brok McFerron, Noshirwan Petigara, and Satwiksai Seshasai. 2005. *The Mathematical Theory of Claude Shannon.* Unpublished ms.

Chomsky, Noam. 1956. Three Models for the Description of Language. *IRE Transactions on Information Theory* 2: 113-24.

— 1965. *Aspects of the Theory of Syntax.* Cambridge, MA: MIT Press.

Church, Alonzo. 1941. *The Calculi of Lambda-Conversion.* Princeton, NJ: Princeton University Press.

Dreyfus, Hubert L. 1991. *Being-in-the-World: A Commentary on Heidegger's Being and Time, Division 1.* Cambridge, MA: MIT Press.

Enfield, N. J. 2009. *The Anatomy of Meaning: Speech, Gesture, and Composite Utterances.* Cambridge: Cambridge University Press.

Engelbart, Douglas C. 1962. *Augmenting Human Intellect.* SRI Summary Report AFOSR-3223.

French, Robert M. 2000. The Turing Test: The First 50 Years. *Trends in Cognitive Science* 4(3): 115-22.

Friedl, J. 2006. *Mastering Regular Expression*. Sebastopol: O'Reilly Media, Inc.
Gibson, James. 1986[1979]. *The Ecological Approach to Visual Perception*. Boston, MA: Houghton Mifflin.
Goffman, Erving. 1981. Footing. In *Forms of Talk*, 124–59. Philadelphia: University of Pennsylvania Press.
   1983. The Interaction Order. *American Sociological Review* 48(1): 1–17.
Gombrich, E. H. 1979. *The Sense of Order*. Ithaca, NY: Cornell University Press.
Halliday, M. A. K., and Ruqaiya Hasan. 1976. *Cohesion in English*. London: Longman.
Haugeland, John. 1998a. The Intentionality All-Stars. In *Having Thought: Essays in the Metaphysics of Mind*, 127–70. Cambridge, MA: Harvard University Press.
   1998b. Mind Embodied and Embedded. In *Having Thought: Essays in the Metaphysics of Mind*, 207–37. Cambridge, MA: Harvard University Press.
Hayles, N. Katherine. 1999. *How We Became Posthuman*. Chicago: University of Chicago Press.
Hill, Jane H., and Bruce Mannheim. 1992. Language and World View. *Annual Review of Anthropology* 21: 381–406.
Hymes, Dell. 1962. The Ethnography of Speaking. In *Anthropology and Human Behaviour*, ed. T. Gladwin and W. C. Sturtevant, 13–53. Washington, DC: Anthropology Society of Washington.
Inoue, Miyako. 2011. Stenography and Ventriloquism in Late Nineteenth Century Japan. *Language and Communication* 31: 181–90.
Jakobson, Roman. 1990a. The Speech Event and the Functions of Language. In *On Language*, ed. L. R. Waugh and M. Monville, 69–79. Cambridge, MA: Harvard University Press.
   1990b. Shifters and Verbal Categories. In *On Language*, ed. L. R. Waugh and M. Monville-Burston, 386–92. Cambridge, MA: Harvard University Press.
Jurafsky, Daniel, and James H. Martin. 2008. *Speech and Language Processing*. 2nd ed. Englewood Cliffs, NJ: Pearson Prentice Hall.
Kernighan, Brian, and Dennis Ritchie. 1988[1978]. *The C Programming Language*. 2nd ed. Englewood Cliffs, NJ: Prentice Hall.
Kittler, Friedrich A. 1989[1986]. *Gramophone, Film, Typewriter*. Palo Alto, CA: Stanford University Press.
   1996[1993]. The History of Communication Media. Online at www.ctheory.net/text_file.asp?pick=45.
Kleene, S. C. 1956. Representations of Events in Nerve Nets and Finite Automata. In *Automata Studies*, ed. C. Shannon and J. McCarthy, 3–41. Princeton, NJ: Princeton University Press.
Kockelman, Paul. 1999. Poetic Function and Logical Form, Ideal Languages and Forms of Life. *Chicago Anthropology Exchange* 29: 34–50.
   2006a. Residence in the World: Affordances, instruments, actions, roles and identities. *Semiotica* 162(1): 19–71.

2006b. A Semiotic Ontology of The Commodity. *Journal of Linguistic Anthropology* 16(1): 76–102.

2007a. Agency: The Relation between Meaning, Power, and Knowledge. *Current Anthropology* 48(3): 375–401.

2007b. Enclosure and Disclosure. *Public Culture* 19(2): 303–5.

2007c. From Status to Contract Revisited. *Anthropological Theory* 7(2): 151–76.

2010. Enemies, Parasites, and Noise: How to Take Up Residence in a System Without Becoming a Term in It. *Journal of Linguistic Anthropology* 20(2): 406–21.

2011. Biosemiosis, Technocognition, and Sociogenesis: Selection and Significance in a Multiverse of Sieving and Serendipity. *Current Anthropology*, 52(5): 711–39.

2013a. Huckleberry Finn Takes the Turing Test: The transformation of ontologies, the virtuality of kinds. *Language and Communication* 33: 15–154.

2013b. The Anthropology of an Equation: Spam, sieves, agentive algorithms and ontologies of transformation. *Hau: The Journal of Ethnographic Theory* 3(3): 33–61.

Kripke, Saul A. 1982. *Wittgenstein: On Rules and Private Language*. Cambridge, MA: Harvard University Press.

Lakoff, George, and Mark Johnson. 1980. *Metaphors We Live By*. Chicago: University of Chicago Press.

Latour, Bruno. 2005. *Reassembling the Social*. Oxford: Oxford University Press.

Lee, Penny. 1996. *The Whorf Theory Complex: A Critical Reconstruction*. Amsterdam: John Benjamins.

Levi-Strauss, Claude. 1969[1949]. *The Elementary Structures of Kinship*. Boston, MA: Beacon Press.

Lucy, John A. 1992a. *Language, Diversity, and Thought*. Cambridge: Cambridge University Press.

1992b. *Grammatical Categories and Cognition*. Cambridge: Cambridge University Press.

ed. 1993. *Reflexive Language: Reported Speech and Metapragmatics*. Cambridge: Cambridge University Press.

MacKay, Donald M. 1969. *Information, Mechanism and Meaning*. Cambridge, MA: MIT Press.

Marx, Karl. 1967[1867]. *Capital*, Vol. 1. New York: International Publishers.

McCarthy, John. 1960. Recursive Functions of Symbolic Expressions and their Computation by Machine. *Communications of the ACM* 3(4): 184–95.

McCulloch, Warren S., and Walter Pitts. 1943. A Logical Calculus of the Ideas Immanent in Nervous activity. *Bulletin of Mathematic Biophysics* 5: 24–56.

McLuhan, Marshall. 1996[1964]. *Understanding Media*. Cambridge, MA: MIT Press.

Mirowski, Philip. 2002. *Machine Dreams*. Cambridge: Cambridge University Press.

Peirce, Charles Sanders. 1955a. Logic as Semiotic: The Theory of Signs. In *Philosophical Writings of Peirce*, ed. Justus Buchler, 98–119. New York: Dover Publications.

———. 1955b. The Principles of Phenomenology. In *Philosophical Writings of Peirce*, ed. Justus Buchler, 74–97. New York: Dover Publications.

———. 1955c. Pragmatism in Retrospect: A Last Formulation. In *Philosophical Writings of Peirce*, ed. Justus Buchler, 269–89. New York: Dover Publications.

Petzold, Charles. 2000. *Code: The Hidden Language of Computer Hardware and Software*. Redmond, WA: Microsoft Press.

Piccinini, G. 2004. The First Computational theory of Mind and Brain. *Synthese* 141(2): 175–215.

Rabin, M.O., and D. Scott. 1959. Finite Automata and their Decision Problems. *IBM Journal*, April: 114–25.

Sapir, Edward. 1949[1924]. The Grammarian and His Language. In *Selected Writings in Language, Culture, and Personality*, ed. David G. Mandelbaum, 150–9. Berkeley: University of California Press.

———. 1985[1927]. The Unconscious Patterning of Behavior in Society. In *Selected Writings in Language, Culture, and Personality*, ed. David G. Mandelbaum, 544–59. Berkeley: University of California Press.

———. 1985[1945]. Grading: A Study in Semantics. In *Selected Writings in Language, Culture, and Personality*, ed. David G. Mandelbaum, 122–49. Berkeley: University of California Press.

Saussure, Ferdinand de. 1983[1916]. *Course in General Linguistics*. La Salle, IL: Open Court Press.

Saygin, Ayse Pinar, Ilyas Cicekli, and Varol Akman. 2001. Turing Test: 50 Years Later. *Minds and Machines* 10: 463–518.

Serres, Michael. 2007[1982]. *The Parasite*. Minneapolis: Minnesota Press.

Shannon, Claude E. 1936. *A Symbolic Analysis of Relay and Switching Circuits*. Cambridge, MA: MIT Department of Electrical Engineering M.S. MIT Institute Archives.

———. 1949. Communication Theory of Secrecy Systems. Declassified Document.

———. 1963[1949]. The Mathematical Theory of Communication. In *The Mathematical Theory of Communication*, 29–125. Urbana: University of Illinois Press.

Sidnell, Jack. 2010. *Conversation Analysis: An Introduction*. London: Blackwell.

Sidnell, Jack, and Nick Enfield. 2012. Language Diversity and Social Action: A third locus of linguistic relativity. *Current Anthropology* 53: 302–33.

Silverstein, Michael. 1976. Shifters, Linguistic Categories and Cultural Description. In *Meaning in Anthropology*, ed. K. Basso and H. Selby, 11–55. Albuquerque: University of New Mexico Press.

———. 1979. Language Function and Linguistic Ideology. In *The Elements: A Parasession on Linguistic Units and Levels*, ed. Paul R. Clyne, William

F. Hanks, and Carol L. Hofbauer, 193–247. Chicago: Chicago Linguistic Society.

Silverstein, Michael, and Greg Urban, eds. 1996. *Natural Histories of Discourse*. Chicago: University of Chicago.

Simon, Herbert A. 1996. *The Sciences of the Artificial*. Cambridge, MA: MIT Press.

Sipser, Michael. 2007. *A Theory of Computation*. New Delhi: Cengage Learning.

Stephenson, Neal. 1999. *In the Beginning Was the Command Line*. New York: Perennial Press.

Suchman, Lucy A. 2007. *Man-Machine Reconfigurations*. Cambridge: Cambridge University Press.

Thompson, Ken. 1968. Programming Techniques: Regular Expression Search Alogorithm Communications. *ACM* 11(6): 419–422.

Tomasello, Michael, and Josep Call. 1997. *Primate Cognition*. New York: Oxford University Press.

Turing, Alan. 2004[1936]. On Computable Numbers, with an Application to the Entscheidungsproblem. In *The Essential Turing*, ed. B. Jack Copeland, 58–90. Oxford: Oxford University Press.

⸺ 2004[1950]. Computing Machinery and Intelligence. In *The Essential Turing*, ed. B. Jack Copeland, 433–64. Oxford: Oxford University Press.

Van Valin, Robert D., and Randy LaPolla. 1997. *Syntax*. Cambridge: Cambridge University Press.

Victor, Bret. 2006. Magic Ink: Information Software and the Graphical Interface. Available at: http://worrydream.com/MagicInk/.

Wardrip-Fruin, Noah and Nick Montfort, eds. 2003. *The New Media Reader*. Cambridge, MA: MIT Press.

Whorf, Benjamin L. 1956[1937]. Grammatical Categories. In *Language, Thought, and Reality: Selected Writings of Benjamin Lee Whorf*, ed. John B. Carroll, 87–101. Cambridge, MA: The MIT Press.

⸺ 1956[1939]. The Relation of Habitual Thought and Behavior to Language. In *Language, Thought, and Reality: Selected Writings of Benjamin Lee Whorf*, ed. John B. Carroll, 134–59. Cambridge, MA: The MIT Press.

Wittgenstein, Ludwig. 1958[1953]. *Philosophical Investigations*. Englewood Cliffs, NJ: Prentice Hall.

⸺ 1961[1921]. *Tractatus Logico-Philosophicus*. London: Routledge and Kegan Paul.

Index

A, agent-like argument of transitive verb, 108
A, transitive subject function, 38, 42
Aboriginal Australia, 56
Aboriginal systems of kinship, 411
absolute frame of spatial reference, 204
abstraction, 716
Abu-Lughod, L., 449
accent, 272
accountability, 12, 13, 60, 331, 390, 427
accusative marking, 42, 196
acquisition, 330
acquisition of phonology, 191
acquisition of sign language, 86
action, 3, 15, 150, 161
action sequencing, 364
actuation, 62
address, 148, 153
address forms, 203
adjacency pairs, 140, 143, 144, 372, 452
adjectives, 41, 160
adolescence, 209
adverbials, 192
aesthetics, 538
affect, 654
affiliation, 170
affordances, 62, 565, 566
Africa, 42, 45, 104, 105, 116, 188, 287
age, 148
agency, 73, 150, 208, 603, 655, 711, 714, 722
agglutinative languages, 192
Agha, A., 72, 411, 486, 489, 492, 494, 503, 612, 630, 649
agreement marking, 195
Ahearn, L., 486
ahistorical linguistics, 230
Aikhenvald, A. Y., 55
Akrich, M., 572
Albert, E., 543
Algeria, 252
algorithms, 718
alignment, 170
allophones, 37
alphabet, 709

Al-Sayyid Bedouin Sign Language, 87, 89, 92, 104, 184, 250
Althusser, L., 591
Altman, S., 402
Alyawarre, 56
Amakalang, 520
Amazon, 33
American Anthropological Association, 2
American anthropology, 27, 229
American families, 201
American languages, 27, 159
American Peace Corps, 159
American pragmatists, 353
American Sign Language, 85, 86, 92, 258, 268
Americas, 116
Amerind, 667, 690
Anakalang, 519
analytic philosophy, 11, 129, 144
anaphoric reference, 274, 319
Anatolia, 316
anatomically modern humans, 311
Ancestry Informative Markers, 688
Andaman islands, 289
Anderson, B., 483, 588
Anderson, J., 233
Andes, 240
animal communication, 6, 401, 404
animator, 563
Annales school, 230
Anscombe, G. E. M., 11, 392, 429
Antaki, C., 448, 452
anthropologists, 29
anthropology, 1, 29, 187, 211, 448
anthropology of language, 3
anti-colonial movement, 230
antithesis principle (Darwin), 51
Anward, J., 489
Apache, 300
ape gestures, 389
apes, 189
aphasia, 83
applicatives, 194
Arabic, 273
Arapesh, 299

Arbib, M., 274, 309
arbitrariness, 3, 344, 401
archaeo-DNA, 185, 310, 313
archaeogenetics, 677
archaeology, 4, 16, 229, 233, 238, 239, 311, 600, 660, 661, 667
architecture of intersubjectivity, 426
argument, 254, 256
argument structure, 196, 255
Aristotle, 481
Aronoff, M., 184
Arrernte, 196
articles, 34, 40
artifacts, 234
artifactualization, 228
artificial intelligence, 350
artificial languages, 716, 720
Asia, 287
assertions, 357
assessments, 489
assimilation, 268, 271
Atkinson, M., 331, 368
attentional state, 389
attunement, 365
Auden, W. H., 516
audience design, 148
Auer, P., 174
Austin, J. L., 11, 12, 13, 130, 131, 144, 150, 384, 385, 392, 424, 425, 426, 427, 428, 429, 432, 433, 441, 457, 485, 495, 496, 497, 499, 503, 504, 523, 604, 608, 614
Austin, P., 286, 288, 291, 297
Australia, 14, 32, 36, 37, 40, 43, 45, 56, 116, 239
Austroasiatic languages, 56
Austronesian languages, 44, 317
authenticity, 722
author, 563
authority, 518, 525
autobiography, 235
automata, 709, 711, 713, 716
automaticity, 272
autonomy of grammar, 28
avoidance, 412, 500
avowals, 348
awareness, 539
Aymaran, 315
Azande, 12

babbling, 191
baby talk, 199, 409, 414
Bakhtin, M., 149, 229, 234, 235, 243, 539
Bali, 252
Banti, G., 487
Bantu, 317
Bantu languages, 116, 194
Baquedano, P., 209
Barker, J., 567
Barthes, R., 627
Basic Child Grammar, 193
basic linguistic theory, 25, 29–47, 112
Basic Oral Language Documentation, 302
basic word order, 274
basic-level categorization, 9
Basque, 45
Basso, E., 521, 522
Basso, K., 233
Bate, B., 481, 482, 487, 552
Bateson, G., 454, 516

Bauman, R., 456, 487, 488, 493, 494, 570
Bayesian phylogenetics, 316
Beach, W., 448, 457
beaver, 310
Bechert, J., 285
Becker, A., 494
bee dances, 401
bees, 400, 401, 404, 416
beneficiary, 434
Benveniste, E., 149, 228, 403, 404, 405, 663
Berber languages, 42
Berson, J., 299, 301
Besnier, N., 463, 653
biased transmission, 61, 62–4
  direct bias, 62
  frequency-dependent bias, 62
  indirect bias, 62
Biber, D., 489
Bickel, B., 27, 274, 317
Bickerton, D., 274, 309, 318
bilingual children, 208
bilingual communities, 204
bilingual learning, 202
binning approach, 434, 437
binomials, 144
bioinformatics, 185, 310, 316
biological anthropology, 16, 601
biological diversity, 291, 686
biological evolution, 315, 330
biology, 16, 70, 114, 198
biology of language, 310
Birdwhistell, R., 26, 454
black-box, 711
Blackhorse, T., 521
Blench, R. M., 600
blind speakers, 79
Bloch, M., 57, 59, 67, 336, 482, 528, 550, 553
Bloomfield, L., 67, 158, 161, 258, 285, 482, 577, 579, 583
Blum-Kulka, S., 457
Blust, R., 666
Boas, F., 3, 229, 238, 285, 454, 481, 482
body torque, 456
body touching, 200
Bohman, J., 486
Bolinger, Dwight, 159
Bonobo, 389
Boole, G., 722
bootstrapping, 195, 196, 197
borrowing, 49, 66, 117
Bourdieu, P., 230, 241, 516, 583, 584, 604, 610, 630, 634
Bowerman, M., 194, 195, 198
Boyd, R., 62, 320, 325, 334
brain, 102, 113, 115
Brandom, R., 343, 347, 431, 610
Brazil, 232
Brazilian Sign Language, 257
Brenneis, D., 528
Brentano, F., 347
Bricker, V., 520
bricolage, 649
Briggs, C., 205, 487, 488, 493, 591
British Sign Language, 85
broadcast range, 312
Brown, E., 493, 494
Brown, P., 183, 325, 330, 365, 388, 393, 411, 456, 465

Brown, R., 9, 193, 411
brute actions, 423
brute facts, 392, 412
Bucholtz, M., 580, 581, 584
Buehler, K., 403
Bunaba, 497, 500
bundling of items in transmission, 70
Burke, K., 546
Burkhart, L., 526
Butler, J., 486
Bybee, J., 160, 162

California, 40, 188
call openings, 456
Cameron, L., 328
Campbell, L., 325
Canadian Royal Commission on Aboriginal Peoples, 292
candidate understanding, 452, 463
Canger, U., 240
caregiver-infant interaction, 199
Caribbean English Creole, 457, 459
case, 107
case marking, 160, 195, 254, 256, 274
case studies, 210
categorization, 9, 129, 136, 162
Caton, S., 505, 528
causal domains, 326
causal mechanisms, 183, 326
causal-conditional mechanisms, 326
causality, 10
Cavalli-Sforza, L. L., 677, 689
Cavell, S., 441
Celtic, 116, 250
Cha'palaa, 462, 465
Chafe, W., 160, 482
Chamula Maya, 520
channel, 139
Chater, N., 62
Chechen, 106
Cheney, D., 401, 417, 418
chess metaphor, 332
child–caregiver interaction, 202
child-centered cultures, 208
child-centered interaction, 198, 201
child-centered methods, 208
child-directed speech, 198, 199, 200, 201
child language acquisition, 110, 113
childhood, 198, 209
childrearing, 198
chimpanzees, 312, 313, 388, 400
Chinese, 104
Chintang, 106, 107, 109, 191
Chomsky, N., 8, 28, 30, 111, 112, 114, 120, 137, 162, 187, 229, 309, 313, 325, 693, 718
Christian evangelization, 242
Christiansen, M., 62, 309
Chronic Otitis Media, 697
chronotopes, 143, 184, 234, 638
chunking, 162, 170
Church-Turing Thesis, 718
citational formulae, 499
Clackamas, 520
Clark, E., 206
Clark, H., 366, 426, 429
Classical Nahuatl, 240
classification, 136
classificatory kinship, 411

classifiers, 31, 319
classroom interaction, 82, 205
clause, 38, 73, 80, 257
Clayman, S., 368
closed versus open class, 39
cloud formations, 160
Clovis, 667
code, 3
code-switching, 204
codices, 233
Codrington, R. H., 501
co-evolution, 227
cognates, 315
cognition, 17, 189
cognitive anthropology, 9
cognitive biases, 10
cognitive development, 193
Cognitive Grammar, 102
cognitive maturation, 193
cognitive preferences, 4
cognitive psychology, 136
Cohen, E., 452
Coleman, B., 565
collateral effects, 9, 50, 425
collective awareness, 228
collective intentionality, 370, 371
collective memory, 227, 232
collectivization, 629
colonial authorities, 241
colonial history, 240
colonial linguistics, 242
colonial rule, 241
colonized peoples, 238
color, 9
color terms, 109
Comaroff, J., 370
combinativeness, 656
combinatorics, 66
commitments, 351, 357
communication, 5, 158, 159, 174
communication systems, 256, 274, 344
communicative competence, 188
community, 254, 577, 588
community of practice, 584
comparative method, 184, 315
comparative psychology, 3, 9
comparison, 194, 210
complementation, 32
complementizers, 274
complexity, 193
compositionality, 137
compounding, 263
compounds, 272, 276, 277
computation, 601, 708, 721
computer languages, 5
computer science, 16, 601, 708, 709, 711
computers, 709, 711, 713
Comrie, B., 159
concatenations, 717
concept formulation, 329
concepts, 351
conceptual unity, 162
conceptualization, 118
conditional relevance, 373, 389
conditionals, 258, 260, 275, 359
conditioning, 330, 600, 608
confirming allusions, 430
Conklin, Harold C., 45

consciousness, 348
constituency, 6, 28, 158, 161–3, 174
constituent exemplars, 164
constituent order, 86, 92, 115, 116, 160, 192, 195
constituent schemas, 164, 165
constituent schematicity, 171
constituent structure, 258
Construction Grammar, 112
constructionism, 187
constructions, 175
contagion (semiotic), 501
content-frame schema, 70
context, 139, 201, 209, 230, 231
context bias, 65, 66
context-free grammar, 611, 715, 717
contextuality, 149
contextualization, 53, 66, 70, 139, 143, 232
contiguity relations, 162
contrastive tone, 320
conventionalization, 264, 272, 276
conventions, 231, 254, 629
conversation, 5, 159, 189, 299, 449, 488
Conversation Analysis, 16, 73, 161, 163, 189, 331, 344, 404, 426, 430, 433, 448, 453, 455, 457, 460, 489
cooperation, 187, 189
coordinate systems, 719
coordination, 258
Coral Gardens and their Magic, The, 481
Corder, 581
corpora, 133
Corpus linguistics, 467
correctness, 352
cortical strip, 311
co-textuality, 140, 142, 146, 148, 149
counting, 83, 297
counting languages, 286, 297
counting speakers, 286
Couper-Kuhlen, E., 27, 185
couplets, 519
Course, M., 517
Craig, C., 159
creaky voice, 166, 168
creole languages, 87
creoles, 263, 274, 318, 672
creolization, 254, 273, 276, 601, 672, 679
critical discourse analysis, 140
critical theory, 240, 241, 599, 603, 722
Croatian, 25, 58, 104
Croft, W., 315
cross cultural pragmatics, 457
cross-cousins, 57
cross-cultural comparison, 449
cross-cultural diversity, 365
cross-domain diagrams, 723
cross-reference, 254
Crystal, D., 288, 291, 295
Csibra, G., 330
cultural anthropology, 16, 67
cultural diffusion, 692
cultural diversity, 198
cultural evolution, 185, 310
cultural knowledge, 452
cultural totality, 58, 59, 61, 67
cultural tradition in humans and other apes, 314
cultural transmission, 48, 331
    centripetal force in, 68

cultural values, 35, 49
cultural variation, 190
culture, 2, 13, 183, 228, 577, 587, 600, 629
    as whole, 26
    causal ontology of, 49
culture words, 239
Cutler, A., 325, 329
cutoff, 170

Danish, 459
Danziger, Eve, 196
Darwin, C., 50, 70, 309, 314, 315, 330
data-mining, 669
Davidson, D., 356
Davis, M, 454
Dawkins, R., 330, 389
De Rocck, M., 405
de Saussure, F., 327, 329, 332, 487, 603, 627
de Vos, C., 319
Deacon, T., 309
deaf, 26, 252
deaf community, 252, 257
deaf community sign language, 87
deafness, 696
declarative, 258, 357
Dediu, D., 185, 250, 312, 317, 600, 601
defeasibility, 499
deixis, 45, 83, 140, 141, 146, 153, 192, 203, 366, 496
delegation, 572
demic diffusion, 668, 692
demographic processes, 689
demography, 63
demonstratives, 44, 45, 141
Demuth, K., 194
Denisovans, 312, 689
denotation, 27, 549
denotational function, 541, 543
denotational view of language, 131, 132
deontic powers, 12
dependency relations, 254
derivation, 30, 31
Derrida, J., 231, 241
Descartes, R., 347, 348, 351, 355
description, 158
descriptive linguistics, 4, 16, 448, 467
design features of language, 401
deterministic, 711
Deterministic Finite Automata, 716
development, 4, 183, 187, 209
developmental milestones, 199
developmental psychology, 199, 211
Dewey, J., 353
diachrony, 3, 160, 163, 174, 186, 229, 232, 326, 327, 331, 604
dialectology, 240
dialects, 102, 103, 153
dialogicality, 184, 234
dictionary definitions, 36
Diessel, H., 403
diffusion, 61, 66, 67, 116, 117, 119, 315, 316, 331
diffusion of innovations, 62
digital media, 565
Dik, S., 159
Dingamanse, M., 404
Dinwoodie, D. W., 237
direct quotation, 405
directional particles, 192

discourse, 3, 193, 229, 230, 239, 257, 604
discourse completion exercises, 457
discourse organization, 160
discourse registers, 411
discreteness, 13, 344, 401
discursive intentionality, 349, 351, 352
discursive norms, 353
displacement, 6, 13, 275, 344, 401
distributed agency, 73
distributed cognition, 73
disturbances, 613
diversity, 1, 5, 27, 102, 103–110
Dixon, R. M. W., 7, 25, 55, 159, 185, 325, 412
DNA, 312
Dobrin, L., 299, 301
doctrine of concepts, 351
doctrine of judgments, 351
doctrine of literal denotation, 132, 136, 145
doctrine of syllogisms, 351
documentary linguistics, 4
dolphins, 400
domination, 612
Donegan, P., 55, 66
Dorian, N., 285, 580
double articulation, 6, 490
Dresher, E., 434
Drew, P., 430
drift, 10
Dryer, M., 118, 159
Du Bois, J., 160, 197, 393, 412, 415, 482, 486, 489, 494, 528
dual inheritance, 185
duality of patterning, 6, 269, 319, 390, 402, 490
Dummett, M., 356
Dunbar, R., 309
Dunn, M., 317
Duranti, A., 2, 369, 384, 385, 387, 388, 392, 448, 463, 486, 528, 547, 548, 582
Durkheim, E., 50, 369, 491, 517, 518
Dutch, 25, 58, 198
Dyirbal, 32, 34, 45
    Girramay dialect of, 33

early adopters, 63
Eckert, P., 57, 66, 147, 325, 331, 415, 584, 600, 647, 648
economy, 118
Edwards, W., 458
Efron, D., 26, 454
Egbert, M., 450, 456
Eibl-Eibesfeldt, I., 454, 465
Eisenlohr, P., 559, 560, 562
elicitation, 332
Elichmann, J., 664
Elyachar, J., 574
embedded structures, 275
embedding, 611
emblems, 153, 540
embodiment, 524
emergent grammar, 160, 161
Emerson, R. W., 243
Emmorey, K., 325
emotion, 17
empathy, 169
enaction, 518, 522
enchrony, 16, 163, 174, 184, 185, 326, 331, 334, 373

enclosure, 601, 708, 721, 722
Enfield, N. J., 10, 11, 26, 28, 163, 185, 290, 315, 325, 364, 366, 373, 384, 390, 392, 452, 456, 457, 462, 464, 465, 493, 503, 522, 678, 697, 715
Engelke, M., 521, 527
Engels, F., 332
Englebretson, R., 489
English, 4, 8, 9, 26, 30, 31, 32, 33, 35, 36, 39, 40, 42, 44, 45, 54, 65, 81, 85, 92, 104, 105, 106, 107, 108, 111, 115, 116, 120, 142, 144, 145, 163, 168, 171, 173, 175, 184, 192, 193, 194, 195, 198, 204
English, British, 37
English, Scottish, 37
Enlightenment, 128, 130, 131, 140, 149, 153
enregistered, 649
enregistered memory, 235
enregisterment, 146, 153, 612
entailment, 144
entextualization, 139, 143, 150, 232, 561
envorganisms, 49
epidemiology of culture and language, 61
epigraphy, 673
epistemology, 517
equivalence classes, 487
equivalence of reference, 721
erasure, 236
ergative languages, 196
ergative marking, 42
ergativity, 108, 119
Erickson, F., 488, 493
Errington, J., 241, 301, 412, 526
Essegbey, James, 196
essentialization, 14
Estonian, 55
ethics, 185, 296, 300
ethnocentrism, 486
ethnographic monograph, 627
ethnographic present, 230
ethnography, 16, 58, 207, 229, 237, 448, 631, 640
ethnography of childhood, 209
ethnography of communication, 183, 188, 457
ethnography of speaking, 3, 209, 456, 488, 545
ethnohistory, 184, 234, 240
ethnology, 229, 238
ethnomethodology, 455
ethnopoetics, 488
ethnopragmatic, 547
ethnopsychology, 17
ethology, 326
Eurasia, 116
Eurocentrism, 238
Europe, 116, 287
European anthropology, 229
Evans, N., 57, 110, 251, 274, 291, 295, 298
Evans-Pritchard, E. E., 12, 336, 392, 518
evidentiality, 149
evidentials, 203
evolution, 70, 185, 238
evolution of language, 113, 189, 309, 330
evolutionary anthropology, 189
evolutionary biology, 189, 686
Ewe, 196
expansion, 174
explanation, 158

explicit performative utterances, 496, 497, 500
externalization, 7
extraposition, 175
eye contact, 198, 199, 206
eyebrow flashes, 465, 466

face-to-face interaction, 147
face-work, 525
facial expression in sign language, 258
fact-making, 231
false consciousness, 519
familylect, 253, 264
family-tree model of diversification, 315
Faudree, Paja, 184
felicity conditions, 485, 496, 614
Ferrara, K., 489
fetishism, 502
fetishization, 616
Field, M., 300, 452, 521
field methodology, 454
fieldwork, 32, 35, 133, 159, 600
figuration, 572, 633, 634
figurational dynamics, 414
figure, 563
Fijian, 31, 40, 42, 44
Filipi, A., 206
Fillmore, Charles, 159
Finegan, E., 489
Finnish, 54, 457
Firbas, Jan, 159
first language acquisition, 183, 187–211
first words, 192
firstness, 713
Firth, R., 481
Fischer, C., 564
Fishman, J., 294, 296
fission and fusion, 331
fission-fusion social organization, 424
Fitch, T., 309, 311, 312, 313, 325
Fleming, 481
Flemish, 25, 58
flexuous movements, 52
Floyd, S., 404
Fodor, J., 8, 356
folklore, 488
Forbidden Experiment, The, 251
form classes, 137
formal completion, 719
formalism, 137, 183
formalization, 482, 528
format tying, 490
Fortes, M., 59
fossil evidence, 310, 312
fossils, 185
Foucault, M., 241, 612
four-stroke engine model of cultural transmission, 63
Fourth position, 383
Fox, B., 172, 462, 463
Fox, J., 519
FOXP2 gene, 312, 693, 695
fractal, 651
fractal recursivity, 578
frame, 609
framing, 71, 72
Frankfurt School, 233, 619
Frazer, J. G., 500, 517, 521, 589

Frederick Kittler, 560
Frege, G., 613
French, 34
frequency, 160, 163, 173, 193, 195
Freud, S., 616
Friedrich, P., 518, 519, 542
Frisch, K., 400, 401
Frog, where are you?, 197
function, 27
function words, 254, 275
functional connection principle (Darwin), 51
functional linguistic relativity, 204
functional relations, 64
functionalism, 140, 158–61, 183
functionalist linguistics, 27

Gal, S., 236, 240, 293, 578, 590, 634, 653
Garfinkel, H., 60, 331, 370, 382, 428, 455
Garibay, A., 520
Garrett, P. B., 209, 293
Gaskins, S., 183, 325, 330
gaze, 200, 375, 456, 464, 465
gaze-following, 366
Geertz, C., 14, 231, 237, 412, 492, 521, 628
Gell, A., 336
gender, 34, 41, 148, 544
gender registers, 662
gender roles, 674
generative capacity, 6
generative linguistics, 7, 29, 229, 720
generativism, 229
generativity, 605
genes, 185
genetic locus, 687
genetic markers, 691
genetic variation, 687, 688
genetics, 4, 253, 601, 676
Geneva Convention, 57
genome sequencing, 677
genre, 232, 519
Gentner, Dedre, 192, 198
geographic distribution of languages, 287
geology, 250
Gergely, G., 330
German, 34, 109
German Sign Language, 257
Gershon, I., 483
gesticulation, 261
gestural emblems, 261
gesture, 7, 27, 78–93, 189, 200, 206, 252, 318, 375, 454, 456, 464
    children's acquisition of, 78
gesture–speech mismatches, 82
Ghana, 250
Giannattasio, F., 487
Gibson, J., 566
Gigerenzer, G., 330, 433
Gilij, 665
Gilman, A., 411
Gimbutas, M., 692
Givón, T., 159, 160, 334
Gleitman, Lila, 195
Glick, D., 486
global warming, 118
globalization, 120
glottal closure, 170
glottochronology, 666
Gluckman, Max, 12

Glyn Daniel, 663
Goffman, E., 12, 60, 325, 331, 336, 344, 365, 366, 386, 415, 418, 425, 426, 438, 464, 489, 503, 522, 525
Gokana, 105, 111, 112, 114, 118
Goldin-Meadow, S., 26, 184, 251, 318
Goodman, N., 493
Goodwin, C., 26, 325, 336, 375, 376, 412, 418, 449
Goodwin, M. H., 375, 418, 490
Goody, J., 336
Gorilla, 389
Gossen, G., 520
Gothic, 250, 317
governmentality, 612
Graham, L., 232, 491
grammar, 3, 4, 203, 253, 274
grammatical agreement, 319
grammatical categories, 261, 262, 316, 496
grammatical criteria, 40
grammatical function, 256
Grammatical parallelism, 482
grammatical relations, 88, 103, 108, 111, 119, 160, 195
grammatical roles, 261, 496
grammatical structure, 276
grammaticalization, 4, 239, 334
grammaticization, 160, 163, 174, 254, 263
Grammer, K., 465
Gramsci, 241
Greek, 120, 250
Greek grammarians, 30
Greenberg, J., 10, 121, 159, 315, 317, 334, 667, 690
greeting sequences, 454
Grenoble, L., 288, 293, 297
Grice, H. P., 331, 355, 384, 385, 392, 610, 616
Groark, K., 393
Guatemala, 191
guided variation, 334
Güldemann, T., 405
Gumperz, J., 3, 188, 230, 456, 482, 578, 580, 584, 605, 644
Guugu-Yimidhirr, 411, 499, 500
Guyanese creole, 458

Habermas, J., 233, 483, 486, 577, 588
Hacking, I., 609
Haiku poetry, 114
Haiman, John, 159
Halbwachs, Maurice, 233
Hale, K., 291, 335
Hale, Kenneth, 10, 14
Hall, E., 454
Hall, K., 486
Halliday, M. A. K., 159
hammers, 66
hand part prominence, 273
Handbook of American Indian Languages, 482
handshape, 268, 271, 273, 277
Hanks, W. F., 242, 325, 418, 526, 529
Hansen, Magnus Pharao, 184
Hanunóo, 44
Harbert, W., 293
harmonic versus disharmonic patterns, 115, 117
Harris, A., 325
Haspelmath, M., 120

Hauser, M., 251, 309, 313, 325
Haviland, J., 411, 412, 499, 520
Hawkins, John, 115, 159
Hayashi, M., 377, 462, 463
head nodding, 465
hearing range, 312
Heath, Shirley Brice, 188
Hebrew, 194, 273
Hegel, G., 352
Heine, Bernd, 116
Heller, M., 301
Herder, 229
heritability, 693, 694, 695
Heritage, J., 331, 364, 368, 370, 375, 439, 440, 448, 449, 455
Hertwig, R., 433
Herzfeld, M., 487
Herzog, M., 331
heteroglossia, 235
heuristics, 8
hierarchical structure, 161
hierarchical syntactic structures, 274
hierarchies in grammar, 4
hieroglyphs, 233
Hill, J., 293, 297, 301, 486, 503, 522
Himmelmann, N., 285, 295, 300, 403
Hinde, R., 344
Hindi, 115, 191, 197
Hinton, L., 294, 296
Hirschkind, C., 528
historical linguistics, 4, 88, 103, 184, 238, 239, 240, 242, 250, 315, 325, 663
historical materialism, 230
historical realism, 114, 115
historicity, 233
historiography, 237
history, 4, 5, 184, 228, 630
Hobbes, T., 12
Hobsbawm, E., 582
Hockett, C., 13, 269, 275, 401, 402
Hodder, I., 648
Holbraad, M., 517
holophrastic, 261
home sign, 89, 91, 318
homeopathic magic, 521
Homo erectus, 313, 314
Homo genus, 312
Homo Heidelbergensis, 312
homonyms, 33
homophone avoidance, 500
honorification, 148, 153
honorifics, 202, 203, 211
Hopi, 8, 236
Hopper, P., 160, 325
Hopper, R., 448, 459
household, 253
How to Do Things with Words, 485
Hull, M., 567
human sociality, 159, 160
Humboldt, W. von, 1, 7, 229
Hurford, J., 309, 319, 325
Husserl, E., 347, 369, 412
Hutchby, 569
hyenas, 400
Hyman, Larry, 111
Hymes, D., 3, 188, 448, 456, 520, 545, 582, 585, 605
hyperarticulation, 648

Ibn Quraysh, Y., 664
iconic, 272, 653
iconicity, 86, 118, 271, 600, 627, 634, 640
iconization, 236, 600, 634, 653
ideal type, 608
identification, 545
identity, 25, 140, 153, 584, 600, 654
ideologies, 3, 4, 103, 149, 150, 152, 184, 232, 236, 237, 238, 240, 241, 538, 617, 630
idiolects, 25, 67, 104
idioms, 144
illocution, 425
illocutionary act, 429
illocutionary force, 145, 428, 485, 497, 498, 502
Ilongot, 458
immediacy, 568
immigrants, 36
imperative, 413
impersonal constructions, 14
implicitness, 655
incorporation, 53, 66, 70
indeterminacy, 518, 528
index, 400
index-finger pointing, 200
indexical dialectics, 149–53
indexical expressions, 496
indexical field, 648
indexical orders, 633, 645, 647, 648, 649
indexical value, 647
indexicality, 139, 140, 141, 144, 146, 149, 152, 370, 600, 627, 640, 647
Indian grammarians, 30
indirect speech acts, 495
individual differences, 201
Indo-European languages, 33, 107, 190, 191, 316, 317, 663, 664
Indonesia, 519
inductive research, 30
inductivism, 132
infancy, 209
inflection, 30, 65, 253
inflectional morphemes, 254
information, 713, 721
information science, 601
infrastructure, 570, 608, 713
innateness, 113, 194, 195, 693
innateness of language, 190
Inoue, M., 563, 638, 716
insert sequence, 452
institutional reality, 11, 12, 370
instrumentalism, 9
instrumentality of language, 128
insults, 458
intensionality, 613
intentional, 343
intentional states, 431
Intentionality, 343, 347, 348, 609
intentions, 66, 547
interaction, 3, 5, 9, 12, 163, 170, 174, 184, 187, 188, 198, 205, 209, 211, 227, 231, 236, 721
interaction engine, 187, 189, 200
interaction order, 725
interactional linguistics, 140, 161
interactional sociolinguistics, 3
interactional style, 192
interdiscursivity, 149, 231
interjections, 65, 502

intermediaries, 571, 711, 713, 714, 715
intermediation, 714, 715, 722
interpellation, 591
interpretants, 51
interpretation, 713, 721
interrogative, 258
intersubjectivity, 12, 67, 233, 343, 364
intertextual relations, 231
intimacy, 715
intonation, 257
intonation unit, 73
intonational phrase, 258
introgression, 689
intuitions, 128, 152
Inuktitut, 191, 192, 194, 197, 201
invariance, 721
invention, 629
involvement, 365
irrealis, 206
Irvine, J., 236, 240, 482, 502, 503, 519, 528, 549, 563, 578, 634, 653
isolated deaf individuals, 318
isolating languages, 192
Israel, 184
Israeli Sign Language, 104, 256, 258, 272
Italian, 92
Italic, 317
item/system problem, 26, 48–71
items, 49, 66
item-utterance fit, 69
iterations, 717
Ito, 570

Jackendoff, R., 251, 263, 274
Jacknis, I., 454
Jackson, J., 525, 550, 551
Jacquemet, M., 425
Jaffe, A., 489
Jakobson, R., 3, 137, 191, 229, 365, 402, 413, 417, 456, 487, 488, 505, 519, 605, 609, 715
James, W., 353
Japanese, 4, 25, 191, 197, 459, 462
Jarawara, 33, 34
Jasperson, R., 172, 462, 463
Javanese, 412
Jefferson, G., 331, 368, 372, 373, 375, 376, 377, 390, 391, 430, 451, 455, 457, 459, 460
Jespersen, O., 417
Johnson, P., 524
Johnstone, B., 489
joint attention, 7, 190, 199, 200, 209, 366, 403, 406, 409
joint attentional behaviors, 366
joint attentional framework, 366
joint object-engagement, 366
Jones, W., 250, 664
Journal of Linguistic Anthropology, 2
judgment, 352
jussive, 413

K'iché Maya, 315, 520
Kalapalo, 521, 522
Kaluli, 191, 409, 522
Kaluli people, 201
Kambaata, 501
Kant, I., 347, 351, 352, 355
    responsible *for*, 352
    responsible *to*, 352

Kapferer, B., 521, 522
Kaplan, M., 518
Kaska, 301
Kata Kolok, 256
Kaufman, T., 68, 315
Keane, W., 520, 526, 527, 528, 561, 566
Keating, E., 450
Keenan, E. O., 524
Kelly, J., 518
Kendon, A., 26, 261, 426, 454, 464
Kevoe Feldman, H., 390
Kharia, 107, 109, 111, 120
khipus, 233
Khoisan languages, 192
Kidwell, M., 206, 366, 456
Kiesling, S., 647
Kiksht, 525
kinesics, 454
kinship, 70, 239, 253
 represented in gestures, 79
kinship terminology, 109, 239
Kinyarwanda, 105
Kirby, S., 69, 309, 319, 325, 334
Kirsch, A., 516
Kita, S., 464, 465
Kitzinger, C., 377
Kockelman, P., 3, 49, 53, 331, 368, 415, 423, 427, 522, 572, 574, 599, 601, 609, 611, 708
Korean, 191, 192, 197, 202
Korowai, 521
Krauss, M., 287, 291
Krebs, J., 389
Kri, 522
Kripke, S., 499, 526
Kristeva, Julia, 231
Kroskrity, P., 240, 300
Ku Waru, 191, 344, 406, 408, 410, 412, 413, 415
Kuipers, J., 519, 529
Kulick, D., 207, 208, 209, 293
Kuna, 465, 523
Kurdish, 289
Kurgan, 316

labels vs. descriptions, 355
Labov, W., 229, 325, 331, 579, 610, 644, 645
ladder of action (Austin/Clark), 429
Ladefoged, P., 697
laggards, 63
Lambek, M., 519, 524
landscape, 637
language, 1, 228, 709
 as opposed to languages, 25
language acquisition, 102, 273, 325
language acquisition device, 187, 199
language automata, 726
language change, 118, 666
language contact, 65, 117, 204, 315, 316
language death, 5, 285
language documentation, 295, 299
language emergence, 87, 254
language endangerment, 185, 285
language evolution, 5, 274, 325
language extinction, 185
language families, 315
language ideologies, 539, 567, 583, 587, 590, 715, 725
language learning, 93

language levelling, 670, 671, 679
language mixing, 673
language of thought, 356
language processing, 115, 118
language restructuring, 672
language revitalization, 236, 296, 669
language shift, 204, 236, 296, 668, 669
language socialization, 203
language standardization, 585
language typology, 28, 185, 190, 192, 317
language universals, 250
language vitality, 5
language–culture relation, 14, 15
language–farming co-dispersal, 692
languages, 2, 58, 103, 153, 183, 228
 vs dialects, 25
language–society–history nexus, 227–243
langue, 3
Lao, 25, 54, 58, 457, 461, 462, 465
Larsen-Freeman, D., 328
larynx, 311, 312, 313
Latin, 39, 40, 41, 42, 250
Latin America, 241
Latour, B., 61, 571, 617, 711
laughter, 368, 376
law, 61
law of the few, 63
Le Page, R. B., 59, 68
Leach, E., 336, 517
learning, 330
Lee, B., 486
legal system, 206
legisigns, 134, 137, 138, 145, 148
legitimation, 648
Leibniz, G., 348
Lemke, J., 328
lemma retrieval, 329
Lempert, M., 481, 489, 491
Leonard, W., 295, 298
León-Portilla, M., 520
Lerner, G., 368, 452, 459
levels of adequacy, 112
Levelt, P., 325, 329
Levinson, S. C., 60, 110, 185, 204, 251, 274, 309, 317, 330, 384, 387, 411, 414, 426, 434, 452, 456, 457, 465, 466, 486, 503, 563, 609
Lévi-Strauss, C., 14, 229, 628
Lewis, O., 582
lexical access, 83
lexical fields, 109
lexical semantics, 432
Lexical-Functional Grammar, 102, 112, 113
lexicalization, 262, 263, 271
lexicography, 239
lexicon, 184, 203, 261, 263
lexicostatistics, 665, 666
Li, Charles, 159
Lieberman, M., 309
life-cycle rituals, 522
lifeworlds, 635
Lindstrom, A., 457
linearization, 80, 88, 91
Linell, P., 175
linguacultural ideologies, 518
linguistic anthropology, 2–6, 16, 17, 131, 184, 185, 229, 230, 233, 236, 237, 240, 243, 539, 604, 610, 626, 708
linguistic description, 257

linguistic diversity, 286, 287, 601, 667, 686
linguistic human rights, 291, 292
linguistic ideologies, 483, 578, 633
linguistic palaeontology, 663, 665
linguistic relativity, 3, 8, 203, 204, 205, 496, 708
Linguistic Society of America, 285, 309
linguistic typology, 27, 73, 159
linguistic variation, 325
linguistics, 7, 187, 211, 229
  as a cumulative science, 29
  defined, 29
linking mechanisms, 14
lip pointing, 465
literary criticism, 235
loanwords, 116, 665
location, 277
Lockean rectangle, 132, 136, 138
Lockhart, James, 240
locutionary act, 131, 429
locutionary force, 13
logic, 129, 359
logical inferential relations, 354
logical positivist, 485
longitudinal methodology, 209
long-term memory, 330
Lorenz, K., 328
Lucy, J., 10, 137, 150, 204, 335, 605, 609, 719
Luke, K. K., 456
Lyell, G., 314
Lyons, John, 136

M.O.P.E.D.S., 186, 326
Maa, 116
Maasai, 116
MacWhinney, B., 327, 328, 333
Madagascar, 519
Mahmood, S., 528
Maine, Henry Sumner, 11
Malinowski, B., 12, 15, 36, 365, 481, 482, 517, 529, 604, 609
Malotki, Ekkehart, 237
Mandarin Chinese, 87, 92, 104, 115, 117, 191, 192, 194
Mandelbaum, J., 448
Mannheim, B., 526
Manning, P., 483
markedness, 118
marriage, 253
Marsaja, G, 256
Marvin, C., 565
Marx, K., 332, 609, 616, 718, 724
material culture, 669, 679
material inferential relations, 354
material qualities, 560
materiality, 232, 233, 559, 561, 568
materialization, 491, 493
math, 84, 85, 92
math learning and gesture, 82
mathematics, 29
Mauss, M., 491
Maya, 238
Maya reducido, 242
Mayan, 144, 191
Mayan languages, 192, 194, 239
Mayan people, 201
McConnell-Ginet, 584
McConvell, Patrick, 57
McHoul, A., 448

McLuhan, M., 572, 616
McNeill, D., 26, 79, 325, 464, 493
Mead, G. H., 11, 604, 610
Mead, M., 454
meaning, 5, 39, 713
Mech, L. D., 370, 389
media, 5, 233, 559
media ideologies, 567
mediation, 184, 232, 568, 600, 603, 605, 606, 608, 639, 713, 715, 721
mediators, 571, 711, 714
Meek, B., 301
megarhetoric, 551
Meir, I., 184
memes, 67
mental rotation tasks, 84
Merlan, F., 409, 410, 412
Mesoamerica, 109, 238, 240
Mesoamerican languages, 191
message, 138, 540
metahistory, 184, 228
metalanguage, 3, 119, 132, 206, 611, 614
metalinguistic description, 27
metalinguistic vocabulary, 428
metalinguistics, 59, 236, 241
meta-mediation, 614, 618
metaphor, 134
metapragmatic, 147, 489, 495, 562
metapragmatic descriptors, 486
metapragmatic icon, 491
metapragmatic regimentation, 148
metapragmatics, 27, 131, 142, 143, 144, 146, 150, 152, 490, 633
method, 211
methodology, 207
metricalization, 143
Mexico, 188, 191
Michael, L., 303
micro-analysis, 209
microgenetic, 186, 326, 329, 334
micro-macro relation, 59
middle-class Americans, 198
Miller, J., 486
Miller, P., 188
Miller, P. J., 206
Millikan, R., 352
Milroy, L., 331, 646
mimesis, 521
mimicry, 518, 521
mind, 2, 7, 17
minimal grasp strategy, 393
minimal pairs, 104, 268
Minimalist Program, 102
Mintz, 230
Mithun, M., 290, 291
mixed languages, 672
Mixe-Zoquean, 239
modality, 26, 78, 87, 92, 93, 130
mode of inheritance, 310
modernity, 549
modifier-head order, 267
Moerman, M., 372, 448, 452, 453, 457, 459, 461
Mondada, L., 331, 456, 464
money, 57, 59
Mongolian, 501
Mon-Khmer languages, 56
Monmonier's algorithm, 691

Moore, E., 650
Moore, R., 297, 301
Mopan Maya, 196
morphology, 7, 88, 105–106, 193, 256, 263, 274, 277, 519
morphosyntax, 175, 462
motherese, 199
motivation, 3
motor cortex, 311
movement, 277
moves, 464
MRI scanning, 185, 310
Muehlmann, S., 297, 298, 482
Mufwene, S., 293, 301
Mukarovsky, J., 488
Muller, M., 663
multi-dimensional scaling, 687
multilingual communities, 204
multilingualism, 71, 586
multi-modal interaction, 207, 456, 633
multimodal practices, 453
multimodality, 206, 454
multiple encoding, 723
Munda languages, 56
Munn, N., 336, 635
mutation, 311, 689
mutual intelligibility, 25, 297
mutual understanding, 458
Mwotlap, 501
Myers, F., 528
my-side telling, 430

Nahuatl, 240, 302, 519, 520, 521, 522, 529
names, 147, 153
name-tabooing, 501
narrative, 205, 275, 299
narrative style, 197
Nash, D., 499
nationalism, 238
nation-state, 153, 585
native metalinguistic vocabulary, 428
native speaker informants, 332
native speakers, 36
natural categories, 192
natural kinds, 423
natural languages, 716
natural meaning, 610
natural selection, 330
naturalization, 634
Navajo, 521
Neanderthal, 311, 312, 314
Neanderthal stone-tool technology, 314
Neanderthal technology, 312
Neanderthals, 688
negative observation, 431
neo-Bloomfieldians, 159
Nettle, D., 286, 453
networks, 64, 68, 184
neurophysiology, 118
Nevins, E., 300
New Guinea, 35
New Philology school, 240
Newell, A., 325, 328, 333
Newmeyer, F. J., 120, 309
next position, 377
Ngarinyin, 497
Nguni languages, 240

Nicaragua, 90, 252
Nicaraguan Sign Language, 88, 90, 252, 255, 257, 318
niche construction, 185, 310, 320
Nichols, J., 315
Nietzsche, F., 229, 241
Nilotic languages, 116
non-alphabetic scripts, 233
nonconformity, 209
non-Indo-European languages, 196
non-natural meaning, 616, 619
non-referential index, 410
nonverbal behavior, 79
non-Western languages, 238
normative accountability, 426
normative concepts, 351
normativity, 145, 351
norms, 9, 11, 12, 60, 66, 67
North America, 45
noun bias, 192
noun phrase, 38
noun/verb distinction, 41, 192
nouns, 39, 40, 54, 120
novel utterances, 274
Nuer, 12
Nukulaelae, 463
number, 204
Nunberg, G., 647
Nyawaygi, 37, 40, 43, 44

O, transitive object function, 38
O, A transitive object function, 42
Ochs, E., 188, 209, 325, 336, 384, 385, 387, 388, 392, 448, 449, 463
Old English, 33
online syntax, 174
ontogenetic, 186, 326, 327, 330, 334
ontogeny, 5, 16
ontological isomorphisms, 723
ontologies, 517, 715, 722, 724
ontology of language, 6
opacity of other minds, 384, 385
open class other-initiated repair, 461
open class repair initiation, 390
operating principles, 193
optative, 413, 414
oral cultures, 230
oral education, 89
orangutan, 389
oratory, 482, 494, 538
ordinary language philosophy, 230
orientalism, 242
Ortner, S., 605
OSV, 256
other-initiated repair, 377, 451, 452, 458, 460, 463
Oto-Manguean, 239
overheard speech, 200, 201
overlap, 375, 451, 456
overshadowing effects, 9

Pachur, T., 433
Pacific, 37, 116
Padden, C., 184
Pagel, M., 10
pain, 348
Paine, R., 542

palaeoanthropology, 661, 688
palaeosociolinguistics, 661, 670, 679
paleontology, 311, 312
Pama-Nyungan, 669
Pandian, A., 636
pantomime, 261, 262
Papua New Guinea, 104, 188, 191, 192, 287, 299, 344, 406
paradigmatic axis, 55, 69, 70
parallel diversification, 689
parallelism, 143, 413, 415, 488, 489, 490, 493, 503, 518, 519, 523
parity problem, 317
Parmentier, R., 232, 491, 630
parole, 3
Parry, J., 57, 59
parsers, 718
Parsons, T., 628
participant roles, 147
participant structure, 198, 565
participation framework, 563
parts of speech, 39, 107, 111, 274, 276
passives, 194
Passivization, 274
paucal, 44
Pavlidou, T.-S., 456
Pedersen, M., 517
peer interactions, 208
Peirce, C. S., 27, 131, 133, 144, 150, 230, 353, 404, 539, 560, 605, 609, 712
performance, 130
performativity, 144, 145, 146, 147, 149, 150, 153, 241, 481, 482, 485, 486, 488, 494, 497, 498, 503, 504
perlocution, 425
perlocutionary act, 429
perlocutionary effects, 429
Perrino, S., 491
person, 548
    grammatical category, 400, 402
person reference and address, 411
personhood, 543, 544, 546
personification, 518, 522
perspective-taking, 408, 409, 410
persuasion, 541
phatic act, 429
phatic communion, 365
phenomenologies, 537, 538
Philippines, 44, 45
Phillipson, R., 292
philosophy, 16
philosophy of mind, 347
phonemes, 37, 86, 103, 104, 115, 191
phonetic act, 429
phonetic practices, 170
phonetics, 7
phonological categories, 190
phonological change, 33
phonological development, 191
phonological encoding, 329
phonological structure, 277
phonological system, 270, 274
phonological variation, 644
phonology, 6, 7, 37, 70, 86, 104–5, 184, 256, 268, 274, 519
phrase structure, 103, 113, 195
phrases, 257

phylogenetic, 186, 326, 327, 330
phylogeny, 5, 16, 230
Piagetian conservation, 81, 83
Piantadosi, 10
Pictet, A., 663
pidgin languages, 5, 87, 263, 274, 672
pidginization, 273, 666, 672
Pinker, S., 195, 251, 274
Pirahã, 107, 111
pirates, 118
place names, 233, 276
place of articulation, 268
Plag, 263
platonism, 350
Podesva, R., 649
poetic function, 487, 489, 494, 633, 715
poetic language, 5
poetic meter, 610
poetic performativity, 503
poetic structure, 142, 491, 492, 494
poetics, 413, 456, 457, 481, 482, 485, 487, 490, 503
poetry, 519
point mutations, 689
point of possible completion, 373
pointing, 7, 90, 200, 366, 464, 465
polarity, 55
political discourse, 494
political economy, 230, 519
political oratory, 487
politics, 537
Pollner, M., 370
Pollock, S., 525
polyphony, 234
polysynthetic languages, 192
Pomerantz, A., 425, 430, 448
Ponapean, 45
population dynamics, 184
population genetics, 239
positivism, 136, 235
possession, 107
    alienable and inalienable, 31, 41
possible pre-closing, 430, 437
post-modernism, 241
post-structuralism, 230
posture, 464
power, 241, 242
power relations, 232
practical intentionality, 349
practical reasoning, 348
practice approach, 3
practices and actions, 430
practice theory, 230, 583, 584
practions, 430
pragmatic semiosis, 631
pragmatics, 7, 103, 130, 131, 138, 140, 149, 184, 188, 197, 231, 275, 485
pragmatism, 350
Prague school, 229
pre-announcement, 383
predication, 137
pre-fab schemas, 165
preferences, 11
Preferred Argument Structure, 197
prelinguistic cognition, 8
preposition, 254
pre-telling, 452

primate grooming, 309
primates, 4, 516
primitives, 8
primordial social situation, 403, 416
principal, 563
principal components analysis, 687
problem of other minds, 364
processing, 325
programming languages, 724, 725
programs, 710, 723
projectability, 173, 373
projection, 164, 166, 173, 174, 175
pronouns, 9, 44, 254, 261, 402
   inclusive versus exclusive, 44
   minimal-type systems, 45
proper names, 319
propositional intentionality, 349, 352
propositions, 254, 351, 357
prosodic salience, 194
prosodic structure, 275
prosody, 164, 165, 168, 173, 257, 258, 259, 260, 277, 519
prosody in sign languages, 258
proto-language, 664
Providence Island Creole, 257
Providence Island, Colombia, 256
proxemics, 454
psycholinguistics, 73
psychological reality, 113
psychological shakiness (Sapir), 65
psychological states, 347
psychology, 16, 114, 187, 365
public, 577
public sphere, 588, 589, 590
publics, 483, 587
purposive action, 344, 424, 426
Putnam, H., 609
Pyers, J., 318

Q'eqchi' Maya, 522
qualisign, 566
quantification, 210, 645
quantitative analysis, 645
quantity, 653
   versus statements, 118
Quine, W. O., 402

racialization, 242
Rączaszek-Leonardi, J., 327, 333
Radcliffe-Brown, 229
Rafael, V., 527
Rannut, M., 292
Rapley, M., 448
Rappaport, R., 517
Rappaport Hovav, M., 497
rationalism, 7, 8
Raymond, G., 377
real imaginaries, 723
receiver, 139
reciprocity of perspectives, 369
recombination, 689
recontextualization, 562
recording technologies, 453
recursion, 6, 54, 103, 107, 111, 114, 228, 229, 236, 275, 717, 718
recursive syntax, 311, 313
Redfield, J., 542

Redfield, R., 582
reducción, 242
reference, 13, 129, 137, 206, 368, 387
reference formulation, 409
referent, 138
referential capacity, 6
referential indeterminacy, 529
referential triangle, 199
reflexive capacity of language, 402
reflexive constructions, 160
reflexiveness, 402
reflexivity, 3, 13, 131, 234, 518, 519, 528
registers, 140, 141, 147, 152, 153, 199, 202, 205, 240, 411, 412, 519, 601, 630, 633, 638, 675, 676, 679
regular expressions, 717
regular languages, 717
Reichenbach, H., 402
reification, 616
Reisman, K., 459
relations-between-relations, 53, 54
relative clauses, 38, 108, 160, 274
relativism, 8, 128
relativity, 721
relayed transmission, 404
relevance, 331
Renfrew, C., 408, 668, 692
repair, 147, 170–173, 174, 189, 331, 364, 390, 460, 463
repair initiation, 170
repair proper, 170
repetition, 143, 390, 493, 518, 519
Replicas, 134
reported speech, 275, 405, 428, 497
representation, 518, 521, 600, 608, 627, 630, 631
representational intentionality, 349, 352
representationalism, 235
represented speech, 405, 408, 409, 414
response offsets, 459
retraction, 174
rhetic act, 429
rhetoric, 130, 131, 301, 537, 538, 539, 541, 715
Riau Indonesian, 108, 111
Rice, K., 185
Richerson, P., 62, 320, 325, 334
Ricoeur, P., 231
rigidity, 499
rigid performativity, 500
ritual, 482, 491
ritual language, 5
ritual textuality, 491
ritualization, 160, 482, 516
Robbins, J., 386, 387, 527
Robinson, J., 390, 430, 463
Role and Reference Grammar, 112
Romaine, S., 286, 287, 297
Roman Empire, 116
Romance languages, 195, 254
Rommetveit, R., 364
Rosaldo, M., 384, 423, 432, 439, 458, 486, 543, 544, 546, 549, 553
Rosch, E., 9
Rossano, F., 389, 456, 464, 465
Rossel Island, 192
Rotinese, 519
Rotokas, 104

Rousseau, J-J, 229
routinization, 160
Ruby, J., 454
rules, 710, 711
Rumsey, A., 384, 386, 387, 412, 429, 497, 522
Ruskin, J., 714
Russian, 14, 106, 107
Russian formalists, 487, 488, 493
Ryle, G., 371

S, argument of intransitive verb, 108
S, 'subject function', 38
Sacks, H., 60, 331, 368, 372, 373, 374, 375, 376, 377, 390, 428, 430, 431, 437, 439, 448, 451, 455, 459, 460
Sadock, Jerold, 146
Sahlins, M., 58, 66, 403, 518, 609
Sallabank, J., 286, 288, 291, 297
salvage anthropology, 454
Samoa, 188, 384, 385, 388, 463
Samoan, 191, 201, 202, 528
sand dunes, 160
Sanders, R., 448
Sandler, Wendy, 184
Sanskrit, 250, 664
Santería, 529
sapience, 348, 349
Sapir, E., 10, 65, 159, 203, 229, 285, 334, 434
Sapir–Whorf Hypothesis, 725
satellite framed constructions, 197
Saussure, Ferdinand de, 13, 54, 229
Savage-Rumbaugh, S., 400
Scandinavian languages, 194
Schegloff, E. A., 325, 331, 336, 343, 364, 372, 373, 374, 375, 376, 383, 384, 387, 390, 425, 426, 430, 431, 433, 434, 437, 439, 440, 448, 449, 451, 452, 453, 455, 456, 459, 460, 462, 464, 465, 486
Schelling, T., 433
schematicity, 173
Schieffelin, B., 188, 207, 208, 209, 325, 409, 449, 522
Schiffrin, Deborah, 235
Schneider, D., 628
schools for deaf, 252
Schrauwers, A., 522
Schutz, A., 331, 344, 369, 412
schwa, 37
science, 231
Scott Kiesling, 647
scrub jays, 400
Searle, J., 11, 12, 72, 330, 347, 370, 371, 384, 392, 400, 423, 424, 425, 431, 432, 457, 458, 485, 486, 495, 503, 518, 609
second-language learning, 189
secondness, 712, 713, 714
secrets, 719, 720
section systems (kinship), 56
sedimentation, 228, 231, 239
segmentation, 80, 86, 88, 91
segmented, 261
self, 211, 544
self-repair, 171, 452, 462
semantic domains, 9
semantic fields, 4
semanticity, 13
semantics, 4, 7, 109–10, 254, 255, 274
semiology, 609

semiosis, 309, 630, 722
semiotic ideologies, 562, 567, 634
semiotic mediation, 627, 628
semiotic processes, 612
semiotic technologies, 232, 614
semiotics, 609
sender, 139
Senghas, A., 255, 318
sensations, 348
sense, 139
sentences, 136
sentience, 348, 349
sequence organization, 161
sequential structure, 465
sequentiality, 162
Serbian, 25, 58, 104
serial-verb constructions, 54
Serres, M., 613, 711
Sesotho, 191, 194
Severi, C., 523
Seyfarth, R., 401, 417, 418
shaming, 205
Shannon, C., 664, 711, 723
shared attention, 365
shared information, 258
shared intentionality, 6, 209, 366
Shattuck, R., 251
Sherzer, J., 456, 465, 523
shibboleths, 147, 153
shifters, 141, 344, 637, 715
Shoaps, R., 527, 528
Shokleng, 491
showing, 366
Sidnell, J., 10, 12, 28, 290, 325, 331, 335, 452, 455, 456, 457, 459, 461, 486, 715
sieves, 709, 711, 726
sign language, 78–93, 104, 250, 276, 318, 696
Sign Language of the Netherlands, 86
sign language 'pronunciation', 269
sign–interpretant relations, 331
Silverstein, M., 3, 15, 27, 411, 412, 414, 417, 425, 429, 486, 487, 488, 489, 490, 491, 494, 495, 496, 497, 498, 503, 520, 529, 539, 540
Simons, G., 498
Simpson, J., 499
Singer, M., 82, 492
single-argument clauses, 255
Sinhalese, 521
Sinsign, 134
situation-centered interaction, 198
Siwu, 450, 461, 462
size-and-shape specifier, 264, 265, 266
Skutnabb-Kangas, T., 292
Slobin, D., 10, 191, 193, 197, 335
Smith, A., 60, 73, 332
Smith, J., 452
social actions, 423
social cognition, 4
social constructivism, 3
social facts, 49, 72
social graces, 211
social interaction, 343
social learning, 190
social life, 11
social norms, 353
social organization, 29
social structure, 118
sociality, 229

socialization, 59, 183, 184, 187–211, 330
Société de Linguistique de Paris, 309
society, 2, 11, 228
Society for Linguistic Anthropology, 2
sociocultural anthropology, 14, 626, 661
socioeconomic factors in language shift, 293
sociolects, 102, 103
sociolinguistic variation, 644
sociolinguistics, 16, 131, 140, 148, 230, 240, 600
sociology, 187, 455
sociometric closure, 68, 70
South America, 45, 287
South Asia, 241
Southeast Asia, 109
southern Africa, 192, 240
SOV, 256, 257
space, 637
Spain, 252
Spanish, 32, 34, 92, 201
spatial prepositions, 198
spatial reckoning, 204
speaker variation, 686
species-uniqueness, 365
speech act labels, 428
speech act theory, 458, 485, 486, 495, 503, 504
speech act verbs, 432, 496
speech acts, 9, 13, 150, 457, 481
speech communities, 147, 578, 579, 581, 583, 605, 663
speech genres, 449, 456, 539
speech levels, 148
speech–gesture mismatches, 92
Sperber, D., 63, 331
Sri Lanka, 521
stack, 718
Stampe, D., 55, 66
stance, 170, 231, 368, 489, 492, 647
stance differential, 489
stance sharing, 368
stance-taking, 494
standardization, 153
Star, S. L., 574
Stasch, R., 491, 521, 530, 600, 636, 637
statistical learning, 330
statistics, 117
status, 12, 144
Steels, L., 327
Steensig, J., 331
stickleback fish, 327
stigma, 253
Stivers, T., 175, 325, 331, 384, 390, 452, 456, 459, 460
Stokoe, W., 268
Stoller, P., 452
story preface, 451
Strathern, M., 409
Streeck, J., 448, 456
stress, 105, 257
    iambic versus trochaic, 56
stress-timed phonology, 192
strings, 709, 711
structural analysis, 161
structuralism, 6, 66, 137, 229
structure, 604
structured elicitation, 299
Struhsaker, T. T., 401
style, 645, 649, 652
stylistic variation, 148

subaltern approach, 241
subcultures, 190
subject, 196
subject (grammatical category), 90
subordination, 258
subsection systems (kinship), 56
Sudnow, D., 455
Summer Institute of Linguistics, 38
Suniyama, 521
supralaryngeal tract, 311
SVO, 256, 257
Swadesh, M., 315, 665
Swedish, 457
syllables, 104, 111, 118
syllable-timed phonology, 192
synchronic structures, 10
synchrony, 3, 28, 163, 174, 186, 229, 326, 327, 332, 604
syncretism, 204
syntagmatic axis, 55, 69, 70
syntax, 7, 106–9, 130, 137, 164, 173, 184, 195, 254, 413, 519
system, 49–61, 183
    defined, 50

taboo, 481, 498
taboo registers, 240
Tabouret-Keller, Andrée, 59, 68
Tagalog, 116
Tahitian, 501
Tai/Lue, 448, 461
Taiap (Gapun), 191
Tai-Lue, 457
Taiwan, 206
Takagi, T., 459
talk-in-interaction, 161, 189, 364
Tambiah, S. J., 481, 486, 517, 518, 519, 521, 524
Tamil, 411
Tannen, D., 488
Tarski, A., 402
Tavárez, D., 481, 482, 527
taxonomy, 33
Taylor, C., 518
teasing, 205
technologies, 14, 49, 70, 231, 233
Tedlock, D., 456, 520
teleosemantic theories, 352
telephone interaction, 456
temporality, 230, 630
tense, 141, 236
tense-aspect, 41
terminology, 2
termite colonies, 160
Tewa, 240
texts, 139, 231, 232, 235, 723
textual analysis, 229
textuality, 184, 230, 231, 232, 488
Thai, 25, 58
thematic roles, 195, 261
theory, 211
    and description, 30
theory of evolution, 314
theory of mind, 202, 209
thesaurus, 36
thick explanation, 210
thinking for speaking, 8, 197
third position, 380

Third Wave, 600, 646
thirdness, 712, 713, 714
Thomason, S., 68, 315
Thompson, D'Arcy, 183
Thompson, S. A., 27, 185
thoughts, 348
Tibetan, 106
time, 236, 517
timescales, 326
Tinbergen, N., 326
tip of the tongue phenomenon, 83
titles, 147
Tok Pisin, 35, 299, 414, 418
token-reflexivity, 402, 404, 405, 416
token-type, 417, 496
Tomasello, M., 7, 199, 309, 325, 327, 330, 366, 388, 389, 403, 405, 516
Tomlinson, M., 527, 529
tone, 105, 194, 698
tool use, 314
topics, 258
totemism, 629
transcription, 456
transformativity, 722
transition function, 709, 710, 715, 717
transition relevance place, 165
transitive, 255, 262
transitivity, 160
transmission, 11
transmission bias, 333, 334
transmission criterion, 26, 49, 60
Traugott, E., 325
Trevarthen, C., 365
tropes, 151
Trouillot, Rolph, 243
Trudgill, P., 325, 646
try-marking, 376
Tuite, Kevin, 240
Turing machines, 709, 716, 718, 719, 720, 723
Turing test, 722
Turkish, 81, 92, 106, 115, 192, 195, 202
turn completion, 165, 167, 169
turn construction, 173, 373
turn constructional units, 73, 373, 375
turn continuation, 167, 170, 173, 174
turn increment, 167
turn organization, 161
turn-taking, 164, 189, 199, 331, 372, 447, 449, 451, 456, 457, 458, 459, 460, 464, 465
Turner, T., 517, 518, 529
turn organization, 375
turns, 464
turns-at-talk, 136, 141, 150, 161, 163, 167, 173, 373
Tylor, E., 500
types of speakers, 298
type-token, 430
typification, 410, 412, 416
typological preference hypothesis, 198
typology, 7, 453
typology of language socialization styles, 202
Tzeltal Maya, 197, 202, 204
Tzotzil Maya, 519, 520, 521

!Ui-Taa languages, 104
unconscious, 613

underspecification, 655
UNESCO, 287
Ungarinyin, 522
uniformitarianism, 666
union, 717
United States, 90, 147, 206, 229
units of analysis, 70
universal grammar, 102, 110, 187, 189, 199, 276, 708, 720
Universal Turing Machine, 718
universalism, 191, 195
universality, 194
universals, 1, 4, 8, 9, 27, 102, 110–119, 131, 159, 174, 189, 199, 239, 719
   absolute, 110–115
   implicational, 121
   statistical, 115–119
Universals Archive, 121
Upper Paleolithic, 311, 312
Urban, G., 227, 491, 562, 605, 715
Urcid, J., 517
Urla, 580
usage-based approach, 163, 187
use-mention, 498
uses of video, 454
Uto-Aztecan languages, 239
utterance, 73

values, 2
van Boxhorn, M., 664
van Reeland, A., 664
variation, 253, 645, 648, 650, 653
variation sets, 202
variationist approach, 148
varieties, 411
Veblen, T., 610
Venkatesan, S., 517
verb agreement, 256, 274
verb framed constructions, 197
verbal art, 456
verb-friendly languages, 192
verb-initial languages, 117
verbs, 39, 40, 54, 255, 262
verbs of speaking, 495, 496
vernacular, 645
vervet monkeys, 400, 401, 404, 416
video recording, 453
Vietnamese, 105, 106, 107, 111
village sign language, 87
village sign languages, 87, 252, 252, 256, 318, 320
violence, 60
virginity, 206
visible behaviour, 458
Viveiros de Castro, E., 523
vocabulary, 253, 261, 263
vocal apparatus, 311
vocal imitation, 4
vocal tract, 313
vocative, 413
voice, 160
voluntary control of vocalization, 313
von Neumann, J., 723
von Roncador, M., 405
vowel contrasts, 311
vowel harmony, 194
vowel quality, 653
Vygotsky, L., 207, 209, 327, 329, 610

Wagner, R., 409, 629
Walker, G., 175
Wallerstein, I., 230
Wardlow, H., 638
Warlpiri, 14, 191, 194
Warner, M., 483, 589, 591
Wasco-Wishram, 301
Washabaugh, W, 256
Watts, J., 525
Weber, M., 524, 608, 612
Weinreich, U., 331, 334
well-formedness constraints, 268
Wells, Rulon S., 162
Welsh, 116, 289
Western Apache, 233
Western Greenlandic, 191
Weweya, 529
whales, 400
Whaley, J., 293, 297
Wharry, C., 527
What is a language?, 274, 298, 309
Whitehead, K., 465
Whorf, B. L., 203, 237, 335, 393, 496
wh-questions, 258
Wierzbicka, A., 10, 14, 335, 423, 429, 432, 433
Wilkins, David P., 196
Wilson, D., 331
Wirtz, K., 235, 529
Wittgenstein, L., 158, 353, 356, 364, 371, 389, 423
wolves, 229, 370
Woodbury, A., 289, 290, 296, 520
Woolard, K., 518
word classes, 39
word meaning, 254

word order, 253, 256, 257, 277, 316, 318, 319
words, 103, 105, 106, 111, 114
  phonological versus morphological, 105, 106
working memory, 84
World Atlas of Language Structures, 116, 317
world systems approach, 230
worldview, 3, 203
Wortham, S., 494
Wotton, W., 664
writing, 601, 662, 679
written-language bias, 175

Xavante, 232
Xhosa, 501
!Xõõ, 104

Yehuda Ibn Quraysh, 664
Yélî Dnye, 109, 192, 466
yes/no question-response sequences, 459
yes/no questions, 258
Yidiñ, 36, 37
Yucatán, 242
Yucatec Maya, 109, 112, 116, 204, 242, 526, 529
Yucatec Mayan families, 201
Yuman languages, 40
Yupik, 519, 520
Yupik cultures, 58

Zhang, 652
Zimmerman, D., 366, 459, 460
Zipf, G. K., 10, 69, 330, 333, 334, 335, 336
Zipf's Law, 186
Županov, I., 527
Zurich German, 109

Printed in the United States
by Baker & Taylor Publisher Services